D1278832

THE EARLY HISTORY OF ISRAEL

THE
EARLY HISTORY
OF ISRAEL

ROLAND DE VAUX

Translated by
DAVID SMITH

THE WESTMINSTER PRESS
PHILADELPHIA

Translated from the French *Histoire ancienne d'Israël: Des Origines à l'Installation en Canaan* (J. Gabalda et Cie, Paris, 1971) and *Histoire ancienne d'Israël: La Période des Juges* (J. Gabalda et Cie, Paris, 1973)

English Translation: © Darton, Longman & Todd Ltd, 1978

PUBLISHED BY THE WESTMINSTER PRESS ®
PHILADELPHIA, PENNSYLVANIA

PRINTED IN THE UNITED STATES OF AMERICA

Library of Congress Cataloging in Publication Data

Vaux, Roland de, 1903-1971.
The early history of Israel.

Translation of Histoire ancienne d'Israël.
Includes indexes.
1. Jews — History — To 953 B.C. I. Title.
DS117.V3813   220.9'5   78-1883
ISBN 0-664-20762-6

CONTENTS

PROLOGUE
The Geographical, Historical, Ethnical
and Cultural Environment

THE ORIGINS OF ISRAEL

Part I
THE PATRIARCHAL TRADITIONS

Part II

THE TRADITIONS OF THE SOJOURN IN EGYPT, THE EXODUS AND SINAI

Part III

THE TRADITIONS CONCERNING THE SETTLEMENT IN CANAAN

Part IV

THE PERIOD OF THE JUDGES

* The Addenda are works which came to the author's notice after the completion of the manuscript. Footnotes citing them are distinguished in the text by an asterisk.

PREFACE
to Volume One of the French edition

FOR a long time I could not decide what was the best title to give to this work. So many books of this kind bear the title 'History of Israel', but this seemed to me to be inadequate, mainly because 'Israel' appears in history only as the collective name given to a group of tribes after their settlement in Canaan. What, then, was this 'Israel'? It became a political entity when the monarchy was established under Saul, a reality which was later reduced to the single Northern Kingdom of 'Israel' after the death of Solomon. It finally ceased to exist politically when this Northern Kingdom became no more than a number of Assyrian provinces after the fall of Samaria. 'Israel' in the wider sense then became a religious entity, combining the traditions of the past and the people's hopes for the future, and to a great extent removed from historical events. In this sense, a 'history of Israel' might be written up to the Roman conquest of the land by Pompey, the capture of Jerusalem by Titus or the revolt of Bar Cochba. It might include virtually everything, even the modern state of Israel. On the other hand, 'Israel' in the religious sense is a term which is used together with, and often in competition with, 'Judaism', to denote a movement which began after the return of the people from exile and which was, despite its many links with the past, sufficiently new to merit a new name.

In this work, however, I do not cover any of these historical periods completely. I begin at a stage which precedes anything to which the name 'Israel' can be given and I only go as far as the conquests of Alexander. I end at this point partly because the later periods have already been adequately dealt with by the authors of other volumes in this series.[1] This was my immediate, practical reason, but I had other and more important reasons as well. Alexander's conquests and the Hellenisation of the Near East brought about a complete transformation of the environment in which the people of Israel lived, changing their political status, their social behaviour and their

---

[1] M.–J. Lagrange, *Le Judaïsme avant Jésus-Christ*, Paris, 1931; F.–M. Abel, *Histoire de la Palestine depuis la conquête d'Alexandre jusqu'à l'invasion arabe*, I–II, Paris, 1952; both in the series Etudes Bibliques.

religious thinking. What is more, the account of events in the historical books of the Hebrew Old Testament ends before Alexander.

This means that it might have been possible to adopt a title, now almost obsolete but much used in the past, 'History of the Old Testament'. But this title would also have been very ambiguous. The Old Testament is a collection of books and I did not wish to write a history of those books. The Old Testament, as opposed to the New, is also a religious concept – God's covenant with his chosen people – and my aim, in which I hope I have succeeded, was to do far more than simply to study the history of this choice and this covenant. But the Old Testament is also the literary record and religious legacy of a nation or people. It tells the history of that people. It was written by that people and preserved by that people. It also mentions that people more than any other subject with the exception of God. Although it does not always use it in exactly the same sense in which it is used by modern historians and sociologists, the word occurs some fourteen hundred times in the Hebrew text. Most important of all, the Old Testament has been my main source and sometimes my only source of information. For this reason, with this idea of 'people' in mind, I seriously considered 'History of the People of the Old Testament' as a title, a history, that is, from the origins on which this source of information, the Old Testament, dwells for so long, up to the period when it ceases to flow. But this title too has its disadvantages, because it might indicate an exclusive concern with the canonical and religious character of the Old Testament. I do not deny that I have always been concerned with this aspect of the Bible, but I am above all a historian and the two should not be confused. What is more, when they spoke of the 'people', the authors of the Old Testament were always referring to Israel in one of the senses which I have so briefly outlined above. So I finally opted for the title 'Early History of Israel', despite the ambiguity inherent in the term 'Israel'. In the original French, of course, the title *Histoire ancienne d'Israël* retains echoes of 'Old Testament' (*Ancien Testament*) which can hardly be preserved in English.

The history of a people is not simply an account of events in chronological order. The historian investigates the past with the aim of obtaining knowledge of that past. But a people's past is much more than a succession of victories and defeats, conquests and subjugations or kingdoms and revolutions. Such events are, in a sense, pure accidents which are only important when seen in relation to the life of the people, the life from which they are derived or in which they bring about a change. Even when they have been explained, they form no more than a framework within which the essential activities of the people – their economy, institutions, literature, philosophy and religion – are developed. As a historian, I shall, of course, try to take all these aspects of the life of the people of the Old Testament into consideration. The unique quality of the history of that people should not, however, be forgotten. Almost our only source of historical knowledge is contained in the religious books of the people of Israel and these books provided above all a norm for religious faith. The history that they present is a religious history, in the course of which the people were again and again brought face to face with their God. A really impartial historian, working within the limits imposed by his special study, must avoid taking sides either for or against that faith. But, because that faith is an essential aspect of the history that he is studying, he must be at pains not to transform the religious history of the people of Israel into a purely profane history. The study of history is a humane science and always open to a degree of uncertainty. This means that the historian's conclusions can only ever be more or less probable. In the case of the religious history of Israel, however, there is also the factor of ultimate ignorance, so that the historian, whether he is a believer or an unbeliever, must often hestitate on the threshold of its mystery.

Since the Old Testament is the main source of our knowledge of this history, it is necessary to study the text, applying the methods of literary criticism. It is not, however, our only source. Going further back than the final text and the known written sources, there are the oral traditions both of the earliest period and sometimes even of more recent periods. These oral traditions have to be disentangled and their accuracy has to be tested before the historian can apply the methods of historical criticism to them, going back to the Old Testament as well and at the same time appealing to external evidence. One element of external evidence will be, for example, the human geography of the region, seen in the context of history. The historian will also study the early texts of the Ancient Near East as external evidence. These texts, which exist in great numbers, provide a great deal of information about Israel's neighbours and enable us to reconstruct their history fairly accurately. Occasionally they even contain a direct reference to a person or an event in the Bible. Some of these texts that have been discovered in Palestine throw light on some fact or situation in the Old Testament. Further external evidence to which the historian will have recourse is, of course, provided by archaeological finds illustrating these ancient non-biblical texts and those of the Bible itself or amplifying these when they are defective.

No historian will deny that it is necessary to take into account both the text of the Bible itself and the contribution made by recent discoveries. This is a rule of research, but it has been applied in different ways. To illustrate this point, I need only to compare two fairly recent 'histories of Israel', both of which are equally to be recommended and both of which soon became classics in this field. M. Noth,[2] who continued the work of A.Alt, has given

[2] M. Noth, *Geschichte Israels*, Göttingen, first edn. 1950, second revised edn. 1954, sixth edn. 1966; inadequate French translation of first edition, Paris, 1954; good English translation of second edn, *History of Israel*, New York and Evanston, 1960.

priority to literary criticism and to a criticism of traditions. His history begins with the federation of tribes, at a point where the texts allow the historian to seize hold of an already formed 'Israel', and goes as far as the revolt of Bar Cochba. Noth has an excellent knowledge of non-biblical texts and of the results of archaeological excavations, but he does not believe that such external evidence will ever help scholars to establish the historicity of the pre-literary biblical traditions, which are, in his opinion, no more than obscure origins. Noth's history can be compared with that written by J. Bright,[3] a disciple of W. F. Albright. Bright has more confidence in the importance of this external evidence, especially that provided by archaeology, which he believes may tip the balance of probability in favour of the historicity of the early oral traditions. His history begins with the patriarchs and ends with the Maccabaean revolt.

The main difference, however, between these two authors is to be found in their judgement of the period before that of the Judges, an epoch which raises very grave problems for the historian. My work covers more or less the same period as that covered by J. Bright, but the reader will soon realise that my method is very close to that of M. Noth, although I have done everything possible to preserve a fairer balance between literary criticism and the use of external evidence. The reader will have to decide for himself whether this path that I have tried to follow, halfway between that followed by M. Noth and J. Bright, really results in a more faithful presentation of the course of Israel's history.

My intention is for this work to extend to three volumes. The present volume takes the people from their origins to their constitution as the 'people of Israel' after the settlement of the tribes in Canaan. The second volume will begin with the period of the Judges and go as far as the destruction of the kingdom of Judah.* The last volume will include the history of the exilic and post-exilic periods and conclude with the conquest of Alexander the Great. This is in fact very much the same plan as that adopted by R. Kittel in his great 'history of the people of Israel'.[4] Kittel was the first scholar to apply, at the end of the nineteenth century, both the discoveries that had been made in the Near East and the results of literary criticism to the study of the history of Israel. He was also the first to write a social and religious history of the people of Israel. His great work, in its revised editions, is still of fundamental importance.

[3] J. Bright, *A History of Israel*, Philadelphia 1959 and London 1960; German translation, Düsseldorf, 1966; a revised edn. in preparation.

* Publisher's Note. Roland de Vaux did not live to complete the second volume that he had planned and Volume Two of the French edition ended with the last of the Judges.

[4] R. Kittel, *Geschichte des Volkes Israel*, Stuttgart, I. Band: *Palästina in der Urzeit. Das Werden des Volkes. Geschichte der Zeit bis zum Tode Josuas*, 1888, 7th edn., 1932; II. Band: *Das Volk in Kanaan. Geschichte der Zeit bis zum babylonischen Exil*, 1892, 7th edn., 1925; III. Band: *Die Zeit der Wegführung nach Babel und die Aufrichtung der neuen Gemeinde*, 1927–1929.

Nonetheless, our understanding and our knowledge in all the branches of this special field of study have advanced to such an extent since Kittel's time that it is now possible to write another work on the same scale and with the same basic plan. In doing this, I have thought it necessary to justify in some detail the solutions to the various problems which I have in fact adopted and to give all the essential references in footnotes, despite the inevitable lengthening of the volumes.

The work of research in this sphere of study will never come to an end. Every year some new hypothesis is put forward or some hitherto unpublished document is revealed. All I hope to do in this work is to give the reader a detailed insight into the present state of this special study and to suggest those solutions which seem to me to be the most probable.[5]

Jerusalem, June 1970

---

[5] I have to thank my students, Jan Mulder, O. Carm, and Daniel Bourgeois, O.P., who have given me so much help in revising the manuscript, correcting proofs and preparing the index.

PREFACE
to Volume Two of the French edition

I N THE preface to the first French volume of his Early History of
Israel, the author, Roland de Vaux, said that the work would be
completed in two further volumes. According to this original plan,
the second volume of the trilogy was to begin at the period of the Judges of
Israel and to end with the collapse of the kingdom of Judah, and the third
was to commence at the Exile, cover the post-exilic period and go as far as
the conquest of Alexandria. This great plan was, however, suddenly interrupted by the author's death on 10 September 1971. After his death, a
good deal of material was found among the late author's papers, some in
typescript but much of it simply written in his own hand, and this was concerned with the period of the Judges. These papers in fact formed the first
part of the second French volume announced by the author on
publication of the first volume. A second part, dealing with the history of
the monarchy as far as the Babylonian Exile, was planned but was unfortunately never written. This second volume,* then, contains no more than
the author's study of the period of the Judges.

Our only source for this period, which extends from the beginning of the
twelfth century until about 1020 B.C., the date when the monarchy was set
up, is the book of Judges. Father de Vaux has studied this book in depth as a
historian, an archaeologist and an exegete and has dealt at length with the
problems of literary criticism and of the history of traditions that arise in it.
He disputes the theory of the Israelite 'amphictyony' and argues that the
system of the twelve tribes represented the ideal structure, at the time of
David, of a great Israel which in fact never existed as a political organisation. At the same time, however, he shows in considerable detail how Israel
gradually became established as a people through struggle and adversity. In
his fascinating search, he follows closely the movements of the different
tribes, paying special attention to the migration of Dan, the tribe about
which we possess most information. He describes their consolidation in Ca-

* Publishers' Note: the French Volume II consisted of Part IV only, included in this book.

naan and discusses their struggle against the neighbouring peoples – Moab, Ammon, Edom, Midian, the Canaanites and finally the Philistines who had recently come to the country. It was against these peoples that the saviours of Israel whom we call the 'great judges' were active – Othniel (against Edom), Ehud (against Moab), Gideon (against Midian), Jephthah (against Ammon) and Samson (against the Philistines). The only battle about which we have any information is the battle of Kishon, in which Deborah and Barak were victorious over the Canaanites on the Plain of Jezreel.

The longest chapter in this volume, Chapter 26 is devoted to the life of the tribes. It is divided into three sections, although the original intention was clearly to include a fourth section. This and the end of the third section, on the story of Samson, are missing. The fourth section was to have dealt with the rivalry between the tribes struggling among themselves for supremacy – Ephraim and Manasseh, Ephraim and Benjamin (Judges 19–21).

Father de Vaux would probably have concluded by providing us with a general survey of the whole of this complex and turbulent period of the Judges which followed the first settlement in Canaan. He would no doubt also have discussed questions of chronology, as he did at the end of the first French volume. All that we find, however, are the simple words: 'impossible to establish a chronology'. We are, of course, inevitably bound to regret the fact that the author was denied the opportunity to justify this negative statement, for, had he lived, he would undoubtedly have provided convincing explanations. On the other hand, however, we can only express our profound admiration for the honesty of a scholar who can admit his ignorance at the conclusion of such an enormous task of research.

The first three chapters were already in typescript and the author had already prepared them for publication.[1] The same cannot, however, be said of the rest of the present volume. Chapter 25, from the section on the 'complexity of the traditions concerning Samuel' (p. 763) onwards, and Chapter 26, from the section on 'Eastern Manasseh' (p. 783) onwards, existed only in the form of rough drafts. There can, of course, be no doubt that Father de Vaux would have wanted to improve a number of passages in these chapters before publication. (That this was his intention can be seen from the footnote following note 65 in Chapter 25; this was originally a marginal note.) Nonetheless, it seemed preferable to publish his text as he had written it, without any alterations.

It should also be pointed out that we are greatly indebted to Father F. Langlamet for his work on the long and difficult task of deciphering the author's manuscripts. In the name of all the readers of this posthumous

---

[1] Chapter II was published originally in the author's 'Studies in Memory of Paul Lapp', *HTR* 64 (1971), pp. 415–436. We are indebted to the editor of the *Harvard Theological Review* for giving us permission to reproduce this article here.

work, I am happy to pay a warm tribute to his patience and wisdom.

Although the great plan as a whole must unfortunately remain un-
fulfilled, it will be generally agreed that this study of the period of the
Judges forms a fitting close to the author's already published history of the
people of Israel from their earliest beginnings up to the time of their settlement in Canaan. For those of us who, as staff and students of the Ecole Biblique de Jérusalem, have for so long enjoyed the great privilege of benefiting
from Father de Vaux' teaching, guidance and fraternal co-operation, this
second French volume represents, despite its modest size, the last important
contribution to the sphere of Old Testament studies made by a man who
devoted his whole life to the Word of God and to the history of the people
of God. May its publication be a homage to his memory!

Jerusalem, November 1972.   R. TOURNAY, O.P.
                                          Director of the Ecole Biblique
                                          Archéologique Française

ABBREVIATIONS

AAA *Annals of Archaeology and Anthropology* Institute of Archaeology, University of Liverpool.

AAS *Les Annales Archéologiques de Syrie*, Damascus; from volume 18 (1968) onwards, the title has been *Annales Archéologiques Arabes Syriennes.*

AASOR *Annual of the American Schools of Oriental Research*, New Haven, Conn., later Cambridge, Mass.

ADAJ *Annual of the Department of Antiquities of Jordan*, Amman.

AFO *Archiv für Orientforschung*, Graz.

AJA *American Journal of Archaeology*, Princeton, N.J.

AJSL *American Journal of Semitic Languages and Literatures*, Chicago; continued by *JNES*.

ALT A. *Kleine Schriften* = A. Alt, *Kleine Schriften zur Geschichte des Volkes Israel*, I, 1953; II, 1953; III, 1959, Munich.

ANEP *The Ancient Near East in Pictures Relating to the Old Testament*, ed. J. B. Pritchard, Princeton, 2nd. edn., 1969.

ANET *Ancient Near Eastern Texts Relating to the Old Testament*, ed. J. B. Pritchard, Princeton, 3rd. edn., 1969.

AnStud. *Anatolian Studies*, London.

ARAB D. D. Luckenbill, *Ancient Records of Assyria and Babylonia*, I–II; *Ancient Records of Assyria*, Chicago, 1926–1927.

ARE J. H. Breasted, *Ancient Records of Egypt*, I–V, Chicago, 1906–1907.

ARM *Archives Royales de Mari*, edited under the direction of A. Parrot and G. Dossin, Paris, 1950–

ArOr *Archiv Orientální*, Prague.

ASAE *Annales du Service des Antiquités de l'Egypte*, Cairo.

ASTI *Annual of the Swedish Theological Institute* (Jerusalem), Leiden.

ATD *Das Alt Testament Deutsch*, Göttingen.

BASOR *Bulletin of the American Schools of Oriental Research*, New

	Haven, Conn., later Cambridge, Mass.
BCH	*Bulletin de Correspondance Hellénique*, Paris.
Bib	*Biblica*, Rome.
BibArch	*The Biblical Archaeologist*, New Haven, Conn., later Cambridge, Mass.
BIES	*Bulletin of the Israel Exploration Society*, Jerusalem; continuation of *BJPES*.
BIFAO	*Bulletin de l'Institut Français d'Archéologie Orientale*, Cairo.
BiOr	*Bibliotheca Orientalis*, Leiden.
BJPES	*Bulletin of the Jewish Palestine Exploration Society*, Jerusalem; continued by *BIES*.
BJRL	*Bulletin of the John Rylands Library*, Manchester.
BKAT	*Biblischer Kommentar. Altes Testament*, Neukirchen-Vluyn.
BMBeyr	*Bulletin du Musée de Beyrouth*, Paris.
BRIGHT J.	*History* = J. Bright, *A History of Israel*, Philadelphia, Pa., 1959.
BSA	*Annual of the British School at Athens*, London.
BZ	*Biblische Zeitschrift*, Paderborn.
BZAW	*Beihefte zur Zeitschrift für die Alttestamentliche Wissenschaft*, Berlin.
CAD	*Assyrian Dictionary of the Oriental Institute of the University of Chicago*, Chicago, 1956–
CAH	*Cambridge Ancient History*, revised edition, volumes I—II, Cambridge, 1961–[1]
CBQ	*Catholic Biblical Quarterly*, Washington, D.C.
ChrEg	*Chronique d'Egypte*, Brussels.
CRAI	*Académie des Inscriptions et Belles-Lettres. Comptes Rendus*, Paris.
DBS	*Dictionnaire de la Bible. Supplément*, ed. L. Pirot, A. Robert, H. Cazelles, Paris, 1928–
EA	J. A. Knudtzon, *Die El-Amarna-Tafeln*, Leipzig, 1908–1915.
EISSFELDT.O	*Einleitung*=O.Eissfeldt, *Einleitung in das Alte Testament*, Tübingen, 3rd. edn., 1964.
	Kleine Schriften=O.Eissfeldt, *Kleine Schriften*, ed. R. Sellheim, F. Maass, Tübingen, I, 1962; II, 1963; III, 1966; IV, 1968.
EstBibl	*Estudios Biblicos*, Madrid.
ETL	*Ephemerides Theologicae Lovanienses*, Gembloux.
EvTH	*Evangelische Theologie*, Munich.
ExpT	*Expository Times*, Edinburgh.
HAT	*Handbuch zum Alten Testament*, Tübingen.

[1] First published in instalments; my numbering of pages in the notes refers to these. The first ten chapters of Vol. 1 have now been bound and have continuous pagination.

HTR	Harvard Theological Review, Cambridge, Mass.
HUCA	Hebrew Union College Annual, Cincinnati.
IEJ	Israel Exploration Journal, Jerusalem.
JA	Journal Asiatique, Paris.
JAOS	Journal of the American Oriental Society, New Haven, Conn.
JbDAI	Jahrbuch des Deutschen Archäologischen Instituts, Berlin.
JBL	Journal of Biblical Literature, Philadelphia, Pa.
JCS	Journal of Cuneiform Studies, New Haven, Conn., later Cambridge, Mass.
JEA	Journal of Egyptian Archaeology, London.
JEOL	Jaarbericht van het vooraziatisch-egyptisch Genootschap, Ex Oriente Lux, Leiden.
JHS	Journal of Hellenic Studies, London.
JJS	Journal of Jewish Studies, London.
JKF	Jahrbuch für Kleinasiatische Forschung, Heidelberg.
JNES	Journal of Near Eastern Studies, Chicago; continuation of AJSL
JPOS	Journal of the Palestine Oriental Society, Jerusalem.
JQR	Jewish Quarterly Review, Philadelphia, Pa.
JRAS	Journal of the Royal Asiatic Society, London.
JSS	Journal of Semitic Studies, Manchester.
JTS	Journal of Theological Studies, Oxford.
KAI	H. Donner, W. Röllig, Kanaanäische und Aramäische Inschriften, I–III, Wiesbaden, 1962–1964.
MDAI	Mitteilungen des Deutschen Archäologischen Instituts. Abteilung Kario, Wiesbaden.
MDOG	Mitteilungen der Deutschen Orient-Gesellschaft, Berlin.
MGWJ	Monatsschrift für Geschichte und Wissenschaft des Judentums, Tübingen.
MIO	Mitteilungen des Instituts für Orientforschung, Berlin.
MJ	Museum Journal, University Museum, Philadelphia, Pa.
MUSJ	Mélanges de l'Université Saint-Joseph, Beirut.
MVAG	Mitteilungen der Vorderasiatisch-Aegyptischen Gesellschaft, Leipzig.
NOTH M.	History = M. Noth, The History of Israel, London, 1958. Überlieferungsgeschichte= M.Noth, Überlieferungsgeschichte des Pentateuch, Stuttgart, 1948. Uberlief. Studien= M.Noth, Überlieferungsgeschichtliche Studien. Die sammelnden und bearbeitenden Geschichtswerke im Alten Testament, Tübingen, 1943.
NRT	Nouvelle Revue Théologique, Tournai and Paris.
NTT	Nederlands Theologisch Tijdschrift, Wageningen.
OLZ	Orientalistische Literaturzeitung, Berlin.

OrAnt	Oriens Antiquus, Rome.
OTS	Oudtestamentische Studiën, Leiden.
PEFQS	Palestine Exploration Fund: Quarterly Statement, London.
PEQ	Palestine Exploration Quarterly, London; continuation of PEFQS.
PRU	Le Palais Royal d'Ugarit; II (C. Virolleaud); III and IV (J. Nougayrol; V (C. Virolleaud) = Mission Archéologique de Ras Shamra, VIII, VI, IX, XI, Paris, 1955–1965.
PW	Pauly-Wissowa, Realencyclopädie der classischen Altertumswissenschaft, Stuttgart.
QDAP	Quarterly of the Department of Antiquities in Palestine, Jerusalem.
RA	Revue d'Assyriologie et d'Archéologie Orientale, Paris.
RAr	Revue Archéologique, Paris.
RB	Revue Biblique, Paris.
REA	Revue des Etudes Anciennes, Bordeaux.
REG	Revue des Etudes Grecques, Paris.
REJ	Revue des Etudes Juives, Paris.
RGG	Die Religion in Geschichte und Gegenwart, Tübingen, 3rd edn., 1957–1965.
RHA	Revue Hittite et Asiatique, Paris.
RHPR	Revue d'Histoire et de Philosophie Religieuses, Paris.
RHR	Revue de l'Histoire des Religions, Paris.
RIDA	Revue Internationale des Droits de l'Antiquité, Brussels.
RLA	Reallexikon der Assyriologie, Berlin; later Leipzig, 1932–
RSO	Rivista degli Studi Orientali, Rome.
RSPT	Revue des Sciences Philosophiques et Théologiques, Paris.
RSR	Recherches de Science Religieuse, Paris.
ST	Studia Theologica, Oslo.
SVT	Supplements to Vetus Testamentum, Leiden.
TLZ	Theologische Literaturzeitung, Leipzig.
TR	Theologische Revue, Münster, Westphalia.
TWNT	Theologisches Wörterbuch zum Neuen Testament, ed. G. Kittel and G. Friedrich, Stuttgart, 1933–
TZ	Theologische Zeitschrift, Basle.
VAUX R.DE	Institutions= R. de Vaux, Les Institutions de l'Ancien Testament, I, Paris, 1961; II, Paris, 1967.
VD	Verbum Domini, Rome.
VT	Vetus Testamentum, Leiden.
WO	Die Welt des Orients, Göttingen.
WZKM	Wiener Zeitschrift für die Kunde des Morgenlandes, Vienna.
ZA	Zeitschrift für Assyriologie und Vorderasiatische Archäologie, Berlin.

ZAS	*Zeitschrift für Ägyptische Sprache und Altertumskunde*, Berlin.
ZAW	*Zeitschrift für Alttestamentliche Wissenschaft*, Berlin.
ZDMG	*Zeitschrift der Deutschen Morgenländischen Gesellschaft*, Wiesbaden.
ZDPV	*Zeitschrift des Deutschen Palästina-Vereins*, Leipzig, later Wiesbaden.
ZTK	*Zeitschrift für Theologie und Kirche*, Tübingen.

PROLOGUE

The Geographical,
Historical, Ethnical
and Cultural Environment

Chapter One

THE COUNTRY OF THE BIBLE

THE history of any people is connected in so many ways with the geography of the region in which they live. The physical structure of the land may attract or repel human settlement. It will determine the frontiers of a state and either favour or threaten the unity and stability of its institutions. The natural resources of the land will similarly determine what the people produce and therefore their trade at home and abroad. The climate will profoundly influence not only the economy and productivity of the people, but also their whole way of life and pattern of behaviour. All these factors will have a decisive effect on the density of the population and on the social psychology of the inhabitants of the land. The country's geographical position within a much wider environment which is largely or slightly [to a greater or lesser extent] different [from itself] will govern the people's peaceful or hostile relationships with its neighbours. It will also make it easier or more difficult to exchange ideas about technical progress, art, culture and religion with those neighbours.

This does not necessarily mean that a people's history can be completely explained in terms of the natural geography of its land. Human history is, after all, shaped by free decisions and by spontaneous actions taken by individuals and groups of men – which is, of course, why so much that is unexpected occurs in history. It is also always determined, especially in the case of the 'chosen people', by God – which is why so much that is mysterious occurs in the history of Israel. Ultimately, however, human will and caprice have to give way to the demands of nature, which God himself uses to carry out his plans. For these and other reasons, then, it is important to give careful attention to the country in which the people of the Bible settled and lived if we are to understand their history fully.[1]

[1] The general works that are essential for a knowledge of the geography of Palestine are: G. A. Smith, *The Historical Geography of the Holy Land, especially in relation to the History of Israel and of the Early Church*, London, 1894, with many later editions (a standard work which is, despite the title, more descriptive than historical in its approach); F.-M. Abel, *Géographie de la Palestine*, Paris, I, 1933, II, 1938, new impression 1967 (a classic work which is above all

I. THE NAME

Every geographical name given to the country raises a number of questions. Both in the Christian tradition and in ordinary usage, the name Palestine has been common and has persisted until the present. This term[2] was first borrowed from the language used by the imperial administration of Rome and Byzantium. After the revolt of Bar Cochba in A.D. 135, the Roman province of Judaea was renamed Palestinian Syria. During the reform of Diocletian, ca. A.D. 295, the southern part of the province of Arabia was added to this province of Palestinian Syria and, round about the year A.D. 400, this enlarged territory was divided into three provinces. The provinces of *Palaestina prima* and *secunda* were west of the River Jordan and the province of *Palaestina tertia* was east of the Jordan and north of the Arnon.

The Romans had not invented this name. Herodotus called the southern region of Syria, from Phoenicia to Egypt and between the sea and the Arab lands, either Palestinian Syria or simply Palestine. The Greek name was derived from *Palastu* (and similar forms), the country of the Philistines as it appeared in Assyrian documents from about 800 B.C. onwards, or from the name for Philistaea as it appears in the Hebrew Bible, *p'lešeth*.[3] In the extended sense in which it was used by the Greeks and the Romans, Palestine meant, broadly speaking, the 'country of the Bible', but it was not used as such by the biblical authors themselves.

In fact, there is no one established name in the Old Testament for the country inhabited by the Israelites. The expression *'eres yiš rā'el*, 'country' or 'land' of Israel, became widespread because of its use in the rabbinical writings and was later raised to an official status when the State of Israel

---

historical); D. Baly, *The Geography of the Bible*, London, 1959 (an excellent guide to the country and its history); E. Orni and E. Efrat, *Geography of Israel, Jerusalem*, 1966 (physical, human and economic geography of the State of Israel); Y. Aharoni, *The Land of the Bible. A Historical Geography*, London, 1967 (almost exclusively historical).

Special aspects of the 'geography' of the Holy Land are dealt with in; F. S. Bodenheimer, *Animal Life in Palestine*, Jerusalem, 1935 (animal ecology and zoogeography); L. Picard, *Structure and Evolution of Palestine*, Jerusalem, 1943 (geology); M. Zohary, *Plant Life of Palestine. Israel and Jordan*, New York, 1962 (vegetation related to types of soil, the climate and man).

For geographical accuracy, the best atlases are: L. H. Grollenberg, *Atlas of the Bible*, New York, 1956 (editions in Dutch, German and French; new revised French edition, *Grand Atlas de la Bible*, Paris, 1962); H. G. May, with R. W. Hamilton and G. N. S. Hunt, *Oxford Bible Atlas*, London, 1962; *Atlas of Israel: Cartography, Physical Geography, History, Demography, Economics, Education*, first published in instalments between 1956 and 1964 by the State of Israel; the most complete atlas of all is D. Baly and A. D. Tushingham, *Atlas of the Biblical World*, New York, 1971 (this is the only atlas covering all the countries of the Bible, but, apart from the title and the list of contents, it is entirely in modern Hebrew).

[2] M. Noth, 'Zur Geschichte des Namens Palästina', *ZDPV*, 62 (1939), pp. 125–144.

[3] Exod. 15:14; Isa 14:29, 31 and in later texts.

was founded. It occurs quite rarely in the Bible, however, and when it is used there it is applied to the whole country and not simply to the Northern Kingdom of Israel.[4] A similar term, *"dk̊math yiśrā'el*, 'land' or 'earth' of Israel, is peculiar to Ezekiel, where it occurs seventeen times. *'Eres* and *ᵃdk̊math yiśrā'el* are not synonymous. The first, when followed by the name of a people, is a term of political geography. The second is more than that – it is a descriptive term, derived from the word *"dhāmah*, earth or ground, and means the good soil or land inhabited by the people of Israel.[5]

The country in which the patriarchs stayed, which was promised to their descendants and which those descendants occupied is known in Genesis, Numbers and Joshua as the 'country' or 'land' of Canaan. This geographical term, which I shall discuss later in this work,[6] covers more or less the whole territory in which the tribes settled or to which they laid claim. This name, however, was never used for the country once the Israelites had occupied it and were governing it.

In the absence of a name, Deuteronomy calls this country, some fifteen times with slightly variant readings,[7] 'the land that I swore to give to your fathers', 'I', of course, being Yahweh. This formula recurs in the Deuteronomic editing of the book of Joshua, Jos. 1:1; 5:6, the editor believing that this promise was fulfilled at the time of the entry into Canaan (cf. Judges 2:1) by the conquest of Joshua and the apportioning of the territory (Jos. 21:43–45). The frontiers of this 'promised land' had already been outlined by the Yahwist author of Genesis as being 'from the wadi of Egypt to the Great River, the Euphrates' (Gen. 15:18). These were the frontiers of Solomon's empire, according to the editor of 1 Kings 5:1; 'from the river to the Egyptian border'.[8] According to Deuteronomy, the promised land had very much the same limits – from the wilderness to the Lebanon and from the River Euphrates to the Western Sea (Deut. 11:24)[9] or the land of Canaan and the Lebanon as far as the Euphrates (Deut. 1:7). In the latter passage, the districts of the 'land of Canaan' are enumerated – the highlands of the Amorites, the 'Arabah, the highlands, the lowlands, the Negeb and the coastland.

---

[4] 1 Sam 13:19; Ezek 40:2; 47:18; 1 Chron 22:2; 2 Chron 2:16.
[5] For the meaning of *'Eres* and *ᵃdhâ mah*, see L. Rost, 'Die Bezeichnungen für Land und Volk im Alten Testament', *Festschrift O. Procksch*, Leipzig, 1934, pp. 125–148 = *Das kleine Credo und andere Studien zum Alten Testament*, Heidelberg, 1965, pp. 76–101.
[6] See below, p. 127.
[7] Deut 1:35; 6:18, 23; 8:1; 9:5; 10:11; 11:9, 21; 26:3, 15; 28:11; 31:7, 20; 34:4.
[8] The 'land of the Philistines' is a gloss in this verse, probably corresponding to the 'Palestine' of the Persian and Greek period from which the duplication in verse 4 dates: 'all Transeuphrates from Tiphsah (on the Euphrates) to Gaza (on the Egyptian border'.)
[9] Repeated in Jos. 1:4; despite the uncertainty regarding the details of the text, this is, I am sure, the basic meaning.

II. FRONTIERS

The frontiers of this land of Canaan which was promised to the Israelites are given in the priestly account (Num. 34:2–12) and in Ezek. 47:15–20, with certain variants. Both of these texts indicate the boundaries of the territory which had to be distributed among the tribes. Since we cannot be absolutely certain about the precise location of the places mentioned, two suggestions have been made concerning the northern limits of the territory. The first does not go beyond Upper Galilee, whereas the other includes part of the Lebanon. The eastern frontier is formed by the Jordan, from Lake Tiberias to the Dead Sea, with the result that the tribes of Reuben and Gad and the half-tribe of Manasseh, which, according to the priestly account (Num. 34:14–15), settled in the land east of the Jordan, were not included in this allocation of land. According to the more utopian distribution outlined in Ezek. 48, on the other hand, they were given their share on the west bank of the river. In both accounts, the territories beyond the Jordan are not included as part of Canaan or the promised land. They are regarded as being outside the 'territory of Yahweh' as described in the story of the construction of the altar by the eastern tribes, the Reubenites, the Gadites and the half-tribe of Manasseh, in Jos. 22:9–34.

The accounts of the apportioning of the land among the tribes in Numbers and Ezekiel come from a different tradition from the account in Jos. 13–19, which provides the best source of information about the distribution of the territory at the period of the Judges that we possess. The lists of towns contained in Jos. 13–19 are of a more recent date, but the outline of the frontiers of the land belonging to each tribe goes back to a document that may well be earlier than the monarchy. The situation described in the book of Joshua is somewhat later and is ideal rather than realistic. In other words, it provides us with a picture of the territory that the tribes were claiming rather than with the reality of the land that they in fact occupied.

The most important aspect of this for us is that this territory represents, in the eyes of the editor, everything that the tribes 'received as an inheritance' (Jos. 14:1), 'all the land he (Yahweh) had sworn to give to their fathers' (Jos. 21:43). The western boundary was the sea. The southern frontier extended from the brook of Egypt (the Wādī el-'Arīsh) to the extremity of the Dead Sea, the line describing a full curve southwards to include Kadesh. The northern frontier was somewhat vaguer. It certainly included Dan at the foot of Mount Hermon, but it is difficult to say precisely whether it was supposed to reach the Mediterranean along the course of the Nahr el-Qāsimīyeh to the north of Tyre or at Rās en-Nāqūrah to the south of Tyre. The tribes which settled to the east of the Jordan received a territory bounded on the south by the Arnon (this separated them from Moab), on the east by the desert or by the frontiers of Ammon and on the north by the land of Bashan. These boundaries were never reached completely by the Israelite occupation – the Phoenicians and the Philistines were never entirely dispossessed – but they were crossed on the north-west and the east during the periods of political expansion, when foreign territories were annexed.

Apart from describing the geographical limits of the whole country, the texts make use of certain distinctive expressions to indicate the extremities of the land in the north and the south. According to Num. 13:21, for example, the scouts sent to reconnoitre the promised land went from the wilderness of Sin to the Lebo'–Hamath, the Entrance to Hamath. This place,[10] which is also named as the northern frontier in Num 34:8, is one of the terms in the formula 'from the Pass of Hamath to the wadi of Egypt', defining the limits of the kingdom of David and Solomon (1 Kings 8:65 = 2 Chron. 7:8). Similarly, it is also one of the two terms defining the extent of the territory reconquered by Jeroboam II, 'from the Pass of Hamath as far as the Sea of the 'Arabah' (2 Kings 14:25). It also recurs, with slight variants, in 1 Chron. 13:5, referring to David, and in Amos 6:14 (Amos prophesied during the reign of Jeroboam II). A more constant formula is 'from Dan to Beersheba'. This marked the limits of the whole territory occupied by the Israelites, the two terms denoting the two sanctuaries farthest away from the centre of the territory, during the period of the Judges and at the beginning of the monarchy (see Amos 8:14).[11] It is possible that this formula was abandoned when these two places of worship were condemned (see the same text in Amos).

We should not be surprised by the failure of the authors of the Old Testament to recognise a specific name for the country in which the history of the people unfolded itself. It was, after all, a history that was always changing. It was in turn the history of a group of tribes, of a unified people, of two different nations and of a religious community living under the yoke of a foreign power. These political variations are, of course, partly explained by the prevailing geographical conditions in a country which was not sharply divided from the surrounding districts and which was itself geographically very diverse.

[10] Although it is generally translated as the 'Entrance to' or the 'Pass of Hamath', it is really the name of a town and not that of a district; see M. Noth, 'Das Reich von Hamath als Grenznachbar des Reiches Israel', PJB, 33 (1937), especially pp. 49–51; B. Maisler (Mazar), 'Lebo Hamath and the Northern Boundary of Canaan', BJPES, 12 (1945–1946), pp. 91–102 (in Hebrew, with an English summary); this place is now called Labweh and is at one of the sources of the Orontes to the north of Ba'albek.

[11] Judges 20:1; Sam. 3:20; 2 Sam. 3:10; 17:11; 24:2, 15; 1 Kings 5:5; in 2 Chron. 30:5, describing events during the reign of Hezekiah, the formula occurs as 'from Beersheba to Dan'.

III. PHYSICAL GEOGRAPHY

The land of Canaan forms the western and southern tip of a great semi-circle of arable land surrounding the Syrian desert and known as the Fertile Crescent. It is, however, the least fertile part of this crescent, which becomes narrower at this point, where it terminates on the verge of another desert, Sinai. The country of the Bible can more exactly be said to form the southernmost third of the descending part of the Fertile Crescent on the west, between the Mediterranean Sea and the desert. It is a wide strip of land with an apparently unified structure and with its main features orientated from the south to the north, thus forming four distinctive and parallel natural regions.

In the extreme west there is the coastal plain, extending in a more or less straight line from Raphia and beyond the land of the Bible as far north as the Gulf of Alexandretta. To the east of this there is a parallel range of subcoastal mountains, including, from south to north, the hill country of Judah and of Galilee, the Lebanon Mountains, Jebel el-Ansārīyeh and the Amanus Mountains, the last link in the chain of the Taurus massif. Thirdly, there is a line of central depressions, forming what is often called the rift valley and extending from the 'Arabah in the south, through the Dead Sea and the Jordan Valley to the Beqā' or 'depressions' and the valley of the Orontes beyond Canaan in the north. Finally, there is a second parallel chain of hills to the east of this rift valley. The chief elevations of this Transjordanian range become more and more widely separated as one proceeds northwards beyond the Holy Land. They include the Sherā', the Jebel, the Belqā, Jebel 'Ajlūn, Mount Hermon, the Anti-Lebanon range, Jebel Zawīyeh and Jebel Sime'ān. These heights form the edge of a great desert plateau which slopes gently down on the eastern side.

Although this small country – it is no more than 500 miles long and 95 miles wide – is clearly divided into several distinct parts, its special character and above all its obvious natural frontiers give it a certain unity. The western boundary is formed by the sea. In the east and south-east, the frontier is the desert, which begins about 25 miles east of the line traced by the Jordan and the Dead Sea. The southern limit of the country is less precise. It is possible to define it either by drawing a line from Gaza through Beersheba to the southernmost end of the Dead Sea, or else by beginning at the mouth of the Wādi el-'Arish, 50 miles south of Gaza, and encircling the Negeb semi-desert. In the north, it is possible to choose between two natural frontiers. The first of these is formed by the course of the Nahr el-Qāsimīyeh and extended as far as the foot of Mount Hermon to include the two main sources of the Jordan. The second is farther south and runs from Rās en-Nāqūrah on the coast to the north of Acco ('Akkā) to the northern tip of Lake Hūleh. These frontiers which are formed by the physical geography of the region are in fact very similar to those indicated in the most sober accounts contained in the Bible, for example, the account of the distribution of the land in Jos. 13–19. The limits indicated in other biblical texts, from Dan to Beersheba or to the Brook of Egypt (Wādi el-ʿArīsh), are also very close to the natural frontiers.

Although the land of the Bible is hardly bigger than Belgium and much smaller than Switzerland, it is geographically much more diverse than both of those countries. The coast runs in a straight line as far as the promontory formed by Mount Carmel and this stretch provides no natural harbour at all, the only fairly good anchorage being at Jaffa. This is in striking contrast to the much more indented coastline of Phoenicia and northern Syria. The first real bay occurs to the north of the Carmel promontory, but even this was too open and sandy to serve as a good harbour until the modern port of Haifa was installed. Even so, there was an ancient trading establishment at Haifa and a port and maritime establishment at Acco (Acre) at the northern extremity of the bay, but neither of these ever belonged to the Israelites. Parallel to the coastline is a long row of dunes, the oldest of which are solidified *kurkar*. Beyond these dunes and further inland there is an alluvial plain which is sufficiently watered to be quite fertile. In the south, this plain is known as the Plain of Philistia. Its northern extremity is broken by the heights of Jaffa and then continues northwards as the Plain of Sharon, when it is again broken by the promontory of Carmel.

Between this alluvial plain and the Cisjordan hill country, there is in the south a range of limestone hills formed in the eocene period. This range is known as the Lowland or the Shephelah in the Bible and is still good farmland where cereals, the olive and the vine are cultivated as basic crops. This transitional zone is separated from the Judaean hills of the Cenomanian level by a fault, within which the intermediary stage of the Senonian level is visible, a soft limestone which has been dug out by the water into a trench which protects the hill country, but which also branches out eastwards. The most important of these branches is the Valley of Aijalon and Bethhoron, which provides access to the highlands.

The crest of the central chain of mountains is reached in three stages after a steep climb. It is a limestone range of the Cenomanian level, predominantly brown in appearance, deeply fissured and with sharp ridges. It has preserved its covering of Senonian limestone with gently sloping whitish undulations in places on the western slopes and almost continuously on the eastern face as low as the Jordan Valley. This Judaean chain rises quite abruptly to the south of Hebron (el-Khalil) after a subsidence which is clearly visible in the Negeb, where the same natural formations are present, but at a much lower altitude and pointing in the direction south-west and north-east.

To the north of Hebron, the altitude is greater, usually more than 3,000 feet. The Mount of Olives, east of Jerusalem for example, is 2,684 feet high, whereas Jebel el-ʿAsūr, north of Bethel, is 3,332 feet above sea level. Water has carved out numerous thalwegs on both sides of the range and has formed small plains where generous alluvia of red soil have made it possible for fields and orchards to be established on the western slope, more copiously watered. There are also vineyards and olive groves on the hills and the peaks are sparsely covered with scrub of the *garrigue* type found in the Mediterranean. The eastern slope is much steeper and drier. It is only when winter is past that it is covered with grass, among which flowers grow. Very soon, however, it reassumes the characteristic appearance of the so-called Wilderness of Judah – brown ridges cut by deep wadis which are dry for most of the season. It is a beautiful landscape, but austere and very poor and unsuited to arable farming. It is a land of shepherds and goatherds.

About 30 miles north of Jerusalem, at Lubban, the countryside changes again on entering Samaria. The central highlands are broken by a series of faults running from the south-east to the north-west and this collision between two systems has resulted in the suppression of the Shephelah in the west and the emergence of small plains enclosed within deeply carved out deposits of the eocene and Senonian levels and now reduced to little whitish hills. Mount Ebal, however, rises to 3,077 feet and it is between this mountain and Mount Gerizim to the south that the pass of Shechem (modern Nāblus) runs. The Cenomanian massif continues further on the eastern slopes, but it is cut by another fault running from the south-east to the north-west, along which the Wādi el-Fārʿah flows down to the Jordan.

A third great fault separates Samaria from Lower Galilee. The Plain of Esdraelon, a very fertile depression consisting of decomposed limestone and basalt rocks, was caused by this third fault. On the west, it is separated from the Plain of Acco by the gorge of Sheikh Abreiq, through which runs the Nahr el-Muqattaʿ (Qishōn), the river which drains the plain. On the east, it is connected by an elevation of only 210 feet at ʿAffūleh with the valley of the Nahr el-Jālūd and along this river valley with the Jordan Valley at Beisān. At this point, there is no sign of the central highlands, which have completely disappeared. Mount Carmel, rising on the southern flank of this great depression, reduces the coastal plain here to a narrow strip of land. The wooded peak of the mountain juts out into the sea, forming the only cape on the coastline.

North of the Plain of Esdraelon, the land rises again, although the peaks are less sharply defined, at least to the immediate north. Mount Tabor reaches the modest height of 1,843 feet and is only conspicuous because of its isolated position on the plain and because the hill on which Nazareth is situated is less than 1,600 feet high. None of the hill country of Lower Galilee is higher than this. The Cenomanian limestone has been gouged out in all directions at this point by deep faults and eaten away by erosion, so all that remains are small hills and fertile plains. The most important of these plains lies east and west and is known as the Sahl el-Baṭṭōf. The countryside is pleasant here, the only dark features being the flows of basalt which spread to the west and south west of Lake Tiberias. Lower Galilee is altogether richer than Judah and much more suited to agriculture.

At the latitude of Acco, there is a sudden elevation to the country of Upper Galilee. The ground rises quickly here to 3,536 feet (Jebel el-'Arūs) and then to the highest point in the Cisjordanian range, Jebel Jermaq, 3,963 feet. Both these mountains are on a watershed which follows the south-north direction of the Judaean range. On the western slopes of the hills are parallel transverse folds which, northwards from Rās en-Nāqūrah, go as far as the sea. On the eastern side, however, the slope has quite a different structure, descending in steps to the upper valley of the Jordan. Upper Galilee is widely afforested. The entire massif descends towards the north and then ceases at a line formed by the course of the Nahr el-Qāsimīyeh, which flows from east to west, and by the depression of Merj'oyūn. The horizon is cut off here by the southern extremity of the Lebanon range and Mount Hermon. This is the point where one geographical region ends and another begins.

The most distinctive feature of the country of the Bible is the rift valley of the River Jordan and the Dead Sea. Although this rift valley forms part of the great fault running from the north of Syria as far south as the African lakes, it has certain distinct characteristics. The Syrian Beqā'to the north is formed from a single geological fault on the western side and has a constant positive elevation. Unlike the Beqā', the Jordan rift is the result of subsidence between two parallel faults. This depression reaches its maximum depth at the Dead Sea, the bottom of which is almost 2,600 feet below the level of the Mediterranean at the deepest point in the northern part of the lake. It is all that remains of an inland sea which once stretched northwards as far as Lake Tiberias, but which gradually dried up in the part now known as el-Ghōr, between the present Dead Sea and Lake Tiberias.

The water of the Dead Sea contains not only an unusual quantity of marine salt, sodium chloride, but also other chlorides such as magnesium, calcium and potassium, as well as bromide. From time to time, almost pure blocks of asphalt float from underwater crevasses to the surface. This, together with the warm and sulphurous springs on the steep east bank of the Sea, is clear evidence of the instability of the subsoil here. No organic life can survive in the Dead Sea. Water enters from the Jordan, from the rivers and wadis that flow into the Sea from the Cisjordanian and Transjordanian hills, from the various underwater springs and from springs along the banks. This inflow, however, is balanced by the intensive rate of evaporation that takes place in this overheated basin, with the result that the water level varies by no more than a few feet, remaining at about 1,280 feet below that of the Mediterranean and following a cycle of almost a century, corresponding to slow variations in the average rainfall.

The floor of the ancient inland lake is now, as I have said, the valley of the River Jordan. This river has several sources at the foot of Mount Hermon and these rivulets flow through the little swampy basin of Lake Hūleh, which was formed by the damming up of the flow of basalt which came down from the volcanic area known as the Jōlān. Here the Jordan is at the same level as the Mediterranean, but, as soon as it leaves Lake Hūleh, it begins to descend in cascades over the basalt until it reaches Lake Tiberias, a lake which abounds in fish and is no less than 685 feet below sea level. After leaving Tiberias and being joined by its tributary, the Wādi Yarmuk (or Sherī'at el-Menādireh), which doubles its volume of water, the Jordan begins to flow much more slowly. It now enters the part of the valley called in Arabic el-Ghōr or 'lowland'.

The first half of this valley, as far as the gorge before the points where the Wādi ez-Zerqā (or Jabbok River) flows from the east and the Wādi el-Far'ah flows from the west into the Jordan, is sufficiently well watered and is therefore not totally uninhabitable. The river is not enclosed between high banks in this northern half of its course through the Ghōr and it can easily be crossed at several points by fords. South of the narrows, however, the distinctive character of the valley is fully revealed. Oases are to be found at the foot of the mountains flanking the river, either where the soil is watered by a spring or else because the shore is a so-called river oasis. The three most important oases in the Jordan valley are Khirbet Fasā'il (Phasaelis), Khirbet 'Auja et-Tahta (Archelais) and, above all, the oasis of Jericho (modern Erīha).

Apart from these oases, pasture land is provided by a strip of steppe, which can also be cultivated if the soil is washed sufficiently to free it of salt and is kept irrigated. Closer to the river, a lunar landscape known as the qattara is entered quite abruptly. This consists of sediment from the ancient inland lake which has not been changed by alluvia, a salty and gypseous marl cut into small mounds and flat surfaces. This land is quite barren. Nearer to the river there is another sharp contrast – the bed of the Jordan itself, known as ez-Zōr. This is a thicket of low brushwood where wild boars wallow in the muddy soil and which was inhabited by lions until the Middle Ages. The turbid river has countless meanders here, making it three times as long as it would be if it flowed in a straight line. It is not wide – when it is not in flood it is only about 60 to 100 feet across – but it is very deep in places, its course is very rapid and there are few fords. The northern part of the valley and the river can be regarded as forming a link between the Cisjordanian and the Transjordanian regions. The desert-like character of the river valley, the impenetrable thicket and the river itself, which is so difficult to ford, however, mean that the southern half serves as a barrier between the west and east banks.

South of the Dead Sea the rift continues as far as the Red Sea. This is, of course, also part of the same geological structure, although a secondary movement has obliterated the western fault here and driven masses of Senonian and Cenomanian limestone towards the eastern flank of the rift. The bottom of the valley rises appreciably some 70 miles south of the Dead Sea at the elevation of Risht el-Hauwār, which is 820 feet above the level of the Mediterranean. It then descends again to el-'Aqabah and the Red Sea about 45 miles farther south. The whole rift formation of desert valley with intermittent points of water and deposits of copper on the sides is known in Arabic as el-'Arabah.

To the east of the 'Arabah rift is the Transjordan plateau. This forms part of the immense Syro-Arabian shelf which, in swinging over to the east, caused the rupture of its opposite edge which ceased, with this movement, to be vertical. It was this tilting movement which resulted in the rift and it also explains why the two sides of the Jordan Valley are so different from each other. Although the geological formations are the same, the eastern side is higher and the lower levels of the deposits in horizontal strata are clearly revealed at the base of this escarpment. From the elevation at Risht el-Hauwār as far as the Red Sea, the rocks which border the rift at these lower levels are crystalline, granite and so on, and this continues well into Arabia. Farther north, the same rocks are also exposed by the transverse fault of the Wādi Dana. Above and behind these rocks, the sandstone is revealed and it is, of course, this that forms the massif of Petra. From the Wādi Dana northwards sandstone is visible everywhere on the Transjordanian side. The cliff along the eastern bank of the Dead Sea and the gully of the Jabbok River of Wādi ez-Zerqā are also of sandstone. The limestone covering is only visible in the Transjordan hinterland from this part of the valley and it is only much farther north when the basalt flows down from the Haurān to the rift that it can be seen closer to the valley.

The Transjordanian plateau has been cut into sections by mountain streams which, in their downward course into the rift valley, have dug out deep gullies running in an east-west direction. The most important of these torrents are the Wādi el-Hesā (the Brook Zered) at the southern end of the Dead Sea, the Seil el-Mōjib (Arnon), which flows into the Dead Sea through a narrow cañon, the Wādi ez-Zerqā (Jabbok) midway between the Dead Sea and Lake Tiberias, and finally the Sherī.'at el-Menādireh (Yarmuk), just south of Lake Tiberias. The plateau is less high at the north of the Jordan Valley than it is at the south, but it is always higher than the corresponding part of the Cisjordanian range. The mountains of Edom south of the Brook Zered are the highest, reaching more than 5,500 feet around Petra. The Moabite plateau between the Brook Zered and the Arnon rises to more than 4,250 feet at the south and 3,250 at the north. In the

Belqa, Mount Nebo hardly tops 2,500 feet, like the Mount of Olives which is almost directly opposite it on the other side of the valley, but Jebel 'Ammān and Jebel Osha' both attain a height of 3,500 feet. North of the Jabbok, the round top of the 'Ajlūn is more than 4,000 feet high, after which the heights become progressively less towards the Yarmuk south of Lake Tiberias. To the north of this river, however, the Transjordan hills become higher again, rising to 3,250 feet or more in a series of cone-shaped basalt mountains which describe an arc round the two lakes, Hūleh and Tiberias.

From a rapid glance at the map, one would think that the streams which divide the Transjordan plateau into sections would at the same time have served to separate the land politically. Generally speaking, however, this has not been the case. With the exception of the Zered, almost all of these natural frontiers have in fact cut into two regions which had the same physical structure and the same economy. All these natural regions have features which are quite different from those on the western side of the rift valley. This contrast becomes more pronounced the farther south one goes. In the north, there is Bashan, extending from the foot of Mount Hermon to the two banks of the Yarmuk. This is a land of great open plains with soil that is mainly composed of volcanic alluvia and particularly suitable for the cultivation of cereals. To the south of Bashan is Gilead, a Cenomanian massif cut into two halves by the valley of the Jabbok, a mountainous region with many natural springs, wooded ridges, slopes covered with good quality vines and valleys where the olive tree, which is rare elsewhere in Transjordan, grows well. The oleander also grows in these valleys. This shrub is common in all the valleys and gorges on the eastern bank of the Jordan, but almost unknown on the other side of the river.

Still farther south, the plateau which borders the Dead Sea and which used to be the territory of Ammon and Moab is again cut in two by the Arnon and the land is very similar on both sides of this river. The river itself descends very rapidly to the sandstone cliff and then plunges into the sea below. It is on this shelf above the Dead Sea that the towns and water points are to be found and the cereals that grow on the flat summit depend on rain which becomes less and less the farther east one goes. Eventually one reaches the steppe, which is covered with grass in the winter, and finally the desert. This country is above all suitable for flocks of sheep and goats, which roam about in search of grazing land and water holes.

South of the Dead Sea, along the 'Arabah, the country changes again. This was the land of the Edomites. The rim of the plateau is sharply raised here, forming a barrier against the clouds and collecting the rain. Deep crevasses have formed, crossing valleys and gullies where springs rise and some agriculture is possible. Because of this rain-collecting barrier, the steppe is closer here than anywhere else in the whole region and Edom in fact gives the impression of being a tongue extended between two deserts. It never has been a region in which either cattle were bred or crops cultivated, but copper has always been mined in the 'Arabah and it has always provided access to the Red Sea and has been the main route for caravans going north from Arabia and westward towards Gaza and Egypt. As a region, Edom's future lay in trade and commerce. This potential was not fully realised until the coming of the Nabateans.

IV. CLIMATE

The climate of the land of the Bible is conditioned by its geographical position and its contours. Because the country is situated between the Mediterranean Sea and the Arabian desert, it is influenced by both. The transition from a maritime climate of the Mediterranean type along the coastline to a continental climate of the Syrian type on the steppe is made less smooth, however, by the series of structural features running parallel to the coast which were discussed in the preceding section. These features above all have the effect of altering the temperature and the distribution of the rainfall.

The rainfall increases as one goes from the south to the north of the country; in other words, as one goes farther away from Arabia and Africa. It also becomes less as one goes from west to east – the farther away one goes from the sea. It increases as one climbs the western slopes of the hills which run the length of the country and decreases on the eastern slopes. The temperature falls as the altitude increases and it tends to rise as one moves towards the south or towards the desert. There are more extreme daily and annual variations in temperature in the highlands and in the east of the land. The climate of the country of the Bible can therefore be grouped conveniently in four different regions, which correspond broadly to the four regions classified above according to physical structure.

1. On the coastal plain and the Plain of Esdraelon, the summers are warm, the average temperature being 25°C. There is no rain, but high humidity on the coastal strip, and the daily variations in temperature are only very slight. In winter, the average temperature is 13°C, but the thermometer can descend as low as 5°C. Snowfall is quite exceptional. The rainfall at Gaza is less than 15 inches, whereas on the plains of Sharon and Esdraelon it is much higher, reaching 20 to 25 inches. The highest rainfall in this coastal region is at Haifa – almost 30 inches.

2. The annual variation in temperature in the Cisjordan range is much greater, the average in summer being 23°C and in winter 10°C. The daily variation in summer at least is greater here than on the coast. Snow is not

unknown. It falls more or less every other year, but hardly ever remains lying for more than a few days. Hebron has about 20 inches of rain, but twice as much each year falls on Mount Jermaq and in Upper Galilee generally. For more than a century, the annual precipitation has been measured in Jerusalem and the average has been calculated over this period at 22 inches. On the eastern slopes of the Judaean hills, on the other hand, the average can be as low as 10 inches.

3. In the rift valley, the mean summer temperatures are 29°C at Lake Tiberias, 30°C at Jericho and 32°C at el-'Aqabah. The mean winter temperatures at the same places are 14°C, 15°C and 16°C respectively. From the north of the central depression to the south, there is a rapid decrease in rainfall. There is an annual precipitation of 15 to 20 inches at Lake Tiberias, mainly because there is no natural barrier against the Mediterranean winds at this point. At Beisān, which is only a little farther south, on the other hand, the rainfall is hardly ever more than 10 inches. South of the confluence of the Jabbok and the Jordan and because it is sheltered by the hills of Judah, the Ghōr has a rainfall of barely 5 inches a year. This is approximately the same rainfall as that of the Negeb. On the shores of the Dead Sea and along the 'Arabah, far less than 5 inches of rain falls each year.

4. Metereological observations in the Transjordan highland have not been carried out for a sufficiently long period for the figures obtained to be entirely reliable. It is therefore difficult to compare temperature and precipitation in this region with those in the Cisjordan region. All that can safely be said is that the winters are much colder and that the road from Amman to Jerusalem, for example, is for a short period blocked by snow almost every year. In summer, on the other hand, although the nights are cool, it is warmer during the daytime than in the hill country of Judah. Since the edge of the Transjordan plateau is higher than the corresponding highland of the Cisjordan region, as much rain falls there as in the country west of the rift valley and it is more evenly distributed. Sometimes, despite the distance from the sea, more rain falls on the Transjordan tableland than on the Judaean hills – for example, it rains more at es-Salt than in Jerusalem. The contrast between the Transjordan and the Cisjordan is even more strik-ing in the territories occupied in biblical times by the Moabites and the Edomites which are opposite to the semi-desert region of the Negeb. In the region of el-Kerak and in that of el-Shōbak, for instance, more than 15 inches of rain fall each year.

These mean temperatures do not, however, give us an exact idea of the climate of the country of the Bible nor of its effects on man. The extreme temperatures have also to be borne in mind, together with the daily and an-nual differences in temperature and the degree of humidity or dryness. The climate at the coast is enervating. In Jericho, it is extremely pleasant in the winter, but exhausting in the summer. In the hill country of Judah, the climate is in every way excellent – never too cold and never too hot, whereas on the other side of the rift valley, on the Transjordan plateau, it is harsher and the seasonal contrasts are more pronounced, with an icy wind from the desert in winter and a constant dry heat in summer.

To judge from the mean annual rainfall – Jerusalem, for instance, receiving as much rain in good years as London or Paris – a great deal of the country of the Bible would seem to have quite sufficient rain. But the mean annual precipitation gives no real picture of the distribution of the rain throughout the course of each year or of its great irregularity. There are, for instance, only two seasons – a wet season, the winter, and a dry season, the summer. The rain begins to fall in October or November, when there are sudden showers followed by days of fair weather. The rainy days increase in number in December until the wettest period is reached in January and February. In March, there is a sharp decrease in rainfall and very little rain at all in April. The light rainfall in March and April guarantees success in the harvest. The wet and dry seasons are separated from each other by transitional periods, the first lasting from the second half of September until the end of October and the second beginning in May and ending in early June. Both the winds and the temperature are very unstable during these periods of transition. Again and again, the wind from the east or south-east blows for two, three or four days, seldom longer, with varying intensity during these periods. This east wind is known as *esh-Sherqīyeh* ('east') or the sirocco. It is hot and sultry and often full of fine dust. It dries everything up, making the vegetation wither and die, darkening the horizon and producing an effect of intense irritation in human beings. As soon as the west wind returns, the sirocco ceases, the temperature falls and, in the first transition period of September and October, there may be rain.

There may be a few rainstorms in May, but these are rare and the month really forms part of the dry season. Summer proper begins in the middle of June and lasts until the middle of September. It is characterised by extreme regularity. Each day, the temperature begins to rise rapidly as soon as the sun has risen, but very soon after this a wind begins to blow from the west or north-west, gently in the morning, but more strongly towards the end of the afternoon and the beginning of the night. This wind has the effect of cooling down the atmosphere. It brings no rain and very few clouds, but it is very damp and this condenses into dew at the beginning and at the end of the dry season especially. In the mornings, this dew can often be seen sparkling on plants and running from the roofs of houses. It plays a very important part in the agricultural life of the country.

Another very important factor is the sunniness of the climate. The sky is seldom completely covered with clouds and when it is, it is only for a short time. Even in a very rainy winter, there are always many sunny days. This means that there is considerable loss of water through evaporation and agriculture and other human needs suffer accordingly. On the other hand, however, days of sun following short periods of rain can and do ensure the rapid growth of plant life at the beginning of the winter season. This has the effect of lessening the possible damage caused by the dry season to agricultural production.

The scientific measurement of rainfall has brought much essential data to light, but it has also concealed great irregularities. For example, the first rains are often delayed until December, with the result that the work of tilling the soil cannot take place until far too late. On the other hand, rain that falls too early in the season may be followed by a period of drought which results in the failure of seed already sown to germinate. Finally, it may happen that the rain at the end of the growing season is too slight to produce a good crop. There are also considerable differences between one year and another. Almost twice as much rain fell, for instance, in 1944–1945 as in 1946–1947. Apart from such extreme and unexpected variations, there are frequent cases of several dry years followed by a series of years which have been unusually wet and vice versa. Between 1958 and 1963, for instance, the rainfall was insufficient for five successive years. Such variations have had a profound effect on the life of a country where, in Old Testament times, irrigation was not known or practised to the extent that it was, for example, in Mesopotamia and Egypt. A fairly prolonged period of drought would lead to famine even in those parts of the country that were rich in cereals. In the semi-desert regions, a few inches of rain more or less than normal, or a different distribution of rainfall, would mean an extension or a reduction of the area of land that could be used for pasture or cultivation. These irregularities in the climate, in other words, resulted in an absence of any certainty about the future among herdsmen and labourers in the fields, especially in biblical times.

The historian, however, is bound to ask whether scientific observations made in recent years can justifiably be applied to the ancient world that forms the object of his studies; whether, that is, there have not been major changes in the climate since biblical times. Various mutually contradictory answers have been given to this question and most of them have been expressed in terms that are too absolute. In the first place, we can be sure that no profound changes have taken place since the beginning of historical times. Sufficient evidence has been provided by archaeologists, by biblical authors and by later writers, that the flora and fauna have continued to be very much the same in the Near East. This does not mean, however, that there may not have been gradual and less striking changes in the climate of the land of the Bible of the kind recognised in Europe and America. We may be certain that such minor changes occurred and that their effect on the population of a land situated at the edge of a desert was far from minor.

Attempts have been made to connect these climatic variations with man's historical development[12] and the historian is bound to take this climatic factor into consideration in his studies. If he formulates hypotheses on the basis of changes in climate, however, he must also recognise that these hypotheses cannot be proved at least until some success has been achieved in establishing a history of the climate of the Near East which is independent of archaeological data and the existing texts. In any case, the part played by the climate in changing the face, the ecology and the history of Palestine has been far less than that played by man himself.[13]

V. HUMAN GEOGRAPHY AND ECONOMY

For centuries, from ancient times until the present settlement of the Jews in Palestine, the country has been progressively empoverished by man. Forest formed the natural vegetation of the highland on both sides of the Jordan and there were great expanses of wooded country during the Old Testament period. There is evidence in the Bible both of the existence and of the clearance of these forests (see, for example, Jos. 17:15–18; 2 Sam 18: 6–10). Deforestation continued at a more rapid pace during the Middle Ages and during the period of Turkish domination. It had only a very slight influence on the temperature and the rainfall as such, but had the very serious consequence of reducing their effectiveness. Once the roots of the trees and the layer of humus which they held together had been removed from the earth, the water began to flow much more quickly down the slopes, taking the soil with it. The soil was absorbed by the mass of porous limestone, springs dried up and the valleys became more arid.

The country of the Bible has, however, never been rich. It has always lacked natural resources which might have been exploited and put to use by ancient processes. The 'Arabah, of course, has always been fairly rich in deposits of copper, but these were seldom in the hands of the Israelites. It has always been a basically pastoral and agricultural economy, but the great area covered either by steppe or by bare or wooded highland has consistently restricted the size of the population.

Reliable figures are always difficult to obtain. It is largely a matter of conjecture and they have also varied so much from period to period.[14] An

---

[12] See, for example, M. Liverani, 'Variazioni climatiche e fluttuazioni demografiche nella storia siriana', Or Ant, 7 (1968), pp. 77–89. This author, who includes Palestine in his survey, is moderate, but places too much trust in K. W. Butzer's conclusions concerning the climatic variations in the Near East.

[13] A. Reifenberg, The Struggle between the Desert and the Town, Jerusalem, 1955.

[14] See R. de Vaux, Institutions, I, pp. 103–105, for more details.

estimate for the first half of the eighth century B.C., which was a period of economic prosperity and political stability, would be at least 800,000 inhabitants in the Northern Kingdom of Israel and about 300,000 in the Southern Kingdom of Judah. (The Northern Kingdom was, of course, three times as large as the Southern Kingdom.) We have no information at all concerning the populations of the kingdoms of Ammon, Moab and Edom in Transjordan, but we may safely assume that they were far smaller. There were almost certainly never more than a million people living in all the territories described above. It is perhaps interesting in this context to compare the population of the country of the Bible with those of two modern countries of a similar size, but with very different physical structures and economies. Belgium has rather more than nine million inhabitants and Switzerland almost six million.

The so-called 'cities' of the Old Testament were, of course, extremely small both in size and in population. The important 'cities' occupied a few acres of land and had a few thousand inhabitants, whereas the others were really no more than villages, covering less than two or three acres and with less than a thousand inhabitants. The two capitals, Jerusalem and Samaria, were an exception to this general rule, but their population hardly ever went beyond 30,000 inhabitants.

It is even more difficult to estimate the relative density of the population in the different parts of the country. All the same, it is possible to say that, in the Israelite period, the most densely populated regions were the edges of the Plain of Esdraelon and of Lower Galilee, the western slopes of the Judaean hill country and the Shephelah. The Plain of Sharon, which was partly sandy and partly marshy, was very little cultivated and had a low density of population before the Persian and Greek periods. Finally, the Jordan Valley was always very thinly populated.

Most of the people living in the land of the Bible were agricultural workers and herdsmen, agriculture predominating in the northern half of the country and the breeding of sheep and goats in the southern half. Cattle were uncommon and the chief crops were wheat and barley, olives, grapes and figs. The villages were often built on the sites of ancient Canaanite towns which had been built close to springs of water or above a sheet of underground water which could be reached by digging a well.

One aspect of the geography of the country above all has had a constant and decisive influence on the life and history of the people. This is its complete lack of geographical unity, the sharp contrasts in the contours, soils and climate in different parts of this small land. The description given above of the physical geography of the country has drawn attention to its longitudinal division into four distinct regions, each of them being subdivided into separate zones. Along the coastal strip, the dry sand-dunes of the Plain of Philistia gave way, in the ancient world at least, to the marshes of the Plain of Sharon farther north. Inland, the Cisjordan range is broken by the transverse folds of the Negeb in the south and by the depression of the Plain of Esdraelon in the north. In between these two extremities, there is the hill country of Judah, the crest of which divides the cultivated land from the steppe. The third prominent longitudinal region, the rift valley of the Jordan, also changes as one follows the river from north to south. In the extreme north, the Jordan drains the marshes of Lake Huleh, but runs through the Ghor without irrigating it. It also flows from the fresh-water Lake Tiberias with its plentiful fish southwards into the salty and absolutely sterile waters of the Dead Sea. Finally, there is a similar sharp contrast between the fertile Plain of Bashan in the north of the Transjordan tableland and the rocky wastes of Edom in the south.

Again, there are even more sharply contrasted zones as one goes from west to east. The distance from Jaffa to 'Ammān, as the crow flies, is 72 miles, but the traveller making this quite short journey leaves the coastal plain, crosses the low hills of the Shephelah, then climbs to 3,250 feet in the Judaean hill country. From Jerusalem to the Dead Sea, he descends almost 4,000 feet every 15 miles and finally rises another 5,000 feet at 'Ammān, only 25 miles to the east. In the course of this journey, he leaves a maritime climate, damp and constant, and passes through a temperate climate at Jerusalem and a tropical climate at Jericho until he enters a region of dry, continental climate at 'Ammān. He also crosses a region where Mediterranean crops flourish (wheat, the vine and the olive), but, on leaving Jerusalem, there are soon no more vineyards or olive groves or even any cultivated fields. On entering the Jordan Valley, he passes the green oasis of Jericho in the surrounding brown waste of el-Ghōr and soon reaches the still water of the Dead Sea. His immediate impression is that he is in a completely different world. On the other side of the rift valley, he finds himself once again in fields of wheat and barley, though there are very few vineyards and almost no olive trees at all. 'Ammān itself is on the edge of the desert.

The geographical conditions, then, clearly divide the country into a patchwork of often quite small zones, each with a different way of life and with varied interests. This division has always been reinforced by the physical difficulties of communication, the main roads having always followed the longitudinal structures of the country which run from north to south.

1. The most important road of all was, of course, the road which ran through the whole country, linking Egypt with Damascus. From Gaza onwards, this road followed the sea as far as Jaffa, where it went further inland to avoid the marshy Plain of Sharon and the obstacle presented by Mount Carmel. The coastal plain to the north of Jaffa was hardly used at all by traffic before the Roman period. The ancient road entered the Plain of

Esdraelon by the Pass of Megiddo, went north-east towards Lake Tiberias, then followed its western bank, crossed the Jordan south of Lake Hūleh and continued towards Damascus along the foot of Mount Hermon. An alternative route was across the river south of Lake Tiberias and then across the Jolan. This is the great highway of international communication used in ancient times by the Egyptian, Assyrian and Babylonian armies and in more recent times by the armies of Napoleon and Ibrahim Pasha. It was partly incorporated into the network of Roman roads and was also marked out by the ruined inns on the Arab caravan routes.

2. Another important road running from south to north followed the crest of the Cisjordan range of mountains, passing through the towns and villages which are mentioned most frequently in the history of Israel from the time of the patriarchs until the end of the monarchy. Beginning in the land of the Bible itself at Beersheba, this road climbed up into the hill country and passed through Hebron, Bethlehem, Jerusalem, Gibeah, Ramah, Mizpah, Bethel, Shiloh, Shechem, Samaria and Dothan. On reaching the Plain of·Esdraelon, it joined the great highway coming from Egypt via the coast.

3. A third major road followed the edge of the Transjordan tableland from Bashan in the north to the Red Sea. This is the road which the four kings must have followed in Gen 14 at the time of Abraham, via Ashtaroth-Karnaim, Ham and Kiriathaim. It is also the 'royal road' through Heshbon, Medeba and Dibon mentioned in Num 21:22. There was never any important traffic through the Jordan Valley itself during the Israelite period – few people lived there, the river itself was not navigable and, because it flowed into the Dead Sea, it led nowhere.

Communications between the different regions would clearly have been improved by good roads running from west to east. These, however, were never reliable and consequently always played a secondary rôle in the history of the people. There were four which were used more than any others.

1. The road from the bay of Acco to Beīsān. This road passed through Megiddo, crossing the great road to the north, Taanach and Jezreel. From Beisan, it was possible to ford the Jordan and continue to Gilead. At its western end, this road gave access to the sea and in its eastern half it merged to some extent with one of the routes followed by the highway to Damascus. It was an important trade route and Israel struggled with the Canaanites and later with the Arameans to control it.

2. The road from the coastal plain to Samaria and Shechem and from there to the Jordan Valley along the wide Wādi el-Fār'ah. The Jordan was crossed by a ford at Damieh and the plateau of Transjordan could be reached from this point. This is the road along which Gideon pursued the Midianites (Judges 8:4–11) and which Jacob followed in the opposite

direction when he left Mesopotamia (Gen 31–33).

3. The road from Jaffa to Lydda and Aijalon, then uphill into the Cisjordan range via Beth-horon and Gibeon to Bethel, where it crossed the road running south to north along the crest of the range. This is the 'descent of Beth-horon' down which Joshua pursued the Canaanite kings in Jos 10: 10–13. It is also the road followed by the Philistines when they were repelled by Saul (1 Sam 14:31). It was possible to follow this road downwards from Bethel to Jericho. Elijah and Elisha took this road in 2 Kings 2:2–4. The Israelites climbed up the same road from Jericho with Joshua according to Jos 7:2 (see also Judges 1:22). From Jericho, the Jordan could be forded and the traveller could reach the steppes of Moab and the territory of the Ammonites. What is remarkable about this route is that it did not go through Jerusalem, but to the north of it. The contours of the land made it difficult to reach Jerusalem both from the west and the coast and from the east and the Jordan Valley. These routes were not actively used until Jerusalem became the capital of a kingdom.

4. The road from Gaza to the Red Sea. This road passed through Beersheba and went down into the 'Arabah by a way known as the 'Ascent of the Scorpions' (Num 34:4; Judges 1:36). The Red Sea was reached along the 'Arabah at Elath on the Gulf of el-'Aqabah. From the 'Arabah, it was also possible to reach the Transjordan plateau along the Wādi el-Hesā or via Petra. This road became one of the main arteries for caravan traffic at the Nabataean period. It might have been an important route for the Israelites as well if they had possessed Gaza. The Ascent of the Scorpions too was at the frontier between Judah and the territory of the Edomites. Finally, the Israelites only intermittently had control of the 'Arabah and of Elath.

The daily life of most of the inhabitants was therefore shaped to a great extent by the physical and human geography of the country, both during the Old Testament period and at the time of the New Testament. Apart from the capital, most of the so-called 'cities' were really no more than villages. The peasants lived from the products of their fields and their flocks, using members of their families as workers. The various craftsmen of the village or of the neighbouring village would look after the other daily needs of the villagers. These men – the potter, the weaver, the carpenter, the builder and the smith – worked with their sons or with a handful of assistants. There was no large-scale industry or trade and, apart from trade in local products, all the trading was done by travelling merchants who were foreigners – generally Phoenicians. Family ties were very close and the traditions of the clan or the tribe were jealously preserved. The central administration interfered very little in the lives of the people, apart from levying taxes or recruiting young men to fight in a war. Internal affairs were in the hands of a council of 'elders'. The people travelled very little from one part of the country to another because it was geographically so divided and the communications were so difficult. The only means of transport for most of the people was the little grey donkey. Horses were kept in the royal stables and were used only to pull war chariots.

This extremely regional way of life had important consequences, of course, in the political sphere and to a great extent determined the history of the people of the Bible. The tribes led largely independent lives until the establishment of the monarchy under Saul. These tribes were unified under David, but this unity did not survive the death of David's successor, Solomon. After Solomon and up to the destruction of Samaria and Jerusalem, the northern state of Israel and the southern state of Judah remained quite distinct and often hostile to each other. Israel was moreover frequently torn by tribal rivalry. There was only one lasting and solid link between the north and the south – religion. It was this which made 'all Israel' into one people, and their country into the country of the Bible.

VI. RELATIONSHIPS WITH THE OUTSIDE WORLD

The geography of the country also had a decisive effect on the people's relationships with the outside world. Of all the roads discussed above, only one was a major international highway – the one running from south to north and linking Egypt with Damascus. But although this road was often used by foreign armies coming from either direction, it was not favoured by traders. The produce of Phoenicia was brought into the country in rather small amounts through the passes of the Ladder of Tyre and Merj'oyūn on each side of the central highlands of Upper Galilee. Throughout history, a long coastline has usually made a people seek profitable adventures beyond their shores. The people of the Bible, however, had no good natural harbours along their coast and they therefore tended to regard it more as a protection against a hostile sea than as an invitation to set out on voyages. The Israelites were never sailors and they never benefited from the sea trade carried out between Egypt in the south and the Phoenician ports of Tyre, Sidon and Byblos in the north. There were also land routes linking Arabia with Syria and Egypt, but these skirted round the land of the Bible, following the edge of the eastern desert or crossing the Negeb.

The Israelites were thus never able to become a trading nation. If they had, what would they have been able to export? In good years, they had a surplus of wheat and oil and it was with these that Solomon, for example, paid for the wood that he bought from the Lebanon to build the temple (1 Kings 5:25). Another bargain that he made with Hiram the king of Tyre, however, cost Solomon twenty of his villages (1 Kings 9:10–14). He was also able to work the copper mines south of the Dead Sea and equip a fleet of ships on the shores of the Red Sea with the help of Phoenician sailors (1 Kings 9:26–28), exchange goods with the Queen of Sheba (1 Kings 10:1–13) and levy taxes from caravans (1 Kings 10:15). But this was only because his power extended to Edom, the 'Arabah and the roads from Arabia. These undertakings, then, were not the result of ordinary trading, but the consequence of great royal strength, possible only at a time of political expansion.

It has been suggested that this little country was destined to form a link between the two worlds of Asia and Africa, a meeting place between these two different cultures, precisely because of its geographical situation. This was not, however, the case and what has already been said about the country's communications and trade is sufficient proof of this. The one great highway was used for the movement of troops more than for the spread of ideas, art or civilisation and in fact it did no more than ring the part of the country that had belonged to Israel for the longest time. There was a fairly active interchange of ideas in the north with Phoenicia where there was a strong tendency towards syncretism. Finally, there was also an influence exerted by Assyria and by Egypt. At certain periods of Israel's history, these two nations quarrelled for political power over the territory lying between their two empires. This influence was never very deep or lasting, however, and the people of Israel lived for the most part in an isolation forced on them by the geographical conditions of their country.

VIII. CONCLUSION

We may conclude by saying that the country of the Bible was both small and poor. Its geography did not in any way prepare it for an important part in the political history of the world. In fact, it only played any part, and even then only a very modest part, when the great powers in the Near East were less prominent. In the thirteenth century B.C., for example, Egypt was weak and had given up her possessions in Asia. This enabled the tribes of Israel to establish themselves in a territory which their masters had lost. Again, in the tenth century, David and Solomon were able to set up an empire and maintain it, at least for a short time, when neither Egypt nor Assyria was in a strong position. Last, and by no means least, this small country presented a constant and living contrast between the poverty of its natural resources and the greatness of its spiritual destiny.

The material poverty of the country, however, was decisive in preparing the people for their spiritual destiny. They could never achieve wealth and prosperity. All that they could do, by working very hard, was to provide for their simple daily needs. They were able to lead a life without luxury within the framework of the extended family and thus develop deep personal relationships and discover truly human values. In many ways, their way of life was similar to that of the ancient Greeks. Both the country of the Bible and ancient Greece had a similarly complicated geographical structure. Both had the same poor soil and equally poor communications between different regions. Yet in both countries a sublime level of spiritual development was reached.

It was not, however, by work alone that man managed to lead the simple way of life that he led in the land of the Bible. That way of life was also dependent, for example, on the rain that made his seed germinate and his crops grow. But rainfall is never completely regular and reliable. There is always an element of doubt and the Israelite had therefore to ask God that it would fall at the right time and in the right quantities. So the country always tended naturally towards the supernatural and the Bible, which was written in that country, preached a spirituality of poverty which was, paradoxically, a wealth.

This spirituality was also nourished by the country's isolation. The very heart of the land of the Bible, the central mountain range, was remote from the great trade routes which the great powers of the Ancient Near East struggled to control. Those powers were never directly interested in the country of the Bible itself, with the result that the people were able to live in peace. Because they were not directly involved in the quarrels that were always taking place between their rich neighbours, they could remain turned towards God. When their prophets opposed the kings' all too human political activities, they were defending not only the people's faith, but also their very existence. Both the poverty of the country and its insignificance prepared the people to receive the word of God and to keep it in their hearts.

In return, the word of God has transformed the country of the Bible. No one can visit the country or live in it, even for a short time, without being reminded constantly of the Bible. Its mountains and valleys, plains and deserts speak again and again of Scripture. On Mount Carmel, one thinks of Elijah, at the Dead Sea of Abraham and Lot, at Mamre and Hebron of Abraham and Sarah. Jerusalem is the city of David and Solomon, and Samaria, modern Sebastiyeh, is the city of Ahab and Jezebel. At Bethlehem and Nazareth and on the shores of the Sea of Galilee, of course, one is inevitably reminded of Jesus. Going along the roads of the Holy Land, one is walking in the footsteps of the patriarchs, the prophets and Jesus himself. The whole country is saturated with the prayers of those early believers, of later pilgrims throughout the history of faith, and of all those who believe in the one God of the Bible. The country itself helps us all to understand the

Bible which came from it. At the same time, the Bible also gives the country its meaning and helps us to love it. In every way, it is the 'country of the Bible'.

Chapter Two

THE EARLIEST PERIODS

I. HUNTING AND GATHERING

THE country which has just been discussed from the geographical point of view and which I propose, for the sake of convenience, to call Palestine, had already had a very long history when the Israelites settled there.[1] The earliest human remains found in the Near East were collected at Tell 'Ubeidiya, which was originally on the shore of the great lake that used to fill a greater part of the Jordan Valley.[2] Two teeth and two fragments of human skull, associated with the most primitive tools known to man, the chipped stones of the so-called 'pebble culture' which go back to the beginning of the quaternary period, were found at this site.

Apart from these finds and a considerable amount of evidence collected at the surface, much of which has proved to be very difficult to interpret, our

---

[1] Because of the speed with which archaeological discoveries are being made and the rapid progress of research in this sphere, it is advisable to turn to the most recent works first. For the subject matter of the whole chapter, see K. M. Kenyon, *Archaeology in the Holy Land*, London, 1960, 3rd edn. with additions, 1970; E. Anati, *Palestine before the Hebrews*, London, 1963, pp. 1–362.

For Sections I, II, III and IV, see J. Perrot, 'Palestine – Syria – Cilicia', in R. J. Braidwood and G. R. Willey, *Courses toward Urban Life*, Chicago, 1962, pp. 147–64; *id.*, 'Préhistoire palestinienne', *DBS*, VIII, Paris, 1968, col. 286–446, which is the best available account.

For Sections I, II and III and within the general context of the Near East, see J. Mellaart, *Earliest Civilisations of the Near East*, London, 1965; D. Kirkbride, 'Der Nahe und der Mittleere Osten', in *Fischer Weltgeschichte*, I, *Vorgeschichte*, Frankfurt a.M., 1966, pp. 229–251.

For Sections I and II, see D. A. E. Garrod and J. G. D. Clark, 'Primitive Man in Egypt, Western Asia and Europe', *CAH*, I, II, 1965; D. A. E. Garrod, 'The Natufian Culture; the Life and Economy of a Mesolithic People in the Near East', *Proceedings of the British Academy*, 43 (1957), pp. 211–227, is an important study concerned with Palestine in particular.

[2] M. Stekelis, L. Picard, U. Baida, G. Haas and P. V. Tobias, *The Lower Pleistocene of the Central Jordan Valley: The Excavations at 'Ubeidiya, 1960–1963*, Jerusalem, 1966; M. Stekelis, O. Bar-Yosef and T. Schick, *Archaeological Excavations at 'Ubeidiya, 1964–1966*. Jerusalem, 1969 (Publications of the Israel Academy of Sciences and Humanities).

information about the earliest cultures in Palestine is extremely imperfect
until we come to the Early Palaeolithic or Old Stone Age. From this period
up to the end of the Mesolithic or Middle Stone Age, our knowledge is
mainly based on a number of soundings made in particular at Jisr Benāt
Yaʻqūb in the upper valley of the Jordan and on the combined stratigraphy
of a number of caves, especially those at Umm Qatafa in the Wilderness of
Judah and at Tabūn and Sukhul at the foot of Mount Carmel.

The application of the European system of great prehistoric periods to
Palestine is fully justified because the cultures in both cases were, in their
first stages, very closely related. The two categories of stone craft found in
Europe are also found in Palestine. These are the craft consisting of tools
fashioned from flakes that had been retouched or trimmed and that in
which flints were cut on two surfaces, the bifacial tools. The series begin
with the so-called Tayacian period of the caves at Tabūn and Umm Qatafa
for the retouched flakes and with the Middle Acheulian Period of Jisr Benāt
Yaʻqūb for the bifacial implements.

These two traditions combined in the Levalloisian-Mousterian Period,
which is the Middle Palaeolithic culture that is most widespread in
Palestine, Syria and the Lebanon and of which there is also evidence in
Anatolia and Iraq. This period also marked the beginning of Egypt's own
distinctive evolution and the point at which the Near East in general began
to develop differently from Europe. It is also the period of the earliest
human fossil remains found in Palestine. The so-called Galilee skull was the
first of these finds. It is also the earliest of all, dating from a pre-Levalloisian
period known as the Yabrudian.[3] Its age has been estimated at 60,000 years.
The Carmel men, a group of a dozen individuals, including four almost
complete skeletons, found in the caves of Tabūn and Sukhul, are later than
this. They are from the Early and Middle Levalloisian-Mousterian periods
and their date is probably 45,000 B.C. Another important group of bones
was found in a cave in the Jebel Qafzeh near Nazareth in 1934–1935, more
discoveries being made on the same site from 1965 onwards. All the information that we have about this group, however, is from preliminary notes.
The same applies to a Neanderthaloid skeleton found in a cave in the Wādi
el-ʻAmūd in 1961 and to a child's skeleton of the Mousterian Period found
in the cave of Kebarah.

These ancient Palestinian men have raised problems which have not yet
been fully resolved, mainly because they present us with a mixture of
Palaeanthropic and neanthropic characteristics, in other words, they are a
mixture of Neanderthal man and of *Homo sapiens*. The scholars who first
presented the Carmel skeletons to the public were of the opinion that they

[3] The name is derived from Yabrūd, a site to the north of Damascus, but the best evidence
is at Tabūn.

were representative of a race in the process of evolution.[4] There was an
immediate reaction on the part of other scholars, who suggested the theory
of a hybrid race from a line of Palaeanthropic men and a line of
Neanthropic men.[5] Many scholars still support this view,[6] but others have
put forward another solution to the problem. Very briefly, this third theory
is that there were two populations in the region of Mount Carmel which
might have been separated by thousands of years. The first was the race of
which remains have been found at Tabūn. This race can be compared with
the Shanidar men found in Iraq and representing a local evolution of a
Neanderthalian type, in other words, a race without any future. The second
race was that found at Sukhul, which is similar to that discovered at Jebel
Qafzeh. These men represent a stage of evolution between the
Palaeanthropic ancestors of man – although they were not Neanderthalian
men – and *Homo sapiens*.[7]

A whole series of remains of the Late Palaeolithic Age[8] was made in the
shelter at Ksar 'Aqil near Antelias in the Lebanon. This age is represented in
Palestine by a less complete series discovered in the Mount Carmel caves of
Maghārat el-Wād and Kebarah, in the Emīreh cave near Lake Tiberias, in
the shelter of 'Erq el-Ahmar and on the terrace of el-Khiam in the Judaean
Wilderness. As in Europe, the principal objects of the Late Palaeolithic Age
are blades and implements with blades and points, such as knives and
burins. The tools belonging to the middle period of this age share many of
the characteristics of those of the Aurignacian culture and would appear to
have been subject to a European influence. The beginning of this age in
Palestine was a period of transition, however, a local development from the
end of the Levalloisian culture, culminating in two phases, the Athlitian and
the Kebarian, neither of which bear any distinct traces of the Aurignacian
culture. The first of these, the Athlitian culture, is a very specialised local
development. The second, the Kebarian, with its high proportion of very
thin blades, should, in the opinion of many scholars, be classified under the

[4] T. D. McCown and A. Keith, *The Stone Age of Mount Carmel, II: The Fossil Human
Remains*, Oxford, 1939.
[5] See, for example, M. F. Ashley Montagu in *Man*, 1940, p. 96.
[6] See especially A. Thoma, 'Métissage ou Transformation? Essai sur les hommes fossiles de
Palestine', *L'Anthropologie*, 61 (1957), pp. 470–502; 62 (1958), pp. 30–52; *ibid.*, 'La définition
des Néanderthaliens et la position des hommes fossiles de Palestine', *L'Anthropologie*, 69
(1965), pp. 519–533.
[7] F. C. Howell, 'Stratigraphie du Pléistocène Supérieur dans l'Asie du Sud-Ouest: âge
relatif et absolu de l'homme et de ses industries', *L'Anthropologie*, 65 (1961), pp. 1–20; R. S.
Solecki, 'Three Adult Neanderthal Skeletons from Shanidar Cave, Northern Iraq', *Sumer*,
17 (1961), pp. 71–96; T. D. Stewart, 'The Skull of Shanidar II', *Sumer*, 17 (1961), pp.
97–106.
[8] D. A. E. Garrod, 'Notes sur le Paléolithique Supérieur du Moyen Orient', *Bulletin de la
Société Préhistorique Française*, 54 (1957), pp. 439–446.

Mesolithic or Middle Stone Age.[9] This is clearly a case of the cultural levels becoming more restricted – Palestine on the one hand and Syria and the Lebanon on the other were at this period very much the same and similar crafts of the Late Palaeolithic Age have also been identified in Anatolia, at Karain near Antalya,[10] at Belbasi and at Beldibi.[11] The Late Palaeolithic Age is, however, very different in Iraq and there is nothing at all that is comparable in Egypt.

These local differences are even more strikingly displayed in the evidence that we have of the Mesolithic or Middle Stone Age, which is expressed in Palestine in the very distinctive Natufian culture.[12] This culture is not found north of a line running from Beirut to Yabrūd or south of the edge of the desert.[13] It is in the main limited to Palestine and traces of it have been discovered in the caves or rock shelters of Mount Carmel and the Judaean hill country, in the open-air sites along the coastal plain, in the Jordan Valley and on the tableland of Transjordania – in other words, in all the four major geographical regions of the country. By this time, the Near East had entered the post-pluvial epoch, which corresponds to the post-glacial period in Europe and which still persists. The contours of the land had become more or less definitively fixed and the fauna and flora were very little different from what they were to be in historical as distinct from prehistoric times. The climate, however, was probably a little less warm and a little less humid than it is today. The Mesolithic Age began about 9,000 B.C., perhaps rather earlier, and lasted about two millennia.

The population of the Middle Stone Age was clearly greater than that during the Palaeolithic. The evidence for this supposition is based not only on the multiplicity and the extent of the buildings of this period, but also on the larger number of human remains that have been discovered. The most notable of these finds include 45 individuals in the cave of Shuqbah in the Wādi en-Natūf, 87 in the Carmel cave of el-Wād, 50 in the Wādi Fellah

---

[9] J. Gonzalez Echegaray, *Excavaciones en la terraza de 'El Khiam' (Jordania)*, I, Madrid, 1964. The bottom of a hut of the Kebarian culture was discovered at 'Ein Geb on the eastern bank of Lake Tiberias; see M. Stekelis, O. Bar Yoseph and A. Tchernov, 'Un habitat du Paléolithique Supérieur à 'Ein Guev', *L'Anthropologie*, 69 (1965), pp. 176–183; *ibid.*, in Hebrew and in much greater detail in *Yediot (BIES)*, 30 (1966), pp. 5–22.

[10] I. I. Kökten, 'Ein allgemeiner Uberblick über die prähistorischen Forschungen in Karain bei Antalya', *Belleten*, 19 (1955), pp. 284–293.

[11] E. Bostanci, 'A New Upper Palaeolithic and Mesolithic Facies at Belbasi Rock Shelter', *Belleten*, 26 (1962), pp. 233–278; 'Researches on the Mediterranean Coast of Anatolia: A New Palaeolithic Site at Beldibi, near Antalya', *Anatolia*, 4 (1959), pp. 124–178.

[12] The word is derived from the Wādi en-Natūf, where the culture was first observed in the Magharat Shuqbah; see D. A. E. Garrod, 'A New Mesolithic Industry: the Natufian of Palestine', in the *Journal of the Royal Anthropological Institute*, 62 (1932), pp. 257–269.

[13] Apart from a simplified form at Beldibi near Antalya in Anatolia and an isolated case at Heluan near Cairo, the 'Natufian' character of which is disputed.

(= Nahal Oren, Carmel) and 62 at 'Ain Mallaha (= 'Einan) in the upper
valley of the Jordan. These men were dolichocephalic and of small stature;
some scholars are of the opinion that they were of proto-Mediterranean
stock, others think that they were Euro-african. To judge from the nature
of the burial places, these groups extended beyond the family and indicate a
movement towards a sedentary way of life.

Further evidence of greater stability at this period is provided by the
appearance of very early buildings. Three levels of round houses cover an
area of more than 1,000 square yards at 'Ain Mallaha, a privileged site
beside Lake Hūleh, which provided an abundance of fish and water birds.
In all probability, this was a permanent habitation. The most typical implements found there are geometrical microliths, often crescent-shaped,
which formed part of composite tools, sickle blades frequently found fixed
in their bone handles, harpoons and fish-hooks made of bone, and several
much larger tools such as picks. These new tools clearly reflect a new type
of economy. Up to this time, man had lived by hunting and gathering his
food. He still lived in this way, but the increase in population forced him to
intensify his search for food. More game could be obtained with the help of
better weapons and fishing yielded another type of food. The presence of
sickles, mortars and grindstones shows at least that crops were harvested and
that the cereals which grew naturally in this region were used systematically. There, is on the other hand, no decisive proof that they were being
cultivated at this time and there were no domestic animals apart from dogs.
Nonetheless, all the factors which combined to bring about the neolithic
revolution were already present.

The Natufian culture of the Mesolithic Age has been divided into four
successive phases, but it would be more exact to distinguish several different
regional movements which were more or less contemporary. The Natufian
culture that is generally regarded as the earliest, Natufian I of the large sites
at el-Wad, Kebarah and 'Ain Mallaha, was already degenerating into
Natufian II on certain sites. Elsewhere it was already developing towards
the pre-pottery Neolithic of the Jericho type. Finally, what has been called
Natufian III-IV and is revealed most clearly at el-Khiam in the Wilderness
of Judah developed from the Kebarian culture and in turn gave birth to the
Tahunian, the pre-pottery Neolithic culture found in the arid regions.[14]

The most interesting of all these Natufian cultures is the first. It emerged
apparently without any real preparation. The cutting and retouching of the
tiny flint tools typical of this tradition was done with considerable technical
confidence. There is abundant evidence of necklaces made of shells and of
pendants of cut bone, of a sudden flowering of animal sculpture, including a
few representations of human figures, and of the practice of elaborate burial

[14] J. Gonzalez Echegaray, *Excavaciones en la terraza de 'El Khiam' (Jordania)*, II, Madrid,
1966.

rites. This early Natufian culture was, however, comparatively short-lived and soon gave way to the second Natufian tradition, Natufian II.

II.HUNTSMEN AND FARMERS

The transition from the Mesolithic to the Neolithic Age can be observed at Nahal Oren (Wadi Fellah) on the western slope of Mount Carmel.[15] A village of circular huts was built on this site above the Natufian level of oval shaped buildings. These round houses are smaller than those found at 'Ain Mallaha ('Einān), but are otherwise similar. The tools found on the site are also in the Natufian tradition, but there are also certain new elements, especially axes for working in the forest and picks for digging the ground. These, together with numerous sickle blades and hafts, testify to the beginnings of agriculture. Taken as a whole, the culture is Neolithic.

A similar development which was to go much further is evident at Jericho.[16] A Natufian I level is covered by a thick layer consisting of numerous basements of huts and containing tools of the Natufian tradition. This layer, which might well be called 'protoneolithic', is followed by a pre-pottery Neolithic level, with the sudden appearance of round houses reminiscent of those at Wādi Fellah, but here constructed of crude bricks. The first attempts at farming in the coastal region (Wādi Fellah) were continued at Jericho in natural conditions which were very favourable. Hunting and the natural resources provided by the oasis were not sufficient to support a sedentary population that has been estimated at 2,000 and the people therefore soon turned to agriculture. The Mesolithic huntsmen also became farmers and it is possible, although by no means certain, that the goat was domesticated at this time. The houses at Jericho seem to have been surrounded by an enclosing wall, including at least one massive round tower on the inside of this wall.

The construction of this settlement and the degree of organisation within the community living there and making use of the oasis have been regarded as clear proof that Jericho was the first town in the world, at least so far as we know. This claim has, however, been disputed.[17] The debate has nonetheless centred to a great extent on terminological problems and the

[15] M. Stekelis and T. Yisraeli, 'Excavations at Nahal Oren', *IEJ*, 13 (1963), pp. 1–12.

[16] See, for example, K. M. Kenyon, *Archaeology in the Holy Land*, 1960, pp. 39–57.

[17] See especially V. G. Childe, 'Civilisation, Cities and Towns', *Antiquity*, 31 (1957), pp. 36–38; R. J. Braidwood, 'Jericho and its Setting in Near Eastern History', *Antiquity*, 31 (1957), pp. 73–81; and K. M. Kenyon's replies: 'Reply to Professor Braidwood', *Antiquity*, 31 (1957), pp. 82–84; 'Some Observations on the Beginning of the Settlement in the Near East', *Journal of the Royal Anthropological Institute*, 89 (1959), pp. 35–43.

most important aspect of this settlement is beyond dispute. This is that Jericho represents a transitional stage from an economy based on food gathering to one based on food production. This is the same stage of development as that reached in the first villages known to us in the Near East – Jarmo in Kurdistan, Çatal Hüyük and Hacilar in Anatolia, Rās Shamrah in Syria and Khirokitia in Cyprus. Men began to cultivate cereals and to domesticate animals independently of each other, yet clearly at about the same time in different regions where the wild grasses from which our wheat and barley were developed grew and where the ancestors of our domestic animals lived. Jericho was undoubtedly neither the first site nor the only one where this process took place in Palestine, but its privileged position gave it a distinct advantage over its neighbours and enabled it to lead in this development towards farming.

It is interesting, in this context, to compare the evolution at Jericho with the situation at el-Khiam, for example, in a semi-desert region of Palestine. Although it was not inhabited continuously, the terrace there was used by groups of people who lived almost exclusively by hunting. They did very little farming or none at all and had probably not even reached the stage of being herdsmen.

Jericho also provides the best evidence that we have in Palestine of the following phase, the so-called Neolithic culture of Pre-pottery B. After having been abandoned for some time, the site was reoccupied by a new population with different tools and different buildings. The rooms of these buildings were square with rounded corners. The foundations and the bases of the walls were covered with a polished and coloured facing, the walls themselves being constructed of a new kind of brick. There is far less certainty as to whether the town was surrounded by a wall, as it had been during the previous phase. The basic industries were still hunting and agriculture, but animals were already being domesticated. These included the goat, two species of dog and the cat. Many pig, cattle and sheep bones have been found at this level on the site and these point to the presence of other species which were still wild, but were capable of being domesticated. Relationships with the outside world were being expanded – obsidian came from Anatolia, turquoise from the Sinai desert and shells from the Mediterranean. Several aspects of the religious life of the inhabitants of Jericho at this time have also been revealed by excavations – a possible explanation of the presence of two buildings is that they were sanctuaries. Another find comprises fragments of two groups of statues modelled in clay, each representing a man, a woman and a child. These are the first known examples of the holy triad which was to have such a long life in Near Eastern worship. Ten skulls have also been found at the same levels. These are interesting because all of them are without the lower jaw and were separated from the rest of the skeletal remains. What is more, in an attempt to make real portraits, the muscles of the face have been modelled in earth. This is an impressive example of the ancestor cult. There had been a certain preparation for this rite in the previous periods, when the skulls of dead people had been buried separately from their bodies.

Jericho is not, however, an isolated case. The site of a village at Beidha near Petra in Transjordan is equally interesting.[18] Six successive levels of building have been excavated here over an area of some 2,500 square yards. The houses are, in turn, polygonal, round and rectangular with concave walls and there is finally a complex of large rooms and chambers arranged along narrow corridors. The foundations and the walls are plastered and painted and the tools that have been found are of flint and stone. These factors and the custom of burying adults' skulls, though never children's, separately from their bodies make it obvious that the settlement at Beidha is very closely related to that at Jericho. Both clearly belong to the Pre-pottery B period of the Neolithic Age.

As at Jericho, the goat was domesticated at Beidha, wheat and barley were successfully grown there and wild pistachios were gathered. All this activity implies that the region had much more water at that period than it has today. Carbon 14 tests have shown that the site was inhabited for a total period of about four hundred years, from about 7,000 until 6,600 B.C. It was probably abandoned after a particularly severe drought. These dates are in accordance with several of those obtained by the same method for similar levels at Jericho.

There is also evidence of the same culture elsewhere in Palestine, especially at Munhata and Sheikh 'Ali in the Jordan Valley south of Lake Tiberias. The farthest north that this culture has been discovered in the Near East is at Tell Ramad near Damascus. Clearly, it did not originate in Palestine and one is tempted to look for its first appearance in the north, possibly even as far north as Anatolia. There are, for instance, square houses with plastered and painted basements and walls at the Anatolian site of Hacilar, which is of the same period. There is also evidence at this site of the same practice of burying skulls apart from the rest of the body, but the domestic tools found there are different from those found at Beidha and Jericho. On the other hand, the presence at both the southern sites of a little obsidian from Anatolia tends to confirm the connection with the north. Finally, Rás Shamrah in Syria, where the deepest level has certain characteristics in common with Jericho, may have been a stage on this road.

The development towards the Neolithic Age in the semi-desert regions was both independent and delayed. Their flint industries had few links with

[18] D. Kirkbride, 'Five Seasons at the Pre-Pottery Neolithic Village of Beidha in Jordan', *PEQ*, 98 (1966), pp. 8–72; 'Interim Report', *ibid.*, 99 (1967), pp. 5–13; 100 (1968), pp. 90–96; 'Beidha: Early Neolithic Village Life South of the Dead Sea', *Antiquity*, 42 (1968), pp. 263–274.

that of Jericho and related sites. They are grouped together under the title of Tahunian,[19] which is a local Mesolithic tradition peculiar to this semi-desert part of Palestine. Many microliths have been found on Tahunian sites and, although arrowheads have been excavated in large numbers, very few sickle blades and hafts have come to light. A great wall was built at this time at el-Khiam and the stone foundations of round huts have been found in the Wādi Dhobai on the Transjordanian steppe.[20] Farther east, the same tools have been discovered at Kilwa [21] near a number of rock carvings of animals, some of which may be just as early. These nomadic or semi-nomadic people were above all huntsmen, but they did a little farming and, ar least at el-Khiam, they also kept goats.

III. FARMERS AND POTTERS

The invention of pottery and the addition of vessels of baked clay to the domestic equipment does not necessarily imply a change in man's way of life or in the economy of his society. All the same, the appearance of pottery does mark the beginning in Palestine of a new period. A long gap separates this new phase, known as Pottery Neolithic, from the end of Pre-pottery Neolithic. The new period was also characterised by a number of important changes.[22]

Some of the Pre-pottery Neolithic sites were not reoccupied and remained permanently uninhibited. In other cases there were new settlements and where life continued as before, as at Jericho, there are signs of an interruption in the stratigraphy. It is not possible to date the end of the Pre-pottery period later than 6000 B.C. or the beginning of the Pottery Neolithic culture of Jericho earlier than 4500 B.C. Nor is it possible for us to tell exactly what brought about the collapse of the Pre-pottery Neolithic culture or why it was followed by such a long interval. It may have been the result of a widespread and serious drought, which led to the abandonment of Munhata, Sheikh 'Ali and Beidha. Whatever might have been the reason, this long period during which the country was deserted does provide a possible explanation for the change in the pattern of man's habitation. The architectural tradition that had persisted throughout the two

[19] The name is derived from the Wādi et-Tahūneh near Bethlehem.

[20] J. d'A. Waechter and V. M. Seton-Williams, 'The Excavations at Wadi Dhobai, 1937–1938, and the Dhobaian Industry', *JPOS*, 18 (1938), pp. 172–186.

[21] H. Rhotert, *Transjordanien. Vorgeschichtliche Forschungen*, Stuttgart, 1938.

[22] For Sections III and IV, see R. de Vaux, 'Palestine during the Neolithic and Chalcolithic Periods', *CAH*, I, IX(b), 1966; P. de Miroschedji, *L'Epoque pré-urbaine en Palestine Revue Biblique*, 13), Paris, 1971.

stages of Pre-pottery Neolithic disappeared completely and the new inhabitants lived in huts which were generally partly sunk in the ground. The almost complete absence of solid buildings persisted until the end of the period. The immigrants did, however, bring the pottery industry with them. The products of this industry can be divided into three groups, although any attempt to place these groups in chronological order remains hypothetical.

The first of these groups is the so-called coastal culture, because it seems to have originated, in Palestine at least, on the Mediterranean coast, where there are sites between Jaffa and Carmel. Other sites have been found in northern Palestine, on the Plain of Esdraelon and in the Jordan Valley from its sources in the north to south of Lake Tiberias. The pottery of this first group is characteristically dark in colour and glossy and it is frequently incised. The decoration of these pots consists of incisions or indentations and quite often of impressions made with the fingernail or with the edge of a shell. Sometimes it is burnished and sometimes not.

Jericho is the main site where pottery of the second group has been found. Two phases have been distinguished within this group. These are known as A and B, although B would seem to have resulted from a mixture with the third group, the so-called Yarmukian culture, which is discussed below. This pottery tends to be very coarse. There is, however, another much more carefully decorated ware of the same culture. This is covered with a cream-coloured slip, often with a decoration of red slip in a pattern of bands and chevrons and finally burnished. In phase B, the slip used is purer and better fired, the pottery appears in a wider variety of shapes and the incised decoration is often combined with painting. This pottery, especially in its more developed forms, has been found outside Jericho at smaller sites in the Jordan Valley, on the coastal plain south of Jaffa and in the Shephelah. It has also been discovered at lower levels in the great tells of the north such as Megiddo, Beth-shean (Tell el-Hisn), Tell el-Far'ah and Shechem. To these sites can be added Ghrubba, opposite Jericho on the other side of the Jordan, which is remarkable because of the distinctive character of the painted decoration of the pottery found there and the absence of incisions.[23]

Sha'ar ha-Gōlan, at the confluence of the Yarmuk and the Jordan,[24] is very typical of the third culture. Many flint and stone tools have been found there as well as a great deal of coarse pottery decorated with incisions. Art and worship are represented by the presence of very many objects — figurines made of fired or even simply dried clay and pebbles carved with human images of a highly schematic kind. This Yarmukian culture has also

[23] J. Mellaart, 'The Neolithic Site of Ghrubba', *ADAJ*, 3 (1956), pp. 24–40.
[24] M. Stekelis, 'A New Neolithic Industry: the Yarmukian of Palestine', *IEJ*, 1 (1950–1951), pp. 1–19.

been found in a very pure form at Munhata just south of Sha'ar ha-Gōlan itself[25] and above all, mixed with the Jerichoan type, at several of the sites where pottery of the Jerichoan culture is found and, mixed with coastal type of pottery, at certain sites on the Plain of Esdraelon.

The earliest of these groups to emerge in Palestine was the coastal culture, but this culture appears to have originated even earlier in the far north. The dark, lustrous pottery is the parent of the pottery known as 'Amuq C found on the Plain of Antioch, and in between these two are the finds at the lowest levels of Rās Shamrah (V A–B, IV C) and, farther south, the Early Neolithic of Byblos and the first pottery level of Tell Ramad. To judge from the dates that have been suggested for these sites, this first group may have settled in Palestine round about 5000 B.C., in which case the gap which occurs between the Palestinian Pre-pottery and Pottery Neolithic Periods would be filled, at least partly.

The Jerichoan group is also connected with this northern culture. It has been suggested that the Jerichoan culture first originated as far north as the Plain of Antioch ('Amuq D), then moved south through Rās Shamrah (IV A–B, III C) and the Middle and Late Neolithic of Byblos. There are also close parallels between Byblos, especially of the Middle Neolithic Age, and the Yarmukian culture of the third Palestinian group mentioned above. This link is most clearly revealed in the products of the stone industry. The same tools have been found at the coastal sites south of Beirut and it would seem as though the Yarmukian culture came to Palestine from the Lebanon through the pass of Merj'oyūn. This double connection would certainly indicate that the two groups of Jericho and Yarmuk existed at the same time. It is therefore possible to give them the same dates as those suggested for Byblos and Rās Shamrah,[26] where the corresponding periods cover the second half of the fifth millennium and the beginning of the fourth B.C.

It is also quite probable that these various groups of immigrants brought other innovations with them into Palestine apart from pottery. One distinct possibility is that the Palestinian peasants began at this time to keep cattle and sheep and perhaps even pigs, as the inhabitants of Syria, their place of origin, were doing. These animals would have been bred in addition to the goat, which had been domesticated since the Pre-pottery Neolithic Age. Whether or not they bred animals, they were certainly farmers who had settled near to springs where they could cultivate a little ground. This explains why there are so many scattered minor sites outside the larger sites which were more favoured. These small sites were inhabited by a family often for a relatively short time.

[25] J. Perrot, 'Les deux premières campagnes de fouilles à Munhata', *Syria*, 41 (1964), pp. 323–345; 'La troisième campagne de fouilles à Munhata', *Syria*, 43 (1966), pp. 49–63.

[26] Including the correction pointed out by H. de Contenson in 'A Further Note on the Chronology of Basal Ras Shamra', *BASOR*, 175 (Oct. 1964), pp. 47–48.

IV. FARMERS, POTTERS AND METAL-WORKERS

The transition from the Neolithic to the Chalcolithic Age, the beginning of the age of metal, which was in the first place copper, was for a long time very tentative in Palestine. None of the sites mentioned in the previous section has provided archaeologists with any metal tools or even with fragments of such tools. All the same, some of these sites have been classified as Chalcolithic because metal-working was already known in other parts of the Near East. The absence of metal on the Palestinian sites has been explained in various ways: by the continual re-use of a material which was still not abundant, by its rapid deterioration when covered with earth and indeed by the poor chances given by past excavations with a very limited range. These explanations are not entirely satisfactory, however, and it is far better in principle to date the beginning of the age of metal in Palestine at a time for which concrete evidence is provided by archaeologists of metal implements being used and even of the presence of a metal industry.

This development was progressive and did not follow the same pattern everywhere. For a long time during the Chalcolithic Age, of course, far more stone and bone implements continued to be used than metal tools. The gradual change which came about in the way of life of these early farmers and potters, however, was due less to the existence of this new equipment than to the demands made by the new industry itself. Centres were established where the ore was mined and the metal was extracted, lines of communication were set up between these centres and a new class of specialised workers arose. These people depended on the farmers for their food, but they furnished products which could be used in trade with the outside world and this led to the emergence of new and more highly organised communities.

What is remarkable is that these innovations first appeared in the more marginal regions such as the approaches to the Dead Sea, the northern Negeb and the southern part of the coastal plain, many of which had previously never had a settled population. The differences in place and time between the sites do not seriously affect the uniform character of this culture, which is known as Ghassulian.

This Chalcolithic culture was in fact given this name because it was first recognised at Teleilāt Ghassūl on the eastern side of the Jordan Valley just north of the Dead Sea.[27] Archaeologists have distinguished four levels in the three mounds which form this site. Only the two highest levels have so

---

[27] A. Mallon, R. Koeppel and R. Neuville, *Teleilât Ghassul, I. Compte-rendu des Fouilles de l'Institut Biblique Pontifical, 1929–1932*, Rome, 1934; R. Koeppel, *Teleilât Ghassul, II. Compte-rendu des Foiulles de l'Institut Biblique Pontifical, 1932–1936*, Rome, 1940; R. North, *Ghassul 1960, Excavation Report*, Rome 1961; J. B. Hennessy, 'Preliminary Report on a First Season of Excavation at Teleilāt Ghassūl', *Levant*, 1 (1969), pp. 1–24.

far been excavated at all extensively. They are intermingled in some places and in others are not found at all. What they certainly reveal is a continuous period of occupation which extended, to judge from the thickness of the deposits, over several centuries. A certain development can be perceived from the finds taken from this site, but as a whole the picture is very homogeneous.

The flint implements found include a large number of sickle blades and hafts, a few arrowheads and some fanscrapers, adzes and chisels. Their presence shows how essential flint still was at this period. The pottery of Teleilāt Ghassūl is rather coarse in texture, but very well fired. In shape it is very varied but quite distinctive and is decorated with incisions or superimposed bands or else painted in geometrical patterns of a very simple kind. The most remarkable artistic finds at Teleilāt Ghassūl, however, are mural frescoes depicting a cultic scene, a star, a number of nightmare figures and real and mythical animals. In the two upper levels, which have been examined more thoroughly, various copper objects have been unearthed, although there is no proof that these metal tools were made at Teleilāt Ghassūl itself. There is, however, evidence of another industry — weaving with a vegetable fibre, possibly flax.[28] It is clear too that Ghassūl was essentially a farming village, because the silos there were found to contain grains of corn and date and olive stones. The great cemetery of 'Adeimeh, a few miles to the east of Teleilāt Ghassūl, where the fleshless bones of the dead were placed in cists or micro-dolmens, was probably the burial place of the inhabitants of Teleilāt Ghassūl.

Other more recent discoveries have shown that Ghassūl was far less isolated than it first seemed to be. The most interesting and the best known of this more recently excavated group of sites is in the region of Beersheba and it is clear that this is the first sign of human habitation there. Digging has revealed the existence of a dozen agglomerations about half a mile away from each other, but connected by isolated habitations. The main ones are Tell Abu Matar,[29] Bir es-Safadi[30] and Khirbet el-Bitar.[31] At first, the people who settled here lived in subterranean or semi-subterranean rooms, but later they built brick houses on stone foundations. As many as a thousand people might have lived in these settlements, and these too were inhabited for at least two or three centuries. During this time, the culture was quite homogeneous. The flint tools and the pottery found there are clearly related to those found at Teleilāt Ghassūl, but there is also a type of pottery which

[28] See G. Crowfoot's note in G. Loud, Megiddo II: Seasons of 1935–1939, Chicago, 1948, p. 140.
[29] J. Perrot, 'The Excavations at Tell Abu Matar', IEJ, 5 (1955), pp. 17–40, 73–84, 167–189; 'Les fouilles d'Abou Matar', Syria, 34 (1957), pp. 1–38.
[30] J. Perrot, 'Bir es-Safadi', IEJ, 9 (1959), pp. 141–142.
[31] M. Dothan, 'Excavations at Horvat Beter', 'Atiqot, 2 (1959), pp. 1–42.

is much finer than that of Ghassūl and lighter in colour. Again, the inhabitants were mainly farmers, cultivating wheat, barley and lentils and raising sheep, goats and cattle. They had several industries, but there was a tendency for each group to specialise. Ivory and bone cutting seems to have been practised above all at Bir es-Safadi, whereas the people of Abu Matar smelted and cast the copper mined in the 'Arabah. Turquoise from Sinai and freshwater shells from the Nile Valley have also been found on these sites.

The same culture extended eastwards as far as Tell 'Arad and westwards as far as the Wādi Ghazzeh, where it did not become established until a little later, so it would seem, and where it had no more than a marginal character. Other quite closely related groups have been found in caves in the Judaean desert, especially in the Wādi el-Murabba'at and in the region of 'Ain Jidi (En-gedi) and Masada (es-Sebbeh), where a cave at Wādi Mahras (Nahal Mishmar) was found to contain Ghassulian pottery and a considerable deposit of copper objects. Near En-gedi, an open-air sanctuary has been identified. A northern offshoot of the Ghassulian culture has also been found at a site in the Jordan Valley, Neve Ur, just to the south of Munhata, which had, by this time, been abandoned.

A number of sites, in particular Hederah[32] on the Plain of Sharon, Benei Beraq[33] and Azor[34] near Jaffa, have produced objects which are even more closely related to those found at Beersheba. The pottery is identical with that of the upper levels of Bir es-Safadi and Tell Abu Matar and it is associated with the burials at the second level. The fleshless bones had been placed in receptacles of fired clay which were in almost every case fashioned in the form of houses. These shapes must be those of the dwellings of the period. These houses were rectangular, they had an arched roof or a double-pitched roof and there was an opening just wide enough to receive the skull in one of the shorter sides. This entrance to the 'house of the dead' is often closed by a hatch. There have been several cases of these house-like ossuaries being found together in great numbers in one cave, often a man-made and subterranean collective grave, which consequently had the appearance of a village of the dead. Where the village of the living was in these cases, however, cannot always be known – the few settlements on the surface with which they might perhaps be associated are often later in date. On the other hand, no such burial places have been discovered in the

[29] J. Perrot, 'The Excavations at Tell Abu Matar', *IEJ*, 5 (1955), pp. 17–40, 73–84, 167–189; 'Les fouilles d'Abou Matar', *Syria*, 34 (1957), pp. 1–38.
[30] J. Perrot, 'Bir es-Safadi, *IEJ*, 9 (1959), pp. 141–142.
[31] M. Dothan, 'Excavations at Horvat Beter', *'Atiqot*, 2 (1959), pp. 1–42.
[32] E. L. Sukenik, 'A Chalcolithic Necropolis at Hederah', *JPOS*, 17 (1937), pp. 15–30.
[33] J. Kaplan, 'Excavations at Benei Beraq, 1951', *IEJ*, 13 (1963), pp. 300–312.
[34] J. Perrot, 'Une tombe à ossuaires du IVe millénaire à Azor près de Tel-Aviv', *'Atiqot*, 3 (1961), pp. 1–83.

caves containing ossuaries found on the coastal plain were used by the inhabitants of the Negeb as cemeteries. These people may have left their villages during the dry season, bringing not only their flocks, but also the bones of their dead with them.

The relative chronology of these various groups is very difficult to ascertain. It would seem as though the earliest were the subterranean dwellings in the vicinity of Beersheba, which were perhaps contemporary with the deepest levels at Teleilāt Ghassūl. The upper levels of this site are probably of the same period as the upper level (with houses) of the Negeb sites and the caves on the coastal plain containing ossuaries. After the sites in the Negeb and at Ghassūl had been abandoned, this culture was, it has been suggested, continued for a time in the surface settlements on the coast and in the caves in the Judaean wilderness. The total duration of this culture would therefore have been about three or four centuries in the middle of the fourth millennium, from about 3600 until 3200 B.C.

This culture, then, established itself in parts of Palestine where, in most cases, there had never been any settled communities. It also introduced the totally new industry of metal-working into the country. There can be no doubt that it came from outside Palestine, but its precise origins remain mysterious. A study of the skeletal remains suggests that the people were brachycephalous and of Armenoid or Anatolian stock.[35] A similar analysis of the copper objects found at Nahal Mishnar points to Anatolia as the source of the metal. The inhumations at the second level, and the ossuaries, are very reminiscent, however, of central and eastern European funerary customs, the closest parallels being the ossuaries found on the banks of the Black Sea. The most probable of all the hypotheses that have been put forward, then, is that this culture originated in the north.

The end of this period is also surrounded by obscurity. Teleilāt Ghassūl was perhaps the first site to be abandoned and was followed by the villages in the neighbourhood of Beersheba, the villages in the Negeb, the caves in the wilderness of Judah and the sites on the coastal plain, probably in that order. There is, however, no indication that they were violently destroyed. What is more, all these regions remained deserted for a long time afterwards and some of them were never inhabited again. The Ghassulian culture, then, arrived unexpectedly, without any apparent preparation, and disappeared without leaving any inheritance.

This culture left hardly any impression in the highlands or in the north of the country. In those regions, the civilisation of farmers and potters described in the preceding section persisted for some time, until it was replaced by another culture which, in turn, made little impact on the south. This northern Chalcolithic culture appeared first at Megiddo, 'Affūleh and

[35] D. Ferembach, 'Le peuplement du Proche-Orient au Chalcolithique et au Bronze Ancien', *IEJ*, 9 (1959), pp. 221–228.

Beisān and has, for this reason, been called the Esdraelon culture. Recent finds, however, have shown beyond doubt that it was far more widely dispersed. Traces of it have been found in the Jordan Valley from Lake Tiberias (Khirbet Kerak) to as far south as the Dead Sea (Jericho and Tulūl Abu el-'Alayiq) and in the hill country between the same latitudes (Tell el-Fār'ah, 'Ai – the modern town of et-Tell – Tell en-Nasbeh, Gezer and Jerusalem). There is also evidence that it penetrated as far north as Kabri and Kafr Gil'adi and as far south as the caves of the Wādi el-Murabba'āt in the Judaean wilderness, the sites in the Wādi Ghazzeh and those on the coastal plain. In these southern sites, this culture is mixed with the last period of the Ghassulian culture of Beersheba.

It is known especially for its very large tombs, some of them containing hundreds of dead. The levels of living habitation, on the other hand, are correspondingly poor. The people would seem to have lived mostly in huts or in pit dwellings – solid buildings have been revealed only very rarely in a few sites. The classification of this culture under the heading of Chalcolithic is justified by the presence of copper implements. Its pottery can be divided into three classes: 1) red pottery, usually burnished; 2) grey burnished pottery and 3) pottery painted with simple geometrical designs using red lines.

The red and the grey burnished pottery have been found mixed together in the tombs of Tell el-Fār'ah and the other northern sites, but the red pottery appears alone at 'Ai, Tell en-Nasbeh, Gezer, Jerusalem and Jericho. The grey pottery, however, has only been found alone at Tulūl el-'Alayiq, just south of Jericho. Finally, there is the painted pottery and this has been excavated in the upper level of a tomb at Jericho, the lower levels of which contained only the red pottery. This would point to a difference in time, but not to a very great one, because the painted and the red pottery have both been found together in tombs at 'Ai, Tell en-Nasbeh and Gezer as well as in a tomb in the Ophel at Jerusalem. A few examples of this painted pottery have been discovered together with red and grey vessels in sites in the north. It is therefore certain that all three classes of pottery belonged to three groups which were more or less contemporary, but were originally distinct from each other and, what is more, were not introduced into the country at exactly the same time. Those who brought the red pottery into Palestine must have arrived before those who introduced the grey pottery and with whom they were associated in the north. They also penetrated farther south than those who came with the grey pottery and, in the south, they were joined by those who introduced the painted pottery.

The origin of these new populations is obscure. Anthropologists have not reached complete agreement, because Mediterranean types, with the exception of one negroid, have been found at Megiddo, proto-Mediterranean dolichocephals and Eurafrican dolichocephals at Jericho and proto-

Mediterranean and Alpine types at Tell el-'Asāwir near Jericho. What is important in this connection, however, is that there has been no indication anywhere of the brachycephals of the Ghassulian culture of Beersheba. The red and grey burnished pottery is very reminiscent of the ware produced in the Neolithic period in Crete, Rhodes and Malta and of a long tradition in Anatolia. It also resembles in certain ways the pottery of the Uruk period in Mesopotamia, and the painted pottery is related to the pottery of northern Syria. It is not yet possible to say whether there is any direct descent or to point to any intermediary stages, but it would seem that this Palestinian culture had many more links with the Eastern Mediterranean basin than with Mesopotamia and that it owed nothing at all to Egypt. On the contrary, some forms of Palestinian pottery were at this time, that is, during the pre-dynastic period of Naqada II, introduced into the Nile Valley.

It is very difficult to place the cultures discussed in this section precisely in one or other of the recognised ages. Some archaeologists have assumed that the culture that produced the painted pottery was a forerunner of the Early Bronze Age and have consequently situated the three groups of red, grey and painted pottery at the beginning of the Early Bronze and have left only the Ghassulian culture in the Chalcolithic Age.[36] Other scholars have also kept the Ghassulian in the Chalcolithic Period, but have classified the three groups of red, grey and painted pottery under a new heading – the Proto-Urban Age.[37] These new classifications are not satisfactory, however, because there is a sharp division between the red and grey pottery on the one hand and the Early Bronze pottery on the other and an even sharper division between the ways of life and patterns of habitation in the two periods. Villages consisting of huts and a few more solid buildings were quite abruptly followed by fortified cities on the great sites of Beisān, Megiddo, Tell el-Far'ah and Jericho. Other sites, like Meser on the Plain of Sharon, were permanently abandoned, whereas yet others, like Tell en-Nasbeh, were left and not reoccupied until much later. What is more, this new grouping into different ages creates an arbitrary division between two cultures which flourished at the same stage of human development – both Beisān, Megiddo and Tell Far'ah on the one hand and Teleilāt Ghassūl and the sites in the vicinity of Beersheba on the other were villages of farmers, potters and metal-workers.

The most decisive reason for keeping to the older classification, however,

[36] G. E. Wright, 'The Problem of the Transition between the Chalcolithic and Bronze Ages', *Eretz-Israel*, 5 (1958), pp. 37*–45*; R. Amiran, *The Ancient Pottery of Eretz Israel*, Jerusalem, 1963, p. 73 (Hebrew), revised English translation, *Ancient Pottery of the Holy Land*, Jerusalem, 1969, p. 41.

[37] See especially, K. M. Kenyon, *Archaeology in the Holy Land*, London, 1960, 3rd edn. 1970, pp. 84–100; *Excavations at Jericho*, I, London, 1960, pp. 84–100; *Excavations at Jericho*, II, London, 1965, pp. 8–32.

is that the two cultures were at least partly contemporary. The culture of Teleilāt Ghassūl and Beersheba was still flourishing in the south when the men who brought the red and grey pottery into Palestine were settling in the north of the land. The distinction is above all geographical. The men who introduced the painted pottery, on the other hand, probably settled first in the central part of the country between Jericho and Gezer, did not penetrate farther into the south and spread, very cautiously at first, throughout the north. It would therefore seem to be better in every way to call the culture of Teleilāt, Ghassūl, and Beersheba, Lower Chalcolithic, and that of the red and grey pottery Upper Chalcolithic. The Upper Chalcolithic Age began in Palestine round about 3400 B.C. – before the end of the Ghassulian period – and may have lasted until about 3100 B.C.

V. The Age of Fortified Cities

The Chalcolithic or Copper-Stone Age was followed by the Early Bronze Age, which suggests that stone was completely replaced by metal in the tool industry. This was not the case, however, in Palestine. The transition was not marked by the abandonment of stone tools, which continued to be used throughout the following age, nor by a widespread employment of metal implements, of which there is relatively little archaeological evidence at this time. The most striking aspects of the change are undoubtedly the emergence of urban life, progress in industry, especially the manufacture of pottery, and the establishment of a civilisation which was to last for a thousand years. This civilisation was remarkably unified, but there is clear evidence of considerable internal growth.[38]

Basing their decisions on changes in pottery, archaeologists have divided the Early Bronze Age into four phases. The painted pottery of one of the groups of the Chalcolithic Age had already prepared the way for the pottery of the Early Bronze Phase I and there is evidence that certain manufacturing techniques and a number of forms survived from the Chalcolithic into this first phase of Early Bronze. There were, however, technical innovations and new shapes in pottery. The Chalcolithic survivals disappeared in Phase II, when more prolonged firing produced the hard 'metallic' ware, so called because it has a metallic ring when struck. The finds of this phase include large plates with flat bases, small jars with

---

[38] See R. de Vaux, 'Palestine in the Early Bronze Age', *CAH*, I xv, 1966; J. B. Hennessy, *The Foreign Relations of Palestine during the Early Bronze Age*, London, 1967 (this work begins at the pre-urban period); P. Lapp, 'Palestine in the Early Bronze Age', *Near Eastern Archaeology in the Twentieth Century, Essays in Honour of Nelson Glueck*, Garden City, New York, 1970, pp. 101–131.*

stump-like bases and elegant larger jars. This ware was either fashioned by hand or turned on the wheel and was decorated by painting, by a beautiful red burnish or by painted triangles. Phase III is characterised by a pottery known as 'Khirbet Kerak ware', because it was first identified at this site at the southern extremity of Lake Tiberias. This pottery is not very well baked and is therefore fragile, but it is coated with a splendid burnish, sometimes uniformly red and sometimes red on the outside and black inside. The effect of this burnishing is sometimes heightened by a decoration in high relief made by grooves or incisions and often by the presence of zones which are not burnished. A fourth phase, Phase IV, has been added by some archaeologists, but it is not well represented and it tends to mark the beginning of the next period. It is above all important to bear in mind, however, that these distinctions are useful for the purposes of classification and of relative chronology, but they should not be allowed to obscure the characteristics shared by the whole period.

The most obvious characteristic of all is the disappearance of village life and the emergence of fortified cities. The dwellings on the sites that were continuously inhabited were grouped much more closely together in the Early Bronze Age and the favourite site for a new settlement in this period was a rocky acropolis. In both instances, the agglomeration was always surrounded by a solid rampart. A good example of this is at Tell el-Fār'ah. Dating from Phase I, a brick rampart more than nine feet thick was built on a foundation consisting of three courses of stones. This rampart was strengthened by bastions and by a projecting wall. It also had at least one gateway defended by two towers, was further reinforced by a stone wall and finally by a bank or glacis which was more than thirty-two feet wide at one point.[39] A second example is at Khirbet Kerak during Phase I or II, where a brick wall, supported on each side by further walls with a marked batter on the outer sides, formed a defence twenty-six feet thick. At Jericho, between the beginning of Phase I and the end of Phase III, the brick defensive walls built on a stone foundation were repaired or rebuilt seventeen times, often on a slightly different line. The houses were grouped very closely together under these walls, but were clearly arranged in order. At Tell el-Fār'ah (the northern site), they were built on each side of streets six and a half feet wide, perpendicular to the rampart, along which a passage was left free. At Khirbet Kerak, the paved streets were eight feet wide and the fortified cities of Tell el-Fā'ah, Beïsān and Megiddo also had drains for waste water.

The geographical distribution of the Early Bronze cities is interesting in itself. Almost all of them are situated in the centre or in the north of the country. Tell 'Arad, in the south and at the latitude of Beersheba, was surrounded by a defensive wall towards the end of Phase I and was abandoned

[39] R. de Vaux, 'Les foiulles de Tell el-Fâr'ah', RB, 69 (1962), pp. 212–215.

during Phase II.[40] It therefore forms an exception, together with Tell Gath near Beit Jebrīn, another Phase I site in the south of Palestine. As for Phase II, two sites at about the same latitude, Tell ed-Duweir and Tell el-Hesi, were clearly not occupied before the beginning of this phase. Another site south of Hebron, Tell Beit Mirsim, was not occupied before the end of the Early Bronze Age, that is, Phase 'IV'. Tell el-'Ajjūl, a site south of Gaza, began during the Intermediate Period between the Early and the Middle Bronze and the southern site of Tell el-Fār'ah was occupied only after the commencement of the Middle Bronze Age. It is important to bear this very slow expansion towards the south of the country in mind in any attempt to determine the origin of this civilisation.

The building methods, materials and plans provide another good indication of the origin and character of this age. Unbaked bricks were the most commonly used material and, at the beginning of the Early Bronze Age, they were employed almost exclusively. This technique must clearly have been introduced into the mountainous part of Palestine at least, where there has always been an abundance of stone, by people who were in the habit of building with bricks and not used to stone-masonry. With regard to the type of construction, houses were sometimes built with an apse on one of the shorter sides, but usually the ground plan was rectangular. Large flagstones were placed in the centre of the room, on the longitudinal axis or against the walls, and provided a base for the posts which supported the roof, which was probably flat and terraced. The thickness or height of some of the walls suggests that there may have been an upper storey. The houses usually consisted of only one room, although there was sometimes an annex. The door opened on to the street or a courtyard. Some of the structures revealed by excavation must have been public buildings. Five connected rooms arranged in two parallel lines between two streets and clearly belonging to Phase I have been unearthed at Tell el-Fār'ah. Three Phase II rooms discovered at Beisān possibly formed part of a more important building and a large hall sixty-five feet long and twenty-one feet wide and divided by a central row of columns has been dug out at 'Ai. It has been suggested that this Phase III structure was either a palace or a temple.

An ancient city such as Ai must have had a temple or even several temples. This great building was more probably a palace. There was a sanctuary in the city, because remains dating from Phase I and showing signs that the building was reconstructed several times at later periods have been discovered close to the defensive wall. At the northern site of Tell Fār'ah there was also a sanctuary, dating from Phase I and consisting of a room for worship and a cella with a dais. The earliest known example of a bāmah, the

[40] Y. Aharoni and R. Amiran, 'Excavations at Tel Arad', IEJ, 14 (1964), pp. 131–147, 280–283; see also IEJ, 15 (1965), pp. 251–252.*

'high place' of Canaanite cultic practice so often mentioned in the Old Testament, has been unearthed at Megiddo (Phase III). It consists of an oval-shaped pile of stones inside a rectangular walled enclosure.

Ancient cities must also have provided resting places for their dead. Very often mortal remains were placed outside the defensive walls of the city in natural caves or in artificial caves dug out of the rock. These tombs were collective burial-places, used for a long time by a family or a group of families. Several hundred individuals have been found in certain collective tombs at Jericho. The size, the number of individual skeletal remains discovered and the long period during which they were used may explain why so few Early Bronze tombs have been found near the great sites. Another explanation has, however, been put forward on the basis of a recent discovery. At Bāb edh-Dhra' in the Lisān below el-Kerak in Transjordania,[41] there is an enormous cemetery containing an estimated number of 20,000 collective burial-places, the earliest being well-tombs and the later ones great charnel-houses specially built to receive the bones of the dead. This great city of the dead is quite out of proportion with the relatively small fortified enclosure on a neighbouring hill where the living sheltered. It is therefore possible that the skeletal remains of the dead were brought to this cemetery and to others which have not yet been excavated from quite distant settlements for a second inhumation.

This development in urban life is clear evidence of a growth in the population and of better living conditions. The main activities were the cultivation of crops and the raising of cattle. Wheat, barley and lentils were grown especially, but evidence has also been found of peas and beans. It is also possible that the almond tree was cultivated and the olive was certainly grown, the local wild species being grafted. The vine was also introduced at this period from abroad.

More is known not only about the products of the pottery industry, but also about the ways in which they were made than about any other industry of this period. Potters' workshops have been discovered, for example, at the northern site of Tell el-Fār'ah.[42] It is certain that slow-turning potters' wheels were widely used for small vases and the necks of jars and pitchers; several small turn-tables have been found at Megiddo, Khirbet Kerak and Tell el-Fār'ah. Firing at a higher and more stable temperature was done in closed kilns, the earliest example of which in Palestine was found at Tell el-Fār'ah. This dates from Phase I.[43]

We have much less information about the metal-working industry,

[41] P. W. Lapp, 'The Cemetery at Bab edh-Dhra' ', *Archaeology*, 19 (1966), pp. 104–111; 'Bab edh-Dhra' Tomb A 76 and Early Bronze I in Palestine', *BASOR*, 189 (Feb. 1968), pp. 12–41; 'Bab edh-Dhra' ', *Jerusalem through the Ages*, Jerusalem, 1968, pp. 1*–25*.

[42] R. de Vaux, 'Les fouilles de Tell el-Fâr'ah', *RB*, 55 (1948), p. 551; 68 (1961), p. 582.

[43] R. de Vaux, 'Les fouilles de Tell el-Fâr'ah', *RB*, 62 (1955), pp. 558–563.

although metal objects have been found on all the sites. Metal was still very precious, however, and therefore carefully guarded and used again and again, so that only small numbers of metal objects have been found. An important hoard of tools and weapons made of copper was nonetheless found by chance on the Plain of Sharon at Kafr Monash.[44] They were made locally from ingots which had come from abroad, some from Anatolia. They can probably be ascribed to Phase I and Phase II. Another and smaller hoard comes from Tell el-Hesi and this dates back to Phase III. Two moulds for casting axes have been discovered at Megiddo.

One important consequence of this increased prosperity was the establishment of economic relationships between the cities of Palestine and with foreign countries, but the extent and the nature of this trade can only be a matter of conjecture. The copper mines of the 'Arabah were not in use at this time and the metal workers had to import their raw materials. Like Syria at the beginning of the Fifth Dynasty, however, Palestine probably exported surplus oil to Egypt. The growth of certain sites was probably due to their situation on trade routes. Khirbet Kerak, for instance, was at the crossroads of two important routes, one running from north to south along the Jordan Valley and the other from east to west, from Damascus and Haurān to the Plain of Esdraelon. One building at Khirbet Kerak has been interpreted as a group of storehouses like those found in Egypt.

In addition to trading relationships, Palestine also had foreign cultural connections at this time. In the first place, her culture was the same as that of southern Syria. The cultural development of Byblos, for example, from its first urban settlement until its destruction at the end of the Fourth Dynasty in Egypt, at about the same time that 'Ai and Khirbet Kerak were destroyed, was parallel to that of the Palestinian cities. The products of the pottery and copper industries in Phoenicia were very similar to those in Palestine, good examples being the jugs with flat ring-shaped handles which were an innovation introduced during Phase II and the Phase III pottery of Khirbet Kerak. These cultural contacts extended to northern Syria[45] and even farther – vases and metal and stone objects similar to those found in Early Bronze Age Palestine have been discovered in central Anatolia[46] and the origins of the pottery of Khirbet Kerak can be traced

---

[44] R. Hestrin and M. Tadmor, 'A Hoard of Tools and Weapons from Kafr Monash', *IEJ*, 13 (1963), pp. 265–288.

[45] These two types of pottery have been found in Phases G and H respectively of the Plain of Antioch at 'Amuq; see R. J. Braidwood and L. S. Braidwood, *Excavations in the Plain of Antioch*, I, Chicago, 1960; for the pottery of Khirbet Kerak especially, see S. Hood, 'Excavations at Tabara el-Akrad', *Anatolian Studies*, 1 (1951), pp. 113–147.

[46] R. Amiran, 'Connections between Anatolia and Palestine in the Early Bronze Age', *IEJ*, 2 (1952), pp. 89–104; M. W. Prausnitz, 'Palestine and Anatolia', *Eleventh Annual Report of the Institute of Archaeology*, London, 1955; P. Parr, 'Palestine and Anatolia: A Further Note', *Bulletin of the Institute of Archaeology*, London, 1 (1958), pp. 21–23.

back, through eastern Anatolia,[47] as far as Transcaucasus.[48]

There were, on the other hand, hardly any contacts at all with Mesopotamia during the whole of the Early Bronze Age. Relationships with Egypt were more active at this time.[49] Objects from the Nile Valley have been found in Palestine, especially offerings made in the sanctuary at Ai. Potters and craftsmen working with bronze in Palestine copied Egyptian models. What is more, vases made in Palestine have also been discovered in tombs of the First Dynasty and occasionally in those of the Second Dynasty. The Palestinian vases date from Phases I and II. Relationships with Egypt seem to have ceased by Phase III, because no Palestinian vases of this period have been excavated in Egypt, although 'Syrian' vases are represented on a Fifth Dynasty relief of Sahu-Re.

A relative chronology of the phases in the Palestinian Early Bronze Age has been based on these connections with Egypt. Phase I began before the First Dynasty in Egypt and the beginning of Phase II coincides with that dynasty, the phase continuing throughout the Second Dynasty and probably also throughout the Third Dynasty. Phase III corresponds to the Age of the Pyramids in Egypt. The final Phase 'IV', which has been added by some archaeologists, and the end of the Early Bronze Age coincide with the beginning of the First Intermediate Period in Egypt. The absolute dates in this chronology depend on the chronology accepted for Egypt. The situation in Palestine and the contacts that can be established with northern Syria would suggest a short chronology, keeping the development of the Early Bronze Age within the limits of a single millennium, that is, between about 3100 and 2200 B.C.

It would not be possible to write the history of Palestine during this period. All that our interpretation of a number of archaeological finds and Egyptian texts has enabled us to do is to sketch out an incomplete and tentative outline of that history. The civilisation of the Early Bronze Age did not develop from the Ghassulian culture, which vanished without leaving any direct successor, nor did it stem from the culture of the Upper Chalcolithic in the north which produced the red and grey burnished ware. Its appearance can only be explained by the influx of a new population. The first immigrants brought with them the painted pottery of the end of the Chalcolithic Age and began to settle in the central part of Palestine. These were then followed by a far greater number of immigrants round about

[47] C. A. Burney, 'Eastern Anatolia in the Chalcolithic and Early Bronze Age', AnStud, 8 (1958), pp. 157–209, especially pp. 173–174.

[48] R. Amiran, 'Yanik Tepe, Shengavit and the Khirbet Kerak Ware', AnStud, 15 (1965), pp. 165–167.

[49] H. J. Kantor, 'The Early Relations of Egypt with Asia', JNES, 1 (1942), pp. 174–213; R. Amiran, 'A Preliminary Note on the Synchronisms between the Early Bronze Age Strata of Arad and the First Dynasty', BASOR, 179 (Oct. 1965), pp. 30–33.

3100 B.C. These Early Bronze Age immigrants did not come from the south
– their civilisation either made less impact there or else only reached the
south at a later phase. On the contrary, it is evident from the close parallel
with the civilisation of Byblos and southern Syria that they entered
Palestine from the north, probably through the Jordan Valley, bringing
with them a tradition of urban life and of building with bricks. Their
origins can therefore be traced back to a region of valleys or alluvial plains.
Contacts with Mesopotamia and northern Syria were probably so tenuous
that it would be fruitless to look for the origins of the Early Bronze immigrants into Palestine in such remote parts. A more reasonable suggestion
would therefore be the Beqaʿ of southern Syria and the Lebanon – a region
which has, moreover, so far been little explored by archaeologists.

Anthropologists have not been able to throw much light on the race to
which this population belonged. Only in the case of two small groups of
human remains have the results of anthropological investigation been
published. In the first place, five skulls of Phases I to III were discovered at
Lachish,[50] but the authors of the study have not distinguished these skulls
from those belonging to the Middle and the Late Bronze Ages and have
simply concluded that there was no striking change between the Bronze
and the Iron Ages. In the second place, nine skulls were excavated at
Megiddo,[51] dating back to the extreme end of the Early Bronze or to the
beginning of the Intermediate Period between the Early and Middle
Bronze Ages. These skulls, which were found in the Lower Tomb 1101 B,
are 'Mediterranean', like the Chalcolithic Age men discovered at Megiddo.

The great unity that persisted throughout the whole of the Early Bronze
civilisation would at least seem to indicate that the population remained
basically the same during the third millennium. The people of this period
spoke a north-west Semitic language. It was from the Palestinians or the
southern Syrians that the Egyptians of the Old Empire borrowed the word
'flour' to denote a kind of bread, qmhw. The inscription on the tomb of
Anta at Deshasheh, which is discussed towards the end of this chapter, contains the Semitic names of two towns. Generally speaking, from the point
of view of the study of place names, Palestine and Syria together make up a
region where many of the early names for mountains, rivers and towns are
of north-west Semitic origin.[52] Some place-names have been shown to date
from the third millennium and others only from the beginning of the
second, but place-names, especially those of mountains and rivers, are
notoriously perdurable. We may therefore conclude by saying that

[50] See M. Giles' contribution to O. Tufnell's *Lachish IV, The Bronze Age*, London, 1958,
pp. 318–322.
[51] A. Hrdlička, in P.L.O. Guy, *Megiddo Tombs*, Chicago, 1938, pp. 192–208.
[52] B. S. J. Isserlin, 'Place Name Provinces in the Semitic-Speaking Ancient Near East',
Proceedings of the Leeds Philosophical Society, VIII ii, 1956, pp. 83–110.

Semites first settled in Palestine at the beginning of the Early Bronze Age. Following the practice of the Bible, it is possible to call these first Semitic settlers 'Canaanites'. Although the authors of the Bible gave this name to those who inhabited Palestine before the arrival of the Israelites, it should not be forgotten that it was a purely conventional name – Canaan is not found in texts before the middle of the second millennium.

Phase II, which began round about 2900 B.C., marks the culminating point of the period. The pottery of this phase clearly reveals new influences which can be traced back to northern Syria but which do not necessarily point to the arrival of a new wave of immigrants into Palestine. The number of cities and their importance are indications of a relatively numerous population at this time and the fact that they were fortified suggests that the country was divided into small states which were frequently at war with each other. The political situation is, however, shrouded in obscurity and we know nothing of the part played by Egypt. Apart from Byblos, where the influence of Egypt was felt at a very early stage because of contacts established by sea, the first pharaohs had a very limited aim when they sent out expeditions by land to Asia – that of defending their turquoise mines in the Sinai desert against bedouins.[53] The Syro-Palestinian vases found in the tombs of the First and Second Dynasties cannot be accepted as evidence that Egypt had political control of Palestine at this time. On the other hand, the stone vases of the Second and Third Dynasties discovered in the sanctuary at Ai and the clay copies of vases of the Fourth Dynasty found with them may have been sent by the pharaohs as a sign of respect paid to a local god and of their authority over those who worshipped that deity. The presence of these vases at 'Ai does in any case prove that there were relationships between the two countries during the Early Bronze Age and it is possible that Egypt wanted to increase her trade with Phoenicia by opening a land route as well as a sea route. This, however, would have meant that she had to control at least part of Palestine. An attempt to do this can perhaps be traced back to Nar-mer, the founder of the First Dynasty. He is represented on a well-known palette[54] as subduing his enemies. Some of these enemies are symbolised by a city surrounded by a rampart with towers, like some of the Palestinian ramparts of Phases I and II, while others are depicted by what would seem to be an enclosure for flocks. This plaque may possibly commemorate a campaign carried out against the Phoenician cities and the nomads inhabiting the Negeb and Transjordania.[55] Epigraphic confirmation of this is provided by

[53] L. Bongrani, "I rapporti fra l'Egitto, la Siria e il Sinai durante l'Antico Regno', OrAnt, 2 (1963), pp. 171–203.

[54] ANEP, fig. 296–297.

[55] Y. Yadin, 'The Earliest Record of Egypt's Military Penetration into Asia?', IEJ, 5 (1955), pp. 1–16. What I believe to be a fortified city seen from above as a ground plan, this author interprets as a ziggurat.*

two ostraca or potsherds used for writing messages found at Tell Gath to the east of 'Asqalān (Ashkalon), with the name Nar-mer inscribed on them.[56] Egyptian control of southern Palestine would have enabled Tell Gath and Tell 'Arad to develop during Phase II and would also explain the presence of Egyptian influences such as those which have been revealed by archaeologists on the two sites. Their abandonment at more or less the same time before the end of Phase II[57] can also be explained by the fact that Egypt lost control of the region at about this period and that the Pharaohs must have had to carry out punitive raids in the Sinai desert from the Third Dynasty onwards.

Round about 2600 B.C., towards the beginning of Phase III, the introduction of Khirbet Kerak ware into the north of the country marked the arrival of the new immigrants, who formed the first wave of a movement which had begun, perhaps a century before this, in Transcaucasus. There were probably far fewer of them at the end of their long migration and they were certainly assimilated very quickly. As for Egypt, the situation is at first not easy to interpret. A scene depicted on the tomb of Anta at Deshasheh (Fifth Dynasty)[58] shows the capture of an Asiatic fortress and the damaged inscription contains two Semitic names of towns, but it is not possible to say with certainty whether they are in Palestine or in Phoenicia. The information that we have about the situation in the Sixth Dynasty is a little more explicit. During the reign of Pepi I, General Uni conducted five campaigns against the Asiatics by land, in the course of which fortresses were destroyed, houses set on fire and fig trees and vines cut down.[59] This cannot have taken place in the Sinai area. Uni must have led his troops into Palestine, in an attempt to establish control, perhaps not for the first time, over the country or more probably in a defensive action against pressure coming from the north and threatening Egypt's frontiers.

Palestine had, by this time, entered a period of serious difficulties. At the end of Phase II and the beginning of Phase III, sites such as Tell el-Fār'ah near Nāblus and Rās el-'Ain at the source of the Jaffa River were deserted. Megiddo was abandoned during the course of Phase III. Towards the end of this phase, the movement was accelerated and Hazor (Tell el-Qedah), Beisān, Khirbet Kerak, 'Ai and Jericho were all destroyed. These disasters did not affect Palestine alone – Byblos[60] was also destroyed by fire during

[56] S. Yeivin, 'Early Contacts between Canaan and Egypt', *IEJ*, 10 (1960), pp. 193–203; 'Further Evidence of Narmer at "Gat" ', *OrAnt*, 2 (1963), pp. 205–213.

[57] A. Ciasca, 'Tell Gat', *OrAnt*, 1 (1962), pp. 23–29; R. Amiran, *IEJ*, 15 (1965), pp. 251–252 (Tell Arad).

[58] Flinders Petrie, *Deshasheh*, London, 1898, p. 5 and plate iv.

[59] *ANET*, pp. 227–228.

[60] *ANET*, p. 441. A much later date has also been suggested for this text; see J. van Seters, 'A Date for the "Admonitions" in the Second Intermediate Period', *JEA*, 50 (1964), pp. 13–23.

the reign of Pepi II and shortly afterwards, the sage, Ipu-wer, complained that trade by sea with Phoenicia had ceased. These were all in fact local aspects of a great migration of groups of people throughout the whole of the Near East, the principal part in this movement being played by the Amorites. But this forms the subject of a new chapter in our history.

Chapter Three

PALESTINE DURING THE FIRST HALF
OF THE SECOND MILLENNIUM

I. THE INTERMEDIATE PERIOD BETWEEN THE EARLY AND MIDDLE
BRONZE AGES

THE collapse of the Early Bronze civilization round about 2200 B.C. marked the end of one era and the beginning of a new one.[1] For a long time now, archaeologists[2] have made a distinction between an Early Bronze IV, as the period during which the Early Bronze Age was declining, and a Middle Bronze I, as the beginning of the following age. It is, however, generally preferable to speak of an intermediate Period between the Early and Middle Bronze Ages. One after another, the fortified cities had been destroyed and urban life appeared again only after an interval of several centuries. At the northern sites of Tell el-Fār'ah, Rās el-'Ain, Megiddo and Beisān these cities began to be repopulated fairly early in the Middle Bronze Age. At Ai, urban life was resumed during the twelfth century B.C., and at Khirbet Kerak it reappeared during the Hellenistic period.

[1] For the general historical background to this period, see, for example: R. T. O'Callaghan, *Aram Naharaim: A Contribution to the History of Upper Mesopotamia in the Second Millennium B.C.*, Rome, 1948; J.-R. Kupper, 'Northern Mesopotamia and Syria', *CAH*, II, I, 1963; G. Posener, J. Bottéro and K. M. Kenyon, 'Syria and Palestine c. 2160–1780', *CAH*, I, XXI, 1965; E. Cassin, J. Bottéro and J. Vercoutter, eds, *Die Altorientalischen Reiche, I, Vom Paläolithikum bis zur Mitte des 2. Jahrtausends* (Fischer Weltgeschichte, 2), Frankfurt a.M., 1965; English translation: *The Near East: The Early Civilisations* (The Weidenfeld and Nicolson Universal History, 2), London, 1967 (Mesopotamia is dealt with in this volume by D. O. Edzard and Egypt by J. Vercoutter; there is virtually nothing about Syria and Palestine); R. Garelli, *Le Proche-Orient Asiatique des origines aux invasions des Peuples de la Mer* (Nouvelle Clio, 2), Paris, 1969.*
[2] For the archaeology of this period, see: R. Amiran, 'The Pottery of the Middle Bronze Age I in Palestine', *IEJ*, 10 (1960), pp. 204–25; W. F. Albright, 'The Chronology of the Middle Bronze I (Early Bronze-Middle Bronze)', *BASOR*, 168 (December 1962), pp. 36–42; K. M. Kenyon, 'Palestine in the Middle Bronze Age', *CAH*, II, III, 1966; ibid., *Amorites and Canaanites*, London, 1966; B. Mazar, 'The Middle Bronze Age in Palestine', *IEJ*, 18 (1968), pp. 65–97.*

This does not mean, however, that all these sites remained completely deserted during this time. Some of them, notably Hazor, Megiddo, Beīan, Jericho and Tell ed-Duweir, continued to be inhabited, but the new inhabitants camped among the ruins or lived in caves. They did not build defensive walls and, at least at the beginning of this intermediate phase, they did not even build houses and, whenever they did, these dwellings were extremely modest. If a group of sanctuaries has to be attributed to this period, then Megiddo must be regarded as exceptional.[3] Other sites with a long history, such as Tell Beit Mirsim, Beth Shemesh, Bethel and Tell el-'Ajjūl, began to be occupied at this time, but, to begin with, there is no evidence of urban life. Pottery of this period has been found at the first three of these sites, but no trace of any buildings. Two cemeteries have been excavated at Tell el-'Ajjūl, but no corresponding level of human habitation. Recent excavations have revealed more tombs and settlements where the same pottery has been found and places which never became urban centres. Examples of these are the tombs at Khirbet Kūfin in the south of Palestine,[4] the area around 'Ain Sāmiyeh in central Palestine[5] and around Ma'ayan Barūkh in the north,[6] the inhabited caves in the Wādi Dahliyah,[7] the open buildings in the Jordan Valley and elsewhere, for instance at Tell Umm Hamed el-Gharbi[8] and Tell Iqtanū.[9] Between the twenty-first and the nineteenth centuries B.C. the Negeb was relatively densely populated – evidence has been found of encampments of round stone huts. These were never surrounded by defensive walls and were probably seasonal.[10]

A number of surface explorations have been carried out in Transjordania,[11] although there have not been enough excavations in that region to substantiate the claims made.[12] Nonetheless, the evidence seems to indicate that the history of Transjordania during this period was different from that of Cisjordania. Pottery similar to that found in the tombs at

[3] K. M. Kenyon, 'Some Notes on the Early and Middle Bronze Age Strata of Megiddo', *Eretz-Israel*, 5 (1958), pp. 51*–60*.

[4] R. H. Smith, *Excavations in the Cemetery at Khirbet Kūfin*, London, 1962.

[5] P. Lapp, *The Dhahr Mirzbaneh Tombs*, New Haven, 1966.

[6] R. Amiran, 'Tombs of the Middle Bronze Age I at Ma'ayan Barukh', *'Atiqot*, 3 (1961), pp. 84–92.

[7] P. Lapp, 'Chronique Archéologique', *RB*, 72 (1965), pp. 408–9.

[8] N. Glueck, 'A Settlement of Middle Bronze I in the Jordan Valley', *BASOR*, 100 (December 1945) pp. 7–16.

[9] An excavation conducted by Kay Wright in 1966, unpublished.

[10] N. Glueck, 'Exploring Southern Palestine (The Negev) ', *BibArch*, 22 (1959), pp. 82–97; ibid., 'The Archaeological History of the Negev', *HUCA*, 32 (1961), pp. 11–18.

[11] N. Glueck, 'Explorations in Eastern Palestine, III (*AASOR*, 18–19), 1939, pp. 251–266; ibid., *The Other Side of the Jordan*, New Haven, 1940, pp. 114–125.

[12] P. Parr, 'Excavations at Khirbet Iskander', *ADAJ*, 4–5 (1960), pp. 128–133; E. Olávarri, 'Fouilles à 'Arô'er sur l'Arnon. Les niveaux du Bronze Intermédiaire', *RB*, 76 (1969), pp. 230–259.

Megiddo has, it is true, been found in a tomb at Hosn on the Transjordanian tableland.[13] There is clear evidence, however, of important settlements consisting of houses and sometimes of ramparts scattered over the whole plateau from the north to the south and these must have been founded at the end of the Ancient Bronze Age and were probably occupied during the Intermediate Period.

Leaving aside the evidence in Transjordania, which has not yet been definitively interpreted, almost everything that we know about the new inhabitants of Palestine is based on their tombs and the contents of these tombs. They built no houses for the living, but clearly took a great deal of care in digging tombs out of the rock for their dead. These were reached by pits which were sometimes very deep and were destined for the remains of a single person. The tombs were grouped in cemeteries which were frequently very large indeed. In the three neighbouring cemeteries at 'Ain Samiyeh, almost a hundred tombs have been excavated. In addition, 75 tombs have been revealed in one of the two cemeteries at Tell el-'Ajjūl, 122 at Lachish and 346 at Jericho.

There is also an astonishing variety of shapes and sizes in these tombs as well as in their furnishings and in the burial customs to which they bear witness. Seven different types have been distinguished at Jericho[14] and five at Lachish. There is a similar variety in the contents of the tombs of this period – some contain only pots, weapons or pearls, whereas others contain a mixture. Sometimes whole bodies have been buried in these tombs and sometimes simply bones without flesh. The pottery is quite distinctive, not at all like that of the Early Bronze Age and even less like that of the Middle Bronze, apart from that at Megiddo. Despite certain shared characteristics, it is possible to distinguish three groups of pottery according to three regions – a northern, a central and a southern zone. As distinct from the Early Bronze Age, many copper objects have been found, especially riveted daggers, javelins with a long point curved at the end and pins with large heads.

All these tombs belong to approximately the same period and it is very difficult to arrange them in chronological order. Their diversity can be attributed to the arrival in Palestine of various groups of people, each retaining its own customs. On the other hand, however, the fact that these new immigrants built no solid houses and that they were so dispersed in their habitat shows that they were semi-nomadic people, who cultivated crops when the occasion arose, but were mainly herdsmen. Their warlike character is clear from the weapons that have been found on these sites. It was undoubtedly these nomads who put an end to the Early Bronze

---

[13] G. L. Harding, *Four Tomb Groups from Jordan*, London, 1953, pp. 1–13.
[14] K. M. Kenyon, *Jericho I*, London, 1960, pp. 180–262; *Jericho II*, 1965, pp. 33–166.

civilisation and who brought about an eclipse of urban life. This eclipse began before 2200 and lasted until about 1900 B.C. During the twenty-second and twenty-first centuries, it was total.

Where did these warlike herdsmen come from? Their pottery and weapons are quite closely paralleled in Syria, both on the coast at Byblos and Rās Shamrah and in the interior, where similar objects have been found in sites along the road from Damascus to Aleppo at Qatna, Khan Sheikhoun, Tell 'As and Tell Mardikh. But it should not be forgotten that Syria experienced the same disorders as Palestine. The country was also invaded by people who were related to but different from those who invaded Palestine and were, moreover, as lacking in unity as the invaders of Palestine at this period. The origins of this movement have to be sought farther afield.

II. The Amorites

The disorders which took place at the end of the third and the beginning of the second millennia were not, however, confined simply to Syria and Palestine. This was also the time of the First Intermediate Period in Egypt and in Mesopotamia it was also an 'Intermediate Period', that is, between the fall of the Third Dynasty of Ur and the reunification of the territory under Hammurabi.[15] These upheavals had different causes in Egypt and in Mesopotamia, but in both cases they were made more serious by the intervention of the desert nomads. It is clear that the events in Palestine have to be considered together with the movement which affected the whole of the Ancient Near East.[16]

The stages in this development can be observed most clearly in Babylonia. At the end of the third millennium the people of the 'West', known in Sumerian as MAR.TU and in Akkadian as Amurru, in other words, the Amorites, began to emerge as a source of danger in the Near East.[17] The penultimate king of the Third Dynasty of Ur, Shu-Sin

[15] This is the name which D. O. Edzard gave to this period; see note 16 below, referring to his book.

[16] For the Amorites, see S. Moscati, *I predecessori d'Israele. Studi sulle più antiche genti semitiche in Siria e Palestina*, Rome, 1956; D. O. Edzard, *Die 'Zweite Zwischenzeit' Babyloniens*, Wiesbaden, 1957; J.–R. Kupper, *Les nomades en Mésopotamie au temps des rois de Mari*, Liège and Paris, 1957; I. J. Gelb, 'The Early History of the West Semitic Peoples', *JCS*, 15 (1961), pp. 27–47; G. Buccellati, *The Amorites of the Ur III Period*, Naples, 1966; M. Liverani, 'Per una considerazione istorica del problema amorreo', *OrAnt*, 9 (1970), pp. 5–27.

[17] The texts will be found in Edzard, *op. cit.*, pp. 31–34 and Kupper has commented on the most important of them, *op. cit.*, pp. 149–150, 156–160. C. Wilcke has expressed certain reservations in his article 'Zur Geschichte der Amorriter in der Ur-III-Zeit', *WO*, 5 (1969), pp. 1–31.

(2048–2039), 'built a rampart (a fortress) against MAR.TU (whom he called) Who-thrust-aside-Tidnum', and another of his inscriptions says that he 'repelled the force of MAR.TU in his steppe land'. Tidnum is a place mentioned later, situated close to the Jebel Bishri on the west of the Euphrates in the direction of Palmyra. More than two centuries before the time of Shu-Sin, Shar-Kali-Sharri had beaten the MAR.TU on their own ground at the Jebel Bishri. The danger therefore threatened from the direction of the Syrian desert. The steps taken against the Amorites proved to be useless, and a letter written to Ibbi-Sin, the last king of the Third Dynasty of Ur (2039–2015), contained a clear warning: 'All the MAR.TU have penetrated into the interior of the country, seizing the great fortresses one after another.'

Further information about these Amorites is also provided by the literary texts dating back to the end of the third millennium. In the epic of Lugalbanda and Enmerkar the wish is expressed that 'the MAR.TU, who do not know wheat, may be thrust out of Sumer and Akkad' and another epic text refers to 'the MAR.TU who know neither house nor city; they are boorish inhabitants of the mountain region'. A lively description can also be found in the myth of the marriage of the god Amurru, the god who gave his name to the Amorites. In this passage, Amurru is called 'a man who unearths truffles at the foot of the mountains, who cannot bend his knee (to cultivate the soil), who eats raw meat, who has no house during his life and who is not buried after his death'. We may therefore conclude that the Amorites were dangerous, unruly nomads living on the fringe of civilization and scorned and feared by their sedentary neighbours.

They did, however, eventually become civilized. When Ur had fallen to the Elamites the empire was divided into a number of principalities, the most important of which, to begin with, was Isin, where Ishbi-Irra settled. Ishbi-Irra had come from Mari on the Middle Euphrates and had rebelled against Ibbi-Sin. Many of the names of the heads of the other principalities are north-western Semitic. The names of the first seven kings of the dynasty which became established at Larsa from Naplanum to Sumu-Ilum, are north-western Semitic in origin. The same applies to Kish, Marad and Sippar in Babylonia and to Eshnunna and Tutub (Khafajeh) to the east of the Tigris. Finally, it was another north-western Semite, Sumu-Abum, who founded the First Dynasty of Babylon. The most famous king of this dynasty was, of course, Hammurabi (1792–1750 B.C.). Hammurabi is another north-western Semitic name.

At the same time as families which were western Semitic in origin were ruling over the little states that had inherited the empire of Ur, hundreds of names of the same kind were appearing in the private documents of Babylonia. These names cannot be regarded as separate from those borne by the MAR.TU of the Third Dynasty of Ur and this new element in the population has clearly to be regarded as Amorite. [18] In fact, the Edict of Ammisaduga, the penultimate king of the Babylonian Dynasty, a document ordering a remission of debts and exemptions from taxation,[19] laid down that these measures applied not only to the Akkadians, but also to the Amorites. This is a clear indication that the Amorites were by this time recognised as an element in the population and that they enjoyed full civil rights. It is therefore with good reason that the Dynasty of Amurru was called, in a late text, the First Babylonian Dynasty.

The same movement took place in Upper Mesopotamia and in northern Syria. Our knowledge of these two regions has been greatly extended by the recent discovery of texts at Tell Harīri (Mari), Chagar Bazar (Ashnakkum[20]) and Tell el-'Atshāneh (Alalaḫ). Our information about the Ur III period, however, is scanty, although we can say with some certainty that the population of Mari was mainly Akkadian. Relatively few of the names are not Semitic and very few indeed are north-western Semitic. To judge from the little information that we have, it would seem to have been the same in Upper Mesopotamia.

A radical change took place, however, during the much better documented period known as the golden age of Mari (1830–1760 B.C.), which coincided approximately with the reigns of Apil-Sin, Sinmuballit and Hammurabi in Babylonia and those of Shamshi-Adad and Ishme-Dagan in Assyria. At this time the kingdom of Mari was ruled by a dynasty, the three kings of which, Yaggid-Lim, Yaḫdun-Lim and Zimri-Lim, all have Amorite names. The population was also overwhelmingly Amorite and the texts that have so far been published contain more than a thousand names which are western Semitic.[21] Yahdun-Lim's opponent and the founder of Assyria's power in the Near East, Shamshi-Adad, had an Akkadian name, but his father was called Ila-Kabkabu. This is an Amorite name and the ruler himself may have originated in Chagar Bazar. The Amorite princes ruled at that time, or were soon to rule, at Carchemish, Yamḫad (Aleppo), Alalah, Rās Shamrah and Qatna. The Chagar Bazar texts have provided us with a small number of Amorite names of private persons and the texts discovered at Alalah have yielded a much greater number.

---

[18] See especially A. Goetze, 'Amurrite Names in Ur III and Early Isin Texts', *JSS*, 4 (1959), pp. 193–203; I. J. Gelb, *op. cit.*, pp. 27–47; G. Buccellati, *op. cit.*; I. J. Gelb, 'An Old Babylonian List of Amorites', *JAOS*, 88 (1968), pp. 39–46 = *Essays in Memory of E. A. Speiser*, New Haven, 1968, same page numbers.

[19] F. R. Kraus, *Ein Edikt des Königs Ammi-Saduqa von Babylon*, Leiden, 1958.

[20] Not Shubat-Enlil, which is at Tell Leilan; see W. J. van Liere, *AAS*, 13 (1963), pp. 119–120; W. W. Hallo, *JCS*, 18 (1964), p. 74.

[21] H. B. Huffmon, *Amorite Personal Names in the Mari Texts*, Baltimore, 1965; in the long list of names given in *ARM* XIII, 1964. No. 1 must be added to Huffmon's list.

Apart from these testimonies to the presence of Amorites in a part of Upper Mesopotamia and in the whole of northern Syria, we also have evidence in the Mari texts of a country called specifically the land of Amurru. One text speaks of this country as neighbouring those of Yamhad and Qatna, while another refers to the messengers of four kings of Amurru at the same time as the messenger of Hazor in northern Palestine.[22] The Alalaḫ texts, which are a little later, also mention the country of Amurru several times as a region that was relatively close.[23] On the basis of all this evidence, then, we may say that Amurru was in central Syria and that the reference to the four kings of the country means that it was politically well organised at the time.

The fact that the Amorites settled in cities and that they gained a certain power does not, however, mean that the movement of nomads ceased altogether. The kings of Mari frequently had to deal with groups of nomads from the steppe land. The most unruly of these nomads were the Suteans, who are also mentioned in Babylonian texts. They were often engaged as mercenaries, but they were above all plunderers who constantly refused to become sedentary. Another group of nomads, living mostly in camps, but sometimes in villages, shepherds who also cultivated the soil and were caravan traders, were the Ḥaneans. Finally, there were the Benjaminites. These people, in whom biblical scholars have been especially interested, remained more attached to the nomadic way of life than the Ḥaneans and less dependent on the kings of Mari. This independence sometimes went as far as open hostility against Mari, frequently ending in alliance or in partial submission. Although their encampments were mainly in the Middle Euphrates around Mari, they also lived in the country surrounding Harran and in Upper Mesopotamia as well as in Syria, to the south of Qatna. The only resemblance between these Benjaminites and the tribe of Benjamin in the Old Testament is the name shared by both. It means, of course, 'Sons of the South' and the Mari texts mention 'Sons of the North' as well. It is necessary to mention a further group of nomads, the Ḥabiru, who will be discussed later in this work.

It is necessary to consult the Egyptian texts of the period to judge the situation in Palestine and southern Syria at the beginning of the second millennium. By the end of the Old Kingdom, Asiatic people were beginning to infiltrate into Egypt and to settle there. At the beginning of the First Intermediate Period which followed the Old Kingdom, the sage, Ipu-wer,

---

[22] Unpublished texts quoted by G. Dossin, 'Kengen, pays de Canaan', RSO, 32 (1957), pp. 37–38; ARM XII 747; A. Malamat, 'Hazor "The Head of All These Kingdoms" ', JBL, 79 (1960), pp. 12–19; ibid., 'Hazor and its Northern Neighbours', Eretz-Israel, 9 (Albright Volume), 1969, pp. 102–108 (in Hebrew).

[23] J.-R. Kupper, op. cit., p. 179; the texts have been published in transcription by D. J. Wiseman in his 'Ration Lists from Alalakh VII', JCS, 13 (1959), pp. 19–33.

who probably lived at this time, complained that the 'foreigners' in Egypt
had become 'people' that is, they had become people of the country and
had learnt all the trades of the Delta.[24] A pharaoh of the Tenth Dynasty,
Akhthoes III, helped the nomarchs of the Delta to rid themselves of the invaders and strengthened the frontier. In the instructions that he left his son
and successor, Meri-ka-Re, he warned the latter against 'the wretched
Asiatic . . . He does not dwell in a single place, (but) his legs are made to go
astray. He has been fighting (ever) since the time of Horus, (but) he does
not conquer, nor yet can he be conquered. He does not announce a day in
fighting, like a thief (?) . . . He may rob a single person (?), (but) he does
not lead against a town of many citizens'.[25] According to the prophecy of
Neferti.[26] Amen-em-het (1991–1962) built a series of fortresses known as
the 'Wall of the Ruler' along the eastern frontier of the land to protect it
against the invaders, although the Asiatics could be authorised to cross the
frontier to let their flocks drink. This wall is also mentioned in the story of
Si-nuhe, an important Egyptian official who went voluntarily into exile in
Syria when Amen-em-het I died.[27] The infiltration of these Asiatic people
continued, but it was controlled.

A painting on the tomb of Khnum-hotep at Beni-Hassan, dating from the
reign of Sesostris II (ca. 1890 B.C), shows the arrival of a caravan of
thirty-seven Asiatics led by 'the ruler of a foreign country Ibsha' (or
Abi-shar) and a scribe recording their entry into Egypt.[28] These Asiatics are
also mentioned in the texts of the Twelfth and Thirteenth Dynasties as
living in Egypt in greater and greater numbers.[29] They remained either
slaves, servants or workers, however, and there was no development in
Egypt that was parallel to the mass immigration of the Amorites into
Babylonia and Upper Mesopotamia and their settlement there.

On the other hand, there are quite striking similarities between the
description given, in the instructions for Merika-Re, of the enemies
threatening Egypt and the accounts provided in the Sumerian texts of the
MAR.TU, between the Wall of the Ruler built by Amen-em-het I and the
wall erected by Shu-Sin against the MAR.TU. Considered on its own,
however, this does not in any way suggest that the invaders of Egypt were
also Amorites. All that it may mean is that both groups were nomads and
that both countries used the same means of defence against them.

In the Egyptian texts, these nomads are called the Amu, a term which

---

[24] *ANET*, pp. 441a, 442a.

[25] *ANET*, p. 416b.

[26] *ANET*, p. 446a; Neferti is known as Nefer-rohu in this prophecy.

[27] *ANET*, p. 19a.

[28] *ANEP*, Fig. 3; the text will be found in *ANET*, p. 229a.

[29] G. Posener, 'Les Asiatiques en Egypte sous les XII et XIII Dynasties', *Syria*, 34 (1957),
pp. 145–163.

was applied to all Asiatics from the Sixth Dynasty onwards. All the same the names of the Asiatics who had settled in Egypt belong to a north-western Semitic group, like the Amorite names.[30] It is, however, even more important to consider the same types of proper name in texts inscribed on bowls and statuettes that were used in magic rites denouncing the pharaoh's enemies. There are in fact three groups of texts which are particularly interesting in this context,[31] all of them probably dating from the end of the Twelfth Dynasty and separated from each other by less than a century. In other words, they go back approximately to a period between 1875 and 1800 B.C.

As far as Asia is concerned, their geographical limits do not extend farther north than the Eleuthera river on the coast and the country around Damascus in the interior. In other words, they cover the whole of Palestine, but only the southern part of Syria. All the names of princes mentioned in these texts are Semitic and all of them might have belonged to Amorites. In the more recent Saqqarah texts, there are also three times as many place names as in the earlier groups (Berlin and Mirgissa). In the early groups, some territories were governed by several rulers, whereas in the recent group almost all the cities or states were ruled by a single prince. These changes point clearly to a measure of progress in the process of settlement and political organisation. They also reflect the same development that has been revealed by archaeological evidence in Palestine dating from the beginning of the Middle Bronze Age – an initially slow resumption of urban life after a long eclipse during the Intermediate Period between Early and Middle Bronze Ages.

We can, however, say that Palestine was affected by the Amorite migrations which extended over several centuries. If the country was in fact affected more profoundly by these movements of nomadic people than Egypt and, apparently, southern Syria, this may have been because the Palestinians resisted the nomads less strenuously. Again, if Palestine was invaded before Babylonia, this was possibly because the country was closer to the centre from which the movement began – the Amorites probably left the Syrian steppes and spread out over the whole of the Fertile Crescent.

Above all, however, it has to be borne in mind that this 'Amorite' theory is no more than a hypothesis.[32] What is more, it is one that has to be

---

[30] W. F. Albright, 'Northwest-Semitic Names in a List of Egyptian Slaves', *JAOS*, 74 (1954), pp. 22–223.

[31] The Berlin texts: K. Sethe, *Die Achtung feindlicher Fürsten, Völker und Dinge auf altägyptischen Tongefäßscherben des mittleren Reiches*, Berlin, 1926; Saqqārah texts: G. Posener, *Princes et pays d'Asie et de Nubie. Textes hiératiques sur des figurines d'envoûtement du Moyen Empire*, Brussels, 1940; texts found at Mirgissa in the Sudan: G. Posener, 'Les textes d'envoûtement de Mirgissa', *Syria*, 43 (1966), pp. 227–287.

[32] See, for example, the rather exaggerated criticism put forward by C. J. J. de Geus in 'De

completely dissociated from the references in the Bible to the Amorites, who have nothing to do with the Amorite nomads of the beginning of the second millennium. The Old Testament authors applied, to part of the pre-Israelitic population of Palestine, the name Amurru which was used in the cuneiform texts of the fourteenth and thirteenth centuries B.C. to denote a state north of Canaan. These people appear in the Egyptian texts written during the reign of Ramses II, where they are called Amor, and it would seem that, from the time of Tiglath-pileser I at the end of the twelfth century B.C., their territory extended over the whole 'western country' from Palmyra to the Mediterranean Sea. If the invaders of the Intermediate Period between the Early and Middle Bronze Ages are identified with the Amorites mentioned in the cuneiform texts of the end of the third millennium and if these people, having become sedentary, are regarded as having been responsible for the Middle Bronze civilisation, then one serious difficulty has still to be overcome. How were these shepherds from the Syrian steppe land able to introduce an already highly developed metal-working industry into the country? How is it that their pottery and their tools were so different from those which followed? Finally, what accounts for the sudden change in burial customs at the beginning of the Middle Bronze Age? The reality of the situation must, in fact, have been much more complicated. It is possible, for example, that the arrival of the Amorites was preceded by the infiltration of other groups coming from a country which produced copper (Anatolia or Caucasia, perhaps) and that these other people were responsible for the destruction of the Early Bronze cities.

III. THE HURRIANS

The Amorites were, however, not the only migratory ethnic group in the Ancient Near East at the beginning of the second millennium. Metal-working became a highly developed industry at Rās Shamrah and Byblos especially because the so-called torque-bearers settled there and their art later spread from these centres into central Europe.[33] These people may have come from the north-east, but this remains purely hypothetical and unsupported by any archaeological evidence.

The Hurrians (or Hurrites) formed a more important group.[34] These

Amorieten in de Palestijnse archeologie: Een recente theorie kritisch bezien', *NTT*, 23 (1968–1969), pp. 1–24.

[33] See F. A. Schaeffer, 'Porteurs de torque', *Ugaritica II*, Paris, 1949, pp. 49–120, together with S. Piggott's remarks in *Ancient Europe*, Edinburgh, 1965, pp. 102–103 and note 62 on p. 111.

[34] For the Hurrians, see I. J. Gelb, *Hurrians and Subarians*, Chicago, 1944; E. A. Speiser,

were non-Semitic people who spoke an agglutinative language which is in
some ways related to the Caucasian languages. These Hurrians came down
from the mountains to the north and east of Upper Mesopotamia. The
earliest text in their language is a foundation tablet in Hurrian and
Akkadian by Tishatal, the king of Urkish, dating from the end of the
Dynasty of Akkad.[35] A little later in date, but still before the Third Dynasty
of Ur, Arisen, the king of Urkish and Nawar, dedicated a temple to the
god Nergal.[36] Urkish was a great religious centre of the Hurrians and was
probably situated at 'Amūda, at the foot of Mount Taurus near the present
Turkish frontier.[37] In this respect, it was exceptional at this time in Upper
Mesopotamia – apart from Urkish, there was no trace of the Hurrians in
this part of the Ancient Near East until they appeared at Mari and northern
Syria towards the end of the third millennium. Hurrian names are found
from time to time to the east of the Tigris and even in Babylonia and they
occur in slightly greater numbers during the Third Dynasty of Ur, but
these are individual occurrences and cannot be compared with the Amorite
penetration, which covered Lower Mesopotamia.

We have much more information about the situation in the north during
the eighteenth century B.C. In a list of names of those working in the palace
of Ekallatum, near where the Upper Zab joins the Tigris, more than half
are Hurrian. Not far from there, to the east of the Tigris at Shusharra (Tell
Shemshāra), the majority of the population was Hurrian.[38] In Upper
Mesopotamia, the princes mentioned in the archives were, as we have seen,
generally Amorites, but four or five have Hurrian names and it is a pity that
it has not been possible to identify the places where they lived. In the
Chagar Bazar texts, rather less than a third of the names are Hurrian. To the
west of the Euphrates in Upper Syria, Hurrian princes ruled at Khashshum
and Urshu, which were north of Aleppo. Hurrians were not ruling at
Alalaḫ at the end of the eighteenth century B.C., but they did occupy certain
important positions and some words of their language entered the Semitic
vocabulary. In the sphere of religion, their influence was felt and the great
goddess Khepat was invoked in a treaty in which Abbael yielded Aleppo to

'The Hurrian Participation in the Civilisations of Mesopotamia, Syria and Palestine', *Cahiers d'Histoire Mondiale*, 1 (1953), pp. 311–327; F. Imparati, *I Hurriti*, Florence, 1964; R. de Vaux, 'Les Hurrites de l'histoire et les Horites de la Bible', *RB*, 74 (1967), pp. 481–503.

[35] A. Parrot and J. Nougayrol, 'Un document de fondation hurrite', *RA*, 42 (1948), pp. 1–20; for the date, see I. J. Gelb, 'New Light on Hurrians and Subarians', *Studi Orientalistici in onore di G. Levi della Vida*, I, Rome, 1956, pp. 378–392.

[36] The so-called tablet of 'Samarra'; see F. Thureau-Dangin, 'Tablette de Samarra', *RA*, 9 (1912), pp. 1–4.

[37] W. J. van Liere, 'Urkiš, centre religieux hurrite', *AAS*, 7 (1957), pp. 91–94.

[38] J. Laessøe, *The Shemshāra Tablets*, Copenhagen, 1959; *ibid.*, 'The Second Shemshāra Archive', *Sumer*, 16 (1960), pp. 12–19.

his vassal Yarim-Lim. In the middle of the seventeenth century, the Hittite king Hattusilis I raided Khashshum and seized the statues of Teshub (Tessub), the great Hurrian god of the storm, who is called in the text the 'god of Aleppo', and of the goddess Khepat, as well as a pair of silver bulls which must have been Sharri and Khurri, the two bulls attributed to Teshub.

The Hurrians were less influential at Mari farther south. Three women working in the place have names containing Khubat, which is probably equivalent to Khepat, the name of the goddess, but they might have been foreigners. The library at Mari contained some Hurrian texts, extracts from rituals, but there was no cult of any Hurrian deity, although one of the kings of the little kingdom of Hana, which followed at Mari, offered a sacrifice to 'Dagan of the Hurrians', that is, Teshub. On the other side of the desert, at Qatna, the earliest inventory of the temple of Nin. E. Gal, dating from the fifteenth century, lists the gifts previously made to the temple and the first donor mentioned has a Hurrian name, Ewir-Sharri. This information does not take us back to a period before the sixteenth century B.C. South of Qatna, there is no trace of the Hurrians at this period – they had not yet reached southern Syria or Palestine and, even in the north, they had penetrated only to a very limited extent. Later, however, they were to penetrate much more deeply until, with the foundation of the kingdom of Mitanni in the course of the sixteenth century B.C., they were to become one of the great Near Eastern powers. Their power was to last for almost two centuries and the part that they played was so important that we shall have to speak of them again later.

The gaps in our information make it seem as though the Hurrian invasion took place in successive stages that were separate from each other, but we can be certain that it was a much more continuous process than it at first sight appears to be. In particular, the existence of a Hurrian kingdom at Urkish dating from before the Third Dynasty of Ur and the presence of Hurrian princes and groups in Upper Mesopotamia and northern Syria during the eighteenth century B.C., indicate – despite the absence of intermediate texts – that the Hurrians were already influential in those regions at the beginning of the second millennium.

IV. THE MIDDLE BRONZE AGE

Palestine itself was not affected by these first Hurrian migrations. The Amorites, who had settled in the country during the Intermediate Period between the Early and Middle Bronze Ages, had, under a strong influence emanating from southern Syria, developed a prosperous civilisation. This was the civilisation of the Middle Bronze Age.

The Middle Bronze Age began modestly with Middle Bronze I.[39] At the northern site of Tell el-Fār'ah, scattered houses rose among the ruins of the Early Bronze defensive wall which had been destroyed several centuries before. In the intervening spaces, tombs were dug large enough for as many as four bodies.[40] Most of the material that we have of this period comes from tombs inside a city wall that was to be built later, for example, at Megiddo, Rās el-'Ain, Jericho and Tell el-'Ajjūl. Of these, Megiddo also had buildings and may even have had a defensive wall at this period. Tell Beit Mirsim certainly had one. The town was surrounded by a very solid wall and houses were built, apparently without any order, against it. No tombs have so far been found in the parts already excavated.

The pottery of this period is quite new. The cooking pots were still fashioned by hand and are bowls with upright walls and the rim emphasised by an applied band and a row of holes. All the other vessels, however, were clearly made on the wheel, with the result that the shapes are different. The vases are frequently rounded and have disc or ring bases. Some have obviously been finely combed, probably in imitation of metal vases, and many are covered by a beautiful red, burnished slip. Those found at Megiddo also have painted bands. The shape and decoration of these vessels are clearly related to those of vases found inland in Syria, especially at Watna. Many more discoveries, which are even more closely related, have been made at sites on the Syrian coast, notably Byblos and Kafr Jarra near Sidon. The finds made at Byblos have been dated and placed – they came, in part at least, from the royal tombs of Amen-em-het III and IV (1842–1790 B.C.), who were ruling in Egypt at about this time. This means that Middle Bronze I has to be extended until the year 1800 B.C. at least.

Not only the pottery, then, but also the pattern of habitat and the burial customs were new and this would seem to point to the arrival of new groups of people. The identity of the immigrants during the Intermediate Period – the first of these immigrants at least – has deliberately been left open.[41] As far as the Middle Bronze Age I is concerned, however, it is possible to speak with great certainty of the presence of Amorites in Palestine, because of the occurrence of Amorite names in the Egyptian inscriptions denouncing the pharaoh's enemies, two of the three groups of these 'execration' texts more or less exactly covering this period. These Amorites, who had also settled in Syria, had made much more rapid progress. The development of their pottery can be followed quite clearly in the finds made in and around Qatna in the interior of Syria and a parallel development can also be observed in northern Palestine, especially at

---

[39] Middle Bronze I is known as Middle Bronze II A in the present nomenclature.
[40] R. de Vaux, 'Les fouilles de Tell el-Fâr'ah', *RB*, 69 (1962), pp. 236–252.
[41] See above, pp. 136–137.

Megiddo, where there are points of contact with Qatna during the
Intermediate Period and Middle Bronze I.

The situation is even more striking at Byblos, where the arrival of the
Amorites did not cause urban life to disappear. All that happened there was
that there was a period of poverty, with indications in the pottery and
weapons of this period of contact with Palestine of the Intermediate Period.
Later on, the city regained its previous prosperity – the improved buildings,
different defensive walls, new pottery and richer furnishings in the tombs
testify to this. This development at Byblos was not, however, due to the
arrival of a new population. It was the result of the creative genius of the
Amorites and their power to assimilate. Similar proofs of this strength are
evident in Mesopotamia, under the 'Amorite' dynasty of Babylon. Palestine
received the benefit of this progress and Megiddo acted as a link, its
relations with Syria and especially with Byblos being closer than with
anywhere else in the Middle Bronze Age as in the Intermediate Period.
Megiddo is also the only site where the pottery found does not reveal a
marked break between these two periods. It is also probable that this influence was brought into Palestine by groups of people coming from
southern Syria.

The seeds that were introduced in this way into the country grew and
bore fruit during the following phase – Middle Bronze II (ca. 1800–1550
B.C.),[42] which was certainly the most prosperous period in ancient
Palestine. One of the most striking aspects of this phase is the emergence or
re-emergence of towns with large populations over the whole of the country. These include Hazor, Taanach, Megiddo, Tell el-Fār'ah (the northern
site), Shechem, Jericho, Jerusalem, Beth Shemesh, Gezer, Tell Beit Mirsim,
Tell ed-Duweir, Tell el-'Ajjūl and Tell el-Fār'ah (the southern site). New
defensive walls were built around all of these cities and the prosperity of the
period is also evident from the number of patrician dwellings as compared
with the relatively few poor houses. That the ruling class was rich at this
time is also clear from the wealthy furnishings of the family tombs grouped
in cemeteries situated outside the city walls and often in burial chambers
dating from previous ages. The dead were not buried in individual tombs as
they had been in the Intermediate Period and, unlike the charnel houses of
the Chalcolithic and the Early Bronze Ages, the Middle Bronze tombs
never contained more than about forty bodies.

Another feature of this new period is its pottery, which reached a peak of
perfection that was never surpassed – slips of fine quality and very well
fired, vases with thin walls and elegant shapes, very little painted decoration
until the latter part of the period and well-prepared surfaces covered with
slip which was at first red, but later cream-coloured or light yellow and

---

[42] In the more recent nomenclature, this period is known as Middle Bronze II B and C.

brightly burnished. The presence of this outstanding pottery – even everyday articles displaying a fine aesthetic sense – in the tombs and the dwellings of the people is indisputable evidence of the high level of civilisation attained in Middle Bronze II.

The same degrèe of progress is also evident in the metal industry of the period. The knowledge of how to make an alloy of copper and tin, in other words, bronze, enabled the people of the period to manufacture far more effective weapons. These new bronze weapons included daggers with blades triangular in section and strengthened by projections, axes with hafts and javelins with sockets. Gold was worked and scarabs were cut and engraved, thus revealing a strong Egyptian influence, which was also felt in other spheres. Alabaster vases were also imported from the Nile Valley and copied in local material.[43] The tombs excavated at Jericho have been exceptionally well preserved and were found to contain wooden furniture closely imitating that of Egypt.

The same civilisation extended all along the Syrian coast as far as Rās Shamrah, but there were, of course, regional differences and certain aspects are peculiar to Palestine. It developed without interruption throughout the whole of the Middle Bronze Age and continued into the Late Bronze Age, although by that time it was decadent. Despite this continuity, however, the country was not always at peace. There is archaeological evidence of four major destructions at Tell Beit Mirsim and five at Megiddo in the course of two and a half centuries. These ruins and the defensive walls built around all the cities give the impression of a country divided into little principalities which were frequently at war. There were also interventions from abroad, which will be discussed later.

The history of these fortifications around the cities of Palestine reveals an increasing concern to guard against means of attack which were becoming more and more effective.[44] The systems employed differ according to the site to be defended, but they all have one important characteristic in common. At the beginning of the period, these ramparts were built vertically and were sometimes furnished with projections, the base of which remained uncovered, and sometimes not. By the end of the eighteenth century and even earlier at Megiddo or the beginning of the seventeenth century B.C., these ramparts were either completely replaced by a glacis or bank of earth surmounted by a defensive wall or else the thrust of the rampart was absorbed by such a glacis. There is evidence of the same type of fortification in Syria and this would appear to be no earlier than the Palestinian fortifications. One not entirely convincing explanation that has been suggested

[43] I. Ben Dor, 'Palestinian Alabaster Vases', QDAP, 11 (1945), pp. 93–112.
[44] P. J. Parr, 'The Origin of the Rampart Fortifications of Middle Bronze Age Palestine and Syria', ZDPV, 84 (1968), pp. 18–45.

is that it was a reply to the battering-ram as a means of attack.[45] The battering-ram is mentioned in eighteenth century Mari texts and an account of the siege of Urshu by Hattusilis I in the middle of the seventeenth century B.C. refers to a battering-ram used 'in the Hurrian manner'.[46]

Into these ramparts were built fortified gates consisting of two or three pairs of projecting pilasters on the inner wall with the same number of tenailles on the outer wall, thus making the way into the city much narrower. This kind of gateway was introduced from the north and it remained predominant in Palestine until the first half of the first millennium B.C. One explanation proposed by many scholars is that these gates were constructed because chariots were widely used during the wars of this period. One chariot, it has been suggested, could pass through the most narrow gate and two abreast could go through a wider gateway. Another equally common view and one which is, despite the apparent contradiction, shared by the same scholars is that the great banks of earth surrounding so many cities of this period were a defence against the chariot. Such surrounding walls are found, for example, at Carchemish and Qatna in Syria and at Hazor and Ashkelon in Palestine. Similar banks of sand are also found at Tell el-Yehudiyeh and Heliopolis in Egypt. All these sites were, it has been suggested, fortified camps for chariots, which could not be accommodated inside the cities and they have consequently been called 'Hyksos camps'.The recent excavations at Hazor in Palestine and the earlier ones at Carchemish in Syria have, however, revealed that these banks of earth enclosed places which were inhabited from the moment that the defences were erected. They were therefore probably extensions of the original 'high city' or acropolis – 'low cities' which could receive citizens when the 'high city' became overpopulated. This explanation also holds good for the other sites in Syria and Palestine. As far as the surrounding walls at Tell el-Yehudiyeh and Heliopolis in Egypt are concerned, these were connected with a sanctuary and not with a city, so that they could not have had a defensive function.[47] We may therefore conclude that these 'low cities' were not associated with the Hyksos or even with chariot warfare, because chariots were not used in Palestine and Egypt until the Hyksos had been expelled, that is, until the end of the Middle Bronze Age.

What is surprising is that this flourishing civilisation did not reach the Negeb, which was quite densely populated during the preceding period. Equally remarkable is the fact that it did not penetrate as far as the southern

---

[45] Y. Yadin, 'Hyksos Fortifications and the Battering-Ram', BASOR, 137 (Feb. 1955), pp. 23–32.

[46] The text will be found in H. G. Güterbock, 'Die historische Tradition und ihre Gestaltung bei Babyloniern und Hethitern', ZA, 44 (1938), p. 117; for the date, see O. R. Gurney, 'Anatolia c. 1,750–1,600 B.C.', CAH, II, VI, 1961, p. 19.

[47] G. R. H. Wright, 'Tell el-Yehudiyah and the Glacis', ZDPV, 84 (1968), pp. 1–17,

half of Transjordania, which was more developed than Palestine in the Intermediate Period. Apart from certain parts east of the Jordan around 'Ammān and Medeba, there was an interruption in the settled life of the central and southern parts of Transjordania until the thirteenth century B.C. and until much later in the Negeb. One reason that has been suggested for this interruption is that there might have been a climatic change in these semi-desert regions. Another possible explanation is that the geographical situation and the natural conditions of both of these regions did not favour the development of urban life. A third and more plausible explanation is based on our observation of the consequence of the process of urbanisation in modern times — the great movement away from the countryside. Very much the same process must have taken place in the Middle Bronze Age. Many of the inhabitants of Transjordania and the Negeb must have been drawn to the cities of Palestine and the population of these cities must have expanded from the beginning of Middle Bronze I onwards. Other people in Transjordania and the Negeb, on the other hand, undoubtedly reverted to a nomadic way of life.

V. PALESTINE AND EGYPT UNDER THE MIDDLE KINGDOM

Although the Middle Bronze civilisation developed in the main peacefully and harmoniously, there were serious disturbances in the Near East as a whole during this period and Palestine was frequently involved in these. One of the most far-reaching of these events was, of course the collapse of the glorious Middle Kingdom of Egypt under pressure from the Hyksos, who in turn ruled Egypt for a century and a half, during the period known as the Second Intermediate. Before considering this period, however, we must give our attention to the situation in which Palestine was placed under the Middle Kingdom.[48]

The first pharaohs of the Twelfth Dynasty had restored internal order and had strengthened the defences along the northern frontier of their kingdom, but neither they nor their successors seem to have made many military expeditions beyond those frontiers. The campaign conducted by General Nesumont against the Asiatics during the co-regency of Sesostris I and his father Amen-em-het I resulted in the destruction of the Asiatic fortresses, but the account provides no geographical details at all.[49] There is,

---

[48] For the relationships existing between Palestine and Egypt, see W. A. Ward, 'Egypt and the East Mediterranean in the Early Second Millennium B.C.', *Orientalia*, 30 (1961), pp. 22–45, 129–155; W. Helck, *Die Beziehungen Agyptens zu Vorderasien im 3. und 2. Jahrtausend v. Chr.*, Wiesbaden, 1962.

[49] *ARE*, I, § 469–471.

moreover, only one text referring explicitly to this event. Sesostris III
(1878–1843 B.C.) also conducted an expedition against Sekmem (probably
Shechem), which was at the head of a Palestinian federation. The Egyptians were victorious, but, on their way back to Egypt, they were harassed
by the Asiatics.[50] On the whole, however, generally peaceful relationships
prevailed between Palestine and Egypt. Intensive mining was carried out in
Sinai during the whole of the Twelfth Dynasty, but the Egyptians felt no
need to resort to arms in order to protect either the mines or the lines of
communication with them.

Si-nuhe, the Egyptian official who went into voluntary exile when
Amen-em-het I died, was warmly welcomed when he went east of Byblos,
into the Syrian Beqā'. He was able to speak the Egyptian language and he
met many Egyptian people, both residents in Asia and messengers from the
court. When he was recalled to Egypt by Sesostris I, he was escorted on his
return by Asiatics who were greeted at the frontier and overwhelmed with
gifts.[51] The situation was very similar in Palestine, which this political
refugee had travelled through before reaching Syria. He had barely crossed
the Egyptian frontier when he was recognised by an Asiatic sheikh who
had been in Egypt. This bedouin at once gave him hospitality. Si-nuhe then
set off for the north, going from tribe to tribe and receiving hospitable
treatment everywhere. There is no mention anywhere, in the entire text, of
the presence of an Egyptian army or of any military activity.

Si-nuhe is simply one example, made famous by an Egyptian text. The
relationships between Egypt and Palestine were, however, continuous
throughout this period. Asiatics with names which, as far as they are known
to us, are Amorite came to Egypt at this time and often stayed there. Their
cattle and livestock are mentioned in several documents. Valuable treasures
were also brought to Egypt from the north. Amen-em-het II (1929–1895
B.C), for example, offered many gifts in the temple of Mantu, the god of
war, at Tôd. These included ingots of gold and silver, cups of wrought
silver and pieces of lapis lazuli cylinders, all contained in four caskets. All
this treasure, collected together for its commercial value, came from
Syria.[52] Egyptian objects also found their way to the north, often as royal
gifts. Among the many artifacts found in the tomb of Abi-shemu, the king
of Byblos, were a vase of ointment made of obsidian set in gold, bearing the
name of Amen-em-het III, and several other Egyptian articles. A casket
made of obsidian and gold and inscribed with the name Amen-em-het IV
was discovered, together with other precious Egyptian objects, in the tomb

---

[50] ANET, p. 230.

[51] ANET, pp. 18–22.

[52] F. Bisson de la Roque, G. Contenau and F. Chapouthier, Le trésor de Tôd, Cairo, 1953;
P. Montet, 'Notes et documents pour servir à l'histoire des relations entre l'ancienne Egypte
et la Syrie', Kêmi, 16 (1962), pp. 76–96.

of Abi-shemu's son, Ib-shemu-abi. The sphinxes of Amen-em-het III and IV, of the daughter of Amen-em-het II and of another princess of the Twelfth Dynasty came from Rās Shamrah, Beirut, Qatna and Byblos. The leading officials of the pharaohs who passed through Palestine and Syria left signs of their presence there behind them. A group of figures representing the vizier Sesostrisankh with his wife and daughter was excavated at Rās Shamrah. A statuette of Thut-hotep, the nomarch of the nome of Hermopolis under Amen-em-het II and Sesostris III, was found at Megiddo.[53] Other statuettes of Egyptians have been dug up at Rās Shamrah, Qatna, Byblos, Megiddo, Gezer and Tell el-'Ajjūl. A chief treasurer and his scribe left their scarabs at Tell el-'Ajjūl[54] and the scarab of a steward responsible for cattle has been found at Megiddo.[55] The impression made by the seal of a scribe of the vizier has been found on jar handles at Jericho[56] and that of a royal major-domo's seal has been discovered at Shechem.[57]

The interpretation of these documents, of which only the most striking have been mentioned here,[58] is disputed. Do they indicate that all the 'Asiatics' were, as Si-nuhe commented, the 'dogs', the docile subjects of the pharaoh? Did Egypt play a politically dominant rôle in Syria and Palestine at this time? Or were there simply diplomatic relationships and trade links? It is difficult to say with certainty. The cattle brought into Egypt may have been booty brought back from a raid into enemy territory; they may have been requisitioned from a subject country; or may have been the result of trading. The steward responsible for livestock may have gone to Megiddo to supervise payment or the delivery of an order. The gifts made by the pharaohs to cities in Syria might have been a way of asserting their authority or of strengthening a friendship. The precious objects found in the royal tombs at Byblos were perhaps presents from the pharaohs to friendly princes with whom they had trading relationships or simply a form of payment for wood which they had bought from them. The vase excavated from the royal tomb of Abi-shemu quite possibly contained ointment to anoint the king, thus making him a vassal of Egypt.[59] In fact, the princes of Byblos called themselves 'governors', a title which was borne in Egypt by heads of provinces. At the same time, however, they also inscribed their names inside oval cartouches as the pharaohs did and as if they were themselves sovereign rulers. The treasure discovered at Tod may

[53] G. Loud, *Megiddo II. Seasons of 1936–1939*, Chicago, 1948, Plate 265.
[54] F. Petrie, *Ancient Gaza I*, London, 1931, p. 7 and Plate XIII.
[55] G. Loud, *Megiddo II*, Plate 149, No. 32.
[56] A. Rowe, *A Catalogue of Egyptian Scarabs*, Cairo, 1936, p. 235.
[57] *ibid.*, p. 234.
[58] The scarabs and the royal cylinders of the Twelfth Dynasty have been discussed by R. Giveon in 'Royal Seals of the XIIth Dynasty from Western Asia', *REG* 19 (1967), pp. 29–37
[59] R. de Vaux, 'The King of Israel, Vassal of Yahweh', *The Bible and the Ancient Near East*, London, 1971, pp. 152–166.

also have been booty seized during a war, tribute claimed from a vassal prince or payment of a debt. The ingots have been stamped with the official mark 'good' by an Egyptian inspector.

The answer to all these questions is bound to be rather subtly shaded. Palestine and Syria had certainly not been integrated into the Egyptian Empire at this time, as the result of conquest. On the other hand, the important officials who left their statues at Rās Shamrah and Megiddo and those of lower rank who left their seals at Megiddo, Shechem, Jericho and Tell el-'Ajjūl were not merely visitors who stayed for a short time, nor could they all have been political refugees like Si-nuhe. On the contrary, they were undoubtedly in Palestine or Syria as official representatives of the pharaohs and had a definite mission to carry out in those countries, a task which may have been either temporary or permanent. Palestine and part of Syria at least would therefore have been Egyptian protectorates during the Twelfth Dynasty.

This would certainly do much to explain the ambiguous attitude of the kings of Byblos. Furthermore, the more detailed knowledge that we have of the situation at Megiddo at this time helps to reinforce this theory. The tomb of the nomarch Thut-hotep who left a statuette of himself at Megiddo has been found in Egypt, where there is a painting of livestock arriving from Retenu, the name which the Egyptians gave to Syria-Palestine.[60] As we have already seen, an overseer responsible for livestock was resident at Megiddo. Surely it is not too bold a conclusion to draw from this that the pharaohs were at this time exploiting the Plain of Esdraelon with its great herds of cattle?

It is also worth while considering the so-called 'execration' texts in this context. Although it was in the first place people or countries who might 'conspire' or 'think of rebelling' against the king of Egypt who were denounced in these texts, these people and countries were not always those that had been effectively subjugated by Egypt. What the texts express above all is a faith in the universal power of the pharaoh, the Son of Re, to govern. They were also closely associated with a rite which was performed at regular intervals as a precautionary measure and may therefore not have had any connection with a situation that was politically threatening. All the same, what is remarkable is that those cities in which the influence of Egypt was, to judge from the archaeological evidence at least, more firmly established do not figure at all in these texts of execration. They contain no denunciation of Byblos, as distinct from its hinterland, Megiddo or Jericho, for example, or of those towns which were properly speaking outside the geographical area covered by the texts, namely Rās Shamrah and Qatna. These cities may not have been named in the texts, of course, because there

[60] P. E. Newberry, *El Bersheh*, I, London, 1894, Plate 18; A. M. Blackman is responsible for the reading 'Retenu' and it is probably correct.

was perhaps no reason for the Egyptians to doubt their faithfulness. Certainly all these texts show that the Egyptians had a very detailed knowledge of Palestine and the Palestinian towns and their leaders and, if the two groups of texts are compared, it can be seen that the Egyptian chancellery kept closely in touch with all changes of government in Palestine. The evident care taken to remain informed is a clear sign of political concern. Very many names are included in the most recent group of texts, dating from the nineteenth century B.C. This may be because a much more complete network of information had been constructed by this time, extending as far as Transjordania. At the same time, it may also reflect Egyptian uneasiness about a growing political threat from a country which was not effectively controlled, but only influenced by Egypt.

Nonetheless, Egypt maintained its position throughout part at least of the Thirteenth Dynasty. The clearest evidence of this comes once again from Byblos. On a cylinder dating from about 1770 B.C., Prince Yakīn-el calls himself the 'servant' of pharaoh Sehetep-ib-Re. On a bas relief, Yantīn, who was probably Yakīn-el's son, had his name inscribed beside that of Nefer-hotep I, who reigned round about 1740–1730 B.C.[61] An incomplete funerary statuette found at Gezer has been attributed to the Thirteenth Dynasty.[62] Several scarabs discovered at Megiddo, Jericho, Tell ed-Duweir and Tell el-'Ajjūl bear names which are almost certainly those of certain pharaohs of this dynasty, in particular those of Nefer-hotep I and Sebek-hotep IV. It has been suggested that an impression made by a seal found at Jericho contains the much later name of Dudimose, but this is certainly not a correct reading.[63]

VI. The Hyksos

This Dudimose was the last independent sovereign of the Thirteenth Dynasty, at least according to Manetho, the late Egyptian priest whose work provides us with our only source of information about the period during which foreigners began to rule Egypt. Manetho was writing fifteen centuries after the event, using sources which have been lost. What he says is that, during the reign of Tutimaios (Dudi-mose),[64] 'an unknown people came unexpectedly from the east and invaded our country and seized it by force without any difficulty, capturing the leaders, burning the towns, raz-

[61] W. F. Albright, 'An Indirect Synchronism between Egypt and Mesopotamia circa 1,730 B.C.', *BASOR*, 99 (Oct. 1945), pp. 9–18.
[62] R. A. S. MacAlister, *The Excavations at Gezer*, II, London, 1912, pp. 312–313.
[63] A. Rowe, *A Catalogue of Egyptian Scarabs*, No. 113; Rowe's reading is rejected by H. Stock, *Studien*, p. 63; see also note 65 below.
[64] This text can be found in Josephus, *Contra Apionem*, I, XIV, 75–82.

ing the temples and treating the inhabitants with terrible cruelty, cutting the men's throats and leading the women and children into captivity. They even made one of their people, Salitis, king. This prince set up his court at Memphis.' A list of five other kings follows, with the comment that they were 'all more and more determined to extirpate the Egyptian people. The whole of this nation is known as the Hyksos, that is, the shepherd kings'.[65]

It was Manetho, then, who first used the name Hyksos. But who were these people? When and how did they enter Egypt? What was the extent of their rule and what were its political and social effects? No historical documents and very few monuments or inscriptions dating back to the period of Hyksos rule itself have been preserved. The lists of kings made by Manetho and his copyists or found on the fragmentary Turin Papyrus show names and reigns divided into four 'dynasties' from the fourteenth to the seventeenth, which were contemporary partly with these dynasties and partly with the end of the Thirteenth Dynasty. But this information is incomplete and almost inextricably confused. The historical texts begin with the war of liberation and are to a great extent spoilt by the style of writing, which is characterised by an extreme hostility towards the foreign rulers. No definitive answers can therefore be given to the questions asked at the beginning of this paragraph. In view of our present lack of information, we can do not more than suggest a few probable answers.

Manetho's own etymological explanation of the Greek word Hyksos, which he himself coined, is clearly not correct. He derived it from the title of the leaders of the invading forces – hq3w ḫ3w.t, 'rulers of foreign countries'. These words were used for several centuries as the name for Bedouin leaders in Syria and Palestine. The people who followed them were called 'Asiatics', 'inhabitants of the sands' or 'people of Retenu' in the Egyptian texts, these names having been used for a long time for the populations of Sinai, Palestine and Syria. Some of the proper names of the Hyksos are undoubtedly Semitic, whatever the precise reading of the second element in these names may be (for example, Yaqub-el or Yaqub-har, 'Anat-el or 'Anat-har), while others are probably Semitic (for example, Khyān and Samuqena). Other names, on the other hand, can hardly be analysed at all in their hieroglyphic or Greek transcriptions and attempts to explain them as Hurrian or Indo-European have proved futile. Others, such

[65] For the Hyksos, see T. Säve-Söderbergh, 'The Hyksos Rule in Egypt', *JEA*, 37 (1951), pp. 53–71; A. Alt, *Die Herkunft der Hyksos in neuer Sicht*, Berlin, 1954 = *Kleine Schriften*, III, 1959, pp. 72–98; H. Stock, *Studien zur Geschichte und Archäologie der 13. bis 17. Dynastie Agyptens,* Glückstadt, 1955; W. C. Hayes, 'Egypt; From the Death of Ammenemes III to Seqenenre II,' *CAH*, II, II, 1962; T. G. H. James, 'Egypt: From the Expulsion of the Hyksos to Amenophis I', *CAH*, II, VIII, 1965; J. von Beckerath, *Untersuchungen zur politischen Geschichte der Zweiten Zwischenzeit*, Glückstadt, 1965; J. van Seters, *The Hyksos: A New Investigation*, New Haven, 1966; D. B. Redford, 'The Hyksos Invasion in History and Tradition', *Orientalia*, 39 (1970), pp. 1–51.

as Apophis, are clearly Egyptian.

The Hyksos adopted Seth as their main god. Seth was an Egyptian god whose cult originated in Upper Egypt and eventually spread throughout the Nile Delta. He was regarded as the ruler of the desert and of foreign countries and as a storm-god.[66] The Hyksos recognised him as their own god and adapted him to suit themselves. When they had left Egypt, Seth was represented in the dress and with the characteristics of a Syrian god and was, in the texts of the period, identified with Baal.[67] Seth's spouse was a naked goddess, who might have been either Anath or Astarte. The obvious conclusion, then, is that most of the Hyksos were Semites.

According to Manetho, they came from the East and in that case they could only have reached Egypt either from or via Palestine. It is clear from the archaeological evidence that Palestine enjoyed a period of exceptional prosperity during the eighteenth and seventeenth centuries B.C. , when the features which were firmly being developed and consolidated. This evolution was so steady and harmonious that Palestine could not have been invaded by foreigners during this period. It is also hardly possible to imagine that the country's development was interrupted by a large-scale migration from north to south, which would undoubtedly have left many traces behind. The only possible conclusion, then, is that the Hyksos came from Palestine itself.

This conclusion has been largely confirmed by the recent excavations at Tell ed-Dab'a, between Khāta'na and Qantūr, about twenty miles south of Tanis.[68] Many tombs containing pottery, weapons and such objects as pins with eye-holes, all of which are very characteristic of the Palestinian Middle Bronze II, have been found there. What is more, a hoard of Palestinian pottery and a scarab of the Hyksos king Khyān have been found only about half a mile away.[69] These finds would seem to confirm that the region of Khāta'na and Qantir, which is so rich from the archaeological point of view,[70] is precisely the area within which a search should be made for the site of the Hyksos capital in the Nile Delta, Avaris.[71]

[66] J. Zandee, 'Seth als Sturmgott', ZÄS, 90 (1963), pp. 144–156.

[67] See H. Bonnet, Reallexikon der ägyptischen Religionsgeschichte, Berlin, 1952, under 'Seth', especially pp. 703–705; S. Morenz, Ägyptische Religion, Stuttgart, 1960, pp. 250–251.*

[68] See, for example, M. Bietak, 'Bericht über die erste Grabungskampagne auf Tell ed-Dab'a im Ostdelta Agyptens im Sommer 1966', Bustan (Vienna), 9 (1968), pp. 20–24; 'Vorläufiger Bericht über die erste und zweite Kampagne der österreichischen Ausgrabungen auf Tell ed-Dab a im Ostdelta Agyptens (1966, 1967)', MDAI, 23 (1968), pp. 79–114; L. Leclant, Orientalia, 37 (1968), pp. 98–100 (first and second campaigns); ibid., 38 (1969), pp. 248–251 (third and fourth campaigns).* A stele bearing the name of a Hyksos princess is thought also to have come from Tell ed-Dab'a; see W. K. Simpson, 'The Hyksos Princess Tany', ChrEg, 34 (1959), pp. 233–239.

[69] Shehata Adam, ASAE, 56 (1959), pp. 220–221 and Plates XV–XVI.

[70] Labib Habachi, 'Khâta'na-Qantīr', ASAE, 52 (1952–1954), pp. 443–562.

[71] ibid., pp. 444, 558–559; J. van Seters, The Kyksos, op. cit., pp. 132–134.

It has been suggested that this movement was set afoot by pressure originating from a point much farther north and making itself felt in southern Syria and Palestine and that the Hurrians and even the Indo-Europeans played a part in these events. The Indo-Europeans, however, did not appear on the near eastern scene until much later and the Hurrians could not have participated in the Hyksos movement because, as we have seen, they had not reached Palestine by the end of the seventeenth century B.C.[72]

The Hyksos movement had in fact begun very much earlier. A stele, according to which the fourth centenary of the inauguration of the cult of Seth was probably celebrated round about the year 1320 B.C., has been discovered at Tanis.[73] On this stele, the god Seth appears as a Syrian Baal and the stone must have been brought from Avaris, if Avaris is not identified with Tanis. The conclusion that has been drawn from this evidence is that the inauguration of the cult of Seth-Baal marked the arrival of the Hyksos four hundred years before this celebration, in other words, round-about 1720 B.C.[74] It will be remembered that, when Manetho called Salitis the first Hyksos king, he said that he set up his court at Memphis during the reign of Tutimaios. This is the Greek name for one of the two pharaohs called Dudi-mose who were among the last rulers of the Thirteenth Dynasty, roundabout 1660 B.C. These two dates, then, approximately mark the stages in the Hyksos invasion.

They settled first in the eastern part of the Nile Delta, taking advantage of the weakness of the central power. No pharaoh of the Thirteenth Dynasty later than Nefer-hotep I 'and his brother Sebek-hotep IV is mentioned in any of the Syrian and Palestinian documents or even on any of the scarabs. The region of Chois in the western part of the Delta had already seceded and had come under a native dynasty, the fourth, which lasted well into the Hyksos period. The gradual infiltration of Asiatics which had begun in the Twelfth Dynasty had certainly helped the Hyksos to enter the Delta and had prepared the way for their settlement there. Later immigrations on a

[72] This conclusion has also been reached by those who have most recently studied the problem of the Hyksos; see, for example, J. von Beckerath, *Untersuchungen, op. cit.*, pp. 113–121; J. van Seters, *The Hyksos, op. cit.*, pp. 181–190; see also R. de Vaux, 'Les Hurrites de l'histoire et les Horites de la Bible', *RB*, 74 (1967), especially pp. 492–496; D. B. Redford, *The Hyksos Invasion, op. cit.*, note 65, p. 6 ff.*

[73] Illustrated in P. Montet, 'La Stèle de l'an 400 retrouvée', *Kêmi*, 4 (1931), Plate XI; the text will be found in *ANET*, pp. 252–253.

[74] This is still a very common interpretation of this stele and can also be found, for example, in W. C. Hayes, *CAH*, II, II, p. 18; J. Vercoutter, *Fischer Weltgeschichte*, 2, pp. 351–352; A. Gardiner, *Egypt of the Pharaohs*, Oxford, 1966, p. 165. On the other hand, other recent authors maintain that there is no connection between this period of four hundred years and the arrival of the Hyksos; see J. von Beckerath, *Untersuchungen, op. cit.*, pp. 84, 161; R. Stadelmann, 'Die 400–Jahre-Stele', *ChrEg*, 40 (1965), pp. 46–60; H. te Velde, *Seth, God of Confusion*, Leiden, 1967, pp. 124–127; D. B. Redford, *op. cit.*, note 65, pp. 23–31.

much greater scale allowed them to seize power. It would, however, be wrong to imagine that they were warlike hordes riding in swift chariots and armed with composite bows. These weapons were not known at the time, at least on the frontiers of Egypt, and Manetho seems to have known that there were no battles. It is also quite probable that some of the 'shepherd kings' included in the Sixteenth Dynasty were Delta princes of this kind prior to the beginning of the Fifteenth Dynasty.

During this dynasty, the Hyksos penetrated into the very heart of Egypt. According to Manetho, there were six 'shepherd kings' who reigned, if we are to believe the Turin Papyrus, for a hundred and eight years. This, then, was the great period of Hyksos supremacy in Egypt. Another dynasty of 'shepherd kings', the Sixteenth Dynasty, was, of course, ruling at the same time in Egypt and there are also many royal scarabs which cannot be classified under either of these two dynasties. These two facts seem to suggest that the Hyksos of Avaris-Memphis were leaders of a federation rather than sovereign rulers of a completely unified state. Their authority extended as far as Upper Egypt – the names of Khyān and Apophis are inscribed on monuments at Jebelein south of Thebes and the last pharaohs of the Thirteenth Dynasty, who had withdrawn to Upper Egypt, were their vassals. Their capital remained at Avaris, however, and this shows that they wanted to maintain contact with Palestine. One general question which often arises in this context is the extent to which they controlled Palestine, but this question is clearly irrelevant if the origin that has been suggested here is correct, in other words, if the Hyksos were originally Palestinians. In this case, the little independent Palestinian states undoubtedly continued to exist and to be sustained by what culture came back to them from their brothers who had moved southwards into Egypt. There is, after all, no evidence of any 'Hyksos' rule or even administration north of Gaza. It would also be quite wrong to suppose that a 'Hyksos' empire covered the Near East at this time. The discovery in Crete, Baghdad and recently at Boghazköy[75] of objects inscribed with the name Khyān cannot necessarily be interpreted as evidence of an extended 'Hyksos' empire. In Egypt, too, the Hyksos clearly came under a strong Egyptian influence, adopting the protocol of the pharaohs, assuming Egyptian names, behaving as if they were the successors of the national pharaohs and making full use of the pharaonic administration. There was, for example, a Hyksos treasurer whose titles were the same as those of his Egyptian counterpart and who even had an Egyptian name, whereas another Hyksos treasurer, with the same titles, had the Semitic name of Hūr. The latter's scarabs have been found at sites as far apart as Kerma in the Sudan and Gaza in the south of Palestine. The Hyksos were able to achieve a degree of political unity for

[75] H. Stock, 'Der Hyksos Chian in Boghazköy', *MDOG*, 94 (1963), pp. 73–80.

which they had not been prepared in their country of origin precisely because they preserved this Egyptian administrative machinery.

In denouncing the cruelty and destructiveness of the Hyksos rulers, Manetho was simply echoing a long tradition. Almost a hundred years after they had been expelled from Egypt, the queen Hat-shepsut, speaking about the temples that she had rebuilt, repaired or founded, said:[76] 'I have restored that which had been ruined. I have raised up that which had gone to pieces formerly, since the Asiatics (Amu) were in the midst of Avaris of the Northland and vagabonds were in the midst of them, overthrowing that which had been made. They ruled without Re.'

These very severe denunciations have been accepted far too unquestioningly by historians. No such judgements are passed on the Hyksos in contemporary historical texts dealing with the war of liberation. All that these texts contain is the accusation, which was obviously made seriously in defence of national honour, that these base Asiatics had subjugated Egypt. As far as we are able to judge, their rule was in no sense catastrophic. Agriculture was not neglected, trade continued to flourish and even increased between the Delta and Palestine, and the economy of the country remained stable. There was no change in the religious life of Egypt, as Manetho and Hat-shepsut said, and they did not recognise only Seth –on the contrary, they included Re in their protocol. The cultural development of Egypt was not interrupted in any way – the copies of many of the great texts, both literary and scientific, date from this period. Hyksos rule also brought two very important improvements into the life of the country. In the first place, it broke down a long tradition of national pride which had caused the Egyptians to believe that they were sacred and untouchable, a nation living in the land of the gods and surrounded by barbarians. In this way, the Hyksos prepared the way for a national revival in Egypt. In the second place, they also made Egypt emerge from her isolation and put her in contact with other peoples and cultures. The Hyksos, who had originated in Palestine and had settled in Egypt, built a bridge between Africa and Asia. Without knowing what they were doing, they prepared the way for the later political conquests and cultural expansion of the Late Kingdom in Egypt.

The national revival began in Upper Egypt. Egyptian princes were ruling at Thebes in the second half of the seventeenth century B.C. and, although they were nominally still vassals of the Hyksos, they had in effect become independent. They formed and trained an army and prepared to reconquer Egypt. These Upper Egyptian rulers were the kings of the Seventeenth Dynasty. According to a semi-legendary account, the penultimate king of this dynasty, Seqnen-Re, received an insulting demand

[76] Inscription of Speos Artemidos, *ARE* II §§ 296–303. The passage on the Hyksos is in *ANET*, p. 231.

from the Hyksos king Apophis who ruled at Avaris, five hundred miles north of Thebes in the Nile Delta, to get rid of the hippopotamus pool at Thebes because the animals prevented him from sleeping.[77] The papyrus is not complete and we do not know how this story ended. Seqnen-Re's mummy has, however, been found and the terrible head wounds from which the ruler died may have been inflicted in combat with the Hyksos. Whether this is so or not, the war of liberation began with Seqnen-Re's son, Ka-mose. This king's actions are narrated on two stelae found at Karnak, the second only quite recently.[78] The effective power of the Hyksos extended at this time no farther than Cusae, halfway between Memphis and Thebes, peace reigned and the Theban rulers were able to collect the taxes due to them from their territories in Lower Egypt. Ka-mose, however, wanted to drive the Asiatics out of the whole country and he seized a city in the Hyksos territory. Panic broke out at Avaris, from which town Apophis (II) sent a letter to the king of Ethiopia, calling on him for help against Ka-mose. This message was intercepted by Ka-mose, who continued to wage war against the Hyksos. Ka-mose's campaign did not apparently lead very far, because the real liberator of Egypt was Ka-mose's brother Amosis, the first pharaoh of the Eighteenth Dynasty.

By what has been called 'an irony of history',[79] our information about the eventual expulsion of the Hyksos comes from autobiographical inscriptions made on the tomb of an obscure officer of a Nile vessel, Ah-mose. He served under Amosis and fought several times at Avaris until the city fell; 'Then I carried off spoil from there: one man, three women, a total of four persons. Then his majesty gave them to me to be slaves.' This personal note is the only evidence that we have concerning the ultimate defeat of the Hyksos rulers in Egypt and the fall of their capital, Avaris. The Hyksos were pursued into Asia and set up a stronghold at Sharuḥen, which may have been the southern site of Tell el-Fārʿah. They were driven out of Sharuḥen after three years and Ah-mose was awarded another two female slaves and a decoration. Egypt was at last free of the foreign invader. One final aspect of the Hyksos rule in Egypt that should be noted is that, in all these texts, the name used is Amu or Asiatics. After Sharuḥen had been taken, Amosis did not pursue these Asiatics any farther, but turned to attack Nubia. The invaders had been driven back to the country from which they had come – Palestine – by the year 1550 B.C.

---

[77] Papyrus Sallier I; see *ANET*, p. 231.
[78] P. Montet, 'La stèle du roi Kamosé', *CRAI*, 1956, pp. 112–120. The first part of the text has been inscribed on another stele, fragments of which were found in 1935. A more complete text is known to us because of a schoolboy's tablet, the so-called Carnarvon Tablet; see *ANET*, pp. 232–233; for the second stele, see *ANET* pp. 554–555.
[79] *ANET*, pp. 233–234.

Chapter Four

PALESTINE DURING THE EIGHTEENTH AND NINETEENTH DYNASTIES IN EGYPT

T HE geographical situation of Syria and Palestine, considered as a single unit, between Anatolia, Mesopotamia and Egypt and its openness to cultural and economic exchanges with the West because of its long coastline, inevitably led to its becoming a region which the various powers struggling for supremacy in the Near East competed with each other to possess. This dispute for the possession of Syria and Palestine did not, however, exist before the middle of the second millennium. Up to this time, Hammurabi's power did not extend westward beyond the frontiers of the kingdom of Mari. Egypt still had not imperial plans and was content to treat the Syrian coastline and hinterland as a protectorate. The Hittites had not crossed the great barrier formed by the Taurus Mountains until the second half of the seventeenth century B.C., when Hattusilis I reduced to vassalage the kingdom of Yamḥad and its capital Aleppo, the most powerful state at the time in northern Syria.[1]

This state of balance was disturbed in 1595 B.C. when Hattusilis' son, Mursilis I, destroyed Aleppo after an uprising and then, following the Euphrates, sacked Babylon. This marked the end of Hammurabi's dynasty and the Cassites, who had come from the mountains in the east a century

[1] For the general historical framework, see G. Steindorff and K. C. Steele, *When Egypt Ruled the East*, 2nd. edn. revised by K. C. Steele, Chicago, 1957; F. Hornung, *Untersuchungen zur Chronologie und Geschichte des Neuen Reiches*, Wiesbaden, 1964 (Hornung's chronology has, generally speaking, been followed here, although M. B. Rowton's criticisms in *JNES*, 25, 1966, pp. 240–258, concerning the Nineteenth Dynasty, have been taken into account); H. Klengel, *Geschichte Syriens im 2. Jahrtausend v.u.Z.*, I. *Nordsyrien; II. Mittel- und Südsyrien*, Berlin, 1965–1969; A. Gardiner, *Egypt of the Pharaohs*, Oxford, 1966, pp. 177–280; E. Cassin, J. Bottéro and J. Vercoutter, eds., *Die altorientalischen Reiche, II. Das Ende des 2. Jahrtausends* (*Fischer Weltgeschichte*, 3), Frankfurt a.M., 1966 (in this work, which is on the whole excellent, H. Otten has dealt with the Hittites and the Mitanni, J. Yoyotte and J. Cerny have written about Egypt and A. Malamat has been responsible for Syria and Palestine); W. Helck, *Geschichte des Alten Agyptens* (*Handbuch der Orientalistik*, I, I, 3), Leiden, 1968, pp. 141–216; P. Garelli, *Le Proche Orient Asiatique des origines aux invasions des peuples de la mer* (*Nouvelle Clio*, 2), Paris, 1969; W. Helck, 'Überlegungen zur Geschichte der 18. Dynastie', *OrAnt*, 8 (1969), pp. 281–327.

before the Hittite raid, assumed full control of Babylonia. For the next five hundred years, Lower Mesopotamia led a very withdrawn existence. The Hittites themselves derived no benefit at all from their daring raid. Mursilis was murdered when he returned to Asia Minor and for more than a century the Hittite kingdom was made impotent and reduced to a state of chaos by internal intrigues and external disasters. Once Mesopotamia and Asia Minor had been eliminated from the Syrian scene, it was possible for a new power to emerge in Syria, where the Hurrians created the kingdom of Mitanni, which came into conflict with the pharaohs of the Eighteenth Dynasty in Egypt, whose policy was one of conquest. The Hittites appeared in Syria once more in the fourteenth century B.C. In the north, they destroyed the power of the Hurrians and in the south of the country they found themselves face to face with the Egyptians. After a short period of stability, the thirteenth century B.C. closed with the invasion of the so-called Sea Peoples who contributed towards the destruction of the Hittite empire, swept through Syria and Palestine and were not halted until they had reached the Egyptian frontier. This marked the beginning of a new stage in the history of the Ancient Near East.

Palestine's geographical position, her limited natural resources and her small strategic importance meant that the neighbouring great powers were not in direct competition with each other to seize the country, which remained within the sphere of Egypt's influence. Nonetheless, these rivalries and struggles among the neighbouring powers had their effect on Palestine and it is to this that we must now turn our attention.

I. THE HURRIAN EXPANSION AND THE KINGDOM OF MITANNI

The early stages of the Hurrian infiltration into northern Syria during the first few centuries of the second millennium have already been sketched out in the previous chapter. The Hittite king Mursilis had to fight against the Hurrians on his way to attack Babylon, and after his death they forced the Hittites to retire across the Taurus Mountains. Among the Hurrian kings mentioned in various Hittite texts, the name of the kingdom of Mitanni occurs during the second half of the sixteenth century B.C.,[2] appearing for the first time on the seal of a certain Shuttarna, the son of Kirta, the king of Mitanni. This seal was used officially several generations later as a means of giving legal status to the ruling dynasty.

[2] For the Hurrian expansion and the kingdom of Mitanni, see R. T. O'Callaghan, *Aram Naharaim, op. cit.*, and the works dealing with the Hurrians mentioned in note 34 in the previous chapter. See also M. Mayrhofer, *Die Indo-Arier im Alten Vorderasien*, Wiesbaden, 1966 (this work includes a full bibliography); A. Kammenhuber, *Die Arier im Vorderen Orient*, Heidelberg, 1968.*

The kingdom of Mitanni was situated in Upper Mesopotamia, in the region which the Hittites and the Assyrians called Hanigalbat and the Egyptians called Naharin, that is, the territory partly enclosed within the great northern bend of the Euphrates. The power of Mitanni, however, extended far beyond these natural boundaries. During the reigns of Parattarna at the end of the sixteenth century B.C. and Saustatar in the first half of the fifteenth century, the kingdoms of Yamhad (Aleppo) and Mukish (Alalah) in the west and Assyria and the kingdom of Arrapkha in the region of Kirkuk in the east were Mitanni's vassals. In other words, Mitanni ruled from the Mediterranean to beyond the Tigris. In the north, they had allies and vassals in Asia Minor, especially the people of Kizzuwatna (Cilicia). In the south, their hegemony extended as far as Hamath on the Middle Orontes, Mitanni's vassals, Aleppo and Alalah, acting as intermediaries. Round about the year 1500 B.C., Mitanni was the most important political power in the Near East, yet very little is known about the history of these people. We know that their capital was called Wassukkani on the Upper Habur, probably at Fekheriyeh, but we have no Mitannian archives and no royal monuments. All our information is derived from the people who were allies or enemies of Mitanni, especially the Hittites and the Egyptians, and our use of these texts is hindered by our uncertainty about the chronology of the period.[3]

One fact, however, emerges clearly. The names of the Mitannian kings were not Hurrian, but either certainly or possibly Indo-Aryan. In the fourteenth century B.C., one of these kings, Mattiwaza, invoked the Indo-Aryan gods Mitra and Uruwana (the Indian gods Mitra and Varuna), Indar (the Indian god Indra) and the Nassattiyana gods (the two Natyas of the Indians) together with many Hurrian deities in a treaty concluded with the Hittite Suppiluliumas. It has also been suggested that Aryan proper names and terms occur in the documents of Nusi near Kirkuk, which date from the fifteenth century B.C. The same kind of names have also been found in texts dating from this period or of a later date and referring to regions which were subjected to Hurrian influences in Asia Minor, Syria and even Palestine. This is clearly the first evidence of the presence of Aryans in the Near East.[4] Living among the Hurrians, they were never

---

[3] For Egypt of the Late Kingdom, I follow the chronology of Hornung, *Untersuchungen, op. cit.*, whose dates are fifteen years later than those of Hayes in *CAH*. For Syria and Asia Minor, I follow the 'average' chronology proposed by S. Smith and accepted by the editors of *CAH*.

[4] See especially R. T. O'Callaghan, *Aram Naharaim, op. cit.*, pp. 56–70 and P. E. Dumont's appendix in the same work on Indo-Aryan names, *ibid.*, pp. 149–155; H. Kronasser, 'Indisches in den Nuzi-Texten', *WZKM*, 53 (1957), pp. 181–192; P. Thieme, 'The 'Aryan' Gods of the Mitanni Treaties', *JAOS*, 80 (1960), pp. 301–317; R. Hauschild, 'Uber die frühesten Arier im Alten Orient', *Berichte über die Verhandlungen der sächsischen Akademie der Wissenschaften*, Leipzig, *Phil.-hist. Kl.*, 106, 6, 1962; M. Mayrhofer, 'Zur kritischen Sichtung

more than a small minority. They never imposed their language or their religion on their environment, but they did become the ruling class.

It has often been suggested that the Hurrians conquered by using the war chariot introduced into the Near East by the Indo-Aryans and revolutionising the art of war. This view is, however, seriously in need of correction.[5] The chariot had been known in Mesopotamia since the third millennium. There is evidence that it was known in the Assyrian trading settlements in Cappadocia in the nineteenth century B.C. About 1800 B.C., Anitta of Kussar, the predecessor of the Old Hittite Empire, confronted the enemy with forty war chariots. In the eighteenth century, the Mari letters refer several times to the horse and chariot. In the seventeenth century, under Hattusilis I, eighty chariots took part in the siege of Urshu. The only possible conclusion, then, that can be drawn is that the war chariot was known long before the kingdom of Mitanni was established. The Indo-Aryans did not introduce the chariot, although it is possible that they developed it, used it widely and perfected the art of breeding war horses. Attention has been drawn to the fact that the Aryan terms contained in the Nuzi texts refer to horses and that the Mitannian aristocracy was composed of *maryannu*. It has for a long time been thought that this word meant 'chariot warrior' and that it was an Aryan word with a Hurrian ending, although the Aryan origin of the words found in the Nuzi texts and of the word *maryannu* especially has recently been called into question.[6] The evidence is late, but it is strong – in the fourteenth century B.C., a man called Kikkuli, calling himself a 'trainer of Mitanni horses', compiled for the use of the Hittites a detailed instruction about the care of war horses in which he included a number of Aryan terms. However this may be, even if the Hurrians or the people of Mitanni were not the first to use war chariots, it is certain that they employed them to establish their empire in Syria and that the chariot

---

vorderasiatischarischer Personennamen', *Indogermanishce Forschungen*, 70 (1965), pp. 146–163; M. Mayrhofer, *Die Indo-Arier, op. cit.*, pp. 14–15, 18–22. In his most recent work, *Die Arier im Vorderen Orient, op. cit.*, A. Kammenhuber greatly restricts the number of Aryan proper names and terms that have been identified in the Hurrian environment. This decision is, of course, one which has to be made by Hurrian and Indo-Aryan specialists, but the historian who is not a specialist in this sphere has nonetheless to be careful not to overestimate the part played by Aryans in the Hurrian expansion and in the whole of the history of the Ancient Near East.

[5] See especially A. Kammenhuber, *Hippologia Hethitica*, Wiesbaden, 1961, with reference to works written previously by this author; M. Mayrhofer, *Die Indo-Arier, op. cit.*, pp. 25–26 and note: W. Nagel, *Der mesopotamische Streitwagen und seine Entwicklung im ostmediterranen Bereich*, Berlin, 1966 (this author's thesis is disputable); A. Kammenbuber, *Die Arier, op. cit.*, especially pp. 219–220, 237–238.

[6] A. Kammenhuber, Die Arier, op. cit., pp. 211–218 (Nuzi), 220–223 (*maryannu*). For the *maryannu* and the Aryan origin of the word, see R. T. O'Callaghan, 'New Light on the *Maryannu* as "Chariot Warriors"', *JKF*, 1 (1950–1951), pp. 309–324; A. Alt, *WO*, 2 (1954–1959), pp. 10–15, 234–237; F. Rainey, *JNES*, 24 (1965), pp. 19–22.

became a very important weapon in battles from the fifteenth century onwards. On the other hand, it does not seem to have played such a vital part in Egyptian warfare when it was mentioned for the first time in documents dating from about 1500 B.C. – two officers in the army of Thut-mose I each carried off a chariot in battle against the Mitanni.[7] There were, however, more than nine hundred chariots and two thousand horses in the booty that Thut-mose III took at Megiddo. Amen-hotep II carried off more than a thousand chariots in his Asiatic campaign and the Hittite Muwatalli employed two thousand five hundred chariots in the battle of Kadesh during the reign of Ramses II and kept a thousand more in reserve.

The increasing use of chariots in war was accompanied by the employment of bronze-plated cuirasses which protected the charioteer and the warrior and which caparisoned the horses. This armour had the same name – with phonetic differences – in Egyptian, Akkadian, Hittite, Ugaritic and Hebrew. The name, together with the armour itself, originated with the Hurrians. Finally, another new weapon of attack, the bow composed of strips of horn and different kinds of wood, was constantly in use at this period. This composite bow, which gave a range and a penetration much greater than those of the simple bow, was the offensive weapon against which the new armour was designed. It was known in the Egyptian texts as the 'Syrian' bow. There is no certain evidence that it was used in Egypt before the Eighteenth Dynasty.[8]

These important new weapons of war gave rise to a new military élite, the *maryannu*, who gave a feudal structure to the little states of the Ancient Near East, whether they were Mitannian vassals or not. The Hurrians, however, also made other important contributions to civilisation. Thousands of cuneiform tablets have been found at Yorghan Tepe, the site of Nuzi in the Kirkuk district. During the fifteenth century, Nuzi belonged to Mitanni and its population was mainly Hurrian. These texts, written in an unlettered form of Akkadian, deal with legal questions and with social customs, especially those relating to the family, which were different from the Mesopotamian law and which were tending to spread with the expansion of the Hurrian influence.

---

[7] *ARE*, III, §§ 81–85; *ANET*, p. 234a. Amosis' chariot (see *ANET*, p. 233b) was really a vehicle in which the ruler travelled. The question concerning the introduction into Egypt of the war chariot and the war horse has recently been raised again by the discoveries at Tell ed-Dab'a (see note 68, p. 164) – the tombs of the Hyksos period have been found to contain skeletons of members of the horse family and pieces of harness. These skeletal remains have not yet been completely identified, however, and we have no proof that these donkeys, wild asses or horses were ever harnessed to war chariots.*

[8] A composite bow in the Metropolitan Museum is believed to have come from a Seventeenth Dynasty tomb, but all that can be said with certainty is that it must be dated before Hatshepsut; see W. E. McLeod, 'Egyptian Composite Bows in New York', *AJA*, 66 (1962), pp. 15–16.

The Hurrians in fact spread farther than the boundaries of the Mitannian empire and we now have to consider their progress into southern Syria and Palestine. Part of the correspondence between the princes of these regions and the pharaohs Amen-hotep III and Amen-hotep IV (Akh-en-Aton) during the first half of the fourteenth century B.C. has been preserved in the Amarna letters. Many of these princes have Canaanite names – especially those from the Phoenician coast – but almost as many have what have been claimed to be Indo-Aryan names.[9] Examples of these are Aitakama and his father Shutatarra at Kadesh on the Orontes, Biryawaza at Damascus, Indaruta at Akshaph, Zurata and Shutatna at Acco, Biridiya at Megiddo and, farther south, Shuwardata at Herbon (?), Widiya at Ashkelon and Shubandu in a city in the south of Palestine. If we add to these the names of others who were not kings and if we limit ourselves simply to Palestine, we find twenty presumably Indo-Aryan and three Hurrian names, including only one name of a prince, 'Abdu Heba of Jerusalem, as opposed to thirty-three Canaanite names on the Amarna tablets. On the twelve Taanach tablets which are dated about five hundred years later, there are five Aryan and four Hurrian names, as against fourteen Semitic names.[10] Finally, there are two Indo-Aryan names as opposed to eight Semitic names on the two Shechem tablets,[11] which belong to more or less the same period as the Taanach tablets. A better knowledge of the Hurrian language might result in a reduction of the number of names at present thought to be Indo-Aryan. In any case, these Indo-Aryans certainly became assimilated by the Hurrians in Syria-Palestine and in the kingdom of Mitanni, and the Egyptians were not mistaken when they named Palestine, among other things, Huru, the land of the Hurrians.[12] This name was seldom used in the Eighteenth Dynasty, but much more frequently in the Nineteenth.

The Hurrian occupation of Syria-Palestine was not, as has often been suggested, simply the consequence of the expulsion of the Hyksos from Egypt, because the Hurrians did not take part in these events. When, then, did they enter Palestine? Thut-mose IV (1412–1402), who reigned just before the period of the Amarna tablets, had the title 'Conqueror of the Huru' and one of the units in his army was known as 'Men-khepru-Re beats the Huru'. During his reign, 'Hurrians' (Huru, Kharu) taken prisoner at

[9] R. T. O'Callaghan, *Aram Naharaim, op. cit.*, pp. 59–63, 151–153; W. F. Albright, *CAH*, II, XX, p. 13; A. Kammenhuber (*Die Arier, op. cit.*) is sceptical about the Indo-Aryan character of the majority of these names.
[10] A. Gustavs, 'Die Personennamen in den Tafeln von Tell Ta'annek', *ZDPV*, 50 (1927), pp. 1–18; 51 (1928), pp. 169–218; W. F. Albright, 'A Prince of Taanach in the Fifteenth Century B.C.', *BASOR*, 94 (April 1944), pp. 12–27.
[11] W. F. Albright, 'A Teacher to a Man of Shechem about 1400 B.C.', *BASOR*, 86 (April, 1942), pp. 28–31; E. F. Campbell, Appendix 3 to G. E. Wright, *Shechem: The Biography of a Biblical City*, New York, 1965, pp. 208–213.
[12] A. Gardiner, *Ancient Egyptian Onomastica*, Oxford, 1947, I, pp. 180*–186*.

Gezer formed a colony at Thebes.[13] During the reign of Amen-hotep II (1438–1412), who was ruling during the period of the Taanach tablets, the plunder taken in the Asiatic campaigns included 36,300 'Hurrians' (Kharu) among a very great number of captives – in addition to the Kharu, there were 15,200 Shasu or Bedouins leading a nomadic existence between Egypt and Syria and 15,070 people from Nukhashshe (Neges) in central Syria.[14] This text does not imply that most or all the people living in Palestine were Hurrians. What it does mean, however, is that the country from which these prisoners came – Palestine and southern Syria – was regarded by the Egyptians as the country of the Hurrians. At a later period, the annals of Thut-mose III, who reigned between 1468 and 1436, refer to the princes of Huru among the pharaoh's adversaries at Megiddo and to a ewer of the Huru.[15] Huru bows were carried off in another campaign.[16] This ewer and these bows might, of course, simply have been of Hurrian manufacture, without any direct reference to a country and we know that the strictly geographical use of the word Huru was rare at this time, the usual name for Palestine and part of Syria being Jahi or Retenu. In any case, these are the first examples of the use of the word Huru that we have in Egyptian texts.

Similarly, it is in texts dating from the reign of Thut-mose III that the *maryannu* are first mentioned. Two cases are especially interesting. In the first instance, *maryannu* were taken prisoner in Galilee.[17] In the second instance, we have a list of *maryannu* sent to the court of Thut-mose III by eleven cities, all of them in northern Palestine, from Taanach to Hazor, together with a messenger from Ashkelon, who had to join the delegation when it went down into Egypt. Their names are not reported in the document, but their title *maryannu* is enough to show that these cities were by this time governed by a Hurrian aristocracy.[18] Before the reign of Thut-mose III, neither Hurrians nor *maryannu* are mentioned in the texts dealing with the expulsion of the Hyksos or in those referring to the Asiatic campaign of Thut-mose I (1506–1494). It would seem therefore that the Hurrians did not reach Palestine until the beginning of the fifteenth century B.C. They apparently arrived on the Palestinian scene when Mitannian military leaders, an Indo-Aryan élite, were extending their power. This may explain why there were so many more Indo-Aryan names than Hurrian names among the princes and leaders in Palestine at this time. These immigrants seized power, but, apart from in a few cities, were never

[13] *ANET*, p. 248a.
[14] *ANET*, p. 247. The figures quoted in this text are, of course, fantastic; see J. J. Janssen, 'Eine Beuteliste von Amenophis II', *JEOL*, 17 (1963), pp. 141–147.
[15] *ANET*, pp. 235b, 237b; *ARE*, II, §§ 420–436.
[16] *ARE*, II, § 501.
[17] *ARE*, II, § 436; *ANET*, p. 237b.
[18] Papyrus de l'Ermitage, 1116A; see also C. Epstein, 'A New Appraisal of Some Lines from a Long-Known Papyrus', *JEA*, 49 (1963), pp. 49–56.

more than a small minority. There is also far too little archaeological evidence and what we possess is contradictory. A study of the Megiddo skulls has obliged archaeologists to conclude that a new, Alpine population appeared in Palestine in the course of the Middle Bronze Age and that this population predominated during the Late Bronze Age.[19] This change in the population has not, however, been observed at Lachish during the same periods[20] or at Jericho, where the series ceases before the Late Bronze Age.[21] However this may be, the population of Palestine undoubtedly remained very much the same and the new rulers soon became assimilated into the life of the country. On the other hand, they imposed their feudal system on Palestine and introduced cuneiform writing and Akkadian as the diplomatic and business language, thus extending the practice that they had found firmly established in Upper Mesopotamia and northern Syria when they arrived there.[22] Their letters to the pharaohs were written for them by native scribes in an Akkadian full of Canaanite expressions and glosses. The Egyptian pharaohs had also to observe this practice – there are several letters in the Amarna collection written in Akkadian at the Egyptian court, two of the Taanach tablets may have been sent by Amen-hotep II and a tablet found at Gezer may have been dispatched by Thut-mose IV.[23]

II. THE EGYPTIAN CONQUEST

Although Egypt must have been interested in these developments taking place in a part of the world which was within her sphere of influence, she did not intervene until the situation began to threaten her directly.[24] Amosis did no more than seize Sharuhen and hold it as a bridgehead in Asia. His successor Amen-hotep I (1527–1506) did not carry out any major military operations in Palestine. Thut-mose I (1506–1494), on the other hand, led a large-scale expedition into Asia, although our only sources of

[19] A. Hrdlička, in P. L. O. Guy, *Megiddo Tombs*, Chicago, 1938, pp. 192–208.
[20] M. Giles, in O. Tufnell, *Lachish IV: The Bronze Age*, London, 1958, pp. 318–322.
[21] D. R. Hughes, in K. M. Kenyon, *Jericho II*, London, 1965, pp. 664–685.
[22] R. Labat, 'Le rayonnement de la langue et de l'écriture akkadiennes au deuxième millénaire avant notre ère', *Syria*, 39 (1962), pp. 1–27.
[23] A. Malamat, 'Campaigns of Amenhotep II and Thutmose IV to Canaan', *Scripta Hierosolymitana*, 8 (1961), pp. 218–231.
[24] For the conquest and the rule of the Egyptians, see W. Helck, *Die Beziehungen Agyptens zu Vorderasien im 3. und 2. Jahrtausend v.Chr*, Wiesbaden, 1962; *ibid*, 'Die ägyptische Verwaltung in den syrischen Besitzungen', *MDOG*, 92 (1960), pp. 1–13; W. C. Hayes, 'Egypt: Internal Affairs from Thutmosis I to the Death of Amenophis III', *CAH*, II, IX (in two parts), 1962; D. B. Redford, *History and Chronology of the Eighteenth Dynasty of Egypt*, Toronto, 1967; M. S. Drower, 'Syria, c. 1550–1360', *CAH*, II, x (in two parts), 1969–1970.*

information are the biographies of two of this pharoah's officers and all that
these men tell us is that they accompanied him as far as Naharin and that
each of them took a chariot.[25] Naharin is the name given by the Egyptians
to the region where the kingdom of Mitanni had just been established –
another inscription of the period of Thut-mose I mentions 'a country called
Mitanni' [26] for the first time, as something quite new. Thut-mose I crossed
the Euphrates and Thutmose III was later to find the stele that his grandfather had erected on the bank of the river. The stele of Thutmose I on the
island of Tombos says that the Egyptians were astonished to find this river
flowing in the opposite direction from the Nile. The pharaoh appears to
have passed through Palestine and Syria without meeting with any opposition and gave himself the pleasure of hunting the elephants in the country
of Niyi, the marshes of the Orontes near Apamea.[27] This bold expedition
has to be dated before the Mitannian expansion under Parattarna and indeed, according to the chronology that we are following here, immediately
before that expansion. Thut-mose I wanted above all to prevent the Mitanni from extending their power. When this in fact took place, his
own success was severely limited and remained short-lived. His immediate successors, Thut-mose II (1494-1490) and the queen Hat-shepsut
(1490–1468), did not intervene in Asia, apart from a very restricted action
by Thutmose II against the Shasu bedouins on the eastern frontier of Egypt.

The outstanding conqueror was Thut-mose III, the greatest sovereign of
ancient Egypt. Kept in a state of dependence and subjection and removed
from public affairs for twenty-two years by his terrible stepmother
Hat-shepsut, he spent his early life in military camps, where he became a
skilled warrior and an accomplished sportsman. Later, he proved to be a
brilliant strategist and an excellent statesman, a great builder and a notable
patron of science and the arts. In a word, he had all the qualities of an
empire-builder.[28] As soon as he had gained freedom and independence on
the death of Hat-shepsut, he set out to conquer Asia, conducting seventeen
campaigns during the first twenty years of his reign (1468–1436). When he
died, he left his son a highly organised empire stretching from the Sudan to
the Euphrates.

His first campaign revealed his mastery of the situation,[29] which had be-

[25] *ARE*, II, §§81 and 85.

[26] H. Brunner, 'Mitanni in einem ägyptischen Text vor oder um 1500', *MIO*, 4 (1965), pp.
323–327.

[27] *ARE*, II, §125; the text certainly refers to Thut-mose I.

[28] One is reminded inevitably of Napoleon, whom this pharaoh even resembled physically
– judging by his mummy, he was only 5 feet 5 inches tall.

[29] The important Egyptian texts have been translated by J. A. Wilson and published in
ANET, pp. 234–241. For their interpretation, see especially H. H. Nelson, *The Battle of
Megiddo*, Chicago, 1913; S. Yeivin, 'A New Egyptian Source for the History of Palestine and
Syria', *JPOS*, 14 (1934), pp. 194–229; R. O. Faulkner, 'The Battle of Megiddo', *JEA*, 28

come very unstable during the reign of Hat-shepsut, who had not troubled the people of Syria and Palestine loyal to Egypt. Indo-Aryan and Hurrian chiefs had settled there, as we have seen, and Egypt had lost control of all the regions north of Gaza that were not on or near the coast. Urged by the Mitanni, who were at this time at the height of their power, the Prince of Kadesh on the Orontes had made himself the leader of a strong coalition. One text, for instance, refers to three hundred and thirty princes, although this must have been an exaggeration. The obvious intention was to march against Egypt and Thut-mose did not lose a moment. In 1468, two months after he had come to power, he set off at the head of his army, passing through Gaza and following the great northern route without at first meeting with any serious resistance. A later account tells how one of his officers took Jaffa by introducing his soldiers into the city in large baskets.[30] The allies gathered at Megiddo, the key position commanding the way into northern Palestine and Syria. Going against the advice of his generals, who recommended that he should follow easier routes terminating south and north of Megiddo, Thut-mose chose the pass of the Wādi 'Ara through the hills opposite the city, thus exposing his army, which advanced across the plain in a long, thin column, to attack from the enemy. The allies were badly informed about the movements of the Egyptian army and were taken by surprise. They were massed in the south and in danger of being cut off from the city. They changed the disposition of their troops too late and were overwhelmed by the first Egyptian charge. The victorious army, however, waited too long before sacking and pillaging the city and the refugees from the battle enclosed themselves inside Megiddo and surrendered only after seven months of siege. During this siege and shortly after the surrender of the city, various detachments of the pharaoh's army conquered Galilee and Jōlān, after which the whole army returned to Egypt. The prince of Kadesh had escaped, the coalition was broken and Thut-mose was able to have a list of one hundred and nineteen districts in Palestine in which his authority was recognized engraved on the pylons of the temple of Amon at Karnak.[31] To judge from the names that can be identified, this list covers, apart from the strategic route from Gaza to Megiddo, the whole of northern Palestine and Transjordan. It does not include the hilly or desert regions of central and southern Palestine, nor

---

(1942), pp. 2–15; M. Noth, 'Die Annalen Thutmoses III als Geschichtsquelle', *ZDPV*, 66 (1943), pp. 156–174; for this and the following campaigns, see M. S. Drower, *CAH*, II, X, Part 1, 1970, pp. 27–41.

[30] *ANET*, pp. 22–23; G. Lefèbvre, *Romans et contes égyptiens*, Paris, 1949, pp. 125–130; see especially also H. Goedicke, 'The Capture of Joppa', *ChrEg*, 43 (1968), pp. 219–233.

[31] J. Simons, *Handbook for the Study of Egyptian Topographical Lists Relating to Western Asia*, Leiden, 1937, pp. 29–44, 109–128; M. Noth, 'Der Aufbau der Pälestinaliste Thutmoses III', *ZDPV*, 61 (1938), pp. 26–65.

does it include southern Transjordan, but these were of secondary importance. Thut-mose III could therefore regard himself as controlling the whole of Palestine.

The only aim of some of the campaigns that followed was to consolidate the conquest and to levy tribute, whereas, in the case of others, it was to extend the power of Egypt gradually into northern Syria. Thut-mose also set up garrisons in the ports so as to retain control of the sea and to safeguard his lines of communication, and kept them supplied by taxes imposed on towns in the interior.[32] The eighth campaign, which Thut-mose conducted in 1457, was undoubtedly the most glorious.[33] The pharaoh first seized Qatna, then fought a battle to the west of Aleppo and finally reached the Euphrates at a point near Carchemish. He had had boats built close to Byblos and these were transported on ox waggons to the Euphrates. With them, the army crossed the river. Having once entered the kingdom of Mitanni – known to the Egyptians as Naharin – Thut-mose hoped to defeat the Mitannian army, but the king, probably Sausatar, refused to fight and fled. Realising that he could not follow the Mitannian king too far from his own base, Thut-mose pillaged the part of the king's territory which bordered the Euphrates, erected his stele alongside that of his grandfather Thut-mose I and crossed back to the other side of the river. On the return journey to Egypt, he had to suppress several uprisings, but he still found time to do what his grandfather had done – to hunt the elephant in the country of Niyi. He almost died when he was attacked by the leader of the herd, an enormous male, and was only saved by one of his officers, Amen-em-heb, who cut off the creature's trunk, which the text calls its 'hand'.

Thut-mose had achieved the goal which he had set himself. He had above all broken the power of Mitanni. He had done this by keeping Mitanni on the far side of the Euphrates, by depriving the people of their allies and vassals on the west of the river and by establishing Egypt as the dominant power in the Near East. This fact was accepted by the Hittites, the Assyrians and the Babylonians and these people sent messengers to Egypt bearing gifts. Thut-mose was able to add two hundred and seventy North Syrian names to the list of cities conquered in Palestine.[34] All the following campaigns up to the year 1448, when the annals cease, had no other aim but to suppress internal uprisings or to make sure that the coastal garrisons were kept supplied.

[32] A. Alt, 'Das Stützpunktsystem der Pharaonen an der phönikischen Küste und im syrischen Binnenland', *ZDPV*, 68 (1950), pp. 97–133 = *Kleine Schriften*, III, pp. 107–140.

[33] *ANET*, pp. 239–241; R. O. Faulkner, 'The Euphrates Campaign of Thutmosis III', *JEA*, 32 (1946), pp. 39–42; A. Gardiner, *Ancient Egyptian Onomastica* I, pp. 153*–171*; 'Notes on Some Campaigns of Thutmosis III and Amenophis II'.

[34] J. Simons, *op. cit* (see note 31 above); M. Astour, 'Place Names from the Kingdom of Alalah in the North Syrian List of Thutmoses III', *JNES*, 22 (1963), pp. 220–241.

It must have been difficult to keep such an empire together even towards the end of the reign of Thut-mose III. Certainly Egypt was beginning to lose territory during the reign of his successor Amen-hotep II (1438– 1412).[35] Even before the death of his father and while he was acting as co-regent,[36] Amen-hotep had to put down a revolt in the land of Takhshi, the Tahash of Gen 22:24, in the valley of the Orontes south of Kadesh, taking seven rebellious leaders captive and putting them to death with his own hands. In the seventh year of his reign, he left for Syria, where there had been a revolt, was acclaimed at Niyi, received the homage of the Prince of Kadesh and probably regained control of the port of Ugarit. On the other hand, Alalah, Aleppo and the Euphrates region were lost to Egypt. On the way back from Syria, on the plain of Sharon, Amen-hotep's troops captured an emissary from the king of Mitanni bearing a clay tablet hung round his neck – clearly a message for a prince in Palestine. The Mitanni were in fact conducting intrigues in this southern part of Syria-Palestine and in the ninth year of his reign Amen-hotep had to carry out a punitive expedition, first in the Plain of Sharon, with its small population, and then in the Plain of Esdraelon. The latter was, of course, much more important and the central point of the Egyptian possessions in Palestine. Amen-hotep took Anaharath, south of Tabor, and the prince of Geba-Shemen, north-west of Megiddo, was punished for revolting by being taken back to the camp of Megiddo, deposed and replaced by one of the pharaoh's puppets.

We have very little information about Amen-hotep's son Thut-mose IV (1412–1402) in Asia. He seems to have preserved what he inherited from his father.[37] He intervened in Palestine and carried off 'Hurrian' prisoners from Gezer.[38] He also visited Sidon.[39] The body of his chariot has been found in his tomb and on it he is shown charging the Asiatics.[40] The accompanying inscription provides a list of the people and places he conquered – Naharin, Babylonia (!), Tunip, the Shasu, Kadesh, Takshi . . .[41] He was given the title 'The Conqueror of the Huru' and a victorious campaign against

---

[35] *ANET*, pp. 245–248; E. Edel, 'Die Stelen Amenophis II. aus Karnak und Memphis', *ZDPV*, 69 (1953), pp. 97–176; A. Alt, 'Neue Berichte über Feldzüge von Pharaonen des Neuen Reiches nach Palästina', *ZDPV*, 70 (1954), pp. 39–62; Y. Aharoni, 'Some Geographical Remarks concerning the Campaigns of Amenhotep II', *JNES*, 19 (1960), pp. 177–183; A. Malamat, *op. cit.* (see note 23 above); W. Helck, *Urkunden der 18. Dynastie, 1287–1316, Ubersetzung*, Berlin, 1961, pp. 28–41.

[36] D. B. Redford, 'The Co-Regency of Thutmosis III and Amenophis II', *JEA*, 51 (1965), pp. 107–122; C. Aldred, 'The Second Jubilee of Amenophis II', *ZÄS*, 94 (1967), pp. 1–6.

[37] R. Giveon, 'Thutmosis IV and Asia', *JNES*, 28 (1969), pp. 54–59.

[38] *ANET*, p. 248a.

[39] *EA*, 85, 69–73.

[40] *ANEP*, Nos. 314–316.

[41] W. Helck, *Urkunden der 18. Dynastie, 2140–2162 (Übersetzung)*, 1961, 1560, p. 150.

Naharin is also mentioned, in passing, in one text. [42] There are references to gifts brought by the people of Naharin on the monuments and on certain inscriptions of his leading officers. These were probably not a form of tribute, because Egypt had given up northern Syria and Thut-mose IV was trying above all to keep peace between Egypt and the kingdom of Mitanni. After several requests had been rejected, he succeeded in marrying a daughter of Artatama, the king of Mitanni.

This rapprochement between the two states had come about on the initiative of Mitanni, because there had been a revival of Hittite power under Artatama's contemporary, Tudhaliyas II, and the Mitannian king did not want a war on two fronts. Friendly relations continued, even though the power of the Hittites weakened under Tudhaliyas' successors. The pharaohs of Egypt and the kings of Mitanni exchanged letters and gifts. The young Amen-hotep III, the son of Thut-mose IV, married a daughter of Shuttarna II, the son of Artatama, then, at the end of his reign, a daughter of Tushratta, the son of Shuttarna. By this time, of course, Egypt was losing the conquering spirit and was withdrawing into herself. Thut-mose IV was the last pharaoh of the Eighteenth Dynasty who made a military expedition into Syria or Palestine. During his long and brilliant reign (1402–1364), Amen-hotep III was content to administer this part of his kingdom from a distance and claim taxes from it – a lack of interest which led to difficulties during the Amarna period.

III. PALESTINE UNDER EGYPTIAN DOMINATION

We must now consider the situation of Palestine in the Egyptian Empire. [44] In addition to the rather scanty information that we have from the Egyptian texts of the Late Kingdom, there are two main sources. The first is the small collection of Taanach texts dating from the fifteenth century B.C. and the second and more important source of information is provided by the fourteenth century Amarna letters.*

With the exception of the relatively small areas which had become the pharaoh's personal property or the property of the temples and to which we shall be returning later, the conquered territory was not directly ad-

[42] W. Helck, *Urkunden*, 1554, p. 147.

[43] *EA*, 29, 16–18.

[44] E. Edel, 'Weitere Briefe aus der Heiratskorrespondenz Rameses' II', *Geschichte und Altes Testament (Festschrift A. Alt)*, Tübingen, 1953, pp. 29–63, especially pp. 55–61 and 63; W. Helck, 'Die ägyptische Verwaltung'; *Die Beziehungen*, pp. 256–267; W. F. Albright, *CAH*, II, XX, pp. 7–11; K. A. Kitchen, 'Interrelations of Egypt and Syria', *La Siria nel Tardo Bronzo*, ed. M. Liverani, Rome, 1969, pp. 77–95; M. S. Drower, *CAH*, II, X, Part 1, 1970, pp. 50–65.*

ministered by Egypt. The pharaoh allowed the native chiefs to remain and to continue to rule after swearing an obligatory oath of loyalty and obedience to himself as sovereign. After the capture of Megiddo by Thut-mose III, for example, the conquered princes had to swear that they would never again harm Menkhepru-ra; they were then reinstated in their cities.[45] The princes of Kadesh and of two other cities swore a similar oath to Amen-hotep II.[46] It was in each case a personal oath which bound one prince to one pharaoh and it had therefore to be renewed every time there was a change of ruler in Egypt or in the principality As a rule, the pharaoh respected the hereditary right of succession, but there was an investiture whenever there was a new prince and the Egyptian ruler could always depose a prince if he found him unsatisfactory.[47] This explains why the Amarna letters are so full of protestations of submission, often expressed with a degrading servility, and why the princes affirm again and again that they owe their power exclusively to the pharaoh. The king of Jerusalem, for instance, declared: 'It was neither my father nor my mother who set me in this place; it was the mighty hand of the king that made me enter the palace of my father'.[48] According to an isolated testimony,[49] the investiture of a prince consisted of anointing with oil and was thus similar to the appointment of the leading Egyptian officers.

Their own people called these princes 'kings', but the pharaoh addressed them as 'the man (chief) ' of a certain city and their official function was that of a *hazanu*, an Akkadian title equivalent to that of burgomaster. They enjoyed a great deal of independence, governing their territories very much as they wanted. Those princes whose territories were larger and who were themselves more powerful even had vassals. They also levied armies, recruited from among their own subjects or composed of mercenaries, and used these to settle local quarrels or to annex new territories. During the Amarna period, Labaya of Shechem built up a kingdom stretching from Lake Tiberias to the frontier of Gaza.[50] In the north, Abdu-Ashirta and his son Aziru made Amurru into a state which included the largest part of cen-

---

[45] *ANET*, pp. 237, 238a.

[46] *ANET*, p. 246a.

[47] The pharaoh was not bound by treaty to these princes, as the Hittite king was to his vassals. He regarded them rather as his functionaries and he appointed them and dismissed them from office at will. For this political conception and its consequences, see M. Liverani, 'Contrasti e confluenze di concezioni politiche nell'età di el-Amarna', *RA*, 61 (1967), pp. 1–18.

[48] *EA*, 286, 9–13, cf. 288, 13–15; this can be compared with Solomon's prayer in 1 Kings 3:7.

[49] *EA*, 51, 4–9.

[50] H. Reviv, 'Regarding the History of the Territory of Shekhem in the El-Amarna Period', *Tarbiz*, 33 (1963–1964), pp. 1–7 (in Hebrew with an English summary); E. F. Campbell, 'Shechem in the Amarna Archive', in G. E. Wright, *Schechem. The Biography of a Biblical City*, New York, 1965, pp. 191–207.

tral Syria.[51] Egypt showed no apparent jealousy. Labaya declared that he
was the pharaoh's faithful servant, 'the dust that he trampled on', and that
he was ready to give him his wife and even to stab himself if he was ordered
to.[52] Aziru also declared his submission and recalled that it was the pharaoh
who had appointed him to be hazanu. The pharaoh himself wrote to Aziru
as 'the man of Amurru'.[53]

It is true, of course, that the Amarna letters which are our main source of
information, date back to a period when Egypt was no longer able to control her empire effectively. The situation had certainly become worse, but it
was not entirely new. Egypt had left Syria-Palestine in the same state in
which she had found it at the time of the conquest – as a mosaic of rival
principalities, among which one would from time to time emerge as
stronger than the others and consequently overpower them. To say nothing
of Syria, Hazor in Palestine was a very powerful kingdom during the Mari
period, in the eighteenth century B.C.[54] It was the same situation that
prevailed when the Israelites settled in Palestine – a great number of 'kings',
but a concentration of forces and alliances. There was, for instance, a strong
alliance of kings formed to fight Gibeon (Jos. 10:3–5) and the king of
Hazor was the leader of a coalition of all the northern kings (Jos. 11:1–2)
and was given the title of 'king of Canaan' (Judges 4:2, 23–24).

So long as these local kings carried out their duties as vassals, and did
not plot against her Egypt was satisfied. The most important of these duties
were the payment of tribute each year, the fulfilment of certain tasks, the
maintenance of garrisons, the quartering of troops passing through and the
despatch of forces when the Egyptian army was going to wage war in
Syria.[55] If a prince failed to carry out his obligations or if he gave rise to
suspicions, he was summoned to the pharaoh's court to give an account of
himself. What is more, the pharaoh kept signs or pledges of the prince's
faithfulness. Thut-mose III, for example, initiated the practice of taking
prisoner the sons of princes whom he had conquered. While they were
waiting to succeed their fathers, they served as hostages.[56]

It is clear from the Amarna letters that many transactions took place
directly between the pharaoh, in other words, between the central administration of Egypt, and the local princes. It is also clear, however, that

---

[51] H. Klengel, 'Aziru von Amurru und seine Rolle in der Geschichte der Amarnazeit',
MIO, 10 (1964), pp. 57–83.

[52] EA, 252–254.

[53] EA, 161–162.

[54] See A. Malamat, 'Hazor, "The Head of all those Kingdoms" ', JBL, 79 (1960), pp.
12–19.*

[55] Compare, for example, the Taanach letters (no. 5 and 6) under Amen-hotep II and,
passim, the Amarna letters.

[56] See the annals of Thut-mose's sixth campaign, ANET, p. 239a, and the heading of the
'Palestinian List', ANET, p. 242a.

the pharaoh had personal representatives in the different countries. These men were called, in Akkadian, *rabisu* or 'provincial administrators' and less frequently *sakin mati*. In Canaanite, they were known as *sokinu* or 'prefects'. They were, in other words, men sent by the pharaoh to represent him in the country. The corresponding Egyptian title was probably 'governor of the foreign countries in the north'. These representatives were usually Egyptians, but several of them had Semitic names and must therefore have been native people who had been educated in Egypt. They were directly responsible to the pharaoh and the local princes owed obedience to them, addressed their requests to them and called on them to testify to their loyalty to Egypt. The pharaoh's representatives, on the other hand, acted as arbitrators in quarrels between princes, sent them rations and troops and ensured that they carried out the sovereign's orders.

At the beginning of the period covered by the Amarna tablets, in the reign of Amen-hotep III, Egypt's possessions in Asia seem to have been divided into three provinces. In the north, there was the province of Amurru, with Sumur as its administrative centre. (Sumur was known as Simyra, in the Hellenistic period and was probably Tell Kazel to the north of the Eleuthera river.[57]) To the east and south-east was the province of Upe (Kingdom of Damascus) with its administrative centre at Kumidi in the Beqāʿ to the north of Hermon. The third province was Canaan in the south; the administrative centre of this province was at Gaza. After Amurru had seceded, the two provinces of Upe and Canaan continued alone and remained distinct until the reign of Ramses II.[58] Gaza, the point of departure for expeditions during the conquest, naturally became the administrative centre and the residence of the *rabisu* of the province. There is evidence of this in the Taanach letters during the reign of Amen-hotep II[59] and elsewhere during the reign of Amen-hotep IV.[60]

Because it was so important, Gaza had been annexed by the pharaoh as his personal possession and Thut-mose III had given it an Egyptian name meaning the city 'which the sovereign has seized'. Jaffa also suffered the same fate and royal granaries were set up there.[61] Wheat-growing lands in this district and on the Plain of Esdraelon were in fact exploited for the pharaoh by Egyptian functionaries using local workers. Other territories too were handed over to the pharaoh. Thut-mose III, for example, appropriated Yanuamma (Yanoam) and two other towns near Lake Tiberias that he had conquered at the same time as Megiddo[62] and gave them later to

[57] M. Dunand and N. Saliby, 'A la recherche de Simyra', *AAS*, 7 (1957), pp. 3–16; M. Dunand, A. Bounni and N. Saliby, 'Fouilles du Tell Kazel', *ibid.*, 14 (1964), pp. 3–14.
[58] See E. Edel, *op. cit.*, note 44.
[59] Taanach, No. 6, 12–14.
[60] *EA*, 289, 30–35.
[61] *EA*, 294, 18–23.
[62] *ANET*, p. 237b.

the sanctuary of Amon of Karnak.[63] Under Ramses III, this sanctuary received income from nine towns of Huru (Palestine) and Ethiopia.[64] There were in addition Egyptian temples in Palestine which were, of course, the property either of the state or of the Egyptian priesthood.[65] A temple of Amon existed in the province of Canaan at the time of Ramses III and received tribute from the inhabitants; clearly, it must have been built before the reign of this pharaoh.[66] It may have been situated at Gaza, the capital of the province. There was also a temple dedicated to Ptah at Ashkelon.[67] Two temples at Beth-shean, revealed in the course of excavations and dating back to the reigns of Ramses II and Mer-ne-Ptah,[68] are built in a style that clearly imitates that of Egypt, but they were dedicated to local deities.

There are also signs of Egypt's military presence in Palestine. Thut-mose III conducted campaigns almost every year and Amen-hotep II conducted three – these point to the need for Egyptian control. There was also a need for more permanent measures to be taken. Thut-mose III had built a fortress in the Lebanon at the time of his first campaign[69] and, when his conquests spread farther into Syria, he organised regular supply lines from ports on the Phoenician coast which served as bases for his troops and points of embarkation and disembarkation. These ports were permanently guarded. In Palestine proper, Gaza, which was not, of course, a port, was not only the administrative centre of the province of Canaan, but also the headquarters of the army of occupation and the Amarna letters mention the troops that left and returned there. Megiddo, further north and further inland, was, in the reigns of Thut-mose III and Amen-hotep II, the great military base.[70] Later, however, under Amen-hotep IV, this base was transferred to Beth-Shean,[71] where it remained until the end of the Egyptian control of Palestine.

The occupation army consisted of infantry and chariots and the troops were mainly Egyptian soldiers and Nubian archers. Apart from the garrisons mentioned above, detachments of troops were quartered in the towns, usually at the request of the princes, who wanted to be defended against their neighbours and their own subjects. These military detachments were often absurdly small in number. The king of Tyre, for example, asked

[63] ARE, II, § 557.

[64] Harris Papyrus, ARE, IV, § 226; cf. ANET, p. 261a.

[65] A. Alt, 'Agyptische Tempel in Palästina und die Landnahme der Philister', ZDPV, 67 (1944), pp. 1–20 = Kleine Schriften, I, pp. 216–230.

[66] ANET, pp. 260a–261b.

[67] G. Loud, The Megiddo Ivories, Chicago, 1939, pp. 12–13.

[68] B. Maisler, 'The Chronology of the Beth-Shean Temples', BIES, 16, 3–4 (1951), pp. 14–19.

[69] ANET, p. 238b.

[70] Taanach, No. 6; see also Y. Aharoni, op. cit. (note 35), pp. 181–183.

[71] EA, 289, 19–20.

for ten foot soldiers on one occasion and, on another, twenty. The king of Jerusalem once complained that the pharaoh's representative had recalled the whole garrison and earnestly requested fifty men because the situation was so critical.[72] At normal times, these troops were simply employed as a police force.

We may conclude by saying that the Egyptian domination of Palestine was always incomplete. There were, of course, certain parts of the country which were of strategic or economic importance to Egypt – the coastline between Gaza and Jaffa, the great route to the north and the Plain of Esdraelon. Apart from these, Egypt was generally satisfied with a purely nominal submission and the collection of taxes, which was often hazardous. After the reign of Thut-mose IV, there were no more military expeditions into Asia and consequently no more demonstrations of Egyptian power in that part of the world. The cities were left to fight their own little wars with each other and to be exploited by the corrupt functionaries of the Amarna period. The country very quickly sank into chaos.

IV. THE HITTITE CONQUESTS AND THE TROUBLES OF THE AMARNA PERIOD

Round about the year 1370 B.C., a sovereign who was to play a very decisive part in the history of the Ancient Near East ascended the Hittite throne. For many years during the early part of his reign, this king, Suppiluliumas, devoted himself to the complete reorganisation of his kingdom and to the reclamation of the territories that had been lost in the course of the disastrous reign of his father, Arnuwandas(?). He then turned his attention to Syria and fought against the people of Mitanni, who were at this time ruled by Tushratta. It is not easy to follow the pattern of events during this period and the dates are particularly difficult to establish exactly, but for the purpose of this work, it is sufficient to recall the main facts and their consequences.[73] Suppiluliumas' first invasion of the country beyond the Taurus range ended in failure – Tusratta repelled his attack and strengthened his control of northern Syria. Suppiluliumas, however, attacked again, this time in the rear, and, coming down from the source of the

[72] EA, 148, 14; 151, 15; 289, 42.

[73] For the Hittite conquests and the troubles of the Amarna period generally, see K. A. Kitchen, Suppiluliuma and the Amarna Pharaohs, Liverpool, 1962; E. F. Campbell, The Chronology of the Amarna Letters, Baltimore, 1964; A. Goetze, 'The Struggle for the Domination of Syria (1400–1300) ', CAH, II, XVII, 1965; W. F. Albright, 'The Amarna Letters from Palestine', CAH, II, XX, 1966; J. Vandier, 'Toutânkhamon, sa famille, son règne', Journal des Savants, 1967, pp. 65–91; H. Otten, Die hethitischen historischen Quellen und die altorientalische Chronologie (Akademie der Wissenschaften und der Literatur in Mainz, Abhandlungen 1968, 3), Wiesbaden, 1968.*

Tigris, eventually reached the Mitannian capital of Wassuganni, which Tusratta had evacuated. Then, turning westwards, he crossed the Euphrates and took Aleppo and Alalah. After this, he moved towards the south, subduing the countries of Nukhashshe and Niyi and the cities of Qatna and Kadesh and finally reaching the region of Damascus, thus making himself master of Syria from the Euphrates to the Lebanon.[74]

Tusratta had not, however, been completely defeated, Carchemish had not been taken and Mitanni had friends and allies among the Hurrian aristocracy and in northern Syria. Suppiluliumas' war against the kingdom of Mitanni therefore lasted for six years, during which time Carchemish fell and Hittite domination was finally established in northern Syria. One of Suppiluliumas' sons was made king of Carchemish and another was given the throne of Aleppo.[75] In Mitanni itself, moreover, a struggle for power was taking place, in which a man called Artatama was favoured by one party as ruler in opposition to Tusratta.[76] Suppiluliumas decided to support Artatama and, when Tusratta was assassinated, he placed Artatama's son Mattiwaza on the throne[77] and made him accept a treaty of vassalage. This was the moment for Assyria, which had been subject to Tusratta and had favoured his successor Shuttarna, to declare her independence. The reign of Ashuruballit I (1365–1330) at this time marks the return of Assyria to the political scene in the Near East. During the reigns of Ashuruballit's successors, Adadnirari I (1307–1275) and Shalmaneser I (1274–1245), Assyria was to reduce Mitanni to vassalage and eventually to conquer it.[78]

The only two powers which confronted each other in Syria-Palestine at this time were the Hittite Empire and the Egyptians. Since his first great campaign there, Suppiluliumas had reached the lands recognised as Egyptian possessions from Ugarit (Rās Shamrah) to Kadesh. After some hesitation, the king of Ugarit became a vassal of the Hittites.[79] The king of Kadesh resisted at first, but was soon conquered by the Hittites.[80] This evoked no reaction from Egypt, where an extraordinary development was taking place. Amenhotep III (1402–1364) had been succeeded by his son Amenhotep IV (1364–1347).[81] The new pharaoh initiated a radical renewal

[74] The most important text that we have is a historical introduction to the treaty between Suppiluliumas and Mattiwaza of Mitanni (see below) and can be found in translation in *ANET*, p. 318.*

[75] Text *KUB*, XIX, 9; English translation in K. A. Kitchen, *op. cit.*, p. 3.

[76] This was, I believe, an interior struggle and not one between the kingdoms of Mitanni and of Hurru, which cannot be situated either in history or on the maps; see M. Liverani, 'Hurri e Mitanni', *OrAnt*, 1 (1962), pp. 253–257. This view is more and more widely accepted.

[77] I preserve this reading of the name, which probably ought to be read as Kurtiwaza.

[78] J. M. Munn-Rankin, 'Assyrian Military Power, 1300–1200 B.C.', *CAH*, II, XXV, 1967.

[79] M. Liverani, *Storia di Ugarit nell'età degli archivi politici*, Rome, 1962, pp. 27–56.

[80] For the text referring to these events, see note 74 above.

[81] Many historians believe that these two pharaohs were for a long time co-regents, but

of the Egyptian religion which consisted of a replacement of the cult of Amon and all the Egyptian gods by the cult of the one god Aten, who was not given a visible form. This one god was the solar disc and the new cult was the worship of the solar disc. In the fifth year of his reign, Amen-hotep IV finally broke with the powerful clergy of Amon at Thebes and established a new capital at Akh-et-Aten, the 'Horizon of the Solar Disc'. The pharaoh took part of his father's archives to the new capital and deposited his own there. It is from Akh-et-Aten that the Amarna letters come – the ruins of the modern Tell el-'Amārna. The pharaoh himself also changed his name from Amen-hotep to Akh-en-Aten, 'the one who is favoured by the solar disc'. He had the idols of Amon destroyed and his own name inscribed on all the monuments. Under his influence and that of the members of the royal court whom he had managed to convert to his faith, Egyptian art and literature were used to express and to spread the new religion. Akh-en-Aten was not, however, simply a mystic or a visionary – his aims were also political. He wanted to free Egypt from the power of the priests of Amon and to unite the empire by providing a form of worship which all his subjects would accept.

Both plans failed. Akh-en-Aten had no sons, but only daughters and for this reason took his son-in-law Semenkh-ka-Re (1351–1347) as his partner at the end of his reign, but Semenkh-ka-Re died very shortly after Akh-en-Aten. The throne passed to a young man, the husband of a royal princess, Tut-ankh-Aten (1347–1338). Tut-ankh-Aten soon had to come to terms with the priests of Amon and, as a result, he returned to Thebes with his court, re-established the cult of Amon and changed his name to Tut-ankh-Amon. He died young, leaving no sons, and power passed to the vizier Aye, who married his widow (1338–1334). Akh-en-Aten, the monotheist and religious reformer, came to be regarded in Egyptian history as the 'heretical' pharaoh. His reforms also met with no success among his subjects, because, under a corrupt administration, Egypt fell into a state of anarchy and the empire collapsed easily when pressed by the Hittites.

When Amen-hotep IV (Akh-en-Aten) came to the throne, Suppiluliumas had sent him a correct but cool letter[82] – Egypt was at that time the partner of the greatest enemy of the Hittites, Tushratta, the king of Mitanni. Relationships between the two allies, however, became rapidly worse. Tushratta sent three letters to Akh-en-Aten, each one sharper in tone than the previous one.[83] After that, the correspondence ceased and Mitanni

---

this is not borne out by the Egyptian documents or the Amarna letters; see E. Hornung, *Untersuchungen, op. cit.,* pp. 71–78; E. F. Campbell, *The Chronology, op. cit.;* J. Vandier, 'Toutânkhamon . . .', *op. cit.,* pp. 67–72; D. B. Redford, *History and Chronology, op. cit.,* pp. 88–169; Redford argues emphatically that they were not even for a short period co-regents.

[82] *EA,* 41.

[83] *EA,* 27–29.

was no longer able to depend on Egypt. The principalities of Asia, which were also Egypt's subjects, were similarly abandoned. Burnaburiash, the king of distant Babylon (*ca.* 1375–1347), was able to write to Akh-en-Aten: 'Canaan is your country and its kings are your servants', but he also complained that his traders had been murdered in the pharaoh's country and that caravans had been held to ransom there by Biryawaza, the prince of Damascus, and even by the pharaoh's representative.[84] The Egyptian empire was in fact breaking up. Most of the Syrian princes were playing a double game. With the Egyptians, they made a great display of their loyalty in order to obtain money and men. These were used either to defend their territory against their neighbours or to enlarge it at their neighbours' expense. Their attitude towards the Hittites, on the other hand, was quite different – they either resisted them or submitted to them, according to the circumstances. Niqmadu of Ugarit, for example, had married an Egyptian princess, but he became subject to the authority of the Hittites. Aitakama of Kadesh, whom Suppiluliumas had reinstated as a vassal king after he had taken the city, went over to the Egyptian camp for a time when the pharaoh's troops had shown evidence of their strength and Suppiluliumas was in difficulties in the north.

The most important example of this double game is that played by the country of Amurru.[85] Abdu-Ashirta had made Amurru the most powerful state in central Syria and Amen-hotep III seems to have recognised him as the protector of the Egyptian province of Amurru, although, in fact, all that Abdu-Ashirta was seeking was his own advantage. After his violent death,[86] his son Aziru pursued the same policy and soon became in effect the sole master in the entire province. Despite the strong protests made again and again by Rib-Addi of Byblos, who felt directly threatened by Aziru, Egypt, which was ruled at the time by Amen-hotep IV (Akh-en-Aten) accepted the situation. It would seem that Egypt did this because she preferred a unified territory controlled by Aziru and nominally subject to the pharaoh at the frontier between Egypt and the Hittite empire to several small principalities quarrelling among themselves. When Aziru was summoned to the Egyptian court, he excused himself on the grounds that he had to defend the pharaoh's country against the Hittites, although he was in fact already in league with them. All the same, he replied to another summons and went to Egypt, where he was kept for a long time answering accusations brought against him. At the same time, however, he continued, despite the great distance, with his intrigues in Syria. He returned to Syria with a letter testifying to his loyalty to the pharaoh, but, when Tut-ankh-Amon had died and the Hittite empire seemed to hold

[84] *EA*, 7–8.
[85] H. Klengel, *MIO*, 10 (1964), pp. 57–83.
[86] W. L. Moran, 'The Death of 'Abdi-Aŝirta', *Eretz-Israel*, 9 (1969), pp. 94–99.

power, he signed a treaty of vassalage with Suppiluliumas.[87] The province of Amurru was finally lost to Egypt.

It is clear that the whole of Egypt very nearly became part of the Hittite empire. When Tut-ankh-Amon died, Suppiluliumas received a surprising letter from his widow, who said that she had no male children and wanted to marry one of Suppiluliumas' sons. Suppiluliumas was suspicious and sent an officer to obtain further information. The officer returned to the Hittite king with another, more urgent message, saying that the Hittite prince would certainly be the queen's husband and the king of Egypt. Suppiluliumas sent off his son Zannanza, but the young man was murdered on the way and the widowed queen was obliged to marry the old vizier Aye. Suppiluliumas sent troops to the Syrian Beqā to revenge this murder, but they brought back prisoners with the plague, which quickly spread through Asia Minor, killing not only Suppiluliumas himself (1336), but also his successor, Arnuwandas II (1335). This plague, which continued to lay the Near East waste for many years, marked a halt in the course of the history of this period.[88]

Palestine had avoided involvement in these conflicts between the Hittites and Egypt, but had been torn by domestic struggles. The Amarna letters which originated in this part of the Near East[89] are full of recriminations on the part of princes, protesting complete loyalty to Egypt, but accusing each other of treachery. They ask for reinforcements to defend their territories. They complain bitterly of the negligence or the excessive demands of the Egyptian officials and of the bad behaviour of the occupation troops – of Nubian archers, for example, making a hole in the roof of the palace at Jerusalem in order to get inside.[90] Only a few of the most important facts included in this long list of grievances can be considered here.

The most noteworthy are grouped around the figure of Lab'ayu, the prince of Shechem, and his sons.[91] Lab'ayu was active towards the end of the reign of Amen-hotep III. He had entered into an alliance with Tagu, a prince of the plain to the south-west of Carmel, and with Milkilu of Gezer, Tagu's son-in-law.[92] Milkilu was apparently one of Egypt's most faithful

[87] The Akkadian text will be found in E. F. Weidner, *Politische Dokumente aus Kleinasien*, Leipzig, 1923, pp. 70–79; the Hittite text is in H. Freydank, 'Eine hethitische Fassung des Vertrags zwischen dem Hethiterkönig Suppiluliuma und Aziru von Amurru', *MIO*, 7 (1959–1960), pp. 356–381.

[88] See the annals of Suppiluliumas compiled by his son in *ANET*, p. 319; H. G. Güterbock, 'The Deeds of Suppiluliuma', *JCS*, 10 (1956), Fragment 28, pp. 94–97, Fragment 31, pp. 107–108; Mursilis II's prayer against the plague in *ANET*, pp. 394–396; see also W. Federn, 'Dahamunzu', *JCS*, 14 (1960), p. 33; J. Vergote, *Toutankhamon dans les archives hittites* (*Publications de L'Institut Historique et Archéologique Néerlandais de Stamboul*, 12), 1961.

[89] Some of these have been translated in *ANET*, pp. 483–490.

[90] *EA*, 287, 33–37; *ANET*, p. 488a.

[91] E. F. Campbell, *op. cit.* (see note 50 above).

[92] *EA*, 249 and 263, but the context is incomplete.

and obedient vassals – so much so that Amen-hotep III was able to order him to supply forty women and, what is more, forty beautiful women, for his harem at forty shekels each.[93] Then Milkilu and Lab'ayu quarrelled. It would seem that Lab'ayu was jealous of Milkilu because the latter had been made exempt from paying tribute and that Milkilu had in turn denounced Lab'ayu to the pharaoh. Lab'ayu used language in his own defence which is exceptionally free in comparison with the language normally encountered in the Amarna letters.[94] He took care, however, not to say that he had seized Shunem, Gath-rimmon and two other towns[95] and that he wanted to possess Megiddo.[96] Probably in pursuit of an order given by the pharaoh, Lab'ayu was captured and sent to Zurata at Acco. Zurata should have sent Lab'ayu by sea to Egypt, but he betrayed the pharaoh and released the prisoner for a ransom.[97]

Lab'ayu died shortly after this adventure, but his two sons were equally turbulent. One of these sons, Mut-Ba'lu, who was prince of Pella in the Jordan Valley, extended his land to include several cities in Jōlān, which is called in the text 'the country of Garu'. These cities revolted against Mut-Ba'lu, but he subdued them with the help of Ayyāb (a Job), the prince of Ashtaroth. Ayyāb was sought by Yanhamu, the Hittite ruler's representative in Canaan, who accused Mut-Ba'lu of keeping Ayyāb hidden at Pella. Mut-Ba'lu denied this and assured the representative of his and of Ayyāb's loyalty.[98]

Lab'ayu's two sons were equally busy in the south of Palestine, where they were associated with Milkilu of Gezer.[99] The letters accusing the prince of Gezer of being in league with the pharaoh's enemies come from 'Abdu-Heba, the prince of Jerusalem. Six of his letters are addressed to Akh-en-Aten during the first years of his reign.[100] They are quite pathetic. They show us this prince as the pharaoh's loyal servant, pressed on all sides by enemies who were at the same time hostile to the pharaoh. These enemies included not only Lab'ayu's sons and Milkilu, but also Tagu, Milkilu's father-in-law, and Shuwardata of Hebron. These men apparently deprived 'Abdu-Heba of Keilah in the region of Hebron, Rubutu in the hill country of Jerusalem and even Bethlehem at the gates of his own city.[101]

---

[93] A letter edited by G. Dossin and published in *RA*, 31 (1934), pp. 125–136 = *EA*, 369; *ANET*, p. 487a.

[94] *EA*, 252–254; *ANET*, p. 486.

[95] *EA*, 250; *ANET*, p. 485b.

[96] *EA*, 244; *ANET*, p. 485a.

[97] *EA*, 245; *ANET*, p. 485.

[98] *EA*, 256; *ANET*, p. 486b; see also W. F. Albright's commentary, 'Two Little Understood Letters from the Middle Jordan Valley', *BASOR*, 89 (Feb. 1943), pp. 7–15.

[99] *EA*, 287 and 289; *ANET*, pp. 488–489. The first of these letters is badly preserved; the other five have been published in translation in *ANET*, pp. 487–489.

[101] This is, of course, assuming that the Bit Ninurta of *EA*, 290 is in fact Bethlehem.

The pharaoh's representative did nothing. Even worse than simply doing nothing, he asked for the garrison than had been stationed at Jerusalem to be sent back, requesting the king to send his archers to save Jerusalem, the city where 'the king had chosen to give his name a home for ever'.[102] If he did not act at once, the whole of the pharaoh's country would fall into the hands of the Habiru, the agitators of whom we shall have to speak later in this work. This loyalty in misfortune would be very touching, were it not for the fact that we also have a letter from Shuwardata insisting that Keilah had been made over to him by the king and that 'Abdu-Heba had annexed it. Lab'ayu is dead, Shuwardata continues in this letter, but 'Abdu-Heba is a new Lab'ayu.[103] It is, of course, impossible for us to make any final decision about these contradictory statements and these mutual accusations and it is quite likely that it was equally impossible for the Egyptian court to do so. All that is quite certain is that Egypt had lost all effective control.

V. THE HABIRU/'APĪRU

The Habiru[104] first became known to us through the letters of 'Abdu-Heba, which still, more than half a century later, present us with two unsolved problems – who were the Habiru and were they related to the Hebrews?

Although the Habiru are not mentioned in any of the other Amarna letters, these do speak in similar terms of people denoted by an ideogram or a pseudo-ideogram, SA.GAZ. It was not long before these SA.GAZ were thought to be the same as the Habiru[105] and this hypothesis was confirmed by the Hittite treaties of the fourteenth and thirteenth centuries B.C. where, in the final invocations, the phrase 'the gods of the SA.GAZ' alternates with the phrase 'the gods of the Habiru'. On the other hand, the Rās Shamrah texts, which date from the same period, have shown that the 'pr of the

---

According to Z. Kallai and H. Tadmor, *Eretz-Israel*, 9 (1969), pp. 138–147 (an article in Hebrew), Bit Ninurta was Beth-horon and the kingdom of Jerusalem stretched as far as the edge of the hill country of Ephraim.

[102] *EA*, 287, 60–63; cf. the formula used in Deut. 12:11; 14:23, etc.

[103] *EA*, 280; *ANET*, p. 487a.

[104] For the Habiru/'Apīru, see J. Bottéro, *Le Problème des Habiru à la 4 Rencontre Assyriologique Internationale*, Paris 1954; M. Greenberg, *The Hab/piru*, New Haven, 1955; R. de Vaux, 'Le problème des Hapiru après quinze années', *JNES*, 27 (1968), pp. 221–228; W. Helck, 'Die Bedrohung Palästinas durch einwandernde Gruppen am Ende der 18. und am Anfang der 19. Dynastie', *VT*, 18 (1968), pp. 472–480.

[105] Compare especially 'Abdu-Heba's accusation of the sons of Lab'ayu of having handed the king's country over to the Habiru, *EA*, 287, 30–33, with Lab'ayu's reply to the pharaoh's request for an explanation, in which he states that he has no knowledge of any association between his sons and the SA.GAZ, *EA*, 254, 31–35.

alphabetic script are the same people as these SA.GAZ and this has in turn enabled us to identify the SA.GAZ-Habiru of the cuneiform texts with the 'Apīru of the Egyptian texts.

All the texts referring to the SA.GAZ – Habiru/'Apīru were published in 1954 and 1955 in two collections, the first French and the second American.[106] These contain altogether one hundred and ninety items and since then another twenty new texts have appeared.[107] These texts come from every part of the Ancient Near East and cover a long period, from the end of the third millennium to the end of the second millennium. Most of them, however, date back to the period between the seventeenth and the thirteenth centuries B.C. The authentic form of the name in question is almost certainly 'Apīru, which is the form that appears in the alphabetic Rās Shamrah texts and in the Egyptian texts. Because there was no sign for 'ayîn in syllabic cuneiform writing, the first syllable of the name was transcribed as ha. The second syllable was transcribed by a sign with two values, bi and pi. The presence of 'ayîn clearly points to the West Semitic origin of the name.

The most common view is that the name applies not to a people, nation or ethnic group with a particular geographical location, but rather to a class of individuals. There are three main reasons for believing this. In the first place, it is very difficult to explain the presence of a people unknown to history for a whole millennium in Upper and Lower Mesopotamia, Asia Minor and Syria-Palestine. Secondly, the personal names of individual 'Apīru are onomastically quite different – there are, for example, Akkadian, Hurrian, West Semitic and other names. Thirdly, the geographical origin of the owners of these names is often indicated in the texts and this varies. There is, however, considerable divergence of opinion as to what the name 'Apīru means. The etymology of the word is widely disputed.

The earliest references to the SA.GAZ in southern Mesopotamia during the Akkadian and neo-Sumerian periods are of no use to us in this context because the ideogram does not or may not have any necessary connection with the 'Apīru in these texts, in which it means 'aggressor', 'aggression' or 'to commit an act of aggression'.[108] In certain neo-Sumerian literary texts, on the other hand, SA.GAZ denotes rebellious and marauding people living in the desert.[109]

[106]J. Bottéro, Le Problème des Habiru, op. cit. (my references to the texts in this chapter follow the numbers in Bottéro's collection); M. Greenberg, The Hab/piru, op. cit.

[107] R. de Vaux, 'Le problème des Hapiru', op. cit.

[108] Bottéro, No. 1–8; F. R. Steele, 'An Additional Fragment of the Lipit-Ishtar Code Tablet from Nippur', ArOr, 18, 1–2 (1950), p. 491; A. Falkenstein, Die neusumerischen Gerichts-urkunden, Munich, 1956–1957, II, Nos. 42, 121, 125; F. R. Kraus, in BiOr, 15 (1958), pp. 77–78.

[109] Bottéro, No. 6 (cf. A. Falkenstein, in ZA, 57, 1965, p. 70, 1. 169 and note on p. 107), No. 8 and above all the text translated by A. Falkenstein in ZA, 53 (1959), p. 286, note 32.

The first example of Habiru, written phonetically, is to be found in a letter in early Assyrian which was discovered at Alishar in Cappadocia. This dates from the nineteenth century B.C. and deals with the question of free men in the service of a prince, kept in captivity – perhaps in Alishar itself – and able to be set free on payment of their ransom.[110] In Babylonia in the eighteenth century B.C., SA.GAZ are said to receive food rations and Habiru soldiers are given tunics.[111] Both must have been in the service of the state. At the same period, Habiru, but, it should be noted, never SA.GAZ, are said to have formed armed bands, sometimes large ones, and to have caused trouble in the districts to the north and the north-west of Mari.[112] These bands sometimes acted on their own initiative and at other times they took part in raids in the service of a prince. They were generally on hostile terms with the king of Mari. A little later, at Alalah, there is reference in one text to the date when the king 'made peace' or 'concluded a treaty' with the Habiru,[113] which may mean that he concluded a treaty with them engaging them as regular soldiers in his army. This hypothesis is borne out by a text of the Early Hittite Kingdom.[114] In the more recent Alalah texts, those of the fifteenth century B.C.,[115] SA.GAZ of different geographical origins are mentioned as troops stationed in certain cities.

The situation during this period was rather more complex at Nuzi, east of the Tigris. There are texts which mention Habiru in the service of the palace and receiving clothes and rations for themselves and barley for their horses.[116] Most of the texts, however, are concerned with Habiru men and women who have given up their freedom by placing themselves, either alone or together with their families, at the service of some rich person. The gods of the SA.GAZ or the Habiru are mentioned, always together with the gods of the Lulahhu, in the final invocations in treaties between the Hittite kings and their vassals in Asia Minor and Syria. These references are found in texts of the Late Hittite Kingdom, dating from the fourteenth and thirteenth centuries B.C.[118] The same association between the Habiru and the Lulahhu can be found in the exorcisms used by certain classes in society.[119]

---

[110] Bottéro, No. 5.
[111] Bottéro, No. 9–16.
[112] Bottéro, No. 18–34; J. R. Kupper, Les nomades en Mesopotamie au temps des rois de Mari, pp. 245–259; ibid., 'Sutéens et Hapiru', RA, 55 (1961), pp. 197–200.
[113] Bottéro, No. 36.
[114] Bottéro, No. 72; H. Otten, 'Zwei althethitische Belege zu den Hapiru', ZA, 52 (1957). pp. 216–223.
[115] Bottéro, No. 38–44.
[116] Bottéro, No. 67–69; E. Cassin, 'Nouveaux documents sur les Habiru', JA, 246 (1958), pp. 226–236.
[117] Bottéro, No. 49–66.
[118] Bottéro, No. 75–86.
[119] Bottéro, No. 88, 91–92.

These Lulahhu were barbarians inhabiting the hill country in the east.[120]

In the Amarna letters, the Habiru (in the letters from Jerusalem) and the SA.GAZ (in the letters from other cities) figure very often and in every part[121] as armed bands which are presented to us as hostile to the pharaoh and to the princes who claim to be loyal to the pharaoh. These SA.GAZ-Habiru are especially associated in the Amarna correspondence with Aziru of Amurru and with Lab'ayu of Shechem and his sons and we may fairly ask whether a letter from Shuwardata of Hebron does not describe Lab'ayu as the 'chief of the SA.GAZ'.[122] Certainly the description of the SA.GAZ-Habiru as the pharaoh's enemies must be interpreted in the light of the mutual accusations made by the princes, whose own enemies are the enemies of the pharaoh. Biryawaza of Damascus, for example, placed himself at the pharaoh's orders together with his men, his chariots, his SA.GAZ and his Sūtū.[123]

Clearly, then, the Habiru were simply mercenaries, offering their services to the highest bidder. They certainly formed quite an important section of the population of Syria-Palestine. Amenhotep II, for instance, brought three thousand six hundred 'Apīru prisoners from the campaign he conducted back from Syria-Palestine in the ninth year of his reign.[124] Under Seti I, who reigned round about the year 1300 B.C., the 'Apīru stirred up trouble in the region of Bethshan.[125] 'Apīru are also mentioned as being employed to carry stones and as working in quarries in Egypt during the reigns of Ramses II and IV and, under Ramses III, 'Apīru were living in a domain of the god Atum at Heliopolis.[126] They were foreigners in Egypt and probably prisoners of war.

Finally, according to the Akkadian texts from Ugarit dating back to the fourteenth and thirteenth centuries,[127] the SA.GAZ had a very bad reputation, but were nonetheless subject to the king. Although they were not settled people, at least they had a quarter in a city named after them. An edict promulgated by the Hittite king Hattusilis III states that he would not accept any fugitive from Ugarit among his Habiru, but that he would send

[120] According to the language of the texts in which they are mentioned, the Lulahhu appear as Lullū, Lullubū, Lullumū etc. See, for example, H. Klengel, 'Lullubum. Ein Beitrag zur Geschichte der altvorderasiastischen Gebirgsvölker, MIO, 11 (1966), pp. 349–371.

[121] Bottéro, No. 93–153.

[122] F. Thureau-Dangin, 'Nouvelles lettres d'Amarna', RA, 19 (1922), pp. 98–99 = EA, 367; ANET, p. 487.

[123] Bottéro, No. 132.

[124] Bottéro, No. 183; ANET, p. 247a; the other figures in this list are fantastic and it is therefore possible that this list of 'prisoners' was really a census of the occupied zones; see J. J. Jansen, JEOL, 17 (1963), p. 143.

[125] Bottéro, No. 184; ANET, p. 255a.

[126] Bottéro, No. 187–190.

[127] No. 158–162; J. Nougayrol, Le Palais Royal d'Urgarit, III, Paris, 1955, pp. 3, 105, 213–214; IV, Paris, 1956, pp. 107–108, 161–163.

any such man back to the king of Ugarit.

The information that we have concerning the Habiru-'Apīru is so varied with regard to date and place of origin that it is not possible to construct a single coherent picture of these people from it. Any attempt to qualify them as a social group can only be made on the basis of the purely negative characteristics that they have in common. They were, for example, *not* members of the local population, they can *not* be identified with one particular class in society and they did *not* all have the same occupation or the same status. Many Assyriologists regard them as foreign fugitives, but others think that they were uprooted people, exiles who were dependent on a patron, either the state or a private person.

The meaning of the words used to name these people ought to help us to know who they were, but this meaning is by no means clear. The ideogram SA.GAZ is explained in the cuneiform vocabularies by *habbatu*, but *habbatu* may have two meanings. The more common meaning is 'bandit' and the less common is 'migrant worker'. The Egyptian texts and the texts from Rās Shamrah have clearly shown that authentic form of the word Habiru was 'Apīru with a p, so that the hypothesis, based on the assumption that the word Habiru comes from *'br* 'to cross', that the Habiru were fugitives who had 'crossed' the frontier is obviously a false one. It is also not possible to trace the name back to a root *'pr*. Some scholars have in fact suggested a western Semitic root *pr* meaning 'to provide', which is the root of the Akkadian word *epēru*. ('*Ayin* was sometimes rendered in Akkadian script by h and sometimes it was simply omitted.) This would mean that the 'Apīru were those who received 'rations', the name thus revealing their state of dependence.[128] There is, however, no evidence that any such root existed in western Semitic.[129] The only root that has been proved to exist is *'pr* in the sense of 'dust', a root which corresponds to the Akkadian *eperu*. If the word 'Apīru is related to this root, then, the 'Apīru were 'dusty' people, bedouins from the sands of the desert,[130] emigrants moving along the great highways[131] or perhaps donkey-drivers in caravans, following their beasts in a cloud of dust.[132] Unfortunately, however, the 'Apīru were never associated, at least according to the texts that we have, with the caravan trade, which is otherwise quite well documented as far as the periods during which the 'Apīru appeared and the districts in which they were found.

[128] W. F. Albright, in *JAOS*, 74 (1954), p. 225; A. Goetze, in Bottéro, p. 162; M. Greenberg, *The Hab/piru*, *op. cit.*, p. 91.

[129] On the other hand, we do know that 'ration' was *hpr* in Ugaritic.

[130] R. de Langhe, *Les Textes de Ras Shamra-Ugarit et leurs rapports avec le milieu de l'Ancien Testament*, Gembloux, II, 1945, p. 465.

[131] E. Dhorme, 'Les Habirou et les Hébreux', in *Revue Historique*, 211 (1954, I), p. 261; R. Borger, *ZDPV*, 74 (1958), p. 131.

[132] W. F. Albright, *CAH*, II, XX, p. 17; *ibid.*, *Yahweh and the Gods of Canaan*, London,

A fairly recent suggestion[133] is that they were discontented people, deserters or fugitives coming from neighbouring cities, from nomadic tribes or from even greater distances and hiding in the great stretches of coppice or brushwood which still covered part of Syria and Palestine and from which they made raids. Another etymology has also been suggested, extending the basic meaning of the Akkadian word *eperu*, 'dust', to include 'earth' or 'land'. According to this hypothesis, the 'Apīru were 'men of the territory', in other words, of the wooded regions which were, from the political point of view, a 'no man's land'. This theory cannot, however, be applied to the other regions where the 'Apīru appeared and behaved differently.

One basic objection can be made to all these explanations. They all presuppose that these people were called by a nickname – 'fugitives', 'receivers of rations' or the 'dusty' people and that they did not call themselves by any such name. It is, however, very unlikely that the same nickname was given and maintained for almost a millennium in many different regions and by people speaking different languages even when this name no longer applied to their way of life or to their activities at that time. There are certain linguistic indications that this nickname was given by people who spoke western Semitic. It is just possible that, once it had been given to the these people known as Habiru-'Apīru, the name remained with them even in countries where the language was non-Semitic, that is, in Egypt and in the Hittite Empire of Asia Minor. It is, however, not probable that, even in the earliest texts, the name 'Apīru would have been written Habiru (which can also be read as Hapiru) by Akkadian scribes from Alishar and Babylonia who must have understood this word in a language related to their own and who, moreover, possessed its equivalent in their own tongue. This equivalent was *eberu*, if the name is derived from '*br* and given the meaning of 'fugitive' or *epēru* and *eperu*, if it is associated with the root '*pr* and understood to mean 'receiver of rations', 'dusty' or man from the 'brushwood' or 'no man's land'.

These difficulties are eliminated as soon as we cease to think of the 'Apīru as a class in society and regard them as a people. This was in fact how the 'Apīru were first regarded when the Amarna letters were discovered, but this opinion was later discredited because the 'Apīru were all too readily identified with the Hebrews of the Bible. It may, however, have been abandoned too lightly.[134] Some documents suggest that the word Habiru

1968, pp. 64–79.
    [133] M. B. Rowton, 'The Topological Factor in the Hapiru Problem', *Studies in Honor of B. Landsberger*, Chicago, 1965, pp. 375–387.
    [134] For what is said in the rest of this section, see R. de Vaux, in *RB*, 63 (1956), pp. 261–267, and 'Le problème des Hapiru', *op. cit.*; A. Pohl, 'Einige Gedanken zur Habiru-Frage', *WZKM*, 54 (1958), pp. 157–160.

should be applied to an ethnic group and others almost compel us to accept this interpretation. The Hittite treaties, for example, speak of the 'gods of the Habiru' and it is difficult to accept as meaningful the gods of a class of people in society or of a band of fugitives or of expatriates. What is more, these texts always name the gods of the Habiru together with the gods of the Lulahhu, who were, as we have seen, a people. Shortly after 1500 B.C., Idrimi fled from the country of Aleppo and, having stayed with the Suteans, he went to the SA.GAZ, with whom he stayed for seven years.[135] In very similar circumstances, Si-nuhe had also stayed with a clan of the Retenu. The SA.GAZ are introduced into the text with exactly the same words as the Suteans and these were nomads in the Syrian desert. They are also mentioned in the Amarna letters at the same time as the SA.GAZ-Habiru – we have, for example, seen that Biryawaza of Damascus declared his loyalty to the pharaoh with his SA.GAZ and his Suteans. Similarly, another prince asks to be delivered from the SA.GAZ and the Suteans.[136] In the Mari texts, the Suteans are never directly associated with the Habiru, but are described in similar terms and one text mentions a clan of the Suteans, the clan of Almatu, one member of which, in a Babylonian list, is a SA.GAZ.[137] The name 'Apīru appears alongside three other names of peoples, the Shasu, the people of Huru and the people Nukhashshe. This text does not identify the Habiru/'Apīru with the Shasu, as has been suggested, but both peoples have certain characteristics in common[138] and there are marked similarities between the Shasu and the 'Hebrews' of the Bible.[139] In any case, the term Shasu denotes an ethnic group, like the name Tayaru, the allies of the 'Apīru on the stele of Seti I at Beth-shean.

We must now briefly reply to the objections to this interpretation of the Habiru/'Apīru as the name of an ethnic group. The fact that these Habiru were found everywhere in the Ancient Near East cannot be accepted as a valid objection to this interpretation. The Suteans, for example, were also found spread over a very wide area, from the Middle Euphrates to Philistia and, in the first millennium, they penetrated as far as Babylonia and even crossed to the east of the Tigris. The Amorites before them and the Arameans after them were also dispersed over an equally vast territory. The variety of proper names met with in the case of the Habiru can also be explained if they adopted, at least in part, the nomenclature of the districts

[135] Bottéro, No. 37, but without the context.
[136] Bottéro, No. 152.
[137] See J.-R. Kupper, 'Sutéens et Hapiru', RA, 55 (1961); Kupper's conclusions are, however, different from ours.
[138] W. Helck, Die Bedrohung Palästinas, (see note 104).
[139] R. Giveon, 'The Shosu of Egyptian Sources and the Exodus', Fourth World Congress of Jewish Studies, Papers I, Jerusalem, 1967, pp. 193–196.*

in which they settled. The geographical names that occur whenever the
Habiru are mentioned can also be accounted for if we think of a modern
parallel – that of Bretons in Paris, Greeks in Smyrna or Chinese in San
Francisco.

Whenever explicit reference is made to the Habiru collectively, it is
always to armed groups or to mercenary soldiers. In the case of individuals
– those at Nuzi, for example – these Habiru are presented as having a special position in society. We may, of course, presuppose in such cases that an
ethnic term came to be used as a name for these Habiru. Once again, a close
parallel can also be found in more recent history. During the Middle Ages
and even later, there were many Swiss hired by almost every court in
Europe. There were Swiss regiments in France as late as 1830 and even today there are Swiss guards at the Vatican. We may go further and point to
the extended meanings of the word *suisse* in French. In the seventeenth century it was a common term in France for doorkeeper – the modern *concierge*
– and nowadays is still used for the person with a similar task in a church.
Finally, we may also ask whether these Habiru/ʿApīru were not originally
one of the ethnic groups leading a nomadic life at the fringes of the desert
regions during the first half of the second millennium and whether the
name given to this ethnic group was not transcribed differently according
to the region.

The most common view nowadays is, as we have said, that the name was
that of a class of individuals and not that of an ethnic group. The arguments
given above cannot finally eliminate that view, of course, but they do at
least oblige us to leave the question open. The second problem, that of the
possible connection between these Habiru/ʿApīru and the Hebrews of the
Bible, will be discussed when we come to consider the origins of Israel.

VI. The Egyptian Resumption of Control
During the Nineteenth Dynasty

Thanks to the efforts of General Hor-em-heb, an army officer who began
his career under Akh-en-Aten, Egypt did not lose all her possessions in
Asia during the Amarna period.[140] During the reign of Tut-ankh-Amon, he
became the strong man of the government and he is represented in the tomb
that he had made for himself at Saqqārah leading the tribute of the Asiatics
back to the pharaoh and receiving from him the reward for his victories.[141]

[140] For the Egyptian resumption of control, see especially R. O. Faulkner, 'Egypt: From
the Inception of the Nineteenth Dynasty to the Death of Ramesses III', *CAH*, II, XXIII,
1966.
[141] *ARE*, III, §§ 1–21; *ANET*, pp. 250–251.

These pictures probably exaggerate his success and his military expeditions no doubt went no further than the south of Palestine, but at least they show that Egypt was not entirely inactive. When he assumed power on the death of Aye and became pharaoh, reigning from 1334–1306, his main concern was to restore order in Egypt and the famous Edict of Hor-em-heb,[142] suppressing abuses and reforming the tribunals, shows how corrupt the administraton had become.

Hor-em-heb was succeeded by his vizier, who became the first pharaoh of the Nineteenth Dynasty under the name of Ramses I. Ramses I only reigned for two years, however, and it was left to his son and successor, Seti I (1304–1290), to make Egypt's presence effective again in Syria. A show of force was all the more urgently needed because, just as Egypt herself had begun to recover as a powerful nation on the international scene, the Hittites, escaping the terrible scourge of the plague, had regained control of Syria under Mursilis II. Between the two hostile powers, the kingdom of Amurru had remained loyal to the Hittites.

Our sources of information about the campaigns of Seti I are geographical lists, a series of reliefs and inscriptions decorating the walls of the temple of Amon at Karnak[143] and the stelae erected at various points reached by his armies. In the first year of his reign, he set off at the head of three divisions, taking the military route to the north marked by fortified walls. He defeated the Shasu bedouins in the land between the Egyptian frontier and the walls of the 'city of Canaan', which was probably Gaza, the administrative centre of the province of that name. He then crossed Palestine without encountering serious resistance and reached the Plain of Esdraelon. We know from information provided by a great stele erected by Seti and found at Beth-shean,[144] that trouble had broken out in the Jordan Valley. The Egyptian garrison at Beth-shean and a city a few miles south of Beth-shean that was loyal to Egypt, Rehob, were both threatened by a coalition of the princes of Hamath (which may be Tell el-Hammeh, a few miles south of Beth-shean) and Pella on the other side of the Jordan. Seti sent the division of Amon to deal with Hamath, that of Re to protect Beth-shean and the uprising was crushed in a day. A second stele found at Beth-shean,[145] the date of which has disappeared, probably refers to another campaign, when a detachment was sent to deal with the 'Apīru in the hill country of Yarmuta, which is possibly Kokab el-Hawa just south of

---

[142] Good translations will be found in K. Pflüger, 'The Edict of King Haremhab', *JNES*, 5 (1946), pp. 260–268; W. Helck, *Urkunden*, pp. 416–423.

[143] *ARE*, III, §§ 80–156; parts reproduced in *ANET*, pp. 254–255.

[144] *ANET*, p. 253.

[145] *ANET*, p. 255a; see W. F. Albright, 'The Smaller Beth-Shan Stele of Sethos I', *BASOR*, 125 (Feb. 1952), pp. 24–32; A. Alt, *ZDPV*, 70 (1954), pp. 62–75.

Beth-shean. Either on his journey to or on his return from his first campaign, Seti destroyed Pella and erected a stele at Tell esh-Shihab in the Hauran.[146] While the Beth-shean operation was taking place, Seti's third division, the division of Seth, had been directed against Yeno'am, which was probably to the south-west of Lake Tiberias. The capture of this town is shown in the reliefs of Karnak. On the coast, Acco and Tyre fell to the Egyptians and a stele erected by Seti has recently been discovered at Tyre.[147] The pharaoh received the submission of the princes of the Lebanon and returned in triumph to Egypt.

It is obvious that Seti followed the same plan as Thut-mose III, the pharaoh who had led the earlier conquest, and that his first intention was to make Palestine submit to his authority, but that he later became more ambitious in his aims. During a second campaign, about which we are less well informed, he occupied Simyra and the coastal region of Amurru and took Kadesh on the Orontes, where a stele bearing his name has been found.[148] He must therefore have penetrated into the territories held by the Hittites. A final campaign brought him face to face with the Hittite king's army in an encounter taking place somewhere to the north of Kadesh and resulting in a victory for Egypt. Seti was wise enough, however, not to press his advantage and it would seem that he made peace with Muwatallis, who succeeded Mursilis II.[149]

Seti's military success led Benteshina of Amurru to break his treaty of vassalage with the Hittites and to go over to Egypt's side, thus causing another war to break out between Egypt and the Hittites.[150] The two adversaries prepared for war and Muwatallis began to mobilise his troops. In Egypt, Seti was succeeded by his son Ramses II (1290–1224). The length of his reign and the care that he took to have it glorified by his scribes, artists and architects gave it a more important place in the memory of the people of the Ancient Near East than in fact it had in history. His activities in Syria took up half of his reign, which lasted for sixty-seven years, and were not particularly beneficial to Egypt. A stele engraved with his name at the mouth of the Nahr el-Kelb to the north of Beirut shows that he was in Phoenicia in the fourth year of his reign. We do not know the extent of this first campaign, but may assume that it was an answer to Muwatallis' preparations and that Ramses carried it out in order to make sure of having

---

[146] G. A. Smith, PEFQS, 1901, pp. 347–349.

[147] The text has not yet been finally published; see J. Leclant, Orientalia, 30 (1961), p. 394.

[148] M. Pézard, Qadesh. Mission archéologique à Tell Nebi Mend, Paris, 1931, pp. 19–21, Plate XXVIII.

[149] The treaty between Ramses II and Hattusilis III refers to this peace; see ARE, III, § 377; ANET, p. 200a.

[150] This is what is said in the historical introduction to the later treaty between Tudhaliyas II and Shaushgawuma of Amurru. The essential text has been translated by A. Goetze, OLZ, 32 (1929), col. 834–835. See also W. Helck, Die Beziehungen, p. 204.

a base for his troops in the war which seemed inevitable. The campaign that he carried out in the fifth year of his reign was decisive and ended with the battle of Kadesh in 1286. We are better informed about this battle than about any other in the ancient world because of the literary account of his exploits that the pharaoh had written in addition to the official report of his victory and the many pictures with which he covered the walls of temples in Egypt and Nubia.

Muwatallis raised troops in every part of his empire and brought them together at Kadesh. In the meanwhile, Ramses had come up from Egypt at the head of four divisions. Each army consisted of some 20,000 men in equal proportions of foot soldiers and chariot-borne troops. The essential aspects of the battle as it concerns us here[151] are as follows. Misled by false reports which assured him that the Hittites had retreated to Aleppo, Ramses allowed his four divisions to become spread out along both banks of the Orontes and delayed crossing the river by the ford at Shabtuna, which may be Riblah. The first division, commanded by the pharaoh himself, the division of Amon, had almost gone beyond Kadesh when the Hittite chariots, hidden to the east of the city, attacked the Egyptian division of Re which was following the first division. The Hittites put the second division to flight and turned on Ramses' troops, among whom panic was soon spread by fugitives and the Hittites pursuing them. The pharaoh and his guard were saved by the arrival of an élite corps that had been sent back to safeguard the Syrian coast and now reappeared at the critical moment. Muwatallis had kept some of his chariots in reserve and tried to save the day by throwing these into the battle, but the Egyptians broke his attack and rejoined the division of Ptah which was just coming on the scene. The tide of fortune changed in favour of the three Egyptian divisions and the Hittites were thrown back to the Orontes. In all this, Muwatallis had, strangely enough, not made use of his infantry. The fourth Egyptian division of Sutekh had, moreover, not taken any part in the action, because it was too far removed from the scene of the battle. Action was resumed on the following day, but, according to the Egyptian documents, Muwatallis soon asked for an armistice and Ramses was in all probability only too glad to accept this.

Although the pharaoh ordered the outcome of this battle to be celebrated as a great victory, it was in fact a real reversal for Egypt. Kadesh, lost again after having been taken by Seti I, had not been regained and Amurru was to submit to the Hittites. The frontier between the two states became again what it had been after the great Hittite advance at the time of Suppiluliumas a century before and Ramses II's later campaigns resulted in no

---

[151] A full bibliography will be found in *CAH*, II, XVII, 1965, p. 62 and an important recent contribution to the study of this battle has been made by R. O. Faulkner, 'The Battle of Kadesh', *MDAI*, 16 (1958), pp. 93–111.

essential change. It is in fact extremely difficult to assess the extent and the results of these campaigns because the documents are so terse and there is so little certainty with regard to places.[152] This is particularly true, for example, of the campaign in the eighth year of the pharaoh's reign, which brought the Egyptians into the territory of Amurru, and of the campaign that took place in the tenth year, of which the only evidence is an almost illegible stele at the mouth of the Nahr el-Kelb. It also applies to our interpretation of the lists of 'conquered' cities and of the Karnak and Luxor reliefs representing the capture of Asiatic cities.

At last, however, the Egyptians came to accept the need to give up all attempts to control northern Syria. At the same time, the Hittites began to look for peace on their southern frontier as the threat from Ashur in the east increased. After sixteen years of indecisive skirmishing, in the twenty-first year of Ramses II's reign, that is, in 1269, an alliance was signed by the pharaoh and Hattusilis III, who had, after a short interval, succeeded his brother Muwatallis.[153] This treaty, which confirmed the *status quo*, established peace between the two states, a peace which lasted until the end of the Hittite empire. What is more, relationships soon became quite friendly between Egypt and the Hittites, to such an extent that, in the thirty-fourth year of his reign, Ramses II married the elder daughter of Hattusilis III and another Hittite princess later joined the pharaoh's harem.

Several documents throw light on the situation in Palestine itself during the reign of Ramses II. There were still uprisings, some of them local. Some of the cities mentioned in connection with Ramses' campaign in the eighth year of his reign – Marom, Salem and the hill country of Beth-'anath – may have been in Galilee.[154] Ramses had to put down a revolt at Ashkelon at an unknown date.[155] A stele erected in praise of Ramses at Beth-shean during the eighteenth year of his reign contains no historical information at all, but merely testifies to the permanent nature of the Egyptian garrison in the city.[156] The citadel of Jaffa, or at least its gate, was built during Ramses' reign.[157] A stele at Karnaim (now known as Sheikh Sa'd) in Bashan, may be evidence of military activity in this region.[158] Several texts also speak of

[152] See, for example, M. Noth, 'Ramses II. in Syrien', ZDPV, 64 (1941), pp. 39–74; W. Helck, Die Beziehungen, op. cit., pp. 219–222.
[153] The Egyptian version will be found in ANET, pp. 199–201 and the Hittite version on pp. 201–203.
[154] ANET, p. 256b.
[155] ibid.
[156] J. Cerny, 'Stele of Ramses II from Beisan', Eretz-Israel, 5 (1958), pp. 75*–82*.
[157] Recent excavations, see RB, 64 (1957), p. 243; 67 (1960), pp. 376–377; J. Kaplan, 'Jaffa's History Revealed by a Spade', Archaeological Discoveries in the Holy Land, New York, 1967, pp. 113–118.
[158] Called in the country the 'stone of Job'; A. Erman, 'Der Hiobstein', ZDPV, 15 (1892), pp. 205–211; see also R. Giveon, 'Two Egyptian Documents Concerning Bashan from the

operations against the bedouins of Seir, a name which is also included in a list of those conquered by Ramses[159] together with three other Shasu tribes which have probably to be situated in the Negeb or the 'Arabah. In addition, Ramses also conducted an important campaign in Moab and took Dibon.[160] It would appear that the Hittites remained loyal to the treaty of 1269 and did not try to stir up trouble in the lands possessed by Egypt. The two provinces of Damascus and Canaan also continued with their administration.

VII. THE SYRIAN INFLUENCE IN EGYPT

Egypt's relationships with her provinces in Asia had important consequences in the religious sphere.[161] We have already seen that several temples were built in Palestine and dedicated to Egyptian gods.[162] These were primarily intended for Egyptians living in Palestine, but that they were also used by native people is borne out by the Palestinian name of a female singer in the temple of Ptah at Ashkelon.[163] The Egyptians also consecrated temples to Semitic deities. The garrison at Beth-shean had temples dedicated to Mikal, the Baal of Beth-shean, and to Astarte, his female partner. Stelae were dedicated there by two Egyptian men and one Egyptian woman to Mikal of Beth-shean, to 'Anat, the 'Lady of the Heavens and Mistress of all the Gods', and to Astarte.[164] The stele at Sheikh Sa'd shows Ramses II making an offering to a Semitic deity.[165] All this clearly indicates that the Egyptians recognised the gods of the countries that they had conquered and that they even incorporated them into their own pantheon.

The Canaanite deities were introduced into Egypt by the Egyptians

---

Time of Ramses II', *RSO*, 40 (1965), pp. 197–200.

[159] See H. W. Fairman, *JEA*, 25 (1939), p. 141 and Plate XIV, 4; W. Helck, *Die Beziehungen, op. cit.*, p. 223 and note 50. This unpublished list of conquered people from west Amara is, however, a copy of a list of Amenhotep III found at Soleb in the Sudan and may have, as its source, Thut-mose III; see R. Giveon, 'Toponymes ouest-asiatiques à Soleb', *VT*, 14 (1964), pp. 239–255.

[160] Certain new texts from Luxor, K. A. Kitchen, 'Some New Light on the Asiatic Wars of Ramesses II', *JEA*, 50 (1964), pp. 47–70.

[161] For the Syrian influence on Egypt, see P. Montet, *Les reliques de l'art syrien dans l'Egypte du Moyen Empire*, Paris, 1937; W. Helck, *Die Beziehungen, op. cit.*, pp. 359–465, 482–514; W. Helck, 'Zum Auftreten fremder Götter in Ägypten', *OrAnt*, 5 (1966), pp. 1–14; R. Stadelmann, *Syrisch-palästinensische Gottheiten in Ägypten*, Leiden, 1967.

[162] See above, p. 98.

[163] W. F. Albright, *Archaeology and the Religion of Israel*,[2] Baltimore, 1946, p. 127.

[164] A. Rowe, *The Topography and History of Beth-Shan*, Philadelphia, 1930, Plate 33, 48, 50; *ANEP*, No. 487.

[165] See above, note 158.

themselves or else by prisoners of war or merchants.[166] These borrowings
began, at the instigation of the pharaohs or of those who formed their immediate circle, at the time of the conquest of Syria. Even when
Amenhotep II was no more than heir to the throne of Egypt, it was said
that Resheph and Astarte 'rejoiced' because of him. Later, he was called the
'beloved of Resheph' and as 'brave as Resheph'. Thut-mose IV was called a
'brave horseman like Astarte' who was often represented, from the reign of
Thut-mose onwards, as a goddess of war on horseback.[167] Tut-ankh-Amon
was called the 'beloved of Horon,' as Amenhotep II had been before him
and Ramses II was after him. Horon was a Canaanite god with more examples in Egypt than in his country of origin. This movement increased in
the Nineteenth Dynasty, when 'Anat and Baal appeared in the Egyptian
court. Seti I, for example, called one of his teams of horses ' 'Anat is glad'
and he himself was known as 'the formidable one of Baal'. Ramses II in particular was much attracted to the gods of Canaan and called one of his
daughters 'Bint 'Anat', the 'daughter of 'Anat', his sword ' 'Anat is victorious' and one of his hounds ' 'Anat in her strength'. He had himself
depicted seated at the right hand side of 'Anat while the goddess was saying
'I am your mother'. He also claimed to have 'sucked the milk' of the
goddess, who had a temple at Pi-Ramses. During the battle of Kadesh,
Ramses was 'like Baal in person'. During the reign of Ramses III, the
pharaoh was compared even more frequently with the Canaanite gods and
goddesses. He was 'like Baal in the hour of his strength', 'powerful as Baal
over foreign countries'; his war-cry was 'like that of Baal in heaven' and his
name was 'like that of Baal'. Ramses III was also compared with 'Anat and
Astarte, who were called his 'shields' and each of his soldiers was likened to
a Resheph.

Apart from the pharaoh's court, which was the most important centre of
lasting devotion to the foreign deities, the cult of these gods was also prominent at Memphis, where Syrian traders had established the worship of Baal
Zaphon, the patron of navigators, and Astarte. It is interesting to note that
Astarte was venerated as the goddess of war at the court of the pharaoh, but
as the goddess of love at Memphis. During the reign of Amenhotep
IV-Akh-en-Aten, there was a prophet of Baal and Astarte with a semitic
name at Memphis. Later on, the prophetic function in the temple of Baal
was handed down from one generation to another within the same family
at Memphis and, even later, there were, according to Herodotus, sanctuaries of the sea-god Proteus and of Aphrodite in the Tyrian quarter of

---

[166] For what follows, see *ANET*, pp. 249–250; J. Černy, *Ancient Egyptian Religion*, London,
1952, pp. 124–129; S. Morenz, *Ägyptische Religion*, Stuttgart, 1960, pp. 248–255; W. Helck,
'Zum Auftreten', *op. cit.*; R. Stadelmann, *Syrisch-palästinensische Gottheiten, op. cit.*
[167] J. Leclant, 'Astarté à cheval d'après les représentations égyptiennes', *Syria*, 37 (1960),
pp. 1–67.

Memphis. Baalat, Kadesh and Baal Zaphon are mentioned among the deities worshipped at Memphis in a papyrus of the period of Ramses II. The goddess Kadesh – another aspect of Astarte – had not been adopted by the pharaohs, but was popular among the ordinary people. She was represented naked, standing upright on a lion and holding snakes or lotus blossoms or both.[168] After the Late Kingdom, these Canaanite deities were no longer worshipped officially, but they continued to be venerated in Phoenician settlements in Egypt or by the ordinary people, who added their foreign sounding names to magic formulae.

Many legends accompanied the cult of these Canaanite gods. Some of the texts of the Late Kingdom betray the clear influence of these Canaanite myths. For example, 'Anat and Astarte intervene as the daughters of Re in the trial between Horus and Seth. In another story, the blood flowing from one of Re's wounds is gathered by 'Anat and used against evil demons. In another myth, 'Anat beseeches Re to cure Seth, who has become poisoned after having violated her.[169] The longest document, one which has unfortunately been very badly preserved, is the myth of Yam, the sea-god, who marries Astarte.[170] All these texts were clearly inspired by Canaanite poems similar to those found at Rās Shamrah.

To complete this picture of relationships between Egypt and Syria-Palestine, we must add the great number of Syrian objects imported at this time into the Nile valley.[171] It should also be remembered that pottery and other articles from Crete and Cyprus and later from Mycenaean Greece came to Egypt via Syria.[172] The conquest of Syria-Palestine thus opened Egypt to various foreign influences and played a large part in giving the civilisation of the Late Kingdom its cosmopolitan flavour.

---

[168] *ANEP*, Nos. 470–474.

[169] The texts will be found in papyrus: the Chester Beatty Papyrus, I, III, 4–5, edited by A. Gardiner, London, 1932; the Leiden Magical Papyrus, edited by A. Massart (*The Leiden Magical Papyrus*, Leiden, 1954), cf. E. Drioton, *BiOr*, 12 (1955), p. 164; Chester Beatty Papyrus, VII, 4–6, edited by A. Gardiner, *Hieratic Papyri in the British Museum, Third Series*, London, 1935, I, pp. 61–63.

[170] G. Lefebvre, *Romans et contes égyptiens*, Paris, 1949, pp. 106–113; *ANET*, pp. 17–18; O. Kaiser, 'Die mythische Bedeutung des Meeres in Ägypten, Ugarit und Israel', *BZAW*, 78, 1959, pp. 78–91.

[171] P. Montet, *Les reliques de l'art syrien, op. cit.* *

[172] F. H. Stubbings, *Mycenaean Pottery*, see note 173 below, pp. 56–58, 90–101; J. Vercoutter, *L'Egypte et le monde égéen préhellénique*, Cairo, 1956; R. S. Merrillees, *The Cypriot Bronze Age Pottery Found in Egypt*, Lund. 1968.

VIII. Palestinian Archaeology of the Late Bronze Age

This cosmopolitanism was in fact a feature of this whole period and is very evident in the Palestinian archaeology with which we are concerned in the final section of this chapter.[173] A suitable point at which to begin our study of the Late Bronze Age is the expulsion of the Hyksos from Egypt round about 1550 B.C., although this event did not have any immediate effect on Palestine. The Middle Bronze traditions in architecture and handicrafts continued uninterrupted in Palestine, but there was a slow but steady decline in technical skill and artistic value. What was new in the Late Bronze Age was the increasing number of contributions from abroad and above all from Cyprus. Until this time, there had been very little Cypriot pottery in Palestine, but now more and more began to arrive.

In addition to this pottery imported from Cyprus, there was also new Late Bronze pottery originating in Palestine itself, red and black in colour and decorated with geometrical patterns which often serve as a framework for figures of birds and fishes and, less frequently, of bulls or goats. This native pottery has been found in considerable quantities at Megiddo and at Tell el-'Ajjūl and to a lesser extent on the Plain of Esdraelon, as far south as Beth-shean and in the north at Hazor. Many vases of this kind have also been discovered in northern Syria, especially at Rās Shamrah, and in Cyprus, several reached Egypt and some have even been found at Aniba in the Sudan. It has been suggested that a Palestinian master potter was at work here,[174] but this explanation cannot be accepted because of the great number of pieces of pottery that have been preserved and their great variety. We should, rather, speak of a Palestinian 'school' of pottery at this time.

The most recent work on this subject [175] favours the view that the Hurrians were responsible for this pottery, but it appeared in Palestine before the Hurrians settled there. The most probable explanation is that this ware was a Palestinian creation combining local traditions with Cypriot elements (the shape of some of the vases and parts of the geometrical decoration are signs of this) and elements from northern Syria and Upper Mesopotamia (the painting and the figures of animals). Its widespread occurrence can also be explained by sea trading, which took it to Egypt on

[173] For Palestinian archaeology of the Late Bronze Age, see F. H. Stubbings, *Mycenaean Pottery from the Levant*, Cambridge, 1951; V. Hankey, 'Mycenaean Pottery in the Middle East', *BSA*, 62 (1967), pp. 107–148; C. Epstein, *Palestinian Bichrome Ware*, Leiden, 1966; H. J. Franken, 'Palestine in the Time of the Nineteenth Dynasty: (b) Archaeological Evidence', *CAH*, II, XXVI (b), 1968; E. D. Oren, 'Cypriot Imports in the Palestinian Late Bronze I Context', *Opuscula Atheniensia*, 9 (1969), pp. 127–150.

[174] W. A. Heurtley, 'A Palestinian Vase Painter in the Sixteenth Century B.C.', *QDAP*, 8 (1939), pp. 21–37.

[175] C. Epstein, *Palestinian Bichrome Ware, op. cit.*

the one hand and to Syria and Cyprus on the other.

This first phase of the Late Bronze Age is not represented in two of the great inland sites, Tell Beit Mirsim and Jericho. Both these cities were destroyed in the middle of the sixteenth century and were not occupied again until about 1400 B.C. There is, moreover, no justification for linking the destruction of Tell Beit Mirsim and Jericho with the expulsion of the Hyksos, since, as we have seen, the Egyptian advance had by that time gone no further than the south of Palestine.

The excavation of a temple rebuilt three times in the moat surrounding the ancient city of Lachish, the modern Tell ed-Duweir, has thrown a great deal of light on the following periods of the Late Bronze Age. The first temple was built at the beginning of the fifteenth century, the second replaced it at the end of the same century and remained until the last third of the fourteenth century and the third temple was destroyed during the second half of the thirteenth century. Late Bronze bichrome pottery has been found in Temple I together with plenty of Cypriot pottery and one of the first pieces of ceramic ware imported from Greece, a chalice belonging to Mycenaean II. Cypriot vases have also been found in considerable quantities in Temples II and III as well as several fragments of Mycenaean III A and the beginning of B. It was round about 1400 B.C. that Mycenaean ware began to arrive in Palestine in some quantity. This influx from Greece was the result of increasing Mycenaean trade with the Levant following the collapse of the Cretan hegemony at about the same time.

These imported vases[176] have, of course, been found in greater quantities in sites near to the coast, such as Tell el-'Ajjūl, the southern site of Tell el-Far'ah, Ashkelon and Gezer. From this Mycenaean ware, it has been possible to date with reasonable certainty the levels at which it has been found and the tombs excavated to the fourteenth and thirteenth centuries B.C. The richest collection of Mycenaean III, combined with imports from Cyprus, comes from a warehouse used by traders set up round about 1400 B.C. at Tell Abu Hawām in the bay of Haifa,[177] which seems to have been the main port at which this Mycenaean ware arrived in Palestine. The boats bringing it certainly put in at Cyprus, although it is still not known whether the bases were manufactured for the most part in Cyprus or whether they came chiefly from the mainland of Greece.[178]

[176] See F. A. Stubbings, *Mycenaean Pottery, op. cit.*, pp. 59–87; V. Hankey, 'Mycenaean Pottery', *op. cit.*

[177] R. W. Hamilton, 'Excavations at Tell Abu Hawām', *QDAP*, 4 (1935), pp. 1–69; E. Anati, 'Excavations at the Cemetery of Tell Abu Hawam', *'Atiqot*, 2 (1959), pp. 89–102; *ibid., IEJ*, 13 (1963), pp. 142–143.

[178] The first of these views has been proposed by F. H. Stubbings in *Mycenaean Pottery, op. cit.* and in 'The Expansion of the Mycenaean Civilization', *CAH*, II, XXII(a), 1964, p. 19; the second by H. W. Catling, 'Cyprus in the Late Bronze Age', *CAH*, II, XXII (b), 1966, pp. 56–58.

In recent years, more and more pieces of this Mycenaean ware have been discovered over a much wider area. Some was excavated, for instance, in 1969 from a tomb at Tell Dan in the extreme north of Palestine. A find of forty vases was made in Late Bronze tombs at Pella in the Jordan Valley. One vase was found recently in a tomb at Tell es-Sa'idiyeh and five were discovered in a room next to the sanctuary of Deir 'Alla. Further east, vases and fragments have been found in the little sanctuary of Amman, which was founded a little before 1400 B.C.[179]

The cosmopolitan character of this period in Palestine is borne out not only by the ceramic ware excavated, but also by the variety of languages and scripts used at the time. The Egyptian conquerors or residents employed hieroglyphic signs or hieratic scripts. The language used in official correspondence between the princes of Palestine and the pharaohs or their representatives was Akkadian, written in syllabic cuneiform (the Amarna letters). The same language and script were also employed in certain private correspondence (the two Shechem tablets and some of the Taanach tablets). The Canaanite language may have been written in alphabetic cuneiform of the Ugaritic type[180] or in a linear alphabet which preceded the 'Phoenician' alphabet.[181] Despite the discovery of certain Hurrian elements in Palestine, the Hurrian language does not seem to have been widespread in the country. The Deir 'Alla tablets, which date from about 1200 B.C. and which have not yet been deciphered, may be connected with the Aegean and the Sea Peoples.[182]

Palestine was not made richer by these foreign contributions and this ethnic diversity – on the contrary, the country became progressively poorer throughout the Late Bronze Age. Moreover, it is precisely in those sites – Tell el-'Ajjūl, Tell el-Fār'ah (the southern site), Tell ed-Duweir, Megiddo and Beth-shean – which have provided archaeologists with precious objects and works of art where there is also other evidence pointing to the presence

---

[179] The material from Tell Dan has not yet been published*; the material from the other excavations has been discussed by V. Hankey, 'Mycenaean Pottery', *op. cit.*, Nos. 31, 34, 37, 41; for the temple at Amman, see J. B. Hennessy, 'Excavations of a Bronze Age Temple at Amman', *PEQ*, 1966, pp. 155–162.

[180] Short texts will be found in the following: the Beth-Shemesh tablet, W. F. Albright, 'The Beth-Shemesh Tablet in Alphabetic Cuneiform', *BASOR*, 173 (Feb. 1964), pp. 51–53; the Mount Tabor tablet, S. Yeivin, 'A New Ugaritic Inscription from Palestine', *Kedem*, 2 (1945), pp. 31–41; the Taanach tablet, D. R. Hiller, 'An Alphabetic Cuneiform Tablet from Taanach', *BASOR*, 173 (Feb. 1964), pp. 45–50; M. Weippert, *ZDPV*, 82 (1966), pp. 311–320; 83, (1967), pp. 82–83; F. M. Cross, *BASOR*, 190 (April 1968), pp. 41–46.

of the Egyptians. In certain districts and at certain times, effective foreign control made for a measure of stability, but the people paid a heavy price for this in high taxes. What is more, Palestine was never entirely free from local disturbances. The Amarna tablets are proof of the existence, at one period at least, of such internal troubles.

---

[181] Especially the ewer and the bowl from Lachish, thirteenth century, and the ostracon from Beth-Shemesh; see F. M. Cross, 'The Evolution of the Proto-Canaanite Alphabet', *BASOR*, 134 (April 1954), pp. 15–24; D. Diringer in O. Tufnell, *Lachish IV. The Bronze Age*, London, 1958, pp. 128–130; F. M. Cross, 'The Origin and Early Evolution of the Alphabet', *Eretz-Israel*, 8 (1967), pp. 8*–24*.

[182] H. J. Franken, 'Clay Tablets from Deir 'Alla', *VT*, 14 (1964), pp. 377–379. The 'Philistine' hypothesis has been suggested by G. E. Wright in *BibArch.*, 29 (1966), p. 73 and W. F. Albright, *CAH*, II, XX, p. 27. M. Weippert, 'Archäologischer Jahrbericht', *ZDPV*, 82 (1966), pp. 299–310, has not come to any decision. G. Sauer, 'Die Tafeln von Deir 'Alla', *ZAW*, 81 (1969), pp. 145–155, has suggested that these tablets were the work of Proto-Arab nomads visiting the sanctuary. Attempts have been made to decipher the tablets by A. van den Branden, 'Essai de déchiffrement des inscriptions de Deir 'Alla', *VT*, 15 (1965), pp. 129–152, cf. pp. 532–535; H. Cazelles, 'Deir Alla et ses tablettes', *Semitica*, 15 (1965), pp. 5–21.

Chapter Five

CANAAN AND THE CANAANITE CIVILISATION

WE must now consider the period when the name 'Canaan' came to be applied to one of the geographical regions under Egyptian control. It was in this 'Canaan' that the Israelites were to settle, either supplanting the original 'Canaanites' or else intermingling with them. Their religion was to be confronted with the 'gods of Canaan' and with the worship of those gods. First of all, however, we must discuss what is meant by the name 'Canaan' itself and by the Canaanite civilisation.[1]

I. THE NAME 'CANAAN'[2]

The first evidence of the name 'Canaan' in Akkadian texts is at the beginning of the fifteenth century B.C. in the Idrimi inscription, which speaks of a flight to the 'land of Kin'ani'. The name is found in the same form three times in the Alalah tablets, which are of a slightly later date. A century later, the 'land of Kinahni' or 'Kinahhi' is mentioned in eleven of the Amarna letters, the same form (Kinahhi) also occurring in a letter written in Akkadian by Ramses II to Hattusilis III.[3] The form Kinahi is found once in the Amarna letters and once at Rās Shamrah.[4] In documents written in

---

[1] See two recent works by the same author: J. Gray, *The Canaanites*, London, 1964; J. Gray, *The Legacy of Canaan. The Ras Shamra Texts and their relevance to the Old Testament* (*SVT* 5)[2], 1965.

[2] For the name 'Canaan' and its geographical application, see, for example, B. Maisler (Mazar), 'Canaan and the Canaanites', *BASOR*, 102 (April 1946), pp. 7–12; S. Moscati, *I Predecessori d'Israele. Studi sulle più antiche genti semitiche in Siria e Palestina*, Rome, 1956; S. Moscati, 'Sulla storia del nome Canaan', *Studia Biblica et Orientalia*, III, Rome, 1959, pp. 266–269; R. de Vaux, 'Le pays de Canaan', *JAOS*, 88 (1968), pp. 23–29 = *Essays in Memory of E. A. Speiser*, New Haven, 1968, also pp. 23–29.

[3] E. Edel, 'KBo I 15 19, ein Brief Ramses' II mit einer Schilderung der Kadešschlacht', *ZA*, 49 (1950), pp. 195–212, see also p. 209, 1. 29.

[4] *EA*, 36, 15; *Ugaritica* V, No. 16, 9.

Egyptian, on the other hand, the form *Kn'n* appears with the article, *p.kn'n*, 'the Canaan', although it appears once without the article. The earliest appearance of this name in Egyptian texts is during the reign of Amenhotep II and the latest is during the Twenty-second Dynasty. The word is used for the land of Canaan and the adjective derived from it is more rare and describes the inhabitants of the country. In a Rās Shamrah list written in alphabetic cuneiform, one individual is called *kn'ny*, 'Canaanite'. A comparison of these different transcriptions shows that the word Canaan was certainly pronounced with an *'ain*, like the Hebrew Kena'an, and that it was a Semitic term.[5]

Various etymologies have been suggested. 1) According to a very early explanation, inspired by the Bible, Canaan is the 'Lowland', in contrast to the hill country inhabited by the Amorites (see Num. 13:29). The root *kn'*, however, means 'to bend', not 'to be low'. 2) In the Akkadian texts from Nuzi, the word *kinahhu* is used with the meaning 'red purple'. This discovery led to the interpretation of Canaan as the 'country of purple dye'. This dye was one of the main products of Phoenicia. What is more, the name 'Phoenicia' is itself derived from the Greek φοῖνιξ 'purple'. It was used in this sense as a translation of 'Canaan'. *Kinahhu* in the sense of 'purple' is only found, however, at Nuzi. Other words were used in the whole of the west and therefore also in Canaan.[6] 3) Because the word 'Canaanite' is used several times in the Bible with the meaning of 'merchant', it has been suggested that Canaan originally meant the 'land of merchants' or 'traders', but there is no known Semitic root to which this meaning can be ascribed. 4) The most recent hypothesis goes back to the etymological argument – Canaan being the country where the sun 'bends' or 'inclines', in other words, the country in the west.[7] This name could, however, only have been given to the country by foreigners, in the same way that the Amorites were called MAR.TU or the 'people of the West' by the inhabitants of Mesopotamia.

On the other hand, it is hardly necessary and might even be impossible to find an etymological explanation of the word 'Canaan' if it is simply a geographical term. If the Hurrians of Nuzi called the purple dye *kinahhu*, it was because this dye was imported from Kinahhi, Canaan – in the same way as we call a fabric originally manufactured at Mosul 'muslin'. Again, if the merchants were known in the Bible as 'Canaanites', it is because the Canaanites or Phoenicians had acquired a kind of monopoly in the import trade in Israel.

[5] See what has been said with regard to Habiru/'Apīru, above pp. 106, 109.

[6] M. Dietrich and O. Lorenz, 'Der Vertrag zwischen Šuppiluliuma und Niqmandu', *WO*, 3 (1966), pp. 205–245; see also pp. 227–232.

[7] M. Astour, 'The Origin of the Terms "Canaan", "Phoenician" and "Purple" ', *JNES*, 24 (1965), pp. 346–350.

II. THE LAND OF CANAAN ACCORDING TO NON-BIBLICAL TEXTS

It is not easy to determine what is meant in the cuneiform and Egyptian texts by the 'land of Canaan'. Very often the country is mentioned simply in passing and without any geographical reference. The extent of the country might also have changed in different periods and according to circumstances. The most suitable approach to this question is to consider only the useful texts in chronological order.

According to the inscription on the statue of Idrimi, the first stopping-place of a fugitive on the way to the land of Canaan is Ammia.[8] This city, which is mentioned several times in the Amarna letters, has been located on the coast or near to the coast, about twelve miles north of Byblos. The earliest Egyptian reference, half a century later, mentions, among the prisoners taken by Amenhotep II, 640 'Canaanites' as well as 550 *maryannu* and 232 'sons of princes'.[9] Although some scholars think differently, many believe that the term may, in this case, denote inhabitants of the land of Canaan. If this is so, then the country thus designated may be very great indeed, since Amenhotep reached Kadesh on the Orontes and the land of Niyi in his campaign. On the other hand, it may simply mean that these prisoners came from only one of the districts subjugated by the pharaoh, a land of Canaan, the precise position of which is not indicated in the text.

The fourteenth century Amarna tablets include one letter from the king of Alashia in Cyprus, who refers to the 'province of Canaan'.[10] Several other letters enable us to situate certain cities in Canaan and this evidence is corroborated by the Idrimi inscription. These cities include Hinnatuna, the Hannathon of the Bible, and Akshapu, the Achshaph of the Bible, in the region of Acco, Hazor in Galilee, Sidon, Tyre and Byblos on the Phoenician coast.[11] Although there are opinions to the contrary, it is generally accepted that no other letter includes as quite certainly in Canaan the whole or part of Amurru or any more remote region.[12] Rās Shamrah (Ugarit) certainly did not form part of Canaan, at least during the reign of Ramses II – a dispute between the people of Ugarit and the 'people of the land of Canaan' was settled in the presence of a special representative whom the pharaoh sent to the Hittites.[13]

[8] S. Smith, *The Statue of Idrimi*, London, 1949, pp. 18–23, 72–73.

[9] E. Edel 'Die Stelen Amenophis' II. aus Karnak und Memphis', *ZDPV*, 69 (1953), pp. 97–126, 132, 167–173. The name appears for the first time used in an undeniably geographical sense of an escutcheon of Soleb in the reign of Amenhotep III.

[10] *EA*, 36, 15: *pehati ša kinahi*.

[11] *EA*, 8, 131, 137, 148; *RA*, 19 (1922), p. 100.

[12] For *EA*, 109 and 162, see S. Moscati, *I Predecessori, op. cit.*, pp. 47 and 50; for *EA*, 151, see A. F. Rainey, *IEJ*, 14 (1964), p. 101.

[13] *Ugaritica* V, No. 36, see J. Nougayrol, *Iraq*, 25 (1963), p. 123; A. F. Rainey, 'A Canaanite

Amurru stretched to the north of Canaan, which was bounded on the east and north-east by the land of Upe, which is the kingdom of Damascus and probably included the Egyptian possessions in northern Transjordania. A prefect of the province of Upe is mentioned in the correspondence of Ramses II, alongside a prefect of the province of Canaan.[14] Central and southern Transjordania were not ruled in any way permanently by Egypt – Ramses II's interventions in Moab and perhaps even in Edom[15] were of short duration. The Jordan Valley formed the eastern frontier of the province of Canaan, which clearly included Palestine as far as Gaza, where the pharaoh's representative resided.

The texts written in Egyptian are not very helpful. They contain no reference at all to Canaan during the Amarna period. Towards the end of the thirteenth century B.C., a text describing the 'limits' of Canaan lists several stopping places between the Egyptian frontier and Raphia and Gaza,[16] so that the limits mentioned must have been the southernmost extremity of Canaan. Another text of the same period refers to Canaanite slaves of Huru[17] and a master scribe had, among his titles, the 'one sent by the pharaoh to princes of the foreign countries of Huru from Sile (on the Egyptian frontier) to Upe'.[18] A possible interpretation of these texts is that the provinces of Canaan and of Upe were merged together after the reign of Ramses II and that the Egyptian possessions in Asia came to be known either as Huru or as Canaan.[19] This is possibly the case in the last reference in an Egyptian text to Canaan, which is of a later date than the Philistine settlement – a statuette was inscribed in the name of a 'royal representative in Canaan and in Philistia'.[20]

III. THE LAND OF CANAAN IN THE BIBLE

The greatest number of references to the land of Canaan are found in the Bible and this applies even to the patriarchal period. Unlike the non-

---

at Ugarit', *IEJ*, 13 (1963), pp. 43–45; *ibid.* 'Ugarit and the Canaanites Again', *IEJ*, 14 (1964), p. 101: *ibid.* 'The Kingdom of Ugarit', *BibArch*, 28 (1965), pp. 105–106.

[14] E. Edel, 'Weitere Briefe aus der Heiratskorrespondenz Ramses' II.', *Geschichte und Altes Testament (Festschrift A. Alt)*, Tübingen, 1953, pp. 29–63, 44–48.

[15] See above, p. 116.

[16] Papyrus Anastasi I, 27, in *ANET*, p. 478b.

[17] Papyrus Anastasi III, A, 5–6 = IV, 16, 4, in R. A. Caminos, *Late Egyptian Miscellanies*, London, 1954, p. 117.

[18] Papyrus Anastasi III, 1, 9–10, in R. A. Caminos, *op. cit.*, p. 69.

[19] See, perhaps, the 'stele of Israel', *ANET*, pp. 376–378; in this text, the names of Palestinian cities are enclosed by those of Canaan and Huru.

[20] G. Steindorff, 'The Statuette of an Egyptian Commissioner in Syria', *JEA*, 25 (1939), pp. 30–33; according to Steindorff, this inscription belongs to the Twenty-second Dynasty.

biblical references, however, none of the biblical texts which mention 'Canaan' dates from the time at which the Israelites settled there. What is more, the texts which deal most explicitly with the geography of Canaan were also edited at a much later date. Finally, the use of the name varied and was influenced by historical circumstances.

One datum, however, remained unchanged – the land of Canaan never extended to the east of the Jordan. The entry of the Israelites into Canaan is characterised by the crossing of the Jordan (Num 33:51; 34:2; 35:10; cf. Deut 32:49; Jos 5:12). The territories of Reuben and Gad were bounded on the west by the Jordan and were outside the land of Canaan (Jos 11:10–11, 25, 32). Only one text – Gen 50:10–11 – is an exception to this general rule in that it mentions 'Canaanites' east of the Jordan. This text can, however, be explained as an attempt to include a tradition which deviated from the norm, that of a tomb of Jacob situated in Transjordania.

As we have already seen, the Jordan was also the frontier of the Egyptian province of Canaan and it is not unreasonable to assume that, when the Israelites settled in the country, they adapted their own terminology to make it agree with this administrative district. In fact, in the two most detailed biblical texts, Canaan has the same frontiers as those which existed during the period of Egyptian control at the end of the thirteenth century B.C. The boundaries of the land of Canaan, the 'inheritance' of Israel, are indicated in the first text, Num 34:2–12, and the frontiers of the land that was to be shared between the tribes of the Israel of the future are delineated in the second of these texts, Ezek 47:15–20; 48:1. In both texts, the southern boundary stretches from the Dead Sea to the Brook of Egypt, the wādi el–'Arīsh. As in the texts mentioned above, the western frontier is formed in these two texts by the Mediterranean and the eastern frontier by the Jordan. The northern boundary according to these two texts has been disputed. Certain exegetes have preferred to stick more closely to the territory in fact occupied by Israel and have therefore suggested a line extending from the mouth of the Nahr el-Qāsimīyeh to the sources of the Jordan and to Mount Hermon.[21] Other scholars, on the other hand, have favoured a frontier much farther north and they are almost certainly right.[22] The points along this frontier which are common to both texts are the Sea, the Pass of Hamath, Zedad and Hazer-enan. These points follow a perfectly normal line if the Pass of Hamath, Lebo'-Hamth, is identified with Lebweh

---

[21] One of the first scholars to support this theory was J. P. van Kasteren, in 'La frontière septentrionale de la Terre Promise', RB, 4 (1895), pp. 23–36, and one of the most recent M.Noth, in Das vierte Buch Mose. Numeri (ATD), 1966, pp. 215–216.

[22] M. Maisler (Mazar), 'Lebo Hamath and the Northern Boundary of Canaan', BJPES, 12 (1945–1946), pp. 91–102; J. Simons, The Geographical and Topographical Texts of the Old Testament, Leiden, 1959, pp. 98–103; see also map IX 4b in the Atlas of Israel, Jerusalem, 1956–1964.

on the Upper Orontes, Zedad with Sadad to the north of Mount Hermon
and Hazer-enan with the well of Qaryatein halfway between Damascus
and Palmyra. The first point mentioned in Numbers after the Mediterranean Sea is Mount Hor. In Ezekiel, it is Hethlon. Mount Hor in this context must therefore be the northernmost mountain of the Lebanese range,
Jebel Akkar. Similarly, Hethlon must be Heitelā, which is situated to the
north-west of Tripoli at the foot of Jebel Akkar and just south of the
Eleuthera River. This river forms a natural frontier. Nowadays, it separates
the Lebanon from Syria. At the period we are now considering, it formed –
if what we have said concerning the position of Simyra is correct – the
frontier between Canaan and the land of Amurru. In both texts,
Hazer-enan was the last point on this northern boundary. From this eastern
extremity, the frontier curved down to Lake Tiberias according to
Numbers and to the Jordan according to Ezekiel. Implicitly in Numbers,
but explicitly in Ezekiel, the kingdom of Damascus is included in this
territory – the northern boundary passes between territory of Damascus
and that of Hamath (see Ezek 47:17; 48:1).

In their details and in their mode of expression, these two passages are so
different that they are without any doubt independent accounts. On the
other hand, however, they are, in their essential data, so closely in accordance with each other and with the historical situation prevailing during
the period that they must go back to a common source or tradition. Ezekiel
47:16–18 refers to the territories of Hamath, Damascus, Gilead and Hauran
– this is the only mention of Hauran in the Bible – but these are all names
of Assyrian provinces set up between 733 and 720 B.C. We may therefore
conclude that the tradition provided by Ezekiel is later than this. Since these
four names do not, however, occur in the account given in Numbers, we
may assume that the tradition or source common to both accounts is prior
to the end of the eighth century B.C. On the other hand, this common
source does not, as has been suggested, represent the situation during the
reigns of David and Solomon, because Philistia and Phoenicia are included
within it, but not Transjordan south of Lake Tiberias. It would therefore
seem that, even though they were edited at a much later date, the accounts
provided by Num 34:2–12 and Ezek 47:15–20 preserve the memory of
what Canaan meant to the Israelites when they settled in the land – it was
the Canaan of the Egyptians after the union of the province of Upe and the
province of Canaan.[23]

The same memory of the Egyptian province is also preserved in other
texts. Jos 13:2–5, for instance, describes the 'country remaining' and notes
the difference between the territory that the tribes were to share and the

[23] See B. Maisler (Mazar), op. cit., pp. 93–96; Views of the Biblical World, Jerusalem, I, 1958
and the map.

Canaan that ought to have been conquered by them.[24] The latter extends to the north as far as the Pass of Hamath, as in Num. 34 and Ezek 47, and as far as the territory of the Amorites, which seems to have been the territory of Amurru. This was immediately to the north of the Egyptian province of Canaan and had at this period come under the control of the Hittites. What is more, these are the same northern and southern boundaries as those mentioned in Num. 23:17 and 21, according to which Moses sent scouts to reconnoitre the land of Canaan 'from the wilderness of Zin to the Pass of Hamath'.[25] This can be compared with the expression 'from the Pass of Hamath to the wadi of Egypt', which denoted the extremities of the land of Canaan during the reign of Solomon (1 Kings 8:65) and during the reign of Jeroboam II (2 Kings 14:25).

The theory outlined above differs from the view that has been expressed by many scholars, namely that the name Canaan was given first only to Phoenicia and was only later extended, in the Old Testament, to the coastal region generally, the Jordan Valley and northern and central Cisjordania and finally to the whole region west of the Jordan.[26] The conclusion reached by these scholars is certainly not justified by the evidence of the non-biblical texts. As for the biblical texts themselves, it is much more probable that the Israelites took over the name Canaan with the meaning that it already had before they settled in the country. The name may have been applied to a more limited geographical area when Canaan came to be identified with the land that had been conquered and not with the 'promised' land of Gen 10:19. On the other hand, the name may have become more limited in its geographical application when the name Canaanite was restricted to the inhabitants of those parts of Canaan that had not been subjugated, as in Jos. 17:11–13 and Judges 1:27–33 or when the part in which they lived was restricted to Phoenicia. The traders were called 'Canaanites' because they came from Phoenicia. Tyre and Sidon were called 'the fortresses of Canaan' (Isa 23:1–14). Sidon was the 'first-born' of Canaan (Gen. 10:15; 1 Chron 1:13). 'Sidonian' meant the same as 'Canaanite' (Deut 3:9; Judges 18:7; 1 Kings 11:5, 33; 2 Kings 23:13), just as the words 'Sidonian' and 'Phoenician' are both used in Homer without any difference in meaning. In the second century B.C., Beirut was called Laodicea in Phoenicia and its coins bore the name Canaan, the only known occurrence of the name in Phoenician inscriptions. During the same period, Canaan was translated

[24] D. Baldi, 'La Terra Promessa nel programma di Giosue', *Studii Biblici Franciscani Liber Annuus*, 1 (1950–1951), pp. 87–106; F.-M. Abel, La prétendue caverne des Sidoniens et la localisation de la ville de Ara', *RB*, 58 (1951), pp. 47–53.

[25] See map 50 in Y. Aharoni and M.Avi–Yona, *The Macmillan Biblical Atlas*, New York, 1968.

[26] B. Maisler (Mazar), *Untersuchungen zur alten Geschichte und Ethnographie Syriens und Palästinas*, Giessen, 1930, pp. 54–74; S. Moscati, *I Predecessori, op. cit.*, p. 67; M. Noth, *The Old Testament World*, London, 1966, pp. 50–51.

several times as Phoenicia in the Septuagint. Finally, in the New Testament, the Canaanite woman mentioned in Matt 15:22 is the same as the Syro-Phoenician woman of Mark 7:26.

IV. THE INHABITANTS OF CANAAN ACCORDING TO THE BIBLE [27]

In accordance with the very wide definition of the land of Canaan inherited from the Egyptian administration, the collective adjective 'Canaanite' is used in many biblical texts for all the inhabitants of Cisjordania before the arrival of the Israelites, without making any ethnic distinctions between them (see, for example, Gen. 12:6; 24:3; Exod 13:11; Num 21:1). In other texts belonging to the same tradition, it indicates the early inhabitants of the country who were dispossessed when the Israelites conquered the land or who escaped from the Israelites (see, for example, Jos. 16:10; Judges 1:1–10, 17, 27–33).

The same chapter of Judges mentioned above, however, goes on at once to speak of the *Amorites* pushing the Danites back into the highlands and holding their ground in the territory of the House of Joseph. In fact, the term 'Amorite' is used in competition with the term 'Canaanite' to designate the early population of Palestine. According to many critical examinations of the Pentateuch 'Canaanite' is the name used in the Yahwistic accounts, whereas 'Amorite' is the term used by the Elohistic editors. As it is difficult, however, to maintain this clear distinction in every case, another explanation has to be found for the use of these two names. In the first place, it is necessary to consider separately the passages in which the early inhabitants of the territories occupied by the tribes of Israel in Transjordan to the north of Edom and Moab – the kingdoms of Sihon, of Og of Bashan and Gilead – are called Amorites. These are Num 21:13; 32:33–39; Deut 3 *passim*; 4:46; 31:4; Jos 2:10; 9:10; 24:8; Judges 10:8; 11:21–23. This is quite in accordance with the geography of Canaan, the eastern boundary of which was the River Jordan – to the east of the Jordan, the people were not Canaanites, but Amorites. On the other hand, other texts refer to Amorites occupying land to the west of the Jordan, either the whole of Cisjordan (Gen. 15:16; Jos. 24:15, 18; Judges 6:10; 2 Kings 21:11) or else only the mountainous region, from southern Palestine and the 'highlands of the Amorites' (Deut 1:7, 19, 20, 44). There were Amorites at Hazazon-tamar (Gen. 14:7) and at Hebron (Gen. 14:13). The king of Jerusalem had formed

---

[27] B. Maisler (Mazar), *Untersuchungen zur alten Geschichte und Ethnographie, op. cit.*; J. C. L. Gibson, 'Observations on Some Important Ethnic Terms in the Pentateuch,' *JNES*, 20 (1961), pp. 217–238; I. J. Gelb, 'The Early History of the West Semitic Peoples', *JCS*, 15 (1961), pp. 27–47; M. du Bruit, 'Populations de Palestine', *DBS*, VIII, 1967, col. 111–126.

an alliance with four other Amorite kings (Jos 10:5 ff) and the Gibeonites were a 'remnant of the Amorites' (2 Sam 21:2). Shechem had been conquered by the Amorites (Gen. 48:22). Other texts make a distinction between these Amorites of the highlands [28] and the Canaanites of the coastal region (Jos 5:1) or of the sea coast and the Jordan Valley (Num 13:29; cf. Jos. 11:3).

Unlike the biblical use of the word 'Canaanite', this use in the Old Testament of the name 'Amorite' has no counterpart in non-biblical texts before the settlement of the Israelites. It cannot be based on a recollection of the Amorite immigration round about 2000 B.C. Nor can it refer to the land of Amurru,[29] which was, according to the Amarna letters and the Egyptian texts, to the north of Canaan. The name is, however, probably derived from the Amurru that occurs in the Assyrian texts from the time of Tiglath-pileser I (1115–1070 B.C.) onwards as a general term for the 'land of the west', from Palmyra to the Mediterranean Sea.[30]

It would seem, then, that the bibilical use of the term 'Amorite' was later than that of the word 'Canaanite' and that it was always subordinate to it. The term 'Amorite' came, as we have already seen, to be applied not only to the people living in Transjordan, but also to those inhabiting the hill country of Cisjordan and then to the inhabitants of the whole region west of the Jordan. At the same time, as we have noted, the reverse process took place with the term 'Canaanite'. To begin with, all the people of the Egyptian province of Canaan were called 'Canaanites'. The use of this term was later restricted to the inhabitants of Cisjordania, later still to those of the coastal region and the Jordan Valley and finally to the Phoenicians. In the Bible, 'Amorite' has no historical or ethnic significance at all.

All the same, the Amorites seem, according to certain biblical texts, to have been a distinctive race of people. In Amos 2:9, Num 13:32 and Deut 3:11, for example, they are described, as the Canaanites never are in the Bible, as being exceptionally tall and strong. This, however, is only because the Amorites were regarded as the successors or the descendants of the legendary giants of prehistory – the Rephaim of Bashan and of Gilead (Deut 3:11, 13; Jos 12:4; 13:12[31]). These Rephaim were related to the Zamzummim of Ammon (Deut. 2:20–21) and the Emim of Moab (Deut. 2:10–11). The Rephaim were also to be found at Jerusalem, where their memory was preserved in the name 'the plain of the Rephaim' (Jos 15:8; 18: 16; 2 Sam 5:18). In Cisjordania, on the other hand, they were known as the

---

[28] The Amorites are situated on the plain in only one text, Judges 1: 34–35, quoted above.
[29] With the possible exception of Jos 13:4; see above, p. 132.
[30] The texts will be found in P. Dhorme, 'Les Amorrhéens, VIII, Amourrou et l'Assyrie', RB, 40 (1931), pp. 172–181 = Receuil Edouard Dhorme, Paris, 1951, pp. 152–162.
[31] See also the Book of Jubilees 29:9 and Jos 17:15, if this verse refers to the settlement of the Manassites in Transjordan.

Anakim and lived in Hebron and the surrounding hill country (Num 13:22, 28, 33; Jos 14:12; 15:13; Judges 1:20), in the whole hill country of Judah and Israel (Jos. 11:21) and, in one text (Deut. 9:2), in the whole of the country to be conquered to the west of the Jordan. This, then, covers all the parts of Canaan in which the Amorites were said to live and the physical qualities attributed to these people cannot be taken literally because of their reputed descent from the legendary Rephaim.

The *Hittites* are also mentioned in another series of texts as other early inhabitants of Palestine. They appear six times at the head of eighteen of the lists of the five, six or seven peoples who are supposed to have occupied Palestine and nine times in the second place. According to Gen 23, the inhabitants of Hebron at the time of Abraham were the 'sons of Heth'. According to Gen. 26:34 and 27:46 (see also Gen. 36:2), Esau married Hittite women at Beersheba. According to Num 13:29, the Hittites lived, together with the Amorites, in the highlands. Later, David is said to have had a Hittite ally (1 Sam. 26:6) and a Hittite officer (2 Sam. 11).

What is quite certain is that the Hittites never controlled Palestine or entered the country in great numbers. It is, of course, possible that individual Hittites settled there, but it is remarkable that all these 'Hittites' mentioned in the Bible – Ephron and his father Zohar at Hebron, Esau's wives and their fathers and David's soldiers, Ahimelech and Uriah – all have Semitic names. They may have been originally Hittite, but they were completely assimiliated.

Attempts have been made to justify the existence of a Hittite enclave at Hebron on the basis of an enigmatic text written by Mursilis II, which refers to a treaty concluded in his presence between the Hittites and Egypt and dealing with the settlement in the 'land of Egypt' of the population of Kurustamma, a city in Asia Minor.[32] At this time, Hebron was situated in country controlled by Egypt. This hypothesis, however, is entirely without historical or archaeological foundation.[33] What is more, a text published after this theory was suggested[34] refers to this agreement and states explicitly that these people were brought into Egypt and 'became Egyptians'. There is, in other words, no question of Hebron playing any part. Similar attempts have been made to uphold the Hittite tradition of Gen 23 by juridical arguments, namely that the purchase of the cave on the field at Machpelah from the 'sons of Heth' took place in accordance with Hit-

[32] E. O. Forrer, 'The Hittites in Palestine', *PEQ*, 1937, pp. 100–115, especially pp. 104 ff. A translation of this text has been published in *ANET*, p. 395a and a translation and commentary have been provided by O. R. Gurney, *The Hittites*, Harmondsworth, 1954, pp. 59–62.

[33] L. Delaporte, 'Les Hittites sont-ils nommés dans la Bible?', *RHA*, 4/32 (1938), pp. 289–296.

[34] H. G. Gütterbock, 'The Deeds of Suppiluliuma as Told by his Son Mursili II', *JCS*, 10 (1956), pp. 75–98, see also p. 96.

tite law and that a Hittite contract was drawn up.[35] Whatever may have happened at the time of the event, it is certainly true to say that the edited text of Gen 23 is not based on Hittite customs, but rather on neo-Babylonian bills of sale.[36]

As in the case of the Amorites, the biblical use of the name 'Hittite' among other early inhabitants of Palestine is entirely without historical or ethnic significance. How, then, was the name introduced? The Hittites, as an ethnic group with a place in history, conquered Syria from the Euphrates to the Mediterranean Sea and Kadesh in the south, but their empire fell round about 1200 B.C. There is, however, no record in the Bible of these authentic Hittites. After the collapse of the Hittite empire, various independent states arose on what had been Hittite territory on both sides of the Taurus Mountains and as far south as Hamath in central Syria. These people used a 'Hittite' hieroglyphic form of writing and modern historians have referred to them as 'neo-Hittite' kingdoms. The term is, however, not accurate, because these states preserved very little of the Hittite inheritance and a great deal of Assyrian practice. When they came into contact with these new states, from the time of Tiglath-pileser I (1115–1070) onwards, the Assyrians called all the territory between the Euphrates and the land of Amurru the land of Hatti. It is possible that it is this practice that is reflected in the difficult text or gloss, Jos 1:4, which states that the 'land of the Hittites' extended from the Lebanon to the Euphrates and in 2 Sam. 24:6, the Greek version of which reads 'to Kadesh in the land of the Hittites'. This Hittite country may have been the native land of Ahimelech and Uriah, whose names occur in the history of David, and of Solomon's Hittite wives (1 Kings 11:1). The 'kings of the Hittites' with whom Solomon traded at the same time as he was trading with the 'kings of Aram' (1 Kings 10:29) were almost certainly princes of northern Syria. These princes were possibly also the 'Hittite kings' who were in alliance with the Aramaeans against Samaria (2 Kings 7:6).

It was during this period, however, that the Assyrian practice was developing and, following the advance of the Assyrian armies, the name Hatti spread to southern Syria and to the whole of Palestine. Shalmaneser III (858–824 B.C.) had to fight several times against a coalition of twelve kings of Hatti, who are also called 'kings of the sea coast' and are listed in connection with the battle of Karkara in 853. Apart from two leaders, the kings of Hamath and Damascus, the kings mentioned in this list include those of Israel, Ammon, Arvad and other principalities in the West and an

---

[35] M. R. Lehmann, 'Abraham's Purchase of Machpelah and Hittite Law', *BASOR*, 129 (Feb. 1953), pp. 15–18.

[36] H. Petschow, 'Die neubabylonische Zwiegesprächsurkunde und Genesis 23', *JCS*, 19 (1965), pp. 103–120. G. M. Tucker, 'The Legal Background of Genesis 23', *JBL*, 85 (1966), pp. 77–84.

Arab king.[37] Almost two centuries later, Esarhaddon (680–669 B.C.) provided a list of 'twenty-two kings of Hatti, the seashore and the islands,' which contains, apart from ten kings of Cyprus (the islands), twelve kings of the sea coast. The countries ruled by these twelve kings, however, are not the same as those given in Shalmaneser's list. They are Tyre, Judah, Edom, Moab, Gaza, Ashkelon, Ekron, Byblos, Arvad, Samsimuruna, Ammon and Ashdod. In other words, they are all territories in the west conquered by Assyria but without the status of provinces.[38]

From this period onwards, the name 'Hittite' disappeared from the cuneiform documents. The term used in the Bible for the early inhabitants of Palestine was certainly derived from this Assyrian practice and could not have been introduced into Palestine before the name Hatti had reached the country. In other words, it could not have been used there before the second half of the ninth century B.C. According to literary criticism of the Old Testament, the use of this term is, moreover, a characteristic of the priestly tradition in the Pentateuch. This may be so, even though it is only possible to check this theory against the few texts of Genesis and the one text of Numbers mentioned above. It is, however, certain that the practice of using this name began before the priestly work of editing was carried out. Two further factors should also be borne in mind. First, the lists of peoples inhabiting Palestine which are prior to the date of this priestly revision give a prominent place to the Hittites. Secondly, the words Hatti and Hittite were no longer used at the time of the priestly revision.

The *Horites* present us with a very different problem.[39] As we have already seen, groups of Hurrians moved south into Palestine and there is evidence to show that they were living there in the fifteenth and fourteenth centuries B.C.[40] The geographical term Huru figures in texts written during the reign of Thut-mose III as a name for Palestine and part of Syria – at the end of the eighth century B.C., it was equivalent to 'Canaan'.[41] Round about 1100 B.C., Wen-Amon set sail from Huru to go to Byblos and sent a messenger from Byblos to Egypt, the messenger eventually returning from Egypt to Huru.[42] The Israelites certainly encountered descendants of these Hurrians when they settled in Palestine and they were also certainly familiar with the name Huru that the Egyptians had given to the country. The Old Testament authors were therefore bound to speak of the Hurrians and in fact mentioned the Horites. There can be no doubt that the two

---

[37] *ANET*, pp. 278b–279a.
[38] *ANET*, p. 291; see also p. 294.
[39] See, for example, R. de Vaux, 'Les Hurrites de l'histoire et les Horites de la Bible', *RB*, 74 (1967), pp. 481–503.
[40] See above, p. 83 ff.
[41] See above, p. 129.
[42] *ANET*, pp. 26a, 28a.

names are philologically identical. The widespread view that the 'Horites' were 'cave-dwellers', because the Hebrew word hôr means 'cave', goes back at least as far as Jerome,[43] but there is no scriptural evidence for this interpretation and it is not in accordance with the geography of Edom. According to the Bible and certainly according to the Hebrew text of the Old Testament, the Horites lived exclusively in Edomite territory (Gen. 14:6; 36:20). They were, however, dispossessed of this land by the Edomites (Deut. 2:12, 22). There is no evidence either in history or in archaeology that the Hurrians entered southern Transjordan, nor is there any indication that the Egyptian name Huru was applied especially to this region. Finally, it has to be admitted that the arguments put forward to explain certain names in the list in Gen. 36:20–30 as Hurrian are not very convincing.[44]

Other inhabitants of Canaan according to the Bible are the *Hivites*. In eighteen lists in the Old Testament, sixteen mention these Hivites alongside the Canaanites, the Amorites and the Hittites as early inhabitants of Cisjordania, in other words, of the region where Hurrians would be expected according to non-biblical texts. It is true that, in Gen. 34:2 and Jos. 9:7, the Septuagint has 'Horite' instead of 'Hivite', which appears in the Hebrew version. On the other hand, both the Hebrew and the Greek versions of Gen. 36:2 have 'Hivite', whereas both versions have 'Horite' in Gen. 36:20, 21, 29 and 30. It would be wrong to correct 'Hivite' everywhere in the Old Testament and replace it with 'Horite' or to regard the two names as identical.[45] Similarly, it would also be wrong to imagine that the biblical authors changed the Hurrians of Cisjordan into 'Hivites' merely in order to distinguish them from the (Semitic) Horites of Transjordania.[46] In the same way, there is no justification for transposing the two names, that is, for putting the Horites in Cisjordania and the Hivites in Edom.[47] The three texts mentioned above can best be explained as errors in transcription, since two Hebrew square letters are very similar and can easily be confused.[48] The two different names used in the Old Testament have therefore to be preserved in a consistent manner (the three textual errors form an exception

[43] In the *Liber de Nominibus Hebraicis;* see under *Chorrai, PL,* XXIII, col. 777.
[44] H. L. Ginsberg and B. Maisler, 'Semitised Hurrians in Syria and Palestine', *JPOS,* 14 (1934), pp. 243–267; W. Feiler, 'Hurritische Namen im Alten Testament', *ZA,* 45 (1939), pp. 216–219; I. H. Eybers, 'Who were the Hivites?', Die Ou Testamentiese Werkgemeenskap in Suid-Afrika. Papers Read at 2nd Meeting, Pretoria, 1959, pp. 6–14.
[45] E. A. Speiser, 'Ethnic Movements in the Near East in the Second Millennium B.C.', *AASOR,* 13 (1933), pp. 26–31; I. H. Eybers, 'Who were the Hivites?' op. cit.
[46] E. A. Speiser, *Genesis (The Anchor Bible),* Garden City, 1964, pp. 282–283.
[47] W. F. Albright, 'The Horites in Palestine', *From Pyramids to Paul (G. L. Robinson Volume),* New York, 1935, pp. 9–26.
[48] In Gen. 34: 2, the Hebrew is supported by the Greek versions of Aquila and Symmachus; in Jos 9:7, the Hebrew text is supported by several manuscripts of the Septuagint and the early Latin, Ethiopian and Syriac versions.

to this, of course) in order to denote two distinct peoples, the Horites in Transjordan and the Hivites in Cisjordania.

Apart from these lists of peoples, only the Hivites are named in the Bible as inhabitants of the hill country with the Amorites and the Jebusites (Num. 13:29; cf. Jos 11:3, Greek) or as inhabitants of the Lebanese highlands (Judges 3:3). The only places mentioned explicitly in this context in the Old Testament are Shechem (Gen 32:2) and Gibeon (Jos. 9:7; 11:19). The people of Shechem, however, have Semitic names and, according to Gen 34:20, they are Canaanites. According to 2 Sam 21:2, the Gibeonites were Amorites. Finally, we must conclude that it is simply not possible to give any ethnic importance to the name 'Hivite' or to ascertain its origin.[49]

The Bible, then, has not preserved any memory of a Hurrian element in the population of Canaan, although the biblical authors clearly recognised the Egyptian geographical term Huru and applied it without any real justification to the Edomite territory, possibly because they had no other name at their disposal to give to this region. These conclusions are confirmed by an examination of the Hurrian proper names that can be found in the Bible. Various attempts have been made, not all with equal success, to identify these names.[50] The most certain are Araunah[51] and Shamgar.[52] Araunah was a Jebusite from Jerusalem (2 Sam 24:18), however, and, although the king of Jerusalem during the fourteenth century B.C., 'Abdu-Heba, has a Hurrian name, the Jebusites were, according to Jos. 10:5 ff, Amorites. The second element in Shamgar's name, ben Anath, son of Anath (Judges 3:31; 5:6) shows that this was a semitised Hurrian name. The names of the 'three sons of Anak', Ahiman, Sheshai and Talmai (Num. 13:22; Jos 15:14; Judges 1:10)[53] cannot be called Hurrian with such certainty. All that can be said is that they were Anakim according to the first two texts and Canaanites according to the third and that they lived in Hebron. According to Gen. 23, moreover, the inhabitants of Hebron were Hittites.

Finally, one people, already mentioned several times in this section, who figure in almost all the lists of inhabitants of Canaan are the *Jebusites*. In the Old Testament, however, they are always situated in Jerusalem (see Jos. 15:63; Judges 1:21; 2 Sam 24:18; see also Jos 15:8; 18:16) and Jerusalem was an

---

[49] According to J. Callaway, *JBL*, 87 (1968), p. 318, G. E. Meldenhall compared the name 'Hivite' with the name Queh (Kue) on the Cilician plain and looked for the origin of the Hivites in Asia Minor. This comparison is without any philological and historical foundation.

[50] See specially the articles mentioned above, note 44.

[51] The name is strictly speaking a title – 'Lord'; see C. H. Gordon, *Ugaritic Textbook*, Glossary, No. 116.

[52] A. van Selms, 'Judge Shamg:.r', *VT*, 14 (1964), pp. 294–309, believed that this name was Semitic.*

[53] W. Feiler, *op. cit.* (note 44 above), pp. 225–228; R. de Vaux, *RB*, 55 (1948), p. 327, note 1.

Amorite city according to Jos 10:5 ff. It was precisely because they were early inhabitants of the capital that they were treated with such favour by the biblical authors. Little is known of these Jebusites – not more than is known of the peoples who accompany them in certain lists, namely the Perizites [54] and the Girgashites.

We may conclude by saying that it is not possible to gain any historical or ethnic information of any value from the biblical references to the early inhabitants of Canaan apart, perhaps, from the fact that the population was mixed – and this is something that we already know from the history of the country. The Israelites themselves were aware of this mixture of races in the country that they entered and their arrival added to this mixture. Ezekiel reminded Jerusalem that she belonged to the land of Canaan, that her father was an Amorite and her mother a Hittite and he declared that Samaria and Sodom had the same origins (Ezek. 16:3, 45).

V. 'CANAANITE' CIVILISATION – SOCIETY [55]

Despite or perhaps even because of this extremely mixed population, the cosmopolitan nature of Palestine at the end of the second millennium B.C. was very similar in many respects to the civilisation of the Mediterranean coast as far north as Ras Shamrah. The majority of the inhabitants of that region were Semitic and those who were not ethnically Semitic had certainly become more or less completely semitised. The languages spoken everywhere were western Semitic dialects. Excavations in Palestine and in Phoenicia, especially at Byblos and even more particularly at Rās Shamrah, have revealed a clear relationship between the architecture, pottery, metal ware and lesser products of the two countries. The sensational discovery of the Rās Shamrah texts – a work which is still continuing – has given life to this silent evidence. [56]

The private and administrative archives of Ugarit have added greatly to

[54] If this word is Semitic, it may mean 'those who live in the country' as opposed to the city. According to a recent hypothesis, the Perizzites were semi-nomadic immigrants of the Intermediate Period between the Early and Middle Bronze Ages; see P. Lapp, 'Bâh edh-Dira, Perizzites and Emim', *Jerusalem through the Ages*, Jerusalem, 1968, especially pp. 24–25.

[55] A. F. Rainey, *The Social Structure of Ugarit. A Study of West Semitic Social Stratification during the Late Bronze Age* (Hebrew), Jerusalem, 1967.*

[56] The Ugaritic texts discovered between 1929 and 1939 have been published in a definitive edition in A. Herdner, *Corpus des tablettes en cunéiforme alphabétique (Mission de Ras Shamra X)*, Paris, 1963. All the texts edited as far as 1965 have been published in transcription in C. H. Gordon, *Ugaritic Textbook*, Rome, 1965. In addition, C. Virolleaud, *PRU*, V, 1965; *Ugaritica*, V (Mission de Ras Shamra XVI), 1968, pp. 545-606. There is no corpus of Akkadian texts, but the texts acquired in recent campaigns have been edited by J. Nougayrol, *PRU*, III and IV and *Ugaritica*, V, pp. 1–446.

the rather scanty knowledge that we have been able to gain from the Amarna letters and other texts originating in Palestine. We have learned from these archives a great deal about the family customs, the legal practices, the state of the economy and the administration of civil affairs of Ugarit and, by extension, of the region as a whole. The religious texts – poems, myths and rituals[57] – have thrown considerable light on what the Bible tells us about the gods and cultic practices of Canaan and on the traditions preserved by later authors in the region of Phoenicia. This underlying geographical unity to some extent justifies the modern practice of grouping this whole complex under the one heading of 'Canaanite' civilisation. All that has to be borne in mind in this context is that it is a conventional term and that similarities should not be assumed to exist if there is no proof of their existence. Archaeological discoveries have, after all, revealed not only many characteristics shared by the various regions, but also many striking variations and it is reasonable to suppose (and has indeed in certain cases been proved) that differences existed also in the social and religious spheres. Because the documents at our disposal are to some extent unbalanced, we are obliged to call this society and its religion 'Canaanite' on the basis of the Rās Shamrah texts, although Rās Shamrah did not, as we have seen, form part of the 'land of Canaan'. It is therefore important not to apply indiscriminately all our conclusions to Palestine and the Bible. Nonetheless, there are aspects which are of general and essential application. Above all, Canaanite civilisation was the civilisation of a sedentary, urban society with an economy based on agriculture and trade.

However large or small they might have been, the Canaanite states were kingdoms and their kings, like the rulers of Ugarit, were very much in control of their own territories, even though they were vassals of Egypt. The king's authority was supreme. There was no appeal against his decisions as judge and he was the leader of the army and the high priest. All administration was ultimately his responsibility. The absolute power which he exercised and the abuses to which this could give rise are listed in the warnings given by Samuel to the Israelites when they demanded a king (1 Sam 8:10–17) and are illustrated in the Palestinian and Syrian texts, especially those of Alalah and Rās Shamrah.[58] The idea that the king himself and his sub-

---

[57] The main religious texts have been translated, though not definitively, in C. H. Gordon, *Ugaritic Literature. A Comprehensive Translation of the Poems and Prose Texts*, Rome, 1949; H. L. Ginsberg, 'Ugaritic Myths, Epics and Legends', *ANET*, pp. 129–155; G. R. Driver, *Canaanite Myths and Legends*, Edinburgh, 1956; J. Aistleitner, *Die mythologischen und kultischen Texte aus Ras Schamra*, Budapest, 1956, 2nd edn., 1964; A. Jirku, *Kanaanäische Mythen und Epen aus Ras Schamra-Ugarit*, Gütersloh, 1962; A. Caquot and M. Sznyzer, 'Textes Ougaritiques', *Les Religions du Proche-Orient. Textes et traditions sacrés babyloniens-ougaritiques-hittites*, ed. R. Labat, Paris, 1970, pp. 350–458.

[58] I. Mendelsohn, 'Samuel's Denunciation of Kingship in the Light of Akkadian Documents from Ugarit', *BASOR*, 143 (Oct. 1956), pp. 17–22.

jects had of the royal status does not emerge from the administrative texts, but it is expressed quite clearly in the Rās Shamrah poems of Keret and Aqhat-Danel. In these poetic texts, the king is presented as a sacred person closely connected with the divine world, embodying the community and acting as the mediator between his people and the gods. It is, however, difficult to say to what extent this image of the king is purely mythological and poetic. All that can be said is that these texts do not enable us to speak of a deification of the king. These early poems were not, or were no longer, an expression of the situation that prevailed in fact at the end of the second millennium. In the heroic era, the king had come down to earth again and had divested himself of some at least of his special privileges.[59] The submission of the kinglets of Canaan to the pharaoh or to the great Hittite king, whom they called their 'god' or 'sun', must have hastened this development.

At the period at present under discussion, the king had at his disposal a senate of eminent men to advise him. The Amarna letters, for example, refer to the elders of the city of Irqata[60] and the 'gentlemen of the city' at Byblos.[61] In the history of Wen-Amon, round about 1100 B.C., the king of Byblos is mentioned as consulting his council and the Egyptian text has a Canaanite word here.[62] The absence of other references in the Amarna letters and the Rās Shamrah documents must be purely accidental, since councils of elders with political or administrative powers were a familiar feature of other monarchical governments in the Ancient Near East. They were known at a very early date in Mesopotamia,[63] a little later in the Hittite kingdom[64] and later still in the kingdom of Israel. King Rehoboam, for instance, consulted the elders of his father Solomon (1 Kings 12:16) and Ahab summoned his elders and followed their advice (1 Kings 20:7–8). In all ordinary matters, then, the king acted through his functionaries. At Rās Shamrah, a 'prefect' or šakin māti administered the whole country,[65] which was divided into districts, each with its 'burgomaster' or hazanu. We have already seen that, in the Amarna letters, the šakin māti or rabisu was the governor of a province and hazanu was the title given to princes in their cities – in other words, Egypt adapted native practices to the needs of her

[59] J. Gray, 'Canaanite Kingship in Theory and Practice', VT, 2 (1952), pp. 193–220.*
[60] EA, 100, 4; read ṣibutu.
[61] EA, 138, 49.
[62] mōʿed, Wen-Amon,, II, 70, ANET, p. 29a; see J. A. Wilson, 'The Assembly of a Phoenician City', JNES, 4 (1945), p. 245.
[63] G. Evans, 'Ancient Mesopotamian Assemblies', JAOS, 78 (1958), pp. 1–11; A. Malamat, 'Kingship and Council in Israel and Sumer', JNES, 22 (1963), pp. 247–253.
[64] H. Klengel, 'Die Rolle der 'Ältesten' im Kleinasien der Hethiterzeit', ZA, 57 (1965), pp. 223–236.
[65] A. Alt. 'Hohe Beamte in Ugarit', Studia Orientalia J. Pedersen . . . dedicata, Copenhagen, 1953, pp. 1–11 = Kleine Schriften, III, 186–197.

empire. Staff at the lower level included provincial administrators, inspectors, collectors and scribes, all of whom were called 'people of the king' or 'servants of the king'.

Many of the administrative texts of Rās Shamrah are inventories – lists of individuals classified according to their status or profession, lists of civilian or military staff, lists of persons entitled to receive rations or bound to perform corvée labour or to pay taxes, and lists of cities or of estates. According to these exact registers, Ugaritic society was not based on blood relationships nor was it organised on the basis of families or clans.[66] It was a feudal society with a ruling class of noblemen to whom the king assigned land or privileges in return for certain personal services. This system was known throughout the whole of the Ancient Near East, but at Ugarit it developed into a feudalism which was tied to the land rather than to the owner of the land, so that the slaves belonged to the land, even if its owner changed.[67] The aristocracy had its origin partly in the military class of *maryannu*, who needed a high income from land in order to maintain their chariots, horses and equipment. In the fourteenth and thirteenth centuries at Ugarit, however, the word *maryannu* was apparently only an aristocratic title and not necessarily connected with military service.[68] A king of Ugarit would, for instance, confer this title on one of his subjects and on his sons and provide them with a fief with exemption from military service and from the tithe, although they would be subject to the authority of the master of the chariots. At Alalah as early as the fifteenth century, the title of *maryannu* was given in perpetuity to a man and to his descendants who were also priests. A woman could inherit the title of *maryannu* left by her husband and hand it on to her children.[69] What took place, then, was a merging of the early military aristocracy with that of the great landowners. This is comparable with the evolution of the title of 'knight', *chevalier* or *Ritter* in the monarchies of Europe.

Apart from the lower functionaries, or officials, and the artisans, the peasants formed the biggest class of people between the noblemen and the slaves, who do not seem in any case to have been numerous. Although their status was low, these peasants were free men, cultivating their plots of land or their vineyards or else working in the king's or the noblemen's domains. They were bound to perform corvée labour, which was known as 'service of the king' or 'service of the palace'.[70] In the census list of Alalah

[66] Compare the reaction based on tribal feeling against David's census in 2 Sam 24:1–4.

[67] G. Boyer, *PRU*, III, pp. 293–299; C. Schwarzenberg, 'L'organizzazione feudale ad Ugarit', *RIDA*, 3rd series, 11 (1964), pp. 19–44.

[68] The texts have been arranged by A. F. Rainey, 'The Military Personnel of Ugarit', *JNES*, 24 (1965), pp. 17–27, see also pp. 19–21.

[69] D. J. Wisemen, *The Alalakh Tablets*, London, 1953, Nos. 15 and 91.

[70] I. Mendelsohn, 'On Corvée Labor in Ancient Canaan and Israel', *BASOR*, 167 (Oct. 1962), pp. 31–35.

and in the correspondence of Rib-Addi of Byblos, the are called *hupsu*, a word which is also found in Hebrew with a more developed meaning, that of 'freed'.[71] The kings recruited their guards and foot soldiers from this lower class of people, whereas service with the chariots was the duty and the privilege of the noblemen. These local troops were supplemented by mercenary soldiers. A distinction is made in the Amarna letters, for instance, between chariot and foot soldiers, who were recruited locally, and the Sūtū or 'Apīru mercenaries.[72] It would seem too that the king of Ugarit had mercenaries, who were 'Apīru and Shardans. Little is known, however, about the military organisation at Ugarit and many of the terms are quite obscure.[73]

Apart from corvée labour and military service, subjects of the king of Ugarit had to pay at least three kinds of tax. In the first place, a tithe on corn, oil and wine. Secondly, to provide common grazing on their land and thirdly, they had to pay a tax in money on real estate and goods in transit. To these have to be added extraordinary taxes and fines payable in case of contravention.[74]

The state's main source of income, however, was trade. The king bought and sold land and took part in financial transactions. Like all the great eastern kings, he had caravans escorted by soldiers and a mercantile fleet. His traders held official rank in the state, received rations and a salary from the palace and acted as business agents and even, when the occasion arose, as diplomatic messengers. Other traders worked for themselves and often became very rich. They had their own ships and donkey transport and went to Egypt, where they had a storehouse at Memphis, Cyprus and even to Crete. On the other hand, foreign merchants also crossed the country with their caravans and, to defend their interests and to increase their profits, formed 'companies' among themselves. Ugarit was placed at the centre of communications between Asia Minor, the Aegean, Syria and Egypt, and was clearly the main trading centre,[75] but the little kingdoms of Canaan, especially those on the coast such as Byblos,[76] as well as others inland such as Taanach,[77] were also important. According to the history of Wen-Amon, the kings of Byblos kept a register of their dealings with the

[71] I. Mendelsohn, 'The Canaanite Term for 'Free Proletarian' ', *BASOR*, 83 (Oct. 1941), pp. 36–39; D. J. Wiseman, *op. cit.* (see note 69 above), pp. 10–11; I. Mendelsohn, 'New Light on the Ḫupšu', *BASOR*, 139 (Oct. 1956), pp. 9–11.
[72] *EA*, 195, 24–29.
[73] J. Nougayrol, 'Guerre et paix à Ugarit', *Iraq*, 25 (1963), pp. 110–123, see also pp. 117–118; A. F. Rainey, 'The Military Personnel of Ugarit', *JNES*, 24 (1965), pp. 17–27.
[74] J. Nougayrol, *PRU*, III, Répertoire I, see under 'Franchises et exemptions', 'Recettes fiscales', 'Services et corvées' and 'Sommes d'argent et d'or'.
[75] A. F. Rainey, 'Business Agents in Ugarit', *IEJ*, 13 (1963), pp. 313–321.
[76] *EA*, 113, 14; 114, 17–20; 126, 4–8.
[77] *Ta'annak*, No. 1, 8–11.

pharaoh. Twenty ships at Byblos were in this way associated – ḫubur (a Canaanite word) – with Smendes the prince of Tanis. In the same text, we read that fifty ships at Sidon were similarly tied to Warkatara, another prince of the coastal region or possibly a powerful shipowner.

The Canaanite civilisation described in this section was totally unlike the way of life led by the groups of Israelites who were later to enter the country. These people were semi-nomadic herdsmen, whose society was based on blood relationships, and they were astonished, perhaps even horrified and in a sense fascinated, by the civilisation that they found in Canaan. This aspect of sharp contrast and compromise between the two societies is something that we shall encounter again and again in the social and religious history of Israel, which it to some extent dominated. On the other hand, however, even the earliest accounts of Israel's settlement in the country contain a strong condemnation of the sedentary life.[78] For example, Abel was a shepherd, whereas his murderer Cain cultivated crops (Gen 4:1–8). Cain also founded the first city and was the ancestor of the craftsmen and artists who made the necessary articles and the luxuries of urban life (Gen 4:17–22). The building of the town and the tower of Babel was a great sin and punished by God (Gen 11:1–9). Cities were regarded as evil places. Sodom and Gomorrah (Gen 18:20 ff.) are typical examples of this. Depravity and passion proved to be more powerful than the sacred law of hospitality in Sodom (Gen 19:1–11). Dinah was violated in Shechem (Gen 34:1–5). The wives of the patriarchs were not safe in cities in Egypt and the Negeb (Gen 12:10–20; 20:1–18; 26:1–11). Finally, the whole of Canaan was regarded by the Israelite immigrants as Noah's evil son (Gen 9:20–24).[79]

VI. 'CANAANITE' RELIGION – THE GODS AND MYTHS

Until the site at Rās Shamrah had been excavated, our knowledge of the early religion of Canaan remained very limited. Archaeologists had provided us with images of the Canaanite gods which were generally anonymous. The names of the patrons of the temples that had been unearthed were seldom known. Objects and buildings were often called 'cultic' simply because no other explanation could be found for them. All the inscriptions found in Phoenicia were of the first millennium B.C. and almost all of them were recent. Most of them merely provided the names of gods or referred to temples. Other texts were more detailed, but they too were very recent and came not from Phoenicia proper, but from the Phoenician colonies of Cyprus and North Africa.

[78] G. Wallis, 'Die Stadt in den Uberlieferungen der Genesis', ZAW, 78 (1966), pp. 133–148.
[79] The reference to Ham in Gen 9:22 is an adaptation to a different tradition.

Before the discoveries at Rās Shamrah, then, we had to rely mainly on indirect evidence. The Old Testament was our most valuable source of information, but it contained only adverse judgement on the Canaanite religion. Some evidence concerning the Canaanite religion can be found in Greek authors such as Lucian of Samosata in the second century B.C., Nonnos of Panopolis in the fifth century and Damascius in the sixth century. The most informative of these Greek authors is Philo of Byblos who, at the end of the first century or at the beginning of the second century A.D., claimed to have translated the work of a Phoenician author, Sanchuniaton, who was, it seems, living and writing before the Trojan war. But we only have fragments of Philo's work and, even if this Sanchuniaton ever existed, all that we have of his writing is a Greek interpretation of it. The whole situation changed, however, with the publication of the religious texts found at Rās Shamrah. These texts were written in the fourteenth and thirteenth centuries in Ugaritic and consist partly of mythological or epic poems and partly of rituals and lists of sacrifices or offerings. They therefore provide us with early and direct evidence.

All the studies that have been written in recent years of the 'Canaanite' religion have been based above all on these documents.[80] It would hardly, of course, have been possible to proceed in any other way, but at the same time it is important to recognize that the conclusions reached by following this procedure are to some extent uncertain and limited. The texts themselves have not yet been fully understood – this is clear from a comparison of the translations that have already been made. They also contain many gaps. The longest and most interesting texts are spread over several tablets and not only is the order of these tablets not known – we also cannot be certain whether they all really belong to the same literary corpus and if so whether they contain all the separate parts of this corpus. On the other hand, it is certain that the great mythological poems represent an earlier stage of religion than the phase reflected in the ritual texts and that the religion revealed is in each case different. We may therefore conclude that the religion of Ugarit was never, in any of its stages, the religion of the whole of 'Canaan'. Each district, each city and even each sanctuary had its

---

[80] For the 'Canaanite' religion see, apart from J. Gray, *The Legacy of Canaan*, *op. cit.* (note 1), the following books and articles: C. H. Gordon, 'Canaanite Mythology', *Mythologies of the Ancient World*, ed. S. N. Kramer, New York, 1961, pp. 181–219; A. Caquot, 'Mythologies des Sémites Occidentaux', *Mythologies de la Méditerranée au Gange*, ed. P. Grimal, Paris, 1963, pp. 84–93; O. Eissfeldt, 'Kanaanäisch-ugaritsche Religion', *Handbuch der Orientalistic*, Part I, VIII, I, Leiden, 1964, pp. 76–91; M. H. Pope, W. Röllig, 'Syrien', *Götter und Mythen im vorderen Orient (Wörterbuch der Mythologie*, I, 1), ed. H. W. Haussig, Stuttgart, 1965, pp. 219–312; A. Jirku, *Der Mythus der Kanaanäer*, Bonn, 1966; A. Caquot, 'Problèmes d'histoire religieuse', *La Siria nel Tardo Bronze*, ed. M. Liverani, Rome, 1969, pp. 61–76, and Caquot's introduction to the translation of the Rās Shamrah texts in the volume edited by R. Labat, *op. cit.* (note 57).*

own favourite gods, its own ritual and its own sacred legends. A unity in religion which had not even been achieved by very centralised states such as those in Mesopotamia and Egypt can hardly have existed in a country as geographically and politically divided as Canaan. In fact, we have clear proof of this religious diversity throughout the Near East. We have, for example, two sacrificial lists from North Africa and they do not agree with each other. The main gods of Carthage were not the same as those of Tyre, the metropolis of Carthage, which shows that gods differed according to the town or else that they were given different names. The fragments of Canaanite myths found in Egyptian texts have analogies in the poems of Rās Shamrah, but there are no exact parallels. For instance, the first Canaanite deities adopted by the pharaohs, Resheph and Astarte, both of whom remained very popular in Egypt, play very little part in the Rās Shamrah poems and had only a very limited place in Ugaritic worship. The goddess 'Anat figured prominently, on the other hand, both at Rās Shamrah and in Egypt, but is never mentioned in the Bible.

Because of these variations, it is impossible to provide a uniform picture of the 'Canaanite' religion, but the sources at our disposal are complementary rather than contradictory. This is illustrated by the example of 'Anat, who is not mentioned in the Bible. Scripture does, however, mention Anathoth and Beth Anath as place names. What is more, Anath-Bethel and Anath-Yaho were venerated in the Jewish colony of Elephantine during the fifth century B.C. so we may conclude that the goddess 'Anat was known in Palestine.[81] The same deities, then, figured, more or less prominently, throughout the whole of Canaanite society, either with the same names or at least with equivalent names and with the same basic characteristics. They also tended to play the same part everywhere. Although they were venerated locally, they were by no means restricted to one place, because they represented universal ideas and aspirations. It would serve no purpose to discuss the Ugaritic myths in detail here, because they are only one of the ways in which religious thought was expressed in that society. It is, however, necessary to make use of them, in connection with the other information that we have, if we are to provide a general outline of the religion of Canaan.

In the first place, it was a polytheistic religion. The proof of this polytheism is contained in the great number of names of gods in all the documents that we have at our disposal. For example, there are two Rās Shamrah tablets, one in Ugaritic writing and the other in Akkadian writing, which provide a list of more than thirty deities who had been included in the pantheon of Ugarit.[82] This list is in no sense exhaustive. In the

[81] For the Canaanite gods who appear in the Old Testament, see M. J. Mulder, *Kanaänietische Goden in het Oude Testament,* The Hague, 1965.

[82] The tablet in alphabetic cuneiform, G 17 = H 29 (the letter G refers to Gordon, *Ugaritic*

second place, it was also an anthropomorphic religion. The gods of Ugarit were born, died and were reborn, married and begot children, ate and drank like human beings and were moved by the same passions as human beings.

All the same, although the list was so long, it is only a few of these deities who were really important. Supreme in the pantheon was El,[83] whose name meant simply 'god' in every Semitic language with the exception of Ethiopian. Among the western Semites, however, El was a personal god. He was the father of the gods and the 'father of men', the 'creator of created things', the 'father of the years' (?), whom we are bound to imagine as an old man with a white beard. He was 'wise', 'benevolent' and 'merciful'. He lived in a mysterious place at the end of the world, 'at the source of the Rivers, in the hollow of the abysses', but he lived there, not in lazy retirement, but rather as the supreme judge and the guardian of the cosmic order, because he was ultimately responsible for all decisions concerning the gods and men. It is possible that El played a more active part at an earlier stage or in another cycle of legends which has not come down to us. One of his titles was the 'Bull El' which would appear to present him as powerful rather than as prolific. At the same time, however, a poem known by its opening words 'The birth of the gracious and beautiful gods', tells how El fertilised two women who gave birth to Dawn and Dusk. El's divine spouse was the goddess Asherah who bore him seventy divine sons, with the result that she was known as the 'Mother of the Gods'. She was also frequently called 'Asherah of the Sea'. She had great influence over El and the other gods used her to mediate between them and El. The Asherah of Ras Shamrah had no more in common with the Asherah of the Old Testament, the goddess of vegetation and the partner of Baal, than the same name.[84]

In the poems of Rās Shamrah, this respectable divine couple are, however, eclipsed by two young and unruly gods, Baal and his sister and lover 'Anat. It is possible that they also became members of the Canaanite pantheon. Baal[85] was certainly regarded as the son of El, who was in any case the father of all the gods, but he was above all known as the 'son of

---

Textbook, op. cit., the letter H refers to Herdner, *Corpus des tablettes, op. cit.*); the tablet in syllabic cuneiform, J. Nougayrol, *Ugaritica* V, No. 18, with the commentary on pp. 42–64; see also No. 170 and pp. 320–322.

[83] O. Eissfeldt, *El im ugaritischen Pantheon*, Leipzig, 1951; M. Pope, *El in the Ugaritic Texts*, Leiden, 1955; P. D. Miller, 'El the Warrior', *HTR*, 60 (1967), pp. 411–431. For the extension of El as the supreme god of the pantheon to the whole of Canaan, see the reservations of R. Rendtorff, 'El, Ba'al und Jahwe', *ZAW*, 78 (1966), pp. 277–292.*

[84] K.-H. Bernhardt, 'Aschera in Ugarit und im Alten Testament', *MIO*, 13 (1967). pp. 163–174.

[85] See A. S. Kapelrud, *Baal in the Rās Shamra Texts*, Copenhagen, 1952; U. Oldenburg, *The Conflict between El and Ba'al in Canaanite Religion*, Leiden, 1969.*

Dagan'. This god Dagan was venerated especially in the country of the Upper and Middle Euphrates and the name 'Anat also appeared at quite an early stage. Baal had the common name of 'the Master' and this also became his personal name. He also had the proper name of Haddu at Rās Shamrah. This is, of course, the same as Hadad, the great Semitic deity, the storm god who brought rain and fertility. Baal was the 'Prince', the 'Master of the Earth', the 'Rider of the Clouds'. He was the god of the mountains where the storms built up, the 'Master of the Heights of Zaphon', which was the place where the gods gathered and which has been located at Jebel el-Aqra' to the north of Rās Shamrah. He was also a warrior god, the 'Omnipotent Hero', represented walking on the mountains and the sea, brandishing a mace and pointing to the earth a lance with lightning at its tip.

Baal's sister and spouse, 'Anat, has the same sharply contrasting characteristics.[86] She was a goddess of war and of love, sometimes atrociously bloodthirsty and violent, but also a typical woman, young, beautiful, desirable and life-giving. In the great poems of Rās Shamrah, the goddess Astarte to some extent duplicates 'Anat and remains rather in the background. In the cultic texts, on the other hand, she is mentioned more often. A recently edited mythological text[87] gives her a position of importance and stresses her warlike character and the part she played in upholding justice and law. In Egypt, she enjoyed a popularity equal to that of 'Anat and was frequently associated with her. Finally, in Palestine, at least according to the Old Testament, she completely eclipsed 'Anat and the two goddesses later became one: the great 'Syrian goddess' Attargatis of the Hellenistic period.

Revolving round these central figures were the deities who, in our texts at least, seem to have played a secondary rôle at Ugarit. These include the sun goddess Shamash and the moon god Yarih,[88] the god of pestilence Resheph and the divine craftsmen or messengers with two names – Koshar-wa-Hasis or 'Clever and Skilful', Gapan-war-Ugur or 'Vineyard and Field' and Kadesh-wa-Amrar or 'Holy and Blessed'. A special place has to be accorded to Baal's adversaries – Mot,[89] who was 'Death', and Yam,[90] the 'Sea Prince and River Ruler'. Mot was the master of the sterile underworld and Yam was the god of the turbulent and useless waters – irriga-

---

[86] U. Cassuto, *La déesse 'Anat*, Jerusalem, 1951 (Hebrew); A. S. Kapelrud, *The Violent Goddess Anat in the Ras Shamra Texts*, Oslo, 1969.

[87] *PRU*, V, No. 1 = G 2001; commentary by W. Herrmann, 'Aštart', *MIO*, 15 (1969), pp. 6–55.

[88] W. Herrmann, *Yariḫ und Nikkal und der Preis der Kuṯarāt Göttinnen. Ein kultisch-magischer Text aus Ras Schamra (BZAW, 106)*, 1968.

[89] T. Worden. 'The Literary Influence of the Ugaritic Fertility Myth in the Old Testament', *VT*, 3 (1953), pp. 273–297.

[90] O. Kaiser, *Die mythische Bedeutung des Meeres in Agypton, Ugarit und Israel (BZAW, 78)*, 1959.

tion was unknown at Canaan. Both fought Baal, the master of the fertile earth, for supreme power.

These, then are the principal stars in the constellation of these ancient myths, disconnected fragments of which have been preserved in the Rās Shamrah poems. Most of these fragments form part of the Baal cycle, in which three main themes have been distinguished. The first describes Baal's struggle with Yam. The god El, whose authority is threatened by Baal, gives Yam a palace and agrees to deliver Baal up to him, but Baal, with the help of two clubs forged by Koshar-wa-Hasis, is victorious over Yam and becomes master of the pantheon. He is acclaimed as king. The second theme describes the building of Baal's palace. Giving way to the violent intervention of 'Anat and to the flattery of Asherah, El finally agrees to have a palace built for Baal, who at first refuses to allow the divine architect, Koshar, to put any windows in the house, perhaps in order to prevent his enemy Mot from entering. Finally, however, he agrees that one window will remain open : the sound of his thunder and of the rain falling on the earth can be heard through this opening. The third theme deals with the fight between Baal and Mot. Having been recognised as king and possessing his own residence, Baal turns to his great enemy, 'Death'. He sends messengers to Mot in his underground domain to announce that he has seized power, but Mot's reply is to summon Baal to join him. Baal is surprisingly submissive and goes to Mot, together with the Clouds, the Winds, the Rain and the whole of his court. Baal dies and is lamented by El and buried by 'Anat, who beseeches Mot in vain to give her back her brother. After seven months of vain pleading, she attacks Mot, seizes him and then treats him like corn, winnowing, parching and grinding him and scattering what is left in the fields. 'Anat then goes in search of Baal, eventually finding him so much alive that he is able to defeat his enemies. Seven years later, Mot again provokes Baal, but is finally defeated.

We are, of course, still very uncertain about the meaning of many of the details contained in these poems and there are many gaps in the text. Despite this, however, and bearing in mind the special forms that these poems might have taken at Ugarit, we can be sure that they contain many characteristics that were common to Canaanite mythology as a whole. On the one hand, there is the cosmic myth of the struggle against primaeval chaos, represented at Ugarit by Yam, who was probably the same as the monsters Lotan (Leviathan) and Tannin, both of which are mentioned in the Rās Shamrah texts. On the other hand, there are the fertility myths. The alternation between seasonal fertility and sterility is represented at Ugarit by Baal's period on earth and his descent into the kingdom of the dead. The cyclical alternation of fertility and sterility, however, is represented by the periods of seven years, at the end of which Mot's intervention threatens to destroy the abundance brought about by Baal. These seasonal and cyclical myths basically only repeat the single original myth of the constant struggle between the powers of life and of death. These themes are, of course, universal, but their expression in the religion of Canaan was adapted to the special aspects of the Canaanite civilisation outlined above. It was a settled society governed by kings and in it the gods fought constantly for the title of king and for the possession of a palace – an aspect which is clearly reflected in the Ugaritic myths of Keret and Aqhat/Danel. At the same time, it was also a peasant society and the adventures of the gods of Canaan expressed and also controlled both the regular phases of life on the land and its fearful risks.

VII. 'CANAANITE' RELIGION – CULT

The mythological poems of Ras Shamrah, with their strongly religious content, were found for the most part in a 'library' close to two temples. Priests certainly dictated them.[91] Although they were undoubtedly connected with public worship, it would be an exaggeration to regard all these 'myths' as necessarily accompanying religious 'rites' or even as scripts of liturgical dramas acted in the temples.[92] In fact, only one text, the 'Birth of the Gracious Gods'.[93] in which the poem is intersected by rubrics indicating the words to be said and the actions to be performed, is clearly intended for ritual use. These poems were obviously recited – this is clear from the notes in the Baal cycle and the epic of Aqhat-Danel indicating that the speaker should repeat certain parts of the text.[94] They were doubtless recited in the temples on certain feasts and we may suppose that these myths of the cosmic struggle, or the disappearance or the return of the fertility god, were associated with the celebration of feasts of the new year and the harvest. This is, however, no more than a hypothesis, since nothing is said explicitly about the ritual of these feasts in the texts themselves – their existence is not even mentioned.

Very little is in fact known about the public worship of Ugarit. Apart from certain lists of gods or of offerings, the cultic texts themselves contain no more than short rituals, all of them fragmentary, prescribing certain sacrifices for certain deities and sometimes indicating the month or the day

---

[91] The colophon of a tablet of the Baal cycle, G 62, 53–7 = H 6, VI, 53–57.

[92] See especially T. H. Gaster, *Thespis, Ritual, Myth and Drama in the Ancient Near East*, New York, 1950, 2nd, edn., 1961; A. S. Kapelrud, *op. cit.* (note 85) and *The Ras Shamra Discoveries and the Old Testament*, trans. G. W. Anderson, Oxford, 1965.

[93] G 52 = H 23.

[94] G 51, col. IV, 104–105 = H 4, col. IV, 104–105; H 19.225 this line is left out by G 1 *Aqht*.

of the month. One of the most important of these texts is a ritual of a public sacrifice offered by the men of Ugarit, including the king, and the women, including the queen, for the expiation of sins confessed.[95] Another important ritual prescribes sacrifices for the day of the new moon in the 'first month of the wine' (or simply the 'first month'), ablutions for the thirteenth day, further sacrifices for the fourteenth, the day of the full moon, and finally similar ceremonies for the same days of another month.[96] The cultic terms used at Ugarit and those used in the Bible have been compared, but the results have been rather arbitrary.[97] The language of sacrifice was different in the two societies, just as it was different again later at Carthage. On the other hand, the sacrificial systems themselves seem to have been very similar. The Rās Shamrah texts contain examples of the holocaust or burnt offering, the peace-offering or communion sacrifice and the expiatory sacrifice, and it is assumed in the Bible that the Canaanite sacrifices and those of Israel had a commmon ritual. An example of this is the same method of preparation followed in the case of the holocaust of the prophets of Baal and that of Elijah on Mount Carmel (1 Kings 18).

According to the ritual text of Ras Shamrah the king had a very active part to play in the cult of Ugarit. The cultic rôle of the king is also stressed in the epics of Ras Shamrah, in which the legendary kings Keret and Danel hold the office of priest. There was, however, also a special priesthood at Ugarit, with a 'chief of the priests' at its head. In the population lists discovered at Rās Shamrah, the priestly families appear as a separate class. In addition to these priests, there are also the q'dhešim, a word which is used in the Bible in association with sacred prostitution. The Ras Shamrah texts, however, do not suggest that the word was used in this sense – at Ugarit these q'dhešim were simply 'consecrated' persons. At a lower level, those responsible for cultic activities at Ugarit included cantors, door-keepers and a group of persons whose name corresponds to that of the n'thînîm or servants of the Temple at Jerusalem.[98]

These cultic texts throw very little light on the feelings which inspired those who belonged to the Canaanite religion. To know this, we should have to have at least some prayers composed by the believers themselves. The mythological poems tend to lead us astray. For example, they portray 'Anat massacring her enemies and 'plunging her knees into the blood of the

[95] G 2 = H 32; see A. Caquot, 'Un sacrifice expiatoire à Ras Shamra', RHPR, 42 (1962), pp. 201–211. To this text must be added the parallel text RS 17.100 A 17.000 B, published by A. Herdner, op. cit., pp. 134–136, Appendix I.

[96] G 3 = H 35 and the duplicate RS 18.56, published by A. Herdner, Syria 33 (1956), pp. 104–112 = Corpus des tablettes, pp. 136–138, Appendix II. See also B. A. Levine, 'Ugaritic Descriptive Rituals', JCS, 17 (1963), pp. 105–111.

[97] See especially T. H. Gaster, 'The Service of the Sanctuary. A Study in Hebrew Survivals', Mélanges Syriens offerts à M.R. Dussaud, II, Paris, 1939, pp. 577–582.

[98] B. A. Levine, 'The Netînîm', JBL, 82 (1963), pp. 206–212.

warriors, her thighs into the discharge from the wounds of the heroes'. They show us 'Ashtar, Baal's comic deputy, sitting on the throne, but 'his feet do not reach the footstool and his head does not reach the top of the seat'. They describe the sexual activity of the gods with intolerable crudeness and using words with double meanings. The busy traders and aristocratic army officers of Ugarit probably regarded them as 'tall stories', but the peasants must have been fascinated by these adventures of their gods and believed that the fertility of their crops and animals depended on these activities.

It is also not difficult to understand how seductive this violent and sensual religion must have seemed to the Israelites when they settled in Canaan. Did their lives not depend on the same forces of nature and did the performance of the same rites not guarantee their survival in the land of Canaan? The Canaanite religion was, however, based on a cyclical return of natural phenomena and could therefore not be reconciled with the religion of the Israelites, which was based on the personal interventions of their god in a linear, progressive movement of history, a god who had chosen them, saved them and led them to the land of Canaan.

The conflict between Yahweh and Baal began as soon as the Israelites entered Canaan.[99] The new religion could not accommodate the Canaanite myths, which provided only literary images for the celebration of the omnipotence of the one deity, Yahweh, and for the consecration to him of the trophies taken from the defeated gods of Canaan. Yahweh also took over the functions of these gods and the same rites with a new and different meaning could be adapted to the cult of Yahweh. There are many elements in the arrangement of Israel's feasts and sacrifices borrowed from the Canaanite religion, but they bear the imprint of inner conflict – that of Baal being fought with his own weapons.

Finally, it should be borne in mind that all the groups of foreigners, including non-Semitic people such as the Hurrians and the Philistines at a later stage, forgot their own religion very soon after their arrival in Canaan, In view of this, surely it is, from the human point of view, extraordinary that the struggle between Yahweh and Baal should have gone on for such a long time and that, in spite of many setbacks and a great deal of unfaithfulness on the part of the Israelites themselves, it should have ended with a victory for Yahwism.

---

[99] For this conflict, see G. Ostborn, *Yahweh and Baal. Studies in the Book of Hosea and Related Documents*, Lund, 1956; N. C. Habel, *Yahweh versus Baal. A Conflict of Religious Cultures*, New York, 1964; F. E. Eakin, 'Yahwism and Baalism Before the Exile', *JBL*, 84 (1965), pp. 407–414; W. F. Albright, *Yahweh and the Gods of Canaan*, London, 1968.

THE ORIGINS OF ISRAEL

INTRODUCTION

WE now have to try to place the origins of the people of Israel within this historical, ethnic and social context in the Ancient Near East during the second millennium B.C. Before we attempt to do this, however, we must ask whether it is legitimate or even possible for the historian to undertake such a task.

In the Bible, 'Israel'[1] is first and foremost the collective name of the twelve tribes regarded as the descendants of the twelve sons of Jacob. At the same time, however, 'Israel' is also the individual name given to Jacob, the ancestor common to those tribes (Gen. 32:29; 35:10). All the members of the twelve tribes were called 'sons of Israel', b'nê yiśrā'el, and formed the 'people of Israel', which, according to most modern historians, did not exist as such until the settlement in Canaan, when its history commenced.[2] For the Israelites themselves, however, the history of their people began with their 'father' Abraham.

There are two words in Hebrew which are usually translated as 'people' and 'nation', although this rendering is far from perfect, because the words 'am and gôy are very different in meaning from our modern words 'people' and 'nation'.[3] In the plural, the word 'am is used to mean close relatives on the father's side. Used collectively in the singular, it only rarely has this meaning and can usually be translated as 'people'. There is no reason to indicate these two uses by employing two different words, as is often done in lexicons and dictionaries, because the 'people' was thought of as an exten-

---

[1] L. Rost, *Israel bei den Propheten*, Stuttgart, 1937; G. A. Danell, *Studies in the Name Israel in the Old Testament*, Uppsala, 1946.

[2] From J. Wellhausen, *Israelitische und Jüdische Geschichte*, Berlin, 1894, 9th edn. 1958, to M. Noth, in his introduction to *The History of Israel*, London, 1958.

[3] L. Rost, 'Die Bezeichnungen für Land und Volk im Alten Testament', *Festschrift Otto Procksch*, Leipzig, 1934, pp. 125–148, especially pp. 137–147 = *Das kleine Credo und andere Studien zum Alten Testament*, Heidelberg, 1965, pp. 76–101; E. A. Speiser, ' "People" and "Nation" of Israel', *JBL*, 79 (1960), pp. 157–163 = *Oriental and Biblical Studies*, Philadelphia, 1967, pp. 160–170; A. Cody. 'When is the Chosen People called a gôy?', *VT*, 14 (1964), pp. 1–6.

sion of the family on the paternal side and as founded, like the family, on
ties of blood. When a man died and was buried in the family tomb, he was
'gathered to his people' or *'ammîm* (Gen 25:8, 17 etc.). If a man transgressed
against certain religious laws, on the other hand, he was 'outlawed from his
people' or *'ammîm* (Ex 30:33, 38 etc.). A priest made himself unclean by
going near the corpse of one of his *'ammîm* (Lev 21:1–2). Jeremiah left
Jerusalem for a sharing of land among his *'ammîm* (Jer 37:12). All Boaz' *'am*
knew that Ruth was a virtuous woman (Ruth 3:11) and Boaz asked all the
'am of Bethlehem to witness his marriage with her (Ruth 4:9). The
marriages between Jacob's clan and the Shechemites would have made 'one
'am' of the two groups (Gen 34:16). The movement from the meaning of
close relation to that of family, clan and people is imperceptible. When
Abraham left Haran with his wife, his nephew Lot and his entire
household, this group already constituted an *'am* and the Israelites were able
to begin the history of their 'people' at that point.

God did not promise that he would make Abraham a great *'am* or
'people', but that he would become a great *gôy* or 'nation' (Gen 12:2,
18:18). The same word is used in the promises made to Jacob (Gen 35:11;
46:3) and to Moses (Ex 32:10; Num 14:12). The fulfilment of these
promises is recalled in a profession of Israel's faith that the little group
which went down into Egypt became a *gôy*, a 'nation, great, mighty and
strong' (Deut 26:5). The same word, *gôy*, is often used to depict the other
'nations' in the world. It is usually applied to Israel especially in connection
with the idea of the 'promised land', first in the promises made to the
patriarchs (Gen 35:11–12) and then at the time of the conquest (Jos 3:17)
and elsewhere. The nation, *gôy*, was a territorial[4] and therefore a political
unit. The two kingdoms of Israel and Judah were two 'nations' which God
wished to unite as one 'nation' under one king (Ezek 37:22). Very rarely,
the word is applied to Israel in a religious context, but even then is still used
politically, in connection with Yahweh's kingship, Israel being the 'nation'
which is 'ruled' by Yahweh (Mic 4:7).In the case of foreign nations, the
two words 'nation' and 'king' (or 'kingdom') very often go together

---

[4] The word is found elsewhere in the Ancient Near East only in the Mari texts, in the
Akkadian word *ga'um* or *gawum*. The translation that was first suggested, by A. Finet, *Répertoire analytique des tomes I à V (Archives Royales de Mari XV)*, Paris, 1954, p. 200, was
'territory'. This, however, was abandoned later in favour of other translations. In the *Chicago
Dictionary*, V, 1965, it is translated as 'group' or 'troop' of workers and W. von Soden
suggests 'people' in his dictionary of 1965. Various scholars have suggested that it might, as a
rare word used in connection with nomads, have signified the sub-division of a tribe; see. J.
Bottéro, *Archives Royales de Mari*, VII, 1957, p. 224; J.–R. Kupper, *Les nomades en Mésopotamie
au temps des rois de Mari*, 1957, p. 20; D. O. Edzard, *ZA*, 56 (1964), p. 144. To this primarily
ethnic meaning of the word, however, can also be added the idea of a common habitat; see
A. Malamat, 'Aspects of Tribal Societies in Mari and Israel', *XVe Rencontre Assyriologique
·Internationale, Liège*, Paris, 1967, especially pp. 133–135.

(1 Kings 18:10; Jer 18:7, 9, etc.). When Israel asked for a king, it was to be like the other 'nations' (1 Sam 8:20).

As a 'nation', Israel was in fact very much like her neighbours and this was a decisive factor in her relationships with them, in her foreign policy, one might say. When the term 'people' is applied to Israel, it refers above all to the mutual relationships existing between the members of the community, which were, of course, based on blood ties, and to their relationships with God, whose 'chosen people' they were. The Israelites believed that God's choice of them had been expressed in the promises made to Abraham and that it had been manifested and achieved in their deliverance from slavery in Egypt, the revelation on Mount Sinai and the conquest of the Promised Land. These were the essential articles of their faith and the account of these events takes up more room in the Bible, from Genesis to the end of the book of Joshua, than the whole history of the 'nation' of Israel and of the two 'nations', Israel and Judah. This historical faith of Israel is an essential aspect of the historical study of comparative religion and is of equal importance to the historian as such, since it is his task to evaluate these traditions and to discover the origins of the people of Israel.

We must, however, ask ourselves two questions – first, whether this quest is at all possible, and secondly, what paths should we follow?[5] In our study of the origins of Israel, the only immediate literary source at our disposal is the Bible. The stories contained in the Old Testament were written down long after the events which they describe had taken place and we cannot at once dismiss the possibility that the authors might have used much earlier texts or reliable oral traditions. We have, however, to recognise that a very complex development, both oral and written, took place before the biblical narratives appeared in their existing form and that they were written in the historical perspective of an Israel which had been united and constituted as a people in Palestine and in the religious perspective of a fully developed form of Yahwism. Various traditions came together to form the traditions of the 'whole of Israel'. Certain additions were made and details were changed in order to accommodate elements of a more recent situation.[6] Finally, modifications were necessitated because narratives

[5] For these questions of method, see especially J. Bright, *Early Israel in Recent History Writing*, London, 1956; M. Noth, 'Der Beitrag der Archäologie zur Geschichte Israels', *Congress Volume, Oxford (SVT*, 7), 1960, pp. 262–282; J. A. Soggin, 'Ancient Biblical Tradition and Modern Archaeological Discoveries', *BibArch*, 23 (1960), pp. 95–100; R. de Vaux, 'The Hebrew Patriarchs and History', *The Bible and the Ancient Near East*, London, 1971, pp. 111–121; ibid., 'Method in the Study of Early Hebrew History', *The Bible in Modern Scholarship*, ed. J. P. Hyatt, Nashville and New York, 1965, pp. 15–29; ibid., 'On Right and Wrong Uses of Archaeology', *Near Eastern Archaeology in the Twentieth Century. Essays in Honour of Nelson Glueck*, ed. J. A. Sanders, Garden City, N.Y., 1970, pp. 64–80.
[6] See G. Wallis, 'Die Tradition von den drei Ahnvätern', *ZAW*, 81, (1969), pp. 18–40:

were recited in the sanctuaries of Israel and used in public worship. It is very difficult indeed to determine precisely what memories lurk behind these composite traditions and which of them are authentic. Study of the internal evidence provided by the biblical texts themselves would seem to lead us to a number of probable conclusions, but these have to be compared with the external, non-biblical evidence. The very many texts as well as the monuments and other objects that have been excavated in the Ancient Near East during the past fifty or so years have added enormously to our knowledge and have also made that knowledge much more complex. We now have abundant evidence of the movements of the different Near Eastern peoples, their struggles against each other, their internal social and political structures and their family, legal and religious practices during the second millennium B.C., which was the period when Israel had its origins. It is, of course, very difficult to interpret with certainty the evidence provided by monuments and other non-textual discoveries. It is also true that Israel is not mentioned in the non-biblical texts until the end of the thirteenth century B.C. Even so, this first allusion to Israel, on the stele of Mer-ne-Ptah, is ambiguous because it contains no explicit reference to the Hebrew patriarchs, the period spent in Egypt, or the conquest of Canaan. It is, moreover, doubtful whether any further light will be shed on this question by new texts. The positive result achieved by these new discoveries, however, is that many parallels have been established between the names and customs found in the Bible and those found in the Ancient Near East generally. These parallels and the many points of similarity between the history of Israel and that of the Near East as a whole that have been revealed by these archaeological finds have enabled historians to place the biblical traditions in their original context. They have also strengthened our confidence in the validity of those traditions.

These two sources of information, the Bible and the non-biblical Ancient Near Eastern texts, have, as far as possible, to be used in conjunction with each other and for mutual verification. Because of their own education, experience or personal inclination, some historians have concentrated their attention on a textual study of the Bible and are consequently more concerned with the difficulties raised by the text itself; they tend to underestimate its content. Other scholars have given more attention to the external context within which the biblical accounts are placed, and their tendency has been to overestimate the historical value of those narratives. A final judgement should, however, be based on a study of the positive contribution made by both kinds of evidence. Undoubtedly the best method to follow is to examine what the Bible says, using all the

---

J' collects together the traditions which concern David's Judaean kingdom, J fills them with a spirit of Israelite nationalism after the division of the two kingdoms and E adds certain theological themes to them, P finally deriving ritual forms from them.

available means of textual and literary criticism as well as the findings of historical research into the Old Testament tradition, at each stage bearing in mind the non-biblical evidence, both textual and non-textual. In this way, the historian should be able to form a balanced judgement and come to clear conclusions. This light thrown from outside on the internal evidence of the biblical texts may result in what has hitherto been regarded as merely possible being revealed as probable. Furthermore, the fact that these conclusions are in accordance with the history of the Near East generally may enable the historian using this method of research to outline the origins of Israel, although his 'history' will inevitably be incomplete and in many respects purely hypothetical. At the outset, however, he will be very conscious of the fact that a true 'history' of the origins of Israel lies far beyond his reach, because his sources are too few and too uncertain.

PART I

The Patriarchal Traditions

Chapter Six

THE PATRIARCHAL TRADITIONS IN GENESIS

THE historian's difficulties increase the further he goes back into the past, the most intractable problem being that of the first ancestors whom Israel claimed to possess, the patriarchs Abraham, Isaac and Jacob, whose 'history' is told in Gen 12–35. The history of Joseph, which occupies the whole of the rest of Genesis with the exception of Gen 38 and 49, belongs to the following period, that of Israel's stay in Egypt.

I. LITERARY ANALYSIS[1]

Despite the enormous amount of work that has been done during the past two centuries in the field of literary criticism, especially in connection with the Pentateuch in general and with Genesis in particular, the conclusions that have been reached are far from unanimous and the foundations on which this literary criticism has been based have been called into question again and again. The view that is still encountered more frequently than any other is based on the documentary hypothesis, according to which the Pentateuch can be traced back to three or four great sources – the Yahwistic source (J), the Elohistic source (E) and the priestly source (P). General agreement has been reached as to how, at least in broad outline, the text

---

[1] A full history of this aspect of biblical scholarship, an account of the most recent standpoints and a good bibliography will be found in H. Cazelles, 'Pentateuque', *DBS*, VII, 1964, col. 687–858; the text of this article has been revised and the bibliography brought up to date in the Italian translation, H. Cazelles and J. P. Bouhot, *Il Pentateuco*, Brescia, 1968. Recent expositions of the documentary theory, with variants, will be found in O. Eissfeldt, *Einleitung in das Alte Testament*,[3] Tübingen, 1964; English translation with an up to date bibliography, *The Old Testament: An Introduction*, Oxford, 1966; with special reference to Genesis, O. Eissfeldt, *Die Genesis der Genesis*,[2] Tübingen, 1961; S. Mowinckel, *Erwägungen zur Pentateuchquellenfrage*, Trondheim, 1964; E. Sellin and G. Fohrer, *Einleitung in das Alte Testament*,[10] Heidelberg, 1965, pp. 112–209.; English translation, G. Fohrer, *Introduction to the Old Testament*, London, 1970, pp. 103–195.

should be divided between these three sources. The smallest share in the compilation of the Pentateuch is attributed to P. The priestly writers, it is maintained, touched up and completed certain accounts and inserted the lists, the genealogies and the details of the births, deaths and ages of the patriarchs, thus providing a chronological framework for the narrative. According to this theory, only two long passages were written in full by the priestly authors. The first is Gen 17, which describes the covenant with Abraham, the promise of numerous descendants and of the land of Canaan, and the institution of circumcision. The second passage, Gen 23, describes how the cave of Machpelah was acquired for the tomb of the patriarchs. Most of the stories are regarded as a combination of J and E. The first evidence of Elohistic material is found in Gen 15, describing the covenant with Abraham and the promise of many descendants and of the land, a chapter which is, of course, parallel to Gen 17 (P). The literary composition of Gen 15 is, however, very complex[2] and to some extent all the other patriarchal narratives are characterised by the same difficulty, that of the combination of two sources. The Elohist's share is most clearly apparent in certain doublets: Abraham and Sarah in Egypt (Gen 12:10–13:1, J) and Abraham and Sarah at Gerar (Gen 20:1–18, E); Hagar and Ishmael in the wilderness (Gen 16:1–14, J)and Hagar and Ishmael at Abraham's house (Gen 21:8–21, E); Abraham and Abimelech (Gen 21:22–34, E) and Isaac and Abimelech (Gen 26:12–23, J). Elohistic material can also be found in short passages in Genesis which have no equivalent in J, for example, Jacob's building of an altar at Bethel (Gen 35:1–7) and the birth of Benjamin and the death of Rachel (Gen 35:16–20). Finally, there is general agreement among scholars that Gen 14, which describes Abraham's victory over the four kings and his meeting with Melchizedek, does not belong to any of these three sources.

Even granted the existence of these different sources, there are still very many questions which have to be asked about the inner unity and the nature of each of these sources and about the period at, and the environment in, which they originated. The only real way of finding a satisfactory answer to these questions is to study, together with Genesis, the other books of the Pentateuch in which material from these sources is also found. All that can be done here is to summarise the most probable conclusions and to apply them to the patriarchal narratives.

No really serious problem is posed by P, which was the work of priests of the Temple of Jerusalem and was edited at the end of the exile or soon after the return from exile. It is, however, possible that earlier traditions

[2] See H. Cazelles, 'Connexions et structure de Gen. XV', *RB*, 69 (1962), pp. 321–349; A. Caquot, 'L'alliance avec Abram (Genèse 15)', *Semitica*, 12 (1962), pp. 51–66; N. Lohfink, *Die Landverheissung als Eid. Eine Studie zu Gen. 15*, Stuttgart, 1967; R. E. Clements, *Abraham and David, Genesis 15 and Its Meaning for Israelite Tradition*, London, 1967.

were incorporated into P. On the other hand, frequent attempts have been made for some time now to distinguish an earlier source in the material regarded as J. The following narratives have been attributed to this earlier J source: the history of Sodom and the daughters of Lot (Gen 18–19), the birth of Jacob and Esau and the story of the lentil soup (Gen 25), Jacob's fight with God at Peniel (Gen 32) and the story of Judah and Tamar (Gen 38) which is included within the story of Joseph. Because it is so concerned with the south of Palestine and Transjordan, this source has been called Kenite or Seirite (= Edom). Because it contains no references to cult, it has been called the 'lay' source and because it is archaic and seldom mentions the sedentary life it has been called 'nomadic'. It may be a first attempt at a history, from man's origins till the entry into Canaan, and it is quite likely that it was written during the reign of David. It cannot be denied that the passages that have been ascribed to this early source have many distinctive features and many common resemblances, but there is no evidence to show that they form a continuous whole, nor is it possible to show that they ever existed as an independent written source. More probably they were special traditions collected by the Yahwist, who respected their particular form. It is also true to say that the proper sphere for the study of this early source is that of the history of traditions rather than that of literary criticism. Finally, it would seem that the Yahwist was a single author, a Judaean at the king's court probably during the reign of Solomon.

More important for the historian is the problem raised by the Elohistic source. From the literary point of view, it is indisputable that the elements attributed to the Elohist were inserted later into the Yahwistic material with which they became merged or which they sometimes completed. According to one very widespread opinion, these Elohistic elements are derived from an oral or written source which was formed and transmitted independently of J before becoming combined with it. There is less general agreement about the period and the environment in which this source originated, the predominant view being that it became established during the eighth century B.C., that it gathered together various traditions that were prevalent in the north and that it was connected with the prophetic movement.[3] From Abraham onwards, E runs parallel to J and, because it is independent of J, many scholars have concluded that the two sources, J and E, go back to a common oral or written source.[4] This common source contained the essential aspects of the story of the patriarchs, that is, the

[3] For a defence of the Elohist as an independent source with its own theology, see H. W. Wolff, 'Zur Thematik der elohistischen Fragmente im Pentateuch', *EvTh*, 29 (1969), pp. 59–72.

[4] This is M. Noth's 'foundation' in his *Überlieferungsgeschichte*, pp. 40–44, and E. A. Speiser's 'tradition' in *Genesis (Anchor Bible)*, 1964, pp. XXXVII ff.

genealogical succession from Abraham to Isaac and Jacob, the oppression and the freedom from slavery in Egypt, the revelation on Mount Sinai and the entry into the Promised Land. In other words, it included all the major themes of the Pentateuch. Since it is earlier than J, it represents a stage in tradition which is prior to the Israelite monarchy. The historian is therefore in a better position to judge the value of the patriarchal narratives than the late date at which they were edited would lead him to expect.

Certain scholars, however, do not accept the existence of an Elohistic source which ran parallel to J and was independent of it.[5] The distinction that has been made between J and E is, in many passages, in no sense striking and, in other passages the fragments attributed to E give the impression of being additions or corrections to the J text, reflecting loftier moral and religious ideas. According to these scholars, the existence of a parallel and independent source (E) cannot be proved and J was revised, completed and corrected orally in the first place and, in the second place, edited with the help of these traditional variants. If this theory is true, we cannot go back to a stage in tradition prior to J.

There are several convincing arguments in favour of this second theory. It has to be admitted that there are many uncertainties in the distribution between two 'sources' of those texts which are regarded as common to both J and E and it should not be forgotten that, taken as a whole, the classical documentary theory is still hypothetical.[6] All the same, the unvarying character of the words used and the ideas expressed in the elements ascribed to E and the fact that they are parallel to those occurring in J certainly tip the balance in favour of the documentary hypothesis. On the other hand, we may accept this fully and still agree that the earlier date suggested for J is correct and that there was a tradition common to and prior to both J and E. Despite this, however, at least in our literary criticism of the Pentateuch, we cannot go back earlier than the period when the tribes, once settled in Canaan, regarded themselves as united by ties of blood and by a common faith. They were, they believed, a single people descended from Abraham. They worshipped one God, who was the same as the God of Abraham, Isaac and Jacob. They inhabited one country, which was the land promised to Abraham, Isaac and Jacob. This threefold unity is proclaimed throughout the whole of the Pentateuch. How did the authors of these books arrive at this conviction and what is the real value of this unified tradition? To answer these questions it is necessary to leave the sphere of literary criticism and enter that of the history of traditions.

[5] P. Volz and W. Rudolph, Der Elohist als Erzähler. Ein Irrweg der Pentateuchkritik? (BZAW, 63), 1933. The same thesis was taken up by S. Mowinckel, Erwägungen zur Pentateuchquellenfrage, op. cit., who has supported it with fresh arguments.

[6] The most respected propounder of this theory today, O. Eissfeldt, has himself said, in his Introduction, op. cit., p. 240, that the whole criticism of the Pentateuch is no more than a

II. The Formation of Tradition[7]

Whether or not we accept the existence of the Elohist, we cannot dispute the fact that the Yahwist made use of an already formed tradition. The only places in which this tradition could have been found or transmitted were the sanctuaries where the tribes worshipped the same God together. The basic article of their faith was that this God had delivered their ancestors from the pharaoh's oppression and had led them into Canaan. Memories of the exodus from Egypt combined with memories of the possession of the land to form part of this primitive tradition, which also included – contrary to the opinion of certain scholars[8] – memories of Sinai, since this encounter with God was at the very beginning of their common faith. On the other hand, we are bound to ask whether the patriarchs were not integrated into this tradition at a later stage, because there is a remarkable break between Genesis and Exodus, that is, between the end of the story of the patriarchs and the beginning of the story of the exodus from Egypt. No memory has been preserved of the intervening period and the editors of the Pentateuch did not try to fill in that gap. It is, of course, possible to quote the confession of faith of Deut 26:5–10 in this context, the 'little creed' of Israel which begins with the words 'My father was a wandering Aramaean . . .' and goes on to recall the deliverance from Egypt and the entry into the land of Canaan. This Israelite creed is regarded as very old and it has been suggested that it links the conquest of the land with the patriarchs.[9] More precisely, however, this conquest is linked in the text with the figure of Jacob, the 'Aramaean' referred to in Deut 26:5 – Jacob was also known as Israel and he was the father of all the *b'nê yiśra'el*, the sons of Israel.[10] Ultimately, the tradition goes back to Isaac and then to Abraham.[11] It is important in this context, however, to remember that according to the literary criticism of Deut 26:5–10, only the

hypothesis, although this is based on 'very significant arguments'.

[7] G. von Rad, *Das formgeschichtliche Problem des Hexateuch*, Stuttgart, 1938 = *Gesammelte Studien*, Munich, 1958, pp. 9–86; M. Noth, *Überlieferungsgeschichte des Pentateuch*, Stuttgart, 1948, 2nd. edn., unaltered, 1960; A. Jepsen, 'Zur Überlieferungsgeschichte der Vätergestalten', *Festschrift Alt*, Leipzig, 1953, pp. 139–155; C. Westermann, 'Arten der Erzählung in der Genesis', *Forschung am Alten Testament*, Munich, 1964, pp. 9–91; R. Kilian, *Die vorpriestlichen Abrahamsüberlieferungen, literarkritisch und traditionsgeschichtlich untersucht*, Bonn, 1966; G. Wallis, 'Die Tradition von den drei Ahnvätern', *ZAW*, 81 (1969), pp. 18–40,

[8] See Part II, Chap. 14, II, pp. 393–452.

[9] See especially G. von Rad, *Das formgeschichtliche Problem, op. cit.*, pp. 2–7, 50–51 = *Gesammelte Studien*, pp. 11–16, 62–64; *ibid., Theologie des Alten Testaments*, I, Munich, 1957, pp. 127–128.

[10] M. Noth, *Überlieferungsgeschichte, op. cit.*, p. 60 ff.

[11] *ibid.*, p. 112 ff.

first words of verse 5, referring to an anonymous ancestor to whom a land is given, and verse 10, are in fact primitive. The rest of the passage is the work of a Deuteronomic editor. We cannot, simply on the basis of this text, identify this ancestor with Jacob, nor can we regard his connection with the events in Egypt as original.[12]

In the Pentateuch in its present form, the story of the patriarchs is linked to the stories of the Exodus and the conquest of the Promised Land by the theme of the promise.[13] In other words, the settlement of the Israelites in Canaan is the fulfilment of the promises made to their early ancestors that they would have many descendants and a land. This theme also unites the various patriarchal narratives, which are set within a framework of the announcement made to Abraham: 'It is to your descendants that I will give this land' (Gen 12:7), and Joseph's last words: 'God will be sure to remember you kindly and take you back from this country to the land that he promised on oath to Abraham, Isaac and Jacob' (Gen 50:24). This link presupposes that the end, that is, the existence of Israel as a people settled in Canaan, was known and that the idea of a history of salvation beginning with Abraham and ending with the conquest of Canaan was already firmly established. It is clearly of secondary literary importance in some, though by no means all, texts in Genesis.[14] It was known by the Yahwist and had already been established in the tradition that he used. The theme of the promise did not originate with the tradition used by the Yahwist. On the contrary, it was received along with other individual traditional elements and transformed by that tradition. The narratives of the promises must, in their earliest form, have included the fulfilment of those promises. The promise of posterity must, for example, have been followed by the birth of a son, as in Gen 18, and the promise of land was certainly followed by an account of the taking of that land – this is clear in Gen 12:7; 13:15; 28:13. In its final form, this link between the promise and its fulfilment is extended to include the period spent in Egypt, the exodus and the conquest. It was explained that this long delay in the fulfilment of the promise had already

---

[12] L. Rost, 'Das kleine geschichtliche Credo', Das kleine Credo und andere Studien sum Alten Testament, Heidelberg, 1965, pp. 11–25; see also M. A. Beek, 'Das Problem des aramäischen Stammvaters', OTS, 8 (1950), pp. 193–212 and especially p. 207 ff.

[13] It is not possible to go into this question in detail here. See G. von Rad, 'Verheissenes Land und Jahwes Land im Hexateuch', ZDPV, 66 (1943), pp. 191–204 = Gesammelte Studien, pp. 87–100; ibid., Theologie des Alten Testaments, I, pp. 169–175; M. Noth, Überlieferungsgeschichte, op. cit., pp. 58–62; W. Zimmerli, 'Verheissung und Erfüllung', EvTh, 12 (1952–1953), pp. 34–59 = Probleme alttestamentlicher Hermeneutik, ed. C. Westermann, Munich, 1960, pp. 69–101; J. Hoftijzer, Die Verheissungen an die drei Erzväter, Leiden, 1956; C. Westermann, 'Arten der Erzählung', op. cit., pp. 11–34; N. Lohfink, Die Landverheissung als Eid, op. cit. (note 2 above); I. Blythyn, 'The Patriarchs and the Promise', Scottish Journal of Theology, 21 (1968), pp. 56–73.

[14] Unlike J. Hoftijzer, who gives a late date to the promises made to the patriarchs, namely under the monarchy or even during the exile.

been announced by God to Abraham (Gen 15:13–16).[15] Later, and in contrast to the early texts, the priestly editors stressed that the patriarchs had been strangers who had settled in Canaan (Gen 17:8; 23:4; 36:7; 38:1).

It is possible to reconstruct the stages by which this tradition became the common property of the whole of Israel, but the result is purely conjectural. Each group forming part of the people of Israel had its own special traditions and above all its own ancestor, whose story was told and who was remembered in the group's cult of the 'god of the father'.[16] Several of these groups later became united and three leading 'patriarchal' figures emerged from this early multiplicity of ancestors – Abraham, Isaac and Jacob. The bonds formed between these enlarged groups were then expressed as a genealogy which showed all the descendants of Abraham, through Isaac and Jacob-Israel, to be the 'sons of Israel'. This prehistory is evident in the many different traditions referring to each patriarch.

The great cycle of traditions around Abraham (Gen 12–25:18) and the cycle of Jacob traditions (Gen 25:19–34) spring at once to mind, but it is more difficult to distinguish a cycle of Isaac traditions. The story of Isaac is in the first place included within the story of his father Abraham (Gen 21; 22; 24) and secondarily in that of his sons Jacob and Esau (Gen 25:19–28; 27; 28:1–9; 35:27–29). It is only in Gen 26 that Isaac is the central figure, yet even here the stories are only about his relationships with the people of Gerar and are all duplicated in the story of Abraham: the testing of Rebekah (Gen 26:1–16; cf. Gen 20:2–18), the matter of the wells (Gen 26:15–25; cf. Gen 21:25–31) and the alliance with Abimelech (Gen 26: 26–33; cf. Gen 21:22–32). These separate passages may possibly be remnants of an independent and earlier Isaac cycle, the various elements of which may have been integrated into, or duplicated in, the story of Abraham once a genealogical connection had been established between Abraham and Isaac and the latter had become the link joining Abraham to Jacob.[17] The geographical links, however, are different – the Abraham tradition is above all established at Hebron and Mamre, whereas the tradition of Isaac is very firmly attached to Beersheba and the neighbouring well of Lahai Roi.

It is also possible that there never was an Isaac cycle. After all, Gen 12–25 form what is essentially a family story, the main interest being the question of posterity, which is what justifies the great emphasis on the women. Sarah and Hagar play almost as important a part as Abraham and more space is devoted to Rebekah than to Isaac. The theme of the promise of descendants, which occurs only generally in the Jacob cycle and as a reminder of the promises made to Abraham, is of primary importance in the

[15] Usually attributed to E.
[16] See below, Chap. 10, 'The Religion of the Patriarchs', p. 267.
[17] Noth, *Überlieferungsgeschichte, op. cit.*, p. 122 ff.

Abraham cycle. The announcement of Isaac's birth (Gen 18:1–15) forms the central story in the cycle. The way is prepared for this by references in the text to two important facts, first, that Abraham is without children (Gen 15:2–3) and secondly, that Sarah is barren (Gen 16:1), both statements being accompanied by a promise of posterity. The central story is also followed by that of the birth of Isaac (Gen 21:1–7). The story of Hagar and Ishmael (Gen 16, J), which has to be considered in conjunction with the Elohist's doublet (Gen 21:8–20), both narratives containing a promise of posterity (Gen 16:10; 21:13), is connected with the statement that Sarah is barren and strengthens the unity of this group of stories. The story of Isaac's marriage (Gen 24) may be regarded as the normal conclusion to this group of narratives. In this concluding story, the continued existence of the race, which is the main theme in this cycle, is assured and Abraham can die in peace (Gen 24:1; 25:11, J). Very little remains in this Abraham cycle if everything that has to do with Isaac is removed from it.[18] A cycle of Abraham and Isaac is in fact the earliest traditional body of narratives to which we can go back and it would probably be futile to try to go back any further in history. The events attributed to Isaac in Gen 26 may therefore be regarded not as remnants of an independent cycle of stories, but rather as an attempt to enrich the figure of Isaac by borrowing from the Abraham cycle and to strengthen the already established link between the cycles of Abraham and of Jacob. Whatever may be the case here, however, the fact remains that the traditions connected with Abraham and Isaac are all situated in the south of Palestine, in the Negeb and at Hebron and Mamre, Beersheba and the well of Lahai Roi and at Gerar, and that they clearly have their origin in groups living in the south.

These traditions are also connected with another story of a different origin, that of Lot.[19] The germinal idea of this story is to be found in a popular tradition concerning a natural disaster which occurred to the south and south-west of the Dead Sea (Gen 19). It is quite possible that the memory of a geological subsidence which took place in historical times is preserved in the tradition of Lot, but its literary *genre* is certainly much more closely related to that of the flood myths than to that of the patriarchal accounts. Just as the flood was explained as a punishment for man's sins, so too was the destruction of Sodom and Gomorrah regarded as a punishment for the perversity of the inhabitants (see, for example, Gen 13:13; 18: 16–32). It is clearly an aetiological account, in certain details at least if not as a whole. Examples of this are the explanation of the name Zoar (Gen

---

[18] Noth comes to the same conclusion. *Überlieferungsgeschichte, op. cit.*, p. 120 ff.

[19] All the explanations that have been suggested concerning the way in which this tradition may be linked to that of Abraham are purely hypothetical; the latest of these hypotheses are those of R. Kilian, 'Zur Überlieferungsgeschichte Lots', *VZ*, n.F.14 (1970), pp. 23–37.

19:10–22) and Lot's wife turned into a pillar of salt (Gen 19:26). Another similarly aetiological account, this time of the origin of the Moabites and the Ammonites (Gen 19:30–38) is added to the story of the destruction of Sodom. They are clearly traditions which originated in Transjordan and which were incorporated into the story of Abraham – Lot was Abraham's nephew (Gen 12:5), Abraham and Lot shared the land between them (Gen 13) and God saved Lot from the disaster that destroyed Sodom because of Abraham (Gen 19:29). There is no parallel to the story of Lot in the Elohistic material of Genesis, but this does not necessarily mean that it was the Yahwist who connected it with Abraham. The link may be even earlier; in other words, it may point to the fact that the Israelites were originally related to their 'cousins' in Transjordania.[20] The purely family interest in the story of Abraham was in this way extended to include relationships between different peoples, so that the scope of the story went beyond Palestine itself.

We must now consider the more complicated Jacob traditions.[21] There are four main cycles of stories which intersect at certain points: 1) Jacob and Esau-Edom; 2) Jacob and Laban; 3) Jacob at Shechem and Bethel and 4) Jacob-Israel. Behind this corpus of stories, there is clearly a pluriform tradition, the development of which is very difficult to reconstruct.

1) The story of Jacob and Esau (Gen 25:19–34; 27; 32–33) is, of course, also a family story, like the story of Abraham and Isaac. It is, however, different from that of Abraham and Isaac in that the centre of interest is not the descent from father to son but the relationships between two rival brothers. The twins fought with each other even when they were in their mother's womb (Gen 25:22). The name Jacob means 'supplanter' (Gen 27:36; cf. Hos 12:4). Jacob in fact deprived his brother of his birthright as the first-born son (Gen 25:29–34) and of his father's blessing (Gen 27:1–40). If Jacob pretended to be reconciled to Esau, it was only in order to deceive him better (Gen 32:4–22; 33:1–17). Jacob was a cunning man and his mother's favourite, whereas Esau was stupid and loved by his father. The strictly family interest in the cycle of stories, however, is transcended in that Jacob and Esau represent two social types of the period. Jacob is a peace-loving herdsman who succeeds not by force but by skill and intelligence, whereas Esau is a nomad, living from hunting and pillage (Gen 25:27; 27:39–40). What is most important is that, although the nomadic hunter was the first inhabitant, he had to give way to the herdsman.[22]

[20] On the other hand, the link between Lot and the campaign of the four great kings (Gen 14) is, like the whole of the chapter, of late date; see Chapter 7, V, below, pp. 216–233.

[21] G. Wallis, 'Die Jacobtradition und Geschichte', Geschichte und Überlieferung, Stuttgart, 1968, pp. 13–44.

[22] There are variants of this sociological theme in the stories of Isaac and Ishmael and of Cain and Abel.

This story of two rival brothers has in this case been modified by the addition of another element, the fact that Esau was at the same time Edom, the ancestor of the Edomites. Originally, however, the two figures were not the same.[23] The district of Mahanaim and Peniel, where Jacob met Esau, cannot be correct if Esau was Edom, which was much farther south.[24] The explanation of the name given to Esau, Edom the 'red' one, because of the 'red' soup that he ate (Gen 25:30) is of secondary importance in the story of the birthright which referred to Esau. Similarly, one would expect to find the name Edom, an inhabitant of the land of Seir, not the name Esau, following the description of the newborn child who was 'red, 'adh'môni, as though he were completely wrapped in a hairy cloak, śe'âr' (Gen 25:25). The account of the birth of the twins cannot be understood if it refers to the birth of Jacob and Edom. What is more, the oracle accompanying this account (Gen 25:23, J) does not apply to two brothers – it refers to the two peoples descended from them. The same is true of the blessings (Gen 27:27–29 and 39) – Jacob was to receive 'the richness of the earth' and Esau was to be excluded from this gift. This points to something beyond the simple rivalry between the herdsman and the hunter in the early story of Jacob and Esau. It refers in fact to the contrast between the fertile land of Palestine where the Israelites lived and the mountainous, desert region of Transjordania inhabited by the Edomites. These two passages proclaim that the older brother will serve the younger brother. David made Edom Israel's subject and this continued for part of Solomon's reign. It was during this period that the story of Jacob and Esau-Edom was given its definitive form and it is possible, though by no means certain, that this combination was the work of the Yahwist himself.

2) The story of Jacob and Laban (Gen 29–31) was originally independent of the story of Jacob and Esau. It is also a composite narrative. In the first place, it is a family story, describing the period which Jacob spent with his uncle and his marriage with Laban's two daughters, his wealth and his flight. This story has to be separated from the account of the birth of Jacob's sons (Gen 29:31–30:24), which forms part of a later phase in this tradition, since it presupposes two facts, namely that Jacob and Israel were one and the same and that the twelve tribes were established as a system. This account is followed by the story of the treaty between Jacob and Laban (Gen 31:43–54), which is presented both as a family agreement with the purpose of safeguarding the position of Laban's daughters and thus continuing the previous narrative (Gen 31:50) and also as a political pact

---

[23] V. Maag, 'Jacob-Esau-Edom', TZ, 13 (1957), pp. 418–429; G. Wallis, 'Die Tradition von den drei Ahnvätern', ZAW, 81 (1969), pp. 18–40, especially pp. 20–22, 36–37.

[24] The problem of the precise location of Seir, where Esau lived, still remains; see J. R. Bartlett's rather unconvincing article, 'The Land of Seir and the Brotherhood of Edom', JTS, n.s.20 (1969), pp. 1–20.

establishing the frontier between Jacob and Laban (Gen 31–52).[25] Clearly, this was a treaty, not between two individuals, but between two peoples, the Israelites or their ancestors and the Aramaeans.[26] Galeed, the 'cairn of witness' marking the frontier, is not Ramoth-Gilead, which was a bone of contention between the Israelites and the Aramaeans in the ninth century B.C. According to the context, it was obviously the Gilead south of the Jabbok.[27] The story therefore describes a historical situation preceding the monarchy. The memory preserved here may perhaps date back to the period of the conquest after the exodus, but we cannot *a priori* exclude the possibility of its going back to a first settlement in the patriarchal period.[28]

3) A third group of stories connects Jacob with the sanctuaries at Shechem and Bethel. There is no mention of Esau or of Laban in these accounts, in which we are told of Jacob dreaming and erecting a monument, a *massebheh*, at Bethel (Gen 28:10–22, JE), setting up an altar and a stele, again at Bethel (Gen 35:7–14, E) and buying a field and erecting an altar at Shechem (Gen 33:19–20, E). The two sanctuaries are brought together in a cultic passage (Gen 35:2–4, E), in which Jacob's family buries the images of the foreign gods under the oak tree near Shechem and goes on a pilgrimage to Bethel to erect an altar there.[29] Another story of quite a different kind is connected with Shechem (Gen 34, J),[30] a narrative in which Jacob's part is minimal and all the action is borne by his sons Simeon and Levi, who were no more than children in the preceding chapter (Gen 33:13–14). Their sister Dinah, who figures in no other story, had been seduced by Shechem, the son of the prince of the town. A marriage alliance might have been concluded, resulting in peace in the land between Jacob's family and the Shechemites, but Simeon and Levi treacherously murdered the inhabitants of Shechem and Jacob's family had to leave the region. It is possible that Simeon and Levi were introduced at a later stage into a narrative which previously only dealt with the 'sons of Jacob', but we may be sure that it is a collective story, preserving the memory of a fruitless adventure carried out by the

---

[25] There is no general agreement among scholars about the division in this passage between J and E.

[26] Laban is called the 'Aramaean' twice in this passage, verses 20 and 24. According to the gloss, verse 47, Laban gave the frontier an Aramaean name, while Jacob gave it a Hebrew name.

[27] R. de Vaux, *RB*, 50 (1941), pp. 29–33 = *Bible et Orient*, pp. 127–134; M. Noth, *ZDPV*, 75 (1959), pp. 41–42.

[28] See below, p. 573.

[29] A. Alt, 'Die Wallfahrt von Sichem nach Bethel', *In piam memoriam A. von Bulmerincq*, Riga, 1938, pp. 218–230 = *Kleine Schriften*, I, pp. 79–88.

[30] For the history of traditions mentioned in this chapter, see especially E. Nielsen, *Schechem, A Traditio–Historical Investigation*, Copenhagen, 1955, pp. 240–264; S. Lehming, 'Zur Überlieferungsgeschichte von Gen 34', *ZAW*, 70 (1958), pp. 228–250; A. de Pury, 'Genèse xxxiv et l'histoire', *RB*, 76 (1969), pp. 5–49. The results are, however, uncertain; see below, p. 533.

Simeonites and the Levites or by other proto-Israelite groups with the aim of settling in central Palestine. This event precedes the settlement of the 'house of Joseph', Ephraim-Manasseh, in the region of Shechem.

4) In Gen 32:29 and 35:10, Jacob's name is changed to Israel and, in Gen 33:20, Jacob erects an altar at Shechem to 'El, God of Israel'. These are the first references in the Bible to Israel and they are often interpreted as taking the collective name of the tribes believed to have descended from a common ancestor back to that single ancestor. 'Israel', however, has the form of a personal name and it certainly seems to have been in the first place the name of the ancestor of a special group with which the group of Jacob became united.[31] In fact, the change of name and the rather clumsy etymological explanation of the name Israel seem to be of secondary importance in the account of Jacob's struggle with the mysterious being at the ford of the Jabbok (Gen 32:23–33). The account itself goes back to a very old legend adopted by the Jacob cycle, in which it interrupts the story of the meeting with Esau. In the second reference (Gen 35:10), the change of the name Jacob into Israel is linked with an appearance of God at Bethel (Gen 35:9–13). This passage has, correctly, been attributed to P, but it is quite possible that verse 10 is a very early element coming from the same Elohistic source from which the whole of Gen 35:1–8 and 14–20 comes. The Elohist reports the 'pilgrimage' from Shechem to Bethel and the passage referring to the building of the altar to El, God of Israel, at Shechem (Gen 33:19–20) may also be attributed to the same source.[32] The memory of Israel and of its connections with Jacob in the region of Shechem and Bethel would in this way have been preserved in the Elohistic tradition. This memory cannot be found explicitly in the Yahwistic tradition, but it was known to the Yahwist, because he associated Jacob closely with Bethel and Shechem (Gen 28:13–16; 34) and he gives the name Israel to Jacob from Gen 35:21–22 onwards and in the story of Joseph. This tradition is connected with the cult of El (the altar of El, God of Israel, and the name of Bethel).

Geographically, the traditions concerning Jacob are divided into two groups. Those about Jacob and Esau and about the treaty with Laban[33] have their situation in a small part of Transjordania, primitive Gilead and the lower course of the Jabbok, Peniel, Mahanaim and Succoth. It is possibly in this district that one tradition situated a tomb of Jacob in Transjordania (Gen 50:10). The traditions concerning Jacob at Shechem and Bethel and concerning Jacob-Israel are situated in central Palestine. The

---

[31] O. Eissfeldt, *OLZ*, 58 (1963), col. 331; H. Seebass, *Der Erzvater Israel*, Berlin, 1966; A. de Pury, *op. cit.* (note 30). This question is discussed again below, pp. 648–649.

[32] This is the view of Noth, Speiser and others, but Eissfeldt attributes these verses partly to his source L (pre-Yahwistic).

[33] For Jacob and Laban in Upper Mesopotamia, see below, pp. 176–177.

Transjordanian tradition is very early and probably has a Reubenite origin.[34] Reuben was regarded as Jacob's first-born and, according to Num 32:1, the tribe settled in Transjordania and more precisely in Gilead. The link between this Transjordanian tradition and the central Palestine tradition was no doubt established by the movement of Reubenite elements to the west of the Jordan, where there was a 'Stone of Bohan son of Reuben' (Jos 15:6; 18:17) and where Reuben committed incest at Migdal-eder, which cannot be located precisely, but which was certainly to the south of Bethel (Gen 35:21–22). This hypothesis about the movement of the Jacobite tradition in fact joins the biblical story of the movement of Jacob from Peniel to Succoth and Shechem to Bethel (Gen 33:17–20; 35:1–4).

This connection was, however, possible only because there was already an early tradition concerning Jacob west of the Jordan and the explanation given is, of course, different from the one previously given.[35] The traditions concerning Jacob probably originated in central Palestine at Shechem, after which they were taken into Transjordania and enriched by the house of Joseph, which had the sanctuaries at Shechem and Bethel, although Ephraim also had connections with the land of Gilead (Judges 12:4),[36] and Machir-Manasseh had been established both to the north of Ephraim in Palestine and to the north of Gilead in Transjordania. All the same, this explanation does not account for the forcefulness of the Transjordanian traditions and would, if it were accepted, delay their emergence until after the 'colonial' expansion of the house of Joseph beyond the Jordan.

Even if this solution to the problem is rejected, it does not mean that there is no connection between the Jacob tradition and the house of Joseph – all that it means is that the connection is different and earlier. We shall be coming back to this difficult question concerning the house of Joseph and its formation in a later chapter.[37] What can be said here is that the story of Joseph begins in the neighbourhood of Shechem (Gen 37) where there was an altar to 'El, God of Israel' and it is possible to reconstruct traces of a tradition, according to which Joseph was the first-born of Rachel and Israel (but not of Jacob). Jacob's adoption of Joseph's sons (Gen 48) marks the merging of this group of Israel with the group of Jacob. This merging, which is denoted by the double name Jacob-Israel, took place only when the tribes settled.

Shared memories going back to the remote past, however, facilitated and prepared the way for this merging together of the two groups. At the time

[34] A. Jepsen, 'Zur Überlieferungsgeschichte der Vätergestalten', Festschrift Alt, Leipzig, 1953, pp. 146–147.
[35] M. Noth, Überlieferungsgeschichte, op. cit., pp. 86–111.
[36] However these connections may be explained, see M. Noth, op. cit., p. 98; H. Seebass, Der Erzvater Israel, op. cit., p. 46. Is it simply by chance, as Noth suggests, Geschichte, op. cit., p. 60, that there was a forest of Ephraim south of the Jabbok (2 Sam 18:6)?
[37] See below, pp. 642–653.

of the patriarchs, in the region of Shechem where Israel first lived, there were also clans of the house of Jacob (Gen 34) who were of the same stock and who practised the same cult of El, associated with the God of the father at Shechem and Bethel. The history of these neighbouring groups was at least partly the same. Just as Simeon and Levi emigrated towards the south, so too was Joseph the Israelite taken into Egypt, to which he drew his 'brothers', and it is probable that certain contacts were always maintained. A little light can be thrown on this obscure early history if the status of the 'tribes' of Israel at this time is recognised. Above all, they had not become separated into individual tribes with distinct names and their relationships with each other were not at this time stable. This happened only after they had become settled. Until then, they were only groups of people vaguely related by blood, a common abode and similar social and religious practices. It is also worth noting in this context that the three sons of Leah, Reuben, Simeon and Levi, head the canonical list of the 'sons of Jacob'. They were the bearers of the earliest traditions concerning Jacob – Reuben in Transjordania and Simeon and Levi in the region of Shechem. Although these groups began by being powerful, however, Reuben and Simeon were quickly absorbed by others and Levi soon changed its status. In any case, the traditions that they handed down must have been extremely early.

However much uncertainty there may be regarding this question, we may be quite sure that the geographical area in which the cycle of Jacob stories is set, that of central Palestine and central Transjordania, is quite different from that in which the Abraham cycle takes place, namely southern Palestine in the case of Abraham and Isaac and southern Transjordan in the case of Abraham and Lot. These two sets of traditions are also different in form and in their central theme. The Abraham cycle is above all the story of a family and its continuity, the ethnological element, that of the ancestor who personifies the group which has descended from him being no more than secondary and appearing only in the figure of Ishmael and in the story of Lot's daughters. In the Jacob cycle, the family element is still present, the relationships in this case being between brothers and not, as in the Abraham cycle, between a father and sons, but the individuals also – or perhaps only – represent groups. For instance, the rivalry between Jacob and Esau is representative of the rivalry between herdsmen and hunters or, in the blessings in Gen 28, between peasants and nomads. Jacob and Edom are the Israelites and the Edomites. The treaty with Laban involves the Israelites and the Aramaeans. Simeon and Levi personify two groups of people and, generally speaking, what is said about the twelve sons of Jacob and even about their birth can be explained only in terms of the twelve tribes of Israel. On the other hand, the central theme is not the same. The theme of the Abraham cycle is the promise, whereas that of the Jacob cycle is the blessing. After wrestling with God, Jacob is given, not a promise but a blessing (Gen 32:27–30). It is this blessing from God which explains his superhuman strength (Gen 32:28) and his success in his encounters with Esau and Laban. The theme of the blessing is also repeated in different forms in this cycle. Jacob receives his father's blessing (Gen 27), Laban is blessed because of Jacob (Gen 30:27, 30) and the dying Jacob blesses Joseph's two sons (Gen 48).

These differences of origin and conception imply that the Abraham-Isaac cycle and the Jacob cycle were in the first place independent of each other. The question then arises where and when they came together. This merging must have taken place in the south, where the traditions of Abraham and Isaac had become firmly rooted, where groups of Jacob's family, Simeon and Levi, had emigrated at a very early stage and where, according to the Bible itself, Jacob went when he left Bethel. To be more precise, Isaac forms the connection between Abraham and Jacob and the figure of Isaac is especially closely linked with Beersheba. It is true, of course, that the priestly account gives, not Beersheba, but Mamre-Hebron as the place where Jacob met Isaac and where Isaac died and was buried (Gen 35:27–29). The priestly source is, however, the only one which gives this information and which also brings the three dead patriarchs together in the cave of Machpelah (Gen 23; 25:9–10; 49:29–32; 50:12–13), despite the fact that the Yahwist and the Elohist have nothing to say about the place where Abraham and Isaac died and despite the tradition of a tomb of Jacob in Transjordania (Gen 50:10–11). It is, however, from Beersheba that Jacob set out for Egypt (Gen 46:5) and it is also at Beersheba that a cultic link was established between Jacob and Isaac – in the sanctuary set up by Isaac (Gen 26:23–25), Jacob has a vision of El, the God of his father (Gen 46:2–4). What is remarkable is that the tribes of central Palestine, with whom the traditions concerning Jacob rested, preserved such a long connection with the sanctuary at Beersheba, whereas the same sanctuary seems to have been neglected in Judah. For example, Samuel's sons were judges at Beersheba (1 Sam 8:2), Elijah passed through Beersheba when he was fleeing to Horeb (1 Kings 19:3) and, according to Amos, the Israelites were still going on pilgrimage to Beersheba in the eighth century (Amos 5:5) and swore by the deity of Beersheba (Amos 8:14). At the same time as this cult at Beersheba, again according to Amos, the memory of Isaac, which had been lost in Judah, was still more alive in the north than the memory of Abraham – the sanctuaries of Israel were called the high places of Isaac (Amos 7:9) and Israel was the house of Isaac (Amos 7:16).

When we consider the period during which the Abraham-Isaac traditions and those concerning Jacob began to merge together, it is only with great difficulty that we can accept the establishment of equally firm links between Beersheba and the northern groups after Judah became a barrier between the two regions. We are therefore bound to conclude that these links go back to a time before the period of the conquest and similarly that the merging together of the traditions dates back to the same period. With its wells and its sanctuary and its function as the gateway to the desert and the junction of several caravan routes, Beersheba was the place where many nomadic and semi-nomadic groups converged and therefore where they could share their traditions. Since Beersheba was also on the way to Egypt and above all since it was from Beersheba that Jacob and his sons set off for Egypt according to Gen 46:5, we may go even further and say that the ancestors of the Israelites who went down into Egypt – whoever they may have been – were quite possibly already known and may also have taken with them an embryonic tradition including the three patriarchs, Abraham, Isaac and Jacob.

One question has been deliberately kept until now. It is this. All the traditions say that the patriarchs were not among the primitive inhabitants of Canaan. According to the Yahwist, Abraham left 'his country, his family and his father's house' to go to Canaan (Gen 12:1–5) and it was in 'his own land' and among 'his own kinsfolk' that he looked for a wife for Isaac (Gen 24:4). The country to which Abraham sent his servant on this quest was Aram Naharaim and the town which the servant visited was Nahor's town (Gen 24:10), where Laban, Rebekah's brother, lived (Gen 24:29). Rebekah sent Jacob to Haran, where Laban was living, to escape from Esau (Gen 27:43). Jacob arrived at Haran and was welcomed there by Laban (Gen 28:10; 29:4). He lived for a long time at Haran and married Laban's two daughters, Rachel and Leah. When he fled from Haran, he crossed the river (Gen 31:21, JE), in other words, the Euphrates, which means that he was still in Upper Mesopotamia. His journey took him into Gilead, where the Transjordanian tradition that we have been considering began. The priestly source reinforces this tradition and makes it explicit. Abraham and Lot left Haran (Gen 12:4–5). The region in which Abraham's family lived, to which Jacob went to visit Laban, where his sons were born and from which he returned, is again and again called Paddan-aram in P (Gen 25:20; 28:2–7; 31:18; 35:9, 26 etc.). Paddan-aram in P is equivalent to Aram Naharaim in J and both are names for Upper Mesopotamia.

This tradition, however, is in conflict with another which presupposes that Israel's ancestors came from a region which was less remote than Upper Mesopotamia. According to Gen 29:1(J), Jacob went to the land of the *b'nê qedhem*, the 'sons of the East', when he visited Laban. According to Judges 6:3, 33; 7:12; 8:10 and other later texts, these *b'nê qedhem* were nomads in Transjordan. Laban learned three days later that Jacob had fled and caught up with him seven days later (Gen 31:22–33, J). It is about five hundred miles from Haran to Gilead and clearly too far for Laban to have covered in seven days or for Jacob to have travelled in ten. The treaty between Jacob and Laban (Gen 31:44–54) shows that they had neighbouring territories,

Gilead forming a common frontier. A frequent conclusion among scholars is that the tradition of Upper Mesopotamia is later and that the patriarchs' country of origin was on the edge of the desert of Transjordania.[38] It was only when Haran became an important caravan centre during the Aramaean expansion that the memory of Jacob and Laban the 'Aramaean' as well as the memory of Abraham himself were taken there.

All the same, if the Abraham-Isaac cycle was originally independent of the Jacob cycle, it is still possible to solve the problem in the following way. Abraham emigrated from Upper Mesopotamia and Jacob came from the desert of Transjordania. When the two traditions merged together and Jacob was called the son of Isaac, son of Abraham, the origin of the story of Jacob and Laban was taken back to Upper Mesopotamia, the home country of Abraham. It was at Haran, from which Abraham had set out, that Laban the brother of Rebekah, Isaac's mother, lived and it was Rebekah who sent Jacob to her uncle Laban, whose two daughters he married. The genealogical tree of Israel's ancestors thus spread its branches in order to include the merging together of proto-Israelite groups and their relationships with the neighbouring groups. In the same way, Lot the Transjordanian became the nephew of Abraham, at least according to P (Gen 11:27), and left Haran with him (Gen 12:4b–5). The same information is provided by the Yahwist (Gen 12:4a; cf. 13:1), although he does not state the precise relationship between Abraham and Lot. What is more, the same source which states that Jacob went to the b'nê qedhem and which can be used as a proof in this case also insists that he arrived at Haran (Gen 29:4, J). Moreover, the term b'nê qedhem, which occurs only once in Genesis (Gen 29:1), may have a wider meaning here than in Judges and be applied to the inhabitants of the whole eastern desert. Furthermore, there is the question of the treaty concluded at Gilead between Jacob and Laban, with its political aspect and its family aspect, which is certainly connected with the narrative of Jacob's stay with Laban in Upper Mesopotamia. Finally, Jacob's group and Laban's group were not always in the desert near Transjordania – they came there from elsewhere. The internal evidence of the biblical traditions can also be adapted to include a migration of Jacob's group from Haran and Gilead and from there into Palestine. Light can also be thrown on this problem, as it can on the question of Abraham's connections with Upper Mesopotamia, by the use of external, non-biblical evidence. It is, however, important to note that a more convincing explanation of the merging of the Abraham-Isaac cycle with the Jacob cycle, based on the study of traditions, is that the two groups were aware of their common origin.

[38] Among recent authors, see especially M. Noth, Überlieferungsgeschichte, op. cit., pp. 95–111; 217–218; O. Eissfeldt, 'Das Alte Testament im Lichte der safatenischen Inschriften', ZDMG, 104 (1954), pp. 88–118 = Kleine Schriften, III, pp. 289–317.

III. THE VALUE OF THE TRADITIONS

The mere age of the patriarchal traditions does not, however, provide a sufficiently firm basis for assessing their historical value, since it is quite possible that they were invented. The stories of the patriarchs are no longer interpreted as astral myths,[39] as they were earlier in this century, nor are the patriarchs themselves interpreted as early Canaanite deities who had been reduced to the level of ancestors.[40] They are, moreover, no longer regarded as the legendary founders of the sanctuaries in Canaan, to which the Israelites were connected by an artificial genealogy which gave them a spurious legal basis for their possession of the land.[41] Other more subtle solutions have been suggested, one of the most interesting being that the patriarchs personified clans or tribes and that their individual histories were in fact collective histories.[42] This theory is to some extent justified, because, in the semi-nomadic world of the Semites from which the Israelites came, each group was regarded as representing the descendants of one ancestor and relationships between the groups were expressed by family relationships. These blood ties were often real, but they might also be imaginary.[43] It is also true to say that the leader represented his own group, that he was at one with it and that the experiences and undertakings of the group might be attributed in tradition to the ancestor. As we have already seen in Genesis, certain figures have a value as social types – Esau, for example, is the hunter and Ishmael is the bedouin – and there are stories with a clearly collective meaning, for instance, those of Simeon and Levi at Shechem and of Jacob and Laban in Gilead. This collective character, however, does not in any sense diminish the value of the stories – on the contrary, it makes them more valuable to the historian. On the other hand, there are too many characteristics which cannot be reduced to a collective interpretation for this explanation to be applied generally. Finally, there is the application of the form-critical method to Genesis. H. Gunkel[44] was the first to use form-criticism in this way, separating the patriarchal

[39] A. Jeremias, *Das Alte Testament im Lichte des Alten Orients*, especially the second edition, Leipzig, 1906, pp. 338–343, following E. Stücken and H. Winckler.

[40] E. Meyer, *Die Israeliten und ihre Nachbarstämme*, Halle, 1906, pp. 249–298.

[41] See especially R. Weill, 'L'installation des Israèlites en Palestine et la légende des Patriarches', *RHR*, 87 (1923 A), pp. 69–120; 88 (1923 B), pp. 1–44; 'La légende des Patriarches et l'histoire', *Revue des Etudes Sémitiques*, 1937, pp. 145–206.

[42] C. Steuernagel, *Die Einwanderung der israelitischen Stämme in Kanaan*, Berlin, 1901; C. F. Burney, *Israel's Settlement in Canaan*, 1918. F. Schmidtke, *Die Einwanderung Israels in Kanaan*, Breslau, 1933 (this author has certain reservations).

[43] R. de Vaux, *Institutions*, I, *op. cit.*, pp. 17–20.

[44] See H. Gunkel's introduction to his commentary on Genesis, *Genesis*, 1901, 4th edn., 1917; published separately as *Die Sagen der Genesis*, 1901; *ibid.*, *Das Märchen im Alten Testament*, Tübingen, 1917; see also H. Gressmann, 'Sage und Geschichte in den Patriarchenerzählungen', *ZAW*, 30 (1910), pp. 1–34.

accounts into elements which were originally independent and no more than popular stories. The Israelites adopted this folklore, merged the episodes together, added aetiological accounts and cultic legends to them and, having associated certain stories with certain places, connected these places to each other by supposed migrations undertaken by the persons in the stories. It was in this way that the 'cycles' came about and, according to this method, these cycles were finally joined together by fictitious genealogical connections between the different heroes.

Modern research is still to a great extent inspired by this method and its conclusions. M. Noth has made considerable use of them in his important studies[45] and has also added to them by critically analysing the origins and the growth of the patriarchal traditions and by developing his own personal views concerning the composition and the aims of the Pentateuch (Tetrateuch). He assumes that the clans which formed Israel had many 'patriarchs' and, if Abraham, Isaac and Jacob were especially remembered, this was because of the special circumstances in which the Pentateuch was given its form. These patriarchs were venerated, Noth believes, as the founders of a cult of the god of Abraham, Isaac or Jacob, in other words, of the 'god of the father'. The essential aspect of these cults was the promise of a country and of descendants. The cults began in the desert, to which these semi-nomadic groups periodically moved their flocks, and were later taken by them into Canaan and established in various sanctuaries. The patriarchs were regarded as the founders of these sanctuaries and the settlement in Canaan seemed to these semi-nomadic groups to be the fulfilment of the promise made to their ancestors. This essential aspect of the promise formed the link between the patriarchal traditions and the principal themes of the Pentateuch – the exodus and the entry into Canaan. According to Noth, Jacob was the first to be introduced because of the dominant part played by the tribes in central Palestine in the formation of a common tradition. Later, Abraham and Isaac, two figures of a similar type venerated in the south, were included. The three patriarchs were then connected genealogically. Certain local traditions which were initially in no way connected with the patriarchs also became attached to them. All this, however, took place after the Israelite tribes had settled in Canaan and Noth concludes that 'we have no evidence . . . for making any definite historical assertions about the time and place, presuppositions and circumstances of the lives of the patriarchs as human beings.'[46]

---

[45] M. Noth, *Überlieferungsgeschichte, op. cit.*, pp. 58–62, 86–127; *History, op. cit.*, pp. 120–126.

[46] *History*, p. 122. It is only fair to note that, in the second and later editions, this negative judgement is followed by a long comment, pp. 122–123, which acknowledges the possibility that the patriarchs were connected with the general history of the Near East in the second millennium B.C., a possibility which became a probability in Noth's later works; see 'Der

It is true that the patriarchal tradition was only given its definitive form in the perspective of 'all Israel' after the conquest and settlement in the Promised Land and we have ourselves tried to distinguish the special traditions used in the patriarchal tradition and to retrace the stages in their composition. However complicated this development may have been, and however obscure it may still be, we should not be justified in concluding that the traditions have no historical value at all, since without evidence it would be wrong to claim that the Israelites had no knowledge at all of their own origins.

The question, then, that arises in this context is whether and how they would have been able to know something of their origins. A people's memory of past events is preserved in its written documents and in its oral traditions. Writing had been known in Mesopotamia and Egypt since about 3000 B.C. and we possess a great number of texts from both, dating from the end of the third millennium and the first centuries of the second. Two systems of writing were known during this period and used in Syria-Palestine and in the course of the second millennium several other systems were invented in the Ancient Near East – the pseudo-hieroglyphs of Byblos, the writing on the proto-Sinaitic inscriptions, the alphabetic cuneiform of Ugarit and the first attempts at 'Phoenician' script to which several short inscriptions found in Palestine bear witness. Biblical traditions would therefore have been able to rely on written documents relating to the patriarchs and perhaps even contemporary with them.

One extremely important factor, however, limits this possibility. The texts used by historians specialising in the Ancient Near East all come from settled civilisations and it is only at a relatively later date that they have the form of ordered accounts of historical events. The nomadic people had no archives and, to take examples only from the same cultural environment, the Aramaeans are known to us only by references to them in cuneiform texts, at least until the period when the Aramaean kingdoms were set up in Syria when the first Aramaean inscriptions appeared and the same applies; at a later date to the Nabataeans. This was also the case even when these nomads were acquainted with writing – the proto-Sinaitic inscriptions of the second millennium, like the many Safaitic texts of the beginning of our own era are really no more than *graffiti* preserving the name of an individual and the memory of one of his actions, certainly not a sufficient basis for the writing of a history. The ancestors of the Israelites were nomads or semi-nomads and, even supposing that they were able to write, they did not commit their recollections of their own times or of the past to

---

Beitrage der Archäologie zur Geschichte Israels', *Congress Volume Oxford* (*SVT*, 7), 1960, pp. 262–282; *Die Ursprünge des Alten Israels im Lichte neuer Quellen*, Cologne, 1961.

writing. The only documents about the patriarchs that can be expected are those which were occasioned by their contacts with people already settled in Palestine. There are only two cases in which this might arise – the story of the campaign of the four kings in which Abraham was involved (Gen 14) and the account of the purchase of the cave of Machpelah (Gen 23). The use of contemporary documents about the patriarchs in these chapters has been suggested from time to time, but, as we shall see, these passages are among the latest in Genesis and the non-biblical texts with which they can be compared are equally late.

We must therefore consider the possibility of oral tradition. The part played by this tradition in the formation of the Old Testament has, in recent years, been the object of many studies, [47] most of which, however, have been mainly concerned with questions of form – the oral transmission of a 'text' before or after it has been written down. One is bound to conclude from all these studies that a relatively stable form is preserved in oral transmission only when the composition handed down in this way is poetic or rhythmic and when it is also supported by a written tradition. We are concerned here less with the form than with the content, or rather with the historical value of the memories transmitted in the first place by a purely oral tradition. Various attempts have been made to find analogies in the Nordic sagas, [48] the Homeric epics and the Arthurian legend, [49] but it is more appropriate to look for a comparison with groups of people who are closer, both racially and socially, to the ancient Israelites, namely the early and the present-day nomadic Arabs. The conflicts between the various Arab tribes before the coming of Islam were narrated orally for a very long time be professional story-tellers, first in single episodes and often in different forms, and later in cycles containing groups of the same episodes. These traditions were eventually collected and edited by authors and editors who selected and harmonised the oral 'texts' and added genealogical,

---

[47] J. van der Ploeg, 'Le rôle de la tradition orale dans la transmission du texte de l'Ancien Testament', *RB*, 54 (1947), pp. 5–41; J. Lassøe, 'Literacy and Oral Tradition in Ancient Mesopotamia', *ST*, 3 (1949), pp. 34–59; H. Ringgren, 'Oral and Written Transmission in the Old Testament', *Studia Orientalia I. Pedersen dedicata*, Copenhagen, 1953, pp. 205–218; E. Nielsen, *Oral Tradition. A Modern Problem in Old Testament Introduction*, London, 1954; G. Widengren, 'Oral Tradition and Written Literature among the Hebrews in the Light of Arabic Evidence, with Special Regard to Prose Narratives', *Acta Orientalia* (Copenhagen), 23 (1958), pp. 201–262; I. Engnell, 'Methodological Aspects of Old Testament Study', *Congress Volume. Oxford* (*SVT*, 7), 1960, pp. 13–30; R. C. Culley, 'An Approach to the Problem of Oral Tradition', *VT*, 13 (1963), pp. 113–125; G. W. Ahlström, 'Oral and Written Transmission', *HTR*, 59 (1966), pp. 69–81; J. R. Porter, 'Pre-Islamic Arabic Historical Traditions and the Early Historical Narratives of the Old Testament', *JBL*, 87 (1968), pp. 17–26.
[48] C. Westermann, *Arten der Erzählungen, op. cit.*, pp. 36–39.
[49] W. F. Albright, *From Stone Age to Christianity*,[2] Baltimore, 1946, pp. 33–43 = pp. 64–76 in the new edition of *Anchor-Books*, 1957.

topographical and chronological notes.[50] This process is very similar to the process by which the patriarchal tradition was formed, according to our analysis. The ordered narrative to which this oral and written tradition finally led has no value for the historian, but he can find in it reliable information about the ethnic, social and religious situation in central Arabia before Mohammed and about the adventures of certain small groups, even though it is not possible to date these events exactly.

Nomadic and semi-nomadic Arabs still narrate in their tents today the traditions, genealogies and stories of their tribes or families. Both adults and children hear the same stories again and again and whenever the narrator omits or adds something, they correct him at once. Different versions of the same story are often found in different families. Everyone knows the history of his tribe or his clan by heart.[51] Verse narrators with a knowledge of the past history and the genealogy of the tribes go from camp to camp and in this way perpetuate the history of the bedouins.[52] The 'historical' memories of a tribe in the process of becoming settled to the east of Bethlehem, the Taʿamira, have recently been committed to writing for the first time.[53] This history is presented in the form of a genealogical tree and the genealogy of the thirteen families which make up the tribe is given in great detail and amplified by biographical and topographical notes. The history claims to cover almost four centuries and it deals with the migrations and adventures of the tribe, its struggles with rival groups and its attempts to gain pasture-land from Medāʿin Saleh to Tebūk and Maʿan and then from Maʿan to Beit Taʿamira to the south-west of Bethlehem. Place names or names of groups within the tribe as well as ancestors' surnames are explained by popular etymology. The anecdotes establish the tribal right to use a certain territory or to enjoy a certain privilege and in them the group to which the narrator belongs plays a leading part.

In all these cases, both in the past and in the present, the historical memories become more and more meagre and are separated by long gaps as one goes back in time. On the other hand, certain pieces of information are preserved and transmitted with great tenacity. This is especially true of the genealogical traditions. The names of Mohammed's ancestors, for example, have been preserved to the twenty-second degree and the genealogical tree of the Yemen tribes goes back to the thirtieth degree at least before Islam, when it was set down in writing.[54] On the basis of an average of

[50] This is the collection known as the 'Days (of Combat) of the Arabs', *'Ayyām al–'Arab;* see W. Caskel, 'Aijaam al–'Arab', *Islamica,* 3, fasc. 5 (1930); G. Widengren, 'Oral Tradition', *op. cit.,* especially pp. 232–243; J. R. Porter, 'Pre-Islamic Arabic Historical Traditions', *op. cit.*

[51] A. Musil, *Arabia Petraea,* III, Vienna, 1908, pp. 232–233.

[52] T. Ashkenazi, *Tribus semi-nomades du Nord de la Palestine,* Paris, 1938, pp. 58–59.

[53] B. Couroyer, 'Histoire d'une tribu semi-nomade de Palestine', *RB,* 58 (1951), pp. 75–91.

[54] F. Wüstenfeld, *Genealogische Tabellen der arabischen Stämme und Familien,* Göttingen, 1852,

three generations per century, this means that the oral tradition goes back for seven hundred years for Mohammed and a thousand years for the Yemen tribes. These traditions are to some extent credible, but they are not entirely reliable. The list of real ancestors of the Yemen tribes, for instance, is preceded by a list which claims to go back to Ishmael, and through Ishmael, to Adam. A Fuqara bedouin was able to recite his genealogy to the sixteenth degree, but the sixteenth ancestor was Adam![55]

The origin of tribes and their mutual relationships are remembered in these traditions, but in addition to this it frequently happens that these facts are expressed by the invention of ancestors who give their names to the tribes or families or by imaginary family ties. There is, for example, a group of small shepherd tribes living on the Middle Euphrates called the 'Agēdāt or 'confederates', but their relationships with each other are explained by means of a common genealogical tree.[56] Another example is that of a tribe known as Khoza'a, the 'separated ones', because they are separated from the Azd, but their genealogists have given both tribes a common ancestor, called Khoza'a.

A recently published Akkadian text shows clearly that this interest in genealogy existed at the beginning of the second millennium among the Amorites, with whom, as we shall see later, Abraham was connected.[57] The first links in this genealogical chain are an artificial composition of names of individuals, tribes and places, with the sole object of connecting the line to the ethnic and geographical environment from which it is derived. There is a striking parallel between this genealogy and that of Abraham's ancestors from Shem to Terah, as given by P in Gen 11:10–26.[58]

Topographical traditions are usually extremely stable, place names persisting in the oral tradition, often in opposition to a different official and written usage. An obvious example of this is the persistence of the early Semitic place names despite the later use of Graeco-Roman names in Palestine. The memory of these early names, frequently of course in rather distorted forms, may be preserved for a very long time indeed, quite apart from any written tradition. One of the chambers cut into the rock at Petra is known locally as Madrase, the 'school' and M. J. Lagrange read there, for

---

with an index, 1853; W. Caskel, *Gamharat an-Nasab. Das genealogische Werk des Hišam, Ibn Muhammad al-Kalbī*, Leiden, 1965.

[55] A. Jaussen and R. Savignac, *Coutumes des Fuqara*, Paris, 1920, p. 4.

[56] H. Charles, *Tribus moutonnières du Moyen Euphrate*, Paris, 1949.

[57] J. J. Finkelstein, 'The Genealogy of the Hammurabi Dynasty', *JCS*, 20 (1966), pp. 55–118 and A. Malamat's commentary, 'King Lists of the Old Babylonian Period and Biblical Genealogies', *JAOS*, 88 (1968), pp. 163–173 = *Essays in Memory of E. A. Speiser*, New Haven, 1968, the same pagination.

[58] For the genealogies of the Pentateuch and especially of Genesis, see C. Westermann, *Genesis, Einleitung*, Neukirchen and Vlyun, 1966, pp. 8–24; M. D. Johnson, *The Purpose of Biblical Genealogies*, Cambridge, 1969, especially Chapter I.

the first time for some two thousand years, the name 'Dushara, god of Madrasa'.[59]

The oral tradition, then, is very faithful in some ways. It does, however, invent a great deal and it is forgetful. To explain the name of a person, a place, a monument, a ruin, a custom or even a natural formation, oral tradition often resorts to telling the story of an action, a situation or an event, the story finishing by recalling the custom or the monument, for example, which survives 'until this day', although this concluding formula may be omitted without changing the character of the story. There are very many examples of this in Genesis alone – personal names such as Abraham, Jacob and Edom, Moab and Ammon, the sons of Lot, place names such as Zoar, Bethel and Gilead, the pillar of salt into which Lot's wife was changed, the traditional reason why the Israelites are forbidden 'to this day' to eat the sciatic nerve, because this is where the mysterious adversary injured Jacob at the ford of the Jabbok. The historian is always suspicious of these 'aetiologies' – false etymologies and false interpretations which are found in every language and every country. Tradition, however, only invents in this way by imitating true explanations. Not all explanations are invented and a whole tradition cannot be based on an aetiology. General agreement has been reached in recent studies[60] regarding the secondary and accidental character of these aetiologies in Genesis. The most obvious aetiologies are found in the Lot cycle, which was not originally part of the patriarchal tradition. Aetiology certainly did not, in any case, play the main part in the formation of this tradition.

It has also been suggested that cult helped to create tradition,[61] in other words, that the stories of the patriarchs, which are grouped around certain sacred places, were cultic legends of these sanctuaries, the foundation of which was attributed to one of Israel's ancestors, following a theophany during which he had received promises or blessings. The movements of the patriarchs from one sanctuary to another reflects the combination of different traditions. It is, of course, true that sanctuaries were places where traditions were preserved and that these traditions might have been modi-

[59] M. J. Lagrange, *La méthode historique*,[2] Paris, 1904, pp. 189–190, new edition, Paris, 1966, p. 146.

[60] This question will be dealt with again in greater detail in connection with the accounts of the 'conquest' in Joshua, in which it plays a more important part from the historian's point of view; see below, pp. 481–482 and the bibliography, note 8.

[61] For the part played by cult in the formation and transmission of traditions, see G. von Rad, *Das formgeschichtliche Problem des Hexateuch, op. cit.*, especially pp. 50–57; M. Noth, *Überlieferungsgeschichte, op. cit.*, especially pp. 58–62, 272–273; G. E. Wright, 'Cult and History', *Interpretation*, 16 (1962), pp. 3–20; A. S. Kapelrud, 'The Role of the Cult in Old Israel', *The Bible in Modern Study*, ed. J. P. Hyatt, Nashville and New York, 1965, pp. 44–56 and especially B. Vawter's reply to Kapelrud, pp. 57–64; S.Herrmann, 'Kultreligion und Buchreligion. Kultische Funktionen in Israel und in Ägypten', *Das Ferne und Nahe Wort. Festschrift L. Rost (BZAW,* 105), 1967, pp. 94–105.

fied by the cult practised at the sanctuaries. Elements might even have been added to these traditions by cultic practice and above all the performance of later rites might have been attributed to the ancestor who founded the sanctuary in question. What is certain, however, is that traditions were not created by cult – cultic practices simply helped to recall traditions. The Passover, which became a commemoration of Israel's deliverance from Egypt, is a rite which antedates the exodus and there are other feasts which were only connected later to historical events. In the patriarchal period, for example, the religion of the god of the father who guided the nomads and preserved the promises that he had made to them, antedates the adoption of the sanctuaries in Canaan. The development, then, is quite the opposite to the development that has been suggested. In the Babylonian religion, in which myths occupied the same place as sacred history in Israel, the traditional rites were explained at a later date by myths which were similarly traditional.[62] In other words, neither myth nor history was created by cult.

But, even if it is not possible to find the origin of these traditions in aetiology or in cult, this does not mean that their historical value is any the less. Internal criticism of the patriarchal traditions has shown how complicated their development has been. Scholars in this field have concluded that a long oral transmission might have been faithful with regard to certain points, but that this faithfulness had its limits. It may also be added that this transmission, in which the sanctuaries certainly played an important part, would be inexplicable if all the elements from which the people of Israel came went down into Egypt and stayed there for four centuries. It is possible to explain it if this stay in Egypt concerned only a part of the Israel that was to be. At the present stage of research, however, all that the historian can say is that it is possible for Israel to have preserved memories of its origins. If he is to go any further than this, he has to go outside the Bible.

[62] W. G. Lambert, 'Myth and Ritual as Conceived by the Babylonians', *JSS*, 13 (1968), pp. 104–112; for Egypt, see S. Herrmann, *op. cit.*, especially p. 98.

Chapter Seven

THE PATRIARCHAL TRADITIONS AND HISTORY

I N the preceding chapter, we analysed the patriarchal traditions found in the Bible itself and concluded that it is quite possible that they contain early memories. We now have to compare these bibilical traditions with extrabiblical and archaeological evidence to discover the extent to which this patriarchal 'history' is in accordance with the history of the Ancient Near East in general.[1] The first problem is that of the origin of the patriarchs. According to the Bible, Abraham came from 'Ur of the Chaldaeans' in Lower Mesopotamia. From there, he went to Haran (Harān)

[1] The following can be mentioned as among the most important of the many books and articles published in recent years: R. de Vaux, 'Les Patriarches hébreux et les découvertes récentes', *RB*, 53 (1946), pp. 321–348; 55 (1948), pp. 321–347; 56 (1949), pp. 5–36; German translation: *Die hebräischen Patriarchen und die modernen Entdeckungen*, Leipzig, 1959, Bonn, 1961; H. H. Rowley, 'Recent Discoveries and the Patriarchal Age,' *BJRL*, 32 (1949–1950), pp. 44–79 = *The Servant of the Lord and Other Essays on the Old Testament*,[2] Oxford, 1965, pp. 281–318; M. Noth, 'Mari und Israel. Eine Personennamenstudie'. *Geschichte und Altes Testament*. *(Festschrift Alt)*, Tübingen, 1953, pp. 127–152; M. Noth, *Die Ursprünge des Alten Israel im Lichte neuer Quellen*, Cologne, 1961; H. Cazelles, 'Patriarches', *DBS*, VII 1961, col. 81–156; W. F. Albright, 'Abram the Hebrew', *BASOR*, 163 (Oct. 1961), pp. 36–54; J. C. L. Gibson, 'Light from Mari on the Patriarchs', *JSS*, 7 (1962), pp. 44–62; A. Parrot, *Abraham et son temps*, Neuchâtel, 1962; S. Yeivin, 'The Age of the Patriarchs', *RSO*, 38 (1963), pp. 277–302; C. H. Gordon, 'Hebrew Origins in the Light of Recent Discoveries', *Biblical and Other Studies*, ed. A. Altmann, Cambridge, Mass., 1963, pp. 3–14; F.M.T. de Liagre Böhl, 'Die Patriarchenzeit', *JEOL*, 17 (1963), pp. 125–140; J. M. Holt, *The patriarchs of Israel*, Nashville and New York, 1964; F. Vattioni, 'Nuovi aspetti del problema dei patriarchi biblici', *Augustinianum*, 4 (1964), pp. 331–337; N. A. van Uchelen, *Abraham de Hebreeër. Een literair–en historisch–kritische studie naar aanleiding van Genesis 14:13*, Assen, 1964; R. de Vaux, 'Les Patriarches hébreux et l'histoire', *RB* 72 (1965), pp. 5–28; German translation; *Die Patriarchenerzählungen und die Geschichte*, Stuttgart, 1965; Italian translation: *I Patriarchi ebrei e la storia*, Brescia, 1967; K. A. Kitchen, *Ancient Orient and Old Testament*, Chicago, 1966, pp. 41–56, 79–81, 154–156; W. F. Albright, *Archaeology, Historical Analogy and Early Biblical History*, Baton Rouge, Louisiana, 1966, Chap. II: 'The Story of Abraham in the Light of New Archaeological Data', pp. 22–41; W. F. Albright, *Yahweh and the Gods of Canaan*, London, 1968, Chap. II: 'The Patriarchal Background of Israel's Faith', pp. 47–95; K. Koch, 'Die Hebräer vom Auszug aus Ägypten bis zum Großreich Davids', *VT*, 19 (1969), pp. 37–81; B. Mazar, 'The Historical Background of the Book of Genesis', *JNES*, 28 (1969), pp. 73–83.

in Upper Mesopotamia and from there to Canaan. What value should be attached to these traditions describing Abraham's migration?

I. THE MIGRATION FROM UR

According to the Yahwistic account (Gen 11:28), Abram's brother Haran died in the presence of their father Terah in their native land, *'ûr kaśĭdîm*. According to the priestly tradition (Gen 11:31), Terah, Abram, Sarai and Lot left *'ûr kaśĭdîm* to go to the land of Canaan, but they settled in Haran. In the Yahwistic-Elohistic (?) account of the covenant, Yahweh says to Abram: 'I am Yahweh who brought you out of *'ûr kaśĭdîm* to make you heir to this land' (Gen 15:7). This tradition is not mentioned again in the Old Testament until Neh 9:7, which clearly echoes Gen 15, and Judith 5:6. It also occurs several times in the Book of Jubilees, chapters 12 and 13. Finally, it is repeated in Stephen's speech in Acts 7:2. The Hebrew version is always *'ûr kaśĭdîm* and the Greek version is 'the land of the Chaldaeans'. It has been suggested that the primitive version was 'Ur in the land of the Chaldaeans' and that this form was abbreviated differently in Hebrew and in Greek.[2] The more likely explanation, however, is that the version in the Septuagint is an interpretation of a name which was no longer understood.

This first migration undertaken by Abraham is generally regarded as having no historical foundation and it certainly gives rise to serious difficulties. The city of Ur in Lower Mesopotamia is well known to us because of the cuneiform texts and L. Woolley's excavations.[3] It was a flourishing city in the third millennium B.C., especially during the Third Dynasty of Ur. After this dynasty had come to an end and the town had been destroyed by the Elamites a little before 2000 B.C., Ur soon rose again from the ruins and remained an important religious and trading centre until some time after the end of Hammurabi's reign. It then passed through a period of almost total eclipse for about a millennium, only prospering again during the neo-Babylonian period. It is clear, then, that Ur was a city that was very much alive during the first centuries of the second millennium, which is the period during which it is probable that Abraham lived. On the other hand, the city could not have been called Ur of the Chaldaeans at that time.[4] The

---

[2] W. F. Albright, *BASOR*, 140 (Dec. 1955), pp. 31–32; *The Biblical Period from Abraham to Ezra*,[4] New York, p. 97, note 1.

[3] Woolley made use of his discoveries to confirm the biblical tradition, but his conclusions are scarcely to be accepted; see *Abraham. Recent Discoveries and Hebrew Origins*, London, 1936.

[4] The Hebrew Bible has *kaśĭdîm*, whereas the Greek Bible has *chaldaioi*, which reproduces the late Akkadian *kaldu*. The change from -*sd*- to -*ld*- is a regular one in neo-Assyrian and neo-Babylonian. The Hebrew form is phonetically the original form, but this does not mean that it occurred early in time; this is, of course, not the view of J. M. Grintz, *JNES*, 21 (1962), p. 190, note 10.

188 I: THE PATRIARCHAL TRADITIONS

Chaldaeans – the Kaldu of the cuneiform inscriptions – were Aramaean tribes who did not appear in the Assyrian texts until the ninth century B.C. and it is not possible to speak of Ur of the Chaldaeans until even later than this, in other words, until after the foundation of the neo-Babylonian empire at the end of the seventh century B.C. It is in fact at this period that the *kaś'dîm* or Chaldaeans are mentioned for the first time in the Bible apart from the book of Genesis.[5] We are therefore bound to recognise the possibility at least of *kaś'dîm* having been added anachronistically to the name of Ur.

It has been suggested, however, that the whole of this tradition might have been invented during the exile by the Jews in Babylonia at a time when Ur had emerged from oblivion, when Nabonidus was restoring the temples and when a close relationship had been established between Ur and Haran. Nabonidus had originally come from Haran and he rebuilt the sanctuaries at Haran like those at Ur. His mother had been a priestess of Sin at Haran and his daughter was a priestess of the same god at Ur.[6] Nonetheless, it is difficult to see why a tradition such as this should have been invented. There is one possible reason, which is ultimately a literary one – Abraham's migration from Ur would have provided a link between the story of the Tower of Babel and the 'scattering of the peoples over the whole face of the earth', that is, in Lower Mesopotamia (Gen 11:1–9) on the one hand and the story of Abraham which begins in Upper Mesopotamia (Gen 12:1–5) on the other. But Gen 11:1–9 and Gen 12:1–4a belong to the Yahwistic tradition and Gen 11:28–30, which states that Abraham's family was present at Ur, also belongs to this tradition. The migration from Ur therefore forms part of the ancient pentateuchal tradition and, what is more, it is mentioned again in Gen. 15:7.[7] It could not therefore have been invented when these traditions were being edited, for Ur was at that time completely forgotten.

Another objection is that, according to a much more reliable tradition (Gen 12:1; 24:4, 7), Abraham's 'native land', *môledheth* or *'res môledheth,* was not Ur, but Haran, so that he must have been born in Upper

[5] The first texts are Jer 21:4 and Hab 1:6; its occurrence in Isa 23:13 is a late gloss, the text of which is itself dubious; see W. Rudolph, 'Jesaja 23.1–14', *Festschrift Fr. Baumgärtel,* Erlangen, 1959, pp. 166–174; J. Lindblom, 'Der Ausspruch über Tyrus in Jesaja 23', *ASTI,* 4 (1965), pp. 56–73.
[6] See S. Smith, *Babylonian Historical Texts Relating to the Capture and Downfall of Babylon,* London, 1924, p. 36 ff; C. J. Gadd, 'The Harran Inscriptions of Nabonidus', *AnStud.,* 8 (1958), pp. 35–92.
[7] It is not relevant to our problem whether this verse is J or E. Even if Gen 15 is thought of as having been composed at the beginning of the monarchy (see A. Caquot, *Semitica,* 12, 1962, pp. 50–66), this is still not at all close to the period of priestly editing, the period, in other words, suggested as that in which the Ur tradition was invented. The reference to *'ûr kaś'dîm* in Gen 11:28 and 15:7 cannot, moreover, be regarded as an attempt to harmonise with P, since *'ûr kaś'dîm* is mentioned only once in the priestly narrative (Gen 11:31).

Mesopotamia.[8] From the etymological point of view certainly, *môledheth* may mean 'birthplace', but, in every case in which this word is used in the Bible, it always can, and often must, be translated as 'descendants' or 'family'.[9] In effect, Upper Mesopotamia is the region where Abraham's family was settled or where his descendants lived.

Attempts have been made, however, to avoid these apparent difficulties by suggesting that Ur of the Chaldaeans was a town not in Lower Mesopotamia, but in Upper Mesopotamia. In the nineteenth century especially, before the fame of Ur had been restored by Assyriologists, the biblical town was commonly identified with Urfa, known in Syriac as Orrhai and now called Edessa, some twenty or so miles north-west of Haran. This opinion, which goes back to a conviction shared by many early Christian writers, is still supported by some scholars today.[10] Another explanation has been suggested by C. H. Gordon,[11] who has pointed out that some of the Rās Shamrah texts refer to a town called Ura in Hittite territory and that merchants came from this Ura to trade at Ugarit. This town, Gordon has argued, is the *'ûr kaś'dîm* of Genesis and Abraham was not a nomadic shepherd, but a merchant prince. In the following chapter, the second part of Gordon's proposition will be discussed more fully;[12] here we will simply consider the geographical aspect. Apart from the interpretation of *môledheth* as 'birth-place', which we have rejected, the main arguments are as follows. In the first place, according to Gen 11:31, Terah left Ur of the Chaldaeans with Abraham to go to Canaan, but they stopped at Haran. A journey from Ur in Lower Mesopotamia to Canaan would only have taken the travellers through Haran if they had made an enormous détour. This itinerary presupposes that this town of Ur was farther away from Canaan than Haran and therefore that it was to the north of Haran. Secondly, as we have seen, Ur of Lower Mesopotamia could not have been called Ur of the Chaldaeans. There were, however, Chaldaeans in the north – Xenophon mentioned them together with the Kardouchoi (or Kurds) as neighbours of the Armenians.[13]

[8] See, for example, C. H. Gordon. *JNES*, 17 (1958), p. 31; F. Vattioni, *Augustinianum*, 4 (1964), pp. 335–336.

[9] U. Cassuto, 'Studi sulla Genesi', *Giornale della Società Asiatica Italiana*, new series I (1926), pp. 205–206; *ibid.*, *A Commentary on the Book of Genesis*, II, Jerusalem, 1964, p. 274. Convincing examples are Gen 43:7, 48:6; Esther 8:6.

[10] See A. Lods, *Israël. Des origines au milieu du VIIIe siècle*, Paris, 1930, 187; J. M. Grintz, *JNES*, 21 (1962), p. 190, note 10; C. H. Gordon regards it as possible, 'Abraham of Ur', *Hebrew and Semitic Studies presented to G. R. Driver*, Oxford, 1963, pp. 77–84, especially p. 83.

[11] C. H. Gordon, 'Abraham and the Merchants of Ura', *JNES*, 17 (1958), pp. 28–31; this hypothesis has been criticised by A. Saggs, 'Ur of the Chaldees. A Problem of Identification', *Iraq*, 22 (1960), pp. 200–209; Gordon has replied to this criticism in 'Abraham of Ur', see above, note 10.

[12] See below, p. 228.

[13] Xenophon, *Anab.*, IV, III, 4; *Cyrop.*, III, I, 34.

These arguments, then, are not convincing. The text of Gen 11:31 which gives Canaan as Terah's destination belongs to the priestly tradition, but the priestly writer was considering, not Terah's intention, but the destination of the migration undertaken by Abraham, Sarah and Lot, who left Ur with Terah (Gen 11:31) and arrived in Canaan (Gen 12:5, P). On the other hand, however, a migration undertaken by herdsmen with small livestock, like Abraham's group, would pass round the desert and would not cross it by a direct route from Ur to Canaan. As for Xenophon's Chaldaeans, they were neighbours of the Armenians and Stephen of Byzantium knew a country of Chaldia which was part of Armenia. Was it from that country that the patriarchs are said to have come?

There was in fact a city called Ura in Armenia, mentioned in the fourteenth century in the Boghazköy archives, but it was about one hundred and ninety miles to the north of Haran and therefore could not have been the city mentioned in the Rās Shamrah texts and used by Gordon, since the merchants of Ura made seasonal journeys to Ugarit.[15] There was, however, an Ura in Cilicia, which has been identified either with Olbia of the Greeks, about fifteen miles from Seleucia,[16] or with Seleucia itself or a place very near to it.[17] This is the town mentioned in the Rās Shamrah texts, but it is a long way from Haran and the route from this Ur to Canaan, in other words, from Seleucia to Palestine, could not have passed through Haran. Gordon's thesis is therefore without any firm basis.

We should, then, only look for Ur of the Chaldaeans in Lower Mesopotamia and show that Abraham's first migration is in accordance with certain historical data. From the onomastic point of view, the patriarchs are connected with the Amorites. The Amorites, however, entered Babylonia from the end of the third millennium onwards and their presence there is better attested by the texts than it is in Upper Mesopotamia.[18] They certainly reached Ur – the documents of the early Babylonian period mention the Amorites, MAR.TU, and several persons there had Amorite names.[19] One text is especially interesting – a Sutean Amorite makes an offering at the temple of Ningal;[20] he is probably not a

[14] See above, A. Saggs, *op. cit.*, note 11.
[15] See J. Nougayrol, *CRAI*, 1954, p. 242, note 2.
[16] D. J. Wiseman, *Chronicles of Chaldaean Kings*, London, 1956, p. 88; E. Laroche, *Syria*, 35 (1958), pp. 270–272.
[17] W. F. Albright, *BASOR*, 163 (Dec. 1961), p. 44, note 42.
[18] See above, pp. 58–59.
[19] For the Ur III period, see L. Legrain, *Ur Excavation Texts*, III, London, 1947, Index; G. Buccellati, *The Amorites of the Ur III Period*, Naples, 1966, pp. 320–321; for the following period, see H. H. Figulla and W. J. Martin, *Ur Excavation Texts*, V, London, 1953, Index. These names are proportionally much rarer at Ur than in the rest of Babylonia.
[20] Figulla No. 564; cf. J.-R. Kupper, *Les nomades en Mésopotamie au temps des rois de Mari*, Paris, 1957, p. 88.

resident of Ur, but a visitor who has come from the neighbouring country. In fact, a letter sent from Ur to Larsa mentions a Sutean encampment at the gates of the town.[21] These Suteans, who were of Amorite stock, were also active in Upper Mesopotamia.[22] They were, moreover, not the only western Semites who were still semi-nomadic – groups of these western Semites have been located both in Upper and in Lower Mesopotamia.[23] What is remarkable in this context is that there is evidence of certain names that occur in the story of the patriarchs in Lower Mesopotamia at the end of the third millennium B.C. and at the beginning of the second, which is before the existence of any such evidence in Upper Mesopotamia.[24] Abraham's great-grandfather is called Serug and a *sa-ru-gi* is mentioned in a document from Tello which dates back to the Third Dynasty of Ur.[25] Abraham's grandfather and one of his brothers were called Nahor and the personal name *Na-ha-rum* occurs in four documents of the same period, probably coming from Nippur.[26] The name Jacob, which is an abbreviation of *ya'qôbh-'El*, appears in several different forms. The two forms *Ya-ah-qú-ub-El* and *Ya-qú-ub-El* appear in four Kish documents, about a century before Hammurabi,[27] *Ya-ah-qú-ub-El* probably still at Kish [28] and *Ya-qú-ub-El* in the two Tell Harmal documents of the same period.[29] It also appears as *Ya-ku-ub-El* and even in the abbreviated form *Ya-ku-bi* in the texts of the First Dynasty of Babylonia.[30]

It has also been known for some time that several of the names that occur in Abraham's family are in some way connected with the lunar cult. Terah *(teraḥ)* has, for example, been compared with *yerah*, the lunar month, and with *yārêaḥ*, the moon.[31] Laban *(lābhān)* means white and *l'bhānāh*, the white one, is a poetic term for the full moon. Sarah is equivalent to *šarratu*, queen, an Akkadian translation of a Sumerian name for Ningal, the female

[21] *Textes cunéiformes du Louvre*, XVII, No. 58; cf. J.-R. Kupper, *op. cit.*, p. 88.

[22] J.-R. Kupper, *op. cit.*, pp. 83–96.

[23] Especially the various 'Benjaminite' tribes; see J.-R. Kupper, *op. cit.*, pp. 47–52; D. O. Edzard, *Die 'Zweite Zwischenzeit' Babyloniens*, Wiesbaden, 1959, pp. 104–108.

[24] N. Schneider, 'Patriarchennamen in zeitgenössischen Keilschrifturkunden', *Biblica*, 33 (1932), pp. 516–522; not all the comparisons are equally valuable.

[25] G. A. Barton, *Documents from the Temple Archives of Tello*, III, Philadelphia, 1914, Index, p. 51.

[26] A. L. Oppenheim, *Catalogue of the Cuneiform Tablets of the Wilberforce Eames Babylonian Collection*, New Haven, 1948, Index, p. 197.

[27] M. Rutten, 'Un lot de tablettes de Mananâ', *RA*, 54, (1960), Index, p. 149.

[28] S. D. Simmons, *JCS*, 14 (1960), p. 122, No. 100, 21.

[29] S. D. Simmons, *JCS*, 13 (1959), p. 114, No. 26, 7; 14 (1960), p. 27, No. 57, 13.

[30] T. Bauer, *Die Ostkanaanäer*, Leipzig, 1926, p. 27. M. Noth's suggested explanation of these names, 'Mari und Israel. Eine Personennamenstudie', *Geschichte und Altes Testament (Festschrift Alt)*, Tübingen, 1953, especially p. 142, is almost certainly correct in the light of the new texts mentioned in the above notes.

[31] The name may, on the other hand, be related to the Akkadian *turahu*, ibex.

partner of the god Sin. Milcah, Nahor's wife, has the same name as Sin's daughter, the goddess Malkatu, the princess. These comparisons have been wrongly used in order to show that the patriarchs were mythological or astrological figures, but they might perhaps show that the patriarchs came from an environment in which the moon was worshipped. The moon-god Sin (known in Sumerian as Nannar) and the moon-goddess Ningal had, after all, always been the patrons of the city of Ur and continued to be its patrons until the end of its history. They were also, however, the main gods of Haran,[32] not simply during the neo-Assyrian and neo-Babylonian periods. In the fourteenth century B.C., the god Sin of Haran was invoked in the treaty between Suppiluliumas of Hatti and Mattiwaza of Mitanni.[33] In the eighteenth century, a letter from Mari refers to a pact made between the Benjaminites and the kinglets in the temple of Sin at Haran.[34] It is almost certain that the cults of Sin and Ningal were introduced at Haran from Ur and it is also probable that this took place as early as the Third Dynasty, when the neo-Sumerian civilisation was spreading far beyond the political frontiers of the empire of Ur.

There were two natural routes connecting Ur and Haran, one along the Tigris and the other along the second great river of Mesopotamia, the Euphrates. Both were widely used at the beginning of the second millennium. The route along the Tigris is described in an itinerary, of which we have two critical revisions.[35] The Euphrates route is borne out by an interpretation of the dreams of a man who saw himself going to Nippur, Babylon, Sippar, Rapiqum and Mari[36] – from there, several roads went to Haran.[37] This second itinerary was the one which a group of western Semites moving from Ur to Haran would follow.

The migration from Ur, then, is in accordance with the prevailing historical and geographical conditions at the time of Abraham. Since it forms part of the earliest literary tradition of Genesis (J) and since it could hardly have been invented at the time when this tradition was being formed, it would be unwise to claim that it is entirely without any historical basis. It must at least be regarded as possible.

[32] See E. Dhorme, 'Abraham dans le cadre de l'histoire', RB, 37 (1928), pp. 379–385, 481–484 = Recueil Ed. Dhorme, Paris, 1951, pp. 205–215, 763.

[33] E. F. Weidner, Politische Dokumente aus Kleinasien, Leipzig, 1923, pp. 32–33, 1. 54.

[34] G. Dossin, 'Benjaminites dans les textes de Mari', Mélanges Syriens ... R. Dussaud, II, Paris, 1939, p. 986.

[35] A. Goetze, 'An Old Babylonian Itinerary', JCS, 7 (1953), pp. 51–72; W. W. Hallo, 'The Road to Emar', JCS, 18 (1964), pp. 57–88.

[36] A. L. Oppenheim, The Interpretation of Dreams in the Ancient Near East, Philadelphia, 1956, pp. 260, 268.

[37] See the map showing the roads in Mesopotamia during the early Babylonian period in W. W. Hallo, op. cit., p. 87.

II. UPPER MESOPOTAMIA

The biblical tradition concerning the patriarchs' links with Upper Mesopotamia is richer, but very complex.

According to the Yahwistic tradition, Abram was commanded by God to leave his country, his family and his father's house and to go to the land that God would show him (Gen 12:1). Everything is very vague and no more precise statement is made by the Yahwist until Gen 24, when we are told that Abraham sent his servant to look for a wife for Isaac in his own land and among his own family (Gen 24:4) and that the servant 'set out for Aram Naharaim and Nahor's town' (Gen 24:10). A final detail is added in the story of Jacob, when Rebekah tells Jacob to go to her brother Laban in Haran (Gen 27:43). Jacob left for Haran (Gen 28:10), arrived in the land of $b^e n\hat{e}$ qedhem, the 'sons of the East' (Gen 29:1)[38] and met the shepherds who were from Haran and who knew Laban in that country (Gen 29:4).

In the priestly tradition, Terah settled at Haran and died there (Gen 11:31–32). Abraham left Haran with Lot to go to Canaan (Gen 12:4b–5). After this, Haran is not mentioned again by the priestly writer. The family of Rebekah and Laban lived at Paddan-aram (Gen 25:20), the country to which Isaac sent Jacob (Gen 28:2, 5–7), where Jacob became rich (Gen 31:18), where his sons were born (Gen 35:26, 46:15) and from which he returned to Canaan (Gen 35:9). One text in which Paddan alone is mentioned (Gen 48:7) may belong either to the priestly account or to the Elohistic tradition.

Almost nothing is found in the Elohistic account. If Gen 48:7 does not belong to E, all that is left is Gen 31: 21, which some scholars believe is part of the Elohistic narrative because of the reference to the river, the Euphrates. According to this verse, Jacob crossed the river in his flight from Laban. The ancestors of the Israelites thus lived beyond the Euphrates – which is in accordance with Jos 24:15.

It is clear, then, that these traditions are linked to two names of countries, Aram Naharaim and Paddan-aram, and with two names of towns, 'Nahor's town' and Haran. Because of its apparently dual form, Aram Naharaim has usually been interpreted as Aram of the two rivers, the country between the Euphrates and the Tigris,[39] or else the country between the Euphrates and its tributary the Balih.[40] The suggestion has been made, however, that Naharaim is not a dual form, but simply a plural form of geographical names, so that Aram Naharaim would in this case be Aram of the rivers, the region between the Tigris and the Euphrates watered by the Balih, the

---

[38] See above, p.177.
[39] See especially R. T. O'Callaghan, *Aram Naharaim*, Rome, 1948, new edition 1961.
[40] M. Noth, *Die Ursprünge des alten Israel im Lichte neuer Quellen*, Cologne, 1961, pp. 31–32.

Habur and their tributaries.[41] It would seem[42] that the Hebrew name may have been an adaptation of an early name for the region surrounded on three sides by the great loop of the Euphrates. This name is Naharin and it designates the kingdom of Mitanni in the Egyptian texts from Thut-mose I onwards; the name that appears, with the same meaning, in the Amarna letters is Nahrima. The country is the 'land of the river' (in the singular) and this river is the Euphrates. It should, however, be noted that this name does not occur anywhere before 1500 B.C. There is no proper name for this region in any of the numerous texts which come from northern Syria and Upper Mesopotamia and which date back to the beginning of the second millennium. In the Mari archives, it is known as the High Land and Shamshi-Adad I, who annexed it, called himself the 'ruler (or conqueror) of the country between the Tigris and the Euphrates'.[43] The only name that can really be compared with the 'land of the river' is found in a document of the First Babylonian Dynasty, the name birit nārim or 'between the river', that is, the region surrounding the river (in the singular),[44] but this is not a proper name, only a descriptive term which is also used of other territories.[45] The term Aram, which goes together with Naharaim in the Old Testament, makes it necesssary for us to go back less far in time, since Aram, as the name of a people or a country, does not appear in any Assyrian text before Tiglath-pileser I at the end of the twelfth century B.C. or in any Egyptian text before Amen-hotep III at the beginning of the fourteenth century. Aram Naharaim is not mentioned again in the Old Testament after Gen 24:10 – its only occurrence in Genesis – until Deut 23:5, where we read that the town of Pethor on the west bank of the Euphrates is in Aram Naharaim. The name occurs next in Judges 3:8, where the value of Aram Naharaim depends on the value given to its king, the enigmatical Cushan-rishathaim.[46] Finally, it occurs in the title of Psalm 60 together with Aram-zobah. This is an allusion to David's wars against the Aramaeans, which situates it in this instance in Syria, to the south-west of the Euphrates. In conclusion, we may say that Aram Naharaim gives rise to the same difficulties as Ur of the Chaldaeans – Aram does not coincide with the patriarchal period and Naharaim might well point to a place other than

[41] R. de Vaux, RB, 55 (1948), p. 323; for place-names ending in ayîm, see H. Torczyner, Die Entstehung des semitischen Sprachtypus, Vienna, 1916, pp. 188–190; W. Borée, Die alten Ortsnamen Palästinas, Leipzig, 1930, pp. 54–56.

[42] J.-J. Finkelstein, 'Mesopotamia', JNES, 21 (1962), pp. 73–92, especially pp. 84–88.

[43] E. Ebeling, B. Meissner and E. F. Weidner, Die Inschriften der altassyrischen Könige, Leipzig, 1926, p. 23.

[44] Quoted by J.-J. Finkelstein, op. cit., p. 74.

[45] CAD, II, 1965, under birit, p. 253.

[46] According to A. Malamat, 'Cushan Rishathaim and the Decline of the Near East around 1200 B.C.', JNES, 13 (1954), pp. 231–242, Aram Naharaim stretched to the west of the Euphrates and to the south, at least as far as the latitude of Aleppo.

Upper Mesopotamia.

The Paddan-aram of the priestly tradition is even less certain. The term Aram gives rise to the same anachronism. Paddan has been interpreted by the Assyrian *padānu*, 'road', so that the name might mean the 'road of Aram'. On the other hand, 'road' is also *harrānu*, which is the etymology of Haran (Harrān). Paddan-aram would in this case be the name of a town, another name for Haran.[47] According to the Syriac and Arabic languages, however, it is more likely that Paddan means the 'plain'.[48] It is the Aramaic equivalent of *s'dhēh 'arâm* (Hos 12:13), the plain to which Jacob fled. This interpretation rules out any possibility of a precise location.

We are fortunately on more solid ground in the case of the two names of towns. A town called Nahuru figures on the Cappadocian tablets.[49] The same town plays an important part in the Mari texts.[50] It was still an administrative centre and the seat of a governor in the twelfth century B.C.[51] After a long period, during which it was abandoned or ruined, it reappeared in the seventh century with the name Til-Nahiri.[52] At that time, it belonged to the district of Haran and was situated to the east of that town, only a short distance away.

The name Haran has been preserved as the name of a district in the Upper Balih (Balikh) in modern Turkey; nearby is Eški Harran or 'old Haran', but it is probable that the ancient city is hidden beneath the Muslim ruins and the present tell of Harran.[53] The city was situated at a junction of caravan routes and the name itself means 'road' and 'caravan' in Akkadian (*harrānu*). The name is found in the Cappadocian tablets of the twentieth and nineteenth centuries B.C.,[54] in the Mari archives of the eighteenth century B.C.,[55] and in the early Babylonian itineraries.[56] It is not found in

---

[47] E. Dhorme, *RB*, 37 (1928), p. 487 = *Recueil Ed. Dhorme*, p. 218; R. T. O'Callaghan, *Aram Naharaim, op. cit.*, p. 96.

[48] W. F. Albright, *From the Stone Age to Christianity*,[2] Baltimore, 1946, p. 180; R. de Vaux, *RB*, 55 (1948), p. 323.

[49] E. Bilgiç, 'Die Ortsnamen der "kappadokischen" Urkunden', *AfO*, 15 (1945–1951), pp. 1–37, cf. pp. 23, 24.

[50] See J.-R. Kupper, *Les nomades, op. cit.*, Index; see also *ARM*, IX, 1960, No. 124, 8.*

[51] According to the legal texts of Ashur, *KAJ*, 109, 8, 10, 16; 113, 27, 30; 121, 7, in the reign of Shalmaneser I; see *AfO*, 13 (1939–1941), p. 118, the reign of Tukulti-Ninurta I (?).

[52] C. H. W. Johns, *Assyrian Deeds and Documents*, Cambridge, 1898–1923, No. 420, 3; *ibid., An Assyrian Doomsday Book*, Leipzig, 1901, p. 71, No. 21, 2.

[53] S. Lloyd, W. Price, 'Harran', *AnStud*, 1 (1951), pp. 77–111, see also p. 96. These inscriptions were used again to pave the floor of the great mosque of Harran; see C. J. Gadd, 'The Harran Inscriptions of Nabonidus', *AnStud*, 8 (1958), p. 35.

[54] E. Bilgiç, *op.cit.*, p. 33 (see above, note 49).

[55] See J.-R. Kupper, *Les nomades, op. cit.*, Index; J. Bottéro and A. Finet, *Répertoire analytique des tomes I–V des Archives Royales de Mari*, Paris, 1954, p. 125.

[56] A. Goetze, *op. cit.*, p. 61 (see above, note 35); W. W. Hallo, *op. cit.*, p. 77 (see above, note 35).

texts for several centuries after this – the god Sin of Haran was known in the new Hittite empire and mentioned in its documents, but the town itself was not.[57] It reappears in the Assyrian texts from the reign of Adadnirari I onwards, that is, from about 1300 B.C. It is clear, then, that the two towns of Nahor and Haran were important during the first centuries of the second millennium and that, in view of the fact that they are unmentioned in later texts, they declined in importance for several centuries afterwards. The biblical tradition would seem to go back to the period of their prosperity.

Other parallels with Genesis are provided by geographical evidence. The name Serug which, as we have seen, appeared as a personal name in Lower Mesopotamia, is also the name of a town in Upper Mesopotamia. This is the Sarûgi of the Assyrian documents of the seventh century B.C.[58] It is the Christian centre of Sarug, the modern Sürüç, halfway between Haran and the Euphrates. The name of Abraham's father, Terah, was preserved in the ninth century B.C. at Til-sa-Turah or Til-Turahi, the 'ruin of Terah',[59] in the Baliḫ basin. Unlike Serug, there is no evidence of Terah as a personal name.[60] It would seem to have been a Hurrian custom to call a place by what was originally the name of a person such as Nahor, Serug and Terah.[16] What is remarkable is that all these geographical names are found in the district of Haran – according to the biblical traditions it is precisely in this region that Abraham's family stayed.

Even the names of the three patriarchs connect them with the same environment. The first patriarch is called Abram until Gen 17:5, which forms part of the priestly account of the covenant. At this point, his name is changed to Abraham. The short form, Abram, has been compared with the name Abam-râma, Aba-râma or Abam-ram that is found in the First Babylonian Dynasty.[62] During the Assyrian period, this name appeared as Aba(AD)-rama (or -ramu or -rame), an eponymous officer of 677 B.C.[63]

[57] Haran is in no way connected with Hurna or Hurrana in the Halys basin; see J. Garstang, *The Geography of the Hittite Empire*, London, 1959, pp. 27–28; F. Cornelius, 'Geographie des Hethiterreiches', *Orientalia*, 27 (1958), pp. 225–251, see also p. 233 ff; nor has it anything to do with Mount Harana; see F. Cornelius, *op. cit.*, p. 240.

[58] C. H. W. Johns, *An Assyrian Doomsday Book*, Index, under 'Sarûgi'.

[59] The inscriptions of Shalmaneser III, *ARAB*, I, §§ 563, 610, 646; see also E. G. H. Kraeling, *ZAW*, 40 (1922), p. 153.

[60] The parallel with *Te-ra*, a name found in a Tello document, see N. Schneider, *op. cit.*, p. 521 (see note 24 above), is very questionable because of the absence of the final aspirant. I suggested a parallel with the Safaitic *trh*, *RB*, 55 (1948), p. 324, but this is a common name meaning 'sadness'. see G. Ryckmans, 'Le nom propre Téraḥ est-il attesté en safaïtique ?' *RB*, 56 (1949), pp. 579–582. The attempt to find Terah in the Rās Shamrah texts as the name of a moon deity has been abandoned. In Ugaritic, *trh* is a common name meaning the price paid for a wife (Akkadian *tirḫatu*) or a verb, meaning to pay the purchasing price.

[61] According to H. Lewy, 'Assyria c. 2600–1816 B.C.', *CAH*, I, XXV, 1966, p. 5.

[62] A. Ungnad, 'Urkunden aus Dilbat', *Beiträge für Assyriologie*, VI, 5, 1909, p. 82.

[63] *Reallexikon der Assyriologie*, II, 1938, pp. 426–427.

and, in the feminine form, Abu(AD)-rami, the sister of Naqi'a, Sennacherib's favourite wife.[64] This name is however, really Akkadian and means 'loves the father',[65] because it comes from the root r'm, 'to love', which does not exist in western Semitic and the name Abram would have to be explained by reference to the latter. In western Semitic, the root rûm means 'to be lifted up, exalted' and Abram therefore means either 'he is exalted as to his father; he is noble by birth' if 'ab is accepted as an adverbial accusative[66] or 'the (my) father is exalted' if Abram is regarded as a shortened form of Abiram ("bhîrām).[67] The possible abbreviation of Abiram to Abram can be compared with the two forms Abner ('abh'nêr) and Abiner ("bhînêr) and the two forms Absalom ('abh'sālôm) and Abishalom ('bhîsālôm) in the Old Testament and the Assyrian transcription Ṣḥiab for the Hebrew Ahab ('aḥ'ābh). The root rûm is used in ●Amorite personal names as well[68] and names formed with abi- are frequent.[69] All the same, the name Abram (or Abiram) has not been encountered so far in the documents of the beginning of the second millennium. The form Abiramu occurs in the Akkadian texts from Rās Shamrah[70] and it may perhaps be evident on a Taanach tablet.[71] We are left, then, with the possibility of explaining the name Abram (or Abiram) by referring to Amorite personal names.

The longer form of the name, Abraham, is simply a variation in dialect and can be explained by the insertion of -h- in a weak root or a long syllable. This is a phenomenon that also occurred in Aramaic,[72] Ugaritic[73]

[64] C. H. W. Johns, Assyrian Deeds and Documents, No. 70. Because Naqi'a has an Aramaic name and was originally a foreigner – see H. Lewy, JNES, 11 (1952), pp. 272–273; J. Mougayrol, Syria, 33 (1956), p. 156 ff – attempts have been made to explain her sister's name as well by reference to western Semitic; see K. Tallquist, Assyrian Personal Names, Helsinki, 1914, p. 5 and more recently H. Cazelles, 'Patriarches', DBS, VII (1961), col. 121. See also J. J. Stamm. Die akkadische Namengebung, Leipzig, 1939, p. 292.

[65] B. Gemser, De Beteekenis der Persoonsnamen voor onze Kennis van het Leven en Denken der ouden Babyloniërs en Assyriërs, Wageningen, 1924, p. 144; J. J. Stamm, op. cit., p. 292 (see note 64 above).

[66] W. F. Albright, 'The Names Shaddai and Abram', JBL, 54 (1935), pp. 173–204; R. de Vaux, RB, 53 (1946), p. 323.

[67] From Gunkel and E. Meyer to E. A. Speiser, Genesis (Anchor Bible), 1964, see comments on Gen 17:5.

[68] H. B. Huffmon, Amorite Personal Names in the Mari Texts, Baltimore, 1965, pp. 261–262; this occurred as early as the Third Dynasty of Ur, see G. Buccellati, The Amorites of the Ur III Period, Naples, 1966, p. 131.

[69] H. B. Huffmon, op. cit., p. 154.

[70] J. Nougayrol, PRU, III, p. 20. The form 'abrm in one text in alphabetic cuneiform should not, however, be included here, as the name designates a Cypriot and an Egyptian on one and the same tablet.

[71] Taanach, 12, 2: a-bi-ra . . .

[72] W. F. Albright, JBL, 54 (1935), p. 203.

[73] bhtm (from bt), the feminine plurals umht, amht, qrht, ilht; see C. H. Gordon, Ugaritic Textbook, Rome, 1965, Grammar, § 8.7 and 8.

and Phoenician.[74] The name may perhaps be represented in an Egyptian transcription by Aburahana in certain execration texts.[75] It should be noted in this context that, at the same time as the name Abram became Abraham, the name Sarai (*šarai*) was changed to Sarah (*šarāh*) (Gen 17:15). It is possible that this twofold change of name reflects a movement from one linguistic zone to another – Sarai can be compared with the divine titles that are found in the Rās Shamrah texts (Pidrai, Tallai and 'Arsai [76]) and the ending -*aya* is found in a class of feminine Amorite names.[77] As we have seen, the short form Abram (or Abiram) was known at Rās Shamrah and the longer form Abraham was paralleled only in an Egyptian text.

To turn now to the name of the second patriarch, Isaac,[78] we find that it is a diminutive form of a name composed of a verb in the imperfect followed by the subject of the verb which is either a divine name or the name of a relation. In the first case, the name *yiṣḥāq-'Ēl* (or the equivalent) meant 'God laughs, is favourable' or 'may God laugh, may he be favourable'. The verb root *ṣāḥaq* (*ṣḥq*) also occurs in the Ugaritic poems, which speak of the god El smiling in favour. If the name Isaac is an abbreviation of *yiṣḥāq-'ābh* (or the equivalent), then it meant 'the father (or the relation) laughs' or 'may the father (or the relation) laugh'. A Hurrian story translated into Hittite depicts a father smiling at a newly born son placed on his knees.[79] There is no evidence of the name outside the Bible, but names composed in this way from a verb in the imperfect form the most typical and the most numerous class of Amorite personal names. On the other hand, Canaanite-Phoenician examples of this type of personal name are rare. In Israel, this type of name was fairly widespread until the time of David, when it disappeared, only emerging again just before the Exile, when, perhaps because of an Aramaean influence, it became quite common.[80]

[74] *dlht*, 'the doors', *KAI*, Nos. 18, 3; 122, 2; see J. Friedrich, *Phönizisch-punische Grammatik*, Rome, 1951, § 240–241, 12.

[75] See W. F. Albright, *BASOR*, 83 (Oct. 1941), p. 34; for the alternation of *m* and *n*, see above, p. 194 – *nahrima* in the Amarna letters = Naharin in the Egyptian texts.

[76] J. T. Milik, *Rivista Biblica*, 6 (1958), pp. 252–254; F. M. Cross, *HTR*, 55 (1962), pp. 246–247.

[77] H. B. Huffmon, *op. cit.*, p. 135 (see note 68 above).

[78] J. J. Stamm, 'Der Name Isaac', *Festschrift A.Schädelin*, Berlin, 1950, pp. 33–37.

[79] *ZA*, 49 (1950), p. 221, 1. 5; cf. E. A. Speiser, *Genesis*, p. 125.

[80] M. Noth, *Die israelitischen Personennamen im Rahmen der gemeinsemitischen Namengabung*, Stuttgart, 1927, pp. 28–29; *ibid.*, 'Mari und Israel. Eine Personennamenstudie', *Geschichte und Altes Testament (Festschrift Alt)*, Tübingen, 1953, pp. 127–152, cf. 138–143; H. B Huffmon, *op. cit.*, pp. 63–85 (see note 68 above). Isaac's brother, Ishmael – *yisˈmāˈel*, 'God hears' or 'may God hear' – has a similar name, but it is not abbreviated. The equivalent form *Ya-ás--ma-ah-El* occurs twice in the Mari texts, as well as the parallel names *Ya-ás-ma-ah-Addu*, *Is-me-Addu*, *Ya-ás-ma-ah-Dagan* and *Is-me-eh-Ba-al*; see Huffmon, *op. cit.*, pp. 44, 249–250. The name *Is-me-ᵈX* also occurs on a jar of eighteenth or seventeenth century B.C. found at Hazor; see Y. Yadin, *Hazor*, II, Jerusalem, 1960, pp. 115–117.

The name Jacob is in the same category. It is an abbreviation of *ya'qôbh-'Ēl* (or the equivalent) and it has been suggested that the complete form is to be found in the difficult text of Deut 33:28.[81] Certainly there is clear evidence outside the Bible that the name existed at an early period, for example in Lower Mesopotamia.[82] As for Upper Mesopotamia, *Ya-ah-qu-ub-El* occurs four times in the Chagar Bazar inscriptions, which date back to a little later than 1800 B.C.[83] and *Ya-a-qu-ub-El* occurs once at Qat(t)una on the Habûr at the end of the eighteenth century B.C.[84] In Egyptian, the name – or at least the first part of it – is found as a royal name on the Hyksos scarabs.[85] On the other hand, *ya'qôbh-'Ēl* is a Palestinian place-name in the geographical list of Thut-mose III and those of Ramses II and Ramses III who copied Thut-mose's list.[86] The root *'qb* forms part of the composition of other Amorite names[87] and has the meaning of 'to protect', a meaning which was not preserved in Canaanite and Hebrew, but which survived in Ethiopian and in southern Arabic.[88] The name Jacob, then, means '(God) protects' or 'May (God) protect.'

No individual was given the name of Abraham, Isaac or Jacob apart from the three patriarchs themselves throughout the whole of the Old Testament period. All three names belong to onomastic types which were well known before the Israelites emerged as a people and, what is more, they appeared in the very regions from which the patriarchs came according to the Bible. The editors of Genesis, not understanding the meaning of these names, had recourse to popular etymology. According to Gen 17:5, for example, Abraham was given this name because he was to be the 'father of a multitude', *'abh hāmôn*, because of the assonance with *hāmôn*, 'multitude'. In the Bible, if Yahweh 'laughs', this is never a sign of his favour – it is because he is scornful or mocking (see, for example, Hab 1:10; Ps 2:4; 36:13). If the

---

[81] D. N. Freedman, 'The Original Name of Jacob', *IEJ*, 13 (1963), pp. 125–126.

[82] See above, p. 191.

[83] C. J. Gadd, *Iraq*, 7 (1940), p. 38.*

[84] J. Nougayrol, *Syria*, 37 (1960), p. 207, 1. 4.

[85] *Y'qb'r* and *Y'qbhr*, which are regarded as two transcriptions of *ya'qôbh-'Ēl*. On the other hand, *Y'qbhr* might be read as a transcription of *ya' qôbh-Har, Har* being used here as a divine title ('mountain god'); see W. F. Albright, *From the Stone Age to Christianity,*[2] Baltimore, 1946, p. 184 = *Anchor Books*, 1957, p. 242. *Y'qb'r* is the equivalent of *ya'qôbh-Ba'al* according to S. Yeivin, *JEA*, 45 (1959), pp. 16–18. Finally, both names might be read as transcriptions of *ya'qôbh-'Al*, a divine name, according to W. F. Albright, *Yahweh and the Gods of Canaan*, London, 1968, p. 50, note, cf. p. 133, note.

[86] J. Simons, *Handbook for the Study of Egyptian Topographical Lists Relating to Western Asia*, Leiden, 1937, pp. 118, No. 102, 158, No. 9, 169, No. 104.

[87] J. B. Huffmon, *op. cit.*, p. 203. One name that might be added is Ya-áq-qú-ub-e-da, found on a cylinder, probably eighteenth century Syrian; see J.-R. Kupper, *Les nomades, op. cit.*, p. 237.

[88] M. Noth, *Die israelitischen Personennamen, op. cit.*, p. 177; W. F. Albright, *JAOS*, 74 (1954), p. 231.

name Isaac is to be explained etymologically by 'laughing', it is because Abraham laughed (Gen 17:17) or because Sarah laughed (Gen 18:12; 21:6) and because there is a good deal of word-play in connection with the name. Ishmael 'played' with Isaac (Gen 21:9) and Isaac 'fondled' Rebekah (Gen 26:8) – 'to play' and 'to caress' are two other meanings of the Hebrew root ṣāhaq. In Hebrew, too, the root 'qb ('āqabh) does not mean 'to protect', but 'to supplant', or, in the noun form ('aqêbh), 'heel'. The conclusion drawn from this is that Jacob was so called because, when he was born, he was holding the heel of his twin brother Esau (Gen. 25:26) and because he later supplanted him (Gen 27:36).

These names, then, were transmitted by a very early tradition. To judge by their structure and their grammatical form, all three may have been Amorite names. The name Jacob in particular could only have been Amorite, introduced by the Amorites into Lower and Upper Mesopotamia during the first few centuries of the second millennium. Bearing in mind too that other names occurring in the stories of the patriarchs, especially Serug, Nahor and Terah, occur as personal or place names during the Amorite period and in the parts of the Ancient Near East occupied by the Amorites – above all in the neighbourhood of Haran as far as the place-names are concerned – one is bound to conclude that these traditions have a firm historical basis. We may go further and say that the migrations of the patriarchs were closely related to the movement of the Amorites.

III. AMORITES OR ARAMAEANS?

It is, however, indisputable that the patriarchs are connected in the biblical tradition not only with the Amorites [89] but also with the Aramaeans. We have already seen that, according to that tradition, the patriarchs came from Aram Naharaim or from Paddan-aram and that Laban, Abraham's great-nephew, Rebekah's brother and the father of Leah and Rachel, is again and again called 'the Aramaean' (Gen 25:20; 28:5; 31:20, 24). Later, the Israelite was obliged to make a confession of faith beginning with the words: 'My father was a wandering Aramaean' (or 'an Aramaean ready to perish', Deut 26:5), when he presented his first fruits. This is a very early biblical tradition, belonging to the Yahwistic source. It could not have been established when the Aramaeans were the enemies of Israel, as they were from the time of David onwards. It troubled the rabbis, who misinterpreted Deut 26:5.[90]

[89] 'Your father was an Amorite' in Ezek 6:3 is scornful. The name is used in the biblical sense; see above, pp. 132–133. The Amorites of the modern historians are, of course, different.

[90] M. A. Beek, 'Das Problem des aramäischen Stammvaters', *OTS*, 8, (1950), pp. 193–212.

Is it, however, possible to speak of Aramaeans during the patriarchal period? The Aramaeans of the first millennium are fairly well known to us through their own inscriptions, the Assyrian texts and the Bible itself. They had already established principalities in Upper Mesopotamia, in the valleys of the Orontes and the Leontes (Nahr el-Lītāni) and in the whole of southern Syria by the eleventh century B.C. This expansion towards the south-west can be seen in the names of the sons of Nahor and his concubine Reumah given in the priestly account (Gen 22:24) – these names are all situated in this region.[91] Apart from Genesis, the earliest references to Aramaeans in the Bible – Num 23:7 (Balaam's coming from Aram) and Judges 3:8 (Cushan Rishathaim, the king of Aram Naharaim) – hardly enable us to go back further in history.[92] The first clear reference to the Aramaeans in the cuneiform texts dates from the time of Tiglath-pileser I, who fought the Ahlamu-Aramaeans along the Euphrates and burnt six of their 'towns' (or encampments) at the foot of Jebel Bishri in the fourth year of his reign, round about 1110 B.C. Altogether, Tiglath-pileser I conducted fourteen campaigns against the Ahlamu-Aramaeans.[93] These two names appear again in several inscriptions made during the reigns of later rulers up until that of Ashurnasirpal II (883–859 B.C.). Finally, Ahlamu sometimes appears alone, until the reign of Ashurbanipal (668–626), when it was synonymous with Aramaean, a name which was used less and less at this period. To this can be added the fact that, in late texts, the adjective or adverb derived from Ahlamu refers to the Aramaic language and writing.[94]

On the other hand, however, the name Ahlamu was sometimes used alone before the two names Ahlamu-Aramaeans appeared together, to designate western nomads who were hostile to the Assyrians. There are examples of this usage during the reigns of Ashurreshishi, the father of Tiglath-pileser (1132–1115),[95] Tukulti-Ninurta I (1244–1208),[96] Shalman-eser I (1274–1245)[97] and Adadnirari I, who recalls the victory gained by his father Arikdenili (1318–1307) over the Ahlamu and the Suteans.[98] During the thirteenth century, the Ahlamu prevented the messengers of the king of Babylonia from reaching Hattu.[99] In the fourteenth and

[91] A. Malamat, *XV Rencontre Assyriologique Internationale, Liège*, Paris, 1967, pp. 130–131.
[92] This, of course, depends on the date of the oracles of Balaam and the interpretation of Judges 3:7–11.
[93] *ARAB*, I, §§ 239, 308 and the text edited by E. Weidner, *AfO*, 18 (1957–1958), p. 344, lines 29–30. For the Egyptian texts which may perhaps provide references which are a little earlier, see below, p. 204.
[94] *CAD*, I, I, 1964, under the headings *ahlamatti* and *ahlamu*.
[95] *ARAB*, I, § 209.
[96] *ibid.*, § 166.
[97] *ibid.*, § 116.
[98] *ibid.*, § 73.
[99] *KBo*, I, 10, line 35 ff. See J. Friedrich, *Aus dem hethitischen Schrifttum* (*Der Alte Orient*, XXIV, 3), 1925. p. 26.

thirteenth centuries B.C., individual Ahlamu, both men and women, appear as immigrants in the region of Nippur.[100] During the reign of Burnaburiash II (1375–1347 ?), Ahlamu who had probably been engaged as workers gave some trouble to the governor of Dilmun, which is now the island of Bahrein and the coastland facing it.[101] At about the same time, the Ahlamu are mentioned in one of the Amarna letters in a mutilated context.[102] It has been suggested that the Ahlamu as a people are mentioned even earlier, in some of the Mari texts in which a functionary responsible for receiving oil for the royal table is called Ahlamu.[103] The name has also been explained as an Amorite personal name and not as an ethnic term,[104] but it appears in a so far unpublished text of the eighteenth century B.C., dating back to the period of Rim-Sin, in a reference to the 'Ahlamu messengers'.[105] This is, of course, the Mari period and that of the patriarchs.

For a long time, it was accepted that Ahlamu was a broken plural meaning the 'confederates' and that the word was related to the Arabic *hilm*, the plural of which is *'ahlam*. The Ahlamu were therefore regarded as a confederation of nomadic groups, of which the Aramaeans themselves formed one group – hence the term 'the Ahlamu-Aramaeans'. The references to the Ahlamu alone made it possible for the history of these people to be regarded as going back to the fourteenth century B.C.,[106] perhaps even to the eighteenth century. This is, however, an incorrect explanation of the name Ahlamu.[107] First, the Arabic word *hilm* is very rarely used in the sense of 'companion' – it is almost exclusively employed to denote a relationship between a man and a woman: in other words, it means 'one who courts a woman'. Secondly, all the Akkadian transcriptions have a short -a- in the second position and not a long -a- which would call for a broken plural. Finally, there is no evidence that the broken plural

[100] A. T. Clay, *Documents from the Temple Archives of Nippur* (BE XIV, 16, 6; XV, 14, 11; 168, 16 etc.).

[101] P. B. Cornwell, 'Two Letters from Dilmun', *JCS*, 6 (1952), pp. 137–145.

[102] *EA*, 200, 8 and 10.

[103] The references will be found in Huffmon, *Amorite Personal Names, op. cit.*, p. 21; to these can be added *ARM*, XII, 1964, Nos. 110, 264, 334, 339, 492, 506, 508, 509. The same individual is referred to in each case. The suggestion that this is connected with the Ahlamu as a people was made by A. Dupont-Sommer, 'Sur les débuts de l'histoire araméenne', *Congress Volume. Copenhagen* (SVT, 1), Leiden, 1953, pp. 40–49. This suggestion was accepted by J.-R. Kupper, *Les nomades, op. cit.*, p. 108; S. Moscati, *The Semites in Ancient History*, Cardiff, 1959, p. 64; *ibid.*, 'The Aramaean, Ahlamu', *JSS*, 4 (1959), pp. 303–307, see also p. 304.

[104] H. B. Huffmon, *Amorite Personal Names, op. cit.*, pp. 147–148, 195–196; see also I. J. Gelb, *JCS*, 15 (1961), p. 28, no. 5.

[105] M. Dietrich, O. Loretz, *OLZ*, 61 (1966), col. 243; *TR*, 65 (1969), col. 365.

[106] R. de Vaux, *RB*, 55 (1948), p. 345, with the previous references; R. T. O'Callaghan, *Aram Naharaim, op. cit.*, p. 95; A. Dupont-Sommer, *Les Araméens*, Paris, 1949, p. 19; M. McNamara, 'De populi Aramaeorum primordiis', *Verbum Domini*, 35 (1957), pp. 129–142, cf. pp. 139–140.

[107] S. Moscati, 'The Aramaean Ahlamu', *op. cit.* (note 103).

existed at this time in western Semitic.[108] We are therefore bound to conclude that Ahlamu is the name of a tribe or people and is, in this respect, similar to the name Aramaean.[109] The binomial expression Ahlamu-Aramaeans has several parallels in the Mari texts and those of the Third Dynasty of Ur – the Haneans-Benjaminites, the Haneans-Iamahamu and the Amorites-Suteans, for example.[110] These names may reflect the uncertainty that the settled people felt with regard to the position of the nomads with whom they came into contact. On the other hand, they may reflect the real relationships existing between groups related to each other by ties of blood and leading the same kind of life in the same districts.

It has been claimed that the 'Aramaeans' can also be found even before the Ahlamu-Aramaeans of Tiglath-pileser I.[111] A late copy of one text, for example, describes Naram-Sin's victory in the twenty-third century B.C. over Harsamatki, the lord of Aram and Am in the mountainous district of Tibar. The editor of this text[112] believed that this Aram – the suggested location in Asia Minor or Upper Syria is very uncertain – had nothing to do with the Aramaeans and there is no reason to suppose that he was wrong. A town called Aram is also mentioned in two tablets of the same period from Tutub (Khafajeh),[113] in a tablet from Drehem during the Ur III Period,[114] and in a text of the First Dynasty of Babylonia.[115] Everything contained in these texts points to the fact that this Aram was in the Dyala basin to the east of the Tigris. It is, however, difficult to recognise Aramaean countries in these two geographical names of the third millennium, if indeed there are two names. The claim that there is a connection between them and the Aramaeans presupposes that the Aramaeans were at this time sufficiently settled to give their name to a town or a country or that they took their name from a town or a country, both of them a long way from the region in which they were to be found leading nomadic lives a thousand years later.[116]

---

[108] The last two reasons can also be applied to refute the explanation offered by W. von Soden, *Akkadisches Wörterbuch*, I, 1965, under the heading *ahlamu*, namely that it is a collective term meaning 'youth' and is similar to the Arabic *ǵlm*.

[109] E. Forrer, *Reallexikon der Assyriologie*, I, 1932, col. 131; A. Alt, *Kleine Schriften*, I, p. 174, note 1; S. Moscati, *op. cit.* (note 103); J. C. L. Gibson, *JNES*, 20 (1961), p. 231.

[110] J.-R. Kupper, *Les nomades*, *op. cit.*, pp. 72–73, 88–89; S. Moscati, 'The Aramaean Ahlamu', *op. cit.*, p. 305; G. Buccellati, *The Amorites of the Ur III Period*, Naples, 1966, p. 333.

[111] N. Schneider, 'Aram und die Aramäer in der Ur III Zeit', *Biblica*, 30 (1949), pp. 109–111; S. Moscati, 'Sulle origini degli Aramei', *RSO*, 26 (1951), pp. 16–22; A. Dupont-Sommer, 'Sur les débuts', *op. cit.*. M. McNamara, *op. cit.* (note 106).

[112] F. Thureau-Dangin, *RA*, 8 (1911), pp. 199–200.

[113] I. J. Gelb, *Sargonic Texts from the Diyala Region (Materials for the Assyrian Dictionary)*, Chicago, 1952, No. 217, 8; 220, 9.

[114] 'The Wengler Text, No. 22', A. Deimel, *Orientalia* (old series), II, 1920, p. 62.

[115] J. J. Finkelstein, *JCS*, 9 (1955), pp. 1–2.

[116] This suggested connection has in fact been rejected by several more recent authors; see,

It is also necessary to set aside the evidence that one might expect to find in personal names. For example, another tablet from Drehem[117] refers to a man called Aramu, but, although he would seem to have come from the town of Aram to the east of the Tigris, he is certainly not one of our 'Aramaeans'. Again, the name Aramu appears in a list of people entitled to receive rations in the Mari documents[118] and the name Arammu occurs several times in the Alalah tablets.[119] Even if it is a semitic name,[120] its etymology is unknown and it would be very unwise to link it with the Aramaeans.[121]

When we come to the Rās Shamrah texts, however, we are on rather more solid ground. The name Bn 'Armi appears several times in the alphabetic cuneiform lists.[122] Should this perhaps be translated as 'the Aramaean'? In the Akkadian texts, a witness of a bill of sale is named as Armeya.[123] Does this perhaps mean 'the Aramaean'? A royal gift includes, among other lands, eqlēti a-ra-mi-ma. Should we translate this, as the editor does rather cautiously, as the 'lands of Aramima',[124] or as the 'field of the Aramaeans'?[125] Even if these are the correct interpretations, however, the Rās Shamrah texts do not take us further back than the fourteenth century B.C.

It is possible to go a little further back in history if an Egyptian document is considered in this context. This is a geographical list compiled during the reign of Amen-hotep III and containing the name p3'rm, which may be interpreted as the 'country of Aram' or, because of the personal determinative, the 'people of the country of Aram', the Aramaeans.[126] The other

---

for example, J. J. Finkelstein, op. cit., p. 2, note 13; J.-R. Kupper, Les nomades, op. cit., p. 114; I. J. Gelb, JCS, 15 (1961), p. 28, note 5; J. C. L. Gibson, JNES, 20 (1961), p. 232; A. Goetze, JCS, 17 (1963), p. 4, note 41. S. Moscati, on the other hand, accepts it; see The Semites in Ancient History, Cardiff, 1959, pp. 66–67.
[117] C. E. Keiser, Cuneiform Bullae of the Third Millennium B.C., New York, 1914, No. 159, 18.
[118] M. Birot, RA, 49 (1955), p. 21.
[119] D. J. Wiseman, The Alalakh Tablets, London, 1953, Index, p. 128.
[120] J.-R, Kupper, Les nomades, op. cit., p. 113. Kupper thinks that Arammu is a Hurrian name and compares it with another Hurrian name found at Alalah, Arammusumi.
[121] H. B. Huffmon, op. cit., p. 143.
[122] Gordon 321 (= Herdner 119), III, 22; Gordon 1046, 7 and 9 and 1064, 10 (= Virolleaud, PRU, II, 46 and 64).
[123] J. Nougayrol, PRU, III, 15, 37, p. 35.
[124] Ibid., PRU, 16. 178, p. 148.
[125] A. Dupont-Sommer translates it as the 'field of the Aramaeans'; see his 'Sur les débuts', op. cit. (note 103), pp. 46–47; Dupont-Sommer is followed here by J.-R. Kupper, Les nomades, op. cit., p. 114.
[126] E. Edel, Die Ortsnamenlisten aus dem Totentempel Amenophis', III Bonn, 1966, pp. 28–29. This makes it necessary to reconsider the Anastasi III Papyrus, reverse 5, 5, which mentions a town called p3 'rm, usually corrected to p3 'mr, the 'country of Amurru', and transcribed as

names appearing on this fragmentary list cannot, unfortunately, be identified and the geographical situation of the group is very uncertain. Whatever may be the case, unless we attribute a later date to the patriarchs, the information that is at present available to us certainly obliges us to conclude that the references to Aram and the Aramaeans in Genesis must be anachronistic.

There is, however, an element of historical truth in this name. It has even been suggested that the Amorites should be called 'Proto-Aramaeans'.[127] Different arguments, some less convincing than others, have been put forward in support of this. The language of the archives found at Mari, where an Amorite dynasty ruled during the eighteenth century B.C. and where most of the population at this time was Amorite, is Old Babylonian, an Akkadian dialect.[128] Certain features of the phonetics, morphology and vocabulary of this language, however, betray a clear influence of the spoken language, western Semitic.[129] In the absence of documentary evidence, this 'Amorite language' is still very little known to us.[130] The little that we do know makes it clear that it is the earliest representative of western Semitic that we have so far been able to trace; in other words, it precedes the separation into the different languages or dialects of the western Semitic group and especially the formation of the Canaanite language.[131] The Mari texts provide only very few of the linguistic characteristics of Aramaic.[132]

Proper names have also been used as evidence. We have already drawn attention to the fact that names formed from a verb in the imperfect are very characteristically Amorite and that they disappeared in Israel after David's reign, but appeared again in considerable numbers just before the

---

p3 irm, 'unknown district', by R. A. Caminos, *Late Egyptian Miscellanies*, London, 1954, p. 113.

[127] M. Noth, *Die israelitischen Personennamen, op. cit.*, pp. 43–47. Noth abandoned this theory in an article in *ZDPV*, 65 (1942), p. 34, note 2, but returned to it later after the Mari texts had been published; see *Die Ursprünge, op. cit.*, especially pp. 29–31. I suggested the name myself, first in *RB*, 55 (1948), pp. 345–346, then in *RB*, 72 (1965), p. 15. It was adopted by J. C. L. Gibson, 'Light from Mari on the Patriarchs', *JSS*, 7 (1962), pp. 44–62, especially p. 51.

[128] A. Finet, *L'accadien des lettres de Mari*, Brussels, 1956.

[129] G. Dossin, *Syria*, 19 (1938); A Caquot, 'Remarques sur la langue et le panthéon des Amorites de Mari', *AAS*, 1 (1951), pp. 206–225.

[130] I. J. Gelb, 'La lingua degli Amoriti', *Accademia Nazionale dei Lincei, Rendiconti*, VIII, 13, 1958, pp. 143–164.

[131] See I. J. Gelb, *JCS*, 15 (1961), p. 44.

[132] The linguistic links have been exaggerated by M. Noth, *Die Ursprünge, op. cit.*, pp. 34–40, which I followed in *RB*, 72 (1965), pp. 14–15; see D. O. Edzard's criticism in 'Mari und Aramäer?' *ZA*, 56 (1964), pp. 142–149; M. Wagner, 'Beiträge zur Aramaismenfrage im alttestamentlichen Hebräisch', *Hebräische Wortforschung. Festschrift W. Baumgartner (SVT*, 16), 1967, pp. 355–371.*

Exile.[133] The reappearance of this type of proper name can be explained by the re-emergence of Aramaean influence. There is sporadic evidence of this onomastic form in imperial Aramaic and in the Nabataean and Palmyrene texts. It is also very common in southern Arabic.[134] It should, however, be noted that it does not appear at all among the fifty or so names contained in the earliest Aramaic inscriptions of the tenth to the seventh centuries or in the biblical texts of the same period.[135] It is also true that certain elements of these Aramaic names appear in Amorite onomastic forms, but they are also encountered in other western Semitic languages and therefore cannot be regarded as specifically Aramaic.

Finally, attempts have also been made to discover Aramaean deities in the Amorite pantheon,[136] but, although this pantheon contains deities that were venerated by the Aramaeans, none of them was exclusively Aramaean or of Aramaean origin.[137] The pantheon of Mari was, moreover, no more closely linked with the Aramaeans than it was with the other western Semites.[138]

Research into the linguistic, onomastic and religious fields has so far yielded results which are almost entirely negative. There are, however, other more general data which ought to be taken into account. There is, for instance, a striking parallel between the movements of the Amorite people and the migration of the Aramaeans. Both originated in the Syrian desert and, even if it may be the result of a pure coincidence in our information, it is particularly striking that the first references to the Amorites – MAR.TU – are found in the locality of the Jebel Bishri,[139] which is, of course, the district where the first Aramaeans mentioned in history had their camp.[140] Both the Amorites and the Aramaeans are described as nomadic herdsmen, first living in the desert but later penetrating into the settled regions and set-

---

[133] See above, p. 198.

[134] M. Noth, *Die israelitischen Personennamen, op. cit.*, pp. 29–30.

[135] Both sets of texts are dealt with by M. Liverani, 'Antecedenti dell'onomastica aramaica antica', *RSO*, 37 (1962), pp. 65–76.

[136] M. Liverani, *op. cit.*, p. 75.

[137] The two most convincing examples of such deities are Mer and 'Atar. Mer – and Itur-Mer – was a storm god who was venerated at Mari and the same deity has been found at Hamath in the inscription of Zakir in the form 'El-Wer. Mer was originally a Mesopotamian deity. See H. B. Huffmon, *Amorite Personal Names, op. cit.*, pp. 271–272 and references. In the case of 'Atar, a name discovered at Mari, 'Attarisaduq, contains the name of the god 'Atar or 'Attar. This deity was venerated especially by the Aramaeans, but he was also honoured elsewhere and seems to have been particularly popular in southern Arabia; see A. Caquot, 'Le dieu Athar et les textes de Râs Shamra', *Syria*, 35 (1958), pp. 45–60; G. Garbini, ' 'Atar dio aramaico?', *RSO*, 35 (1960), pp. 25–28; J. Fitzmyer, *JAOS*, 81 (1961), p. 188; M. Höfner, *Wörterbuch der Mythologie*, ed. H. W. Haussig, I, Stuttgart, 1965, pp. 497–501.

[138] See A. Caquot's conclusions, *op. cit.* (note 129), p. 224.

[139] See above, p. 58.

[140] See above, p. 201. The Jebel Bishri was known, during the reign of Tukulti-Ninurta I, as the 'hill country of the Ahlamu'; see J.-R. Kupper, *Les nomades, op. cit.*, p. 136.

ting up little kingdoms there. Many of the districts occupied by the Aramaeans were the same as those inhabited by the Amorites, the region which is of special interest to us being Upper Mesopotamia. In central Syria,[141] the land of Amurru of the Mari texts in the eighteenth century B.C. then became the Egyptian province of Amurru during the fifteenth and fourteenth centuries and this was in turn succeeded by the state of Amurru. Aziru, the first ruler of this state, had an Amorite name which might equally well have been Aramaic.[142] This state of Amurru survived until the end of the thirteenth century. Less than two centuries later, the Aramaean states of Hamath, Zobah and Beth Rehob were established.

Running parallel to this geographical continuity is a certain overlapping of ethnic terms. The Hiranu, for instance, figure in the list of Aramaean tribes which appeared during the reign of Tiglath-pileser III.[143] They were already active in Upper Mesopotamia and in the state of Mari round about 1300 B.C.[144] The first undisputed example of the name 'Aramaeans' is provided by the Ahlamu-Aramaeans round about 1100 B.C., but it is possible to trace the history of the Ahlamu back at least two centuries earlier. They were also associated with the Suteans during the reign of Arikdenili at the end of the fourteenth century B.C.[145] A document possibly dating from the reign of Ashurbelkala in the eleventh century speaks of campaigns against the Aramaeans and then mentions, in a passage that is unfortunately mutilated, both the Suteans and the Ahlamu.[146] The Suteans are named several times after the Aramaeans or after a list of Aramaean tribes by Sargon II (720–704 B.C.).[147] These Suteans formed the most permanent and perhaps even the most important group of nomads in the Syrian desert.[148] They appeared during the First Babylonian Dynasty and, as we have already seen, one document discovered at Ur refers to a Sutean Amorite.[149] The Mari archives frequently mention them and they appear in the Alalah, the Boghazköy and the Rās Shamrah tablets and above all in the letters excavated at Tell-el-ʿAmārna. We have quoted just some of the texts in which they are mentioned; to these should be added an Assyrian text dating back to the reign of Esarhaddon, in which the name appears for the last time.[150]

[141] See above, pp. 61, 97, 102.

[142] The Amorite name is Aziru or Haziru at Mari and Chagar Bazar; the Aramaic name may be Hadadezer of Zobah or Adad-idri of Damascus.

[143] *ARAB*, I, § 788.

[144] According to a letter published by O. R. Gurney, *Iraq*, II (1949), pp. 139–141.

[145] See above, p. 201. There is also a much later reference to them in one of Sennacherib's inscriptions; see *ARAB*, II, § 325.

[146] E. Weidner, *AfO*, 6 (1930–1931), p. 92, lines 8–14.

[147] *ARAB*, II, §§ 82, 96, 99.

[148] See especially J.-R. Kupper, *Les nomades, op. cit.*, pp. 83–147.

[149] See above, pp. 190–191.

[150] *ARAB*, II, § 585.

We may therefore conclude that they took part in the Amorite migrations and that they were associated with the Aramaean movement. There is, of course, no question of regarding the names – Suteans, Ahlamu, Aramaeans – as interchangeable because they appear together in the same documents. On the other hand, there can be no doubt that the continued association and succession of these names points to a relationship and a racial continuity between these groups. The basic population of the Syrian desert, from which they all came and where they lived very similar lives, did not necessarily change during the four centuries which separate the Amorites of Mari from the Ahlamu – or Aramaeans – of the fourteenth century B.C. and we have seen that there is possible evidence of the Ahlamu from the eighteenth century B.C. onwards. The pressure exerted by the nomads certainly never ceased throughout the second millennium, but they only forced their way into the settled countries when those countries were no longer dominated by a strong power. The Amorite 'invasion' followed the collapse of the kingdom of Ur about 2000 B.C. and the Aramaean 'invasion' was made possible by the ruin of the Hittite and Egyptian empires about 1200 B.C.

Having admitted the existence of a continuity, we must go a stage further and recognise that 'Amorite' is not an ethnic term, but a geographical one. MAR.TU in Sumerian and Amurru in Akkadian mean the 'country of the west' or the 'people of the west' and it has been suggested that they should be called 'Canaanites'.[151] This name, however, goes against the traditional usage of the name 'Canaanite' inherited from the Bible and, even if this usage is extended to include, among the people called Canaanites by convention, the first Semites who inhabited Palestine and part of Syria before 3000 B.C., it is still not possible to give the people we are considering here the name Canaanites.[152] A distinction must be made between these early inhabitants and those who began to arrive from about 2000 B.C. onwards. Here we can draw on the classical distinction made in the western Semitic dialects between Canaanite and Aramaic and use the term 'Proto-Aramaeans'. It is, however, important to stress that this is a purely conventional name, because the difference between Canaanite and Aramaic becomes apparent only at the end of the second millennium. We have no knowledge at all of the language spoken by the 'Canaanites' in the third millennium and very little indeed of that spoken by the Amorites.

[151] 'Canaanites of the East' according to T. Bauer, *Die Ostkanaanäer. Eine philosophisch-historische Untersuchung über die Wanderschicht der sogenannten 'Amoriter' in Babylonien*, Leipzig, 1926, following B. Landsberger, *ZA*, 35 (1924), p. 238, who continued to insist on this name, *JCS*, 8 (1954), p. 56, note 103. Simply 'Canaanites' according to D. O. Edzard, *Die 'Zweite Zwischenzeit' Babyloniens*, 1957, p. 30, note 127 and *passim*; W. von Soden, *Propyläen Weltgeschichte*, ed. G. Mann and A. Heuss, I, Berlin, 1961, p. 568.
[152] See above, pp. 51–52.

What is more, it is quite legitimate to criticise the classification of a linguistic group in terms of ethnology. All the same, the term 'Proto-Aramaeans' has the great advantage of showing that there was a continuity between the Amorites of the patriarchal age and the Aramaeans of the eleventh and tenth century B.C.

This is, of course, the period when the traditions of Genesis became established and were set down in writing. A precise memory of the coming of Israel's ancestors from Upper Mesopotamia had been preserved as well as a memory of the blood-ties connecting the patriarchs with the Semites already settled in this district. The new names that had been received were naturally enough given to the country and its inhabitants – it was, for example, Aram Naharaim where Laban the Aramaean lived.[153] This may be an anachronism, but it is unconsciously linked with a reality, so that the Israelite could truthfully say: 'My father was a wandering Aramaean . . .'

IV. THE 'HEBREWS' AND THE 'HABIRU'

Although we use such terms as the Hebrew language, the Hebrew people and the Hebrew patriarchs, these and similar phrases are unknown in the 'Hebrew' Old Testament itself,[154] in which the language of the Israelites, for example, is called the 'language of Canaan' (Isa 19:18), the 'Judaean language' (2 Kings 18:26; Isa 36:11) or the 'language of Judah' (Neh 13:24; 2 Chron 32:18). The term 'Hebrew language' appears for the first time, in Greek, in the prologue or 'translator's foreword' to Ecclesiasticus and in several apocryphal writings of more or less the same date – the Book of Jubilees, the Letter of Aristeas and the Testament of Nephthali – and later, in the New Testament and in the work of Philo of Alexandria and Josephus. In Semitic, the term 'Hebrew' language – or 'Hebrew' writing – is found exclusively in the rabbinical texts, although the expression 'holy language' occurs more frequently in those texts. The Greek word Ἑβραῖος, in the plural Ἑβραῖοι, appears at more or less the same period, that is, at the end of the second century or in the first century B.C. in the books of Judith and 2 Maccabees and then three times in the New Testament and again in Philo and Josephus. It is used to denote a Jew, the Jewish people or the Jews. It is moreover, in these cases, an archaic and noble term, synonymous with Ἰουδαῖος and the pagan authors usually employed it to designate the Jews

[153] Compare the 'Philistines' in the stories of Abraham (Gen 21) and Isaac (Gen 26) with the biblical use of 'Canaan' and 'Canaanites' in the sense of the Egyptian administration; see above, p. 128 ff.

[154] Exact references in this section will be found in the article Ἰσραήλ TWNT, III, 1938, pp. 366–370, 374–376, 391–394; Mary P. Gray, HUCA, 29 (1958), pp. 188–193.

of Palestine as distinct from those in the Diaspora. During the Old Testament period, the word 'Hebrew' is not found in any extrabiblical source as a term denoting the Israelites or the Jews. The Moabite Stone, containing King Mesha's inscription, and the Assyrian texts, speak of Israel or the king of Israel and of Judah or the king of Judah.

In the Hebrew Old Testament, apart from two isolated examples (Gen 14:13; Jonah 1:9), the words 'ibh'rî and 'ibh'rîm ('Hebrew' or 'Hebrews') occur in three distinct groups, each referring to three different subjects. The first and most common use of these words is in connection with the period spent by Israel in Egypt, that is, in the stories of Joseph and Moses. The words are employed in these stories in three different ways. In the first place, they are used when an Egyptian speaks of the Israelites (Gen 39:17; 41:12; Exod 1:16, 22 – in this last case not in the Targum – 2:6). Secondly, they are used when an Israelite speaks to Egyptians (Gen 40:15; Exod 1:19, 2:7; 3:18; 5:3; 7:16; 9:1, 13). In the last five references, it should be noted, the word 'Hebrews' is associated with 'God': '(Yahweh) God of the 'ibh'rîm'. Thirdly, the words 'Hebrew' and 'Hebrews' are used four times by the editor himself to distinguish the Israelites from the Egyptians (Gen 43:32; Exod 1:15; 2:11, 13). All these texts belong to the early traditions, either J or E, and none to the priestly source. The second use of these words can be found in the narratives dealing with Saul's wars against the Philistines, when the name 'Hebrew' is either spoken by the Philistines themselves (1 Sam 4:6, 9; 13:19; 14:11; 29:3) or employed by the editor (1 Sam 13:3, 7; 14:21). The third and least common use of the name 'Hebrew' is found in the laws concerning the emancipation of slaves, in this case the 'Hebrew' slave, in the Book of the Covenant (Exod 21:2–6; this is repeated in the Deuteronomic Code, Deut 15:12–17 and in Jer 34:9, 14).

It should be noted in this context that, apart from the texts in Deuteronomy and Jeremiah, in which the earlier formulae are repeated, all the cases in which the word 'Hebrew' occurs refer to periods preceding the monarchy. After this time, the word disappears, only reappearing after the Exile, when it occurs once in the book of Jonah and in the late midrash of Gen 14.[155]

Two questions have to be answered. Does the word 'ibh'rî always have an ethnic meaning and does it always refer exclusively to the Israelites?

In the first place, the ending -î does not always indicate a people in the sense of an ethnic group, as it does, for instance, in mô' ābhî, Moabite, or k'na''nî, Canaanite. It is often used to denote a certain category of people, as in nokh'rî, stranger, ragh'lî, foot soldier, or hoph'sî, a freed man. In the two isolated cases mentioned above, Jonah 1:9 (cf. 1:8) and Gen 14:13,[156] it

[155] For the date, see below, p. 218–219.

[156] It should, however, be noted that the name is twice translated instead of being

clearly has an ethnic meaning, but these are both deliberate archaisms. The word also seems to have had an ethnic meaning in the group of texts relating to Israel's stay in Egypt. It is true that Joseph is called a 'Hebrew' insofar as he was a slave and that he was no longer called this after his promotion by the pharaoh, which might mean that *'ibh rî* pointed to a social status. On the other hand, in Gen 40:15, Joseph says that he was 'kidnapped from the land of the Hebrews' and here the ethnic meaning is beyond doubt. In the story of Moses, *'ibh'rî* is the name used by the Egyptians to denote the Israelites and by the Israelites of themselves when they are speaking to the Egyptians, but there is no indication that they used the name among themselves. We may go further and say that there is also no indication in the Bible that any other people, apart from the Israelites, were called *'ibh'rîm* in Egypt.[157]

In the accounts of the wars against the Philistines, the word can be explained as an ethnic usage and as denoting the Israelites, at least in the five cases where it is spoken by Philistines. The other three cases (1 Sam 13:3, 7; 14:21), where it is used by the editor, are more difficult to explain and a clear interpretation is hindered by the variants in the Greek translation. The clearest of these three texts is 1 Sam 14:21 – the Hebrews who had been in the service of the Philistines defected and joined the Israelites who were with Saul. This would seem to indicate that there were Hebrews who were not Israelites known to the source of 1 Sam 13–14.[158] This in turn might perhaps mean that some Israelites were called 'Hebrews' because they were in the service of the Philistines.[159] If this is true, the term does not have an

transcribed as Ἑβραῖος in the Septuagint. In Jonah 1:9, it appears as δοῦλος κυρίου, either because the translators read *'ebhedh Y(ah'weh)* or because they interpreted *'ibh rî* according to the verse 'I worship Yahweh'. The second case is to be found in the Septuagint version of 1 Sam 13:3; 14:21, where *'ibh'rîm* is translated as δοῦλοι. In Gen 14:13, περάτης is a creation on the part of the Septuagint – Abraham is the one 'from beyond the river' (cf. Jos 24:3). This was the commonest explanation of the word *'ibh'rî* among the rabbis; see *Bereshith Rabba*, 42, 8, quoted by M. Greenberg, *The Hab/piru*, New Haven, 1955, p. 5, note 24.

[157] Mary P. Gray, *HUCA*, 29 (1958), p. 179, and N. A. van Uchelen, *Abraham de Hebreeër*, Assen, 1964, pp. 15–16. Both of these authors have come to the conclusion that the expression 'A Hebrew, one of his countrymen' (Exod 2:11) indicates that there were other Hebrews apart from the Israelites. The contrast, however, is between the Hebrews, who were Moses' 'countrymen' or 'brothers', and the Egyptians referred to in the same verse. There is possibly implicit evidence in Exod 12:38, which refers to a very mixed crowd of different people joining the Israelites when they left Egypt.

[158] See A. Guillaume, *PEQ*, 1946, p. 68; M. P. Gray, *HUCA*, 29 (1958), pp. 180–182; H. Cazelles, *Syria*, 35 (1958), pp. 203–204; J. P. Oberholzer, 'The 'ibrim in I Samuel', *Studies on the Books of Samuel (Papers read at the Third meeting of Die O.T. Werkgemeenskap in Suid-Afrika)*, Pretoria, 1960, p. 54; cf. A. H. van Zyl, *ibid.*, p. 70. N. A. van Uchelen, *op. cit.* (note 157), pp. 18–19; J. Weingreen, 'Saul and the Habiru', *Fourth World Congress of Jewish Studies, Papers*, I, Jerusalem, 1967, pp. 63–66.

[159] A. Alt, *Die Ursprünge des israelitischen Rechts*, Leipzig, 1934, p. 21 = *Kleine Schriften*, I, p. 292.

ethnic meaning, at least here. This explanation is, however, rather improbable.

The same problem arises in the case of the law concerning the emancipation of 'Hebrew' slaves (Exod 21:2–6; Deut 15:12–18; Jer 34:9, 14).[160] A slave who was 'ibh'rî could be kept for no more than six years. After this period of slavery, he was 'emancipated' or set free, ḥoph'šî, but, if he asked to remain with his master, he would be a slave 'to perpetuity', l''ôlām ('he shall be in his master's service for all time', Exod 21: 6; cf. Deut 15:17). The law of Deut 15, quoted in Jer 34:14, is concerned with a 'fellow Hebrew' sold to an Israelite master. In Jer 34:9, the question of the need to set all 'Hebrew' slaves free is raised and it is stated that no one has the right to keep a 'brother Jew' in slavery. Both in Deuteronomy and in Jeremiah, there can be no doubt that these slaves were Israelites who had 'sold' themselves because they had been driven to this by misery or debt. The early law of Exodus 21 does not state explicitly that the 'Hebrew' slave is necessarily an Israelite – the whole question is in fact omitted. The word 'ibh'rî is contrasted in this passage with two common names, ḥoph'šî and l''ôlām and we have therefore to regard it also as a common and not a proper name. It expresses a state of temporary slavery and must have been borrowed from Israel's neighbours before the time of the monarchy. In this case, it would have been an archaic term in the language of the law.

On the other hand, according to the biblical tradition, Abraham was descended from Eber ('ēbher), so that 'ibh'rîm would be the correct ethnic term for the descendants of Eber, who was, according to Gen 10:21, 24–25 (J), Shem's great-grandson. Eber had two sons, Peleg and Joktan. Joktan was the ancestor of the tribes of southern Arabia (Gen 10:26–30, J) and Peleg was the ancestor, six generations later, of Abraham (Gen 11:20–26, P). It is clear from the Old Testament tradition, then, that Eber was the ancestor of many peoples apart from the Israelites and this has led many scholars to conclude that the Israelites were conscious that they belonged to a much wider group of people, the 'Hebrews'.[161] Apart from the southern Arabs who were descended from Joktan this group included all the northern Arabian tribes descended from Abraham through Ishmael and the sons of Keturah (Gen 25:1–4), all the Aramaean tribes descended from Nahor (Gen 22:20–24), the Moabites and the Ammonites descended from Lot (Gen 19:30–38) and the Edomites descended from Esau-Edom (Gen 36:10–14). The Israelites knew that they were related to these other peoples, but what is remarkable is that they never thought of calling them 'Hebrews'. The reference to Eber and his position in the line of Shem is no more than an

---

[160] A. Alt, op. cit., pp. 19–23 = pp. 291–294; A. Jepsen, 'Die "Hebräer" und ihr Recht', AfO, 15 (1945), pp. 55–68; H. Cazelles, Syria, 35 (1958), pp. 200–201; M. P. Gray, HUCA, 29 (1958), pp. 182–185; R. de Vaux, Institutions, op. cit., I, p. 129.

[161] This opinion is shared by many authors, including myself; see RB, 55 (1948), p. 344.

artificial classification of certain ethnic data and is in this respect rather like the series of names at the beginning of the early Babylonian genealogies.[162]

Apart from the case of Exod 21, then, the word 'ibh rî' seems always to have had an ethnic meaning and, apart from 1 Sam 14:21, it seems always to have referred to the Israelites. If, however, we exclude the isolated cases of Gen 14:13 and Jonah 1:9, the use of this word is confined to the early period between the sojourn in Egypt and the reign of Saul. What is more, this use of the word is limited to Israel's relationships with foreigners and even further restricted to her relationships with the Egyptians and the Philistines. Apart from Gen 14:13, which, as we have seen, is generally accepted as a late text, the word never appears in the patriarchal accounts, even in connection with Abraham's stay in Egypt, nor does it occur, either in these accounts or in later texts, when Israel's relationships with the Canaanites, the Aramaeans or other people are involved. This would seem to indicate that the word originated outside Israel and that geographical and historical circumstances play a part in its application to Israel.

We have already seen that the Habiru-'Apīru are mentioned frequently in the documents of the second millennium B.C.[163] Is there perhaps a connection between these people and the 'Hebrews'? Many scholars deny that there is any connection at all,[164] but the problem has to be discussed and it is certainly not an easy one. As we have seen, the word Habiru-'Apīru has generally been regarded as a common name, but it may in many cases have had an ethnic meaning and, in certain cases, it *must* have had this meaning. With regard to the word 'Hebrew', on the other hand, we have just seen that it has in most cases to be interpreted ethnically, but that it must be regarded as a common name in the case of the law concerning the emancipation of 'Hebrew' slaves (Exod 21). We have therefore to compare two uncertain factors.

In addition, we are confronted here with a philological difficulty – how can *habiru* or *'apīru* be related to *'ibh rî*? This is not insurmountable. As we have seen, the Akkadian transcription *habiru* was imperfect and the Ugaritic and Egyptian forms of the word show that the initial consonant was *'ain*.[165] On the basis of the same evidence, the middle consonant was -p-, but an alternation between -p- and -b- was fairly frequent in

---

[162] See A. Malamat, *JAOS*, 88 (1968), pp. 166–167; see also M. Greenberg, *The Ḫab/piru*, op. cit., p. 93.

[163] See above, pp. 105–112.

[164] See especially C. H. Gordon, 'Marginal Notes on the Ancient Middle East', *JKF*, 2 (1952–1953), pp. 50–61; cf. p. 51; E. Dhorme, 'Les Habirou et les Hébreux', *Revue Historique*, 211 (1954 A), pp. 256–264; B. Landsberger, in J. Bottéro, *Le problème des Habiru*, Paris, 1954, p. 161; M. Greenberg, *The Hab/piru, op. cit.*, pp. 91–96; M. G. Kline, 'The Ha-BI-ru-Kin or Foe of Israel?', *Westminster Theological Journal*, 1956–1958, pp. 1–24, 170–184; 1957–1958, pp. 47–70, especially the second article.

[165] See above, p. 105.

Ugaritic itself or between Ugaritic and other Semitic languages including Hebrew.[166] As far as the morphology of the word is concerned,[167] if 'ap/bīru is a common name or appellative, it has a form used in Akkadian for names of categories. The Hebrew equivalent would be the segolated form 'ebher, which could easily become 'ibh'rî if the word developed an ethnic meaning. What is more, we have seen that the form ending in -i is also used in Hebrew to denote a category of people rather than an ethnic group and we quoted hoph'sî, nokh'rî and ragh'lî as examples. If 'ap/bīru was, on the other hand, originally an ethnic term, the relationship with 'ibh'rî can be more easily established, since this is the ordinary form denoting people in the ethnic sense in Hebrew. There can therefore be no fundamental objection to the fact that the two words are parallel, but they can only be accepted as equivalent if other arguments are found to support this.

In the first place, there are certain general situational analogies. The basic characteristic shared by all the 'Apīru everywhere is that they were strangers who were not fully integrated into the population among whom they lived. The Hebrews were similarly strangers in Egypt and the Philistines regarded them as strangers in Palestine. The second characteristic of the 'Apīru is that they were mobile and ubiquitous – there is evidence that they appeared at different periods and in different places. These times and places correspond, to some extent at least, to those given in the Old Testament in connection with the movements of Israel's ancestors. For instance, the SA.GAZ-Habiru of Lower Mesopotamia during the dynasty of Larsa correspond in this respect with the clan of Terah at Ur, the Habiru of Upper Mesopotamia during the Mari period with Abraham's family at Haran, the Habiru-'Apīru of Syria-Palestine with the patriarchs in Canaan and the 'Apīru in Egypt with the Israelites in the Delta. The Habiru-'Apīru cease to appear in the extrabiblical texts at about the same time as the 'Hebrews' disappear from the biblical texts. The last references to the Habiru in Mesopotamia were made in the twelfth and eleventh centuries B.C. and to the 'Apīru in Egypt in the twelfth century. Similarly, the last reference to the 'ibh'rîm in the Bible (1 Sam 29:3) occurs at the end of the eleventh century. In some texts, the 'Apīru are portrayed as settled people, but others describe them as having been nomadic or semi-nomadic or as still leading this kind of existence. They have been presented as 'coming from western Semitic groups and heading for the edges of the Fertile Crescent'.[168] This description could certainly be applied to the ancestors of the Israelites.[169]

[166] C. H. Gordon, *Ugaritic Textbook*, Rome, 1965, Grammar, § 5. 28, and the lists in J. Aistleitner, *Untersuchungen zur Grammatik des Ugaritischen*, Berlin, 1954, pp. 11–12.

[167] See W. F. Albright, *BASOR*, 125 (Feb. 1952), p. 32; 163 (Oct. 1961), p. 53; S. Yeivin, *RSO*, 38 (1963), pp. 277–278.

[168] J.-R. Kupper, who included the Habiru in his study of the Mesopotamian nomads at the time of the kings of Mari, *Les nomades, op. cit.*, p. 259.

[169] I said almost exactly the same about the very early Israelites in *RB*, 55 (1948), p. 343.

There are also particular situational analogies. The Hebrews came to Egypt from Canaan, like the 'Apīru who had been brought into Egypt as prisoners by Amen-hotep II. Like the 'Apīru, the Hebrews were employed in various tasks for the pharaohs. They built the city of Ramses (Exod 1:11), whereas the 'Apīru transported stones for the great gateway of Ramses Miamun.[170] In Canaan, although the term 'ibh'rîm is not used in this context, the surprise attack carried out by Simeon and Levi against Shechem (Gen 34) and the band of outlaws whom David gathered around him (1 Sam 22:1–2) and with whom he held Nabal to ransom (1 Sam 25) and later made raids in the Negeb (1 Sam 27) bear a strange resemblance to the movements of the warlike and looting Habiru who figure in the texts of Mari and Amarna. What is more, David's position in the service of the Philistines (1 Sam 27:5–7) and that of his men, whom the Philistines regarded as mercenaries and called 'the Hebrews' (1 Sam 29:1–4), are almost exactly parallel to that of the companies of Habiru who served the princes of Alalah, the Hittites and various rulers in Palestine during the Amarna period.[171] Finally, in the Nuzi texts, the situation of the Habiru man or woman, either as slaves or as servants, is very similar to that of the 'Hebrew' slave in Exod 21.

Although there are many parallels, however, there are also certain differences. There is, for instance, no case of an extrabiblical text dealing with the 'Apīru which is at the same time directly concerned with the Hebrews.[172] Above all, it is impossible to identify the Habiru of the Amarna period with the groups of Israelites who took part in the conquest of Canaan. On the other hand, the Habiru-'Apīru are said to have been in parts of the Ancient Near East where Israel's ancestors never penetrated, regions such as Asia Minor (the Alishar texts and those of the Old and Late Hittite Kingdoms) or the territory to the east of the Tigris (the Nuzi texts). There were also 'Apīru in districts which the ancestors of the Israelites had left – for example, Egypt in the twelfth century B.C.

These similarities and differences can be explained if Israel's ancestors were part of a much wider group of people, in other words, the Habiru-'Apīru. The Philistines would clearly have given the Israelites who attacked them from the hill country of Palestine the same name as the Habiru who were already living in that hill country during the Amarna period. Similarly, it is not unreasonable to suppose that the Egyptians would have identified Joseph, who was sold in their country as a slave, and

---

[170] Leiden Papyrus, 348; R. A. Caminos, *Late Egyptian Miscellanies*, London, 1954, p. 491.

[171] See O. Eissfeldt, 'Ugarit und Alalach', *Forschungen und Fortschritte*, 28, 3 (1954), pp. 80–85 = *Kleine Schriften*, III, pp. 270–279.

[172] This shows that I do not accept the exaggerated conclusions of A. Jepsen, 'Die "Hebräer" und ihr Recht', *AfO*, 15 (1945), pp. 55–68; A. Jirku, 'Neues über die Habiru-Hebräer', *JKF*, 2 (1952–1953), pp. 213–214.

the Semites who were descended from him, with the 'Apīru against whom they had fought in Canaan and whom they had taken prisoner. The use of these names in the Bible is justified if the suggestion that has been made here is accepted, namely that Habiru-'Apīru was an ethnic term describing a group or groups of western Semites, 'Amorites' or 'Proto-Aramaeans', with whom the patriarchs were connected.[173]

V. ABRAHAM AND THE FOUR GREAT KINGS OF THE EAST

The first of the patriarchs is, of course, called 'Abram the Hebrew' in Gen 14:13, but this is one of the most disputed chapters in the whole of the Bible. It contains an account of the campaign conducted by four kings, Chedor-laomer of Elam, Amraphel of Shinar, Arioch of Ellasar and Tidal, king of the Goiim, against five minor kings whose territories were south of the Dead Sea – Bera of Sodom, Birsha of Gomorrha, Shinab of Admah, Shemeber of Zeboiim and the king of Bela (Zoar). These five kings had been Chedor-laomer's vassals, but had revolted. They were defeated by the four kings and Abraham's nephew, Lot, who lived at Sodom, was taken prisoner. Abraham pursued the four kings, defeated them at Dan, followed them as far as Hobah, to the north of Damascus, and took Lot, his family and all his possessions back.

Many scholars of good reputation regard this military campaign and Abraham's share in it as historically authentic, at least in essence.[174] Other authors, especially exegetes and literary critics, think that it is a late composition which possibly contains some genuine elements, but which cannot be used as an authentic basis for the story of Abraham or the history of the Ancient Near East as a whole.[175] Why has this chapter given rise to such

[173] K. Koch's 'Die Hebräer vom Auszug aus Ägypten bis zum Großreich Davids', VT, 19 (1969), pp. 37–81, is important in connection with the biblical references to the 'Hebrews', but his conclusions are often risky, the most notable being that the earliest tradition concerning the sojourn in Egypt, the exodus and the adoption of Yahwism was linked with the Hebrews and not with the Israelites.

[174] See especially F. M. T. de Liagre Böhl, Der Zeitalter Abrahams (Der Alte Orient, XXIX, 1), 1930; a revised edition appears in the author's Opera Minora, Groningen, 1953, pp. 26–49; J. H, Kroeze, Genesis Veertien, een exegetisch-historisch studie, Hilversum, 1937; W. F. Albright, BASOR, 88 (Dec. 1942), pp. 32–36; 163 (Oct. 1961), pp. 49–54; F. M. T. de Liagre Böhl, King Hammurabi of Babylon in the Setting of his Time, 1946 = Opera Minora, pp. 339–363; F. Cornelius, 'Genesis XIV,' ZAW, 72 (1960), pp. 1–7; E. A. Speiser, Genesis, 1964, pp. 105–109; K. A. Kitchen, Ancient Orient and Old Testament, Chicago, 1966, pp. 43–47. I have also argued in favour of the historical authenticity of this passage in RB, 55 (1948), pp. 327–336, but compare this with RB, 73 (1966), p. 590.

[175] Among recent authors, the most notable are M. Noth, Überlieferungsgeschichte, op. cit., p. 170; ibid., History, op. cit., p. 122–123; G. von Rad, Das erste Buch Mose (ATD), Göttingen, 1952, p. 147; O. Eissfeldt, Introduction, op. cit., pp. 211–212.

divergent opinions? It is probably because it contains a curious mixture of both early and more recent details and of both possibly authentic and apparently invented elements.

There is, for example, a word used in Gen 14:14, *hanîkhîm*, which occurs nowhere else in the Bible, but has been found in the Egyptian execration texts of the nineteenth century B.C. and in one of the fifteenth century Taanach letters, where it means 'armed supporters'.[176] In this text in Genesis, *hanîkhîm* is explained by the phrase *y'lîdhê bêthô*, 'born in his house', or 'members of his household from birth', which may in this case be an archaic expression denoting servants tied to their master by military obligations.[177] On the other hand, *r'khûs*, 'possessions', which occurs in verses 11, 12, 16 and 21, is a late word which is only used in the priestly editing of the Pentateuch and in the post-exilic books. The term 'Abram the Hebrew' in verse 13 is a deliberate archaism, similar to that found in Jonah 1: 9.[178]

The chapter provides an accurate and detailed geographical description of the invasion, containing place-names some of which occur only in the Old Testament and which are in some cases explained by a name that is better known. They are situated along the central mountain ridge of Transjordania, according to Deut 1–3 a route followed in the opposite direction by the Israelites on their way from Sinai, the 'king's highway' of Num 20: 17, and the later Roman road of Trajan from Busra to Eilat. This was the recognised route for military expeditions and trading caravans going between Syria and the Red Sea – another probable sign of authenticity. We should note, however, that it was on this historical highway that the four kings defeated the legendary Rephaim, Zuzim-Zamzummim, Emim and Horites, who, according to the scholarly notes in Deut 2:10–12, 20–22 and 3:11–13, were the prehistoric inhabitants of these regions.

It is the only text in which the names of the five towns south of the Dead Sea are gathered together and it is from this source that the pentapolis or 'five cities' of Wis 10:6 is derived. Only the first four names are recorded in Gen 10:19[179] and in Deut 29:23 (exilic). Elsewhere in the Bible, these cities are mentioned in pairs, the more usual being Sodom and Gomorrha. Admah and Zeboiim only occur in Hos 11:8. It is probable that in Hosea the tradition is that of northern Israel, whereas that of Sodom and Gomorrha came from the south. The fifth city is Zoar, which was given its name only after the others had been destroyed (Gen 19:20–22). The 'early' name, Bela, only appears in Gen 14 and it is quite possible that it was in-

[176] T. O. Lambdin, *JAOS*, 73 (1953), p. 150.
[177] See F. Willesen, 'The Yālīd in Hebrew Society', *ST*, 12 (1958), pp. 192–210.
[178] See above, p. 210.
[179] This verse – or at least the list of *four* towns – is an addition to the Yahwist's table of nations.

vented, since *bela'* means 'swallowed' or 'devoured'. In the history of
traditions, the account comes between the final editing of Deuteronomy,
the four towns destroyed by Yahweh (Deut 29:22), and the Book of
Wisdom, the five cities devastated by fire (Wis 10:6). The name of the king
of Bela is not given in Gen 14. The names of the kings of Sodom and
Gomorrha are invented — Bera means 'in evil' *(bera')* and Birsha means 'in
wickedness' *(bir'sa')*. The name of the king of Zeboiim is Shemeber *(šem
'ebher)* in the Massoretic text, but *šem 'abhadh* in the Samaritan text and
s^eˇmîyôbhedh or *s^eˇmî 'abhadh* in the Qumran Genesis Apocryphon, which can
be interpreted as 'the (my) name is lost'.

The names of the four kings of the East are quite different. The leader of
the coalition, Chedor-laomer of Elam, has a name which is composed of
two authentically Elamite elements, but no king of Elam with this name is
known in history. Amraphel of Shinar has been identified with Hammurabi
of Babylon,[180] but this is not in accordance with the laws of philology and
all that can be said with certainty is that the name is Amorite.[181] In the rest
of the Bible, Shinar is used to denote Babylonia or Mesopotamia
generally,[182] but it has been suggested that Amraphel's country is the same
as the Singar that occurs in the Assyrian texts, the region of the Jebel Sinjar
to the east of Mosul.[183] The king of Ellasar clearly has a Hurrian name,[184]
but the name of Arioch's kingdom, Ellasar, cannot be satisfactorily
explained.[185] Tidal is obviously the equivalent of Tudhaliyas and four
Hittite kings had this name. According to Gen 14, Tidal was the king of the
Goiim or 'nations' *(gôyîm)*. This vague term is reminiscent of the Umman-Manda, the 'people of Manda' of the cuneiform texts, a name applied
to the warlike hordes of the north who were never named precisely. In the
first millennium, the name was given first to the Cimmerians, then to the
Medes. They are first mentioned in a historical text in the middle of the

---

[180] This suggestion was first made in 1887 by Schrader; the theory was abandoned later,
but taken up again recently by F. Cornelius (see note 174 above).
[181] The original form may have been Amar-pi-El (see *Amarphal*, LXX). The two parts are
found in Amorite onomastic forms; *RB*, 55 (1948), pp. 331–332; H. B. Huffmon, *Amorite
Personal Names, op. cit.*, pp. 128, 168, 254; see especially A-mu-ud-pi-ila, king of Qatna, according to Böhl, *King Hammurabi, op. cit.*, p. 18 = *Opera Minora*, p. 353, and K. Jaritz, 'Wer
ist Amraphel in Genesis 14?', *ZAW*, 70 (1958), pp. 255–256. Amraphel is possibly the same
name as Amudpiel (*r* for *d*) and the two persons may be identical.
[182] Like Sangar in Egyptian and Sanhar in cuneiform texts; see A. H. Gardiner, *Ancient
Egyptian Onomastica*, I, Oxford, 1947, pp. 209*–212*.
[183] R. de Vaux, *RB*, 55 (1948), pp. 332–333, with the references.
[184] The name appears as Arriyuk or Arriwuk in the Mari archives and as Ariukki in the
Nuzi texts. M. Noth opposes the identification of Arioch with the name in the Mari texts;
'Arioch-Arriwuk', *VT*, 1 (1951), pp. 136–140.
[185] Possible explanations are Ilansura between Carchemish and Haran, Alzi at the source
of the Tigris, or even Assyria; in the Genesis Apocryphon of Qumran, it is interpreted as
'Cappadocia'.

seventeenth century B.C. as the enemies of the Hittite king Hattusilis I.[186] They could not, then, have had a Hittite, Tidal-Tudhaliyas, as king. The names of these four kings were not invented and they might therefore have been those of real persons living in the first few centuries of the second millennium B.C. All attempts to identify these kings, however, either certainly or merely probably, with any person known in history have so far failed. The authors who argue in favour of the historicity of this story in Genesis either give this 'historical event' an indeterminate date somewhere between the twentieth and the seventeenth centuries B.C. or else date it precisely within this period. These precise dates vary, however, from one author to another and each author has tried to relate this account to a different historical context.

These attempts to manipulate Gen 14 are, however, not justified. If the account is regarded as authentically historical, it is necessary to accept what it says. In essence, it says that four great kings of the East, an Elamite, a western Semite, a Hurrian and a Hittite, formed a coalition headed by the king of Elam and that these four kings waged war against five towns south of the Dead Sea because these towns had been subjected to the king of Elam, but had revolted against him. There are certainly gaps in our knowledge of the history of the Ancient Near East,[187] but we know quite enough to be able to say that it is historically impossible for these five cities south of the Dead Sea to have at any one time during the second millennium been the vassals of Elam, and that Elam never was at the head of a coalition uniting the four great near eastern powers of that period.

This account, then, cannot be regarded as historically useful, but it is necessary to explain its origin and its character. The mixture of early and more recent terms and of genuine and invented names can be explained by the fact that it is a late scholarly composition. It cannot be related by literary criticism to any of the known sources of the Pentateuch.[188] It postdates both the merging of the tradition of Lot at Sodom with the Abraham tradition of Gen 18–19, the tradition of Sodom and Gomorrha with that of Admah and Zeboiim (Deut 19:22) and the work of the priestly editor, whose precise chronology (Gen 14:4–5) and vocabulary (for example, the word rᵉkhûs) are imitated. The author was inspired by pseudo-historical Assyro-Babylonian texts expressing a certain historical

---

[186] For the Umman-Manda, see H. Klengel, OLZ, 57 (1962), col. 460-461 and note; F. Cornelius, 'ERIN-Manda', Iraq, 25 (1963), pp. 167–170; J.-R. Kupper, CAH, II, I (1963), pp. 40–41.

[187] K. A. Kitchen uses this argument to defend the historical authenticity of the passage, op. cit. (note 174), p. 44.

[188] M. C. Astour's recent suggestion in 'Political and Cosmic Symbolism in Genesis 14 and in its Babylonian Sources', Biblical Motifs. Origin and Transformation, ed. A. Altmann, Cambridge, Mass., 1966, pp. 65–112, that it was composed by the 'second Deuteronomist' round about 550 B.C. is not acceptable.

philosophy or theology, such as those referring to Sargon of Agade and Naram-Sin.[189] Certain links have been established between Gen 14 and the Spartoli tablets, which have been called the Chedor-laomer texts[190] and which list four kings who were opposed to Babylonia. Attempts have been made to discover in the names of these kings the names of the four kings of Gen 14. There is no certainty about the parallels between the two sets of names, but we may be fairly sure that the author of Gen 14 used a text of this kind as a source for his early names. Whatever this original cuneiform text may have been, however, it certainly did not connect these early kings with the five Dead Sea towns. These come from the biblical tradition of Lot and the towns of Sodom and Gomorrha, with the result that Abraham would not have entered this story in the extrabiblical version. This intervention by Abraham was clearly the work of the author of Gen 14, who wanted Abraham to play a decisive part in the story and, in this way, to gain a military glory which he otherwise lacked.

[189] For this *naru* literature, see H. G. Güterbock, 'Die historische Tradition und ihre literarische Gestaltung bei Babyloniern und Hethitern', *ZA*, 42 (1934), pp. 19–20, 62–79; E. A. Speiser, in *Idea of History in the Ancient Near East*, ed. R. C. Dentan, New Haven, 1955, pp. 55–60.
[190] A. Jeremias, 'Die sogenannten Kedorlaomer Texte', *Orientalische Studien Fr. Hommel . . . gewidmet* (*MVAG*, XXI), 1917, pp. 69–97; W. F. Albright, *BASOR*, 88 (Dec 1942), pp. 33–36; M. C. Astour, 'Political and Cosmic Symbolism', *op. cit.* (note 188); the great merit of this author's work is that he stresses the relationship between these texts and Gen 14 as far as their literary *genre* and content are concerned; his detailed exegesis is, on the other hand, not acceptable.*

Chapter Eight

THE PATRIARCHS AND EASTERN SOCIETY

W E HAVE spent some time examining the relationship between
the patriarchal traditions and, on the one hand, history in general and, on the other, the movements of people in the Ancient
Near East during the first half of the second millennium B.C. We must now
see how these traditions fit into the general social and juridical framework
of the Near East at this period.

I. THE NOMADIC LIFE OF THE PATRIARCHS [1]

In Genesis, the patriarchs are depicted as nomadic herdsmen. They live in
tents (Gen 12:8; 13:3, 18; 18:1–10; 24:67; 31:25, 33, 34), they raise sheep and
goats (30:32–43) and dig wells (21:30; 26:15–22). They move from one
camp to another (12:9; 13:3) with their flocks. Their great migrations are
from Upper Mesopotamia to Canaan, from Canaan into Egypt and then
from Egypt back to Canaan. Inside Canaan itself, they went from Shechem
to Bethel, Hebron, Beersheba and the Negeb. They observe the unwritten
law of the desert, preserving purity of blood (24:3–4; 28:1–2), keep the law
of hospitality (18:1–8; 19:28–32) and take collective revenge (34:25–31).
Since, however, there are so many different nomadic ways of life, it is
necessary to try to define as precisely as possible the nomadic life of the

---

[1] M. von Oppenheim, E. Brünlich and W. Caskel, *Die Beduinen*, I–IV, Wiesbaden,
1939–1968; R. de Vaux, 'Les Patriarches hébreux et les découvertes modernes', *RB*, 56
(1949), especially pp. 5–16; J.-R. Kupper, *Les nomades en Mésopotamie au temps des rois de Mari*,
Paris, 1957; F. Gabrieli, ed., *L'antica società beduina*, Rome, 1959; R. de Vaux, *Institutions*, I,
pp. 15–35 and the bibliography, pp. 323–325; H. Klengel, 'Zu einigen Problemen des alt-
vorderasiatischen Nomadentum', *ArOr*, 30 (1962), pp. 585–596; M. Rowton, 'The Physical
Environment and the Problem of the Nomads', *XVe Rencontre Assyriologique Internationale.
Liège, 1966*, Paris, 1967, pp. 109–121; J. Henninger, *Über Lebensraum und Lebensformen der
Frühsemiten*, Cologne, 1968; J. Henninger, 'Zum frühsemitischen Nomadentum',
Viehwirtschaft und Hirtenkultur. Ethnographische Studien, ed. L. Földes, Budapest, 1969, pp.
33–68.

patriarchs. Many ethnological studies have been carried out among the nomadic populations of the Near East, the majority before the lives of these people were radically changed by industrialisation and twentieth-century economic and political structures. The results of these studies can be helpful to us insofar as they are concerned with groups of Semitic people living as herdsmen in the parts of the Near East where the patriarchs used to live. We have, however, to be careful not to exaggerate the similarities, above all because there is no historical continuity between the ancestors of the Israelites and the nomadic Arabs of today. The bedouins in the full sense of the word are a relatively recent phenomenon, very different in character from the nomads of patriarchal times. Apart from the Bible itself, the Mari texts have shown us how great this difference is and the results of modern ethnological research are less valuable to our understanding of the way of life of the patriarchs than these texts.[2]

1. The patriarchs were not 'great' nomads

The true bedouin – the name means 'man of the desert' – raises camels. The camel can live for several days without drinking or eating, can cover very long distances and carry very heavy loads. With the camel, man can live in districts which would otherwise be inaccessible and uninhabitable. The camel-raising bedouin derives all that is essential in his life from his animals – milk, for example, hair for his clothes, skin for his tents and oc- casionally meat, though this is exceptional. The bedouin is, however, of necessity a 'great' nomad, because he has to travel with his flock to pasture land that is still green and to the rare sources of water in the desert. Camel-raising bedouin tribes living in winter quarters in the Nejd, for in- stance, lead their flocks and herds great distances – between three hundred and seventy-five and five hundred miles – to summer pastures in northern Syria. Their contacts with people living settled lives are very limited. They buy things they need in towns situated at the edge of the steppe and are from time to time in touch with the small populations of the oases and little desert towns or villages, since they have to pay a 'brotherhood tax' in the form of dates or grain.

This way of life was unknown during the patriarchal period. It did not really begin to develop fully until the beginning of the modern era, and was first practised in northern Arabia.[3] The great camel-breeding tribes first

[2] The most important work is J-R. Kupper's book, Les nomades, op. cit.; see also H. Klengel, 'Zu einigen Problemen', op. cit.; M. Weippert, Die Landnahme der israelitischen Stämme, Göttingen, 1967, pp. 102–123, taken in conjunction with W. L. Moran's comments in CBQ, 30 (1968), pp. 644–645; J. Henninger, Über Lebensraum, op. cit., pp. 28–30; ibid., 'Zum frühsemitischen Nomadentum', op. cit., pp. 35–38.

[3] W. Dostal, in F. Gabrieli, L'antica società beduina, pp. 11–34; see also RB, 67 (1960), pp. 472–474; J. Henninger, 'Zum frühsemitischen Nomadentum', op. cit., pp. 35–38.

entered Syria in the seventeenth century A.D. This development was, however, the end, or perhaps the resumption, of a long process of evolution. A
very similar way of life existed in the ancient world. At the time of Gideon,
that is, at the beginning of the eleventh century B.C, the Midianites came
with their camels 'past counting', pillaging the whole of central Palestine. [4]
According to a number of authors, this is the first authentic reference to the
camel in the Bible, the one-humped camel or dromedary having become
domesticated one or two centuries earlier. [5] Certainly camels are not mentioned at all in the Rās Shamrah texts, the Amarna letters or the Mari documents, all of which provide us with a good deal of information about the
nomads. [6] Other authors, however, believe that the camel was domesticated
at a much earlier date. They support this claim by archaeological evidence
– excavations have revealed skeletal remains as well as illustrations of
camels at the levels of the third and second millennium B.C. [7] The dating and
identification of these skeletal remains and the interpretation of the illustrated documents are often uncertain, but there is sufficient reliable evidence for us to conclude that the camel was known and that it was domesticated in the Near East at least from the end of the second millennium B.C.
onwards. On the other hand, there is no evidence before the end of the
second millennium of the breeding and keeping of cattle or small livestock
and of the use of the camel for caravans and war.

[4] Judges 6:5; 7:12; 8:21, 26. It should, however, be noted that in the first of these references
(Judges 6:5), the Midianites have herds of cattle as well as camels – they are not purely
camel-breeding people.

[5] One of the first scholars to put forward this view and to continue to defend it was W. F.
Albright, *From the Stone Age to Christianity*, Baltimore, 1940, 2nd edn, 1946, p. 120; *The
Biblical Period from Abraham to Ezra*, New York and Evanston, 1963, p. 7; *History,
Archaeology and Christian Humanism*, New York and Toronto, 1964, p. 158, note 2;
Archaeology, Historical Analogy and Early Biblical Tradition, Baton Rouge, 1966, p. 36, note 6;
Yahweh and the Gods of Canaan, London, 1968, pp. 62, 156; *JBL*, 87 (1968), p. 390. The same
view was accepted and developed by, among others, R. Walz, 'Zum Problem des Zeit-
punkts der Domestikation der altweltlichen Cameliden', *ZDMG*, 101 (1951), pp. 29–51;
'Neue Untersuchungen zum Domestikationsproblem der altweltlichen Cameliden', *ZDMG*,
104 (1954), pp. 45–87; 'Beiträge zur ältesten Geschichte der altweltlichen Cameliden unter
besonderer Berücksichtigung des Problems des Domestikationszeitpunktes', *Actes du IV*
Congrès International des Sciences Anthropologiques et Ethnologiques, Vienna, 1952, III (1956), pp.
190–204.

[6] A text from Alalah dating back to the eighteenth century B.C. would appear to refer to a
domesticated camel; see No. 269, 59, cf. *JCS*, 13 (1959), p. 29 (cf. pp. 33, 37); on the other
hand, this has also been interpreted as a reference to a stag; see W. G. Lambert, *BASOR*, 160
(Dec. 1960), pp. 42–43.

[7] R. de Vaux, *RB*, 56 (1949), pp. 8–9; C. Rathjens, *Sabaeica II (Mitteilungen aus dem Museum
für Völkerkunde in Hamburg*, 24), 1955, pp. 114–117; A. Pohl, *Orientalia*, 19 (1950), pp.
251–253; 21 (1952), pp. 373–374; 23 (1954), pp. 453–454; 26 (1957), pp. 165–166; W. Dostal,
op. cit. (note 3); W. Nagel, *Frühe Tierwelt in Werden im Orient. Ein archäologischer Beitrag zur
Zoologie*, Wittenberg, 1965, pp. 54–57.

It is in the light of these studies that the references to camels in the patriarchal accounts have to be judged. The scholars who believe that the camel was domesticated at a later date regard these references as anachronistic,[8] whereas others defend their authenticity.[9] Several scholars, on the other hand, admit the possibility of the patriarchs having made limited use of the camel, because the animal had already been domesticated by this time, although it was still very little used at the beginning of the second millennium.[10]

It is very difficult to decide between these different opinions. The references to camels in the lists of the patriarchs' possessions (Gen 12:16; 30:43; see also Gen 32:8, in which the Greek version does not include camels) can, of course, be attributed to an editor. A more audacious solution is to suppress them in certain accounts. Camels are, however, mentioned fifteen times in the story of Rebekah's marriage (Gen 24) and the camel plays an essential part in the story of Rachel and the teraphim or household gods (Gen 31:34). It is, moreover, not simply a case of individual camels in Genesis. Abraham's servant, for example, sets off for Haran with ten of his master's camels (Gen 24:10). In the story of Joseph, the Ishmaelites (Midianites) use camels in their trading caravans (Gen 37:25). Jacob has camels to carry his wives and children (Gen 31:17) and he is prepared to give Esau, among other animals, thirty camels together with their calves (Gen 32:16). He has a herd and he breeds camels. Rachel hides the teraphim or household gods of Laban in her camel's saddle or litter (it is difficult to ascertain the exact meaning of the Hebrew *kar* here). This points to a fairly advanced stage in the use of camels, which were originally ridden without saddles.[11] We may therefore conclude, on the basis of this argument, either that these accounts are anachronistic or else that the extrabiblical texts of the second millennium provide us with an incomplete picture.

This second solution is quite possible and, as a consequence, the question must remain open. It is, however, important to note in this context that these biblical accounts contrast strongly with others in the Bible, in other words, that there is no mention of camels in any of the other patriarchal stories. When Abraham and Lot parted company, for example, only cattle and small livestock are mentioned (Gen 13:5). The same applies to

[8] W. F. Albright, in the books mentioned above in note 5; J. Bright, *History of Israel, op. cit.,* pp. 72–73.
[9] J. P. Free, 'Abraham's Camels', *JNES,* 3 (1944), pp. 187–193; J. Morgenstern, 'The Ark, the Ephod and the Tent', *HUCA,* 17 (1942–1943), pp. 255–258, note 174; K. A. Kitchen, *Ancient Orient and Old Testament,* Chicago, 1966, pp. 79–80.
[10] R. de Vaux, *RB,* 56 (1949), pp. 9–10; 72 (1965), p. 16; O. Eissfeldt, 'Achronische, anachronische und synchronische Elemente in der Genesis', *JEOL,* 17 (1963), p. 157; *CAH,* II, XXVI (a) 1965, p. 6; W. Weippert, *op. cit.* (note 2), pp. 107–108; J. Henninger, 'Nomadentum', *op. cit.,* pp. 41–44.
[11] W. Dostal, *op. cit.* (note 3), pp. 15–20.

Abimelech's dealings with Abraham (Gen 20:14; 21:27). When Jacob arrives at Laban's home, he meets shepherds (Gen 29:1–11) and he becomes rich by raising and tending his uncle's sheep and goats (Gen 30:32–42). The fact that camels are not mentioned in this second story strengthens the impression that the mention of camels in the verse that follows (Gen 30:43) is the work of an editor. Again, only cattle and small livestock are mentioned in the story of Jacob's meeting with Esau (Gen 32:6, 8 – in the Greek version; 33:13), whereas camels are only mentioned in the list of animals that Jacob chose as a gift for Esau (Gen 32:16).

If the patriarchs did in fact possess camels, it is remarkable that there are no references to them precisely where we should expect to find them. For instance, Abraham leaves with an ass to sacrifice Isaac (Gen 22:3). Jacob's sons, too, went down to Egypt in search of corn with donkeys (Gen 42:26–27; 43:18, 24; 44:3, 13). Finally Joseph sent gifts from Egypt to his father on donkeys (Gen 45:23). We may therefore conclude that it is probable that the reference to camels in Genesis reflects the situation prevailing at the time when the traditions became established, not the life of the people during the patriarchal period. What is more, even if we accept that the patriarchs may have possessed a number of camels, this does not necessarily mean that they were 'great' nomads. It would, moreover, be entirely wrong to think of the patriarchs of Israel as bedouin sheikhs.

2. The patriarchs were not caravan traders

More recently,[12] the patriarchs have been described as breeders of donkeys and leaders of caravans, in other words, as 'donkey nomads'. It has been suggested, for example, that the name 'Hebrew', like the name Habiru/ʿApīru, really meant 'dusty'[13] and denoted the donkey drovers who followed their animals (the leaders of camel caravans walked ahead of their beasts). In this context, it has been pointed out that the places where the patriarchs broke their journey were all on caravan trails. Nonetheless, the term 'donkey nomad' can only be used if it is subjected to certain qualifications.[14] Unlike the camel, the donkey does not provide man with

---

[12] W. F. Albright, *Archaeology and the Religion of Israel,*[2] Baltimore, 1946, pp. 97–101; 'Abram the Hebrew. A New Archaeological Interpretation,' *BASOR,* 163 (Oct. 1961), pp. 36–54; *Yahweh and the Gods of Canaan, op. cit.,* pp. 62–64 and *passim* (see also the report in *RB,* 76, 1969, p. 118); 'Midianite Donkey Caravans', *Translating and Understanding the Old Testament (H. G. May Volume),* New York and Nashville, 1970, pp. 187–205.

[13] See above, pp. 109–110.

[14] R. Walz, 'Gab es ein Esel-Nomadentum im Alten Orient?' *Akten des XXIV. Internationalen Orientalisten-Kongresses, Munich, 1957,* Wiesbaden, 1959, pp. 150–152.

food or clothing – its flesh is not eaten, it yields little milk and its hair cannot be woven. The donkey-breeding nomads must also have had sheep or goats. Otherwise, they must either have been hunters or leaders of caravans or else have practised certain minor industries.

The donkey is above all a means of transport: in other words, it is ridden or it is loaded with goods. It was certainly only used in this way in the east until it was replaced by the camel and the horse. The nomadic herdsmen with their small livestock always required a few donkeys to carry their camping equipment, their provisions, their wives and small children. Until the end of the second millennium, all caravan trade was carried on by means of donkey transport.[15] A well-known painting in a tomb at Beni Hasan, dating from the beginning of the nineteenth century B.C,[16] depicts the arrival in Egypt of thirty-seven Asiatics, who were hunters, musicians and metalworkers.[17] Among them are two donkeys bearing loads and, according to the accompanying text, they are bringing eye-paint. According to the Egyptian texts of the Old and Middle Kingdoms, as many as five or six hundred or even a thousand donkeys were included in the caravans that went to Sinai or to the Sudan.[18] Donkeys are often mentioned too in the Assyrian texts from the trading colonies in Cappadocia dating from the nineteenth century B.C. They were used as a means of transport between the towns of Asia Minor as well as in the caravans coming from Assyria.[19] These caravans assembled at Ashur, where the representatives of Cappadocian firms bought, for gold or silver, donkeys and goods such as textiles and metals, especially lead, tin and copper. The accounting unit was the 'donkey load' and this became a measure of capacity for corn in Assyria and continued to be a measure in Israel, the *hômer*. Transactions were usually concerned with the rather small quantities that could be carried by a few donkeys, but much larger orders requiring as many as two hundred donkeys have been recorded.[21] Caravans were generally very large and almost always escorted by guards to protect them.

This is, of course, very interesting, but it has nothing to do with any way of life led by the 'donkey nomads'. The donkeys were known as 'black asses' and probably originated in the country around Damascus, which

[15] W. F. Albright, *BASOR*, 163 (Oct. 1961), p. 40 ff.
[16] *ANEP*, No. 3; text in *ANET*, p. 229.
[17] W. F. Albright has interpreted two objects among the donkeys' load as bellows; see *Archaeology and the Religion of Israel*,[2] pp. 98, 200.
[18] W. F. Albright, *Yahweh and the Gods of Canaan*, p. 62; note 42.
[19] J. Lewy, 'Some Aspects of Commercial Life in Assyria and Asia Minor in the Nineteenth Pre-Christian Century', *JAOS*, 78 (1958), pp. 89–101; P. Garelli, *Les Assyriens en Cappadoce*, Paris, 1963, Part III and the index under 'Ânes' and 'Caravanes'.
[20] J. Lewy, 'The Assload, the Sack and Other Measures of Capacity', *RSO*, 39 (1964), pp. 181–197.
[21] J. Lewy, *op. cit.* (note 19), pp. 92–93.

became known in the later Assyrian texts as the 'land of the donkeys'.[22] They were bought in Assyria and sold again on arrival in Asia Minor, since nothing was exported from Asia Minor and all that could be taken out was the gold or silver given in payment. All trading was done by Assyrians and even the leaders of the caravans usually had Assyrian names. It has been suggested that the Amorites played a part in organising these caravans, especially since the caravans assembled in a suburb of Ashur known as Amurru.[23] This, however, can be no more than a hypothesis, because these Amorites were no longer nomadic at this time, but had been assimilated into the settled way of life of the Assyrians. There is, in other words, nothing in the Cappadocian texts which can throw light on the patriarchal way of life.

We must also consider the references to donkeys and caravans in the Mari texts of the eighteenth century B.C.[24] The caravans were at the disposal of the kings of Mari or their representatives. The texts provide us with a few figures — ten, a hundred or two hundred donkeys[25] — and, in one case, the transportation of three or four hundred 'donkey loads' of corn presupposes a much more important caravan.[26] One text is quite exceptional in referring to three thousand Hanean donkeys which returned without loads because of a refusal to deliver the goods.[27] This text is also unusual, first, because it mentions such a large number of donkeys, and secondly, because it is the only Mari document which makes a direct connection between donkeys and caravans on the one hand and nomads on the other, whereas other texts indicate that the Haneans were above all sheep-raising people. These Haneans were the contracting party in a treaty concluded in the presence of the king's representative by the sacrifice of a young ass.[28] It would, however, be wrong to deduce from this that the donkey played an important part in the lives of these nomads, because this rite was performed at the insistence of the king's representative, replacing the rite suggested by the contracting party, by whom a young animal, perhaps a dog, and a lettuce were generally used.[29] The official term in the Mari documents for

[22] J. Lewy, *HUCA*, 32 (1961), pp. 72–74.

[23] J. Lewy, *ibid.*, pp. 61–72.

[24] See E. Nielsen, 'Ass and Ox in the Old Testament', *Studia Orientalia, I. Pedersen dedicata*, Copenhagen, 1953, pp. 263–274, especially pp. 272–274; J. Bottéro and A. Finet, *Répertoire analytique des tomes I à V (ARM XV)*, Paris, 1954, pp. 288 (*âne, ânesse*), 294 (*caravane*).

[25] Mentioned respectively in *ARM* I, 17; *ARM* II, 123; *ARM* V, 70; *ARM* II, 126.

[26] *ARM* II, 52.

[27] Partly and rather badly edited by C-F. Jean, *Semitica*, I, 1948, pp. 21–22; see also M. Greenberg, *The Hab/piru*, New Haven, 1955 No. 15. The correct reading has been provided by J.-R. Kupper, *Les nomades, op. cit.*, p. 253, note 2; H. Klengel, *ArOr*, 30 (1962), p. 593; W. F. Albright, *Yahweh and the Gods of Canaan*, p. 63, note 43.

[28] *ARM*, II, 37.

[29] G. Mendenhall, 'Puppy and Lettuce in North-West Semitic Covenant Making', *BASOR*, 133 (Feb. 1954), pp. 26–30; *CAD*, 6 (1956), p. 128, under *ḫassu*.*

'entering into a covenant' was 'to kill a young ass',[30] but this does not necessarily imply the survival of a nomadic custom. It is not possible to find any proof either in the Mari or in the Cappadocian texts that there were 'donkey nomads' or that nomads took part in caravan trading, although they may have done so incidentally. Furthermore, as we have already seen, the Habiru too were not donkey drovers who led caravans.[31]

As we should expect then, we find that those texts in Genesis in which donkeys are mentioned as part of the patriarchs' flocks or herds (Gen 12:16; 24:35; 30:43; 32:6, 16) always show that they were used as mounts or as beasts of burden.[32] This is, of course, fully in accordance with the needs of people who keep small livestock and does not in any way imply that the patriarchs went in for trading. There is not a single biblical text which suggests that they were donkey-drovers who led caravans. The routes which they followed might have been the same as the established caravan trails, but this was no doubt because the needs of both groups of people were the same – pasture and springs. On the other hand, there is no evidence that they broke their journey in Canaan at points along the caravan trail between Syria and Egypt. During the patriarchal period, caravans must have travelled, as they did later, through Damascus, Megiddo and Gaza on their way into Egypt.

In spite of this, however, certain scholars have insisted that the patriarchs were in fact traders.[33] One argument put forward in favour of this theory is that the verb *sḥr* in Gen 34:10, 21 and 42:34 means 'to trade', so that these three texts show that Jacob's sons were able to settle, first, near Shechem and secondly, in Egypt and to trade there. The verb, these scholars argue, was certainly understood in this sense in the early versions and the participle of the verb means 'merchants' in classical Hebrew and in Gen 23:16 and 37:28. Quite apart from the caravan hypothesis, the same view has been defended on the basis of a Rās Shamrah text dealing with merchants from Ura in Asia Minor, namely that Abraham of Ur was a merchant prince.[34] We have, however, already discussed this idea that Ura and Ur were identical and have rejected it.[35] We may add here that the social situation of the

---

[30] G. Dossin, *Syria*, 19 (1938), pp. 108–109; M. Noth, 'Das alttestamentliche Bundschließen im Lichte eines Mari-Textes', *Annuaire de l'Institut de Philologie et d'Histoire Orientales et Slaves*, 13 (1953), pp. 433–444 = *Gesammelte Studien zum Alten Testament*, Munich, 1957, pp. 142–154.

[31] See above, pp. 109–110.

[32] See the texts quoted in the previous section.

[33] W. F. Albright, *BASOR*, 163 (Oct. 1961), p. 44; 164 (Dec. 1961), p. 28; *Yahweh and the Gods of Canaan*, op. cit., p. 78, note 92.

[34] C. H. Gordon, 'Abraham and the Merchants of Ura', *JNES*, 17 (1958), pp. 28–31; 'Abraham of Ur', *Hebrew and Semitic Studies Presented to G. R. Driver*, Oxford, 1963, pp. 77–84; L. R. Fisher, 'Abraham and his Priest-King', *JBL*, 81 (1962), pp. 264–270.

[35] See above, pp. 187–190.

patriarchs was not in any way similar to that of the merchants of Ugarit during the fourteenth and thirteenth centuries B.C. or to that of the Babylonian merchants at the beginning of the second millennium.[36] As far as the verb *shr* is concerned, its basic meaning is 'to travel' or to 'go around', which is also the meaning of the same root in Akkadian and in Aramaic, for example in the Qumran Genesis Apocryphon. This basic meaning of 'to move about' is perfectly acceptable in the three texts of Genesis quoted above as well as in the two other cases in which the verb is used in a finite form in the rest of the Old Testament (Jer 14:18; Ps 38:11). The meaning of the participle in Hebrew – and in Phoenician – is clearly a derivative, since travelling merchants were known everywhere in the Ancient Near East.[37]

We may therefore conclude that the patriarchs were not 'great' nomads who raised camels. Nor were they donkey drovers who led caravans, or merchants.

3. *The patriarchs kept sheep and goats and were beginning to lead a settled life*[38]

In Genesis, whenever the patriarchs' possessions are listed, their small livestock, that is to say, their sheep and goats, are always mentioned and, what is more, with one exception, these animals are mentioned first. Rachel, for example, was a shepherdess (Gen 29:9). Jacob was a herdsman looking after Laban's sheep and goats and the tricks that he employed to increase his own livestock show that he knew all about breeding these animals (Gen 30:25–42). Jacob's sons pastured their father's flock (Gen 37:12, 17) and it was as shepherds and goatherds that they settled in Egypt (Gen 46:31–34; 47:1–6).

The raising of sheep and goats is, of course, dependent on certain geographical and climatic conditions. It is, after all, not possible to keep small livestock in the desert – but it is possible to do so in country bordering the desert, where the animals can graze and find water more easily. The sheep-breeding tribes of today move their flocks much less than the camel-keeping tribes move their beasts from one pasture to another. They may travel long distances, but they do so in very short stages and the route that they follow is marked by springs. In the Near East, the type of country which seems to suit such tribes best is one where between ten and twenty

[36] A. F. Rainey, 'Business Agents at Ugarit', *IEJ*, 13 (1963), pp. 313–321; W. F. Leemans, *The Old Babylonian Merchant. His Business and his Social Position*, Leiden, 1950. So far, very little has been found in the Mari texts that have already been published.
[37] E. A. Speiser, 'The Verb *shr* in Genesis and Early Hebrew Movements', *BASOR*, 164 (Dec. 1961), pp. 23–28; R. de Vaux, *RB*, 72 (1965), pp. 18–19.
[38] R. de Vaux, *RB*, 56 (1949), pp. 12–16; 72 (1965), pp. 16–17; J. Henninger, 'Nomadentum', *op. cit.*, pp. 44–50.

inches of rain fall each year. On a precipitation map of the Near East, this zone would be on the edge of the desert and would be shown as a wide strip cutting across the north of Mesopotamia, curving in towards the south from Aleppo onwards, becoming narrower as it approaches Damascus, Transjordan and Palestine and wider again towards the Negeb.[39] It is interesting to note that all the places where the patriarchs halted on their journey, Haran, Shechem, Bethel, Hebron and Beersheba, are situated within this zone.

These sheep-breeding tribes living on the fringe of the desert are often in touch with the towns and with people whose main industry is agriculture, with the result that they naturally tend towards a settled way of life. They add cattle to their flocks and these larger, less mobile animals restrict their movements. They acquire land and begin to cultivate it. They build huts of mud and branches or even stone houses. In the winter and spring, part of each tribe will set up tents in the grazing land where the flocks are, but for the rest of the year, these flocks are entrusted to shepherds.[40] By a process of natural evolution, then, these shepherds become people who are no longer nomadic, but at the same time not completely sedentary. Their society is dimorphous, one in which urban and tribal characteristics are either merged with each other or else opposed to one another.[41]

It is possible to observe this double morphology in certain tribes in Syria and Palestine even today and it was undoubtedly present among the semi-nomadic people of Upper Mesopotamia during the Mari period.[42] These sheep-raising people had flocks in grazing land, *nāwum*[43] and enclosures or encampments, *haṣārum*,[44] but they also had fields and they gathered in harvests. They also concluded treaties and covenants with settled peoples. They had 'villages', *kaprātum*, and 'towns', *ālānû*, both of which were clearly more or less permanent settlements occupied by a tribe or by part of

[39] See, for instance, the map published in *RB*, 56 (1949), p. 13.

[40] H. Charles, *Tribus moutonnières du Moyen-Euphrate (Documents d'Etudes Orientales de l'Institut Français de Damas*, VIII), 1939; *La sédentarisation entre Euphrate et Balik*, Beirut, 1942; A. Jaussen, *Coutumes des Arabes au pays de Moab*, Paris, 1908, new edn, 1948; T. Ashkenazi, *Tribus semi-nomades de la Palestine du Nord*, Paris, 1938; L. Haefeli, *Die Beduinen von Beerseba*, Lucerne, 1938; J. Sonnen, *Die Beduinen am See Genesareth*, Cologne, 1952.

[41] M. Rowton, 'The Physical Environment and the Problem of the Nomads', *XVe Rencontre Assyriologique Internationale, Liège, 1966*, Paris, 1967, pp. 109–121.

[42] J.-R. Kupper, *Les nomades, op. cit.*; A. Malamat, 'Mari and the Bible. Some Patterns of Tribal Organization and Institutions', *JAOS*, 82 (1962), pp. 143–150; *ibid.*, 'Aspects of Tribal Societies in Mari and Israel', *XVe Rencontre Assyriologique* (see above, note 41), pp. 129–138.

[43] The word means grazing land, flock and encampment; see J.-R. Kupper, *Les nomades, op. cit.*, pp. 12–13; D. O. Edzard, 'Altbabylonisch *nawûm*', *ZA*, 53 (1959), pp. 168–173; cf. *ZA*, 56 (1964), p. 146; A. Malamat, *JAOS*, 82 (1962), p. 146; M. Weippert, *Die Landnahme, op. cit.*, p. 115, note 1.

[44] M. Noth, *Die Ursprünge des alten Israel im Lichte neuer Quellen*, Cologne, 1961, p. 37; A. Malamat, *JAOS*, 82 (1962), p. 147.

a tribe near one of the towns permanently inhabited by settled people.[45] According to one letter, the Benjaminites left their 'towns' at Sagaratum and went towards the high land because there was no more grazing land.[46] In another letter, we read that the Haneans came from the grazing land, *nawum*, and lived in the 'towns', *ālānû*.[47] The sharing by a stranger of a field jointly owned by a clan of the Rabbeans is regulated by a contract,[48] the clan being represented by thirteen heads of families, five of whom live, according to the text, in the town of Appum, not far from Mari, while the other eight together form a group camping in the grazing land.

The patriarchs, then, followed a way of life which was transitional, halfway between a nomadic life and a settled one. It is, moreover, very probable that the various stages in this evolutionary process from a nomadic to a settled way of life were compressed in the patriarchal tradition. Cattle are mentioned as well as small livestock whenever the patriarchs' possessions are listed and, in Egypt, Jacob's sons are seen as men who keep both sheep and cattle (Gen 45:10; 46:32; 47:1), but there are only two stories in which cattle play a concrete part – a heifer is used in the rite of the Covenant (Gen 15:9) and a calf is immolated by Abraham at Mamre for his three visitors (Gen 18:7). Sheep and goats, however, figure far more frequently and they alone occur in the stories which are connected with Upper Mesopotamia (Gen 29–31). In the Mari texts concerned with the same region, cattle are, however, mentioned, but never in connection with nomadic people.[49] These would appear to have owned no animals apart from sheep. Like the people of Mari and indeed like the semi-nomadic tribes of the Near East today, the patriarchs began to cultivate the soil. Isaac, for instance, sowed crops and harvested them (Gen 26:12) and Joseph dreamed of sheaves while he was tending his brothers' flocks (Gen 37:2, 7). These are, however, both exceptional cases, since Isaac's experience as a farmer took place at Gerar, in a cultivated region, while the story of Joseph belongs to the end of the patriarchal age. The patriarchs were not really settled peasants.[50]

---

[45] J.-R. Kupper, *Les nomades, op. cit.*, pp. 13, 56; D. O. Edzard, *ZA*, 53 (1959), pp. 170–171; M. Noth, *Die Ursprünge, op. cit.*, pp. 16–17; J. C. L. Gibson, *JSS*, 7 (1962), pp. 56–58; M. Weippert, *Die Landnahme, op. cit.*, pp. 115–118.

[46] *ARM*, II, 102, 5–16, with W. L. Moran's corrected translation, *CBQ*, 30 (1968), pp. 644–645; cf. *ARM*, III, 58, 5–10 – the 'towns' men of Benjamin went back to their houses from the highland.

[47] *ARM*, II, 48, 8–9.

[48] *ARM*, VIII, 11, with G. Boyer's juridical commentary, *ibid.*, pp. 190–193; A. Malamat, *JAOS*, 82 (1962), pp. 145, 147–148; *XVᵉ Rencontre Assyriologique, op. cit.*, p. 135.

[49] I am not, of course, taking *ARM* IV, 80, 5–6 into account here, that is, the story of the Haneans' raid on the palace and their seizure of the sheep and bulls.

[50] The patriarchs' sedentary and agrarian way of life has been exaggerated by B. D. Eerdmans in 'Der Ackerbau in den Vätersagen', *Alttestamentliche Studien*, II, *Die Vorgeschichte*

The words used in the Mari texts for more or less permanent settlements of semi-nomadic peoples are not found in any of the stories in Genesis, but they remained in the Hebrew language and were employed later. *Nâweh* is used, generally poetically and above all in connection with Jacob-Israel, for example, in Jer 10:25; Lam 2:2; Ps 79:7 etc., for 'home'. *Ḥāṣēr* is the word employed for the encampments of Ishmael in Gen 25:16 (P), of the Avvites in Deut 2:23, of Kedar in Isa 42:11 and elsewhere for other types of habitation. It is more generally used for a village that is not fortified (Lev 25:31) or for a village that is dependent on a town (*passim* in Jos 15 and 19). In the south of Judah and in the Negeb, where a form of semi-nomadic existence continued, geographical names formed from or with *hāṣēr* were very frequent.[51] The word meaning 'villages' in the Mari texts, *kaprātum*, disappeared almost completely in classical Hebrew – it is only found as *kâphar* in 1 Sam 6:18 and as *kôpher* in 1 Chron 27:25 – but it reappeared in Aramaic and many place-names in Palestine were formed from it. An example of the latter usage is Chephar-ammoni (*kᵉphar hā'ammônî*, the 'village' of the Ammonites', one of Benjamin's towns, Jos 18:24).

Quite apart from the question of the vocabulary used, however, the patriarchal mode of habitation is described in Genesis in a way which is to some extent similar to that of the Mari texts. The patriarchs, for example, set up their encampments, which could also be called *nāwum*, in the neighbourhood of existing urban centres. Abraham pitched his tents between Bethel and Ai (Gen 12:8). He left this site and returned to it (Gen 13:3). Leaving it again, he established his camp at Mamre near Hebron (Gen 13:18), where he was to be buried. He also lived as a nomad in the Negeb (Gen 20:1). Jacob camped near Shechem (Gen 33:18) and later at Mamre (Gen 35:27), but he moved his flocks from there to Shechem and Dothan (Gen 37:12, 17). The patriarchs concluded treaties with city dwellers – Abraham, for instance, with Abimelech (Gen 20:15) and with the people of Hebron (Gen 23), Isaac with Abimelech (Gen 26:30) and Jacob with the people of Shechem (Gen 33:19; 34).

All the same, if the traditions in Genesis are compared with the whole body of Mari texts, the only possible conclusion that can be reached is that the Genesis stories depict a less advanced stage on the way towards a settled

---

Israels, Giessen, 1908, pp. 38–48; A. Eberharter, 'Betrieben die Patriarchen Abraham, Isaak und Jakob auch Ackerbau?', *Theologische Quartalschrift*, 97 (1915), pp. 1–16; S. D. Goitein has made the same error more recently in *Jews and Arabs. Their Contacts through the Ages*, New York, 1955, pp. 19–32; See also G. Mendenhall, *BibArch*, 25 (1962), p. 69.

[51] Archaeologists have established that these sites go back to the eleventh and tenth centuries B.C.; see R. Gophna, 'Sites from the Iron Age between Beersheba and Tell el-Far'a', *Yediot*, 28 (1964), pp. 236–246 (Hebrew series); *ibid.*, 'Iron Age I haserim in Southern Philistia', '*Atiqot* (Hebrew series), 3 (1966), pp. 44–51, with English summary, pp. 5*–6*; M. Kochavi, 'Excavations at Tell Esdar', '*Atiqot* (Hebrew series), 5 (1969), pp. 14–48, with English summary, pp. 2*–5*.

life. As we have seen, there is nothing in Genesis that can be compared with the *ḥaṣārum*, the 'villages' and the 'towns' of Mari,[52] and the Haneans and Benjaminites of Mari had much more frequent and complex contacts with the cities and those who governed them. But the difference between Genesis and the Mari documents in this instance may perhaps be the result of their very diverse nature – in the case of the first, we have to do with traditions relating to private families, whereas in the second case, we are concerned with archives of a centralised administration.

What is more, the biblical tradition made a clear distinction between the way of life led by the patriarchs and that followed by other groups of nomads.[53] Isaac, for example, is contrasted in Genesis with Ishmael (Gen 16:12; 25:16–18) and Jacob with Esau (Gen 25:27; 27:39). The patriarchal way of life is shown to be quite different from that of the Midianites or the Amalekites, with whom the Israelites came into contact later in their history. We may therefore conclude that the patriarchs were originally shepherds or goatherds and that they entered Canaan and lived on the fringe of cultivated land, and in contact with settled people, they too began to lead a settled life.

II. Patriarchal Society According to Genesis[54]

The sagas of the patriarchs are fundamentally family histories. It has often been said that the original form of the family among the Semites was the matriarchy, which is a very widespread form of society in so-called primitive communites. In such societies, the mother does not, as is commonly supposed, exercise authority, but she does determine the relationships within the family. The child, for example, belongs to his mother's clan and

---

[52] There is one exception – according to Gen 24:10, cf. 13, Laban lived in the 'town' of his father Nahor and he had a 'house' there (Gen 24:31–32). It is possible that the word for 'town', '*ir*, is the equivalent here of the *ālānû* or 'towns' of Mari and that 'house', *bêth*, has the meaning of 'tent', which *bītum* might have at Mari; see J.-R. Kupper, *Les nomades, op. cit.*, p. 15, note 2; J. C. L. Gibson, *JSS*, 7 (1962), p. 60; but this story is the one in which the most important part is played by the camels and we have said that it reflects a situation later than that of the patriarchs.

[53] J. Henninger, *Lebensraum, op. cit.*, p. 27; 'Nomadentum,' *op. cit.*, p. 50.

[54] I. Mendelsohn, 'The Family in the Ancient Near East', *BibArch*, 11, pp. 24–40; *ibid.*, 'On the Preferential Status of the Eldest Son', *BASOR*, 156 (Dec. 1959), pp. 38–40; J. Henninger, 'La société bédouine ancienne', in F. Gabrieli, ed., *L'antica società beduina*, Rome, 1959, pp. 69–93; A. Malamat, 'Mari and the Bible. Some Patterns of Tribal Organization and Institutions', *JAOS*, 82 (1962), pp. 143–150; J. M. Holt, *The Patriarchs of Israel*, Nashville and New York, 1964, Chap. III: 'Patriarchal Family Life', pp. 91–126; A. Malamat, 'Aspects of Tribal Societies in Mari and Israel', *XVᵉ Rencontre Assyriologique Internationale, Liège 1966*, Paris, 1967, pp. 129–138; J. Henninger, *Lebensraum, op. cit.*, note 1, pp. 34–38.

he is not related to those related by marriage to his father. The rights of inheritance are also determined by descent on the mother's side. It has been claimed that traces of a matriarchal way of life remained in Israel.[55] In Gen 20:1–12, for example, Abraham is forgiven for having let Abimelech think that Sarah was his sister because she was in fact his half-sister and he married her quite legitimately (cf. 2 Sam 13:13). The conclusion that has been drawn by some scholars from this is that in primitive societies the relationship was determined by the mother. Similarly, in such societies and according to certain scholars it was the mother who normally named the newly born son, the biblical examples of this are the naming of all Jacob's sons born in Mesopotamia (Gen 29:31–30:24), and of Benjamin (Gen 35:18; see also Hannah's naming of Samuel, 1 Sam 1:20). On the other hand, the reservations felt by most ethnologists nowadays with regard to matriarchy in general and their reluctance to acknowledge it as the primitive form of the Semitic family should be taken into account here.[56] As far as the patriarchs are concerned, the story of Abraham, Abimelech and Sarah (Gen 20:1–12) can be quite adequately explained by the influence of a non-Semitic practice that was not properly understood later. In the second case, that of mothers naming their sons, there are several examples in Genesis which show that it was not always the mother who chose the child's name (Gen 16:15; 17:19; see also Gen 35:18).[57]

Other authors have claimed that it is possible to discover traces of a fratriarchy in the patriarchal way of life. In this type of family, authority is exercised by the eldest brother and is handed on from brother to brother as something inherited, the inheritance passing to the eldest son of the first brother on the death of the last brother. This system is believed to have existed, in a mitigated form at least, in Asia Minor among the Hurrians and the Elamites.[58] The institution of the levirate (Gen 38), the initiative taken by Jacob's sons, Simeon and Levi, to revenge the rape of their sister Dinah (Gen 34) and the part played by Laban in the marriage of his sister Rebekah (Gen 24) are cited as examples showing traces of a fratriarchal system in Genesis.[59] It has to be admitted, however, that it is doubtful whether this type of family relationship ever existed among the Semites[60] and, as far as

---

[55] V. Aptowitzer, 'Spuren des Matriarchats im jüdischen Schrifttum', *HUCA*, 4 (1927), pp. 207–240; 5 (1928), pp. 261–297.

[56] J. Henninger, 'La société bédouine ancienne', *op. cit.*, pp. 88–90; *Lebensraum, op. cit.*, pp. 36–37, with references.

[57] See, in general, W. Plautz, 'Zur Frage des Mutterrechts im Alten Testament', *ZAW*, 74 (1962), p. 9–30.

[58] P. Koschaker, 'Fratriarchat, Hausgemeinschaft und Mutterrecht in Keilschriftrechten', *ZA*, 41 (1933), p. 1–89.

[59] C. H. Gordon, 'Fratriarchy in the Old Testament', *JBL*, 54 (1935), pp. 223–231.

[60] J. Henninger, 'Zum Erstgeborenenrecht bei den Semiten', *Festschrift W. Caskel*, ed. E. Gräf, Leiden, 1968, pp. 162–183, cf. pp. 180–181.

the three stories in Genesis given as examples are concerned, the influence of Assyrian and Hurrian practices has to be recognised in the levirate and in certain of the features present in the story of Laban and Rebekah. (We shall come back to this later.)

We may therefore conclude that the family portrayed in the accounts in Genesis is of the patriarchal type. The head of this family is clearly the father, whose authority is apparently boundless. He decides, for example, whom his sons shall marry (Gen 24:3–9; 28:2). Abraham drives Hagar and the son he has had by her away (Gen 21:8–14). He sacrifices his wife's honour to his own safety (Gen 12:11–13; 20:2; see also Isaac's calling his wife Rebekah his sister, Gen 26:7). Lot is also ready to sacrifice his daughters' honour in order to protect his guests (Gen 19:8). Finally, Abraham bequeaths all his possessions to Isaac and sends away the sons whom he has had by his concubines (Gen 25:5–6).

The descent in the family was determined according to the father's line and the first-born had precedence over the other brothers.[61] In other words, he enjoyed *b'khôrah,* the birthright or the right of primogeniture (Gen 25:31–34; 27:36; 43:33). In the case of twins, the first to emerge from his mother's womb was the first-born (Gen 25:24–26; 38:27–30). The eldest son could, however, lose his right of primogeniture as the result of a serious fault, as in the case of Reuben (Gen 35:22; 49:3–4; 1 Chron 5:1) or he could, like Esau, relinquish it (Gen 25:29–34).

On the other hand, it would seem that the patriarch could choose his 'eldest' son and the theme of the youngest son who takes the place of the eldest occurs frequently in Genesis. Abraham's inheritance passed to Isaac instead of to Ishmael (Gen 21:10; 25:5). Jacob supplanted Esau (Gen 25:23; see also the etymology of the name Jacob given in Gen 27:36). Joseph was his father's favourite son and, in a dream, he saw himself dominating his brothers (Gen 37:5–11). According to one tradition, he had all the prerogatives and even the title of first-born (Gen 48:22; 1 Chron 5:1–2). Jacob put Ephraim before Manasseh (Gen 48:18–19).

It has been suggested that these examples betray traces of a practice of ultimogeniture, in which the inheritance passes to the youngest son – a practice that has been observed among other shepherd peoples. The explanation of these texts is, however, quite different.[62] They are examples of the common law and may express a conflict between juridical practice and human feeling, that of a father for the son 'of his old age' (Gen 37:3; 44:20). From the theological point of view, they reflect the gratuitous nature of

---

[61] For the right of the first-born among the Semites in general, see J. Henninger, *op. cit.* (note 60); *ibid.,* 'Premiers-nés', *DBS,* VIII, 1968, col. 467–482. For the birthright in the Old Testament, see H. Cazelles, 'Premiers-nés', *DBS,* VIII, 1969, col. 482–491.

[62] R. de Vaux, *Institutions,* I, p. 42; J. Henninger, *op. cit.* (note 60), pp. 179–180; *DBS,* VIII, col. 480.

God's choice (Gen 21:12; 25:22–23) – God loved Jacob and hated Esau (see Mal 1:2–3; cf. Rom 9:13). Finally, according to the history of traditions and historical criticism, these texts reveal the changing destinies of groups of people personified by their ancestors.[63]

Several cases of adoption are mentioned in the stories in Genesis.[64] Sarah, for example, gives her servant Hagar to Abraham so that she might be able to have children through her (Gen 16:1–2).[65] Similarly, Rachel gives her servant Bilhah to Jacob so that she may give birth on her knees and so that she, Rachel, might have children through her. What is more, it is Rachel who names the two sons born in this way (Gen 30:1–8). In the same way, Leah names the two sons whom her servant Zilpah has conceived by Jacob (Gen 30:9–13). Jacob also declares that the two sons of Joseph, Ephraim and Manasseh, are to be his sons (Gen 48:5) and he took them 'between his knees' (Gen 48:12). The children of Machir, the son of Manasseh, 'were born on Joseph's lap' (Gen 50:23). These cases can be compared with that of Naomi taking the newly born son of Ruth on her lap and those who were present saying 'A son has been born for Naomi' (Ruth 4:16–17).

These are all clearly cases of adoption accompanied by an expressive rite, evidence of which exists among other peoples. This rite consists of the child being taken between or on the knees of the man or woman who is adopting him. They are, moreover, the only explicit cases of adoption in the Bible and they are all confined to the patriarchal age, with the single exception of the story of Ruth and Naomi, which, in any case, recalls, in its late editing, much older customs. These cases of adoption are, it will be noted, never concerned with children of foreign blood. They always take place within the family and in a direct line. In other words, the child is adopted by the step-mother, the grandfather or the grandmother. There is, however, one case which is different – if Abraham, who was still without children, anticipated leaving his possessions to a servant (Gen 15:3) this would be

---

[63] See below; for Reuben, see pp. 576–581; for Joseph and for Ephraim-Manasseh, see pp. 650–652.

[64] M. David, 'Adoptie in het oude Israël', Mededelingen der Koninklijke Nederlandse Akademie van Wetenschappen, Afdeling Letterkunde, new series, 18, 4, 1955, pp. 85–103; R. Yaron, 'Varia on Adoption', Journal of Juristic Papyrology, 15 (1965) = Volume V. Arangio-Ruiz, pp. 171–183; M. H. Prévost, 'Remarques sur l'adoption dans la Bible', RIDA, 3rd series, 14 (1967), pp. 67–77. On the other hand, H. Donner, in his article 'Adoption oder Legitimation? Erwägungen zur Adoption im Alten Testament auf dem Hintergrund der altorientalischen Rechte', OrAnt, 8 (1969), pp. 87–119, believes that adoption was never practised in Israel and interprets the cases that are quoted in this chapter as acts of legitimation. This may, of course, be simply an argument about words, the consequence of a too rigid application of modern juridical concepts.

[65] Adoption may have been a remedy against sterility or infertility; see, for example, the medical evidence collected by S. Kardimon in his article 'Adoption as a Remedy for Infertility in the Period of the Patriarchs', JSS, 3 (1958), pp. 123–126. Whether this is the case or not, it is still adoption.

because he had already adopted that man. If this is the correct explanation of this text, then there must have been some influence exerted by a foreign custom. (This will be discussed more fully later.[66])

This rather limited part played in patriarchal society by adoption, which was practised much more widely among the settled peoples of Mesopotamia and Syria, can be explained by the desire to keep the blood pure, since purity of blood was the real bond of tribal life. It was because of the need for purity of blood too that marriages between blood relations were preferred. Abraham, for instance, sent his servant to look for a wife for Isaac among his family in Mesopotamia (Gen 24:4). Isaac also sent Jacob to Mesopotamia to choose a wife (Gen 28:2) and Laban declared that he would prefer to give his daughter to Jacob rather than to a stranger (Gen 29:19). Marriages between cousins were frequent and two obvious examples are the marriage between Isaac and Rebekah and Jacob's marriage with Leah and Rachel. Bearing in mind his father's preferences, Esau married a daughter of his uncle Ishmael (Gen 28:8–9) but he had, of course, already married two Canaanite women against his parents' wishes (Gen 26:34–35).

Monogamy was after all not a strict rule at the time of the patriarchs.[67] At first Abraham had only one wife, Sarah, but because she was unable to have children, he took Hagar – at the suggestion of Sarah herself (Gen 16:1–2). According to Gen 25:1, he also married Keturah and there is reference in Gen 25:6 to his several concubines. These two texts, however, represent special traditions of uncertain origin. Nahor, who had children by his wife Milcah, also took a concubine, Reumah (Gen 22:20–24). Similarly, Eliphaz, Esau's son, had both a wife and a concubine (Gen 36:11–12). Jacob married the two sisters, Leah and Rachel, and each of them gave him her slave-girl (Gen 29:15–30; 30:1–9). Esau had three wives who are placed at the same level in Gen 26:34; 28:9 and 36:1–5, but all these texts are in the priestly tradition. The patriarchs seem to have been less strict in their practices with regard to marriage than the people of Mesopotamia during the same period, who recognised only one habitual spouse. Their marital practices were, on the other hand, also different from the polygamy practised at a later period by the leaders of Israel. Gideon, for example, had 'many wives' and at least one concubine (Judges 8:30–31) and the kings had harems which were often very large.

One question which has to be asked in this context is, however, whether these multiple marriages and relationships with women and these distinctions made between wives and concubines really express historical or geographical relationships between related groups.[68] It cannot be denied

---

[66] See below, p. 249.

[67] W. Plautz, 'Monogamie und Polygamie im Alten Testament', *ZAW*, 75 (1963), pp. 3–27.

[68] See A. Malamat's comments in the *XV⁴ Rencontre Assyriologique Internationale, op. cit.*, pp.

that actual marital practices are described in these multiple relationships, but these practices may well be those which were current at the time when the traditions were established and not those prevailing during the patriarchal age. This is a doubt which arises in connection with every picture of the patriarchal way of life provided by Genesis and the particular problems involved in it can only be solved if we have recourse to evidence outside the Bible itself.[69]

Practically nothing at all is known about the wider framework within which the family had its place, and the boundaries of the family itself are similarly very vague. In Genesis, the family is called the 'house', *bêth*, or the 'paternal house', *bêth 'abh*, which implies both a community tied by blood relationships and a community living together in a house or tent. Around the patriarch in this 'house' or 'household' were grouped the patriarch's wives, his sons and daughters, the wives of his sons and their children. The 'house of Jacob' in Egypt included three generations (Gen 46:27; cf. 5:31; 48:12). Esau also migrated with his wives, sons and daughters and 'all the members of his household' (Gen 36:6), since the 'household' also included the servants (Gen 15:3; 24:2). If a son married and lived separately, he set up his own 'house', so that, in Gen 50:8, for example, the 'house' of Joseph in Egypt is distinguished from that of his father Isaac. Yet both Abraham in Canaan and Jacob in Mesopotamia still felt that they were tied to their father's 'house' (Gen 20:13; 31:30). Rachel and Leah say that they are no longer entitled to any share in their father's 'house' (Gen 31:14), but, when Laban joins Jacob who has fled with his 'house', he says: 'These daughters are my daughters and these sons are my sons' (Gen 31:43). We may therefore conclude that the use of the word 'house' was as flexible at the time of the patriarchs as the use of the word 'family' today. In the extended sense, the limits of the family or of kin were established by the prohibitions of Lev 18, the basis of which is very ancient. These prohibitions also take both blood relations and the community of those living together into account.[70]

Between the paternal house and the tribe, there was also, according to Jos 7:16–18, the 'clan', 'kinsfolk' or 'family', the *mis'pāhāh*. Although this word points to a larger unit than the family in the more limited sense, its usage is uncertain.[71] In Genesis especially, it tends to be used together with 'paternal

---

129–130.

[69] See below, pp. 244 ff.

[70] K. Elliger, 'Das Gesetz Leviticus 18', *ZAW*, 67 (1955), pp. 1–25; G. Fohrer, 'Das sogenannte apodiktisch formulierte Recht und der Dekalog', *Kerygma und Dogma*, 11 (1965), pp. 49–74 = *Studien zur alttestamentlichen Theologie und Geschichte (BZAW*, 115), 1969, pp. 120–148, especially pp. 124–126; J. R. Porter, *The Extended Family in the Old Testament* (*Occasional Papers in Social and Economic Administration*, No. 6), London, 1967.

[71] J. Pedersen, *Israel, Its Life and Culture*, I–II, London, 1946, pp. 46–51; C. H. Wolf, 'Terminology of Israel's Tribal Organisation', *JBL*, 65 (1946), pp. 45–49.

house' (Gen 24:38–40) and must therefore have the same meaning. The word *môledheth*, 'descendants' or 'family', is also used alongside 'paternal house' (Gen 12:1; 24:7).

What is more, these great patriarchal families appear as entirely independent units. Not only were they not subject to any political authority exercised by sedentary groups of people – they were also not connected in any way with any wider group leading the same semi-nomadic way of life. These 'paternal houses' seem not to have formed part of any tribe – the Hebrew words for 'tribe' do not occur once in Genesis. This fact calls for an explanation.

In the Mari archives, several terms are used for the nomadic tribal units of Upper Mesopotamia – *gāyum/gāwum*, *ummatum* and *hibrum*.[72] The precise value of these terms is, unfortunately, very difficult to determine and it might have been affected by a certain amount of interference in the lives of these tribal groups on the part of the central administration of the kingdom of Mari.

The first of these words, *gāyum/gāwum*, seems to have been the name given to a group of families with the same ethnic origin, but it is also used in the Mari texts with a geographical meaning. The Hebrew equivalent, *gôy*, developed in meaning in the same way and was later to be used for a whole nation.

The second of these terms, *ummatum*, seems to have denoted the largest social group of nomads. In one inscription, *ummat Hana* is parallel with 'all the "fathers" of Hana'[73] and the Haneans were, of course, one of the principal groups of nomads during this period. The Hebrew equivalent, *'ummāh*, only occurs three times in the Old Testament. In Ps 117:1, it is parallel with *gôyîm*. The other two texts are more interesting in this context, because they are concerned with nomads. Zur, the father of the Midianite woman killed at Peor, was the chief of *'ummôth* of Midian (Num 25:15). The word is explained in this text by a gloss, *bêth 'abh*, 'patriarchal house', and this gives it a more important meaning, since this Zur is called, in Num 25:18, a 'prince', *nâsî'*, and, according to Num 31:8, he is said to be one of the five 'kings' of Midian. These five men were the leaders of great branches of the Midianites (cf. the five 'sons' of Midian, Gen 25:4). In Gen 25:13–16, the 'sons' of Ishmael are listed according to their encampments, *hâserîm*, and their duars, *tîrôth*, twelve princes, *n'sî'îm*, according to their *'ummôth*. These are, of course, the twelve Ishmaelite tribes. The word *nâsî'* was also to be the title of the leaders of the twelve tribes of Israel.

The third term, *hibrum*, meant a more restricted unit, but one which was

---

[72] For what follows, see A. Malamat, *JAOS*, 82 (1962), pp. 143–146; *ibid.*, *XV* *Rencontre Assyriologique, op. cit.*, pp. 133–135.

[73] G. Dossin, 'L'inscription de Iahdun-Lim, roi de Mari', *Syria*, 32 (1955), pp. 1–28, col. III, 28; *ANET*, p. 556.

greater than the family. A text to which we have already referred[74] applies the word to a group of eight families of the 'house' of Awîn, a branch of the Rabbeans. The equivalent Hebrew term, *hebher*, means various kinds of associations, but it is possible that the first meaning, that of tribe, may be present in the personal name Heber, given to the leader of a group of semi-nomadic Kenites (Judges 4:11, 17) and to the ancestor of a group of families of Asher (1 Chron 7:31–32).

All this tells us very little about the organisation of patriarchal society beyond the family. There was, however, an awareness within the patriarchal tradition of certain links uniting the ancestors of Israel to other groups of people, but these were always expressed genealogically.[75] Lot, for example, was Abraham's nephew. He went with him from Ur to Haran (Gen 11:31) and from Haran to Canaan (Gen 12:5). He then separated from him (Gen 13:5–12) and became the father of the Moabites and the Ammonites (Gen 19:30–38). Again, Nahor, Abraham's brother, had twelve sons who were the ancestors of the Aramaean tribes (Gen 22:20–24). As we have already seen, Ishmael, Isaac's brother, was the ancestor of twelve *'ummôth,* the equivalent of tribes (Gen 25:13–16). Finally, Jacob's brother Esau was the 'father' of the Edomites (Gen 36:6–9), who were divided into clans or *'allûph* (Gen 36:15–19, 40–43).

These genealogies express the relationships between the various groups and also their geographical distribution. All these groups are outside Canaan, which is, of course, the country of the patriarchs themselves, but it was not only the family of Abraham, Isaac and Jacob that had to lead a semi-nomadic way of life as shepherds and goatherds in Canaan. Within each group, genealogies were given to explain the division of the group into branches which were less important, the equivalent of the twelve 'sons of Jacob', the ancestors of the tribes of Israel. These were not formed until after the settlement in Canaan which followed the exodus, but they took their origin from groups which were already in the country during the patriarchal period. It is within this whole complex of relationships, which cannot at present be made more precise, that the family stories of Abraham, Isaac and Jacob have been set. These stories have been preserved, among others, by the patriarchal traditions and arranged in a genealogical series.[76]

---

[74] *ARM*, VIII, 11; see also above, note 48.

[75] M. D. Johnson, *The Purpose of the Biblical Genealogies,* Cambridge, 1969, pp. 3–5, 77.

[76] See what has been said above about the formation of the patriarchal traditions, pp. 165–177.

III. THE PATRIARCHS AND THE LEGAL PRACTICES
OF THE ANCIENT NEAR EAST

The discovery of the Code of Hammurabi in 1902 was a piece of extra-ordinary good fortune for biblical scholars. The family practices of the patriarchs – marriage, concubinate, inheritance and so on – were shown to be in accordance with the rules of this code. Several scholars went so far as to claim that patriarchal society was governed by the laws of the great Babylonian sovereign. Since the beginning of this century, however, our knowledge of the laws and legal practices of the Ancient Near East has improved considerably and our views have become much more subtly shaded.

1. The eastern laws

The various collections of laws, which have incorrectly been called 'codes', are our main source of knowledge of these laws of the Ancient Near East.[77] The Akkadian Code of Hammurabi is the most complete text,[78] but we now have in our possession several other collections which antedate this code. First, we have fragments of the Sumerian Code of Ur-Nammu, the first king of the Third Dynasty of Ur.[79] Secondly, there is the Sumerian Code of Lipit-Ishtar, the king of Isin at the end of the twentieth century B.C.[80] and thirdly, there are the laws of the city of Eshnunna,

---

[77] The two most recent analyses are R. Haase, *Einführung in das Studium keilschriftlicher Rechtsquellen*, Wiesbaden, 1965, and the articles under 'Gesetze' (laws) in the *Reallexikon der Assyriologie*, III, 4, Berlin, 1966, pp. 243–297, the article on Babylonian laws is by J. Klima and H. Petschow, that on Assyria is by G. Cardascia and that on the Hittites by V. Korošec. R. Haase has made a convenient collection of the texts in translation in *Die keilschriftlichen Rechtssammlungen in deutscher Übersetzung*, Wiesbaden, 1963 (quoted in the footnotes to this section as Haase) and almost all of the texts have also been published in English translation in *ANET*, pp. 159–198, 521–530.

[78] Abbreviated here as *CH*; see Haase, pp. 23–55; *ANET*, pp. 163–180; commentary by G. R. Driver and J. C. Miles, *The Babylonian Laws*, I–II, Oxford, 1952, 1955; see also J. J. Finkelstein, 'A Late Old Babylonian Copy of the Laws of Hammurapi', *JCS*, 21 (1967) = *Volume A*. Goetze, 1969, pp. 39–48; *ibid.*, 'The Hammurapı Law Tablet BE XXXI 22', *RA*, 63 (1969), pp. 11–27.

[79] Abbreviated here as *CU*; see Haase, p. 1; *ANET*, pp. 523–525; see also S. N. Kramer, 'Ur-Nammu Law Code', *Orientalia*, 23 (1954), pp. 40–48, see also pp. 49–51; O. R. Gurney and S. N. Kramer, 'Two Fragments of Sumerian Laws', *Studies in Honor of B. Landsberger*, Chicago, 1965, pp. 13–19; E. Szlechter, *RA*, 49 (1955), pp. 169–177; 61 (1967), pp. 105–126.*

[80] Abbreviated here as *CL*; see Haase, pp. 17–20; *ANET*, pp. 159–161; see also F. R. Steele, 'The Code of Lipit-Ishtar, *AJA*, 52 (1948), pp. 425–450; R. Szlechter, 'Le Code de

which are slightly earlier than the Code of Hammurabi.[81] Related to these 'codes' of law are the 'edicts' proclaimed by the kings of the First Dynasty of Babylon at the beginning of their reigns and afterwards at intervals. These edicts are acts of 'equity', mišarum, aiming to provide a remedy for economic and social unrest by remitting debts under certain conditions and by returning lands to their original owners.[82] Two of these royal edicts have been found. The first is the Edict of Ammisaduga, the penultimate king of the dynasty[83] and the other, of which we have only a fragment, is the Edict of Samsu-Iluna, Hammurabi's successor.[84] To these official texts two schoolboys' exercises may be added. These provide us with the wording of legal cases relating to family law.[85]

In addition to these Babylonian texts, we also have at our disposal a collection of Assyrian laws preserved on tablets dating back to the end of the twelfth century B.C., but in fact representing Meso-Assyrian laws existing several centuries before this.[86] A collection of Hittite laws found on tablets dating from the thirteenth century B.C. has also been preserved. These laws from Asia Minor reflect a process of development extending over several centuries, although it is not possible to give any precise date.[87]

We have no private legal documents concerning the Hittites, but the picture that can be formed from these Babylonian and Assyrian legal texts is made more complete by the existence of countless contracts, bills and other documents illustrating the practice of the law. A very important group of texts comes from Arrapha and another comes from Nuzi, both in the region

---

Lipit-Ishar', RA, 51 (1957), pp. 57–82, 177–196; 52 (1958), pp. 74–90; M. Civil, 'New Sumerian Law Fragments', Studies in Honor of B. Landsberger, pp. 1–6; E. Szlechter, RA, 62 (1968), pp. 147–154.

[81] Abbreviated here as CE; see Haase, pp. 9–16; ANET, pp. 161–163; see also E. Szlechter, Les lois d'Eshnunna, Paris, 1954; A. Goetze, The Laws of Eshnunna (AASOR, 31), 1956; J. Bottéro, Ecole Pratique des Hautes Etudes, IV⁴ Section, Annuaire, 1965–1966, pp. 89–105; R. Yaron, The Laws of Eshnunna, Jerusalem, 1969.

[82] This can be compared with the sabbatical year in Israel (Deut 15:1–18).

[83] Haase, pp. 57–60; ANET, pp. 526–528; see also F. F. Kraus, Ein Edikt des Königs Ammisaduqa von Babylon, Leiden, 1958.*

[84] F. R. Kraus, 'Ein Edikt des Königs Samsu-Iluna von Babylon', Studies in Honor of B. Landsberger, Chicago, 1965, pp. 225–231; for the promulgation and application of these edicts, see J. J. Finkelstein, 'Some New misharum Material and its Implications', ibid., pp. 233–246.

[85] A tablet of Yale, Clay 28 (Sumerian); see Haase, pp. 5–6; ANET, pp. 525–526; in the ana ittišu series (Sumerian and Akkadian), a section of 'family laws'; see Haase, pp. 3–4; G. R. Driver and J. C. Miles, The Babylonian Laws, II, op. cit., pp. 308–313.

[86] Abbreviated here as LA; see Haase, pp. 95–116; ANET, pp. 180–188; G. R. Driver and J. C. Miles, The Assyrian Laws, Oxford, 1935; J. Bottéro, Ecole Pratique des Hautes Etudes, IV⁴ Section, Annuaire, 1966–1967, pp. 81–100; 1967–1968, pp. 89–104; G. Cardascia, Les lois assyriennes, Paris, 1969.

[87] Haase, pp. 61–94; ANET, pp. 188–197; J. Friedrich, Die hethitischen Gesetze, Leiden, 1959; V. Korošec, 'Les lois hittites et leur évolution', RA, 57 (1963), pp. 121–144.*

of Kirkuk east of the Tigris.[88] They date from the fifteenth century B.C., when the population of this district was mainly Hurrian. The fact that many of the practices outlined in these texts are different from those in Mesopotamia is explained by their Hurrian origin and this makes the connections that can be established between them and the patriarchal practices more valuable, because the patriarchs were in touch with the Hurrians in Upper Mesopotamia.[89]

No code or collection of laws has so far been found in Syria or Palestine and relatively few private legal documents or contracts have come to light there. They form only a small part of the Mari archives – no more than about a hundred legal texts have been published.[90] Several hundred texts have been found at Alalah, between Aleppo and Antioch, and these have been divided into two groups, the first dating from the seventeenth century and the second from the fifteenth century B.C.[91] The excavations at Rās Shamrah have yielded several documents from private archives and one important group has been found in the royal palace.[92]

In comparing these legislative or juridical texts with the legal practices found in the accounts in Genesis, several questions concerning method have to be borne in mind. As we have seen, these texts were either codes or edicts produced by royal legislators or they were, like the collections of Assyrian and Hittite laws, the work of legal experts or advisers. In both cases, however, they are neither well organised nor complete, even if they have been preserved in their entirety. Above all they deal with cases of jurisprudence. Those legal documents which are contemporary or which are a little earlier or later than one another do not have recourse to each other as to obligatory 'laws' and often provide different solutions for the same cases. Although they are all in cuneiform, they are, leaving aside the question of dialects, written in three quite different languages, with the result that it is often very difficult to establish the exact meaning of the juridical terms used. They also cover a wide geographical area stretching

[88] R. Tournay, 'Nouzi', DBS, VI (1960), col. 646–674, with bibliography; see also Excavations at Nuzi VII. Economic and Social Documents = Harvard Semitic Studies (HSS), XVI, 1958; VIII, Family Law Documents = HSS XIX, 1962; cf. E. Cassin, 'Nouvelles données sur les relations familiales à Nuzi', RA, 57 (1963), pp. 113–119.

[89] The connections between these texts and the Old Testament have often been the object of study; see, for example, the biliography in R. Tournay, op. cit., col. 673–674 and the summary in C. J. Mullo Weir, 'Nuzi', Archaeology and Old Testament Studies, ed. D. Winton Thomas, Oxford, 1967, pp. 73–86.

[90] ARM, VIII, with an introduction and a legal commentary by G. Boyer.

[91] D. J. Wiseman, The Alalakh Tablets, London, 1953 and JCS, 8 (1954), pp. 1–30; 12 (1958), pp. 124–129; 13 (1959), pp. 19–33, 50–62; ibid., 'Alalakh', Archaeology and Old Testament Studies (see above, note 89), pp. 119–135.

[92] J. Nougayrol, PRU, III, Paris, 1955, with an important juridical study by G. Boyer, 'La place des textes d'Ugarit dans l'histoire de l'ancien droit oriental', pp. 283–308; J. Nougayrol, Ugaritica V, Paris, 1968, pp. 2–16, 172–187.

from the Persian Gulf to Asia Minor and from east of the Tigris to the Mediterranean Sea in the west. They also cover a great period of time – eight centuries lie between the Code of Ur-Nammu and the juridical texts of Rās Shamrah. Finally, these laws applied to settled people, were promulgated by kings or princes and are only to a very limited extent appropriate to the social conditions of the patriarchs.

These eastern laws, then, differ according to time and place, but, in addition to the fact that they are all written in cuneiform, there are many other similarities between them. They are, for example, all based on the one shared common law of the Ancient Near East, one of the products of the mixture of peoples and societies characterising the second millennium B.C. This shared background justifies any attempt to compare the laws of the Ancient Near East with the legal practices of the patriarchs, although care has to be taken in view of the differences of time, place and social conditions and any tendency to exaggerate these parallels has to be avoided.[93]

2. Marriage

Because of the nature of the sagas of the patriarchs, these comparisons have above all been concerned with family customs. Abraham's marriage with Hagar, Sarah's servant, and Jacob's marriage with Bilhah, Rachel's servant and then with Zilpah, Leah's servant, have, for instance, been compared with certain articles in the Code of Hammurabi which make provision for a barren wife to give a slave to her husband so that he can have children by her.[94] These articles, however, have the special case of the *nadītu* in mind, in other words, of a 'hierodule' or priestess who was not permitted to have children.[95] A better comparison therefore with marital practice in the patriarchal era is a contract made in the Assyrian trading colony of Kültepe in Asia Minor in the nineteenth century B.C., confirming the

[93] C. H. Gordon, 'Parallèles nouziens aux lois et coutumes de l'Ancien Testament', RB, 44 (1935), pp. 35–41; ibid., 'Biblical Customs and the Nuzu Tablets', BibArch, 3 (1940), pp. 1–12 = The Biblical Archaeologist Reader, ed. E. F. Campbell and D. N. Freedman, II, Garden City, 1964, pp. 21–33; R. de Vaux, 'Les Patriarches hébreux et les découvertes modernes', RB, 56 (1949), esp. pp. 24–35; R. Tournay, 'Nouzi', DBS, VI, 1960, col 663–670; J. M. Holt, The Patriarchs of Israel, Nashville, 1964, pp. 91–126; R. de Vaux, 'Les Patriarches hébreux et l'histoire', RB, 72 esp. pp. 22–25; R. Martin-Achard, Actualité d'Abraham, Neuchâtel, 1969, pp. 27–32.
[94] CH §§144–147; see also G. R. Driver and J. C. Miles, The Babylonian Laws, I, op. cit., pp. 304–306, for a legal commentary.
[95] For the nadītu, see R. Harris, 'The Nadītu Woman', Studies Presented to L. Oppenheim, Chicago, 1964, pp. 106–135; J. Renger, 'Untersuchungen zum Priestertum in der altbabylonischen Zeit', ZA, 58 (1967), especially pp. 149–176.

marriage of an Assyrian to a native woman. This marriage contract states that the wife must buy a slave for her husband if she has not given birth to children after two years and, when the slave girl has given birth, she is to be sold again.[96] This clause emphasises the part played by the concubine – the only function that she has is to provide offspring for the husband who, according to the contract, is not entitled to take a second wife. The cases in Genesis, however, are different, in that the wife always urges the husband to take a concubine and then adopts the children born as a result of this relationship. Neither is the continuity of the father's line in question in either case – Abraham was able to take a second wife (he married Keturah, Gen 25: 1) and Jacob already had four sons by Leah when Rachel gave him her slave-girl. One contract from Nuzi which has often been quoted in this context stresses the obligation on the part of a wife who has not given her husband any children to obtain a slave of the best birth for him and the fact that she may not drive away any children whom this slave has by him.[97] This has been compared with the situation in Gen 21: 10–13, where Sarah asks Abraham to drive away Hagar and her son Ishmael. Sarah, in other words, does not claim any right here and Abraham is reluctant to give way to her demand. Any similarity between the story in Genesis and the Nuzi document is, therefore, only external and the two cases are quite different. In the Nuzi document, the conditions governing the marriage form part of an act of adoption – the husband is the adopted son of his step-father and the principal aim of the contract is to keep the inheritance within the line of descent of the adoptive father.

The best parallels are to be found in much earlier documents.[98] In Egypt, round about 1100 B.C, for example, a couple without children acquired a slave-girl who gave the husband three children, which were adopted by the wife and became legitimate heirs.[99] An Assyrian marriage contract from Nimrud (seventh century B.C.) makes provision for the barrenness of the wife by stating that the husband should take a servant and that the servant's children should be recognised as those of the wife.[100] Both these texts, however, are very difficult to interpret.

Abraham twice allows his wife Sarah to be taken for his sister – once at the pharaoh's court (Gen 12:10–13) and once when he is with Abimelech at

[96] ANET, p. 543a; see also J. Lewy, HUCA, 27 (1956), pp. 9–10; H. Hirsch, Orientalia, 35 (1966), pp. 279–280.
[97] HSS, V, 67; translation in E. M. Cassin, L'adoption à Nuzi, Paris, 1938, pp. 285–288; ANET, p. 220; see also C. H. Gordon, RB, 44 (1935), p. 35; BibArch, 3 (1940), p. 3; E. A. Speiser, Genesis, p. 120 (the last words are differently translated).
[98] J. van Seters, 'The Problem of Childlessness in Near Eastern Law and the Patriarchs of Israel', JBL, 87 (1968), pp. 401–408.
[99] A. H. Gardiner, 'Adoption Extraordinary', JEA, 26 (1940), pp. 23–29.
[100] B. Parker, 'The Nimrud Tablets, 1952 – Business Documents', Iraq, 16 (1954), pp. 37–39 (according to J. van Seter's interpretation, op. cit., p. 407).

Gerar (Gen 20:1–17). Also at Gerar with Abimelech, Isaac pretends that Rachel is his sister (Gen 26:1–11). Both early and recent commentators have been troubled by these three episodes. A modern scholar has attempted to explain them by reference to a similar custom mentioned in the Nuzi texts.[101] The wife could at the same time be adopted by her husband as his 'sister' and, even more than this, a woman given in marriage by her brother – either natural or adoptive – would legally become her husband's 'sister'. These 'sister-wives' enjoyed certain special privileges from the social and legal point of view and the practice was above all favoured at the higher social levels. According to Gen 20:12, Sarah was Abraham's half-sister and, if she was Terah's adopted daughter, she was well qualified for the position of wife-sister. As for Rebekah, she was given in marriage to Isaac by her brother Laban, so that she became a wife-sister and, as in the Nuzi contracts, her consent was asked for and obtained (Gen 24:57–58). It is therefore possible to claim that the Hurrian practice, to which the Nuzi texts bear witness, lay behind the wife-sister situation in the Genesis stories. A memory of this special status of 'wife-sister' may have been preserved in the patriarchal tradition, but the real meaning of this status may have been lost, with the result that it was interpreted rather differently. The original, primitive meaning of these episodes in Genesis may well have been different and Abraham and Isaac may even have wanted to boast in the presence of their hosts of the honourable rank that their wives held.

This explanation, however, is not very convincing because of its dependence on the rather doubtful theory of a primitive 'fratriarchy' at Nuzi – and in the society of Israel's ancestors – and because the documents dealing with this adoption as a sister, ahatūtu, are so difficult to interpret. Another and very different solution to the problem has therefore been suggested.[102] In Islamic law, in addition to the formula used in divorcing a wife, 'You are no longer my wife', there is another declaration: 'You are as a sister to me'. Abraham and Isaac seem to have repudiated their wives, but only for the period that they spent in Egypt and at Gerar respectively. On the other hand, there is no case of any parallel situation, that is, of a temporary divorce, either in Islam or in the Ancient Near East. The interpretation of these three narratives has therefore to be left to those specialising in exegesis and the history of traditions.

When Abraham sent his servant to Mesopotamia in search of a wife for Isaac, it was envisaged that the young woman might refuse to come to Canaan and that Isaac might have to go back to Mesopotamia to join her (Gen

---

[101] E. A. Speiser, 'The Wife-Sister Motif in the Patriarchal Narratives', *Biblical and Other Studies*, ed. A. Altmann, Cambridge, Mass., 1963, pp. 15–28 = E. A. Speiser, *Oriental and Biblical Studies*, Philadelphia, 1967, pp. 62–82; *Genesis, op. cit.* (note 97), pp. 91–94, 184–185.

[102] L. Rost, 'Fragen zum Scheidungsrecht in Gen 12, 10–20', *Gottes Wort und Gottes Land (Festschrift H. W. Hertzberg)*, Göttingen, 1965, pp. 186–192.

24:5). After his marriage with Leah and then with Rachel, Jacob stayed with his wives' family. It has therefore been suggested that there was a form of marriage in the patriarchal period by which the wife continued to live with her husband in her paternal house.[103] This type of marriage, the so-called *errēbu* marriage, is not mentioned in the Code of Hammurabi, but there is evidence of its existence in Lower Mesopotamia in the series known as *ana attišu*[104] and seven articles of Assyrian law are apparently devoted to it, since they are concerned with the wife who is 'in her father's house'.[105] This Assyrian parallel cannot be accepted however, because in Assyrian society the wife normally lived in her husband's house and became an integral member of his family. Although this was the only type of marriage in Assyria, it might happen that the wife would continue to live with her father, so that the intention of these articles would be to protect the rights of the husband.[106] As far as the stories in Genesis are concerned, it should not be forgotten that Abraham refused to allow Isaac to go and live in Mesopotamia (Gen 24:6, 8) and that Jacob always intended to go back to Canaan (Gen 27:44; 28:2–4, 21) and, when he expressed his desire to go back to his own country, Laban did not raise the question of the obligations that would have been imposed on him by that type of marriage (Gen 30:25–28).

3. Adoption

The legal formulae in the series *ana ittišu* which have just been quoted above refer to the case of an adopted son who has married the daughter of the adoptive parent and who is living with him. It has also been suggested that Jacob had been adopted by Laban and a comparison has been made between this situation and some of the Nuzi documents.[107] It has, moreover, been noted that Laban's own natural sons are only mentioned in passing towards the end of this story, when Jacob had already been living for

---

[103] C. H. Gordon, 'The Story of Jacob and Laban in the Light of the Nuzi Tablets', *BASOR*, 66 (Apr. 1937), pp. 25–27; M. Burrows, 'The Complaint of Laban's Daughters', *JAOS*, 57 (1937), pp. 259–276.

[104] *Ana ittišu*, 3, IV, 32–46.

[105] *LA*, A §§ 25, 26, 27, 32, 33, 36, 38.

[106] A. van Praag, *Droit matrimonial assyrio-babylonien*, Amsterdam, 1945, pp. 181–190; G. Cardascia, *Les Lois Assyriens*, *op. cit.*, p. 64; for this question and several of the parallels that have been examined in this section, see also J. van Seter's justified reservations in 'Jacob's Marriages and Ancient Near East Customs. A Reexamination', *HTR*, 62 (1969), pp. 377–395.

[107] C. H. Gordon and M. Burrows, *op. cit.*, (note 103); C. H. Gordon, *BibArch*, 3 (1940), pp. 6–7.

twenty years with his step-father (Gen 30:35; 31:1). One supposition is that these sons were born after Laban and Jacob had made their arrangement, Laban having adopted Jacob because he had no sons of his own at the time, with the result that, according to the law of Upper Mesopotamia, Jacob became Laban's heir. When Laban's sons were born, however, they became the natural heirs and Jacob, together with Leah and Rachel, were frustrated. This would explain the sons' bitterness and what Rachel and Leah say to Jacob: 'Have we any share left in the inheritance of our father's house?' (Gen 31:14). As an adopted son, however, Jacob remained, with his wives, subject to Laban, and Laban's authority over Jacob as his father would clearly justify the statement that he made when he had caught up with the fleeing Jacob: 'These daughters are my daughters and these sons are my sons . . .' (Gen 31:43).

All the same, the hypothesis that Jacob was adopted by Laban is not in accordance with Laban's offer to Jacob of wages (Gen 29:15), with the fourteen years that Jacob served Laban in order to marry Leah and Rachel (Gen 29:18, 27), and with the contract that Jacob concluded afterwards with Laban (Gen 30:28ff). What is more, Jacob also speaks of his own 'house', as distinct from that of Laban (Gen 30:30). None of these data are compatible with the position of an adopted son[108] and for this reason we may conclude that the comparison between these Genesis narratives and the Nuzi documents referring to adoption cannot be justified.

Another hypothesis has, however, been suggested, one which does not have recourse to external evidence such as the Nuzi texts.[109] When Laban greeted Jacob, he said to him: 'Truly you are my bone and flesh' (Gen 29:14). This may not be an explicit formula of adoption, but it is certainly an affirmation expressing a bond with certain legal consequences, that is, Jacob's union with Laban's family. In fact, 'Jacob stayed with him for a month' (Gen 29:14). After this, however, Laban's attitude seems to have changed and, according to this hypothesis, his words (Gen 29:15) should be translated as: 'Are you my brother? And are you to serve me for nothing?', meaning 'You are not my brother and you are not to serve me for nothing'. In other words, Laban thus breaks the family tie which unites him to Jacob and Jacob becomes his paid employee. This theory is certainly worth considering, but, according to the grammatical structure of verse 15, the translation 'Because you are my kinsman (brother), are you to work for me without payment?', which is also basically that of the Septuagint and the Vulgate, is fully justified. This translation of the verse does not imply that Jacob's status had changed in any way, nor that he had in the first place been adopted by Laban. All that we can infer from it is that he is still related

[108] See also Z. W. Falk, *Hebrew Law in Biblical Times*, Jerusalem, 1964, p. 125.
[109] D. Daube and R. Yaron, 'Jacob's Reception by Laban', *JSS*, 1 (1956), pp. 60–62.

to Laban, as his kinsman. Nonetheless, like the theory discussed at the beginning of this section on adoption, this hypothesis is open to the general criticism that an attempt is made to discover a juridical statement in a narrative which is fundamentally only seeking to express personal feelings. What Jacob, Laban and his daughters say in this story should clearly be interpreted in this sense.

According to Gen 15:1–3, if Abraham had no children, his heir should be one of his servants. At Nuzi, those who had no children adopted a stranger so as to ensure that they would be supported when they were old and to safeguard their funeral rites and the survival of their family and their inheritance. The adopted son was the 'indirect heir',[110] but, if a natural son was born, the adopted son would forfeit his right to the main share in the inheritance. Thus, if Abraham had adopted a member of his household, the practice of Nuzi would explain Yahweh's reply: 'He shall not be your heir; your heir shall be of your own flesh and blood' (Gen 15:4).[111] All the same, in the Nuzi texts that are usually quoted in this instance, it would appear that it was only very rarely that slaves were adopted; adopted sons were almost always of free birth.[112] One Nuzi document that has been commonly quoted in this case,[113] is in fact not a good parallel with Genesis, because the adopted son is not the 'slave' of the man adopting him, but someone in the service of a great person and thus occupying a higher status than that of slave. He was entitled to use his adoptive father's property during his lifetime; in other words, he had the right of usufruct, but not of possession or inheritance. This Genesis text (Gen 15:1–3), then, can be explained most simply as a will and testament which Abraham wanted to make – if he had no heir, he would leave his possessions to a servant whom he trusted and whom he would set free.[114] The only real cases of adoption in the stories of the patriarchs are those which took place within the family and which have been discussed earlier in this chapter. These can be compared with the case of a grandson adopted by his grandfather on the mother's side in a Rās Shamrah text, the aim of which was to ensure that the adopted grandson had the right of succession.[115]

[110] ewuru; see E. A. Speiser, JAOS, 55 (1935), pp. 435–436.
[111] C. H. Gordon, BibArch, 3 (1940), p. 2; E. A. Speiser, Genesis, p. 112.
[112] A. Saarisalo, New Kirkuk Documents Relating to Slaves (Studia Orientalia, V, 3), 1934, p. 73.
[113] HSS, IX, 22; A. Saarisalo, op. cit., pp. 23–24; E. M. Cassin, L'adoption à Nuzi, op. cit., pp. 280–282.
[114] Z. W. Falk, op. cit. (note 108), p. 166, which can be compared with Prov 17: 2.
[115] RS, 16. 295, in J. Nougayrol, PRU, III, Paris, 1955, pp. 70–71, with G. Boyer's legal commentary, ibid., p. 303.

4. Birthright

According to the texts from Genesis discussed above,[116] it would seem that the eldest son in patriarchal society had precedence over his brothers, but that the patriarch could also choose his 'eldest son' (as in the case of Isaac, Jacob, Joseph and Ephraim), a practice which might possibly result in the son who was eldest by birth rather than by paternal choice having to renounce his birthright, as in the case of Esau. This case has been compared with cases in two Nuzi documents. In the first of these, a man acquires the preferential share from another, who is content with the ordinary share,[117] but this is not a good parallel because these two men are not natural brothers. In the second text, a man gives up his right to inherit an orchard to his younger brother for three sheep.[118] There is, however, no question here of the older brother giving up his birthright and this contract is one of the fictitious adoptions which occurred at Nuzi and which concealed the transference from one person to another of property or land which could not be legally transferred.

The father's – or the widowed mother's – power to determine which of the sons was to enjoy the birthright emerges fairly clearly from several of the documents from Arrapha and Nuzi.[119] In one of these, the father gives back to his eldest son the right which he had taken from him.[120] According to a marriage contract of the fifteenth century B.C. from Alalah, a decision is made between the sons of two different wives as to which is the eldest.[121] A document from Rās Shamrah provides for the widowed mother's choice of the principal heir.[122] In Israel, the law of Deuteronomy withdrew from the father's disposal the right of the first-born over another son (Deut 21: 15–17).

This same law stipulates that the eldest son must receive a double share of the inheritance (cf. Elisha's request to inherit a double share of Elijah's spirit, 2 Kings 2:9). According to the Codes of Lipit-Ishtar[123] and of

---

[116] See above, p. 235.

[117] *HSS*, V, 99 = *AASOR*, X, pp. 48–49; see also E. A. Speiser, *AASOR*, XIII, p. 44.

[118] *N* 204 = E. M. Cassin, *L'adoption à Nuzi*, pp. 230–231; see also C. H. Gordon, *BibArch*, 3 (1940), p. 5 and a similar transaction in the same family = E. N. Cassin, *op. cit.*, pp. 232–233.

[119] Gadd 12 = *RA*, 23 (1926), p. 67; *HSS*, V, 27 = *AASOR*, X, p. 31; *HSS*, V, 73 = *AASOR*, X, p. 51.

[120] *HSS*, V, 21 = *AASOR*, X, p. 39.

[121] D. J. Wiseman, *The Alalakh Tablets*, London, 1953, No. 92 and I. Mendelsohn's interpretation, 'On the Preferential Status of the Eldest Son', *BASOR*, 156 (Dec. 1959), pp. 38–40.

[122] F. Thureau Dangin, 'Trois Contrats de Ras-Shamra', *Syria*, 18 (1937), pp. 249–251.

[123] *CL* §§ 24, 31 (36); see also *Studies in Honor of B. Landsberger, op. cit.*, p. 3; *RA*, 62 (1968), p. 152.

Hammurabi,[124] a father's sons inherited equal shares, but the eldest son could keep the gift that his father had given him during his lifetime by a sealed deed. On the other hand, the legal documents from Lower Mesopotamia[125] which antedate these codes and the *ana ittišu* series[126] all state that the eldest son should receive the preferential share. According to a testament from Rās Shamrah, the eldest son inherited a supplementary share.[127] Again, according to Assyrian law the eldest son inherited a double share,[128] a law which appears in a contemporary deed.[129] The same law was applied in the Hurrian community at Nuzi and at Arrapha.[130] There is also evidence of this law at Mari in the eighteenth century B.C.[131] These texts throw light on the origin of the law of Deuteronomy and suggest that this practice probably existed among settled peoples at the time of the patriarchs. The patriarchs, themselves, however, as semi-nomadic shepherds, do not seem to have practised it. Ishmael, who was the first-born, was simply disinherited (Gen 21:10) and Abraham left all his possessions to Isaac, apart from the gifts that he had already given during his lifetime to his concubines' sons (Gen 25:5–6). On the other hand, one Genesis text that should not be overlooked in this context is Gen 48:22, which says that Joseph was given Shechem as a share 'more than his brothers' – according to one tradition at least, Joseph was regarded as the first-born.[132]

5. The teraphim

When Jacob and his family left Upper Mesopotamia, Rachel, unknown to Jacob, took her father's *teraphim* or household idols (Gen 31:19) and, when he had caught up with Jacob, Laban reproached him for having

[124] *CH* §§ 165–170.
[125] References in G. R. Driver and J. C. Miles, *The Babylonian Laws*, I, p. 331.
[126] *ana ittišu*, 3, IV, 8–9, 6, I, 1.8.
[127] *RS*, 17. 36 = *Ugaritica*, V, pp. 10–11; see also the incomplete text 17. 38, *ibid.*, p. 12.
[128] *LA* B §1; 0 § 3.
[129] E. Weidner, 'Eine Erbteilung in mittelassyrischer Zeit', *AFO*, 20 (1963), pp. 121–124.
[130] C. J. Gadd, *RA*, 23 (1926), No. 5 and 6, pp. 90–93; *HSS*, V, 67, 21, 72 = *AASOR*, X, No. 2, 8, 21; E. M. Cassin, *L'adoption à Nuzi*, *op. cit.*, pp. 286, 292. This was not, however, a law which had to be obeyed – one will (*HSS*, **XIX**, 17) divides an inheritance equally between three sons and says that 'none will be the eldest', E. A. Speiser, 'A Significant New Will from Nuzi', *JCS*, 17 (1963), pp. 65–71.
[131] *ARM*, VIII, 1, with G. Boyer's legal commentary, pp. 178–182; I. Mendelsohn, *op. cit.* (note 121); *ANET*, p. 545b; see also M. Noth, *Die Ursprünge des alten Israel im Lichte neuer Quellen*, Cologne, 1961, pp. 19–20, who, instead of using the translation 'double share', has 'two thirds', which is not in accordance with the Assyrian laws and the Nuzi texts.
[132] See below, pp. 647–648.

stolen his 'gods' (Gen 31:30). In good faith, Jacob protested against this and asked Laban to look for his 'gods'. Laban searched the camp, but found nothing, because Rachel, claiming that she had a monthly period, remained seated on the camel's saddle in which she had hidden the teraphim (Gen 31: 31–35). These teraphim were household idols and are mentioned in other biblical texts.[133] Laban calls them his 'gods' and they have quite legitimately been compared with the family gods, ilâni, mentioned in the Nuzi texts. In particular, a contract of adoption stipulates that the 'gods' of the adoptive father should be handed on to his natural son if he had one or to his adopted son if he had no natural son.[134] This text, together with other references to the ilâni in the Nuzi documents, has been used to clarify the story in Genesis.[135] Certain scholars have maintained that the possession of these idols meant entitlement to inheritance, which would explain why Rachel stole them and why Laban, who was not upset by the loss of his daughters and his livestock, was inconsolable because of the loss of his 'gods'.

This theory is, however, not very convincing and another explanation of the story has to be sought.[136] The 'gods' of Nuzi are never connected directly with inheritance, and entitlement to an inheritance is not brought about by possessing them. They are penates or domestic gods and therefore belong to the paterfamilias. When he dies, they normally pass to the new head of the family, the eldest son, and possession of them is tied to the birthright. All this is implicit in the contract quoted and is explicit in other documents.[137] Even if Jacob had been Laban's adopted son, he would not have had any right to possess these idols during Laban's lifetime and their theft would not have given him the right to inheritance after Laban's death. Rachel's theft of the teraphim, then, cannot be explained by juridical reasons. This text in Genesis has therefore been compared[138] with another extrabiblical text, according to which, during the first century A.D., a Parthian woman married to a Jew took with her, secretly, the images of her dead husband's ancestral deities, because, Josephus says, 'it is the custom of all the people of this region to have cultic objects in their houses and to take them with them when they go abroad'.[139] It would, moreover, seem

---

[133] P. R. Ackroyd, 'The Teraphim', ExpT, 62 (1950–1951), pp. 378–380; A. R. Johnson, The Cultic Prophet in Ancient Israel,² Cardiff, 1962, pp. 32–33, with bibliography.

[134] Gadd 51 = RA, 23 (1926); ANET, pp. 219b–220a.

[135] S. Smith, JTS, 33 (1932), pp. 33–36; C. H. Gordon, BASOR, 66 (Apr. 1937), pp. 25–27; BibArch, 3 (1940), pp. 5–6; A. E. Draffkorn, 'Ilâni/Elohim', JBL, 76 (1957), pp. 216–224; E. A. Speiser, IEJ, 7 (1957), p. 213; id., Genesis, pp. 249–251.

[136] M. Greenberg, 'Another Look at Rachel's Theft of the Teraphim', JBL, 81 (1962), pp. 239–248.

[137] Gadd 5; HSS, XIV, 108, quoted by A. E. Draffkorn, op. cit.; see also HSS, XVII, 7: the ilâni are entrusted to the widow, after which they are passed on to the eldest son, cf. RA, 57 (1963), p. 115.

[138] M. Greenberg, op. cit., (note 136).

[139] Ant. XVIII, IX, § 344. For the whole story, see J. Neusner, A History of the Jews in

advisable to compare Gen 31 with Gen 35:2, according to which Jacob, having come back from Mesopotamia, tells his family and all those who are with him to get rid of the foreign gods which they have brought with them. Both these texts may go back to a common tradition, used in Gen 31 to hold Laban up to ridicule.[140]

6. The patrimony

In Gen 31:14, Rachel and Leah complain that they no longer have any share in the patrimony, *nah⁽ᵉ⁾lāh*, of their father's house and, according to Gen 48:6, the sons born after Ephraim and Manasseh were to bear their brothers' names for the purpose of the *nah⁽ᵉ⁾lāh*. This word, which occurs again and again in later passages in the Old Testament, is applied not only to individuals and to groups of people, but also to God and is generally, but rather inadequately, translated as 'inheritance'.[141] Used for the first time in these two texts in Genesis, both the noun, and the verb too, are peculiar to western Semitic. They are unknown in Akkadian, but, apart from Hebrew, they are found in the dialect of Mari, in Ugaritic and in Phoenician.

The most important references in our present enquiry are those which occur in the Mari texts.[142] The *nahâlum* is land or property, real estate belonging to a group of people, to the state or to an individual. It is inherited and cannot, in principle, be transferred to someone outside the family. This is also the basic definition of the *nah⁽ᵉ⁾lāh* in Israel. Two Mari texts are particularly interesting because they deal with semi-nomadic peoples. In a document that has already been mentioned in this chapter,[143] the representatives of the clan of Awīn, which is only leading a partly settled life, make over part of their domain to a person who, by a legal fiction, has become their 'brother'. In a second text, the king grants land to a nomad chief in order to make him lead a settled life and give up raiding.[144] The concept *nahâlum*, then, corresponds to a tribal and patriarchal system; it is the tribal or family patrimony and has to remain within the tribe or family.

Babylonia; I. The Parthian Period, Leiden, 1965, pp. 51–54.

[140] As we have already seen, the reference to the camel, especially in the episode of the *teraphim*, does not square with life at the time of the patriarchs; see above, pp. 223–225.

[141] F. Horst, 'Zwei Begriffe für Eigentum (Besitz) ', *Verbannung und Heimkehr (Festschrift W. Rudolph)*, Tübingen, 1961, pp. 135–152.

[142] ARM, VIII, 11–14, with G. Boyer's commentary, pp. 190–197; see also ARM, I, 91, 6; X, 90, 31 and possibly the letter published by G. Dossin in *Studies in Old Testament Prophecy Presented to T. H. Robinson*, Edinburgh, 1950, pp. 103–110; M. Noth, *Die Ursprünge, op. cit.*, quoted above in note 131, pp. 18–19; A. Malamat, *JAOS*, 82 (1962), pp. 147–150.

[143] ARM, VIII, 11; see also above, notes 48 and 74.

[144] ARM, I, 91, with G. Boyer's revised translation, *op. cit.*, p. 197.

The Hebrew *naḥ⁽lāh* similarly denotes the territories made over to the different tribes of Israel in the distribution of the Promised Land. The ruling made in the case of Zelophehad's daughters (Num 27:1–11; 36:1–2) was intended to prevent the patrimony of land from leaving the tribe or clan (see especially Num 36:9).[145] That this idea of land as an inalienable patrimony should only have been made explicit in connection with the definitive settlement of the tribes in the Promised Land is, of course, perfectly normal. The comparable references in the Mari documents, however, mean that it is reasonable to suppose that the practice of *naḥ⁽lāh* may have existed during the patriarchal period. Even when they were leading a mainly nomadic way of life, the tribes had their own grazing lands and, when Abraham and Lot parted company, each leader acquired rights to the land which was to become what could be called the *naḥ⁽lāh* of their descendants (Gen 13:5–18; see especially verse 15).

7. Economy

There is no parallel in the documents of the Ancient Near East to the way in which Jacob increased his sheep and goats (Gen 30:37–42). That narrative is a piece of herdsman's folklore. On the other hand, the conditions of Jacob's employment as a shepherd by Laban are made clearer by a number of extrabiblical texts. Seven articles in the Code of Hammurabi are devoted to the wages and the duties of the shepherd.[146] He is responsible for any losses among the animals caused by his negligence – if a beast dies of disease or is killed by a wild animal, the shepherd has to prove his innocence by taking an oath and to produce the body of the dead beast. This was normal practice in the Near East,[147] but Jacob declared that he had not taken advantage of the law. He had not brought back to Laban the sheep that had been mauled by wild animals, but had 'borne the loss himself' (Gen 31:39). The word used for this in the Hebrew is the piel of the verb *ḥāṭā'* and this is the only case of this use in the Old Testament.[148] It is a borrowing from the very early vocabulary of the law – in early Akkadian, for example, *ḥitītum* or *ḥītum* meant only 'damage' or 'loss'. The word *ḥītum* occurs especially in a contract made at the time of Samsu-Iluna and con-

---

[145] F. Horst, *op. cit.*, pp. 138–139; A. Malamat, *op. cit.*, pp. 149–150; N. H. Snaith, 'The Daughters of Zelophehad', *VT*, 16 (1966), pp. 124–127.

[146] *CH* § 261–267, especially § 266, with G. R. Driver's commentary in G. R. Driver and J. C. Miles, *The Babylonian Laws*, I, *op. cit.*, pp. 453–461.

[147] See the Code of the Covenant (Exod 22:12), which is not directly dependent on the Code of Hammurabi.

[148] The piel of *šalam* is used in Exod 22:12.

cerning the taking over of a flock by a sheep breeder. If the Old Testament story is compared with this contract or with other similar Akkadian texts, in which the shepherd's wages and so on are established, it is at once clear that Jacob agreed to work under conditions which were in no sense favourable to him.[149] This background has to be borne in mind in any attempt to understand what the biblical account says about Jacob's astuteness (Gen 30:37–42, J) or about the favour that God bestowed on him (Gen 31:4–16, E).

With regard to the buying and selling of land, a number of comparisons have been made between the purchase of the cave of the field of Machpelah by Abraham (Gen 23) and other, non-biblical texts. This transaction is reported in the Old Testament in the form of a dialogue between Abraham and Ephron the owner of the land. The price is paid in silver 'according to the current commercial rate' (Gen 23:16) and finally the conveyance of the land is stated in precise legal terms: 'Thus Ephron's field at Machpelah opposite Mamre, the field and the cave that was on it, and all the trees that were on it, the whole of its extent in every direction, passed into Abraham's possession in the sight of the sons of Heth and of all the citizens of the town' (Gen 23:17–18). It should be noted in passing that in the older translation this text ends: 'in the presence of the Hittites, before all who went in at the gate of his city'.

The juridical nature of this Old Testament passage has led to comparisons with certain Nuzi texts, especially those dealing with the transfer of land. These often end with the formula: 'This tablet was written after proclamation at the gate'.[150] Attempts have also been made to explain a linguistic peculiarity of this chapter in Genesis by referring to the Hurrian language, which would, it has been suggested, have been spoken by the 'sons of Heth' at Hebron.[151] The silver 'at the current commercial rate' has also been compared with an Akkadian technical term in the Code of Eshnunna which speaks of selling beer 'at the current price'.[152]

Above all, however, Abraham's first plan, to buy no more than the cave, and Ephron's insistence that he had to buy the whole field with the cave on it, have been explained by reference to Hittite law, according to which the partial transfer of a fief, *ilku*, leaves all the charges attached to this fief to be borne by the vendor, while passing them on to the purchaser if the whole fief is conveyed to him.[153] This hypothesis has been widely accepted as a

[149] For all this, see J. J. Finkelstein, 'An Old Babylonian Herding Contract and Genesis 31: 38 f' in *JAOS*, 88 (1968), pp. 30–36 = *Essays in Memory of E. A. Speiser*, New Haven, 1968, with the same page numbering.

[150] R. de Vaux, *RB*, 56 (1949), pp. 24–25.

[151] C. Rabin, 'L- with Imperative (Gen XXIII) ', *JSS*, 13 (1968), pp. 113–124.

[152] *CE* § 41; see also E. A. Speiser, *Genesis, op. cit.*, p. 171. This usage is limited to Old Babylonian and Middle Assyrian.

[153] *LH* §§ 46–47; M. Lehman, 'Abraham's Purchase of Machpelah and Hittite Law',

reason for Abraham's wanting to buy only part of the estate, but there are serious objections to it. In the first place, the Hittites, as we know them in history, never occupied Hebron or any other part of Canaan[154] and it is very doubtful whether any of their particular practices had any influence there. It is moreover not known if the system of fiefs presupposed by the Hittite laws of the New Kingdom was already in existence during the Old Kingdom, the period during which Abraham was presumably living. What is more, this feudal land system was not peculiar to the Hittites. Although it existed in many different forms, it was basically common to the states of the Ancient Near East and there is very good documentary evidence of it in particular at Ugarit.[155] It is, however, very difficult to see how Abraham could have fitted into this system if we are to accept as correct the biblical presentation of his way of life. Finally, there is no mention in the biblical account of the charges which would have encumbered the estate, while Abraham agreed very readily to buy the whole field. Whatever the historical background to the story in Genesis may be, it is clear that it makes use of the terminology found in contracts of the sale and purchase of land and property. The texts which reveal the greatest similarity with Abraham's purchase of the cave at Machpelah, however, are the so-called 'dialogue contracts', which were used from the end of the eighth century onwards and especially during the neo-Babylonian period.[156] These late parallels are certainly entirely in accordance with the date when this chapter of Genesis was edited, since it is generally accepted that it is a priestly document.

All this goes to show that the various comparisons that have been suggested are unequal in value. Some are justified and these help us to understand the biblical texts and show the way in which the patriarchal narratives form an integral part of the general pattern of social and juridical practices in the Ancient Near East of the time. Some of these comparisons are in accordance with the presumed antiquity of the patriarchal traditions, but others – and these are among the best – make use of parallels outside the Bible which do not belong to the patriarchal period itself, but rather to the time when the traditions of the patriarchs were edited. Above all, however, they can neither prove nor disprove the historical truth of these traditions, nor can they help us in any way to establish the date of the patriarchs.

BASOR, 129 (Feb. 1953), pp. 15–18; C. H. Gordon, *JNES*, 17 (1958), p. 29; L. R. Fisher, 'Abraham and his Priest-King', *JBL*, 81 (1962), pp. 264–270; B. Perrin, *Revue Historique de Droit Français et Etranger*, 1963, pp. 5–19, especially pp. 12–13; K. A. Kitchen, *Ancient Orient and Old Testament*, Chicago, 1966, pp. 154–156.

[154] See above, p. 134 ff.

[155] G. Boyer, quoted in note 92 above, pp. 293–299.

[156] H. Petschow, 'Die neubabylonische Zwiegesprächsurkunden und Genesis 23', *JCS*, 19 (1965), pp. 103–120; G. M. Tucker, 'The Legal Background of Genesis 23', *JBL*, 85 (1966), pp. 77–84; see also J. J. Rabinowitz, 'Neo-Babylonian Documents and Jewish Law', *Journal of Juristic Papyrology*, 13 (1961), pp. 131–175, especially pp. 131–135.

Chapter Nine

THE DATE OF THE PATRIARCHS

AT THIS stage in our investigations, a proposed date for the patriarchs is to be expected. This question would not, of course, arise if the accounts in Genesis simply presented us with the historical situation at the period when these accounts were edited[1] or at a period immediately preceding that editing.[2] What is certain, however, is that the Genesis narratives bear the imprint both of the age when they were written and of the age when the traditions which they relate were established. Sufficient examples of this have been provided in the foregoing chapters. It has also been demonstrated that the patriarchal traditions may have preserved early memories which were quite authentic. They show the patriarchs leading a way of life which was not the same as that led by the Israelites when they had settled in Canaan. Quite often they refer to customs of which there is early evidence outside the Bible and which were not followed later in Israel. There is, then, sufficient basis for an attempt to establish at least an approximate date for the patriarchs.

I. WAYS OF APPROACHING THE PROBLEM

1. Within the Bible

There are undeniably certain chronological indications in the Bible itself. The age of the patriarchs Abraham, Isaac and Jacob is stated in certain P texts (Gen 12:4; 16:16; 17:1, 24; 21:5; 25:7, 20, 26; 35:28; 37:2; 41:46; 47:9,

---

[1] This was the position represented by the early school of literary criticism; see, for example, B. Stade, *Geschichte des Volkes Israel,* I, Berlin, 1885, pp. 9–10; J. Wellhausen, *Prolegomena zur Geschichte Israels,*[3] Berlin, 1886, especially p. 331; *Israelitische und jüdische Geschichte,*[9] Berlin, 1958, p. 10.

[2] This was suggested quite recently by B. Mazar, 'Historical Background of the Book of Genesis', *JNES,* 28 (1969), pp. 73–83. In the same way, G. Wallis, in 'Die Tradition von den

28). The length of the period spent in Egypt is given in Exod 12:40–41 (P) as four hundred and thirty years and in Gen 15:13 (an addition to E?) as four hundred years. Finally, according to 1 Kings 6:1 (D), the time that elapsed between the exodus from Egypt and the building of the temple by Solomon was four hundred and eighty years. Various attempts have been made to establish a historically justified chronology on the basis of these biblical data, the most notable being that of the seventeenth-century Irish archbishop, James Ussher. His detailed chronology included, among others, the date of Abraham's birth in 1996 B.C., the date of Isaac's birth in 1896 B.C., that of Jacob's birth in 1836 B.C. and the date when Joseph entered Egypt as 1728 B.C.[3] All these figures are, however, artificial, the result of later calculations and of no use to the historian.[4]

More recently, however, two texts containing precise references to the history of the Near East have been examined in an attempt to give a date to the patriarchs. The first of these is the story of the campaign of the four great kings of the East (Gen 14). We have, however, already seen that this chapter was a late, scholarly composition and that Abraham's place in it was the result of an arbitrary connection made between him and more or less authentic memories of a distant past.[5] What is more, different dates, extending over several centuries, have been attributed to the data reported in this story by those who have argued in favour of its historical authenticity.

The second of these texts is Num 13:22, which says that 'Hebron was founded seven years before Tanis in Egypt'. The well-known stele dating back to the year 400, discovered at Tanis,[6] would appear to fix the establishment of the cult of Seth at Tanis and the settlement of the Hyksos there at approximately 1730 B.C. This 'Tanis period' has been used to calculate the four hundred and thirty years which the Israelites spent in Egypt (Exod 12:40–41) and to provide a date for the end of the patriarchal age.[7] The patriarchs lived before the 'foundation' of Hebron, however, and Hebron was known during the patriarchal period as Kiriath-arba (see Gen

---

drei Ahnvätern', *ZAW*, 81 (1969), pp. 18–40, has linked the formation of the patriarchal traditions with the development of the history of Israel. According to Wallis, the earliest layer of J reflects the contemporary preoccupation with territory in David's first kingdom, J itself represents the political situation in the united kingdom of David and Solomon and E, after the division into the Northern and Southern Kingdoms, emphasises the theological aspect. He explicitly sets aside, however, the problem of the historicity of the traditions; see p. 20.

[3] Jacobus Usserius, *Annales Veteris et Novi Testamenti*, I–II, London, 1650–1654.

[4] See below, pp. 317–318, with reference to the sojourn in Egypt.

[5] See above, pp. 216–220.

[6] See above, p. 78.

[7] W. F. Albright, *BASOR*, 58 (April 1935), p. 16; *From the Stone Age to Christianity*,[2] Baltimore, 1946, pp. 184, 195; J. Bright, *A History of Israel, op. cit.*, p. 76, note 36, p. 111; see

23:2; 35:27). These two texts, on the other hand, belong to the priestly tradition. Num 13:22 is a very early text, attributed to the Yahwist, but it cannot refer to a 'Tanis period', which – if it ever really existed – could only have been very limited in its use.[8] In the context of Num 13:22, it is not associated either with the period spent in Egypt or with the patriarchal age. The most probable explanation is that this chronological indication simply reflects a Judaean tradition which attributed to Hebron, David's first capital, the glory and honour of being older than Tanis, which was at that time the capital of Egypt.

2. Outside the Bible

None of the patriarchs is mentioned in any of the extrabiblical documents of the second millennium B.C. and it is extremely unlikely that this situation will be changed by any new discoveries. All that can be done at present is to try to find which period provides the best historical framework of documentation outside the Bible for those elements in the stories of the patriarchs that are acknowledged to be of early date. The various arguments that have been put forward are based on the history of the Near East in general, archaeological evidence, onomastics and a study of Ancient Near Eastern social and legal customs. All these aspects have been discussed in the preceding chapters and we have seen that there are only very few real points of contact and similarity between the biblical and the extrabiblical data and that, in most cases, these are separated by too great a distance in time. It is not surprising, then, that the scholars who have followed this way of approach to the problem have, according to their own preference, argument or interpretation, come to very divergent conclusions.

II. RECENT VIEWS

Nelson Glueck has made extensive use of archaeological evidence. His surface explorations in Transjordania have led him to conclude that settled life there ceased suddenly, about 1900 B.C, and was not resumed until the end of the thirteenth century B.C. He has attributed this to the campaign described in Gen 14, the historical character of which he accepts, and has

---

also the criticism of H. H. Rowley, *From Joseph to Joshua*, London, 1950, pp. 75–77; S. Mowinckel, 'Die Gründung von Hebron', *Orientalia Suecana*, 4 (1955), pp. 67–76.

[8] J. von Beckerath, *Tanis und Theben*, Glückstadt, 1951, pp. 38–41; R. Stadelmann, 'Die 400-Jahr-Stele', *ChrEg*, 40 (1965), pp. 46–60, who holds an even more radical opinion.

therefore given this as the date of Abraham.[9] He has moreover found evidence in the Negeb which has confirmed this opinion – he has brought to light there a great number of settlements founded in the twenty-first century B.C. and abandoned in the nineteenth century, a period which corresponds to Middle Bronze I in the current terminology and which we have called the Intermediate Period between the Early and Middle Bronze Age. In Glueck's opinion, this period is the only one which fits the situation described in Gen 12 and 13 and which he calls the Age of Abraham.[10] We, however, have not accepted Gen 14 as historical for even if it were historically authentic, it would not satisfactorily explain the end of a whole civilisation. As far as the Negeb is concerned, there is nothing in the stories of the patriarchs which might support or deny the existence of the settlements which have been revealed by archaeological explorations and which were also probably seasonal. It is, after all, a region that has at all times in history been frequented by herdsmen such as the patriarchs. What is more, it is neither the only nor the most important region in which the patriarchs were traditionally supposed to have lived.[11]

W. F. Albright has not only accepted this archaeological argument, but has also enlarged it and combined it with other elements which he has previously used. Although it is not very convincing, there is evidence that Shechem, Bethel, Hebron and Gerar were occupied at this time. In Albright's opinion, these cities, which are mentioned in Genesis, and the contemporary settlements in the Negeb and in Sinai, marked stages along the caravan trails used by the patriarchs, who were, he believed, leaders of donkey caravans. (It will be remembered that we do not accept this view.[12]) Albright also believes that the campaign outlined in Gen 14 is historically authentic and that it may have taken place in the nineteenth century B.C. or a little later and that this, then, was the period of Abraham. What is very significant in this context, however, is that Albright has consistently refused to give precise dates in his recent works and has only said that the recent dates that have been suggested – the fourteenth and fifteenth centuries B.C. – are unacceptable.[13]

J. Bright has also decided in favour of a wide chronology and has con-

[9] N. Glueck, *The Other Side of the Jordan*,[2] Cambridge, Mass., 1970, p. 140; *Rivers in the Desert: A History of the Negev*,[2] New York, 1968, pp. 68–76.

[10] N. Glueck, 'The Age of Abraham in the Negeb', *BibArch*, 18 (1955), pp. 2–9; *BASOR*, 152 (Dec. 1958), p. 20; *BibArch*, 22 (1959), pp. 87–89; 'The Archaeological History of the Negeb', *HUCA*, 32 (1961), pp. 11–18, especially p. 12; *Rivers in the Desert, op. cit.*, pp. 66–70.

[11] See also Y. Aharoni, *Archaeology and Old Testament Study*, ed. D. Winton Thomas, Oxford, 1967, p. 387.

[12] See above, pp. 225–229.

[13] W. F. Albright, *Recent Discoveries in Bible Lands*,[2] New York, 1955, pp. 72–78; 'Abraham the Hebrew. A New Archaeological Interpretation', *BASOR*, 163 (Oct. 1961), pp. 36–54, especially p. 44ff; *The Biblical Period from Abraham to Ezra*,[3] New York and Evanston, 1963, pp. 6–9; *Yahweh and the Gods of Canaan*, London, 1968, pp. 47–95.

cluded that the date of the stories of the patriarchs is most suitably situated between the twentieth and the seventeenth centuries B.C.[14] Similarly, after carefully considering all the arguments, K. A. Kitchen has suggested as a general date the period between the twentieth and the eighteenth centuries B.C.[15]

Also relying on the historicity of Gen 14, F. Cornelius has followed Schrader's suggestion, first made in the late nineteenth century but later rejected, that Amraphel the king of Shinar was in fact the Babylonian king Hammurabi. According to the short chronology that he favours, the campaign of the four kings took place towards the end of Hammurabi's reign, shortly after 1700 B.C. He has explained the destruction of the cities to the south of the Dead Sea, which occurred after the period when Abraham was alive, as the result of an earthquake which shook the whole of the Near East round about 1650 B.C. The campaign described in Gen 14 was, Cornelius believed, directed against Egypt and formed part of the migration which took the Hyksos into the Nile Valley.[16] It is, however, rather disturbing to find the midrash of Gen 14 being used in this way to rewrite history.

A. Rasco has connected Abraham's arrival in Canaan with the Hurrian expansion towards the south which began in 1700 B.C. In his view, it is not possible to date Abraham later than 1600 B.C. because of the historical and social situation reflected in the texts and the archaeological evidence. The parallels that have been established between the patriarchs and the Hurrian practices at Nuzi can, he believes, be justified at a period beginning at 1650 B.C. and he has therefore suggested this date as a reasonable one for Abraham. The camels and the Philistines mentioned in Genesis also strike a less anachronistic note, Rasco believes, if this date is accepted.[17] On the other hand, there is no indication that the migration led by Abraham formed part of the Hurrian migration — the Hurrians did not reach Palestine until after 1500 and there were never very many of them.[18] What is more, it is not a very good chronological argument to claim that Abraham should not be dated too many centuries before the Nuzi texts of the fifteenth century B.C. or too many centuries before the widespread use of the domestic camel and the arrival of the Philistines.

[14] J. Bright, A History of Israel, op. cit., pp. 74–78.

[15] K. A. Kitchen, Ancient Orient and Old Testament, Chicago, 1966, pp. 41–56.

[16] F. Cornelius, 'Genesis XIV', ZAW, 72 (1960), pp. 1–7; ibid., Geistesgeschichte der Frühzeit, Leiden, II, 1, 1962, p. 144; II, 2, 1967, pp. 87–88, 90–91, 181 and the notes on pp. 302, 327–328. In BASOR, 163 (Oct. 1961), p. 50, note 68, W. F. Albright has linked this campaign with the fall of the Middle Kingdom in Egypt at the beginning of the eighteenth century B.C. For the tradition of Sodom and Gomorrha, see above, pp. 168–169, 217.

[17] A. Rasco, 'Migratio Abrahae circa a. 1650', Verbum Domini, 35 (1957), pp. 143–154.

[18] R. de Vaux, 'Les Hurrites de l'histoire et les Horites de la Bible', RB, 74 (1967), pp. 481–503; see also above, p. 83 ff.

C. H. Gordon's arguments are more logical.[19] According to the Old Testament, the sojourn in Egypt was to last for four generations (Gen 15:16) and there were to be five generations between Jacob and the conquest (Exod 6:16–20; Josh 7:1). This would mean that Jacob lived in the middle of the fourteenth century and Abraham during the Amarna period. This late date can, Gordon claims, be confirmed by further arguments – the parallels with the Nuzi texts, which Gordon was one of the first scholars to use, the linguistic and literary affinities with the Rās Shamrah poems and the similarity between Abraham and the Hittite and Ugaritic merchants of the fourteenth and thirteenth centuries B.C. In this light, Gordon believes, the camels are not an anachronism in Genesis,[20] nor are the 'Philistines', who appear in the region of Gerar and Beersheba but not in the part of the land which they were to occupy later. There are, however, certain important aspects of the problem which are not taken into account in Gordon's argument, especially the early forms of the names of the patriarchs and their ethnic and linguistic connections with the Amorites of the Mari period. The Amarna period and, generally speaking, the period of the Late Kingdom in Egypt do not form a really suitable framework for the stories of the patriarchs.

O. Eissfeldt is openly sceptical with regard to all the solutions that have so far been suggested and is of the opinion that it is impossible to come to any firm conclusions concerning the period during which the patriarchs lived. On the other hand, though, he believes that the stories of the patriarchs point more probably to the two centuries before the final settlement of the Israelites than to an earlier period in the second millennium.[21]

The great diversity of data has led other authors to distinguish various phases in the patriarchal history and to conclude that it spanned a very long period of time. H. H. Rowley has dated Abraham's migration into Canaan at about 1650 B.C., the entry of Jacob's group at about 1400 and the descent into Egypt at about 1360.[22] F. M. T. de Liagre Böhl has made use of Gen 14 to date Abraham in the first half of the seventeenth century and Jacob's entry during the Amarna period, in connection with the activity of the

[19] C. H. Gordon, in several works, especially 'The Patriarchal Age', Journal of Bible and Religion, 21 (1953), pp. 238–243; 'The Patriarchal Narratives', JNES, 13 (1954), pp. 56–59; 'Hebrew Origins in the Light of Recent Discovery', Biblical and Other Studies, ed. A. Altmann, Cambridge, Mass., 1963, pp. 3–14.

[20] C. H. Gordon has drawn attention to a mounted camel on a Syrian cylinder in the Mitannian style, Iraq, 6 (1939), plate VII, No. 55, but this is a Bactrian camel with two humps and unknown in Palestine.

[21] O. Eissfeldt, CAH, II, XXVI (a), 1965, pp. 8–10.

[22] H. H. Rowley, From Joseph to Joshua, pp. 111–116 and the plate on p. 164; 'Recent Discovery and the Patriarchal Age', BJRL, 32 (1949–1950), pp. 44–79, especially p. 63; this article has been included, with different notes, in The Servant of the Lord,[2] Oxford, 1965, pp. 303–304.

Habiru.[23] H. Cazelles believes that the patriarchs Abraham, Isaac and Jacob should be placed towards the end of the Middle Kingdom of Egypt, that is, the eighteenth century B.C. This date, he thinks, is most closely in accordance with the early forms of the names of the patriarchs and with the connections between the patriarchs and the Amorite migration, the Mari texts bear witness. Members of both these groups, Cazelles maintains, were, like Joseph, taken as prisoners into Egypt and this is in accordance with the tradition that the sojourn in Egypt lasted for four generations (Gen this first wave, which he thinks was 'more Semitic Amorite', was added, during the Amarna period, another wave which was 'more Aramaean' and composed of Semitised Hurrians bringing the customs to which the Nuzi texts bear witness. Members of both these groups, like Joseph, were, Cazelles maintains, taken as prisoners into Egypt and this is in accordance with the tradition that the sojourn in Egypt lasted for four generations (Gen 15: 16).[24] It should be noted in fairness to the author that he is aware of the hypothetical nature of his reconstruction.

The most detailed chronology, which is at the same time the most extended in time, has been suggested by S. Yeivin. According to this scholar, the patriarchal period began with the departure from Ur after the fall of the Third Dynasty, that is, shortly after 1950 B.C. The sojourn at Haran lasted from 1950 until 1750, when the Abrahamites arrived in Canaan, the campaign described in Gen 14 occurring between 1717 and 1696. The periods of Isaac and Jacob extended over the seventeenth century and the descent into Egypt took place at the end of the Hyksos period, not later than 1580.[25] The character of the biblical traditions and the uncertainty of the external evidence, however, make it impossible for us to be so precise.

III. AN ATTEMPT TO SOLVE THE PROBLEM [26]

There is in fact no way of establishing the exact dates of the patriarchs. The best that can be done is to try to ascertain the most probable period to which the patriarchal traditions appear to point. In this attempt, some of the findings and suggestions discussed in the preceding chapters can be put to practical use.

[23] F. M. T. de Liagre Böhl, 'Der Zeitalter Abrahams', Opera Minora, Groningen, 1953, pp. 26–49.

[24] H. Cazelles, 'Patriarches', DBS, VII, 1966, col 136–141; this section of the dictionary was first published separately in 1961.

[25] S. Yeivin, 'The Age of the Patriarchs', RSO, 38 (1963), pp. 277–302, especially pp. 290–302.

[26] The position that I take up here is much more reserved than the point of view that I held some years ago in RB, 55 (1948), pp. 326–337 and even fairly recently in RB, 72 (1965), pp. 25–27.

The names of the three patriarchs are very old.[27] In its complete form, *ya'qôbh-'El*, the name Jacob occurs several times in Lower Mesopotamia, where it also occurs once in its shorter form, one century before Hammurabi and during the First Babylonian Dynasty. It is also found four times at Chagar Bazar in Upper Mesopotamia at the beginning of the eighteenth century B.C., once at Qat(t)una on the Habur at the end of that century and also on Hyksos scarabs. The name Isaac has not yet been found in any extrabiblical texts, but it has the same onomastic form as the name Jacob – a verb in the imperfect followed by the subject, which is a divine name or a name of a relative. Names formed in this way are the most frequently encountered and the most characteristic of all Amorite personal names, whereas they are unusual in Canaanite and very uncommon in early Hebrew. The original form of the name of the first patriarch, Abram, is composed of two elements used in the formation of Amorite proper names. The longer form, Abraham, can be compared with the name Aburahana found in the Egyptian execration texts of the nineteenth century B.C. There is also evidence outside the Bible of other family names from the stories of the patriarchs – for example, the name of Abraham's great-grandfather Serug, during the Third Dynasty of Ur, and the name of Abraham's grandfather and brother, Nahor, during the same period. The name Ishmael is found twice in the Mari texts. The names of the three patriarchs, Abraham, Isaac and Jacob, were never again given to anyone in Israel during the whole of the Old Testament period and at quite an early period they were no longer understood and had to be explained by popular etymology. In the case of Abraham, the name was explained by assonance; in the case of Isaac and Jacob, the verb forming the basis of the name was given the meaning that it had taken in Hebrew, a meaning which was different from the original, primitive sense.

The language also preserved other traces which had survived from the period when the ancestors of the Israelites did not speak Hebrew, although the meanings of these words were somewhat changed. In the Mari documents, *nawum* (= *nâweh*) and *hasārum* (= *hâsér*) are both words meaning encampments of semi-nomadic people.[28] In the same texts, the terms *gāyum/gāwum, ummatum* and *hibrum* were used to denote tribal units of these herdsmen and these words became, in Hebrew, *gôy, 'ummāh* and *hebher*.[29] These sheep-raising people in Upper Mesopotamia belonged to the same ethnic group as the immigrants who, at the beginning of the second millennium, founded new dynasties in the cities in the north of Syria and in Mesopotamia – like them, they were Amorites, but they had by that time not become settled. They certainly belonged to the same social type as the

---

[27] See above, p. 191, and pp. 196–200, where the references will be found.
[28] See above, pp. 230–231.
[29] See above, pp. 239–240.

patriarchs.[30] They lived in the region which Abraham left to go to Canaan, from which Isaac and Jacob took their wives and where Jacob stayed. The biblical traditions are in accordance with these onomastic, linguistic and sociological factors and it is very probable that the arrival of the first ancestors of the Israelites ought to be connected with the Amorite migration.

This migration extended to the whole periphery of the Syrian desert, assuming different aspects according to the particular region and lasting for several centuries.[31] In Palestine, it began quite early and possibly violently, if the destruction of the Early Bronze Age towns at the end of the third millennium can be attributed, at least partly, to a first invasion by the Amorites.[32] The patriarchs, on the other hand, did not enter Canaan as conquerors. On the contrary, they camped peacefully[33] near towns which were at that time inhabited, arriving after the collapse of urban life, the way of life which characterised what we have called the Intermediate Period between the Early and the Middle Bronze Ages. They may have arrived during the second half of the nineteenth century B.C., that is, during our Middle Bronze I, at a time when the cities were becoming repopulated and when peace and prosperity were beginning to be enjoyed. At this time, Egyptian military intervention was not troubling Asia and the roads between Palestine and Upper Mesopotamia were open. Hazor, for example, enjoyed good relationships with Mari[35] and the same Mari texts speak of large-scale movements of groups of herdsmen who lived the same kind of life as the patriarchs. According to the information which we have at our disposal at present, then, it would seem that during the whole of the second millennium, the nineteenth and eighteenth centuries B.C. formed the most suitable period for Israel's ancestors' first settlement in Canaan.

Quite apart from the fact that they do not take all these facts into account, the arguments that have been put forward in favour of a much later date for the patriarchs – the fourteenth or even the thirteenth century B.C. – are not in any way convincing. If the links made in the Bible between the patriarchs and the Aramaeans are regarded as valid, then it is necessary to give an even later date to the patriarchs, since the Aramaeans did not appear outside the Bible until the end of the twelfth century B.C. We have already tried in this volume to show the racial continuity between the Amorites and the Aramaeans and to justify the biblical terminology.[36] As for the legal practices of the Hurrian population at Nuzi during the

---

[30] See above, pp. 229–231.

[31] See above, pp. 58–64.

[32] See above, pp. 63–64.

[33] The conflict described in Gen 34 only broke out after a settlement which was at first peaceful (See Gen 33:18–20).

[34] See above, pp. 66–68.

[35] See above, p. 61.

[36] See above, pp. 205–208.

fifteenth century, they cannot be regarded as having served as a model for the patriarchs. Not all the comparisons that have been made are valid and, insofar as they are, they may point to practices going as far back as the eighteenth century B.C., when the Amorites and the Hurrians lived together in Upper Mesopotamia, the region which the patriarchs left to go to Canaan.[37]

All that we have tried to do in this chapter has been to find a possible date for the first entry of Israel's ancestors into Canaan. The biblical tradition presents this entry in a very simple form – Abraham's family entered Canaan and the entire people of the Twelve Tribes descended, through Isaac and Jacob, from that family. This tradition was, however, the result of a process of unification and selection – the reality was certainly much more complex. We have to recognise that there were originally several groups belonging to the same ethnic environment and the same sociological background, but that these groups might not have arrived at the same time or in the same way. The study of this tradition would seem to have proved this in one very important respect at least, namely that the Jacob cycle was originally independent of the Abraham-Isaac cycle.[38]

It is no easier to date the end of the patriarchal period. Some scholars have suggested that it lasted until the descent into Egypt, but as we shall see this was also a very complex process.[39] On the other hand, there are traditions in Genesis which are later than the patriarchs. This may be so in the case of the story of Simeon and Levi at Shechem (Gen 34), which may date from the Amarna period. This may also be the case with the story of the treaty between Jacob and Laban (Gen 31), which may refer to the settlement of the tribes in the thirteenth century B.C. It is undoubtedly so in the case of the story of Judah and Tamar (Gen 38), which reflects the expansion of the tribe of Judah after the time of Joshua. We may therefore conclude that it is only possible to speak in very general terms of an 'age of the patriarchs' and that it is impossible to give exact dates either to the beginning or to the end of that period.

---

[37] See above, pp. 64–66; see also E. A. Speiser, *Oriental and Biblical Studies*, Philadelphia, 1967, p. 67.

[38] See above, pp. 169–175.

[39] See below, pp. 319–320.

Chapter Ten

THE RELIGION OF THE PATRIARCHS

THE NATURE of the Genesis traditions and the relatively late date
at which they were edited make any investigation into the religion
of the patriarchs as difficult as a study of their historical context and
their date. In this field too, authors have tended to take up extreme
positions. L. Rost, for example, has come to the conclusion that the early
traditions were severely expurgated and that each of the three sources, J, E
and P, provided an idealised image of the religion of the patriarchs, each
one with its special emphases, and that we cannot go back beyond these
sources to the point of historical truth.[1] V. Maag, on the other hand, has
given quite a detailed outline of the patriarchal religion.[2] The truth,
however, must surely lie somewhere between these two extremes of radical
scepticism and exaggerated confidence.[3]

It is, of course, true that the religion of the patriarchs was identified with
that of the people of Israel in biblical tradition, in other words, that
Abraham worshipped the same god as Moses. Each of the three sources expresses this conviction in its own way. According to the Elohist, the god
who revealed himself to Moses as Yahweh was the god of the fathers, 'the
God of Abraham, the God of Isaac and the God of Jacob' (Exod 3:6, 15).
According to the priestly author, Yahweh was the same god as the god who
appeared to Abraham, Isaac and Jacob as El Shaddai (Exod 6:3). The

[1] L. Rost, 'Die Gottesverehrung der Patriarchen im Lichte der Pentateuchquellen',
Congress Volume, Oxford (*SVT*, 7), 1959, pp. 346–359.
[2] V. Maag, 'Der Hirte Israels. Eine Skizze von Wesen und Bedeutung der Väterreligion',
Schweizerische Theologische Rundschau, 28 (1958), pp. 2–28; 'Das Gottesverständnis des Alten
Testaments', *NTT*, 21 (1966–1967), pp. 161–207 (corrections, pp. 459–460).
[3] The following authors all tend, in varying degrees, towards this middle position: H.
Ringgren, *Israelitische Religion*, Stuttgart, 1963, pp. 15–24; T. C. Vriezen, *The Religion of An-
cient Israel*, London, 1967, pp. 119–123, W. H. Schmidt, *Alttestamentlicher Glaube und seine
Umwelt*, Neukirchen and Vluyn, 1968, pp. 17–30; G. Fohrer, *Geschichte der israelitischen
Religion*, Berlin, 1969, pp. 11–27. A rather conservative attitude is maintained by M.-H.
Segal, *The Pentateuch, its Composition and its Authorship and other Biblical Studies*, Jerusalem,
1967, pp. 124–170.

Yahwist therefore used the name Yahweh in all the patriarchal stories from the call of Abraham onwards (Gen 12:1) and even made the worship of Yahweh go back to the very origins of man himself, to the time of Enosh, Seth's son (Gen 4:26).

The Elohist and the priestly writer, however, both emphasise quite strongly the difference; in other words, that Yahweh was a new name which was to replace those used by the patriarchs. At the same time, no mention is made at the patriarchal period in either of these sources, or even in the Yahwistic account, of the cultic practices of the later religion of Israel; and all three sources have preserved the memory of practices which were either condemned or abandoned by official Yahwism. We are told in Genesis that the ancestors worshipped other gods than Yahweh – Jacob ordered his family to get rid of the idols that had been brought from Upper Mesopotamia (Gen 35:2–4). We also read in the book of Joshua that when he was suggesting that those groups of people who did not yet know Yahweh should believe and serve him, Joshua told them to put away the gods that their ancestors had served beyond the river and still served (Josh 24: 2, 14–15).[4] It would therefore seem a worthwhile task to try to discover the essential characteristics of this religion which preceded Yahwism.[5]

I. THE GOD OF THE FATHER[6]

The most important aspect of the religion of the patriarchs is the cult of the 'god of the father', who was invoked or referred to or who manifested himself as the 'god of my, your or his father' (Gen 31:5, 29, correction according to the Greek; 43:23; 46:3; 50:17; Exod 3:6; 15:2; 18:4).

This formula in the singular is much earlier than the similar formula in the plural, the 'god of our, your, their fathers', which only occurs accidentally in the early sources and never in Genesis (Exod 3:13, 15, 16; 4:5) and which was used frequently only later, by the Deuteronomist and especially

---

[4] V. Maag, 'Sichembund und Vätergötter', *Hebräische Wortforschung. Festschrift W. Baumgartner*, (*SVT*, 16), 1967, pp. 205–218.
[5] This chapter is basically an elaboration and a modification of a study of 'El et Baal, le Dieu des pères et Yahweh' which was originally published in *Ugaritica VI (Mélanges offerts à Cl.F.A. Schaeffer)*, Paris, 1969, pp. 501–517.
[6] The standard work on this subject is by A.Alt, *Der Gott der Väter. Ein Beitrag zur Urgeschichte der israelitischen Religion*, Stuttgart, 1929 = *Kleine Schriften*, I, pp. 1–78 = *Essays on Old Testament History and Religion*, Oxford, 1966, pp. 1–77. Alt's work has been subjected to criticism, to which Alt has replied in 'Zum "Gott der Väter" ', *PJB*, 36 (1940), pp. 53–104. More recently, his conclusions have been rejected, especially by J. Hoftijzer, *Die Verheißungen an die drei Erzväter*, Leiden, 1956, pp. 84–96; M. Haran, 'The Religion of the Patriarchs. An Attempt at a Synthesis', *ASTI*, 4 (1965), pp. 51–52, note 34; O. Eissfeldt, 'El

by the Chronicler.[7] Other formulae make use of a proper name, with or without the addition of 'father'. Among these are the 'god of Abraham' (Gen 31:53), the 'god of your father Abraham' (Gen 26:34; 28:13; 32:10), the 'god of Isaac' (Gen 28:13), the 'god of my, his father Isaac' (Gen 32:10; 46:1) and the 'god of Nahor' (Gen 31:53). The formula 'god of Abraham' occurs not only in the traditions concerning Abraham,[8] but also in those concerning Isaac and the formula 'god of Isaac' is used not only in the Isaac traditions, but also in the Jacob traditions. On the other hand, the formula 'god of Jacob' is never used in isolation. These formulae which include the proper name of a father are, however, later – they presuppose the genealogical order of the three patriarchal figures. They develop into the 'god of my father Abraham and the god of my father Isaac' (Gen 32:10) or the 'god of Abraham your father and the god of Isaac' (Gen 28:13) and finally the 'god of Abraham, the god of Isaac and the god of Jacob' (Exod 3:6, 15, 16), in apposition to the 'god of your father' (Moses) or the 'god of your fathers'. Here we are clearly at the end of a process of evolution.

This development was quite justified, since the 'god of the father' was originally the god of the immediate ancestor, whom the son recognised as his god, but because this cult was transmitted from father to son, this god became the god of the family and the 'father' became perhaps a more remote ancestor, the one from whom the whole clan had descended. Thus Jacob invoked the 'god of my father Abraham and the god of my father Isaac' (Gen 32:10; cf. 28:13) and Laban suggested that Jacob should place the treaty that they had just concluded under the protection of the god of Abraham, Jacob's ancestor, and the god of Nahor, Laban's father, but Jacob preferred to swear by the kinsman – or the fear – of his father Isaac (Gen 31:53).

The comparison which has sometimes been made[9] with the Mesopotamian god of personal protection at the beginning of the second

---

and Yahweh', *JSS*, 1 (1956), pp. 25–37, especially pp. 35–36 = *Kleine Schriften*, III, pp. 395–396; *Wissenschaftliche Zeitschrift der Martin-Luther-Universität* · (Halle), 17 (1968), p. 53, note 26, in which Alt is not explicitly mentioned. Alt's work is valuable in that it has thrown light on a very real and important aspect of the religion of the patriarchs; it has, however, been corrected, amplified and modified by, among others, H. G. May, ' "The God of my Father". A Study in Patriarchal Religion', *Journal of Bible and Religion*, 9 (1941), pp. 155–158, 199–200; J. P. Hyatt, 'Yahweh as "The God of my Father" ', *VT*, 5 (1955), pp. 130–136; K. T. Andersen, 'Der Gott meines Vaters', *ST*, 16 (1962), pp. 170–188; H. Seebass, *Der Erzvater Israel*, Berlin, 1966, pp. 49–55.

[7] See especially H. G. May and K. T. Andersen, *op. cit.*, note 6.

[8] There is, of course, Gen 24:12, 27, 42, 48: 'Yahweh, God of my master Abraham', but this is a special case – in this Yahwistic account, the servant justifies his use of the name Yahweh by calling him the 'God of his master'.

[9] H. Cazelles, 'Patriarches', *DBS*. VII, 1966, col 142; J. P. Hyatt, *JBL*, 86 (1967), p. 377. For the Mesopotamian patron god, see H. Hirsch, *Untersuchungen zur altassyrischen Religion*, Graz, 1961, pp. 35–45.

millennium B.C. is not a good one, since although the Mesopotamian god was certainly the god of a person, he was not the 'god of the father'. A better comparison can be made with the Nabataean and Palmyrene inscriptions which mention the 'god of Un-Tel', this Un-Tel being different from the dedicator, Un-Tel – certainly one of his ancestors or the first ancestor of the clan.[10] These references, however, occur much later than the patriarchal age and the anonymous formula 'god of my, your, his father' is never found in them. This formula does, however, occur in the Cappadocian tablets of the nineteenth century B.C.[11] As witnesses to their contracts, traders of the Assyrian colonies in Asia Minor sometimes took the god Ashur and a god who was called the 'god of my father', the 'god of your father', the 'god of his father', the 'god of our father' or, quite simply, 'my god' or 'your god'. This god might remain anonymous, but the formula might also be in apposition to a divine name. In this function, four deities occur – Ilabrat, Amurru, Ishtar-Star and Ishtar-KA.ZAT. The formulae in this case were 'Ilabrat, the god of our father', 'Amurru, the god of my father',[12] 'Ishtar-Star, the deity of our fathers', 'Ishtar-KA.ZAT, the deity of your father' and so on. In one of the letters in the Mari archives of the eighteenth century B.C. the king of Qatna refers to the 'god of my father'.[13] In the fourteenth-century Amarna letters, a king of the same city of Qatna also mentions several times 'Shamash, the god of my father'.[14] What is more, the inventories of the temple at Qatna, which come between these two dates, mention offerings to the 'god of the father', a phrase which alternates with the 'god of the king'.[15]

[10] A. Alt, *Der Gott der Väter, op. cit.* and appendix; see also D. Sourdel, *Les cultes du Hauran à l'époque romaine,* Paris, 1952, pp. 54–56, 95–96; J. Starcky, 'Palmyre', *DBS,* VI, 1960, col. 1097; *ibid.,* 'Pétra', VII, 1966, col. 987–988.

[11] J. Lewy, 'Les textes paléo-assyriens et l'Ancien Testament', *RHR,* 110 (1934–B), pp. 50–59; B. Landsberger, *Belleten,* 14 (1950), p. 258; *CAD,* VII, 1960, p. 95 under *il abi*; according to P. Garelli, *JSS,* 3 (1958), pp. 298–300, this view has to be corrected and amplified; L. Matous, *ArOr,* 32 (1964), pp. 134–135; P. Garelli, 'La religion de l'Assyrie ancienne', *RA,* 56 (1962), pp. 191–210, especially pp. 207–208; H. Hirsch, 'Gott der Väter', *AfO,* 21 (1966), pp. 56–58.

[12] In all these cases, the same grammatical construction might lead us to hesitate between the two translations: 'the god, my father' or 'the god of my father', see H. Hirsch, *AfO,* 21 (1966), p. 56, note 8, but the references in the Qatna texts quoted here clearly point to the translation that I have adopted, along with all Assyriologists.

[13] *ARM,* V, 20, 16.

[14] *EA,* 55, lines 53, 57, 59, 63.

[15] J. Bottéro, *RA,* 43 (1949), pp. 178, 42–43, cf. p. 174, 1. For the translation 'the god' instead of 'the gods', despite the writing DINGIR.MEŠ, see J. Bottéro, *op. cit.,* pp. 33–34. The parallel with Rās Shamrah, where *'il 'ib* in the pantheon of Ugarit has been translated as 'god of the father', see A. Caquot, in *La Siria nel Tardo Bronzo,* ed. M. Liverani, Rome, 1969, p. 72, has to be rejected – the Akkadian version *il a-bi* is best translated as 'father-god', see J. Nougayrol, *Ugaritica V,* Paris, 1968, pp. 45–46, and the Hurrian transcriptions make this interpretation quite certain, see E. Laroche, *ibid.,* pp. 518–527, especially p. 523. In the poems

Outside the Bible, then, this 'god of the father' may be anonymous or may also be called by a proper name which is that of a god who is known in another connection. In Cappadocia, the gods thus named were minor deities. Ilabrat, also written as NIN.SUBUR, has been identified with PAP.SUKKAL, a divine messenger and an intercessory god. Amurru, whose name is the same as that of the Amorites and is written with the same ideogram, is an indeterminate figure of whom there is little evidence among the Amorites themselves.[16] Ishtar-Star was connected with the worship of Amurru[17] and Ishtar-KA.ZAT was another form of Ishtar of which nothing is known. On the other hand, the king of Qatna's 'god of the father' has been identified with the great god Shamash. In Nabataea, Dushara, who became the chief god of the Nabataeans, was the god of the royal line from the time of the Aslah inscription onwards, that is, round about the year 95 B.C. In this inscription, Dushara is called the 'god of Malikatu', who was probably one of the first kings of the dynasty.[18] Later, in the same environment, the 'god of Un-Tel' was identified with Baalshamin, the great god of heaven, or, in the Greek texts, with his equivalent, Helios.

In Genesis, the god of the father is only rarely given a name. The term *pahadh yiṣʿḥāq*, which is usually translated as 'fear of Isaac', but which really means 'kinsman of Isaac',[19] appears twice in the same story (Gen 31:42, 53). A similar name, 'shield, *māghen*, of Abraham', cannot possibly be derived from the expression 'I am your shield' (Gen 15:1). This is simply a metaphorical term signifying divine protection. It also occurs in Deut 33:29 and frequently in the psalms.[20] In an early text which is not one of the

---

of Rās Shamrah, the term *tr.abh* joined to El does not, as C. H. Gordon, *Journal of Bible and Religion*, 21 (1953), p. 239 believes, mean 'the Bull (a divine epithet) of the father', but 'the Bull, his father', see J. P. Hyatt, *VT*, 5 (1955), p. 132.

[16] For this enigmatic deity, see J.-R. Kupper, *L'iconographie du dieu Amurru*, Brussels, 1961, pp. 81–88, who concludes, p. 88, that 'Amurru owes nothing to the Amorites'; see also J. Lewy, 'Amurritica', *HUCA*, 32 (1961), especially p. 34 ff.

[17] J. Lewy, *op. cit.*, pp. 42–46.

[18] J. Starcky, *Studi Orientalistici in onore di G. Levi della Vida*, II, Rome, 1956, p. 523; *RB*, 64 (1957), p. 208.

[19] W. F. Albright, *From the Stone Age to Christianity*,[2] Baltimore, 1946, pp. 188–189, according to the Palmyrene and the Arabic. It is unlikely that 'fear of Isaac' is an allusion to Gen 22, see N. Krieger, 'Der Schrecken Isaaks', *Judaica*, 17 (1961), pp. 193–195; E. A. Speiser, *Genesis*, 1964, p. 247. L. Kopf's hypothesis, the 'refuge of Isaac', *VT*, 9 (1959), p. 257, is not sufficiently supported by the Arabic.

[20] The name is connected with the ideology of the holy war, at least according to O. Kaiser, *ZAW*, 70 (1958), p. 113. It can also be compared with the phrase 'my grace is your shield', which occurs in an oracle of Ishtar to Esarhaddon, *ANET*, p. 450a. The reading *môghen*, 'he who gives', has also been suggested; see M. Kessler, 'The "Shield" of Abraham', *VT*, 14 (1964), pp. 494–497, the 'benefactor', see M. Dahood, 'Ugaritic Lexicography', *Mélanges E. Tisserant*, Vatican City, 1964, p. 94.

stories of the patriarchs, that is, the passage in which Jacob blesses Joseph and makes his will known to him (Gen 49:24–25), the 'god of the father' is placed in parallel with *"bhîr ya"qôbh*, the 'Mighty One' or 'Bull' of Jacob[21] and with the 'Shepherd' or 'Stone' of Israel,[22] and with El Shaddai. We shall be discussing El Shaddai more fully later. Here we may simply note that, with the exception of El Shaddai, these names of God are not proper names of the deity – originally, the god of the father was anonymous.

On the other hand, if it is admitted that Israel was in the first place an independent patriarchal figure who later became merged with the figure of Jacob, then the name 'Shepherd' would have been kept for the god of Israel (see Gen 48:15, where God is called 'my Shepherd', following the reference to Israel in 48:14), just as the name 'Mighty One' or 'Bull' was reserved for the god of Jacob and the name 'Fear' or 'Kinsman' was given to the god of Isaac. Each clan had its family god and, if it is accepted that the ancestors of the people of Israel belonged to several of these groups, then they must have had several gods of the father, just as the groups that were related to them had theirs. Laban, for example, called the 'god of Abraham and the god of Nahor' (Gen 31:53) to witness.[23] Each clan worshipped its own god and disregarded others. This was not, of course, monotheism, but rather a form of 'monolatry'. The veneration of a god of the father did not, however, exclude attachment to minor deities or guardian spirits – Laban swore by the god of his father Nahor (Gen 31:53), although he complained that he had lost his 'gods' (Gen 31:30).

This religion of the god of the father is the earliest form of patriarchal religion of which we can have any knowledge. It is the religion which the ancestors of the people of Israel brought with them into Canaan. It is possible to outline some of its characteristics.[24] The god of the father was not tied to any sanctuary – he was above all connected with a group of men. He had revealed himself to the ancestor of these men and had been recognised by that ancestor. This link, which extended from the ancestor to the group descended from him, was regarded as a kind of kinship. As we have observed, the probable meaning of *pahadh* in the term *pahadh yiṣˁhâq* is 'kinsman'. There is also the evidence of a very early group of proper names which became rare after the tenth century B.C. These names were formed

[21] The term the 'Mighty One of Jacob' is also found in Ps. 132:2, 5; Isa 49:26; 60:16 and the 'Mighty One of Israel' is found in Isa 1:24. For the translation 'Bull', see F. Dumermuth, *ZAW*, 70 (1958), pp. 85–86; M. Weippert, *ZDPV*, 77 (1961), p. 105.

[22] For this difficult text, see V. Maag, 'Der Hirte Israels', *op. cit.* note 2; M. Dahood, 'Is 'Eben Yisrā'ēl a Divine Title?', *Bib*, 40 (1959), pp. 1002–1007.

[23] A gloss, which is not found in the Greek version, attempts to conceal this duality by adding 'the god of their fathers'.

[24] Here I have made use, with certain reservations, of V. Maag's analysis in 'Der Hirte Israels', *op. cit.*, note 1, pp. 10–15 and that of G. Fohrer, *Geschichte der israelitischen Religion, op. cit.*, note 3, pp. 23–27.

with 'am, uncle or more generally kinsman on the father's side, 'abh, father, or 'ah, brother, signifying the deity. These names were common in north-western Semitic,[25] but were rare in Akkadian.[26] They occur with particular frequency in Amorite proper names[27] and undoubtedly reflect the religious ideas that were current during the nomadic period.[28]

The god of the father, then, was really a nomadic deity, leading, accompanying and guarding the group that was faithful to him, deciding where the people should go and keeping them safe on their way. 'Leave your country . . . for the land I will show you', the god of Abraham said at the beginning of the story of the patriarchs (Gen 12:1). The god of his father told Jacob to go back to Canaan (Gen 32:10; cf. 31:3). The god of Abraham went with the first patriarch from Haran to Canaan (Gen 12:7) and from Canaan to Egypt (Gen 12:17). Abraham's servant invoked the god of his master when he was in Upper Mesopotamia (Gen 24:12). The god of Jacob kept him safe wherever he went (Gen 28:15, 20; 35:3), protected him from Laban's dealings (Gen 31:42) and saved him from danger when Esau threatened him (Gen 32:12). In other words, the god of the father was deeply involved in the history of the group and guided it.

This god, who had revealed himself to the ancestor of the people and who remained 'with him', was committed to those who were faithful to him by virtue of his promises. The theme of the promise recurs frequently in the stories of Genesis,[29] appearing in various forms – as the promise of posterity, the promise of land or the promise of both posterity and land at the same time. In their final edition, these stories extend the promise of posterity to include the whole people of Israel and the promise of land to include the whole of the 'Promised Land', but they make use of early traditions.[30] Each of the patriarchal cycles contains promises of this kind. In the Abraham cycle, the most important text in this respect is Gen 15. This chapter describes the sealing of God's solemn commitment, his b rîth, (which

[25] M. Noth, 'Gemeinsemitische Erscheinungen in der israelitischen Namengebung', ZDMG, 81 (1927), pp. 1–45; ibid., Die israelitischen Personennamen im Rahmen der gemeinsemitischen Namengebung, Stuttgart, 1928, pp. 66–79. To these studies of Semitic proper names must be added an investigation into those of Ugarit by F. Gröndahl, Die Personennamen der Texte aus Ugarit, Rome, 1967, Glossary I under 'B, 'H, 'MM.

[26] J. J. Stamm, Die akkadische Namengebung, Leipzig, 1939, pp. 53–58.

[27] H. B. Huffmon, Amorite Personal Names in the Mari Texts, Baltimore, 1965, pp. 154, 160, 196.

[28] M. Noth also came to this conclusion; see ZDMG, 81 (1927), p. 45; see also his Die israelitischen Personennamen, op. cit., p. 66.

[29] See especially C. Westermann, 'Arten der Erzählung in der Genesis, I, Verheißungserzählungen', Forschung am Alten Testament, Munich, 1964, pp. 11–34; Westermann discusses and assesses previous studies of this question.

[30] In this, I disagree with J. Hoftijzer, Die Verheißungen an die drei Erzväter, Leiden, 1956, who believes that this theme dates back only to a period during which the existence of the people was threatened and perhaps only during the Exile; see his conclusion, p. 99.

is incorrectly translated as covenant) by the very ancient rite of animals cut in half.[31] This oath made to Abraham is renewed with Isaac (Gen 26:3–4). In the Jacob cycle, a similar promise is made in the dream at Bethel (Gen 28:13–15). Although the promise of land is not mentioned before Abraham's entry into Canaan (Gen 12:7), the guarantor of these promises is not the Canaanite god El,[32] but the god of the father. This is stated explicitly in Gen 26:3, 24 in the case of Isaac and in Gen 28:13; 32:13, cf. 10 in the case of Jacob. These promises are completely in accordance with two fundamental desires experienced by semi-nomadic herdsmen – the desire for posterity which will ensure continuity in the clan and the desire for land where they hope to settle.

II. The God of the Father and El

When the nomadic clans came into contact with the settled people, they used their sanctuaries and worshipped the gods of the country, even though they did not give up the cult of their own god as their patron and protector. The process of becoming settled led to a religious syncretism and to the giving of a personal name to the god of the father. It will be clear from the parallels that have been made between the religion of the patriarchs and that of their neighbours that there was no uniform process of assimilation. In Cappadocia, for instance, the early Amorite nomads, who had become merged with the Assyrians and were possibly also specially responsible for the transport of goods,[33] used to invoke both the great god Ashur and the god of their father or fathers. As we have seen, this god of the father was known as Amurru, the ethnic deity to some extent imposed on the Amorites by the settled people of Mesopotamia,[34] or else Ishtar, under two forms, or Ilabrat, who might have been an early god of Asia Minor,[35] or finally an artificial creation, the deity of the community.[36] The god of the

---

[31] N. Lohfink, *Die Landverheißung als Eid. Eine Studie zu Gen. 15*, Stuttgart, 1967, especially pp. 89–100; G. Fohrer, *TLZ*, 91 (1966), col. 897–898; R. E. Clements, *Abraham and David. Genesis 15 and its Meaning for Israelite Tradition*, London, 1967; S. E. Loewenstamm, 'Zur Traditionsgeschichte des Bundes zwischen den Stücken', *VT*, 18 (1968), pp. 500–506.

[32] I believe this in spite of R. E. Clements, *op. cit.*, especially p. 33 and O. Eissfeldt, 'Der kanaanäische El als Geber der den israelitischen Erzvätern geltenden Nachkommenschaft- und Land-besitz-Verheißungen', *Wissenschaftliche Zeitschrift der Martin-Luther-Universität* (Halle), 17 (1968), pp. 45–53.

[33] H. Lewy, 'Anatolia in the Old Assyrian Period', *CAH*, I, XXIV (b), 1965, p. 17.

[34] J.-R. Kupper, *op. cit.*, (note 16).

[35] W. von Soden, *Orientalia*, 26 (1957), p. 314.

[36] This suggestion has been made by T. Jacobsen in F. M. Cross, *HTR*, 55 (1962), p. 229, and note; see also *Assur u il e-ba-ru-tim* in a Cappadocian text, H. Hirsch, *Untersuchungen zur altassyrischen Religion, op. cit.*, p. 74.

father was identified by the Amorite dynasty at Qatna with the great god Shamash. The Nabataeans, who had become a settled state with a monarchy, made Dushara their national deity and this god was recognised by the Nabataean kings as the god of their ancestors. Later, the Nabataeans identified the god of the father with Baalshamin-Helios.

In the same way, when they arrived in Canaan, the semi-nomadic ancestors of the Israelites came in contact with a new form of religion. In addition to the god of the father, the stories of the patriarchs include names formed with the element *'el* followed by a noun. Names formed in this way are El Elyon (Gen 14:18–22), El Roi (Gen 16:13), El Shaddai (Gen 17:1; 27:3; 35:11; 43:14; 48:3; 49:25, corr.), El Olam (Gen 21:33) and El Bethel (Gen 31:13; 35:7). The word *'el* is the usual noun for 'god' in all Semitic languages apart from Ethiopian and it is for this reason that these names were for a long time regarded as names of different deities. Now, however, it is generally accepted that they are different forms of the same great god El, a deity whom the Rās Shamrah texts have made better known.[37]

These titles are not easy to interpret.[38] In the first place, El Elyon has to be eliminated from the religion of the patriarchs, since in Genesis the name only occurs in the incident involving Melchizedek (Gen 14), which is of late date, and, apart from Genesis, in Ps 78:35. Used alone without *'el*, the word *'elyôn*, most high, is common in the rest of the Bible as a title or a substitute for Yahweh. There is no evidence anywhere of El Elyon outside the Bible.[39] In fact, El and Elyon are two different deities in the Canaanite-Phoenician pantheon and were arbitrarily combined in Gen 14.[40]

El Bethel can be understood in the sense of El of the local sanctuary of Bethel. On the other hand, the second word can be understood as a divine name in apposition and there is evidence in the Bible itself of a god Bethel [41] in the proper name Bethel-Sharezer (Zech 7:2) and possible evidence of this god in Jer 48:13. Outside the Bible, there is evidence of a god Bethel in the Elephantine papyri [42] and earlier in cuneiform texts.[43]

---

[37] See above, p. 147.

[38] A good general work has been written by F. M. Cross, 'Yahweh and the God of the Patriarchs', *HTR*, 55 (1962), pp. 225–259, especially with regard to El Olam, El Elyon and El Shaddai, pp. 232–250. Other references will be given in the notes that follow.

[39] For the possible appearance of El Elyon in southern Arabic inscriptions, see A. G. Loundine, *Le Muséon*, 76 (1963), pp. 207–209.

[40] R. Lack, 'Les origines de Elyon, le Très Haut, dans la tradition cultuelle d'Israël', *CBQ*, 24 (1962), pp. 44–64; R. Rendtorff, 'The Background of 'El 'Elyôn in Gen XIV', *Fourth World Congress of Jewish Studies, Papers*, I, Jerusalem, 1967, pp. 167–170; *ibid.*, 'El, Baal und Jahwe', *ZAW*, 78 (1966), pp. 277–292.

[41] O. Eissfeldt, 'Der Gott Bethel', *ARW*, 28 (1930), pp. 1–30 = *Kleine Schriften*, I, pp. 206–233; J. P. Hyatt, 'The Deity Bethel and the Old Testament', *JAOS*, 59 (1939), pp. 81–98.

[42] B. Porten, *Archives from Elephantine*, Berkeley, 1968, pp. 163–170 and Appendix V, pp. 328–331; *ibid.*, 'The Religion of the Jews of Elephantine in the Light of the Hermopolis

El Roi may possibly mean 'El of the Vision' or 'El sees me'. The explanation given in Gen 16:13 is incomprehensible and the text is in any case probably corrupt. El Olam means either 'El of eternity' or 'El, the Eternal One'. The name has been read in a proto-Sinaitic inscription,[45] but the decipherment of these texts is as yet very uncertain. More certain is the comparison that has been made between the 'Eternal Sun' in an unedited text from Rās Shamrah, 'Shamash the Eternal One' in a Karatepe inscription of the eighth century B.C. and 'Elath the Eternal One' in an Aramaic incantation of the seventh century.[46]

The name El Shaddai, however, is the one which raises the most interesting questions.[47] According to the priestly account of the call of Moses (Exod 6:3), El Shaddai was the name of the god of Abraham, Isaac and Jacob. Also according to the priestly account, God revealed himself to Abraham as El Shaddai (Gen 17:1). The name is in fact found frequently in the priestly narrative (see Gen 28:3; 35:11; 43:14; 48:3). It is, however, a very old name, because it is also found in Jacob's will (Gen 49:25).[48] The shorter form šaddai also occurs five times in the psalms and the prophets, twice in Ruth and thirty-one times in Job, but this is also an early name, because it appears twice in the oracles of Balaam, in parallel with El (Num 24:4) and in parallel with 'el'yôn (Num 24:16). These references do not provide sufficient evidence for us to decide which of the two forms was the earlier and, because of this doubt, it is possible that Shaddai was a divine name which was at first independent, but which was later combined with El. The same uncertainty prevails with regard to the meaning of the name. The hypothesis that is most widely accepted nowadays is that it was derived from the Akkadian šadū, mountain, so that the meaning is '(El) of the Mountain'.[49]

Papyri', JNES, 28 (1969), pp. 116–121.

[43] R. Borger, VT, 7 (1957), pp. 102–104; J. Starcky, Syria, 37 (1960), pp. 104–105.

[44] Apart from F. M. Cross, op. cit., see E. Jenni, Das Wort 'ôlam im Alten Testament, Berlin, 1953, pp. 52–57; O. Eissfeldt, Forschungen und Fortschritte, 39 (1965), pp. 298–300 = Kleine Schriften, IV, pp. 193–198.

[46] These references will be found in F. M. Cross, op. cit., p. 237; a further comparison can be made with the 'Eternal King' as a divine title (cf. Jer 10:10) in a Rās Shamrah text, Ugaritica, V, p. 553.

[47] In addition to F. M. Cross, op. cit., pp. 244–250, see especially M. Weippert, 'Erwägungen zur Etymologie des Gottesnamens 'El Saddaj', ZDMG, 111 (1961), pp. 42–62.

[48] According to several Hebrew manuscripts and the Syriac text, it should be read as w''el sadday instead of w''et sadday; E. A. Speiser, however, preserves the Massoretic text in Genesis, op. cit., 1964, as does W. H. Schmidt, Alttestamentlicher Glaube, op. cit., p. 27.

[49] See especially W. F. Albright, 'The Names Shaddai and Abram', JBL, 54 (1935), pp. 173–193; F. M. Cross, op. cit. Two recent hypotheses have to be rejected – a derivation from the Sumerian, with the meaning of 'omniscient', see N. Walker, 'A New Interpretation of the Divine Name "Shaddai" ', ZAW, 72 (1960), pp. 64–66 and a suggestion that the three divine names, Shaddai, Hadad and 'Addu, come from a root dd, meaning 'he who gives power', see E. C. B. MacLaurin, 'Shaddai', Abr-Nahrain, 3 (1961–1962), pp. 99–118.

It would, however, be more advisable to look for an etymological explanation of the name El Shaddai in north-western Semitic and the suggestion has in fact been made that it may be derived from the Hebrew *śādheh/śâdhay*. If this etymology is correct, then El Shaddai would mean 'El of the Plain', 'El of the Fields' or 'El of the Steppe'.[50] The philological objection that has been raised is that the initial consonant is different – that of *śādheh/śâdh ay* being *śîn*, whereas that of *śaddai* is *šîn*.[51] It is, however, possible that Shaddai preserved a pronunciation which was earlier than that of Hebrew and that the name was no longer understood in Hebrew. In Ugaritic, the word for 'field' was pronounced *śd* and a gloss is provided in a letter from Jerusalem in the Amarna correspondence on the Akkadian word for 'field', *śa-de-e*.[52] While agreeing that these forms may not be in accordance with the original phonetics of the word, it has to be admitted that the word was pronounced in this way in the fourteenth century B.C. at Ugarit and at Jerusalem. On the other hand, El Shaddai can be compared with *bêl ʿsadê*, which is the most common title given to the god Amurru in the early Babylonian texts.[53] This title has been translated as 'Lord of the Mountain', but the real meaning is 'Lord of the Steppe' – the word *śadū* has two meanings in Akkadian[54] and Amurru was also called *bêl sêrim*, which could not mean anything other than 'Lord of the Steppe'.[55] Amurru was the god of the Syrian steppe, where the Amorites lived as nomads. It will be remembered in this context, on the one hand, that the patriarchs were connected with the Amorites and, on the other, that the god of the father was also called Amurru in the texts of the Assyrian colonies of Cappadocia. Because of these similarities, it is probable that Shaddai, 'the One of the Steppe', was a name – or the name – of the god of the father, brought by the ancestors of the people of Israel from Upper Mesopotamia. This would also explain why, unlike El Roi or El Olam, El Shaddai was not linked to a special sanctuary. The theophany described in Gen 17:1, which is the first mention of the name, clearly took place in a special sanctuary or holy place, but the site is not precisely stated. It may possibly have been Mamre. El Shaddai also manifested himself, however, at Bethel (Gen 35:11; see also

[50] M. Weippert, *op. cit.* (note 47).

[51] *ibid.*, pp. 51–54; F. M. Cross, *op. cit.*, p. 245, note 25.

[52] *EA*, 287, 56.

[53] L. R. Bailey has made this comparison in 'Israelite 'El Sadday and Amorite Bel Sadê', *JBL*, 87 (1968), pp. 434–438, but his conclusions are different. I agree more with J. Ouellette, 'More on 'El Sadday and Bel Sadê', *JBL*, 88 (1969), pp. 470–471.

[54] A. Heidel, 'A Special Usage of the Akkadian Term *śadû*', *JNES*, 8 (1949), pp. 233–235; Heidel concludes that *'śadû* occasionally ... corresponds, both etymologically and semantically, to Hebrew *śâdê*'. The Akkadian adjective *śad(d)û'â'u* (the equivalent of the Hebrew *ʿsadday*) has been translated by W. G. Lambert as 'belonging to the plain', in *Babylonian Wisdom Literature*, Oxford, 1960, pp. 177, line 15, 179, line 29; see also p. 332.

[55] G. Dossin, *L'antica società beduina*, ed. F. Gabrieli, Rome, 1959, pp. 42–43; J.-R. Kupper, *L'iconographie du dieu Amurru*, Brussels, 1961, pp. 62–68, 73.

48:3). If this hypothesis is correct, the name El Shaddai must mean that Shaddai, the god of the father, was identified with El. This identification might already have taken place in Upper Mesopotamia, where the cult of the great god El is attested by reliable evidence, at the beginning of the second millennium B.C. Nonetheless, the god El is never associated with any other land but Canaan and it is probably there that the relationship was established.

It is a striking fact that the name Baal is never mentioned in the stories of the patriarchs and that there is no personal name formed with Baal in those stories. The explanation of this fact must be sought in the history of Canaanite religion. El plays a rather modest part in the poems of Rās Shamrah and his authority is undermined by the increasing power of a young god, Baal. Baal might possibly have been regarded as El's son, because El was the father of all the gods, but he is explicitly called the son of Dagan, the god of the Middle Euphrates. He was, in other words, a new-comer to the pantheon of Ugarit. It is not possible to judge from the original texts of Rās Shamrah when Baal appeared on the scene, but there is external evidence which enables us to come to a probable conclusion.[56]

The name Baal appears for the first time in the Egyptian texts during the reign of Amen-hotep II, that is, in the fifteenth century B.C., but Baal was not accepted by the pharaohs until the nineteenth dynasty. The Egyptians recognised Baal as the great god of the Hyksos, but there is evidence of this identification only after the expulsion of the Hyksos. The Hyksos scarabs contain possible onomastic evidence of a Ya'qub-Ba'al[57] and there is also the evidence in a nineteenth-century execration text of a name formed with Baal among a list of Syrian slaves in Egypt in the eighteenth century B.C.[58] There are two or three references to Baal in the Cappadocian texts, which are a little earlier. In these tablets, the name, which is written as Bêlum, forms part of several personal names, in which it may have been the name of a god and not simply a divine title.[59] Among the Amorite personal names of the eighteenth and seventeenth centuries B.C., there are several names formed with the element ba'al,[60] but it is not easy to say whether this element has, either in the case of these Amorite names or in that of the names occurring in the Egyptian texts mentioned above, the usual meaning of 'master', used as a divine title, or whether what we have here is the per-sonal name of a god. All that can be said is that this second usage was excep-tional. These ambiguous and occasional references to Baal are in striking

[56] U. Oldenburg, The Conflict between El and Baal in Canaanite Religion, Leiden, 1969, pp. 143–145; Oldenburg's arguments and conclusions are, in my opinion, not very satisfactory.
[57] S. Yeivin, JEA, 45 (1959), pp. 16–18.
[58] See W. F. Albright, JAOS, 74 (1954), pp. 231–232.
[59] H. Hirsch, Untersuchungen zur altassyrischen Religion, op. cit., pp. 22–24.
[60] H. B. Huffmon, Amorite Personal Names in the Mari Texts, Baltimore, 1965, pp. 100 and 174.

contrast to the predominant part played by Baal in the Rās Shamrah poems during the fourteenth century B.C., in Egypt from the same period onwards and in the Bible, after an initial reference to the cult of Baal in Num 25, from the age of the Judges onwards.

If the evidence relating to the god El is studied, however, a development in the opposite direction will be observed. In the execration texts, there are several names formed with *ilu* and, in the Cappadocian texts, there are several formed with *ilum* (AN). Apart from certain exceptions, in these texts the word must have the usual meaning of 'god'.[61] The situation is much clearer in the Mari archives, in which the god Ilum (written as AN, but also as *i-lu-um*) is called the founder of the city and is therefore the supreme god in his pantheon.[62] We are therefore justified in recognising the god El at least in some of the many proper names from Mari and the rest of the Amorite domain formed with the element *ilum*.[63] When the Canaanite gods were adopted by the pharaohs of the eighteenth and nineteenth dynasties, however, El was no longer the supreme god and he was not worshipped in Egypt. He finally lost his pre-eminent position in Syria in the first millennium – in the lists of gods which have so far been found he appears in the second place, after Hadad at Zenjirli and Sfire and after Baalshamim at Karatepe, although at Karatepe he has the title of 'creator of the earth'. All this evidence would seem to indicate that Baal was not an important figure in Canaan before the middle of the second millennium, although he may have become important a little earlier at Ugarit.[64] The stories of the patriarchs, in which El is mentioned but not Baal, reflect an early state of the Canaanite religion. If we are correct in believing that the patriarchs preceded the Hyksos period, then the ancestors of the people of Israel did not find Baal worshipped when they arrived in Canaan, but El.

The nomadic and semi-nomadic peoples frequented the sanctuaries of those who had already settled in Canaan. The Benjaminites of Mari, for instance, concluded a treaty in the temple of Sin at Haran and a Sutaean

---

[61] P. Garelli, *RA*, 56 (1962), pp. 199–200.

[62] G. Dossin, 'L'inscription de fondation de Iahdun-Lim, roi de Mari', *Syria*, 32 (1955), pp. 1–28, especially p. 25.

[63] H. B. Huffmon, *op. cit.*, pp. 162–165; A. Finet, 'Iawi-Ilâ, roi de Talhayûm', *Syria*, 41 (1964), pp. 117–142, especially pp. 118–120 (it is difficult to accept, however, the author's identification of Iawi with Yahweh); M. Liverani, *OrAnt*, 9 (1970), pp. 20–21.

[64] U. Oldenburg, *op. cit.* (Note 56) believed that the cult of Baal was introduced at Ugarit at about 2000 B.C. or even earlier, basing this on the date given by W. F. Albright for the formation of the Baal cycle, *BASOR*, 150 (Apr. 1958), p. 36; see also his *Yahweh and the Gods of Canaan*, London, 1968, p. 101 ff. M. Liverani is more correct in suggesting the period 1800–1500, *Atti della Accademia Nazionale dei Lincei. Rendiconti*, VII, XIX, 5–6 (1964), p. 1. The language of these poems is certainly archaic, but it is not possible to date them precisely.

Amorite, camped in the vicinity of Ur, made an offering to the goddess Ningal in her temple.[65] The patriarchs undoubtedly encountered El in the sanctuaries of Canaan.[66] We have already seen that El Shaddai was connected with an anonymous holy place and with Bethel. The god of Beersheba was El Olam, whom Abraham invoked (Gen 21:33) there, who revealed himself to Isaac there as the god of his father Abraham (Gen 26:23–25) and to Jacob as the god of his father (Gen 46:1–3). It was at Bethel too that the god of Abraham and Isaac appeared to Jacob (Gen 28:13) and the same 'god of my father' (Gen 31: 5b) declared that he was El of Bethel (Gen 31:13; cf. 35:7). Shechem was the sanctuary of 'El, God of Israel' (the patriarch) (Gen 33:20) and Mamre must have had a similar tradition. Abraham, for instance, erected an altar there (Gen 13:18) and, since the early narrative continues immediately after the interruption of the story of the four great kings (Gen 14), it is probable that the divine promises were also made to Abraham at Mamre (Gen 15). It is explicitly stated that he received the divine visitors there (Gen 18). Following a hypothesis made in an earlier work, it is quite possible that Shaddai, the 'god of the father' who revealed himself to Abraham, was assimilated to El at Mamre – the revelation of the name El Shaddai opens Gen 17, which is the priestly parallel to Gen 15. The sanctuary at Mamre, however, seems to have been deliberately condemned to oblivion – it is not mentioned again in the Bible and even in Genesis there is some confusion between Mamre and Hebron.[67]

In the same way, the editors of the Deuteronomistic history from Judges to Kings reduced the importance of the sanctuary at Shechem and the sanctuaries at Bethel and at Beersheba were explicitly condemned by orthodox Yahwism. The traditions associating the patriarchs with these four sanctuaries were therefore very early, but they also developed – in becoming unified, these patriarchal traditions connected Abraham and Jacob with Shechem and Bethel and Abraham, Isaac and Jacob with Beersheba. Originally, each patriarch was probably associated with only one sanctuary – Abraham with Mamre, Isaac with Beersheba, Jacob with Bethel and Israel with Shechem.

The patriarchs are shown as the founders of these sanctuaries – they are the places where they erected an altar and invoked the name of God, or of Yahweh in the Yahwistic tradition. In fact, however, they were really early Canaanite sanctuaries where the patriarchs discovered the cult of the great god El practised in the various forms outlined above. It is interesting in this context to observe that the divine revelations were made to the patriarchs during a dream or in a nocturnal vision (see Gen 15:5, 17; 26:24; 28:13;

[65] J.-R. Kupper, Les nomades en Mésopotamie au temps des rois de Mari, Paris, 1957, pp. 56, 88–89.

[66] R. de Vaux, Institutions, pp. 289–294.

[67] ibid., p. 120.

31:13; 46:2) and that at Ugarit El was the only deity who was associated with dreams.[68] The stories claiming that the patriarchs founded these sanctuaries really mean that the patriarchs adopted them and that the patriarchal god of the father, the private god of the nomadic group, was assimilated to the god of the settled people with whom the nomads came into contact.

El was the highest god in the Canaanite pantheon. At Ugarit, he was called the father of the gods and of men and the 'creator of creatures'. This 'creation', however, was a procreation, since El procreated rather than created. In one text, El is described copulating with two women in order to procreate the gods Shahar and Shalem and then a series of other gods. El did not, in other words, create the gods and there is no myth of creation at Ugarit.[69] The nearest Ugaritic parallel to a creation myth is the myth of Baal's struggle against the powers of chaos, but it would be unjustified to apply this aspect of Baal to El.[70] Outside Ugarit, however, El was entitled the 'creator of the earth' during the fifteenth and fourteenth centuries B.C. in the Hittite adaptation of a Canaanite myth (Ilkunirsa), in the Phoenician inscription of Karatepe in the eighth century B.C., in a neo-Punic inscription at Leptis Magna and in an inscription on a tessera found at Palmyra and dating from the Roman period. It is therefore probable that El was a creator god in ancient Canaan.[71] In any case, he was the lord and master of the world and it was because of this that he was given the title of Bull, which clearly shows him as the powerful one rather than as the begetter.[72] As the head of the pantheon, he was also given the title of king and he presided over the assembly of the gods in his palace, which was situated at the farthest limits of the world. He was the ideal king, wise and kind, showing sadness and happiness, but never anger. The Canaanite religion of El was very different from the religion of the god of the father.[73] It was above all the religion of a settled people – El was the head of a pantheon, a king living in a palace and surrounded by a court of other gods, the master of the

---

[68] A. Caquot, Canaan et Israel, in Les songes et leur interprétation (Sources Orientales, II), Paris, 1959, pp. 103–106; V. Maag, Syrien-Palästina, in H. Schmockel, Kulturgeschichte des Alten Orients, Stuttgart, 1961, p. 569.
[69] For this question, see M. H. Pope, El in Ugaritic Texts (SVT, 2), 1955, pp. 49–54; A. Caquot, 'La naissance du monde selon Canaan', La Naissance du Monde ('Sources Orientales, I), Paris, 1959, pp. 177–184; W. Schmidt, Königtum Gottes in Ugarit und in Israel (BZAW, 80), 1961, pp. 49–52; L. R. Fischer, 'Creation at Ugarit and in the Old Testament', VT, 15 (1965), pp. 313–324.
[70] As P. D. Miller has done in 'El the Warrior', HTR, 60 (1967), pp. 411–431.
[71] In spite of W. F. Albright's claim, in The Biblical Period, op. cit., p. 13, there is insufficient proof that the Canaanite god El was identified with Ptah, the creator god of Memphis; see also ibid., The Proto-Sinaitic Inscriptions and their Decipherment, Cambridge, Mass., 1966, pp. 4, 22; F. M. Cross, HTR, 55 (1962), p. 238; P. D. Miller, HTR, 60 (1967), p. 431.
[72] P. D. Miller, op. cit., pp. 418–425, gives good reasons for holding this view.
[73] V. Maag, NTT, 21 (1966–1967), pp. 173–179.

world who never intervened in human history.

In assimilating El into the religion of the god of the father, the ancestors of Israel in no sense abandoned their nomadic religion, [74] but rather enriched it. In this process of assimilation, it is difficult to distinguish precisely which characteristics were borrowed from the religion of El. According to the stories of the patriarchs and the progress of Israel's religious history, of all El's mythological aspects and other characteristics, including his aspect as king, none was borrowed. It is possible, however, that his aspect of supreme power was borrowed and it is tempting to attribute the title of 'bhir, the Mighty One or Bull, which was given to the god of Jacob, to the influence of the religion of El the Bull. This title of the Mighty One was, after all, a very considerable one, since it qualified El as the all-powerful cosmic god, enlarging the idea of God to include the whole world, rather than simply the family or clan.

In recent years, certain authors have attempted to trace knowledge of the name Yahweh back to the patriarchal age, maintaining, for example, that all that was revealed to Moses was the hidden meaning of the name, [75] that it was originally a cultic title of El, like Olam, Elyon or Shaddai [76] or that it was the name of Moses' 'god of the father'. [77] These theories, which are based on the use of the name in the Yahwistic material, go counter to the evidence of the other two traditions, the Elohistic and the priestly accounts, both of which affirm that Yahweh was a new name revealed to Moses. All three traditions, moreover, affirm that the God of the patriarchs was the same as the Yahweh who revealed himself to Moses. Although it is possible to accept that one of these traditions may have extended the use of this name, it is hardly possible to believe that the other two traditions would have denied that it was known to the patriarchs if they had not been compelled to do so by an early and authentic memory. This question will be discussed more fully in connection with the origin of Yahwism. [78]

III. RELIGIOUS PRACTICES

Genesis has very little to tell us about the external observances of this

---

[74] O. Eissfeldt has interpreted Gen 35:2–4 as an abandonment of the god of the father; see his article in *JSS*, 1 (1956), p. 36; see also K. T. Andersen, *ST*, 16 (1962), pp. 170–188; V. Maag, *Hebräische Wortforschung. Festschrift W. Baumgartner* (*SVT*, 16), 1967, pp. 213–214.

[75] S. Mowinckel, 'The Name of the God of Moses', *HUCA*, 32 (1961), pp. 121–133; M. Haran, *ASTI*, 4 (1965), pp. 38–39.

[76] F. M. Cross, *HTR*, 55 (1962), pp. 225–259.

[77] J. P. Hyatt, *VT*, 5 (1955), pp. 130–136; 'The Origin of Yahwism', *The Teacher's Yoke* (*Volume H. Trantham*), ed. E. J. Vardaman, J. L. Garrett, Waco, Texas, 1964, pp. 85–93; *JBL*, 86 (1967), pp. 376–377.

[78] See below, p. 338 and 456–457.

religion of the god of the father, either before or after it had become assimilated with the religion of El and the little information that it does provide may well reflect later customs. A few archaic factors can, however, be distinguished. It is also possible to have recourse to comparisons with other ancient societies of the same racial and sociological characteristics. Unfortunately, however, we have almost no knowledge at all of the religious practices of the Ancient Near Eastern nomadic or semi-nomadic peoples. Only a little more is known about the practices of pre-Islamic Arabs and this is possibly of little value to our understanding of the patriarchal age. What is suggested in this section, then, will inevitably be incomplete and hypothetical.

1. Altars and sacrifices

According to Gen 12:7, 8; 13:18; 26:25; 33:20; 35:7, the patriarchs erected altars. As we have already said, however, this was a way of saying that they adopted sanctuaries that were already in existence. This thesis is confirmed by the fact that the patriarchs' altars served no practical purpose — we are never told that they made sacrifices on them, apart from the case of Gen 22, an exception to which we shall be returning. In northern and central Arabia before the coming of Islam, no altars were built and sacrifices were made on rock surfaces or on large, rough stones.[79] The patriarchs, we may conclude, had no need of altars.

Although the patriarchs, like these nomads in Arabia, sacrificed animals, these sacrifices occur rarely in the Genesis stories — there is a simple reference to sacrifices, z'bhahîm, found in Gen 46:1 and in Gen 31:54 we read that Jacob sealed his treaty with Laban by offering a sacrifice, zebhah, followed by a meal. There is only one detailed account of a sacrifice — the sacrifice of Isaac (Gen 22:1–19) — and this took place on a mountain which cannot be identified. There, Abraham built an altar in order to sacrifice his son as a burnt offering, 'ôlah, but a ram was offered in Isaac's place. The Elohist[80] clearly intended this sacrifice to be seen as a test of Abraham's faith and obedience — in the person of Isaac, the whole of the future people of Israel was bound on the altar and could only survive by their ancestor's submission and the goodness of their God, who gave life and took it away. What may underlie this account of the sacrifice of Isaac is a story justifying

[79] In contrast to the more developed Arabian kingdoms in the south of the country; see G. Ryckmans, 'Sud-arabe mdbht – hébreu mzbh et termes apparentés', Festschrift Werner Caskel, Leiden, 1968, pp. 253–260.

[80] Gen 22:15–18 are usually regarded as additional; see R. Kilian, Die vorpriesterlichen Abrahamsüberlieferungen, Bonn, 1966, pp. 263–278. Verse 14 or at least v. 14b is disputed. Count Reventlow believes that it is of early date; see his Opfere deinen Sohn. Eine Auslegung von Genesis 22, Neukirchen and Vluyn, 1968, pp. 25–31.

the substitution of an animal victim for a human offering, or narrating the establishment of a sanctuary where human victims were not sacrificed. [81] The early aspect of this story is, however, no longer apparent and it probably never belonged to the very earliest Abraham tradition, [82] so that nothing can be derived from it which will tell us anything about the religion of the patriarchs. It does contain the word 'ôlah six times and the burnt offering is a type of sacrifice which does not seem to have been borrowed from the Canaanites until after the definitive settlement of the tribes. [83] The first references in indisputably early texts date from the period of the Judges.

Probably only a simple form of blood offering, zebhah, of the type of the paschal sacrifice, was known in the patriarchal religion. This sacrifice preserved the characteristics of its nomadic origin [84] and its closest parallels have been found, not in Canaan, where it was not known, but among the nomadic peoples of northern and central Arabia. These were family sacrifices, like those mentioned in the Safaitic inscriptions of the first few centuries A.D. [85] These offerings were made outside sanctuaries, without an altar or a priest and in places where the people were camped. Each man immolated his own victim for himself after taking it from the flock. It was not burnt and it was eaten communally by the sacrificer and his family. In central Arabia, the victim was immolated in front of an upright stone symbolising the divine presence and the blood was either poured out over the stone or else allowed to spill into a pit dug at the foot of the stone. [86] Sacrifices of this kind were made above all at the feasts celebrated by these nomadic Arabs during the first month of spring in order to ensure the fertility and prosperity of their flocks. [87] The ancestors of the people of Israel, who were also semi-nomadic herdsmen, probably celebrated a similar feast. The book of Exodus presupposes the celebration of Passover from the time

[81] R. de Vaux, Les sacrifices de l'Ancien Testament, Paris, 1964, pp. 61–62. According to Reventlow, op. cit., pp. 32–65, it is not an aetiological, but a popular story.

[82] M. Noth, Uberlieferungsgeschichte, pp. 125–126. The original was, possibly a Canaanite narrative, according to Reventlow, op. cit., p. 65.

[83] L. Rost, 'Erwägungen zum israelitischen Brandopfer', Von Ugarit nach Qumran (Festschrift O. Eissfeldt), Berlin 1958, 2nd edn, 1961, pp. 177–183 = Das kleine Credo und andere Studien zum Alten Testament, Heidelberg, 1965, pp. 112–119; R. de Vaux, Les sacrifices de l'Ancien Testament, op. cit., pp. 21–22, 41–48.

[84] R. de Vaux, op. cit., pp. 7–27.

[85] G. Ryckmans, 'Le sacrifice dbh dans les inscriptions safaitiques', HUCA, 23, 1 (1950–1951), pp. 431–438.

[86] J. Henninger, 'La religion bédouine préislamique', L'antica società beduina, ed. F. Gabrieli, Rome, 1959, pp. 135–136; G. Ryckmans, 'Les religions arabes préislamiques', M. Gorce and R. Mortier, Histoire générale des religions, IV, 1960, p. 203.

[87] J. Henninger, 'Les fêtes de printemps chez les Arabes et leurs implications historiques', Rivista do Museu Paulista (Sao Paolo), new series 4 (1950), pp. 389–432; 'Über Frühlingsfeste bei den Semiten', In Verbo Tuo. Festschrift zum 50-jährigen Bestehen des Missionpriesterseminars St. Augustin bei Siegburg, Rheinland, 1963, pp. 375–398.

before the exodus from Egypt. Without any explanation, the Yahwistic
narrative of Exod 12:21 begins with the words: 'Go ... and kill the
Passover victim', as though this were something that was already well
known. Apparently it was a 'feast in honour of Yahweh' that the Israelites
wished to celebrate in the wilderness (Exod 5:1; cf. 3:18; 4:23, etc.).

2. Sacred stones and trees

The practices attributed to the patriarchs, for which they were not
originally blamed, but which were later condemned by the official
representatives of Yahwism, may be regarded as early.[88] From the
etymological point of view, the *mass'bhāh* was an upright stone which might
have various purposes. The stone which Jacob set up in Gilead established a
boundary and witnessed to the treaty between him and Laban (Gen 31:45,
51–52). A *mass'bhāh* was also erected as the monument of Rachel's tomb
(Gen 35:20). Other *mass'bhôth*, however, had a more directly religious
significance, recalling a theophany and acting as the sign of God's presence.
After his dream at Bethel, Jacob set up the stone that he had used for a
pillow as a *mass'bhāh*. It was a 'house of God', *bêth 'el*, and became the object
of a cult. Jacob even poured oil over it (Gen 28:18, 22 and the doublet Gen
35:14). These *mass'bhôth*, however, also became a symbol of Baal and
associated with the 'high places' of the Canaanite religion, with the result
that they were condemned (Exod 34:13; Deut 7:5; 12:3; Hos 10:1; Mic
5:12, etc.). There was a widespread cult of such stones in pre-Islamic Arabia
and the word *nusb*, in the plural *'ansâb*, which comes from the same root as
mass'bhāh, denotes the upright stones which were venerated as idols: victims
were immolated at their feet and they were anointed with the blood of the
sacrificed animals.[89]

The memory of the patriarchs was also linked with certain trees. The
Oak of Mamre marked the holy place of Shechem, Abraham's first stopping place in Canaan (Gen 12:6). The name means the 'Oak[90] of the
Teacher or the Diviner'. The same tree is mentioned in Deut 11:30 and it is
probably the same as the anonymous tree of Gen 35:4, the 'Diviner's Oak'
of Judges 9:37 and the tree under which Joshua set up a 'great stone', a
mass'bhāh (Jos 24:26; cf. Judges 9:6, corr.). Deborah, Rebekah's nurse, was

[88] H. Ringgren, *Israelitische Religion*, Stuttgart, 1963, pp. 21–23.
[89] J. Wellhausen, *Reste arabischen Heidentums*,[2] Berlin, 1897, pp. 101–103; M.–J. Lagrange,
Etudes sur les religions sémitiques,[2] Paris, 1905, pp. 187–210; M. Höfner, *Götter und Mythen im
Vorderen Orient* (*Wörterbuch der Mythologie*, I), ed. H. W. Haussig, Stuttgart, 1965, p. 450.
[90] Here and in all the references to this tree that follow, the translation 'oak' is only
approximate. Other authors are in favour of 'terebinth'. In any case, what we have here is a
very large tree.

buried under the Oak of Tears near Bethel (Gen 35:8). Abraham planted a tamarisk at Beersheba and invoked El Olam there (Gen 21:33). He also built an altar under the Oak of Mamre (Gen 13:18) and received the three divine visitors there (Gen 18:1; see also Gen 14:13). In the later tradition, attempts were made to lessen the importance of these trees because superstition played such a large part in the cult practised there. We have already noted that Mamre was not mentioned again in the Bible after Genesis and to this can be added the fact that the Oak of Mamre disappears from the Genesis Apocryphon of Qumran in Chapter XIV. In Gen 13:18; 14:13; 18:1, the plural 'the oaks' appears in the Massoretic text, despite the evidence of the versions and the indication in Gen 18:4 and 8. In the same way, the Oak of Moreh appears in the plural in Deut 11:30. The Jewish interpreters went even further. In the Targum of Onkelos, for example, 'oak' is replaced by 'plain' (or 'valley') in Gen 12:6; 13:18; 14:13; 18:1; 35:8. The same replacement is found, at least partially, in the other Targums. This interpretation had its effect on Jerome's translation of the Bible – the Oak of Moreh is called *convallis illustris* in Gen 12:6 and *vallis* in Deut 11:30, while the Oak of Mamre appears in the Vulgate as *convallis Mambre* (Gen 13:18; 14:13; 18:1). The trees of the patriarchs were included, then, in the general condemnation of all Canaanite places of worship set 'on high mountains, on hills, under any spreading tree' (Deut 12:2). The same condemnation appears in other passages edited by the deuteronomist (1 Kings 14:23; 2 Kings 16:4, etc.) and in the prophets (Hos 4:13; Jer 2:20; 3:6, etc.). Finally, it should be noted that, in addition to stones, sacred trees played an important part in the religion of the pre-Islamic Arabs.[91]

3. *Circumcision*

It is also very likely that the ancestors of the people of Israel practised circumcision,[92] although the circumstances in which this practice was introduced are not clearly known.[93] It is unlikely that it was brought from Egypt, as has been suggested, because it was not universally practised there. Nor is it probable that it was borrowed from the Midianites – a conclusion drawn from an obscure text, Exod 4:24–26.[94] In fact, circumcision was

[91] J. Wellhausen, *op. cit.*, pp. 104–105; M.-J. Lagrange, *op. cit.*, pp. 169–180; M. Höfner, *op. cit.*, pp. 430–431.

[92] M. Haran, *ASTI*, 4 (1965), p. 44.

[93] R. de Vaux, *Institutions*, pp. 46–48; E. Isaac, 'Circumcision as a Covenant Rite', *Anthropos*, 59 (1964), pp. 444–456.

[94] See H. Kosmala, 'The "Bloody Husband" ', *VT*, 12 (1962), pp. 14–28; J. Morgenstern, 'The "Bloody Husband" (?) Once Again', *HUCA*, 34 (1963), pp. 35–70; H. Schmid, 'Mose, der Blutbräutigam', *Judaica*, 22 (1966), pp. 113–118

practised before the descent into Egypt, at least according to Gen 34, and the use of a flint knife (Exod 4:25; Jos 5:2–3) points to the archaic nature of the rite. In Jos 5:2 ff and Gen 17:9–14, 23–27 (P), it is connected with the land of Canaan. An ivory engraved in the fourteenth or thirteenth century B.C. and found at Megiddo shows Canaanite prisoners who are circumcised.[95] It is possible, then, that the ancestors of the people of Israel adopted the ritual practice when they entered Canaan. On the other hand, however, bronze statuettes found at Tell el-Judeideh provide evidence of the practice of circumcision in northern Syria from round about 2800 B.C. onwards.[96] According to Jer 9:24–25, the Edomites, the Ammonites, the Moabites and the Arabs living in the desert were all circumcised, just as the pre-Islamic Arabs were according to their poets. Circumcision, then, was a very ancient rite, practised outside Canaan by peoples who were related to the patriarchs or who led the same kind of life as the patriarchs. It is therefore quite possible that the ancestors of the people of Israel were acquainted with circumcision and practised it before they entered Canaan. At that time, it had the primitive significance of an initiation into marriage and into the communal life of the clan (this is the sense in which it has to be understood in Gen 34:14–16) and it was not until later that it became the sign of the covenant between God and his people, although the priestly author of Gen 17 refers this meaning back to the period of Abraham.

The historian can draw only very limited, and at the most probable, conclusions with regard to the religion of the patriarchs, but he can say enough to enable the continuity of that religion with the religion of Moses to be recognised, despite the fact that there were also new developments in the latter.

---

[95] *ANEP*, No. 332.

[96] R. J. Braidwood, L. S. Braidwood, *Excavations in the Plain of Antioch*, I, Chicago, 1960, pp. 300–305, Fig. 240–243, Plate 56–59; J. M. Sasson, 'Circumcision in the Ancient Near East,' *JBL*, 85 (1966), pp. 473–476.

PART II

The Traditions of the Sojourn
in Egypt, the Exodus and Sinai

Chapter Eleven

THE SETTLEMENT IN EGYPT
THE STORY OF JOSEPH

IN EXODUS 12:40 (P), we read that the sojourn in Egypt lasted for four hundred and thirty years, whereas in Gen 15:13 (E?) God tells Abraham that his descendants were to be slaves in a foreign land for four hundred years. We shall return to these figures and discuss them more fully when we try to establish the chronology of this period. All that we need to point out here is that, according to the biblical tradition, the ancestors of Israel stayed for a very long time in Egypt.

Nothing, however, is said in the Bible about these four centuries or more in Egypt. The traditions regarding the origins of Israel are summarised in the little 'historical credo'[2] of Deut 26:5–9, which passes abruptly from the descent of Israel's ancestors into Egypt to the oppression of the people by the Egyptians as a prelude to the exodus. Another short confession of faith (Deut 6:20–24) begins with the oppression of the Israelites: 'Once we were Pharaoh's slaves in Egypt, and Yahweh brought us out of Egypt by his mighty hand'. In the summaries given in Jos 24:2–13 and 1 Sam 12:8–11 of

[1] Apart from commentaries on Genesis, see H. Gunkel, 'Die Komposition der Joseph-Geschichte', ZDMG, 76 (1922), pp. 55–71; H. Gressman, 'Ursprung und Entwicklung der Joseph-Saga', Eucharistèrion H. Gunkel, Göttingen, 1925, pp. 1–55; H. H. Rowley, From Joseph to Joshua, London, 1950; G. von Rad, 'Josephsgeschichte und ältere Chokma', Congress Volume. Copenhagen (SVT, 1), Leiden, 1953 = Gesammelte Studien zum Alten Testament, Munich, 1958, pp. 272–280; G. von Rad. Die Josephsgeschichte (Biblische Studien, 5), Neukirchen and Vluyn, 1954; J. M. A. Janssen, 'Egyptological Remarks on the Story of Joseph in Genesis', JEOL, 14 (1955–1956), pp. 63–72; J. Vergote, Joseph en Egypte, Genèse chap. 37–50 à la lumière des études égyptologiques récentes, Louvain, 1959; S. Morenz, 'Joseph in Ägypten', TLZ, 84 (1959), col 401–416; S. Herrmann, 'Joseph in Ägypten. Ein Wort zu J. Vergotes Buch "Joseph in Ägypten" ', TLZ, 85 (1960), col 827–830; O. Kaiser, 'Stammesgeschichtliche Hintergründe der Josephsgeschichte', VT, 10 (1960), pp. 1–15; S. Herrmann, 'Israel in Ägypten', ZAS, 91 (1964), pp. 63–79; L. Ruppert, Die Josephserzählung der Genesis. Ein Beitrag zur Theologie der Pentateuchquellen, Munich, 1965; B. J. van der Merwe, 'Joseph as Successor of Jacob', Studia Biblica et Orientalia Th. C. Vriezen dedicata, Wageningen, 1966, pp. 221–232; R. N. Whybray, 'The Joseph Story and Pentateuchal Criticism', VT, 18 (1968), pp. 522–528.*

[2] This term was first used by G. von Rad in Das formgeschichtliche Problem des Hexateuch, Stuttgart, 1938 = Gesammelte Studien zum Alten Testament, Munich, 1958, pp. 9–86, see also

the history of salvation, the story of the descent of Jacob and his sons into Egypt is followed immediately by the exodus led by Moses and Aaron.

There is in fact no biblical tradition dealing with the sojourn in Egypt. There is a tradition concerning the descent into Egypt – the story of Joseph and his brothers (Gen 37–50) – and there is also a tradition concerning the exodus from Egypt (Exod 1–15), which opens with a portrayal of the oppression of the Israelites (Exod 1:8–22). These two traditions are juxtaposed in the early Yahwistic and Elohistic traditions of the Pentateuch – there is a break between the death of Joseph in the last verse of Genesis and the coming to power of the pharaoh 'who knew nothing of Joseph' in the first verse of the Yahwist's account in Exod 1:8. The priestly editor has connected the two together by saying that the seventy persons who went with Jacob into Egypt had increased greatly in number after the death of Joseph (Exod 1:1–7). Instead of filling in the gap between the end of Genesis and the beginning of Exodus, however, the priestly editor has made it more obvious – the 'sons of Israel-Jacob' (verse 1) became, over an undefined period of time, the people of Israel (verse 7). What is more, like the authors of the historical summaries and the confessions of faith that we have mentioned above, the priestly editor does not say what took place during this period of increasing population. The Israelites did not preserve any memories of the period that their ancestors spent in Egypt – all that they remembered was their entry into Egypt and their departure from it. These are two traditions which have to be examined separately.

The Israelites' settlement in Egypt is narrated within the framework of the story of Joseph. This occupies the whole of the end of Genesis (Gen 37–50), with the exception of the story of Judah and Tamar (Gen 38, J), which is a special tradition concerning the origins of the tribe of Judah, and the story of Jacob's will and blessing (Gen 49), which is a collection of sayings about the tribes and does not form part of any of the major sources of the Pentateuch.

I. LITERARY ANALYSIS OF THE STORY OF JOSEPH

Only a few interventions on the part of the priestly editor are taken into account in the classic literary criticism of the Joseph story, which is divid-

pp. 11ff. It has since become widely accepted. The very early date given by von Rad to this confession of faith and the conclusions that he has drawn from it with regard to the composition of the Pentateuch have recently been severely criticised. For the date, see L. Rost, 'Das kleine geschichtliche Credo', *Das kleine Credo und andere Studien zum Alten Testament*, Heidelberg, 1965, pp. 11–25; for the problem of the Pentateuch, see A. Weiser, *Einleitung in das Alte Testament*,[5] 1963, pp. 81 ff; C. H. W. Brekelmand, 'Het "historische Credo" van Israël', *Tijdschrift voor Theologie*, 3 (1963), pp. 1–10; C. Carmichael, 'A New View of the Origin of the Deuteronomic Credo', *VT*, 19 (1969), pp. 273–289.*

ed as a whole between the Yahwistic and the Elohistic sources.

1. The plots made by the sons of Israel (J) or of Jacob (E) against Joseph, who is defended by Judah (J) or Reuben (E) and is sold to the Ishmaelites (J) or carried off by the Midianites (E).

2. Joseph's early period in Egypt as the slave of an anonymous Egyptian who has him put in prison when his wife denounces him (J) or as the slave of Potiphar, the commander of the guard, who puts him in charge of the prisoners (E).

3. Joseph's promotion by Pharaoh, who makes him the governor or administrator of the whole land of Egypt (J) or who appoints him chancellor or lord of his household (E).

4. The first journey during the famine into Egypt made by the sons of Israel (J) or of Jacob (E), whom Joseph recognises, but whom he pretends to accuse of coming to explore the country (J) and of being spies (E).

5. The return to Canaan on the part of Joseph's brothers, who find in their sacks at one stage of the journey (J) or on their arrival (E), the money that they had brought to buy corn.

6. The second journey into Egypt and the meeting between Joseph and his brothers at which he makes himself known to them and they are invited by Pharaoh (J) or by Joseph himself (E) to settle in Egypt with their father (E).

7. The dying Jacob's blessing of Ephraim and Manasseh (JE).

8. Jacob's funeral (JE).

There is general agreement among scholars that the Yahwist was responsible for the stories of the woman's attempt to seduce Joseph (Gen 39:7–20), of Judah's intervention and of Joseph's cup in Benjamin's sack (Gen 43–44) and for the description of Joseph's agrarian policy (Gen 47:13–26). Joseph's interpretation of the dreams of Pharaoh's officials and of Pharaoh himself (40:2–41:32), the account of Joseph's generous behaviour towards his brothers after the death of Jacob and the story of Joseph's own death (Gen 50:15–26) are attributed to the Elohist.

Apart from these accounts, however, there is little agreement among the critics as to how the text should be divided between the two sources. There is, moreover, less and less certainty with regard to this division as the story of Joseph proceeds. It is only at the beginning of the story that the two sources can be precisely distinguished by clear criteria – the Yahwistic elements by means of the words Israel, Judah and the Ishmaelites, and the Elohistic elements by the terms Jacob, Reuben and the Midianites.[3] After

---

[3] The validity of this criterion has been disputed recently by M. Anbar, 'Changement des noms des tribus nomades dans la relation d'un même événement', *Bib*, 49 (1968), pp. 221–232. The parallels given do not, however. explain the two different accounts of Joseph's abduction by the Midianites in Gen 37:21, 25aα, 28a, 29–30, 36 and of the sale to the Ishmaelites, Gen 25aβ–27, 28b and 39:1bβ.

Gen 37, it is impossible to divide all the elements of the text between two 'documents', J and E, without encountering almost insuperable difficulties.[4] Arbitrary separation of this kind has rightly been criticised[5] and it is clear that a purely 'documentary' approach to the story of Joseph is not practicable and leads to very doubtful conclusions. It is one of the most striking instances in the whole of the Pentateuch of a purely 'documentary' form of literary criticism ending in failure.[6] Those scholars who favour this approach have themselves insisted on the artistic way in which these 'documents' have been 'combined' to form a continuous narrative. This unity is in striking contrast with the very fragmented stories of Abraham and of Jacob, to say nothing of the story of Isaac. The priestly editor was responsible for making a 'story of Jacob' (Gen 37:2), following a 'story of Isaac' (Gen 27:19) and ending with the death of Jacob (Gen 49:29–33) and his burial in the cave at Machpelah (Gen 50:12–13). The story of Joseph thus became the last part of the story of the patriarchs. It did not really belong to the patriarchal story, however, and is in fact a new element. It was composed in quite a different way from the stories of Abraham and of Jacob. Unlike them, it is not a cycle into which traditions with different origins were integrated.

Neither is it a free literary composition in which various themes of universal folklore or different popular stories were gathered together – the young brother persecuted by the older brothers, the slave who reaches a high position, the wife who attempts to seduce the young man and so on – which had nothing to do with Joseph or the tribes of Israel.[7] It may have used some of these elements, but only in order to illustrate an already existing tradition – it was known that 'Jacob and his sons went down into Egypt' (Jos 24:4). This tradition and the story of Joseph which develops it were certainly not invented in order to make a connection between the two main themes of the Pentateuch – the patriarchs and the exodus from

---

[4] M. Noth, *Überlieferungsgeschichte*, pp. 29–31, 38; Noth has only reached this conclusion by accepting numerous editorial corrections; he has not ventured to suggest anything for Gen 48, *ibid.*, p. 38, note 136. H. Cazelles, 'Pentateuque', *DBS*, VII, 1966, col. 780 and 804, has suggested a different division and admits that the editor JE has harmonised a great deal.

[5] W. Rudolph, 'Die Josephsgeschichte', at the end of P. Volz and W. Rudolph, *Der Elohist als Erzähler. Ein Irrweg der Pentateuchkritik?*, Giessen, 1933. S. Mowinckel agrees with him; see his *Erwägungen zur Pentateuchquellenfrage*, Trondheim, 1964, pp. 61–63.

[6] R. N. Whybray, *VT*, 18 (1968), pp. 522–528.

[7] See H. Gunkel, *ZDMG*, 76 (1922), pp. 55–71; H. Gressmann, *Eucharistèrion Gunkel*, pp. 1–55. The story of Potiphar's wife may, some scholars believe, have been influenced by the 'Story of Two Brothers' found on an Egyptian papyrus of the end of the thirteenth century B.C.; see G. Lefèbvre, *Romans et contes égyptiens*, Paris, 1949, pp. 136–158; *ANET*, pp. 23–25. In this story, the younger brother is approached with a proposal of adultery by his sister-in-law, who falsely accuses him to her husband when she is rejected. There is no doubt that the situations are very similar, but the analogy is confined to the initial theme. The Egyptian story soon enters the realm of magic and marvellous adventure.

Egypt.[8] As we have seen, the story of Joseph leaves a gap between these two themes, a gap which is really the sojourn in Egypt.

The story of Joseph, then, is not a carefully constructed combination of two 'documents'. It is the work of a single author who worked with previously existing traditions. His genius, his psychological understanding, his sense of local colour, his exotic taste, his wisdom and his religious purpose are all found not only in the texts attributed to E, but also in those ascribed to J. The recent praiseworthy attempt to derive a Yahwistic 'theology' and an Elohistic 'theology' from this supposed division of the text could only lead to very arbitrary results.[9] This story, which is in striking contrast with the other patriarchal stories and with all the other narratives in the Pentateuch, originally existed independently and, what is more, as a written work, before it was incorporated into the Yahwistic narrative.[10]

II. LITERARY GENRE AND DATE OF COMPOSITION

Seen from the literary point of view, this story has often been called a 'novel' or a 'tale' and it cannot be denied that it has many of the characteristics of this literary form. It has a clear plot which is gradually unravelled from the beginning when the brothers scheme to get rid of their father's favourite, to the end when they are forgiven. It has a hero, Joseph. whose adventures are narrated from youth until death in a series of dramatic episodes which keep the reader in suspense – Joseph is carried off, lives as a slave and is raised to a position of high honour. His brothers go twice to Egypt and meet him and the story culminates in the great scene when the hero makes himself known to them. It does not make use of the device of divine intervention to further the action, but appeals to human sentiments such as the hostility of the brothers, Jacob's tender feelings for Joseph and Benjamin and Joseph's generosity. Dialogue is used frequently and in these scenes actors with clearly-drawn features confront each other and reveal themselves. The story takes those who read it – or listen to it – from the pasture of Canaan to the land of Egypt and shows them something of its strange customs, its complicated administration, its court life and the officials, magicians and wise men in the service of the great Pharaoh. It is

[8] See M. Noth, *Überlieferungsgeschichte*, pp. 226–232; G. Fohrer, *Geschichte der israelitischen Religion*, Berlin, 1969, p. 58.
[9] L. Ruppert, *Die Josephserzählung der Genesis, op. cit.*, note 1; O. Eissfeldt has expressed certain reservations in *TLZ*, 91 (1966), col. 820–821; see also N. Lohfink, *Bib*, 49 (1968), pp. 298–302.
[10] W. Rudolph, *op. cit.*, pp. 180–183, finds further evidence of this prior existence in the use of divine names; see also A. Jepsen, 'Zur Überlieferungsgeschichte der Vätergestalten', *Festschrift Alt*, Leipzig, 1954, pp. 139–155, cf. p. 154.

undoubtedly a polished work of art, but this does not mean that everything in it was invented by the author. On the contrary, whatever part was played in its composition by the literary genius of the writer, the important question remains – was this an 'historical' novel?

Certainly its aim was not simply to entertain the listeners. Its principal purpose was didactic. It is related to the ancient wisdom literature.[11] Joseph's forbearance is echoed, for example, in Prov 14:29; 15:18, his readiness to forget injuries in Prov 24:29 and his chastity can be compared with the theme of the 'alien woman' in the Books of Wisdom. All these characteristics made Joseph a model to be imitated. It is above all Joseph's humility which leads him to high honour (see Prov 15:33; 22:4) and humility is founded in the fear of God (see Prov 15:33). Above all, Joseph 'fears God' (Gen 42:18), which means that he submits to the will of God. Despite its profane appearance and its links with Eastern wisdom, this ancient Israelite wisdom is above all religious. 'Yahweh guides a man's steps', Prov 20:24 declares and, although God neither appears nor speaks in the story of Joseph, as he does in the stories of the patriarchs, he guides everything that happens.

The key to this long narrative is to be found in Gen 45:8: 'It was not you who sent me here' and Gen 50:20: 'The evil you planned to do to me has by God's design been turned to good'. These two texts clearly express the lesson contained implicitly in the story of Joseph. This sapiential teaching is also linked to the history of salvation. The result of the special providence shown by God to Joseph is the establishment of Joseph's brothers in Egypt and it is at the same time a sign and a security that God will continue to guide them. Joseph's last words to his brothers are: 'God will be sure to remember you kindly and take you back from this country to the land that he promised on oath to Abraham, Isaac and Jacob' (Gen 50:24).

The story of Joseph has breadth and grandeur. It reaches a high level of literary perfection with its dramatic sense of situation, its acute psychological understanding of character, its universal wisdom and its exotic flavour. All these qualities mean that it could not have been written before the reign of Solomon. It was, after all, during this period that the wisdom literature of Israel emerged. Israel was most open during Solomon's reign to foreign culture and especially to that of Egypt. Finally, it was at this time that the first great literary work of Israel was written – the story of David's accession to the throne (2 Sam 9–1 Kings 2), a story of comparable quality.

---

[11] G. von Rad, 'Josephsgeschichte' and *Die Josephsgeschichte, op. cit.*, note 1; *ibid., Das erste Buch Mose*, Göttingen, 1953, pp. 379–384. Von Rad's argument has not been seriously affected by the criticisms made by L. Ruppert in *Die Josephserzählung, op. cit.*, note 1, *passim*, or by J. L. Crenshaw, 'Method in Determining Wisdom Influence upon "Historical" Literature', *JBL*, 83 (1969), pp. 129–142, especially pp. 135–137.

III. The Egyptian Character of the Story

There is, however, another important aspect of the story of Joseph. On the one hand, it is an account not of almost contemporary events, but rather of something that happened in the distant past. On the other hand, however, the story takes place almost entirely abroad – in Egypt; indeed it introduces its readers or listeners to that country. Ever since the rise of Egyptology as a serious study, biblical scholars have been fascinated by the Egyptian aspect of the story of Joseph and the interest has not diminished in recent years.[12] Scholars have continued to examine it in search of proof for the historical value of the story and of a method of dating the arrival of Israel's ancestors in Egypt. As we shall see, the Egyptian character of the story of Joseph merely confirms the date of its composition.

1. The position of Joseph

The Bible does not tell us the name of the pharaoh who took Joseph into his service and welcomed his brothers. This does not mean, however, that the whole story was invented, since the pharaoh who figures in the account of the exodus is referred to only by his title. It should also be noted in this context that this title, which means 'the great house' and was originally applied to the palace and its departments, was only used to designate the sovereign himself from the reign of Thut-mose III onwards.[13]

The Semitic name, Joseph, and the Egyptian name that Joseph was given (Zaphenath-paneah; Gen 41:45) are not found in any Egyptian text. As for his position in Egyptian society, according to the Bible Joseph was the first man in the country after the pharaoh, with authority over all the people and the whole country (see Gen 41:39–44; 45:8). For a long time, it was generally believed that Joseph was therefore the pharaoh's vizier. His name does not, however, appear among the very many names of viziers known to us. It has been suggested that, like other high-ranking persons, he might have been given two Egyptian names and that he concealed himself under the name of one of the viziers known to us. This is theoretically possible as a

[12] J. M. A. Janssen, *JEOL*, 14 (1955–1956), pp. 63–72; J. Vergote, *Joseph en Egypte*. From the Egyptological point of view, this book was acclaimed almost without reservation by S. Morenz, *TLZ*, 84 (1959), col 401–416; K. A. Kitchen, *JEA*, 47 (1961), pp. 158–164; serious reservations were expressed, however, by B. Couroyer, *RB*, 66 (1959), pp. 582–594; strong objections were raised by S. Herrmann, *TLZ*, 85 (1960), col 827–830 and *ZAS*, 91 (1964), pp. 63–79; W. Helck, *Die Beziehungen Ägyptens zur Vorderaisen im 3. und 2. Jahrtausend v. Chr.*, Wiesbaden, 1962, pp. 385, 612. For the opinion of exegetes, see especially O. Eissfeldt's measured criticism, *OLZ*, 55 (1960), col 39–45.
[13] The two first references will be found in *Urkunden*, IV, 1248, 16 and 1265, 11; see E. Hornung, *MDAI*, 15 (1957), p. 122.

solution to the problem, but it is also an admission of ignorance. What is more, the biblical description of Joseph's position only partly coincides with the status and functions of the vizier in Egyptian society.[14] Joseph, the Bible tells us, had authority over the whole land of Egypt, but, from 1500 until 850 B.C. at least, there were almost always two viziers, one for the south and the other for the north. Joseph was the holder of the royal seal (Gen 41:42), but the vizier shared this privilege with officials of lower rank. The only administrative tasks carried out by Joseph that are described in any detail in the Bible are concerned with the storing of corn in the royal granaries, the distribution of wheat and the imposition of taxes on agricultural products (Gen 41:34–36; 47:13–26), but these functions were fulfilled in Egypt by the inspector of granaries.[15] Joseph, on the other hand, was appointed to the pharaoh's house as his 'chancellor' (Gen 41:40) or 'lord of all his household' (Gen 45:8) and this office might correspond to the Egyptian title of administrator of the crown possessions. The relationship between this function and those of the vizier is not clear,[16] but Joseph's office might also correspond to some extent to the Israelite position of *ser 'al–habbayith*, which later became that of prime minister, but at the time of Solomon was simply that of superintendent of the royal palace and estate.[17] It is difficult not to believe that the author of the story of Joseph wanted to glorify his hero and to make him the most important person in Egypt after the pharaoh – this is what the vizier, of course, was – with the result that he added to his narrative characteristics which would correspond individually to one or other real position in Egyptian society, but which would collectively form an unreal figure.

This does not, however, mean that Joseph might not have been able to reach a position which would have enabled him to carry out high functions in Egypt, as indeed other Semites did. The pharaohs of the Middle Kingdom employed Asiatic officials.[18] These must have been more numerous during the Hyksos period, but we have very little information about this period generally. We do at least know that they employed as treasurer a Semite called Hûr, whose sphere of activity extended from the Sudan as far as southern Palestine.[19] Semites were also employed in the service of the pharaohs of the Late Kingdom.[20] Some were equerries and

[14] See J. Vergote, *Joseph en Egypte*, pp. 102–114; J. M. A. Janssen, *Chr. Eg.*, 26 (1951), pp. 59–62; W. A. Ward, 'The Egyptian Office of Joseph', *JSS*, 5 (1960), pp. 144–150.

[15] G. Steindorff and K. C. Seele, *When Egypt Ruled the East,*[2] Chicago, 1957, p. 88.

[16] For this function, see W. Helck, *Der Einfluß der Militärführer in der 18. ägyptischen Dynastie*, Hildesheim, 1964, pp. 43–54.

[17] R. de Vaux. *Institutions*, pp. 125, 129–130.

[18] W. Helck, *Die Beziehungen Ägyptens, op. cit.*, p. 82.

[19] H. Stock, *Studien zur Geschichte und Archäologie der 13. bis 17. Dynastie Ägyptens*, Glückstadt, 1955, p. 68.

[20] J. M. A. Janssen, 'Fonctionnaires sémites au service de l'Egypte', *Chr. Eg.*, 26 (1951), pp.

others held the position of major-domo and cup-bearer especially during the Nineteenth and Twentieth Dynasties, but even as early as the reign of Thut-mose III. They were entrusted with confidential missions and tasks such as the supervision of officials and the undertaking of delicate legal enquiries, as in the case of the harem plot during the reign of Ramses III.

Some of these Semites who rose to a high position in the Egyptian hierarchy are fairly well known to us. A tomb discovered at Tell el–'Amārna was that of a man called Tûtu,[21] who acquired a great number of titles during the reign of Amen-hotep IV (Akh-en-Aten) – he became the first servant of the king in the Temple of Aten, the first servant of the king in the boat, the inspector of all the king's undertakings, the inspector of the treasure of the Temple of Amarna and finally the 'highest mouth' in the whole country. This last title meant that he had total authority in the special tasks that he was given and was responsible only to the pharaoh. It is one of the titles that Joseph is supposed to have had. The wall paintings on the tomb at Tell el–'Amārna show Tûtu's appointment by the pharaoh, who is putting the golden necklace of office around his neck; they also show him leaving the palace, getting into his chariot and riding off as the people prostrate themselves before him in acclamation. This is altogether an excellent illustration of what must have taken place when Joseph was appointed chancellor in Egypt, in charge of the pharaoh's household (Gen 41:41–43). Similar scenes are illustrated elsewhere, but what is particularly interesting in this case is that the person whom the pharaoh is honouring is a Semite. In his biographical inscription Tûtu himself says,[22] 'I was the "highest mouth" in the whole country, in expeditions, works and undertakings and for all people, living and dead. As for messengers from foreign countries, I took all their words to the palace, where I was every day. I went out to meet them as the king's representative invested with his majesty's authority'. This text enables us to identify this Tûtu with the senior official called Dûdu in the Amarna letters, whose name was certainly Semitic (Dôd).[23] Aziru of Amurru wrote twice to Dûdu, calling him his lord and father, and asking him to plead on his behalf with the pharaoh. He seems, moreover, to have benefited from Dûdu's intervention when he was obliged to stay in Egypt. Another Semite, Yanhamu, fulfilled several important functions in Palestine at the same period. He is frequently mentioned in the Amarna letters and it would seem that his special task was the administration of the royal granaries.[24]

50–62; W. Helck, *Die Beziehungen Ägyptens, op. cit.*, pp. 369–371, 385–386.
[21] N. de G. Davies, *The Rock Tombs of El Amarna*, VI, London, 1908, pp. 7–15, plates XIX-XX.
[22] *ibid.*, p. 27.
[23] *EA*, 158, 164, 167, 169.
[24] *EA*, 85, 22 ff; 86, 15–16; see also W. Helck, *Die Beziehungen Ägyptens, op. cit.*, p. 259.

During the reigns of Ramses II and Seti II, foreigners, including Semites, settled in the Fayum and were given an Egyptian education there to equip them, if the need arose, to carry out official functions in the country.[25] One of them, Ben-Azen, came originally from Ziribashani in northern Transjordan. He was given two Egyptian names, Ramses-em-per-Re, which must have been given to him by Ramses II, and Meri-ûnu. During the reigns of Ramses II and then during that of Mer-ne-Ptah, he was first herald, first major-domo, first cup-bearer of the royal beer and fan-bearer at the king's right hand. Together with the vizier, he had the task of fitting out Mer-ne-Ptah's tomb.[26]

Later, during the troubled period at the end of the Nineteenth Dynasty round about 1200 B.C., full power in Egypt was in the hands of a Syrian. The whole affair is very obscure, but according to the Harris papyrus,[27] before Seth-nekhte, the founder of the twentieth dynasty and the father of Ramses III, came to the throne, a 'Syrian' or *Huru* called Irsu made himself prince and subjected the whole country to his rule. The name seems to have meant 'the one who made himself' and it might have been a pseudonym, used in a disparaging sense, that was given to him by others. He has been identified with Siptah, the last pharaoh of the Nineteenth Dynasty, who might have been an Asiatic employed at first in the service of the court.[28] Another suggestion is that Irsu was a usurper who ruled during an interregnum between the Nineteenth and the Twentieth Dynasties.[29] Most probably, however,[30] the nickname Irsu denotes the 'great chamberlain of all the country', Bay, who on two inscriptions is given the title 'the one who sets the king on the throne of his father'. Bay was effectively the ruler of the country during the first few years of Siptah's reign, while Siptah was still a child, and it is possible that he came originally from Palestine.

[25] S. Sauneron and J. Yoyotte, 'Traces d'établissements asiatiques en Moyenne Egypte sous Ramsès II', *Revue d'Egyptologie*, 7 (1951), pp. 67–70.
[26] A. Rowe, 'Stelae of the Semite Ben-Azen'. *ASAE*, 40 (1940), pp. 45–46; J. Capart, 'Un grand personnage palestinien de la cour de Merneptah', *Chr. Eg.*, 11 (1936), pp. 32–38; J. Cerný, *Ostraca hiératiques (Catalogue Général du Musée du Caire)*, I, 1935, No. 25504; S. Sauneron and J. Yoyotte, *op. cit.*, p. 68.
[27] *ANET*, p. 260a. The Harris papyrus dates from the end of Ramses III's reign.
[28] J. von Beckerath, *Tanis und Theben*, Glückstadt, 1951, pp. 76–79; W. Helck, 'Zur Geschichte der 19. und 20. Dynastien', *ZDMG*, 105 (1955), pp. 27–52, especially pp. 44ff; J. von Beckerath, 'Die Reihenfolge der letzten Könige der 19. Dynastie', *ZDMG*, 106 (1956), pp. 241–251.
[29] See J. A. Wilson, *ANET*, p. 260a. Following this hypothesis, A. Malamat has suggested that Irsu was the oppressor mentioned in Judges 3:7–11; see his article 'Cushan Rishathaim and the Decline of the Near East about 1200 B.C.', *JNES*, 13 (1954), pp. 231–242.
[30] This is the last opinion, suggested by A. Gardiner, 'Only One King Siptah and Twosre not his Wife', *JEA*, 44 (1958), pp. 12–22, especially p. 21; J. von Beckerath, 'Queen Twosre as Guardian of Siptah', *JEA*, 48 (1962), pp. 70–74; R. O. Faulkner, 'From the Inception of the Nineteenth Dynasty to the Death of Ramesses III', *CAH*, II, XXIII, 1966, pp. 26–27.

It is clear from these examples that Joseph's promotion to a high position was historically possible and that there are other parallel cases in the Ancient Near East. All the same, these parallels are very diverse and are spread over a period of some five centuries and they do not allow us to be precise about the functions that Joseph fulfilled in Egypt nor about the date.

2. The political and geographical framework

We may, however, continue our search in another direction. The Egyptian character of the story of Joseph is particularly striking. It is evident in the political situation presupposed in the story, in the descriptions of Egyptian customs and institutions and in the use of Egyptian words and personal names. Can it be used to help us to determine the date of Joseph himself or at least the period when his story was edited? Recent attempts have been made to show that all this evidence takes us back to the Nineteenth Dynasty and especially to the reign of Ramses II. It has also been concluded that the author of the Joseph story might have been Moses and that Joseph himself lived during the Eighteenth Dynasty,[31] but in my opinion these conclusions are unacceptable.

It is certain that the author had a very wide knowledge of Egypt; it is equally certain from what we have seen with regard to Joseph's position and functions in Egyptian society, that his knowledge was not exact and he was not an eyewitness. In other words, he was not writing in Egypt for Egyptians. He wrote from the vantage-point of a Palestinian who was fascinated by his country's powerful neighbour. One detail stands out – in the pharaoh's dream the author refers to the ears of corn scorched by the east wind (Gen 41:23, 27). An Egyptian author would have spoken of the south wind. Some of the titles can be explained just as well and perhaps even better by Semitic usage than by Egyptian usage. As we have seen, Joseph's function as 'chancellor' or 'lord of the household' (Gen 41:40; 45:8) might be a reflection of the Israelite title *'ăśer 'al-habbayith*, which is used elsewhere in the Joseph story in its original sense – in Gen 39:4 (Joseph in the Egyptian's house) and Gen 43:16 and 44:1, 4 (Joseph's 'chamberlain'). In the same way, instead of looking for an Egyptian equivalent for *śar hattabahîm*, the 'commander of the guard' (Gen 37:36; 39:1; 40:3 ff; 41:10, 12), it is perhaps better to compare this title with another of which there is a good deal of evidence in Mesopotamia and in the Bible itself. This is *rabh hattabahîm*, which is found seven times in 2 Kings 25:8–20 and seventeen times in Jer 39; 40; 41 and 42. In the Genesis story of Joseph itself, Joseph says that he was appointed lord (*'adhôn*) of all Pharaoh's household and administrator (*môšel*)

[31] J. Vergote, *Joseph en Egypte*, conclusions, pp. 203–213.

of the whole land. There is therefore no need to look for close Egyptian counterparts. The Hebrew terms used are not precise, but they indicate that Joseph had great power in Egypt, although he was not equal to the pharaoh.

As for the geographical framework within which the Joseph story takes place, we are first of all told that the sons of Jacob settled in the land of Goshen (Gen 45:10; 46:28–29; 47:1 etc.). This place name is not found in any Egyptian text and it is probably not Egyptian, but Semitic. There was a town called Goshen (Jos 15:51) and a land of Goshen (Jos 10:41; 11:16) in the south of the hill country of Judah. This is transcribed in the Septuagint as Gesem[32] and in two texts it is called more precisely 'Gesem of Arabia' (Gen 45:10; 46:34). During the Graeco-Roman period, the nome of Arabia was one of the nomes of the eastern Delta, with its capital at Faqus. In the third reference to this place in the Joseph story (Gen 46:28–29), the Septuagint has replaced Goshen by Herōopolis, which is the Greek name for Pithom. The name Pithom is used in the Bohairic version and it also appears in Exod 1:11. Pithom means the temple of Atum (Pr-Itm) and it is the religious name of Teku, which has been located at Tell el-Maskhûtah. [33] These details taken from different versions of the Old Testament only reflect, of course, the tradition prevalent in the Diaspora in Egypt, but they are interesting in this context because they are in agreement with the data given at the beginning of Exodus and they are probably accurate. Pithom-Teku is situated at the mouth of the Wādi Tumilāt near the Bitter Lakes, not far from the modern Ismailia and close to the ancient frontier of Egypt, in a district that was attractive and favourable to the semi-nomadic herdsmen of the Sinai and from even farther afield. It is clear from a model letter which is supposed to have been sent by an official serving on the frontier during the eighth year of Mer-ne-Ptah's reign that a number of semi-nomadic people certainly came there. According to this letter, the Egyptians had 'finished letting the Bedouin tribes of Edom (the Shasu) pass the Fortress of Mer-ne-Ptah . . . which is in Tjeku (Teku), to the pools of Per-Atum (Pithom) . . . which are in Tjeku (Teku), to keep them alive and to keep their cattle alive'.[34] The land of Goshen can therefore be identified

[32] This Greek form was probably influenced by the name Geshem the Arab, the king of Kedar and Nehemiah's contemporary (Neh 2:19; 6:1, 2). This name has been found on a silver bowl discovered at Tell el-Maskhûtah-Pithom (see below); see I. Rabinowitz, JNES, 15 (1956), pp. 5–6; W. F. Albright, BASOR, 140 (Dec. 1955), p. 31.

[33] W. Helck, 'Ṯkw und die Ramses-Stadt', VT, 15 (1965), pp. 35–48, who criticises D. B. Redford, 'Exodus I, 11', ibid., 13 (1963), pp. 401–418; H. Cazelles and J. Leclant, 'Pithom', DBS, VIII, 1967, col 1–6. The biblical Pithom is not and cannot be the Heliopolis near Cairo, as suggested by E. P. Uphill, 'Pithom and Raamses: Their Location and Significance', JNES, 27 (1968), pp. 291–316; 29 (1969), pp. 15–39.

[34] ANET, p. 259a; R. A. Caminos, Late Egyptian Miscellanies, London, 1954, pp. 293–296; W. Helck, Die Beziehungen Ägyptens, op. cit., pp. 38–40.

beyond doubt with the Wādi Tumilāt or at least with its eastern half. In referring to the 'Land of Rameses' (Gen 47:11), instead of to the land of Goshen, then, the priestly editor was allowing himself to be inspired by Exod 1:11 and was thus committing an anachronism.

The proximity of the place where Joseph's brothers settled to the usual residence of the pharaoh is presupposed in the biblical account (see especially Gen 45:10 and 46:28–29 compared with 47:1). The Hyksos, it will be remembered, had their capital in the Delta at Avarus (Tanis). During the Eighteenth Dynasty the capital was Thebes in Upper Egypt, at least until the Amarna period, and Amarna was a long way from the Delta. At the beginning of the Nineteenth Dynasty, Ramses II had a new capital built in the Delta, Pi-Ramses, probably at Qantir, south of Tanus. It was here that the pharaohs of the Nineteenth and Twentieth Dynasties lived, at least until the time of Ramses III.[35] During the Twenty-first Dynasty, the capital was Tanis. During the Twenty-second dynasty it was Bubastis, and during the Twenty-third Dynasty it was once again Tanis. If this aspect only of the problem is borne in mind, together with the historicity of the story of Joseph, then we must regard the Hyksos period as possible for the Joseph story and the Eighteenth Dynasty as impossible. If, on the other hand, the period of the editing of the Joseph story is considered, then any date from the time of Ramses II onwards would be possible.

3. The dreams

We must now turn to the question of the Egyptian customs and institutions in the story of Joseph. All the people of the Ancient Near East attached a very great importance to dreams and their interpretation.[36] We have, for Egypt especially, a large number of accounts of dreams[37] and guides for their interpretation from the Middle Kingdom[38] until the Roman period.[39] The dreams of the pharaoh and his officials (Gen 40–41)

[35] The pharaohs had several residences and did not always live at Thebes; see W. Helck, Zur Verwaltung des Mittleren und Neuen Reiches, Leiden, 1958, pp. 1-9.

[36] A. L. Oppenheim, The Interpretation of Dreams in the Ancient Near East, with a Translation of an Assyrian Dream-Book (Transactions of the American Philosophical Society, New Series, 46, 3), Philadelphia, 1956; Les songes et leur interprétation (Sources Orientales), a symposium published in Paris, 1959.

[37] S. Sauneron, Les songes et leur interprétation dans l'Egypte ancienne, in the symposium noted above, pp. 17–61.

[38] A. H. Gardiner, Hieratic Papyri in the British Museum, III, Chester Beatty Gift, I, Text, London, 1935, pp. 9–23. The text may date from the Middle Kingdom, but the papyrus dates from the thirteenth century B.C.

[39] A. Volten, Demotische Traumdeutung, Copenhagen, 1942.

have a very strong Egyptian flavour. The officials have dreams that are closely related to their functions at court. The pharaoh dreams first of cows feeding among the rushes on the banks of the Nile and the succession of fat cows and thin cows is clearly connected with the flooding of the river. It has even been suggested that the word used for this food of rushes, *ăhû*, is Egyptian, but the form shows that the word entered western Semitic at a very early stage, perhaps during the third millennium.[40] There is evidence of its existence in Ugaritic *('ah)* and it became completely adopted in Hebrew, since it is also found in Job 8:11. It also entered Aramaci.[41] As far as the dreams of the full and ripe ears of corn and those which were meagre and scorched by the wind, it will be recalled that the Egyptians attributed the variations in the level of the waters of the Nile and therefore the floods and the drought to the changes in the wind. According to the prophecy of Nefer-rohu,[42] 'the rivers of Egypt are empty . . . The south wind will oppose the north wind'. The south wind is the wind which burns and dries everything up in Egypt, but, as we have seen, the author of the biblical account replaced it with the east wind.[44]

The pharaoh consulted *har'tummîm* and 'wise men' for the interpretation of his dreams (Gen 41:8, 24). The word *har 'tôm* comes from the Egyptian[45] and meant 'chief reader' in Egypt. These members of the clergy were trained in the House of Life where they received a higher education than the scribes. They were educated scribes or 'wise men'. The second Hebrew term used in these texts does not refer to a different category of men, but merely explains the first term. These wise men were trained to interpret dreams and to study magicians' books of spells. In certain Egyptian texts, they figure as magicians. It is in this sense that the word is used in Ex 7:11, 22; 8:3, 14, 15; 9:11, the stories of the plagues of Egypt. The word was adopted by Hebrew and it is also used in Dan 1:20; 2:22. It is also found in Assyrian, where it occurs as *hartibi*. This form is closer to the original than the Hebrew form. In one Assyrian text, three *hartibi* with Egyptian names and described as 'Egyptian scribes' are mentioned.[46]

---

[40] J. Vergote, *op. cit.*, pp. 59–66; T. O. Lambdin, *JAOS*, 73 (1953), p. 146.

[41] The Inscriptions of Sfire, I, 28–29; *KAI*, No. 222.

[42] *ANET*, 445a.

[43] See G. H. Stricker, *De overstroming van de Nijl*, Leiden, 1956, especially p. 16.

[44] It is interesting to note that the Septuagint, which was written in Egypt, does not mention the east wind (Gen. 41:6, 23, 27) and simply says that the ears of corn were *anemophthoroi*, 'destroyed by the wind'; in Ex 10:13 (the plague of locusts) and 14:21 (crossing of the sea) the Septuagint has *notos*, the south wind, instead of east wind.

[45] See J. Vergote, *Joseph en Egypte*, *op. cit.*, pp. 80–84.

[46] See A. L. Oppenheim, *op. cit.*, note 36, p. 238.

4. The famine and agrarian policy

Joseph interpreted the pharaoh's dreams as the announcement of a famine. This scourge struck Egypt when the flooding of the Nile was not sufficient or when it did not come in time.[47] One non-biblical text is of special interest in this context. A decree, which it is believed Djoser, a pharaoh of the Third Dynasty, promulgated after a famine lasting seven years, is inscribed on a stele found on the island of Sehet, between Elephantine and the first Nile cataract.[48] It is, however, certain that this inscription dates back to the Ptolemaic period. It may perhaps be a pseudonymous inscription made by Ptolemy V in 187 B.C. to mark the return to the crown of the southern provinces which the pharaoh gives as an appanage to the god Khnum, the lord of the cataract and of the inundation of the Nile. Since this inscription was found in a place quite near to Elephantine, where there was a Jewish colony, it has been suggested, as a hypothesis, that this reference to a famine lasting seven years – unique in Egyptian literature – was inspired by the story of Joseph. It is also possible that the text is a reflection of an Egyptian tradition of seven years of drought, of which there is no other textual evidence. Finally, it is also possible that this figure, both in the Bible and in the inscription of Sehel, is connected with a tradition common to the whole of the Ancient Near East, since there are references to seven lean years both in Mesopotamia and at Ugarit.[49]

Joseph's advice to the pharaoh was to prepare for the famine by setting aside one fifth of the harvest in the whole country in the form of a tax during the good years and storing the corn in the royal granaries (Gen 41:34–36). When the famine came, Joseph distributed the corn in exchange for money, then for livestock and finally for land. As a result of this policy, all the land became the property of the pharaoh and all the people became his serfs. The land was leased out and the people had to give a fifth of their crop to the pharaoh. Only the priests were exempt from this. They were able to keep their land and they received an allowance from the pharaoh. What is more, 'Joseph made a statute' of this which is 'still in force today' (Gen 47:13–26). However important it may be to substantiate these facts by reference to Egyptian texts, it is not possible to do so, at least as far as the details which might be most useful to us in establishing a date for Joseph or for the editing of the Joseph story are concerned. This is simply because the measures taken by Joseph are said to be 'still in force today'. There is enough evidence that the pharaoh regarded himself as the owner of the whole land of Egypt. It is possible that the crown confiscated the estates of all the noble families at the beginning of the Eighteenth Dynasty, when the Hyksos had

---

[47] See J. Vandier, La famine dans l'Egypte ancienne, Cairo, 1936.

[48] ANET, pp. 31–32; see especially P. Barguet, La stèle de la famine à Séhel, Cairo, 1953.

[49] C. H. Gordon, 'Sabbatical Cycle or Seasonal Pattern?' Orientalia, 22 (1953), pp. 79–81.

been expelled.[50] There are also signs that the priests were exempted, at least in theory. During the Roman period, Diodorus of Sicily, I 73, said that the whole land of Egypt was divided into three lots – the lands of the priests, the pharaoh's lands and the military fiefs. This was undoubtedly the situation in general, but the reality seems to have been very much more complex.[51] The tax of a fifth does not appear in any Egyptian document. It differed according to the period, the type of farming and the class of land. Royal granaries had existed since the very beginning of Egyptian history. The measures taken to prevent or to relieve famine are mentioned in certain texts, but these are not the same as those attributed to Joseph. On the contrary, they refer to free distribution of corn, loans of grain between different towns and exemptions from taxes.[52]

Although we cannot give a precise date to the story of Joseph on the basis of this description of the Egyptian land system, it cannot be denied that the essential aspects of the outline are correct. Two facts that are established beyond doubt, for example, are the sovereign right of the pharaoh over the whole land and the extent of the crown domains and of those belonging to the priests, between them covering almost the whole of the land of Egypt. The most striking characteristic of this system was 'that the principal landowners were institutions and that the right of private ownership was apparently of secondary importance and was indeed hardly developed at all.'[53]

The Israelites must have been struck by the difference between the situation in Egypt and that in their own country, where the usual system was that of family ownership, and this undoubtedly explains why the author of the story of Joseph was so interested. In claiming that Joseph was responsible for introducing measures which in fact originated in Egypt, the author was obviously exalting his hero, one of the ancestors of his people. On the other hand, however, the fact that he seems to have regarded the Egyptian land system as better and to have approved of the seizing of land and the reduction of the people to serfdom certainly requires an explanation. This is especially necessary because the same measures were condemned by Samuel, although it is clear that these measures were less extreme. In his address to the people of Israel when they asked for a king, Samuel said: 'He will take the best of your fields, of your vineyards and olive groves and

[50] G. Steindorff and K. Seele, *When Egypt Ruled the East*,[2] Chicago, 1957, p. 88, with reference to the Joseph story.

[51] See A. Gardiner, *The Wilbour Papyrus, II, Commentary*, Oxford, 1948, conclusions, pp. 202 ff; W. Helck, *Zur Verwaltung des Mittleren und Neuen Reiches*, Leiden, 1958, pp. 89–170 and *Materialien zur Wirtschaftsgechichte des Neuen Reichs (Akademie der Wissenschaften und der Literatur in Mainz, Abhandlungen)*, 1960 ff.

[52] J. Vandier, *La famine dans l'Egypte ancienne, op. cit.*, note 47, pp. 55–56.

[53] W. Helck, *Materialien*, I, *op. cit.*, p. 7; see also II, p. 237 ff.

give them to his officials. He will tithe your crops and vineyards to provide for his eunuchs and his officials. He will take the best of your manservants and maidservants, of your cattle and your donkeys and make them work for him. He will tithe your flocks, and you yourselves will become his slaves' (1 Sam 8:13–16). This was commonly done by the Canaanite kings who were Israel's neighbours.[54] If a practice condemned in this early text[55] is recommended in the story of Joseph, it must surely be because the accounts were composed at different times and in different environments. We have already pointed out that the story of Joseph has clear connections with the Wisdom literature, which first emerged in Israel from the reign of Solomon onwards and in the king's circle. While Solomon was on the throne, the kingdom of Israel was moving towards the idea of an empire. The administration was modelled on that of Egypt and more and more land was being added to the crown domains. A system of taxation had been set up to support the king and his household. *Corvée* labour had been instituted to carry out the grandiose programme of building and especially the construction of the temple. The status of the clergy was greatly enhanced by the splendour of the temple. There was a general movement in Israel at this time towards an extension of the part played by the state and it is quite possible that some of the wise men at the court thought that the Egyptian land system was an ideal one.[56]

5. *Personal names and expressions*

Confirmation of the fact that the story of Joseph was written during the reign of Solomon can be found in a study of the Egyptian personal names that figure in the story. In accordance with an established practice,[57] Joseph was given an Egyptian name, Zaphenath-paneah (Gen 41:45). For a long time now this name has correctly been explained by reference to the Egyp-

[54] I. Mendelsohn, 'Samuel's Denunciation of Kingship in the Light of the Akkadian Documents from Ugarit', *BASOR*, 143 (Oct. 1956), pp. 17–22.

[55] See A. Weiser, *Samuel, seine geschichtliche Aufgabe und religiöse Bedeutung*, Göttingen, 1962, pp. 38–42.

[56] It is not necessary, however, to say, as K. H. Henry has in 'Land Tenure in the Old Testament', *PEQ*, 1954, pp. 5–15, cf. p. 13, that the Joseph story reflects an Israelite situation. The Genesis description does not apply to any period in the history of Israel; see A. Alt, 'Der Anteil des Königtums an der sozialen Entwicklung in den Reichen Israel und Juda', *Kleine Schriften*, III, 1959, pp. 348–372; A. Weiser, *Samuel, op. cit.*, note 55, pp. 39–40.

[57] In the list of Asiatic slaves contained in the Brooklyn Papyrus, W. C. Hayes, *A Papyrus of the Late Middle Kingdom*, New York, 1955; *ANET*, pp. 553–554, dating from the thirteenth dynasty, an Egyptian name in each case faces a Semitic name. For a name given by the king, see the Varzy Papyrus: 'the name that the pharaoh his lord gave him when he already had a name of humble servant', quoted by J. Vergote, *op. cit.*, p. 142, note 1.

tian 'The god has said: he will live'. There is no evidence of this name in any Egyptian text in the exact form in which it occurs in the Joseph story, but there is certainly evidence of equivalents containing the name of a special god, as, for example, 'Isis, or Amon, or Osiris etc. has said: he will live'.[58] These names, it should be noted, did not appear until the Twenty-first Dynasty, although there is one case, a doubtful one, in the Twentieth Dynasty. Names of this kind, moreover, were only meaningful when they were given to a newly born child, perhaps as the result of an oracle obtained for the mother before her confinement.[59] Joseph could not have been given the name 'The god has said: he will live' as an adult. It must therefore have been attributed to him by the editor of the story.

Joseph's Egyptian wife was called Asenath (Gen 41:45, 50; 46:20). The name means 'May she belong to Neith' (the goddess) and can be compared with masculine names such as 'May he belong to Amon, or Mut, or Chons' in the middle of the Twentieth Dynasty[60] or with the woman's name 'May she belong to Mut'.[61]

Asenath was the daughter of Potiphera, priest of Heliopolis (Gen 41:45, 50; 46:20) and this name means 'The one whom the (god) Re has given'. It belongs to an onomastic type which was especially frequent from the Twenty-first Dynasty onwards. The biblical name itself, P3–dj–p3–r‛, has been found once on a stele which cannot be earlier than the Twenty-first Dynasty[62] and twice in rather late texts.[63] Most scholars agree that this name is the same as that of Joseph's master Potiphar, though the second is an abbreviated form (Gen 37:36; 39:1).[64]

The three proper names that occur in the story of Joseph, then, belong to onomastic groups which only go back as far as the Twentieth and Twenty-first Dynasties; and the only name of which there is direct evidence in Egyptian texts, Potiphar, goes back no further than the Twenty-first Dynasty, in other words, to the time when Solomon was reigning.

This date is confirmed by the evidence of the expressions and common names of Egyptian origin found in the Joseph story. If the word 'ahu is Egyptian, it was, as we have seen, a very early borrowing.[65] The Egyptian prototype of harôm appeared during the reign of Ramses II. The

[58] H. Ranke, Die ägyptischen Personennamen, Glückstadt, 1935, pp. 409–412.

[59] H. Ranke, 'Zur Namengebung der Ägypter', OLZ, 29 (1926), col. 733–735.

[60] H. Ranke, Die ägyptischen Personnenamen, op. cit., p. 14, 13–17.

[61] H. Ranke, ibid., p. 15, 3.

[62] H. Hamada, 'Stela of Putiphar', ASAE, 39 (1939), pp. 273–276.

[63] References in J. Vergote, op. cit., p. 147.

[64] Y. M. Grintz, however, believes that they are different, 'Potiphar – the Chief Cook', Leshonenu, 20 (1965–1966), pp. 12–17 (in Hebrew, with an English summary). Potiphar, he thinks is a transcription of an Egyptian title (the chief cook) and the equivalent of the Hebrew title śar hattabahîm.

[65] See above, p. 304.

enigmatical exclamation 'abrek' that the people cry before Joseph after he has been invested (Gen 41:43) presents difficulties. It has been explained by reference to the Egyptian ib r.k., 'the heart to you!' (= 'attention!'), which is found three times in texts at the end of the Ramesside period. This is a possible explanation, but one which is regarded as very doubtful by a number of reputable Egyptologists.[66] Another suggestion that has been made is that it is the imperative of the Semitic verb brk, to kneel down, which was borrowed by the Egyptians during the reign of Ramses III. In that case, 'abrek' would mean 'pay homage!',[67] but the addition of aleph as a prefix is not a regular feature of the imperative in Egyptian verbs consisting of three consonants. These two explanations are both in accordance with the date that we have suggested for the story of Joseph.

Going outside Egypt, the Akkadian abarakku has also been suggested.[68] This is the name of the superintendent or major-domo of a private house or the royal palace. The abarakku of the palace was, of course, one of the great men in the state.[69] Joseph's position was very similar to that of the abarakku and after his investiture it is conceivable that he would have been greeted by his new title. The main objection to this thesis is that he would have been addressed by an Egyptian title, although we have suspected the presence of other Semitic titles in the story of Joseph, namely 'ăšèr 'al-habbayith and šar hattabahîm. An even more serious objection is, however, that it is very improbable that there would be any loan words in Hebrew from Mesopotamia and, in particular, from Assyria, especially borrowed titles, before the ninth and eighth centuries B.C., since Israel had no contacts with Assyria before that time.

There is no exact equivalent of the oath taken 'as sure as the pharaoh lives' (Gen 42:15, 16) until the Twenty-second Dynasty.[70] But there is surely no need to look for an Egyptian parallel, since the formula of this oath is certainly Hebrew (cf. 2 Sam 15:21, during the reign of David), the word 'pharaoh' replacing 'my lord the king', to give a touch of local colour.[71]

Joseph lived for a hundred and ten years (Gen 50:22, 26). According to

---

[66] T. O. Lambdin, JAOS, 73 (1953), p. 146; A. Gardiner, 'Minuscula Lexica', Agyptische Studien (Festschrift H. Grapow), ed. O. Forchow), Berlin, 1955, p. 2; J. Vergote, Joseph en Egypte, op. cit., pp. 136–138.

[67] J. Vergote, Joseph en Egypte, op. cit., pp. 138–141; B. Couroyer, RB, 66 (1959), pp. 591–594.

[68] J. D. Croatto, 'Abrek "Intendant" dans Gen. 41.43', VT, 16 (1966), pp. 113–115. This hypothesis had already been suggested by H. de Genouillac, Tablettes Sumériennes Archaiques, Paris, 1909, p. LVIII.

[69] E. Klauber, Assyrisches Beamtentum (Leipziger Semtische Studien, V 3), 1910, pp. 80–87; CAD, I, pp. 31–35.

[70] J. Vergote, Joseph en Egypte, op. cit., p. 165; B. Couroyer, RB, (1959), pp. 589–590.

[71] J. M. A. Janssen, JEOL, 14 (1955–1956), p. 68.

Egyptian texts, this was an ideal age.[72] The great majority of examples date from the Ramesside period (seventeen out of twenty-seven) and of these eleven or twelve occur in the Nineteenth Dynasty. They are mentioned less and less frequently from the Twenty-first Dynasty onwards.

One final feature is worth discussing briefly. The embalming of Jacob (Gen 50:2–3) is another Egyptian touch. The process of mummification took seventy days. This is the figure given in the Joseph story for the period of mourning. The figure given for the embalming process is forty days. This is not, however, borne out by the Egyptian texts and this first half of verse 3 may perhaps be a gloss. In the last verse of the Genesis story of Joseph (Gen 50:26), another custom which was alien to Palestine in its early history is mentioned – the laying of Joseph in a coffin.

6. *Conclusion*

Because of the literary genre and the content of the story of Joseph and above all the Egyptian personal names found in the story, it cannot have been composed before the reign of Solomon. There is, moreover, nothing to indicate that it was written after this time. The author clearly had a very wide knowledge of Egyptian things, but his knowledge was imperfect and he was uncertain about some points. He certainly knew no more than any wise man living in the royal circle in Jerusalem could have known. The Egyptian princess whom Solomon married (1 Kings 3:1) would not have come to Jerusalem without followers and these would have spoken about their country. David's and Solomon's secretary might have been an Egyptian[73] or might have had an Egyptian name.[74] Solomon traded with Egypt (1 Kings 10:29) and his people went to and from Egypt. The flight and the return of Hadad, the Edomite prince (1 Kings 11:17–24) and of Jeroboam after his revolt against Solomon (1 Kings 11:40; 12:1) are extreme examples of relationships between Israel and Egypt which must have been very common.

---

[72] G. Lefebvre, 'L'âge de 110 ans et la vieillesse chez les Egyptiens', *CRAI*, pp. 106–119; J. M. A. Janssen, 'On the Ideal Lifetime of the Egyptians', *Oudheidkundige Mededelingen uit het Rijksmuseum van Oudheiden te Leiden*, No. 31, 1950, pp. 33–43.

[73] R. de Vaux, 'Titres et fonctionnaires égyptiens à la cour de David et de Salomon', *RB*, 48 (1939), pp. 394–400 = Bible et Orient, pp. 192–196.

[74] A. Cody, 'Le titre égyptien et le nom propre du scribe de David', *RB*, 72 (1965), pp. 381–393.

IV. THE HISTORY OF THE TRADITIONS

The author made the story of Joseph into a fine literary work enhanced by many Egyptian touches, but he did not invent it. The question, which is not well posed in terms of written sources, comes ultimately within the scope of the history of traditions.[75] There were two traditions or rather two forms of one oral tradition concerning Joseph in Egypt and these can be distinguished most clearly at the beginning of the story. According to one form of this oral tradition, the sons of Israel plotted against Joseph, who was defended by Judah and sold to the Ishmaelites, who in turn sold him to an anonymous Egyptian. According to the other form, the sons of Jacob plotted against Joseph, who was defended by Reuben and thrown into a well. He was taken out of the well, according to this second form, by the Midianites and sold by them to Potiphar, the commander of the guard. The first tradition of Israel, Judah and the Ishmaelites, can be called 'Yahwistic' and the second tradition of Jacob, Reuben and the Midianites, can be called 'Elohistic' insofar as they are connected with the two streams of tradition running from Genesis to the end of Numbers, the Yahwistic tradition originating in the south and the Elohistic tradition originating in the north of the country. The author of the Joseph story has taken these two traditions into account and has respected their differences. They have, in other words, imposed themselves on him with a kind of canonical authority.[76] Despite their differences, however, these two forms of tradition are basically in agreement with regard to the broad outline of the story of Joseph, with the result that we may say that they both go back to a single tradition.[77] If our suggested date for the composition of the Joseph story is correct, and if the two forms were distinct at the time of Solomon and had each acquired an independent authority, the original tradition must go back at least to the period of the Judges.

The fact that the most important part in the story is played by Joseph means that this original tradition must have been preserved in the 'house of Joseph', which was established in central Palestine. The story of Joseph begins at Shechem (Gen 37:12) and at Dothan (Gen 27:17) – this is, incidentally, the only mention of this town in the Old Testament apart from

---

[75] This is the opinion of S. Mowinckel, *Erwägungen zur Pentateuchquellenfrage*, Trondheim, 1964, p. 62; A. Jepsen, 'Zur Überlieferungsgeschichte der Vätergestalten', *Festschrift Alt*, Leipzig, 1954, pp. 139–155, cf. p. 139.

[76] See, for example, the remarks made by E. A. Speiser in *Genesis*, 1964, p. 294. On the other hand, however, S. E. Loewenstamm has suggested, in 'Reuben and Judah in the Joseph-Cycle', *Fourth World Congress of Jewish Studies, Papers, I*, Jerusalem, 1967, pp. 69–70 (Hebrew), that there never was an independent 'Judah' tradition, but that Judah was introduced into the earlier tradition which ascribed the principal part to Reuben.

[77] This is M. Noth's 'foundation' (*Grundlage* or 'G'), *Überlieferungsgeschichte*, pp. 40–42, and E. A. Speiser's 'Tradition' or 'T', *Genesis*, pp. xxxvii–xxxix.

2 Kings 6:13 and Joseph was buried at Shechem (Jos 24:32). We may therefore expect the Elohistic tradition, which originated in this region, to be the closer of the two to the primitive form. This hypothesis is confirmed by the part played by Reuben in the Elohistic tradition. According to the tradition of Gen 29:32 and Jacob's blessing and will (Gen 49:3), Reuben was the eldest of Jacob's sons and in fact Reuben figures in the story of Joseph as the first-born. He loses this pre-eminent position, however, in the passage in which Jacob blesses his sons (Gen 49:3–4) and, after the Song of Deborah (Judges 5:15b–16), he disappears completely from the historical books.[78]

The other tradition gives a certain prominence to Judah. This is certainly in accordance with the predominant position occupied by the tribe of Judah during the reign of Solomon at the time when the story of Joseph was being written. But the author of the story did not introduce Judah in order to replace Reuben. If this had been his intention, he would simply have suppressed Reuben. What is more, the part which the author gives to Judah is not at all the same as the part given in the other tradition to Reuben; and Judah is, as we have seen, associated with other special characteristics. The author was therefore following a tradition which was earlier. The predominance of Judah was the work of David; the name of Israel given to Jacob in this Judaean form of tradition presupposes the completion of the grouping of the tribes of Israel at the time of the Judges. It may, on the other hand, be a more direct reflection of the union between Israel and Judah during the reign of the Judaean king David. The form of tradition which used Israel-Judah was much later, probably becoming established at the time of David. Its emergence did not, however, lead to the disappearance of the earlier form of Jacob-Reuben and the author of the story of Joseph, writing at the time of Solomon, undoubtedly knew it and must have taken it into account.

We can even try to go back to an earlier period for the origin of the Joseph story. The focal point for the story in Palestine is the region of Shechem and Dothan and this is where an early group known as Machir lived. This name appears alongside other names of tribes in the Song of Deborah (Judges 5:14).[79] This group may perhaps have been the first custodian of the tradition concerning Joseph. The name Machir has been explained[80] as 'the one who hires himself', the 'mercenary' and it would appear to have been the name of a group which placed itself at the service

---

[78] For the story of the tribe of Reuben, see below, pp. 576–580.

[79] For Machir, see E. Meyer, *Die Israeliten und ihre Nachbarstämme*, Halle, 1906, pp. 516–519; E. Täubler, *Biblische Studien. Die Epoche der Richter*, Tübingen, 1958, pp. 190–193; O. Kaiser, 'Stammesgeschichtliche Hintergründe der Josephsgeschichte', *VT*, 10 (1960), pp. 1–15, cf. pp. 9:11; H.–J. Zobel, *Stammesspruch und Geschichte (BZAW*, 95), 1965, p. 65; see also below, pp. 586–587.

[80] E. Täubler, *op. cit*, p. 190; O. Kaiser, *op. cit.*, p. 8.

of the Canaanites, in the same way that Issachar was a group which 'hired itself for payment' to do agricultural work. This is quite possible, but it is also possible to translate Machir as 'the one who is sold'[81] and this is, of course, Joseph's situation (Gen 37:28; 45:5), the same verb being employed in these two texts (*mākhar*). Were the Machirites not connected with an ancestor who had been 'sold' – Joseph?

The tradition of the descent of the sons of Jacob-Israel into Egypt, which is an integral part of the story of Joseph, is connected with Beersheba. It was from this town in the south that Jacob left with his family for Egypt (Gen 46:1-5). All attempts to analyse the 'sources' of this passage have proved disappointing, but there is no reason to doubt that it is part of the early Elohistic form of the tradition, since it was in the north that the traditions concerning Beersheba were best preserved.[82] It was also at Beersheba that memory of Isaac was preserved and it has been suggested that Joseph should be connected with the Isaac tradition,[83] but this hypothesis is affected by the same doubt as that concerning the existence of an independent Isaac cycle. It is possible at least to think that the Josephites of Machir had at a very early stage come into contact at Beersheba with groups of kinsfolk settled in the south.[84] Beersheba is, after all, on the way to Egypt and, if a group of Israel's ancestors ever went down into Egypt, it was certainly Joseph's group. One is inclined to admit that the tradition which was to become common both to the north and to the south – where it was to be adapted to give prominence to Judah – originated at Beersheba and that this origin at Beersheba coincided with the events which were transmitted as a memory – Joseph's arrival in Egypt, followed by that of his brothers.

V. HISTORICAL INTERPRETATION

This early tradition must have a historical basis. There is no reason to doubt that a person called Joseph really existed. The name is an abbreviated form of *Yôseph–'el* (or a divine equivalent) and there are two etymological explanations for the name in the biblical traditions. The Elohistic explanation is 'God has taken away (*'āsaph*) Rachel's shame' (Gen 30:23) and the Yahwistic etymology is 'May God "add" (*yôseph*) another son' (Gen 30:24). The second is the correct explanation and it shows that the name Joseph could not have been the name of a hero or a god or even of a group, but that it was given to a child at the moment of its birth.[85] It was only

---

[81] See E. Meyer, *op. cit.*, p. 516; this is rejected by E. Täubler, *op. cit.*, p. 190, note 1.
[82] See above, p. 175.
[83] A. Jepsen, *op. cit.*, note 75, p. 145.
[84] O. Kaiser, *op. cit.*, note 79, pp. 6-7.
[85] M. Noth, *Die israelitischen Personennamen*, Stuttgart, 1928, p. 212.

extended to cover a group of tribes, the 'house' of Joseph or the northern kingdom or even at times the whole of Israel. Unlike the names of the three patriarchs, Abraham, Isaac and Jacob, the name Joseph was also given to others, although only in post-exilic texts (Num 13:7, P; Ezra 10:42; Neh 12:14; 1 Chron 25:2, 9). It also occurs in the form Josiphiah (*yôsiph'yāh*) in Ezra 8:10. Like the names Isaac and Jacob, the name Joseph also belongs to a very early Amorite onomastic type,[86] but there is no evidence of it in any extrabiblical texts of the second millennium B.C.[87]

Joseph was taken into Egypt in a caravan by traders carrying spices and was sold as a slave to a private person. It is not easy to situate this episode in Egyptian history, especially because our knowledge of slavery and even more particularly our information about the way in which slaves were acquired in Egypt are very restricted.[88] In the Late Kingdom, during the Eighteenth and Nineteenth Dynasties, slaves were above all prisoners of war and the pharaoh could make them over either to the temples or to private persons. There were already, however, many Asiatic slaves in Egypt during the Middle Kingdom;[89] there were very few military campaigns in Asia during this period and it is therefore highly probable that some at least of these slaves were brought into Egypt by merchants. We have, however, very little information about the slave trade and none at all prior to the Late Kingdom. The only text that gives any explicit information is a papyrus dating back to the reign of Ramses II.[90] In a tomb of the period of

---

[86] See above, pp. 198–199.

[87] The name Joseph is different from the Amorite name Ya šub-ilu (Ya šub-AN, cf. Ya šub-IM, Ya šub-Dagan and so on); see the references in T. Bauer, *Die Ostkanaanäer*, Leipzig, 1926, p. 30; H. B. Huffmon, *Amorite Personal Names in the Marit Texts*, Baltimore, 1965, pp. 48, 266. The Hebrew equivalent of this Amorite name is *Yašûbh* or Jashub (Num 26:24). The name Joseph is also different from the place name 'Išipi or Jšipi in the execration texts of the nineteenth century B.C.; see K. Sethe, *Die Ächtung feindlicher Fürsten*, Berlin, 1926, p. 58, f. 21; G. Posener, *Princes et pays d'Asie et de Nubie*, Brussels, 1940, p. 71, E 12, cf. p. 108; cf. W. F. Albright, *JPOS*, 8 (1928), p. 249. It is also different from the place name Y-š-p-i-r in the geographical list of Thut-mose III, No. 78; see J. Simons, *Handbook for the Study of Egyptian Topographical Lists Relating to Western Asia*, Leiden, 1937, p. 118; W. Borée, *Die alten Ortsnamen Palästinas*, Leipzig, 1930, p. 99; 9; A. Jirku, *Die ägyptischen Listen palästinicher und syrischer Ortsnamen*, Leipzig, 1937, p. 14. This name corresponds to the Canaanite Yašub-il(a). The name Joseph would be transcribed in Egyptian as Y(w)tp; see W. F. Albright, *op. cit.* and *The Vocalization of Egyptian Syllabic Orthography*, New Haven, 1934, p. 34.

[88] A. Bakir, *Slavery in Pharaonic Egypt*, Cairo, 1952, especially p. 109 ff; W. Helck, *Materialien, op. cit.*, note 51, III, 1963, pp. 316–339.

[89] See the list dating back to the middle of the eighteenth century B.C. published by W. C. Hayes, *A Papyrus of the Late Middle Kingdom in the Brooklyn Museum*, New York, 1955; *ANET*, pp. 553–554; see also G. Posener, 'Les Asiatiques en Egypte sous les XIIᵉ et XIIIᵉ Dynasties', *Syria*, 35 (1957), pp. 145–163.

[90] A. H. Gardiner, 'A Lawsuit Arising from the Purchase of Two Slaves', *JEA*, 21 (1935), pp. 140–146.

Amen-hotep III, there is a scene showing Syrian merchants unloading their cargo in Egypt; among jars of oil and other goods, there are two women, a child and a man who may be interpreted as slaves for sale.[91] In the Amarna letters, there are several references to the delivery or the sale of slaves, especially women, to the pharaoh by the princes of Canaan,[92] but this was not a private transaction. There is no real documentation of the slave trade between Palestine and Egypt until the Greek period.[93]

The Ishmaelites had 'camels laden with gum, tragacanth, balsam and resin' (Gen 37:25) and these were also included among the gifts that Jacob had taken to Joseph (Gen 43:11). They were certainly Palestinian products, but we have very little information indeed about the date of their arrival in Egypt. The reference in Genesis is the earliest to resin, which is not mentioned again until the first century A.D., by the Elder Pliny.[94] The balsam of Gilead and Egypt are first juxtaposed in the period of Jeremiah (Jer 46:11) and gum tragacanth is not mentioned in Egypt before the Greek period, when it occurs in medical prescriptions.[95] None of these products, then, can help us in any way to date the story of Joseph. As in the case of the slave trade, the importation into Egypt of Palestinian products may have begun early,[96] but, as we have seen, the camel caravan reflects a situation which is later than that of the period when the story of Joseph is presumed to have taken place.[97]

We may assume that Joseph ceased to be a slave because of his successful career in Egypt and his marriage to the daughter of a priest of Heliopolis. We know practically nothing, however, about the laws governing the emancipation of slaves in Egypt. We have only one clear text of the Twentieth Dynasty relating to this question,[98] although an earlier text at least implies that a slave was given his freedom.[99] This silence about emancipation generally may be because slaves had no rigidly fixed legal status in Egypt and could pass, without any legal formalities, from a state of

---

[91] N. de G. Davies and R. O. Faulkner, 'A Syrian Trading Venture into Egypt', *JEA*, 33 (1947), pp. 40–46; *ANEP*, No. 111.

[92] References in W. Helck, *Materialien, op. cit.*, III, pp. 319–320.

[93] The slave trade was a prominent feature of this period, slaves being the main merchandise that Zeno, for example, brought into Egypt during the middle of the third century B.C.; see V. Tscherikover, 'Palestine under the Ptolemies', *Mizraim*, 4–5 (1937), pp. 9–90, especially pp. 16–20; C. Préaux, *L'économie royale des Lagides*, Brussels, 1939, pp. 361, 561. Zeno also imported spices from Palestine, as the Ishmaelites did in Genesis; see V. Tscherikover, *op. cit.*, pp. 25–29.

[94] A. Lucas and J. R. Harris, *Ancient Egyptian Materials and Industries*,[4] London, 1962, p. 94.

[95] J. Vergote, *Joseph en Egypte, op. cit.*, pp. 12–13.

[96] The Asiatics depicted in the tomb of Khnum-hotep III at Beni Hassan in the nineteenth century B.C. (*ANEP*, No. 3) are bringing lead glance, which was used to prepare eye-paint.

[97] See above, pp. 223–225.

[98] The 'Papyrus of Adoption'; see A. Bakir, *op. cit.*, note 88, pp. 122–123.

[99] W. Helck, *op. cit.*, note 88, pp. 332–333.

slavery to one in which they were regarded as servants. It is noticeable in this context that there is no mention in the Joseph story of emancipation.

We have already given several examples of Semites who rose to high positions in Egyptian society[100] and who might originally have been slaves. At the same time, however, we have already seen that these parallel cases, which extend over a very long period, are of no help in the quest of a date for Joseph. One problem, moreover, still remains – it is not easy to see how Joseph, a young herdsman from Palestine, could suddenly have become an important Egyptian official without having been educated for administration – and the Bible has nothing to say about this.[101]

Even in the very earliest form of the tradition, the story of Joseph is inseparably linked with the story of his brothers. If he did in fact exist and if he really went to Egypt, then we are bound to accept that he was followed there by a group of blood relations. The conditions under which this group entered Egypt, however, were different from those governing other groups. According to the biblical tradition, Abraham went down into Egypt because of the famine in Canaan (Gen 12:10). The well-known painting in the tomb of Khnum-hotep at Beni Hassan, made during the reign of Sesostris II at the beginning of the nineteenth century B.C., shows the arrival of thirty-seven Asiatics, men, women and children, led by their chief Ibsha (which should perhaps be read as Abi-shar).[102] An even more striking parallel is the report of a frontier official during the reign of Mer-ne-Ptah, quoted above,[103] authorising the Shasu of Edom to enter Egypt 'to keep them alive and to keep their cattle alive'. This is something that must have happened again and again, if the people arriving at the frontier were known to have peaceful intentions. When there was a less powerful government in Egypt and frontier supervision was less strict, more and more of these Bedouins came into Egypt and became a danger. This happened especially at the end of the Old Kingdom and during the First Intermediate Period, when the question of the invasions of the Asiatics was discussed in several literary texts.[104] These took the form of raids or of disordered, irregular movements of flocks to parts of the desert where the

[100] See above, pp. 298–301.

[101] J. M. A. Janssen, JEOL, 14 (1955–1956), p. 67. Joseph might, however, have received such an education in Egypt; see above, p. 300, note 25.

[102] P. E. Newberry, Beni Hasan I, London, 1893, Plate XXVIII, XXX-XXXI. This tomb painting has been reproduced very frequently, for example in ANEP, No. 3; the text will be found in ANET, p. 229a.

[103] See above, p. 302.

[104] The Admonitions of Ipu-wer, ANET, pp. 441–444, J. van Seters, however, has suggested a much later date for this text; see his 'A Date for the "Admonitions" in the Second Intermediate Period', JEA, 50 (1964), pp. 13–23. See also the Prophecy of Nefer-rohu, ANET, pp. 444–446; see also G. Posener, Littérature et Politique dans l'Egypte de la XIIe Dynastie, Paris, 1956, pp. 21–60. See also the Instructions for Meri-ka-Re, ANET, pp. 414–418.

frontier was shared. Some of these Asiatic groups, however, penetrated further into the Nile Delta and settled there, at least for a time.[105] During the Second Intermediate Period, settlements of this kind played a part in the Hyksos' seizure of power.[106] To judge by these parallel cases, the 'sons of Jacob' could have arrived in Egypt at any time during the second millennium.

To summarise the evidence supplied by these extrabiblical documents, then, they would seem to point to the probable arrival in Egypt of a Semite called Joseph who rose from the status of slave to a position in which he exercised very high functions. They also show that a group of Semites probably settled in the Delta. These, of course, are the essentials of the story of Joseph and his brothers. The evidence outside the Bible does not, however, enable us to establish a date for Joseph or for the coming of his 'brothers' to Egypt.

Going back once more to the Bible itself, it is obvious that the data it provides are apparently irreconcilable. According to Ex 12:40–41, the Israelites stayed in Egypt for four hundred and thirty years, counted day by day. In the Samaritan text of the Pentateuch and the Septuagint, the phrase 'and in the land of Canaan' is added. This means that the whole story of the patriarchs is included in this period of time and this is the tradition followed by Paul in Gal 3:17. According to the few shreds of information given in Genesis, two hundred and fifteen years elapsed between Abraham's arrival in Canaan and Jacob's departure for Egypt. This leaves only two hundred and fifteen years, exactly half the period, for the sojourn in Egypt. The Massoretic text is certainly to be preferred, but it is a P text and one is bound to suspect that, like all the priestly chronology, this period of four hundred and thirty years is artificial. According to Gen 15:13, Abraham was told that his people would have to stay in Egypt for four hundred years. This could be regarded as a round figure and equivalent to the four hundred and thirty years stated in Ex 12:40, but only three verses later (Gen 15:16), we read that Abraham's descendants would return 'in the fourth generation (dôr)'. Attempts have been made to overcome this contradiction by attributing the two verses to different sources, J and E,[107] by supposing the existence of a very early text giving the correct length of the sojourn in Egypt as three generations, but having been wrongly interpreted in Ex 12:40 and Gen 15:13[108] and finally by explaining the word dôr in Gen 15:16

[105] G. Posener, op. cit., p. 40.

[106] See above, pp. 78, 79.

[107] H. Cazelles, RB, 69 (1962), pp. 340–341; 'Patriarches', DBS, VII (1966), col. 772, 803–804.

[108] N. H. Tur-Sinai, BiOr, 18 (1961), pp. 16–17; the early text 'three generations (šillēšîm) extending over a hundred and four years' became, according to this theory, 'four hundred and thirty (šᵉlōšîm) years' in Ex 12:40 and 'four hundred years' in Gen 15:13, šillēšîm having been omitted.

not as a 'generation', but as a cycle in time representing the ideal length of a man's life and possibly equivalent to a century.[109] None of these theories can, however, be regarded as certain.

What is, however, quite certain is that the genealogies in the Pentateuch point to a period of time that is much less than four centuries. Thus Moses was Levi's great-grandson by his father (Ex 6:16, 18–20; Num 26:57–59) and Levi's grandson by his mother (Ex 6:20; Num 26:59). Judah's grandson, Hezron, was born before the descent into Egypt (Gen 46:12) and Hezron's grandson, Amminadab, was Aaron's father-in-law (Ex 6:23). Reuben's grandsons, Dathan and Abiram, rebelled against Moses in the wilderness (Num 16:1). According to Jos 7:1, there were only four generations between Judah and Achan, who lived at the time of the taking of Jericho by Joshua.[110] Further examples could be provided of the incomplete nature of all these genealogies and of the fact that they miss out stages between the last generations that were well-known and the first ancestor of the family in question.[111] Both modern ethnology and the documents of the Ancient Near East provide good and comparable examples of this practice, which deprives us of the possibility of dating the descent into Egypt by means of genealogies.

On the other hand, although the tradition of Gen 15:13 and of Ex 12:40 points to a very long period spent in Egypt, a very short period is apparently indicated at the end of Genesis and in the first verses of Exodus. Joseph died when he was a hundred and ten (Gen 50:26); he died and with him died all the generation that came into Egypt (Ex 1:6); a new king came to power in Egypt who knew nothing of him (Ex 1:8). This would seem to point to the fact that the pharaoh who oppressed the people of Israel was the immediate successor of the pharaoh who gave such a high position to Joseph and who welcomed his brothers.

Neither the extrabiblical evidence nor the very contradictory information provided by the Bible itself, then, enable us to date the descent into Egypt. We have to fall back on conjecture and there is a variety of opinions here. This descent is often associated with the migration of Hyksos.[112] One view that has been put forward is that Semites certainly came to Egypt during the Hyksos period, when the capital, Avaris, was in

---

[109] H. H. Rowley, *From Joseph to Joshua*, London, 1950, p. 69; W. F. Albright, *The Biblical Period from Abraham to Ezra*,³ New York and Evanston, 1963, p. 9. This theory was accepted by E. A. Speiser, who has suggested the translation 'in the fourth time span'; see also K. A. Kitchen, *Ancient Orient and Old Testament*, Chicago, 1966, p. 54.

[110] See H. H. Rowley, *op. cit.*, pp. 71–2.

[111] W. F. Albright, *op. cit.*, p. 9 and note 26; J. Bright, *History*, pp. 75, 125; K. A. Kitchen, *op. cit.*, note 109, pp. 54–55.

[112] See, for example, W. F. Albright, *op. cit.*, p. 10; P. Montet, *L'Egypte et la Bible*, Neuchâtel, 1959, pp. 15–23; J. Bright, *History*, p. 78; R. de Vaux, *RB*, 72 (1965), p. 26.

the Nile Delta, and that it is consequently possible that a Hyksos ruler who was himself a Semite welcomed Joseph and his brothers. This opinion has, however, been sharply disputed.[113] It is true that this peaceful entry of a group of Semites is not in accordance with the picture that has usually been painted of a Hyksos 'invasion', but this picture is, on the other hand, in need of correction and, in any case, groups of Semitic peoples infiltrating into Egypt prepared the way for the Hyksos seizure of power. Where this hypothesis really encounters difficulties is in the question of explaining the continuation and even the growth of an important Semitic enclave in the Delta after the expulsion of the Hyksos and during the Eighteenth and Nineteenth Dynasties. The Amarna period has also been suggested both for the patriarchs and for Joseph[114] or simply for Joseph, allowing for a fairly long break between Joseph and the three patriarchs,[115] but, like the Hyksos Semitic theory, this hypothesis has also met with strong opposition;[116] what is more, from the same quarter. The Eighteenth Dynasty has been very generally suggested,[117] but, during that period, the pharaohs lived at Thebes and this is not in accordance with the data given in the biblical account. Finally, a very short period of no more than a few decades has been suggested as the most likely interval between the descent into Egypt and the exodus.[118]

If all the various possibilities provided by the history of ancient Egypt and the different and often contradictory data furnished by the Bible are taken into account, the solution to the problem is a complex one. As we shall see later, we may be reasonably certain the exodus from Egypt under Moses that took place during the thirteenth century B.C.[119] As we have already seen, the patriarchs probably lived in the nineteenth and eighteenth centuries B.C.[120] The tradition of Gen 15:13 and Ex 12:40 would therefore seem to be justified. This long 'sojourn', however, was not necessarily a sojourn which was continuous, made by the same group and involving the whole people. The diptych of the twelve sons of Jacob going into Egypt and the twelve tribes of Israel coming out of

[113] See especially S. Herrmann, ZAS, 91 (1964), p. 70.

[114] See C. H. Gordon, especially his article 'Hebrew Origins in the Light of Recent Discoveries', Biblical and Other Studies, ed. A. Altmann, Cambridge, Mass., 1963, pp. 3–14.

[115] H. H. Rowley, op. cit., note 109, pp. 116–120; H. Cazelles, 'Patriarches', DB S, VII, 1966, col. 140–141.

[116] S. Herrmann, op. cit., note 113, pp. 71–72.

[117] J. Vergote, Joseph en Egypte, p. 212.

[118] M. Noth, Geschichte, p. 114; S. Herrmann, op. cit., p. 74; O. Eissfeldt, Stammessage und Menschheitserzählungen in der Genesis (Sitz der Sächsischen Akademie der Wissenschaften zu Leipzig, 110, 4), 1965, p. 19; ibid., 'Palestine in the Time of the Nineteenth Dynasty', CAH, II, XXVI (a), 1965, p. 17.

[119] See below, pp. 388–392.

[120] See above, pp. 263–266.

Egypt cannot be an expression of a historical truth, even if four centuries are allowed for this development. There was no 'people of Israel' in Egypt. The tribes took a very long time to become formed, differentiated and federated. The 'system of the twelve tribes' was the last expression of this very slow process. There is therefore no real need to ask which tribes went down into Egypt and stayed there.[121]

Some of the elements which ultimately went to form the people of Israel may have gone to Egypt at an early period and have left again later, as other Semitic groups did and as Abraham is said to have done according to Gen 12. We can, in this context, call to mind especially certain constitutive groups of Judah-Simeon, whose settlement in Canaan began in the south and followed a path that was different from that of the other tribes.[122] Other elements entered Egypt and settled there and, if our analysis of the history of traditions is correct, this would apply in the first place to the group known as Machir. In any case, whatever the history of its formation may have been in detail, the 'house of Joseph' included elements which had been in Egypt. The part played by Moses in the exodus and his Egyptian name, as well as the names of other members of his family, mean that elements of the tribe of Levi also went to Egypt. Various groups with a similar past might have been integrated into other tribes. These movements into Egypt may have been spread over several centuries. From the historical point of view, it is not impossible, and bearing in mind the date that we have suggested for the patriarchs it is even quite probable, that the first entry into Egypt took place just before or at the beginning of the period of Hyksos rule and that the last entry may have occurred shortly before the period of oppression.

It is therefore possible to explain in this way the uncertainty and the great variety of biblical traditions. Some of the elements which went to form the future people of Israel would also have had memories of Egypt. These groups were probably not numerous, but it is quite possible that they shared and combined their memories. The factor that played a decisive part, however, in the formation of a unified tradition occurred later than the history of Joseph and his brothers. The experiences of the group led by Moses during the exodus from Egypt and in Sinai became decisive in the formation of the people of Israel and the establishment of their religion. Together with their memory of a period spent in Egypt, these experiences became the inheritance of 'all Israel'.

---

[121] J. Bright, *History*, pp. 125–126, is in agreement with M. Noth, *History*, pp. 118–119.
[122] See H. H. Rowley, *op. cit.*, note 109, p. 101 ff and below, p. 526 ff.

Chapter Twelve

THE MISSION OF MOSES

I. LITERARY ANALYSIS OF EXODUS 1–15

THE ONLY immediate source that we have for the exodus from Egypt, which was to remain in the minds of the people of Israel as their most important historical and religious memory, is the Bible itself. The first fifteen chapters of the book of Exodus are the primary source of this memory, the few other texts in the Old Testament being no more than parallels or utilisations of the Exodus text. The account in Exodus can be divided into the following six episodes:

1. The oppression of the Israelites by the Egyptians (Ex 1)
2. Moses: his birth, youth, call and mission (Ex 2:1–7:7)
3. The struggle between Moses (and Aaron) and the Pharaoh (Ex 7:8–10:29)
4. The tenth plague and the passover (Ex 11:1–13:16)
5. The departure, the pursuit and the crossing of the sea (Ex 13:17–14:31)
6. The song of victory (Ex 15).

This whole account forms an indisputable unity. It is above all an account of a deliverance which God wanted and brought about, using Moses as mediator. The people of Israel interpreted the event as God's will to deliver or bring his people up out of Egypt, the 'house of slavery'. This affirmation occurs again and again throughout the Bible, from the Pentateuch to the latest books of the Old Testament, Daniel and Wisdom, and in every literary form found in the Old Testament – in the historical books, the prophetic books and the psalms. It is, in fact, the basic article of Israel's faith.

This unity, however, was the result of literary composition. The account as a whole clearly includes many different literary elements. There are, for example, elements of legend in the story of Moses' birth and the plagues of Egypt. There is a certain epic quality as well as mythical memories in the story of the crossing of the sea and in the song of victory. The account also incorporates a liturgy of the Passover and cultic laws relating to the Passover, the feast of Unleavened Bread and the first-born. There are two stories of the call of Moses (Ex 3–4 and 6:2–7:7) and these are separated by the beginning of the conflict between Moses and the Pharaoh (Ex 5:1–6:1). It is also difficult to determine the part played by Moses as distinct from that played by Aaron. In Ex 3:20; 11:1 and 13:31, the departure of the Israelites from Egypt seems to be the result of a concession gained from the Pharaoh. According to Ex 14:5 and other texts, however, it seems to be a flight unknown to the Pharaoh and even made against his will. The present account, in other words, clearly has a long history behind it.

Literary critics of the passage in question have no hesitation in separating the song of victory (Ex 15:1–19). It is also quite easy to distinguish certain priestly contributions, although these may be the work of P or that of a later priestly editor. The most important of these are the bare indications in Ex 1:1–5, 7 and 13–14[1] the second account of the call of Moses (6:2–7:13); the plague of mosquitoes (8:12–15) and the plague of boils (9:8–12); the law of the Passover and the Unleavened Bread (12:1–20, 40–51) and the law of the first-born (13:1–2). There is also some priestly editing in several other parts of the account and especially in the story of the crossing of the sea (Ex 14), which forms the climax of the account of the exodus.

The task of distinguishing which elements go back to J and which go back to E is much more difficult. The two sources are acknowledged in the account of the exodus by classical literary criticism, but no two authors can agree as to the detailed distribution.[2] Other critics do not accept the existence of a separate Elohistic source in the exodus account and believe that, apart from P, there is only one source, that of J, which is a combination of different traditions with a number of additions[3] or else was 're-edited' with corrections and supplementary material.[4] According to the most recent literary criticism, there are two sources, J and E, but their distribution is different. Most of the account has, therefore, to be attributed to E and the Yahwist-Elohist editor was responsible for considerable changes.[5]

This uncertainty about the J and E sources has led to a search for another explanation of the composition of the account of the exodus. The one that has been most widely accepted is the cultic explanation,[6] according to

[1] T. C. Vriezen, 'Exodusstudien. Exodus 1', VT, 17 (1967), pp. 334–353.

[2] Compare, for example, three recent analyses – M. Noth, Überlieferungsgeschichte, pp. 18, 31–32, 39; O. Eissfeldt, Introduction, pp. 183–190 and G. Fohrer, Überlieferung und Geschichte des Exodus. Eine Analyse von Ex. 1–15 (BZAW, 91), 1964, table on pp. 124–125.

[3] W. Rudolph Der 'Elohist' von Exodus bis Josua (BZAW, 68), 1938, pp. 1–32 and table on pp. 274–275. See also the literary criticism of O. Eissfeldt, 'Die Komposition von Exodus 1–12. Eine Rettung des Elohisten', Theologische Blätter, 18 (1939), col. 224–233 = Kleine Schriften, II, pp. 160–170.

[4] S. Mowinckel, Erwägungen zur Pentateuchquellenfrage, Trondheim, 1964, pp. 64–65.

[5] A. Besters, 'L'expression "Fils d'Israël" en Ex i–xiv. Un nouveau critère pour la distinction des sources', RB, 74 (1967), pp. 321–355.

[6] J. Pedersen, 'Passahfest und Passahlegende', ZAW, 52 (1934), pp. 161–175; ibid., Israel. Its

which Ex 1–15 is thought to be the sacred legend of the feast of the Passover. This feast of farmers and herdsmen was linked to the exodus from Egypt, perhaps because of a historical coincidence, although this is pure conjecture and cannot be verified. The cultic act itself brought the deliverance from Egypt to life again and the accompanying story was composed to explain the celebration. This story presented the event as a struggle between God and the pharaoh and extended it in the concluding poem to cosmic dimensions in describing it as a mythical combat between Yahweh and the powers of evil. On the other hand, the rites that were celebrated also influenced the story. According to this theory, it is not possible to trace the stages in the composition of the account, but it is possible to say that it is not a simple combination of various literary sources. In other words, it is not the work of J, nor is it the work of E. It is not even the work of P, because it is basically not a historical but a cultic text.

There are, however, several difficulties in connection with this theory. It has to be borne in mind that Ex 1–15 is not isolated – it is linked with what precedes it and with what follows it in the Pentateuch and forms part of a great history of salvation – and it is above all intended to be history. The same varieties of style and of intention that are found in Genesis and in the rest of the book of Exodus are found in this account, which show that it is still a literary composition.[7] The question whether there are two sources (J and P) or three (J, E and P) is secondary. On the other hand, if this story was composed to provide an explanation of the Passover, the celebration of the feast ought then to follow the climax of the story. But the account culminates with the crossing of the sea and the destruction of the Egyptians and the Passover is celebrated, in this account, before this culminating event.[8] In fact, the only explanation provided of the Passover in the earliest tradition (Ex 12:26–27) is that it is a 'passing over', but not a passing over of the sea. According to this text, it was a passing of Yahweh over the houses of the Israelites, sparing them, during the tenth plague. There is clearly a link between the Passover and the history of Israel's salvation, but there is no explicit connection with the exodus until Deut 16:1–6. The 'historicisation' of the feast was therefore progressive.[9] Finally, according to 2 Kings 23:22 and 2 Chron 35:18, the Passover was not celebrated by Israel as a whole between the period of the Judges and the reform of Joshua. It is therefore unlikely that a sacred legend would have been composed for a feast which was no longer celebrated in the central sanctuary of Israel.[10]

Life and Culture, III-IV, London, 1940, pp. 384–415, 728–737; 2nd. edn, 1959, *ibid.*, and pp. 794–795.

[7] S. Mowinckel, 'Die vermeintliche "Passahlegende", Ex 1–15', *ST*, 5 (1951), pp. 66–88.

[8] M. Noth, *Überlieferungsgeschichte*, p. 71 ff.

[9] R. de Vaux, *Les sacrifices de l'Ancien Testament*, Paris, 1964, pp. 20–23.

[10] G. Fohrer, *Überlieferung, op. cit.* (see note 2), pp. 90–96.

There is another more general reason. The faith of Israel was based on the interventions that the people believed God made in their history and their cult was the expression of that faith and the commemoration of that history of their salvation. In other words, we may accept the principle that tradition precedes cult, which does not create history. [11] It is clear however, that the formulation of tradition is influenced by cult – this is especially evident in Ex 12–13. The historian therefore, while bearing literary criticism in mind, has to try to ascertain the facts underlying this tradition and its cultic expression.

II. THE OPPRESSION (Ex 1:8–22; 5:6–23)

The oppression of the Israelites is attributed in Exodus to a new king 'who knew nothing of Joseph' (Ex 1:8), in contrast to the pharaoh who had welcomed Joseph and his brothers. The reason for the oppression was the great increase in the number of the Israelites, who had become a danger to the Egyptians (Ex 1:9–10). The promises made to the patriarchs were, in other words, being fulfilled.

This oppression took place in three stages – first, the slave labour of building (Ex 1:11–12), secondly, the killing of the newly born boys (1:15–22) and thirdly, the worsening of the conditions of slave labour (5:6–23). The first and the third stages are in accordance with each other, but the second stage is out of tune with the others. The killing of all newly born boys was, after all, contrary to the intention of the pharaoh, who wanted workers to carry out his building plans. Moreover it does not prepare for the third stage, the worsening of conditions. What is more, the story, as narrated in Ex 1:15–22, is not in accordance with the datum that the Israelites were increasing in number, which was presumably the reason for oppressing them, because, according to the story, there were only two midwives. The names of these midwives are also interesting, because they are Semitic names of an early type. Shiphrah, the name of the first, is also found in a list of Asiatic slaves in Egypt in the eighteenth century B.C.[12] and Puah, the second name, is also found in the Rās Shamrah poems as the name of one of the daughters of Danel, pġt, which is, in Ugaritic, also a common name meaning simply 'girl'.[13] This story of the 'second stage' in the oppression belongs to an early tradition, but one which was different

---

[11] G. E. Wright, 'Cult and History', *Interpretation*, 16 (1962), pp. 3–20; A. S. Kapelrud, 'The Role of the Cult in Old Israel', *The Bible and Modern Scholarship*, ed. J. P. Hyatt, New York, 1965, pp. 44–56. See also W. G. Lambert, 'Myth and Ritual as Conceived by the Babylonians', *JSS*, 13 (1968), pp. 104–112.

[12] W. F. Albright, *JAOS*, 74 (1954), pp. 222–233, see also p. 229.

[13] C. H. Gordon, *Ugaritic Textbook*, Rome, 1965, Glossary No. 2081; J. Aistleitner, *Wörterbuch der ugaritischen Sprache,*[2] Berlin, 1965, No. 2246.

from the tradition of the slave labour. The story moreover prepares for that of the birth of Moses (Ex 2:1–10).

The oppression to which the Israelites were subjected, then, was to have been employed in building the store cities or garrison towns of Pithom and Rameses (Ex 1:11). There is no reason for regarding these details as late.[14] Pithom is Pr-Itm =Teku, in the district where Joseph's brothers settled.[15] Rameses is Pi-Ramses, the city of Ramses, the precise situation of which is the subject of discussion. The two most probable sites of this ancient city are Tanis[16] and Qantîr,[17] which is about twelve miles south of Tanis. Both of these sites have monuments named after Ramses and both have a serious claim to be regarded as Pi-Ramses. The most convincing objection to Tanis is a reference, in a text dating back to the end of the Ramesside period, to Tanis and Pi-Ramses as two different places.[18] A possible solution to this problem is that both Tanis and Ramses formed part of a great domain on which Ramses built Qantîr, where remains of a palace of Ramses II have been found, being the residential quarter and Tanis the religious city.[19] The problem is, however, of secondary importance to the historian. The important aspect of the question is that the name Pi-Ramses disappeared from Egyptian texts before the end of the Twentieth Dynasty, which shows that the biblical tradition was very old and that it undoubtedly had a historical basis. It enables us to name the pharaoh who oppressed the Israelites in Egypt as Ramses II (1290–1224). We know that he built a great deal in the Nile Delta and that he transferred his residence and the capital of Egypt to the Delta. This is, of course, in accordance with the data provided in the Exodus account.

It would appear that Egypt had no regularly organised corvée labour, that is, work which had to be done for the state each year without payment, of the kind that existed in Mesopotamia and in Canaan.[20] It is quite certain,

[14] I do not agree with D. B. Redford, 'Ex 1, 11', *VT*, 13 (1963), pp. 401–418; see also W. Helck, 'Tkw und die Ramsesstadt', *VT*, 15 (1965), pp. 35–48.

[15] See above, pp. 301–303.

[16] See especially P. Montet, 'Tanis, Avaris et Pi-Ramsès', *RB*, 38 (1930), pp. 5–28 and frequently afterwards; A. Gardiner, 'Tanis and Pi-Ra'messe. A Retraction', *JES*, 19 (1933), pp. 122–128; *ibid.*, *Ancient Egyptian Onomastica*, II, London, 1947, pp. 171*–175*, 278*–279*.

[17] See especially B. Couroyer, 'La résidence ramesside du Delta', *RB*, 43 (1945), pp. 75–98; L. Habachi, 'Khatâ na-Qantir', *ASAE*, 52 (1954), pp. 479–559; E. P. Uphill, 'Pithom and Raamses. Their location and Significance', *JNES*, 27 (1968), pp. 291–316; 28 (1969), pp. 15–39.

[18] The onomasticon of Amenope, in A. Gardiner, *Ancient Egyptian Onomastica*, II, No. 410 and 417.

[19] A. Alt, 'Die Delta-Residenz der Ramessiden', *Festschrift Fr. Zucker*, Berlin, 1954, pp. 3–13 = *Kleine Schriften*, III, pp. 176–185; J. von Beckerath, *Untersuchungen zur politischen Geschichte der zweiten Zwischenzeit in Ägypten*, Glückstadt, 1965, especially the excursion 'Die Delta-Residenz der Ramessiden', pp. 157–159.

[20] I. Mendelsohn, 'On Corvée Labor in Ancient Canaan and Israel', *BASOR*, 167 (Oct.

however, that, with certain exceptions, every one of the pharaoh's subjects could be impressed when the need arose. The ordinary workers who were employed in great public undertakings were supplied by the army or else were prisoners of war or serfs attached to the temples and the royal domains.[21] These serfs were themselves captives or descendants of captives.[22] A tomb painting of Rekh-mi-Re during the Eighteenth Dynasty shows Nubians and Syrians making and carrying bricks and the inscriptions read: 'The captives whom his majesty has brought to build the temple (of Amon at Thebes) . . . making bricks to reconstruct the stores (of Amon)'.[23] In the same way, David made the conquered population of Rabbah, the Ammonite town, do construction work and brickmaking (2 Sam 12:31). Similarly, Mesha, the king of Moab, used Israelite captives for his buildings.[24] An expedition sent to the quarries at Wadi Hammamat during the reign of Ramses IV included, in addition to the specialist workers, five thousand soldiers, two hundred sailors, eight hundred 'Apīru and two thousand men from the sacred and royal domains.[25] In two papyri dating from the reign of Ramses II, there are orders to distribute rations to the soldiers and the 'Apīru who were transporting stones for the buildings being erected around Memphis.[26] These 'Apīru were almost certainly prisoners of war who came originally from Canaan, like the three thousand six hundred 'Apīru whom Amen-hotep II brought back from his campaign in Asia.[27]

It is, moreover, in the texts which refer to the sojourn in Egypt and especially those referring to the period of oppression that the name *'ibh'rîm*, for the Israelites, occurs most frequently in the Old Testament and as we have already seen, the terms 'Hebrew' and 'Habiru/'Apīru' coincide to some extent.[28] In the present case, because of the similar race and origin, the ancestors of the Israelites, who had entered Egypt freely, became assimilated to the 'Apīru prisoners of war and were also forced to work on the

---

1962), pp. 31–35.

[21] See the texts quoted by W. Helck, *Der Einfluß der Militär-führer in der 18. ägyptischen Dynastie*, Hildesheim, 1964, p. 21; similarly in Mesopotamia, I. Mendelsohn, *Slavery in Ancient Near East*, New York, 1949, pp. 92–99.

[22] G. Posener, 'Une liste de noms propres étrangers', *Syria*, 18 (1937), pp. 183–197.

[23] N. de G. Davis, *The Tomb of Rekh-mi-re' at Thebes*, New York, 1943, I, p. 55; II, pl. lviii-lix. For the brickmaking, see C. F. Nims, 'Bricks without Straw?' *BibArch.*, 13 (1950), pp. 22–28.

[24] Stele, lines 25–26; *KAI*, No. 181; *ANET*, p. 320.

[25] L. Christophe, 'La stèle de l'an III de Ramsès IV au Ouâ di Hammâmât,' *BIFAO*, 48 (1949), pp. 1–38, lines 16–17; see also J. Bottéro, *Le problème des Habiru*, Paris, 1954, No. 190.

[26] Leiden Papyrus, 348 and 349, J. Bottéro, *op. cit.*, Nos. 187–188. A new translation of the first text will be found in R. A. Caminos, *Late Egyptian Miscellanies*, London, 1954, p. 491.

[27] *ANET*, p. 247a = Bottéro, *op. cit.*, No. 183.

[28] See above, pp. 209–216.

buildings of Ramses II in the Delta. It is not difficult to understand that semi-nomadic herdsmen would have bitterly resented this change in their conditions of employment and would have wanted to resume their free way of life in the desert. On the other hand, the Egyptians would have been reluctant to lose this unpaid labour force and would have regarded opposition to corvée labour as an uprising of slaves and flight as an escape of prisoners.

III. Moses' Childhood and Youth

It is at this point in the Bible that Moses appears. From his birth to his death, it is he who dominates all the stories in the Pentateuch from the beginning of Exodus until the final chapter of Deuteronomy. He was long regarded as the author of the Pentateuch, the founder of the religion of Israel, the announcer of the Law, the organiser of the people and of their worship, a charismatic leader, a prophet and a priest. Modern critics have, however, deprived Moses of almost all of these prerogatives and have even gone so far as to doubt whether he really existed or at least to doubt whether anything of historical value can be said about his person or the part that he played in the history of Israel.[29] He was, it has been suggested, introduced into the traditions concerning the exodus from Egypt, the journey through the desert and the events of Sinai when these memories, which had been peculiar only to certain groups, became the common property of 'all Israel'.[30] He cannot, moreover, be regarded as a founder of Israel's religion.[31]

There has, however, been a reaction recently against these extreme theories and certain authors have recognised that the figure of Moses has a greater degree of historicity.[32] In the first place, it has to be acknowledged

---

[29] For the history of research into Moses, see C. A. Keller, 'Vom Stand und Aufgabe der Moseforschung', *TZ*, 13 (1957), pp. 430–441; R. Smend, *Das Mosebild von H. Ewald bis M. Noth*, Tübingen, 1959; E. Osswald, *Das Bild des Mose in der kritischen alttestamentlichen Wissenschaft seit Julius Wellhausen*, Berlin, 1962; H. Schmid, 'Der Stand der Moseforschung', *Judaica*, 21 (1965), pp. 194–221; R. J. Thompson, *Moses and the Law in a Century of Criticism since Graf (SVT, 19)*, Leiden, 1970.

[30] According to M. Noth, *Überlieferungsgeschichte*, pp. 172–191, Moses could not have been an original figure in all the different 'themes' of the Pentateuch, which were, in the first place, independent of each other. He played a secondary part in the themes of the exodus, the journey through the desert and Sinai. Only one traditional element seems reliable – the memory of a tomb of Moses in the land of Moab (Deut 34:6). Noth believes that Moses played a part in the preparatory phase before the occupation of Canaan by the tribes of central Palestine and that the details were lost when the figure of Moses was expanded to include 'all Israel'; see also M. Noth, *History*, pp. 134–136.

[31] M. Noth, *History*, p. 135, note 3; K. Koch, 'Der Tod des Religionsstifters', *Kerygma und Dogma*, 8 (1962), pp. 100–123, with F. Baumgärtel's reply, *ibid.*, 9 (1963), pp. 223–233.

[32] In the second edition of his 'History', M. Noth acknowledges that Moses, because of his

that, if Moses is suppressed, the religion and even the existence of Israel are impossible to explain. It has been said that 'if tradition told us nothing about Moses, it would be necessary to invent him'.[33] But this is not all. It is also necessary to establish the links between the traditions and history.

The pharaoh's command to kill all the male children (Ex 1:15–22), which, as we have seen, is not in accordance with the tradition concerning the corvée labour, prepares the way for the story of Moses' birth (Ex 2:1–10). This story has been compared with other, similar legends about the early childhood of certain heroes. In particular, it has been compared with the Mesopotamian legend of Sargon of Agade.[34] In this legend, Sargon's mother put the baby in a basket of rushes, sealed the lid with bitumen and placed the basket in the river. It was taken out by Akki, a drawer of water, who raised Sargon as his own son and later employed him as his gardener. The boy became a great king. This is, of course, quite a common theme in folklore.

Another interesting comparison has been made[35] with a Sumero-Akkadian text relating to adoption. In this document, a child is found and given to a nurse, who keeps him for three years, for which she receives a salary. He is afterwards adopted and is educated as a scribe.[36] The parallel between this legal text and the biblical account is striking. It is probable that, together with the folklore theme of the child who is found, the biblical story was inspired by the customs of adoption in the Ancient Near East. It might have come from the same environment as the story of Joseph. The story of the birth of Moses, like the Joseph story, shows a certain familiarity with Egypt – the thick reeds along the banks of the Nile, the basket of papyrus coated with bitumen and pitch and made in the shape of an Egyptian barque. It also reveals a certain lack of knowledge, especially in its presentation of a pharaoh's daughter bathing in the river, which is something to which Egyptologists have objected. What we have, in fact, is another example of Egypt seen through the eyes of a Palestinian. The pharaoh's daughter, for instance, speaks Hebrew – she calls the child *Môšeh*,

---

Egyptian name, might have played a part in the exodus, that of a messenger of God announcing the divine intervention, *History*, p. 135, note 1. More positive views will be found in R. Smend, *Jahwekrieg und Stämmebund. Erwägungen zur ältesten Geschichte Israels* Göttingen, 1963, pp. 87–97; G. Fohrer, *Überlieferung und Geschichte des Exodus. Eine Analyse von Ex. 1–15* (*BZAW*, 91), 1964; S. Herrmann, 'Mose', *EvTh*, 28 (1968), pp. 301–328; H. Schmid, *Mose, Überlieferung und Geschichte*, Berlin, 1968; G. Widengren, 'What do we know about Moses?', *Proclamation and Presence (Volume G. Henton Davies)*, London, 1970, pp. 21–47.

[33] N. Söderblom, *Das Werden des Gottesglaubens*, 1916, p. 310; this saying has often been repeated, for example, by J. Bright, *History*, p. 116.

[34] *ANET*, p. 119.

[35] B. S. Childs, 'The Birth of Moses', *JBL*, 84 (1965), pp. 109–122.

[36] The text is in B. Landsberger, *Die Serie ana ittišu (Materialien zum sumerischen Lexikon*, I), Rome, 1937, pp. 43–47.

because she drew him out (*māšah*) of the waters. This is, of course, only an approximate explanation, because the name 'Moses' has the form of an active participle and means 'drawing' rather than 'drawn'.

The name Moses is, of course, really Egyptian.[37] It is comparable to those names bearing the name of a god, for example, Ah-mose, Thut-mose or Ptah-mose, meaning 'the god . . . is born', and given to children born on the anniversary of the god. The short form *mśy* or *mśw* is also found in Egyptian and occurs quite frequently in documents of the Late Kingdom. Attempts have even been made to identify one of these persons with Moses.[38] In a papyrus dating from the end of the Nineteenth Dynasty, a complaint is made against the vizier before 'Mose', who punishes the vizier.[39] But, since only the pharaoh was above the vizier in Egyptian society, this Mose must have been the king himself and his name would, in that case, have been a short form of Amen-mose, one of the successors of Mer-ne-Ptah.[40] Another papyrus, however, which is a little earlier in date and is a copy of a literary work, speaks about soldiers who have not been given their rations and who threaten to have the guilty party punished by 'Mose'.[41] This may still be the pharaoh, but it cannot be Amen-mose. It is possible, therefore, that 'Mose' was a familiar name given to the reigning pharaoh and derived from Ramses, the royal name *par excellence* during the Ramesside period.[42] In any case, it is certainly not possible to identify this Mose with Moses, although his name is undoubtedly Egyptian, like the names of other members of his family,[43] the most clearly Egyptian being Merari (Ex 6:16), *Mrry*, 'beloved', and Phinehas (Ex 6:25), *P'-nḥsy*, 'the negro'.[44] These names show that there was a group of Levites in Egypt and that Moses was one of them. According to the priestly genealogies (Ex 6:20; Num 26:59), Moses' father was Amram and his mother was Jochebed. He was Levi's grandson on his mother's side and his great-grandson on his father's side. He had an elder brother, Aaron, and a sister, Miriam, who, according to the story in Ex 2:1–10, was older than Moses.

---

[37] A. Gardiner, 'The Egyptian Origin of Some English Personal Names', *JAOS*, 56 (1936), pp. 189–197; J. G. Griffiths, 'The Egyptian Derivation of the Name Moses', *JNES*, 12 (1953), pp. 225–231; P. Montet, *L'Egypte et la Bible*, Paris, 1959, pp. 34–36; S. Herrmann, *op. cit.* (note 32), pp. 303–304.

[38] See, for example, F. Cornelius, 'Moses urkundlich', *ZAW*, 78 (1966), pp. 75–78.

[39] Pap. Salt 124, rect. 2, 17–18, re-edited by J. Černy, *JEA*, 15 (1929), pp. 243–258.

[40] J. Černy, *op. cit.*, p. 255; W. Helck, 'Zur Geschichte der 19. und 20. Dynastie', *ZDMG*, 105 (1955), pp. 27–52, cf. p. 40; C. Aldred, 'The Parentage of King Siptah', *JEA*, 49 (1963), pp. 41–48, cf. p. 43.

[41] Pap. Anastasi, I, 18, 1–2, A Gardiner, *Egyptian Hieratic Texts*, I, Leipzig, 1911, p. 20.*

[42] R. O. Faulkner, 'Egypt from the Inception of the Nineteenth Dynasty to the Death of Ramesses III', *CAH*, II, XXIII, 1966, p. 22.

[43] T. Meek, 'Moses and the Levites', *AJSL*, 56 (1939), pp. 113–120.

[44] A P'-nhsy was vizier during the reign of Mer-ne-Ptah.

He was, again according to this story, adopted by the pharaoh's daughter (Ex 2:10) and he stayed at the court until he reached manhood (Ex 2:10–11). Tradition has concluded from this that he 'was taught all the wisdom of the Egyptians' (Acts 7:22). There is also the case of the Asiatics who were educated at this period on the instructions of the pharaohs so that they could be entrusted with administrative duties.[45] There are, however, no indications that this is what happened in Moses' case. According to tradition, Moses, having come back to see his brothers and having killed an Egyptian slave-driver, had to flee to Midian, where he stayed for a long time, married, had a son and, after Yahweh had revealed himself to him, went back to deliver his brothers (Ex 2:11–4:31).

IV. MOSES AND THE MIDIANITES [46]

This story of Moses' stay in Midian, in which both the Yahwistic and the Elohistic sources have been distinguished by literary critics, is continued in Ex 18 (E), which describes the meeting between Moses and Jethro. The Midianite tradition is certainly early and there is no reason for us to believe that the figure of Moses was introduced at a later stage.[47] It must, in other words, have a historical basis.[48] We only have to recall the hostility towards the Midianites that is apparent in the stories of Baal Peor (Num 25:6–9), of the holy war against Midian (Num 31) and of Gideon (Judges 6–8) to realise that the tradition that Moses had a Midianite wife and had a vision of Yahweh in Midian and that a Midianite had taken part in the organisation of the people was not an invention. It should be noted in this context that the priestly editor transposed the scene of the revelation of the divine name to Egypt (Ex 6:2–9).

Moses' family relations with the Midianites are very confused in the texts of the Bible. According to Ex 2:21, Moses married the Midianite woman Zipporah. According to Num 12:1, on the other hand, he married a

---

[45] See above, p. 298–301 and the reference in S. Sauneron and Y. Yoyotte, *Revue d'Egyptologie*, 7 (1951), pp. 67–70.

[46] This section is a resumption of my study 'Sur l'origine kénite ou madianite du yahvisme', *Eretz-Israel*, 9 *(Albright Volume)*, 1969, pp. 28–32.

[47] This is A. H. J. Gunneweg's view, 'Mose in Madian', *ZTK*, 61 (1964), pp. 1–9. He follows M. Noth's theory on the composition of the Pentateuch from 'themes' which were originally independent. In his opinion, the Midianite tradition and the tradition of Sinai were concurrent and Moses was alien to both. He had an authentic and original place in the tradition of the exodus from Egypt, which did not know Yahweh.

[48] See R. Smend, *Jahwekrieg und Stämmebund. Erwägungen zur ältesten Geschichte Israels*, Göttingen, 1963, p. 96; G. Fohrer, *op. cit.* (note 32), p. 27; H. Seebass, *Der Erzvater Israel und die Einführung der Jahweverehrung in Kanaan (BZAW*, 98), 1966, pp. 86–87.

Cushite woman. Some scholars have rejected this datum as late.[49] If it is regarded as early, however, and retained, then this Cushite woman would have been an Ethiopian, at least according to the usual meaning of Cush in the Bible. More probably, however, Moses' wife came from the tribe of Cushan, which is placed in parallel with Midian in Hab 3:7, either because the two names were equivalent or because the two peoples were united by a blood relationship or by a common abode. In that case, all that we would have would be a variant of the Midianite tradition. According to Judges 1: 16 (corrected according to the Greek version) and 4:11, Moses' mother was a Kenite woman, the daughter of Hobab, 'the father-in-law of Moses'. According to Num 10:29, however, this Hobab was the son of Reuel the Midianite, 'the father-in-law of Moses'. It has been suggested that the term 'father-in-law' referred to Reuel and not to Hobab, who would in that case have been Moses' brother-in-law. Reuel is, however, called Moses' father-in-law, without any ambiguity at all, in Ex 2:18. But, in the same story (Ex 3:1) and several times in Ex 18, the Midianite Jethro is named as Moses' father-in-law. There is general agreement that Reuel is secondary in Ex 2:18 and Num 10:29 may represent an attempt to reconcile this tradition with that of Judges 1:16; 4:11.[50] Literary critics attribute Hobab to the Yahwistic source and Jethro to the Elohistic source. It has also been suggested that Jethro was Moses' father-in-law ('hôten), that Hobab was his son-in-law (ḥātān) and that both came from the clan of Reuel. In Judges 1:16; 4:11, 'Kenite' is, some scholars believe, the name of a status and means 'smith', so that Hobab was a member of a group of metal-workers belonging to the Midianites.[51] We may conclude that there were two parallel traditions – the tradition of Exodus, according to which Moses married the daughter of the Midianite Jethro and the tradition of Judges, according to which he married the daughter of the Kenite Hobab. Both proper names occur in the Rās Shamrah texts[52] and it is therefore possible that both traditions were early. Attempts have been made to reconcile them by regarding the Kenites as a branch of the Midianites,[53] but the only text that supports this argument is Num 10:29. There is no other place in the Bible where the Kenites are assimilated to the Midianites or even associated with them.

[49] Wellhausen was of this opinion and more recently H. Seebass, *VT*, 14 (1964), p. 111, note 3 and *Der Erzvater Israel, op. cit.*, p. 84, note 139.

[50] For the composite character of Num 10:29–36, see H. Seebass, 'Zu Num. X, 33 f', *VT*, 14 (1964), pp. 111–113; M. Noth, *Das vierte Buch Mose, Numeri (ATD)*, 1966, pp. 69–70.

[51] W. F. Albright, 'Jethro, Hobab and Reuel', *CBQ*, 25 (1963), pp. 1–11.

[52] C. H. Gordon, *Ugaritic Textbook*, Rome, 1965, Glossary No. 918, Hbb at No. 1170, Ytr.

[53] This is a common view; see H. H. Rowley, *From Joseph to Joshua*, London, 1950, pp. 152–153; K.–H. Bernhardt, *Gott und Bild*, Berlin, 1956, p. 127, with bibliographical references; more recent authors include B. Mazar, 'The Sanctuary of Arad and the Family of Hobab the Kenite', *JNES*, 24 (1965), pp. 297–303, cf. p. 300.

The tradition of Moses' marriage with the Kenite woman originated in southern Palestine, where the Kenites had settled with Judah in the region of Arad (Judges 1:16). It was there that Saul encountered the Kenites (1 Sam 15:6). At the time of David, there was, in the same district, a 'Negeb of the Kenites' (1 Sam 27:10) and 'towns of the Kenites' (1 Sam 30:29). These contacts between the Israelites and the Kenites were always friendly and they must have resulted in a number of family ties. On the other hand, groups of Levites had settled at quite an early stage in this region (see especially Num 26:58; Judges 17:7; 19:1). It is possible that this tradition provided the southern Palestinian version of Moses' marriage with a foreign woman. It is, in any case, independent of the Midianite tradition and is not connected with the tradition of the exodus from Egypt.[54]

The tradition of Moses' Midianite marriage, on the other hand, is closely connected with Egypt. According to both the Yahwistic and the Elohistic traditions, Moses came from and returned to Egypt. It is also tied to the exodus from Egypt – it was in Midian that Moses was told by Yahweh that he would bring the Israelites up out of Egypt (J) or that he would bring them out of the country (E). What is more, Jethro the Midianite 'rejoiced at all Yahweh's goodness to Israel in rescuing them from the Egyptians' hands' (Ex 18:9–10, E?). This connection, which is confirmed by the two early sources, forms part of the primitive tradition and it must be in accordance with history. We said at the beginning of this section why the tradition of Moses' sojourn in Midian could not have been invented and Moses' Egyptian name is also a confirmation of his links with the Nile valley and of the part he played in the exodus from Egypt.

Geographers place Midian in Arabia, to the south-east of the Gulf of 'Aqabah. According to both the topography and the folklore of the Arabs, Moses stayed in this region with Jethro, who is known as Shu'aib in Arabic. Eusebius speaks of a city of Madiane in Arabia, which also figures in Ptolemy's writings and which was perhaps in Josephus' mind when he spoke of Moses going to the city of Madianē near the Red Sea.[55] This location may not, however, be applicable to an earlier period and the Bible is much vaguer, presenting the Midianites above all as 'great' nomads. The Israelites encountered them to the north-east of the Dead Sea (Num 22:4; 25:6 ff; 31). They came from Transjordan, mounted on their camels, to pillage central Palestine (Judges 6–8). The only precise information concerning their own territory is found in 1 Kings 11:18, in which we read that the young Edomite prince Hada passed through Midian and then through

[54] In 1 Sam 15:6, the friendliness shown by the Kenites towards the Israelites when they came up from Egypt is recalled. This is not, however, a memory of Moses' stay in Midian and of the exodus, but an echo of Num 10:31–32.

[55] The references will be found in F.–M. Abel, Géographie de la Palestine, I, Paris, 1933, p. 285.

Paran on his flight from Egypt. The road from Edom to Egypt did not, however, pass through Arabia and the wilderness of Paran stretched to the south of the Negeb, from Kadesh to Egypt. Ishmael made his home there (Gen 21:21) and it was from Paran that the men were sent out to reconnoitre Canaan (Num 12:16; 13:3, 26). All these data point to the fact that Midian was situated to the east of the wilderness of Paran, but in the Sinaitic peninsula. What is more, Jethro is presented in the Bible from Ex 2:16 onwards as a nomadic herdsman and after his meeting with Moses he returns to his own country (Ex 18:27). Moses took his flock far from where Jethro was staying (Ex 3:1). These last two episodes took place on the 'mountain of Elohim'. There is therefore no reason either for making Moses go into Arabia or for situating the revelation of God there.

We can, in any case, regard it as historically authentic that Moses had relationships with the Midianites. Attempts have been made to go further than this. Moses' father-in-law is several times called the 'priest of Midian' (Ex 2:16; 3:1; 18:1) and he offers a sacrifice (Ex 18:12). It is, of course, true that the patriarchs also offered sacrifices, but they are never called priests and this title given repeatedly to the father-in-law of Moses shows that he was more than a tribal chief and that he clearly had a religious function.[56] It should be remembered that the name of Yahweh was revealed to Moses while he was in Midian (Ex 3:13–15), that Jethro himself invoked the name of Yahweh (Ex 18:10) and that he apparently offered his sacrifice to Yahweh and presided at the sacred meal which followed it (Ex 18:12). The conclusion that has been drawn by most scholars, both exegetes and historians, is that Yahwism originated in Midian.[57]

Other arguments have also been used to connect the Kenites and the ancestors of Israel, especially by those scholars who believe that the Kenites and the Midianites were related. (Attempts have even been made to link the Kenites with Moses himself, following the tradition of Judges.) Cain, who gave his name to the Kenites, bore the 'mark of Yahweh' (Gen 4:15) and was therefore a worshipper of Yahweh.[58] The Rechabites, who were fervent Yahwists (2 Kings 10:15–27; Jer 35:1–11), were, according to 1 Chron 2:55, the descendants of the Kenites. The Genesis text, however, is the work of the Yahwist, with the result that it really says no more than

---

[56] I believe this despite the theory of C. H. W. Brekelmans, 'Exodus xviii and the Origins of Yahwism in Israel', *OTS*, 10 (1954), pp. 215–224.

[57] See H. H. Rowley's bibliography and arguments in *From Joseph to Joshua*, pp. 149–155; 'Moses and Monotheism', *From Moses to Qumran*, London, 1963, pp. 48–57; K.–H. Bernhardt, *Gott und Bild*, Berlin, 1956, pp. 125–128; O. Eissfeldt, 'Jahwe, der Gott der Väter, *TLZ*, 88 (1963), cols. 481–490, cf. col. 486–487 = *Kleine Schriften*, IV, pp. 85–86.

[58] This opinion has been widespread since the time of B. Stade, 'Das Kainzeichen', *ZAW*, 14 (1894), pp. 250–318 and W. Vischer, *Yahwe, der Gott Kains*, Munich, 1929; more recently, H. Heyde, *Kain, der erste Jahwe-Verehrer*, Stuttgart, 1965.

334 II: TRADITIONS OF THE SOJOURN IN EGYPT, THE EXODUS AND SINAI

that God put a mark on Cain to protect him, this mark being the sign of a clan in which vengeance was taken in a particularly terrible way (Gen 4:15, 24). Apart from the editing of the Yahwist, there is nothing to say that this was the 'mark of Yahweh'. As for the Rechabites, the late genealogy of the Chronicles only shows that the Rechabites and the Kenites were assimilated because their way of life was similar. There is no really clear indication in the Bible that the Kenites worshipped a god called Yahweh or by any similar name.

Indirect and extrabiblical evidence can, of course, be used. A geographical list, dating from the period of Amen-hotep III and found in the temple at Soleb in Nubia, contains, in addition to other 'lands of the Shasu', a 'land of the Shasu Yhw3' and the same name appears in a copy of this list made during the reign of Ramses II in a temple at Amara West (also in Nubia).[59] The only other name that can be identified with certainty in this group is, at Amara, that of the 'land of the Shasu S'rr', which is apparently Seir in Edom. The bedouins who led a nomadic existence in southern Palestine and Transjordania to the east of the Egyptian frontier of the Delta were called by the Egyptians 'Shasu'. It is probable that the Kenites, the Midianites and some of the other tribes which preceded Israel were included within this generic term and the Egyptians only distinguished them according to their usual pasture land. Like Seir, Yhw3 is a geographical name, but it would be arbitrary to regard it as the equivalent of a Beth Yhw3, a 'temple of Yahweh'.[60] A simpler supposition is that the name of the district was the same as the name of the deity who was worshipped there, but this is pure hypothesis. A final theory is that there was, in the region where the Kenites lived and where the ancestors of the Israelites met them, a geographical name which was very similar to that of the God of Israel. This is an interesting theory, but it is not sufficiently substantiated for us to be able to speak of a cult of Yahweh among the Kenites.[16]

Another argument has been based on the discovery in the excavations at Tell Arad of an Israelite sanctuary, apparently Yahwistic, which was built in the tenth century B.C. This sanctuary was probably constructed on the site

---

[59] Neither of these texts has yet been definitively edited. For Soleb, see J. Leclant, *Orientalia*, 32 (1963), pp. 203; R. Giveon, 'Toponymes ouest-asiatiques à Soleb', *VT*, 14 (1964), pp. 239–255. For Amara West, B. Grdseloff, *Revue de l'Histoire Juive en Egypte*, 1 (1947), pp. 79–83; S. H. Horn *JNES*, 12 (1953), p. 201; K. A. Kitchen, *JEA*, 50 (1964), p. 67; H. H. Rowley, *From Moses to Qumran*, pp. 53–54.*

[60] R. Giveon, 'The Shosu of Egyptian Sources and the Exodus', *Fourth World Congress of Jewish Studies, Papers*, I, Jerusalem, 1967, pp. 193–196, cf. p. 193; *ibid.*, *JBL*, 83 (1964), pp. 415–416.

[61] S. Herrmann, 'Der Name Jhw3 in den Inschriften von Soleb. Prinzipielle Erwägungen', *Fourth World Congress, op. cit.* (Note 60), pp. 213–216; *ibid.*, 'Der alttestamentliche Gottesname', *EvTh*, 26 (1966), pp. 281–293.

of a holy place used by the family of Hobab the Kenite which, according to Judges 1:16, had settled at Arad.[62] This hypothesis is possible so long as the theory that the Kenites worshipped Yahweh is regarded as established, but it cannot be used as an argument to prove that theory. If, on the other hand, the Kenites and the Midianites are regarded as distinct and the different traditions of a Kenite and a Midianite marriage made by Moses are accepted, then it is very improbable that Yahwism had a 'Kenite' origin.

The arguments based on the Midianite tradition seem at first sight to be more convincing. In Ex 18, Moses and his father-in-law, the priest of Midian, meet in the desert at the 'mountain of Elohim'. The priest of Midian offers a sacrifice and presides at a meal which is eaten 'in the presence of God'. The incident takes place, in other words, in a holy place and a priest of Midian officiates. But this priest blesses Yahweh for having delivered the Israelites and declares that Yahweh is 'greater than all the gods'. This Midianite priest is therefore clearly a priest of Yahweh. The 'mountain of Elohim' where he offers a sacrifice is also a Midianite sanctuary. But it should not be forgotten that it was on the 'Mountain of Elohim' where, according to the same Elohistic source, Moses received his revelation of the name of Yahweh, (Ex 3:1b) and his mission (Ex 3:12). These are the arguments put forward.

Jethro's declaration (Ex 18:10–11), however, is open to several different interpretations. It may be a confession of his own faith, strengthened by the wonders performed by Yahweh on behalf of the Israelites, just as, after her son had been raised to life by Elijah, the widow of Zarephath said: 'Now I know you are a man of God' (1 Kings 17:24) – she already knew it. After centuries of Yahwism, the expression 'You will know that I am Yahweh' was often addressed to the Israelites and it is met with frequently in Ezekiel.[63] On the other hand, the Syrian Naaman, after he had been cured by bathing in the Jordan, confessed: 'Now I know that there is no God in all the earth except in Israel' (2 Kings 5:15). This shows that he had been converted to Yahweh. Several authors have concluded that this is the meaning of Ex 18, namely that Jethro had been converted to the Yahwism of Moses.

Another explanation is, however, more obvious. It is simply that Jethro recognised that Yahweh, the god of Moses, was more powerful than the other gods. There are many parallels in the Old Testament. For instance, when Abimelech came to Isaac with the suggestion of a covenant, he said: 'It became clear to us that Yahweh was with you' (Gen 26:28). Again, at Jericho, Rahab said to the Israelite spies: 'We have heard how Yahweh dried up the Sea of Reeds . . . Yahweh your God is God both in heaven

---

[62] B. Mazar, op. cit. (note 53).

[63] See W. Zimmerli, *Erkenntnis Gottes nach dem Buche Ezechiel*, Zürich, 1954 = *Gottes Offenbarung*, Munich, 1963, pp. 41–119.

above and on earth beneath' (Jos 2:9–11). Neither Abimelech nor Rahab were Yahwists, nor were they converted to Yahwism. It is simply that this recognition of the God of Israel by the gentiles is a theme that recurs in the Old Testament from the story of Balaam (Num 22–24) and that of the Gibeonites (Jos 2:9–10) up to the discourse of Achior in the story of Judith and Holofernes (Judith 5:5–21).

It also has to be remembered that Ex 18 has not preserved the tradition in its primitive form.[64] The frequency of the name Yahweh (six times in verses 1–10) in this text, which is attributed to the Elohist, and the doublets contained in the same verses show that the text in its present form is the endproduct of a long development. Jethro's declaration concerning the greatness and power of Yahweh has to be compared with the texts which precede this declaration and in which the plagues which strike the Egyptians are presented as proofs of the presence and the power of God.[65] The most explicit texts in the early sources are those in the Yahwistic tradition. Before the water of the Nile is turned into blood we read: 'That I am Yahweh you shall learn by this' (Ex 7:17, J). Before the plague of gadflies, we read: 'So that you may know that I, Yahweh, am in the midst of the land' (Ex 8:18, J) and before the locusts: 'To let you know that I am Yahweh' (Ex 10:2, J additional). When Jethro learned 'all that Yahweh had done to Pharaoh and the Egyptians' (Ex 18:8), he cried out: 'Now I know that Yahweh is greater than all the gods' (Ex 18:11).

Verse 11 is, of course, the climax of the story and verse 12 might be a final stage in the tradition, or else it might have a different origin. Jethro offered a holocaust and zᵉbhahî, the victims being eaten in common afterwards. This form of holocaust and sacrifice of communion was Canaanite, however, and apparently not known in Israel during the period in the desert.[66] It is significant too that Moses is not mentioned in verse 12 and that the meal is shared by Aaron and the elders, who have not figured in the story so far. It is possible that Jethro's recognition of Yahweh's greatness was interpreted in the biblical tradition as a conversion and that the first consequence of that conversion would have been this offering of a sacrifice as a testimony to Jethro's faith. It should, however, be borne in mind that, when he pretended to be converted to Baal, Jehu also offered zᵉbhahîm and holocausts to him (2 Kings 10:18–24) and that, on his conversion, Naaman promised that he would 'no longer offer holocaust or sacrifice (zebhah) to any god except Yahweh' (2 Kings 5:17).

---

[64] M. Noth, Das zweite Buch Mose. Exodus (ATD), 1959, in loco; R. Knierim, 'Exodus 18 und die Neuordnung der mosaischen Gerichtsbarkeit', ZAW, 73 (1961), pp. 146–171; H. Seebass, Der Erzvater Israel, pp. 70, 84.

[65] W. Zimmerli, op. cit. (note 63), pp. 19–27.

[66] R. de Vaux, Institutions, p. 429; Les sacrifices de l'Ancien Testament, Paris, 1964, pp. 21, 47; R. Schmid, Das Bundesopfer in Israel, Munich, 1964, pp. 75–99; A. Cody, Bib, (1968), pp. 162–164.

It is therefore not possible to prove that Jethro had always been a worshipper of Yahweh, nor is it possible to say whether the 'mountain of Elohim' had been a Midianite sanctuary served by Jethro. In Ex 18:5, Jethro came to Moses at the mountain of Elohim, camped there and then returned from the same place to his own country (Ex 18: 27). According to Ex 3:1, the mountain of Elohim was a long way from the place where Jethro usually lived.

We must now briefly consider whether Moses's father-in-law was a 'priest of Midian'. We know nothing about the Midianite priesthood and nothing about the priesthood of the early nomadic Semites of northern Arabia and Sinai. The traditions of central Arabia before the coming of Islam show that there was no separate class of priests as distinct from the ordinary people and that there were no sacrificing priests.[67] One religious figure occurs in these traditions, however, the *kāhin*,[68] who was a soothsayer, transmitting oracles, consulted in all the important affairs that concerned the tribe and acting as judge in disputes between individuals, when his decisions were accepted as divine judgement. It should be noted in this context that the advice that Jethro gave to Moses in his administration of justice was that he should bring the more serious disputes between the people to God and to teach them the statutes and laws of God (Ex 18:19–20). Was Jethro not in fact advising Moses to reserve for himself the very functions that he, Jethro, exercised as a Midianite *kāhin*?

Certain difficulties are encountered in this explanation. All the information that we possess concerning the Arab *kāhin* is almost two thousand years later than the period of Moses, when the situation must have been different. The name, which is quite isolated in Arabic, may have been borrowed, with a degraded meaning, from the north-western Semitic languages or from the Canaanites, Hebrews or Aramaeans, among whom *kôhen* or *kahna* meant 'priest'.[69] There is also another, equally serious, difficulty. Even if verses 21b and 25b are discounted as additions to the text, the steps which Jethro advised Moses to take and which he in fact took presuppose a people which was large and already sedentary. (It should be noted that, after his case had been settled, each man went home satisfied, v. 23.) What this passage indicates, then, is that a decentralisation of legal power which took place at a later date was attributed to Moses.[70] It is therefore necessary to leave the real character and functions of this 'priest' of Midian undefined.

[67] J. Wellhausen, *Reste arabischen Heidentums*,[2] Berlin, 1897, p. 130; H. Lammens, *L'Arabie occidentale avant l'hegire*, Beirut, 1928, pp. 107–108.

[68] J. Wellhausen, *Reste, op. cit.*, pp. 134–136; A. Fischer, 'kâhin', *Encyclopédie de l'Islam*, II, 1927, pp. 665–666; J. Henninger, 'La religion bédouine préislamique', *L'Antica società beduina* (ed. F. Gabrieli), Rome, 1959, p. 138; T. Fahd, *La divination arabe*, Leiden, 1966, pp. 91–97; A. Cody, *A History of the Old Testament Priesthood*, Rome, 1969, pp. 14–18.

[69] W. F. Albright, *From the Stone Age to Christianity*,[2] Baltimore, 1946, p. 18.

[70] B. Knierim, *op. cit.* (note 64) believes that this happened during the reform of

There is, however, no reason to believe that this legal reform was the consequence of an intervention on the part of a Midianite, once this is not required to satisfy an early tradition which insists on an influence exerted by the Midianites during the early period of organisation of the people. Some scholars have even interpreted Ex 18 as the memory of a covenant between Jethro's and Moses' groups.[71] This conviction is based above all on verse 12, which describes a meal similar to that shared in the covenant between Isaac and Abimelech (Gen 26:28–30) and a sacrifice and a meal like that in the treaty between Jacob and Laban (Gen 31:54). This is possible if we accept that verse 12, without the mention of the holocaust and of Aaron, belongs to the primitive tradition. It does not, however, change the conclusion – it cannot be proved that Jethro acted as a priest of Yahweh,[72] nor can it be demonstrated that he transmitted his faith to Moses. We do not know which deity was the object of Midianite worship and we know nothing about their cult or their priesthood. It is important to know what the Midianites were able to give to the Israelites before we can judge whether or not the Israelites borrowed anything from them. We are therefore bound to conclude that the suggestion that Yahwism originated among the Midianites or among the Kenites is no more than a hypothesis which cannot be proved.

V. THE REVELATION OF THE DIVINE NAME [73]

According to the Yahwistic tradition, the name Yahweh was invoked by the first human beings, by Enosh, the son of Seth (Gen 4:26). This is why only the theophany of the burning bush (Ex 3:1–5) and the mission of Moses (Ex 3:16–20) were retained in the Yahwistic account of God's appearance to Moses in Midian.

According to the Elohistic tradition of Ex 3:6, 9–15, God revealed to Moses the name by which he wished to be invoked from that time forward, the name of Yahweh.[74] In an attempt to reconcile these two traditions, it

---

Jehoshaphat, as outlined in 2 Chron. 19:5–11; see W. F. Albright, 'The Judicial Reform of Jehoshaphat', *Alexander Marx Jubilee Volume*, New York, 1950, pp. 61–82.
[71] C. N. W. Brekelmans, *op. cit.* (note 56); F. C. Fensham, 'Did a Treaty Between the Israelites and the Kenites Exist?', *BASOR*, 175 (Oct. 1964), pp. 51–54; A. Cody, 'Exodus 18, 12: Jethro Accepts a Covenant with the Israelites', *Bib*, 49 (1968), pp. 153–166.
[72] A. Cody, op. cit., pp. 159–161, has drawn attention to the fact that the text says literally that Jethro 'received' the sacrifices, not that he 'offered' them – being one of the contracting parties, he 'accepted' a part of the sacrifice of the covenant.
[73] In this section, I am summarising, with a number of changes and modifications, what I said in 'The Revelation of the Divine Name YHWH', in *Proclamation and Presence. Old Testament Essays in Honour of G. H. Davies*, London, 1970, pp. 48–75.
[74] The attribution of this text to the Elohist has recently been called in question. See

has been suggested that Moses did not receive a revelation of the name of
Yahweh, which he knew, but simply an explanation of the name.[75] This, of
course, weakens the implication of the text, because verse 15 forms part of
the early account[76] and states clearly that Yahweh is a new name.

The priestly tradition affirms this even more clearly. In the priestly account, the scene is transferred to Egypt, where God reveals himself as
Yahweh, a name that was unknown to the patriarchs and which was to
replace the name El Shaddai, by which the patriarchs invoked God.*

1. The form of the name

Yahweh was to remain the name of the God of Israel from the time that it
was revealed to Moses. It is used in the Bible almost always in the long form
of Yahweh but, sometimes in poetry and in the liturgical acclamation
hallluyāh, in the short form of Yah. This divine name is also used in various
short forms in personal names containing it – *Yʰô–*, *Yô–*, *Yʿ–* etc. at the
beginning of a name and *–yah*, *–yahû* at the end.[77] The longer form is the
earliest form (although this has been disputed[78]). This longer form is almost
invariably used in the Old Testament when the divine name does not occur
in combination to form a proper name. It is this form which is explained
in Ex 3:14.

The name of the God of Israel is also found outside the Bible, notably as
Yhwh in the Mesha stele (ninth century B.C), on an eighth century seal,[79] in

especially S. Mowinckel 'The Name of the God of Moses', *HUCA*, 32 (1961), pp. 121–133;
ibid., *Erwägungen zur Pentateuchquellenfrage*, Trondheim, 1964, p. 64 (the text is J); A. Besters,
'L'expression 'Fils d'Israel' en Ex i-xiv', *RB*, 74 (1967), pp. 321–355, especially pp. 328–333
(the text is J, rewritten by a priestly editor, who was especially responsible for verse 15).

[75] This solution is particularly favoured by those scholars who reject the idea of an
independent Elohistic tradition; see S. Mowinckel, *HUCA*, 32 (1961), p. 126. It is also
favoured by those who reject all documentary criticism; see M. H. Segal, 'The Revelation of
the Name JHWH', *Tarbiz*, 12 (1940–1941), pp. 97–108 (Hebrew); *The Pentateuch. Its Composition and its Authorship and Other Biblical Studies*, Jerusalem, 1967, pp. 4–8. One argument
which some scholars have regarded as decisive is that Moses' mother had a name composed
with Yahweh – Jochebed. This name, however, is given in late genealogies (Ex 6:20; Num
26:59) and it is not certain whether it contains the name Yahweh; see M. Noth, *Die
israelitischen Personennamen*, Stuttgart, 1928, p. 111; Koehler and Baumgartner, *Lexikon, sub
voce*.

[76] See M.Noth, *Exodus (ATD)*, p. 30; G. Fohrer, *Uberlieferung und Geschichte des Exodus
(BZAW*, 91), 1964, p. 40.

[77] Apart from the Bible, the short terminal form has been found on seals and ostraca as
–yw.

[78] See the recent publication by H. Cazelles, *XVᵉ Rencontre Assyriologique Internationale,
Liège, 1966*, ed. J.-R-Kupper, Paris, 1967, pp. 82–86.

[79] F. M. Cross, *HTR*, 55 (1962), p. 251.

the ostraca of Tell 'Arad at the end of the seventh century,[80] frequently in the Lachish letters[81] at the beginning of the sixth century and in graffiti which may be pre-exilic.[82] The shorter form has been found on a Samaritan ostracon of the eighth or seventh century as *lyh*[83] and on a seventh century ostracon from Megiddo as *lyw*.[84] These two readings are, however, uncertain. The two letters *yh* found in post-exilic stamps do not represent the divine name.[85] They are in fact an abbreviation of *Yhd*, the name of the province of Judaea during the Persian and Hellenistic periods.[86] In the Elephantine papyri, the short form *Yhw* occurs every time except once, when it appears as *Yhh*. In the ostraca of Elephantine, on the other hand, the form is always *Yhh*.[87] The longer form is certainly the commonest and the earliest form encountered outside the Bible. A contradiction of this long form can, however, be explained more easily from the philological point of view than a lengthening of a shorter form.

How was the name pronounced? We know that the Massoretes gave the divine name the vowels of *ʾdhōnai*, 'my Lord', which was to be read instead of the Tetragrammaton itself. The pronunciation of Yahweh is based on the etymological interpretation given in Ex 3:14, on analogy with the Amorite names Yawi-ilā, Yawi-Addu, Yawi-Dagan etc. which we shall consider later in this chapter, and on the Greek transcriptions *Iaove* and *Iaβε*. The pronunciation *Yahwo* has been suggested and this pronunciation has recently been defended with good arguments.[88] In the first place, the form *Yhw*, found at Elephantine, may have been pronounced *Yaho*, which is one of the abbreviated forms assumed by the divine name in combination with personal names. Secondly, there is the transcription *Iaō* found in the works

[80] Y. Aharoni, 'Hebrew Ostraca from Tell Arad', *IEJ*, 16 (1966), pp. 1–7; 'Three Hebrew Ostraca from Arad', *Eretz-Israel*, 9 (1969), pp. 10-21 (Hebrew).
[81] The two examples of *Yhw* in the Lachish letters quoted by A. Murtonen in *A Philological and Literary Treatise on the Old Testament Divine Name*, Helsinki, 1952, p. 43 are errors in reading made by the first scholar to publish them.
[82] J. Naveh, 'Old Hebrew Inscriptions in a Burial Cave', *IEJ*, 13 (1963), pp. 74–92.*
[83] G. A. Reisner and C. S. Fisher, *Harvard Excavations at Samaria*, Cambridge Mass., 1924, p. 238, No. 65, Plate 55b. (It is possible that the three letters are the end of a name containing the name of God separated because of the break in the fragment.) Another example of *lyh*, in Aramaic writing, suggested by E. L. Sukenik, *PEQ*, 1936, pp. 34–27, has to be set aside; see S. A. Birnbaum, in J. W. Crowfoot and others, *Samaria-Sebaste III. The Objects*, London, 1957, p. 28.
[84] H. G. May, 'An Inscribed Jar from Megiddo', *AJSL*, 50 (1933–1934), pp. 10–14; R. S. Lamon, G. M. Shipton, *Megiddo I*, Chicago, 1939, Plate 115, 5 (although the reading of *waw* is very dubious).
[85] I disagree here with L.–H. Vincent, *RB*, 56 (1949), pp. 286–291.
[86] Y. Aharoni, *IEJ*, 6 (1956), pp. 148–149; ibid., *Excavations at Ramet Rahel*, Rome, 1962, pp. 6, 30; 1964, pp. 20, 44; F. M. Cross, *Eretz-Israel*, 9 (1969), pp. 22–26.
[87] A. Dupont-Sommer, *RHR*, 130 (1945–B), pp. 22–23; *Semitica*, 2 (1949), p. 34.
[88] W. Vischer, 'Eher Jahwo als Jahwe', *TZ*, 16 (1960), pp. 259–267.

of some of the Church Fathers and in the historical writings of Diodorus of Sicily (I, 94). The name *Iaō* is also found on gnostic gems and amulets and in the magic papyri of the first five centuries A.D. The argument based on the Greek transcriptions is the most convincing, but it loses much of its cogency as soon as we remember that *Iaō* may only have been, at least originally, a material transcription of the Hebrew *Yaw*, which could not substantiate the pronunciation *Yao*.[89] Taking everything into consideration the generally accepted pronunciation *Yahweh* is preferable.

2. The name of Yahweh outside Israel?

This divine name was new to Israel and was used only by Israel, but it may possibly have existed before elsewhere. Attempts have in fact been made to find evidence of its existence outside Israel and before the period of Moses.[90] The early Babylonian names *Yaum-ilum* or *Yawum-ilum* have been cited and translated as 'Yahweh is God'. The short form *Yaum* has also been noted, although it is now accepted as meaning 'mine'.[91] It was believed that a god *Yw* was mentioned in a mythological text of Rās Shamrah, in which the god El says– 'The name of my son *yw-ilt* . . .'[92] The reading has been disputed, but it is certain.[93] The text, on the other hand, is badly preserved and obscure. The first publisher of this text suggested that there was a connection between this god and Yahweh and this is still accepted by certain specialists in Ugaritic.[94] Other scholars, however, have rejected it or else

---

[89] In the same way, *Iaη*, found in Origen, *Selecta in Psalm.*, Ps ii, PG, XII, 1104, is simply a transcription of *Yah*.

[90] A. Murtonen, *The Appearance of the Name YHWH outside Israel* (*Studia Orientalia*, XVI, 3), Helsinki, 1951, resumed in *A Philological and Literary Treatise* (see note 81), whose theory has to be corrected and amplified in certain points. The name *Aḫi-yawi*, read on a Taanach tablet (fifteenth century B.C.) ought to be read as *Aḫi-yami*; see W. F. Albright, *BASOR*, 94 (April 1944), p. 20. I do not include, among the possible cases of the occurrence of the divine name outside Israel, the names Azriya'u of Ya'udi (Samal) in the reign of Tiglath-pileser III and Ya'ubidi (also known as Ilubidi) of Hamath in the reign of Sargon II. Both of these are of later date than Moses and both reflect an Israelite influence.

[91] See *CAD*, sub voce *ja'um*, with references, and B. Landsberger, *ZA*, 35 (1924), p. 24, note 2; J. Lewy, *Orientalia*, 15 (1946), pp. 362 and 393; W. von Soden, *WO*, 3 (1964–1966), p. 178. H. Cazelles, *op. cit.* (note 78) has used this pronoun to explain the name Yahweh in the short form Yaw, which is, in his opinion, primitive and meant 'mine'. The pronoun *yaum*, however, is peculiarly Akkadian and does not exist in western Semitic. This does not, moreover, explain the long form, which is, we believe, original.

[92] C. Virolleaud, *La déesse 'Anat*, Paris, 1938, tablet VI AB IV 14 = Gordon *'nt* Plate X (*Ugaritic Textbook*, p. 255) = *Corpus Herdner*, No. 1.

[93] A. Herdner, Corpus, p. 4.

[94] C. H. Gordon, *Ugaritic Textbook*, Rome, 1965, Glossary, No. 1084 (p. 410). J. Aistleitner, *Wörterbuch der ugaritischen Sprache*, Leipzig, 1965, No. 1151.

regard it as extremely uncertain.[95] This possible divine name does not, in any case, apppear anywhere else in the Rās Shamrah texts. Immediately after mentioning Yw, this poem goes on to speak of the god Ym = Yam, the god of the sea or of the rivers, a deity who was well known at Rās Shamrah. It is therefore possible that Yw may be a different way of writing Ym or else part of a title of the same god. It would nonetheless be very difficult to establish that Yam was equivalent to Yahweh.[96] If the primitive form of the divine name is the long form $Yhwh$, this would exclude any possibility of a borrowing.

This long form of the divine name has also been compared with the element $Yawi-$ or $Yahwi-$ in the Amorite proper names $Yawi-ila$, $Yahwi-ila$, $Yawi-Addu$, $Yawi-Dagan$ and $Yahwi-Nasi$. We shall ourselves use these Amorite names later in this chapter to throw light on the etymology, the form and the meaning of the name Yahweh. There have, however, also been recent attempts to see in them the name of the God of Israel. The translation that has been suggested is: 'El (or Addu or Dagan) is Yahweh' and these names point to the adoption of a god Yahweh by the Amorites at the beginning of the second millennium B.C. as the assimilation of that god into the Amorite pantheon.[97]

This explanation is unlikely, however, for several reasons. The names belong to the numerous class of Amorite names formed from a verb and a divine name. In the case in question, the problem is to decide which verbal root is used and what tense.[98] There is no letter $h\bar{e}$ in Akkadian, which either does not transcribe it or else expresses it by ha. The forms Yawi-N and Yahwi-N may therefore both contain the same root hwy = 'to be'. There is also no letter in Akkadian corresponding to $heth$, which is transcribed again by ha or else omitted. The consequence of this is that both forms of the name may contain the root hwy = 'to live'. As far as the form of the verb is concerned, it would seem that Amorite had preserved the simple qal common to all Semitic verbs, with the forms *$yaqtal$, *$yaqtil$ and *$yaqtul$ for the perfect-present aspect and the forms *$yaqtalu$, *$yaqtilu$ and *$yaqtulu$ for the imperfect-future aspect. The forms of the causative $hiphil$ are *$yaqtil$ and *$yaqtilu$ respectively. But, in the case of the verbs which have *$yaqtil$ in the simple qal and in the case of the verbs in the third radical w/y,

---

[95] Recent works include J. Gray, 'The God YW in the Religion of Canaan', *JNES*, 12 (1953), pp. 278–283, summarised in *The Legacy of Canaan* (*SVT*, 5),[2] 1965, pp. 180–184. M. Pope, in *Götter und Mythen im vorderen Orient*, ed. H. W. Haussig, Stuttgart, 1965, pp. 291–292.

[96] Despite the theory of A. Murtonen, *op. cit.* (Note 81); W. E. C. B. MacLaurin, *VT*, 12 (1962), pp. 449–451.

[97] A. Finet, 'Iawi-ilâ, roi de Talhayum', *Syria*, 41 (1964), pp. 117–142, especially pp. 118–122.

[98] H. B. Huffmon, *Amorite Personal Names in the Mari Texts*, Baltimore, 1965, pp. 70–72; W. von Soden, *WO*, 3 (1964–1966), pp. 179–181.

the writing does not allow us to distinguish between the simple and the causative.

Leaving aside the uncertainty of the aspect, then, there are several possible translations of these names in theory – 'N lives' or 'N causes to live', 'N exists' or 'N causes to exist'. Furthermore, the divine name may also be in the vocative – 'He exists (the child), O N' or 'He lives (the child), O N'. Finally, it is possible that two series of names have to be distinguished – *Yahwi-N* formed with the root *hwy* = 'to live' and *Yawi-N* formed with the root *hwy* ='to be'.

Bearing in mind Amorite onomastics, especially the formation of many other names with the root *hwy* and the frequent use of the causative *hiphil*, and the fact that *h* is usually transcribed as *ḫ* in Akkadian, the most likely explanation of the name *Yahwi-N* is 'N causes to live'. This is fully in accordance with the requirements of a name given to a newly-born child. If the name *Yawi-N* is in fact different and contains the root *hwy* = 'to be', it would be the only Amorite name formed with this root. It would, however, be equivalent to the Akkadian formation of names such as *Ibašši-Ilum, Ibašši-Ilani* and *Ibašši-Adad* and, in the stative form, *Baši-Ilum*. These names mean 'The god or the gods or Adad exists'. This is not simply a statement of fact or even a confession of faith. It is a sign of recognition and respect with regard to the god in question, who has revealed himself as a god who exists and acts.[99] If this is correct, then, *Yawi-N* must mean 'N exists' rather than 'N causes to exist', although the second meaning is still possible. We may in any case conclude that the elements *Yawi-* and *Yahwi-* are not a divine name.

The only name found outside the Old Testament and before the period of the exodus that can be legitimately compared with the name Yahweh is *Yhw3*, the name of a Shasu country, which we have already discussed in connection with the suggestion that Yahwism originated in Midian. [100] There is, however, no evidence that this geographical or ethnic name may also have been the name of a deity. The only conclusion to which we can come, then, is that it is possible and even probable that the divine name *Yhwh* existed outside Israel before Moses – particularly because its form is, as we have seen, archaic – but we have no certain evidence of this.

3. *The etymology and the meaning of the name Yahweh*

An Egyptian etymology was suggested almost a century ago for the first time and this possibility has been taken up again recently and developed

[99] J. J. Stamm, *Die akkadische Namengebung*, Leipzig, 1939, p. 179.
[100] See above, pp. 334–335.

II: TRADITIONS OF THE SOJOURN IN EGYPT, THE EXODUS AND SINAI

further,[101] but it has to be rejected, because the name could not have been composed of two Egyptian words, *Yah*, the Egyptian moon god, and *we3*, 'one'. We also feel bound to reject three other possible explanations. The first is that the name has an Indo-European origin – that *Dyau-s*, which became Zeus in Greek and Jupiter in Latin, became *Yaw* in Hebrew.[102] The second explanation is that the Hurrian *ya*, meaning 'god', was enlarged by the addition of the Hurrian suffixes *-ha* or *-wa*.[103] Finally, there is the suggestion that the name Yahweh is connected with the god Yae or Yaue, apparently mentioned in a so far undeciphered inscription found in the Indus valley and dating back to the third millennium B.C.[104]

We have therefore to confine our search for the etymology of the name to the Semitic sphere. One suggested explanation is that it was a exclamation that occurred in worship, formed from the interjection *ya*, which is common in Arabic, and the personal pronoun *hūwa*, 'he'. *Ya-hūwa* would therefore mean 'O he!' and this is, according to this theory, the origin both of the long form of the name, *Yhwh*, and the form *Yhw*.[105] The pronoun in the third person does in fact seem to have been used sometimes in the Bible as a substitute for the divine name or as its equivalent.[106] An example of this is the personal name Abihu (*'bhîhû'*), which is parallel to the names Abiel (*'bhî'ēl*) and Abijah (*'bhîyyāh*). in the same way, Elihu (*'lîhû'*, sometimes written *'lîhû*) is equivalent to Elijah (*'ēlîyyāhû* or *'ēlîyyah*). Similarly, the name Micah, Micahu (*mîkhāh* and *mîkhāhû* without the final *aleph*, cf. *'lîhû*) is comparable to Michael (*mîkhā'ēl*) and Micaiah (*mîkhāyāhû* and *mîkhāyāh*). Finally, there is the name Jehu (*yēhû*), which is composed of the divine name in the abbreviated form *yô-* (becoming *yē-* before the sound *û*) and the pronoun *hû'*. In the Deutero-Isaiah, the formula *'nî hû'*, (I am) he' (Isa 43:10, 13; cf. 41:4; 48:12 and perhaps 52:6; see also Deut 32:39). This formula can be compared with *w''attāh hû'*, 'thou art he' (Ps 102:28). In a Qumran paraphrase of Isa 40:3, the Tetragrammaton is replaced by *hw 'h*' [107]

---

[101] N. Walker, *The Tetragrammaton*, West Ewell, 1948; *ZAW*, 70 (1958), pp. 262–265; *JBL*, 79 (1960), p. 277; *ZAW*, 75 (1963), p. 226. It is an Egyptologist who has criticised this theory; see J. Vergote, *ETL*, 39 (1963), pp. 447–452.

[102] E. Littmann, *AfO*, 11 (1936), p. 162.

[103] J. Lewy, 'Influences hurrites sur Israël', *Revue des Etudes Sémitiques*, 1938, pp. 49–75, especially pp. 55–61.

[104] B. Hrozný, 'Inschriften und Kultur der Proto-Inder von Mohenjo-Daro und Harappa', II, *ArOr*, 13 (1942), pp. 1–102, especially p. 52 ff.

[105] M. Buber, *Moses*, Amsterdam, 1953; see especially S. Mowinckel, 'The Name of the God of Moses', *HUCA*, 32 (1961), pp. 121–133, especially pp. 131–133.

[106] See S. Mowinckel, *op. cit.* (note 105) and H. Kosmala, 'The Name of God (YHWH and HU')', *ASTI*, 2 (1963), pp. 103–106; see also N. Walker, 'Concerning HÛ' and 'ANI HU' ', *ZAW*, 74 (1962), pp. 205–206.

[107] *Man. Disc.*, VIII, 13, cf. III, 17, 25; IV, 25, in which hw 'h' takes the place of 'God'. One explanation which must be rejected is that of E. Katz, *Die Bedeutung des Hapax legomenon der*

and the rabbis also used the pronoun *hû'* in the same way. Outside Israel, but in the same Semitic environment, the *dhikr* of the Islamic religious brotherhoods consists of a simple, constant repetition of the divine name in various forms, especially *Allah-hû* followed by a title or merely *huwa*, 'he'.[108]

A few remarks on these names and words are appropriate here. In the personal names mentioned above, the personal pronoun refers to God and means that God, Elohim or Yahweh, is the God of the man who bears the name. These names, then, mean 'It is he my father' (Abihu), 'It is he my God' (Elihu), 'Who is like him (God)?' (Micah, *mîkhāhû*), 'It is he Yahweh' (Jehu).[109] In the same way, the invocation used by the Arabs, Allah-hu, means 'It is he Allah'. It is, however, not possible to say that *hû'* is a divine name or even that it is a substitute for the divine name – in the case of Jehu (*yēhû'*), *hû'* is clearly not a substitute for Yahweh. In the texts quoted in the previous paragraph, this idea of the personal God develops into that of the one God (see especially Isa 43:10; Deut 32:39) and of the God who always remains consistent (see especially Isa 41:4; 48:12; Ps 102:28). This can be compared with Job 3:19, according to which 'the high and the low are *hû'* ', that is, 'the same'.[110] In Isa 52:6, it is necessary to translate 'It is I who ... ' and this can be compared with Isa 51:9: 'It is you who ... '

It is much more probable that the name contains the root of a verb, which, according to the writing, must be *hwh*, the earlier form being *hwy*, In Hebrew, the root *hwh* exists, with the meaning of 'fall'. The verb is used once in the Old Testament (Job 37:6) and two nouns are derived from it – *huwwāh*, 'destruction', and *hôwāh*, 'disaster'. The parallel root *hwy* exists in Arabic, meaning to 'throw from above to below' or to 'fall'; hence the suggested explanation of the name Yahweh as the deity of the storm, thunder and lightning.[111] Arabic also has a root *hwy* meaning to 'love' or 'to act with passion' and Hebrew has a comparable noun *hawwāh*, 'desire'. This has led to the explanation that *Yhwh* is the one who loves and acts with passion, the passionate one.[112] The verb is, however, not used in Hebrew, which employs the related root *'wh* for 'to desire' and the noun *hawwāh* is rare (Mic 7:3; Prov 10:3; 11:6) and always has the depreciatory sense of

---

Qumraner Handschriften HUAHA, Bratislava, 1967.
[108] See L. Gardet, 'dhikr', *Encyclopédie de l'Islam* II, pp. 230–233 and 'Un problème de mystique comparée: la mention du nom divin *(dhikr)* dans la mystique musulmane', *Revue Thomiste*, (1952), pp. 642–679, especially p. 653.
[109] M. Noth, *Die israelitischen Personennamen*, Stuttgart, 1928, pp. 143–144. The Ugaritic name *hwil = Huwa'il*, 'It is El (or God)', can be compared with Jehu; see C. H. Gordon, *Ugaritic Textbook*, Glossary, No. 754.
[110] This is the meaning given by Koehler and Baumgartner's lexicon to all these texts; cf. Mal. 3:6: 'I am Yahweh; I do not change'.
[111] P. de Lagarde, J. Wellhausen; also H. Bauer, P. Leander, *Historische Grammatik der hebräischen Sprache*, I, Halle, 1922, p. 24, note 2.
[112] S. D. Goitein, 'YHWH The Passionate', *VT*, 6 (1956), pp. 1-9.

'cupidity'. These two theories, however, are made less convincing because the Arab roots have a much more diverse and developed meaning than that used in these hypotheses.

Almost all scholars who have considered this question in recent years believe that the name *Yhwh* is derived from the north-western Semitic root *hwy*, 'to be'. The existence of this root has been conjectured in Amorite – it has been suggested that its found in the proper names of the group Yawi-ilā. Its existence is also very doubtful in Ugaritic.[113] The usual root meaning 'to be' both in Amorite and in Ugaritic is, in any case, *kwn*. This is the only root of which there is evidence in the Canaanite of the Amarna letters and in Phoenician. In Akkadian, the phonetic equivalent *ewi/emu* means 'to be changed into', 'to become like' and, in the causative, to 'change into' or 'to make like'. The root is, however, common in Aramaic and its dialects, occurring in the earliest inscriptions[114] as well as in biblical and post-biblical Aramaic, Nabataean, Palmyrian and Syriac, in the forms *hwh, hw'* and *hwy*. In biblical Hebrew, the Aramaic root *hwh* is exceptional,[115] being found in Gen 27:29; Isa 16:4; Eccles 2:22; 11:3; Neh 6:6. The first reference is to an early poetic text which may have preserved the primitive form; in the other cases, *hwh* is an Aramaism. In Hebrew, the same verb became *hyh*, so that the name Yahweh probably preserves the early form of the root. We now have to determine the grammatical form of the word.

Attempts have been made to explain the name Yahweh as a participle and reference has accordingly been made to certain strange forms in a Phoenician inscription found at Karatepe and dating back to the eighth century B.C., in which a form of the verb *yqtl* is followed by an independent pronoun in the first person: this is believed to be a causative participle with a preformative *y* instead of the usual *m*. In this case, the name Yahweh would mean 'the one who sustains, supports, establishes'.[116] This explanation

---

[113] It is never found in the texts. It has been pointed out in a vocabulary in four languages, in which the Akkadian *ú-wi* transcribes the Ugaritic **hwy*; see C. Virolleaud, *Comptes-Rendus du GELCS*, VIII, 1959, p. 66; see also C. H. Gordon, *Ugaritic Textbook*, Glossary, No. 754a. The text has been published by J. Nougayrol, *Ugaritica*, V, 1968, No. 137, R° II, 28, who translates it by a noun – a '(living) being'. The Sumerian and Akkadian columns are missing at this point and the Hurrian column has *ma-an-ni*, which may in fact be the verb 'to be', but may also be a demonstrative pronoun; see E. A. Speiser, *Introduction to Hurrian* (*AASOR*, XX), 1941, pp. 86:87. F. M. Cross, *HTR*, 55 (1962), p. 254, note 124, notes that the Akkadian *u* does not transcribe the Ugaritic *h*, but *hu*. he therefore suggests the reading *huwa*, 'he'.

[114] References in C. F. Jean, J. Hoftujzer, *Dictionnaire des Inscriptions Sémitiques de l'Ouest*, Leiden, 1965, p. 63.

[115] M. Wagner, *Die lexikalischen und grammatikalischen Aramaismen im alttestamentlichen Hebräisch (BZAW*, 96), 1966, p. 45.

[116] J. Obermann in several publications: 'The Divine Name YHWH in the Light of Recent Discoveries', *JBL*, 68 (1949), pp. 301–323; 'Phoenician *yqtl'nk*', in *JNES*, 9 (1950), pp. 94–100; 'Survival of an Old Canaanite Participle and its Impact on Biblical Exegesis',

cannot, however, be accepted[117] and the forms in the Karatepe inscriptions are generally regarded as infinitives followed by a personal pronoun.[118] An infinitive without a pronoun governing it could never have become a proper noun, naming a person or a god.

Another suggestion is that *Yhwh* is a descriptive noun formed with the prefix *ya-* and several analogous formations in Hebrew have been quoted to support this theory. Examples of these are *yaḥmûr*, a species of antelope (the 'red one'), *yalqût*, a shepherd's bag ('the receptacle'), *yanšûf*, a bird, perhaps the barn owl (the 'whistler')[119] and *yārîbh*, the adversary in justice (the 'plaintiff'). Yahweh could therefore be described, if this theory is correct, as 'the Being' or 'the Existing'.[120] This type of noun is, however, very rare and this form can be explained as a verb in the imperfect used as a noun, [121] and this is the solution that we prefer for the problem of the name Yahweh.

In Hebrew, there are several personal names which can be explained as verbs in a finite form which are not used hypocoristically like the names Jacob (-El) and Isaac (-El). This explanation has been suggested in the case of the names of Esau's sons Jeush and Jalam (*yᵉ'ûs; ya'lām*; Gen 46:5, 14, 18), the name of one of Judah's descendants, Idbash (*yidbāš*; 1 Chron 4:3) and finally that of a descendant of Issachar, Ibsam (*yibḥšām*; 1 Chron 7:2). It is in no way strange that a divine name should also be formed in this manner. In pre-Islamic times, the Arabs, for example, worshipped a god called Yagut̠ (the name is the same as that of Esau's son, *yᵉ'ûs*), meaning 'he helps' and a god Ya'uq, 'he prevents (misfortune)'.[122] What we have to ascertain is whether the name Yahweh contains the verb 'to be' in the simple *qal* ('he is') or in the causative *hiphil* ('he causes to be').

Several authors favour the second explanation, [123] saying that the form Yahweh is that of a causative (*yaqtil*), the simple form being Yihweh (*yiqtôl*), with the result that the name means 'he causes to be', in other words, 'he is the creator'. The short form Yahû would therefore be the corresponding jussive.

---

[117] *JBL*, 70 (1951), pp. 199–209 and other articles.

[118] G. R. Driver, 'Reflections on Recent Articles', *JBL*, 73 (1954), pp. 125–131.

[119] J. M. Sola-Solé, *L'infinitif sémitique*, Paris, 1961, pp. 110–118.

[120] G. R. Driver, 'Birds in the Old Testament, I', *PEQ*, 1955, p. 15.

[121] L. Koehler, 'Jod als hebräische Nominalprefix', *WO*, 1 (1950), pp. 404–405; *Lexikon*, op. cit., pp. 357a and 369a; R. Meyer, *Hebräische Grammatik*, I, 1952, § 40, 3.

[122] See W. von Soden, *WO*, 3 (1964–1966), p. 182.

J. Wellhausen, *Reste arabischen Heidentums*, 1897, pp. 19–24; M. Höfner, in *Götter und Mythen im vorderen Orient* (see note 95), pp. 478–479; T. Fahd, *Le panthéon de l'Arabie centrale à la veille de l'hégire*, Paris, 1968, pp. 191–197.

[123] See especially W. F. Albright, *JBL*, 48 (1924), pp. 370–378; *From the Stone Age to Christianity*,² Baltimore, 1946, pp. 197–199; *JBL*, 67b (1948), pp. 379–380; *CBQ*, 25 (1963), p. 10; see also Albright's disciples, especially D. N. Freedman, *JBL*, 79 (1960), pp. 151–156; F. M. Cross, *HTR*, 55 (1962), p. 253.*

One objection that has been made to this suggestion is that it is too abstract and too philosophical an idea for such an early period [124] and another objection is that it is not in accordance with the biblical idea of God. [125] These objections are not, however, convincing because they deny that the Israelites could have had ideas which had been widespread for a long time among the peoples surrounding them.

The philological objections are more serious. In this theory, the name of Yahweh is compared with the Amorite names Yaḫwi-ila and Yawi-ila, which are, it is claimed, causative forms. We have seen, however, that it is not possible to distinguish, simply by the form of the verb, between the simple *qal* and the causative *hiphil* of verbs with a weak radical, since the movement from the preformative *ya-* to *yi-*, from **yaqtul(u)* to *yiqtôl*, which is a characteristic of Hebrew, was not perfected in Amorite, at least in personal names. [126] It is true, of course, that this change was taking place in Ugaritic and in the Canaanite of the Amarna letters and that it had taken place definitively in classical Hebrew, but this preformative *ya-* might, in the name Yahweh, be a sign of archaism, like the use of the root *hwh* in place of the root *hyh*. It has been pointed out in this context also that the verb *haya*, 'to be', is never used in Hebrew in the causative and that other roots are used for 'to make', 'to create' and so on. [127] This argument is not convincing, because both Aramaic and Syriac use the causative of *hwy/hw'*. The most serious objection to this hypothesis is that it insists on a correction to the text of Ex 3:14, which provides an explanation of the name Yahweh. (This is something to which we shall return later.)

The most probable solution to the problem of the divine name, then, in our opinion, is that it is formed from the root *hwy/hwh,* used in the imperfect of the simple form *qal* and therefore meaning 'he is'. But this root had become *hyh* in Hebrew and the vocalisation of the verb form had become changed, so that an explanation of the name cannot be provided on the basis of the Hebrew that we know. The interpretation given in Ex 3:14 is to some extent obstructed by it and this is a good reason for believing that the name is pre-Israelite. On the other hand, there is as yet no evidence that it existed outside Israel and before the period of Moses.

---

[124] S. Mowinckel, *HUCA,* 32 (1961), p. 128, among others.

[125] W. von Soden, *WO,* 3 (1964–1966), p. 182.

[126] H. B. Huffmon, *Amorite Personal Names* (note 98), p. 64.

[127] This is W. Eichrodt's main objection in *Theologie des Alten Testaments,* I[6] Stuttgart, 1959, p. 118.

4. The Biblical Interpretation of the Name Yahweh

What is of special importance to us, however, is the interpretation of this name given in the theophany of the burning bush (Ex 3:13–15). The text reads:

[13] Then Moses said: 'I am to go, then, to the sons of Israel and say to them, "The god of your fathers has sent me to you". But if they ask me what his name is, what am I to tell them?'
[14]Elohim said to Moses, *"eh'yeh "ser 'eh'yeh*. This', he added, 'is what you must say to the sons of Israel: "*'eh' yeh* has sent me to you".' [15] Elohim also said to Moses, 'You are to say to the sons of Israel: "*Yhwh*, the God of your fathers, the God of Abraham, the God of Isaac, and the God of Jacob, has sent me to you." This is my name for all time; by this name I shall be invoked for all generations to come.'

This is the only formal explanation of the name Yahweh in the whole of the Old Testament. It is also in accordance with the philological interpretation that we regard as the most likely in that it points to the root 'to be' in the imperfect *qal* in the divine name. Those scholars who have favoured the causative of the root 'to be' have had to resort to various devices, some of them changes in the text. One suggestion is that the earliest formula was *'ah'yeh "ser yih'yeh*, meaning 'I cause to be who comes into existence.'[128] Egyptian parallels have been employed to justify this reconstruction, the most notable being 'He is the one who causes to exist him who will exist' in a hymn to Amen-em-het III[129] and the invocation of 'the one who makes everything exist' repeated several times in the great hymn to Amon.[130] Another suggestion is simply to change the vocalisation of the formula to *'ah'yeh "ser 'ah'yeh*, giving it the meaning of 'I cause to be whom I cause to be' or 'I create whom I create'.[131] It has been argued that the formula originally had this vocalisation, which was changed when the early causative of *hayah* ceased to be used. There, is, however, no philological justification for believing that the name Yahweh contains a causative and it it therefore quite arbitrary to correct the Massoretic text in order to make it conform to a pure hypothesis. It is the Massoretic text that we must try to explain.

The first reading gives the impression that one is present at the formation of the divine name. God is Being. Speaking of himself, he cannot,

[128] P. Haupt, *OLZ*, 12 (1909), col. 211–215; W. F. Albright, *JBL*, 48 (1924), pp. 376–377; *From the Stone Age to Christianity*, p. 198.
[129] An inscription found on a stele in the Cairo Museum, *ASAE*, 40 (1940–1941), p. 217.
[130] *ANET*, pp. 365–367.
[131] D. N. Freedman, *JBL*, 79 (1960), pp. 152–153.

of course, say 'he is', because this would be an admission of another Being apart from himself. He is therefore bound to say 'I am' and it is precisely this 'I am' who is to send Moses. Moses, however, cannot say 'I am', because he is not the Being, so he is to say 'he is'.

The text is clearly very heavily charged. In verse 13, Moses asks for the name of the god of the fathers, but verse 14 is not a reply to this question, because the God of Israel has never been called *'eh'yeh*. What is more, there are repetitions:[14] Elohim said . . . he added . . .[15] Elohim also said . . .

It would seem as though verse 15 is very early, that verse 14a was added to provide an interpretation of the name and that verse 14b, in which the same words are used as in verse 15, with the exception of *'eh'yeh*, which replaces the *Yhwh* of verse 15, forms a link between the personal name and its explanation.[132] It would also seem that the name Yahweh had been accepted in Israel simply as a personal name – whatever its meaning and its origin may have been – and that it was explained afterwards.[133]

What is the explanation that is given? In Hebrew, the early form of the perfect-present aspect **yaqtul* disappeared and was replaced by the *wayyiqtôl* and the early form of the imperfect-future aspect **yaqtulu* became *yiqtôl*. However difficult the problem of the 'tenses' or 'aspects' of the Hebrew verb may be,[134] the use of the verb *hāyāh* is clear enough. The *yiqtôl* of the verb *hāyāh* as a verb of action, 'to happen', 'to become', is sometimes used to express a frequentative past, as in Num 9:16, 20, 21: 'it happened that . . .', and less commonly to express a frequentative present, as in Eccles 1:9 'it happens'. The *yiqtôl* of *hāyāh* as a static verb, meaning simply 'to be', always has the future sense 'he will be'.[135] In ordinary Hebrew usage, then, the formula should be translated as 'I shall be who I shall be' and this is precisely how it has been translated by Aquila and Theodotion — ἔσομαι ὅ ἔσομαι.

This meaning of the divine name has been received with favour in recent years.[136] In the verses immediately preceding the revelation of the name,

[132] I agree here with M. Noth, *Exodus (ATD)*, p. 30 and disagree with those who regard verse 15 as secondary or later. Verse 14, however, is an early development of the Elohistic tradition (according to M. Noth), It is not a late gloss, as E. B. Eerdmans believed; see his *Alttestamentliche Studien*, III, Giessen, 1910, pp. 12–13. The text of Ex 3:14 was also known to Hosea; see below.

[133] See W. Zimmerli, *Gottes Offenbarung*, Munich, 1963, p. 290; R. C. Dentan, *The Knowledge of God in Ancient Israel*, New York, 1968, pp. 131, 256, note 7.

[134] C. Brockelmann, *Hebräische Syntax*, Neukirchen, Kreis Moers, 1956, pp. 37–45, with references to previous works. T. Rundgren, *Das althebräische Verbum, Abriß der Aspektlehre*, Stockholm, 1961, and R. Meyer's review *OLZ*, 59 (1964), col. 117–126; A. Sperber, *A Historical Grammar of Biblical Hebrew*, Leiden, 1966, especially pp. 587–592. A negligible contribution is made by D. L. Barnes, *A New Approach to the Problem of Hebrew Tenses*, Oxford, 1965.

[135] P. Joüon, *Grammaire de l'Hébreu Biblique*, Rome, 1923, §§ 111 h and 113 a.

[136] R. Abba, 'The Divine Name Yahweh', *JBL*, 80 (1961), pp. 320–328.

God says to Moses: 'I shall send you . . . to bring my people out of Egypt' (Ex 3:10) and, a little later, 'I shall be with you' (Ex 3:12). Later still, God tells Moses twice: 'I shall be with your mouth' (= 'I shall help you to speak', Ex 4:12, 15). In this context of salvation and promise, the name Yahweh means that God will always be present for Israel. The same perspective is preserved in the priestly account of the revelation of the name to Moses: 'I will adopt you as my own people, and I will be your God. Then you will know that it is I, *Yhwh* your God, who have freed you from the Egyptians' burdens' (Ex 6:7). The formula 'I shall be your God and you will be my people' was to become as it were a summary of the covenant and it is especially frequent in Jeremiah and Ezekiel.[137] As we shall see, these ideas of being present, of promise and of the covenant are all contained in the theophany of Ex 3, but it is apparently difficult to accept the fact that, in Ex 3:14, *'eh'yeh* must be translated by a future tense, 'I shall be'. In all the parallel texts quoted, 'I shall be' has a complement such as 'I shall be this or that' or 'I shall be with . . . ', but it is not possible to say, in the first person, simply 'I shall be', which would presuppose that the person who is speaking is no longer. The formula 'I shall be what I shall be' is not, of course, absolute, but has a complement, but this is the explanation of the name which is itself absolute and cannot be translated by 'I shall be'. It would seem as though this future is merely apparent and that it comes from the attempt made to interpret the name Yahweh by the same grammatical form in Hebrew, even though that form no longer expressed the perfect-present aspect of the earlier *yaqtul*. This is the meaning that should be retained here rather than the usual meaning in Hebrew. It is in this sense too that it was understood in the Septuagint, 'Εγώ εἰμί, and by almost all modern translators of the Old Testament.

The stylistic device used in the formula of Ex 3:14 has sometimes been called, not altogether correctly, 'paronomasia',[138] which is a bringing together of words which resemble each other either etymologically or else purely formally or externally, but which do not have the same meaning.[139] What we have, in fact, is a repeated use of the same root with the same meaning and, in this particular case, the same verb used in the same person in the main clause and in the relative clause depending on it. This linguistic

---

[137] The texts have been brought together by K. Baltzer, *Das Bundesformular*, Neukirchen, Kreis Moers, 1960, p. 46; J. L'Hour, *La morale de l'alliance*, Paris, 1966, p. 35; see also R. Smend, *Die Bundesformel*, Zürich, p. 5 ff.

[138] P. Joüon, *Grammaire de l'Hébreu Biblique*, § 158; H. Reckendorf, *Über Paronomasie in den semitischen Sprachen*, Giessen, 1909.

[139] J. Marouzeau, *Lexique de la terminologie linguistique*, Paris, 1933. Paronomasia is understood in its correct sense with regard to the Hebrew language by I. M. Casanowicz, *Paronomasia in the Old Testament*, Boston, 1894; E. König, *Stilistik, Rhetorik, Poetik*, Leipzig, 1900, p. 291 ff.

device is one that is particularly popular among Arab authors, but it is common to all the Semitic languages and is used for many different purposes.[140] In biblical Hebrew it is found occasionally and expresses uncertainty. Examples of this are 'Send whom you will send' (Ex 4:13); 'Bake what you want to bake, boil what you want to boil' (Ex 16:23) 'They went where they went' (1 Sam 23:13); 'I am going where I am going' (2 Sam 15:20) and 'Live where you will live' (2 Kings 8:1).

Several authors[141] are of the opinion that this vague meaning is what is intended in the formula of Ex 3:14, 'I am the one that I am' or 'I am what I am' being an evasive reply, showing that Yahweh refused to reveal the mystery of himself, as the one who could not be named, understood or determined. In the light of this interpretation, Ex 3:13–15 has been compared with similar scenes in the Old Testament. At Peniel, Jacob asked the name of the mysterious being with whom he had been wrestling, but the latter said: 'Why do you ask my name?' (Gen 32:30).[142] Manoah asked the angel of Yahweh the same question and the angel gave a similar reply: 'Why ask my name? It is a mystery' (Judges 13:18). It should be noted, however, that, whereas the deity refuses to give his name in these two cases, he reveals it as Yahweh in Ex 3:13–15. The formula must therefore have a positive meaning. This conclusion is strengthened if we accept the explanation that verse 15 is early and verse 14 is later in date. In this case, the formula 'I am who I am' is not an evasive reply, but an attempt to explain the divine name that has been revealed and this explanation must be positive.

The same stylistic device of paronomasia is also used to indicate totality or intensity. For example, Yahweh's words to Moses: 'I have compassion on whom I have compassion, and I show pity to whom I show pity' (Ex 33:19) mean 'I am truly the one who has compassion and shows pity'. Similarly, 'I will say the word that I shall say and it will come true' (Ezek 12:25) means 'All my words will come true'. A further example can be found in Ezekiel: 'They have gone among the nations where they have gone and they have profaned my holy name' (Ezek 36:20). This means: 'Among all the nations where they have gone, they have profaned my holy name'. The intensifying effect of this figure of speech can be compared with an expression found in an Egyptian document dating back to the end of the third millennium B.C. In his instructions to his son Meri-ka-Re, the pharaoh Achthoes

[140] H. Reckendorf, op. cit., pp. 156–157; T. C. Vriezen, Festschrift Bertholet, Tübingen, 1950, pp. 498–512.
[141] A.–M. Dubarle, 'La signification du nom de Iahweh', RSPT, 35 (1951), pp. 3–21, with references to earlier works; G. Lambert, 'Que signifie le nom divin YHWH?'. NRT, 74 (1952), pp. 897–915; O. Eissfeldt, 'Jahwe, der Gott der Väter', TLZ, 88 (1963), col. 481–490, especially col. 483 = Kleine Schriften, IV, pp. 80–81.
[142] This parallel has been developed by O. Eissfeldt, 'Jakobs Begegnung mit Jahwe', OLZ, 58 (1963), col. 325–331 = Kleine Schriften, IV, pp. 92–98.

III, speaking about his victories over the bedouins who were threatening the frontiers of his country, said: 'I am as I am'.[143] This means that he is and that he acts powerfully.

We may go a step further. More than a century ago, the German biblical scholar, Knobel, and the French exegete Reuss suggested the translation: 'I am the one who is',[144] appealing to a rule in Hebrew syntax which lays down that, whenever the subject of the main clause is in the first or second person, the corresponding word in the subordinate, relative clause must also be in the first or second person.[145] This translation has been taken up again recently and supported with further arguments.[146] It can be compared with 'I am Yahweh who brought you out of Ur of the Chaldaeans' (Gen 15:7); the stereotyped phrase 'I am Yahweh your God that brought you out of the land of Egypt' (Ex 20:2; 29:46; Lev 19:36; 25:38; Deut 5:6, etc.); 'Are you the man of God who came from Judah?' (1 Kings 13:14); 'Was it not I that have sinned and have done this most wicked thing?' (1 Chron 21:17) If the text of Ex 3:14 had been *'eh'yeh 'ʾašer yih'yeh*, we should have no hesitation in translating it as 'I am (the one) who is' and it is possible to believe that this was the meaning that the editor had in mind, since he attempted to explain the name Yahweh as the verb 'to be' in the third person, although this particular rule of Hebrew syntax prevented him from doing so. It should be noted that the translators of the Septuagint, who knew Hebrew, kept this meaning: Ἐγώ εἰμί ὁ ὤν.

Whichever translation is accepted, this version, 'I am who is' or the more usual one, 'I am who (I) am', the formula certainly explains the name Yahweh in terms of being. We have therefore to be careful not to introduce into this explanation the metaphysical idea of Being in itself or Aseity as elaborated in Greek philosophy. It is not certain whether the translation of the Septuagint was influenced by the Greek idea of Being, but this influence was undoubtedly present in the book of Wisdom, for example, when the whole of creation is contrasted with 'Him who is' (Wis 13:1). This metaphysical idea of Being was taken up by the scholastic theologians of the Middle Ages and is present in a number of theologies of the Old Testament,[147] but it is undoubtedly foreign to the biblical view of God, according to which 'being' was first and foremost 'existing'. God's

---

[143] On the back, line 95, *ANET*, p. 416b; A. Alt, *ZAW*, 58 (1940), pp. 159–160.

[144] A Knobel, *Kurzgefaßtes exegetisches Kommentar zum AT. Die Bücher Exodus und Leviticus*, Leipzig, 1857; E. Reuss, *La Bible*, Paris, 1879.

[145] C. Brockelmann, *Hebräische Syntax*, § 153a.

[146] E. Schild, 'On Exodus iii 14, 'I am that I am''', *VT*, 4 (1954), pp. 296–302; J. Lindblom, 'Noch einmal die Deutung des Jahwe-Namens', *ASTI*, 3 (1964), pp. 4–15. O. Eissfeldt, however, had certain reservations; see his article in *Forschungen und Fortschritte*, 39 (1965), pp. 298–300 = *Kleine Schriften*, IV, pp. 193–198.

[147] P. Heinisch, *Theologie des Alten Testaments*, Bonn, 1940, pp. 19–21; F. Ceuppens, *Theologia Biblica*, I[2], Rome, 1949, pp. 27, 30.

being in the Bible was above all an existence or, to use the existentialist term, a *Dasein* or 'being there', which was realised in many different ways, so that there is a danger of investing the formula in Ex 3:14 with all its possibilities and of regarding it as the quintessence of the whole of the biblical doctrine of God.[148]

It would be impossible to discuss all the attempts that have been made to explain this formula. We have above all to consider the ordinary sense of the verb *hāyāh* and its function in the Hebrew language. In the sentence *'eh'yeh "šer 'eh'yeh*, the relative clause *"šer 'eh'yeh* is the predicate of *'eh'yeh* and, like many relative clauses, it is equivalent to a participle. This brings us once more back to the translation of the Septuagint. With another verb and in a different context, the pronoun *"nî* would be used, followed by a participle. The participle of *hayah* is never used, however, in Hebrew and, in the formula of Ex 3:14, the first *'eh'yeh* takes the place of *"nî* because this explanation plays on the etymology of the name Yahweh and it was necessary to emphasise the verb *hāyāh*. If the relative clause is replaced by the divine name that it attempts to explain, however, it becomes obvious that the formula of Ex 3:14 is equivalent to *"nî Yhwh*, 'I am Yahweh'. This expression[149] is used again and again in the priestly account that is parallel to this Elohistic passage (Ex 6:2, 6, 7, 8) and it is also very common in the priestly narrative of the Pentateuch generally and especially in the Code of Holiness, the Deutero-Isaiah and Ezekiel. The same expression, 'I am Yahweh', is also found in the Yahwist (Gen 15:7; 28:13) and in the Elohist (Ex 20:2). Finally, it is also used by Hosea, in a reference to the divine name of Ex 3: 'I am Yahweh, your God since the days in the land of Egypt' (Hos 12:10; 13:4).

We may conclude by saying that the formula of Ex 3:14 can be translated best as 'I am the Existing One'. Yahweh, then, is the God whom Israel had to recognise as really existing.[150] The exegesis of this verse can therefore rest content with this and it is also important to bear in mind that the aim of this text is to explain the divine name and not to define God himself.

For a Semite, however, a personal name is a definition of the person who bears that name and we are bound to ask the meaning that the Elohist gave to the name Yahweh when he explained it as 'the Existing One'. In attemp-

---

[148] C. H. Ratschow, *Werden und Wesen. Eine Untersuchung des Wortes* hajah *als Beitrag zur Wirklichkeitserfassung des Alten Testaments (BZAW,* 66), 1941, p. 81; T. Boman, *Das hebräische Denken im Vergleich mit dem griechischen,* Göttingen, 1965, p. 37: Ex 3:14 means, according to this author, that there is no other *hāyāh* like the *hāyāh* of God, this *hāyāh* including Being, Becoming, Existence and Action. See also J. Barr's cogent criticism in *The Semantics of Biblical Language,* London, 1961, pp. 68–72, although this does not refer specially to our text.

[149] W. Zimmerli, 'Ich bin Jahwe', *Geschichte und Altes Testament (Festschrift Alt),* Tübingen, 1953, pp. 179–209. K. Elliger, 'Ich bin der Herr – euer Gott', *Theologie als Glaubenswagnis (Festschrift K. Heim),* Hamburg, 1954, pp. 9–34.

[150] J. Lindblom, *ASTI,* 3 (1964), p. 12.

ting to answer this question, of course, it is important not to take as a point of departure a philosophy of Being, the possible uses of the verb *hāyāh* in Hebrew or the general idea of God in the Bible. Our point of departure must be either the immediate or the nearest context in the same source. We may consider the Elohistic tradition as a whole, but we must not go beyond its limits.

As for the context, just before the revelation of the divine name, God calls Israel his people (Ex 3:10) and tells Moses that it is this people that he must bring out of Egypt (Ex 3:11) and that he, God, will be with him for that task (Ex 3:12). When the Elohistic narrative is resumed after the revelation of the name, Yahweh says to Moses: 'I shall be with your mouth' (= 'I shall help you to speak', Ex 4:12) and then 'I shall be with your mouth and with his mouth' (= I shall help you to speak and Aaron too', Ex 4:15). According to Ex 4:22-23 – and there is no reason to doubt that this passage should be attributed to the Elohist [151] – Moses had to tell the Pharaoh: 'This is what Yahweh says: Israel is my first-born son ... Let my son go'.

Yahweh, then, was 'with Moses', just as the god of the patriarchs was with Abraham (Gen 21:22, E), with Isaac (Gen 26:3, 28, J) and with Jacob (Gen 28:15; 3, J). A personal or family relationship existed between them and he was the god of the father. In this context, Yahweh is with Moses to serve his people, with whom he is united in a very special way – Israel is his first-born son. Yahweh's care of his people is primary – he sends Moses to bring them out of Egypt and he commands the pharaoh to let them go. It is also for the benefit of his people that he reveals his name. The implicit consequence of all this is that Israel must recognise that Yahweh is, for Israel, the only Existing One and the only Saviour. This is not a dogmatic definition of an abstract monotheism, but a commandment to observe monotheism in practice. [152] From then onwards, Israel was to have no other God but Yahweh. What is more, the fundamental article of Israel's faith is also included in this revelation – it is Yahweh who is to bring the people out of Egypt (Ex 3:9–11; cf. Deut 26:5–9). Finally, the covenant is prepared – Israel is the people of God.

These ideas are also found in a more explicit form in the same Elohistic tradition of the theophany on Mount Sinai, which is a counterpart of the theophany of the burning bush, depending on and prepared for in the account of the burning bush (Ex 3:12. cf. verse 1). It was on Sinai that Yahweh bound himself solemnly to his people, through the mediation of Moses and the covenant, and the decalogue is the document of that covenant. It opens with the words: 'I am Yahweh',which correspond to the formula of Ex 3: 14, and with the memory of the salvation from Egypt, the

---

[151] G. Fohrer, *Überlieferung und Geschichte des Exodus (BZAW,* 91), 1964, p. 41.
[152] See J. Lindblom, *op cit.;* G. W. Anderson, *History and Religion of Israel,* London, 1966, p. 37.

words which were announced in Ex 3:9–10: 'I am Yahweh your God, who brought you out of the land of Egypt' (Ex 20:2). The first commandment is: 'You shall have no gods except me' (Ex 20:3). Yahweh calls for exclusive worship, because he is a 'jealous God' (Ex 20:5), the only Existing One. In Ex 33,[153] Moses asks God to reveal his *derekh* to him, his 'way' or 'mode of being' (Ex 33:13) and Yahweh replies: 'I will pronounce before you the name Yahweh. I have compassion on whom I have compassion, and I show pity to whom I show pity' (Ex 33:19). This would seem to be an interpretation of Ex 3:14, in that the same stylistic device is used in both passages. The commentary on this declaration is found in Ex 34:6, although the critical attribution is disputed: 'Yahweh passed before him (Moses) and proclaimed: 'Yahweh, Yahweh, a God of tenderness and compassion'.

Turning now from the immediate context of the revelation of the divine name and to the whole of the Elohistic tradition and the difference between its teaching and that of the Yahwistic tradition,[154] we find elements of the revelation of the name (Ex 3:9–15) in that tradition. In particular, we find an interest in the people, a feeling of the transcendence and mystery of God and a sense of God's manifestation and activity being brought about by the mediation of Moses.

We may also include Hosea as a witness to the Elohistic tradition.[155] There are several reminiscences of the revelation of the divine name and a kind of commentary on the theophany of the burning bush in Hosea, who, in the first place, calls Moses a prophet (Hos 12:14), which recalls Ex 4:12, 15, cf. 16 and is resumed in Deut 18:15. Hosea also situates in Egypt the beginning of Israel's faith in Yahweh: 'I have been Yahweh, your God, since the days in the land of Egypt' (Hos 12:10) and points to the consequence of this fact: 'I am Yahweh, your God since the days in the land of Egypt; you know no God but me, there is no other saviour' (Hos 13:4). Since the days in Egypt, Yahweh has called Israel his son (Ex 4:22), but the more he called to him, the more he offered sacrifices to the Baals (Hos 11:1–2). Finally, Hosea contains the only explicit reference in the whole of the Old Testament to the formula of Ex 3:14: 'Name him *lô' 'ammî* (No-People-of-Mine), for you are not my people and I shall not be (*lô'*

---

[153] Generally speaking, this chapter has not been divided between J and E. M. Noth sees no trace of E in it; *Überlieferungsgeschichte*, p. 33, note 114. H. Seebass recognises E in the texts considered here and believes that they are in accordance with Ex 3: 13–15, which is, in his opinion, a summary of the Sinai tradition; see his *Mose und Aaron, Sinai und Gottesberg*, Bonn, 1962, p. 18ff, 23 ff; *Der Erzvater Israel und die Einführung der Jahweverehrung in Kanaan* (*BZAW*, 98), 1966, pp. 58, 61.

[154] L. Ruppert, 'Der Elohist – Sprecher für Gottes Volk', *Wort und Botschaft*, ed. J. Schreiner, Würzburg, 1967, pp. 108–117.

[155] See O. Procksch, *Das nordhebräische Sagenbuch. Die Elohimquelle*, Leipzig, 1906, pp. 248–255; S. Herrmann, *Die prophetischen Heilserwartungen im Alten Testament*, Stuttgart, 1965, p. 108.

'*eh'yeh*) for you' (Hos 1:9).[156] The parallel with *lô' 'ammî* gives to *(lô' 'eh'yeh*
the value of a personal name. Just as the 'my people' of Ex 3:10 becomes
'not my people', so too does the *'eh'yeh* of Ex 3:14b become 'not *'eh'yeh*'.
Israel's unfaithfulness broke the covenant that was foretold in the theophany
of the burning bush and was concluded on Sinai. The covenant was,
however, restored — Hosea says that, instead of being called 'no people of
mine', they would be called 'sons of the living God' (Hos 2:1).

Viewed within the immediate context of the revelation of the divine
name and within the much wider context of the Elohistic tradition as a
whole, the explanation of the name Yahweh can be interpreted in the
following way. Yahweh was the only 'Existing One'. He was a mystery to
his people and he transcended them, but at the same time he was active in
their history and Israel was bound to recognise him as its only God and
saviour. The account of Ex 3:9–15 emphasises both the continuity of this
faith and that of the fathers and also the new aspect of that faith as expressed
by the divine name interpreted in this way. It was by adhering to this faith
that the people of Israel was constituted. The religion of Israel was to be
founded on it. Israel was united by belief in a God who did not have a
divine history like that of the gods of mythology, because he was simply,
totally and constantly the 'Existing One', Yahweh was, however, a God
who directed man's history and who manifested himself not in the
phenomena of nature taking place in a cycle of seasonal events, like the
fertility and vegetation gods, but in historical events following one another
in time and moving towards an end.

This is, of course, a concept of religion which was totally different from
that which the Hebrews encountered in Egypt and were later to meet in
Canaan. The historian of religions can do no more than simply recognise
the extraordinary novelty. The believer, on the other hand, can see in it a
divine intervention. The essence of the later developments within the
history of revelation is contained in Ex 3:14, which, seen in this perspective,
is a passage that fully justifies the theological claim that its meaning is
profound and inexhaustible. We do not have to go outside the Bible itself
to hear an echo of, and a commentary on, the statement 'I am the Existing
One', which is found at the beginning of Scripture; in the last book,
Revelation: 'I am the Alpha and the Omega,' says the Lord God, who is,
who was, and who is to come, the Almighty' (Rev 1:8).

---

[156] See H. W. Wolff, *Dodekapropheton, I, Hosea*,[6] Neukirchen-Vluyn, 1965, pp. 23–24; E.
Jacob, *Osée*, Neuchâtel, 1965, p. 22. The correction 'I shall not be your God', which many
critics have adopted, including A. Weiser, *Die Phopheten: Hosea (ATD)*,[6] Göttingen, 1967;
R. Smend, *Die Bundesformel*, p. 38, note 73, is supported only by a few cursive minuscule
manuscripts of the Septuagint.

Chapter Thirteen

THE EXODUS FROM EGYPT

I. THE DISPUTES BETWEEN MOSES AND THE PHARAOH
(Ex 7:8–10:29)

THE revelation of the name of Yahweh (Ex 3:9–15) is connected with the mission of Moses, who had to obtain the Pharaoh's permission for the Israelites to leave Egypt (Ex 3:10; cf. 4:23, E). The revelation of the divine name is not included in the Yahwistic account, although this is also a description of Moses' mission (Ex 3:18–20). Both traditions agree that it was only after Yahweh had manifested his power that the Pharaoh gave way.

These manifestations of power are, of course, known as the 'plagues', although the word for plague, *maggephāh*, appears only once and then in a text which is generally regarded as late. The word *negheph*, from the same root, is also found only once (Ex 12:13), for the plague of the first-born. The cognate verb, *nāghaph*, to strike, occurs only three times (Ex 7:27; 12:23, 27) and the noun *negha'* is only found once (Ex 11:1), in connection with the first-born. In most cases, these plagues are generally called either 'wonders' (*môpheth*, Ex 11:9) or 'signs' ('*ôth*, Ex 10:1, 2, which may be an addition). The same words are used for the signs and wonders that Moses was given the power to perform ('*ôth*, Ex 4:8, 9, 17, 28, 30; 21; *môpheth*, 7:9). The purpose of these signs and wonders was to enable Moses to be believed by the Israelites and the Pharaoh. We shall see later whether the 'plagues' were not destined to make Yahweh believed, in other words, to have his power recognised by the Pharaoh.

Various attempts have been made to explain these plagues as natural phenomena causing disasters. Here, we shall confine ourselves to the most recent of these attempted explanations. The first can be grouped under the heading of 'cosmic explanations'.[1] In the course of the second millennium, a comet is believed to have made contact with the earth on two occasions, thus explaining the exodus and the theophany on Sinai. Red dust caused the discolouration of the waters of the Nile and irritated the skin of animals and

[1] I. Velikovsky, *Welten im Zusammenstoß*, 1951, pp. 63–106; G. Fohrer, *Überlieferung und Geschichte des Exodus (BZAW, 91)*, 1964, p. 76

men, causing boils. The plague of hail was caused by small meteorites, the darkness by clouds of dust and ashes, while the death of the first-born can be explained by earthquakes and the crossing of the sea by movements of the waters. All these events bewildered the people and gave rise to the account of marvels that we possess.

The second explanation is geological.[2] A violent eruption of the volcano of Santorini round about 1447 B.C. is thought to have caused a tidal wave which destroyed the Egyptian army in the lagoon of Sirbonis (the Sea of Reeds). The plagues have been explained as the after-effects of these eruptions and tides.✳

According to what may be called the natural explanation,[3] the plagues correspond to a series of natural phenomena, each one producing the next. An exceptionally large flood in July and August gives the waters of the Nile a red colour, caused by silt and intensified by the presence of small organisms, *Euglana sanguinea*, and their bacteria, brought down by the White Nile. This organism absorbs a great deal of oxygen from the water. In the case of the first plague of Egypt, the fish in the river died and their dead bodies infested the banks of the Nile and the reeds that grow there. The frogs which normally inhabit the reedy banks of the river left and sought refuge in places where it was cool and damp – the houses of the people. They were, however, infected with microbes *(Bacillus anthracis)* and died. This second plague took place in August. The exceptional inundation of the Nile also caused the mosquitoes to multiply in October and November (the third plague). When the flood subsided, there was an enormous number of flies, *Stomoxys calcitrans*, a tropical and sub-tropical species which bites both animals and men. This fourth plague took place in December and January, the flies disappearing, as they do, almost as quickly as they came. After the death of the frogs and the rotting of their bodies, the grass and the soil became full of the microbe *Bacillus anthracis*, which infected the cattle when they were put out to graze in January. In the Delta, however, the cattle are put out to graze later and the soil is washed much more by the rains, with the result that the Israelites' cattle were spared. (This is the natural explanation of the fifth plague.) The boils were symptoms of anthrax, carried by the fly *Stomoxys calcitrans*, which attacks both men and cattle in their houses and sheds at the end of December and in January. (The sixth plague of boils.) At the beginning of February, the flax and the barley were destroyed by an extremely violent hailstorm, but the later crops of wheat and spelt were not (the seventh plague). In the year of the plagues, the weather was exceptionally damp and very many locusts left

[2] A. G. Galanopulos, 'Die ägyptischen Plagen und der Auszug Israels aus geologischer Sicht', *Das Altertum*, 10 (1964), pp. 131–137; criticised by W. Krebs, *ibid.*, 12 (1966), pp. 135–144; reply by A. G. Galanopulos, *ibid.*, 13 (1967), pp. 19–20.*
[3] G. Hort, 'The Plagues of Egypt', *ZAW*, 69 (1957), pp. 84–103. 70 (1958), pp. 48–59.

northern Arabia and were driven by the east wind to Egypt (the eighth plague). The exceptional flood left behind a thick deposit of red, powdery soil. This was blown by the first sirocco of the year, at the beginning of March, and caused the plague of darkness. The Israelites were spared because the Wādi Tumilāt, where they lived, is a depression in the Nile valley and is therefore protected from the force of the sirocco which blows there. (This is the natural explanation given for the ninth plague.) The tenth plague is explained in the following way. It was originally not the death of the first-born, the b'khôrîm, but the destruction of the first-fruits, the bikkûrîm, in other words, of what remained of the wheat and the spelt after their destruction by the hail and the locusts. This final destruction was caused by the sirocco; the Israelites were again protected from the effects of the sirocco as they had been in the ninth plague. This tenth plague took place in March or April.

The natural explanation of the ten plagues outlined above is ingenious, but improbable.[4] What is omitted in this explanation is precisely what is overlooked in the cosmic and the geological explanations – the essentially 'wonderful' aspect of the stories and the fact that they taught the pharaoh something. It ought also to be remembered that these stories make use of natural phenomena, some of which are known in Egypt, but unknown in Palestine (the red Nile, the frogs and the black sirocco), others known both in Egypt and in Palestine (the locusts) and others again which are known in Palestine, but exceptional in Egypt (hail).[5]

Folklore, and especially Egyptian folklore, also finds its place in the stories of the plagues.[6] The stories of the serpent changed into a staff, of the hand covered with leprosy and of the water transformed into blood are reminiscent of the tricks performed by Egyptian magicians.[7] These powers were given to Moses to prove that he was sent by Yahweh (Ex 4: 1–9, J). They also indicate, together with the other data used in the stories of the plagues, that these accounts originated in an environment in which there was some knowledge, albeit clearly imperfect, of Egyptian matters. This, as we have seen, also applies to the story of Joseph and to the story of the childhood of Moses.

On the other hand, however, there is also evidence of literary composition in the account of the plagues of Egypt.[8] There are, for example, several

[4] It is, however, favoured by K. A. Kitchen, *Ancient Orient and Old Testament*, Chicago, 1966, p. 157.
[5] In November 1966, there were disastrous falls of rain and hail in the Delta.
[6] F. Dumermuth, 'Folkloristisches in der Erzählung von den ägyptischen Plagen', *ZAW*, 76 (1964), pp. 232–325.
[7] P. Monet, *L'Égypte et la Bible*, Paris, 1959, pp. 90–98; I. S. Katznelson, 'The Westcar Papyrus and the Biblical Legend of Moses' (in Russian), *Palestininski Sbornik*, 13 (76), (1965), pp. 38–46.
[8] Only the following need to be mentioned: M. Noth, *Das Zweite Buch Mose. Exodus*

repetitions – the mosquitoes (the third plague) and the gadflies (the fourth plague) as well as the cattle epidemic (the fifth plague) and the epidemic affecting both men and cattle (the sixth plague). Repetitions are also found inside the same story (in this case, the first plague – it was impossible to drink the water of the Nile, first because it had been changed into blood and secondly, because the dead fish had poisoned it). There are certain impossible elements in the order of the plagues – if all the cattle had died of the fifth plague, how could they be afflicted by boils in the sixth plague and by the hail that fell in the seventh plague? Incompatible elements are also found within the story of a single plague in at least two cases – if all the water had been changed into blood in the first plague; (Ex 7:19), how could the magicians perform the same wonder (Ex 7:22)? Again, if frogs swarmed over the whole land of Egypt (in the second plague; Ex 8:2), how could the Egyptian magicians make frogs swarm over the whole land as well (Ex 8:3)?

The book of Exodus is, moreover, not the only place containing the tradition of the plagues of Egypt. In at least two psalms, there is evidence of different traditions. In Ps 78:43–51, the 'signs' ('ŏthôth) are given in the following order: the water changed into blood, the flies, frogs, locusts, hail (and frost), cattle plague, fire and finally the plague killing men and the death of the first-born. There is, it should be noted, no darkness in this list. In Ps. 105:27–36, the signs ('ŏthôth) are: darkness, the water changed into blood, death of the fish, frogs, insects, mosquitoes, hail, fire, locust larvae and locusts and finally the death of the first-born.

It would appear, then, that a great deal was in fact said about these 'plagues', and that only one tradition, providing one selection, is contained in Exodus, which is clearly a literary composition of the type known as midrash.[9] Literary critics of the Old Testament agree that the third and the sixth plagues (the mosquitoes and the boils) are the work of the priestly editor, but they disagree about the others. M. Noth believes that they are only J; O. Eissfeldt and G. Fohrer think that they are predominantly J and E; whereas A. Besters attributes the other plagues especially to E. What is more important is that a distinction is made in literary criticism between the accounts of the first nine plagues (Ex 7:14–10:29) and the tenth account. The latter consists of a proclamation (Ex 11:1–9) and the accomplishment

---

(ATD). Göttingen, 1959; Überlieferungsgeschichte, pp. 70–77; O. Eissfeldt, Hexateuch-Synopse, Leipzig, 1922, pp. 106–128*; 'Die Komposition von Exodus 1–12. Eine Rettung des Elohisten', Theologische Blätter, 18 (1939), col. 224–233 = Kleine Schriften, II, pp. 160–170; G. Fohrer, Überlieferung und Geschichte (note 1); A. Besters, 'L'expression 'Fils d'Israel', en Ex I–XIV', RB, 74 (1967), pp. 321–355.

[9] G. M. Camps, 'Midras sobre la historia de las plagues', Miscellanea Biblica B. Ubach, Montserrat, 1953, pp. 97–113. This midrash was developed at the end of the Old Testament period, in Wis. 15–19.

of the plague itself (12:29–34), joined to the account of the Passover (12:1–27). Neither the vocabulary nor the plan of the story of the tenth plague, the death of the first-born, are the same as those of the first nine. These differences have often been observed, but, in the present order of the text, the tenth plague clearly appears to be the culminating point of the narrative, the scourge which ultimately forces the Pharaoh's hand, and for this reason several scholars (especially Noth and Fohrer) have concluded that this was originally the only plague, the others having been invented as a preparation for the increasingly serious disasters.

In fact, the stories are not closely linked together. The account of the first nine plagues concludes by saying that the Pharaoh remained inflexible and that Moses would not see him again (Ex 10:28–29). This was, in other words, the end, and since the pharaoh would not give the Israelites permission to leave Egypt, all that they could do was to go without his knowledge (see Ex 14:5a). This is a tradition of the flight or exodus from Egypt which is independent of the tradition of the tenth plague, according to which the Israelites were driven out of Egypt (Ex 12:31–33; cf. 4:21; 6:1; 11:1). After Ex 11–13, the account of the plagues is continued in the pursuit of the fugitives and the miracle of the crossing of the sea (Ex 14).[10]

An examination of the first nine plagues, without taking the tenth into account, reveals a very careful literary composition which in fact defies analysis by the methods of literary criticism. There is, for instance, little agreement about the style of this composition. The Jewish exegetes – Rashbam (Shemuel ben Me'ir) in the ninth century and Abrabanel in the fifteenth, followed by various modern Jewish scholars [11] – have noted that these nine plagues are divided into three groups of three plagues each. Within each group, each plague opens with the same formula. In the first, fourth and seventh plagues, Moses is told to find the Pharaoh the next morning on the river bank and to announce the plague to him. In the second, fifth and eighth plagues, he is told to find the Pharaoh at his home and to proclaim the plague to him. Finally, in the third, sixth and ninth plagues, the Pharaoh is given no warning. Moses – together with Aaron – has to make a gesture which will result in a plague. Each of these three cycles of stories is moreover characterised by certain peculiarities of style.

Other critics have added to this account of the first nine plagues the story of the meeting between the Pharaoh and Moses and Aaron, when the latter's staff was changed into a serpent (Ex 7:8–13), since this story uses very much the same formulae. This results in ten 'wonders', divided into

[10] D. J. McCarthy, 'Plagues and Sea of Reeds, Exodus 5–14', *JBL*, 85 (1966), pp. 137–158.
[11] U. Cassuto, *A Commentary on the Book of Exodus*, Jerusalem, 1967, pp. 92–93 (English translation of a work in Hebrew); M. Greenberg, 'The Thematic Unity of Exodus III–IX', *Fourth World Congress of Jewish Studies, Papers*, I, Jerusalem, 1967, pp. 151–154, and in detail in *Understanding Exodus*, New York, 1969, pp. 151–192.

three groups. In the first group of four wonders (the staff changed into a serpent and the first three plagues), the agent is Aaron. In the second group, which consists of the fourth and fifth plagues, Yahweh is the agent. Finally, in the third group (four plagues – the sixth to the ninth), Moses is the agent. The stories are, according to this theory, constructed in three types which alternate systematically.[12]

Again considering these ten 'wonders' (Ex 7:8–10:29), it has been suggested that they are arranged concentrically or rather as a series of inclusions, each episode having a counterpart of approximately the same length and using the same formulae. The first five wonders correspond to the last five in reverse order. The first wonder (of the staff changed into a serpent) is short and corresponds to the tenth wonder (the darkness). Again, the second wonder of the waters of the Nile changed into blood is long and corresponds to the ninth long wonder of the locusts and so on.[13]

All these attempts to explain the plagues of Egypt are based on the correct assumption that the story is not a historical account, but a literary composition. The fact that so many different analyses have been suggested, however, shows that the structure of this literary composition is by no means clear. What is undeniable, on the other hand, is that there is an element of progress in the narrative. The Pharaoh's magicians, for example, also perform the wonders of changing a staff into a serpent and the waters of the Nile into blood and they also follow Moses and Aaron in producing a plague of frogs. On the other hand, they fail to produce mosquitoes (the third plague) and are themselves covered with boils (the sixth plague). As for the Pharaoh, his heart is hardened after the wonder of the staff changed into a serpent and the first plague, but he says nothing. In the case of the plague of frogs, he asks Moses to rid Egypt of the creatures. After the plague of gadflies, he allows the Israelites to go into the wilderness, but they are obliged to return. After the hail, the Pharaoh admits his guilt. After the locusts, he allows the men only to leave and, after the darkness, he allows all the people to go, but they have to leave their flocks and herds behind. There is, then, a clear progression of events. Finally, the Pharaoh himself becomes stubborn in the first five plagues, whereas, in the sixth, eighth and ninth plague, it is Yahweh who hardens his heart.

The account of the plagues, then, is in fact a series of disputes between Moses and the Pharaoh and the aim of this contest is to make the Pharaoh recognise the existence and the power of Yahweh (Ex 7:17; 8:6, 18; 9:14, 16, 29). This, of course, is the reply to the question first asked by the Pharaoh when he met Moses for the first time: 'Who is Yahweh, that I should listen to him?' (Ex 5:2).[14] It is not important, in this contest, that

[12] See E. Galbiati, *La struttura letteraria dell'Esodo*, Alba, 1956, pp. 111–133.

[13] D. J. McCarthy, 'Moses' Dealings with Pharaoh', *CBQ*, 27 (1965), pp. 336–347.

[14] H. Eising, 'Die ägyptischen Plagen', *Lex Tua Veritas (Festschrift H. Junker)*, Trier, 1961,

Moses and Aaron appear to have been defeated and that the Pharaoh refuses to give way, because this story of the nine plagues – if it does in fact form a literary unit – is not the whole story. It is a preparation for what follows – the Pharaoh's stubbornness gives rise to an even more striking manifestation of Yahweh's power, the crossing of the sea and the wonder that accompanies it (Ex 7:4–5; 14:17–18). This same hardening of the Pharaoh's heart, which leads to further wonders, is also directed towards the Israelites themselves; they too are to know 'that I am Yahweh' (Ex 10:2) and they too were convinced by the wonder of the crossing of the sea and put their faith in Yahweh (Ex 14:31; 15:1, 21).

II. THE TENTH PLAGUE AND THE PASSOVER
(Ex 11:1–13:16)

As we have seen, most literary critics of the Old Testament regard the tenth plague, the death of the Egyptian first-born, as different from the first nine plagues and as closely connected with the account of the Passover, which in turn is closely connected with the deliverance of the Israelites from Egypt. The night that God struck the first-born of Egypt the Israelites also celebrated the Passover and the rite protected them from this scourge (Ex 12:13, 23, 27). The same night, the Israelites left Egypt (Ex 12:31, 41–42). The conclusion that has been drawn from this by certain scholars [15] is that the whole of Ex 1–15 had its centre in the Passover and that the whole story was a cultic legend of the feast, a historical justification of its rites. The most obvious objection to this theory is that a historical tradition is not created by cult. [16] In this particular case, moreover, it is worth pointing out that the climax of the whole story is not the Passover, but the miracle of the sea. What is more, if this story is in fact a sacred legend of the Passover, then the feast ought to be celebrated after the miracle that it is thought to commemorate. [17]

These chapters of Exodus, then, have to be examined on their own. Because of the important position that the Passover came to assume in worship, they were thoroughly edited. They constitute our main source for

---

pp. 75–87; D. J. McCarthy, *op. cit.* (note 13), pp. 345–346; M. Greenberg, 'The Thematic Unity', p. 153 and *Understanding Exodus, op. cit.*, p. 169 (note 11).

[15] I. Pedersen, *ZAW*, 52 (1934), pp. 161–175; *ibid., Ancient Israel. Its Life and Culture,*[2] London, 1959, pp. 384–415, 728–737, 794–795; I. Engell. 'Paesah–Massôt and the Problem of "Paternism" ', *Orientalia Suecana*, I, 1952, pp. 39–50.

[16] See, for the question that concerns us here, S. Mowinckel, *ST*, 5 (1951), pp. 66–68; see also above, pp. 322, 323; in general, see G. E. Wright, 'Cult and History', *Interpretation*, 16 (1962), pp. 3–20.

[17] See M. Noth, *Überlieferungsgeschichte*, pp. 70–77.

any study of the feast itself and of its origins The additions to the text are fairly easy to isolate and literary critics more or less agree about them. The deuteronomic additions[18] include Ex 12:24–27a; 13:3–16 and perhaps also 13:1–2, unless this is a much later addition. The priestly additions are those connected with the ritual laws and the meaning of the Passover. Two separate levels can be distinguished in the priestly narrative: (1) Ex 11:9–12:20, 28, 40–41 and (b) 12:42–51.

What is left in the account of the tenth plague and the Passover, then, as the early narrative is: Ex 11:1–8; 12:21–23, 27b, 29–39. This account is not, however, homogeneous. Some critics believe that it contains elements written by the Elohist (11:1–3; 12:21–23 according to Eissfeldt; 11:1; 12:31, 39b according to Fohrer); but this is not certain (Noth does not accept it) and, in any case, not important. The whole of this early narrative is in the Yahwistic tradition, but there are two levels – the earliest (J[1] of the classical school of criticism – Eissfeldt's so-called *Laienquelle*, Fohrer's 'nomadic source') and a later level. In this composite Yahwistic source, there is already a connection between the tenth plague and the exodus (Ex 11:4–8, 31–33) and between the tenth plague and the Passover (Ex 12:23). The problem that confronts us is to discover whether this early tradition has a historical basis.

1. *The Passover*[19]

This was a feast of nomadic or semi-nomadic herdsmen. This is clearly indicated by its essential rites. It was celebrated without any sanctuary, without a priest and without any altar. The victim was taken from the flock or herd and roasted, not boiled. It was eaten with the unleavened bread of the bedouins and with desert herbs. It was also eaten in a dress which was that worn by herdsmen. It was moreover celebrated at night time, when the

---

[18] This does not mean that these additions were later than Deuteronomy or that they were directly inspired by it. They are part of the same movement as Deuteronomy, which is the main representative, but which is a later product of this tendency. See N. Lohfink, *Das Hauptgebot. Eine Untersuchung literarischer Einleitungsfragen zu Dtn 5–11*, Rome, 1963, *Exkurs*, pp. 121–124; M. Caloz, 'Exode XIII, 3–16, et son rapport au Deutéronome,' *RB*, 75 (1968), pp. 5–62.

[19] See R. de Vaux, *Institutions*, pp. 484–492 and bibliography, pp. 550–551; *ibid, Les sacrifices de l'Ancien Testament*, Paris, 1964, pp. 7–26. According to J. B. Segal, *The Hebrew Passover from the Earliest Times to A.D. 70*, London, 1963, the Passover was always associated with matsôth and was originally a feast of the new year or the spring among settled people. This theory has not been accepted, especially by G. Fohrer, *Überlieferung*, p. 92, note 29; H. Kosmala, *VT*, 14 (1954), pp. 504–509. M. MacRae, *CBQ*, 26 (1964), pp. 123–126; B. Childs, *JBL*, 83 (1964), pp. 94–95.*

people were not concerned about their flocks or herds, and, what is more, on a night of full moon, because this enabled them to see.

This paschal sacrifice also has close links with that of the pre-Islamic Arabs. Especially interesting in this context is the sacrifice of the month of Rajab, when the victims were offered and eaten in order to ensure that the flock or herd was preserved and remained fertile.

It was also a pre-Israelitic sacrifice. The etymology of the word *pesah* is not known. The explanation offered in Ex 12:13, 23, 27 is that, on the night of the Passover, Yahweh 'passed over', 'left out' or 'protected'[20] the houses of the Israelites. This is, however, a later explanation. The Passover celebrated before the exodus from Egypt was not in fact the first Passover that the Israelites had ever celebrated – it is introduced into Ex 12:21 as a feast that was already known. It may perhaps be the feast or the sacrifice that Moses and the Israelites wished to celebrate in the desert, when they asked the Pharaoh for permission to do this (Ex 3:18; 5:3; 7:16, 26; 8:4, 16, 23; 9:1, 13; 10:3, 7, 11, 24, 26; all these texts are J).

The Passover was also an annual feast, celebrated during the first full moon in the spring, when the lambs and kids were born and when the flocks and herds were taken to their summer pasture.[21] This was, of course, an important time of year, full of dangers – the roads, the uncertain state of the summer pastures and the many threats to the lives of the young animals. These dangers are personified in the Exodus account as a demon, the 'destroyer', *maš^ye hîth*, mentioned in Ex 12:23 (J). The houses were smeared with blood – in early times the tents were treated in this way – in order to protect them and their inhabitants from these forces.

2. The Passover and the tenth plague

If the Passover was prior to the exodus from Egypt, then its connection with the tenth plague was accidental or coincidental, the exodus happening at the same time as the Passover. It is true that a connection between the two events has been suggested, owing to the fact that the first-born sons of the Egyptians were killed just as the first-born lambs of the flocks belonging to the Israelites were, no doubt, sacrificed for the Passover. It

[20] For the meaning of 'protect' here, see the various commentaries, especially S. Liebermann, *Hellenism in Jewish Palestine*, New York, 1950, pp. 50–51; T. F. Glasson, 'The "Passover", a Misnomer: the Meaning of the Verb *pasach*', *JTS*, new series, 10 (1959), pp. 79–84.

[21] L. Rost, 'Weidewechsel und alttestamentlicher Festkalendar', *ZDPV*, 66 (1943), pp. 205–215 = *Das kleine Credo und andere Studien zum Alten Testament*, Heidelberg, 1965, pp. 101–112.

should be noted, however, that it is not stated in any text that the victims of the Passover were the first-born lambs or kids.[22] The law of the first-born, as laid down in Ex 13:1–2, 11–16, is an addition to the early text. It is, moreover, attached not to the account of the Passover itself, but to that of the deaths of the first-born of the Egyptians. In the Code of the Covenant (Ex 22:28–29), it is independent of the Passover.

The connection between the Passover and the tenth plague is established by the rite of the blood. This is the most important rite in the feast. It is the rite which was performed to protect the people and their animals from the destroyer, the *mašʿḥîth* of Ex 12:23; this blood rite protected the houses of the Israelites while the destroyer was striking the first-born of Egypt (Ex 12:23, J; 12:11b-13, P). This connection is made explicit in the addition, which bears the imprint of the hand of the deuteronomist, of Ex 12:27: 'It is the sacrifice of the Passover in honour of Yahweh who passed over the houses of Israelites in Egypt, and struck Egypt but spared our houses'. (In this passage, we would substitute for 'passed over' 'protected' or 'passed in front of'.) The death of the first-born is the only plague in one of the two forms of the tradition, that of the exodus-expulsion, and the text of Ex 11:2–3 means that there could not have been other plagues before this one.[23]

Is this tradition based on historical fact? In Ex 4:23, Yahweh says that the Pharaoh's son only will die. We know that Mer-ne-Ptah was not the eldest son of Ramses II, whose eldest son in fact died before him. We also know that the Pharaoh of the exodus was probably Ramses II.[24] It would, however, be wrong to use the death of his eldest son as a proof and to connect this with the tenth plague. Ramses II was more than eighty years old when he died. He also had about a hundred sons, twelve of whom died before him. Furthermore, Mer-ne-Ptah was more than fifty years old when he succeeded his father.[25] Nonetheless, the tradition of the tenth plague must have a historical basis – one spring, while the Israelites were celebrating the Passover, a scourge struck the Egyptians and spared the Israelites. It may have been an epidemic, resulting in panic and confusion, which would have favoured the departure of the Israelites.[26] There is an

---

[22] See R. de Vaux, *Institutions*, p. 489; E. Kutsch, 'Erwägungen zur Geschichte der Passafeier und des Massotfestes', *ZTK*, 55 (1958), especially pp. 5–9; G. Fohrer, *Überlieferung*, op cit., p. 91.

[23] G. Fohrer, *Überlieferung*, p. 82. The theme of the plundering of the Egyptians, here and in Ex 3:21–22; 12:35–36, was, in Fohrer's opinion, a special tradition of the 'N' source. This is possible, but it is connected with the exodus-expulsion rather than with the exodus-flight; see G. W. Coates, 'Despoiling the Egyptians', *VT*, 18 (1968), pp. 450–457.

[24] See A. Gardiner, *Egypt of the Pharaohs: An Introduction*, Oxford, 1961, p. 267.

[25] See Flinders Petrie, *A History of Egypt*, III, 1905, pp. 83–87, 107; R. O. Faulkner, 'Egypt from the Inception of the Nineteenth Dynasty to the Death of Rameses III', *CAH*, II, XXIII, 1966, p. 18.

[26] See G. Beer, *Exodus*, Tübingen, 1939, p. 60ff; G. Fohrer, *Überlieferung*, p. 90, regards this

effective link of cause and effect between the tenth plague and the exodus from Egypt in Ex 11:5–8; 12:31–33 (J), but this link is not clearly expressed in what follows. In Ps 105:36–37, the tenth plague and the exodus are simply juxtaposed and the same applies to Ps 78:51–53.

3. The Passover and the exodus from Egypt

As we have said, however, the blood rite of the Passover is presented, in the deuteronomistic addition of Ex 12:24–27, as the commemoration of the salvation of the Israelites, who had been spared from the tenth plague. The whole of the feast of the Passover is also explained in the same tradition as the memorial of the exodus from Egypt (Ex 13:3–10). This is, of course, what the Deuteronomist himself did in Deut 16:1–3. In the same way, the priestly tradition relates the blood rite and the whole ritual of the Passover to the tenth plague and the exodus from Egypt (Ex 12:11b–14, 42). Giving a historical value in this way to the Passover does not mean that the story of the tenth plague and the exodus was invented to provide an explanation for the feast as a 'cultic legend'. The cult, on the other hand, served to preserve the memory of the historical event because of the temporal link – the exodus from Egypt took place when the Passover was celebrated. Although it was made explicit in Deuteronomy, this meaning of the feast as a commemoration does not simply date from the period of Deuteronomy.[27] Even in the early account (Ex 12:34, 39), the rite of the unleavened bread was related to the exodus. This unleavened bread was not the same as that eaten in the Canaanite feast of *massôth* which was borrowed by the Israelites when they became settled in Canaan. It was in fact the unleavened bread of the early Passover in the desert. After the settlement in Canaan, the feast of the Passover continued to be celebrated by families, but, through the mediation of the common rite of the unleavened bread, its significance as a commemoration was extended to the feast of the *massôth*, which was originally different, but to which the commemorative meaning is attributed in the calendars of religious feasts in the book of Exodus (Ex 23:15 and 34:18), which antedate Deuteronomy. This common rite and this connection with the history of salvation made it easy to join together two feasts which were celebrated in the same month of the year. This combination of the two feasts was fully put into effect after Deuteronomy and the reform of Josiah.

The account of Ex 11–12 therefore combines two themes, both referring to the same event, but each independent of the other. The first is the theme

---

explanation as improbable, but agrees that there may have been a link in time between this plague and the exodus, *ibid.*, pp. 96–97.

[27] I believe this, contrary to G. Fohrer, *Überlieferung*, p. 92.

of the tenth plague which allowed the Israelites to leave Egypt and the second is the theme of the Passover which was the temporal background of the exodus.[28] The link between these two themes and historical events modified the meaning of the ancient rites of this feast, which was originally one of shepherds and herdsmen, and this giving of a historical value to the cult has noticeably influenced the text of Ex 11–12. In particular, we may observe this influence in the interpretation of the name *pesaḥ* as Yahweh's 'jumping', 'passing over', 'sparing' or 'protecting' the houses of the Israelites marked by the blood of the paschal victim (Ex 12: 23, J; 12: 27, 'D'; 12: 13, P). The destroyer, *mašḥith,* became the one who carried out the tenth plague (Ex 12:23, J; 12: 13, P). The dress worn by the shepherds and herdsmen became that worn by travellers ready to depart (Ex 12:11, P) and the unleavened bread became the sign of a hasty departure (Ex 12:34, 39, J).

The historical memory handed down in this account can be summarised in the following way. One spring, when the feast ensuring the well-being of the flocks and herds before they were taken to their summer pastures was being celebrated, at a time when a scourge was laying Egypt waste, the Israelites left Egypt, led by Moses in the name of their God, Yahweh.

III. THE EXODUS FROM EGYPT
(Ex 13:17–15: 21)

1. *The biblical traditions*

The order of events leading to the exodus is presented in the account as we have it in the following way. The Israelites are oppressed and they want to leave Egypt. In order to obtain the Pharaoh's permission, they put forward the plea that they have to offer a sacrifice to their God in the desert. Despite the wonders of the first nine 'plagues', however, the Pharaoh refuses to let them go. Yahweh then inflicts the tenth plague and the Egyptians let them go, even urging them to leave. They depart, but the Pharaoh changes his mind and pursues them. Yahweh intervenes with the miracle of the sea. This, in brief, is the outline of the story, but it is important to note that it contains elements with different themes and a different vocabulary. There are, in fact, two distinct presentations of the exodus story, the exodus-flight and the exodus-expulsion.

(a) *The exodus-flight.* Carrying out the mission that he has received from Yahweh (Ex 3.18), Moses asks the Pharaoh to let the Israelites go (*šillaḥ*) on a three day's journey into the desert to offer a sacrifice there to their God,

---

[28] E. Kutsch, *ZTK*, 55 (1958), pp. 10, 34.

Yahweh. This theme is fundamental to the account of the first nine plagues (see Ex 5:3; 7:16, 26; 8:4, 16, 21–23; 9:1, 13; 10:3, 7, 11, 24–26; all these texts are J). Either Moses was deceiving the Pharaoh with regard to the reason for and the aim of this exodus or else this tradition was not directed towards the occupation of Canaan, but towards a return to the place where Yahweh revealed himself. The second solution to the problem is the more probable and it means that this tradition was originally connected with that of Sinai. In fact, there are only three camps – or three 'days' – between leaving Egypt and Sinai – Elim (Ex 15:27; the Israelites did not camp at Marah); the wilderness of Sin (Ex 16:1; 17:1); Rephidim (Ex 17:1) and the wilderness of Sinai (Ex 19:2). The reason for the pilgrimage is taken up again in the account of the tenth plague (Ex 12:31–32), but these verses interrupt the story, which breaks off at verse 30 and continues at verse 33, with the theme of the expulsion. Verses 31–32 are an addition to the text, connecting the story of the first nine plagues with the story of the tenth.[29]

The Pharaoh does not give way – he refuses to see Moses again and Moses does not see him any more (Ex 10:27–29, J). The matter is closed; the Israelites know that they cannot leave freely and that they can only flee. This is precisely what they do (Ex 14:5a, J; verse 5b, which resumes the theme of 'letting go', is from another source). This is the only explicit reference to a flight, although this is implied in the pursuit described in Ex 14:6–9.

(b) *The exodus-expulsion.* The Pharaoh drives the Israelites out (*gāraš*). This expulsion is announced in Ex 6:1b (E?) and it forms the theme of the tenth plague (Ex 11:1; 12:39). It is true, of course, that, in Ex 6:1; 11:1, *gāraš* is in parallel with *šillaḥ*, which is the key-word of the exodus-flight. The two verbs are partly the same in meaning, a factor which helped the two traditions to become merged. The verb *šillaḥ* not only means 'to let go' – it also means 'to send' (Ex 12:33). The two verbs are in parallel in Gen 3:23–24 – God 'sends' and 'expels' Adam and Eve from the garden of Eden. An even closer text is Gen 12:17–20; when God inflicted 'plagues' *nᵉghaʿim* (cf. *negha*ʿ, Ex 11:1), on the Pharaoh, Abraham was 'sent', *šillaḥ*, from Egypt, The same verb is used in the juridical sense of 'repudiating' a wife (Deut 22:19, 29; 24:1, 3–4),as is *gāraš* in Lev. 21:7; 22:13; Num. 30:10.

The verb *šillaḥ* has another juridical meaning, that of 'setting free'[30] (see Deut 15:12–13, 18; Jer 34:9–16). Cyrus 'sets free' the exiles, *šillaḥ* (Isa 45:13) – the Deutero-Isaiah, it should be noted, presenting the return from exile as a new exodus. This juridical meaning is also quite clear in Ex 14:5b (the source of this text is not certain). There is also another juridical term for the emancipation of a slave. This is the verb *yaṣaʾ*, used in the *qal* of the one who

---

[29] See A. Besters, *RB*, 74 (1967), p. 348.
[30] D. Daube, *The Exodus Pattern in the Bible*, London, 1963, pp. 29–30.

is set free and in the *hiphil* of the one who sets free.[31] This is the most frequently used term in the later texts for God's action in the exodus from Egypt. The formula 'God brought Israel out of Egypt' or an equivalent formula is found eighty-three times, including twenty-one times in Deuteronomy alone. It is not found at all in any of the prophets before Jeremiah. In the story of Exodus, it is found four times in the deuteronomistic addition (Ex 13:3–16) and frequently in the P texts (Ex 6, five times; 7:4, 5; 12:17, 42, 51). It also occurs in the Elohistic source – Moses brings Israel out (Ex 3:10, 11, 12) and Yahweh brings Israel out (Ex 18:1). One is bound to ask whether the verb is used in its juridical sense in this ancient source. It is never found in the Yahwistic narrative of the nine plagues – only *šillaḥ* is used there. In our opinion, it was an Elohistic term which was canonised by the deuteronomistic tradition and amplified a little in that tradition, according to which Yahweh brought Israel out of Egypt 'by his mighty hand'. It was also taken up again in the priestly tradition. In Deuteronomy and other related texts, another formula is sometimes added: 'Your own eyes have seen the signs and wonders' of Yahweh or the equivalent. Some of these texts clearly refer to the plagues, which were called 'signs' (Ex 10:1, 2) and 'wonders' (Ex 11:9), and Yahweh's bringing the Israelites out 'by his mighty hand' refers to the miracle of the sea. In other texts, the formulae are used in a wider sense and apply to all the interventions of Yahweh which accompanied the deliverance from Egypt.[32]

This theme of setting free is associated with the sojourn in Egypt regarded as a period of slavery (which first appeared in Gen 15:14) and this link is stressed by the formula used: God has brought Israel out of 'the house of slavery', *mibbêth 'abhadhîm*, in the deuteronomistic passage in Ex 13:3–16 and later six times in Deuteronomy. The different words used to express this setting free – *šillaḥ* in J and *hôšî* in E – correspond to two different stages or to two different points of view. In other words, Moses asked the Pharaoh, in the name of Yahweh, to let his people go, to set them free, *šillaḥ*, and the Pharaoh refused. Yahweh then 'brought them out', *hôšî*, by his power. The

---

[31] See D. Daube, *op. cit.*, pp. 31–34; H. Lubsczyk, *Der Auszug Israels aus Ägypten. Seine theologische Bedeutung in prophetischer und priestlicher Überlieferung*, Leipzig, 1963; P. Humbert, 'Dieu fait sortir. Hiphil de *yāṣā'* ', *TZ*, 28 (1962), pp. 357–361, 433–436; especially J. Wijngaards, '*hôsi*' and *hē'ēlah*. A Twofold Approach to the Exodus', *VT*, 15 (1965), pp. 91–102; B. S. Childs, 'Deuteronomic Formulae of the Exodus Traditions', *Hebräische Wortforschung. Festschrift Baumgartner (SVT*, 16), 1967, pp. 30–39; W. Richter, 'Beobachtungen zur theologischen Systembildung in der altestamentlichen Literatur an Hand des "Kleinen geschichtlichen Credo" ', *Wahrheit und Verkündigung, I (Festschrift M.Schmaus)*, Munich, 1967, pp. 175–212.

[32] B. S. Childs, *op. cit.* (note 31) believes that to confine them to the plagues and to the miracle of the crossing of the sea in this way is to restrict more general formulae. This narrower sense, however, is the one in which it is used in the early sources of Exodus and in which it was to be used in P.

great action performed by this power of Yahweh was the miracle of the sea, which is called, in the prose narrative, a saving act, y'šū'āh (Ex 14:13, J) and which is celebrated in the poem of victory (Ex 15) as a y'šū'āh, verse 2, of the people whom Yahweh has redeemed, gā'al, verse 13, and purchased for himself, qānah, verse 16. In the story, the oppression of the Israelites by the Egyptians (Ex 1 and 5) prepares for this act of setting free, and it is the reason for Yahweh's intervention and for the mission of Moses (Ex 3:9–10, E; 3:16–17, J). This is, moreover, the theme which was to be stressed throughout the whole of the deuteronomic and the priestly traditions, especially in its juridical aspect.

In addition to hôsi', another, less common term is used. This is he'elah, to 'cause to go up', which is employed forty-one times in connection with the exodus. It is encountered in the early sources (Ex 3:8, J) and several times in the course of the book of Exodus, including five times in Ex 32 (JE?). It is also found as an announcement in Gen 46:4; 50:24 (E). Outside the Pentateuch, it is used by the early prophets, Hosea, Amos and Micah, and in the pre-deuteronomic texts. It is found only once in Deuteronomy itself (20:1) and only very rarely afterwards. It does not express the idea of slavery and setting free, but rather looks forward towards the future, a 'going up' to Canaan, an anabasis instead of an exodus. It is the opposite to the 'going down' into Egypt (Gen 46:3–4). It is also found in the story of the golden calf (Ex 32) and in the parallel story of Jeroboam's golden calves (1 Kings 12) as well as in Hosea and Amos. This would seem to show that it was a liturgical term employed in the sanctuaries in the north.[33] It refers to the exodus, but sees it from the point of view of Canaan, where the conquest has already taken place (see Jos 24:17; Judges 2:1; 6:8, 13). It is clear that the groups of people who took part in the exodus did not experience it as a 'going up', but rather as a 'going out', a deliverance, and the later tradition was right to insist more on this aspect of the experience.

It would seem, then, that there were certainly two traditions, one of the exodus-flight and the other of the exodus-expulsion. The distribution of the texts between these two traditions, however, corresponds only very imperfectly to the division of the same texts between the various early sources. In other words, it would seem as though these two traditions merged together at a very early stage and that they had a deep influence on each other. The tenth plague especially, in which the theme of the exodus-expulsion is most explicit, was directly connected to the exodus-flight of the group around Moses.

---

[33] See J. Wijngaards, VT, 15 (1965), pp. 98-101.

2. The historical interpretation

We must now consider the historical interpretation of these traditions. Was this deliverance from Egypt obtained by a flight from the country or was it the result of an expulsion? Even in the early accounts, these two explanations are merged together, despite the fact that they appear to be mutually exclusive. The historian would to have to choose, it seems, between whether the Israelites fled or whether they were driven out of Egypt.

The most probable interpretation of the exodus is that it was a flight. We have already pointed to the historical probability that the Israelites were forced to perform corvée labour in the Delta. For people who had led lives as nomadic and semi-nomadic shepherds and herdsmen and were continuing to lead such lives, this corvée labour seemed to be an unendurable form of slavery from which they longed to free themselves. It is also easy to understand that the Pharaoh did not want to lose a cheap source of labour which he very much needed to carry out his ambitious construction plans. His refusal to let the Israelites go is therefore perfectly understandable. The Israelites consequently ran away.

There is a striking parallel to the flight from Egypt in modern times.[34] At the beginning of the nineteenth century, Mohammed Ali of Egypt settled various bedouin tribes from the Nejd and Mesopotamia in the wādi Tumilāt (where the Israelites had settled long before) and gave them good lands. They grew mulberry trees and raised silkworms, spinning and weaving silk. They were also exempt from taxes and from military service. After Mohammed Ali's death, attempts were made to make them pay taxes and to conscript them. They protested, but to no avail. One night, the whole bedouin population fled with their flocks, leaving their houses empty and with the doors open.

Where, then, does the other theme, that of the exodus-expulsion, come from? Is it perhaps a memory, preserved in a rather distorted form, of the expulsion of the Hyksos? A connection was established in Egypt, during the Greek period, between the Hyksos and the Hebrews and this provided fuel for anti-Semitic polemics. Manetho, in the third century B.C, quoted by Josephus (*Contra Apionem*, I, § 86–90), said, that the so-called 'shepherd kings' (a translation of 'Hyksos') were driven out of Egypt and besieged at Avaris. After they had been honourably defeated, they left Egypt, crossed the desert and built a city in Judah which they called Jerusalem. Manetho also narrated a second story, the story of the the 'impure ones' who were associated with the Hyksos and who were, it has been suggested, the

---

[34] A. H. Sayce, *The 'Higher Criticism' and the Verdict of the Monuments*, London, 1894, pp. 249–250.

Israelites. This 'calumny' was refuted at considerable length by Josephus (*Contra Apionem*, I, § 228–287). Manetho's second story is also related in a much more sober form by a fourth century Greek author, Hecataeus of Abdera.[35] According to this version of the exodus, 'A pestilential sickness had been declared in Egypt and the rabble believed that it had been caused by the anger of the deity. The country was in fact peopled with many different kinds of foreigner who practised, in their religion and their sacrifices, certain special rites ... The natives became convinced that they would never be delivered from their ills unless they drove out these foreigners. They therefore set about expelling them ... The mass of this foreign rabble emigrated into the land known as Judah ... The leader of this colony was a person known as Moses, who founded, among other towns, the city of Jerusalem in the land of Judah.' This tradition cannot be traced back any earlier than the Greek period and it was clearly inspired by the Bible itself. The fact that the sons of Jacob were presented as 'shepherds' when they arrived in Egypt and the comment in Gen 46:34 that the Egyptians had a horror of all shepherds has also been used as a proof.[36] This is, however, unacceptable, because the explanation that the Hyksos were 'shepherd kings' is not correct – it only goes back to Manetho, who invented it. It has also been suggested that the association was made by Egyptian scribes at Solomon's court. These men may have known the story of the Hyksos and had certainly listened to accounts of the exodus from Egypt, and consequently they may have influenced the editing of tradition.[37] It is also possible to ask whether there is not a parallel here with the tradition of Abraham 'driven out' of Egypt after the 'plagues' inflicted on the Pharaoh (Gen 12:17–20).

The solution to this problem may perhaps be more easily found if we look in a different direction. Just as there were several entries into Egypt, so too is it possible that there were several exoduses, some groups being expelled, others fleeing from Egypt. These two exoduses might therefore explain the duality of the ensuing traditions – the northern route and the southern route for the exodus from Egypt, the tradition of Kadesh and the Sinai tradition and the conquest of Canaan by the south and the conquest from Transjordania. According to this theory, the tradition of the exodus-expulsion continued with the journey by the northern route, Kadesh and entry into Canaan by the south. The tradition of the exodus-flight, on the other hand, continued with the journey by the East, the pursuit, the miracle of the crossing of the sea, Sinai and the conquest of Canaan

---

[35] In his *Egyptiaca*, quoted by Diod. Sic., XL, 3 = *FHG*, II, pp. 391–392 = Jocoby, *FGrHist*, III, a, p. 46ff. This text forms part of Hecataeus' authentic fragments; cf. B. Schaller, *ZNW*, 54 (1963), pp. 15–31.

[36] I used to believe this; see *RB*, 62 (1955), p. 102 and the notes in the Jerusalem Bible.

[37] H. Cazelles, *RB*, 62 (1955), p. 364.

from Transjordania. The firm basis of this working hypothesis will be revealed in the course of our study.

3. The route of the exodus[38]

The following texts provide information about the route by which the Israelites left Egypt:

Ex 12:37, J (Noth), L (Eissfeldt), N (Fohrer, apart from 37b, which Fohrer believes to be an addition):
from Rameses to Succoth;
Ex 13:17–18a, E (Noth, Eissfeldt, Fohrer):
'God did not let them take the road to the land of the Philistines, although that was the nearest way . . . but the roundabout way of the wilderness, the Sea of Sûph';
Ex 13:20, J (Noth), L (Eissfeldt), N (Fohrer):
from Succoth to Etham;
Ex 14:2, P (Noth), JE (Eissfeldt), N (Fohrer):
Yahweh orders the Israelites to turn back and camp 'in front of Pi-hahiroth, between Migdol and the sea, facing Baal-zephon . . . beside the sea' (cf 14:9);
Num 33:5–8 mentions all these place names in a list of stages; the text is, however, one of the latest in the Pentateuch.

Is it possible to situate these names on a map, retrace the route followed by the Israelites and thus establish the place where the miracle of the sea took place?

The Israelites did not take 'the road to the land of the Philistines', but 'the way of the wilderness' (Ex 13:17–18). The 'land of the Philistines' is undoubtedly an anachronism, but we may be sure that what the Elohist had in mind here was the military and trade route to Palestine which left Egypt at Tjaru = Sile (Zilu) near Qantarah, ran along the south of Lake Sirbonis and continued along the coast as far as Gaza. This road was marked by military stations and guarded even during peace-time. It is clear that the fleeing Israelites would have avoided it. God made them take 'the roundabout way

[38] See the following recent works: H. Cazelles, 'Les localisations de l'Exode et la critique littéraire'. RB, 62 (1955), pp. 321–364; criticised by J. Prado, 'Las primeras etapas del Exodo. De Rameses al mar rojo', Sefarad, 17 (1957). pp. 152–168; P. Montet, L'Egypte et la Bible, 1959, pp. 59–64; J. Simons, The Geographical and Topographical Texts of the Old Testament, Leiden, 1959, pp. 234–251; J. Botterweck, 'Israels Errettung im Wunder am Meer', Bibel und Leben, 8 (1967), pp. 8–33.*

of the wilderness, the Sea of Sûph'. The last words in this text are in apposition. They may be an addition or they may be a geographical definition.

The name 'Sea of Sûph' is an ambiguous term in the Bible. In the first place it can mean the place where the miracle of the sea occurred (Ex 15:4, 22; Deut 11:4; Jos 2:10; 4:23: 24:6; Neh 9:9; Ps 106:7, 9, 22; 136:13–15). Only the first of these texts (Ex 15:4) is early and it is, of course, poetic. What is particularly striking is that only the sea is mentioned in the prose narrative of the miracle, never the Sea of Sûph. In the second place, the Sea of Sûph may mean the Gulf of Suez or the Red Sea, as, for example, in Ex 10:19, Num 33:10–11, which is different from the crossing of the 'sea' in Num 33:8. In the third place, it may signify the Gulf of 'Aqabah, certainly in 1 Kings 9:26, fairly clearly in Num 14:25; 21:4; Deut 1:40 and Jer 49:21 and without any certainty in Judges 11:16.

The translation 'Εϱυθϱὴ Θάλασσα found in the Septuagint includes not only the Red Sea with its two great gulfs, the Gulf of Suez and the Gulf of 'Aqabah, but also the Persian Gulf. An Egyptian word, tjoufy, 'papyrus', used in this sense in Ex 2:3, 5 and Isa 19:6, has been recognised in sûph by modern biblical scholars.[39] Papyrus does not, however, grow in the Gulf of Suez or in the Gulf of 'Aqabah, but it grows in abundance in the marshes at the north of the Delta, to such an extent that the district between Tanis and Zilu was known as pa-tjouf(y), 'the land of the papyrus'.[40]

If the Sea of Sûph in fact points to this district, then the words 'Sea of Sûph' (Ex 13:18) are contradictory to the words 'the way of the wilderness' and must therefore be an addition. If, on the other hand, the Sea of Sûph is the Gulf of 'Aqabah, then the words must point to the end of the journey in the desert which led the Israelites to the Gulf of 'Aqabah after Kadesh (Num 21:4; cf. Deut 2:1; cf. 2:8) or after Sinai and before Kadesh (Num 33:35; Ezion-geber). On the other hand, however, this Sea of Sûph cannot be the place where the miracle of the sea occurred, because the Egyptians did not pursue the Israelites acrosss the whole of the Sinai peninsula.

It is, however, possible that the term yām sûph does not mean either 'Sea of Papyrus' or 'Sea of Reeds'. The reading yām sôph has been suggested[41] and this would mean 'Sea of the End', the extremity or the end of the world, with its abysses and mysteries. It has moreover been observed that the earliest reference to this sea (Ex 15:4) is found in a text in which the miracle of the sea is raised to the level of a cosmic struggle. One major difficulty in connection with this theory is that sôph is an Aramaic word which was introduced into Hebrew at a late date.[42]

[39] H. Cazelles, op. cit., pp. 340–343.
[40] A. Gardiner, Ancient Egyptian Onomastica, II, 201*s; R. Caminos, Late Egyptian Miscellanies, London, 1954, p. 79.
[41] N. H. Snaith, 'Yam-sôp, the Sea of Reeds: the Red Sea', VT 15 (1965), pp. 395–398.

These uncertainties with regard to the meaning and the location of this Sea of Sûph on the one hand and the fact that it is not mentioned explicitly in the story of the miracle of the sea on the other makes it clear that we should not attach too much importance to this term in considering the problem of the route of the exodus.

In any case, the words 'Sea of Sûph' in Ex 13:18 must be regarded as an addition. Only very general information is given in the Elohistic tradition, namely that the Israelites did not take 'the road to the land of the Philistines', in other words, the northern route, but 'the way of the wilderness', which went towards the east or the south east.

The route indicated by the Yahwist, or by the Yahwist and the priestly editor if Noth is right and Ex 14:2 is the work of the latter, is as follows.

Rameses: in the region of Tanis–Qanṭir.[43]

Succoth: this is usually identified with the Egyptian Ṭeku, the present Tell el-Maskhūtah at the mouth of the Wādi Tumilāt near the modern town of Ismailia. It was one of the gateways to the desert and was perhaps the gateway through which the sons of Jacob came into Egypt.[44] During the reign of Mer-ne-Ptah, the Shashu of Edom certainly entered Egypt this way.[45] What is more interesting, however, is that this was the way used by escaping slaves.[46] A model letter written at the end of the thirteenth century B.C., which is believed to have been the work of a frontier official at Ṭeku, tells us that, having been sent to pursue two runaway slaves, this official learned at Ṭeku that they had been seen in the south. He apparently followed them in this direction, but, when he arrived at the 'fortress', *htm*, he received news that they had crossed the fortifications to the north of the Migdol of Seti and he therefore abandoned the chase. What we have in this account is, presumably, three of the names of places on the route of the exodus and, what is more, in the same order: Ṭeku = Succoth; *htm* = Etham; Migdol of Seti = Migdol. The Egyptian story is also a close and striking parallel to the story of the fleeing, pursued Israelites. There are, however, certain difficulties.

Etham: from the philological point of view, it is not entirely satisfactory to equate Etham and *htm*. Furthermore, the best and most obvious fortress in this district was that of Sile. The information given on the Egyptian papyrus is, according to certain Egyptologists, incorrect, when it refers to the south. As far as the Bible is concerned, if Etham was really the fortress of Sile, then the Israelites would have followed the 'road to the land of the

---

[42] M. Wagner, *Die lexikalischen und grammatikalischen Aramaismen im alttestamentlichen Hebräisch* (*BZAW*, 96), 1966, p. 87.

[43] See above, p. 325.

[44] See above, p. 302.

[45] *ANET*, p. 259a.

[46] Pap. Anastasi, V, **XIX**, 2-XX, 6; *ANET*, p. 259b; R. Caminos, *op. cit.*, pp. 254–259.

Philistines', since Sile was situated at the beginning of that road. According to Ex 13:17 (E), however, the Israelites did not take that road, so that the question must remain open.

Migdol: the Israelites who were at Etham (Ex 13:20) had to turn back (Ex 14:2) and camp 'in front of Pi-hahiroth, between Migdol and the sea.' This Migdol is the Migdol mentioned in the list of place names in Num 33:7, but four prophetic texts also speak of a Migdol where a Jewish colony existed at the time. This second Migdol is usually located at Tell el–Ḥeir, about eight miles south of Pelusium,. Apart from the Migdol of Seti mentioned in the papyrus from which we have quoted, however, at least three other places called Migdol are referred to in the Egyptian texts and all of them have been located along the road from Egypt into Canaan. We are therefore brought back once more to the 'road to the land of the Philistines' which the Israelites were to avoid. On the other hand, the Migdol of Seti of the papyrus would seem to have been to the south of Ṭeku = Succoth, although none of the other texts points to a Migdol in the south of the isthmus of Suez, nor is there any archaeological evidence of this. Once again, then, the question must remain open, although some light may be thrown on the problem by considering the other places mentioned in the same verse (Ex 14:2; see also 14:9) – Pi-hahiroth and Baal-zephon.

Pi-hahiroth: the name, *pî-haḥîrôth*, may be the consequence of folk-derivation ('mouth of the channels') applied to an Egyptian term. We do not know what this term was, but it may have been *P(rt)–hathrt*, the 'house of Hat-Hor' or *p(i)Hrt*, the 'house of Hrt', who may have been a Syrian goddess.[47] It may also have been *pa-hwjr*, which was the name of the branch of the Nile near Pelusium. Finally, it was possibly *p(a)-ḥrw*, a stretch of water near Tell el-Maskhūtah. .

Baal-zephon.[48] This is the Baal of Ras Shamrah. The worship of this Baal was introduced into Egypt by Canaanite sailors. At Rās Shamrah, he was later identified with Zeus Kasios and the same identification also took place in Egypt, where he was worshipped in a Phoenician temple of Zeus Kasios. This temple has been located near Lake Sirbonis, either at Mahammediyeh (Eissfeldt) or at Rās Kasrūn (Cazelles). There is no evidence of this cult, however, before the Greek period. In an Aramaic letter of the sixth century B.C.,[49] Baal-zephon figures, on the other hand, among the gods honoured at Daphne in the north-east of the Delta, where he must have had a temple. What is more, the early name of Daphne may also have been

---

[47] W. F. Albright, *BASOR*, 109 (February 1948), p. 16. This Syrian goddess, however, seems to be known only to Albright, who gives no references.
[48] O. Eissfeldt, *Baal Zaphon, Zeus Kasios und der Durchzug der Israeliten durchs Meer*, Halle, 1932; W. F. Albright, 'Baal-Zephon', *Festschrift Bertholet*, Tübingen, 1950, pp. 1–14; M. Dothan, *op. cit.* (note 39).
[49] *KAI*, No. 50.

Baal-zephon.[50] The cult of Baal-zephon, then, existed in the northeast of the Delta. It also existed at Memphis.[51] There is no evidence that it existed in the south of the isthmus of Suez, nor is it likely that it was widespread there, because the worship of this god only reached those places which were visited by Phoenician sailors.

We can draw no certain conclusions from this investigation of the problem. In favour of the route by the east or the south-east, it is possible to appeal to the fact that the Israelites were told not to take 'the road to the land of the Philistines', but 'the way of the wilderness'; to the papyrus which refers to Teku = Succoth, $\d{h}tm$ = Etham (?) and Migdol in an order north-south; and to the possibility of a Migdol in the south and a location of Sinai, as the end of the journey, in the south of the peninsula.

In favour of a route by the north, it is possible to point to the location of Baal-zephon, to that of the Migdol of the prophetic texts and to the iden-tification of the 'Sea of Sûph' with the Egyptian pa—tjouf(y) in the north-east of the delta, as well as to the location of Sinai in the north of the peninsula and the importance of Kadesh in the exodus tradition.[52]

This contradiction corresponds to two literary traditions – the Elohistic tradition describes the exodus from Egypt by the 'way of the wilderness', the route following the south or the south-east, whereas, in the Yahwistic tradition, the Israelites left by the northern route, which is, in fact, the 'road to the land of the Philistines', which is excluded by the Elohistic tradition.[53] These two traditions may, however, present the memory of two different exoduses, taking the following form.[54] Elements of the tribes of Leah may have been the first to leave Egypt, following the northern route. They would have settled in the south of Palestine. Elements of the tribes of Rachel may have left later, led by Moses and following the southern route. If this hypothesis is correct, this second group of Israelites would have made the long journey through the desert and have had the experience of Sinai.

[50] W. F. Albright, op. cit. (note 49), p. 14.

[51] Papyrus Sallier, IV, verso, 1, 6; ANET, p. 250a; R. A. Caminos, Late Egyptian Miscellanies, pp. 333, 338.

[52] To this can be added the recent exploration of the shores of Lake Sirbonis; see M. Dothan, 'An Archaeological Survey of Mt. Casius and Vicinity', Eretz-Israel, 9 (Albright Volume), 1969, pp. 47–59 (in Hebrew); 'Lac Sirbonis', Chronique Archéologique, RB, 76 (1969), pp. 579–580 : there are traces of settlements at the beginning of the Iron Age on the narrow strip of land which encloses Lake Sirbonis in the north and on the road which runs along the coast in the south. According to Dothan, the Israelites may have travelled along the northern strip of land, following a different path from the 'road to the land of the Philistines', which was to the south. Mount Casius or Ras Kasrun may therefore have been Baal-zephon and Lake Sirbonis may have been the 'sea'. But this is not the 'way of the wilderness' of Ex 13:18 and the Israelites would have encountered the Egyptian military posts at Succoth, Etham and Migdol.

[53] H. Cazelles, op. cit., 'Conclusion'.

[54] J. Botterweck, op. cit., p. 25.

Certainly this hypothesis is fully in accordance with the two ways in which the exodus is presented in the Old Testament. The exodus-expulsion was, according to our hypothesis, the experience of the first group of Israelites, who were driven out of Egypt in the course of police operations during the Eighteenth Dynasty. The exodus-flight was the experience of Moses' group. Just as the various entries into Canaan were merged together in the final narrative, so too were these two exoduses combined by the editors of the Old Testament.

In any case, the miracle of the sea occurred only once and it is associated with the exodus of the second group of Israelites, the exodus-flight led by Moses. Because of the existence of these two traditions of the exodus, however, and because of the editorial work that we have described, we shall never know precisely where it took place. This would be so even if the place names could be located with accuracy.

4. *The miracle of the sea* (Ex 14:10–31)[55]

Despite a number of uncertainties, there is general agreement among literary critics of the Old Testament that this miracle is presented in two ways in the book of Exodus.[56]
1. Moses is told to raise his staff, stretch his hand out over the sea and part it, 'for the sons of Israel to walk through the sea on dry ground' (Ex 14:16). Moses does this, the waters part and the Israelites cross on dry ground (verses 21 aα, bβ, 22). The Egyptian chariots pursue them (verse 23). Yahweh then orders Moses to stretch out his hand, 'that the waters may flow back on the Egyptians' (verse 26). Moses does this (verse 27a), the Egyptians are drowned (verse 28) and the Israelites are saved (verse 29). Broadly speaking, this presentation of the miracle of the sea is in accordance with the priestly source (Noth) or with the Elohistic source (Eissfeldt and Fohrer).
2. The Israelites are being pursued. They believe that they are lost and, in their terror, they revolt against Moses, who tells them to stay where they are and watch (Ex 14:10–14). The pillar of cloud protecting them changes its position, coming between the Israelites and the Egyptians (verse 19a, 20;

[55] In addition to the works mentioned in note 8 above, see A. Lauha, 'Das Schilfmeermotiv im Alten Testament', *Congress Volume, Bonn (SVT, IX)*, Leiden, 1963, pp. 32–46; L. S. Hay, 'What Really Happened at the Sea of Reeds?', *JBL*, 83 (1964), pp. 397–403; R. Schmid, 'Meerwunder – und Landnahmetradition', *TZ*, 21 (1965), pp. 260–268; J. Botterweck, 'Israels Errettung im Wunder am Meer', *Bibel und Leben*, 8 (1967), pp. 8–33; G. W. Coats, 'The Traditio-Historical Character of the Reed Sea Motif', *VT*, 17 (1967), pp. 253–265; F. E. Eakin, 'The Reed Sea and Baalism', *JBL*, 86 (1967), pp. 378–384.
[56] K. von Rabenau, 'Die beiden Erzählungen vom Schilfmeerwunder, Ex 13, 17–14, 31', *Theologische Versuche*, ed. G. Schiller and P. Wätzel, Berlin, 1966, pp. 7–29.

19b is a doublet, replacing the pillar of cloud by the 'angel of Yahweh'). During the night, Yahweh makes a strong easterly wind blow and this dries the sea (verse 21aβ, bα). During the morning watch, Yahweh looks down on the Egyptians from the pillar of fire and cloud, throws them into confusion and clogs the wheels of their chariots (verses 24–25). At daybreak, the waters return and Yahweh overthrows the Egyptians who are crossing (verse 27aβ, b). 'That day, Yahweh rescued Israel . . . and Israel saw the Egyptians lying dead on the shore' (verse 30). Broadly speaking, this tradition has been attributed to J (Noth), L and J (Eissfeldt) or N (Fohrer).

Attempts have been made to explain this miracle by natural phenomena. In the course of our discussion of the plagues of Egypt, [57] we mentioned, for example, the hypothesis that it was a tidal wave caused either by a comet striking the earth or else by a violent eruption of a distant volcano. There are other, less extreme, explanations. The Israelites may, for example, have been trapped between the Egyptian chariots and a stretch of water, which was dried by a very strong wind, so that the Israelites were able to escape by crossing it on foot. Pursuing them, the Egyptian chariots became bogged down. Then the waters returned and the Egyptians were drowned. Another possible explanation is that the crossing was made to the south of the Bitter Lakes, which are connected with the Gulf of Suez and might have been affected by winds and tides. There might, then, have been an unusual coincidence of an exceptionally low sea and an exceptionally long-lasting and violent wind, although that is rare in this district. [58] The waters divided by Moses' staff and the two walls of water can be seen as embellishments to what was fundamentally a natural event, used by God to save his people Israel. [59]

It would, however, be wrong to invent a tidal wave or even an exceptional tide, neither of which are mentioned in the text, which refers only to Moses' gesture and to the natural event of the east wind. There is also an inner contradiction in the text. Only a very shallow 'sea' could be dried even by a very strong wind. On the other hand, only a fairly deep sea could return and engulf the Egyptians' chariots. We are therefore bound to conclude that the story cannot be explained by natural phenomena.

The question is, however, incorrectly asked. Let us consider the second account that we have distinguished above. What is remarkable about it is that there is no reference to the crossing of the Israelites, who are presented as camping at the side of the sea and watching the Egyptians approach (Ex 14:9–10). Yahweh tells them to keep still and watch – they have nothing to do (14:13). After this, everything that happens takes place between Yahweh and the Egyptians and, on the following day, the Israelites see the Egyptians

[57] See above, pp. 359–361.
[58] C. Bourdon, 'La route de l'Exode', RB, 41, (1932), especially pp. 547–548.
[59] J. Botterweck, op. cit., p. 29.

lying dead on the shore (14:30). This is Yahweh's 'great act' (14:31). In this tradition, then, the miracle is not the crossing of the Israelites, but the destruction of the Egyptians. This is, in fact, all that is mentioned in the very early song of Miriam (Ex 15:21): 'Sing of Yahweh: he has covered himself in glory; horse and rider he has thrown into the sea'. In the longer poem, which is, in our opinion much later, this is also the only aspect of the miracle that is developed (Ex 15:1–18). Finally, it is the destruction of the Egyptians that is mentioned in two other references to the event, Deut 11:4 and Jos 24:7.[60]

One conclusion that has been drawn from this[61] is that there was a military engagement in which the Israelites were victorious over the chariot troops of the Pharaoh who was pursuing them. In this encounter, they succeeded in putting the 'sea' between themselves and the Egyptians. At this time, this 'sea' was exceptionally low and may even have been dried by unusual atmospheric conditions. The Egyptian chariots entered this damp and shifting zone and became bogged down. They were therefore an easy target for the Israelite archers. Against this theory, however, there is the fact that, according to the text, the Israelites did nothing and that Yahweh destroyed the Egyptians while they looked on. It was undeniably a war, but it was a war in which Yahweh played the leading part as a warrior.[62]

Each story is complete in itself. Each has its own framework and its leading actor, who is different in each case. In the first story, it is Moses who acts. Yahweh tells him to stretch out his staff and divide the sea. Moses does this and the sea parts in two. Again, Yahweh orders Moses to stretch out his staff and close the sea again. He does this and the sea closes together again. In the second story, it is Yahweh who acts. During the night, he makes the wind blow and dries the sea. During the morning watch, he spreads panic among the Egyptians. At daybreak, he overthrows the Egyptians in the sea. During the day, the Israelites see the Egyptians dead on the shore.

The impression that Yahweh is conducting a war is underlined by the text itself. 'Yahweh is a warrior' is stated explicitly (Ex 15:3) and the whole poem (Ex 15:1–8) is a song of victory in honour of Yahweh,[63] This

[60] F. M. Cross, 'The Song of the Sea and Canaanite Myth', *Journal for Theology and the Church*, 5 (1968), pp. 1–25, especially pp. 16–19.

[61] L. S. Hay, *JBL*, 83 (1964), pp. 397–403.

[62] See G. von Rad, *Der Heilige Krieg im alten Israel*, Zürich, 1951, pp. 45–47; H. Fredriksson, *Jahwe als Krieger*, Lund, 1945, pp. 83–86; R. Smend, *Jahwekrieg und Stämmebund*, Göttingen, 1963, pp. 79–81; F. M. Cross, 'The Divine Warrior in Israel's Early Cult', *Biblical Motifs*, ed. A. Altman, Cambridge, Mass., 1966, pp. 11–30.

[63] N. Lohfink, *Das Siegeslied am Schilfmeer: Christliche Auseinandersetzungen mit dem Alten Testament*, Frankfurt a.M., 1965, pp. 102–128; J. Muilenburg, 'A Liturgy on the Triumphs of Yahweh', *Studia Biblica et Semitica (Festschrift Th.C. Vriezen)*, Wageningen, 1966, pp. 233–251; F. M. Cross, *op. cit.* (note 60).

poem can be compared with the Song of Deborah (Judges 5), which is parallel to the prose narrative of Judges 4, just as the poem of Ex 15 is parallel to the prose account of Ex 14 and contains the same transposition. In the desert stories, Yahweh figures as a warrior in the early song of Num 10:33–36: 'Arise, Yahweh, may your enemies be scattered and those who hate you run for their lives before you!' The battle against the Amalekites (Ex 17:8–16, E) is also a battle fought by Yahweh.

Moreover this is connected with the idea of the exodus as a going out from Egypt under the leadership of Yahweh – the terms 'go out' and 'bring out' are also military terms. The 'armies', *ṣᵉbhā'ôth*, of Israel are mentioned frequently (Ex 6:26; 7:4; 12:41, 51) and Israel goes out of Egypt in military formation, 'fully armed' (Ex 13:18). It is true, of course, that all these texts are either P or else additions, but the idea that Yahweh was a warrior is nonetheless very early. It is in fact a continuation and a development of the part played by the god of the fathers in protecting the clan against its enemies. There is no reason to believe that the influence of Baal the warrior or even of El, if in fact this god was also regarded as a warrior,[64] was felt in Israel at this stage of its history.

As in the Song of Deborah, Yahweh called the natural elements into active service and used them to gain a victory. In other words, he used wind, cloud and fire. Bearing the epic character even of the prose account of Ex 14 in mind, it would be foolish to try to discover what really happened. The fleeing Israelites are shown to be in a desperate situation and their rescue is attributed by them to a powerful and miraculous intervention by their God. This act of salvation strengthens their faith in Yahweh (Ex 14:31). The same 'great act' became a fundamental article of faith for all those who became associated with Yahwism. It forms an explicit part of the 'professions of faith' of Deut 11:4 and Jos 24: 7 and the confessions of Deut 6:21–22; 26:7–8 also refer above all to this act. There is, in these texts, no question of the Israelites simply crossing the sea.

What, then, are we to say about the first account of the crossing of the sea that we distinguished from this second presentation? One of the main characteristics of this first account is the parting of the waters and the crossing of the Israelites between two walls of water.

It has to be compared with another 'crossing' which forms a counterpart to the crossing of the sea in the book of Exodus and occurs at the other end of the exodus story – the crossing of the Jordan. This connection is in fact established by the biblical texts themselves. In the poem of Ex 15, the victory of Yahweh in the miracle of the sea, which it should be noted, is not described simply as a crossing (verses 4–10), is followed by the description of a crossing which can only be the crossing of the Jordan (verses 15–16).

[64] P. D. Miller, 'El the Warrior', *HTR*, 60 (1967), pp. 411–431.

The link is made explicitly in Jos 4: 22–23 and the two crossings are in parallel in Ps 66:6; 74:13, 15; 114:3, 5. This connection has often been the object of study and most scholars have concluded that the account in the book of Joshua was influenced by that in Exodus. The nature and the extent of this influence has, however, been widely debated. Certain scholars take an extreme view, claiming that the account in Jos 3–4 is no more than a replica of the crossing of the sea in Exodus without the poetic quality and meaning of the latter and presented in the manner of a liturgical procession.[65] Other authors have explained the story of Jos 3–4 as the sacred legend of a festival in which the exodus and the conquest of Canaan were celebrated and commemorated and in which the crossing of the sea was made present and actual in a procession along the Jordan at Gilgal.[66] Others have simply agreed that the composition of Jos 3–4 was influenced by the account in Exod 14.[67] Several scholars have, however, insisted on the differences that undoubtedly exist between the two accounts and have concluded that there were two traditions which were independent of each other and which referred to two different crossings,[68] although some have admitted a later influence by the account of the crossing of the sea on the story of the crossing of the Jordan.[69] Recently, this connection has been considered in reverse, the suggestion being that it was the story of the crossing of the Jordan which influenced that of the crossing of the sea.[70]

It may be necessary to go a step further than this and say that the tradition itself of the crossing of the sea, not simply the story or its editing, is dependent on the crossing of the Jordan. Literary criticism of Jos 3–4 has proved to be extremely difficult[71] and many exegetes have distinguished several levels of editing, some as many as five or six. There is fairly general agreement about the content of the earliest tradition of all, which is Joshua's proclamation that the waters of the Jordan, flowing down, would be 'cut', *karath*, and would be piled up into one mass or 'dyke', *nedh* (Josh 3:13). When the Israelites struck camp to cross the river, (3:14a), the waters flow-

---

[65] S. Mowinckel, *Tetrateuch-Pentateuch-Hexateuch (BZAW, 90)*, 1964, p. 35.

[66] H.–J. Kraus, 'Gilgal, Ein Beitrag zur Kultusgeschichte Israels', *VT*, 1 (1951), pp. 181–199. *ibid., Gottesdienst in Israel,*[2] Munich, 1962, pp. 181–187; with certain reservations, H. Wildberger, *Jahwes Eigentumsvolk*, Zürich, 1960, pp. 59–62; J. A. Soggin, 'Gilgal, Passah und Landnahme' *Volume du Congrès, Genève (SVT*, 15), Leiden, 1966, pp. 263–277, especially pp. 270–276; F. M. Cross, 'The Divine Warrior', *op cit.*, pp. 26–27.

[67] M. Noth, *Das Buch Josua,*[2] Tübingen, 1953, p. 33; O. Kaiser, *Die mythische Bedeutung des Meeres in Ägypten, Ugarit und Israel (BZAW*, 78), 1959, pp. 139–140.

[68] R. Schmid, *TZ*, 21 (1965), p. 266.

[69] A. R. Hulst, 'Der Jordan in den alttestamentlichen Überlieferungen', *OTS*, 14 (1965), especially p. 179–184.

[70] G. W. Coats, *VT*, 17 (1967), pp. 260–261. R. Schmid, *op. cit.*, p. 267, shows signs of accepting this hypothesis.

[71] F. Langlamet, *Gilgal et les récits de la traversée du Jourdain (Jos iii–iv)*, Paris, 1969, See also below, Chap. 19, III.

ing downstream 'stood still and made one heap' or dyke *(nedh)* 'over a wide space . . . while those flowing down to the Sea of the 'Arabah . . . stopped running altogether' and 'the people crossed opposite Jericho' (3:16). 'All Israel continued to cross dry-shod' (3:17ba).

This is obviously a miracle, but it is told in a very sober way. It is fully in accordance with the geographical conditions prevailing in the Jordan Valley. An event which took place on the night of the 7–8 December 1267 and is recorded by the chronicler Nowairi has often been mentioned in this context – the dunes upstream of the bridge at Damieh collapsed, causing the river to stop in its course from midnight until ten o'clock in the morning. It would seem, then, that the story of the crossing of the Jordan is founded in reality. It is unlikely to have been invented on the basis of the marvellous story of the first tradition of the miracle of the sea in Ex 14, according to which Moses made a gesture and the sea divided, forming two walls between which the Israelites crossed. The essential element of the crossing of a stretch of water dry-shod is the same in both accounts, but the action is different. In the book of Joshua, the miracle is announced by Joshua, but takes place without his intervention. In the Exodus account, Yahweh orders Moses to accomplish the miracle and he does so.

The words used in each account are also different. Set out below are the key-words of Jos 3–4 and Ex 14, to which are added those of Ex 15:8 (the miracle of the sea) and 16 (the crossing of the Jordan) as well as those of Ps 78:13 (the crossing of the sea).

Jos 3:13–17; 4:7		Ex 14:21–23, 29		Ex 15:8,16	Ps 78:13
the waters	*mayîm*	the sea	*yam*	*yam*	*yam, mayî*
were cut	*karath*	parted	*baqa'*		*baqa'*
stopped	*'amadh*			*nasabh*	*nasabh*
stood up	*qûm*			*ne'et mû*(hapax)	
in a dyke	*nedh*	two walls	*homāh*	*nedh*	*nedh*
crossed	*'abhar*	went into	*bô'*	*'abhar*	*'abhar*
dry-shod	*beharabhāh*	on dry ground	*bayyabāsāh*		
			leharabhāh		

This clearly reveals the different structure of the two accounts. It also shows that the two are not dependent on each other from the literary point of view. It is therefore possible to maintain that Jos 3–4 and Ex 14 represent two different and independent traditions and that there were also perhaps two different crossings. There are, however, other factors to be considered. The two versions of the miracle of the sea in Ex 14 cannot be harmonised and the one that has to be considered especially in this connection is the account which portrays the miracle as a destruction of the Egyptian army. The crossing of the sea in the other account would seem to be a replica of the crossing of the Jordan as narrated in the earliest tradition, but with a different vocabulary and some exaggeration of the miraculous character. The word *nedh*, for example, is used twice in this account of the crossing of the Jordan and elsewhere it is found in the Bible only in Ex 15:8 and Ps 78:13. In the first of these two cases (Ex 15:8), it describes the miracle presented not as a crossing, but as the destruction of the Egyptian army. In the second case (Ps 78:13), it is used together with the noun *mayîm*, the waters, and the verb *nāsabh*, to stop, as in Ex 15:8, but also in parallel with *yam* and *bāqa'*, as in Ex 14:16. *Nedh* can be translated as 'mass', 'heap' or 'dyke' (Arabic *nadd*), in which case its use in the singular in Jos 3 is quite suitable, since the miracle is presented there as the stopping or damming of a flow of water. It is not suitable, however, in Ex 15:8, where the miracle is described as the drying of a stretch of water by the wind. Nor is it suitably employed in Ps 78:13, where the miracle is presented as a crossing between two masses of water. It is notable, in this connection, that *nedh* is not used in Ex 14, which speaks of two walls, *hômah*, of water (Ex 14:16, 29). In the account of Joshua, the word *nedh* is primitive and Ex 15:8 and Ps 78:13 are dependent on this early tradition.[72]

This complicated situation cannot have been due to a merging at the editorial stage. It can only be satisfactorily explained in the light of contacts made at the level of the oral traditions. In the poem of Ex 15, the miracle of the exodus is the destruction of the Egyptian army (verses 4–10) and the crossing of the Jordan is mentioned in addition (verses 15–16). In this second description, the people of Yahweh 'pass' and the rulers of the surrounding territories are frightened as they were after the crossing of the Jordan in the account given in Jos 5:1. What is more, the destruction of the Egyptian army is described in the poem of Ex 15 like the crossing of the Jordan : the waters stopping, piling up and standing up like a *nedh* (Ex 15:8). There is, then, a clear parallel between the two great interventions on the part of God which mark the beginning and the end of the sojourn of the Israelites in the desert, their exodus from Egypt and their entry into Canaan. This parallel is emphasised by a tradition which transferred a replica of the crossing of the Jordan at the end of the story back to the exodus from Egypt at the beginning. This tradition was formed without any influence being exerted by the text of Jos 3 – this is clearly the case since the words used are different – and became combined, in the poem of Ex 15, with the miracle of the sea in the version describing the destruction of the Egyptians. The two crossings of the sea and of the Jordan, canonised by tradition, are combined together in Jos 4:23–24; Ps 66:6; 74:13, 15; 114:3, 5. In Ps 78:13, all that is retained is the crossing of the sea, but the vocabulary both of Jos 3 and of Ex 14 is combined in it. Finally, it should be noted that the crossing

[72] I do not agree here with W. F. Albright, *Yahweh and the Gods of Canaan*, London, 1968, pp. 40–41.

of the Jordan was overshadowed by the crossing of the sea – in later texts the crossing of the Jordan is never mentioned alone, whereas the crossing of the sea is (see Ps 106:9–11; 136:13–14; Isa 63:12–13; Neh 9:11; Wis 10:18–19; 19:7–8).[73]

Certain scholars have attributed the theme of the parting of the sea to the influence of Baalism,[74] but Baal is never represented as parting the sea. It is true, of course, that the miracle was described afterwards as a victory on the part of Yahweh over the sea and cosmic enemies and that certain aspects of this description were borrowed from the Canaanite myth of the struggle between Baal and Yamm, the god of the sea and rivers.[75] It is also impossible to deny that the myths of the struggle between the supreme god and the powers of chaos at the beginning of time in general influenced the biblical theme of the miracle of the sea. This cosmic struggle is frequently recalled in the poetic texts of the Old Testament and is found, in connection with the miracle of the exodus from Egypt in Ps 74:13–14, the Sea, Tannîn, Leviathan; Ps 89:10–11, the Sea, Rahab *(rāhābh)*; Ps 114:3, 5, the Sea personified; Isa 51:9–10, Rahab, the great Abyss, *Tehôm*. This cosmic transposition is already obvious in Ex 15,[76] but it is not present in the prose account of Ex 14.

IV. THE DATE OF THE EXODUS

Whatever the case may be concerning the hypothesis of a double exodus, the only exodus that we shall consider seriously here is the one led by Moses. This group bore the faith in Yahweh that was to be handed down and experienced the miracle of the sea. It was the experience of this group that was remembered traditionally as the real exodus.

[73] I am in partial agreement here with G. W. Coats, 'The Song of the Sea', *CBQ*, 31 (1969), pp. 1–17.

[74] F. E. Eakin, *JBL*, 86 (1967), pp. 378–384.

[75] O. Kaiser, *Die mythische Bedeutung des Meeres in Ägypten, Ugarit und Israel (BZAW*, 78), 1959, pp. 44–77; M. H. Pope, in *Götter und Mythen im vorderen Orient (Wörterbuch der Mythologie*, I), ed. H. W. Haussig, Stuttgart, 1965, pp. 258–260, 289–290.

[76] F. M. Cross, *op. cit.* (note 60).

[77] This problem has been studied at length by H. H. Rowley, *From Joseph to Joshua*, London, 1950; this author provides an analysis, a full discussion of the various opinions and a good bibliography. More recent works include M. B. Rowton, 'The Problem of Exodus', *PEQ*, 85 (1953), pp. 46–60, and H. H. Rowley's reply, 'A Recent Theory on the Exodus', *Orientalia Suecana*, 4 (1955), pp. 77–86; E. Drioton, 'La date de l'Exode, *RH PR*, 35 (1955), pp. 36–49; C. de Wit, *The Date and the Route of the Exodus (The Tyndale Biblical Archaeology Lecture*, 1959), London, 1960; S. Herrmann, 'Israel in Ägypten', *ZAS*, 91 (1964), pp. 63–79; K. A. Kitchen, *Ancient Orient and Old Testament*, Chicago, 1966, pp. 57–75; S. Mowinckel, *Israels opphav og eldste historie*, Oslo, 1967, pp. 75–84.

According to 1 Kings 6:1, Solomon began to build the temple in the fourth year of his reign and this was four hundred and eighty years after the exodus from Egypt. This would mean that the exodus took place in the middle of the fifteenth century B.C. and the entry into Canaan under Joshua round about 1400. These dates are in accordance with the reference in the Amarna letters to the 'Apīru in the fifteenth century, and the excavations at Jericho which have revealed that the Late Bronze city was destroyed round about 1400 would seem to confirm them. The 'Apīru of the Amarna letters could not, however, have been the Israelites led by Joshua and the situation described in the letters is not in accordance with the conquest of Canaan. (We shall be returning to the problem raised by the excavations at Jericho in a later chapter.[78]) In any case, the information provided by 1 Kings 6:1 is without value, since the figure 480 is artificial. Various explanations have been put forward for this figure,[79] the most probable being that the deuteronomic editor constructed it on the basis of certain data provided in his sources.[80]

In the same way, no satisfactory conclusion can be drawn from Judges 11:26, which states that three hundred years passed between the war against Sihon and the time of Jephthah. If Jephthah is placed in the middle of the period of the Judges, then the Israelites would have arrived in Transjordan about 1400 B.C. Judges 11:26 occurs in a passage (Judges 11:12–28) which was introduced later into the story of Jephthah, however,[81] and we do not know where this chronological detail comes from. The difficulties applying to 1 Kings 6:1 therefore also apply to this figure of three hundred years.

There is only one reliable datum in the Bible which can help us to date the exodus. According to Ex 1:11, the Israelites built the store-cities of Pithom and Rameses. This information is undoubtedly early and it is authentic.[82] The exodus therefore took place later than the accession of Ramses II to the throne in 1290 B.C., although it is difficult to say precisely how much later. According to Ex 2:23a, the king of Egypt died while Moses was in Midian, so that the exodus must have taken place after the long reign of Ramses II, from 1290–1224, during the reign of his successor, Mer-ne-Ptah. The text Ex 2:23a is early, probably J, but it is isolated, being followed by a P text. It would seem that, in its source, it was intended to prepare for the story of Moses' return to Egypt. It has a parallel in Ex 4:19 (J), in which Yahweh says to Moses: 'Return to Egypt, for all those who

---

[78] See below, pp. 608–612.
[79] See the discussion in H. H. Rowley, *From Joseph to Joshua, op. cit.*, pp. 86–98.
[80] M. Noth, *Überlief. Studien*, pp. 18–27; *Könige (BKAT)*, 1968, p. 110.
[81] See W. Richter, 'Die Überlieferungen um Jephtah, Ri 10, 17–12, 6'. *Bib*, 47 (1966), pp. 485–556, especially pp. 522–547.
[82] See above, p. 325.

wanted to kill you are dead' (cf. Ex 2:15a, E?). This is a way of indicating divisions in the narrative. Another example is the statement that 'a new king who knew nothing of Joseph' came to the throne (Ex 1:8). This does not, it should be noted, provide a historical framework. In any case, Ramses II began to carry out his grandiose building plans in the Delta and especially the construction of his new residence, Pi-Ramses, at the beginning of his reign and it is therefore likely that the exodus took place during the first half or towards the middle of his reign. It is almost impossible to be more precise. The chroniclers of the Egyptian court have not recorded any memory of the flight of Semitic groups in an attempt to avoid corvée labour in the service of the pharaoh and successfully escaping from the pursuing Egyptian police. This flight was clearly no more than an insignificant episode, too small and lacking in glory to find any place in the accounts of the great achievements of the Pharaoh, whom the Egyptian chroniclers had to immortalise.

One Egyptian text has, however, been used to establish the date of the exodus. This is the stele of Mer-ne-Ptah, dating from the fifth year of his reign and mentioning Israel.[83] Israel is the only geographical name in the hymn inscribed on this stele which is followed by the determinative of people instead of that of land. The conclusion that has been drawn from this is that the Israelites were at this time not a settled people with their own land; having just left Egypt, they were leading a nomadic life in the desert. On the basis of this text, then, the date of the exodus has been fixed during the reign of Mer-ne-Ptah.[84] On the other hand, in the hymn itself, Israel is situated in Canaan. This would mean that the Israelites might have left Egypt during the reign of Ramses II and have entered Canaan while Mer-ne-Ptah was pharaoh without having settled there.[85] It should, however, be noted that the determinative 'people' attached to Israel is not decisive, because it might well be a case of carelessness on the part of the scribe – there are several such errors in the text. It is also important to know what the name Israel might have meant at the time of Mer-ne-Ptah. It could not have meant the whole of Israel, that is, the twelve tribes, because 'all Israel' had not been constituted at that time. It must therefore have meant Israel in a much narrower sense. Between the names Canaan and Huru, which are synonymous,[86] four geographical names are mentioned on the stele – Ashkelon–Gezer and Yenoam–Israel. The first two, which must be seen as a pair, are places situated in the south of the country and Yenoam is

[83]   ANET, pp. 376–378; see also below, p. 490.

[84]   See E. Drioton, RHPR, 35 (1955), p. 45; C. de Wit, op. cit., p. 10.

[85]   See J. Bright, History, p. 104; K. A. Kitchen, Ancient Orient, pp. 59–60; W. Helck, Geschichte des Alten Ägyptens, Leiden, 1968, p. 190; see also, however, Helck's article in VT, 18 (1968), p. 479.

[86]   See above, p. 128.

in the north, so that Israel must be in the north or in the centre. We have already seen that the tradition of the patriarch Israel originated in Shechem (and perhaps Bethel?)[87] and, in a later chapter, we shall also see that the group of Israel-Rachel settled in central Palestine.[88] The stele may therefore point to a group which had not become settled at the time of the inscription, in which case the determinative 'people' would certainly apply to their situation. What we have, then, is the fact that a group of people known as Israel existed in Canaan in 1220 B.C. and was known to the scholars at the court of Mer-ne-Ptah. If the tradition of the sojourn in the desert is borne in mind, this would confirm our supposition that the exodus took place before the middle of the thirteenth century B.C.

Other archaeological evidence has been sought in an attempt to date the destruction of the Canaanite towns mentioned in the accounts of the conquest and their reoccupation by the Israelites. When we come to consider the settlement of the tribes in Canaan, we shall see how difficult this archaeological evidence is to interpret. Among the many factors that have to be borne in mind are the literary genre of these accounts, the nature of the 'conquest' itself, the uncertainty of some of the locations and the imprecise nature of almost all archaeological dates. It also has to be remembered that great changes were taking place in the whole of the Near East at this time and that the settlement of the Israelites was only one of them. In the course of the fourteenth and thirteenth centuries B.C., all the cities of the Late Bronze Age were destroyed, some of them several times. This was something that went far beyond the limits of Palestine, and other peoples as well as the Israelites were responsible for this destruction. It is not, moreover, possible to ascertain beyond doubt, on the basis of archaeological evidence alone, whether it was the Israelites who destroyed certain cities or whether their subsequent re-occupation is a certain sign of settlement on the part of the Israelites. All the same, we can say in general that the decline of the Late Bronze civilisation, which took place at the end of the thirteenth century, and the modest beginnings of the new Iron Age, undoubtedly form the most favourable framework for the entry of the Israelites into Canaan and their settlement in the central part of the country.

The situation in Transjordania has also been used as a proof. There are clear archaeological indications that the southern half of the land went through a long period of eclipse as far as town life was concerned and that settlement only began again in the towns in the thirteenth century B.C. The Bible itself tells us that on their way from Kadesh the Israelites had to go round the territories of Edom and Moab (Num 20:21; Deut 2:1–9; Judges 11:17–18). The kings of Edom and Moab are also mentioned in the Bible (Num 20:14; 22–24; Judges 11:17). The first king of Moab was conquered

[87] See above, pp. 171–173.
[88] See below, pp. 648–649.

by Sihon, the king of Heshbon, who wanted to prevent the Israelites from passing through his land (Num 21:26). In Gen 36:31–39 = 1 Chron 1: 43–50, there is a list of eight kings who reigned over Edom before the time of Saul (or David), which would indicate that the kingdom of Edom was founded in the thirteenth century B.C. This agreement between textual and archaeological evidence would seem to confirm the date that we have suggested for the exodus, but despite the impressive character of the argument there is no certainty in any of its component factors. In the first place, the list of the kings of Edom may be a list of chiefs of principalities who were at least partly contemporary with each other. It is not necessarily a list of monarchs reigning in succession.[89] Again, it is not certain in the biblical texts that the Edomites and the Moabites were settled at that time – the 'kings' mentioned might well, like the king of the Amalekites (1 Sam 15:8, 20, 32),[90] have been leaders of nomadic groups of people refusing another nomadic group the right to cross their pasture. Thirdly, the route skirting Edom and Moab as described in the texts mentioned above is a detail that does not form part of the early tradition.[91] Finally, it is still not possible, on the basis of archaeological evidence, to give a precise date to the settlement of the Edomites and the Moabites. The very few excavations that have so far taken place in the regions where they lived have yielded nothing that can without doubt be dated back to the thirteenth century B.C. Despite all this uncertainty, however, there is one positive indication in the Egyptian texts which refer to Ramses II's plundering of the town of Dibon and another Moabite town which has not been identified.[92] This piece of evidence may perhaps make good what is lacking at present from the archaeological point of view and justify the biblical tradition.

In conclusion, we may say that the exodus took place during the reign of Ramses II, probably round about 1250 B.C. or a little earlier.

---

[89] See below, pp. 517–519.
[90] See the other biblical and extrabiblical references below, p. 517.
[91] See below, pp. 563–564.
[92] K. A. Kitchen, 'Some New Light on the Asiatic Wars of Ramesses II', *JEA*, 50 (1964), pp. 47–70.

Chapter Fourteen

THE SINAI TRADITIONS

AFTER the exodus from Egypt, the most important event set by the Bible in the origins of the people of Israel is the sojourn at Sinai. The account of this sojourn occupies the whole of the central section of the Pentateuch, from the arrival at Sinai (Ex 19:1) to the departure (Num 10:28). In other words, it includes the second half of the book of Exodus, the whole of Leviticus and a good deal of Numbers. Much of decisive importance occurred there. Yahweh made Israel his own people at Sinai. He concluded a covenant with them. He also gave them their laws. These laws and instructions given to Israel at Sinai include the decalogue (Ex 20 and perhaps 34), the civil and religious laws of the Code of the Covenant (Ex 21–23), the instructions concerning the sanctuary and its ministers (Ex 25–31 and 35–40) and the cultic law contained in Leviticus and supplemented in Num 1–10. It is obvious that the final editing of the Pentateuch projected all the later developments in Israel back to the origins of the people and that the Pentateuch, in its ultimate form, provides us with the law of the Jewish community as it was after the Exile. All these legal texts, to which must be added Deuteronomy, are connected, more or less closely, with the events described in the early sources of Ex 19–34, namely, Israel's encounter with God at Sinai and the conclusion of the covenant. These are the traditions which we must consider in this chapter.

I. LITERARY ANALYSIS OF EXODUS 19–34

It is not difficult to distinguish the work of the priestly editor in this section of the book of Exodus. The date of the Israelites' arrival at Sinai (Ex 19:1–2a) is part of the priestly material,[1] which is resumed at Ex 24:15b and

---

[1] Verse 1 is certainly P; verse 2a is usually attributed to P, but is connected with 17:1 and 8–16 (Rephidim) and may be read before verse 1.

continues then until 31:18a. In this priestly narrative, God manifests himself in a cloud on the mountain and calls Moses, who climbs the mountain and is given Yahweh's commandments regarding the building of the sanctuary in the desert, the tabernacle, and the organisation of the priesthood and of worship.

The only interruption in the block of priestly material is Ex 24:18b: 'Moses stayed on the mountain for forty days and forty nights', which is connected with verse 13b and ought to be immediately in front of 32:1, after 31:18b, which is connected with 24:12 and which prepares for the story of the golden calf (Ex 32), in which the tablets of the law play an important part, in 32:15–16. The priestly account continues at Ex 34:29–35,[2] when Moses comes down from the mountain with the tablets of the 'Testimony' and carries out the commandments of Yahweh (Ex 35–40). When the tabernacle was completed, Yahweh took possession of the sanctuary and his glory filled the tabernacle (Ex 40:34–35).

These priestly texts from a whole without any gaps, the main purpose of which would seem to be to provide a parallel account to the narrative of the early sources between which the priestly texts are inserted (Ex 19:3–24:15a and 31:18b–34:28). The framework of the story is basically the same, that of a theophany on the mountain where Moses encounters Yahweh and hears his words, which he then communicates to the Israelites. What is particularly striking, however, is that there is no question of the conclusion of a covenant or of the imposition of a law, which are the two essential aspects of early narratives. The commandments which are given to Moses and which he then hands on to the Israelites (Ex 34:32) are concerned only with the institution of the cult, the building of the sanctuary and the organisation of the priesthood (Ex 25–31). There is a text on the sabbath (Ex 31:13–17), but this is not the promulgation of a law, which existed, according to this tradition, since the creation (Gen 2:3). It is rather a reminder of an observance which had to be respected even during the building of the tabernacle,[3] as the addition of Ex 35:1–3 notes. To judge from what follows this passage on the sabbath, these instructions were apparently contained in the two tablets that Moses brought down from the mountain (Ex 31:18a and 34:29). This, however, is no more than apparent. In the first place, it is unlikely that such a long text should have been written on only

---

[2] Recent critics generally attribute this to P because of its vocabulary, but the story of Moses' face shining and of the veil that he puts over his face is not in the style of P. We are bound at least to recognise that, in verses 30–35, the priestly editors were following an independent tradition; see M. Noth, *Das zweite Buch Mose (ATD)*, p. 220; T. Dumermuth, 'Moses strahlendes Gesicht', *TZ*, 17 (1961), pp. 240–248. According to O. Eissfeldt, *TLZ*, 91 (1966), col. 2–3 = *Kleine Schriften*, IV, pp. 209–210, this is a late addition.

[3] See M. Noth, *in loco*. Verses 15–17 are certainly are additions and verse 14 may perhaps be an addition.

two tablets. In the second place, and more important, these two brief references to the tablets are both found at points of intersection between the priestly narrative and earlier sources. Ex 31:18a is situated just before the story of the golden calf, in which, in the text known to P, the tablets are mentioned, and Ex 34:29 is placed immediately after the reference to the tablets at the end of the account of the covenant (Ex 34:28). The priestly editor clearly felt bound to mention the tablets, but he did not attach a great deal of importance to them and changed their name. In the early accounts,[4] they were simply called the 'tablets' or the 'tablets of stone'. In Deuteronomy, they are also known as the 'tablets of the covenant' (*b'rîth*, Deut 9:9, 15). In P, on the other hand, they are called the 'tablets of the testimony, *'edhûth*. (We shall be returning to this word later.) The priestly editor was acquainted with the deuteronomic tradition, according to which the tablets bearing the 'ten words' or decalogue were placed in the ark, which, in this tradition, is called the ark of the covenant, *b'rîth* (Deut 19:8). In P, however, it is only called the ark of the testimony, *'edhûth*. This name is used twelve times in the passages that refer to Sinai and, the tabernacle of the testimony, *'edhûth*, in which the ark of the testimony is sheltered, is mentioned four times in the same texts. According to P, the ark does not contain the tablets of the covenant, the *b'rîth* of Deuteronomy, but the testimony, *'edhûth* (without 'tablets'). The narrative of the conclusion of the covenant at Sinai does not appear in P and, what is more, the priestly editor had deliberately avoided using the word *b'rîth* in this context.[5]

This clearly calls for an explanation. The priestly editor does not deny that a covenant was concluded at Sinai; as we shall see, he alludes to it. What he does in fact is to give it a different meaning. The priestly account of the revelation of the divine name (Ex 6:2–8) prepared for this covenant – Yahweh recalls his covenant, *b'rîth*, with the fathers in this account (verse 4) and says: 'I will adopt you as my own people, and I will be your God' (verse 7), which is regarded as the outstanding formula of the covenant.[6] Elsewhere, the same priestly tradition recalls the covenant that Yahweh concluded after the exodus from Egypt 'in order to be their God', at the end of the Law of Holiness (Lev 26:45). In the Exodus texts themselves, the sabbath is called by Yahweh 'a sign between myself and you' (Ex 31:13), in other words, a sign of the covenant, just as the rainbow was the sign of the covenant with Noah after the flood (Gen 9:12–16, P) and circumcision was the sign of the covenant with Abraham (Gen 17:11, P). The priestly editor, then, knew and accepted the document of this covenant at Sinai – it was the

---

[4] For the tablets of the law, see O. Eissfeldt, 'Lade und Gesetztafeln', *TZ*, 16 (1960), pp. 281–284 = *Kleine Schriften*, III, pp. 526–529; S. Lehming, *VT*, 10 (1960), pp. 32–40.
[5] The only place where *b'rîth* is found is in Ex 31:16, in an addition; see note 3 above.
[6] R. Smend, *Die Bundesformel*, Zürich, 1963, especially p. 27; see also N. Lohfink's criticisms, 'Dt 26, 17–19 und die "Bundesformel"', *ZTK*, 91, (1969), pp. 517–553.

ʿedhûth which was written on the tablets and placed in the ark (Ex 25:16, 21; 40:20).

The name ʿedhûth is one that is peculiar to the priestly editor. It is an extremely interesting word,[7] wrongly translated as 'testimony'. The word undoubtedly has the same meaning as the Akkadian adû, which is used, always in the plural, for a pact imposed by a superior on a partner of inferior rank. It is, in other words, a term used for a treaty of vassalage. The same word is found in Aramaic, again always in the plural and often in the construct, ʿdy, although once in the absolute, ʿdn, on the Sfire steles, which are treaties of vassalage imposed on the king of Arpad during the eighth century B.C. This meaning is quite appropriate in these biblical texts. The other cases where the word is used in the Bible, not in P material, confirm the correctness of this translation. ʿEdhûth is found in parallel or in connection with bʿrîth, covenant, huqqîm, decrees, or misʿwôth, commandments, and in every case can be translated by 'solemn pact' or 'undertaking'. In parallel with bʿrîth (Ps 128:12), for example, it qualifies the covenant with David, and used alone (2 Kings 11:12)[8] it points to the treaty binding the Davidic king to Yahweh. There is no doubt that this treaty or pact, ʿedhûth, was, for the priestly editor, the same as the document of the covenant, bʿrîth, of the other traditions, the 'ten words' or the decalogue.

The priestly editor, then, acknowledged the covenant and the law associated in the other traditions with Sinai. But the question still arises – why did the priestly author have so little to say about the covenant and why did he use a different vocabulary?[9] To answer this question, we must consider the whole of his work. He was acquainted with two covenants before the covenant concluded on Sinai – the covenant with Noah and the whole of mankind (Gen 9:8–17) and the covenant established with Abraham and his descendants (Gen 17). The covenant with Abraham was also known to the authors using the early traditions of the Pentateuch (Gen 15) and we shall see how this was connected in their accounts with the covenant of Sinai. Finally, the covenant with Abraham, Isaac and Jacob was known to the Deuteronomist, who frequently recalls it in the introductory discourses of Deut 1–11. The covenant of Horeb – the name which the Deuteronomist gives to Sinai – is, however, placed in the foreground in

---

[7] For ʿedhûth, see R. de Vaux, 'Le roi d'Israel, vassal de Yahvé', Mélanges Eugène Tisserant, I, Rome, 1964, pp. 127–128 = Bible et Orient, Paris, 1967, pp. 295–296; to the bibliography, add I. Gelb, BiOr, 19 (1962); CAD, I, 1, 1964, sub voce adû, pp. 131–134; R. Frankena, OTS, 14 (1965), pp. 134–136; J. A. Fitzmyer, The Aramaic Inscriptions of Sefire, Rome, 1967, pp. 23–24.

[8] See especially A. R. Johnson, Sacral Kingship in Ancient Israel,[2] Cardiff, 1967, pp. 23–24, 67.

[9] For this point, see W. Zimmerli, 'Sinaibund und Abrahambund. Ein Beitrag zum Verständnis der Priesterschaft', TZ, 16 (1960), pp. 268–280 = Gottesoffenbarung. Gesammelte Aufsätze, Munich, 1963, pp. 205–216, which modifies the conclusions that I have made concerning ʿedhûth. N. Lohfink, Rivista Biblica, 15 (1967), pp. 403–406, takes a different view.

Deuteronomy and presented as the fulfilment of the covenant concluded
with the fathers and of the promises contained in that early covenant.
Indeed, the whole of the law of Deuteronomy is fundamentally the document of this covenant established on Mount Sinai[10] and renewed on the
plains of Moab.[11] It is in Deuteronomy that the idea of the covenant with
all its juridical implications and its perspectives of being broken and
restored is developed.[12] This Sinai covenant overshadows the earlier
covenant with Abraham and makes the covenant with David useless.

The priestly editor was in fact reacting against this attitude taken by the
Deuteronomist. What he does is to insist on the pre-eminence of the covenant, *b'rîth*, concluded with Abraham, which was a *b'rîth 'ôlām*, a 'covenant
in perpetuity' (Gen 17:7, 13, 19), not a bilateral pact, but a gracious initiative on God's part, a personal commitment in which he binds himself to
a promise: 'I will give to you and to your descendants after you the land
you are living in . . . and I will be your God' (Gen 17:8; cf. 17:19). When
the descendants of Abraham, Isaac and Jacob became a people, they were
integrated, as a people, into the covenant made with their fathers. The
reference to the covenant concluded on Mount Sinai at the end of the Law
of Holiness (Lev 26:45) is preceded by a reminder of the covenant with
Abraham (Lev 26:42). In Ex 6:2–8, Yahweh recalls explicitly the promises
that he made to the fathers and is now about to fulfil: 'I will adopt you as
my own people and I will be your God . . . I will bring you to the land I
swore that I would give to Abraham, and Isaac, and Jacob' (verses 7–8).
This act of integration into the covenant takes place at Sinai, where the
people receive the pact, the *'edhûth*, which binds them to their God. For the
priestly author, however, the essential element is that the people of Yahweh
should receive a theocratic constitution: 'I will remain with the sons of
Israel, and I will be their God' (Ex 29:45). The Tent of Meeting of the early
tradition, *'ohel mô'edh*, became the Dwelling, *miš'kān*, which appears almost
fifty times in Ex 25–31, 35–40; cf. 25:8. Provided with a sanctuary and a
priesthood, this community is enabled for the first time to practise a cult. It
becomes a holy community, the offerings (28:38), the altar (29:37), the tent,
the ark and its furnishings, all of which were holy. Whatever touched
them was holy (30:25–29) and indeed the whole community was holy 'It is
I, Yahweh, who sanctify you' (31:13). The priestly editor does not simply
project the image of the second Temple and its priesthood and cult back to

---

[10] See R. E. Clements, *God's Chosen People. A Theological Interpretation of the Book of
Deuteronomy*, London, 1968, pp. 37–45.

[11] See N. Lohfink, 'Der Bundesschluß im Land Moab', *BZ*, new series, 6 (1962), pp.
32–56.

[12] This idea is developed at the different editorial levels of Deuteronomy itself; see N.
Lohfink, 'Die Wandlung des Bundesbegriffs im Buch Deuteronomium', *Gott in Welt
(Festschrift K. Rahner)*, I, Freiburg, 1964, pp. 423–444.

Sinai. He also projects the ideal of the post-exilic Jewish community back to Sinai.

The text that we have now to consider is the long Code of the Covenant (Ex 20:22–23:33). This name is taken from the text itself – in Ex 24:7, we are told that Moses took the 'Book of the Covenant', *sēpher habbⁿrîth*, and 'read it to the listening people'. There is, however, almost complete agreement now among scholars that the collection of laws outlined in Ex 20:22:23:33 is not this 'book of the covenant' from which Moses read, and that Ex 20:22–23:33 was added at a later period.[13] The extremely colourless introduction to this passage is clearly editorial. What is more, the preceding text (Ex 20:18–21) is not in its right place. It ought to be read immediately after the description of the theophany on Mount Sinai (Ex 19) and before the decalogue (Ex 20:1–17). It was clearly moved to a different position to make the insertion of the Code of the Covenant easier and to provide a suitable transition from the decalogue to the Code. Another more probable explanation is that it was moved when the decalogue was inserted into its present position. The connection between this Code and what follows it is even less certain. It is usual to regard this Code as going as far as Ex 23:33, the concluding passage being Ex 23:20–33. This passage, however, has certain similarities, as far as its vocabulary and its thought are concerned, with Deuteronomy and with Ex 32–34. It is, in other words, an addition and it is not easy to say whether it was added before or after the insertion of the Code of the Covenant into the book of Exodus. Some scholars believe that it contains elements of J and E and that it should be read after Ex 34:28, at the conclusion of the covenant of Sinai.[14] Another indication of the insertion of the Code can be found in Ex 24:3, according to which Moses tells the people all the words, *dᵇhārîm*, and all the ordinances, *mišᵖāṭîm*, of Yahweh. These *mišᵖāṭîm* refer to the *mišᵖāṭîm* of the Code of the Covenant (Ex 21:1) and the word was added. In what follows Ex 24:3, there is no reference even in the second half of verse 3 and in verses 4 and 8, to *mišᵖāṭîm*, but only to *dᵇhārîm* (words, commands, rules), which refers us back at once to the introduction to the decalogue (Ex 20:1) – the *dᵇhārîm* are the 'ten words'. The *sēpher habbⁿrîth* of Exod 24:7, then, is not the Code of the Covenant, but the decalogue, seen as the document of the covenant of Sinai.

The Code of the Covenant was inserted into the book of Exodus after Deuteronomy – according to Deut 5, which reveals a knowledge of the texts of Ex 19–20 in the order in which we now have them, including the

---

[13] Apart from the various introductions to and commentaries on this passage, see W. Beyerlin, *Herkunft und Geschichte der ältesten Sinaitraditionen*, Tübingen, 1961, p. 8; J. L'Hour, *RB*, 69 (1962), pp. 350–361; E. Nielsen, *Die Zehn Gebote. Eine traditionsgeschichtliche Skizze*, Copenhagen, 1965, pp. 45–48.

[14] O. Eissfeldt, *Einleitung*, p. 217; *ZAW*, 73 (1961), p. 137.

change of position of Ex 20:18–21, and no knowledge of any law other than the decalogue (cf. Deut 5:22). The Code of the Covenant was clearly known to the authors of Deuteronomy and was the inspiration for the deuteronomic legislation, but this Code was known in a different context. The suggestion has, for instance, been made that a Mosaic code promulgated on the plains of Moab and replaced by the code of Deuteronomy was at the basis of this Code of the Covenant,[15] but this Code has too many references to the settled way of life for it to be given such an early date. Another suggestion is that it was the document of the covenant of Shechem and that its correct position is therefore after Jos 24. in other words, according to this opinion, it is the law, the mišpat, written in the 'Book of the Law of God' that Joshua gave to the people (Jos 24:25–26).[16]

Having discussed the priestly texts and the Code of the Covenant, we must now turn to Ex 19:2–20:21; 24:1–15a; 31:18b–34:28. These are difficult passages especially with regard to literary criticism and most scholars are in a state of despair, so great is the uncertainty concerning them.[17] A great variety of different conclusions is clear evidence of this – only a few points emerge with any clarity. There is, for example, general agreement that Ex 19:3b–8, which includes an announcement of the covenant and of Yahweh's choice of Israel as a 'kingdom of priests' and a 'consecrated nation', is a later text.[18] Although it is difficult to decide whether this addition is part of one of the earliest traditions (Eissfeldt and Beyerlin think that it is E) or whether it is an independent tradition (Wildberger), deuteronomistic (Noth) or post-deuteronomic (Haelvoet and Fohrer), it is probable that it is late.

The same question arises in connection with Ex 33:12–23, Moses' prayer and his meeting with Yahweh. This text also has nothing to connect it with the context. Noth believed that it was an addition, but could not give a precise date or origin to it. He was of the opinion, however, that it is related to the story of Elijah (1 Kings 19:9–18) and that it might include a local Sinai tradition. Eissfeldt, on the other hand, thought that it was a

---

[15] See, for example, Caspari and H. Cazelles, *Etudes sur le Code de l'Alliance*, Paris, 1946.

[16] See R. de Vaux, *Institutions*, p. 143; J. L'Hour, 'L'Alliance de Sichem, ' *RB*, 69 (1962), pp. 5–36, 161–184, 350–368; A. Weiser, *Einleitung in das Alte Testament,⁵ Göttingen, 1963, pp. 112–113.* Other scholars place this passage at the beginning of the period of the kings; see G. Fohrer, *Introduction to The Old Testament*, London, 1970, pp. 136–137.

[17] M. Noth, *Überlieferungsgeschichte*, p. 33, note 114 and 115; see also p. 157.

[18] M. Haelvoet, 'La théophanie du Sinaï', *ETL*, 29 (1953), pp. 374–397; H. Wildberger, *Jahwes Eigentumsvolk*, Zürich, 1960, pp. 9–16; G. Fohrer, 'Priesterliches Königtum', *TZ*, 19 (1963), pp. 359–362 = *Studien zur alttestamentlichen Theologie und Geschichte (BZAW, 115)*, 1969, pp. 149–153; W. Beyerlin, *Herkunft und Geschichte*, pp. 13–16, 78–90; W. L. Moran, 'A Kingdom of Priests', *The Bible in Current Catholic Thought (Gruenthaler Memorial Volume)*, New York, 1962, pp. 7–20.

development of the L source and Beyerlin believes that it was later than J. More important, however, is that these authors are all agreed that the decalogue of Exodus 20:1–17 was inserted into its present position at a later date. This is almost certainly correct, but it does not mean, as we shall see when we return to this question, that the decalogue of the Sinai tradition has to be suppressed.

Furthermore, it would undoubtedly be mistaken to try to divide these texts between the Yahwistic and Elohistic sources. It would seem certain that a theophany and a covenant were contained in both these early sources. They are closely interwoven in the account of the theophany in Ex 19. The Elohist's version of the covenant is to be found in Ex 24 and the Yahwist's in Ex 34. These two accounts of the covenant are separated by the story of the golden calf (Ex 32). This tells of a breaking of the covenant, expressed by the breaking of the tablets of the law. The Yahwistic account of the covenant in Ex 34, with its reference to the making of two new tablets of stone, would seem to present us with a renewal of the covenant. One is tempted to think that this is an artificial arrangement, the episode of the golden calf – whatever its origin may have been – having been placed here in order to separate the two accounts of the covenant and to make it possible to retain both.

There is one final question of literary criticism which must be considered in connection with the Sinai traditions – the question of isolating the earliest account of the covenant of Sinai.[19] The following order has been suggested: Ex 24:1–2, 9–11, 13a, 14–15a; 34:10–13, 14b–16; 32:17–18, 25–29; 33:3b–4. This yields the following story. Moses and the seventy elders of Israel climb the mountain, see the God of Israel and they eat and drink. Moses and Joshua alone climb the mountain to Yahweh. Joshua promises to drive out the inhabitants of Canaan and the Israelites must not enter into a pact with the Canaanites. Joshua hears a noise in the camp that he takes to be the sound of battle. Moses tells him that it is a rebellion. He calls to those who are on Yahweh's side to save the situation and the Levites kill three thousand men. Yahweh then refuses to go in person with the Israelites. (He will be with them in the ark.)

This is still a covenant, but without any legal text. In this very early version of the covenant, Yahweh commits himself by word of mouth to get rid

---

[19] O. Eissfeldt, 'Die älteste Erzählung vom Sinaibund', *ZAW*, 73 (1961), pp. 137–146 = *Kleine Schriften*, IV, pp. 12–20; 'Sinai-Erzählung und Bileam-Sprüche', *HUCA*, 32 (1961), pp. 179–190 = *Kleine Schriften*, IV, pp. 21–31; 'Das Gesetz ist zwischeneingekommen. Ein Beitrag zur Analyse der Sinai-Erzählung', *TLZ*, 91 (1966), co. 1–6 = *Kleine Schriften*, IV, pp. 209–214; *Die Komposition der Sinai-Erzählung, Exodus 19–34 (Sitzungsberichte der Sächsischen Akademie der Wissenschaften zu Leipzig, Phil.–hist. Kq.*, 113, 1), 1966. See also H.–J. Zobel, 'Ursprung und Verwurzelung des Erwählungsglaubens Israels', *TLZ*, 93 (1968), col. 1–11, especially col. 7.

of Israel's enemies so that they will be able to settle in Canaan. This commitment on Yahweh's part finds its response in the Israelites' agreement not to come to terms with the Canaanites.

It is a very interesting hypothesis and is certainly quite in accordance with one way of presenting the covenant of Sinai in the very primitive tradition. It cannot, however, be based mainly on literary criticism. The texts isolated by Eissfeldt are attributed by him to the source which he calls L.[20] The existence of the pre-Yahwistic written source has, however, been disputed and it would seem to be difficult to attribute Ex 32:25–29 to it. The investiture of the Levites as priests as a reward for their zeal in defending Yahweh would, moreover, seem to be based on the investiture of Phineas and his descendants after the Israelites' worship of the Baal of Peor (Num 25:10–13) and it cannot be understood within the framework of a story which, according to Eissfeldt, did not include that of the golden calf.

The results achieved by literary criticism alone, then, are very uncertain. The content and the meaning of the Sinai traditions have therefore to be understood in the light of factors other than the written documents. Before going on to consider this question, however, we must examine the connection between these Sinai traditions and the other traditions of the Pentateuch, especially the tradition of the exodus and the conquest and that of Kadesh.

II. THE SINAI TRADITION AND THE TRADITION OF THE EXODUS-CONQUEST

Many literary critics are of the opinion that these two traditions were originally independent. This thesis has been brought to our attention by G. von Rad's work on the composition of the Hexateuch.[21] According to von Rad, the Hexateuch is a development of a confession of faith. The formula of this confession of faith is, von Rad believed, the creed that every Israelite had to recite when he offered his first-fruits (Deut 26:5–9): ' [5]My father was a wandering Aramaean. He went down into Egypt to find refuge there; but there he became a great nation, great, mighty and strong. [6]The Egyptians ill-treated us, they gave us no peace and inflicted harsh slavery on us. [7]But we called on Yahweh, the God of our fathers. Yahweh heard our voice and saw our misery, our toil and our oppression; [8]And Yahweh brought us out of Egypt with mighty hand and outstretched arm, with

[20] O. Eissfeldt, *Introduction*, p. 195.

[21] G. von Rad, *Das formgeschichtliche Problem des Hexateuch*, Stuttgart, 1938 = *Gesammelte Studien zum Alten Testament*, Munich, 1958, pp. 9–86 (*The Problem of the Hexateuch and Other Essays*, Edinburgh, 1966, pp. 1–78). My references to von Rad are taken from his *Gesammelte Studien*.

great terror, and with signs and wonders. [9] He brought us here and gave us this land, a land where milk and honey flow.'

The style of this confession of Israel's faith is undoubtedly deuteronomic, especially in the second half, but von Rad was convinced that it was ancient. What is above all remarkable is that it recalls the exodus from Egypt and the entry into Canaan, but says nothing at all about the revelation on Mount Sinai. The same is true of the confessions of faith in Deut 6:21–23 and Jos 24:2–13. The second text lists God's interventions in the history of Israel's salvation from the call of Abraham until the settlement in Canaan and again there is no mention at all of Sinai. The same tendency can be observed in Samuel's summary of his 'farewell discourse' (1 Sam 12:8): 'When Jacob came to Egypt the Egyptians oppressed them, and your ancestors cried to Yahweh who sent Moses and Aaron; they brought your ancestors out of Egypt and gave them a settled home there'. Similarly, the great works of Yahweh are celebrated in Ps 78, 105, 135 and 136, which cover the period from the monarchy to after the Exile, but none of these psalms mentions Sinai. The exilic psalm, Ps 106:19–20, recalls the making of the golden calf at Horeb (Sinai), but says nothing about the law given there. Only in the penitential liturgy of Neh 9:13–14 do the theophany of Sinai and the giving of the law appear between the exodus and the entry into Canaan. If we consider the Pentateuch itself, the Sinai narratives (Ex 19–34) interrupt the accounts relating to Kadesh (Ex 17 and 18),which are continued from Num 10:29 onwards.[22] The Sinai tradition is therefore independent of the tradition of the exodus-conquest. According to von Rad, the Yahwist took a bold initiative in combining them and thus uniting the message of salvation and the expression of God's grace, in other words, the 'gospel' of the tradition of the exodus-conquest, with God's revelation of himself and of his will, in other words, the 'law', of the Sinai tradition. In doing this, however, he acted in opposition to different and already firmly established attitudes which continued until after the Exile. This is clear from the evidence in the Old Testament of the confessions of faith and their various lyrical adaptations.[23]

The two traditions, von Rad has argued, have different cultic connections. The Sinai tradition was the cultic legend of a feast of the covenant and its renewal and the pattern of this cult is outlined in Ex 19–24:

1. Parenesis and historical exposition of the events at Sinai (Ex 19);

2. Recitation of the law, the decalogue and the Code of the Covenant (Ex 20–23);

3. Promise of blessings (Ex 23:20–33);

4. Ceremony of the covenant (Ex 24).

[22] G. von Rad, *op. cit.*, pp. 11–22.
[23] *ibid.*, pp. 60–62.

This renewal of the covenant was celebrated at the feast of Tabernacles, the great autumn festival. A later text which reflects the earlier practice (Deut 31:10–11) states that the law had to be read every seven years at the feast of Tabernacles. Ezra also read the law at the same feast (Neh 8). During the period before the monarchy, this feast of the renewal of the covenant was celebrated at Shechem. The pattern of this cult (Ex 19–24) is also found, von Rad believed, in the account of the covenant of Shechem (Jos 24), to which it is necessary to add Deut 27:15–26 and Jos 8:32–35.[24]

The tradition of the exodus-conquest, on the other hand, was the cultic legend of a feast of Gilgal, where the crossing of the Jordan and the entry into Canaan were celebrated, together with the memory of the exodus from Egypt. It coincided with the feast of Weeks (Ex 34:22) or the feast of Harvest (Ex 23:16), the Pentecost when the first-fruits were offered. This was precisely the time prescribed for the recitation of the creed of Deut 26:5–9.[25]

M. Noth accepted the essential elements of von Rad's thesis and gave them additional emphasis by integrating them into his own thesis concerning the composition of the Pentateuch as a coming together of previously independent 'themes'. In Noth's opinion, the theme of Sinai is independent of the theme of the exodus from Egypt. It originated among the southern tribes, but later was accepted by the whole of Israel and found a place in worship in the great autumnal feast that was celebrated at the central sanctuary of Shechem. On the other hand, however, Noth does not believe that the tradition of the exodus-conquest should be linked to the sanctuary of Gilgal, as von Rad thought. He is troubled by the very few references to this feast in the Old Testament and asks why not only the memory of Sinai, but also the memory of the exodus and the sojourn in the desert are both linked with the feast of Tabernacles in Lev 24:42–43. He also asks why, apart from the Pentateuch, Sinai-Horeb is mentioned so rarely, independently of the exodus. Leaving aside Deut 33:2 ff, it is possible to quote, in this connection, Ps 68:8–9, 18; Judges 5:5, 1 Kings 19:9–14 and Mal 3:22. This is, Noth suggests, because the Sinai tradition was very early and had been overshadowed by the later tradition of the exodus-conquest.[26] In the fundamental oral or written tradition which preceded the editorial work of the Yahwist and the Elohist and which Noth called G *(Grundlage)*, these two traditions were already one.[27]

Noth's thesis is supported by H.–J. Kraus, who, unlike von Rad, believes that the celebration of the exodus-conquest at Gilgal took place at the Passover rather than at the feast of Weeks. The combination of these

---

[24] *ibid.*, pp. 28–48.
[25] *ibid.*, pp. 48–55.
[26] M. Noth, *Überlieferungsgeschichte*, pp. 54–58, 63–67.
[27] *ibid.*, pp. 42–43.

traditions resulted, in his opinion, in the feast of Shechem taking place at the sanctuary at Gilgal.[28]

Other authors have made useful contributions to the solutions of this problem. There is general agreement that there were originally two distinct traditions, but none concerning the way in which they were combined in the Pentateuch. This thesis has also been seriously criticised in recent years from various vantage points. Above all, however, there is the criticism that the problem has been wrongly approached. It is, in other words, necessary to reverse the problem, taking as our point of departure not the existence of two separate traditions in the beginning, but the original unity of both traditions. This gives rise to the need to explain why and how they became – or seem to have become – separated.

We shall first criticise the arguments in favour of this thesis and then go on to give positive arguments for the combination of the two traditions. Finally, we shall attempt to explain their apparent separation and the reason why the Old Testament preserves silence with regard to the Sinai tradition.

1. *Criticism of the thesis of the independence of the two traditions*[29]

(a) *The 'historical creed'* It is not possible for the Hexateuch to have been composed as a development of the confession of faith or creed of Deut 26:5–9, because the traditions dealing with the history of Israel's salvation precede these confessions of the people's faith, which summarise that history. On the other hand, there is no proof that the creed outlined in Deut 26:5–9 in fact preserves a very early confession of faith within a deuteronomic framework. The vocabulary of this creed is closely related to that of the discourses in Deuteronomy and to the language found in the biographical chapters of Jeremiah. The creed does not in fact belong to the body of deuteronomic laws, but is an addition made at the time of Josiah.[30] It is, moreover, not connected in any way with the celebration of any

---

[28] H.-J. Kraus, 'Gilgal. Ein Beitrag zur Kulturgeschichte Israels', *VT*, 1 (1951), pp. 181–199; *Gottesdienst in Israel*, Munich, 1954, 2nd and enlarged, improved edition, 1962.

[29] See E. Osswald, *Das Bild des Mose in der kritischen alttestamentlichen Wissenschaft seit Julius Wellhausen*, Berlin, 1962, pp. 249–252 (von Rad), 274–285 (Noth); A. S. van der Woude, *Uittocht en Sinaï*, Nijkerk, 1961; H. Seebass, *Der Erzvater Israel* (*BZAW*, 98), 1966, pp. 56–73; J. M. Schmidt, 'Erwägungen zum Verhältnis von Auszugs – und Sinaitradition', *ZAW*, 82 (1970), pp. 1–31; J. P. Hyatt, 'Were There an Ancient Historical Credo in Israel and an Independent Sinai Tradition?', *Translating and Understanding the Old Testament. Essays in Honor of H. G. May*, Nashville and New York, 1970, pp. 152–170; see also the specialised works mentioned below.

[30] L. Rost, 'Das kleine geschichtliche Credo', *Das kleine Credo und andere Studien zum Alten Testament*, Heidelberg, 1965, pp. 11–25.

special feast or sanctuary. The 'first-fruits, rēšíth, of the produce of the soil' mentioned after the creed (Deut 26:10) were offered throughout the course of the farming year at the feasts of the Passover, Weeks (Pentecost) and Harvest (Tabernacles). The gift of land is stressed in this liturgical formula (Deut 26:9–10) precisely because it accompanied an offering of the first-fruits of the land. It incorporates into the history of Israel's salvation a rite borrowed from the Canaanites and claims for Yahweh the blessings that were attributed by the Canaanites to Baal (see Hos 2:7, 10). It is certainly not a summary of the whole of Israel's faith.[31]

The other confessions of faith which can be compared with the creed of Deut 26:5–9 and which also make no reference to Sinai are placed in a context which recalls the covenant and the promulgation of the law.[32] Deut 6:21–23 is a reply to the question in verse 20: 'What is the meaning of the decrees and laws and customs that Yahweh our God has laid down for you?' and it is followed by verse 24: 'And Yahweh commanded us to observe all these laws'. Again, Jos 24:2–13 is followed by verses 14–26, in which the people of Israel commit themselves to the exclusive service of Yahweh and also by verses 25–28, which are connected with the conclusion of the covenant and the reading of the law. Finally, 1 Sam 12:8 forms part of a renewal of the covenant at a time when a completely new period in the history of Israel was beginning with the institution of the monarchy.[33]

(b) *The links with cultic practice.* Several preliminary remarks of a general nature have to be made here. The Sinai tradition and the tradition of the exodus cannot be called 'cultic legends', in the sense that they were invented in order to explain certain cultic rites.[34] Tradition is not, as we have said, created by cult.[35] On the other hand, it is quite reasonable to suggest that these traditions were recited during a feast celebrating and commemorating the events that were narrated in the traditions and that the stories themselves were influenced by being used in cultic practice. This is almost certainly the case in the narrative of the tenth plague and the Passover (Ex 12–13).[36] It is also true that the liturgical calendars contained in the Old Testament include only the feasts which had been canonised by official worship and there must have been, as indeed there were, other

---

[31] T. C. Vriezen, *The Religion of Ancient Israel,* London, 1967, p. 127. A. Weiser, *Einleitung in das Alte Testament,*⁵ Göttingen, 1963, p. 82.
[32] A. Weiser, *op. cit.,* p. 81 ff.
[33] J. Muilenburg, 'The Form and Structure of Covenantal Formulations', *VT,* 9 (1959), especially pp. 360–365; A. Weiser, *Samuel, seine geschichtliche Aufgabe und religiöse Bedeutung,* Göttingen, 1962, p. 83; K. Baltzer, *Das Bundesformular,* Neukirchen and Vluyn, 1960, pp. 73–76.
[34] This is what S. Mowinckel has suggested, *Le Décalogue,* Paris, 1927.
[35] See above, pp. 321–323 with regard to the Passover and in general pp. 184–185.
[36] See above, pp. 367–369.

feasts, both very early feasts and local ones, which were not mentioned there; but there is a recent tendency in Old Testament scholarship which would lead us to accept rather too easily the existence of feasts not mentioned in the Bible or to endow those feasts which are mentioned with rites or meanings which are not mentioned in the texts.[37]

The Sinai tradition is therefore often linked with a feast in which the covenant was renewed. This feast is not mentioned in the Bible, but, according to this theory, it goes back to the feast of Tabernacles.[38] The main argument used to support this theory is the text of Deut 31:10–13, which lays down that the law, in this case Deuteronomy, should be read every seven years at the feast of Tabernacles.[39] This is a recent text, however, and the only meaning that it can have is that there was no annual renewal of the covenant – all that had to take place was the reading of the law every seven years. This is the essential aspect of this commandment – the connection with the feast of Tabernacles is fortuitous. Until the end of the monarchy, the feast of Tabernacles was, the most popular of the three annual feasts drawing pilgrims to Jerusalem. It was for this reason as well as to apply the law of Deuteronomy that Ezra chose the feast of Tabernacles to read the law (Neh 8). The argument in favour of the feast of Tabernacles has also been based on Ps 81 which, in the Jewish tradition, was sung at the feast of Tabernacles and refers to the theophany and to the decalogue (verse 8b–10). This reference, however, is preceded and followed by two reminders of the deliverance from Egypt (verses 6b–8a and 11), so that we are bound to conclude that this psalm is really evidence of the combination of the two traditions in the cult.[40] Finally, Lev 23:42–43 states explicitly that the exodus from Egypt was to be commemorated at the feast of Tabernacles.

Despite this evidence, attempts have been made to connect the tradition of the exodus-conquest with the feast of Weeks. As we have seen, the argument based on the creed of Deut 26:5–9 is not convincing. On the other hand, it is certain that the covenant of Sinai was commemorated at the feast of Weeks during the Jewish period. This is stated explicitly in the Book of Jubilees, according to which all the covenants found in the Old Testament, from the covenant concluded with Noah up to that made on Sinai, are dated back to this feast, at which the renewal of the covenant was to be

---

[37] E. Kutsch, 'Feste und Feier, II, in Israel', *RGG*,[3] II, 1958, col. 914–196.

[38] This idea was originally suggested by S. Mowinckel, *Le Décalogue*, pp. 114–129, who believed that the feast of Tabernacles was also a feast of the new year, of the enthronement of Yahweh and of the renewal of the covenant.

[39] It should be noted, in passing, that verse 13 ends by reminding the Israelites of the crossing of the Jordan. Once again, then, we find both traditions combined in the same text.

[40] A. Weiser, *Die Psalmen*, II (ATD), 1950, *in loco*; H.–J. Kraus, *Psalmen* II (*BKAT*), 1960 agrees with this, but believes that the Sinai tradition is in the foreground (with reference to Ps 50:4–7).

celebrated. This was, in fact, practised by the Qumran community.[41] This connection between the covenant of Sinai and the feast of Weeks, however, certainly goes back even further. According to Ex 19:1a (P), the Israelites reached Sinai at the third new moon after the exodus from Egypt[42] and, according to the same source, the revelation on the mountain occurred a week afterwards (Ex 24:16). Since the Israelites left Egypt during the night of the Passover, in the middle of the first month, seven weeks must have passed between this exodus and the revelation on Sinai, in other words, the period separating the Passover from the feast of Weeks (Lev 23:15).[43] The chronicler must have been thinking of the same feast when he established the renewal of the covenant in the third month during the reign of Asa (2 Chron 15:10–15).

There is in fact only one clear and at the same time early link between these traditions and cultic practice. It is that between the tradition of the exodus-conquest and the Passover and the maṣṣôth, the feast of Unleavened Bread. It is stated explicitly in the accounts of Ex 12–13, not only in the priestly source (Ex 12:11b–14, 40–42), but also in other texts which are earlier, but are difficult to date (Ex 12:24–27; 13:3–10).[44] The maṣṣôth are linked with the exodus in Ex 12:34, 39 (J) and in the calendars (Ex 23:15; 34:18). Outside the book of Exodus, this link between the exodus from Egypt and the Passover is confirmed by Deut 16:1 and presupposed by Jos 5:10–11, according to which the Passover was celebrated after the crossing of the Jordan. The second text is, moreover, not a priestly addition.[45] On the contrary, it is an early text (apart from the mention of the day in verse 10) and refers to a rite of the Passover celebrated in the sanctuary at Gilgal commemorating the entry into Canaan (and the exodus).[46]

We may therefore conclude by saying that it is not possible to prove the existence of a feast of the renewal of the covenant in Israel or of a connec-

---

[41] B. Noack, 'The Day of Pentecost in Jubilees, Qumran and Acts', *ASTI*, 1 (1962), pp. 73–95, especially pp. 81–90; A. Jaubert, *La notion d'alliance dans le Judaisme aux abords de l'ère chrétienne*, Paris, 1963, pp. 101–104, 214–215.

[42] For this interpretation, see M. Noth, *Das Zweite Buch Mose, Exodus (ATD)*, in *loco*; U. Cassuto, *A Commentary on the Book of Exodus*, Jerusalem, 1967, in *loco*.

[43] This matter is complicated by the later controversy that arose in connection with the way in which these seven weeks ought to be counted; see R. de Vaux, *Institutions*, II, pp. 393, 396; J. van Goudoever, *Biblical Calendars*, Leiden, 1959, pp. 58–60, 139–140; French translation of the third edition, *Fêtes et Calendriers bibliques*, Paris, 1967, pp. 88–89, 199–203.

[44] They are regarded as deuteronomic or pre-deuteronomic (at least Ex 13:3–16) by M. Caloz, *RB*, 75 (1968), pp. 5–62; O. Eissfeldt attributed them to his Laienquelle, *Hexateuch-Synopse*, Leipzig, 1922; Einleitung, p. 258.

[45] E. Kutsch, 'Erwägungen zur Geschichte der Passafeier und des Massot-festes', *ZTK*, 55 (1958), pp. 1–35, especially pp. 20–21.

[46] H.:J. Kraus, 'Zur Geschichte des Passah-Massot Festes im Alten Testament', *EvTh*, 18 (1958), pp. 47–67, especially pp. 58–60; J. Gray, *Joshua, Judges and Ruth*, London, 1967, pp. 70–71.

tion between the Sinai tradition and the feast of Tabernacles excluding the tradition of the exodus-conquest. The cultic practice of these two traditions cannot therefore provide us with any proof of their having been distinct.

(c) *The context of the Sinai tradition in the book of Exodus.* It is true that the stories of Sinai and the laws added to them (Ex 19 to Num 10) are preceded (Ex 18) and followed (Num 10:29–32, Hobab the Midianite; especially Num 20) by stories centred on Kadesh. The problem raised by this context is not that of the connection between the Sinai tradition and that of the exodus-conquest, but rather the problem of the link between the Sinai tradition and the tradition of Kadesh. This is something that we shall have to consider separately.

(d) *The combination of traditions in the Pentateuch.* All the texts that have been used to show that the traditions were different – the confessions of faith and the various psalms – are later than the Yahwistic and Elohistic narratives in the Pentateuch, in which the Sinai tradition and that of the exodus are combined. Those who insist on the distinction between them have therefore to explain how it was that they were combined in the earliest sources of the Pentateuch. G. von Rad attributed the insertion of the Sinai tradition to the Yahwist. This was, von Rad maintains, a purely literary undertaking. He gives no evidence to support his claim, which was made on the basis of his attitude towards the connection between the traditions and cultic practice. If these two traditions had been associated with two different feasts celebrated in two different sanctuaries, von Rad argued, they could not have been combined at the level of oral tradition. Von Rad's view has not been accepted by other scholars. M. Noth was of the opinion that the tradition of the exodus-conquest was already combined with the Sinai tradition in the *Grundlage* or G source which he believes underlies the editing of the Yahwist and the Elohist. S. Mowinckel, who does not accept the existence of an independent Elohistic source, thought that the two traditions were already combined in the oral *Vorlage* of the Yahwist.[47]

This brings us to two of Noth's most important arguments – those of the amphictyony and of the composition of the Pentateuch on the basis of independent 'themes'. Noth is of the opinion that the people of Israel did not exist and that there were not even any Israelite tribes before the 'League of Tribes'. Some tribes brought the exodus tradition into Canaan, others brought the Sinai tradition. These two traditions were merged together in Canaan. It is even possible, Noth suggests, that certain members of these groups of people who brought the traditions into Canaan found themselves

---

[47] S. Mowinckel, *Erwägungen zur Pentateuchquellenfrage,* Trondheim, 1964, p. 53.

together in the same tribes and that this made the combination of the traditions easier.

This view of the way in which the people of Israel was formed is not, however, in accordance with what we know of the formation of semi-nomadic tribes, the grouping of those tribes and the development from the tribal stage to that of people and nation as the nomadic life is renounced in favour of a settled way of life. It is, of course, true that not all the elements that were to form the future people of Israel were in Egypt and experienced the exodus and Sinai. It is, however, equally true that all these groups were united by a common faith in Yahweh. This common faith was not the consequence of the union of the various tribes – it was the basis of that union. We have shown that there were probably two exoduses. We have also established that there were certainly two entries into Canaan, one in the south and the other through Transjordan. This means that after settling in Canaan the tribes lived separately throughout the whole period of the Judges until the reign of David. They were both territorially and politically distinct and all that they had in common were ties of blood and religious faith. It is therefore impossible for elements which are fundamentally characteristic of Yahwism to have been combined at that time. According to the earliest texts that we have in our possession – texts which are earlier than the Yahwistic and Elohistic narratives of the Pentateuch – Yahweh was both the God of the exodus (Ex 15:21) and the God of Sinai (Deut 33:2; Judges 5:5; Ps 68:8–9, 18). The exodus and Sinai traditions were therefore merged before the settlement in Canaan. They formed part of the one tradition of a group of people who experienced both the exodus from Egypt and the revelation on Mount Sinai. The unity – and this means in the first place the religious unity – of the people of Israel came into being round this group and this tradition.

The same arguments prevail against other ways of explaining the combination of the two traditions which have been regarded as different. H.-J. Kraus thought that it was probable[48] and later thought that it was at least possible[49] for the traditions to have been combined when the place of worship was changed from Shechem to Gilgal.[50] R. Smend attributed the two traditions to the groups of Leah and Rachel respectively, the tribes of Leah bearing the tradition of the amphictyony, the Sinai (covenant) tradition, and the tribes of Rachel bearing the tradition of Moses, that is, the holy war of Yahweh (the exodus) and the entry into Canaan. The union of

---

[48] H.-J. Kraus, 'Gilgal. Ein Beitrag zur Kultusgeschichte Israels', *VT*, 1 (1951), pp. 181–199, especially pp. 193–194.

[49] H.-J. Kraus, *Gottesdienst in Israel,*[2] 1962, p. 193.

[50] The historical connections between these two sanctuaries are very complex; see W. H. Irwin, *RB*, 72 (1965), pp. 170–175; J. A. Soggin, *Volume du Congrès. Genève (SVT,* 15), Leiden, 1966, pp. 263–277.

these two groups of people led, Smend believes, to the merging together of the traditions.[51] Smend agrees that the members of Rachel's group might have gone on pilgrimage to Sinai and might therefore have come to know the other tradition at Sinai before settling in Canaan.

2. Positive arguments for the unity of the Exodus-Sinai tradition

(a) *Outside the narratives of the Pentateuch.* Several arguments in favour of the unity of the two traditions have been put forward in the course of the previous section, in which the thesis of two distinct traditions was criticised. For example, Yahweh was both the God of the exodus (Ex 15:21) and the God of Sinai (Deut 33:2; Judges 5:5; Ps 68:8–9, 18). The theme of the exodus-conquest was associated with the theme of the law and the covenant in the confessions of faith of Deut 6:20–24 and Jos 24 as well as in 1 Sam 12. In Deut 31:10–13, the idea of keeping the law is linked to the possession of the land. Finally, there is evidence of the unity of the two traditions in worship in Ps. 81.

We have also seen[52] that a formula denouncing the covenant is combined with a reference to the revelation of the divine name in Hos 1:9. Also in the book of Hosea the tradition of the exodus-conquest is connected with that of being led out into the desert and meeting God, when special relationships were formed between Yahweh and Israel (Hos 2:16–17; 11:1–4; 12:10; 13:4–6).[53] It is, of course, true that Hosea never refers explicitly to the covenant of Sinai,[54] but this fundamental relationship is clearly more important than an explicit reference in view of the fact that Hosea is quite original in his use of the historical traditions of Israel especially with regard to the Pentateuch.

(b) *Grace and the law.* The two traditions also have a unity which is based on their content, the content of the one complementing the other. The contrast between grace, as represented in the tradition of the exodus-conquest, and the law, as represented in the Sinai tradition, is an artificial one. This apparent dualism is in accordance with the two ways in which

---

[51] R. Smend, *Jahwekrieg und Stämmebund*, Göttingen, 1963, pp. 79–97.

[52] See above, pp. 356–357.

[53] For these texts, see the recent commentaries by H. W. Wolff, *Dodekapropheton, I, Hosea (BKAT),*[2] 1965, and A. Weiser, *Das Buch der zwölf Kleinen Propheten, I I (ATD),*[2] 1967.

[54] For this point and the use of *bᵉrîth* in Hosea, see G. Fohrer, 'Prophetie und Geschichte,' *TLZ*, 89 (1964), especially col. 488–489 = *Studien zur alttestamentlichen Prophetie (BZAW, 99)*, 1967, pp. 265–293; H. W. Wolff, *op. cit.,* pp. 155, 176; E. Kutsch, 'Der Begriff *bᵉrît* in vordeuteronomischer Zeit', *Das ferne und nahe Wort. Festschrift L. Rost (BZAW, 105)*, 1967, especially pp. 138–139.

God reveals himself in the Old Testament. On the one hand, he reveals his existence by his actions in history. On the other hand, he manifests his will by the words that he speaks in his theophanies or that are handed on by his authorised messengers.[55] The formula of the revelation of God, the personal declaration 'I am Yahweh', is common to both these manifestations and makes them valid.[56] Grace and the law, in other words, Israel's election and the commandments, are united in the special relationship established between Yahweh and his people which we call by the inadequate name of covenant.[57]

This covenant is not a bilateral pact by which two partners undertake mutual obligations. The full formula of the covenant is 'I will take you as my people and I will be your God', but the two partners are not equal. God takes the initiative. He takes Israel as his people and he commits himself to them by a solemn promise. This promise does not, however, bind him with regard to the people; it only binds him with regard to himself. The behaviour of the people does not play a direct part in God's resolve, which is an act of pure grace. This is clear in the covenant with Abraham (Gen 15) and it is also, as we shall see, apparent in the early form of the Sinai covenant. The result – not the condition – of this divine choice and promise is that the people, having become the personal property of Yahweh, must not have any other gods apart from him. They must serve Yahweh and obey his commandments. The people thus commit themselves. This commitment is to God and is imposed by God. It is expressed in the law. Grace and the law are the two inseparable elements of the covenant.

It is significant that God's gracious acts in delivering the Israelites from Egypt are presented as having been done for 'his people'. This phrase is used again and again and corresponds to the first part of the covenant formula: 'I

[55] See, in connection with this question, A. Weiser, *Einleitung in das Alte Testament,*[5] 1963, pp. 85–87.

[56] W. Zimmerli, 'Ich bin Jahwe', *Geschichte des Alten Testament (Festschrift Alt)*, Tübingen, 1953, pp. 179–209 = *Gottes Offenbarung. Gesammelte Studien*, Munich, 1963, pp. 11–40; *ibid.*, *Erkenntnis Gottes nach dem Buch Ezechiel*, Zürich, 1954 = *Gottes Offenbarung*, pp. 41–119, especially pp. 61–66; K. Elliger, 'Ich bin der Herr – euer Gott', *Theologie als Glaubenswagnis (Festschrift K. Heim)*, Hamburg, 1954, pp. 9–34.

[57] For what follows, see M. Noth, *Die Gesetze im Pentateuch*, Halle (Saale), 1940 = *Gesammelte Studien zum Alten Testament*, Munich, 1957, pp. 9–141, especially Chapter II and pp. 52–58; W. Zimmerli, 'Das Gesetz im Alten Testament', *TLZ*, 85 (1960), col. 481–498 = *Gottes Offenbarung*, pp. 249–277; N. W. Porteous, 'Actualization and the Prophetic Criticism of the Cult, *Tradition und Situation (Festschrift A. Weiser)*, Göttingen, 1963, pp. 63–105, especially p. 95 = *Living the Mystery*, Oxford, 1967, pp. 127–141; W. Eichrodt, 'Bund und Gesetz. Erwägungen zur neueren Diskussion', *Gottes Wort und Gottes Land (Festschrift Hertzberg)*, Göttingen, 1965, pp. 30–49; N. Lohfink, 'Gesetz und Gnade', Das Siegelslied am Schilfmeer, Frankfurt am Main, 1965, pp. 151–173; D. J. McCarthy, *Der Gottesbund im Alten Testament*, Stuttgart, 1966, pp. 80–82; E. Kutsch, 'Gesetz und Gnade,' *ZAW*, 79 (1967), pp. 18–35; E. W. Nicholson, *Deuteronomy and Tradition*, Oxford, 1967, pp. 42–43.

will take you as my people'. It is also significant that all of Israel's laws, the decalogue the Code of the Covenant and Deuteronomy, are connected with the theophany on Mount Sinai, which corresponds to the second part of the covenant formula: 'I will be your God'. In Israel, the law did not exist apart from grace. This is stressed in the introduction to the decalogue: 'I am Yahweh your God who brought you out of the land of Egypt, out of the house of slavery. You shall have no gods except me' (Ex 20:2–3). The law and grace are the two poles of the religious life of the people of the Old Testament and there was constant tension between those poles because of Israel's lack of submission.[58] The two traditions of the exodus-conquest and of Sinai are meaningful only if they are combined.

(c) *The Exodus narratives are orientated towards Sinai.* The two traditions are in fact combined in the earliest Yahwistic and Elohistic editions. Whether we think in this case of Eissfeldt's L source, Noth's G source or Mowinckel's *Vorlage*, these two traditions were already in existence very early and in a united state. The important factor is that they were not juxtaposed in this early state, but closely connected with each other.

The stories of Israel's deliverance from Egypt (Ex 1–15) are not complete in themselves. They are no more than a part of a much longer story.[59] The miracle of the sea, for example, is not an end in itself – it is simply a stage, the first stage on the road to Sinai. In Ex 3, the revelation of the divine name (E) or the theophany of the burning bush (J) take place in the desert. The Elohist states that Moses came 'to the mountain of God' (Ex 3:1). The addition of the name 'Horeb' as a gloss is of little importance – the 'mountain of God', 'Horeb' and 'Sinai' all point to the same place. What is more, the term *s'neh*, 'bush', which is only found in the Yahwistic passage (Ex 3:2, 4) of the 'burning bush' and in Deut 33:16 which refers to that passage, but nowhere else in the Old Testament, was most probably chosen because it sounds similar to *sinai*. The burning of the bush is also parallel to the fire of the theophany on Mount Sinai. In the Elohistic account (Ex 3:12), moreover, Moses is given the task of bringing the people out of Egypt and of leading them to this mountain in order to worship God. From the very beginning of the story of the exodus, then, we find a connection with Sinai that goes back to the earliest tradition.[60]

Moses has to ask the Pharaoh to let the Israelites go into the desert, making three days' journey, in order to offer a sacrifice to Yahweh (Ex 3:18, J;

---

[58] See W. Zimmerli, *Das Gesetz und die Propheten*; English translation, *The Law and the Prophets*, Oxford, 1965, chap. 3–4.

[59] See G. Fohrer, *Überlieferung und Geschichte des Exodus*, pp. 221–122; T. C. Vriezen, *The Religion of Ancient Israel*, London, 1967, pp. 127–128.

[60] G. Fohrer, *Überlieferung*, p. 35; for *s'neh*, see R. Tournay, 'Le nom du "buisson ardent"', *VT*, 7 (1957), pp. 410–413.

cf. 5:3, J). This petition was to become a basic theme in the story of the first nine plagues of Egypt (always in the texts attributed to J). We have linked these texts to the tradition of the exodus-flight,[61] which continues with the miracle of the sea (Ex 14). Leaving aside the suggestion that Moses deceived the Pharaoh on Yahweh's orders, we must assume that this tradition is not orientated towards the conquest, but towards the holy place in the desert where Yahweh revealed himself to Moses, in other words, towards Sinai. A possible objection is that in Ex 3:8, which is also the work of the Yahwist, Yahweh promises to deliver the people from the Egyptians and to take them to Canaan and that there is no mention of Sinai in this text. On the one hand, however, this promise was, as we have seen, given at Sinai itself and, on the other hand, the text is, as it were, played in a different register – that of the promise rather than that of service – these two registers corresponding to the two themes of election and commandment or grace and the law. The various summaries of the history of Israel's salvation, the 'confessions of faith' to which we have already alluded, are also played in this same register – Sinai is similarly not mentioned in these confessions of faith. The first part of the promise was fulfilled in the miracle of the sea and the destruction of the Egyptians. The Israelites then had to go to the place where Moses was given this promise and prepare themselves there to fulfil the second part. Once again, the two traditions appear to be linked closely together.[62]

(d) *The Sinai stories refer to the exodus-conquest.* Just as the stories about the deliverance of the Israelites from Egypt are orientated towards Sinai, so too are the narratives concerning Sinai directed on the one hand towards the exodus and, on the other, towards the entry into Canaan. It is, of course, true that the only reference to the exodus is in the introduction to the decalogue: 'I am Yahweh your God who brought you out of the land of Egypt' (Ex 22:2). There is, however, another text which is important in this context – Ex 19:3b–8. This text is regarded as the best existing expression of the Sinai covenant[63] and has in fact been called the charter of Israel's election.[64] Verse 4 contains a reminder of how Yahweh dealt with the Egyptians and this datum is given as the reason why the Israelites had to respect the covenant and to put Yahweh's commandments into practice (verses 5 and 8). As we have seen, however, the literary criticism of this passage presents us with serious difficulties. It is usually attributed to the

---

[61] See above, pp. 371–372.

[62] G. Fohrer, *Überlieferung*, p. 97.

[63] J. Muilenburg, *VT*, 9 (1959), pp. 351–359; K. Baltzer, *Das Bundesformular*, Neukirchen and Vluyn, 1960, pp. 37–38; W. Beyerlin, *Herkunft und Geschichte der ältesten Sinaitraditionen*, Tübingen, 1961, pp. 78–90.

[64] H. W. Wildberger, *Jahwes Eigentumsvolk*, Zürich, 1960, pp. 9–16.

Elohist, but, because of its rhythmic style and language, it is also clearly related to both the deuteronomistic and the priestly sources. Most scholars now believe that it is an addition to the early Sinai narratives.[65] This means that it is of no use to us in this instance.

On the other hand, the link between Sinai and the conquest is obviously stressed in Ex 34:10–11: 'I am about to make a covenant with you . . . Mark, then, what I command you today. I mean to drive out the Amorites before you, the Canaanites .. ' This text is usually attributed to the Yahwist and, according to O. Eissfeldt, it forms part of the earliest account of Sinai, the source which this scholar called L.[66] The promise to drive out the inhabitants of Canaan is a new aspect of the promise associated with Sinai – both before and in Ex 3:8, the promise spoke only of a gift of land. The same promise to drive out the Canaanites recurs in Ex 33:2 (J) and Ex 23:23, 27–30, the latter passage being now placed at the end of the Code of the Covenant, after having been moved, according to Eissfeldt, from its original position in the Sinai covenant.[67]

(e) *The parallel with the treaties of vassalage.* One final argument which has recently been put forward in favour of the unity of the two traditions of the exodus and of Sinai must be briefly discussed here, because it has been presented as conclusive.[68] It is based on a presumed connection between the Sinai covenant and the treaties of vassalage which date back to the fifteenth to the thirteenth centuries B.C. and which open with a historical summary and then go on to list the various clauses in the treaty in question. This historical introduction corresponds, the proponents of this theory claim, to the 'historical creeds' of Israel and the clauses to the laws. As we shall see, however, this comparison between the covenant and these Eastern treaties of vassalage is exaggerated. What is more, it is not a justifiable comparison in the case of the Sinai covenant in its earliest form.

---

[65] M. Noth, *Das zweite Buch Mose, Exodus (ATD), in loco* (D); W. Wildberger, *op. cit.*, p. 14 (an independent tradition); W. L. Moran, 'A Kingdom of Priests', *The Bible in Current Catholic Thought (Gruenthaler Memorial Volume)*, New York, 1962, pp. 7–20 (the tradition of the amphictyony, incorporated in the Elohistic tradition). G. Fohrer, ' "Priesterliches Königtum", Ex 19, 6', *TZ*, 19 (1963), pp. 359–362 = *Studien zur alttestamentlichen Theologie und Geschichte (BZAW*, 115), 1969, pp. 149–153 (the end of the monarchy); D. J. McCarthy, *Treaty and Covenant*, Rome, 1963, pp. 152–167 (not originally in the Sinai accounts). It is in my view not possible for the text to be earlier than Deuteronomy. It is not a text containing the very early meaning of the covenant.

[66] O. Eissfeldt, *ZAW*, 73 (1961), especially p. 144.

[67] The texts of Ex 33:2 and 23:23, 27–30 are regarded by M. Noth as additions. Was this judgement not influenced, then, by his thesis that the two traditions were different?

[68] W. Beyerlin, *Herkunft und Geschichte, passim* and pp. 190–191; H. B. Huffmon, 'The Exodus, Sinai and the Credo', *CBQ*, 27 (1965), pp. 101–113.

3. The apparent difference between the two traditions outside the Pentateuch

(a) *The two traditions are not distinguished, but the Sinai tradition is passed over in silence.* We have already shown how some of the texts used to prove that the two traditions were separate point, on the contrary, to the fact that they were united (see Deut 6:20–24; Jos 24; 1 Sam 12; Deut 31:10–13; Ps 81). On the other hand, if grace and the law were the two aspects of the tradition of the exodus-Sinai, if they were, in other words, the two opposite poles of the covenant, it must have been possible to emphasise one of those aspects or one pole without speaking of the other, but at the same time without denying its existence. This is above all a natural process in hymns, and Pss 78, 105, 125 and 126, for example, praise the works of God's salvation without mentioning the law, which belongs to another sphere.[69]

The problem, then, is not so much one of the difference between the two traditions, as that the Sinai tradition was apparently forgotten throughout almost the whole of the period of the monarchy. This silence with regard to Sinai is in striking contrast to the importance given to the events of the exodus – Yahweh was not the God who revealed himself on Mount Sinai, but the God who brought Israel out of Egypt. This was the great event in the history of the people of Israel and the basis of their faith in Yahweh. (It should incidentally be noted in this context that this silence with regard to Sinai does not lend support to the argument that there was an annual feast at which the covenant was renewed in Israel and the events of Sinai were commemorated.) It is, however, clearly necessary to explain this silence and I should like to suggest two possible ways.

(b) *A series of covenants.* The group of people which left Egypt led by Moses became the 'people of Yahweh' at Sinai through a covenant which continued the tradition of the God of the fathers and which was comparable to the covenant with Abraham (Gen 15). This action was unique, unrepeatable and constitutive. It could never be done away with and its effects were lasting. The relationships established by this covenant between the people and their God, however, had to be adapted to historical developments and, as soon as the people settled in Canaan, a change came about in their conditions.[70] Various groups of people who did not

---

[69] See A. Weiser, *Einleitung in das Alte Testament,* p. 84 ff. This conclusion remains valid even though we may not necessarily be in agreement with Weiser, who believed that these hymns were sung during a ceremony of renewal of the covenant of the law was also read.

[70] R. Smend, *Die Bundesformel*, Zürich, 1963, pp. 11ff, 18ff. G. Fohrer, 'Altes Testament – "Amphiktyonie" und "Bund"?', *TLZ*, 91 (1966), especially col. 898–899 = *Studien zur alttestamentlichen Theologie und Geschichte (BZAW, 115)*, 1969, pp. 103–119. G. Fohrer does not, however, discuss the Shechem covenant and doubts whether there ever was a Davidic 'covenant'.

experience the exodus or Sinai joined the Yahwistic group and the 'people of Yahweh' became the people of Israel at the great assembly of Shechem and Yahweh became the God of Israel. This change was recorded in the covenant at Shechem (Jos 24). The covenant of Sinai was rejected at the second level as something that had taken place in the past, but its effects were transferred to the new entity, Israel, and the spirit of this earlier covenant continued. There are several references, for example, in the Song of Deborah, to Israel and to Yahweh, the God of Israel, but this Israel is also called the 'people of Yahweh' (verse 13; see also verse 11). This 'people of Israel' is identified with the 'house of Israel' in 2 Sam 1:12 and Israel is also called 'Yahweh's people' in 2 Sam 6:21. This is, of course, the period of David, when another change took place, the people of Israel becoming a kingdom. This change in circumstances was reflected in a new expression of the relationship between God and his people, the Davidic covenant.

(c) *The Davidic covenant and the Sinai covenant.* Different explanations have been suggested to account for the relationship between these two covenants. According to L. Rost,[71] the Sinai covenant remained valid in the Northern Kingdom, whereas it was replaced by the Davidic covenant in the Southern Kingdom of Judah after the political schism. The intentions of these two covenants were different and Josiah tried to combine them in his reform. Noth thought that Rost's explanation was too simple, because the ark of the Sinai covenant was kept at Jerusalem and the promises made to David concerned the whole of Israel.[72] H.-J. Kraus[73] was of the opinion that both covenants were combined in the cult at Jerusalem, this combination having come about by the transference of the feast of the covenant from Shechem and its transformation into a feast of Zion celebrated at the feast of Tabernacles. Against this theory, however, is the fact that there is no proof of the existence of any such feast at Jerusalem.

I have tried to show elsewhere[74] that the two covenants had the same object – the Sinai covenant made Israel the vassal of Yahweh, whereas the Davidic covenant made the king his vassal, although the people were also involved. My view of the Davidic covenant as a treaty of vassalage was accepted and further developed with the help of Nathan's prophecy (2 Sam 7).[75] It has also been criticised.[76] I am personally less inclined now than I

---

[71] L. Rost, 'Sinaibund und Davidsbund', *TLZ*, 72 (1947), col. 129–134.

[72] M. Noth, 'Gott, König, Volk im Alten Testament', *ZTK*, 47 (1950), pp. 157–191 = *Gesammelte Studien*, pp. 188–229, especially pp. 224–225.

[73] H.-J. Kraus, *Die Königsherrschaft Gottes im Alten Testament*, Tübingen, 1951; *Gottesdienst in Israel*, Munich, 1954, pp. 77–91; 2nd edn. 1962, pp. 222–234.

[74] R. de Vaux, 'The King of Israel, Vassal of Yahweh', *The Bible and the Ancient Near East*, London, 1971, pp. 152–166, especially pp. 157–160.

[75] P. J. Calderone, *Dynastic Oracle and Suzerainty Treaty*, Manila, 1966.

[76] D. J. McCarthy, *Der Gottesbund im Alten Testament*, Stuttgart, 1966, pp. 75–76.

was then to acknowledge the formal presence of treaties of vassalage in the Sinai and the Davidic covenants, but I still insist on the basic connection that exists between the two. The Davidic covenant concerns both the people and the dynasty – the fact that the people are involved is quite clear from Nathan's oracle: 'I will provide a place for my people Israel; I will plant them there and they shall dwell in that place' (2 Sam 7:10). David's prayer, which follows this oracle, also refers implicitly to the Sinai covenant: 'You have constituted your people Israel to be your own people for ever; and you, Yahweh, have become their God' (2 Sam 7:24). This link between the two covenants is also expressed in the renewals of the Davidic covenant. After Athaliah had been deposed and Jehoash had been enthroned, the priest Jehoiada 'made a covenant between Yahweh and king and people, by which the latter undertook to be the people of Yahweh' (2 Kings 11:17). The early name 'people of Yahweh' is, by way of exception, found in this text. During the reign of Josiah, 'the king . . . stood . . . in the presence of Yahweh' and 'made a covenant to follow Yahweh and keep his commandments and decrees and laws . . . in order to enforce the terms of the covenant as written in that book [Deuteronomy]. All the people gave their allegiance to the covenant' (2 Kings 23:3). It is, of course, true that Josiah's reform was a reaction, just as the enthronement of Jehoash had been, but both marked a return to the real meaning of the Davidic covenant. According to Ps 89, which is a commentary on this covenant, it was made in favour of the people (verse 4) and despite all the faults committed by individual kings the dynasty was to continue because of the people (verse 34).

Although there is a difference, then, between the two political situations, the situation before the establishment and that which existed afterwards, there is none between the two covenants. The aim of the Davidic covenant was to incorporate the monarchy into the early tradition of the covenant of Shechem and Sinai.[77] The glory of the dynasty of David, however, with its capital and temple at Jerusalem, overshadowed the memory of Sinai. On the other hand, this memory was kept alive in the north. Elijah, for instance, went to Horeb to encounter God (1 Kings 19) and to complain to him about Israel's abandonment of his covenant (verses 10 and 14).[78] The only prophet whose writings contain any reference to Sinai was a prophet from the north, Hosea.[79] Deuteronomy also originated in the north and the

[77] A. H. J. Gunneweg, 'Sinaibund und Davidsbund', VT, 10 (1960), pp. 335–341; in general, J. R. Porter, Moses and Monarchy, Oxford, 1963, pp. 12–13.

[78] The Massoretic texts only, the versions having only 'the sons of Israel have deserted you', which comes to the same thing.

[79] See above, p. 410. It has been claimed that there are references to Sinai in other prophetic books: W. Beyerlin, Die Kulttradition Israels in der Verkündigung des Propheten Micha, Göttingen, 1959 (Micah); H. Graf Reventlow, Das Amt des Propheten bei Amos, Göttingen,

Sinai covenant was restored to favour there. The memory was also preserved in the Kingdom of Judah and possibly even at the court of Jerusalem, at least among the 'people of the land', the *'am ha'ares* who supported the movements for the reform of national and religious life and who seem to have been the custodians of the ancient Yahwistic tradition.[80] Whatever relationships he may have had with Deuteronomy, Jeremiah was certainly a prophet who preached above all the Sinai covenant (see Jer 11:1–10; 24:7; 32:39–40) and the new covenant that he proclaimed (Jer 31:31–34) was a renewal and a deepening of the Sinai covenant, in which there was no reference at all to the Davidic covenant.[81]

(d) *Jerusalem, the new Sinai.* Another reason why the Sinai covenant was passed over in silence during the period of the monarchy is that Jerusalem replaced the 'mountain of God'. The ark, in which the 'ten words' were kept, was set up in Jerusalem. In Ps 132, the covenant with David is presented as God's reply to the transfer of the ark to Zion, which Yahweh chose as the place where he would rest (Ps 132:3–5, 11–13). Nathan's oracle (2 Sam 7) also follows the story of the transfer of the ark to Jerusalem (2 Sam 6), but this literary order of events cannot be used as proof because it is of a later date. It has been suggested that Nathan's prophecy was a protest against the theory of Ps 132, that the Davidic covenant was not the consequence of David's initiative, but a pure act of grace on Yahweh's part.[82] The fact remains, however, that the ark of the covenant was at Jerusalem. When it was brought into the temple, Yahweh's cloud, *'arāphel*, and his glory, *kābhôdh*, filled the sanctuary (1 Kings 8:10–11). Yahweh revealed himself on Mount Sinai in a cloud, *'arāphel* (Ex 20:21, E) and when it was set up in the desert, the Tent of Meeting was covered with Yahweh's cloud, *'anān*, and his glory filled the tabernacle. (Ex 40:34–35, P). This text is so similar to 1 Kings 8:10–11 that the latter has been attributed to a gloss inspired either by the Exodus text or by a tradition from the same priestly environment.[83] Whatever the case may be, the poetic couplet which

---

1962 (Amos); H. Wildberger, 'Jesajas Geschichtsverständnis', *SVT*, 9, 1963, pp. 104–105 (Isaiah). The word *b'rîth*, however appears in none of them and none contains any clear reference to the events of Sinai.

[80] R. de Vaux, *RA*, 58 (1964), p. 170.

[81] M. Sekine, 'Davidsbund und Sinaibund bei Jeremia', *VT*, 9 (1959), pp. 47–57; R. Martin-Achard, 'La nouvelle alliance selon Jérémie', *RThPh*, 12 (1962), pp. 81–92. According to Jer 33:14–26, Yahweh promised to fulfil the Davidic and the priestly covenants permanently, but this passage is not accepted by the whole biblical tradition; it is lacking, for example, in the Septuagint.

[82] H. Gese, 'Der Davidsbund und die Zionserwählung', *ZTK*, 61 (1964), pp. 10–26.

[83] M. Noth, *Könige (BKAT)*, Neukirchen and Vluyn, 1968, *in loco*. Several scholars have, however, argued that the text is early; see H. Schmid, *ZAW*, 67 (1955), p. 193; J. Schreiner, *Sion-Jerusalem, Jahwes Königssitz*, Munich, 1963, p. 149.

follows immediately and which is undeniably very early (1 Kings 8:12–13) also says that Yahweh 'dwells in the thick cloud, *ᵃrāphel*' and this is clearly an allusion to the theophany on Mount Sinai.

In the accounts of the exodus, Sinai was called the 'mountain of God'. During the monarchy, Jerusalem became the 'mountain where God has chosen to live . . . Yahweh has left Sinai for his sanctuary' (Ps 68:17–18). As in the past, so too during the monarchy, Yahweh speaks and commands at Jerusalem, as, for instance, in Amos 1:2: 'Yahweh roars from Zion, and makes his voice heard from Jerusalem'. Isaiah proclaimed that 'the Law will go out from Zion, and the oracle of Yahweh from Jerusalem' (Isa 2:3).[84] Jerusalem, then, where Yahweh lived, revealed himself and spoke, was the new Sinai. This may perhaps be the real reason why Sinai seems to have been forgotten during the period of the monarchy.

III. The Sinai Tradition and the Kadesh Tradition

One of the arguments put forward for separating the Sinai tradition from the tradition of the exodus is that the stories about Sinai were introduced into a complex of traditions centred on Kadesh. These traditions are found in Ex 15:23 to 18:27 on the one hand and in Num 10:29 to 20:22 on the other. Some scholars have regarded this Kadesh tradition as very important,[85] maintaining that the Israelites went straight to Kadesh from Egypt and spent almost the whole of the time that they stayed in the desert there. It was at Kadesh, they believe, that they were given their religious institutions and from Kadesh that they tried to enter Canaan, some groups of the people in fact succeeding. If Sinai was really different from Kadesh and if there is any historical authenticity in the Sinai stories, these exegetes claim, then Sinai was no more than a very short episode which took place after Kadesh.

According to this theory, the Israelites went direct to Kadesh. In fact, they went from the Sea of Reeds into the 'wilderness of Shur', which stretched out eastwards from the Egyptian frontier in the north-west of the Sinai peninsula, and 'they travelled there for three days without finding water' (Ex 15:22). This is certainly in accordance with what they asked the

---

[84] This text is, of course, resumed in Mic 4:2 and its origin and age have been frequently discussed. There is, however, no reason to doubt that it is genuinely Isaian; see H. Wildberger, *Jesaja (BKAT)*, 1965, pp. 78–80.

[85] H. Gressmann, *Mose und seine Zeit*, Göttingen, 1913; S. Mowinckel, 'Kadesj, Sinai, og Jahve', *Norsk Geografix Tidsskrift*, 11 (1942), pp. 1–32; idem., *Israels opphav og eldste historie*, Oslo, 1967, pp. 45ff; E. Auerbach, *Moses*, Amsterdam, 1953; W. Beyerlin, *Herkunft*, 1961, *passim* and pp. 165–171.

Pharaoh again and again to let them do – to travel for three days in the desert in order to offer a sacrifice to their God. They wanted to go to a sanctuary and Kadesh, as its name indicates, was a holy place. There is confirmation of this in Judges 11:16–18, in which Jephthah says that Israel, coming up from Egypt, reached Kadesh and stayed there until leaving for Moab. There is, in other words, no mention of Sinai.[86] A text in Deuteronomy (Deut 1:46) also says that the Israelites had to stay 'for many a day' at Kadesh. It has even been suggested that, out of the forty years that the Israelites spent in the desert (Deut 1:3; 2:7; 8:4), they remained for thirty-eight years at Kadesh and Deut 2:14 has been used to support this theory.[87] According to this text, however, the thirty-eight years do not point to the period spent at Kadesh, but to the time spent wandering in the desert between Kadesh and the entry into Transjordan, which is clearly quite different. What is more, according to Deut 2:1, the Israelites wandered 'for many days' in the mountain district of Seir – the words are the same as those used in Deut 1:46 to describe the period spent at Kadesh.

Leaving aside the question of the length of the stay at Kadesh, we may be certain that this stay took place after crossing Sinai, at least according to the Pentateuch in its present state. The name Kadesh occurs for the first time in Num 13:26 and the Israelites arrived there from Sinai, as in the summary in Deut 1:2, 19 and in the list of stopping places (Num 33:36). It has been suggested that Kadesh was not mentioned earlier in the Pentateuch because the overwhelming importance of Sinai and its tradition led to the suppression of the Kadesh tradition.

What, however, has been attributed to this Kadesh tradition? The texts relating to this tradition are very heterogeneous. Many have to be set aside – the long priestly texts, such as Num 15 and 18–19, which deal with cultic laws, a great deal of Ex 16 (the manna), Num 13–14 (the reconnaissance in Canaan and the people's rebellion) and Num 16, in which Korah's rebellion is combined with the early account of the rebellion of Dathan and Abiram. What is more, it would be wrong to relate the encounter with Jethro and the conversation with Hobab (Num 10:29–32), which belong to the Midianite cycle, to the Kadesh tradition. Some episodes are repeated both before and after the Sinai stories and their connection with Kadesh is either vague or secondary. These include the story of the manna and the quails (Ex 16, J and P; Num 11, J and E), the miracle of the water from the rock at (Massah) Meribah (Ex 17:1–7, J and E; Num 20:1–13, J and P) and the appointment of the judges (Ex 18:21–26, E; Num 11:16–17, addition). The story of the manna and the quails presents us with a special problem.

[86] In this historical summary, only the events from Kadesh onwards are described; it is also dependent, in the literary sense, on Num 20–21; see W. Richter, 'Die Überlieferungen um Jephthah', *Bib*, 47 (1966), pp. 485–556, especially pp. 531–534.
[87] H. H. Rowley, *From Joseph to Joshua*, London, 1950, p. 105 *et alia*.

These were two natural phenomena which took place at Sinai, but in different parts of the desert. The manna of Sinai is the secretion of two insects, *Trebutina mannipara* and *Najacoccus serpentinus*, which live on the tamarisk. The harvest is made at the end of May and in June. Tamarisk grows everywhere in the Sinai desert, but the insects that produce manna live only in the central area. The northern limit of the zone where manna is found is the Wādi Gharandal.[88] There is no manna in the region of Kadesh. The quails migrate to Europe in the spring and return in the autumn. Exhausted after crossing the Mediterranean, they come down near the coast and are very easily caught. Great quantities of these birds are captured every year over a large area, from Gaza in the north to Egypt in the south. This is the migration referred to in Num 11:31, which says that 'a wind . . . drove quails in from the sea'. The priestly chronology, however, dates the two arrivals of the quails at the end of the spring (Ex 16:1; Num 10:11). The quails arrive in great numbers and are very easily caught only on the north-west coast of the Sinai peninsula; it would therefore be unjustified to relate this episode (or these two episodes) to Kadesh or even to the journey to Kadesh.[89] From what we know of the natural phenomena of the manna and the quails, we can say with certainty that these could not have taken place in the same part of the desert. Manna is a natural phenomenon occurring in central Sinai and the arrival of the migrating quails is a phenomenon of the north-west coastline. It would therefore seem as though these two phenomena, peculiar to Sinai, were known to the Israelites and had perhaps even been experienced by various groups among the Israelites' ancestors. This knowledge and this experience were then used to illustrate God's providence during the sojourn in the desert.

In the same way, the two miracles of the water are also doublets.[90] They are closely linked with the theme of the murmuring of the people in the desert. In Ex 17:1–7 (JE), two geographical names are given and two etymologies are provided – Massah, the people put Yahweh 'to the test', and Meribah, the people 'contended' with Yahweh. It is probable that Massah is later and, in any case, it cannot be located. Only Meribah is mentioned in Num 20:1–13 (P), in which it is linked in an obscure way with the punishment of Moses and Aaron, who were to die before the entry into

---

[88] F. S. Bodenheimer and O. Theodor, *Ergebnisse der Sinai Expedition 1927*, Leipzig, 1929, pp. 45–88; F. S. Bodenheimer, 'The Manna of Sinai', *BibArch*, 10 (1947), pp. 2–6.

[89] C. J. Jarvis, *PEQ*, 1938, pp. 30–31; J. Gray, *VT*, 4 (1954), p. 148ff.

[90] For these two texts, see J. R. Porter, 'The Role of Kadesh-Barnea in the Narrative of the Exodus', *JTS*, 44 (1943), pp. 139–143; E. Arden, 'How Moses Failed God', *JBL*, 76 (1957), pp 50–52; A. S. Kapelrud, *ibid*, p. 242; S. Lehming, 'Massa und Meriba', *ZAW*, 73 (1961), pp. 71–77; J. Koenig, 'Sourciers, thaumaturges et scribes', *RHR*, 164 (1963–B), pp. 17–38, 165–180; G. W. Coats, *Rebellion in the Wilderness*, Nashville and New York, 1968, pp. 53–82; V. Fritz, *Israel in der Wüste. Traditionsgeschichtliche Untersuchung der Wüstenüberlieferung des Jahwisten*, Marburg, 1970, pp. 51–55, 97.

the Promised Land. In Ex 17, the miracle is situated at Rephidim, which was the last stopping-place before Sinai. In Numbers, the incident would appear to have taken place at Kadesh (Num 20:1aβ), but these words come from another source and are not in their proper place in this priestly narrative which refers to the desert of Zin. It is also true that Kadesh is also the location of the following incident (Num 20:14) and this connection has in fact been stressed – the name became Meribah of Kadesh in Num 27:14, which is a gloss, and in the later texts in Deuteronomy and Ezekiel (Deut 32:51; Ezek 48:28; Deut 33:2, in which it is sometimes restored conjecturally). It is, in any case, clear that this incident, in which the people complain that they were led into the desert and deprived of water and land (Num 20:2–5), can have nothing to do with the oasis at Kadesh, where there was a great deal of water and cultivation.[91]

All that remains, then, that can be directly linked with Kadesh according to the early sources, are the following texts: the death and the tomb of Miriam (Num 20:1b, E or J), if this text really follows verse 1aβ; the account of a reconnaissance in Canaan which was made from Kadesh and in which Caleb played the most important part and learned that he would be given the land that he had visited (Num 13–14, J or JE and P); the story of the attempt to enter Canaan and the defeat of the people of Israel at Hormah by the Amalekites and the Canaanites (Num 14:39–45, J); the account of the sending of messengers from Kadesh to Edom to request that the Israelites should be allowed to cross the land of the Edomites and the refusal to grant this request (Num 20:14–21, J).

To these texts, one further and very important passage must be added, even though Kadesh is not mentioned explicitly in it – the story of the victory over the Amalekites (Ex 17:8–16).[92] The text is certainly very early and is attributed to the Yahwist. It is situated at Rephidim (Ex 17:8), but this word may have been added later, according to Ex 17:1. The place is, in any case, unknown. The Amalekites led a nomadic life in the Negeb to the south of Palestine. It was there that Saul (1 Sam 15) and David (1 Sam 30) encountered them in battle and it is in connection with Kadesh that they are mentioned in Num 14:39–45.

It was the Judaeans who were in contact for the longest time with these Amalekites and they too were the most involved in the story of Caleb. The most persistent traditions concerning Kadesh were therefore the traditions originating in the south of Palestine and these were possibly preserved above all at Hebron.[93] They were brought there by groups which entered Canaan directly from Kadesh and it is to these groups that the victory over

[91] See also below, pp. 531.
[92] J. Grønbaek, 'Juda und Amalek', ST, 18 (1964), pp. 26–45.
[93] See M. Noth, Überlieferungsgeschichte, pp. 143–150.

the Canaanites at Hormah[94] can probably be attributed. The capture of Hormah marked the entry of these groups into Canaan and the passage describing it is undoubtedly in a context to which it does not really belong (Num 21:1–3).

The groups of Israelites who entered Canaan by the more roundabout route through Transjordan also had a tradition concerning Kadesh. At the end of a stay in Kadesh, they met with the refusal of the Edomites to allow them to pass through their territory (Num 20:14–21). If, as we have tried to show, the Sinai tradition is connected with the tradition of the exodus on the one hand and with that of the conquest on the other, then what follows in the order indicated in the text is very probably true – Moses' group came from Sinai to Kadesh and on leaving Kadesh, reached Canaan by a very roundabout route. As we have seen, none of the incidents that occurred between the exodus from Egypt and Sinai (Ex 16–18) is unquestionably connected with Kadesh, apart from the victory in the battle with the Amalekites which belongs to the Judaean tradition of Kadesh. This is not part of a firm tradition of Kadesh interrupted by the introduction of a number of stories concerning Sinai. They are rather elements of varied traditions or repetitions which were used to give substance to the journey from Egypt to Sinai.[95]

There is therefore no Kadesh tradition in contrast to a Sinai tradition. Kadesh has a rightful place within the one tradition of the exodus-Sinai-conquest which was the tradition of the group led by Moses. Kadesh also has a place within the special tradition peculiar to the southern tribes of Palestine. What, then is the connection between these two Kadesh traditions?

In several texts, Kadesh is called Kadesh-barnea. The meaning of this name is not known – it may possibly be that of a person. It is, however, certain that both names point to the same place, the location of which has been fairly firmly established.[96] The name is preserved at the spring of 'Ain

[94] Hormah is probably situated at Tell el–Mshash between Beersheba and Arad = Tell el-Milh; see Y. Aharoni, *The Land of the Bible*, London, 1967, p. 184; M. Naor, 'Arad et Horma dans le récit de la conquête', *Yediot*, 31 (1967), pp. 157–164 (in Hebrew); see below, p. 490.

[95] I believe this, in contrast to M. Noth, *Überlieferungsgeschichte*, pp. 181–182, who maintains that there was a real 'tradition of Kadesh' and goes too far in rejecting alternatives.

[96] R. de Vaux, 'Nouvelles recherches dans la région de Cadès', *RB*, 47 (1938), pp. 89–97; see especially Y. Aharoni in B. Rothenberg, *God's Wilderness*, New York, 1961, pp. 117–140. According to one tradition, of which the leading representatives were Josephus and Eusebius, Kadesh was situated at Petra in Transjordan. This location was later accepted by A. Musil, *The Northern Heğâz*, New York, 1926, pp. 262–266 and more recently by H. Bar-Deroma, 'Kadesh-Barne'a', *PEQ*, 1964, pp. 101–142, who believes that Kadesh-barnea was different from Kadesh. The former, he believes, was Medain Saleh, about 300 miles south-east of 'Aqabah. The latter was Petra. These theories are, however, impossible to accept because Kadesh is mentioned in several texts (Num 34:4; Ezek 47:19; Jos 15:3) as a

Qedeis about fifty miles south-south-west of Beersheba. This is, however, the least important of a number of springs spread out over a distance of about twelve miles to the north-west. The most important of these springs is 'Ain Qedeirāt. This is followed by 'Ain Qeseimeh and finally 'Ain Muweileh. The sheet of water supplying these springs is not far to seek and can be reached by wells varying between eight inches and six and a half feet deep. The name Kadesh must, however, be applied to the whole of this region, which is the main oasis in the north of the Sinai peninsula. There are tracks leading from the oasis to Egypt, the Gulf of Aqabah and Beersheba. It was densely populated during the Intermediate Period between the Early and Middle Bronze Ages, that is, especially round about the twentieth century B.C. It was also cultivated when the Israelites lived there and later by the Nabataeans and the Romans and during the Byzantine period. The kings of Judah built a fortress there, at 'Ain Qedeirāt, in the ninth century B.C., and maintained it until the sixth century. Caravans passed through this oasis at all periods and the Israelites must have done so when they led their herds to pasture in the desert. It is very likely that they lived there for a time or that they used it as a centre for the seasonal movements of their flocks and herds. Very probably too, Kadesh was the base from which they set off in an attempt to invade Canaan.

There is, however, no evidence of their having come directly from Egypt to Kadesh. They went out into the desert in order to offer sacrifice to their God and it is undeniably true that the name Kadesh, 'holy', points to the fact that the place was associated with holiness. This group of springs was normally evidence of divine providence. The name, however, existed before the Israelites came there and for them it was a name like all other names. No particular religious or cultic importance is attached to it either in the Pentateuch or in later texts. According to the Exodus texts, it took three days to reach the place where sacrifice was to be made (Ex 3:18; 5:3 and in the stories of the plagues). What is more, the Israelites travelled in the wilderness of Shur for three days without water (Ex 15:22). Both these texts, it has been suggested, point to Kadesh. It is, however, one hundred and twenty-five miles from the Egyptian frontier to Kadesh and the first stopping place mentioned in the biblical account is not Kadesh, but Marah (Ex 15:23).

Another group, however, may possibly have left Egypt under the leadership of Moses and have arrived at Kadesh without going to Sinai. According to the hypothesis suggested earlier,[97] there were two exoduses and the exodus-flight of the group led by Moses may have followed the

---

place at the southernmost limit of Canaan or Judah between the southern end of the Dead Sea and the Mediterranean.

[97] See above, pp. 370–373.

exodus-expulsion of the other group of Israelites, who first went along the coast, where the miracle of the quails took place, and then went down to Kadesh. It is therefore possible that it was this group of Israelites who entered Canaan from Kadesh. These Israelites would thus have formed the nucleus of the tribes of Leah. Just as the two different exoduses were merged in the one Exodus story, so also may two distinct traditions concerning Kadesh have been combined together in the same story.

This is a very plausible hypothesis, but it has been carried too far by certain scholars.[98] The traditions concerning Kadesh refer, these scholars claim, not only to two different groups of people, but also to two quite different periods, the Judaean-Calebite group having moved from Kadesh to Palestine some time before Moses' group. There is one essential reason for rejecting this theory – it depends on the explanation offered for both of these groups having the same faith in Yahweh. The usual explanation given is that they received their faith in different ways – the Judaean-Calebite group through their neighbours the Kenites who worshipped Yahweh, and Moses' group through Jethro, the Midianite priest who was Moses' father-in-law. The theory that Yahwism originated among the Midianites and Kenites has, however, not yet been sufficiently proved and therefore cannot be accepted. Furthermore, whatever the origin of the divine name may have been, it is certain that Moses' Yahwism was something quite new and was, in addition, the faith of settled groups of people in the south of Palestine. We have insisted more than once that the later religious unity that came about between the northern and the southern tribes which originally entered Palestine by different routes and were separated for quite a long time, means that there was a single basic tradition common to all the tribes before they settled in Canaan. This is also the meaning of the general agreement that exists between the earliest written sources, the Elohist's work in the north and the Yahwist's in the south. The two groups of Israelites must therefore have been in contact with others in the desert and it is quite possible that they met at Kadesh. We can do no more than suggest hypotheses, but the most probable are those which most take into account the texts that we possess and the traditions that they represent.

Some of the difficulties that we have encountered in this discussion about the Sinai and the Kadesh traditions would have been diminished if Sinai could be located in the same region as Kadesh. Where, then, was Sinai?

---

[98] This theory has often been put forward by H. H. Rowley, *From Joseph to Joshua*, p. 190ff; *Men of God*, London, 1963, pp. 16–19; *From Moses to Qumran*, London, 1963, pp. 50–55; *Worship in Ancient Israel*, London, 1967, p. 43, note 1.

IV. THE LOCATION OF SINAI

One fact is beyond dispute – the theophany and the covenant are both connected with a mountain. The word occurs again and again in Ex 19, 24, 32 and 34. Where, then, was this mountain situated?

1. *The mountain of God – Horeb – Sinai*
(a) The theophany of the burning bush took place on the mountain of God (Ex 3:1). Aaron met Moses at the mountain of God (Ex 4:27). Jethro visited Moses on the mountain of God (Ex 18:5). Moses and Joshua went up the mountain of God (Ex 24:13) and Elijah went to the mountain of God (1 Kings 19:8).

In Ex 3:1 and 1 Kings 19:8, the mountain of God is identified with Horeb, but 'Horeb' is an addition in the first of these two texts and it may also be in the second. On the other hand, the use of the word *s'neh* for bush is probably the Yahwist's allusion to Sinai, and the fire in the bush also probably recalls the theophany on Mount Sinai, as we have already noted. In Ex 24, the words 'mountain of God' (verse 13) alternate with the words 'mountain of Sinai' (verse 16). Finally, the mountain of God to which Elijah went is without doubt the mountain on which Yahweh revealed himself – Horeb-Sinai.

The term 'mountain of God' is most frequently found in the group of Midianite traditions and in those texts which are usually ascribed to the Elohist or are thought to be influenced by him. Some scholars have concluded from this purely literary datum that this 'mountain of God' was different from Sinai-Horeb.[99] They have, however, based their reasoning on no more than a generalised theory that the traditions of the Pentateuch were independent of each other and this is a theory which we have criticised.

(b) It is generally accepted that Horeb is the name used in the E and D sources, whereas the name Sinai was used by the Yahwist and then adopted by the priestly editor. This opinion is in need of revision.[100] In Deuteronomy, for example, the word Horeb appears only once in the code of laws and then in a passage which does not form part of the earliest material in the book (Deut 18:16). On the other hand, however, it occurs very often in the narrative sections of Deuteronomy (Deut 1:2, 6, 19; 4:10, 15: 5:2; 9:8; 28:69) and in the historical work of the Deuteronomist (1

---

[99] M. Noth, *Überlieferungsgeschichte*, pp. 150–155; H. Seebass, *Mose und Aaron, Sinai und Gottesberg*, Bonn, 1962; H. Schmid, *Mose, Überlieferung und Geschichte* (*BZAW*, 110), 1968, pp. 61–69.
[100] See M. Noth, *Überlief, Studien*, p. 29.

Kings 8:9 = 2 Chron 5:10; 1 Kings 19:8). The word Sinai is never used in Deuteronomy itself, (apart from the early text Deut 33:2), or by the Deuteronomist.

Horeb occurs only three times in texts ascribed to the Elohist. These are Ex 3:1, which is a gloss; Ex 17:6, in which 'at Horeb' is also a gloss; Ex 33:6, which is a difficult text and would appear to be an addition.

Apart from these texts, there are only two other references in the Old Testament to Horeb – Mal 3:22, the law, and Ps 106:19, the golden calf.

It is therefore not correct to say that the name Horeb is used in the Elohistic source. In fact, the name is not found in the early documents of the Pentateuch and its use is later than that of the name Sinai.

(c) Sinai was used exclusively by the Yahwist and was later adopted by P. This use varies, however. 'Sinai' alone appears only in Ex 16:1. Here it is used as a landmark and may point to a region. The phrase 'wilderness of Sinai' occurs frequently (Ex 19:1, 2; Num 1:1, 19; 3:4, 14; 9:1, 5; 10:12; 26:64; 33:15, 16). The words 'mountains of Sinai' are also common (Ex 19:11, 18, 20, 23; 24:16; 31:18; 34:2, 4, 29, 32; Num 3:1; 28:6).

It is clear from the way in which the word 'Sinai' is used that it points primarily to a region, a desert or wilderness, within which a particular mountain is situated. What is more, apart from one case, that of the doubtful text Ex 33:6, the word 'Horeb' is never preceded by the word 'mountain'. The question that arises, then, is whether 'Horeb' was not the name of the particular 'mountain of Sinai' of the Yahwistic source and of the 'mountain of God', or simply the 'mountain' of the Elohistic source.

Since Horeb does not occur either in those texts which are purely Elohistic or in the early parts of Deuteronomy, it is not possible to conclude that two traditions existed in the earliest period: a northern tradition in which the word Horeb was used and a southern tradition using the term Sinai, Horeb and Sinai referring in each case to a different place.[101] We have therefore to try to explain why 'Horeb' never appears in the earliest traditions and why the Deuteronomist seems to have avoided the word 'Sinai'. I have to admit that I cannot answer the first question and as for the second, the answer can only be conjectural. Is it perhaps because the memory of Sinai was obliterated at Jerusalem? Or is it, on the other hand, possibly because the name 'Sinai' gave rise to unfortunate associations with the name of the Assyro-Babylonian god Sin?

2. *Was Sinai near Kadesh?*

The suggestion has been made that Sinai was situated in the north of the Sinai peninsula. The following arguments have been put forward in sup-

---

[101] G. Hölscher, 'Sinai und Choreb', *Festschrift R. Bultmann*, Stuttgart, 1949, pp. 127–132.

port of this theory.[102] The arrival of the quails, mentioned twice in the biblical narrative, is a natural phenomenon occurring in the north-west of Sinai. The victory at Rephidim, the last stopping-place before Sinai, was gained over the Amalekites, who lived in the north of the peninsula. There are also many early texts outside the Pentateuch in which Sinai is associated with the region to the south of Palestine. These include Judges 5:4, according to which Yahweh left Seir and went to the fields of Edom; Deut 33:2, which says that Yahweh came from Sinai, after Seir and after Mount Paran; Hab 3:3: 'Eloah is coming from Teman and the Holy One from Mount Paran' and Hab 3:7, which proclaims the terror that has struck the tents of Cushan and Midian as God passes. To this can be added the argument that the Israelites stayed in the district of Kadesh for almost the whole time that they remained in the desert. The attempt was made therefore to find a mountain in the region of Kadesh, and Jebel Halal, about twenty-five miles to the west of Kadesh, was regarded as the Sinai of the Bible.

As we have seen, however, it would be wrong to exaggerate the importance of Kadesh in the early biblical traditions. The victory gained over the Amalekites should not, as we have also seen, be associated with Sinai (and Rephidim), but with a Judaean tradition concerning Kadesh. The incident of the quails, moreover, probably had nothing to do with Sinai or with Kadesh. The three poetic texts that are usually quoted to support this hypothesis are also interrelated, the text of Habakkuk depending on the other two – they describe Yahweh's coming from the point of view of Canaan and all that they can mean is that he came from the far south. If these texts are still used in support of the hypothesis, the references to Seir, Edom, Teman and Midian would not take us to the north of the Sinai peninsula, but to the south-east, on the other side of the 'Arabah.[103] (We shall have to return to this question later.)

On the other hand, Kadesh was never associated with the Sinai desert. According to Num 13:26 (cf. Num 13:3), Kadesh was in the 'Wilderness of Paran', and, according to Num 33:36, in the 'wilderness of Zin'. Several texts point to the possibility that Sinai was a long way from Kadesh. There were three stages in the journey between Sinai and Kadesh according to Num 11–13, and according to the list given in Num 33, there were twenty-

---

[102] C. S. Jarvis, *The Forty Years' Wanderings of the Israelites*, PEQ, 1938, pp. 25–40; J. Gray, *The Desert Sojourn of the Hebrews and the Sinai-Horeb Tradition*, VT, 4 (1954), pp. 148–154.

[103] N. Glueck, 'The Boundaries of Edom', HUCA, 11 (1936), pp. 141–157, believed that the 'Arabah was the old western frontier of Edom. He was conscious of the difficulty presented by these texts if Sinai was located in the peninsula and concluded that the texts were post-exilic, dating back to a time when the Edomites lived to the west of the 'Arabah and the region was known as Idumaea. These texts are, however, undoubtedly pre-exilic. For these texts, see J. Jeremias, *Theophanie. Die Geschichte einer alttestamentlichen Gattung*, Neukirchen and Vluyn, 1965, pp. 7–11, 38 ff.

one stopping-places. In Deut 1:2, we read that it was eleven days' march between Horeb and Kadesh, through a 'vast and terrible wilderness' (Deut 1:19). Elijah travelled for forty days and forty nights from Beersheba to Sinai (1 Kings 19:8). All these pieces of information come from different sources and they differ among themselves, except insofar as they all indicate clearly that Sinai was a long way from Kadesh.

3. Was Sinai in the south of the peninsula?

The name 'Sinai peninsula' is modern. It is derived from the Christian tradition, according to which Sinai was located in the south of the peninsula. This Christian tradition goes back to the fourth century, to the time when the Spanish pilgrim Egeria (or Etheria) visited Sinai in A.D. 383.[104] From this time onwards, Christians grouped all the Old Testament memories round the Jebel Mūsa.[105] To the north of this mountain (7,362 ft) are the three peaks of the Rās Safsafeh (6,738 ft), at the foot of which stretches the plain er-Rāha, where the Israelites are believed to have camped. The country is extraordinarily impressive and forms a most appropriate framework for a theophany. The memory of St Catherine is linked with that of Moses at the top of the neighbouring mountain, which is at the same time the highest of the group, Jebel Katherina (8,550 ft). This tradition was finally canonised when Justinian had the monastery and the basilica of St Catherine erected at the foot of Jebel Mūsa, the 'mountains of Moses', in the middle of the sixth century.

Another but much less strong tradition situated Sinai at Jebel Serbal, near the oasis of Feirān, about thirty miles to the north-west of Jebel Mūsa. This tradition appeared for the first time in Cosmas Indicopleustes' 'Christian Topography' (ca. A.D. 540). This author situated Horeb-Sinai at a site about six miles from Pharan which was, according to him, the modern name for the ancient Rephidim.[106] This location, however, is based only on the gloss of Ex 17:6, in which the miracle of the water at Rephidim is situated 'at Horeb'.

This tradition which situates Sinai at Jebel Mūsa cannot be traced back any earlier than the fourth century A.D. Nothing useful can be derived either from Eusebius' vague reference in his Onomasticon or from the annotated translation by Saint Jerome.[107] Certain Nabataean inscriptions dating back to the second and third centuries A.D. have been found in the Sinai massif

---

[104] For this date, see P. Devos, 'La date du voyage d'Egérie', Analecta Bollandiana, 85 (1967), pp. 165–194.

[105] Itinerarium Egeriae, I-V, ed. Aet. Franceschini and R. Weber, Turnhout, 1958; ed. O. Prinz, Heidelberg, 1960; text and translation, H. Pétré, Ethérie, Journal de Voyage (Sources Chrétiennes), Paris, 1948, I-V.

[106] PG, LXXXVIII, § 196, at the beginning.

[107] Eusebius, Onomasticon, ed. Klostermann, p. 173.

and in even greater numbers in the Serbal massif in the south of the peninsula; it is clear from these that both mountains had a sacred character and were places of pilgrimage.[108] Their holy character might go back to the Israelite period. There are altogether more than two thousand five hundred of these inscriptions. They are very short, very seldom contain the name of a god and never mention any cultic act.[109] They are similar to all the *graffiti* scratched by Nabataeans here and there on rocks along their caravan routes and at their stopping-places. The existence of these inscriptions in this particular region, however, is something of a mystery, since it is a long way from good pasture land and not on any trade route.[110] It should, however, be noted that all these inscriptions are later than the reduction of the Nabataean kingdom to a Roman province in A.D. 106. Various Nabataean groups probably went back into Sinai at that time and they possibly carried on an independent caravan trade there between Arabia and Egypt; no longer following the route from Petra to Gaza, which was occupied by the Romans, but travelling along another route from the Gulf of 'Aqabah to the Gulf of Suez, going round the desert of Tiy to the south. This road was longer, but there were springs and small oases along it.[111] It would also have enabled the Nabataean caravans to trade directly between the port of Dahab on the eastern coast of Sinai facing Arabia and the ports of Markha or Tor on the western coast, opposite Egypt. Dahab was on the same latitude as Jebel Mūsa, Markha was situated farther north and Tor farther south. All these places and the oasis of Feirān were connected by tracks. It is true that we can learn very little from the Nabataean inscriptions about the location of Sinai, but the routes followed by the Nabataeans and marked out by their inscriptions may also have been followed by the Israelites.[112]

Most modern atlases of the Bible follow the ancient Christian tradition with some degree of certainty and show Sinai in the Jebel Mūsa massif. Their authors justify this by recourse to biblical texts. This location of Sinai is, they argue, in accordance with the eleven days' march from Horeb to Kadesh (Deut 1:2). In 1906, for example, the caravan of the Ecole Biblique

[108] B. Moritz, *Der Sinaikult in heidnischer Zeit* (*Abhandlungen*, Göttingen, XVI, 2), 1916; see also M. Noth, *Das Zweite Buch Mose. Exodus (ATD)*, p. 125.

[109] J. Koenig, *RHPR*, 43 (1963), pp. 4–11.

[110] J. Cantineau, *Le Nabatéen*, I, Paris, 1930, pp. 24–25; J. Starcky, 'Pétra et la Nabatène' *DBS*, VII, 1966, col. 935–936, who nonetheless thinks that it is possible that these inscriptions are connected with a place of worship at Feiran.

[111] J. Koenig, *op. cit.* (note 109). These Nabataean routes have been explored by B. Rothenberg, 'An Archaeological Survey of South Sinai', *Museum Haaretz Bulletin*, 11 (1969), Rothenberg thinks, however, that the Nabataeans used these routes not for caravan trading, but for the exploitation of copper and turquoise mines; see p. 38.

[112] It is true that recent exploration has brought nothing to light along these routes with regard to the Late Bronze Age or the early Iron Age (see B. Rothenberg, *op. cit.*, p. 36), but illiterate nomadic shepherds and herdsmen could not leave any written traces.

took exactly this time to go from Jebel Mūsa to 'Ain Qedeis.[113] Attempts have also been made to establish the intermediate stages on the journey between the exodus from Egypt and Sinai and then between Sinai and Kadesh, making use of the information given in the stories in Exodus and Numbers and in the list of stopping-places in Num 33.[114]

The hypotheses that have been suggested are all possible, but the obstacle is that very few biblical names can be found among the modern place-names in the region. The oasis of Feirān at the foot of Jebel Serbal clearly recalls the name of the desert, the 'wilderness of Paran' mentioned in Exo-dus and Numbers, and of the mountain of Paran mentioned in the poetic texts. There is evidence that this region was occupied almost continuously from the ninth or eighth century B.C. (Israelite *ostraca*) until the Arab period. The name of the town of Pharan was known to Ptolemy in the second cen-tury A.D. and the name Paran may even have been the early name for the whole peninsula. This would explain why the information given in the Bible about the 'wilderness of Paran' is so vague and why the name does not appear in the Old Testament as a special stage in the journey.[115] It would also make it possible for us to situate Sinai in the south of the peninsula, but would not enable us to locate it precisely. The name Rephidim, the last stage on the journey to Sinai (Ex 17:1; 19:2; Num 33:14), has been com-pared with the name of the wādi Refayied, an oasis to the north-west of Jebel Mūsa. Hazeroth, the second stage after Sinai on the way to Kadesh (Num 11:35; 12:16; 33:17) has been identified with 'Ain Huḍra or 'Ain Huḍeirāt on a track from Jebel Mūsa to 'Aqabah. Together with Hazeroth, Deut 1:1 mentions Dizahab, which may be the port of Ḏahab on the eastern coast of Sinai[116] and the Jothbathah of Num 33:33, which is the penultimate halting-place before Ezion-geber, may perhaps be Tabeh, which is about eight miles to the south of Elath.[117] Finally, Ezion-geber itself (Num 33:35) must surely be Tell el-Kheleifeh at the end of the Gulf of 'Aqabah.

Apart from Ezion-geber, however, none of these identifications is at all certain and at least one of them must be rejected. From the point of view of phonetics, Hazeroth bears little relationship to 'Ain Huḍra and moreover the meanings of the two names are quite different. Hazeroth, *ḥaṣerôth*, means 'encampments', whereas the Arabic place name means 'green spring'. In view of these difficulties it is understandable that a recent author should prefer to indicate these place names on a map, but not to connect them

[113] F.–M. Abel, *Géographie de la Palestine*, I, p. 393.

[114] F.–M. Abel, *Géographie*, II, pp. 210–215; J. Simons, *The Geographical and Topographical Texts of the Old Testament*, Leiden, 1959, pp. 251–259.

[115] Y. Aharoni, in B. Rothenberg, *God's Wilderness*, 1961, pp. 165–169.

[116] Y. Aharoni, *op. cit.*, pp. 144, 161.

[117] F.–M. Abel, *Géographie*, II, p. 366; Y. Aharoni, *op. cit.*, p. 166 ff.

together in an itinerary.[118] In any case, it would be an exaggeration to claim, as some scholars have in fact done, that this thesis is the only one that can be reconciled with the texts of the Bible.[119] We have, after all, to consider one other question very seriously – are we not obliged by certain texts to situate Sinai outside the Sinai peninsula?

4. Was Sinai in Arabia?

On the basis of various biblical texts other authors have in fact looked for Sinai in northern Arabia to the east of the Gulf of 'Aqabah. They have used several arguments in support of this claim.[120]

(a) *The theophany of Sinai was a description of a volcanic eruption.*[121] According to the Yahwistic source, 'the mountain of Sinai was entirely wrapped in smoke, because Yahweh had descended on it in the form of fire. Like smoke from a furnace the smoke went up' (Ex 19:18). Again, according to Deuteronomy, 'the mountain flamed to the very sky, a sky darkened by cloud, murky and thunderous. Then Yahweh spoke to you from the midst of the fire' (Deut 4: 11b-12a); 'Now when you heard this voice coming out of the darkness, while the mountain was all on fire . . . you said, "See how Yahweh our God has shown us his glory and his greatness and we have heard his voice in the middle of the fire" ' (Deut 5:23–24); 'So I went down the mountain again and it was blazing with fire' (Deut 9:15). Finally, according to the priestly source, 'the cloud covered the mountain, and the glory of Yahweh settled on the mountain of Sinai . . . To the eyes of the sons of Israel the glory of Yahweh seemed like a devouring fire on the mountain top' (Ex 24:15b–17).

These texts from the Yahwistic, the Deuteronomistic and the priestly sources all describe, these authors maintain, a volcanic eruption. To this has to be added the sign of an active volcano present in the pillar of cloud by day and the pillar of fire by night in the Yahwistic tradition, which dissociated this sign from its volcanic origin and made it the sign guiding the Israelites on their journey and the symbol of Yahweh's presence.

On the other hand, the Elohist described the theophany as a storm; 'There were peals of thunder on the mountain and lightning flashes, a dense cloud, and a loud trumpet blast' (Ex 19:16); 'Louder and louder grew the

---

[118] Y. Aharoni, *op. cit.*, p. 170 and *The Macmillan Bible Atlas*, New York, 1968, map 48.

[119] J. Simons, *op. cit.* (note 114), p. 253.

[120] These arguments have been developed recently by J. Koenig in a series of articles; see his 'La localisation du Sinaï et les traditions des scribes', *RHPR*, 43 (1963), pp. 2–30; 44 (1964), pp. 200–235; 'Itinéraires sinaïtiques en Arabie', *RHR*, 166 (1964–B), pp. 121–141; 'Le Sinaï, montagne de feu dans un désert de ténèbres', *RHR*, 167 (1965–A), pp. 129–155; 'Aux origines des théophanies iahvistes', *RHR*, 169 (1966–A), pp. 1–36; 'Tradition iahviste et influence babylonienne à l'aurore du judaïsme', *RHR*, 173 (1968–A), pp. 1–42.

[121] In addition to J. Koenig, in the previous note, see J. Jeremias, *op. cit.* (note 103), pp. 100–111.*

sound of the trumpet; Moses spoke and God answered him with peals of thunder'.[122]

One element is missing from the descriptions of the Yahwist, the Deuteronomist and the priestly editor – the flow of lava, an essential element in any volcanic eruption. The scholars who have put forward this theory, however, insist that this flow of lava is found outside the Pentateuch, in other theophanies. Two such theophanies are especially mentioned in this context: 'Yahweh treads the heights of earth. The mountains melt as he goes ... like wax before the fire, like water poured out on a steep place' (Mic 1:3–4) and 'Oh, that you would ... come down – at your presence the mountains would melt, as fire sets brushwood alight, as fire causes water to boil' (Isa 63:19–64:2). Other texts that have been quoted to support this claim are Judges 5:5; Hab 3:6; Nahum 1:5; Ps 97:3–6, etc. The flow of lava was dissociated from the other phenomena common to volcanic eruption, just as the column of smoke or fire was detached from the volcano itself. These other theophanies also include characteristics of the storm – there are 'stormy eruptions' and 'volcanic storms', according to whether the storm or the volcanic activity predominates.[123]

(b) *There are no volcanoes at Sinai, but there are in northern Arabia.* The theory was first suggested by E. Meyer, then by Gunkel and Gressmann, but the region in which these scholars thought that Sinai should be located was little known at the time. Concrete evidence was, however, provided by A. Musil's exploration in 1910.[124] Musil himself elaborated the theory in the appendices to his story of the expedition,[125] but used the biblical texts in an uncritical way. The question was also taken up again by J. Koenig.

Koenig believes that Sinai was an extinct volcano called Hala el-Bedr, the 'crater of the full moon', which has already been described by Musil[126] and is situated about two hundred miles as the crow flies to the south-east of 'Aqabah. Musil thought first of Hala el-Bedr in his preliminary report,

---

[122] J. Koenig regarded this mention of the 'sound of the trumpet' as a sign of volcanic action and quoted Cassius Dio Cocceianus who, in his monumental history of Rome, said that the sound of trumpets was heard during the eruption of Vesuvius; see *RHR*, 169, (1966), p. 26.

[123] See J. Koenig, especially *RHPR*, 44 (1964), pp. 213–223; *RHR*, 166 (1964–B), pp. 122–124; J. Jeremias, *Theophanie*, pp. 7–15, on the other hand, finds no evidence of volcanic activity in these texts. J. Koenig, 'Tradition iahviste et influence babylonienne à l'aurore du judaisme', *RHR*, 173 (1968–A), pp. 1–42, also thinks that the texts dealing with the new exodus in Deutero-Isaiah also contain volcanic elements.

[124] A preliminary account will be found in *Anzeiger der kaiserlichen Akademie der Wissenschaften*, Phil.-hist. Kl., 48, Vienna, 1911, pp. 139–159, then in *The Northern Ḥeǧâz*, New York, 1926.

[125] A. Musil, *The Northern Ḥeǧâz*, especially pp. 267–272, 275–298.

[126] *ibid.*, pp. 214–216.

but later decided on a more northerly site, in what he believed was the centre of the country of the Midianites. The Bedr has been active during historical times and the bedouins have a memory of its throwing out stones and flames at one time. They regard it as forbidden territory and point out the 'cave of the servants of Moses' nearby, where, they say, Moses' servants stayed while their leader conversed with Allah. In another place, there are twelve stones known as el-Madbah, the altar, where the bedouins offer sacrifice.

(c) *The place-names of Exodus and Numbers are found in this region.* [127] Among the great number of place-names collected by Musil, there are in fact many which are very similar to those occurring in the biblical texts and sometimes they are even found in the bedouin territory in the same order as the stages mentioned in the long list in Numbers. This list is the most useful of the biblical texts in this case. M. Noth has called it an itinerary of the pilgrimage to Sinai. [128] The story of Elijah would be evidence that this pilgrimage was observed during the period of the monarchy.

Topographical data from all the sources of the Pentateuch are found in Num 33, which is a late text, dating back to the fifth century B.C. Num 33:18–36 is an additional document, containing new names, with the exception of the section Num 33:30b–34a, in which the names mentioned in Deut 10:6–7 appear in a different order and with certain differences. Deut 10:6–7 is itself of a later date and is clearly a fragment of an itinerary which is parallel to Num 33. The names listed in Num 33:18–36 form an itinerary from Sinai to Ezion-geber. It would seem to begin at a point to the south-east of 'Aqabah = Ezion-geber. This theory is made to some extent plausible by the fact that some of the biblical names have been identified with place-names situated between the volcano of Bedr and Aqabah. The distances do not constitute a serious objection. As A. Musil has pointed out, the stages on the pilgrimage to Mecca in the north of the Hejāz are on the average about thirty miles apart, [129] which is much more than the normal distance between stopping-places made by a tribe on an ordinary journey. The eleven days' march from Horeb to Kadesh (Deut 1:2) would therefore be about three hundred and forty miles, which is the distance between the volcano of Bedr and 'Ain Qedeis.

(d) *Other biblical texts point to north-western Arabia.* According to Judges

[127] J. Koenig, *RHPR*, 44 (1964), pp. 200ff and the map, P.203; *RHR*, 166 (1964–B), pp. 129–140.

[128] M. Noth, 'Der Wallfahrtsweg zum Sinai', *PJB*, 36 (1940), pp. 5–28; he has also included his conclusions in *Das vierte Buch Mose. Numeri (ATD)*, 1966, *in loco*. See also H. Gese, *Das ferne und nahe Wort. Festschrift L. Rost (BZAW,* 105), 1967, pp. 81–94, especially pp. 85–88.

[129] A. Musil, *The Northern Heğâz*, pp. 322, 328.

5:4–5, Yahweh came from Seir and Edom; according to Deut 33:2, he came from Sinai, Seir and Mont Paran; according to Deut 1:2, the mountain of Seir was crossed between Horeb and Kadesh; according to Hab 3:3, God came from Teman and Mount Paran and according to Hab 3:7, the tents of Cushan and Midian were struck with terror when he passed them. Seir, Edom and Teman have been situated to the east of the 'Arabah and Midian has been located to the south of Edom.

(e) *The volcanic landscape* of this region, which is a desert of lava or *harra*, explains why Sinai, the mountain of fire, was associated with the term 'desert of darkness'.[130]

(f) *According to a Jewish tradition, Sinai was in Arabia.*[131] Demetrius, a Jewish historian living in the Egyptian Diaspora in the third century B.C., stated that Dedan was Jethro's ancestor. According to Gen 25:3 Dedan was Abraham's descendant by his wife Keturah, like the other Arab tribes, and, as a place name, Dedan must be identified with the oasis of el-'Ela. Similarly, Demetrius said that when Moses went to Midian, he stayed in fact in Arabia.

During the reign of Augustus, Trogus Pompeius placed Sinai in the kingdom of Damascus. He must have been thinking of the Nabataean kingdom, which at one time included Damascus but did not extend as far as the Sinai peninsula.[132] The nature and the length of Nabataean rule at Damascus have, however, been seriously discussed.[133]

It is difficult to reconcile the evidence provided by the Jewish historian Josephus. He placed Sinai in the land where the city of Madiane was (see his *Antiquities*, II, 264; III, 76). This town was also known to Ptolemy and was to the east of the Gulf of 'Aqabah, near the mouth of the gulf. Elsewhere, however, Josephus said that Sinai was between Egypt and Arabia, which points to the Sinai peninsula (see *Against Apion*, II, 25).

Finally, in his allegory on the two covenants represented by Hagar and Sarah (Gal 4:21–31), Paul says: Τὸ δὲ Ἁγὰρ Σινᾶ ὄρος ἐστὶν ἐν τῇ Ἀραβίᾳ. It is a difficult text, frequently disputed, but this would seem to be the best version of it and the meaning is: 'for Hagar is Mount Sinai which is in Arabia'.

This sentence of the apostle Paul has never been explained satisfactorily,

---

[130] J. Koenig, *RHR*, 167 (1965–A), pp. 130–155.
[131] H. Gese, *op. cit.*, pp. 88–93.
[132] H. Gese, *op. cit.*, p. 89.
[133] R. North, 'The Damascus of Qumran Geography', *PEQ*, 1955, pp. 34–48, especially pp. 41–43, has drawn some very daring conclusions. His article also contains a valuable bibliography. See especially J. Starcky, 'Pétra et la Nabatène', *DBS*, VII, 1966, col. 907–909, according to whom the Nabataeans controlled Damascus only between 84 and 72 B.C.

but it would appear to form the basis of Paul's allegory. It can be understood if Hagar is compared with *Eγϱα* (Ptolemy) = Hegra (Pliny) = Hegra (Nabataean) =el-Hejr (Arabic), that is, Medain Saleh, which was, together with Petra, the most important centre in the Nabataean kingdom. The tradition which Paul followed, then, located Sinai in northern Arabia.

Taken as a whole, these arguments are very impressive. Individually, however, they can only be regarded as hypothetical and several of them can be interpreted in various ways. I propose to consider them now more or less in the reverse order, that is, beginning with the Pauline text.

Leaving aside the philological difficulties involved in identifying Hagar with Hegra, it cannot be denied that Hegra = Medain Saleh is not a mountain and that there are no mountains nearby with which the memory of Sinai could be associated. All that we know, then, is that Paul, like Josephus, at least in some of his texts, and Demetrius, situated Sinai in Arabia. It would seem too that the itinerary given in Num 33:18–36 locates Sinai to the south-east of el-'Aqabah. The Jewish tradition of a Sinai situated in the north-east of Arabia apparently goes back to the fifth century B.C.

On the other hand, however, it is very much open to question whether the list provided in Num 33 is really a pilgrimage route, particularly in view of the insertion into this list of verses 41b–47a, which provide another itinerary, peculiar to this list of place-names, apart from the names Oboth and Iye-abarim (verses 43–44), which are also found in Num 21:10–12. This itinerary, leading from Kadesh to Mount Nebo and crossing the 'Arabah and Moab by the great route of Dibon, conflicts with the texts of Num 20:14–21; 21:10–20; Deut 2:8–9 and Judges 11:17–18. These agree with each other insofar as they all mention the refusal of the rulers of Edom and Moab to allow the Israelites to pass through their territory and the fact that the Israelites skirted round these two countries and passed through the eastern desert. The document used here in Num 33 describes a road going from Kadesh to the north of Moab and has nothing to do with a pilgrims' way to Sinai or to anywhere else. There is, in other words, no reason for interpreting the list of places in Num 33:18–36 as the itinerary of a pilgrimage. The analogy with Num 33:41–47 and the partial parallel with the information given in Deut 10:6:7 show that this list of place-names belongs to a class of documents which must have existed in Israel just as they existed in Mesopotamia and in Egypt. They were, so to speak, travel documents.

In the fifth century B.C, Jews might well have known and wanted to use the road to north-western Arabia. There were Jewish colonies, for example, in northern Arabia, especially at Dedan (el-'Ela) and at Hegra (Medain Saleh). We can now say that these colonies originated as military settlements set up by Nabonidus in the sixth century B.C.[134] These settlers kept in contact with Judah and it is possible to ask whether it was not these Jews who brought Sinai and the memories of Moses that are found in Arab folklore into this region. This hypothesis is certainly in accordance with the date that is generally given to Num. 33.

This list is not, however, sufficient to enable us to prove that there was at that time a pilgrimage to this Arabian Sinai, nor is it possible to appeal to the story of Elijah to show that this practice went back to the period of the monarchy. If it was said that Elijah took forty days and forty nights to walk from Beersheba to Horeb, it is because Sinai seemed to be a very long way away in the south. It is quite possible that its whereabouts were not known. If indeed there was a regular pilgrimage to Sinai, then the fact that Sinai was forgotten throughout the whole of the period of the monarchy is even more difficult to explain.

The precise locations that have been suggested in northern Arabia for the stages on the journey mentioned in Num 33 are no more and no less valid than those proposed in the Sinai peninsula for the stopping-places in other texts. The suggestion that Hala el-Bedr is the site of Sinai is quite arbitrary – there are other extinct volcanoes in the region and the question has not yet been fully explored.

The earliest texts appealed to in this context (Judges 5:4–5; Deut 33:2; Hab 3:3) do not point to this part of the Near East – Edom and Teman are to the east of the 'Arabah, but to the north of the Gulf of 'Aqabah. The mountain of Seir has been located in Edom to the east of the 'Arabah in the early texts, although it is situated to the west in Deuteronomy.

The references to Midian in these texts and in the Midianite tradition about Moses are more important, since Midian was, from the Graeco-Roman period onwards, a geographical entity in north-western Arabia. As we have already seen, however, in connection with this Midianite tradition,[135] the Midianites were much less firmly located during the early period and the only text giving fairly precise information regarding the location of Midian is 1 Kings 11:18, according to which they lived in the north of Sinai.

We have now to consider the volcanic aspects of the theophany on Sinai in the Yahwistic tradition and in the priestly and deuteronomistic traditions

---

[134] The question has arisen again in connection with the discovery of the inscriptions of Nabonidus at Haran; see C. J. Gadd, 'The Harran Inscriptions of Nabonidus', *AnStud.*, 8 (1958), pp. 35–92. For the Jewish colonies, see R. de Vaux, ' "Lévites" minéens et lévites israélites', *Lex Tua Veritas (Festschrift H. Junker)*, Trier, 1961, pp. 265–273 = *Bible et Orient*, Paris, 1967, pp. 277–285; I. Ben-Zvi, 'Les origines de l'établissement des tribus d'Israël en Arabie', *Le Museon*, 74 (1961), pp. 143–190, especially pp. 145–149; R. Meyer, *Das Gebet des Nabonid (Sitzungsbericht Sächs. Akademie der Wissenschaften zu Leipzig, Phil.–Hist. Kl.*, 107, 3), 1962, pp. 67–81.

[135] See above, pp. 332–333.

which depend on the earlier source. This argument has been weakened rather than strengthened by the almost exaggerated use that has been made of it to explain textual details. It has also and above all been weakened by its extension to include other theophanies and a whole series of texts. It is certainly going too far to apply it to the other theophanies. On the other hand, it is remarkable how little influence the Sinai theophany as a fundamental event in the past had on the accounts of Yahweh's appearances in the holy war or of his eschatological coming. An essential element in these theophanies which does not exist in the theophany of Sinai and which therefore gives them an entirely different character, is the fact that the whole natural order is overthrown.[136]

It cannot be denied that the Yahwist's account of the theophany on Mount Sinai has many volcanic aspects, but it is possible that they were borrowed. There was a great deal of interest in the natural phenomena that took place in foreign countries at the period of Solomon. We have given this interest as the reason for the existence of certain characteristics in the story of Joseph; for example, the accounts of the plagues of Egypt and the stories of the manna and the quails. There were also contacts with Arabia – the visit of the Queen of Sheba to Solomon's court is a notable example (1 Kings 10:1–13) and the caravan trade mentioned in 1 Kings 10:15 may also be included. The Arabs told stories of volcanic eruptions in their own countries and these impressive phenomena were no doubt used in the Yahwist's description of Yahweh's descent on Sinai. It is possible to go even further and say that some Israelites may also have experienced a volcanic eruption, although it is very unlikely that they camped at the foot of an erupting volcano – the natural reaction would have been to go as far away from it as possible. During Solomon's reign, there was, it will be recalled, an expedition made to Ophir. Even though Ophir may not be in Arabia, the expedition would certainly have followed the coast, near which there were volcanoes. The description in the Yahwistic account is clearly of an eruption seen from afar – the plume of smoke and the fire without any lava flow or rocks and stones thrown up – and it is obviously wrong to look for a mention of lava and rocks in other theophanies. The pillar of cloud and fire moving can also be explained in the same way: in other words, as an illusion of moving smoke and fire seen from a moving ship.

This, then, might well be the correct explanation of the way in which the theophany of Sinai was described by the Yahwist in the environment of Jerusalem; in contrast to the Elohist, who represented the theophany in an impressive way which was more familiar to him, in other words, as a storm. This means therefore that we shall never know what really happened at Sinai.

[136] J. Jeremias, *Théophanie*, 1965, pp. 105–111; 154–155.

We shall also never know where Sinai was situated. Quite apart from the possibility that Sinai was connected with a volcanic eruption, the arguments for locating it in Arabia are to some extent convincing. If I personally prefer to locate it in the Sinai peninsula, it is mainly because of the degree of cohesion prevailing among the various traditions of the Pentateuch. Sinai could be located in northern Arabia only if the Sinai tradition had in the first place been different from the tradition of the exodus and the conquest and also of the Midianite tradition about Moses. We have already suggested that the exodus tradition is linked to that of Sinai and that the Midianite tradition is also connected with Sinai by the reference to the mountain of God. We have also seen that Moses has an authentic place in the exodus and the Midianite traditions and that there is no reason why he should be excluded from the Sinai tradition. In the light of all these factors, Sinai must have been quite near to Egypt. It was not in the north of the peninsula because it was a long way from Kadesh. It must therefore have been in the south of the peninsula, although not necessarily in the exact place determined by later tradition. It is indeed very likely that at a very early stage it was no longer known where the holy mountain was to be found.

V. The Covenant of Sinai

1. The eastern treaties of vassalage

For about fifteen or more years now, the various Old Testament 'covenants' and the idea of 'covenant' itself have been interpreted in the light of the eastern treaties of vassalage and especially those treaties that were concluded between the great Hittite king and his vassals in Asia Minor and in northern Syria during the fifteenth to the thirteenth century B.C. The comparison was made first of all by G. E. Mendenhall.[137] He was followed by K. Baltzer, who derived a 'covenant formula' from these texts which he discovered also in the Old Testament texts relating to the conclusion, restoration or confirmation of the covenant between God and his people.[138] The same comparison was renewed, refined and extended to include the treaties more recently discovered in Syria and Mesopotamia and

---

[137] G. E. Mendenhall, *Law and Covenant in Israel and the Ancient Near East*, Pittsburgh, 1955; German translation, *Recht und Bund in Israel und dem Alten Vordern Orient*, Zürich, 1960. E. Bikerman, 'Couper une alliance', *Archives du Droit Oriental*, 5 (1950), pp. 153–154, drew attention briefly to the relationship between these treaties and the 'covenant' before Mendenhall.

[138] K. Baltzer, *Das Bundesformular*, Neukirchen and Vluyn, 1960, 2nd edn., 1964.

covering a longer period, that is, from the seventeenth to the thirteenth century.[139] The form of these treaties would, it has been argued, have been familiar to the Israelites and they therefore made use of them to express the relationships between their God and his people. This thesis has been generally accepted and has given rise to many detailed studies.[140] There have, however, been reactions against it, both with regard to details and against the thesis as a whole.[141]

What cannot be denied is that this comparison with the treaties of vassalage has been used to excess to explain texts, including, for example, prophetic texts, which could be explained differently and perhaps ought to be elucidated in another way. On the other hand, however, it is probable that the composition of certain biblical texts was influenced by the form of these treaties and it is even possible that the idea of the covenant was thus influenced at a certain period. It is, for instance, fairly clear that Deuteronomy was influenced in this way,[142] and attempts have been made to explain the covenant of Shechem (Jos 24) by reference to the Near Eastern treaties.[143] All that we are concerned with here, however, is whether and how the thesis can be applied to the Sinai covenant.

The vassalage treaties which are most likely to have influenced the form of the Sinai covenant date back to the second half of the second millennium B.C. They include two fifteenth-century treaties from Alalaḫ in Syria, the group of Hittite treaties between 1450 and 1200 B.C. and the Rās Shamrah treaties which come within the previous category because they were imposed by the Hittite king on his vassal at Ugarit. Despite certain differences, all these treaties have the same basic structure. They consist of the following elements:

I. Preamble: name and title of the Great King;
II. Historical prologue recalling all that has preceded the treaty and the past actions of the Great King;
III. Conditions imposed on the vassal;

---

[139] D. J. McCarthy, *Treaty and Covenant. A Study in Form in the Ancient Oriental Documents and in the Old Testament*, Rome, 1963.

[140] The situation to the end of 1965 is summarised, with a bibliography, by D. J. McCarthy in *Der Gottesbund im Alten Testament*, Stuttgart, 1966; see also the more recent work by R. Martin-Achard, 'La signification de l'alliance dans l'Ancien Testament d'après quelques récents travaux', *RThPh*, 18 (1968), pp. 88–102.

[141] The most useful studies are F. Nötscher, 'Bundesformular und "Amtsschimmel,"' *BZ*, new series 9 (1965), pp. 181–214; G. Fohrer, 'Altes Testament – "Amphiktyonie" und "Bund"?', *TLZ*, 91 (1966), col. 893–904 = *Studien zur alttestamentlichen Theologie und Geschichte (BZAW 115)*, 2969, pp. 103–119.

[142] R. Frankena, 'The Vassal-Treaties of Esarhaddon and the Dating of Deuteronomy', *OTS*, 14 (1965), pp. 122–154.

[143] J. L'Hour, 'L'alliance de Sichem', *RB*, 69 (1962), pp. 5–36, 161–184, 350–368; see also below, pp. 669–670.

IV. Clause regarding the preservation of the document of the treaty and its reading aloud in public.

V. List of gods invoked as witnesses;

VI. Curses and blessings.

2. *Was the Sinai covenant in the form of a treaty of vassalage?* [144]

(a) Ex 19:3b–8. This text is regarded as a summary of all the texts on the covenant in the Old Testament and as their source.[145] It has been claimed that it contains the first three elements found in vassalage treaties:

I. The preamble (verse 3b);

II. The historical prologue (verse 4);

III. The conditions (verses 5–6).

The parallel is in no sense perfect, however, and the last three elements common to such treaties are lacking, especially the essential curses and blessings. What is more, this text is not one of the earliest traditions of Sinai. It contains deuteronomistic and priestly influences and was certainly not composed before the Exile.[146]

(b) Ex 20 and 24:3–8. According to G. E. Mendenhall, the decalogue is the document of the Sinai covenant in the form of a covenant of vassalage.[147] A comparison with other vassalage treaties of the Ancient Near East has been made by W. Beyerlin,[148] who has found the first three elements of these treaties in Ex 20:2: 'I am Yahweh your God who brought you out of the land of Egypt' is, in his opinion, equivalent to the preamble (I) and the historical prologue (II) and the ten commandments are the conditions (III). As in Ex 19:3b–8, the three final elements of such treaties of vassalage are missing. Beyerlin, however, believes that they can be found in Ex 24:3–8, according to which Yahweh's 'words' were written (IV) and the twelve steles were erected to take the place of witnesses (V).

There is clearly a connection between Ex 24:3–8 and the decalogue and we shall return to this question later. In the meantime, however, it is impor-

---

[144] W. L. Moran, 'Moses und der Bundesschluß am Sinai', *Stimmen der Zeit*, 170 (1961–1962), pp. 120–133.*

[145] J. Muilenberg, 'The Form and Structure of Covenantal Formulation', *VT*, 9 (1959), pp. 347–365, 'It is *in nuce* the *fons et origo* of the many covenantal pericopes which appear throughout the Old Testament', (P. 352); K. Baltzer, *Das Bundesformular*, pp. 37–38: '*In nuce*, it is a complete covenant'.

[146] G. Fohrer, 'Priesterliches Königstum', *TZ*, 19 (1963), pp. 359–362 = *Studien zur alttestamentlichen Theologie und Geschichte (BZAW*, 115), 1969, pp. 149–153; see also the other references mentioned above, note 18.

[147] G. E. Mendenhall, *Law and Covenant, op. cit.*, pp. 5, 38–40.

[148] W. Beyerlin, *Herkunft und Geschichte der ältesten Sinai-traditionen* (note 63), pp. 59–78, especially p. 74 ff.

tant to note that, according to another tradition, the tablets of the covenant containing the Ten Words were placed in the ark in the same way as the Hittite treaties were placed in the temple. In Ex 24:3–8, however, the setting of the document in writing and the erection of the twelve stelae were actions, not parts of the treaty itself. Finally, the curses and blessings of the Hittite and other treaties are absent.

What is more, the formula of revelation or personal confession, 'I am Yahweh your God' (Ex 20:2)[149'] cannot really be compared with the preamble of the Hittite treaties, an example of which is 'Thus speaks the Sun Mursilis, the Great King, the king of the land of Hatti, the favourite of the god Teshup, the son of . . . ' In these treaties, the prologue is often quite long; in Ex 20, on the other hand, it is reduced to a simple relative clause: 'who brought you out of the land of Egypt'. Its very grammatical structure means that it cannot be a historical summary. It simply qualifies Yahweh. Many scholars have regarded it, in any case, as an addition.[150] Again, the ten commandments are not comparable to the conditions of the Hittite and similar treaties, in which the absolute and apodeictic form, 'you shall . . . ' or 'you shall not . . . ' is seldom used, the preferred and usual form being conditional: 'If it happens that . . . ' The most important difference between the Hittite treaties and the decalogue, however, is that the former presuppose a knowledge and acceptance of the general rules of conduct between the suzerain lord and the vassal. Only general, universal precepts which are outside time and apply to the whole of moral life are, on the other hand, given in the decalogue.[151] Finally, the conditions imposed in the treaties govern the relationships between two partners. Apart from the first two commandments, on the other hand, the decalogue regulates the behaviour of the Israelites towards each other, but not their relationship towards their God.[152]

(c) Ex 34:10–28. There is little in common between this renewal of the covenant with its 'cultic' decalogue and the Ancient Near Eastern treaties. There is no preamble, the historical prologue is replaced by a proclamation

---

[149] See D. J. McCarthy's criticisms, *Treaty and Covenant*, pp. 158–162; see also F. Nötscher, BZ, new series, 9 (1965), pp. 195–196; G. Fohrer, *TLZ*, 91 (1966), col. 896.

[150] See especially A. Jepsen, 'Beiträge zur Auslegung und Geschichte des Dekalogs', *ZAW*, 79, (1967), pp. 277–304, especially p. 291, on which Jepsen rejects the comparison with the Hittite treaties. But is the rejection of this sentence in Ex 20: 2 perhaps not simply due to a wish to preserve the idea that the Sinai tradition was independent of the exodus tradition?

[151] H. Gese, 'Der Dekalog als Ganzheit betrachtet', *ZTK*, 64 (1967), pp. 121–138, especially p. 124; English summary, 'The Structure of the Decalogue', *Fourth World Congress of Jewish Studies, Papers* I, Jerusalem, 1967, pp. 155–159.

[152] E. Gerstenberger, 'Covenant and Commandment', *JBL*, 84 (1965), pp. 38–51, especially p. 47.

of the marvellous deeds that Yahweh will perform (verses 10b–11), there are no witnesses and no curses or blessings. The only parallel is the order given to Moses to record the words of the covenant in writing (verses 27–28) and this is, of course, far too little.

Because there are so few points of similarity, we are bound to conclude that the covenant of Sinai was not in the form of a treaty of vassalage in the earliest sources. The structure of these treaties can only be found in the covenant by accepting very imperfect parallels and adding elements from various sources in an arbitrary way.[153] Such hasty comparisons have been used at various times in attempts to prove the historicity of the Sinai covenant or to show that the decalogue is traceable to Moses. Seen from the historical point of view, it is very unlikely that the semi-nomadic group of people led by Moses would have known the treaties made between the great Hittite kings and their vassals in Asia Minor and northern Syria. It is also most unlikely that they would have taken these political treaties used by settled peoples as their model in their attempt to express their relationship with their God.[154]

One comment which has so far not been made, moreover, points to the uncertain character of these comparisons between treaties made between a sovereign and a vassal prince and the covenant of Sinai concluded between God and his people. It is that it is necessary to examine not only the treaties between ruler and vassal in the light of the covenant, but also those treaties imposed by the Hittite kings on small tribes or groups of semi-barbarians who did not have a monarchy, such as the Kashka in the north of Asia Minor, or on countries ruled by a group of aristocrats or elders. The treaties imposed on these groups do not have the same form as those discussed above; they have no historical prologue and the list of the gods acting as witnesses follows the preamble, but precedes the list of conditions. They also include a list of the individuals taking the oath.[155] The conclusion that we are bound to draw, then, is that there was more than one 'covenant formula'.

---

[153] K. A. Kitchen, *Ancient Orient and Old Testament*, Chicago, 1967, pp. 101, note, and 128. This scholar makes use of the outline of the covenant given in Ex 19–24 taken as a whole and of the fact that it is parallel to the vassalage treaties to point out an error in documentary criticism.

[154] G. Fohrer, *TLZ*, 91 (1966), col. 896.

[155] E. von Schuler, 'Staatsverträge und Dokumente hethitischen Rechts', *Neuere Hethiterforschung*, ed. G. Walser (*Historia, Einzelschriften*, 7), 1964, pp. 34–53, especially pp. 38–39; ibid., 'Sonderformen hethitischer Staatsverträge', *Gedenkschrift für H. Th. Bossert*, Istanbul, 1965, pp. 445–464. The treaties imposed on the Kashka have been translated by E. von Schuler in *Die Kaskäer*, Berlin, 1965.

3. The forms of the Sinai covenant in the early sources

It is therefore important to study the forms of the Sinai covenant themselves in the early sources. We used the word 'forms' advisedly, since there are several. We may set aside the late text of Ex 19:3b–8 and consider the two different ways of presenting the covenant in Ex 24:1–11 and the third form in Ex 34:10–28.

(a) Ex 24:1a and 9–11. Most exegetes agree that there are two stories of the conclusion of the covenant in Ex 24. The first is found in verses 1a and 9–11.[156] Verses 1b–2, which contradict verses 10–11, are an addition. There is less agreement regarding the literary analysis of this passage,[157] but it is generally accepted that it goes back to an early tradition. According to this tradition, Moses, Aaron, Nadab, Abihu[158] and seventy elders of Israel[159] went up to Yahweh. They saw the God of Israel and they ate and drank. This meal is the climax of the story and it has to be interpreted as a meal of the covenant, similar to those which sealed pacts between human beings.[160] Clearly, God did not take part in this covenant meal, which was, however, eaten in his presence. No reference is made in this account either to the content of this covenant or to God's 'words'. The word *b'rîth* is not even used. All that we have here, in fact, is the remnant of a tradition, according to which the covenant was concluded on the mountain with a group of men representing the whole people.

(b) Ex 24:3–8. The scene depicted in this account is very different. Moses tells the assembled people Yahweh's words. They give their consent and Moses then puts the words into writing, builds an altar at the foot of the mountain and erects twelve stelae. He then has holocausts and communion sacrifices offered by young Israelites. Half of the blood of the sacrifices is poured on the altar and the other half is put into basins. The *sēpher habb'rîth*, the 'book of the covenant', is next read to the people, who promise to obey its decrees. Moses sprinkles blood from the basins over the people and says:

---

[156] For the literary criticism of this passage, see M. Noth, *Das zweite Buch Mose. Exodus (ATD)*, in loco; W. Beyerlin, *Herkunft und Geschichte*, p. 19–23, 33–42; O. Eissfeldt, *ZAW*, 73 (1961), pp. 137–146, and *TLZ*, 91 (1966), col. 1–6; H. Schmid, *Mose Überlieferung und Geschichte*, note 99, pp. 64–73.

[157] Usually attributed to J; L (Eissfeldt) or N (Fohrer), but E according to Noth.

[158] It is only in the earliest sources that Nadab and Abihu are mentioned in this text. According to Ex 6:23 etc., they were two of Aaron's sons.

[159] According to M. Noth, *Das zweite Buch Mose, in loco*, and *Überlieferungsgeschichte*, p. 178, there were only these seventy elders in the earliest tradition. This forms one of Noth's main arguments for eliminating Moses from the Sinai tradition.

[160] Gen. 26: 30; 31:54, cf. 44 etc. and J. Pedersen, *Israel, Its Life and Culture*, I–II, London, 1946, p. 305 ff.

'This is the blood of the covenant that Yahweh has cut with you, according to all these words'.

Here too, no certain conclusions have been drawn from literary analysis. M. Noth attributes this passage neither to J nor to E. A widely held opinion is that it is a conclusion to the Code of the Covenant if this Code is linked to the events at Sinai and this conclusion belongs immediately after Ex 23:19. The conclusion was, however, replaced by Ex 23:20–33 and used again here.[161] The sēpher habb'rîth of Ex 24:7 is, in Noth's view, the Code of the Covenant.[162]

Noth thought that this text was quite early. J. L'Hour agreed that it was connected with the Code of the Covenant and that it was composed when the Code of the Covenant was introduced into the accounts of Sinai. Believing that this took place later than the composition of Deuteronomy, he dated this passage to the period of the Exile and looked for evidence in the vocabulary and thought of the passage to confirm this date.[163]

It is, however, widely accepted that Ex 24:3–8 was the work of the Elohist and should immediately follow the decalogue, that is, after Ex 20:17 and before the Code of the Covenant. 'All the commands – d'bhārîm, words – that Yahweh has decreed' (Ex 24:3) corresponds to the opening statement of the decalogue– 'God spoke all these words, d'bhārîm (Ex 20:1). It is true that Ex 24:3 adds the words 'and all the ordinances, mišp̄āṭîm', but this addition takes into account the introduction of the Code of the Covenant which opens, after the initial section containing the law concerning the altar, with the words: 'This is the ruling – these are the ordinances, mišp̄āṭîm – which you are to lay before them' (Ex 21:1). In what follows, however, all that is mentioned are the d'bhārîm (Ex 24:3b, 4, 8). The conclusion that must be drawn from this, then, is that the sēpher habb'rîth of verse 7 is the decalogue.[164]

The word sēpher may, however, may point to any kind of document and in particular it can mean a juridical text such as a bill of divorce (Deut 24:1) or a deed of purchase (Jer 32:11ff). The treaty between Bar-Gaiah of KTK and Mati'el d'Arpad engraved in Aramaic on the stelae of Sfire often describes this text by the word spira', which can be translated not only as 'inscription', but also as 'document', perhaps even the document of the treaty. The sēpher habb'rîth is therefore the 'document of the covenant', in other words, the decalogue. The objection cannot be made that this document was written by Moses, when the decalogue was also to be written later on the tablets of stone by God himself (Ex 24:12; 32:16; 34:1).[165] The

---

[161] Apart from the commentaries, see especially W. Beyerlin, Herkunft und Geschichte, pp. 44–57; J. L'Hour, RB, 69 (1962), pp. 355–361.

[162] M. Noth, Das zweite Buch Mose. Exodus, p. 161.

[163] RB, 69 (162), pp. 355–361.

[164] See especially O. Eissfeldt, Introduction, pp. 212–213.

[165] J. L'Hour, RB, 69 (1962), p. 357.

tablets of the covenant form part of a different tradition.

Was the connection between Ex 20:1–17, the decalogue, and Ex 24:3–8 itself primitive? It cannot be regarded as early if it is accepted that the decalogue was introduced into its present position at a late stage. In that case, it would be a conclusion to the Elohist's version of the theophany, elements of which are contained in Ex 19, the theophany continuing in Ex 20:18–21. (The Elohistic theophany was displaced by the introduction of the decalogue). It should be noted also that Ex 20:19 presupposes that Moses transmitted God's 'words' mentioned in Ex 24:3–8.

This text is, however, superfluous. Yahweh's words are communicated twice and accepted twice by the people (verses 3 and 7). The second time (verse 7) is an interruption of the blood rite. Some scholars insist that this verse is an addition and should therefore be suppressed. Other exegetes prefer to retain everything except 'all the ordinances' in verse 3 and explain the repetition as Moses' oral reporting of Yahweh's commandments and the people's submission to them. This was followed, these scholars believe, by the ceremony of the conclusion of the covenant – the editing of the document, the sacrifice and the blood rite. Two actions take place in the blood rite, the blood sprinkled on the altar expressing God's participation and the blood sprinkled on the people signifying the part they had to play in the covenant. These two actions are separated by the reading of the document, which binds the people. It is therefore possible that two parallel stories were combined here, both fundamentally the same – God's commandment, the people's acceptance and a blood rite. This rite is, of course, an essential aspect of the story, because it was the 'blood of the covenant'.

The essential element in Ex 24:1a, 9–11, however, is the meal. This version appears to be later than the other version. It clearly does not precede the settlement in Canaan, since the twelve stelae point to the fact that the people had been constituted. They recall the twelve stones of Gilgal (Jos 4:4–9, especially verse 8, cf. verse 20). The altar and the sacrifice are reminiscent of the altar and the sacrifices made on it at Shechem (Jos 8:30–31). It was at Shechem that Joshua also read the words of the law (Jos 8:34), just as Moses read the document of the covenant in the passage we are considering here. What is more, a part is also played in the account of this covenant at Shechem by stelae. One stone was set up as a witness to the covenant (Jos 24:26–27), the law was written on stones (Deut 27:8; Jos 8:32) and, according to Deut 27:2–4, these stones were the twelve stones brought from Gilgal. This is, however, a development which is later than the tradition which is presented in a simpler form in Ex 24:4. The part played by the young men in the sacrifice is an early element, but the sacrifices offered were holocausts and communion sacrifices and these two forms of offering were borrowed from the Canaanites.

The essential element, the blood rite, is, however, early. There is no other place in the Bible describing a double sprinkling, one of the altar and one of the people. This blood rite is, on the other hand, similar to the blood rites practised by the ancient Arabs.[166] It is possible to trace this use of blood back to an even earlier period. The form of a pact made between Arabic people was described by Herodotus (III, 8): 'When men wish to pledge themselves to each other, a third man stands between the two and, with a sharp stone, cuts each man's hand on the inside near the thumb. He then takes a piece of fluff from the garment of each of the parties and smears seven stones placed between them with blood, invoking Dionysius and Urania'. There is also a brief description of this blood rite dating back to the same period as Moses on a Ramsesside *ostracon*; in this text, a father reproaches his son for binding himself, in the Delta or in Sinai, with Semites: 'You associated with Amu by eating bread mixed with your blood'.[167] The blood of the partners themselves or of a sacrificed animal created a bond, strengthened an oath or sealed a pledge between men.

A primitive tradition, then, is preserved in Ex 24:3–8. According to this tradition, the covenant first includes commandments, and secondly, was concluded with Moses acting as intermediary, and sealed by a blood rite which pointed to the union between Yahweh and his people. This blood rite and the covenant meal (Ex 24:11) are parallel and both have the same meaning. In this primitive tradition, however, the obligations entailed in the covenant are expressed.

(c) Ex 34:1–28. In its present form, this account describes the renewal of the covenant and the preparation of the new tablets of stone. This is because of the insertion into the narrative of the story of the golden calf. It is generally accepted that the Yahwistic story of the covenant of Sinai figures in this chapter of Exodus. Additions have, however, been made to the basic story and there is less agreement among scholars about these. The most important area of disagreement concerns Ex 34:10–16. M. Noth[168] prefers to separate the promises in verses 10b, 11b–13 and 15–16 and regard them as belonging to the deuteronomistic tradition, because they interrupt the proclamation and the promulgation of the commandments in verses 10a, 11a, 14 and 17 and the verses that follow. O. Eissfeldt, on the other hand,[169] believed that these verses belonged to the earliest source, which he called L. Thus, whereas Noth thought that only the aspect of 'commandment' should

---

[166] W. Robertson Smith, *Religion of the Semites*,[2] London, 1894, pp. 314ff, 479ff, *Kinship and Marriage*,[2] London, 1903, pp. 56–62.

[167] J. Cerný, 'Reference to Blood Brotherhood among Semites in an Egyptian Text of the Ramesside Period', *JNES*, 14 (1955), pp. 161–163.

[168] M. Noth, *Das zweite Buch Mose, in loco.*

[169] O. Eissfeldt, 'Die älteste Erzählung vom Sinaibund', *ZAW*, 73 (1961), pp. 137–146 = *Kleine Schriften*, IV, pp. 12–20.

be retained, Eissfeldt was of the opinion that only the aspect of 'promise' belonged to the primitive Sinai tradition and that the aspect of commandment was subsequent. This, of course, is the central problem of the Sinai covenant – did it include a 'promise' or a 'commandment' or did it include both? In our opinion, the covenant included a promise and a commandment; it had the twofold aspect of a pledge undertaken by God and an obligation imposed on the people.[170]

In contrast to the 'ethical' decalogue of Ex 20, the commandments of Ex 34:14–26 have often been called the 'ritual' decalogue. It cannot be denied that these commandments have a religious and cultic character, nor can it be disputed that they are called, in verse 28, the 'ten words'. There are, however, more than ten commandments in Ex 34:14–26 and all attempts to reduce them to ten have proved unsatisfactory. It is possible that the editor of verse 28 had a different text in front of him or that he interpreted the text that we have now as ten commandments. On the other hand, it is possible that the phrase 'the ten words', coming at the end of the verse after the phrase 'the words of the covenant' (verse 28), is a gloss. The expression 'the ten words' is not used anywhere else in the book of Exodus. It only appears again in Deut. 4:13 and 10:4.

Some exegetes believe that this 'decalogue' is older than the decalogue of Ex 20 and that it can even be dated before the exile and was borrowed from the Kenites at the same time as the Israelites borrowed the Kenite god Yahweh.[171] This theory is, however, impossible, since all the commandments listed in verses 18–26 presuppose that the Israelites were already settled in Canaan, leading an agrarian life and celebrating agrarian feasts borrowed from the Canaanites. The 'cultic' commandments are partly parallel to the commandments of Ex 23:12–19 at the end of the Code of the Covenant, although the two passages are not dependent on each other from the literary point of view. In the same way, Ex 34:18–26 is, like Ex 23:12–19, a religious calendar.[172]

Apart from this difficulty, there is also the commandment not to bow down to any other god but Yahweh (verse 14) and not to make images of gods (verse 17), both of which correspond to the first two commandments of the decalogue (Ex 20:3–6). In both cases, too, there is reference to the same 'jealous God', 'El qannā', This title describes Yahweh as the God who reacts passionately, forcefully and energetically to his people's behaviour, the God who will not let himself be imprisoned within an image and who

---

[170] A. Jepsen, *ZAW*, 79, (1967), p–301. For the theme of 'Grace and Law', see above, pp. 410–411 and the bibliography above (note 57).

[171] J. Morgenstern, 'The Oldest Document in the Hexateuch' (a 'Kenite' document), *HUCA*, 4 (1927), pp. 1–138; H. H. Rowley, 'Moses and the Decalogue', *Men of God*, London, 1963, pp. 7–13, 18; *Worship in Ancient Israel*, London, 1967, pp. 44–46.

[172] H. Kosmala, 'The So-called Ritual Decalogue', *ASTI*, 1 (1962), pp. 31–61.

will not tolerate another god beside him.[173] Despite these close similarities between Ex 34:14, 17 and Ex 20:3–6, however, the two passages are not dependent on each other from the literary point of view. It would, moreover, seem as though these two commandments, which are in reality only one single commandment, form the fundamental commandment of the covenant. There is no reason at all why it should not go back to Sinai and to Moses.[174]

There is also no reason why the other eight commandments of the decalogue should not go back to the time of Moses, although they may then have had a form which would be impossible to find now in the two versions that we have, namely Ex 20 and Deut 5.[175] The only element that might give rise to doubts is the use of the word 'house' in the tenth commandment. The word *bêth*, however, also had a meaning for nomadic people and it was connected as well with the the sabbath rest on the seventh day, although it would seem that the institution of the sabbath went back to the very origins of Yahwism.[176]

If, however, the decalogue is really very old, how can we explain from a literary point of view its introduction into the Sinai accounts? The most plausible explanation is that it belonged to a special tradition. In its composition and its transmission, this tradition did not belong to a legal category consisting of 'apodeictic' laws nor did it result from cultic practice. The short, rhythmic formulae of the decalogue, which go together in pairs, were clearly meant to be learnt by heart and are also obviously related to the maxims found in the wisdom literature.[177] The other device used in the decalogue as an aid to memorisation is the number ten, which corresponds to the fingers of both hands and is also found elsewhere in the Old Testament collections of laws and precepts.[178] The decalogue was transmitted orally among the groups of people who shared the experience

---

[173] A. Jepsen, *ZAW*, 79 (1967), p. 289; see also B. Renaud, *Je suis un Dieu jaloux*, Paris, 1963, pp. 27–46.

[174] According to R. Knierim, 'Das erste Gebot', *ZAW*, 77 (1965), pp. 20–39, these commandments were put into practice from the time of the desert onwards, but they were not formulated until Shechem, where the tribes became united in the knowledge that Yahweh was their God and the other gods were rejected.

[175] It is becoming accepted more and more commonly that the decalogue is very old and that it may well go back to the time of Moses; see J. J. Stamm, *Der Dekalog im Lichte der neueren Forschung,*[2] Berne, 1962; H. Graf Reventlow, *Gebot und Predigt im Dekalog*, Gütersloh, 1962; H. H. Rowley, 'Moses and the Decalogue', *Men of God*, London, 1963, pp. 1–36; A. S. Kapelrud, 'Some Recent Points of View on the Time and Origin of the Decalogue', *ST*, 18 (1964), pp. 81–90; A. Jepsen, 'Beitrage zur Auslegung und Geschichte des Dekalogs', *ZAW*, 79 (1967), pp. 277–304.

[176] See R. de Vaux, *Institutions*, II, p. 377; H. H. Rowley, *Men of God*, pp. 27–32.

[177] H. Gese, 'Der Dekalog als Ganzheit betrachtet', *ZTK*, 64 (1967), pp. 121–138.

[178] E. Auerbach, 'Das Zehngebot – Allgemeine Gesetzes-Form in der Bibel', *VT*, 16 (1966), pp. 255–276.

of Sinai and it was probably the 'elders' of those groups who were responsible for this transmission.[179] These precepts preserved the religious and social stability within the groups and ensured that the members of each group remained in good relationships with God and with each other. The decalogue already had a fixed, independent form in the oral tradition of the Elohist, but it was known that it contained the 'words' of Sinai, so that, when this Elohistic tradition came to be edited, the decalogue was inserted after the account of the theophany, as this seemed to be the most suitable place.

4. Is it necessary to speak of a 'covenant'?

The Hebrew word *b'rîth* is almost always translated as 'covenant', but this leaves a great deal to be desired. If, by 'covenant', we mean a mutual contract between two partners, then the *b'rîth* which governs relationships between God and his people is clearly not a covenant. This question has recently been subjected to considerable discussion.[180]

The etymology and the origin of the word are obscure and comparisons with Akkadian have yielded few tangible results.[181] The Hebrew term for concluding a covenant is *kārath b'rîth*, 'to cut a covenant'. The *b'rîth* is a solemn pledge that is taken or imposed. The word 'swear', which is used in the same contexts and is parallel with *b'rîth*, shows that the latter was a form of oath. It was accompanied by a rite, the one who pronounced the oath passing between animals 'cut' in half and thus showing that, if he broke his oath, he would suffer the same fate. This rite is mentioned in the Bible (Gen 15 and Jer 34:18-21) and there are clear parallels outside the Bible – at Mari in the eighteenth century B.C. and in various treaties at the beginning of the first millennium. It was, then, clearly an oath involving a curse. In profane practice, a man could use this *b'rîth* to commit himself personally to another man. He could also commit another man without committing himself to him. There were also mutual pledges and this is what most closely resembles the 'covenant' of the Old Testament, but in this case each of the partners commits himself and there are consequently two *b'rîth*. There are

[179] A. Jepsen, *ZAW*, 79 (1967), p. 303.

[180] A. Jepsen, 'B'rîth. Ein Beitrag zur Theologie der Exilszeit', *Verbannung und Heimkehr (Festschrift Rudolph)*, Tübingen, 1961, pp. 161–179; G. Fohrer, 'Altes Testament – "Amphiktyonie" und "Bund"?' *TLZ*, 91 (1966) col. 893–904; E. Kutsch, 'Der Begriff b'rith in vordeuteronomischer Zeit', *Das ferne und nahe Wort. Festschrift L. Post (BZAW*, 105), 1967, pp. 133–143; N. Lohfink, *Die Landverheißung als Eid. Eine Studie zu Gen. 15*, Stuttgart, 1967; E. Kutsch, 'Von "berit" zu Bund', *Kerygma und Dogma*, 14 (1968), pp. 159–182.*

[181] See O. Loretz, 'B'rît – 'Band – Bund' ', *VT*, 16 (1966), pp. 239–241; J. A. Soggin, 'Akkadisch *TAR beriti* und Hebräisch *Karat b'rît*', *VT*, 18 (1968), pp. 210–215.*

several examples of this in the Bible. In the case of the treaty between Solomon and Hiram, 'the two of them cut a b'rîth' (1 Kings 5:26b). There was also 'an alliance, b'rîth, between myself and you', that is, between Damascus and Israel (1 Kings 15:19), and David and Jonathan 'cut a b'rîth' (1 Sam 23:18).

This mutual commitment by means of b'rîth, however, is never found in the early texts of the Bible when it is is a question of relationships between God and his people. The people never 'cut a b'rîth' – only Yahweh does that. In Ex 34:10, Yahweh 'cuts a b'rîth' and commits himself to the promises that he then gives. In Ex 34:27, Yahweh again 'cuts a b'rîth' with Moses and the people and imposes his commandments on them.

5. The Sinai covenant and the covenant with Abraham[182]

The Sinai b'rîth, then, has the twofold meaning of a pledge undertaken by God and an obligation imposed on the people. It therefore has certain similarities with the covenant made with Abraham in Gen 15. The framework in both cases is a theophany, in which God reveals himself. In Gen 15, God manifests himself to Abraham and 'cuts a b'rîth' with him (verse 18). The promise that he makes is to give the whole country to Abraham's descendants. A list of the inhabitants of the land follows (verses 19–21) and this list is early, because it begins with the Kenites-Kenizzites, who do not appear in later lists because they were absorbed by Judah. The Sinai promise is also accompanied by a list of dispossessed peoples (Ex 34:11; cf. 23:22–23, J, and Ex 13:5, pre-deuteronomistic), The difference, however, is that Yahweh not only promises to give to the land of the Canaanites, the people of Israel – he also promises to drive the Canaanites out before the Israelites. It is clear that these promises are made in the perspective of the holy war.[183] Finally, the personal declaration made by God in Gen 15:7: 'I am Yahweh . . . who brought you out of Ur of the Chaldaeans' can be compared with the declaration in Ex 20:2: 'I am Yahweh your God who brought you out of the land of Egypt'.

This promise of land is, as we have seen, a characteristic of the religion of the god of the father, so that what we have here is another link, indeed an

---

[182] For the covenant with Abraham, see G. Fohrer, TLZ, 91 (1966), col. 897–899; N. Lohfink, Die Landverheißung. For its relation to the Sinai covenant, see W. Zimmerli, 'Sinaibund und Abrahambund', TZ, 16 (1960), pp. 268–280 = Gottes Offenbarung, 1963, pp. 205–216; N. Lohfink, Revista Biblica, 15 (1967), pp. 403–406.

[183] F. C. Fensham thinks that this is an element which is comparable with the Hittite treaties; 'Clauses of Protection in Hittite Vassal–Treaties and the Old Testament', VT, 13 (1963), pp. 133–143; 'Covenant, Promise and Expectation in the Bible', TZ, 23 (1967), pp. 305–322.

important link, between the religion of the patriarchs and primitive Yahwism. The Sinai covenant is in a direct line with the covenant made with Abraham.

There is, however, an important difference. Yahweh made a promise to Abraham, but Abraham did nothing. He slept while Yahweh, in the form of a smoking furnace and a firebrand, went between the divided animals, thus committing himself by an oath involving a possible curse. What is more, no commandment is imposed on Abraham. What is implied, however, is that Abraham is bound to acknowledge as his special God the one who pledges himself to him by means of the solemn promise. At Sinai, this obligation was explicitly imposed on Israel at the same time as the commandment not to make images of God, and the basic rules of social life. As a revelation of the divine name, the Sinai covenant deepened and enriched the religion of the fathers.

Chapter Fifteen

THE RELIGION OF MOSES

WE have shown in the foregoing chapters that there was continuity between the early traditions concerning the mission of
Moses, the exodus from Egypt, and Sinai. There is, as we have
seen, no impelling reason for eliminating Moses from any of these traditions; on the contrary, there is positive evidence for believing that they are
closely interconnected. The historian has therefore to recognise the leading
part played by Moses in the events described in these traditions, even
though he may not be able to ascertain the details. In the latest of these
traditions, all of Israel's civil and religious legislation and the whole of the
people's cultic practice were associated with the person of Moses and the
events outlined in the traditions. It is clear from literary and historical criticism that various developments that were in fact much later than Moses
were retrojected, in successive levels, to the period of Moses, but these
accretions were added to an already existing nucleus. The whole process
cannot be explained without accepting the historical basis of the earliest
traditions. In other words, it was during the period of Moses that Yahweh
was recognised as the God who saved the people at the time of the exodus
and who established special relationships between himself and that people at
Sinai. There is no doubt, then, that Moses played an essential part in the
origins of the religion of Israel.

Moses has often been called the 'founder' of a religion. Certain scholars,
of course, believe that he was inserted into the Sinai tradition and that he
did not originally figure in the tradition of the exodus; naturally enough
they do not give him the title of 'founder'.[1] But even if it is accepted
that Moses originally figured in the traditions, it is still doubtful whether
the title of 'founder' is a correct one. The whole person of Moses exceeds
the rather narrow categories within which authors, past and present,
have tried to enclose him. He was not a thaumaturge, nor was he a
judge, a priest or a prophet. He was all these and he was more than all

[1] M. Noth, *Geschichte*, p. 128, note 3; K. Koch, 'Der Tod des Religionsstifters', *Kerygma
und Dogma*, 8 (1962), pp. 100–123.

these. He was the man who received Yahweh's revelation of himself and who communicated that revelation to the people. He was the mediator of the covenant between Yahweh and his people and the leading charismatic figure of the people of Yahweh. He did not, in other words, 'found' a religion in the sense of establishing its institutions and its teaching. What he did is nothing compared with what God did. He was no more than the instrument used by God and, what is more, he was the instrument used by God only in the first stages of the history of Israel's salvation. At the time of Moses' death, before the people of Israel had entered the Promised Land, Yahwism was still the religion of a small group of semi-nomadic people. It was only in the course of a long process of development that it became a world religion, other men of God and God himself playing a part in this development. Moses, however, was at the beginning of this movement. It was he who planted the seed which proved to be extremely fertile.[2] He was the first of Yahweh's 'servants' (Ex 14:31) and it is with all this in mind that it is possible to speak of a religion of Moses and to attempt to outline the characteristics of this primitive form of Yahwism.

I. THE RELIGION OF MOSES AND THE RELIGION OF THE PATRIARCHS

The Elohist and the priestly editor stressed both the new aspect of the name of Yahweh revealed to Moses and the continuity of this new faith with the religion of the fathers. Yahweh revealed himself to Moses as 'the God of your father, the God of Abraham, the God of Isaac and the God of Jacob' (Ex 3:6), as 'the God of your fathers' (Ex 3:13, 15, E) and as the God who appeared to Abraham, Isaac and Jacob as El Shaddai (Ex 6:3, P). This was a basic faith in Israel. It was this faith that inspired the Elohist when he ascribed the promises which Yahweh was to fulfil to the god of the fathers (Gen 46:3–4; 50:24). Moses called his second son Eliezer because, as he said, 'The God of my father is my help and has delivered me from the sword of Pharaoh' (Ex 18:4, E). In the song of victory (Ex 15), 'the God of my father ... Yahweh is his name' is exalted (verses 2–3). This is what gave the Yahwist the right to use the name Yahweh in the whole of the story of the patriarchs up to the story of the burning bush (Ex 3:16, J), where he joined the Elohist. The question confronting the historian is above all whether this affirmation of Israel's faith was in accordance with the reality and whether there was, either certainly or probably, a continuity in cult between the patriarchal period and the time of Moses.

---

[2] See especially W. Eichrodt, *Theologie des Alten Testaments*, I,[6] Stuttgart and Göttingen, 1959, pp. 190–195; G. Fohrer, *Geschichte der israelitischen Religion*, Berlin, 1969, pp. 62–63.

1. *The God of the father and Yahweh*

This continuity is clearly manifested in various ways.[3] First of all, Yahwism originated in an environment of shepherds and herdsmen and began to develop in the desert. The prophetic call to return to pure Yahwism was presented as a call to return to the desert; this was the prophets' 'nomadic ideal' and it resulted in the activity of a group of fervent Yahwists, the Rechabites.

Yahweh was also the God of Sinai. In the Song of Deborah (Judges 5:5) and in Ps 68:9, Yahweh is called *zeh Sînai,* 'the one of Sinai', (These words should not be simply suppressed as glosses.) He was not, however, the god of a mountain. In the Yahwistic and the Elohistic traditions, as we have seen, features taken from a volcanic eruption or from a storm were simply two different images used to describe the theophany. Yahweh did not therefore live on Sinai. He 'descended' on it and manifested himself there (Ex 19:18, 20; 34:5, J). According to the early tradition of Ex 24:10, he lived in heaven, which is an affirmation that was to be made again later. There was no need to go back to the mountain on which Yahweh had appeared to Moses in order to encounter him again. There is also no indication at all, apart from the episode involving Elijah, that Sinai was a place of pilgrimage. Yahweh's activities were never linked with a special place. Before the theophany on Sinai, he manifested his presence and his power in Egypt, in the miracle of the sea, at Marah (Ex 15:25) and at Massah-Meribah (Ex 17:6). After the theophany, Yahweh left Sinai with his people, making his presence visible above the ark of the covenant, which marked the stages of their journey through the desert (Num 10:33–36). He also encountered Moses in the Tent of Meeting (Ex 33:7–11). Yahweh also 'came from Sinai' (Deut 33:2, Ps 68:18, correction: see also Judges 5:4; Hab 3:3). Like the god of the fathers, Yahweh was not tied to any special place. He went with his people. He guided them and was together with them wherever they went. He also had a special bond with Moses, the leader of this group of people, just as the god of the fathers had a particular connection with the patriarchs, the leaders of their clan.

There are, however, certain differences. In the first place, the god of the fathers was anonymous, whereas Yahweh is a personal name. In the second place, this name and the explanation of it given in Ex 3:14 define Yahweh as the 'Existing one'. He is transcendent and he remains a mystery to man, but he reveals his transcendence in his actions. In the stories of the patriarchs, there is nothing to compare with the miracle of the sea and the theophany on Sinai in brilliance and power. In the third place, there is a

---

[3] V. Maag, 'Das Gottesverständnis des Alten Testaments', *NTT,* 21 (1966–1967), pp. 161–207, especially pp. 165–173; H. Seebass, *Der Erzvater Israel (BZAW,* 98), 1966, pp. 76–82.

striking change in emphasis between the relationships of the god of the father and the people and those of Yahweh and his people. In the biblical texts, the term 'god of the father' is replaced by the term 'people of Yahweh'; in the earlier accounts, the 'god of the father' was tied to a group, whereas in the later accounts it is the group of people who are tied to their god. In the fourth place, there is a new concept of divine election. In the case of the patriarchs, the god of the father called Abraham (Gen 12:1–3) and made certain promises to him. These promises were renewed when they were made to Isaac and Jacob. This is one of the aspects of the patriarchal religion. On the other hand, it was when God revealed his name that he called the descendants of the patriarchs 'my people' for the first time (Ex 3:7,10) and this term is used a dozen times in the conflict with the Pharaoh (Ex 5–8). It was the people whom Yahweh redeemed (Ex 15:13) and whom he purchased (Ex 15:16). This is essentially what is expressed in a later text (Ex 19:5): 'You of all nations shall be my very own', in other words, Israel was Yahweh's personal property, s'ghullāh.

In every way, then, Yahwism deepened and enlarged the religion of the patriarchs and, although it was quite new, it did not mark a break with the earlier faith.[4]

2. Yahweh and El

When we discussed the religion of the patriarchs, we saw that the god of the father became assimilated to the great god El. According to Gen 46: 3–4, El, the god of the father of Jacob, told Jacob that he would go down to Egypt with his people, make a great nation of them there and then bring them back from Egypt. This corresponds to 'El brings you out of Egypt' in the oracles of Balaam at the end of the wanderings in the desert (Num 23:22; 24:8).[5] In between these two, however, the religion of El seems to have been absent from the early sources;[6] it is as though El, the god of the settled people whom the patriarchs had known in Canaan and whom their descendants found in Moab had in the meantime been forgotten. The

---

[4] In this, I partly disagree with O. Eissfeldt, 'Jahwe, der Gott der Väter', *TLZ*, 88 (1963), col. 481–490 = *Kleine Schriften*, IV, pp. 79–91. According to Eissfeldt, Yahweh was assimilated into the god of the fathers, but this was an initiative taken by Moses and the continuity if artificial; the deities and the cultic practices were different.

[5] For the translation by the personal name El and not by the common name of God, see W. F. Albright, *JBL*, 63 (1944), pp. 207–233; L. M. von Pákozdy, 'Theologische Redaktionsarbeit in der Bileam-Perikope', *Von Ugarit nach Qumran. Festschrift O. Eissfeldt (BZAW, 77)*, 1958, pp. 161–176.

[6] There are several cases in which El is used in the sense of 'God'; the only case in which the word might be a proper name (Num 16:22) is P.

groups of people who went down into Egypt apparently had only the simple religion of the god of the father. In fact, the god who revealed himself to Moses was not El, but the god of his father, 'the God of Abraham, the God of Isaac and the God of Jacob' (Ex 3:6; cf. 3:13, 15) and that God revealed his name, which was not El, but Yahweh.

It is, however, possible that the worship of El is present in the episode of the golden calf, which is presented as 'Here is your God, Israel, who brought you out of the land of Egypt' (Ex 32:4,8). This, of course, is reminiscent of Gen 46:3–4 and Num 23:22; 24:8, to which we referred above. This image of a young bull undoubtedly symbolises Yahweh, but it also recalls the title 'Bull' given to El in the texts of Rās Shamrah and the bull figures representing El discovered in excavations made there.[7] It is, of course, true that the formula used in Ex 32:4, 8 and again in 1 Kings 12:28, contains the plural form *'lōhîm*, which is not the personal name of El, but the common name God, here used for Yahweh (Ex 32:5). This still leaves us, however, with the bull figure.

The story of the 'golden calf' certainly bristles with difficulties. There is no agreement regarding its literary analysis, its religious interpretation or its connection with the story of Jeroboam's 'calves'.[8] I believe that it is possible to say that this story is really linked to an event that took place during the sojourn in the desert. There may, for example, have been a rival group or a group of dissidents who had broken away from Moses' group who had, or who wanted to have, a bull figure instead of the ark of the covenant as their symbol of the presence of God.[9] It was not, after all, the bull of Baal,[10] but the bull of El and, in accordance with the process of assimilation that had taken place in Canaan, El the Bull would fulfil the function of the god of the fathers – he would go at the head of the group (Ex 32:1). It is possible that there are signs, outside the Bible, of a cult of El in the Sinai peninsula. Canaanites, who were employed by the Egyptians during the fifteenth cen-

[7] C. F. A. Schaeffer, 'Nouveaux témoignages du culte de El et de Baal à Ras Shamra-Ugarit et ailleurs en Syrie-Palestine', *Syria*, 43 (1966), pp. 1–19.

[8] M. Noth, *Das zweite Buch Mose. Exodus (ATD)*, 1959, pp. 200–202; I. Lewy, 'The Story of the Golden Calf Reanalyzed', *VT*, 9 (1959), pp. 318–322; S. Lehming, 'Versuch zu Ex XXXII', *VT*, 10 (1960), pp. 16–50; H. Seebass, *Mose und Aaron, Sinai und Gottesberg*, Bonn, 1962, pp. 32–45; J. Dus, 'Ein richterzeitliches Stierbildheiligtum zu Bethel?' *ZAW*, 77 (1965), pp. 268–286, especially pp. 276–284; M. Aberbach and L. Smolar, 'Aaron, Jeroboam and the Golden Calves', *JBL*, 86 (1967), pp. 129–140.

[9] O. Eissfeldt, 'Lade und Stierbild', *ZAW*, 58 (1940–1941), pp. 190–215 = *Kleine Schriften*, II, pp. 282–305. We feel bound to reject J. M. Sasson's hypothesis, 'Bovine Symbolism in the Exodus Narrative', *VT*, 18 (1968), pp. 380–387, namely that the image of the calf was originally a substitute for Moses who had brought the people up from Egypt and had then disappeared (Ex 32:1).

[10] The story in Num 25, with which the story of the golden calf has sometimes been connected, is different and the 'feast in honour of Yahweh' (Ex 32:5–6) has nothing at all to do with the debauchery at Peor in honour of Baal.

tury B.C. in the mines at Ṣerābīt el-Khādem in the Sinai peninsula, left inscriptions which, according to the most recent attempts made to decipher them,[11] contained the name of El and once the name of *El ḏû 'olâm*, which is precisely the form of the name El which had become assimilated with the God of Abraham, El 'Olām, the 'everlasting God' (Gen 21:33). If these readings are correct, then they may help to confirm our interpretation of the story of the golden calf.

In view of the assimilation that had taken place between the god of the fathers and El, what was the situation with regard to El and Yahweh? According to some recent authors, a relationship existed between them even in the patriarchal period. It has, for example, been suggested that 'Yahweh' was an abbreviated form of 'Yahweh-El', which would therefore mean 'El causes to be', or 'El creates'.[12] Attempts have been made to show that this full name is found in Ps 10:12; 31:6 and, if the Massoretic vowels are changed, in Jer 10:2. Both elements are also found in parallel in Gen 16:11 and in several of the psalms.[13] According to another hypothesis,[14] the name 'Yahweh' is the remnant of a liturgical formula *'El ḏû yahwî*, 'God who causes to be' or 'God who creates'. As this formula usually takes a complement, this would explain the title Yahweh S'bhā' ôth, since the full formula would have been *'El ḏû yahwî saba'ōt*, 'El who creates the (celestial) armies'. In both cases, however, the name Yahweh is regarded as the causative of the verb 'to be' and we have already rejected this possibility.[15] It is also very difficult indeed to explain the title Yahweh S'bhā'ôth itself, which is an integral part of the second hypothesis,[16] especially insofar as the interpretation of the divine title does not take into account the fact that it never appears in the Pentateuch or in the books of Joshua and Judges. In fact, it appears for the first time in 1 Sam 1:3; 11; 4:4, in connection with the sanctuary at Shiloh and the ark. It is therefore unlikely to have been derived from a liturgical formula dating back to the patriarchal age.

We are bound to conclude that although Yahwism had a different origin from the religion of El a process of assimilation undoubtedly took place. As

[11] F. M. Cross, *HTR*, 55 (1962), p. 258; W. F. Albright, *The Proto-Sinaitic Inscriptions and their Decipherment*, Cambridge, Mass., 1966, p. 24, No. 358.

[12] D. N. Freedman, *JBL*, 79 (1960), p. 156.

[13] M. Dahood, *Bib.*, 46 (1965), p. 317. 47 (1966), p. 410; 49 (1968), pp. 87–88.

[14] F. M. Cross, 'Yahweh and the God of the Patriarchs', *HTR*, 55 (1962), pp. 225–259, especially pp. 255–259; this theory was also taken up by P. D. Miller, 'El the Warrior', *HTR*, 60 (1967), pp. 411–431.

[15] See above, pp. 357–348.

[16] See B. N. Wambacq, *L'épithète divine Jahve S'ba'ōt*, Rome, 1947; O. Eissfeldt, 'Jahwe Zeboath', *Miscellanea Academica Berolinensia*, II, 2, 1950, pp. 128–150 = *Kleine Schriften*, III, pp. 103–123; V. Maag 'Jahwäs Heerscharen' *Festschrift L. Koehler* (= *Schweizerische Theologische Umschau*, 20, 3–4), 1950, pp. 27:52; J. P. Cross, 'Yahweh S'ba'ōt in Samuel and Psalms', *VT*, 17 (1967), pp. 76–92; M. Liverani, 'La preistoria dell'epiteto 'Yahweh seba'ōt', *Istituto Orientale di Napoli, Annali*, new series, 17 (1967), pp. 331–334.

we have already said, this possibility would help to explain the episode of the golden calf. It certainly emerges clearly from the oracles of Balaam in Num 23–24 that there was an assimilation of Yahweh and El. These oracles have come down to us through the two early traditions, those of the Yahwist and the Elohist, and, apart from a few additions, they undoubtedly go back to the period prior to the monarchy.[17] Two examples of parallelisms between El and Yahweh placed together in these oracles are:

'How shall I curse when El does not curse?
How shall I denounce when Yahweh does not denounce?' (Num 23:8)

and, with a reference to the bull of El:

'Yahweh his God is with him . . .
El brought him out of Egypt,
he is like the wild ox's horns to him' (Num 23:21–22; cf. 24:8).

This assimilation of Yahweh and El took place without conflict, partly because the way had been prepared for it by the assimilation that had come about between the god of the father and El. Certainly it is not possible to discover any conflict between Yahweh and El.[18] It was from El that Yahweh derived his cosmic character and his title as king. This is, of course, presupposed in the oracles of Balaam (Num 23:21b) and in the early poems (Ex 15:8; Deut 33:5; Ps 68:25). It was also from the religion of El that Yahwism derived the idea of the divine court formed by the *b'nê 'lōhîm*.[19] It is, however, not exactly true that El gave his gentleness and compassion to Yahweh or that Yahweh was originally a cruel and violent god.[20] In Ex 34:6, which is probably very early, Yahweh describes himself as 'a God of tenderness and compassion' (cf Ex 33:19). This would have made the process of assimilation easier, since at Ugarit El was called *ltpn il dpid*, 'El beneficent and good'.

---

[17] See especially J. Coppens, 'Les oracles de Biléam, leur origine littéraire et leur portée prophétique', *Mélanges E. Tisserant*, I, Rome, 1964, pp. 67–80, which includes all the previous bibliography; M. Noth, *Das vierte Buch Mose, Numeri (ATD)*, 1966, pp. 145–169. It is difficult to accept W. F. Albright's early date (1200 B.C. or earlier) for these texts in *Yahweh and the Gods of Canaan*, 1968, pp. 13–14.

[18] O. Eissfeldt, 'El and Yahweh', *JSS*, 1 (1956), pp. 25–27; in German, 'El und Jahwe', *Kleine Schriften*, III, pp. 386–397.

[19] F. M. Cross, 'The Council of Yahweh in Second Isaiah', *JNES*, 12 (1953), pp. 274–277; W. Herrmann, 'Die Göttersöhne', *Zeitschrift für Religions– und Geistesgeschichte*, 12 (1960), pp. 242–251; O. Cooke, 'The Sons of (the) God(s)', *ZAW*, 76 (1964), pp. 22–47.

[20] O. Eissfeldt, *JSS*, 1 (1956), p. 37; F. Løkkegaard, 'A Plea for El, the Bull, and Other Ugaritic Miscellanies', *Studia Orientalia I. Pedersen*, Copenhagen, 1953, pp. 218–235, especially p. 232.

3. Yahweh the warrior

This brings us to a characteristic which would seem at first sight to mark a difference between Yahwism and the religion of the fathers. As we have seen, the deliverance from Egypt was presented as a war fought by Yahweh, both in the prose account of Ex 14 and in the poetic account, the song of victory of Ex 15.[21] The story of the war against the Amalekites ends with the cry: 'Yahweh is at war with Amalek from age to age' (Ex 17:16). The song of the ark in Num 10:35–36 is an appeal to Yahweh to defeat his enemies, who are also the enemies of Israel. There is reference in Num 21:14 to a 'book of the wars of Yahweh'. This characteristic of Yahweh as a warrior is an aspect of primitive Yahwism, which is linked by this to the following period of Joshua and Judges, when the idea of the holy war was to be developed[22] and was also possibly to be expressed in cultic practice.[23]

On the other hand, this warlike aspect of the deity seems not to have been present in the religion of the patriarchs and it is partly because of this that the suggestion has recently been made that this new element was borrowed from the religion of El.[24] El is not presented in the Rās Shamrah texts as a warrior, certainly, but this aspect of the god is found in the 'Phoenician History' of Sanchuniaton, used by Philo the Elder, who was quoted by Eusebius.[25] (El-Kronos and his allies the 'Eloim' waged war against Uranos, the father of El-Kronos, and seized power from him.) This is in accordance with the title 'Bull' given to El, which describes him above all as a warrior. This warlike character was softened down at Ugarit when Baal gained a pre-eminent position in the pantheon. This did not, however, happen in the south of Canaan. This hypothesis is quite possible, but even if it is correct, it does not mean that the Israelites' idea of Yahweh was influenced by this presumably warlike character of El; there is nothing to indicate that there was any connection between El's mythological struggle against Uranos and Yahweh's wars against the enemies of his people.

Here too, Yahweh continued to play the part of the god of the father who protected and saved his people (compare, for example, Gen 31:42, 32:12 with Ex 15:2; 18:4). What is new is that there were many divine

[21] See above, pp. 383–384 and the bibliographical references given there.

[22] This continuity has been emphasised by W. H. Schmidt, *Alttestamentlicher Glaube und seine Umwelt*, Neukirchen and Vluyn, 1968, pp. 34, 92–95. According to R. Smend, *Jahwekrieg und Stämmebund*, Göttingen, 1963, those who handed down the tradition were the 'tribes of Rachel' coming from Egypt and settling in central Palestine.

[23] F. M. Cross, 'The Divine Warrior in Israel's Early Cult', *Biblical Motifs*, ed. A. Altmann, Cambridge, Mass., 1966, pp. 11–30.

[24] P. D. Miller, 'El the Warrior', *HTR*, 60 (1967), pp. 411–431.

[25] Philo of Byblos, Fr 2 = *Praep. Ev.*, I, 10, §§ 17–21, ed. K. Mras, in the *Corpus* of Berlin, *Eusebius Werke*, VIII, I, 1954, pp. 47–48; ed. F. Jacoby, *F GR HIST*, III, C, 1958, pp. 809–810.

interventions. The idea of Yahweh the warrior was born at the same time as faith in him from the powerful experience of the deliverance from Egypt (Ex 14:31; 15:3, 21). To this may be added the fact of a change in Israel's conditions of life. The earliest ancestors infiltrated peacefully into the fringe areas of the cultivated lands of Canaan. Life in the desert was rougher and struggles took place between rival groups in their efforts to establish themselves among the settled peoples. Cain, expelled from Eden, cried out: 'Whoever comes across me will kill me!' (Gen 4:4) and it was said of Ishmael that he would be 'against every man, and every man against him' (Gen 16:12). The Bible speaks of the raids that the Amalekites and the Midianites made into Canaan. Outside the Bible, we read of the life of the Asiatic nomad as fighting since the time of Horus, neither conquering nor being conquered.[26] The Benjaminites of Mari were especially warlike.[27] At a later period, the rulers of Mesopotamia had to increase the number of expeditions against the Aramaeans living in the Syrian desert and threatening their frontiers.

It is hardly surprising, then, that Moses' group should have been so belligerent and that the wars undertaken by these Israelites should have had a religious aspect. At Mari, for example, no campaign was ever undertaken without ensuring the favour of the gods for the venture. The prophets were asked to give oracles of victory and sometimes they even accompanied the army on the expeditions. The booty was subject to a religious interdict similar to the biblical *herem*.[28] Among the pre-Islamic Arabs, the soothsayer, the *kāhin* or *kāhina*, was consulted before the army left and often took part in the expeditions. These soothsayers sometimes even led the military expeditions and they always guarded the sacred tent that accompanied the warriors and housed the betyles or sacred stones symbolising the deity.[29] It is therefore quite justifiable to do as the texts suggest and date the title of Yahweh the warrior and the idea of the holy war back to the period of primitive Yahwism when the Israelites were leading a semi-nomadic life and to reject any possible influence of the religion of 'El. Once again, however, we are aware of the originality and the vitality of Yahwism. The above examples of Mari and of the Arabs before the coming of Islam show

---

[26] Instructions for Meri-ka-Re, *ANET*, p. 416b.

[27] J.–R. Kupper, *Les nomades en Mésopotamie au temps des rois de Mari*, Paris, 1957, pp. 65–68.

[28] A. Malamat, 'The Ban in Mari and in the Bible', *Biblical Essays. Proceedings of the 9th Meeting. Die Ou-Testam. Werkgemeenskap in Suid-Afrika*, Pretoria, 1966, pp. 40–49; J. M. Sasson, *The Military Establishments at Mari (Studia Pohl, 3)*, Rome, 1969, pp. 36–37; J.–G. Heintz, 'Oracles prophétiques et "'guerre sainte" selon les archives royales de Mari et l'Ancien Testament', *Congress Volume, Rome, 1968 (STV, 17)*, Leiden, 1969, pp. 112–138.

[29] A. Fischer, 'kāhin', *Encyclopédie de l'Islam*, II, Paris, 1927, p. 665; H. Lammens, 'Le culte des bétyles et les processions chez les Arabes préislamites', *BIFAO*, 17 (1920), pp. 39–101, reprinted in *L'Arabie occidentale avant l'hégire*, Beirut, 1928, pp. 101–179, especially pp. 106–116.

that war had a religious significance in at least two different environments, both of which were similar ethnically and sociologically to that of the ancestors of Israel. There is, however, nothing comparable in the whole of the Ancient Near East to the personal, extremely important and sometimes even unique rôle that Yahweh played in the holy wars of Israel.

II. MOSES AND MONOTHEISM

According to one theory that is especially associated with the name of J. Wellhausen, Israel moved from the stage of animism to that of polytheism and only then to monotheism, a stage that was not reached until the period of the prophets in the eighth century B.C. and perhaps not until the period of Deutero-Isaiah. This theory of the evolution of Israel's religion has, of course, been abandoned, but even now there is no agreement about the date of the appearance of monotheism in Israel. We have described the religion of the patriarchs as a monolatry. Some scholars believe that true monotheism began with Moses. It was in connection with Moses that Y. Kaufmann, for example, spoke of the 'monotheistic revolution' and the 'death of the gods'.[30] W. F. Albright was convinced that the founder of Yahwism was a monotheist.[31] Appeals have frequently been made to the authority of Albright in this context, but certain reservations have, in general, been placed on that authority, with the result that the full significance and extent of his affirmation have been considerably restricted.[32] If, as Albright says, the term monotheist means someone who teaches the existence of only one God,[33] ... then Moses was not a monotheist, since we have no indication at all that he professed to believe in one God. On the contrary, everything points to the fact that this was not the teaching of primitive Yahwism. In the song of victory (Ex 15:11), we read, for example, the question: 'Who among the gods is your like,

[30] Y. Kaufmann, *The Religion of Israel. From its Beginnings to the Babylonian Exile*, translated by M. Greenberg, Chicago, 1960, p. 290 229 ff.

[31] W. F. Albright, *From Stone Age to Christianity*,[2] Baltimore, 1964. The sub-title of this book is *Monotheism and the Historical Process*. See especially pp. 196–207.

[32] See, for example, G. E. Wright, *The Old Testament Against its Environment*, London, 1950, p. 39, who says that, if the term 'monotheism' is used for the faith of Israel, we should always make it quite clear that we are not using it in the speculative sense in which it was used by the Greeks; J. Bright, *A History of Israel*, Philadelphia, 1959, p. 139, who insists that it is not a monotheism in any philosophical sense; P. van Imschoot, *Théologie de l'Ancien Testament*, I, Tournai, 1954, p. 37: 'A practical rather than a theoretical monotheism'; E. Jacob, *Théologie de l'Ancien Testament*, Neuchâtel and Paris, 1955, p. 51 is prepared to accept the idea of monotheism on condition that by this term is meant a conviction of faith, not the result of reflection. When, then, one is bound to ask, should the term be retained at all if it no longer conveys its only possible meaning?

[33] *op. cit.*, p. 207.

Yahweh?' and, after hearing the story of the deliverance from Egypt, Jethro cries out: 'Now I know that Yahweh is greater than all the gods' (Ex 18:11).

The existence of other gods is not denied in the first commandment of the decalogue itself;[34] in fact, it presupposes their existence and forbids the Israelites to worship them. It is not really a teaching about the unique nature of God, but a practical rule of life, expressing the exclusive claim made by Yahweh to the worship of the people. The same is expressed in the 'cultic' decalogue (Ex 34:14), in Hos 13:4 and in the Code of the Covenant (Ex 22:19;23:13). The reason for this prohibition is given in the additions to the decalogue (Ex 20:5–6; Deut 5:9–10), namely that Yahweh is a 'jealous God'.[35] The same expression is used in Deut 4:24; 6:15; Jos 24:19 and it is always employed as a justification of the prohibition against worshipping other gods. Leaving aside the question as to when this theological explanation was explicitly formulated, we may say that together with the first commandment it represents a primitive and fundamental aspect of Yahwism. Yahweh was, in other words, an exclusive and jealous God.

It would not, however, be quite true to say that the struggle against the other gods began with Moses and in the earliest stages of Yahwism.[36] There is no trace of any opposition to other gods in the whole of the book of Exodus apart from Ex 12:12: 'I shall deal out punishment to all the gods of Egypt', but this is a late text. The prophets were later to present the sojourn in the desert as a time of unbroken love between Israel and Yahweh (see Hos 2:17; 13:4–5; Amos 2:10–11; Jer 2:2). The concurrent and later tradition of rebellion and complaints in the desert does not mention other gods apart from Yahweh, nor does the story of the golden calf. The struggle against false gods did not, in fact, begin until after the Israelites had left the desert and had reached Peor (Num 25). According to Hosea, Israel became

---

[34] R. Knierim, 'Das erste Gebot', *ZAW*, 77 (1965), pp. 20–39, says nothing about the earliest possible formulation of the first commandment, but believes that it was not expressed in its existing formula until the assembly at Shechem, although he admits that it must have been implicitly accepted and put into practice by the group that came from Egypt. This group did not, however, have to wait until it had settled in Canaan before it learned that other groups worshipped other gods. There must also have been, Knierim thinks, a minimum number of 'commandments' practised in the religion of this group from the very beginning. It should be pointed out, however, that Knierim exaggerates the importance of the assembly at Shechem; see also below, pp. 671–672.

[35] W. Zimmerli, 'Das zweite Gebot', *Festschrift A. Bertholet*, Tübingen, 1950, pp. 550–563= *Gottes Offenbarung. Gesammelte Augsätze*, Munich, 1963, pp. 234–248, has shown that this development is connected with the first commandment by way of the prohibition of images. For the meaning of this term 'a jealous God', see G. von Rad, *Theologie des Alten Testaments*, I, Munich, 1957, pp. 203–211; B. Renaud, *'Je suis un Dieu jaloux'*, Paris, 1963, pp. 27–46.

[36] See, for example, Y. Kaufmann, *The Religion of Israel, op. cit.* (note 30), pp. 222, 224 ff, 230; B. Gemser, *OTS*, 12 (1958), p. 19 ff. See also H. Seebass' comments in *Der Erzvater Israel*, pp. 81–82.

unfaithful to Yahweh for the first time at Baal-peor, where the struggle against idolatry really began: 'It was like finding grapes in the desert when I found Israel ... but when they reached Baal-peor they devoted themselves to shame' (Hos 9:10). As we shall see later, however, the incident at Baal-peor represents a situation that prevailed during the period of the Judges.[37]

The religion of Israel was distinguished from all other religions in the Ancient Near East by this exclusiveness and this intolerance of all other gods. In the Near East generally, it was possible to regard one or other god as pre-eminent, but other deities were always worshipped at the same time. Individual attempts were made from time to time on the initiative, for example, of Amen-hotep IV (Akh-en-Aten) in Egypt and Nabonidus in Mesopotamia, to unify worship, but they always ended in failure. In contradistinction, Yahweh demanded that his people worship him alone and he even refused to have any goddess in association with him, as the great gods of the Near East had. This meant that Israel was prevented from having anything comparable to the mythology of the Ancient Near East.

This exclusiveness in cult, however, is not the same as monotheism or the affirmation of one God. It is, of course, possible to speak of a 'practical' monotheism or a 'monolatry', but in using such terms there is a danger of enclosing within a static definition an impulse which undoubtedly carries in itself the germ of future dynamic growth. It was on the basis of the first commandment that Israel's religious experience and theological thought reached the point where they could be expressed as monotheism in the true sense of the word. Israel, in other words, came to realise that these other gods, who meant nothing to Israel, were equally impotent towards those who believed in them. It was then that the Israelites were able to deny their existence.[38]

III. THE MOSAIC CULT

1. *The prohibition of images*[39]

Another characteristic of Yahwism which distinguishes it sharply from the other religions of the Ancient Near East is that it prohibited the use of images of God or of gods. This prohibition is formulated in the second

---

[37] See below, pp. 568–570.

[38] H. H. Rowley, 'Mose und der Monotheismus', *ZAW*, 69 (1957), pp. 1–21; revised English text: 'Moses and Monotheism', *From Moses to Qumran*, London, 1963, pp. 35–63, which includes a full bibliography up to this date; W. H. Schmidt, *Alttestamentlicher Glaube und seine Umwelt*, Neukirchen and Vluyn 1968, pp. 68–76.

[39] W. Zimmerli, 'Das Zweite Gebot', *op cit.* (note 35); K.–H. Bernhardt, *Gott und Bild. Ein Beitrag zur Begründung und Deutung des Bildverbotes im Alten Testament*, Berlin, 1956; G. von Rad, *Theologie des Alten Testaments*, I, pp. 211–218; J. Ouellette, 'Le deuxième command-

commandment (Ex 20:4; Deut 5:8). It is also found, in different formulae, in the introduction to the Code of the Covenant (Ex 20:23), the 'ritual' decalogue (Ex 34:17), in the curses of Deut 28:15 and in the laws of holiness (Lev 19:4; 26:1). Some of these texts are very late and in them the prohibition against images is associated with the commandment not to worship foreign gods. They are not condemnations of all images as art forms, but condemnations of cultic images and above all of representations of the deity. There can be no valid reason for not attributing this prohibition to the period of Moses at least in its most simple form: 'You shall not make yourself an image'. Images of foreign gods were not prohibited in this commandment, because this was the content of the first commandment and there was no need for it to be repeated or clarified here. What was forbidden in the second commandment was the making of images of Yahweh. The later texts, and those of the prophets, which also condemned – or condemned only – the making of images of other gods, belonged to periods when the absence of images in the worship of Yahweh was taken for granted or else at the peak of the struggle against foreign 'idols'. What is more, it was images and representations of Yahweh himself that were prohibited in this commandment, not every image associated in one way or another with the cult of Yahweh. The prohibition did not, in other words, apply to the cherubs of the sanctuary at Shiloh and the temple of Jerusalem, since these were symbolic figures guarding and supporting the throne on which Yahweh was seated but invisible. It did not even apply to the golden calf in the desert or to Jeroboam's calves, insofar as these were, in accordance with the purpose of those who made them, only the pedestal of the invisible deity. Despite individual transgressions, the most obvious of these being the idol of Micah (Judges 17), the cult of Yahweh was from the very beginning, and it always continued to be, a cult without images. This was something which constantly surprised the gentiles, who always filled the temples of their own gods with statues.

It is, however, not easy to discover the precise meaning of this prohibition against images. The homiletic commentary of Deut 4:9–20 explains it by reference to the theophany of Sinai, when the Israelites heard Yahweh's voice speaking 'from the midst of the fire', but 'saw no shape', with the result that they were not to make any image of Yahweh. The commandment is in this way connected with a fact, but its religious meaning is not in any sense defined. Various interpretations have been suggested by modern authors, but they are generally speaking unsatisfactory. Above all, it is important not to look for a sign here of Yahweh's spiritual nature, because the idea of 'pure spirit' meant nothing to the Israelites, who thought of their

ment et le rôle de l'image dans la symbolique religieuse de L'Ancien Testament. Essai d'interprétation', RB, 74 (1967), pp. 504–516; W. H. Schmidt, Alttestamentlicher Glaube, op. cit. (note 38), pp. 76–83.

God as being in the image of man. It was, after all, in a human form that he had always appeared to them (Ex 24:10–11; 33:21–23). It is paradoxical that he could be seen, but that he could not be represented.

It has also been suggested that man could obtain power over his god by enclosing him within an image that could be treated badly or deprived of offerings. It is true that it may have been a popular practice to identify a god with the statue of that god and this would certainly have given fuel to the prophets and sages of Israel in their polemics against idolatry. This popular conviction, however, was not in the true spirit of paganism, according to which the statue was not the god himself, but the place where he lived and the sign of his presence. If it was harmed or broken, this was a religious offence, but it did not touch the person of the god himself.

It is possible to find a more valid reason in the development of the second commandment. According to Ex 20:4 = Deut 5:8, it was forbidden to look for a likeness to Yahweh in anything that was 'in heaven or on earth or in the waters' and this is repeated in greater detail in Deut 4:16–19. In other words, there is nothing in the whole of nature that can be compared to Yahweh and nothing that can represent him. God made himself known to man through the revelation of his word and through his activity in the world. He revealed himself in this way as both near and far, but he remained both outside nature and a mystery to man. The prohibition against images was therefore the consequence of his transcendence and this was precisely the meaning of the name of Yahweh, by which he revealed himself.[40]

2. The desert sanctuary[41]

This sanctuary is described at great length in the priestly tradition (Ex 26; 36:8–38) and, apart from these long descriptions, it is mentioned frequently by the priestly editor, who calls it the 'tabernacle' or mišᵉkān, a term which is peculiar to it, or the Tent of Meeting, 'ōhel mô'ēdh, as it was also called in the other traditions. This dwelling housed the ark of the Testimony, 'ārôn hâ-'ēdhûth, which is described as a chest of acacia wood.

[40] See above, p. 357.

[41] R. de Vaux, Institutions, pp. 294–302 and the bibliography, pp. 442–443 (in the second French edition); R. E. Clements, God and Temple. The Idea of the Divine Presence in Ancient Israel, Oxford, 1965, pp. 28–39; M. H. Woudstra, The Ark of the Covenant from the Conquest to Kingship, Philadelphia, Pa., 1965; S. Lehming, 'Erwägungen zur Zelttradition', Gottes Wort und Gottes Land (Festschrift H.–W. Hertzberg), Göttingen, 1965, pp. 110–132; V. W. Rabe, 'The Identity of the Priestly Tabernacle', JNES, 25 (1966), pp. 132–134; M. McKane, 'The Earlier History of the Ark', Glasgow University Oriental Society, Transactions, 21 (1965–1966), pp. 68–76; G. Henton Davies, 'The Ark of the Covenant', ASTI, 5

The Tent of Meeting is mentioned only once in Deuteronomy (Deut 31:14–15), but the ark is mentioned four times in this book and called the ark of the covenant, *'arôn habb'rîth*, which is also described as a chest of acacia wood, containing the tablets of stone on which the 'ten words' are inscribed (Deut 10:1–5). It was entrusted to the Levites (Deut 10:8; 31:9) and the law of Deuteronomy was placed beside it (Deut 31:26).

The Tent of Meeting is mentioned four times in the earliest traditions of the Pentateuch. It is pitched outside the camp by Moses, who consults Yahweh in it (Ex 33:7–11). It is in the Tent of Meeting that the seventy elders receive some of the spirit of Yahweh (Num 11:16–17, 24–25). Finally. Aaron and Miriam are condemned in it (Num 12:4–10). The ark is mentioned only twice in the early traditions. In the first case, it precedes the Israelites in their travels and seeks out a stopping-place for them (Num 10:33–36). In the second case, it does not leave the camp when the Israelites go out to attack the Canaanites and are beaten by them (Num 14:44). Neither the ark nor the Tent of Meeting are described in these very early texts, which, like Deuteronomy, do not relate the ark in any way to the Tent. (This is done in the priestly tradition.) This laconic manner of dealing with the ark and the Tent raises two questions. First, do they really go back to the period spent in the desert? Secondly, if the reply to this first question is in the affirmative, what was their relationship to each other?[42]

It has been suggested that the priestly editor's description of the Tent of Meeting was based on the tent that David pitched at Jerusalem to house the ark (2 Sam 6:17).[43] It has also been suggested that this description incorporates both aspects of the Temple built by Solomon and features of the sanctuary at Shiloh, which could not have been a 'temple', as, for example, 1 Sam 1:7, 9; 3:15 indicate, but was undoubtedly a tent, as indicated in 2 Sam 22:7; Jos 18:1; 19:51 and in the prophecy of Nathan (2 Sam 7:6).[44]

Neither of these two theories can, however, be justified. It is only the Temple of Jerusalem that could have been the priestly editor's inspiration,

---

(1966–1967), pp. 30–47; M. Görg, *Das Zelt der Begegnung. Untersuchung zur Gestalt der sakralen Zelttraditionen Altisraels,* Bonn, 1967; T. E. Fretheim, 'The Ark in Deuteronomy', *CBQ,* 30 (1968), pp. 1–14; D. R. Hiller, 'Ritual Procession of the Ark and Ps 132', *ibid.,* pp. 48–55; O. Eissfeldt, 'Die Lade Jahwes in Geschichtserzählung, Sage und Liede', *Das Altertum,* 14 (1968), pp. 131–145; J. Dus, 'Herabfahrung Jahwes auf die Lade und Entziehung der Feuerwolke. Zu zwei Dogmen der mittlerer Richterzeit', *VT,* 19 (1969), pp. 290–311.*

[42] In what follows, I make use of the conclusions to which I came in an earlier study, 'Ark of the Covenant and Tent of Reunion', The Bible and the Ancient Near East, London, 1971, pp. 136–151. These conclusions have not been seriously affected in my opinion by later studies.

[43] F. M. Cross, 'The Tabernacle', *BibArch,* 10 (1947), pp. 45–68; V. W. Rabe, *JNES,* 25 (1966), pp. 132–134.

[44] M. Haran, 'Shilo and Jerusalem. The Origin of the Priestly Tradition in the Pentateuch', *JBL,* 81 (1962), pp. 14–24; for the tent at Shiloh, see O. Eissfeldt, *Das Altertum,* 14 (1968), pp. 134–135.

but his desert temple was a model of this, reduced in size and capable of being taken down. The tent structure was preserved. Sheets, for example, were to be made 'to form a tent over the tabernacle' (Ex 26:7), which is further covered with skins (Ex 26:14). In other words, it is the Tent of Meeting of the early traditions, the memory of which could not be forgotten. There is, then, no reason to doubt that the Israelites really had a sacred tent in the desert. The comparison that has been made between this and the Arabs' prayer-tents or palanquins, the *'utfah* of the modern Arabs and the *qubbah* of the pre-Islamic Arabs, is fully justified.

It has often been disputed that the ark itself was very early and several scholars think that it was borrowed from Canaan. It is mentioned twice in the early sources of the Pentateuch, but these texts are regarded as additions and it is also widely believed that the ark was introduced at a later period into the story of the crossing of the Jordan (Jos 3–4).[45] This literary criticism is, however, not justified, In Num 14:44, the ark plays the same part in battle as it did in the much earlier story described in 1 Sam 4. In the case of Num 10:33–36, it is true that this text is situated in a chapter which is composite from the literary point of view and that the ark is mentioned only in the prose framework enclosing the two distichs, verses 35 and 36, in which the ark is not in fact named. On the other hand, however, the ark is given the same meaning in these two warcries as it is given in Num 14:44 and this is not compatible with the part that it plays in Num 10:33, where it acts as a guide. Because of the dangers involved in any movement on the part of a nomadic group of people in the desert, this movement always took on the aspect of a military displacement. This, then, is an aspect of very early Yahwism.[46] Like the god of the father, Yahweh went with his people as a leader and guide and the cultic symbol of his presence, the ark in this case as the visible pedestal of the invisible deity, would have been quite normal. The ark, then, was very old and another proof of this is that the whole idea of the ark was changed when the people had settled in Canaan and the ark appeared in the full light of history. It was brought from the sanctuary at Shiloh on to the field of battle and 'God came to the camp' (1 Sam 4:3–8). This is certainly in accordance with Num 14:44 and 10:33–36, but here there is a certain difference in that it is the 'ark of Yahweh Sabaoth, him who is seated on the cherubs' (verse 4). The influence here is certainly Canaanite and Yahweh is thought of as sitting on a royal throne flanked by winged sphinxes. This new symbol is combined with the earlier symbolic value of the ark, which, from having been a simple resting place, became the steps leading up to the divine throne.[47]

---

[45] See especially, among more recent authors, J. Maier, *Das altisraelitische Ladeheiligtum* (*BZAW*, 93), 1965, pp. 4–39.

[46] See above, p. 460.

[47] R. de Vaux, 'Les chérubins et l'arche de l'alliance, les sphinx gardiens et les trônes divins

Both the tent and the ark, then, went back to the nomadic period. We now have to try to determine the relationship between them. According to the priestly tradition, the ark was sheltered in the tent, just as it was placed in Solomon's temple. This appears to contradict the date provided by the earlier traditions, in which the tent and the ark are never mentioned in the same context. It has therefore been suggested that they belonged to two different groups of traditions. The priestly editor, however, only preserved fragments of the early traditions concerning cultic practice in the desert and we should not draw too hasty conclusions from the sparsity or absence of information. These early traditions are, after all, silent about the origin and the appearance of the tent and the ark.

One text can, however, be used to show that there was some relation between the tent and the ark. The Elohistic fragment, Ex 33:7–11, which refers to the Tent of Meeting, opens abruptly and simply says 'Moses used to take the Tent and pitch it outside the camp for him'. The words 'for him' are generally taken to refer to Yahweh or to Moses in recent commentaries, but they may refer to the ark itself, since this is masculine in Hebrew and was possibly intended in the original context from which this passage was taken.[48] This theory has not been established, but it has much to recommend it. Certainly the conviction that the ark was placed in the tent was present before the priestly editor began his work. It was expressed in the prophecy of Nathan (2 Sam 7:6) and it explains why David pitched a tent to house the ark when it was brought to Jerusalem (2 Sam 6:17). Finally, it is difficult to imagine that a tent used for cult would be completely empty and that the ark would not be under a shelter, which among nomadic people must have been a tent. The *qubbah* of the pre-Islamic Arabs sheltered the tribal idols.

We cannot be certain, but we can regard it therefore as highly likely that both the tent and the ark go back to the Mosaic period, that the ark was housed in the tent and that the tent was the meeting place with Yahweh precisely because it contained the ark, which was the symbol of the divine presence.

3. The priesthood and the sacrifices

There was at this time no organised priesthood.[49] The only priest to appear in the early stories is a Midianite, Jethro (Ex 18) and we do not

---

dans l'ancien Orient', *MUSJ*, 37 (1960–1961), pp. 91–124 = Bible et Orient, pp. 231–259.

[48] Among recent authors, see especially O. Eissfeldt, 'Lade und Steinbild', *ZAW*, 58 (1940–1941), pp. 190–215, especially pp. 191–192 = *Kleine Schriften*, II, pp. 283–284; G. Henton Davies, *ASTI*, 5 (1966–1967), pp. 34–39; M. Görg, *op. cit.* (note 41), pp. 156–157; see also J. Maier's long criticism, note 45, pp. 13–18.

[49] C. Hauret, 'Moïse était-il prêtre?' *Bib*, 40 (1959), pp. 509–521; A. Cody, *A History of Old Testament Priesthood*, Rome, 1969, pp. 39–52.

really know what is meant by this name.[50] It is true that Moses was a mediator, interceding for the people, receiving and transmitting oracles and teachings from God, as priests normally did (Deut 33:8–10), but he is never called a priest in any text and he transcended the priesthood just as he was far more than a prophet (Num 12:6–8). In the ceremony of the covenant (Ex 24:3–8), Moses built an altar and had victims sacrificed by young men, but he himself sprinkled the blood of the victims on the altar and on the people. In a sacrificial ritual, the blood rite was always performed by the priest, but here the blood rite was not so much a sacrificial rite as a covenant rite. What is more, although he built an altar and had sacrifices offered, Moses was doing no more than the patriarchs had done and they were not priests.

According to the priestly tradition, the priest at the time of the sojourn in the desert was not Moses, but Aaron. In the early traditions, however, Aaron is a very vague figure.[51] As Moses' assistant in Ex 4:13–16, 27–31 and especially in the story of the plagues of Egypt (Ex 5:1–5; 7–10), Aaron seems to have played a secondary rôle and the conflict between Moses and Aaron (Ex 32; Num 12) would seem to reflect later polemics. Certainly Aaron does not act as a priest in the early accounts and he too is never called a priest. He is, it is true, called a 'Levite' (Ex 14), but this passage does not belong to the earlier tradition and a 'Levite' was not the same as a 'priest'.

The members of the group of Levi never have priestly functions outside the priestly sources. In Ex 32:25–29, the sons of Levi put to the sword the Israelites who had offered sacrifices to the golden calf, not even sparing their closest relatives. This action is presented as an 'investiture as priests of Yahweh'. The passage is, however, an addition explaining why the Levites formed a separate group (see also Deut 33:9). It may be that the special status which was always to be accorded to the priestly tribe of Levi went back in fact to the period of Moses. It may also be that Moses entrusted the care of the moveable desert sanctuary to his kinsmen who were, like him, members of the secular tribe of Levi, which had broken up. (Certain families in pre-Islamic Arabia were entrusted with the task of guarding the sanctuaries.) The memory of this was preserved by later traditions and these traditions set the Levites aside for the transport of the tent and the ark (Num 1:50–51; 3:8; 10:17, 21; Deut 10:8).

The fact that there was no organised priesthood at this time does not mean that the Israelites did not offer blood sacrifices in the desert. These formed an essential part of the religion of shepherds and herdsmen. In this

[50] See above, pp. 335–338.

[51] A. H. J. Gunneweg, *Leviten und Priester. Hauptlinien der Traditionsbildung und Geschichte des israelitisch–jüdischen Kultpersonals*, Göttingen, 1965, pp. 81–98; A. Cody, *op. cit.*, pp. 146–156; E. Auerbach, 'Das Aharon-Problem', *Congress Volume. Rome, 1968* (STV, 17), 1969, pp. 37–63.

context, it is interesting to contrast two prophetic texts. According to the first, Amos 5:25, the Israelites did not offer God either sacrifices or oblations during their forty years in the desert. According to the second text, Jer 7:22, God gave the Israelites no orders at all regarding holocaust and sacrifice when he brought them out of Egypt. Both of these texts have been discussed at length.[52] The text of Amos 5:25 may be deuteronomistic interpolation,[53] but it is in any case in the same tradition of thought as Jer 7:22. Both point to the same ideal, that of the time spent in the desert, in contrast to settled life, during which Israel had borrowed so much from the abundance of Canaanite worship. In the desert, the Israelites had been unconditionally faithful to God (see Hos 2:16–17; 9:10; Jer 2:2), without being enslaved to rites which closely resembled the rites practised by gentiles.[54]

We know very little about the sacrifices that were offered in the desert. They are seldom mentioned in the early accounts. In Ex 18:12, the Midianite Jethro offers a holocaust, 'ôlāh, and sacrifices, z'bhāhîm, and these were followed by a meal. When the covenant had been concluded (Ex 24:5–8), Moses ordered young men, who were neither priests nor Levites, to offer holocausts and communion sacrifices, which are given the exceptional double name of z'bhāhîm s'lāmîm.[55] He then performed a covenant rite with the blood of the victims. In the story of the golden calf, the Israelites offered holocausts and communion sacrifices, s'lāmîm, then ate and drank (Ex 32:6). The formulation of these texts was undoubtedly influenced by later practices, the holocaust and the communion sacrifice having been borrowed from Canaan.[56] It would appear that only one form of sacrifice, the zebhah, was known in the Mosaic religion and this consisted of the immolation of the victim, the sprinkling of its blood and the eating of its flesh. There is evidence that this form of sacrifice was performed in northern Arabia and in central Arabia before the coming of Islam and it belonged to family worship. The same form of sacrifice was preserved in the ritual of the Passover and we have already drawn attention to the archaic nature of that rite.[57] It was perhaps also continued in the family and clan sacrifices (see 1 Sam 1:21; 2:19; 9:12; 20:6).[58]

[52] Apart from commentaries, see R. Hentschke, *Die Stellung der vorexilischen Schriftpropheten zum Kultus (BZAW,* 75), 1957, pp. 86–88, 114–118; H.–J. Kraus, *Gottesdienst in Israel,*[2] Munich, 1962, pp. 134–135; A. Strobel, 'Jeremias, Priester ohne Gottesdienst? Zu Jer. 7, 21–23', *BZ,* new series, 1 (1957), pp. 214–224; P. Reymond, 'Sacrifice et "spiritualité" ou sacrifice et alliance? Jer 7, 22–24', *TZ,* 21 (1965), pp. 314–317; S. Erlandsson, 'Amos 5:25–27, ett crux interpretum', *Svensk Exegetisk Arsbok,* 33 (1968), pp. 76–82.

[53] See H. W. Wolff, *Dodekapropheton. Amos (BKAT),* 1969, *in loco.*

[54] H.–J. Kraus, *op. cit.* (note 52). I give a slightly different emphasis here to the view that I expressed in *Institutions,* II, pp. 308–309.

[55] This double name is found elsewhere only in 1 Sam 11:15.

[56] R. de Vaux, *Les sacrifices de l'Ancien Testament,* Paris, 1964, pp. 41–48.

[57] See above, pp. 366–367.

[58] M. Haran, "Zebaḥ hayyamîm' *VT,* 19 (1969), pp. 11–22. R. Rendtorff, *Studien zur*

4. The Sabbath[59]

The Sabbath probably goes back to the very origins of Yahwism. It was prescribed in the Code of the Covenant (Ex 23:12) and in the yahwistic 'ritual decalogue' (Ex 34:21). In both of these texts, a settled, agrarian way of life is presupposed, but they are both adaptations of an earlier law. The sabbath is also found in both forms of the decalogue (Ex 20:8–11; Deut 5:12–15). In both cases, it is the central commandment and the most developed. These developments are late, but they date back to a period when the sabbath had become one of the leading religious observances. The reasons given for the sabbath law are different in Exodus and in Deuteronomy, however. In the first, the sabbath is said to be an imitation of Yahweh, who rested after his creation (Ex 20:11). In the second, it serves to remind the people of the slavery in Egypt (Deut 5:15). The fact that there are two different explanations shows that the law was very old. In its simple form, every seventh day was 'sanctified' and a day of rest for Yahweh. It was not a feast, nor was it marked by any special rite. It was simply a day when everyday activities ceased.

It has been said that the sabbath was borrowed from the Kenites. It is forbidden to light a fire in Ex 35:2–3 and it is also forbidden to gather wood on the sabbath in Num 15:32–36. This was, of course, something that metal-workers did every day and 'Kenite', qeni, means 'smith'.[60] This is not a very firmly based hypothesis, especially if it is dissociated from the overall theory of the Kenite origin of Yahwism, which is, in our opinion, incapable of being proved.[61] The Israelites did not adopt the practice of the sabbath in Canaan, where it was unknown. They certainly observed the practice before entering Canaan. One possible objection is that this practice would have been impossible for people keeping sheep and goats, which needed attention every day. We do not, however, know precisely how the sabbath was observed in its primitive form. It may simply have been a day that was 'sanctified' or set aside for God, a day when the people did not move camp. This would certainly be in accordance with the apparent meaning of the word in its most primitive sense, that is, 'halt'. But here too, we can only conjecture.

Geschichte des Opfers im Alten Israel, Neukirchen and Vluyn, 1967, pp. 119–168, has tried to prove that *zebhaḥ* and *s'lamîm* were two types of sacrifice which were different for a long time. All the same, unlike Rendtorff, I believe that the *zebhaḥ* included from its very beginning a blood rite; see S. McEvenue, *Bib,* 50 (1969), pp. 115–121.

[59] R. de Vaux, *Institutions,* pp. 475–482 and the bibliography, p.550; see also J. J. Stamm, *Der Dekalog im Lichte der neueren Forschung,* Berne and Stuttgart, 1962, pp. 47–51; N. Lohfink, 'Zur Dekalogfassung von Dt 5', *BZ,* new series, 9 (1965), pp. 17–32; W. H. Schmidt, *Alttestamentlicher Glaube, op. cit.* (note 38), pp. 83–87.

[60] H. H. Rowley, 'Moses and the Decalogue', *Men of God,* London, 1963, pp. 30–31, with the bibliography,

[61] See above, pp. 333–334 and R. de Vaux, 'Sur l'origine kénite ou madianite du Yahvisme', *Eretz-Israel,* 9 *(Albright Volume),* 1969, pp. 28–32.

PART III

The Traditions Concerning the Settlement in Canaan

INTRODUCTION

T HE PROBLEM raised by the settlement of the Israelites in Canaan and the growth of the system of the twelve tribes is the most difficult problem in the whole history of Israel.

The picture that first emerges from a reading of the Bible, however, is apparently quite simple. After first attempting and failing to enter Canaan by the south (Num 13–14), the twelve tribes which left Egypt under the leadership of Moses make a long detour through the desert and arrive in Transjordan. They beat Sihon, the king of Heshbon, and Og, the king of Bashan, seize their countries and camp in the plains of Moab (Num 20–25). The conquered land is divided between Gad and Reuben (Num 32). Joshua leads the twelve tribes across the Jordan. Jericho and Ai are taken and the way into the centre of Canaan lies open (Jos 1–9). First the south and then the north of Palestine are conquered (Jos 10–11) and this enables the Israelites to subdue the whole country. All that remains is for the land to be divided among the tribes (Jos 13–19). The settlement in Canaan is thus presented as a speedy military conquest of the whole country, a joint operation carried out by all the tribes under the high command of Joshua.

Even the Bible itself, however, reveals that this is a highly simplified picture. The fact that not all of the tribes took part in the exodus from Egypt and the conquest of Canaan is presupposed in the account of the pact made at Shechem (Joshua 24 and especially verses 14–15). The treaty with the Gibeonites (Jos 9) and the fact that there were no military operations in the hill country of Ephraim and before Shechem point to a peaceful settlement in some parts of Canaan at least. Finally, it is clear from Jos 13:1–6 and Judges 1 that the conquest was not completed, and theological explanations for this are given by the deuteronomistic editor (Judges 2:1–6, 20–23; 3:1–6).

It is clearly necessary, then, to review the biblical accounts in the light of literary criticism and the history of traditions and to compare them with the extrabiblical evidence provided by archaeology and general history. This has, of course, been done by several scholars, who have come to varying conclusions, based to a great extent on the relative importance they have attached to these factors.

1. Y. Kaufmann's theory[1]

Kaufmann recognised the need for literary criticism, but rejected the solutions that had already been suggested, both the theory that Joshua and Judges were a continuation of the documents of the Pentateuch and the hypothesis that these books formed part of a great deuteronomistic history from Deuteronomy to the end of Kings. In his opinion, the book of Joshua was written very soon after the events themselves had taken place by an author who had collected together the memories of a living tradition and had also made use of written sources. He also used a 'deuteronomistic' style of writing which had in any case existed long before the book of Deuteronomy itself. Kaufmann also accepted that the stories of the conquest were shrouded in legend, but nonetheless insisted that they were in accordance with the historical reality. The conquest was, in other words, undertaken as a joint operation by all the tribes, which had been united since their sojourn in the desert by a religious and national covenant. Joshua himself was a man of exceptional qualities who realised that the conquest would only be carried out successfully if the tribes remained united in battle and if their morale remained high. This is why, Kaufmann maintained, he did not allow the settlement to take place until the fighting was over or permit any of the conquered cities to be occupied or rebuilt, but insisted on the people remaining in camp and returning to camp after each campaign. He kept the morale of the people high by making them absolutely confident of victory in various ways. For example, after the crossing of the Jordan, he set up the twelve stones at Gilgal. After Jericho had been taken, he cursed the city. After taking and destroying Ai, he hanged its king. He had an altar built on Mount Ebal, killed the five kings at Makkedah after their defeat near Gibeon and hamstrung the horses and burnt the chariots of the northern kings after the victory at Merom. Joshua not only understood the psychology of his people – he was also an excellent strategist, Kaufmann believed. He maintained the camp at Gilgal because by so doing he could lay the country waste as he conquered it. He could also obtain supplies in Transjordan, in the friendly territories of Reuben and Gad and the half-tribe of Manasseh, where he bought provisions with the silver and gold he had taken as booty. He had also to protect his people against a possible

---

[1] Y. Kaufmann, *The Biblical Account of the Conquest of Palestine*, Jerusalem, 1953; 'Traditions Concerning Early Israelite History in Canaan', *Scripta Hierosolymitana* (Jerusalem), 8 (1961), pp. 303–334.

attack in the rear by the Ammonites or the Moabites. Finally, Kaufmann has also pointed to his remarkable ability as a tactician – always taking the offensive, making surprise attacks, taking advantage of the territory, giving no rest to the enemy in flight and taking one city after another without giving any of them time to recover.

The picture provided by Judges 1, Kaufmann has pointed out, is no different. It is an early account of the events that took place at the beginning of the period of the Judges after Joshua's death. All the land to be conquered had already been shared out in advance in a national agreement made between the tribes – this is the 'geographical' document of Jos 13–19. Each tribe settled in the territory assigned to it, but the conquest had not been completed and the tribes had to continue to fight individually in order to make sure of their land. Judges 1, then, Kaufmann insisted, was the historical continuation of Joshua. He made a distinction between four different kinds of war following in succession. The first were the wars of conquest (Num 21 to Judges 1), the last war of conquest being the capture of Bethel (Judges 1:22–26). These were followed by a short period of wars in which the Canaanites were not conquered and driven out, but were compelled to do forced labour (Judges 1:27–35). The period of the Judges and of the beginning of the monarchy was a time of wars of liberation (Judges 3–1 Sam 31) and the period of David and Solomon was a time of imperial wars. The whole of the territory had been conquered by a joint action undertaken by all the tribes by the time that Joshua and Caleb had died. There was no time at all, Kaufmann was convinced, when Canaan was occupied peacefully. The picture provided by Joshua and Judges 1, he believed, is historically authentic and all the other theories are simply scholarly inventions.

Kaufmann's theory cannot, however, be accepted,[2] because it does not take into account the results of literary criticism, the findings of the history of traditions and the achievements of historical criticism. The book of Joshua cannot be regarded as the work of a single author writing at the beginning of the period of the Judges in the style of the Deuteronomist. It is also not possible to accept that so little time elapsed between the events described. The way in which they are described is also indicative of more than one author. The biggest section of the story of the conquest is occupied by the accounts of the taking of Jericho and Ai (Jos 2–8) and these accounts can only be the end-product of a long traditional development. Kaufmann also minimises the importance of elements which contradict his theory or else ignores them completely. Among these elements are the treaty with the Gibeonites, the situation at Shechem and the fact that the conquest was not

---

[2] O. Eissfeldt, 'Die Eroberung Palästinas durch Altisrael', *WO*, 2 (1954–1959), pp. 158–171; A. Alt, 'Utopien', *TLZ*, 81 (1956), col 521–528; J. Bright, *Early Israel in Recent History Writing*, London, 1956, pp. 56–78.

completed. It is paradoxical to date the description of the tribes and the lists of cities (Jos 13–19) to the period of Joshua. Finally, Kaufmann does not consider at all the extrabiblical and archaeological evidence.

2. The theory of A.Alt and M. Noth

A. Alt and M. Noth have put forward a hypothesis based on the history of traditions and of territorial distribution[3] which is diametrically opposed to that suggested by Kaufmann.

The change that took place in the population of Canaan with the arrival of the Israelites did not basically affect the distribution of larger and smaller territorial units. It is in fact possible to explain how they settled in Canaan if we compare the situation that existed in the country before their arrival and the situation after they had settled there. From the beginning of the second millennium (according to the literary evidence of Egyptian execration texts) or from the beginning of the third millennium onwards (according to archaeological finds), Canaan had been divided into a great number of city-states. This situation had not changed under Egyptian rule, but disorder prevailed when Egypt lost power. This occurred in the Amarna period. The situation in the plains, where most of the city-states were grouped, was different from that in the hill districts, where there were fewer city-states and bigger states had developed. Hazor was the great state in the north during the period of Egyptian domination, Shechem was the state in central Canaan and the Garu mentioned in the Amarna letters was possibly the state in the hill country of Judah. With the collapse of Egyptian rule, the situation changed completely. New states bearing the names of peoples – Edom, Moab and Ammon in Transjordania and Judah-Israel and Philistia in Cisjordan – appeared in Canaan. The older system of city-states continued on the fringe – there was a line of Canaanite cities from Acco to Beth-shean and another from Gezer to Jerusalem which included the Gibeonite tetrapolis. The Israelite tribes first entered Canaan for the most part peacefully. There were local exceptions, of course, but, generally speaking, they infiltrated, in search of new pasture for their flocks and herds, into the lands which were not incorporated into the system of city-states or were less heavily populated. This peaceful settlement is con-

---

[3] A. Alt, *Die Landnahme der Israeliten in Palästina*, Leipzig, 1925 = *Kleine Schriften*, I, pp. 89–125; 'Josua', *Werden und Wesen des Alten Testaments* (*BZAW*, 66), 1936, pp. 13–29 = *Kleine Schriften*, I, pp. 176–192; 'Erwägungen über die Landnahme der Israeliten in Palästina', *PJB*, 35 (1939), pp. 8–63 = *Kleine Schriften*, I, pp. 126–175; M. Noth, *Das Buch Josua* (*HAT*),[2] 1953; *Geschichte*, pp. 67–82. This theory has been taken up again by M. Weippert in *Die Landnahme der israelitischen Stämme in der neueren wissenschaftlichen Diskussion*, Göttingen, 1967, pp. 14–51.

firmed by various data provided in the Bible itself, especially, for example, the treaty with the Gibeonites and the absence of fighting in central Palestine.

The question that arises, then, is where did the tradition of the 'conquest' come from? Each of the conquest stories in Jos 2–11 is connected with a particular place. They are aetiological stories, in other words, they explain the origin of or the reasons for a situation which had existed 'until this day', that is, until the time of the narrator. An attempt is made to explain, for example, why Jericho was in ruins, why Ai was called 'a ruin' and why there was a great cairn near the ruined city gate and why the cave near Makkedah had its entrance closed with great stones.

No part or almost no part at all was played in this by Joshua. He was an Ephraimite and originally had nothing to do with traditions which were not connected with his own tribe. According to A. Alt,[4] Joshua figured originally in Jos 10:10–14, which is not an aetiological text and which describes events that took place in Ephraimite territory. Joshua's authority was confirmed in this local victory and this enabled him to act as arbitrator in tribal disputes (Jos 17:14–18, in which only the 'house of Joseph' was involved). He may also have played this part in the pact at Shechem (Jos 24). Finally, it has been suggested that he was Moses' successor. M. Noth believes also that he did not originally figure in Jos 10, but that his name may have replaced that of a local hero. He may, in Noth's opinion, have been connected with the events described in Jos 17:14–18 and he certainly played an important part in uniting the tribes (Jos 24) and it was from this point that he entered the other traditions in the book of Joshua.

The peaceful settlement of the Israelites in the less populated regions of Canaan and their transition from a semi-nomadic to an agrarian way of life took place uneventfully and left no deep impressions on tradition, Noth believed. Their occupation of Canaan (the *Landnahme*) took a long time and fighting broke out again and again with the Canaanites whenever the clans already occupying the country tried to extend their territory by seizing land from the city-states that surrounded them. This period of intermittent war was that of the settlement proper (the *Landesausbau*). Noth tried to establish precisely how each tribe took possession of and settled in its land by considering carefully the territory assigned to each of the tribes and evaluating the few data provided in the Bible. He concluded that the occupation took a very long time and the movements differed according to the groups of people and the parts of the country. He believed that it was impossible to give precise dates and that it was only possible to suggest the approximate beginning, the second half of the fourteenth century B.C., after the Amarna period, and the approximate end of this occupation, round

[4] A.Alt, 'Josua', quoted in the previous note.

about 1100 B.C. It is possible, however, that two hundred years is too long a time and that the occupation began in the thirteenth century B.C.

Noth believed that the conclusions that he had drawn from the internal evidence of the Bible were not affected in any way by external, archaeological evidence.[5] In support of their argument in favour of a military conquest of Canaan, many scholars have appealed to the destruction at the end of the thirteenth century of certain Canaanite cities mentioned in the book of Joshua. These ruins may, however, have resulted from the repeated struggles that took place between the cities of Canaan themselves or possibly, from 1200 onwards, from the Sea Peoples' attacks. Noth was convinced that the archaeological evidence had to be subjected to as close a scrutiny as the textual evidence and that each case had to be considered separately. Jericho, for example, had been destroyed in the 14th century and was deserted during what is generally assumed to be the period of Joshua. Ai was in ruins from the second half of the third millennium B.C. onwards and Bethel was destroyed towards the end of the thirteenth century, although, according to Judges 1:22–26, it was taken without fighting, through treason on the part of an inhabitant. Lachish (Tell ed-Duweir) and Debir, if Debir is really Tell Beit Mirsim, were destroyed during the last quarter of the thirteenth century B.C., but the conquest of Lachish and Debir is attributed to Joshua only in the list given in Jos 10:28–30. Joshua concluded a pact with the inhabitants of Gibeon according to the Old Testament, but no remains of any Late Bronze town have been discovered in the excavations at el-Jîb. Noth accepted only one positive archaeological contribution – the destruction of Hazor and the burning of the town at the end of the thirteenth century, which have been borne out by the excavations carried out at the site and are at the same time in accordance with the account given in Jos 11:10–13. To be more precise, Noth upheld the historical authenticity of this account on the basis of his assessment of the internal evidence, but rejected as aetiological the accounts of the destruction of Jericho and Ai. The archaeological evidence, in his opinion, did not confirm the historicity of the Joshua accounts of the conquest – it only really confirmed the results of literary criticism.

This hypothesis that the Israelites occupied Canaan peacefully, at least to begin with, has recently been taken up again by M. Weippert, with certain modifications. He concluded[6] that the first, peaceful settlement was carried out by the tribes of the group of Leah and those associated with it, the groups of Bilhah and Zilpah. The group of Rachel, which introduced the

---

[5] M. Noth, 'Grundsätzliches zur geschichtlichen Deutung archäologischer Befunde auf dem Boden Palästinas,' *PJB*, 34 (1938), pp. 1–22; 'Hat die Bibel doch Recht?', *Festschrift G. Dehn*, Neukirchen and Vluyn, 1957, pp. 8–22; 'Der Beitrag der Archäologie zur Geschichte Israels', *Congress Volume, Oxford* (*STV*, 7), 1960, pp. 262–282.

[6] M. Weippert, *op. cit.* (note 3), especially the conclusion, p. 140.

cult of Yahweh and the idea of the holy war, came later, in Weippert's opinion, and initiated the period of armed occupation which plays such an important part in the texts. Weippert, in other words, re-emphasised the traditions of the house of Joseph concerning an armed conquest of Canaan and the part played by Joshua.

The theory of a peaceful occupation has also been sharply criticised.[7] Some of these criticisms are not justified – it is, for example, wrong to call the attitude taken by Alt and Noth 'nihilistic' simply because their positive solution is not in accordance with the impression gained from reading the biblical texts themselves. The two most serious criticisms of this theory, however, are that Alt and Noth appear to have recourse too frequently to aetiology and that they either neglect or minimise the external evidence provided by archaeology.

Several recent authors have thrown a good deal of light on the concept of aetiology.[8] The word means the 'study of causes', but nowadays it is used almost exclusively for a branch of medical science concerned with the causes of diseases. In biblical studies since Gunkel, the texts which provide an explanation for the name of a person, a nation or a place, for a natural event, a monument, a custom or a rite which has existed 'until this day' have been called 'aetiological'. These texts are a natural answer to the question 'why?' and etymological, cultic, historical and ethnological aetiologies are frequently found in the earliest texts of the Bible, but much less frequently in the later texts. Close parallels to the biblical aetiologies are also found in other literatures.

The phenomenon is diverse and complex. What is very often implied in the use of the word 'aetiology' is an invented explanation. Originally, however, the reply was regarded as just as serious as the question. The narrator certainly regarded it as true. Childs has proved convincingly that the formula 'until this day' only very rarely had the aetiological function of justifying an existing fact. In most cases, it simply served as a personal testimony which was added to a tradition which the narrator was reporting and which was confirmed by his testimony. What is more, the aetiological

[7] W. F. Albright 'The Israelite Conquest of Canaan in the Light of Archaeology', *BASOR*, 74 (April 1939), pp. 11–23, and the works mentioned in note 9; Y. Kaufmann, *The Biblical Account, op. cit.*, pp. 70–74; J. Bright, *Early Israel*, pp. 79–110.

[8] J. Bright, *Early Israel*, pp. 91–100; J. Fichtner, 'Die Ätiologie in den Namengebungen der geschichtlichen Bücher des Alten Testaments', *VT*, 6 (1959), pp. 372–396; I. L. Seeligmann, 'Aetiological Elements in Biblical Historiography', *Zion*, 26 (1961), pp. 141–169 (in Hebrew, with an English summary); B. S. Childs, 'A Study of the Formula "Until this Day" ', *JBL*, 82 (1963), pp. 279–292; A. Ibañez Arana, 'La narración etiológica como género literario bíblico. Las etiologías etimológicas del Pentateuco', *Scriptorium Victoriense* (Victoria, Spain), 10 (1963), pp. 161–176, 241–275; C. Westermann, 'Arten der Erzählung in der Genesis', *Forschung am Alten Testament*, Munich, 1964, pp. 39–47; S. Mowinckel, *Tetrateuch – Pentateuch – Hexateuch (BZAW, 90)*, 1964, Excursus pp. 78–86; B. O. Long, *The Problem of Etiological Narrative in the Old Testament (BZAW, 108)*, 1968.*

elements usually referred only to certain details in the narrative. An example of this is the mention of cairns and great stones. Achan's tomb and the tomb of the king of Ai were marked by cairns which had lasted 'until this day' (Jos 7:26; 8:29) and both references occur at the end of the stories of the violation of the ban under which Jericho had been placed and of the taking of the city of Ai. There is also the case of the cave with its mouth closed by great stones 'until this day' (Jos 10:27) at the end of the story of the war against the five Amorite kings. But, since there were so many cairns and caves with stones blocking their mouths in Canaan, why was it especially necessary to explain these two cairns and this one cave, when no tradition had originally been connected with these places? What has to be recognised is that, in many of these stories, the aetiological elements were later and also that there are very few stories which were solely aetiological. It can be said in general that, if there had never been any fighting between the Israelites and the Canaanites and if there had never been any armed conquest, there would never have been any need to explain these local phenomena in this way. The aetiological aspect of a story does not of necessity make it into a fiction. The historical authenticity of a tradition is not dependent on the aetiological elements that may be attached to it.

Alt and Noth have also been criticised for not taking the external evidence sufficiently into account, especially archaeological evidence. In fact, neither Alt nor Noth entirely overlook the findings of archaeology, but they are certainly critical of the evidence produced and the conclusions drawn by archaeologists. Their criticism may be too negative, but it is a healthy counterbalance to the excessive dependence on archaeology that characterises the theory that we are now about to examine.

3. W. F. Albright's theory[9]

Albright was of the opinion that, however difficult the story of the conquest of Canaan might be because of the uncertainty of the biblical accounts, it was undoubtedly possible to say that a conquest really took place and to establish the approximate date (the second half of the thirteenth century) on the basis of archaeological evidence. The last Canaanite cities, Debir (Tell Beit Mirsim) and Bethel, were destroyed, he believed, in the thirteenth century. Lachish was destroyed round about 1220 B.C. and the last occupation during the Late Bronze Age at Hazor ceased at the end of the thirteenth century. In each of these cases, these important Canaanite

---

[9] In addition to *BASOR*, 74 (April 1939), mentioned above in note 7 and to the detailed articles on various biblical sites, see *The Biblical Period from Abraham to Ezra,* New York, 1963, pp. 24–34; *Archaeology, Historical Analogy and Early Biblical Tradition*, Baton Rouge, 1966, pp. 3–21.

cities were followed, with or without an interruption in habitation, by a much less prosperous form of occupation. They were, in other words, settled by Israelites, who may also have been responsible for their destruction. There is, in Albright's view, no valid evidence against the destruction of Jericho in the fourteenth century – the last Late Bronze layers were eroded by the wind and the rain during the four centuries between the destruction of the city by Joshua and its reoccupation at the time of Ahab. In the biblical tradition, Albright thought, the story of the capture of the neighbouring city of Bethel was transferred to the 'ruins' of Ai. Shechem and Gibeon played an important part in the stories of the book of Joshua, but they were not conquered – the Israelites found kinsmen there and these became their allies. The theory of a gradual and peaceful entry into Canaan on the part of nomadic groups of Israelites was rejected by Albright. He remained convinced that the Israelites conquered Canaan and that Joshua played a part in that conquest, although his part was certainly magnified by tradition, in which conquests that took place later were ascribed to him.

Albright's conclusions have been widely accepted, especially in America by his own disciples, who have completed them in many respects or added to them certain shades of meaning or emphasis. G. E. Wright, for example,[10] has tried to reconcile the account given in Jos 1–11 with that of Judges 1 by appealing to Albright's theory. In his view, Joshua attacked only a certain number of key cities in the south of Canaan and the conquest was completed later by local engagements. J. Bright[11] followed very much the same line, but laid less emphasis on the importance of the archaeological evidence, which he believed could not be regarded as absolute, although it did tip the balance in favour of the historical authenticity of the biblical accounts. Bright called this the 'balance of probability', a conclusion which was also accepted by J. A. Soggin,[12] and Bright himself concluded that 'However complicated the Israelites' occupation of Palestine may have been and however schematised the narrative of Joshua may have been, it may be regarded as certain that a violent irruption into the land took place late in the thirteenth century'. More recently, P. Lapp[13] has carefully examined the results of archaeological excavations in Palestine and Transjordan and

---

[10] G. E. Wright, *The Westminster Historical Atlas to the Bible,*[2] Philadelphia, 1956, pp. 39–40; *Biblical Archaeology,*[2] Philadelphia, 1962, pp. 69–84; 'Archaeology, History and Theology', *Harvard Divinity School Bulletin,* 28 (1964), pp. 85–96; 'The Literary and Historical Problem of Joshua 10 and Judges 1', *JNES,* 5 (1946), pp. 105–114.

[11] J. Bright, *Early History,* pp. 87–89; *History,* pp. 117–120.

[12] J. A. Soggin, 'Ancient Biblical Traditions and Modern Archaeological Discoveries', *BibArch,* 23 (1960), pp. 95–100; 'Alttestamentliche Glaubenszeugnisse und geschichtliche Wirklichkeit', *TZ,* 17 (1961), pp. 385–398, especially pp. 396–397.

[13] P. Lapp, 'The Conquest of Palestine in the Light of Archaeology', *Concordia Theological Monthly,* 38 (1967), pp. 283–300; *Biblical Archaeology and History,* New York and Cleveland, 1969, pp. 107–111.

has admitted that Albright and his disciples may have exaggerated the importance of the archaeological evidence. On the other hand, however, he has affirmed that he feels more inclined to accept this solution than Noth's, because it is more in accordance with the biblical tradition.

In contrast to the complete agreement of some scholars and the more reserved acceptance of another, various specialists in the Old Testament, in particular M. Noth himself and M. Weippert,[14] have opposed Albright's theory. Noth and Weippert believe that there are no archaeological facts as such, but only interpreted facts. Because no written documents have been found among the ruins excavated, archaeology can tell us nothing about the causes of the destruction of these cities or about who destroyed them. They may have been destroyed by an earthquake, a fire or enemy attack. In the latter case, the enemy may not have come from outside the country, especially during a period of purely nominal Egyptian rule and constant strife between the different cities. If the enemy was in fact a foreign invader, it should not be forgotten that the Israelites were not the only people who were entering Canaan at that time. There were also the Sea Peoples. This period was in fact one of great change in the whole of the eastern basin of the Mediterranean and it is not easy to define the precise part played by the Israelites. The clash that took place between different societies at the end of the Late Bronze Period and the beginning of the Iron Age cannot be taken as evidence of an Israelite invasion. It was a general phenomenon and it was not necessarily the Israelites who caused this change in the whole social and political structure in Canaan – they simply benefited from it. As a result, there can be little weight in the archaeological evidence to tip the 'balance of probability' in favour of an armed conquest of Canaan by the Israelites. The last word, then, must remain with literary criticism and the history of traditions, which also had the first word.

The most serious criticisms of Albright's theory, which is based almost entirely on archaeological evidence, have come, however, from archaeologists themselves, including several who have excavated the sites. Kathleen Kenyon's final opinion with regard to Jericho is: 'It is impossible to associate the destruction of Jericho with such a date (from the exodus to the thirteenth century B.C.). The town may have been destroyed by one of the other Hebrew groups, the history of whose infiltrations is, as generally recognised, complex. Alternatively, the placing at Jericho of a dramatic siege and capture may be an aetiological explanation of a ruined city. Archaeology cannot provide the answer.'[15] In the case of Ai, Judith

<hr />

[14] M. Noth, 'Der Beitrag der Archäologie' (note 5); M. Weippert, *Die Landnahme*, (Note 3), pp. 124–132.

[15] K. M. Kenyon, *Archaeology and Old Testament Study*, ed. D. Winton Thomas, Oxford, 1967, p. 273; see also her assistant in the excavation, H. J. Franken, 'Tel es-Sultan and Old Testament Jericho', *OTS*, 14 (1965), pp. 189–200.

Marquet-Krause has concluded that chapters 7 and 8 of the book of Joshua, which might possibly have been regarded as historical, in fact form part of a legend.[16] The last archaeologist to take part in excavations at Ai, J. Callaway, believes that the long account of the taking of the town in the Bible is based simply on the seizure by the Israelites, after they had settled in Canaan, of a little village founded by other immigrants on the ruins of the Early Bronze city of Ai. He has concluded that it can no longer be regarded as an established fact that the conquest of Canaan by the Israelites included the destruction of the Late Bronze towns at Lachish, Tell Beit Mirsim or Hazor.[17] Finally, J. B. Pritchard is convinced that, on the basis of existing archaeological evidence, there was no city of any importance at the time of Joshua on the site of Gibeon. He has concluded that 'the apparent anomalies found in the archaeological results derived from the three sites which figure so prominently in the narratives in the first part of the book of Joshua (Jericho, Ai and Gibeon) suggest that we have reached an impasse on the question of supporting the traditional view of the conquest with archaeological undergirding'.[18]

4. G. E. Mendenhall's theory[19]

Since there would seem to be no way of reconciling the opposition between the theory suggested by Alt and Noth and that of Albright, G. E. Mendenhall has approached the question from a different point of view and put forward an original hypothesis. The ancestors of the Israelites were, he believes, not nomads or even semi-nomadic people. What is more, before the coming of the great camel-breeding tribes, the contrast between nomadic people and those living in villages did not exist in the Ancient Near East. The so-called nomads were in fact, according to Mendenhall, shepherds and herdsmen associated with the life of the villages. The 'tribe' was not the result of genealogical descent. It was a social unit which went beyond the purely village group. On the one hand, the members of the 'tribe' were loyal to their social unit and, on the other, the unit protected them collectively. The conflict was not between settled farmers and semi-nomadic herdsmen, but between villagers and city-dwellers. This conflict also existed in Canaan, where the Habiru/Hebrews formed groups subject to the authority of the cities. In the Bible, the Israelites are treated as the

[16] J. Marquet-Krause, Les fouilles de 'Ay (Et-Tell), Paris, 1949, p. 24.
[17] J. Callaway, 'New Evidence on the Conquest of 'Ai', JBL, 87 (1968), pp. 312–320.
[18] J. B. Pritchard, 'Culture and History', The Bible in Modern Scholarship, ed. J. P. Hyatt, Nashville and New York, 1965, pp. 319.
[19] G. E. Mendenhall, 'The Hebrew Conquest of Palestine', BibArch, 25 (1962), pp. 66–87.

same as the Habiru and therefore have the same origin as the Habiru. There was, Mendenhall believes, no movement of peoples or large-scale immigration, but a revolt among the peasants, the farmers and herdsmen, against the Canaanites who lived in the city-states. This conflict was brought to a head by the arrival of a group of prisoners who had escaped from Egypt and who were at the same time united in their belief in a new god, Yahweh, with whom they had entered into a covenant and to whom they attributed all the characteristics of human rulers. When these people reached the west bank of the Jordan and entered Canaan, all the various resistance movements in the country became polarised – kings were expelled or killed and cities were destroyed. Israel, in other words, was, in Mendenhall's opinion, not an ethnic group which became a religious community. It was, on the contrary, a religious community which, in the course of time, acquired a degree of ethnic unity by marriage within the community and by resistance to ethnic additions from outside the community.

Relatively few scholars have criticised this theory,[20] but it is certainly difficult to accept. It disregards, for example, the conviction which was fundamental and constant in Israel, namely that the people were strangers to the population of Canaan and that they lived as shepherds and herdsmen for a long time. Mendenhall has also overlooked not only the tradition of the sojourn in the desert that followed the exodus from Egypt, but also the whole tradition of the patriarchs. This is in accordance with what we know about the Syrian nomads in the second millennium from the Mari documents. Mendenhall, however, gives a false picture of these nomads. Furthermore, his idea of the tribe as based on a community of interest and religion and not on blood ties is quite contrary to all the biblical data and all modern sociological analyses.[21] It is also difficult to justify the claim that the Israelites were the same as the Habiru. What is more, the Habiru of the Amarna period did not play the part that Mendenhall ascribes to them.

Some aspects of Mendenhall's theory, however, are worthy of serious consideration. The group of people who brought faith in Yahweh from the desert into Canaan formed only part of the future people of Israel. They had a certain ethnic unity, however, and gathered around them related groups of people who had come from outside Canaan and had already settled there. Mendenhall's hypothesis most probably holds good for some of the northern tribes. These people had probably become closely intermingled with the Canaanites and were the hired servants of various princes.

[20] The only justified criticisms that I know are those of M. Weippert, *Die Landnahme, op. cit.*, pp. 59–123; P. Lapp, *Concordia Theological Monthly, op. cit.* (note 13), pp. 298–299. I have not been able to study J. A. Soggin's criticism in the appendix to his article, 'La conquista israelitica della Palestina nei sc. XIII e XII e le scoperte archeologiche', *Protestantismo*, 17 (1962), pp. 194–208.

[21] For the Arabs in particular, see T. Ashkenazi, 'La tribu arabe: ses éléments', *Anthropos*, 41–44 (1946–1949), pp. 657–672.

It is also quite possible that they rose against these rulers when Joshua's group arrived in Canaan. It was this group which brought the religion of Yahweh and the ideology of the holy war. (We shall be returning to this question later.)

In the meantime, we may conclude that the controversy is concerned with two opposing views. Alt and Noth have based their opinion primarily on the internal evidence of the Bible itself, whereas Albright and his school have developed a theory which makes almost exclusive use of external, archaeological evidence. This controversy between the men of the texts, the literary critics, and the men of the monuments, the archaeologists, is not, of course, confined to this particular problem or even to the interpretation of Old Testament history in general. It extends to other spheres as well and it is especially interesting in this context to compare the opposing views outlined here in connection with Israel's settlement in Canaan with the debate between those scholars who have defended the historical authenticity of the Trojan War and those who have rejected it. The different stages which separate this war from the 'canonical' edition of the Iliad and the Odyssey in the sixth century B.C. cover as long a period and are of very much the same nature as the stages separating the 'conquest' of Canaan in the thirteenth century B.C. from the final editing of the book of Joshua by the Deuteronomist. In both controversies, the same points of disagreement are found expressed in strangely similar language.[22]

We are therefore bound to look for a solution to this problem which will take both the evidence of the texts and the archaeological evidence equally into account. The first task is to examine critically the textual and the archaeological evidence separately and then go on to consider each in the light of the other. We shall attempt to do this here, but our conclusions will be no more than hypothetical, because the origins of Israel, like the origins of all ancient peoples, are wrapped in obscurity. To a very great extent they are beyond the reach of the historian.[23]

[22] For the method in general and in particular with regard to this question, see my two articles: 'Method in the Study of Early Hebrew History', *The Bible in Modern Scholarship* (note 18), pp. 15–29, especially p. 29; in greater detail: 'On Right and Wrong Uses of Archaeology', *Near Eastern Archaeology in the Twentieth Century. Essays in Honor of Nelson Glueck*, ed. J. A. Sanders, Garden City, New York, 1970, pp. 64–80.
[23] See J. A. Soggin, 'Alttestamentliche Glaubenszeugnisse', *op. cit.* (note 12).

Chapter Sixteen

THE HISTORICAL FRAMEWORK

IF WE are to understand the phenomenon of the settlement of the
Israelites in Palestine, we must try to situate it within its historical
framework. It was an extremely troubled period of history, during
which a complete change took place in the Near East. Until that time, the
second millennium B.C. had been characterised by a struggle between the
great powers – Egypt, the Hittites, the Mitanni and Assyria – culminating
in a degree of balance brought about by the peace treaty between Ramses II
and Hattusilis III. In Syria-Palestine, Egypt and the Hittites were equally influential. During the particular period which we must consider in this
chapter, Egyptian rule came to an end in Syria, the Hittite Empire collapsed, the Sea Peoples invaded Palestine and the Assyrian Empire was
extended by military force towards the west, an expansion which was followed by a retreat. By the end of the period under review, Syria-Palestine
had assumed an entirely new appearance. Neo-Hittite kingdoms had been
established in northern Syria, Aramaean states were flourishing in central
Syria and Transjordan and the Phoenicians, the Philistines and the Israelites
who had settled in Palestine had become important sea powers.

I. The End of Egyptian Rule[1]

This period covers most of the Nineteenth Dynasty, the whole of the
Twentieth and the beginning of the Twenty-first Dynasties. Any detailed
chronology of this period inevitably depends on the precise date when

[1] Among the most recent works on this question are J. Černý, 'Egypt from the Death of
Ramesses III to the End of the Twenty-first Dynasty', *CAH*, II, XXXV, 1965; R. O.
Faulkner, 'Egypt from the Inception of the Nineteenth Dynasty to the Death of Ramesses
III', *CAH*, II, XXIII, 1966; J. Vercoutter, *Die Altorientalischen Reiche, II. Das Ende des 2. Jahr-
tausends (Fischer Weltgeschichte, 3)*, 1966, pp. 267–293; W. Helck, *Geschichte des Alten Ägypten
(Handbuch der Orientalistik, I, 1, 3)*, 1968, pp. 184–205. The special problem discussed in this

Ramses II began his long reign of sixty-six years and two months and this date has been disputed. If it is correct that the sign of a full moon corresponds to one day in the Egyptian calendars, then the two possible dates of Ramses' accession according to astronomical calculations are 1304 or 1290 B.C. Scholars are not in agreement about which of these dates is correct and opinions have varied frequently. In my opinion, there is more evidence in favour of 1290.[2] So far, no totally convincing arguments have been put forward,[3] but most scholars who have examined this question in recent years have come to accept this second date.[4]

On the basis of 1290 as the date of Ramses' coming to the throne, then, the peace concluded between the Egyptians and the Hittites in the twenty-first year of his reign would have occurred in 1269. It was respected by both sides and was strengthened thirteen years later by the marriage that took place between Ramses II and the eldest daughter of Hattusilis III. Later, Ramses II certainly married another of Hattusilis' daughters.[5] In 1224, Mer-ne-Ptah succeeded his father Ramses II and reigned at least until 1214, since there is evidence in the documents of the tenth year of his reign. He may even have reigned until as late as 1204, if the number of years of his reign attributed to him by Manetho is to be believed. The glorious years of the empire were over and Egypt had to adopt a defensive attitude. By the end of his aged father's reign, the Egyptians were less vigilant on their frontiers, their army had fallen into neglect and bands of Libyan marauders, driven from the west by hunger, had penetrated into the Delta. In the fifth year of Mer-ne-Ptah's reign,[6] the Libyans, led by their prince, Maraye, made a massive attack against Egypt. It is clear that they intended to settle in the Delta, because Maraye was accompanied on this expedition by his

---

section is considered in W. Helck, *Die Beziehungen Ägyptens zu Vorderasien im 3. und 2. Jahrtausend v. Chr.*, Wiesbaden, 1962, pp. 240–255; A. Malamat, 'The Decline of Egyptian Rule in Canaan', *The World History of the Jewish People* (Hebrew), II, 1967, pp. 139–147, notes 333–336.

[2] See especially E. Hornung's study *Untersuchungen zur Chronologie und Geschichte des Neuen Reiches*, Wiesbaden, 1964.

[3] K. A. Kitchen, *ChrEg*, 40 (1965), pp. 310–322 (a review of Hornung's study); *ChrEg*, 43 (1968), pp. 321–322 (a review of Redford's work); M. B. Rowton, 'The Material from Western Asia and the Chronology of the Nineteenth Dynasty of Egypt', *JNES*, 25 (1966), pp. 240–258.

[4] D. B. Redford, *History and Chronology of the Eighteenth Dynasty*, Toronto, 1967, pp. 183–208; J. von Beckerath, *ZDMG*, 118 (1968), pp. 18 ff; W. Helck, *Geschichte des Alten Ägypten*, 1968, p. 141. The date 1304, however, is favoured by H. L. Thomas, 'Archaeological Implications of Near Eastern Chronology', *Opuscula Atheniensa*, 8 (1968), pp. 11–12, especially pp. 21–22, because of the synchronisms with Mesopotamia.

[5] K. A. Kitchen and G. A. Gaballa, 'Ramesside Varia, II, 1. The Second Hittite Marriage of Ramesses II', *ZÄS*, 96 (1969), pp. 14–18.

[6] An attack which took place in the fourth year of his reign is mentioned in an Amad text; see A. Abd-el-Hamid Youssef, *ASAE*, 58 (1964), pp. 273–280, but this must be an error.

twelve wives and their children. The allies of the Libyans were the Meshwesh and the Qahaq, certain related tribes, and various groups of people from the north who had come by sea. This is the first reference in the Egyptian texts to the 'Sea Peoples', to whom we shall have to return later in this chapter. The allies were beaten and the prisoners were treated with a cruelty unusual in Egypt.

This victory was celebrated in several texts, but only one of them merits our attention here, the famous Israel stele discovered in 1895 by Flinders Petrie in the funerary temple of Mer-ne-Ptah at Thebes and housed now in Cairo Museum.[7] It is a commemorative hymn or series of hymns celebrating the victory over the Libyans. Nothing new is found on the stele that is not found elsewhere in the historical texts, but it expresses the relief felt by the Egyptians on being delivered from the threat of invasion, and the severe punishment inflicted on the prisoners shows how serious the danger was. The final text on the stele is a hymn which is not directly connected with the victory over the Libyans, but which celebrates the real or imaginary triumphs of the pharaoh:

> The princes are prostrate, saying 'Mercy!' (or 'peace', *shalam*)
>   Not one among the Nine Bows raises his head
> Desolation is for Tehenu (Libya); Hatti is pacified;
>   Plundered is the Canaan with every evil;
> Carried off is Ashkelon; seized upon is Gezer;
>   Yanoam is made as that which does not exist;
> Israel is laid waste, his seed is not;
>   Hurru is become a widow for Egypt!
> All lands together, they are pacified;
>   Everyone who was restless, he has been bound . . .

This is the first reference to Israel in an extrabiblical text. It is also the only reference to Israel in the whole of Egyptian literature. The text raises two problems for us. The first is, does it prove that Mer-ne-Ptah conducted a campaign in Palestine? The second is, what does this reference to Israel really mean? The possibility of a military expedition into Canaan led by Mer-ne-Ptah has been ruled out because the text is poetic and because it mentions Yanoam and Ashkelon, which are also found in the texts of Seti I and Ramses II. A military action in Canaan on the part of Mer-ne-Ptah is, however, confirmed by the title 'the one who reduced Gezer' on the Amada inscription.[8] We have already discussed the reference to Israel on this stele when we were considering the date of the exodus.[9] It is not

[7] Text in *ANET*, pp. 376–378; illustrations in *ANEP*, Nos. 342–343.
[8] J. Breasted, *ARE*, III, § 606; better: *ASAE*, 58 (1964), p. 273 ff.
[9] See above, p. 390.

possible to conclude from this text that there was a military engagement against Israel conducted by Mer-ne-Ptah. Quite apart from the fact that there is no reference to such an engagement anywhere in the Old Testament, the hymn itself is written in conventional and stereotyped language and the obvious intention is to maintain the fiction that Egypt was effectively ruling Canaan, hence the stylised phrases attached to Ashkelon, Gezer and Yanoam.

The reference to the Hittites (Hatti) alongside the Libyans (Tehenu) at the beginning of the hymn has led some scholars to believe that Mer-ne-Ptah also fought the Hittites or that the Hittites at least encouraged the Libyans and the Sea Peoples to attack Egypt. All that the text tells us, however, is that the Hittites were at peace. What is more, the most extensive historical text that we have relating to the war against the Libyans also says that Mer-ne-Ptah sent wheat to the Hittites who were suffering from famine.[10] It was clearly advisable for the two states to be reconciled as they were both threatened by the Sea Peoples and had to make a common stand against them. The sword marked with Mer-ne-Ptah's scroll which was discovered at Ras Shamrah, where it had been sent as a gift, is also evidence of the interest that this pharaoh took in affairs in the north.[11]

Apart from the Israel stele, there are other documents which show that Mer-ne-Ptah retained some degree of control over Syria-Palestine. We have in our possession, for example, a report by an Egyptian official on the eastern frontier of the country dating back to the third year of Mer-ne-Ptah's reign.[12] He states that, in the space of eleven days, he saw two messengers leaving Egypt and bearers of three communications, one of which was destined for the prince of Tyre. Another entry in this official's diary refers to an officer coming from the springs of Mer-ne-Ptah 'which are in the hills'. Attempts have been made to locate this site at the Waters of Nephtoah, mei neph'tôah, which are given in Jos 15:9; 18:15 as the point on the frontier between Judah and Benjamin and now known as Liftah, near Jerusalem, which would at that time have been an Egyptian post.[13] This hypothesis is, however, difficult to maintain[14] and the name probably refers to a spring on the military road between Egypt and Gaza. As in the time of the Middle Kingdom, groups of herdsmen looking for better pasture for their flocks and herds were allowed to enter Egypt – in a schoolboys' model letter dating back to the eighth year of Mer-ne-Ptah's reign, there is

[10] Great inscription at Karnak, line 24: J. Breasted, ARE, III, §580; cf. G. A. Wainwright, 'Merneptah's Aid to the Hittites', JEA, 46 (1960), pp. 24–28.

[11] C. F. A. Schaeffer, Ugaritica, III, Paris, 1956, pp. 169–178.

[12] ANET, pp. 258–259; R. A. Caminos, Late Egyptian Miscellanies, London, 1954, pp. 108–113.

[13] M. Noth, Das Buch Josua (HAT),³ 1953, p. 88; J. Gray, Joshua, Judges and Ruth (The Century Bible), 1967, p. 143; Y. Aharoni, The Land of the Bible, 1967, p. 173.

[14] D. Leibel, Yediot, 28 (1964), pp. 255–256 (Hebrew).

evidence of the entry and the registration of the clans of the Shasu of Edom at Mer-ne-Ptah's fortress.[15] It frequently happened that slaves escaped from Egypt and searches were made beyond the frontiers.[16] There is also archaeological evidence of the presence of the Egyptians. Among the finds that have been made in Palestine are a portable sundial bearing the scroll of Mer-ne-Ptah, discovered at Gezer,[17] a bowl with a hieratic inscription dating back to the fourth year and probably Mer-ne-Ptah's, found at Tell ed-Duweir (Lachish) [18] and a citadel built at Beth-shan, probably during the reign of Mer-ne-Ptah.[19] All this evidence is, however, confined to those places where the Egyptians maintained garrisons. The safety of the country was less certain where there were no such garrisons. One text, written for the use of schoolboys, gives an exaggerated and amusing account of the misadventures suffered by a royal messenger crossing Canaan by the extremely bad roads infested with thieving bedouins.[20]

Mer-ne-Ptah was followed by several less important pharaohs. The last ruler of the Nineteenth Dynasty was Queen Ta-Usert, who reigned at the beginning of the twelfth century B.C., the exact dates of her reign being unknown. A vase with her name has been found at Deir 'Alla.[21] The end of this dynasty was chaotic. According to the historical conclusion of the Harris Great Papyrus,[22] an Asiatic named Irsu ruled the country. Irsu[23] may have been another name for the great chancellor Bay, who was probably a foreigner and who exercised great power at the end of the dynasty.[24]

The founder of the Twentieth Dynasty, Set-nakht, resumed control, but, after ruling for only two years, handed over power to his son Ramses III, who reigned for thirty-two years. There is no certainty regarding the precise dates of this pharaoh's reign, but, according to the most recent suggestions, he ruled from about 1184 until about 1153 B.C.[25] Ramses III was the last of the great warrior pharaohs and his reign formed a brilliant end to

---

[15] *ANET*, p. 259a; R. A. Caminos, *op. cit.*, pp. 293–296; W. Helck, *VT*, 15 (1965), pp. 38–40. This letter could not have been written during the reign of Seti II, as Caminos and others claim, because his reign only lasted for six years.

[16] *ANET*, p. 259b; R. A. Caminos, *op, cit.*, pp. 254–258.

[17] E. J. Pilcher, 'Portable Sundial from Gezer', *PEFQS*, 1923, pp. 85–89.

[18] O. Tufnell, *Lachish IV*, London, 1958, p. 133.

[19] For the date, see B. Maisler, *BIES*, 16 (1951), pp. 14–19 (Hebrew).

[20] Anastasi Papyrus, I, transl. *ANET*, pp. 475–479. For the date, see A. Gardiner, *Egypt and the Pharaohs*, Oxford, 1961, p. 274; R. O. Faulkner, *op. cit.* (note 1), p. 21.

[21] J. Yoyotte, *VT*, 12 (1962), pp. 464–469.

[22] J. Breasted, *ARE*, IV, § 398.

[23] There is evidence of this personal name at Ras Shamrah and in Egypt; see W. A. Ward, *JNES*, 20 (1961), pp. 32–33.

[24] A. Gardiner, *Egypt of the Pharaohs*, p. 282; J. Yoyotte, *VT*, 12 (1962), p. 468; W. Helck, *Geschichte*, p. 191 and note; see above, p. 300.

[25] This is the date which E. Hornung has given to the reign of Ramses III. J. Vercoutter has suggested 1182–1151 and W. Helck, *Geschichte*, 1183–1152.

the Egyptian Empire. He consciously imitated his glorious predecessor Ramses II, even to the extent of having his military achievements narrated and illustrated in exactly the same way on his funerary temple at Medinet Habu. These inscriptions contain, for example, several lists of conquered countries which almost exactly copy the lists of countries conquered by Ramses II and Thut-mose III. They are important because they provide us with a certain amount of historical information.

In the fifth year of the reign of Ramses III, there was a war against the Libyans, who were trying, as they had done during the reign of Mer-ne-Ptah, to occupy the Nile Delta. The Peoples of the Sea are not mentioned in this context, apart from one text in the inscriptions of Medinet Habu, in which the two campaigns of the fifth and the eighth years of Ramses III's reign are merged together.[26] The enemies of the Egyptians were beaten in this first campaign. The danger confronting the Egyptians in the eighth year, however, was much more serious. Arriving all along the coast in boats and convoys, the Peoples of the Sea made a powerful thrust into the interior, but were beaten both at sea and on land. The reliefs at Medinet Habu show an extremely vivid naval battle, but the text accompanying these reliefs is not only stilted, but also very imprecise, with the result that historians have been unable to agree about where these sea and land battles took place. Some scholars believe that they occurred in Syria and off the Syrian coast as far north as Arvad. Others have suggested, on the other hand, the frontier of Egypt, the mouths of the Nile and along the southern coast of Palestine as the most likely site. (We shall be returning to this problem when we deal specifically with the Sea Peoples.) Some of the conquered peoples, the Philistines and the Zakkala at least, settled in Palestine, or rather were settled there by Ramses III, who entrusted them with the maintenance of these territories, which nonetheless remained under Egyptian rule.

Ramses III had also to repel a fresh attack by the Libyans in the eleventh year of his reign. Accompanied by the Meshwesh and five tribes not mentioned elsewhere, the Libyans, after achieving some initial successes, were finally driven back, in a decisive battle fought on the edge of the western desert. Battle scenes in Syria, Hatti and Amurru are also illustrated on the reliefs of Medinet Habu. It is generally believed that these campaigns are without any historical basis and the battle scenes are regarded as copies of the battles fought by Ramses II. Nonetheless, the scenes portrayed in Syria also appear in the little temple of Mut at Karnak. There is more certainty regarding a campaign against the Shasu of Seir, which is mentioned in the Harris Papyrus,[27] although the campaign took place in the desert close to

[26] W. F. Edgerton and J. A. Wilson, *Historical Records of Ramses III*, Chicago, 1936, pp. 19–34.
[27] J. Breasted, *ARE*, IV, § 404.

Egypt and to the south of Palestine. Egypt furthermore continued to exploit the copper mines in the 'Arabah, as during the reigns of Seti I and Ramses II.[28]

The Egyptians also made their presence felt at various strategic points in the rest of Canaan. Beth-shean, for example, had a garrison and some of the troops stationed there were mercenaries drawn from the Sea Peoples. The commander of this garrison was called Ramses-Weser-Khepesh – the name is inscribed on blocks of stone coming from his home and these blocks also bear the scroll of Ramses III.[29] The pharaoh's statue was also at Bethshean.[30] An ivory model pencase has been found at Megiddo; this is in the name of a 'royal envoy to all foreign countries' and bears the scroll of Ramses III.[31] This scroll is also found on a fragment of vase found at Gezer.[32] Scarabs of Ramses III have also been collected at Beth Shemesh and Tell el-Fār'ah (the southern site), as well as at Lachish. According to the Harris Great Papyrus, Ramses III had a funerary temple built for himself near a temple of Amon at Gaza. The income from nine Canaanite towns was offered to Amon.[33]

This Great Papyrus was revised at the death of Ramses III and placed in his tomb. The pharaoh died in 1153, in the thirty-second year of his reign. He was followed by eight kings bearing the same name (Ramses IV to Ramses XI) and Egypt's power declined very rapidly during their reigns. All her Asiatic possessions were lost at this time. It is, of course, true that scarabs of Ramses IV have been found at Tell es-Safī, Tell ez-Zakarīyeh and Gezer; a scarab of Ramses XI has been found at the southern site of Tell el-Fār'ah; and an enamelled plaquette of Ramses IX (or perhaps Ramses X) has been discovered at Gezer. These objects are, however, of no significance. More important is the base of a bronze statue of Ramses VI (dating back to about 1140 B.C.) unearthed at Megiddo.[34] This is the last evidence of the presence of the Egyptians in Canaan. It was also during the reign of Ramses VI that the turquoise mines of Sinai ceased to be exploited and Egypt's frontier was taken back to the Suez isthmus.

The country experienced a serious internal crisis in the second half of the reign of Ramses XI, the last ruler of the twentieth dynasty. This was caused by the fact that the smouldering conflict between the central power in

---

[28] B. Rothenberg, *Bible et Terre Sainte,* 123 (July-August, 1970), pp. 6–14.

[29] Frances M. James, *The Iron Age at Beth Shan,* Philadelphia, 1966; Appendix D by W. A. Ward, pp. 161–175.

[30] A. Rowe, *The Topography and History of Beth-Shan,* Philadelphia, 1930, p. 38 and Plate 51.

[31] G. Loud, *The Megiddo Ivories,* Chicago, 1939, p. 11 and Plate 62–63.

[32] R. A. S. Macalister, *The Excavations of Gezer,* II, London, 1912, p. 235 and Figure 388 (wrongly attributed to Ramses II).

[33] J. Breasted, *ARE,* IV, §§ 219, 384.

[34] G. Loud, *Megiddo II,* Chicago, 1948, p. 135.

Egypt and the high priests of Amon at Karnak burst into flame at this time. The high priest Heri-Hor seized power in Upper Egypt and, although he did not dare (apart from a few exceptions) to arrogate to himself the title of king, he did initiate a new era of dating. At the same time, another Egyptian, Ne-su-Ba-neb-Ded, whom historians since the time of Manetho have called Smendes, seized power in the Delta and took up his residence at Tanis. He too did not assume the title of king, although at that time the pharaoh's power was no more than nominal. Egypt had, in fact, ceased to be a great power.

We possess very interesting evidence of the weakening of Egypt's position at this period and the situation in Syria-Palestine in general in the form of a description of a journey undertaken by an official of the temple at Karnak, Wen-Amon.[35] It is a romanticised, but basically true story, written very soon after the events described in it. While Ramses XI was still on the throne, Wen-Amon was sent by Heri-Hor to Byblos to obtain wood for the repair or the remaking of the sacred barque of the god Amon. To increase his prestige when he undertook this mission, a statue of Amon-of-the-Road had been sent with him on the journey. He arrived at Tanis Dor. Beder, the Prince of Dor, treated him quite well, but refused to intervene in the case of one of his sailors who had stolen gold and silver from him. Wen-Amon left Dor on another ship belonging to the Zakkala (Tjeker). It seems from the text as though he was recompensed for his loss, but only by stealing from the Zakkala. After a short stay at Tyre, he arrived at Byblos. For a month, the king of Byblos, Zakar-Baal, refused to receive him and only agreed to do so after a young man who was possessed had insisted that he should receive him and his god. Zakar-Baal, however, continued to behave arrogantly towards Wen-Amon, saying that he was the master in his own country and that he would supply nothing without payment. Wen-Amon was therefore obliged to send a messenger to Egypt and to wait until a whole consignment of goods had arrived for the prince. He was finally given his timber and was about to leave Byblos, but, at that moment, some ships belonging to the Zakkala (Tjeker) came in to the port, clearly with the intention of recovering the silver Wen-Amon had taken. Zakar-Baal refused to arrest Wen-Amon, but sent him away in a ship, thus handing him over to his enemies. He did not, however, fall into their hands, but was driven by a storm on to the coast of Cyprus. The inhabitants wanted to kill him, but he sought justice from the Queen of Cyprus, Heteb. At this point, the narrative breaks off. It is clear from it that Egypt had lost

---

[35] *ANET*, pp. 25–29; G. Lefèbvre, *Romans et Contes Egyptiens,* Paris, 1949, pp. 204–220; J. Leclant, 'Les relations entre l'Egypte et la Phénicie du voyage d'Ounamon à l'expédition d'Alexandre', *The Role of the Phoenicians in the Interaction of Mediterranean Civilisations,* ed. W. Ward, Beirut, 1968, pp. 9–31.

both power and prestige at this time in Asia. Wen-Amon, the messenger of Amon, was badly treated at Dor, Byblos and Cyprus. It is obvious that the King of Byblos did not acknowledge Egypt's sovereign power and that he wanted to deal commercially with Egypt on an equal footing. The eastern Mediterranean, which had been an Egyptian sea, had become a sea infested by Syrian ships and the pirate ships of the Zakkala or Tjeker.

When Ramses XI died in about 1070 B.C., Smendes became the first pharaoh of the Twenty-first Dynasty and was recognised, nominally at least, by Heri-Hor. Egypt remained divided, however, and passed through a period of obscurity and trouble, during which the high priests of Amon, who were members of the same family, succeeded one another in a dynasty parallel to the twenty-first pharaonic dynasty and retained power in the south. Very soon afterwards, other internal dissensions broke out in the country.[36]

From the end of the reign of Ramses II, then, the Egyptians began rapidly to lose control in Palestine and this loss of power continued despite all attempts by Ramses III to recover it. All the same, Mer-ne-Ptah asserted his sovereignty over Canaan and recognised the existence of a group of people known as Israel. Ramses III also maintained a garrison at Beth-shean until his death in 1152 B.C. and may have kept occupation forces elsewhere in the country. There is also evidence that there were Egyptians at Megiddo in the reign of Ramses VI, about 1140 B.C.

This was, of course, the period during which the Israelites were settling in Canaan and it also covers part of the period of the Judges. It may therefore cause surprise that neither Joshua nor Judges contains a single reference to Egyptian troops or even to Egypt itself. The reason for this can only be that there was no occasion when the Israelites came into contact with the Egyptians. Only the coastal plain, including Gaza and the strategic route to the north, and the plain of Jezreel and Beth-shean were effectively controlled by the Egyptians. As we shall see later, none of the cities where evidence of Egypt's presence has been found – Gaza, Gezer, Megiddo, Beth-shean and even Lachish – was occupied by the Israelites at the time of their settlement in Canaan. In the rest of Palestine, moreover, Egyptian rule was purely nominal.

II. The Collapse of the Hittite Empire [37]

The Egyptian domination of Asia came to an end after the collapse of the Hittite Empire. After the end of the thirteenth century, there is no more

[36] For this period, see H. Kees, *Die Hohenpriester des Amun von Karnak von Herihor bis zum Ende der Äthiopenzeit*, Leiden, 1964 and the review of this work by E. Hornung, *OLZ*, 61 (1966), col 437–442; J. Černý, *CAH*, II, XXXV, 1965; S. Wenig, 'Einige Bemerkungen zur

evidence of Hittite documents, but, on the contrary, there is clear evidence of the total destruction of the great Hittite sites – Boghazköy, the site of the Hittite capital, Kültepe, Alaca and Alishar – that have been thoroughly excavated. The Hittites, who had been one of the great powers in the Ancient Near East and the frequently successful rivals of Egypt, were obliterated from the map at this time and disappeared for ever from the historical scene. The Hittite chronology and history of this period are so uncertain, there are so few written documents and such a veil of anonymity surrounds those who brought about the destruction of the Empire that the conditions in which the catastrophe came about remain obscure. However some light has been thrown on the mystery of the last days of the Hittite Empire by recent discoveries at Boghazköy and Rās Shamrah.

Hattusilis III, who had signed a peace treaty with Ramses II in 1269, was succeeded by his son Tudhaliyas IV (*ca* 1250–1220). The Hittites remained at peace with Egypt and continued to control northern Syria. Their position was, however, threatened by Assyria.[38] During the reign of Tukulti-Ninurta I (*ca* 1244–1208), the Assyrians had entered the northern part of Mesopotamia, had subjugated Babylonia and had tried to advance towards the west. Tudhaliyas, who had been friendly towards Tukulti-Ninurta I when he came to the throne, then declared that he was hostile towards him and established a blockade in trade against Assyria. It would, however, seem that the conflict between the two countries simply took the form of Assyrian raids to the west of the Euphrates and small military operations close to the frontier. An uprising in Assyria in which Tukulti-Ninurta was assassinated, and a series of less powerful kings, put an end to the threat from this country.

In Asia Minor, Tudhaliyas IV extended the Hittite Empire towards the north-west and incorporated the land of Assuwa, which later became part of the Roman province of Asia, a name which came to be applied to the whole continent. In the thirteenth century B.C., however, it was in the west

---

Chronologie der frühen 21. Dynastie', *ZAS*, 94, (1967), pp. 134–139.

[37] E. Laroche, 'Suppululiumas II', *RA*, 47 (1953), pp. 70–78; H. Otten, 'Neue Quellen zum Ausklang des Hethitischen Reiches', *MDOG*, 94 (1963), pp. 1–23; A. Goetze, 'The Hittites and Syria (1300–1200 B.C.)', *CAH*, II, XXIV, 1965, pp. 49–61. The chronology and the history of this whole period have, however, been subject recently to questioning. See especially H. Otten, *Die hethitischen historischen Quellen und die altorientalische Chronologie (Akademie der Wissenschaften, Mainz, 1968, 3)*, Wiesbaden, 1968; *ibid., Sprachliche Stellung und Datierung des Madduwata-Textes (Studien zu den Boğasköy-Texten,*11), Wiesbaden, 1969; O. Carruba, 'Die Chronologie der hetitischen Texte und die hetitische Geschichte der Großreichzeit', *ZDMG*, Supplement I, 1969, pp. 226–249. In particular, these scholars believe that some of the texts which have been dated as thirteenth century and to which we refer here go back to the fifteenth century. Other scholars reacted to this suggestion: A. Goetze, *JCS*, 22 (1968), pp. 46–50; A. Kammenhuber, *Orientalia*, 38 (1969), pp. 548–552.*

[38] J. M. Munn-Rankin, 'Assyrian Military Power 1300–1200 B.C.' *CAH*, II, XXV, 1967.

of Asia Minor that the clouds were gathering. Attarissiya, a man from the land of Ahhiyawa, was trying to build an empire for himself out of the western provinces of the Hittite Empire. When the texts were discovered in 1924, E. Forrer[39] put forward the suggestion that Ahhiyawa was the land of the Achaeans and Attarissiya was Atraeus, the king of Mycenae. He also suggested that a number of other personal names occurring in the Boghazköy texts corresponded to names found in pre-Homeric Greece. He was sharply criticised by F. Sommer,[40] who rejected the comparisons made by Forrer as being linguistically unacceptable. What is more Sommer believed that, according to the texts themselves, Ahhiyawa was not necessarily a country on the other side of the Mediterranean. It is rather a region in the north-west of Asia Minor itself. Nonetheless, the reference to Ahhiyawa in the texts coincides with the expansion of Mycenae in the eastern Mediterranean and with the settlement of the Achaeans in the islands, in Crete, at Rhodes, in Cyprus and at certain points along the coast of Asia Minor. Many recent historians agree that Ahhiyawa may possibly have been Achaea and Attarissiya Atraeus of Mycenae, but several do not.[41] The most recent hypothesis[42] is that the Achaeans of Greece had originally emigrated from Asia Minor and developed the Mycenaean civilisation in Greece, while those who remained in Asia Minor became the Ahhiyawa of the Boghazköy. The question must remain open. One fact that must, however, be considered in this context is that this Attarissiya drove a man called Madduwatta into exile (the name is reminiscent of those of the first kings of Lydia, Alyattes and Sadyattes) and that Madduwatta sought refuge with Tudhaliyas, who gave him a small kingdom in the west of Asia Minor, which he held as a vassal.

The situation deteriorated during the reign of Tudhaliyas' successor, Arnuwandas III. Madduwatta deserted and became an ally of Attarissiya, seizing hold of the whole of Arzawa in the south-west of Asia Minor. At the same time, a man called Mita became powerful in the north-east. (His name has been compared with that of the Phrygian Midas who, according to the Greek tradition, lived during the eighth century B.C. 'Mita' may in fact be a dynastic name pointing to the arrival of the Phrygians.) In the north of Asia Minor, the Kashka barbarians, the traditional enemies of the Hittites, threatened the very centre of the empire. In addition to these

[39] E. Forrer, 'Vorhomerische Griechen in den Keilschrifttexten von Boghazköi', MDOG, 63 (1924), pp. 1–22.

[40] F. Sommer, Die Ahhijawa-Urkunden, Munich, 1932.

[41] G. Steiner, 'Die Ahhijawā-Frage', Saeculum, 15 (1964), pp. 365–392. The philological objections to this identification have, however, been rejected by J. Harmatta, 'Zur Ahhiyawā-Frage', Studia Mycenaea (The Mycenaean Symposium, Brno, 1966), ed. A. Bartonek, Brno, 1968, pp. 117–124.

[42] J. G. MacQueen, 'Geography and History in Western Asia Minor in the Second Millennium B.C.', An Stud, 18 (1968), especially pp. 178–185; J. Mellaart, ibid., pp. 189–190.

threats, there were also economic difficulties. As we have seen, Mer-ne-Ptah had sent a consignment of wheat to the Hittites to alleviate the famine in their country.

The brother and successor of Arnuwandas was Suppiluliumas II, the last king mentioned in the recent documents coming from Rās Shamrah and Boghazköy.[43] The situation became even worse during Suppiluliumas' reign. Three letters sent to the last king of Ugarit, 'Ammurapi, refer to consignments of wheat sent to the Hittite lands. One of these letters states that it was a question of life or death and another, written just before the destruction of Rās Shamrah, is a translation into Ugaritic of a message from the Hittite king.[45] It asks for provisions and adds 'the enemy has risen against me'. Other texts also provide information about these enemies. The Hittites had established control over Alashiya, which is almost certainly Cyprus.[46] In the reign of Suppiluliumas II, three engagements took place at sea, according to one text,[47] with the 'enemies of Alashiya' and the 'ships of Alashiya'. Neither the Cypriots nor the king of Cyprus were, however, involved in this encounter at sea. The foreign invaders must have been either the Achaeans who colonised part of Cyprus at the end of the thirteenth century or else the Sea Peoples who, according to the inscription of Ramses III at Medinet Habu, went via Cyprus.[48]

The Hittites, moreover, had no navy, so that this war at sea must have been fought with the help of their allies or vassals. We know that Ugarit had ships operating in these waters and three letters dealing with Cyprus and naval affairs have been found at Rās Shamrah. In one of them,[49] the governor of Cyprus writes to the King of Ugarit about the 'transgression' of his sailors and this may mean that they had gone over to the enemy. He also says that twenty enemy ships have set sail for an unknown destination. Another letter[50] is addressed by the King of Cyprus to 'Ammurapi of

---

[43] H. Otten, op. cit. (note 37); M. C. Astour, 'New Evidence on the Last Days of Ugarit', *AJA*, 69 (1965), pp. 253–258.

[44] *Ugaritica*, V, No. 33.

[45] *PRU*, V, No. 60.

[46] During the reign of Tudhaliyas IV according to H. G. Güterbock, 'The Hittite Conquest of Cyprus Reconsidered', *JNES*, 26 (1967), pp. 73–81; A. Goetze, op. cit. (note 37), pp. 51–52; during the reign of Suppiluliumas II according to H. Otten, op. cit. (note 37); G. Steiner, 'Neue Alašija Texte', *Kadmos*, I, 2 (1962), pp. 130–138. See also C. F. A. Schaeffer, *Ugaritica*, V, Paris, 1968, pp. 744–753.

[47] Texts KBo XII, 38, Rev III, translated with a commentary by H. Otten, op. cit. (note 37), pp. 20–21.

[48] For the archaeological aspect of the presence of the Achaeans and the Peoples of the Sea in Cyprus, see especially V. R. d'A. Desborough, *The Last Mycenaeans and Their Successors*, Oxford, 1964, pp. 196–202, 238–239; F. C. F. A. Schaeffer, 'Götter der Nord- und Inselvölker in Zypern', *AfO*, 21 (1966), pp. 59–69.

[49] *Ugaritica*, V, No. 22.

[50] *Ugaritica*, V, No. 23.

Ugarit and is the reply to a letter that has been lost, in which the King of Ugarit stated that enemy ships had been seen at sea. The King of Cyprus advises the King of Ugarit to rely on his troops and chariots and to wait resolutely for the enemy. 'Ammurapi's reply (?) [51] confirms that the enemy ships came and that towns were destroyed. This letter also states that all of Ugarit's troops were in Hittite territory and all her ships were on the Lycian coast and the southern coast of Asia Minor to the west of Cilicia. The land of Ugarit itself had been abandoned. Only seven enemy ships had brought this about, but there was fear that others might come and the King of Ugarit asks his colleague in Cyprus to keep him informed.

These incidents are clearly connected with the invasion carried out by the Sea Peoples and Ugarit mobilised her troops and ships in order to help the Hittites keep the enemy out. Their efforts were, however, in vain. The documents come to an end at this point; there is clear archaeological evidence of the destruction of the majority of sites in Cyprus, of Tarsus on the coast of Asia Minor, of Ugarit, Alalah (to the east of Ugarit) and Tell Sukas (to the south of Ugarit) in Syria. This is in accordance with the inscription of Ramses III at Medinet Habu to which we have already referred: 'No land could stand before their arms, once Hatti, Kode (Cilicia?), Carchemish, Arzawa, and Alashiya had been cut off at one stroke. A camp was set up in one place in Amor (Coele-Syria?). They destroyed its people, and their land was as though it had never been'. [52]

The destruction of the great Hittite sites in the interior of the country is not, however, explained by the invasion of the Sea Peoples. These sites were destroyed by other peoples, the Kashka coming from the north, [53] the Phrygians from the north-west and the Mushki (the Moskhoi of the Greeks) from the north-east. [54] All these invaders took advantage of the weak state of the Hittite Empire at the time and they and others destroyed it for ever. [55]

[51] *Ugaritica*, V, No. 24.

[52] *ANET*, p. 262b; W. E. Edgerton and J. A. Wilson, *Historical Records of Ramses III*, Chicago, 1936, p. 53.

[53] E. von Schuler, *Die Kaškäer*, Berlin 1965, especially p. 66.

[54] R. D. Barnett, 'Phrygia and the Peoples of Anatolia in the Iron Age', *CAH*, II, XXX, 1967, pp. 3 and 6.

[55] C. F. A. Schaeffer has given a very different explanation for these events in *Ugaritica* V, 1968, especially pp. 753–768 (Schaeffer's conclusions). Ugarit and the other great sites in Asia Minor and Syria at the end of the Late Bronze Age were destroyed, Schaeffer believes, not by the Sea Peoples, but by an earthquake or a series of earthquakes at the beginning of the twelfth century. Ugarit was not sacked by the invaders because it had been abandoned by the Hittites and had become allied to the Sea Peoples in the struggle against Egypt. The battles fought by Ramses III on the land and at sea took place not on the Egyptian frontier, but in northern Syria near the southern frontier of Ugarit. Schaeffer bases his argument mainly on an Akkadian letter found at Rās Shamrah. This letter was sent by a man called Sumiyanu or Sumitti, the 'General' commanding the troops stationed to the south of Ugarit. In this letter, the 'General' speaks of an imminent attack by Egypt. The scholar who edited

III. THE SEA PEOPLES [56]

According to the inscription at Medinet Habu, the enemies from the north left their camp in Amor, which was possibly Coele-Syria, and marched towards Egypt. Ramses III responded by mobilising his troops at the garrisons in Djahi (the Phoenician coast of Palestine) and by massing his navy in the 'river-mouths'. He boasts in this inscription that he annihilated all those who reached the Egyptian frontier and those who came by sea. [57] Ramses III's power, however, did not extend as far as the north of Palestine and the term 'river-mouths' usually means the mouths of the river Nile in the Delta. It is therefore probable that the naval battle, which is illustrated so vividly in the reliefs of Medinet Habu, took place in one of the mouths of the Nile and that the land battle was engaged somewhere along the Palestinian coast. The invasion of the Peoples of the Sea was therefore halted at the very gates of Egypt. According to the chronology that we have adopted, this victory, which occurred during the eighth year of the reign of Ramses III, took place in 1175 B.C.

1. The Sea Peoples

The Sea Peoples are one of the great enigmas of this period, which is itself shrouded in obscurity. In various Egyptian texts, they are called the 'foreigners who came from their lands and the islands in the middle of the Great Green' or the 'foreigners from the north who were in their islands'. The first to appear in history were the Shardans, who, according to the Amarna letters,[58] served as mercenaries at Byblos in the reign of Amen-hotep IV. Ramses II[59] had Shardans with him at the battle of Kadesh; they were sea pirates who had been taken prisoner. During the reign of

---

this text, however, attributed this letter to the Amarna period, thus dating it back to the fourteenth century B.C. (See J. Nougayrol, *Ugaritica*, V, No. 20 and more explicitly *Iraq*, 25, 1963, pp. 119–120). It would therefore seem to have had nothing to do with the Invasion of the Sea Peoples. What is more, Schaeffer's theory cannot be reconciled with the other texts, which certainly date back to the last days of Ugarit.*

[56] For the Sea Peoples in general, see P. Meurtens, 'Les Peuples de la Mer', *ChrEg*, 35 (1960), pp. 65–88; G. A. Wainwright, 'Some Sea-People', *JEA*, 47 (1961), pp. 71–90; W. Helck, *Die Beziehungen Ägyptens zu Vorderasien im 3. und 2. Jahrtausend v. Chr.*, Wiesbaden, 1962, pp. 240–245; W. F. Albright, 'Syria, the Philistines and Phoenicia', *CAH* II, XXXII, 1966, pp. 24–33; R. D. Barnett, 'The Sea Peoples', *CAH*, II, XXVIII, 1969.

[57] *ANET*, p. 262; W. E. Edgerton and J. A. Wilson, *Historical Records of Ramses III*, Chicago, 1936, pp. 53–55.

[58] *EA*, 122 and 123.

[59] J. Breasted, *ARE*, III §§ 307 and 491; for the second text, see J. Yoyotte, *Kemi*, 10 (1949), p. 63 and the note pp. 68–69.

Mer-ne-Ptah, they were allied to the Libyans in the struggle against Egypt. In the reign of Ramses III, they were in the service of Egypt. It has been suggested that their name is the same as the modern Sardinia, written in the ninth century B.C. in the inscription of Nora as *šrdn* and there is archaeological evidence in support of this comparison.[60]

The Peoples of the Sea first entered history in impressive numbers, however, during the reign of Mer-ne-Ptah. In the war that took place in the fifth year of his reign, they were allied to the Libyans. They reached the Libyan coast by sea and they certainly did not at that time invade by land along the Syro-Palestinian coast. Various names are mentioned in the texts. The Shardans are named, together with the Lukka, who have been identified with the Lycians, but have also been located by other authors[61] in the north-west of Asia Minor. During the Amarna period, for example, the King of Cyprus complained that they were raiding his towns.[62] The Aqyawasa (or Aqwayasa), who should be compared with the Ahhiyawa, whether these were the Achaeans or not, the Tursha, who may have been the Tyrsenoi, which is the name that the Greeks gave to the Etruscans,[63] and finally the Shekelesh, who have been compared with the Siculi, the inhabitants of Sicily (this is not certain), are all mentioned.

As we have already seen, a second wave of Sea Peoples came during the reign of Ramses III by sea and by land as far as the Egyptian frontier. The peoples forming the confederation are listed in order. We shall be returning to the first in the list, the Peleset or Philistines. The next people mentioned are the Tjeker, who may have been the Teukroi or Teucrians, who, according to the Greek tradition, inhabited Troy and founded Salamis in Cyprus. This name may also be interpreted as Zakkala, in which case it may be compared with that of the Sicilians. The Shekelesh are mentioned third in this list and these are the only people already named in the reign of Mer-ne-Ptah. The Denyen or Danuna may possibly be the same as the Danaoi of the Greek tradition or the Dnnym of the Phoenician inscriptions of Zenjirli in the ninth century B.C. and of Karatepe a century later.[64] The fifth and last people in this list are the Weshesh. These are also mentioned in the Great Harris Papyrus together with the Shardans as prisoners in the service of the Egyptians.

The Sea Peoples, then, are clearly presented as a group of various peoples who, coming in different waves, disturbed life in the eastern basin of the Mediterranean. The most valid parallels that have been made —

---

[60] R. D. Barnett, *CAH*, II, XXVIII, p. 12.

[61] J. G. MacQueen, *AnStud*, 18 (1968), pp. 174–175 and 178 note 74.

[62] *EA*, 38.

[64] W. F. Albright, 'Some Oriental Glosses on the Homeric Problem', *AJA*, 54 (1950), p. 162 ff; E. Laroche, 'Etudes sur les hiéroglyphes hittites, 6: Adana et les Danouniens', *Syria*, 35 (1958), pp. 263–275; M. C. Astour, *Hellenosemitica*,[2] Leiden, 1967, pp. 1–112.

Aqyawasa/Ahhiyawa, Lukka/Lycians, Denyen/Danaoi – show that there may have been a connection between these Sea Peoples and Asia Minor, but they do not prove that these peoples originally came from Asia Minor, since they may well have been immigrants there. The other parallels that have been made – Tursha/Etruscans, Shardans/Sardinia, Zakkala/Sicily (?) – point to the possibility that these groups, or related groups, of people had settled in the western Mediterranean basin, either because they had been driven there from Egypt or else because they had taken part in a general movement or migration. We do not know the economic or human pressures that lay behind these movements of peoples.

2. The Philistines[65]

We must now consider one of these groups of Sea Peoples which became established in Palestine and indeed gave its name to the country and played an important part at one time in the history of Israel. This group is moreover the one about which we have most information from the Bible and the excavations that have been made in Palestine.

The first reference to the *Prst*, the Philistines, in the Egyptian documents is found in the reign of Ramses III. The Akkadian equivalent, *palastu*, is even later. In the Bible, however, the Philistines and the land of the Philistines are mentioned from the time of the patriarchs onwards (see Gen 21:32, 34; 26:1, 8, 14–15). Attempts have been made to establish the historical authenticity of these references to the Philistines in patriarchal times by relating them to an earlier wave of invasions on the part of the Sea Peoples.[66] The Amarna letters and the Egyptian texts earlier than Ramses III do not, however, mention the Philistines, and the 'king of the Philistines' whom Abraham and Isaac met had a semitic name, Abimelech. These references to the Philistines in the patriarchal period are clearly anachronistic, like the mention of 'the road to the land of the Philistines' in the story of the Ex-

---

[65] In addition to the general works given in note 56 and the special works later, see T. Dothan, 'Archaeological Reflections on the Philistine Problem', *Antiquity and Survival*, 2 (1957), pp. 151–164; *ibid.*, 'Philistine Civilisation in the Light of Archaeological Finds in Palestine and Egypt', *Eretz-Israel*, 5 (1958), pp. 55–66 (Hebrew); G. A. Wainwright, 'Some Early Philistine History', *VT*, 9 (1959), pp. 73–84; B. Mazar, *The Philistines and the Rise of Israel and Tyre* (*Proceedings of the Israel Academy of Sciences and Humanities*, I, 7), 1964; B. Hrouda, 'Die Einwanderung der Philister in Palästina', *Festschrift Moortgat*, Berlin, 1964, pp. 126–135; C. Nylander, in *Berliner Jahrbuch für Vor-und Frühgeschichte*, 6 (1966), pp. 206–209; M.–L. and H. Erlenmeyer and M. Delcor, 'Philistins', *DBS*, VII, 1966, col 1233–1288; G. E. Wright, 'Fresh Evidence for the Philistine Story', *BibArch*, 29 (1966), pp. 70–86; T. Dothan, *The Philistines and their Material Culture*, Jerusalem, 1967 (Hebrew, with English summary).

[66] C. H. Gordon, *Introduction to Old Testament Times*, Ventnor, N. J., 1953, p. 108; *ibid.*, 'The Rôle of the Philistines', *Antiquity*, 30 (1956), pp. 22–26; K. A. Kitchen, *Ancient Orient and Old Testament*, Chicago, 1966, pp. 80–81.

odus (Exod 13:17). The list of the 'regions of the Philistines' and of their five chiefs among the districts which Joshua had not conquered (Jos 13:2–3; *cf.* Judges 3:3) belongs to a late level of editing. The first real reference to the Philistines in the Old Testament, then, is found in the story of Samson (Judges 13–16), which takes place in a part of the country shared by Israel and the Philistines.

They are called 'uncircumcised Philistines' (Judges 14:3; *cf.* 1 Sam 17:26–36) or simply the 'uncircumcised' (Judges 15:18; cf. 1 Sam 14:6; 31:4; 2 Sam 1:20). They are also distinguished from the Canaanites and are not Semites. In fact, according to the Bible itself, they came from Caphtor (Amos 9:7; Jer 47:4). In Deut 2:23, we read of 'the Caphtorim, coming from Caphtor' and driving out the original inhabitants of the district of Gaza. Finally, in the so-called Table of Peoples (Gen 10:14; *cf.* 1 Chron 1:12), the gloss 'from which the Philistines came' should be connected to the Caphtorim and not to the previous name, as occurs in the Massoretic text.

This name Caphtor is undoubtedly the Kaptaru of the Akkadian texts, at least from the Mari period onwards, the *kptr* and the Kabturi of the alphabetic and syllabic texts of Rās Shamrah and the Keftiu of the Egyptian texts, in which the name occurs round about 2000 B.C. for the first time, but is above all used between 1520 and 1350, after which it disappears.

Most Egyptologists, Assyriologists and biblical scholars believe that Caphtor was the island of Crete.[67] Those who have specialised in the history of Crete have been reserved in their response to this suggestion, but are on the whole favourable to it.[68] Attempts have been made to prove that the Philistines came from Crete by appealing to the disc found at Phaistos, on which, it has been suggested, the name Philistia can be read. This is, however, an incorrect reading and the argument cannot therefore be accepted.[69] More frequently, comparisons have been made between the feathered helmets or crowns worn by the Philistines on the reliefs at Medinet Habu and one of the signs that appears on the same disc, a human head with curled hair or feathers. Most scholars, however, agree now that this disc certainly came originally from Crete itself and that the closest parallels with it have been found in Crete and date back to the Middle Minoan period.[70] It is very unlikely that there was any connection with the

---

[67] The best argument in favour of this interpretation is that of J. Vercoutter, *L'Égypte et le monde égéen préhellénique*, Cairo, 1956, whose conclusion is no more than a 'favourable assumption'.

[68] R. W. Hutchinson, *Prehistoric Crete*, Harmondsworth, 1962, pp. 106–111.

[69] B. Schwartz, *JNES*, 18 (1959), p. 226.

[70] F. Schachermeyr, *Die minoische Kultur des alten Kreta*, Stuttgart, 1964, pp. 245–247; C. Davaras, 'Zur Herkunft des Diskos von Phaistos', *Kadmos*, 6 (1967), pp. 101–105; E. Grumach, 'The Origin of the Disc of Phaistos' (in Russian), *Vestnik drevnei istorii*, 104 (1968), pp. 14–28.*

Philistines. It is in fact difficult to know how much credit should be given to much later information, such as the identification, during the Graeco-Roman period, of the god of Gaza, Marnas, with Zeus Kretagenes and the claim made by Stephen of Byzantium that Gaza was first called Minoia because it had been founded by Minos.

The Bible itself would seem to lend some support to this theory that the Philistines were the same as the Cretans. In Ezek 25:16 and Zeph 2:5, the Philistines and the Cherethites are mentioned in parallel and the names would appear to be synonymous. The Cherethites, it has been asserted, were the Cretans. All the same, long before the time of Ezekiel and Zephaniah, the Cherethites were named together with the Pelethites as members of David's personal bodyguard (2 Sam 8:18; 15:18; 20:7, 23; 1 Kings 1:38, 44). In this stereotyped expression, *hakkᵉretî wᵉhappᵉletî*, 'the Cherethites and the Pelethites', the second name is usually interpreted as being the same as *happᵉlištî*, the Philistines, but assimilated phonetically to *hakkᵉretî*, the first name of the pair. If this interpretation is valid, the fact that there are two names would clearly prove that the Cherethites and the Philistines were different peoples. It is, however, difficult to accept this interpretation[71] and the 'Pelethites' remain an enigma. As for the Cherethites, they lived in fact in the south of Palestine – in 1 Sam 30:14, for example, we read of a 'Negeb of the Cherethites'. They may have been Cretans from Crete itself, but, unlike the Philistines, they are not connected anywhere in the Bible with Caphtor. We are therefore bound to conclude that the Bible itself does not permit us to identify Caphtor with Crete.

G. E. Wainwright has suggested that Caphtor/Keftiu was situated in the southern part of Asia Minor.[72] His main arguments for this hypothesis are that, in the Egyptian geographical lists, the Keftiu are associated with Asia Minor and northern Syria and that the Keftiu personal names in the Egyptian texts have a clearly Asiatic character. He also appeals to the Greek legend of Kabdaros (= Caphtor), the King of Cilicia,[73] and draws attention to the fact that the place name Prostanna, on the borders of Cilicia and Pamphylia, has, without the Asiatic ending -*anna*, the consonants *prst*, which is the name of the Philistines in the Egyptian texts.

In the case of this second theory as well, it is possible to find support in the Bible. The Philistine prince of Gath during the reign of David was called Achish (1 Sam 27:2 ff). This name has been compared with that of

---

[71] L. M. Muntingh, 'The Kerethites and the Pelethites – A Historical and Sociological Discussion', *Studies on the Books of Samuel*, Pretoria, 1960, pp. 43–53; H. Schult, 'Ein inschriftlicher Beleg für "Plethi"?', *ZDPV*, 81 (1965), pp. 74–79.

[72] G. E. Wainwright, especially 'Asiatic Keftiu', *AJA*, 56 (1952), pp. 196–212; 'Keftiu and Karamania (Asia Minor)', *AnStud*, 4 (1954), pp. 33–48; 'Caphtor-Cappadocia', *VT*, 6 (1956), pp. 199–210.

[73] See A. Furumark, *Opuscula Archaeologica*, 6 (1950), pp. 239–246, especially p. 243.

the Trojan father of Aeneas, Anchises, and with *3kš, 3kšt* in a list of Keftiu names in the Eighteenth Dynasty of Egypt. The name Goliath is also comparable to that of Alyatte, the King of Lydia and the father of Croesus. Finally, in Deut 2:23 and Amos 9:7, Caphtor is translated in the Septuagint as Cappadocia. This is, however, very uncertain evidence and, in the case of the personal names, it is important to know whether they are really Aegean or Asiatic. The same applies to the other comparisons with the Keftiu names that Wainwright has made. Finally, it is impossible to accept the name Prostanna as evidence, because the Egyptian transcription of the name 'Philistine' by *prst* was simply because there was no way of rendering the sound *l* in Egyptian script.

There are, then, both advantages and disadvantages connnected with both these theories, Caphtor/Crete and Caphtor/ part of Asia Minor. An attempt has been made by J. Prignaud to reconcile them[74] by assuming that the name was applied to different places. The Keftiu of the Egyptian texts, Prignaud believes, is certainly Crete, but the name disappeared round about 1350 B.C., when relations between Crete and Egypt came to an end as the result of the collapse of Cretan rule. Some of the inhabitants of Crete emigrated to Asia Minor and took the name of their country with them. Immigrants settled in the island of Crete, giving it the name by which it is now known. The Philistines came from the new Caphtor/Asia Minor to Palestine and were later joined there by some of their kinsmen who had remained on the island and had become Cretans. These latter people are the Cherethites of the Bible.

This is an interesting theory, but, like Wainwright's, it gives too much prominence to comparisons between personal names and contains too little proof of a Philistine migration from Crete to Asia Minor. Finally, neither Wainwright nor Prignaud explain the silence preserved in the Hittite texts from the fourteenth to the thirteenth centuries. These contain many references to the political geography of Asia Minor, but never mention the name Caphtor. The Egyptian texts are also silent from 1350 onwards with regard to Caphtor, but this was because relations between Egypt and Crete had ceased by this time. Ugarit, however, was still trading in the thirteenth century with Kabturi/Caphtor and this trade was conducted by sea.[75] This does not mean that Caphtor was not situated on the southern coast of Asia Minor, but it would be mcre understandable if Caphtor had been the name of the island of Crete.

All in all, it is very probable that Caphtor always denoted Crete. The texts of Amos and Zephaniah, according to which the Philistines came from Crete, are five or six centuries later than the last references to the name in the Egyptian texts or the Akkadian texts of Ugarit. They may, of course,

[74] J. Prignaud, 'Caftorim et Kerétim', *RB*, 71 (1964), pp. 215–229.
[75] J. Nougayrol, *PRU*, III, 1955, p. 107.

have preserved a very early memory, but what they say finds no archaeological support. Apart from the very doubtful evidence provided by the disc of Phaitos, no special link can be established between the Philistines and Crete by archaeology.[76]

Certain links have, however, been revealed by archaeology between the Philistines and another island in the Aegean Sea, Cyprus. At the beginning of the Iron Age, during the twelfth and eleventh centuries B.C., there was a class of pottery in Palestine which was distinctive by virtue of its workmanship, shape and decoration. This type of pottery is known as 'Philistine' ware and the title is fully justified because it has only been found in any quantity in those regions which were occupied by the Philistines and because it was only made at the time when the Philistines were important manufacturers of pottery in Palestine. Various influences can be detected in this ceramic ware, the most marked being late Mycenaean, Myc III C lb. In addition, there are also indications of an Egyptian influence, a Canaanite influence inherited from the Late Bronze Age, which is clear from certain shapes and the two-coloured decoration, and a Cypriot influence revealed in other shapes and a certain arrangement of the decoration.

It is above all with the Cypriot variety of Late Mycenaean ware that this pottery has most affinities. The closest parallels – and indeed the only exact parallels – come from the excavations carried out at Enkomi, Sinda and Nicosia. Various points of contact with Cilicia (Tarsus) can be explained not by the Cilician origin of this style, as Furumark has suggested, but by the links established between Cyprus and the coast of Asia Minor. It would seem, then, very likely that this 'Philistine' pottery originated in Cyprus.

Two factors, however, would appear to modify this conclusion. First, this pottery was manufactured locally. Secondly, as far as we can judge, it did not appear at the very moment that the Philistines settled in Palestine, but a little later. (The interval between the arrival of the Philistines and the appearance of the pottery was very short.)

It is clear from these two factors that the Philistines did not bring this pottery with them. It does, however, bear clear witness to contacts between them and Cyprus. This relationship can perhaps be explained by the fact that the Philistines possibly broke their journey previously in Cyprus or that a group of Philistines may have stayed behind in Cyprus and joined their kinsmen later in Palestine. It has even been suggested that this Philistine ware was the work of a potter or a group of potters who had come from Cyprus in order to work in Philistia.[77]

[76] See the lengthy study by M.–L. and H. Erlenmeyer, 'Über Philister und Kreter', *Orientalia*, 29 (1960), pp. 121–150, 241–272; 30 (1961), pp. 269–293; 33 (1964), pp. 199–237. See also the same authors in the archaeological part of the article on 'Philistins', *DBS*, VII, 1966, col 1233–1252. These authors do not, however, make any really convincing contribution.

[77] J. L. A. Benson, *JNES*, 20 (1961), pp. 73–84, especially pp. 81–84; V. R. d'A.

Pottery does not, however, provide the only link between the Philistines and Cyprus. An ivory has been found at Enkomi depicting a hunting scene and a man with feathered head-dress and loin-cloth or kilt similar to those worn by the Philistines in the reliefs of Medinet Habu.[78] A seal, also from Enkomi, shows a warrior with the same Philistine head-dress and a round shield, again like those of the Philistines at Medinet Habu.[79] A hero fighting a gryphon carries a round shield and a long sword like the Philistines', but does not wear the Philistine head-dress, on the ivory handle of a mirror found at Enkomi,[80] and another ivory handle from Kouklia-Palaipaphos shows a similarly armed hero fighting a lion.[81] Instead of the feathered head-dress of the Philistines at Medinet Habu, these two figures wear helmets with bands set with pearls, similar to that worn by one of the figures on the anthropoid clay sarcophagi found at Beth-shean, to which we shall return later.[82]

These objects all date from about 1200 B.C. or a little later. They are in accordance with the Egyptian and Ugaritic texts, which show that the Sea Peoples, including the Philistines, came to Palestine via Cyprus. They did not, however, originally come from Cyprus, just as they did not originate in Crete. Where, then, did they come from?

Various theories have been suggested. One is that, because of certain personal names and Hebrew words which are presumably Philistine, these people were originally Caucasian.[83] This hypothesis is quite unacceptable. The theory that the Philistines had a Hittite origin is also improbable.[84] A third theory, that they came from Illyria,[85] has to be taken more seriously. Certain proper names are also found in Illyria and some common names that might perhaps be regarded as Philistine, seren, the five chiefs of the Philistines, qôbha', helmet, 'ar'gāz, ark, seem to belong to a pre-Indo-European dialect of the centum group, like Illyrian. This is a possible solution, but it would seem to be too restricted. A very early hypothesis,

Desborough, The Last Mycenaeans and their Successors, 1964, p. 214.

[78] Y. Yadin, The Art of Warfare in Biblical Lands in the Light of Archaeological Discoveries, London, 1963, p. 338; a better study in our context is C. de Mertzenfeld, Inventaire commenté des ivoires phéniciens, Paris, 1954, Plate LXIX, 788b.

[79] P. Dikaios, Archäologische Anzeiger, 1962, col 4–5, Figure 11.*

[80] C. de Mertzenfeld, op. cit., Plate LXXII.

[81] V. Karageorghis, Treasures in the Cyprus Museum, Nicosia, 1962, Plate XLI, 1.

[82] The bronze figurines studied by C. F. A. Schaeffer, 'Götter der Nord- und Inselvölker in Zypern', AfO, 21 (1966), pp. 59–69, do not seem to me to have any special connection with the Philistines or even with the Sea Peoples generally.

[83] H. R. Hall, 'The Caucasian Relations of the People of the Sea,' Klio, 22 (1929), p. 335; F. Bork, 'Philistäische Namen und Vokabeln', AfO, 13 (1939–1941), pp. 226–230.

[84] M. Riemschneider, 'Die Herkunft der Philister', Acta Antiqua (Budapest), 4 (1956), pp. 17–29.

[85] A. Jirku, 'Zur illyrischen Herkunft der Philister', WZKM, 49 (1943), p. 13 ff; see especially G. Bonfante, 'Who were the Philistines?', AJA, 50 (1946), p. 251–262.

put forward again recently with more positive arguments,[86] is based on a comparison between the Philistines and the Pelasgians. These were the ancient, pre-Greek inhabitants of Thessaly and Epirus, which are not far from Illyria, and they spread from Greece itself to the islands (Lemnos), to Asia Minor (Troas) and even as far as Crete. According to a scholion on the Iliad, XIX, 176–177, the title Zeus Pelasgikos could also be read as Pelastikos and, according to Hesychius, the Pelasgic wall at Athens was also called the Pelastic wall. The Pelasgians may therefore originally have been called the Pelastians, which may be the same word as Philistines. The only word that we know which is undoubtedly Philistine is *seren* and this was regarded a long time ago as parallel to *turannos,* which is pre-Greek and must therefore have been Pelasgian. Both words mean 'chief'. As far as the Philistine personal names for which parallels exist in Asia Minor are concerned, these may equally well have been Aegean names and therefore Pelasgian. Unfortunately, very little is known about the Pelasgians. Since the beginning of the Greek tradition, it has been almost impossible to establish any historical, ethnic or linguistic data concerning them.[87] We may well say that the Philistines were originally Pelasgians, but this still tells us nothing at all about their origin, which must inevitably remain a mystery until new documents are discovered which may throw some light on it.

According to the Bible, the Philistines certainly settled on the Palestinian coastline from Jaffa to Gaza and formed a confederation of five towns, Gaza, Ashkelon, Ashdod, Ekron and Gath. They also moved into the interior of Palestine and became a danger which threatened Israel until the reign of David. These biblical data are confirmed by the use of the geographical term Philistia in the Egyptian texts and later in the Assyrian texts even after the Philistines had ceased to be an important political power. It is generally recognised nowadays that these Philistine cities originated as colonies of mercenaries recruited from prisoners taken after the defeat of the Sea Peoples in the eighth year of the reign of Ramses III. After the collapse of Egyptian rule in Asia, these Philistine towns became independent. In the story of Wen-Amon's journey at the beginning of the eleventh century B.C., there is reference to three princes who must have been the rulers of the three Philistine ports, Ashdod, Ashkelon and Gaza. One of these princes, Warkatara, who was probably the prince of Ashkelon, was associated with the King of Sidon in sea trade.[88] Although

[86] G. Georgiev, 'Sur l'origine et la langue des Pélasges, des Philistins, des Danéens et des Achéens', *JKF,* 1 (1950–1951), pp. 136–141; J. Bérard, 'Philistins et Préhellènes', *RAr,* sixth series (1951–1), pp. 129–142; W. F. Albright, *CAH,* II, XXXIII, 1966, pp. 29–30.

[87] F. Lochner-Hüttenbach, *Die Pelasger,* Vienna, 1960, considers the problem of the Philistines on pp. 141–177; cf. also E. Laroche, in *RHA,* instalment 68 (1961), pp. 40–42; D. A. Hester, in *Minos,* 9 (1968), pp. 228–231.

[88] B. Mazar, *op. cit.* (note 65), pp. 3–6; W. F. Albright, *op. cit.* (note 86), pp. 30 and 32. The name Warkatara has also, however, been interpreted as a Semitic name, Berkat-El,

we must leave the question of the Philistines now, we shall return later to consider their political and territorial structures in connection with the part they played in the history of Israel during the period of the Judges.

3. *Other Sea Peoples in Palestine*

The problem of the Philistines is made even more complicated by the fact that the movement of the Sea Peoples continued for at least two hundred years (the Shardans, the Lukka and the Ahhiyawa appearing in Palestine from the fourteenth century onwards) and that certain 'Philistine' elements may have reached Palestine before they were mentioned for the first time during the reign of Ramses III. Finally, they may have been confused in the Bible with other groups of Sea People.

We have already mentioned the Cherethites and these may possibly have been one of these groups who were distinct from the Philistines. In any case, there was another group of people who settled at Dor on the Palestinian coast to the south of Carmel. According to the story of Wen-Amon, the port of Dor was in the hands of the Tjeker/Zakkala, who are mentioned in the inscription on the temple of Ramses III at Medinet Habu immediately after the Philistines. It has been suggested that it was this group of people who were responsible for the tombs excavated just south of Dor at Tell Dhurur (Tell Zeror). These tombs consist of large rectangular boxes made of and covered with slabs of limestone, six and a half to ten feet long and capable of holding as many as ten bodies. This type of tomb was otherwise unknown in Palestine. The furnishings of these tombs are eleventh century B.C. and no 'Philistine' pottery has been found at the site.[89] The theory has been suggested that another group of Sea Peoples settled between the Philistines and the Tjeker/Zakkala, that is, between Jaffa and Dor, the Denyen/Danuna mentioned in the same list at Medinet Habu and therefore the Danaoi of the Greek tradition. According to this tradition, it was on the Mediterranean coast at Jaffa that the Danaean hero Perseus delivered Andromeda and another Danaean, Mopsos, arrived at Ashkelon from Asia Minor and died there. These Danaeans, it has been suggested, settled on the Palestinian coast, were pushed back by the Philistines and eventually became the tribe of Dan, which was integrated into Israel at a late date.[90]

---

which would mean the 'blessing of El'.

[89] K. Ohata, *Tel Zeror II. Preliminary Report of the Excavations. Second Season 1965*, Tokyo, 1967. This type of tomb is frequently found in Greece in the Submycenaean period, but they are individual tombs and much smaller; see C.-G. Styrenius, *Submycenaean Studies*, Lund, 1967, index under 'Cist tomb'.

[90] C. H. Gordon, *SVT*, 9, 1962, p. 21; Y. Yadin, 'And Dan, why did he abide with the

We shall examine at a later stage in this work precisely how this theory fits into the biblical tradition.[91] It is possible that another group of people occupied the bay of Acco and part of the plain of Jezreel. The greatest battle fought during the period of the Judges, at the time of Deborah and Barak, took place near Tabor and was conducted against a man called Sisera, 'who lived at Harosheth-ha-Goiim' (see Judges 4–5). This place name, *hᵃrošeth haggôyîm*, 'Harosheth of the Gentiles', would seem to point to a population which was not Canaanite and the name Sisera is also certainly not Semitic.[92] It is also noteworthy that, in the biblical account of this battle, the only adversaries of the Israelites are Canaanites.

At the time of Saul, there were, according to the Bible, 'Philistines' at Beth-shean and archaeological finds have shown that Philistines may have been there even earlier. The most interesting discoveries in this context at Beth-shean have been coffins made of fired clay and approximately cylindrical in shape. The parts of these coffins corresponding to the head and shoulders of the corpse have been cut off to form a lid, on which very stylised representations of a face and arms have been modelled.[93] Out of more than forty of these coffins of which remains have been preserved, five show a full face with a feathered head-dress bearing one or two bands of pearls or a single band of pearls and a zig-zag band. This is the same as the head-dress worn by some of the Peoples of the Sea on the Medinet Habu reliefs. All three variations of the Beth-shean head-dress are represented at Medinet Habu. Scholars have therefore concluded that these coffins were Philistine coffins. This conclusion, however, needs to be made a little less definite.

Similar coffins have also been found in other parts of Palestine; these portray rather stylised masks and arms, but without the featured head-dress. Two lids and part of a cylindrical sarcophagus bearing an incomprehensible Egyptian inscription have, for example, been found in a tomb at Tell ed-Duweir (Lachish). These finds, which are without Philistine pottery, date back to the period of transition between the Late Bronze and the Iron Ages.[94] Two lids have been discovered in two twelfth or eleventh century

ships?', *Western Galilee and the Coast of Galilee*, Jerusalem, 1965, pp. 42–55 (Hebrew); English version: 'And Dan, why did he remain in ships?', *The Australian Journal of Biblical Archaeology*, I, 1 (1968), pp. 9–23.

[91] This question is discussed in detail below, pp. 775 ff, in connection with the migration of Dan.

[92] A. Alt, *ZAW*, 60 (1944), p. 78 = *Kleine Schriften*, I, p. 266, and note 3.*

[93] Y. Yadin, *The Art of Warfare in Biblical Lands, op. cit.* (note 78), pp. 344–345; T. Dothan, articles in *Antiquity and Survival* and *Eretz-Israel* (note 65); G. E. Wright, 'Philistine Coffins and Mercenaries', *BibArch*, 23 (1959), pp. 54–66, revised in *The Biblical Archaeologist Reader*, 2, Garden City, N.Y., 1964, pp. 59–68; T. Dothan, *The Philistines and their Material Culture, op. cit.* (note 65), Chapter IV.*

[94] O. Tufnell, *Lachish IV: The Bronze Age*, London, 1958, pp. 36, 60–61, 131–132, 248–249.

tombs at the southern site of Tell el-Fār'ah, together with Philistine ware mixed with local pottery and vases revealing an Egyptian influence.[95] At Sahab in Transjordan, to the south-west of Amman, a lid has been found bearing a mask with a short beard but without a head-dress. This has been dated round about 900 B.C., before rather than after this date.[96] A sarcophagus with no more than a stylised mask without head-dress at the top has been found at Dībān. The date of this find is towards the end of the ninth century B.C.[97] Finally, a sarcophagus with a mask without a head-dress was excavated at Amman, where it was found in a tomb containing pottery of Iron II.[98]

Many similar coffins have also been found in Egypt, from the Delta to as far south as Aniba in Nubia and dating from the beginning of the Eighteenth Dynasty to as late as the Graeco-Roman period. The sarcophagi bearing the closest resemblance to those found in Palestine as far as the period and the style are concerned come from Nebesheh and Tell el-Yehūdiyeh in the Delta and from Aniba in Nubia. They have been found with a mixture of pottery – mostly Egyptian, and some Syro-Palestinian vases, but no Philistine pottery.

Three conclusions can be drawn from the survey of this type of sarcophagus. The first is that it was quite unknown in Crete, the Aegean and Asia Minor. The second is that these coffins were common in Egypt during the Eighteenth, Nineteenth and Twentieth Dynasties. They could not have contained the bodies either of prisoners or of mercenaries serving in Egypt. If, however, they are connected with the Sea Peoples, they should yield positive evidence as far as their contents are concerned. No such evidence exists at Aniba and, although there is a fair amount of foreign pottery at Nebesheh and Tell el-Yehūdiyeh, it is Syro-Palestinian, not Aegean. We are therefore not justified in connecting these Egyptian sarcophagi with the Peoples of the Sea and especially with the Philistines.

The third conclusion that we may draw from this type of coffin is that it was introduced into Palestine under the influence of Egypt. The three examples from Transjordania – Sahab, Dībān and Amman – certainly testify to this influence, but their geographical location and their late date mean that they cannot be connected with the Philistines. The sarcophagi found at Tell ed-Duweir cannot be considered either, in this context, because the tomb in which they were discovered antedates the great invasion of the Sea Peoples and the pottery found there is Palestinian. What is more, Tell ed-Duweir is a site where the Egyptians appear to have stayed for the longest time, and

---

[95] Flinders Petrie, *Beth-Pelet I*, London, 1930, p. 6 and Plates XIX–XX, XXIII–XXV.

[96] W. F. Albright, *AJA*, 36 (1932), pp. 295–306.

[97] F. V. Winnett and W. L. Reed, *The Excavations at Dibon (Dhibân) in Moab* (*AASOR*, 36–37), 1964, pp. 58–60, Plates 52–53, 97.

[98] *ADAJ*, 11 (1966), p. 103; *ANEP*, No. 853.

consequently this tomb may have belonged to an Egyptian family that had settled at Lachish. It is more likely, however, since the hieroglyphic inscription is incomprehensible, that it belonged to a Canaanite family that had been influenced by Egyptian fashions.[99] The lids found in the tombs at Tell el-Fār'ah, on the other hand, merit closer attention, since this is the only site at which Philistine pottery has been found and where the Philistines are known to have been. The masks on these lids, however, are without the feathered head-dress associated with the Philistines.

We are therefore left with the finds made at Beth-shean.[100] The sarcophagi have been dated at the sixth level, which covers the whole of the twelfth century. Beth-shean was the main base from which the Egyptians ruled Palestine and the Egyptian influence was strongly felt there. The pottery found at Beth-shean has many points in common with the Egyptian pottery of the twentieth dynasty. This type of sarcophagus is clearly Egyptian in origin and for this reason the coffins and the tombs at Beth-shean may have been those of Egyptian officers stationed there. The masks on the lids have, however, feathered head-dresses, the type ascribed to the Philistines in the inscriptions accompanying the reliefs at Medinet Habu. This type of head-dress was, on the other hand, not exclusive to the Philistines and was also worn by the Tjeker and the Denyen or Danuna.[101] A final factor to be borne in mind is that no 'Philistine' pottery has been found with these sarcophagi. We may therefore conclude that the Beth-shean coffins contained the bodies of Sea Peoples recruited by Ramses III as mercenaries, but that they were not necessarily – and were probably not – Philistines. As we have seen, groups of people related to the Philistines had settled along the Palestinian coast. When the Bible refers to the Philistines at Beth-shean (1 Sam 31:8, 12; cf. 1 Chron 10:8, 12), then, the name of the Philistines of the five cities is extended to include a related group.

The shape of these tombs has been used as another argument in favour of the presence of the Philistines.[102] The anthropoid sarcophagi at Tell el-Fār'ah were found in rectangular tombs with a bench along two or three sides; they are reached by descending several steps. Similar tombs are found at Beth-shean. This type is different from the classical tomb of the Middle

---

[99] G. E. Wright's reservation, *The Biblical Archaeologist Reader*, 2, 1964, p. 68, is fully justified.
[100] Frances W. James, *The Iron Age at Beth Shean*, Philadelphia, 1966, especially pp. 136–137.
[101] W. F. Edgerton and J. A. Wilson, *Historical Records of Ramses III*, Chicago, 1936, p. 45, note 19a; G. A. Wainwright, *JEA*, 47 (1961), p. 74 ff.
[102] G. E. Wright, *BibArch*, 29 (1966), p. 74; T. Dothan, *The Philistines and their Material Culture, op. cit.* (note 65), Chap. IV; Jane C. Waldbaum, 'Philistine Tombs at Tell Fara and their Aegean Prototypes', *AJA*, 70 (1966), pp. 331–340. Another tomb of the same type has also been found at Tell 'Aitun near Lachish; this contains 'Philistine' vases; see *Hadashôt Archiologiôt*, July 1968, pp. 5–6; *Qadmoniôt*, 1 (1968), p. 100; *RB*, 76 (1969), p. 578.

and Late Bronze Ages, which is more or less round in shape. The type found at Tell el-Fār'ah and Beth-shean became common only in the Iron Age, an innovation which has been ascribed to the Philistines. Another burial place at Tell Fār'ah, No. 900, contains similar tombs, but these are without anthropoid sarcophagi or Philistine pottery. They contained Mycenaean pottery of the Myc III B type of the thirteenth century, which is associated with the local Late Bronze ware. Another tomb of the same type also exists at Tell el-'Ajjūl. This is also rectangular, but it has no bench. It dates back to the second half of the Late Bronze Age. All these tombs are perhaps in some way connected with a first wave of Sea Peoples.

What is certain is that these rectangular 'chamber tombs' are of a classical Mycenaean type that is found not only in Greece, but also in all the regions where the Mycenaeans settled or where their influence was felt.[103] This type of tomb was also used, however, in the sub Mycenaean period[104], and the 'Philistine' tombs of Palestine reveal certain important differences, notably the bench, which is a regular feature, and the replacement of the *dromos* by steps. What is more, it is clear that none of these tombs can be ascribed to the Sea Peoples, whether they are found in Greece or outside Greece. It is possible that this type of tomb was introduced into Palestine by groups of Sea People who had been influenced by the Mycenaean culture, in view of the fact that the Philistines imitated Late Myceanean pottery. This may be so, but it would still be wrong to ascribe these tombs to the Philistines rather than to another group of Sea People. The conclusion to which we have come with regard to the anthropoid sarcophagi at Beth-shean may also be considered in this context. The fact that there is evidence that this type of tomb existed in Palestine at the end of the Late Bronze Age – notably at Tell el-'Ajjūl and in cemetery 900 at Tell el-Fār'ah – may point to a first wave of Sea Peoples who must inevitably remain anonymous. This type of tomb, however, would seem rather to have been a local development of the tombs with a *dromos* or entrance passage and two lobes in the ground plan of the type found at Tell el-Fār'ah, Tell el-'Ajjūl and elsewhere and dating from the end of the Middle Bronze Age. They may possibly bear witness to an influence coming from Cyprus, where these tombs with two lobes appeared at an earlier date. What has, in any case, to be ruled out is a connection with the Sea Peoples.[105]

Another possible sign of an arrival of the Sea Peoples before the great invasion that took place during the reign of Ramses III is perhaps provided by the results of excavations at Deir 'Alla in the Jordan Valley.[106] During the

[103] V. R. d'A. Desborough, *The Last Mycenaeans*, *op. cit.* (note 48), p. 32 ff.

[104] C.–G. Styrenius, *Submycenaean Studies*, Lund, 1967, Index under 'Chamber tombs'.

[105] W. H. Stiebing, 'Another Look at the Origins of the Philistine Tombs at Tell el-Fār'ah (S)', *AJA*, 74 (1970), pp. 139–143.

[106] H. J. Franken, 'Palestine in the Time of the Nineteenth Dynasty. (b) Archaeological

second half of the thirteenth century, this sanctuary was visited by a new group of people with a different kind of pottery. The sanctuary was destroyed by an earthquake and burnt and this brought this stage to an end, but various finds have been made, including a vase bearing the scroll of Queen Ta-Usert, the last ruler of the Nineteenth Dynasty (*ca.* 1200 B.C.). At the same level, excavations have yielded three clay tablets inscribed in a form of writing which has so far resisted all attempts at decipherment. This writing shows some signs of a relationship with the Cypro-Minoan texts found on Cyprus and at Rās Shamrah which are derived from Cretan Linear A. Several scholars have therefore spoken of a 'Philistine' writing in this context.[107] The scholar who has given the most serious attention to these texts[108] has not ruled out the possibility that this writing was Aegean. There were, after all, several kinds of writing about which we know very little at that time in the Aegean.[109]

The next level at Deir 'Alla, that of the second half of the twelfth century, reveals, in the opinion of archaeologists, the arrival of a new group. This new group had pottery with the same shapes, but the techniques were different. Fragments of Philistine ware have also been found with this pottery. Archaeologists have therefore concluded that there were two successive waves of Peoples of the Sea who came to the Jordan Valley: the first group, which was responsible for the inscribed tablets, settling there in the thirteenth century and the second group, which had trade links with the Philistines or were people who were originally Philistines, and therefore knew the Philistine pottery, arriving in the twelfth century. There is of course no certainty about this interpretation of the finds at Deir 'Alla.

These discoveries do, however, throw some new light on a text of the Bible. The people of Deir 'Alla who had this Philistine pottery were also metal-workers. Their furnaces have been found and, at Tell es-Saʿīdīyeh, a few miles to the north of Deir 'Alla, a number of bronze objects, some of which are clearly related to those produced in Cyprus and the Aegean, have been found in thirteenth and twelfth century tombs.[110] There was a

Evidence', *CAH*, II, XXVI (b), 1968, pp. 8–9; H. J. Franken and J. Kaalsbeek, *Excavations at Tell Deir Alla*, I, Leiden, 1969. In this first volume of the definitive publication, an analysis is provided of the levels containing 'Philistine' pottery, but not of the level which has yielded the inscribed tablets.

[107] G. E. Wright, *BibArch*, 29 (1966), p. 73; W. F. Albright, *CAH*, II, XXXIII, 1966, p. 27.

[108] M. Weippert, *ZDPV*, 82 (1966), pp. 299–310; cf. *Kadmos*, 6 (1967), p. 154.

[109] Maurice Pope, *Aegean Writing and Linear A* (*Studies in Mediterranean Archaeology*,8), Lund, 1964; O. Masson, 'Ecriture et langues de la Chypre antique', *Archäologischer Anzeiger*, 1967, pp. 615–619.

[110] J. B. Pritchard, provisionally in *RB*, 72 (1965), pp. 260–262; *BibArch*, 28 (1965), pp. 14–17; *Expedition*, 7, 4 (1965), pp. 26–30. Of particular interest is a sword of a type that has been found at Ugarit and at Alalaḫ and which is ascribed to the Sea Peoples; this is N. K.

continuing tradition of metal-working in this district and it is relevant to recall that it was here that the bronze furnishings were made for Solomon's temple (1 Kings 7:46). What is of particular interest in our present context, however, is that, according to 1 Sam 13:19–22, the Philistines had a monopoly in metal-working and that the Israelites had to 'go down' to them to have their tools and weapons sharpened. It used to be thought that the Israelites always 'went down' into Philistia along the coastal plain, since archaeologists have unearthed evidence of a metal-working industry at Ashdod, Tell Mor, Tell Jemmeh, Tell Qasıleh and Tell Zeror, but it is now known that they may also have 'gone down' into the Jordan Valley.

It is clear, then, that the problem of the Philistines and the Sea Peoples is far from being solved. It would seem at least that they certainly occupied an important place in Palestine at the time when the Israelites were settling there, during the period of the Judges, and that the Philistines or related peoples were there from the time of the 'conquest'.

IV. EDOM – MOAB – AMMON

We are not well informed with regard to the ethnic and political situation in Transjordan at the end of the second millennium B.C. At the beginning of the first millennium, there seem to have been three kingdoms. These were, from south to north, Edom, Moab and Ammon. They were national kingdoms and, like Israel, each was named after a people. According to the biblical traditions, these three peoples were all related to Israel. Edom's ancestor was Edom-Esau, Jacob's twin brother. Ammon and Moab were the children of Lot's sleeping with his daughters and Lot was Abraham's nephew. Very few inscriptions by these peoples have been found, but the few that we have show that they spoke the same language as the Israelites, with certain differences of dialect. It is also probable that they formed part of the same movement of peoples which brought the ancestors of the Israelites into Canaan and that, like the Israelites, they too spent a long time as nomads or semi-nomads. N. Glueck, who systematically explored Transjordania, was convinced that there was no urban civilisation in the whole of central and southern Transjordania, from Amman to the Gulf of 'Aqabah, between the nineteenth and the thirteenth centuries B.C. The few excavations that have been carried out recently in Edom and Moab have done nothing to change this conclusion – on the contrary, they have tended to reinforce it, because they have revealed no sign of a reoccupation going back to the thirteenth century. The question is, however, slightly

---

Sandars' Group H, see 'Later Aegean Bronze Swords', *AJA*, 67 (1963), pp. 117–153; cf. V. Hankey, *BSA*, 63 62 (1967), p. 130.

different in the case of central Transjordania, where several Middle Bronze tombs have been found in the neighbourhood of Medeba and Amman as well as a Late Bronze temple, at Amman airport, which was used at the end of the fourteenth century and for part of the thirteenth century. Up till now, it has proved impossible to connect these finds with any centre of settled civilisation.[111] It is just possible to imagine that these tombs and even the sanctuary were used by semi-nomadic peoples, except for the fact that there are other signs of Canaanite settlement in this part of the Near East at the end of the Bronze Age. It is precisely in this region that the only geographical names formed with Baal in the whole of Transjordania are to be found and the kingdom of Sihon, with its capital Heshbon, was, according to the biblical tradition, established before the arrival of Moses' group and before the kingdom of Moab was set up.[112]

No national traditions regarding the settlement of the Edomites, the Moabites or the Ammonites are known to us and we have therefore to rely on the Bible for our information. The Edomites seem, according to the Old Testament, to have been settled in Transjordan when the Israelites arrived. According to Num 20:14–21, the King of Edom refused to allow the Israelites to pass through his territory, with the result that they had to go round the land of Edom (Num 21:4). They then went through the desert bordering Moab to the east (Num 21:11; this and the previous quoted text are, however, late). Finally, the king of Heshbon, Sihon, refused to let them pass through his land, but the Israelites fought and beat him, seized hold of his kingdom and went 'as far as the sons of Ammon' (Num 21:24; cf. Judges 11:17–21). According to Deut 2:1–13, Yahweh ordered them to respect the territory of Edom and of Moab.

Gen 36:31–39 (= 1 Chron 1:43–50) provides a list of eight kings 'who ruled in the land of Edom before an Israelite king ruled', in other words, before Saul. Eight generations would take us back to the thirteenth century B.C., so that we may say that this was the century when the first king of Edom reigned, at least according to the biblical tradition. The list contains some very early data, which may, however, have been edited. It should be noted too that none of the kings listed was succeeded by his son and that each came originally from a different city. This list may therefore not be chronological. It may simply be a list of little Edomite kingdoms similar to the Canaanite city-states on the west of the Jordan. Another fact to be noted is that both Edomite and Moabite cities are mentioned in this list.[113] Because

---

[111] J. B. Hennessy, 'Excavations of a Late Bronze Age Temple at Amman', PEQ, 1966, pp. 155–162; E. F. Campbell and G. E. Wright, 'Tribal League Shrines in Amman and Shechem', BibArch, 32 (1969), pp. 104–116.

[112] See below, pp. 565–566.

[113] J. R. Bartlett, 'The Edomite King-List of Genesis xxxvi. 31–39 and 1 Chron i. 43–50', JTS, new series, 16 (1965), pp. 301–314.

of these facts, we cannot know with any certainty when Edom became a kingdom; nor can we know the precise nature of its political structure. Even according to the biblical account, the Edomites may not necessarily have been a settled people when the Israelites arrived, since the 'kings' mentioned in the list of Gen 36 may, like the 'king' in Num 20, have been chiefs of nomadic groups. Other examples of this are the 'kings' of the nomadic Midianites (Num 31:8; Judges 8:12) and the 'king' of the Amalekites, who were also nomads (1 Sam 15:8, 20, 32). The great list of the kings of Ashur begins with 'twenty-seven kings' living in tents.[114] At Mari, the semi-nomadic Haneans and Benjaminites also had kings.[115]

Moab[116] also had a king at that time. There had not been a king of Moab for very long, since, according to Num 21:26, Sihon had taken all the territory that the first king of Moab had occupied north of the Arnon.[117] The deep valley of the Arnon formed a natural frontier which the Moabites tried from time to time to cross because they were attracted by the fertile plains of Medeba. They occupied this territory later when Balak, the king of Moab, called on Balaam to curse the Israelites, an episode which describes a situation existing at the time of the Judges.[118] Also at the period of the Judges, Eglon, the king of Moab, seized Jericho (Judges 3:12–30) and the plain to the north-east of the Dead Sea was called 'ařbhôth mô'abh by the priestly author.

The Ammonites lived to the north-east of Moab and of the kingdom of Sihon, in the upper basin of the Jabbok around their capital Rabbah or 'Rabbah of the Ammonites' (rabbat b'nê 'ammôn, Deut 3:11), the modern city of Amman.[119] It is possible that the Ammonites only became a kingdom after Edom and Moab, since the song of Moses' victory (Exod 15) and the oracles of Balaam (Num 23–24) refer only to Edom and Moab and do not mention Ammon, although this failure to mention Ammon may be explained by the fact that it was farther away. According to Judges 3:13, the Ammonites were the allies of Eglon the Moabite, but they took no part in the action. The Ammonites are said to have a king for the first time in Judges 11:12–28, but Jephthah speaks to the king of the Ammonites through his messengers in this passage as though he was the king of Moab;

---

[114] ANET, p. 564b; F. R. Kraus, Könige, die in Zelten wohnten (Mededeelingen der koninklijke Akademie, 28, 2), Amsterdam, 1965.

[115] J.-R. Kupper, Les nomades en Mésopotamie au temps des rois de Mari, Paris, 1957, pp. 32, 59.

[116] M. Noth, 'Israelitische Stämme zwischen Ammon und Moab', ZAW, 60 (1944), pp. 11–37; ibid., 'Ammon und Moab', ZDPV, 68 (1946–1951), pp. 36–50; A. H. van Zyl, The Moabites, Leiden, 1960.

[117] This is the correct translation; 'the former king of Moab' is not correct.

[118] See below, p. 568.

[119] M. Noth, ZDPV, 68 (1946–1951), pp. 36–50; W. F. Albright, 'Notes on Ammonite History', Miscellanea Biblica B. Ubach, Montserrat, 1953, pp. 131–136.

the message is clearly an added element, dependent on Num 20–21.[120]

Little is added by extrabiblical sources to the information provided by the Bible itself about the origins of Edom, Moab and Ammon. The only reference to Edom in the Egyptian documents is found in a papyrus of the reign of Mer-ne-Ptah, authorising a group of Shasu of Edom to cross the frontier and to settle in the Delta – the name Edom is preceded in this text by the determinative used for foreigners.[121] The geographical name Seir, which is associated in the Bible with Edom, is found in texts dating back to the reigns of Ramses II and Ramses III.[122] Like the name Edom, the name Seir is always found in conjunction with the Shasu bedouins and we cannot conclude from these texts that the Edomites were a settled people at that time. There is also a vague reference to the 'lands of Seir' in the Amarne letters.[123]

Moab is only mentioned twice in the Egyptian texts, once in a geographical list of Ramses II[124] and once in the narrative of the same pharaoh's campaign in Transjordania.[125] In the second of these texts, the reference to 'cities' and in particular to Diban shows that the Moabites had become settled by this time, although they may not have formed a unified state.[126] Finally, it is worth noting that Ammon appears nowhere in any Egyptian text and that it is mentioned in the Assyrian texts only from the ninth century B.C. onwards.

V. The Aramaeans

Another ethnic group, the Aramaeans, settled on the fringe of Palestine at the end of the second millennium B.C. Their origin is very obscure. According to the biblical traditions, they were closely related to the ancestors of the Israelites, but these traditions are very complicated. According to Gen 10:22, Aram was the son of Shem, but, according to Gen 22:21, he was the grandson of Nahor, Abraham's brother and finally there is the

---

[120] See especially Judges 11:19–22 and Num 21:21–25. According to W. Richter, 'Die Überlieferungen um Jephtah', *Bib*, 47 (1966), pp. 485–556, especially pp. 522–547, this text dates from the time of Jeremiah, before Deuteronomy, and belongs to the *genre* of prophetic discourse on history.

[121] Anastasi Papyrus, VI, 51 ff; see *ANET*, p. 259a.

[122] J. Janssen, 'Les monts Seir dans les textes égyptiens', *Bib*, 15 (1934), pp. 537–538; B. Grdseloff, *Revue de l'Histoire Juive en Egypte*, 1 (1947), pp. 69ff; K. A. Kitchen, *JEA*, 50 (1964), pp. 66–67; J. R. Bartlett, *JTS*, new series, 20 (1969), pp. 1–2.*

[123] *EA*, 288, 26 = *ANET*, p. 488b.

[124] J. Simons, *Handbook for the Study of Egyptian Topographical Lists relating to Western Asia*, Leiden, 1937, p. 156.

[125] K. A. Kitchen, 'Some New Light on the Asiatic Wars of Ramesses II', *JEA*, 50 (1964), pp. 47–70, especially pp. 50, 53–55.

[126] M. Noth, *ZDPV*, 68 (1946–1951), p. 45.

Israelite's confession of faith (Deut 26:5): 'My father was a wandering Aramaean'. Abraham came from Paddan-aram or Aram Naharaiim ('Aram of the rivers'), where Nahor lived (Gen 24:10). Isaac married Rebekah, Nahor's daughter (Gen 24:48) – or, according to a later tradition (Gen 24:47), Rebekah, Bethuel's daughter, Bethuel being the son of Nahor. Rebekah was Laban's sister and Laban, Nahor's son (Gen 29:5), is again and again called 'Laban the Aramaean'. What is more, this same Laban was Jacob's uncle and he became his father-in-law (Gen 29:15 ff). All this took place, according to the Old Testament, in Upper Mesopotamia, but, according to Gen 31:43–54, Laban and Jacob concluded a treaty which established a frontier between their lands at Mizpah of Galeed in Transjordania. This was, moreover, a treaty between two peoples, not a treaty between two individuals. This may have preserved the memory, transferred to the age of the patriarchs, of an agreement between Aramaeans and Israelites at the time of the settlement or a little later. On the other hand, it may be an account of the situation before the Exodus.[127] The Aramaeans were also in contact with the Moabites – it was from Aram that Balak called the soothsayer Balaam (Num 23:7). According to Judges 3:7–11, the first judge, Othniel, delivered Israel from oppression by Cushanrishataim, the king of Aram or Aram Naharaiim. The historical interpretation of this episode is, however, very difficult and it has frequently been suggested that 'Edom' should be read instead of 'Aram' in this context.[128] According to Judges 18:9, 28 (Greek), the Danites managed to take hold of Laish quite easily because the town had no relations with the Aramaeans; this, of course, presupposes that there were Aramaeans in the district. In a brief survey of Saul's military achievements (1 Sam 14:47 ff), there is reference to a war against the king of Zobah, but it is not possible to check the historical authenticity of this statement. The Aramaeans really entered the history of Israel only during the reign of David and then as Israel's enemy (see 2 Sam 8:3–8; 10:6–14 and 15–19). At that time, the king of Zobah, Hadadezer, was at the head of a coalition which included not only Zobah, but also the Aramaeans of Beth-rehob and the kingdoms of Maakah and Tob. What is more, Hadadezer's power extended from the slopes of the Anti-Lebanon mountains as far as the Euphrates.[129] This Aramaean empire was not built in a day and the Aramaeans must first have entered the regions to the north and the north-east of Palestine as nomads in the twelfth century B.C. at the latest.

---

[127] See below, for the settlement of Gad, pp. 573–574.

[128] See below, p. 536.

[129] A. Malamat, 'The Kingdom of David and Solomon in its Contact with Egypt and Aram Naharaim', *BibArch,* 21 (1958), pp. 96–102 = The Biblical Archaeologist Reader, 2, 1964, pp. 89–98; B. Mazar, 'The Aramaean Empire and its Relations with Israel', *BibArch,* 25 (1962), pp. 97–120 = The Biblical Archaeologist Reader, 2, 1964, pp. 127–151.

It was certainly in the twelfth century, during the reign of Tiglath-pileser I of Assyria, that the Aramaeans appeared for the first time in documents outside the Bible itself. References to Aram and the Aramaeans have been found in Mesopotamian texts dating back to the third millennium and to the beginning of the second as well as in Mari and Rās Shamrah documents,[130] but they are doubtful. The reference to Aram in a new geographical list of Amen-hotep III at the beginning of the fourteenth century B.C.[131] is far more certain. Here the name is accompanied by the determinative 'man', so that it clearly points to a people, the nomadic Aramaeans. There can be no doubt in the case of Tiglath-pileser, who had to fight against enemies whom he called Ahlamu-Aramaeans. From the fourth year of his reign onwards he was fighting these people in the Middle Euphrates, from Carchemish in the north as far as Rapiqum on the northern frontier of Babylonia. He crossed the river twenty-eight times, which means that he must have conducted fourteen campaigns. He burnt towns and villages in the Jebel Bishri between Palmyra and the Euphrates and pursued them as far as Palmyra and the foothills of the Lebanon.[132]

The Ahlamu-Aramaeans are not mentioned in Assyrian texts before Tiglath-pileser, but the Ahlamu are mentioned alone in earlier texts as western nomads who were hostile to Assyria from the end of the fourteenth century onwards.[133] They are also mentioned in a mutilated text of an Amarna letter.[134] In the thirteenth century, the Ahlamu prevented the messengers of the king of Babylon from reaching Hatti.[135] In the fourteenth and thirteenth centuries, individual Ahlamu appear in the documents. The relationship between these Ahlamu and the Aramaeans is disputed. It is possible that 'Ahlamu' was a very general name which later came to be used in a more precise sense, or it may be that the two terms, Ahlamu and Aramaean, were to some extent the same. In any case, it is certain that the Ahlamu lived, generally speaking, in the same districts as the Aramaeans and that they had certain characteristics in common. There must therefore have been a relationship between them.[136]

[130] A. Dupont-Sommer, 'Sur les débuts de l'histoire araméenne', *Congress Volume, Copenhagen* (*SVT*, 1), 1953, pp. 40–49; S. Moscati, 'Sulle origini degli Aramei', *RSO*, 26 (1951), pp. 16–22. See also the references given above, Chapter 7, note 103, page 202.

[131] E. Edel, *Die Ortsnamenlisten aus dem Totentempel Amenophis III*, Bonn, 1966, pp. 28–29.

[132] Summary and references in J. A. Brinkman, *A Political History of Post-Kassite Babylonia*, Rome, 1968, pp. 277–278.

[133] D. D. Luckenbill, *ARAB*, I, §§ 73, 116, 166, 209.

[134] EA, 200, 8 and 10, in connection with the king of Babylon. The Ahlamu are also, it would seem, mentioned in an unpublished text of the period of Rim-Sin in the eighteenth century B.C.; see above, Chapter 7, note 105, page 202.

[135] J. Friedrich, *Aus dem hethitischen Schrifttum* (*Der Alte Orient*, 24, 3), 1925, p. 26.

[136] For the relationship between the Aramaeans and the Amorites, see above, Part I, Chapter 7, Section III, page 200.

VI. Conclusion

The settlement of the Israelites in Canaan has to be seen within this general framework of the Near East in the last centuries of the second millennium B.C. The final collapse of the Hittite Empire and the weakening of Egypt's position, resulting in the eventual loss of her territorial possessions in Asia, left the field clear for new peoples. It is, however, important to remember that the Israelites were not the only people to take advantage of this situation. The withdrawal of the Egyptians from Palestine left the Canaanite cities intact and Egyptian control no more than nominal. Sea Peoples settled in certain parts of Palestine and the Philistines grew to become a rival power, almost more powerful than the Israelites during the reign of Saul. Moab had become a settled people, Edom had probably become settled and possibly Ammon as well. In the north and the north-east the Aramaeans were infiltrating into Palestine.

The Israelites were able to acquire land at this time precisely because of this disturbance in the balance of political power in Syria-Palestine. They were not, however, able to gain possession of certain parts, such as Edom, Moab and the plain of Philistia, because of the competition from these new powers. No one power was predominant and this explains why, as soon as the first groups of Israelites had settled in Palestine, they were engaged in armed conflict (the period of the Judges), and why Canaanite groups persisted until the time of David.

The biblical traditions concerning the settlement in Canaan have to be considered within this historical framework. As we commented at the beginning of this part of the book, when we were discussing the various theories of the settlement in Canaan, these biblical traditions have to be studied first of all on their own, with the help of literary criticism and the history of traditions. They then have to be compared with the external evidence of general history in the Ancient Near East and of archaeology. These biblical traditions must, however, have had different local origins, and for this reason we shall follow a definite geographical order – the settlement in southern Palestine, in Transjordania, in central Palestine and in the north of Palestine.

Chapter Seventeen

THE SETTLEMENT IN THE SOUTH OF PALESTINE
THE TRIBES OF JUDAH, SIMEON AND LEVI [1]

ACCORDING to Jos 10:28–43, the conquest of the south of Palestine was the work of Joshua and 'all Israel', but, according to Judges 1:1–20, it was the work, after the death of Joshua himself (Judges 1:1), of Judah and Simeon and of Calebite and Kenite groups associated with Judah and Simeon. The conquest of Hebron, which was the main city in the territory of Judah and was to be David's first capital, was in particular attributed to Caleb (see Judges 1:20; Jos 15:13–19). This was the fulfilment of a promise made to Caleb in the desert (Jos 14:6–14) at the time of the abortive attempt to enter the south of Palestine from Kadesh (Num 13–14; cf. Deut 1:19–46). It is clear from any comparison of these texts that this is a difficult problem. Apart from Jos 10, which is pan-Israelitic, the other texts represent south Palestinian and above all Calebite traditions. It is these that we have to study first.

I. THE RECONNAISSANCE OF CANAAN AND THE ROLE OF CALEB
(Num 13–14; Deut 1:19–46; Jos 14:6–14; Num 32:6–15)

Num 13–14 forms part of a group of traditions connected with Kadesh. Twelve scouts, one from each tribe, including Joshua from the tribe of Ephraim and Caleb from the tribe of Judah, are sent into Canaan. They report that the country is good, but that it is inhabited by a powerful people. Although they are encouraged to do so, first by Caleb and then by Joshua and Caleb, the people refuse to enter the country and want to go back to Egypt. God decides to strike the rebellious people, but spares them at the intercession of Moses, saying only that none of the men present, with the exception of Caleb or of Caleb and Joshua, will enter the Promised

[1] This chapter has already been published in English in *Translating and Understanding the Old Testament. Essays in Honour of H. G. May*, Nashville and New York, 1970, pp. 108–134.

Land. The people repent and go up to the highlands to attack, but, because God is not with them, they are defeated.

This is a composite text.[2] There are several doublets, which contain differences. According to Num 13:17 and 22–24, the scouts went only to the Negeb and the highlands of Hebron, but, according to 13:21, they went from the wilderness of Zin to the Pass of Hamath, in other words, they covered the whole of the Promised Land. According to 13:30, Caleb was the only one of the envoys to urge the Israelites to fight, whereas, according to 14:6 ff, both Joshua and Caleb encouraged the people. According to 14:24, only Caleb entered the land, but, according to 14:30, it was Joshua and Caleb. Literary critics are generally speaking in agreement, in view of these differences and certain differences in style, that this passage contains priestly and other texts. The priestly narrative includes 13:1–17a, 21, 25–26, 32–33; 14:1–3, 5–10, 26–38. Peculiar to it are the detailed list of the twelve scouts, the addition of Joshua to Caleb in the task of urging the people to enter the land and in the promise of entering the land and finally the proclamation that the Israelites would spend forty years in the desert and that they would die there, except for Joshua and Caleb. The rest of the passage belongs, in the opinion of most scholars, to the earlier traditions: 13:17b–20, 22–24, 27–31; 14:4, 11–25, 39–45. It would seem to be almost impossible to divide this earlier narrative exactly between the J and the E sources or between the L, J and E sources. Num 14:11–23a must, however, be regarded as a special case. This text contains Moses' intercession and his dialogue with God and is written in a style which is that of the Deuteronomist and has parallels in Exodus. It is clearly an addition to the early account, which had an introduction that was lost and later replaced by the priestly introduction. This early account, moreover, describes only a reconnaissance carried out in the Negeb and the highlands of Hebron as far as the Valley of Eshcol and is only concerned with Caleb. I will discuss the conclusion to this early account, the story of the defeat at Hormah (14:39–45), a little later.

This early narrative, that is, the account without the priestly additions and the addition of 14:11–23a, is also used in Moses' introductory discourse (Deut 1:19–46).[3] The story in Deuteronomy is much less concrete than the earlier account in Numbers. It is above all a dialogue between Moses and the people, the scouts sent to reconnoitre the land play a subordinate rôle and Moses' intercession is omitted. It has a different theological intention,

[2] S. Wagner, 'Die Kundschaftergeschichten im Alten Testament', ZAW, 76 (1964), pp. 255–269; V. Fritz, Israel in der Wüste. Traditionsgeschichtliche Untersuchung der Wüstenüberlieferung des Jahwisten, Marburg, 1970, pp. 19–24, 79–86, 99.

[3] For the relationships between the two accounts, see N. Lohfink, 'Darstellungskunst und Theologie in Dtn 1, 6–3, 29', Bib, 41 (1960), pp. 105–134; G. von Rad, Das fünfte Buch Mose. Deuteronomium (ATD),[2] 1968, in loco; J. L. McKenzie, 'The Historical Prologue of Deuteronomy', Fourth World Congress of Jewish Studies, Papers, I, Jerusalem, 1967, p. 97.

but it reproduces the essential elements of the early account. For instance, the rebellion of the people and their punishment are described. Caleb is exempted from this punishment and is promised 'the land he has set foot on'. I believe that this verse, 36, is early,[4] unlike verses 37–38, which mention Joshua as well and which are, in my opinion, additions.[5] Joshua, it should be noted, is described in verse 38 not as one of the scouts, but as Moses' servant and, according to verse 37, Moses too is not to enter the Promised Land; cf. Deut 3:26; 4:21. What is peculiar to Deuteronomy is that Moses seems to have been punished because he pleased the people (Deut 1:37: 'on your account'). They had asked for scouts to be sent out to explore the land; this was a sign of their failure to trust God (Deut 1:22). According to Num 13:2, on the other hand, these scouts were sent out at the command of Yahweh and this source (Num 20:12, 24 and Deut 32:50–52) gives a different reason for the death of Moses (and Aaron) before the entry into the Promised Land – their lack of faith at the waters of Meribah.[6]

We must now briefly consider a third parallel text, Jos 14:6–14, which tells how, when the land was being allotted, Caleb reminded Joshua of the promise that had been made to him in the desert, namely that he would possess the land that he had set foot on, and how he received Hebron as his portion. This narrative is the work of the deuteronomic editor and it derives from the account in Deuteronomy. The concluding verse, 'Hence Hebron down to the present day has remained the possession of Caleb son of Jephunneh the Kenizzite, because he did the whole will of Yahweh the God of Israel' (Jos 14:14) gives the reason for this tradition. It explains why Hebron, which is situated in the very centre of Judah, was occupied by the Calebites, who were not of pure Israelitic stock.

One final text, Num 32:6–15, recalls the rôle of Caleb in the desert. This text is late and is derived from the priestly account in Num 13-14 – Caleb and Joshua and the forty years in the desert are, for instance, mentioned in both accounts. It would also seem that it derives from Jos 14, since Caleb the Kenizzite occurs in both texts.

All these different literary forms of the Calebite tradition, including the early account in Num 13–14, from which the other texts are derived, belong to a stage at which the special traditions had already been gathered around the various traditions of the house of Joseph, which was to enter Canaan by the roundabout route via Transjordania. Caleb took part in forty years of wandering in the desert, he entered the Promised Land with Joshua and he was eighty-five years old when Joshua allotted him Hebron

---

[4] I believe this contrary to Steuernagel and von Rad, but together with Noth, *Überlieferungsgeschichtliche Studien*, pp. 31–32, especially p. 32, note 1.

[5] I share this opinion with Steuernagel, von Rad and Noth.

[6] E. Arden, 'How Moses Failed God', *JBL*, 76 (1957), pp. 50–52; A. S. Kapelrud, same reference, p. 242.

as his portion (Jos 14:10).

There may, however, have been a preliterary form of this tradition, according to which the Calebites entered Canaan directly and independently of the other groups by the south. Deut 1:20–21 may represent the beginning of the early narrative of Num 13–14 which disappeared as the priestly editors improved on their sources. According to these verses, Moses commanded the Israelites to take possession of the highlands which God had 'given' to his people and, according to Num 14:24 (cf. Deut 1:36), Caleb was in fact to possess the land that he had reconnoitred. One would therefore expect as a consequence that he would enter the land, but instead we have the story of the defeat at Hormah (Num 14:39–45).

A theological meaning is given to the story of the reconnaissance of the land in its present form by this concluding episode.[7] When the Israelites reached the land which according to God's promise they would conquer, they lacked faith and, frightened by the report brought back by those who had reconnoitred the land, they wanted to go back to Egypt. Nonetheless, they attacked, going against the will of God and setting out without the ark and without Moses. What we have here is a complete reversal of the themes of the exodus and the holy war, in other words, the themes are a non-holy war and an anti-exodus.[8] The outcome was bound to be disastrous.[9] At the same time, however, the position of this story of the Israelites' failure in the narrative as a whole makes it possible to link the tradition of the Calebites with the traditions of the house of Joseph. In other words, it explains why Israel had been driven back into the desert and were able to enter Canaan only by following a long and difficult roundabout route. This pattern could only be obtained, however, by combining the Calebite tradition and a tradition which was centred in southern Palestine and had been used and adapted in Num 14:39–46. Originally, this tradition was concerned with other groups of Israelites.

II. THE SETTLEMENT OF THE SIMEONITE AND LEVITE GROUPS

The part of Palestine in which the episode described in Num 14:39–46 takes place is not around Hebron, but in the south of the hill country of Judah on the borders of the Negeb. This region was inhabited by

[7] S. J. de Vries, 'The Origin of the Murmuring Tradition', *JBL*, 87 (1968), pp. 51–58, especially pp. 55–57, who criticises the position taken by G. W. Coats, *Rebellion in the Wilderness*, Nashville and New York, 1968, pp. 137–156. Very little of interest is contained in W. Beltz, *Die Kaleb-Traditionen*, Budapest and Berlin, 1966.

[8] See W. L. Moran, *Bib*, 44 (1963), pp. 333–342.

[9] S. J. de Vries, *op. cit.*, p. 58; S. Lehming, *ZAW*, 73 (1961), p. 71 ff.

Amalekites and Canaanites. The account in Num 14:39–46 should therefore be compared with the story of the defeat of the Amalekites in Ex 17:8–13, which also belongs to the Kadesh cycle.[10] These traditions concerning the Amalekites originated in Judah, where the people had to go on fighting against Amalek until the reigns of Saul and David (1 Sam 15; 30). These Judaean traditions, however, brought together the memories of several different groups living in the south and we are therefore bound to ask whether the tradition concerning Hormah was not originally a Simeonite tradition.

According to Num 14:39–46, the Israelites were defeated and harried 'all the way to Hormah' (verse 45). Hormah is probably Tell el-Mshāsh, to the east of Beersheba, and therefore about fifty miles north of Kadesh on the boundary between the Negeb and the hill country. Since the Israelites had reached 'the heights of the highlands' (verse 44), they must have advanced to the north of Hormah and were therefore thrown back to the south 'all the way to Hormah' (verse 45). They must therefore have conquered Hormah. This conquest is in fact narrated in Num 21:1–3, although this brief description is clearly not in its proper chronological and geographical context. The reference to the king of Arad (verse 1) is a gloss on the early text which did not originally contain the name of the king, but only the word 'Canaanite', which would have been a perfectly legitimate gloss, since Arad is near to Hormah. The conquest, then, must have been made from the southern approach, the Israelites going up 'by way of Atharim'. This road has not been identified with any certainty. It may be the road from Kadesh to Arad which was marked at a later stage by small forts during the Iron Age.[11] It may, however, have been the road which went up to Arad from south of the Dead Sea, if there is no direct connection in this episode with Kadesh.

The correctness of this second hypothesis would seem to be borne out if a parallel account (Judges 1:16–17) is taken into consideration. According to this narrative of the taking of Hormah, the Kenites went up with the sons of Judah from the 'city of palms' as far as the Negeb of Arad and settled there. Judah and Simeon defeated the Canaanites who lived in Zephath, destroying the town, which then took the name Hormah (ḥērem, anathema). This 'city of palms' cannot be Jericho here (as it is in other texts).[12] It is Tamar in 1 Kings 9:18; Ezek 47:19, the present 'Ain Hosb, some twenty miles south-west of the Dead Sea in the 'Arabah.[13] This is clearly another entry

[10] H. Grønbaek, 'Juda und Amalek. Uberlieferungsgeschichtliche Erwägungen zu Exodus, 17, 8–16', ST, 18 (1964), pp. 26–45; Grønbaek considers Num 14:39–46 on pp. 35–37.

[11] Y. Aharoni, IEJ, 10 (1960), p. 109.

[12] B. Mazar, JNES, 24 (1965), p. 300 and note 17; R. Schmid, TZ, 21 (1965), p. 263; V. Fritz, ZDPV, 82 (1966), p. 331.

[13] Y. Aharoni, 'Tamar and the Roads to Elath', IEJ, 13 (1963), pp. 30–42. It has even been suggested that the ha'atārîm of Num 21:1 is a corruption of the hatt mārîm of Judges 1:16.

into Canaan from the south which resulted in the conquest of Hormah by Judah and Simeon. However, the text was originally concerned only with Simeon since Hormah was allotted to Simeon in Jos 19:4 = 1 Chron 4:30. In time, since Simeon had been absorbed by Judah and the lands inherited by the tribe of Simeon were 'encircled' by the lands belonging to Judah (Jos 19:1), the conquest of Hormah was consequently attributed to Judah and Simeon and Hormah was regarded as one of the towns of Judah (Jos 15:30).

In the two narratives, Num 21:1–3 and Judges 1:16–17, the name Hormah is explained as 'anathema', because the town was 'placed under ban', ḥerem. This is, of course, a popular explanation of the origin of the name; there is already a probable mention of the town in the execration texts of Egypt dating back to the nineteenth century B.C. and in the Sinai inscriptions of Amen-em-het III.[14] Despite the popular character of the explanation, however, the fact remains that Num 21:1–3 comes from the Yahwistic source and Judges 1:17 forms part of a summary of the conquest according to the Yahwistic tradition.[15] The two texts preserve the memory of an invasion of groups of the tribe of Simeon from the south. It is in the south of the land, too, that we find the tribe of Simeon settled in the geographical section of the book of Joshua. The frontiers of the territory belonging to the Simeonites are not defined because the tribe was integrated into the tribe of Judah, but, in Jos 15:21–32, there is a list of the towns of Judah situated in the Negeb and the second part of this list (verses 26b–32) is parallel to a list of Simeonite towns given in Jos 19:2–8 and 1 Chron 4:28–32. Different biblical scholars have come to different conclusions regarding these two parallel lists. Alt[16] dated the lists of Jos 15–19 back to the period of Josiah, but thought that the memory of a very early settlement on the part of the tribe of Simeon was preserved in the Negeb. Noth[17] also dated the lists of towns in Joshua back to the same period, but regarded Jos 19:2–8 as the artificial construction of an editor whose aim, from Jos 15 onwards, was to compose a list of 'Simeonite' towns. Cross and Wright[18] were of the opinion that these lists were composed during the reign of Jehosaphat and that Jos 19:2–8 and 1 Chron 4:28–32 were not derived from Jos 15, but went back to an independent list of Simeonite towns. Kallai[19] thought that this list was composed during the period of

---

[14] B. Mazar, *JNES*, 24 (1965), p. 298. According to V. Fritz, *Israel in der Wüste*, quoted in note 2, pp. 89–93, the text is an aetiological explanation of the name based on the battles against towns in southern Canaan.

[15] S. Mowinckel, *Tetrateuch – Pentateuch – Hexateuch* (*BZAW*, 90), 1964, pp. 17–33.

[16] A. Alt, 'Judas Gaue unter Josia', *PJB*, 21 (1925), pp. 100–116 = *Kleine Schriften*, II, pp. 276–288, especially pp. 285–286.

[17] M. Noth, *Josua (HAT)*,[2] 1953, p. 113; *Geschichte*, p. 58.

[18] F. M. Cross and G. E. Wright, 'The Boundary and Province Lists of the Kingdom of Judah, *JBL*, 73–75 (1956), pp. 202–226, especially pp. 209 and 214–215.

[19] Z. Kallai, 'The Town Lists of Judah, Simeon, Benjamin and Dan', *VT*, 8 (1958), pp.

David and was revised during the reign of Hezekiah. Aharoni,[20] who dated the revised lists at the period of Uzziah, was of the opinion that the land allotted to Simeon was the territory known during the reign of David as the Negeb of Judah (1 Sam 27:10; 30:14; 2 Sam 24:7), with Beersheba as its centre. One last opinion that must be mentioned in this context is that of Talmon,[21] who has suggested that the list of the towns of Simeon was not later than David's reign. He has based his opinion on the statement in 1 Chron 4:31b: 'These were their towns (i.e. the towns of Simeon) until the reign of David'. It was during David's reign that Simeon became integrated into Judah and indeed the Simeonites disappeared from the history of Israel from the time of David onwards.

We still have to try, however, to establish the time when the Simeonites settled in the extreme south of Palestine. According to the biblical tradition, the history of Simeon followed a parallel course to that of Levi. Both Simeon and Levi were Leah's sons and according to Gen 34 the two groups of their descendants lived in central Palestine, but left the region after coming into conflict with the inhabitants of Shechem – this episode is connected with the prehistory of Israel, long before the exodus and the conquest of Canaan. Simeon and Levi are also brought together in Jacob's final blessing of all his sons (Gen 49:5–7), in which they are not blessed, but cursed because of their violence, and 'scattered among Israel'.[22] According to this text, they were struck by some undefined catastrophe. We can only be sure that this had nothing to do with what took place at Shechem, for that story is narrated in quite different terms and the Simeonites and Levites emerged unscathed from the episode, at least according to Gen 35:5.[23] Neither tribe had its own territory at the period when Gen 49:5–7 was composed. As we have seen, Simeon had become integrated into Judah in the Negeb or was at least in the process of being integrated.

We must now turn to Levi. According to Gen 49: 5–7, Levi may have been a profane group of Levites, like that that described in Gen 34 or it may have been the priestly tribe of Levi. There is, however, evidence that Levi had very early connections with the south and that it was probably there that it became a priestly tribe, provided that it is accepted that there was a continuity between the two groups. Alongside the canonical division of the Levites into three families, descending from the three sons of Levi, Gershon,

---

134–160, especially pp. 156–159; ibid., Les tribus d'Israël, Jerusalem, 1967, pp. 295–303 (Hebrew).

[20] Y. Aharoni, 'The Negeb of Judah, IEJ, 8 (1958), pp. 26–38.

[21] S. Talmon, 'The Town Lists of Simeon', IEJ, 15 (1965), pp. 235–241.

[22] H. J. Zobel, Stammesspruch und Geschichte (BZAW, 95), 1965, pp. 65–72; A. H. J. Gunneweg, Leviten und Priester, Göttingen, 1965, pp. 44–52.

[23] This matter should now be regarded as settled; see especially S. Lehming, 'Zur Überlieferungsgeschichte von Gen 34', ZAW, 70 (1958), pp. 228–250; A. de Pury, 'Genèse XXXIV et l'histoire', RB, 76 (1969), pp. 5–49.

Kohath and Merari, there is another division of the Levites into five clans, the Libnites, Hebronites, Mahlites, Mushites and Korahites (Num 26:58a).[24] The Libnite clan and the Hebronites are obviously the inhabitants of Libnah and Hebron. The Korahite clan may possibly be connected with Korah, a name that appears in a list of the 'sons' of Caleb in 1 Chron 2:43. This list consists above all of place names, Korah being juxtaposed with Hebron. The other two names listed in Num 26:58a are not at all clear. According to this undoubtedly very early list, the Levites appear to have lived first in the south of the territory of Judah. According to Judges 17–18; 19: 1 ff, from the period of the Judges onwards they spread towards the north. An additional datum is supplied by the tradition which seems to have originated in southern Palestine and according to which Moses' father was Hobab the Kenite. Hobab's family had settled near Arad, which may point to the presence of Levites in that district at a very early period.[25]

The settlement of groups of Levites in the south of Judah may possibly be confirmed by the list of levitical cities given in Jos 21:1–42 and 1 Chron 6:39–66. This list is based on an earlier document which, it is believed, provided an account of the settlement of the Levites just after the schism[26], during the reign of David[27], or during the time of Solomon.[28] The Levites did not, however, settle in these towns at any of these times – they were already settled in them.[29] What is particularly striking is that these towns are not equally distributed. On the contrary, they are situated in groups separated by gaps. There is, for instance, no levitical city in the hill country of Judah between Hebron and Jerusalem. They are all in the south – Hebron and Libnah (two of the Levite clans mentioned in Num 26:58a have the names of these two towns) and five other towns farther south. Of these, Debir, Juttah, Eshtemoa and Jattir have been located and two, Holon (Hilen?) and 'Ain (Ashan?), have not been located, but were undoubtedly also in the south.[30]

[24] R. de Vaux, Institutions, p. 370; M. Noth, Das Vierte Buch Mose. Numeri (ATD), 1966, in loco; A. Cody, A History of Old Testament Priesthood, Rome, 1969, pp. 56–57; J. M. Miller, The Korahites in Southern Judah', CBQ, 32 (1970), pp. 58–68.

[25] For the connection between the traditions concerning Moses' Kenite marriage and those concerning his Midianite marriage, see R. de Vaux, 'Sur L'origine kénite ou midianite du Yahvisme', Eretz-Israel, 9 (Albright Volume), 1969, pp. 28–32 and above, pp. 623–637, especially pp. 624–625.

[26] R. de Vaux, Institutions, II, pp. 366–367.

[27] W. F. Albright, 'The List of Levitic Cities', Louis Ginsberg Jubilee Volume, I, New York, 1945, pp. 49–73.

[28] B. Mazar, 'The Cities of the Priests and Levites', Congress Volume, Oxford (SVT, 7), Leiden, 1960, pp. 193–205.

[29] M. Haran, 'Studies in the Account of the Levitical Cities', JBL, 80 (1961), pp. 45–54, 156–165.

[30] Y. Aharoni, The Land of the Bible, London, 1967, pp. 268–273. Attempts have been made to discover evidence in the Egyptian geographical lists that the Levites settled in the Negeb.

It has often been pointed out that there were close links between the Levites and Kadesh. In the passage containing Moses' blessings (Deut 33:8), Levi is given the Urim and the Thummim, the sacred charms which as a priest he is privileged to possess, after having been put to the test at Massah and having striven with God at the waters of Meribah.[31] Massah and Meribah are found as a double name in Ex 17:1–7, as the place where the miracle of the water occurred, at Rephidim on the way to Sinai (verse 1) or at Horeb (verse 6). Another version of this story, however, is given in Num 20:1–13 and here the miracle of the water takes place at Kadesh. This text, which is mainly the work of the priestly editor, derives from the same early tradition as the text in Ex 17, but there are two major differences – the miracle occurs at Kadesh and the name Massah is not mentioned. The consequence of this is that Meribah is called Meribah of Kadesh in the late texts (Num 27:14; Deut 32:51; Ezek 68:28).

It is, however, not easy to make use of this tradition of the waters of Meribah in order to prove that the Levites were connected with Kadesh. Although the reason for the miracle was the fact that the people were suffering from a shortage of water (Ex 17:1; Num 20:2), it is true to say that the Kadesh region is better supplied with water than anywhere else in the peninsula. A possible reply to this objection is that it was precisely after the miracle performed by Moses that there was water at Kadesh, but this is not stated by any tradition. What is more, the Levites are not mentioned either in Ex 17 or in Numb 20. The people put God to the test (*massāh*) and engaged in strife (*m'ríbhāh*) with him. This is, of course, an aetiology, an example of folk etymology. The name Meribah had in fact been given to a spring near which lawsuits were conducted (*ríbh*) and the same spring must also have had a sacred character (this is, of course, the meaning of the name Kadesh). It is also interesting in this context to note that, in Gen 14:7, the early name for Kadesh is used – *'ēin miš'pāt*, the 'Spring of Judgement'. In Deut 33:8, in which the Levites are mentioned, however, there is no reference to the miracle of the water of Exod 17 and Num 20 and clearly this text must refer to an episode which is unknown to us. It is even possible that no geographical name at all is contained in this

---

One suggestion is *w rwy*, 'the territory of Levi', in a list of Ramses III; see J. Simons, *Handbook for the Study of Egyptian Topographical Lists Relating to Western Asia*, Leiden, 1937, p. 165, Nos. 30 and 94. Another suggestion is *ngb rwy*, the 'Negeb of Levi', in a list of Palestinian and Syrian towns of Sheshonk I; see J. Simons, *op. cit.*, p. 180, No. 74. See also S. Yeivin, 'The Exodus', *Tarbiz*, 30 (1960–1961), p. 6. These suggestions have been accepted by S. Mowinckel, *Israels opphav og eldste historie*, Oslo, 1967, p. 146.

[31] For this text and its connections with Exod 17 and Num 20, see the commentary by G. von Rad, *Das fünfte Buch Mose. Deuteronomium (ATD),*[2] 1968, *in loco*; S. Lehming, 'Massa und Meriba', *ZAW*, 73 (1961), pp. 71–77; J. Koenig, 'Sourciers, thaumaturges et scribes', *RHR*, 164 (1963–B), pp. 17–38, 165–180; H. J. Zobel, *Stammesspruch und Geschichte*, pp. 32–34; H. Schmid, *Mose. Überlieferung und Geschichte (BZAW*, 110), 1968, pp. 91–93.*

text and that the translation should read: 'Your Urim and your Thummim (you give) to the one you favour, whom you have put to the test, with whom you have striven on the day (reading *l'yôm* instead of *'al mē*) of strife.[32] What is certain is that Deut 33:8 was given a geographical interpretation in the biblical tradition and it was in this way that Massah found its way into Ex 17. If these two texts are taken in conjunction with the third text that we have taken into account, Num 20, it can be concluded that there was a tradition according to which Levi was especially linked with Kadesh. What I have said in this context, however, shows that this tradition was probably not an early one. What is more, the view put forward which associates with Kadesh the whole of Israel's religious and civil organisation and especially the levitical institution is probably an exaggeration.

There were, then, groups of Simeonites in the extreme south of Palestine and groups of Levites in Judah and possibly at Kadesh, but it is extremely difficult to know when they settled there. According to Judges 1:1, the taking of Hormah by the Simeonites (Judges 1:17) took place after the death of Joshua, in other words, during the period of the Judges. Judges 1:1–26, however, is a collection of data which were not given a place in the book of Joshua because they were not in accordance with the plan of the book or its theological purpose. These data must therefore be derived from a Yahwistic account of the conquest.[33] The introduction 'After the death of Joshua' is clearly an editorial device and is connected with Jos 24:29–31, but these verses are themselves additional and come from Judges 2:8–10, where they are found word for word. In the early account, Jos 24:28 would have been continued by Judges 2:6. The settlement of the Simeonites in the south of Palestine took place before the period of the Judges.

Their settlement and the settlement of the Levites are sometimes linked with Gen 34, according to which the two tribes left for the south after the incident at Shechem, with the result that they had become settled there long before the Exodus and that they had not gone down into Egypt. There is, however, no justification for this theory in the texts themselves. In Gen 34, the two groups are shown to be forced to leave central Palestine at the time of the patriarchs, but no indication is given of where they went. According to the other texts, they were in the south of Palestine at the time of the conquest, but nothing is said about what had happened to them in the meantime. What is more, it has recently been pointed out that Simeon and Levi appear only in verse 25 and at the end of the story of the affair at Shechem, Gen 34:30–31, and that they must have been introduced into the story at a later stage, the account having originally been concerned only with 'Jacob's

---

[32] See Lehming, *op. cit.*
[33] S. Mowinckel, *op. cit.* (note 15).

sons'.[34] Finally, according to Num 21:1–3 and Judges 1:16–17, the Simeonites at least acquired their land when they came from the south.

This entry into Canaan by the south, in which Simeon is associated, in Judges 1:16–17, with Judah and the Calebites, is clearly different from the conquest ascribed to Joshua.[35] According to Num 21:1–3 and 14:39–45, however, the capture of Hormah and the abortive attempt to advance northwards are connected with the story of the group which left Egypt with Moses. This connection may have been made later, but it may also have a historical basis. The reference to Simeon kept as a hostage in the story of Joseph (Gen 42:24) – and one is bound to ask why Simeon is mentioned in particular here – may perhaps contain a memory of a stay on the part of the Simeonites in Egypt. In the case of Levi, Moses' connections with the tribe and the Egyptian names of Moses himself and of several of the 'sons of Levi', Phinehas, Hophni and Merari at least, certainly have to be taken into account.

In the biblical tradition, then, not only were certain individual traditions preserved; they were also simplified and extended to enable them to be applied to the whole people. In normal circumstances, relations between Palestine, Sinai and Egypt were easy and semi-nomadic groups were always coming and going between Palestine and Egypt. The evidence provided by the stories of Abraham, Joseph and his brothers and Moses in Midian is supported and confirmed by extrabiblical texts. There were several 'descents into Egypt' and Simeon and Levi might have gone down into Egypt at any time. There were also several 'exoduses from Egypt'.[36] As we have already seen, the exodus stories combine two versions of the exodus, one of an exodus-expulsion from Egypt and the other of an exodus-flight. Two different routes are also combined in the same biblical accounts, one to the north and the other to the east, the exodus-expulsion following the northern route and the exodus-flight following the eastern route. We think that it is possible that the groups of the tribe of Simeon (and perhaps of Judah) and part of the Levite group took part in the exodus-expulsion and halted in the Kadesh region, near the Calebites, the Kenites and other groups. The group which fled from Egypt, on the other hand, under the leadership of Moses first halted at Sinai. We have certainly to accept the fact that Moses' group came into contact with the other groups at Kadesh, either for the first time or else making renewed contact, after leaving Sinai. The biblical tradition certainly insists very firmly on the fact that the

---

[34] S. Lehming and A. de Pury, *op. cit.*, note 23 and above, p. 171. It is more doubtful whether these 'sons of Jacob' took the place of a clan of the 'sons of Israel' which had nothing in common with Jacob, as de Pury suggests.

[35] H. Haag, 'Von Jahwe geführt. Auslegung von Ri 1, 1–20', *Bibel und Leben*, 4 (1963), pp. 103–115.

[36] See above, p. 380.

Israelites stayed at Kadesh and it is difficult to explain otherwise the deeply rooted attachment to the religion of Moses, Yahwism, among the tribes of southern Palestine. The groups of Simeon and Levi (and perhaps also Judah) continued, however, to follow their own course in history and, together with the Calebites, settled in their lands as they came up from the south. This is, of course, no more than a hypothesis, but it is one which takes as fully as possible into account the biblical texts, the traditions used in those texts and the history of the Near East in general.

III. THE SETTLEMENT OF THE CALEBITE GROUPS IN THE HEBRON DISTRICT

1. *Caleb*

As we have already seen, Hebron was, according to one tradition, promised to Caleb (Num 13–14; Deut 1:19–46; Jos 14:6–14). What is more, it is probable that the early tradition of Num 13–14 was completed by the story of the taking of Hebron by the Calebite group.[37] This is plainly stated by the story in Jos 15:13–19. In the parallel passage, Judges 1:10–15, it is Judah which benefits. According to Jos 15:13–14, it was Caleb who took Hebron and a link is established between this passage and Jos 14:13, in which Hebron is promised to Caleb as his inheritance, in verse 13. The taking of Hebron by Caleb is also mentioned in Judges 1:20, but, according to Judges 1:10, it was taken by Judah and, according to Jos 10:36–37, by Joshua. These are three stages in the development of the tradition.

The Calebites continued to occupy land to the south of Hebron. According to 1 Sam 25:1–3, for example, Nabal the Calebite kept his sheep at Carmel (= Khirbet Kirmil) and lived at Maon (=Kh. Maʿin). These places are between eight and ten miles south of Hebron. According to 1 Sam 30:14, there was a Negeb of Caleb, which may have been the same region or else a district south of the hill country of Judah. The pattern of Calebite settlement can be completed by the genealogical lists of Judah in 1 Chron 2 and 4, which we have already taken into consideration in connection with the Simeonites.[38] In these lists, various data and dates are brought together and personal and place names are found side by side. There are three lists containing the descendants of Caleb: 1 Chron 2:18–24 and 42–50; 4:11–20. The second of these, 1 Chron 2:42–50, is the most homogeneous and it adds to Hebron and Maon, which we have already mentioned, several places in-

---

[37] R. Schmid, *TZ*, 21 (1955), pp. 263–264.

[38] For these lists, see M. Noth, 'Eine Siedlungsgeographische Liste in 1 Chron 2 und 4', *ZDPV*, 55 (1932), pp. 97–124; J. Myers, *1 Chronicles (Anchor Bible)*, *in loco.*; Y. Aharoni, *The Land of the Bible*, 1967, pp. 224–227.

cluding Ziph between Hebron and Carmel, Tappuah or Beth Tappuah (= Taffuh) to the west of Hebron, Bethzur, about four miles to the north of Hebron, Madmannah, which also appears in Jos 15:31 as a town in the south of Judah (= Umm Deimneh?—about twelve miles to the north-east of Beersheba) and several other places which have not been identified. This is a very early list preserving the memory of the Calebite occupation before Caleb was integrated into the group of Judah. The extent of this occupation, then, was from a point a little to the north of Hebron (Bethzur) southwards to the limits of the hill country of Judah north of Beersheba (Madmannah).

According to 1 Chron 2:24, Caleb married Ephrathah. She bore Ashhur, the father of Tekoa. Ephrathah was the Judaean clan from which David descended. It had settled at Bethlehem (Ruth 1:2; 1 Sam 17:12) and Bethlehem is called Ephrathah in Ruth 4:11; Jos 15:59 (LXX) and Mic 5:1. This marriage and the birth of Tekoa (= Khirbet Tekuʿ, five miles south of Bethlehem) point to a peaceful merging together of Calebite and Judaean elements in the district between Bethlehem and Hebron.

2. *Othniel*

Caleb was ultimately absorbed into the genealogies of Judah. In other texts, however, the memory of Caleb as a Kenizzite was preserved (see Jos 14:6 and 14 and its derivative Num 32:12). According to Gen 36:11, 15, 42, the Kenizzites were related to the Edomites, but, according to Jos 15:17, Caleb was Kenaz's brother. According to Judges 1:13; 3:9, Kenaz was Caleb's younger brother. The conquest of Debir, which was originally called Kiriath-sepher, is ascribed, in Jos 15:16–19 and, with slight differences, in Judges 1:12–15, to Kenaz's son, Othniel, who was therefore Caleb's nephew. Albright located Debir at Tell Beit Mirsim, that is, about twelve miles to the south-west of Hebron on the edge of the Shephelah. This site has been thoroughly excavated. This identification has been questioned by several scholars, who have suggested Khirbet Rabud, which is about eight miles from Hebron to the east of the road between Hebron and Beersheba.[39] According to the biblical account, Caleb promised his daughter Achsah to the man who conquered Debir and, when she was married to Othniel, she asked her father to give her some *gullôth*, some 'bowls' or springs of water and he gave her 'the upper springs and the

[39] K. Galling, 'Zur Lokalisierung von Debir', *ZDPV*, 70 (1954), pp. 135–141; M. Noth, *ZDPV*, 72 (1956), pp. 35 ff; H. J. Stoebe, *ZDPV*, 80 (1964), p. 13; H. Donner, *ZDPV*, 81 (1965), pp. 24–25: Late Bronze and Iron Age I pottery. Y. Aharoni now believes this, although he has not stated this view in writing. W. F. Albright still insists on Tell Beit Mirsim; see *Archaeology and Old Testament Study*, ed. D. Winton Thomas, Oxford, 1967, p. 209.

lower springs' (Jos 15:19; 1:15), the district of the springs of Seil ed-Dilbe about five miles south of Hebron on the present road.[40]

No more than this is known of the possible expansion of the group of Othniel, although Othniel himself, the son of Kenaz the younger brother of Caleb, appears again in the Old Testament as Israel's first 'judge' in Judges 3:7–11. According to this passage, Othniel delivered Israel from the king of Aram Naharaiim, Cushan-rishataim. This story contains a number of strange elements. The name of the oppressor, *kûšan rišᵉ 'āthayîm*, means 'Cushan of double wickedness' and must have been either invented or altered in some way and his country, Aram of the Two Rivers (*ᵃrām naharayîm*) was in Upper Mesopotamia. Attempts have been made to prove the historical authenticity of the story by identifying Cushan-rishataim with a Syrian, Irsu, who seized power in Egypt round about 1200 B.C. and was later overthrown by Set-nakht, the father of Ramses III,[41] who was the first pharaoh of the Twentieth Dynasty. This is, however, pure conjecture, since the identity of the Syrian Irsu is as uncertain in the Egyptian texts as the identity of the 'king of Aram' in the Bible. The suggestion made by certain recent commentators on Judges[42] is generally speaking more acceptable. According to these scholars, 'Aram' should be read as 'Edom' and the *naharayîm* of verse 8 is an addition. (This argument is strengthened by the fact that *naharayîm* does not occur in verse 10.) It is also quite possible that elements of the people of Edom, with whom the Kenizzites were, according to Gen 36:11, 15, 42, closely related, may have tried to settle in southern Palestine as well. Another suggestion that has been made is that Cushan-rishataim was Husham of the land of the Temanites. According to the list given in Gen 36:34–35, this Husham was the third king of Edom.[43] Whether this is so or not, it would certainly seem as though the deuteronomist made use of a Kenizzite tradition concerning Othniel for the purpose of according a place to the tribe of Judah in his survey of the judges who liberated Israel.

3. Jerahmeel

Another group related to the Calebites is the group of Jerahmeel who was Caleb's brother according to 1 Chron 2: 42 and his elder brother according to 1 Chron 2:9. It would seem as though only personal names are con-

[40] In the work mentioned in note 39, W. F. Albright has suggested that *gullôth* should be understood as underground bowls fed by springs; these are found in the district surrounding Tell Beit Mirsim.

[41] A. Malamat, 'Cushan Rishathaim and the Decline of the Near East around 1200 B.C.', *JNES*, 13 (1954), pp. 231–242.

[42] R. Tamisier, 1949; A. Vincent, 1952; H. W. Hertzberg, 1953; J. Gray, 1967.

[43] See, for example, Klostermann and, more recently, A. Vincent and J. Gray in their

tained in the list of Jerahmeel's descendants (1 Chron 2:25–33) and this would suggest that the Jerahmeelites were nomads. In any case, we cannot locate their lands from this list. On the other hand, the Negeb of Jerahmeel is mentioned in 1 Sam 27:10 alongside the Negeb of Judah and the Negeb of the Kenites. The 'towns' of the Jerahmeelites are also mentioned, together with those of the Kenites, in a list in 1 Sam 30:29 of places to which David sent parts of the booty that he had taken from the Amalekites. These references would seem to indicate that the lands of the Jerahmeelites extended into the south of Palestine. Finally, in the geographical list of Sheshonk, several forts in the Negeb are mentioned, including 'rd rbt, that is, Arad the Great, which is probably the recently excavated fortress at Tell 'Arād, and 'rd n bt yrhm or Arad of the House of Yerahm (Jerahm), which may be the ancient town of Arad, located at Tell el-Milh. The Egyptian name of the second would seem to point to a settlement of Jerahmeelites in this district.[44] This would at least provide us with a fixed point in the territory of the Jerahmeelites.

4. Kenites[45]

According to 1 Sam 27:10; 30:29, the Kenites were the neighbours of the Jerahmeelites. According to Judges 1:16, they went up from Tamar in the 'Arabah and settled in the Negeb of Arad. According to the Arabic, the word 'Kenites' means 'smiths'. They may well have been metal-workers and this would certainly be in accordance with their going up from the Arabah, where there were copper mines. They apparently remained nomads for a long time – according to Judges 4:11, 17; 5:24, Heber the Kenite camped in Galilee and, according to 1 Sam 15:6, the Kenites intermingled with the Amalekites, who were nomadic. The Kenites who had settled in the Arad district, however, were more stable; their 'towns' are mentioned in 1 Sam 30:29 and a zanôah haqqayîn, Zanoah of the Kenite,[46] in

---

commentaries, in which they suggest that husvam ro's hattemanîm should be changed to kûšan iš 'athayîm.

[44] Y. Aharoni, *Archaeology and Old Testament Study*, ed. D. Winton Thomas, p. 401; *The Land of the Bible*, p. 289. For Arad, see M. Weippert, *ZDPV*, 80 (1964), p. 185; V. Fritz, Arad in der biblischen Überlieferung und in der Liste Schoschenks I', *ZDPV*, 82 (1966), pp. 331–342; M. Naor, 'Arad and Horma in the Conquest Narrative' (Hebrew), Yediot *(BIES)*, 31 (1967), pp. 157–164.

[45] For the Kenites, see N. Glueck, *Rivers in the Desert*,[2] New York, 1968, especially pp. 132–134; F. C. Fensham, 'Did a Treaty between the Israelites and the Kenites Exist?', *BASOR*, 175 (Oct. 1964), pp. 51–54; B. Mazar, 'The Sanctuary of Arad and the Family of Hobab the Kenite', *JNES*, 24 (1965), pp. 297–303.

[46] M. Noth, *Josua (HAT)*,[2] *in loco*; A. Alt, *Kleine Schriften*, II, p. 286.

the district of Maon, is mentioned in Jos 15:56–57. The Kenites, then, settled in the district to the south east of Hebron on the fringe of the settled country. According to one tradition, they also had blood-ties with Israel – Moses had married a Kenite woman (Judges 1:16; 4:11).

Let us now briefly summarise our findings so far in our investigation into the population of southern Palestine at this time. As far as a point to the north of Hebron, the whole hill country of Judah was populated by different groups of people. The most important of these were the Calebites, who occupied the Hebron district. Their neighbours in the south-west were the Kenizzites of Othniel at Debir and in the south-east the Kenites, between Tell 'Arād and Maon. There were also groups of Levites scattered in this hill country. In the Negeb, there were Simeonites in the region of Beersheba (Hormah) and the Jerahmeelites led a nomadic life in the extreme south, although they may have settled at Tell el-Milh. There was also a certain amount of overlapping between these various territories. This can be presumed from the fact that Tell 'Arād (the Kenites), Hormah (Tell el-Mshāsh, Simeon) and Tell el-Milh (Jerahmeel) were so close to each other. This part of Palestine was not simply peacefully occupied. The memory of several military conquests has been preserved in the biblical tradition (Hebron, Debir and Hormah) and there is also the memory of the defeat to the north of Hormah. Finally, these groups came from the south – the Calebite occupation is linked to the story of the scouts in Num 13–14 and the Simeonites and the Kenites came up from the 'Arabah (Judges 1:16–17).

These, then, are the data provided by the biblical tradition. We cannot so far find archaeological confirmation of these conquests or archaeological evidence of the exact date of this occupation. The site of Hebron is in the course of being excavated, but so far nothing has been revealed between the Middle Bronze Age and a period as advanced as Iron I.[47] The excavations at Tell Beit Mirsim have often been used to establish the date of the conquest at about 1234–1230 B.C.[48] The site was certainly ruined at this period, but, as we have pointed out, there is no certainty that Tell Beit Mirsim was in fact the site of Debir and we can only conclude that it is not possible to find archaeological confirmation of the biblical tradition in this case. Tell 'Arād was not occupied between the Early Bronze Age and the end of the eleventh century B.C. Tell el-Milh may be the site of the ancient Canaanite town of Arad and evidence of tenth and ninth-century occupation is found immediately above Middle Bronze Age ruins.[49] At Tell el-Mshāsh, which,

---

[47] See the preliminary reports by P. C. Hammond, *RB*, 72 (1965), pp. 267–270; 73 (1966), pp. 566–569; 75, (1968), pp. 253–258.
[48] From the very beginning of the excavations at Tell Beit Mirsim, W. F. Albright has always held this view. He has restated it several times; the last time was in *Archaeology and Old Testament Study*, ed. D. Winton Thomas, pp. 207–219, with the precise date, p. 218.

it has been suggested, is the site of Hormah, Middle Bronze and perhaps even Late Bronze potsherds have been found on the surface, but the site has not yet been excavated. Both these sites are in the valley to the east of Beersheba which formed the boundary of the occupied zone of Canaan. Further south, in the Negeb, settling does not seem to have begun before the eleventh century B.C.[50] At a site known as Tell Esdar, about twelve miles south-east of Beersheba, a village founded in the eleventh century has been unearthed.[51] This may be one of the Jerahmeelite 'towns' mentioned in 1 Sam 30:29.

It would, however, be unwise to conclude from this lack of archaeological evidence that the biblical tradition is entirely without any historical basis. An invasion from the south by the groups of people that have been discussed in this section is very much in accordance with the principles of economic geography and with at least one general law of history, the fact that groups of shepherds and herdsmen who are anxious to find land will settle in good agricultural regions. It is probable that the entry of these particular groups was made easier by the decline or even collapse of settled civilisation in this region, but it is also probable that these groups had to overcome resistance by armed force. What is significant is that the first data concerning the 'conquest' are given in the biblical traditions at the same period as the invading groups reached the limits fixed by contemporary archaeologists for the settled lands. We can, however, do no more than provide an approximate date for the settlement of the groups of Simeon and Levi and of the groups associated with them in the hill country of Judah and its southern limits. If it is accepted that, as we have suggested, these groups came into contact with the group that fled from Egypt under the leadership of Moses before they entered this region and if this exodus is dated, again as we have suggested, round about the middle of the thirteenth century B.C., then the settlement of these groups occurred after this date. It was before the eleventh century, since, according to the story of Saul and David, these groups would seem to have been established in their lands at that time and, according to archaeological evidence, the towns in the hill country of Judah had new populations and villages had been built in the Negeb by this century. We may therefore conclude that the settlement of the Simeonites and the Levites in the south of Palestine

---

[49] For the excavations at Tell el-Milh, see the provisional report by M. Kochavi, *RB*, 75 (1968), pp. 392–395; *ibid.*, 'The First Season of Excavations at Tell Malhata', *Qadmoniot*, 3 (1970), pp. 22–24 (Hebrew).

[50] Y. Aharoni, *Archaeology and Old Testament Study*, ed. D. Winton Thomas, p. 389ff; R. Gophna, 'Sites from the Iron Age between Beer-Sheba and Tell el-Far'a', *Yediot*, 28 (1964), pp. 236–246 (Hebrew); *ibid.*, 'Iron Age haserim in Southern Philistia', *'Atiqot* (Hebrew series), 3 (1966), pp. 44–51, with an English summary, pp. 5*–6*.

[51] M. Kochavi, 'Excavations at Tel Esdar', *'Atiqot* (Hebrew series), 5 (1969), pp. 14–48, with English summary, pp. 2*–5*.

must have occurred at about the same time as the group of Israelites led out of Egypt by Moses entered Canaan by way of Transjordania.

IV. THE SETTLEMENT OF THE JUDAEAN GROUP

As we have indicated, Caleb's marriage to Ephrathah (1 Chron 2:24) led to a peaceful expansion on the part of the Calebites towards the north of Palestine, where they intermingled with the group of Ephrathah, with their centre at Bethlehem. According to certain genealogies (Num 26:21; Ruth 4:18; 1 Chron 2:4–5; Gen 46:12), Ephrathah was the wife of Hezron the son of Perez, who was Judah's son, before she became Caleb's wife. This would indicate a Judaean line.

In the lists given in 1 Chron 2 and 4, the descendants of Hezron and Ephrathah are confused with literary interventions, but it would at least seem as though Hur was born of Ephrathah's first marriage with Hezron and not of her marriage with Caleb.[52] The 'descendants' of Hur were, according to 1 Chron 2:50–55; 4:2–4, 16–19, a list of places between Bethlehem and Bethzur (Etam, Gedor), to the north and the north-west of Bethlehem (Nephtoah, Kiriath-jearim, the Valley of Sorke, Eshtaol, Zorah) and in the Shephelah (Soco, Keilah).

Another Judaean lineage is that of Shelah, the son of Judah (1 Chron 4:21–23). The only place that has been identified with any certainty is Mareshah = Tell Sandahanneh in the Shephelah to the north-east of Lachish.

Even if this list of the population of Judah is dated as early as the ninth century B.C., as Noth recommends, it still clearly points to a gradual movement from the Bethlehem region towards the west. To begin with, then, Kiriath-jearim was one of the four Gibeonite cities (Jos 9:17) that had concluded a treaty with the house of Joseph (or Benjamin?). In the same way, Eshtaol and Zorah could only have been occupied by the Judaeans after the movement of the Danites (Judges 18) and these two places were allotted to the tribe of Dan (Jos 19:41).

In fact, the Judaean group was able to expand only towards the west; it was impossible to advance northwards because of the line of Canaanite towns of Jerusalem, Aijalon and Gezer and southwards because of the Calebites in the Hebron district.

The Judaeans would seem to have settled peacefully in their earliest territory, the region of Bethlehem. Bethlehem, which was not a fortified Canaanite town, was not conquered. According to the Amarna letters, it

---

[52] According to M. Noth's reconstruction, *op. cit.* (note 38), which J. M. Myers and Y. Aharoni have accepted, but W. Rudolph has rejected, *Chronikbücher (HAT)*, 1955. I am, like Noth, in favour of the list of descendants of Hur.

was simply a place that belonged to the king of Jerusalem.[53] Jerusalem itself was conquered only by David (2 Sam 5:6–9) and the story in Judges 19:11–12 shows clearly enough that it did not belong to Israel during the period of the Judges. In fact, according to the outline of the tribal frontiers, it lay outside the territory of Judah (Jos 15:8; 18:16). Later, when it was integrated into the administrative structure of the monarchy, it was included among the towns of Benjamin (Jos 18:28). It was not forgotten, however, that it had not been conquered and the Benjaminites had not been able to drive out the Jebusites, who were still living in Jerusalem with the Benjaminites 'to this day' (Judges 1:21). The reference to the Judaeans was added to the list of towns in Judah, where it replaces the Benjaminites (Jos 15:63). Because of all these texts, we are bound to reject the statement made in Judges 1:8, according to which the Judaeans attacked Jerusalem and set fire to it. Attempts have been made to safeguard the historical authenticity of this text, by claiming that the Judaeans did in fact take Jerusalem and destroy it, but that they were unable to keep it.[54] Another solution that has been suggested is that it was a victory which took place under the walls of Jerusalem, allowing the Judaeans to take possession of the lands belonging to the town.[55] Both these suggestions, however, are unjustified.

This verse, Judges 1:8, is in fact a gloss, inserted to explain the strange story narrated in the previous verses (Judges 1:4–7). According to this narrative, Judah and Simeon fought the Canaanites and the Perizzites at Bezek and defeated them. The king Adoni-bezek was captured and mutilated. He was then taken (by his own people or by the Israelites?) to Jerusalem, where he died. It was the reference to Jerusalem that led to the gloss in verse 8, but the name Jerusalem itself was introduced into the story (verses 4–7) because of a confusion between the names of the king Adoni-bezek and that of the king of Jerusalem, Adoni-zedek of Jos 10, who figured in a different story. As a result of this, some commentators have corrected Adoni-bezek here, changing it to Adoni-zedek without any evidence in the versions. There is, however, only one Bezek in the Old Testament, a place mentioned in 1 Sam 11:8 that has been located at Khirbet Ibziq on the road between Shechem and Beth-shean.[56] The Perizzites lived, according to the Bible, in the hill country of Ephraim (Jos 17:15) and in the Shechem district (Gen 34:30). All these places are a long way from Jerusalem. It has been suggested that, before going down into the south, Judah and Simeon

[53] Letter 290, 15 f, *ANET*, 489b, if Bit Ninurta is in fact Bethlehem and not Beth Horon, as Z. Kallai and H. Tadmor have suggested, 'Bit Ninurta = Beth Horon', *Eretz-Israel*, 9 (*Albright Volume*), 1969, pp. 138–147 (Hebrew, with an English-summary).

[54] Y. Aharoni, *The Land of the Bible*, 1967, p. 197.

[55] H. W. Hertzberg, *Josua, Richter, Ruth (ATD)*, 1953, p. 150; J. Gray, *Joshua, Judges and Ruth (The Century Bible)*, 1967, p. 247.

[56] P. Welten, 'Bezeq', *ZDPV*, 81 (1965), pp. 138–165, especially pp. 140–141.

fought in the hill country of Ephraim after their presumed arrival with Joshua's group,[57] but we have already seen that Simeon entered Canaan by the southern route. Most probably what we have here is a memory of the prehistory of Simeon, who stayed in the centre of Palestine during the time of the patriarchs.[58] The introduction of Simeon (and Levi) into the story narrated in Gen 34[59] also belongs to the same group of memories.

There is, however, a tradition concerning Judah which is linked in the Bible to the patriarchal period, but which is more probably related to the period when the tribes were settling in Canaan. This is the story of Judah and Tamar in the Yahwistic tradition of Gen 38. This story not only provides us with an example of levirate marriage; it also explains the development of the tribe of Judah by means of a personal adventure on the part of the tribal ancestor. Leaving his brothers, Judah goes down to Adullam = Tell esh-Sheikh Madhkūr in the Shephelah, about four miles to the south-east of Soco. Judah's flocks were at Timnah, four miles to the north-east of Adullam. The other places mentioned in this story, Kezib and Enaim, have not been identified, but they must be in the same region. Judah married the daughter of a Canaanite called Shua, who gave him three sons, Er, Onan and Shelah. Er married Tamar, who was in all probability also a Canaanite. Tamar became a widow when Er died, but because of Onan's fault and then because of Judah's refusal to give her Shelah as her husband, the law of levirate marriage was not applied in her case. By a trick, however, she had intercourse with Judah, her father-in-law, and bore him twins, Perez and Zerah. This story clearly illustrates the way in which the groups of Judah expanded towards the plains, the family links formed with Canaanites and the formation of the clans of Er and Onan which died out and of the three Judaean clans listed in Num 26:20 – the Shelanite, Perezzite and Zerahite clans. This peaceful penetration into the lowlands is fully in accordance with the conclusion that we have already drawn from our study of the genealogies in 1 Chron 2 and 4.

There is therefore nothing in the biblical traditions to justify the general statement made in Judges 1:9: 'After this, the sons of Judah went down to attack those Canaanites living in the highlands and in the Negeb and the lowlands'. This text is no more than an editorial introduction to the various traditions given in Judges 1:10–20, which have been ascribed to Judah and which we have restored to the groups which were finally absorbed by

---

[57] Y. Aharoni, *The Land of the Bible*, p. 197. Settlement in this region seems, however, to have taken place peacefully; see below, pp. 635–640.

[58] H. W. Hertzberg, 'Adonibezek', *JPOS*, 6 (1926), pp. 213–221 = *Beiträge zur Traditionsgeschichte und Theologie des Alten Testaments*, Göttingen, 1962, pp. 28–35; *ibid., Josua (ATD)*, 1953, p. 149; J. Gray, *Joshua*, pp. 246–247. Basing his argument on verse 7b, P. Welten, *op. cit.*, pp. 144–145, suggests that there was a powerful Canaanite kingdom in the Shechem region which inherited the kingdom of Lab'ayu at the Amarna period.

[59] See above, pp. 532–533.

Judah. These traditions include the taking of Hebron by Caleb (verse 10; cf. verse 20), the taking of Debir by Othniel (verses 11–15) and the occupation of the Negeb of Arad by the Kenites and the taking of Hormah by Simeon (verses 16 and 17).

Finally, according to verse 18, Judah took Gaza, Ashkelon, Ekron and, in the Septuagint, Ashdod. This statement is, however, the opposite to what is said in several texts. According to verse 19, Judah was not able to drive out the inhabitants of the plain and, according to Jos 13:2–3 and Judges 3:3, all the Philistine lands had still to be conquered. In fact, this part of Palestine never belonged to Israel, except perhaps partially and for a short time during the reign of Josiah.[60] What is more, the site which is presumably that of Ekron seems not to have been occupied before the Philistines lived there.[61] The only text that can be mentioned in support of Judges 1:18 is Jos 15:45–47, which includes Ekron, Ashdod and Gaza among the towns of Judah, although it should be pointed out that this text is clearly an addition.[62] Various scholars have defended the authenticity of Judges 1:18 by arguing that the coastal towns were conquered by Judah, but were soon relinquished when the Philistines exerted pressure.[63] This contradiction has been resolved in the Septuagint by the use of a negative statement: 'Judah did not take Gaza, Ashkelon, Ekron and Ashdod'.[64] These attempts to justify Judges 1:18 are unacceptable, however, since, like Judges 1:8, Judges 1:18 is an addition, made with the purpose of enhancing Judah's reputation. Judges 1:2–20 as a whole was written for this purpose – Yahweh delivered the country into Judah's hands (verse 2) and, at the end of the passage, Yahweh 'was with Judah, and Judah subdued the highlands' (verse 19). Judah's success is contrasted with the failure of Benjamin (verse 21) and that

[60] The only evidence of an Israelite occupation in this region is the fortress at Mesad Heshavyahu, about fifteen miles south of Jaffa. Here the Israelites appear to have occupied the site after the Greeks had used it as a trading post; see J. Naveh, 'A Hebrew Letter from the Seventh Century B.C.', *IEJ*, 10 (1960), pp. 129–139; ibid., 'The Excavations at Mesad Heshavyahu', *IEJ*, 12 (1962), pp. 89–113.

[61] J. Naveh, 'Khirbat al-Muqqannaʿ-Ekron. An Archaeological Survey', *IEJ*, 8 (1958), pp. 87–100, 165–170.

[62] F. M. Cross and G. E. Wright, *JBL*, 75 (1956), p. 204; Y. Aharoni, *VT*, 9 (1959), p. 240.

[63] G. E. Wright, *JNES*, 5 (1946), p. 109, accepts this as a possibility and Y. Kaufmann affirms it more positively in his Hebrew commentary on Judges, Jerusalem, 1968, pp. 82–83. Several Old Testament scholars have made use of the findings of the excavations at Ashdod to argue in favour of this theory. (According to the archaeologists, Ashdod was destroyed in the second half of the thirteenth century and remained abandoned until it was occupied by the Philistines.) See D. N. Freedman, *BibArch*, 26 (1963), p. 136; M. Dothan, *IEJ*, 14 (1964), p. 84 = *Archaeological Discoveries in the Holy Land*, New York, 1967, p. 132; M. Dothan and D. N. Freedman, *Ashdod I*, Jerusalem, 1967 (Atiqot, 7), p. 9; T. C. Mitchell, *Archaeology and Old Testament Study*, ed. D. Winton Thomas, pp. 411–412.

[64] Several exegetes prefer this text to the Hebrew text and believe that verse 18 should be placed between verses 19a and 19b. There are, however, strong suspicions that the translators of the Septuagint tried to harmonise verse 18 with verse 19.

of the other tribes (verses 27–34).

According to Jos 10:28–39, however, several towns which are included within the land belonging to Judah (Makkedah, Libnah, Lachish, Eglon, Hebron and Debir) were not conquered by Judah, but by Joshua and all Israel. G. E. Wright has tried to reconcile this account with the account in Judges 1 and has suggested that Joshua conducted a lightning campaign against the royal cities of Canaan which were key points in the occupation of the land and that this was followed, after Joshua's death, by a period of struggles.[65] K. Elliger regarded the capture of Makkedah as an appendix to the story of the battle of Gibeon (Jos 10:1–15) and suggested that Libnah, Lachish and Eklon were destroyed by the Calebites and the Kenizzites, who were unable to maintain their position there and consequently went up to Hebron and Debir, where they settled.[66] M. Noth, on the other hand, was of the opinion that these were the towns of the five kings mentioned in the story of the cave of Makkedah and were therefore different from the kings who took part in the campaign of Gibeon.[67] Whatever may be the case, it is not possible for a historian to conclude very much of importance from these references, nor is it possible to claim, on the other hand, that Joshua and all Israel conducted this campaign in the south of Canaan. Basing our opinion on the Old Testament itself, we concluded that Hebron was taken by Caleb and Debir by Othniel and we are now bound to ask whether the other towns in the Shephelah, Libnah, Lachish and Eglon, were not conquered by Judah at the time of the settlement in Canaan. Everything that we have said so far about the peaceful infiltration on the part of the Judaeans into the Shephelah and especially in connection with the account in Gen 38, points to the contrary.

What archaeological evidence is there to support this argument? Libnah was for a long time identified with Tell es-Safī, but it is now usually located at Tell Bornat, five miles further south. Exploration of the surface has shown that this site was occupied at the end of the Late Bronze Age and at the beginning of the Iron Age, but no excavations have as yet been made. Most authors nowadays site Eglon at Tell el-Hesi, which was excavated between 1890 and 1893 by Flinders Petrie and F. J. Bliss.[68] It appears that the town was destroyed at the end of the Late Bronze Age, but that it remained abandoned during most of the period of the Judges. Lachish was undoubtedly at Tell ed-Duweir, which has been excavated very well, though not completely. The town was destroyed at the end of the Late

[65] G. E. Wright, 'The Literary and Historical Problem of Joshua 10 and Judges 1', *JNES*, 5 (1946), pp. 105–114; *ibid.*, *Biblical Archaeology*, Philadelphia, 1957, pp. 69–70, 81–83.

[66] K. Elliger, 'Josua in Judäa, *PJB*, 30 (1934), pp. 47–71.

[67] M. Noth, 'Die fünf Könige in der Höhle von Makkeda', *PJB*, 33 (1937), pp. 22–36, and *Josua (HAT)*,[2] *in loco*.

[68] F. J. Bliss, *A Mound of Many Cities, or Tell el Hesy Excavated*, London, 1894.

Bronze Age, but the precise date is not known. A hieratic inscription on a bowl discovered there gives the date as the fourth year of the reign of an unnamed pharaoh. If this pharaoh was Mer-ne-Ptah, as seems likely, then the date would be 1220 B.C., according to the chronology followed in this work. This would not, however, be the date of the destruction of the city. It only provides a possible end point, a *terminus ad quem*, but we are bound to take into account the scarab of Ramses III found at the ruined level. [69] This would seem to indicate that the city was destroyed much later, perhaps during the first years of the twelfth century B.C. [70] and therefore after Joshua and at the beginning of the Philistine period. There is no way of establishing precisely who destroyed Lachish. It might have been destroyed by Israelites, Egyptians, Sea Peoples (Philistines) or other Canaanites. In any case, the site remained abandoned for more than a century afterwards, in other words, during the period of the Judges. We may therefore conclude that, on the basis of this archaeological evidence, it is possible that the reference to Libnah, Eglon and Lachish in Jos 10 points to an expansion in Judah's territory during the reigns of David or Solomon. It should also be noted that Eglon is not mentioned outside the book of Joshua and that Libnah and Lachish are mentioned only at a late stage during the period of the monarchy. Libnah is mentioned during the reign of Jehoram (2 Kings 8:22) and Lachish during the reign of Amaziah (2 Kings 14:19).

We are therefore bound to conclude that there is no really early tradition enabling us to say with certainty that Judah conquered these or other towns in the south of Canaan. On the basis of these traditions, we can only say that Judaean groups settled peacefully in the region of Bethlehem, were on good terms with the Calebites at Hebron and penetrated peacefully into the Shephelah.

It is not easy to know how these groups came to the Bethlehem region. They may have come from the south, like the Simeonites with whom they became merged, in which case we should have to accept literally the statement made in Judges 1:16, that the Judaeans came up with the Kenites.What is more, if they came down from the north, they would have encountered the obstacle of the Canaanite cities of Jerusalem, Aijalon and Gezer. On the other hand, the statement that 'Judah left his brothers' (Gen 38:1) may reflect precisely the memory of Judah's having become separated from the other tribes after crossing the Jordan, in which case the Judaean group would have reached Bethlehem after crossing the desert between Jerusalem and the Dead Sea.

In this region there was in fact, a tradition concerning Judah connected with the conquest of Jericho and Ai by Joshua's group. This is the story of

---

[69] O. Tufnell, *Lachish IV. The Bronze Age*, London, 1958, pp. 37, 98.

[70] This is Miss Tufnell's final opinion; see *Archaeology and Old Testament Study*, ed. D. Winton Thomas, p. 302.

Achan (Jos 7:1–26), who belonged to the Judaean clan of Zerah and violated the ban under which Jericho had been placed. His action led to the defeat of the Israelites when they attacked Ai for the first time. He was burnt, together with all his family and possessions, as a punishment and a cairn was erected over him and the place was called the 'Vale of Achor', the Vale of Misfortune (*'ākhôr*), because he had brought misfortune to Israel. This valley formed the boundary between Benjamin and Judah, but it lay within the territory belonging to Judah. It is undoubtedly the plain known as el-Buqe'ah, which lies to the west of the cliffs of Qumran.[71] This is a local tradition which was at first independent. It might have been Judaean in origin, but was more probably Benjaminite, since it damages Judah's reputation. The fact that it was attached – artificially – to the stories of Jericho and Ai can also be satisfactorily explained by a Benjaminite origin, since these stories were Benjaminite traditions.[72]

All that we can really learn from the story of Achan in our present context is that this region was in the possession of the clan of Zerah and this in fact completes the survey of the settlement of the Judaean group that we have deduced from 1 Chron 2 and 4 and Gen 38. We still do not know how the Zerahite group entered this territory, which lies to the east and north-east of Bethlehem. If the Judaean group entered Canaan by crossing the Jordan, the clan of Zerah may have stayed in the plain (or 'vale') of Achor while the rest of the group went on towards Bethlehem. If, on the other hand, Judah entered by the southern route with the Simeonites and the other groups and if the central point of the zone in which the Judaeans settled was Bethlehem, where the clan of Ephrathah lived,[73] then this Zerahite occupation may well have been the result of a later expansion from Bethlehem. (It is interesting to note in this connection that the Buqe'ah is nowadays occupied by the Ta'amira bedouins from Bethlehem.) This later occupation would seem to be confirmed by the fact that, according to Gen 38:30, Zerah was born in the Shephelah and had a Canaanite mother. All in all, it is most probable that the Judaean group entered Canaan by the southern route at the same time as the Simeonites with whom they are so closely associated in the biblical tradition.

V. THE ORIGINS OF THE TRIBE OF JUDAH

Uncertainty with regard to the route followed by the Judaeans into Canaan is only one aspect of the mystery surrounding the origins of the tribe.

---

[71] M. Noth, *ZDPV*, 71 (1955), pp. 42–55.

[72] M. Noth, *Josua (HAT)*,[2] 1953, pp. 43–46; H. W. Hertzberg, *Josua (ATD)*, 1953, pp 48–49; J. Gray, *Joshua (The Century Bible)*, 1967, pp. 80–81.

[73] See above, p. 540.

The etymology of the name 'Judah' is not known. It has been suggested that it was a personal name,[74] but it is more likely that it was first of all a geographical name and especially the name of a region, like Ephraim or Naphthali.[75] There are traces of this very early use of the name. Bethlehem in Judah is mentioned several times in Judges 17 and 19, just as places such as Jabesh in Gilead and Kedesh in Galilee are mentioned elsewhere (cf. Judges 21:8ff and Jos 20:7; 21:32 respectively). In 1 Sam 23:3, David's men say to him: 'We go in fear here in Judah; how much more, then, if we go to Keilah?', but Keilah was inhabited by 'Judaeans'. There is reference to the hill country of Judah alongside the highlands of Ephraim and of Naphthali (Jos 20:7) and to the wilderness of Judah (Judges 1:16), which can be compared with the wildernesses of Ziph (1 Sam 26:2), Maon (1 Sam 23:25) or Tekoa (2 Chron 20:20). Judah, then, is the hill country which stretched from north of Bethlehem to south of Hebron. It was not the tribe which gave its name to the geographical region, but the region which gave its name to the tribe that lived there. The tribe then found for itself an ancestor who was presumed to have given his name to the tribe – Judah, the son of Jacob.

In fact, in the whole of Genesis, Judah only plays the part of a person in two stories. The first is in Gen 38, in which Judah personifies a group of men in a story which, as we have already seen, refers to the period following the settlement and not to the patriarchal period. The second is, of course, the story of Joseph, in which Judah takes the place of Reuben in the southern Palestinian version of the account.

The Song of Deborah (Judges 5), which was written at about the same time as the events themselves and may date back to the third quarter of the twelfth century B.C., mentions neither Judah nor Simeon. This may, of course, mean that these tribes, because they lived in isolation in the south of the country, were not interested in this war and did not have to decide whether or not to take part in it. On the other hand, it may point to the fact that they had not yet become part of Israel. Because there is no reference to these tribes in Judges 5, however, we cannot determine whether Judah existed at that time as a tribal entity with its own name.

It is also significant that Judah and Simeon are not mentioned as tribes in the list of Jacob's blessings (Gen 49) and that only Judah is mentioned in Moses' blessings (Deut 33). The language and the poetical style of both these passages have led some scholars to claim that they were composed before the period of the monarchy,[76] but, according to literary criticism of

---

[74] See especially W. F. Albright, 'The Names "Israel" and "Judah" ', *JBL*, 46 (1927), pp. 151–185, especially pp. 168–178.

[75] L. Waterman, *AJSL*, 55 (1938), pp. 29–31; M. Noth, *The Old Testament World*, London, 1966, pp. 55–56; *History*, pp. 55–56.

[76] W. F. Albright, *Yahweh and the Gods of Canaan*, London, 1968, p. 15 (Deut 33 before the destruction of Shiloh), p. 17 (Gen 49 after the destruction of Shiloh); F. M. Cross and D. N. Freedman, 'The Blessings of Moses', *JBL*, 67 (1948), pp. 191–210 (Deut 33 to the eleventh

the forms in which they are written, both these poems would seem to include elements from different periods.[77] Any attempt to establish the date of what is said about Judah and Simeon by examining the historical situations presupposed by these statements may well draw us into a vicious circle, because it is precisely on the history of these tribes that we have to try to throw some light. It is, however, possible to claim that, according to the statement about Simeon (and Levi) in Jacob's blessings (Gen 49:5–7), the tribe of Simeon was already scattered throughout Israel and had lost its individual character. Similarly, it is also possible to argue from the passage about Judah (Gen 49:8–12), which emphasises that Judah's brothers will 'do him homage' and that 'the sceptre shall not pass' from him, that Judah began to occupy a predominant position only at the time of David. Simeon is not mentioned in Moses' blessings (Deut 33) and this can only be explained by the tribe's having already become absorbed by Judah by this time. Judah on the other hand is mentioned in Deut 33:7, which expresses the desire that he will be brought back to his people. This may be an allusion to the statement that Judah 'left his brothers' at the time when the tribes were settling in Canaan (see Gen 38:1) or possibly to Judah's individual conquest of its land (Judges 1). This may, however, portray the situation that came about as a result of the political division which followed Solomon's death. We may therefore conclude that these early texts can tell us nothing certain about the tribe of Judah before the time of David.

Several scholars have come to the conclusion that the tribe of Judah was not constituted before the reign of David.[78] A possible objection to this theory is that Judah formed part of the system of twelve tribes and that, because of this, its land was as described in Jos 13–19, since this definition of the tribal frontiers, certain exegetes have argued, goes back to the period before the monarchy, although the list of towns does not.[79] This theory of an 'amphictyony' during the period of the Judges has, however, been seriously called into question and, even if it is accepted that a very early document in fact underlay the text of Jos 13–19, it is generally acknowledged nowadays that the frontiers of the tribal territories as defined in this text are not all of exactly the same period. A particular example of this is the description of the frontiers of the land belonging to Judah, the southern, eastern and western frontiers being the ideal boundaries of the land of

century).
[77] H. J. Zobel, *Stammesspruch und Geschichte (BZAW*, 95), 1965; A. H. J. Gunneweg, 'Über den Sitz im Leben der sogenannten Stammessprüche (Gen 49, Deut 33, Jdc 5) ', *ZAW*, 76 (1964), pp. 245–255.
[78] S. Mowinckel, *Von Ugarit nach Qumran (BZAW*, 77), 1958, 1961, pp. 137–138; *Tetrateuch – Pentateuch – Hexateuch (BZAW*, 90), 1964, p. 66; *Israels opphav og eldste historie*, Oslo, 1967, pp. 139–140; see also M. A. Cohen, *HUCA*, 36 (1965), pp. 94–98.
[79] See especially A. Alt, 'Das System der Stammesgrenzen im Buche Josua', *Sellin Festschrift*, Leipzig, 1927, pp. 13–24 = *Kleine Schriften*, I, pp. 193–202.

Canaan and the northern frontier, which is the only one that is defined in detail, being the limit of Judah's territory during the reign of David.[80]

On the other hand, it would seem that even during the reign of Saul Judah was not simply the name of a territory, but was also the name of the tribe occupying that territory and, moreover, that tribe was part of Saul's kingdom.[81] It is, however, possible that Judah had not been part of Israel for very long at that time and this would, of course, explain why Judah is not mentioned in the Song of Deborah (Judges 5). We do not know unfortunately what form the tribe of Judah took at the time of Saul and we know even less about it before Saul. There may have been an 'amphictyony' in the south of Canaan consisting of six member groups (Judah, Caleb, Othniel, Jerahmeel, Simeon and the Kenites) gathered around the sanctuary at Hebron, but this is a pure hypothesis and cannot be proved. It would, however, confirm the supposition that the predominant position occupied by Judah was a late development. It certainly seems as though Judah did not find its own real identity until the reign of David and that it was in fact David who gave the tribe that identity. Various heterogeneous elements – the Calebites, Kenizzites and Jerahmeelites – went to form the genealogy of Judah, which also absorbed the Simeonites. The three main clans of Judah, moreover, were the result of Judah's merging with the Canaanites – the clan of Shelah resulted from Judah's marriage with a Canaanite woman and the clans of Perez and Zerah came from his incestuous relationship with the Canaanite woman Tamar. Then David, the Judaean from Bethlehem, prepared the way for all these various elements to be merged together by conquering their common enemy, the Amalekites and by the gifts that he made to 'his friends' (1 Sam 30:26).[82] The list that follows this reference to David's distribution of the booty taken from the Amalekites (1 Sam 30:27–31) gives a clear indication of the different groups that he was to unite under his sceptre. It is also most significant that, as soon as Saul had died, David settled, not at Bethlehem where he himself had come from, but at Hebron, the Calebite town.[83] It was at Hebron that he was acknowledged as king over the 'House of Judah'. The tribe of Judah, formed in this way, was therefore identified with David's first kingdom at Hebron.

[80] The two most recent works written about the geography of the tribes are in agreement here; see Y. Aharoni, *The Land of the Bible*, 1967, pp. 227–235; Z. Kallai, *Les territoires des tribus d'Israël* (Hebrew), Jerusalem, 1967 and *Les frontières nord de la tribu de Juda* (Hebrew), Jerusalem, 1960.

[81] K.–D. Schunk, *Benjamin* (*BZAW*, 86), 1963, pp. 124–126; *Volume du Congrès, Genève* (*SVT*, 15), p. 257, no. 6; R. Smend, 'Gehörte Juda zum vorstaatlichen Israel?', *Fourth World Congress of Jewish Studies, Papers, I*, Jerusalem, 1967, pp. 57–62.

[82] This is the Greek version (in the plural), which is in contrast with the Hebrew (in the singular). It is not correct to read either the Hebrew (or the Greek) as 'proportionate to their towns'. 'The elders of Judah', the preceding phrase, has no grammatical connection and must

be a gloss.
[83] It is amusing to note, but it would be unwise to accept the hypothesis of H. Winckler in *Geschichte Israels,* I, Leipzig, 1895, p. 25, who suggested that Abner said, not 'Am I a dog's head?' (*roš kelebh*), but 'Am I a prince of Caleb? (*roš kālēbh*), with an allusion to David at Hebron. S. Mowinckel clearly favours this hypothesis in the three passages quoted (note 78).

Chapter Eighteen

THE SETTLEMENT IN TRANSJORDANIA
THE TRIBES OF REUBEN, GILEAD-GAD AND
MANASSEH–MACHIR

THE TRADITIONS concerning an invasion by groups which were later to form the tribe of Judah and which entered the south of Palestine (these were studied in the previous chapter) were eclipsed by the traditions concerning those groups which entered Canaan from the east. This entry into Canaan was preceded by the settlement of certain groups in Transjordania.

I. THE ISRAELITES' ROUTE FROM KADESH TO THE PLAINS OF MOAB [1]

According to the biblical narratives, the group of Israelites led by Moses was pushed back into the desert after having made an abortive attempt to enter Canaan by the south from Kadesh. These Israelites stayed in the desert for a long time before they reached the plains of Moab opposite Jericho, from which point they entered the Promised Land. Their journey from Kadesh to the plains of Moab is described in several texts, the most complete being the list of stages along the route of the exodus in Num 33:37–49. Only the last part of this route is given in detail in the account in Num 21:10–20. The account given in Deut 2 indicates the directions, the territories crossed or skirted and a number of geographical points, but it does not provide a list of the stopping-places.

Attempts have often been made to reconcile these different texts and to reconstruct the journey made by the Israelites. Many scholars agree that they went down from Kadesh to the Gulf of 'Aqabah, then went up again along the eastern side of the 'Arabah to the south of the Dead Sea. Passing between Edom and Moab, they then went up the Wadi el-Hesā, and

---

[1] In this section, I make use of a previous article written for *Mélanges ... A. Dupont-Sommer*, Paris, 1971. See also M. Haran, 'The Exodus Routes in the Pentateuchal Sources', *Tarbiz*, 40 (1970–1971), pp. 113–143 (Hebrew with an English summary), who distinguishes three routes according to the three sources J, ED and P.

round Moab following the eastern desert route and in this way reached the Arnon.[2] Three different routes, from the Arnon onwards, have been distinguished by some of these scholars (Num 33; Num 21; Deut 2). These three itineraries may reflect three different traditions or they may reflect the fact that at this point the Israelites divided into several groups.[3] Other geographers and historians, however, believe that, from the point of departure at Kadesh onwards, it is impossible to reconcile the routes given in Num 33 and Deut 2 – the first route crosses the 'Arabah, Edom and Moab, whereas the second goes down the 'Arabah to the Gulf of 'Aqabah, then skirts Edom and Moab. These scholars therefore argue that there were two waves of immigrants: the tribe of Rachel, led by the house of Joseph (and Joshua) following the route outlined in Num 33 in the fourteenth century B.C. before the kingdoms of Edom and Moab had been set up; the second route being followed by the tribes of Leah with Judah (and Moses) at their head in the thirteenth century, after the establishment of the kingdoms of Edom and Moab, which they were forced to pass round.[4] This difficult problem cannot, however, be solved either by trying to harmonise the texts or by appealing to a historical theory that is not based on the texts themselves. It is above all a problem of literary criticism and of the history of traditions. I shall deal with it as such, taking the texts in the order in which they were composed.

1. *Numbers 20:14–22a and 21:21*

When he was at Kadesh, Moses sent messengers to the king of Edom to ask for permission to cross his land, following the 'king's highway'. Edom refused and threatened to attack him. Israel therefore passed round his

[2] With individual variations, F.–M. Abel, *Géographie de la Palestine*, II, Paris, 1938, pp. 215–217; L. H. Grollenberg, *Atlas of the Bible*, New York, 1956, p. 56 and map 9; G. E. Wright and F. V. Filson, *The Westminster Historical Atlas to the Bible*,[2] Philadelphia, 1956, p. 39 and map V; D. Baly, *The Geography of the Bible*, New York and London, 1957, pp. 212–213; J. Simons, *The Geographical and Topographical Texts of the Old Testament*, Leiden, 1959, pp. 257–262; P. Lemaire and D. Baldi, *Atlas Biblique*, Louvain and Paris, 1960, pp. 92–93 and map 20, p. 86; H. G. May and R. W. Hamilton, *Oxford Bible Atlas*, London, 1962, pp. 58–59 (with an alternative route); H. H. Rowley, *Student's Bible Atlas*, London, 1965, map 3.

[3] F.–M. Abel, *op. cit.*, p. 217; J. Simons, *op. cit.*, pp. 261–262.

[4] B. Mazar, *Encyclopaedia Biblica*, Jerusalem, I, 1950, col 694 ff; II, 1954, col 144 ff (Hebrew); Y. Aharoni, *Antiquity and Survival*, II, 2/3 (1957), p. 142 and *The Land of the Bible*, London, 1967, pp. 287–288 and map 14; Y. Aharoni and M. Avi-Yonah, *The Macmillan Bible Atlas*, New York and London, 1968, p. 41 (in which all the references to Exod can be restored to Num) and map 52; cf. A. Malamat, *Die altorientalischen Reiche*, II (*Fischer Weltgeschichte*, 3), Frankfurt a.M., 1966, pp. 209–210.

territory. This is clearly a composite text. The Israelites' request is repeated twice, in verses 17–18 and in verse 19. The two sources must be J and E, although it is not possible to decide which texts belong to which source. According to verses 14 and 16, the message is sent to the king of Edom from Kadesh, but this is not easy to accept, since Kadesh is not a city, nor is it on the frontier of Edom. No king of Edom, moreover, ever ruled over the south of Palestine, either at the time of Moses or at the time when the J and E traditions were being edited.

The continuation of the journey in the early traditions is found in Num 21:21, according to which Israel had reached the land belonging to Sihon, the king of Heshbon. In fact, Num 20:22b–29, Aaron's death at Mount Hor, is without doubt a priestly text and Num 21:10–20 is, as we shall see, a very late composition. The story of the capture of Hormah (Num 21:1–3) is an early tradition, but it is reported here out of its proper context. According to Judges 1:16–17, Judah and Simeon came up from the south of Palestine with the Kenites and conquered Hormah.[5]

The story of the bronze serpent has also to be taken into account here. The story in Num 21:4b–9 is clearly connected with the datum provided in 2 Kings 18:4, that Hezekiah smashed the bronze serpent which Moses had made and which the Israelites worshipped under the name of Nehushtan. There can be no doubt that this serpent to which the Israelites offered sacrifices in Jerusalem was a Canaanite cultic object which the Israelites had borrowed, but which they claimed went back originally to Moses. It is possible to say that the story given in Num 21:4b–9 was invented in order to explain the fact that the serpent was ascribed to Moses[6] and it has at least to be recognised that the story in Numbers antedates the story of Hezekiah, because the serpent is treated quite favourably in it.[7] It is possible, on the other hand, to regard the connection between this Canaanite serpent and Moses as having been inspired by an old tradition preserved in Num 21. According to this tradition, the Israelites made a bronze serpent as a charm to protect themselves from the dangerous desert creatures, the 'fiery serpents', ṡārāph (verse 6), which are also mentioned in Deut 8:15; Isa 14:29; 30:6.[8] The incident is not given a precise situation in the text, but is recorded rather as something that happened on the way (Num 21:4b). If it is accepted that it is an early tradition, then it can very suitably be connected with the work of copper mining in the 'Arabah. It has been suggested that

---

[5] See above, pp. 527–528.

[6] H. H. Rowley, 'Zadok and Nehushtan', *JBL*, 58 (1939), pp. 113–141, especially pp. 138–139; V. Fritz, *Israel in der Wüste*, Marburg, 1970, pp. 93–96.

[7] M. Noth, *Überlieferungsgeschichte*, pp. 133–134 and, with certain shades of meaning, *Das Vierte Buch Mose. Numeri (ATD)*, 1966, pp. 136–138; G. W. Coats, *Rebellion in the Wilderness*, Nashville, 1968, pp. 115–124.

[8] K. R. Jones, 'The Bronze Serpent in the Israelite Cult', *JBL*, 87 (1968), pp. 245–256.

the mining centre referred to here is that at Punon, which is mentioned in Num 33:42–43. This is the modern Feinān, which is at the same latitude as Kadesh on the other side of the 'Arabah, or, to be more precise, it is Khirbet en-Nahās (the 'copper ruins') about eight miles to the north of Feinān.[9] Another and better suggestion is that the copper mining tradition was situated to the west of the 'Arabah in the mining centre of el-Meneʿiyeh or Timnaʿ, where copper was certainly mined in the thirteenth century B.C. A recent discovery there is a little Egyptian sanctuary which was used by the miners during the reigns of Seti I, Ramses II and Ramses III. A copper serpent partly covered in gold has also been found on this site.[10] This serpent was probably also used, like the serpent in Num 21:4–9, to guard against disease and the parallel with the biblical text may be accidental, but it is certainly striking.

This location of the copper mines is, moreover, entirely in accordance with the only piece of information about the route that the Israelites followed which is provided in the earliest sources – the order given by Yahweh to 'go back into the wilderness, in the direction of the Sea of Suph' (Num 14:25). The Sea of Suph here must be the Red Sea in the Gulf of 'Aqabah, as in Deut 2:8 (Elath and Eziongeber) and in 1 Kings 9:26 and Jer 69:21. The usual way from Kadesh to el-'Aqabah was, however, not directly eastward and then south down the 'Arabah, in which traffic from north to south and south to north was always very restricted. On the contrary, it went south-east and reached the 'Arabah a little to the north of el-Meneʿiyeh about twenty-five miles north of the gulf. The Israelites therefore reached the limits of the land of Edom and it was there that they sought permission to follow the 'king's highway'. When the Edomites refused to allow them to cross their territory, they were obliged to avoid Edom and follow the way of the desert to the east of the country. This was precisely the conclusion reached by the editor of Num 21:4,[11] namely that the Israelites 'took the road to the Sea of Suph, to skirt the land of Edom'. This road was quite open, since the Edomites do not seem to have reached the Gulf of 'Aqabah at that time and the first buildings in Ezion-geber (Tell el-Kheleifeh), the city at the northern point of el-'Aqabah, date from the period of Solomon.[12]

All that we can learn, then, from the early sources is that the group of Israelites led by Moses followed the way of the Gulf of 'Aqabah (Num

[9] N. Glueck, Explorations in Eastern Palestine, II (AASOR, XV) New Haven, 1935, pp. 26–29; Y. Aharoni, The Land of the Bible, pp. 51 and 188.

[10] B. Rothenberg, 'Un temple égyptien découvert dans la Arabah', Bible et Terre Sainte, No. 123 (July–August, 1970), especially pp. 3 and 8–9.

[11] Num 21:4 is a connecting verse between the priestly narrative of the death of Aaron at Mount Hor and the story of the bronze serpent.

[12] N. Glueck, 'Ezion Geber', BibArch, 28 (1965), pp. 70–87; Y. Aharoni, Archaeology and Old Testament Study, ed. D. Winton Thomas, Oxford, 1967, pp. 437–438.

14:25) and skirted the land of Edom (Num 20:21) and that the episode of
the bronze serpent took place on the way (Num 21:4b–9). No details of
stopping-places on the route between Kadesh and north of the Arnon are
given, however, in these early sources. What is more, the beginning and
the end of the journey are described in the early tradition in the form of an
antithesis. At the beginning, Israel asks the king of Edom for right of way;
Edom refuses and threatens to attack and the Israelites turn away from
Edom (Num 20:14:21). At the end of the journey, Israel asks Sihon, the
king of Heshbon, for right of way; Sihon refuses and threatens to attack,
but the Israelites win the battle and conquer his land. This is the beginning
of the 'conquest' (Num 21:21–25). The parallel between the two passages is
made even more striking by the use of the same terms, especially, for example, in Num 20:17, which is echoed almost exactly in Num 21:22.

According to this early tradition too, after leaving Kadesh the Israelites
remained a long time in the desert until all those who had been unfaithful to
Yahweh had died (Num 14:23b–24, J). The chronology of a sojourn of forty years in the desert, that is, a sojourn lasting the whole of a generation,
was based on this text by the later tradition. According to the
deuteronomistic tradition, these forty years began when the Israelites left
Egypt (Deut 2:7; 8:2, 4;29:4; see also Amos 2:10; 5:25;[13] Ps 95: 10–11 and
Neh 9:21, which are dependent on the texts of Deuteronomy). According
to Deut 2:14, which is more precise, the Israelites wandered for thirty-eight
years between Kadesh and the Wādi Zered, after having stayed 'for many a
day' at Kadesh (Deut 1:46). The priestly editor lengthened this period of
wandering from thirty-eight to forty years and emphasised that it was a
punishment (Num 14:33–34; 32:13). All the traditions are, in any case, in
agreement that there was a long period between leaving Kadesh and
arriving in the plains of Moab. During this period, the Israelites led a
nomadic life with their sheep and goats. It would therefore be an impossible
task to try to establish one single, continuous route.

2. Deuteronomy 2:1–25

An attempt was, however, made in the biblical tradition to establish a
single and continuous route of the exodus into Canaan. The first attempt
was made by the Deuteronomist in the first discourse which he attributed to
Moses and with which he began his account. Certain elements in this account (Deut 2:1–25) have been rejected by literary criticism as additions.
These include not only the scholarly notes (verses 10–12 and 20–23), but
also verse 7, in which the singular 'thou' is used, verse 9, which mentions

[13] For the later, deuteronomistic character of Amos 2:10 and the final words of Amos 5:25,
see W. H. Schmidt, 'Die deuteronomische Redaktion des Amosbuches', ZAW, 77 (1965),
pp. 168–193, especially pp. 180 and 189, note 60.

Moab (although the first three words are usually retained), verses 18–19, which deals with Ammon, and verses 24b–25, which anticipate verse 31.[14] In my opinion, the only verses which should be rejected as later additions are verses 10–12 and 20–23 and perhaps also verse 7.[15]

In any attempt to interpret this text, the meaning of certain geographical terms must be taken into account. For example, *g*ʰ*bhûl*, 'frontier,' must be distinguished from *ʼres*, 'country' or 'land.' Two other important terms are *derekh* followed by a geographical name, meaning 'in the direction of' and *midderekh*, which means 'passing through' or 'coming from'. In obedience to God's commandment, (Deut 1:40), the Israelites left Kadesh and went in the direction of the Sea of Suph (Deut 2:1), then wandered for a long time around the highlands of Seir (verse 2), until Yahweh ordered them to turn towards the north (verse 3). They then crossed the frontier of the land belonging to the sons of Esau, who lived in Seir, but received none of their territory, which had been given to Esau as his property. They paid for the food they ate and the water they drank there (verses 4–6). In verse 8, the command is carried out – the Israelites passed beyond the sons of Esau, coming from the 'Arabah, Elath and Ezion-geber, and they followed the direction of the wilderness of Moab.

The early account of this journey in Numbers is presented differently; the request that was made to pass through Edom's territory is refused in that account and the Israelites have to go round it. In the Deuteronomist's account that we are considering here, however, God orders the people to cross the frontier of the territory belonging to the sons of Esau, but to respect that territory. The Deuteronomist did not, however, necessarily have any other source apart from the account given in Numbers. He knew that account – this is clear from the fact that Deut 1:40, which is recalled in Deut 2:1, is a quotation from Num 14:25 and that the theme of water appears in both texts (Deut 2:6 and Num 20:19). The Deuteronomist, however, changed the early narrative of Numbers for theological reasons (we shall return to these later) and also because the political geography of the region had altered. Elath/Ezion-geber, which is not mentioned in Numbers, had been in the hands of the Edomites since the reign of Ahaz (2 Kings 16:6) and the Israelites' turning away or going round Edom, which is suggested in Num 20:21 and made explicit by the editor of Num 21:4, made it necessary for the Israelites at this later stage to cross the frontier of Edom in order to follow the route through the wilderness of Moab.

---

[14] C. Steuernagel, *Das Deuteronomium,*[2] Göttingen, 1923, pp. 56–59; M. Noth, *Überlieferungsgeschichtliche Studien,* pp. 32–35; G. von Rad, *Das fünfte Buch Mose. Deuteronomium (ATD),*[2] 1968, pp. 30–31; J. G. Plöger, *Literarkritische, formgeschichtliche und stilkritische Untersuchungen zum Deuteronomium (Bonner Biblische Beiträge,* 26), Bonn, 1967, pp. 54–55.

[15] N. Lohfink, *Bib,* 41 (1960), p. 127, note 2.

We must now consider the difficult problem of the highlands of Seir, where the sons of Esau lived.[16] It would seem as though the name Seir referred both to a region to the east of the 'Arabah and to a region to the west. The two names, Seir and Edom, seem to have been interchangeable or else to have been placed in parallel (Num 24:18; Judges 5:4; Isa 21:11, corr.). The land that belonged to Edom was the hill country to the south-east of the Dead Sea and in Gen 32:4; 33:14, 16 and 36:8, 30, Seir is certainly to the east of the 'Arabah. It is, however, equally clear that Seir is (also?) in Deuteronomy located to the west of the 'Arabah. According to Deut 1:2 the route from Horeb to Kadesh, for example, passed, through the hill country of Seir: and the Amorites who lived in the hill country of Judah conquered the Israelites in Seir, following them to Hormah (Deut 1:44).[17] According to the pre-deuteronomic collector of the traditions assembled in the book of Joshua, the southernmost extent of the conquest of Canaan was 'Mount Halak, which rises towards Seir' (Jos 11:17; 12:7). This Mount Halak is the Jebel Halaq, which is situated to the north-north-east of 'Abdeh.

At a later period, the Chronicler was also thinking of the western side of the 'Arabah when he recorded the settlement of the Simeonites in the highlands of Seir after having conquered the Amalekites who lived there (1 Chron 4:42–43). The name Seir is very early. There is a reference to it in the Amarna letters; the king of Jerusalem complains in one letter that war is being waged against him from the land of Seir (še-e-ri) in the south as far as Gath-carmel in the north.[18] It cannot be Transjordan to which this document is referring. During the reigns of Ramses II and III, there are also references in the Egyptian texts to the hill country of Seir, the people of Seir and the bedouins (šasu) of Seir.[19] Seir here may also be a district near Egypt, on the western side of the 'Arabah.

It is therefore probable that the highlands of Seir which the Israelites skirted, according to Deut 2:1, were the broken mass of mountains rising to the east and south-east of Kadesh. According to Deut 2:4, 8, this hill country was inhabited by the sons of Esau. In the course of history, the Edomites

---

[16] J. B. Bartlett, 'The Land of Seir and the Brotherhood of Edom', JTS, new series 20 (1969), pp. 1–20. I do not think that this author has solved this problem in his article.

[17] The reference to Seir alongside Moab in Deut 2:29 is dependent on verses 4 and 19. In the additions, verses 12 and 22, Seir is identified with the ancient territory of the Horites, who were dispossessed by the Edomites (Gen 36:21, 29).

[18] EA 288, 26. The full form of the name Gath-carmel (see also 289, 18) has been found on a jar of Shiqmona; see F. M. Cross, IEJ, 18 (1968), pp. 226–233. It was probably situated on the plain of Acco. According to the letter, the whole country was opposed to the king of Jerusalem and the pharaoh.

[19] J. Janssen, 'Les monts Se'ir dans les textes égyptiens', Bib., 16 15 (1934), pp. 537–538; B. Grdseloff; 'Edom dans les sources égyptiennes', Revue de l'histoire juive en Egypte, 1 (1947), pp. 69–99.

tried to extend their territory to the west of the 'Arabah by taking land from Judah. During the reign of Ahaz (736–716 B.C.), the Edomites took Elath/Ezion-geber (2 Kings 16:6) and, according to 2 Chron 28:17, they invaded Judah and conquered the Judaeans. They also probably occupied part of the Negeb after Sennacherib's campaign in 701 B.C.[20] After the collapse of the kingdom of Judah, the Edomites moved to a point north of Hebron and the whole region was called Idumaea. Evidence of the Edomites' advance northwards has been provided by a recent discovery. An ostracon found at Tell 'Arād gives orders that a contingent of troops should be sent from the garrison at Arad to the fortress at Ramath-Negeb, which may be Khirbet Ghazzeh, about five miles to the south-east of Arad, as a precaution against an attack by the Edomites.[21] This fortress guarded the frontier between Judah and Edom. The text dates back to the last years of the kingdom of Judah, before Nebuchadnezzar's attack in 598 B.C. During the period of the Deuteronomist, the sons of Esau in fact occupied the hill country of Seir on the western side of the 'Arabah.

The road which skirted round these highlands and which the Israelites must have followed was the normal road from Kadesh to south of the 'Arabah, as outlined above in our commentary on the texts in Numbers. Despite the difference in presentation, this first part of the journey as described by the Deuteronomist does no more than make explicit the data provided by the early sources.

The Deuteronomist also goes farther along the route followed by the Israelites. They started in the direction of the wilderness of Moab. Yahweh, however, forbade them to attack Moab, since he would give them none of that land (Deut 2:9). The Israelites then crossed the Brook Zered. This is mentioned only here and in Num 21:11, which is in any case probably derived from Deut 2:13. The brook Zered is the Wādi el-Hesa which, at its southern end, enters the Dead Sea and formed the frontier between Edom and Moab. The Israelites then arrived at the northern frontier of Moab (Deut 2:18), the Arnon (verse 24), without any stopping-place in between, a normal procedure, since at this stage they were on the desert road. They were now near to the Ammonites, but, according to the Deuteronomist, Yahweh forbade them to attack the Ammonites, because he would give them none of their land either (verse 19). Yahweh then ordered them to cross the Arnon and they found themselves confronted by Sihon, the king of Heshbon. Here, the situation was quite different from that when they faced the Edomites, the Moabites and the Ammonites. The Israelites now had to attack and conquer Sihon (verses 24–25).

[20] H. L. Ginsberg, 'Judah and the Transjordan States, 734–582 B.C.', *Alexander Marx Jubilee Volume*, ed. S. Liebermann, New York, 1950, p. 323. 353.

[21] Y. Aharoni, *BibArch*, 31 (1968), pp. 17–18; *ibid.*, *Eretz-Israel* 9 (*Albright Volume*), 1969, pp. 10–15 (Hebrew).

At this point the Deuteronomist's account runs parallel to that of Numbers 21:21 ff: the Israelites ask for right of way, this is refused and they wage war against Sihon and are victorious (Deut 2:26–36). In the early sources, however, there is nothing comparable to what is said in Deuteronomy concerning Moab and Ammon. I do not think that this was a later development,[22] nor do I believe that the Deuteronomist had at his disposal certain early traditions which had been left out by J and E.[23] Up to the confrontation with Sihon, the Deuteronomist's route follows the boundaries of Edom and Moab along the border of the eastern desert and this is perfectly acceptable assuming that the Edomites and the Moabites were settled peoples by this time. What is important to recognise here, however, is that this route, like the whole historical prologue to Deuteronomy,[24] reflects theological views.

(a) The most important theme in Moses' discourse is that of the gift of the country and of the fulfilment of the promise (see Deut 1:6–8). Indeed, this theme predominates in the whole of the deuteronomistic history. The fact that it was God himself who allotted the various territories to the different peoples explains why the Israelites had to skirt the land of Edom. Their detour was not, as in Numbers, the consequence of the Edomites' refusal to allow them right of way so much as their carrying out of the commandment given by God who had made a gift of the land of Edom to the sons of Esau. Peoples who were related to Israel had, in other words, to be spared. The Edomites were the Israelites' brothers, because they were the sons of Esau (Deut 2:4). Moab and Ammon were the sons of Lot (verse 9), so they too had to be spared. God, moreover, had given them their lands (verses 5, 9, 18). This is also the reason why the Deuteronomist included the Ammonites in this list, even though the route followed by the Israelites did not come near to their land. Sihon and later Og were Amorites, however, and Yahweh therefore let them be conquered by the Israelites.

(b) Yahweh in fact delivered Sihon and his country over to Israel and spread terror and fear of the Israelites among all the peoples (Deut 2:24–25). The whole generation of men who had incurred guilt at Kadesh had disappeared (Deut 2:14–16; cf. 1:35) and the situation that had existed before the revolt prevailed (Deut 1:21). The war against Sihon was therefore the beginning of the conquest of Canaan. The deuteronomic editor nonetheless made a distinction here. The lands in Transjordan were given to Reuben

---

[22] See above, p. 555–556 and note 14.

[23] W. A. Sumner, 'Israel's Encounters with Edom, Moab, Ammon, Sihon and Og according to the Deuteronomist', *VT*, 18 (1968), pp. 216–228.

[24] N. Lohfink, 'Darstellungskunst und Theologie in Dtn 1, 6 – 3, 29', *Bib*, 41 (1960), pp. 105–134; W. L. Moran, 'The End of the Unholy War and the Anti-Exodus', *Bib*, 44 (1963), pp. 333–342; J. L. McKenzie, 'The Historical Prologue of Deuteronomy', *Fourth World Congress of Jewish Studies, Papers*, I, Jerusalem, 1967, pp. 95–101.

and Gad and to the half-tribe of Manasseh by Yahweh (Deut 3:18; cf. Jos 1:13) or by Moses (Deut 3:12, 13, 15, cf. 19; cf. Jos 1:14–15), without any reference to a previously made promise. The 'Promised Land', on the other hand, was given as the fulfilment of a vow made to the patriarchs (Deut 1:7–8, 35; Jos 1:6). This Promised Land was the land of Canaan (Deut 1:7), bounded by the Jordan (Jos 1:2–4) and Moses was not to enter it (Deut 34:4–5; cf. 3:25–27: 4:21).

3. Judges 11:17–18

According to Jephthah's message to the king of the Ammonites, Israel had first asked the king of Edom, then the king of Moab, for permission to pass through their countries, but both had refused. The Israelites therefore went round the countries of Edom and Moab and camped on the other side of the Arnon. It was from Arnon that Israel sent messengers to Sihon (Judges 11:17–18). The whole of this historical summary (Judges 11:12–28) is a later composition in which the editor has made use of various passages from the Pentateuch, in particular Num 20:14–22a for the request for right of way made to and refused by Edom and Deut 2:1–25 for the reference to Moab in addition to the reference to Edom.[25]

4. Numbers 33:37, 41–49

The fullest itinerary is given in the long list of stopping-places in the exodus and the desert found in Num 33. The section describing the journey from Kadesh to the plains of Moab occupies verses 37, 41–49. This chapter belongs to a later level of priestly editing. It sets out in sequence the geographical data contained in the books of the Pentateuch, but at least half of the names included are new and were taken by the priestly editor from one or more of the documents that he used. The suggestion has been made that this list contains an itinerary of a pilgrimage to Sinai,[26] but this

---

[25] M. Noth, Überlieferungsgeschichtliche Studien, p. 53, note 5; E. Täubler, Biblische Studien. Die Epoche der Richter, Tübingen, 1958, pp. 290–293; W. Richter, 'Die Überlieferungen um Jephtah. Ri 10, 17–12, 6', Bib, 47 (1966), pp. 485–556, especially pp. 522–547.

[26] M. Noth, 'Der Wallfahrtsweg zum Sinaï, PJB, 36 (1940), pp. 5–28 and, with more caution, in his commentary on Numbers (see note 7), pp. 210–213, and his History, p. 130. This hypothesis has been accepted by J. Koenig, who has elaborated on it in a series of articles: 'La localisation du Sinaï et la tradition des scribes', RHPR, 43 (1963), pp. 2–31; 44 (1964), pp. 200–235; 'Itinéraires sinaïtiques en Arabie', RHR, 166 (1964–B), pp. 121–141; 'Le Sinaï montagne de feu dans un désert de ténèbres', RHR, 167 (1965–A), pp. 129–155; and

'pilgrimage' has not been proved, nor is it very likely.[27] Reference has been made in this connection to the story of Elijah (1 Kings 19), but, if there ever was a regular pilgrimage to Sinai, the oblivion into which Sinai sank during the time of the monarchy and the uncertainty that still surrounds its location would be very difficult to explain. It is more probable that the editor used Num 33:16–25 for his outline of the journey from Sinai to Ezion-geber, which includes twenty stopping-places. The additions found in Deut 10:6–7 seem to have been derived from this 'road map' in Numbers.

If certain suggestions concerning the location of places on this 'road map' are accepted, the route begins in a region in the north-west of Arabia. This way was known at Jerusalem, at least since the time of Nabonidus' settlement of colonies of Jews in oases in northern Arabia.[28] If these colonies are taken as a reliable indication, Sinai was situated in the volcanic region to the south-east of the Gulf of 'Aqabah.[29] The route outlined in Num 33 continues from Ezion-geber straight on to Kadesh (verse 36), then on to Mount Hor on the frontier of the country of Edom, where Aaron died (verses 37–39). (These verses are derived from Num 20:22–29, P.) Finally, the list of stopping-places between Kadesh and the plains of Moab is given in Num 33:41–49. It is useful to reproduce them here, at the same time indicating parallel passages in the other routes.

Mount Hor	Num 20:22 (P); 21:4 (editorial)
Zalmonah	only here
Punon	only here
Oboth	Num 21:10; see below
Iyim or Iye-abarim	Num 21:11; see below
Dibon-gad	only here (in the itineraries)
Almon-diblathaim	only here
Abarim Mountains	Num 27:12 (P); Deut 32:49 (P)
Plains of Moab	Num 22:1 (editorial, P?)

Between Mount Hor and the Abarim mountains, both of which are

---

more recently, H. Gese, *Das ferne und nahe Wort. Festschrift L. Rost*, ed. F. Maass (*BZAW*, 105), 1967, pp. 81–94.

[27] See also H. Schmid, *Mose. Überlieferung und Geschichte* (*BZAW*, 110), 1968, pp. 17–22.

[28] R. de Vaux, ' "Lévites" minéens et lévites israélites', *Lex Tua Veritas* (*Festschrift H. Junker*), Trier, 1961, pp. 265–273 = *Bible et Orient*, Paris, 1967, pp. 277–285; (*The Bible and the Ancient Near East*, London, 1972); I. Ben-Zvi, 'Les origines de l'éstablissement des tribus d'Israël en Arabie', *Le museon*, 74 (1961), pp. 143–190, especially pp. 145–149; R. Meyer, *Das Gebet des Nabonid* (*Sitzungsberichte der Sächsischen Akademie der Wissenschaften zu Leipzig, Philologisch-historische Klasse*, 107, 3), Berlin, 1962, pp. 67–81.

[29] This does not, however, mean that a genuine memory is necessarily preserved in this sixth or fifth century tradition; see above, pp. 436–437.

borrowed from P, then, there are six stopping-places in this list, which are in fact peculiar to it. (As we shall show later, Num 21:10–11 comes from Num 33.) Of these, only two can be identified with any degree of certainty. They are Punon, which has been located at Khirbet Feinān, about twenty-five miles south of the Dead Sea at the foot of the mountain range overlooking the 'Arabah on the eastern side, and Dibon, which is known to us apart from the desert routes and located at Dībān to the north of the Arnon. Dibon, however, lay on the 'king's highway' which the Israelites did not follow, according to Num 20:17–18, and this route presupposes that, after leaving Kadesh, the Israelites went due east – Punon is at the same latitude as Kadesh – and not in the direction of the Sea of Suph, as described in Num 14:25. It also presupposes that they crossed Edom and Moab, although they did not do this according to Num 20:14–22a and Deut 2:1–25. Finally, according to this route, the Israelites could have crossed the Arnon and reached Dibon without confronting Sihon, which contradicts what is said in Num 21:21ff, see especially verse 24, and Deut 2:24. We are therefore bound to conclude that the route described in Num 33 cannot be reconciled with that given in the earliest source (Num 20:14–22a) or with the roundabout route outlined in Deut 2:1–25. Num 33 does, on the other hand, provide the most direct and the best route between Kadesh and a point to the north of Arnon. Following the wādi Fiqreh, this route descends into the 'Arabah, where Zalmonah, which was probably Calamona, a Roman station mentioned in the *Notitia Dignitatum,* was situated. It then crosses the 'Arabah, reaches Punon (Feinān) and from there goes up on to the plateau where it joins the main road along the ridge of the highlands, the so-called 'king's highway'.[30] In his outline of this journey, the editor was clearly able to make use of another 'road map' or else he may simply have drawn on the general knowledge of geography available at the time, since this route would certainly have been known.

5. *Numbers 21:10–20*

The route outlined in Num 21:10–20 is inserted between the episode of the bronze serpent and the story of the request sent to Sihon. The stages on the journey are given below, with their parallels in the other texts.

Oboth	Num 33:44
Iye-abarim	Num 33:44
Wadi Zered	Deut 2:13

[30] Y. Aharoni, *The Land of the Bible,* p. 186, map 14; *The Macmillan Atlas of the Bible,* p. 42, map 52.

Arnon	Deut 2:24
Beer	only here
Mattanah	only here
Nahaliel	only here
Bamoth	? Bamoth-baal, Num 22:41
Pisgah	Num 23:14.

A short poetic passage is inserted between the reference to the Arnon and the mention of Beer. This speaks of the Arnon and appears to have been taken from a 'Book of the Wars of Yahweh', which is quoted only in this text.[31] A short song of the well is inserted between the references to Beer and Mattanah.

According to the classical literary criticism of this text, the whole passage (Num 21:10–20) or at least the greater part of it (verses 12–20) was composed by the Elohist, verses 10–11 perhaps having been introduced by P. It would seem, however, that the entire passage was late.[32] It contains some elements of very early Hebrew poetry, certainly, but the route described in it is partly borrowed from other texts and partly invented. Oboth and Iye-abarim are taken from Num 33:44.[33] The editor of Num 21:10–20 took the journey as described in Num 33 as far as this point, that is, just beyond Punon, possibly because he wanted the episode of the bronze serpent to be situated at the mining centre at Punon. (This is the reason that has been suggested not only by several modern scholars, but also by the Byzantines in the Map of Medeba.) After this point beyond Punon, he no longer followed the route of Num 33 and this may be because it crossed Edom and Moab and he wanted to remain faithful to the tradition of Numbers and Deuteronomy, according to which the Israelites avoided these two countries. As a result of this, he located Iye-abarim 'in the wilderness to the east of Moab, towards the sunrise', thus basing himself on Judges 11:18. It was also because of his desire to remain faithful to the tradition that he borrowed the next two stopping-places, the wadi Zered and the Arnon, from Deut 2:13 and 2:24 respectively. He also stated specifically that the Arnon was 'in the desert'. The reference to the Zered was made too late, since the editor had already located Iye-abarim in the desert to the east of Moab and the Zered formed the southern boundary of the land of Moab. As in Deuteronomy too, there is no stopping-place in this account between the Zered and the Arnon.

---

[31] See Tur-Sinai, *BIES*, 24 (1959/1960), pp. 146–148 (Hebrew), who translates this text as 'Hence it is written in the book: there were wars of Yahweh...'

[32] M. Noth, 'Num 21 als Glied der "Hexateuch"–Erzählung', *ZAW*, 58 (1940), pp. 161–189, especially pp. 170–178, and his commentary on Numbers, *in loco*.

[33] And not by the editor of Num 33 from Num 21:10, 11, as H. Gese, *op. cit.* (note 26), p. 87, and H. Schmid, *op. cit.* (note 27), p. 22, claim.

Beer is not known and it is believed that it may have been taken from the song of the well (*b'ēr*) quoted in this passage. It is even more clear that this song led to the invention of the stopping-place of Mattanah, which does not exist. The editor did not understand the final words of the poem in verse 18b: 'and of the desert it is a gift (*mattānāh*)', words that were necessary for the metre. Nahaliel is also not known and neither is Bamoth, unless it is the same as the Bamoth-baal mentioned in the story of Balaam (Num 22:41). The 'height of Pisgah which looks down on the desert' (Num 21:20) in fact brings together two other texts from the story of Balaam (Num 23:14 and 28). The whole of this verse is in fact overburdened and confused. It is, for example, difficult to see how the 'height of Pisgah' can be placed alongside the 'valley that is in the country of Moab' and this 'country of Moab' is, in any case, a vague term referring to the whole of the Moabite territory and is not a precise geographical name. We may conclude, then, that a real route is not provided by Num 21:10–20 and that the editor simply wanted at all costs to fill in the gap left in the book of Numbers between the episode of the bronze serpent and the encounter with Sihon.

Our final conclusion must be that we cannot retrace the route followed by Moses' group from Kadesh to north of the Arnon. All that we are told by the early sources is that this group went in the direction of the Gulf of 'Aqabah (the Sea of Suph), did not cross Edom and was nomadic for a long time. The route suggested by the Deuteronomist went via Ezion-geber and then through the desert to the east of Edom and Moab. The editor of Num 33 described the normal route from Kadesh to north of the Arnon, crossing the 'Arabah. Finally, the editor of Num 21:10–20 went back to the early tradition and then worked out a fictitious route which avoided Edom and Moab.

II. THE WARS AGAINST SIHON AND OG

1. *The war against Sihon, king of Heshbon*

In dealing with Israel's war against Sihon, the king of Heshbon, we are on much firmer ground. Both Deut 2:26–26 and Judges 11:19–21 are derived from Num 21:21–31, the first simply adding a theological interpretation to the story and the second summarising the longer earlier account. We will therefore leave these later texts on one side and consider principally the early document of Num 21:21–34.[34] It has been ascribed to the Elohist

---

[34] For this text, see W. Rudolph, *Der 'Elohist' von Exodus bis Josua* (*BZAW*, 68), 1938, pp. 89ff; R. de Vaux, *RB*, 50 (1941), pp. 19–25 = *Bible et Orient*, 1967, pp. 118–127; M. Noth, *ZAW*, 58 (1940), pp. 162–170; 60 (1944), pp. 37–341; commentary on Numbers, pp.

because the word 'Amorites' is used instead of 'Canaanites', but this has little meaning beyond the Jordan, which defined the boundary of Canaan.

The historical meaning of this passage depends to a very great extent on how the poem contained in verses 27b–30 is interpreted. Unfortunately, the crucial verse 30 is corrupt. Three different hypotheses have been suggested:

(a) This poem was originally an Amorite song of victory celebrating the defeat of the Moabites by Sihon, inserted as a commentary on verse 26b.[35] This theory would mean that verse 30 has to be radically corrected and verse 27 would have to be subjected to a forced translation.

(b) It was a song of victory celebrating the defeat of the Moabites by a king of Israel, either Omri[36] or David.[37] This hypothesis does nothing to explain the references in the poem to Sihon.

(c) It was a song of victory celebrating the Israelites' success in the period of the conquest. This is the most plausible theory. The Israelites' victories during the conquest are proclaimed not only in verse 26, but also in verse 25. Their victory over Sihon is celebrated in verses 27b and 30 and, in this context, Sihon's victory over Moab is also proclaimed in verses 28–29, which declare that Heshbon has devoured the Moabite towns, but that the Israelites have destroyed Heshbon.[38]

It is important to survey the historical situation briefly at this point.[39] A small Canaanite kingdom had been established around Heshbon, the capital, to the north of the Arnon. It is not known when this kingdom was founded. Surface explorations at Hesbān have revealed no evidence of settlement before the Iron Age. Excavations have recently been carried out at the site and so far these too have yielded nothing but potsherds dating from the same period. There is no sign of any settlement of a lasting kind or of any earlier civilisation and the archaeological surveys made at Medeba further south have produced equally negative results. On the other hand, Late Bronze pottery has been found at Jalūd, about six miles to the south-east of Medeba[40] and a Middle Bronze tomb has been discovered near Nebo.[41] The Canaanite kingdom centred on Heshbon was threatened when

---

140–145; P. D. Hanson, 'The Song of Heshbon and David's NIR', *HTR*, 61 (1968), pp. 297–320; J. B. Bartlett, 'The Historical Reference of Numbers XXI, 27–30', *PEQ*, 1969, pp. 94–100.

[35] See H. Cazelles, *Les Nombres (BJ)*,[2] 1958; N. H. Snaith, *Leviticus and Numbers (The Century Bible)*, 1967; P. D. Hanson, *op. cit.*, (note 34).

[36] This has been a common view since it was first suggested by E. Meyer, B. Stade and B. Baentsch.

[37] J. B. Bartlett, *op. cit.* (note 34).

[38] This opinion is favoured by W. Rudolph, M. Noth and myself, *op. cit.* (note 34).

[39] Little of value can be obtained from J. Simons' study, 'Two Connected Problems Relating to the Israelite Settlement in Transjordan', *PEQ*, 1947, pp. 87–101.

[40] W. F. Albright, *BASOR*, 49 (February 1933), p. 28; N. Glueck, *AASOR*, 14 (1934), p. 5.

[41] S. Saller and B. Bagatti, *The Town of Nebo*, Jerusalem, 1949, pp. 24–29, Plates 4–6.

the Moabites, who were in the process of becoming a state, tried to extend their territory to the north of the Arnon. Sihon was victorious against the 'first' king of Moab (verse 26). The Moabites had always laid claim to this rich tableland, the *mîšôr*. They were to possess it during the period of the Judges, when Eglon the king of Moab seized Jericho (Judges 3:12–30), lose it again during the reign of Omri and then take it back again when Mesha was king of Moab. After his victory, Sihon's territory stretched from the Arnon to the Jabbok, at least according to Num 21:26 and Jos 12:2–3. These two texts, however, have probably been adapted to provide an idealised frontier.[42]   According to Num 21:32, Jazer and Gilead were reconnoitred after Sihon's kingdom had been conquered by the Israelites – they are quoted in Num 32:1 without any mention of Sihon. We may conclude that his kingdom did not extend very far to the north of Heshbon and probably had the Wādi Hesbān as its northern frontier. This was no doubt the situation when the Israelites came and conquered Sihon.

We are, however, bound to ask here who it was who gained this victory, in other words, whether it was the whole group of Israelites under Moses' leadership or only part of that group. Moses is not mentioned in this account of the conquest and the conclusion has therefore been drawn that it was only the group of Reuben-Gad involved[43] or simply the group of Gad.[44] The Gadites were in fact settled in this part of Transjordan (Num 32:34–36; Jos 13:24–28) and, on the Moabite Stone, Mesha, the king of Moab, says 'the men of Gad had always dwelt in the land of Ataroth' (line 10). The Reubenites, however, were also settled there according to Num 32:37–38; Jos 13:15–23. (We shall return to this problem concerning the settlement of these two tribes in a later section of this chapter.)

It has been suggested that Gad, having first settled in the Jazer district, extended its territory towards the south, by taking land from Sihon.[45] This theory is, however, contradicted by the only precise datum provided in Num 21:21–31 concerning the geography of the war waged against Sihon, namely that he was beaten at Jahaz (verse 23), the site of which is uncertain. According to this text in relation to Heshbon, Jahaz is in the direction of the desert, although not necessarily in the desert itself. At the time when Eusebius was writing (Onom 104, 11), Jahaz was believed to have been between Medeba and Dibon and, according to the Moabite Stone (1. 19–20), Mesha took it back and attached it to Dibon. This points to a site to

[42] R. de Vaux, *RB*, 50 (1941), pp. 19–21 = *Bible et Orient*, pp. 118–121.

[43] H. Gressmann, *Mose und seine Zeit*, Göttingen, 1913, pp. 305–306; M. Noth, *ZAW*, 60 (1944), pp. 37 ff.

[44] M. Noth, *Geschichte*, p. 138.

[45] M. Noth, *ZAW*, 60 (1944), pp. 39 ff; *Die Welt des Alten Testaments*,[4] Berlin, 1962, p. 68 (*The Old Testament World*, London, 1966, p. 75).

the south-east of Heshbon, so that the Israelites must have attacked from the south and the attacking group must have come from the desert. We have no reason to doubt that this was the group led by Moses and that these Israelites reached the plain to the north-east of the Dead Sea by this route and crossed the Jordan from that point.

2. The war against Og, king of Bashan

The story of a conquest of the kingdom of Og, the king of Bashan, is added in Num 21 to the account of the conquest of the kingdom of Sihon, the king of Heshbon. This addition was clearly borrowed from Deut 3:1–7 and duplicates the story of the victory gained over Sihon. It is not based on any early tradition and Og is not a historical person, nor is the name even a personal name.[46] He is called the king of Bashan, which is the name of a geographical region and was never the name of a kingdom – in fact, in the second millennium B.C., there were several small kingdoms in Bashan. In fact, Og had several 'royal towns', including Edrei, Ashtaroth and Salecah (Deut 3:10; Jos 13:12, 31). He gave battle at Edrei = Der'a on the frontier between Jordan and Syria, at least according to Num 21:33, but, according to Deut 3:11, his bed could be seen at Rabbah of the Ammonites = Amman, sixty or more miles to the south. This bed was fourteen and a half feet long and must have been one of the dolmens in the vicinity of Amman. According to the same text (Deut 3:11), Og was the 'last survivor of the Rephaim', a mythological race of giants who lived in Palestine. The clear intention of this story is to justify the claims made by the half-tribe of Manasseh to a district which the Israelites never in fact possessed.[47]

III. THE ORACLES OF BALAAM AND THE AFFAIR OF THE BAAL OF PEOR

Two episodes are attached to the narrative in Numbers of the journey from Kadesh to Moab and are described as taking place in the plains of Moab. These are the story of Balaam (Num 22–24) and the story of the Baal of Peor (Num 25:1–5). They are not directly connected with the epic of the conquest of Canaan, but they are of importance to us in this context

---

[46] See C. Rabin, *Eretz-Israel*, 8 (1967), pp. 251–254.

[47] M. Noth, 'Beiträge zur Geschichte des Ostjordanlandes', *ZDPV*, 68 (1949), pp. 1–50, specially pp. 2–18; *Geschichte*, pp. 147–148; J. L. McKenzie, 'The Historical Prologue of Deuteronomy', *Fourth World Congress of Jewish Studies, Papers, I*, Jerusalem, 1967, especially p. 99–100.

because they tell us something about the conditions of the geography of Palestine at the time.

1. The story of Balaam

The oracles of Balaam and the story which forms a framework for them are composed of both J and E, the latter predominating. The oracles themselves may be even earlier. According to the narrative itself, Balaam declaimed his oracles in different places. The first place was Bamoth-baal (Num 22:41). The second was on the 'Field of Spies' at the summit of Pisgah (Num 23:14), which is the mountain or the mountain range overlooking the northern tip of the Dead Sea. Thirdly, Balaam offered sacrifice and declaimed an oracle 'at the summit of Peor, dominating the *y'šimôn*', the steppe (Num 23:28). Balaam, accompanied by Balak, the king of Moab, journeys northwards, in other words, along the edge of the tableland which overlooks the steppe to the north-east of the Dead Sea.

This, however, is far to the north of the Arnon, in the land which, according to Num 21:21–31, belonged previously to Sihon and had been conquered by the Israelites. At the time of the formation of this tradition, this ridge was the frontier between the Moabites and the Israelites and the two peoples were hostile towards each other, although this hostility had not resulted in armed conflict. This must have been the real situation in history, although it is not possible to know exactly what the situation was during the period following the settlement of the tribes and preceding the reign of David. The frontiers between the two peoples must have changed from time to time and the population of the whole region to the north of the Arnon and in the plain to the north-east of the Dead Sea must have consisted of Canaanite-Amorites, remnants of Sihon's kingdom and Israelites and Moabites.[48]

2. The episode of the Baal of Peor

The same situation is presented in the episode of the Baal of Peor (Num 25:1–5). The Israelites, according to this story, gave themselves over to debauchery with the Moabite women, who invited them to take part in the sacrifices of their god or their gods and they made themselves subject to the Baal of Peor. This is without any doubt an early tradition, already known

[48] For this problem, see J. Liver, 'The Wars of Mesha, King of Moab', *PEQ*, 1967, pp. 14–31, especially pp. 15–18; M. Noth, *History*, pp. 154–155.

to Hosea (Hos 9:10). Peor was the name of a mountain (Num 23:28) and of the god who was worshipped on that mountain and was therefore called the Baal of Peor or Baal Peor. The place-name Beth-peor (Deut 3:29; 4:46; 34:6) must be the name of the sanctuary of the Baal of Peor. Although the precise location is not known, it is believed that Beth-peor was situated a little to the north of Mount Nebo.[49] This god, Peor, is a local form of the Canaanite, not the Moabite god (Baal) and the sanctuary of Beth-peor must, like the sanctuary of Bamothbaal (Num 22:41), have been one of the sanctuaries in the Canaanite kingdom of Sihon (see Deut 4:46). According to Num 23:28, however, it was on the Moabite frontier and used both by the Moabites and by the Israelites.

The picture is complicated by the verses that follow, verses 6–18. Concluding with a clear reference to the preceding account of the episode of the Baal of Peor (verse 18), this story narrates the events that follow the fault committed by an Israelite with 'the Midianite woman' in the *qubbāh*, the pavilion, tent or alcove which was possibly used for sacred prostitution. This story bears all the signs of priestly editing and it glorifies Phinehas and his descendants, but it makes use of an early tradition. The question that inevitably arises is, is it simply parallel to the tradition of the 'Moabite' women in Num 25:1–4 or does it preserve a memory of the presence of nomadic Midianites living in this region and using this sanctuary? The latter is quite possible, since the Midianites feature in the story of Balaam alongside the Moabites (Num 22:4 and 7).

This Midianite version of the affair of the Baal of Peor, and verses 16–18 especially, gave rise to the long story in Num 31, which tells of a war against Midian with the aim of exterminating the Midianites and which is followed by detailed instructions concerning purification and the sharing of the booty at the end of the campaign. The soothsayer Balaam, who had blessed the Israelites in Num 22–24, is shown in this account as having led them to be unfaithful to Yahweh and to worship the Baal of Peor here (verse 16), which is why he was put to death (verse 8).

This is one of the late passages in the Pentateuch, although O. Eissfeldt has recently defended its historical authenticity.[50] In his view, the references to Midian in Num 22 and 25 point to the fact that Midian exercised the function of a protectorate with regard to Edom, Moab and the kingdom of Sihon and that, despite its recent form, Num 31 preserves an authentic historical memory, the names of the Midianite kings defeated by Moses Num 31:8 and Jos 13:21, which is derived from it) being also authentic. W. F. Albright[51] has argued that the Midianites were donkey-raising

[49] See O. Henke, 'Zur Lage von Beth Peor', *ZDPV*, 75 (1959), pp. 155–163.

[50] O. Eissfeldt, 'Protektorat der Midianiter über ihre Nachbarn im letzten Viertel des 2. Jahrtausends v. Chr.', *JBL*, 87 (1968), pp. 383–393.

[51] W. F. Albright, in correspondence with O. Eissfeldt, quoted *op. cit.* (note 50), pp.

caravan traders in the thirteenth century B.C. (Num 31). He bases this view on the statement that the Midianites possessed sixty-one thousand donkeys according to Num 31:34, but no camels, whereas according to Judges 6–8, in the twelfth century B.C. they had camels but no donkeys. However, it is not easy to accept Albright's opinion.

Both Eissfeldt and Albright believe that the form of the text is recent. Albright dates the editing of the text at the seventh century, but this is in fact too early, since it belongs to a late level of P. Both scholars agree – Eissfeldt explicitly – that the figures given in the text regarding the booty are fantastic, but we are impelled to ask whether it is possible to draw any conclusions from the nature of the booty. The kings were Midianites according to Num 31:8, but princes of Sihon according to Jos 13:21. Their names are interesting. Zur comes from Num 25:15, Rekem is a place-name and is, in fact, the Semitic name for Petra,[52] Hur is the eponym of the Horites, who preceded the Edomites (Deut 2:12; Gen 36:26–30, etc.), Evi[53] may be the eponym of the Emim, the early inhabitants of Moab (Deut 2:10) and the last name, Reba, which means a quarter (*rebha'*), can hardly be accepted as a personal name. Num 31 must therefore be regarded as a late composition, adding nothing to what is contained in Num 22 and 25, namely that there were Midianites in the region.

IV. THE SETTLEMENT OF REUBEN AND GAD[54]

1. Numbers 32

In this section, we shall discuss the settlement of the first tribes of Israel in Transjordan. Literary criticism of this passage (Num 32) is very difficult because although it is late in form and in style it resembles Deuteronomy, with traces of priestly editing, it appears to have an early basis. The tribes of Reuben and Gad saw that the land of Jazer and the land of Gilead were ideal for raising stock and therefore asked Moses to be allowed to settle there (verses 1–4, in part), while at the same time promising to take part

---

389–390, and in 'Midianite Donkey Caravans', *Translating and Understanding the Old Testament. Essays in Honor of H. G. May*, New York and Nashville, 1970, pp. 197–205.

[52] J. Starcky, *RB*, 72 (1965), pp. 95–97.

[53] The name '*w*' has been found on an Ammonite seal; P. C. Hammond, 'An Ammonite Stamp Seal from Amman', *BASOR*, 160 (Dec. 1960), pp. 38–41.

[54] R. de Vaux, *RB*, 50 (1941), pp. 16–47 = *Bible et Orient*, pp. 115–118, 124–129; M. Noth, 'Israelitische Stämme zwischen Ammon und Moab', *ZAW*, 60 (1944), pp. 11–57; ibid., 'Gilead und Gad', *ZDPV*, 75 (1959), pp. 14–73; E. Täubler, *Biblische Studien. Die Epoche der Richter*, Tübingen, 1958, pp. 218–245; H.-J. Zobel, *Stammesspruch und Geschichte (BZAW*, 95), 1965, especially pp. 62–65, 97–101.

with the other tribes in the conquest of Canaan (verses 16–19). The rest of Num 32 is editorial.

The essential aspect of the settlement of Reuben and Gad is that it was peaceful and not a conquest. The datum given in Num 21:32, namely that Jazer and all the towns dependent on it were conquered, is an addition. Part of Num 32:1–4, namely verses 2b–4a, is also additional. These verses contain a list of towns conquered between Jazer and the Arnon. The names in this list are taken from the lists in Num 32:34–38 and they contradict the place-names given in verse 1, Jazer and Gilead, both lands said to be favourable to raising stock. We must now look more closely at this region and try to define it more precisely.

2. Jazer and Gilead[55]

I have already suggested[56] that Jazer was situated at Khirbet Jazzir in the wadi which comes down from es–Salt a little below the spring of 'Ain Hazer, in a district known as 'Ard Jazzir.'[57] This location was rejected by M. Noth[58] because he thought that it was too far to the north and therefore separated from the land of Gad, which was, in his opinion, between Heshbon and the Arnon in a district that must have been difficult to cross. He suggested that it was, in other words, in the region of Nāʿūr. R. Rendtorff[59] has suggested Tell 'Areimeh, about two miles to the north-west of the modern Nāʿūr, whereas Y. Aharoni[60] has declined to locate it exactly. Even if there is no general agreement as to its precise location, however, it was certainly north of Heshbon and, according to the data provided by the Bible itself, the 'land of Jazer' stretched to the north of the kingdom of Sihon and to the west of the territory of the Ammonites.

The land of Gilead must have been to the north of the land of Jazer, from which it is distinguished in the biblical tradition. According to 2 Sam 24:5, David's officers who were given the task of making a census of the people set out from Aroer on the Arnon and then went towards Jazer and into Gilead. The name Gilead was used without any precise geographical sense. It could be used for the whole of the territory belonging to the Transjordanian tribes (Jos 22:9, 15; 2 Kings 10:33) and it was also applied more generally to the hill country between the Wādi Hesbān and the Yarmuk,

[55] This question has recently been considered again by M. Ottosson, Gilead. Tradition and History, Lund, 1969; S. Mittmann, Beiträge zur Siedlungs- und Territorialgeschichte des nörd-hen Ostjordanlandes, Wiesbaden, 1970.
[56] See Bible et Orient, pp. 124–127.
[57] This hypothesis was accepted by F.–M. Abel, Géographie de la Palestine, II, pp. 356–357.
[58] M. Noth, ZDPV, 75 (1959), pp. 63–72.
[59] R. Rendtorff, 'Zur Lage von Jazer', ZDPV, 76 (1960), pp. 124–135.
[60] Y. Aharoni, The Land of the Bible, p. 189.

that is, from the ancient kingdom of Sihon as far north as Bashan (Jos 13:10–12). The territory was divided by the Jabbok into two 'halves', at least according to Deut 3:12–13; Jos 12:2, 5; 13:31, and the name Gilead was sometimes applied to only one of these halves. The northern half was the territory of Machir-Manasseh (Num 32:39–40; Deut 3:15; Jos 17:5–6) and the southern half was the land allotted to Reuben and Gad (Num 32:1; Jos 13:25).

This second use of the term Gilead is earlier and Gilead was originally employed in an even more restricted sense. Strictly speaking, the land of Gilead was to the north of the land of Jazer (see Num 32:1) and did not go beyond the Jabbok, which was a natural frontier from the point of view both of physical and of economic geography. To the south of the Jabbok, according to Num 32:1, 4, there was good land for grazing, while, to the north, the mountainous district, now known as 'Ajlūn, was in biblical times covered with forest, some of which still remains today, and was well populated. The name Gilead is found in modern place-names to the south of the Jabbok – part of this region is now called Jebel Jel'ad and there is a Khirbet Jel'ad and a Khirbet Jal'ūd. The name was later extended to cover the northern half of the territory. This took place when the Israelites were entering the valley of the Jordan and the half-tribe of Manasseh was settling in this region. Apart from the geographical texts in Deuteronomy and the book of Joshua, which we have already mentioned, certain historical texts also reflect this extension of the name to the north. The first clear example of this is the reference to Jabesh-gilead (Tell el-Maqlūb in the Wādi Yābis, which has its source in the Jebel 'Ajlūn) at the time of Saul (2 Sam 2:1–10) and perhaps also during the period of the Judges, if Judges 21:8–9 really reflects a tradition of that period. The other obvious example is the reference to Ramoth-gilead = Tell Ramith on the table land which goes down to the Yarmuk. This is mentioned for the first time as the administrative centre of one of Solomon's districts (1 Kings 4:13).

Reuben and Gad asked for permission to settle in the land of Jazer and the land of Gilead because they owned large herds (Num 32:1). At the time of the establishment of the tribes, however, the groups arriving were all at the same pastoral stage of life. This information can therefore only mean that Reuben and Gad only slowly became settled people. Archaeological research in this district in fact shows that the sedentary occupation of the land began just after the beginning of the Iron Age.

3. The treaty between Jacob and Laban

The fact that Israelitic or pre-Israelitic groups settled peacefully in the

Gilead region at an early date is confirmed by a very different tradition. According to Gen 31:44–54, Jacob concluded a treaty with Laban the Aramaean on Mount Gilead. According to the Yahwist, a frontier was defined by this treaty and a cairn, *gal,* was set up as a witness, *ʿedh,* with the result that Jacob called it *galʿēdh,* Galeed.[61] This is, of course, a case of folk etymology explaining the place name Gilead, *gilʿādh,* but it is connected with a historical memory. Jacob and Laban represent two groups in this story, the Israelites and the Aramaeans, both of whom were still leading the life of shepherds and herdsmen, with a frontier between their lands running to the east of Jebel Jelʿad. During the period of the Judges, and in particular during the time of Jephthah, which we shall be discussing in detail later, this frontier separated the Israelites from the Ammonites. When Moses' group arrived in Transjordan, the Ammonites were already occupying their land, even though they had not become a kingdom, as the Edomites and the Moabites apparently had. We may therefore possibly conclude from this that Gen 31 provides us with an episode in the settlement of the tribes during the thirteenth century, namely an agreement made with the Ammonites, who are included within the very general term of Aramaeans.

It is also possible, however, that this story portrays a situation prior to the exodus. In the Bible itself, it is in fact situated within the period of the patriarchs. What is more, according to the biblical tradition, Gad was a son of Zilpah, Leah's slave-girl. This might point to the fact that Gad's origin was different from that of the Israelite tribes of pure blood. Zilpah's other son, moreover, was Asher and he settled at the other end of the Promised Land. Both names have the same basic meaning, Asher meaning happiness and Gad good fortune. I cannot discuss here the question whether they were originally names of deities later applied to regions or whether they were personal names which later became the eponyms of tribes. What is relevant to our present discussion is that Gad and Asher, who were, according to the biblical tradition, the sons of the same concubine and who both had names of the same basic type, must also have had a similar prehistory. As we shall see later, Asher settled at an early stage in the north of Canaan, did not go down into Egypt and did not take part in the exodus or the conquest. The same hypothesis can also be applied to Gad. This group of shepherds and herdsmen settled in the region between the kingdom of Sihon and the Jabbok, in other words, in the land of Jazer and the land of Gilead. When Moses' group arrived from the east and forced their way through this region after conquering Sihon, they encountered the Gadites. They recognised the Gadites as their kinsmen and the Gadites adopted Yahwism, the religion of the group that had recently arrived. They were not allotted land at this time, nor did they seize land; in fact they kept the

[61] See especially D. J. McCarthy, 'Three Covenants in Genesis', *CBQ,* 26 (1964), pp. 179–189; F. O. Garcia-Treto, 'Genesis 31, 44 and "Gilead" ', *ZAW,* 79 (1967), pp. 13–17.

land that had belonged to them for a long time. From this time onwards, the story of Gad became closely interwoven with that of Reuben and we shall discuss this later in the chapter.

4. Was there a tribe of Gilead?

The same early land of Gilead south of the Jabbok is discussed in the story of Jephthah (Judges 10–12). Jephthah fought the Ammonites who had invaded Gilead and, according to the account in the book of Judges, he lived at Mizpah in Gilead or simply Mizpah, which is clearly the same Gilead as the one in the Yahwistic version (Gen 31:47–48) and which is called Mizpah in the Elohistic version (Gen 31:49). What is remarkable here, however, is that there is no question of Gadites in the story in Judges and that Jephthah is several times called the 'Gileadite' (Judges 11:1, 40; 12:7). When he was running away from Absalom, David sought refuge in the same region and was helped by an old man, Barzillai the 'Gileadite'. In this case, the word clearly related to a people in the ethnic sense, like the terms Benjaminite, Ephraimite and so on. The term 'men of Gilead' is also used in the book of Judges (Judges 12:4–5). This is comparable to the term 'men of Judah' used elsewhere. The term 'elders of Gilead' is also found in Judges 11, passim, and can be compared with the 'elders of Judah'. One of the lesser judges, Jair, is called the 'Gileadite' (Judges 10:13). At a much later period, Pekahiah, the king of Israel, was murdered by Pekah. In this, Pekah was helped by fifty 'sons of Gileadites' or 'sons of Gilead' (2 Kings 15:25). (This text is uncertain.) The term used here is similar to the 'sons of Reuben', the 'sons of Manasseh' and so on. Gad is not mentioned in the song of Deborah, but, in the list of tribes, Gilead is in fact mentioned after Reuben and the song says that 'Gad stayed beyond the Jordan' (Judges 5:17). According to 1 Sam 13:7, the Israelites, fleeing from the Philistines, crossed the Jordan and went to the territories of Gad and Gilead, which seem to have been similar, but distinct. Finally, in Judges 12:1–6, the Ephraimites criticised the Gileadite leader Jephthah for not having called on them to fight with him and kept saying: 'You are no more than deserters from Ephraim, you Gileadites in the heart of Ephraim and Manasseh' (verse 4). (The word translated as 'deserters' is *pālîṭ*.) Taken as a whole, does this not point to the fact that there was a tribe of Gilead, separate from the tribe of Gad and following a different development?

M. Noth[62] thought that this last text was clear proof that Gilead was a group which had separated from Ephraim and had settled in Transjordania after following the route leading from the west. The whole accusation of the Ephraimites, however, is open to doubt. It is absent from several manuscripts and in the Syro-Haxaplar this text is marked with an asterisk. What is more, the word *pālīt* does not really mean 'deserter', which it would have to mean to satisfy Noth's argument, but rather 'escaped' or 'survivor'. The sentence in verse 4 is in any case paralleled in verse 5, which contains the same words: 'Whenever the Ephraimite fugitives said . . .' at the beginning and is completed to form an unintelligible text.[63] E. Täubler, on the other hand, thought that the whole episode, Judges 12:1–6, was a late legend and that verse 4 was an allusion to the origin of Machir. (We shall be discussing this question later.[64])

Several authors have, on the basis of other texts and in particular the Song of Deborah (Judges 5–17), insisted that at the time of the Judges there was a tribe of Gilead in Transjordan and that this tribe formed part of Israel, whereas the tribe of Gad did not exist at that time. Gad was a Gileadite group, living in the south of the territory. According to this theory, the Gadites became independent later – hence the statement concerning Gad in Jacob's blessings (Gen 49:19) – and quickly became powerful – hence the statement in Moses' blessings (Deut 33: 20–21). Both entities, however, existed side by side, according to this hypothesis, at the beginning of the period of the kings (see 1 Sam 13:7, above).[65]

Good, but not entirely convincing arguments have been put forward in support of this theory. There is no doubt that Gilead was originally a place-name and we have already distinguished its first meaning and then its extended meanings. An inhabitant of the land of Gilead might also have been called a Gileadite without reference to a tribe of Gilead, in the same way that an inhabitant of Canaan, Philistia or Hebron could be called a Canaanite, a Philistine or a Hebronite. In the great majority of cases where it occurs, the word Gilead is preceded by the definite article and the Old Testament thus usually speaks of 'the Gilead' and very often of the land, the highlands or the towns of 'the Gilead'. This is not the case with names of tribes.[66] In this context, too, the expression 'the Gilead and the Bashan' occurs frequently (Deut 3:10; Jos 17:1, 5; 2 Kings 10:33). Without the article, 'Gilead' is certainly the name of a region and not the name of a tribe (Judges 10:18; 11:8; 1 Kings 17:1); where the term the 'inhabitants of

---

[63] See G. F. Moore's commentary, 1895, and those of C. F. Burney, 1918, and J. Gray, 1967; and C. A. Simpson, *Composition of the Book of Judges*, Oxford, 1957, pp. 50–51; E. Täubler, *Biblische Studien*, pp. 293–294.

[64] See below, p. 585.

[65] E. Täubler, *Biblische Studien*, pp. 230–235; J. Hoftijzer, 'Enige opmerkingen rond het israëlitische 12-stammensysteem,' *NTT*, 14 (1959–1960), pp. 241–263, especially pp. 244–252; H.–J. Zobel, *Stammesspruch und Geschichte*, pp. 97–98.

[66] With the exception of 'the half of the tribe of Manasseh', in which Manasseh sometimes takes the article, which is the article of '*the* half' carried over to the proper name; see P. Joüon, *Grammaire*, § 137b. 'The' Gad, *haggādh*, in 2 Sam 24:5 is erroneous.

Gilead' is used, as in the two texts of Judges just mentioned, it is certainly never the name of a tribe, nor is it when it is preceded by the preposition of direction, 'to Gilead' (Num 32:39; cf. 2 Sam 24:6, with the article). Finally, it is also the name of a region in the expression 'the land of Jazer and the land of Gilead' (Num 32:1).

It is, furthermore, incorrect to say that Gad and Gilead are quoted as separate entities with the same character in 1 Sam 13:7. In good, classical Hebrew, this passage would read, not 'the territory of Gad and Gilead', but 'the territory of Gad and the territory of Gilead', as in the text of Num 32:1 already quoted. In accordance with the original meaning of the name outlined above, 'Gilead', is here the name of the region to the north of the Jabbok, as it is in Num 32:39–40; Deut 3:15; Jos 17:5–6, whereas the 'territory of Gad' is here the region to the south of the Jabbok, called by the name of the tribe living there. Finally, in the Song of Deborah, Gilead certainly refers to a tribe. In the light of what we have said about the term Gilead, however, it is probable that the name of the region is used here for the name of the tribe inhabiting that region.[67]

5. The tribe of Reuben

We must now return to consider Num 32 again, since this narrative speaks not only of Gad, but also of Reuben, the land of Jazer and the land of Gilead being allotted to both of them in common. A list of the towns of Gad and a list of those of Reuben are given in verses 34–38. Almost all of these towns can be located on the map and the result is clear. Dibon, Ataroth and Aroer were situated in the south, in the territory that Sihon obtained from the Moabites, and these belonged to Gad. Jazer, Jogbehah, Beth-nimrah and Beth-haran were situated in the north, in the land of Jazer and Gilead, and these also belonged to Gad. Reuben's towns were Heshbon, Elealah, Kiriathim, Nebo and Baal-meon and these were situated in what had been the original kingdom of Sihon. Reuben, in other words, lived between the two territories occupied by Gad. We are not sure of the date of the editorial composition of Num 32:34–38 or of its historical authenticity. It is possible that Reuben formed part of Moses' group and, as the eldest tribe, played the leading rôle in the war against Sihon and also gained the greatest prize from the victory, occupying the land of the conquered king.

---

[67] This opinion is held by many recent authors, including H. W. Hertzberg, *Die Bücher Josua, Richter, Ruth (ATD),*[4] 1969, p. 180; S. Mowinckel, *Von Ugarit nach Qumran. Festschrift Eissfeldt (BZAW,* 77), 1958, p. 137; S. Cohen, *Interpreter's Dictionary of the Bible,* II, 1962, p 397. A different point of view regarding the use of the name Gilead and its extended geographical application is defended by M. Ottosson, *Gilead. Tradition and History,* Lund 1969.

If the hypothesis which I have suggested is correct, Gad had settled in the early Gilead to the south of the Jabbok before the arrival of Moses' group and had expanded towards the south into the territory between Reuben and the Arnon. Num 32:34–38 reflects this situation at some time during the period of the Judges.

A different geographical description is given in Jos 13:15–28.[68] The distribution of land is more logical in this account. Reuben received the whole of the southern territory, from Aroer on the Arnon as far as Heshbon. Gad was allocated the whole of the north, from Heshbon to the Jabbok as well as an extension in the Jordan valley, through Succoth and Zaphon as far north as the southern extremity of the Sea of Chinnereth. According to the teaching of the book of Joshua, Reuben had to be given land which was quite distinct from that given to Gad. The deuteronomistic author, however, did not dare to draw a clear frontier between Reuben and Gad. The early account of the tribal frontiers which he used in his description of the distribution of land west of the Jordan did not include Transjordania.[69] According to a recent view,[70] the frontier was to the north of Heshbon and this description dates back to the reign of Solomon, when the land allotted to Reuben would have been Solomon's twelfth district. This district is, however, called Gilead in the Hebrew Bible or Gad in the Septuagint in 1 Kings 4:19, the Greek reading being generally preferred. What is more, Solomon's districts, and especially those in Transjordania, would seem to have changed the early tribal territories quite radically.[71] We cannot therefore form any clear idea of the situation during the period preceding the monarchy.

We may go further and say that the whole history of the tribe of Reuben is lacking in certainty. According to one quite firm tradition, Reuben was Leah's first child and Jacob's eldest son (Gen 29:32; 46:8). Reuben is always named first in any list of the tribes, which means that it was a very early group and was at first very important. According to three texts, however, it is clear that Reuben lost this position of pre-eminence. The earliest of these texts is to be found in the Song of Deborah (Judges 5:15b–16):

[68] For this text, see M. Noth. 'Israelitische Stämme zwischen Ammon und Moab', *ZAW*, 60 (1944), pp. 11–57; *ibid., Josua (HAT)*,[2] 1953, pp. 78–83; R. de Vaux, *Bible et Orient*, pp. 135–137.

[69] R. de Vaux, *Bible et Orient*, p. 137; Y. Aharoni, *The Land of the Bible*, p. 231, as opposed to M. Noth, *ZDPV*, 58 (1935), p. 230ff; *PJB*, 34 (1938), p. 25ff. Some years later, Noth came to the conclusion, in *ZAW*, 60 (1944), especially pp. 54–57; *Josua (ATD)*,[2] 1953, p. 83, that the division of the land between Reuben in the south and Gad in the north was the estimate of an editor.

[70] Z. Kallai and Kleinmann, *VT*, 8 (1958), pp. 135–136; Z. Kallai, *Les tribus d'Israël* (Hebrew), Jerusalem, 1967, pp. 204–228, 266–269 and the map.

[71] G. E. Wright, *Eretz-Israel*, 8 *(Sukenik Volume)*, 1967, pp. 58*–68*; Y. Aharoni, *Bib*, 49 (1968), pp. 406–408.

> Where the clans of Reuben are,
> men hold their long debate.
> Why did you linger among the sheepfolds
> listening to the pipes amid the flocks?[72]

There is no hint in this text that Reuben occupied a less important position. All that is said is that the tribe did not take part in the coalition, but decided to remain with its flocks. The situation, however, is different according to a text included in the Testament of Jacob (Gen 49:3–4):

> Reuben, you are my first-born,
> my vigour, and the first-fruit of my manhood,
> foremost in pride, foremost in strength,
> uncontrolled as a flood; you shall not be foremost,
> for you mounted your father's bed,
> and so defiled my couch, to my hurt (or on mounting it).

It is clear from this text that Reuben has lost his right of primogeniture and this is because of his incestuous relationship with Bilhah (Gen 35:22, J). The historical meaning of this fragment of tradition is otherwise not known, but what is proclaimed in it would appear to have been fulfilled in Moses' blessings (Deut 33:6):

> May Reuben live and not die,
> live too, his small band of warriors!

It should be noted that, after the period of the Judges, there was no further reference – in the historical books – to Reuben as a tribe that was still in existence.

It has therefore been concluded that Reuben was a tribe which was originally powerful, but which later disappeared. Reuben's fate may have been similar to that of Simeon and Levi, two other sons born to Leah and named immediately after Reuben in the list of the tribes or sons of Jacob (Gen 29:34; 46:11; Ex 1:2; 6:16). In Jacob's blessings, Simeon and Levi also immediately follow Reuben, but they are said in this text to be scattered among Israel (Gen 49:5–7).

According to a widely accepted interpretation of Gen 34,[73] Simeon and Levi first settled in central Palestine and it has been suggested that Reuben did the same.[74] The following arguments have been put forward in support

---

[72] For the translation of this last line, see O. Eissfeldt, *Forschungen und Fortschritte*, 25 (1949) pp. 9–11 = *Kleine Schriften*, III, pp. 61–66.

[73] See also above, pp. 532–533.

[74] Steuernagel held this view and, more recently, M. Noth, especially in his *History*, pp. 70–71; O. Eissfeldt, *The Hebrew Kingdom*, CAH, II, XXXIV, 1965, p. 12; J. Gray, *Joshua Judges and Ruth (The Century Bible)*, 1967, p. 51 on Jos 1:12–18.

of this theory. In the Song of Deborah, it is after the mention of Reuben that we hear of anyone to the east of the Jordan and that is said of Gilead (Judges 5:17), Reuben being still on the western side of the river. According to Jos 15:6; 18:17, there was a landmark on the frontier between Benjamin and Judah which was called the Stone of Bohan son of Reuben and this was a memorial to the fact that part of the tribe had lived in that region. Nearby was a cairn raised over the body of Achan, the son of Carmi (Jos 7:1, 18). According to this text, Carmi belonged to the tribe of Judah, but, according to Gen 46:9; Num 26:5–6, he was also a member of the clan of Reuben. In the same way, Hezron, another of Reuben's clans (Num 26:6), was also regarded as being one of the clans of Judah (Num 26:21). According to 1 Chron 5:8, the clan of Bela was one of the clans of Reuben, whereas, according to 1 Chron 8:1; Num 26:38, it was one of Benjamin's clans. Finally, according to Gen 35:21, Reuben committed incest at Migdal-eder, which is impossible to locate exactly, but which would seem, according to the context, to have been in the neighbourhood of Jerusalem. The inevitable conclusion is that, after the catastrophe which decimated the tribe of Reuben, the remnants were scattered and part of the original tribe emigrated to Transjordania, where it became merged with the tribe of Gad.

These arguments are very sound, but they are not decisive.[75] Nothing conclusive can be drawn from the fact that, in the Song of Deborah, Reuben is not explicitly situated in Transjordania, as is Gad, which follows immediately in the text of the Song. The description of Reuben in the Song is certainly in accordance with the situation in Transjordan and with the life led by this tribe of shepherds and herdsmen. Reuben is, moreover, said to have stayed 'among the sheepfolds'. The word used here is *miš p'tayîm*. It is in the dual form and is a technical term for sheepfolds consisting of two walls in the shape of a V and leading into an enclosure where the sheep were penned when danger threatened. The 'pipes amid the flocks' (Judges 5:16) were the danger signal used to gather the sheep together (cf. Isa 5:26; 7:18; Zech 10:8). Sheepfolds of this kind were in use from the time of the Old Kingdom in Egypt until the first centuries A.D. at least. Several have been found by archaeologists in the 'Arabah and in the steppe of Transjordania, but nowhere else.[76] Reuben stayed close to the tribal sheepfolds (see

[75] A. Jepsen, *Wissenschaftliche Zeitschrift der Karl-Marx Universität, Leipzig*, III (1953–1954) *(Festschrift Alt)*, pp. 146–147; E. Täubler, *Biblische Studien*, 1958, pp. 226–229; B. Oded, 'The Settlement of the Tribe Reuben in Transjordania', *Studies in the History of the Jewish People and the Land of Israel in Memory of Zvi Avneri*, The University of Haifa, 1970, pp. 11–36 (in Hebrew with an English summary). According to Oded, the nomadic tribe of Reuben came from the east into Transjordania and its clans gradually settled there from the end of the period of the Judges onwards.

[76] Y. Yadin, *IEJ*, 5 (1955), pp. 3–10; G. L. Harding, *ADAJ*, II (1953), pp. 8–56, cf. Fig. 8 and plate VI; *ibid., Antiquity*, 28 (1954), pp. 165–167; B. Rothenberg, 'An Archaeological Survey of the Eloth District and the Southernmost Negev', *Museum Haarez Bulletin* (Tel

Num 32:16, 24, 36, where the more common word *g'dhērāh* is used) in order to protect the flocks against raids made by nomads. Gad too was also alert, according to Gen 49:19: 'Gad, robbers rob him, and he, he robs and pursues them'.

The other texts which testify to the presence of Reubenites on the west bank of the Jordan and to their integration by Judah or Benjamin point, it has been argued, to the fact that after the ordeal that the tribe had undergone (Deut 33:6), Reubenite groups sought refuge in the west.[77] Others remained in Transjordania in the territory belonging to Gad (see the towns allotted to them in Num 32:37–38), and, if what is said in 1 Chron 5:8–10 can be believed, on the edge of the eastern desert where they still were at the time of Saul, when they ultimately succumbed under the attacks of the Hagrite nomads. These Reubenites living in Transjordania were finally integrated into the tribe of Gad. David's census (2 Sam 24:5) only mentions Gad to the north of the Arnon. Solomon's twelfth district, which included this territory, was known as Gad (1 Kings 4:19, in the Greek version). Finally, the stele of Mesha (the Moabite Stone) of the ninth century B.C. refers only to the Gadites in this region.

What was the historical event which led to this decline of the tribe of Reuben, a decline confirmed by the geography of the region and borne out by the oracles of Gen 49 and Deut 33? One theory is that this decline was the result of a Moabite attack.[78] At the time of the judge Ehud, the Moabites' territory stretched as far as Jericho and its surrounding district (Judges 3:15b–30) and must therefore have included the land which belonged to Reuben. An objection made to this theory is that the story of Ehud is at the beginning of the period of the Judges, before the Song of Deborah, which does not mention the decline of Reuben. In fact, however, we do not know whether the story of Ehud should be placed before or after the Song of Deborah.

Recently, another hypothesis has been suggested.[79] Reuben's loss of importance and ultimate absorption into the tribe of Gad was, according to this hypothesis, the result of conflicts between the two tribes. The statement about Gad in Moses' blessings (Deut 33:20) gives clear support to this theory, although the text is difficult to translate:

Aviv), No. 10 (1968), p. 67. According to Rothenberg, these 'sheepfolds' were used not to protect flocks or herds, but for hunting. G. L. Harding's very clear presentation of the data, *op. cit.*, contradicts Rothenberg's theory. For the application of Judges 5:15b–16 to the text, see O. Eissfeldt, *Forschung und Fortschritte*, 25 (1949), pp. 9–11; 28 (1954), = *Kleine Schriften*, III, pp. 61–70.

[77] A. Jepsen, *op. cit.* (note 75); Y. Aharoni, *The Land of the Bible*, pp. 190–191.

[78] J. Bright, *History*, p. 157.

[79] H.–J. Zobel, *Stammesspruch und Geschichte*, p. 64.

> Blessed is he who gives Gad space enough!
> He lies there like a lion;
> he has savaged arm and face and head.
> He took the first portion for himself;
> there a leader's share was kept for him.

On the basis of this text, then, it is possible to say that Gad became more powerful by violent means and in this way gained the position of pre-eminence that Reuben had once possessed, but had lost (Gen 49:3–4). Reuben, in a word, lost land to Gad.

In conclusion, I would like to suggest the following outline of the situation. The tribe of Reuben, which was originally powerful, arrived with Moses' group and settled in territory from the Arnon in the south as far as the northern frontier of the ancient kingdom of Sihon, where its neighbours were the tribe of Gad. Weakened by its struggles with the Moabites, with Gad or even with both at the same time, the tribe finally became absorbed by Gad. This took place before the middle of the eleventh century B.C., in other words, before the reign of Saul.

6. Did Reuben and Gad take part in the 'conquest' of the land to the west of the Jordan?

According to Num 32, Reuben and Gad promised Moses that they would cross the Jordan with the other tribes and take part in the conquest of Canaan (cf. Deut 3: 18–20). Joshua reminded them of this promise and insisted on their keeping it (Jos 1:12–18). After Canaan had been conquered, Reuben and Gad were sent home to their tents, but, before they crossed the Jordan, they built an altar beside the river. This almost caused war to break out between them and the other tribes of Israel (Jos 22). This obviously requires elucidation.

Let us begin by examining the last text mentioned above, Jos 22. It is obviously composite. Verses 1–6 are the work of the Deuteronomist and they form the counterpart to Jos 1:12–18; the Transjordanian tribes which took part in the conquest of Canaan are now dismissed. Verses 7–9 relate to the half-tribe of Manasseh, which originally played no part in the story about Reuben and Gad, and are additions. Verses 10–34 also bear clear marks of editing by the priestly author. The most striking aspect of this part of the narrative is that Joshua no longer plays a part in it, but the priest, Phinehas, and the n^eśî'îm of the community, 'ēdhāh, of Israel. At the centre of the controversy is the law of the one altar as proclaimed by Deuteronomy, but in addition there is also the question of cultic impurity on the part of the land to the east of the Jordan as opposed to the country on the western side of the river, which is the territory, *'ªhuzzāh* (P), of Yahweh, where he had established his tabernacle, *miš'kān* (P). An early tradition referring to an altar erected by the people of Reuben and Gad is, however, employed in this account, although the one verse which might provide us with the key to this enigma, verse 34, is incomplete: 'The Reubenites and the Gadites named the altar . . ., "Because", they said, "it will be a witness between us that Yahweh is God" ' (*cf.* verse 27). Was there perhaps another explanation of the name Gilead, similar to the explanation given in Gen 31:47 ff?

J. Dus has interpreted this chapter of the book of Joshua in a new and startling way.[80] He agrees that the Deuteronomist and the priestly editor shared in the composition of Jos 22, but believes that the book of Deuteronomy and its law concerning the altar date back to the period of the Judges and refer to the moveable sanctuary of the ark. He also thinks that the priestly document dates back to the second part of the period of the Judges and was the work of the priests of Shiloh, after the ark had been placed in the temple at Shiloh, which had become the permanent habitation or tabernacle, *miš'kān*, of Yahweh. Here Dus makes use of a theory which he has frequently discussed in the past, namely, that until the temple had been built at Shiloh, the sanctuary of the ark changed every seven years. The ark was placed on a new cart and this was drawn by two cows, which were allowed to go wherever they wanted. The place where they stopped was the place that Yahweh had fixed for his new sanctuary. This, in brief, is Dus's interpretation of the story of the return of the ark from Philistine territory (1 Sam 6). This, in turn, is the explanation, according to Dus, of the formula in Deuteronomy: 'The place Yahweh himself will choose from among all the tribes' (Deut 12:5, etc.).

Dus believes that this theory can be used to explain Jos 22 and that Jos 22, in its turn, is a striking confirmation of the theory. In his opinion Jos 22 describes an episode which took place during the time of the Judges; according to the early account, the Reubenites and the Gadites built an altar for themselves in Gilead and their reason for doing so was that the Jordan lay between them and the other tribes. If the ark was carried on a cart, the cows pulling it would not have been able to cross the river by swimming and the Reubenites and Gadites would have been condemned to remain without the tribal sanctuary. To prevent a war between brothers, the decision was made to keep the ark in one place, that is, in the sanctuary at Shiloh, which the Reubenites and Gadites could reach as well as the other tribes.

This hypothesis is, of course, unacceptable and the chapter remains an enigma. A. Menès thought that it reflected the situation that existed at the time of the exile,[81] when there was tension between the priests in Palestine

[80] J. Dus, 'Die Lösung des Rätsels von Jos 22', *ArOr*, 32 (1964), pp. 529–546.
[81] A. Menès, 'Tempel und Synagoge', *ZAW*, 50 (1932), pp. 268–276.

who believed that they alone possessed Yahweh because they lived in his land (see Ezek 11:14 ff; 33:23 ff) and the Jews who lived outside Palestine, but who still wanted to give honour to Yahweh. The solution to this problem, Menès believed, was found in a form of cult without sacrifices (Jos 22:26–29), about which all parties were agreed (verses 30–33). In other words this institution of the principle of synagogue worship went back to the period of the conquest. On the basis of the book of Ezekiel, however, another and even more radical solution has been suggested, namely, that since the Jordan was the frontier of the Promised Land, Israel's inheritance, the tribes of Reuben and Gad were given their portion of the land on the western side of the Jordan (Ezek 48:6, 27). It is quite possible that the meaning which Menès has derived from these texts is the same as that intended by the priestly editor of Jos 22, who changed an early tradition by introducing into it the idea of an altar without sacrifices (verses 26–27), which is, of course, a contradiction in terms.

What, then, was the early tradition? K. Möhlenbrink,[82] believed that it was a tradition which was slightly later than the settlement of the tribes itself and that it contrasted two cultic amphictyonies, the amphictyony of Shiloh and that of Gilgal, where there was presumably an altar named Gilead (verse 34), which was used by the Benjamites and by Reuben and Gad already settled on the western side of the Jordan. This theory of Möhlenbrink's does not, however, seem to be justified by the text of Jos 22 itself and it is quite contrary to the conclusions suggested in this work regarding the history of the two Transjordanian tribes.

J. Vink[83] believes, on the other hand, that the altar built on the side of the Jordan represents a situation that existed at the time of Ezra and that this can be justified by an early aetiology. He bases his argument on inscriptions found recently at Deir Alla on the eastern bank of the Jordan which bear witness to a sanctuary belonging to the Israelites which was still in use during the Persian period.[84] It is, however, still too early for these documents to be used and there is so far no evidence to show beyond doubt that this sanctuary belonged to Israel.

M. Noth[85] has not suggested any solution to this problem – neither he nor Bright mentions this episode in their Histories. All that I would venture to say about it is that, in my opinion, the story preserves the memory of conflicting cults. On the one hand, there was the sanctuary at Shiloh (verses 9 and 12) and its priests (see especially Phinehas, verses 13 ff, 30 ff, who was

---

[82] K. Möhlenbrink, *ZAW*, 56 (1938), pp. 246–250.

[83] J. G. Vink, 'The Date and Origin of the Priestly Code in the Old Testament', *OTS*, 15 (1969), pp. 1–144, especially pp. 73–77.

[84] H. J. Franken, 'Texts from the Persian Period from Tell Deir Alla', *VT*, 17 (1967), pp. 480–481.

[85] M. Noth, *Josua (HAT)*,² 1953, p. 135.

associated with this sanctuary in one tradition; see 1 Sam 1:3; 4:4) and, on the other, the Transjordanian tribes, who were regarded as living outside the Promised Land. Jordan was the frontier of Canaan and Canaan was, after all, the Promised Land.[86]

It is, of course, quite possible that Reuben and Gad were even more profoundly separated from the other tribes. They both asked to be allowed not to cross the Jordan (Num 32:5) and this is surely a historical statement. Participation in the conquest, as expressed in the rest of Num 32, which is a late composition, as we have seen, and in Jos 1:12–18; 22:1-9, both of which passages are also late, is surely the result of the predominant idea in the book of Joshua, namely a conquest of Canaan by all the tribes. It is noticeable that in the accounts of the settlement of Israel in the land to the west of the Jordan, in the narrative of Jos 1–11 and in Judges 1, no part at all is played by Reuben and Gad.

V. THE HALF-TRIBE OF MANASSEH-MACHIR [87]

In the context of the settlement of the Israelites in Transjordania, several of the texts in Numbers and the book of Joshua add part of the tribe of Manasseh to those of Reuben and Gad. According to these texts, Manasseh settled in territory to the north of those of Reuben and Gad, in other words, north of the Jabbok. According to Deut 3:13, Manasseh received the 'rest' of Gilead (taken in the widest sense) and the whole of Bashan, the kingdom of Og. According to Jos 13:30, it received a portion stretching from Mahanaim on the Jabbok and the whole of Bashan. In the biblical tradition too, it was assumed that this half-tribe was given its portion of land at the same time as Reuben and Gad, that is, before the crossing of the Jordan (Num 32:33), but that, like Reuben and Gad, it also took part in the conquest of Canaan (Jos 1:12; 4:12) and then returned, with Reuben and Gad, to Transjordania (Jos 22:1, 9).

The situation was, however, more complicated than this. We have

[86] R. de Vaux, 'Le pays de Canaan', *JAOS*, 88 (1968), pp. 23–30; see also above, pp. 128–129.

[87] The only really important study of the half-tribe of Manasseh is A. Bergman, 'The Israelite Tribe of Half Manasseh', *JPOS*, 16 (1936), pp. 224–256. For the history of Transjordan in this context, see M. Noth, 'Beiträge zur Geschichte des Ostjordanlandes', *ZDPV*, 68 (1949),pp. 1–50, especially pp. 2–18. It is also useful to consider the house of Joseph in general, for example, in O. Kaiser, 'Stammesgeschichtliche Hintergründe der Josephgeschichte', *VT*, 10 (1960), pp. 1–15; E. Täubler, *Biblische Studien*, 1958, pp. 176–203; 246–252; H.–J. Zobel, *Stammesspruch und Geschichte*, 1965, pp. 112–126. For Machir, originally in Transjordan, see J. L. McKenzie, *Fourth World Congress of Jewish Studies, Paper, 1*, Jerusalem, 1967, pp. 99–100.

already seen that the conquest of the kingdom of Og is probably not historically authentic and that the Jabbok was undoubtedly the farthest limit reached in this first settlement by Moses' group. It is, in other words, certain that the Israelites' penetration was halted by the great mass of heavily wooded mountain, the Jebel 'Ajlūn.

What is more, only Reuben and Gad are mentioned in the basic text of Num 32. The reference to the half-tribe of Manasseh in verse 33 is an addition. The Samaritan's repeated addition of Reuben and Gad is, moreover, propaganda in favour of Shechem, which belonged to Manasseh. Similarly, in Jos 22, verses 7–9 are additions referring to Manasseh and the references to the half-tribe in the rest of this chapter are editorial.

A brief account of the activities of Manasseh is added to the story of the settlement of Reuben and Gad in Num 32:39–42.[88] In this short passage, the sons of Machir, the son of Manasseh, take Gilead and drive out the Amorites who live there. Secondly, Jair, the son of Manasseh, takes the *hawwôth* and gives them his own name, *hawwôth ya'îr*. Finally, according to this text, Nobah seizes Kenath and calls it Nobah after himself. The half-tribe of Manasseh is also mentioned in Deut 3:13 and its land is said there to be 'the rest of Gilead and the whole of Bashan, Og's kingdom'. The same text adds that this represents 'the whole *hebhel* of Argob' and that it was Jair who seized hold of it (verse 14). According to verse 15, it was Machir who possessed Gilead. Similarly, in Jos 13:29–31, there is a brief note on the Manassites: 'The land they received stretched from Mahanaim right through Bashan', to which is added 'the whole kingdom of Og . . . all the *hawwôth* of Jair . . . half of Gilead, with Ashtaroth and Edrei, . . . were allotted to the sons of Machir son of Manasseh, to half of the sons of Machir according to their clans'. Finally, there is a reference to the portion given to the tribe of Manasseh on the western side of the Jordan in Jos 17:1 ff. According to this text, 'To Machir, Manasseh's eldest son and father of Gilead, there fell, as was right for a fighting man, the country of Gilead and Bashan'.

According to these texts, then, the settlement of the half-tribe of Manasseh was carried out by Machir, Jair and Nobah. What does this mean? The fact that these data are provided in texts which are generally acknowledged to be additional does not necessarily mean that they were invented. They were more probably remnants of early traditions which were preserved in or reintroduced into the canonical description of the settlement of the tribes.

---

[88] E. Taübler, *op. cit.*, pp. 190–193; O. Kaiser, *op. cit.*, pp. 8–10; K.–D. Schunck, *Benjamin* (*BZAW*, 86), 1963, p. 13; *ibid.*, 'Erwägungen zur Geschichte und Bedeutung von Mahanaim', *ZDMG*, 113 (1963), pp. 34–40, see also p. 35. For the settlement of the Israelites in northern Transjordan, see S. Mittmann, *Beiträge zur Siedlungs- und Territorialgeschichte des nördlichen Ostjordanlandes*, Wiesbaden, 1970, especially pp. 208–231. The study of traditions plays a secondary rôle in Mittmann's book.

1. *Machir*

In the genealogies, Machir is seen to be the son of Manasseh and the father of Gilead (see Num 26:29; 27:1; 36:1; Jos 17:1; 1 Chron 2: 21, 23; 7:14–17). According to Gen 50:23 (E) the sons of Machir, the son of Manasseh, were born 'in Joseph's lap', in other words, they were adopted by him. This shows that, according to the biblical tradition, the group of Machir was regarded as having been in Egypt and as belonging to the 'house of Joseph'.

In the Song of Deborah (Judges 5:14b), Machir is placed as a tribe after Ephraim-Benjamin and before Zebulun-Issachar-Naphtali. If the groups which responded to the call are listed in a geographical order, then Machir settled on the western side of the Jordan between Ephraim and Zabulun. This position corresponds to the territory occupied by Manasseh, which is not named in the Song of Deborah. We should not, however, be in too much of a hurry to conclude from this that Machir, is, in this text, just another name for Manasseh. The story of Joseph at Dothan (Gen 37) begins in the region to the north-west of Shechem, between Ephraim and Zabulun. The name Machir may mean that the Machirites 'sold' *(mkhr)* their services to the Canaanites or to Egyptian masters, just as Issachar did according to his name *(śākhār,* wages) and to Gen 49:15. It may also refer to the story of Joseph, 'sold' *(mkhr)* by his brothers (see Gen 45:4). Far from being a separated branch of the 'house of Joseph', Machir was, according to this theory, the germ.[89]

It has also been suggested that Machir was finally integrated into Manasseh, just as Simeon was integrated into Judah and Reuben into Gad. If, moreover, the story of Joseph at Dothan is connected with Machir and if it preserves a memory of the age of the patriarchs, then Machir-Joseph went south and down into Egypt in the same way as Simeon and Levi did. Having gone down into Egypt, Machir would, in this case, have left Egypt later with Moses' group and returned to its old territory, either crossing the Jordan at Jericho with Benjamin-Ephraim or following the northern route and crossing by the ford at Damieh.

This connection between Machir and the tradition of Joseph may be unacceptable and another solution to the problem may be preferred. Like Issachar, whose name is similar, Machir may not have gone down into Egypt, but have joined the groups which came up from Egypt and have settled with them in the neighbourhood of Shechem. The result is, of course, the same – at the time of Deborah, Machir was still living to the west of the Jordan.

After this period, nothing more is said in the Old Testament about Machir west of the Jordan. To the texts that have been mentioned above,

[89] H.–J. Zobel, *op. cit.,* pp. 112–115.

we can add 2 Sam 9:4–5, according to which Saul's crippled son, Merib-baal, was received by a certain Machir at Lo-debar and this Machir was one of the men who brought food to David at Mahanaim (2 Sam 17:27). The site of Lo-debar is not known, but it must be north of the Jabbok in the land of the half-tribe of Manasseh, in other words, in the territory allotted to Machir in Num 32:39–40; Deut 3:15.

Machir migrated towards the east beyond the Jordan after the period of Deborah, but before the end of the period of the Judges. According to Num 32:39–40, Transjordania was conquered by the tribe of Machir and, according to Jos 17: 1, Machir was a 'fighting man'. This is very probable. Only one royal city situated on the eastern side of the Jordan is mentioned in the Amarna letters. This is Pihil and it is in the Jordan Valley itself – it has been located at Khirbet Fahil (Pella). The other Canaanite towns were all north of the Yarmuk and the Egyptian occupation did not go south of this river or east of the Jordan. There is, however, archaeological evidence that men began to settle once more in the northern territory of Gilead round about 1500 B.C. and increasingly at the beginning of the Iron Age.[90]

Manasseh, then, replaced Machir in Cisjordania and became more impor-tant than Machir. Because of this, the name Manasseh was extended to the groups that had emigrated to Transjordania and these became known as the other half of the tribe of Manasseh. Machir thus became the son of Manasseh and, as he had settled in Gilead in Transjordania, he became the father of Gilead. This is, in brief, the explanation of the genealogies. There still remains, however, the question of the original relationships between Machir and Manasseh. Were they originally two different groups and was Machir forced to emigrate because of pressure exerted by the stronger group of Manasseh or because of the need to avoid being dominated by the Manassites?[91] Or was Manasseh originally a clan of Machir and did the Manassites stay in Cisjordania and, having become more powerful, extend their name to the territory in Transjordania?[92] We shall be returning to these questions in connection with the 'house of Joseph' in a later chapter.[93]

2. Jair

According to Num 32:41; Deut 3:14; 1 Kings 4:13, Jair was the son of

[90] N. Glueck, *AASOR*, 25–28 (1951), p. 423. S. Mittmann, in *Beiträge zur Siedlungs- und Territorialgeschichte, op. cit.* (note 88) has pointed out that Late Bronze sites are rare in this part of Transjordania, whereas there are many more of Iron Age I and these may indicate settle-ment on the part of the Israelites.

[91] H.–J. Zobel, *op. cit.*, pp. 114–115.

[92] M. Noth, *Das System der zwölf Stämme Israels*, Stuttgart, 1930, p. 36; *History*, pp. 61–62 and 72, note 3; J. Hoftijzer, *NTT*, 14 (1959–1960), p. 243, who favours this theory.

[93] See below, pp. 642–643.

Manasseh. On the other hand, however, according to 1 Chron 2:18–22, he was the son of Segub, the son of Hezron the Judaean and his wife, the daughter of Machir. Jair's connection both with Judah and with Machir-Manasseh may, of course, represent a claim on the part of Judah to the north of Transjordania. It may, on the other hand, be no more than an invention on the part of the Chronicler.

According to Num 32:41, Jair conquered 'their encampments', which would be *ḥwwthyhm*, that is, *ḥawwôthehem*, their *ḥawwôth*'. On the other hand, it should perhaps be read as *ḥwwth ḥm*, that is *ḥawwôth ḥam*, 'the *ḥawwôth* of Ham'. This Ham may be the place mentioned in Gen 14:5, about five miles south of Irbid.[94] Jair not only seized these *ḥawwôth*; he also gave them his name, calling them the *ḥawwôth yāʾir*. According to Deut 3:14, these *ḥawwôth yāʾir* formed the 'whole *ḥebhel* of Argob', which is identified with Bashan in a gloss. According to the addition of Jos 13:30, there were as many as sixty towns in these *ḥawwôth yāʾir*! On the other hand, according to Judges 10:4, the *ḥawwôth yāʾir* consisted of thirty towns belonging to the thirty sons of the judge Jair (see below). According to 1 Chron 2:22, Jair had twenty-three towns in Gilead, but, according to 1 Chron 2:23, 'Aram and Geshur took from them the *ḥawwôth yāʾir* and Kenath and his daughters, sixty towns'. These sixty towns come from Deut 3:4 and are those of the *ḥebhel* of Argob belonging to Og of Bashan. The figure 23 in 1 Chron 2:22 must be original. As for the figure 30 in Judges 10:4, this clearly comes from the thirty sons of Jair who rode on thirty donkeys' colts (see Abdon, Judges 12:14).

The situation is obviously very confused. A rather far-fetched explanation was suggested by J. Heller,[95] who translated *ḥawwôth yāʾir* as 'tents of light' and thought that a sanctuary of Heba (= Eve!), the Hurrian goddess, was involved here. Although it would seem that he was not acquainted with this hypothesis, H. Cazelles also believed that Hurrians were involved here.[96] In his view, Argob was originally a personal name, indeed the name of a Hurrian whom Solomon appointed as administrator in Transjordan (1 Kings 4:13, 19; Cazelles corrected these texts). Argob's family was still entrusted with this task of administration during the reign of Pekah (2 Kings 15:25; this text is, however, incomplete). I am unable to accept either Heller's or Cazelle's theory.

From the various data provided in these texts, I would like to draw especial attention to the following. Jair is the name of a person, but it may

[94] The correction of *ḥawwôthehem* into *ḥawwôth ham* was suggested by A. Bergman, *JAOS*, 54 (1934), p. 176, and has been accepted by J. Simons, *The Geographical and Topographical Texts of the Old Testament*, Leiden, 1959, § 302; N. Snaith, *Leviticus, Numbers (The Century Bible)*, 1967, *in loco*.

[95] J. Heller, *ArOr*, 26 (1958), pp. 646–649.

[96] H. Cazelles, 'Argob biblique, Ugarit et les mouvements hurrites', *Studi sull' Oriente e la Bibbia (Volume Rinaldi)*, Genoa, 1967, pp. 21–27.

also be the name of a group of people, like Machir. *Hawwôth* has been interpreted as 'tents', 'encampments' or 'duar',[97] but it may also be a geographical name.[98] The *ḥawwôth yā'îr* are identified with the *ḥebhel* of Argob in the addition of Deut 3:14 and the two additions placed side by side in 1 Kings 4:13 may also be similarly interpreted. On the other hand, this text above all has led certain authors to make a distinction between the *ḥawwôth yā'ir* in Gilead and Argob in Bashan.[99] In all the texts mentioned in this context, however, the reference to Bashan is later and occasioned by the memory of Og of Bashan, which is sometimes made explicit. The meaning of *ḥebhel* is not certain. Baumgartner has suggested that it may mean a strip of land, Noth thought that it was a portion of land measured out by means of a line and Cazelles was in favour of the translation 'confederation'. Argob is not a personal name, but a geographical name for a territory which, according to Deut 3:14, bordered on the Aramaean lands of Geshur and Maakah on the eastern side of Lake Tiberias. The *ḥawwôth yā'ir* = Argob, then, was probably the part of Transjordan situated between the massif of the Jebel 'Ajlūn and the Yarmuk.[100] Neither Jair nor Argob were, however, to the north of the Yarmuk, which the Israelites never crossed.

It is also very likely that Jair was a clan of Machir-Manasseh. The occupation of the extreme north of Transjordan must have been the last to take place, occurring at the end of the period of the Judges.

The whole question is, of course, complicated by the fact that there was a lesser judge called Jair, who had thirty sons who rode on thirty donkeys' colts and possessed thirty towns called *ḥawwôth yā'ir* (Judges 10:3–5). For a long time, it was thought that this figure of the judge Jair had been invented on the basis of the clan of Jair in Num 32:41 in order to supply a judge for the northern territory of Gilead.[101] It is possible, however, and may even be quite probable that there was in fact a 'lesser' judge called Jair.[102] In this case, the reference to the *ḥawwôth* would be an addition to which the name Jair was attributed and the figure 30 would be similar to the forty sons and thirty grandsons who rode on seventy donkeys' colts in Judges 12:14.

[97] W. Baumgartner, *Lexikon*,[2] 1968, with references; the French *Bible de Jérusalem* translates it as *douar*, which can be defined as 'an agglomeration of Arab tents'.

[98] M. Noth, *Könige (BKAT)*, 1968, p. 57.

[99] J. Simons *Geographical and Topographical Texts*, § 21; Y. Aharoni, *The Land of the Bible*, map 23 and p. 278; M. Noth, *Könige*, p. 72.

[100] See E. Täubler, *op. cit.*, p. 252.

[101] See O. Eissfeldt, *CAH*, II, XXXIV, 1965, p. 20.

[102] M. Noth, 'Das Amt des "Richters Israels"', *Festschrift Bergholet*, Tübingen, 1950, especially pp. 410–411; J. Gray, *Joshua, Judges (The Century Bible)*, 1967, p. 328.

3. Nobah

Nobah, which is mentioned only in Num 32:42, is the name of a town which was originally called Kenath and was consequently given the name of its conqueror, Nobah. The name Kenath has been compared with the word *q-n-i* in the Egyptian execration texts, *q-nw* in the list of Ramses III and Qanu in the Amarna letters and has been identified with Qanawat in the Jebel ed-Drūz (Aharoni) and with Kerak Kaneta, in Greek Kanata, which is also in the Jebel ed-Drūz (Abel), about fifteen miles to the west of Qanawat. Both these sites are, however, too far away from the land that was occupied by the Israelites. A Nobah is also mentioned in Judges 8:11 together with Jogbehah = Jubeihāt, on the road from es-Salt to Amman, but this Nobah is south of the Jabbok, so that this information about the town cannot be used by the historian.

The Israelites, as we have already said, settled in the north of Transjordania only towards the end of the period of the Judges, and it was the ancient tribe of Machir which left the part of Cisjordania to the north of Shechem and emigrated to northern Transjordania. The clan of Jair played a special part in this migration.

To conclude this section, we must mention that certain Old Testament scholars have suggested that Jos 17:14–18 contains an allusion to this movement from the west to east of the Jordan.[103] According to this text, the house of Joseph asked Joshua for additional territory because of an increasing population in the original land. There are two variants of this story. In the earlier version, verses 16–18, Joshua tells them to clear the mountain (of Ephraim) and, in the later version, verses 14–15, he sends them to clear the forest of the country of the Perizzites and the Rephaim. The Rephaim were the ancient inhabitants of northern Transjordania. Og was the last survivor of the Rephaim (Deut 3:11) and the half-tribe of Manasseh had been given the country of the Rephaim (Deut 3:13). In the later variant of Jos 17:14–15, an allusion to Transjordania is possible but it should be noted that 'the country of the Perizzites and the Rephaim' is absent from the Septuagint.

VI CONCLUSION

I would like to conclude this chapter on the settlement in Transjordania, in which several hypotheses have been put forward, by summarising the contents under seven headings.

---

[103] M. Noth, *Josua (HAT)*,[2] *in loco; Geschichte*, p. 61; J. Bright, *History*, p. 156; O. Eissfeldt, *CAH*, II, XXXIV, 1965, p. 12. It should be noted that, according to S. Mittmann, *Beiträge zur Siedlungs- und Territorialgeschichte, op. cit.* (note 88), pp. 209–211, both variants contained in this text refer to Transjordania.

1. We do not know how Moses' group of Israelites went from Kadesh to the plains of Moab. No exact memory was preserved in the early tradition of Num 20, which tells us only that Edom refused to allow the Israelites right of way and that they followed the way of the Sea of Suph = the Gulf of 'Aqabah. In Deut 2, which was followed by Judges 11, a roundabout route avoiding Edom and Moab by passing through the eastern desert is outlined. The priestly editor has enumerated the stopping-places along the customary route from the 'Arabah to north of the Arnon (Num 33).

2. The first event in the conquest of Transjordania was the war against Sihon, the leader of a little Canaanite kingdom centred in Heshbon. Their victory over Sihon enabled the members of Moses' group to penetrate as far as the plains of Moab. The war against Og, the king of Bashan, would seem to be entirely without historical foundation apart from Israel's claim to the land to the north of the Yarmuk after the settlement of the half-tribe of Manasseh.

3. The oracles of Balaam, the narrative framework within which they are set and the story of the Baal of Peor are not directly connected with the conquest of Transjordania. They represent a situation during the period of the Judges when the Israelites who were settled in the southern part of the Jordan Valley were in contact with the Canaanites who had survived the collapse of the kingdom of Sihon, the Moabites who were trying to extend their territory to north of the Arnon and the nomadic Midianites. The story of the holy war against the Midianites is late and cannot be considered by the historian in this context.

4. Num 32 is the basic text for the settlement in Transjordania, but only for its earliest and most essential aspect. Gad settled peacefully in the lands of Jazer and Gilead, which stretched between Heshbon and the Jabbok. The name Gilead was later extended to include the land as far north as the Yarmuk; this coincided with the gradual occupation of this land by the Israelites. Israelites settled very early in the original territory of Gilead south of the Jabbok. There is evidence of this occupation in the story of the treaty between Jacob and Haban the Aramaean. It may go back to the age of the patriarchs and may have come about because the tribe of Gad settled there, did not go down into Egypt and therefore played no part in the exodus. This tribe may, if this hypothesis is correct, have become integrated with Moses' group when the latter reached the plains of Moab after the defeat of Sihon. There never was a tribe of Gilead. In the Song of Deborah and in other texts, Gilead is equivalent to Gad, the tribe being named after the land that it occupied.

5. Reuben was initially an important tribe which belonged to Moses' group and may have played a leading part in the victory over Sihon. The Reubenites settled in the kingdom of Sihon and in the land that Sihon had taken from the Moabites to the north of the Arnon. Reuben decreased in

importance during the period of the Judges, either in conflict with the Moabites or in struggles against Gad, which had settled in territory just north of Reuben's land. Just before the reign of Saul, the Reubenites were finally absorbed by Gad.

6. Neither Reuben nor Gad took part in the conquest of Canaan on the western side of the Jordan. The story of the altar which the Reubenites and the Gadites set up near the Jordan may be attributable to rivalry in worship between the priests at Shiloh and the Transjordanian tribes which were regarded perhaps as living outside the Promised Land as defined by the Jordan.

7. The half-tribe of Manasseh did not settle in Transjordania, between the Jabbok and the Yarmuk, before the second half of the period of the Judges, when the ancient tribe of Machir came there from the west. This settlement of the region north of Jebel Ajlūn may have been at least partly carried out, as the biblical tradition insists, by force of arms. Finally, in this occupation, the clan of Jair played a special part.

Chapter Nineteen

THE SETTLEMENT IN CENTRAL PALESTINE
BENJAMIN AND THE HOUSE OF JOSEPH

I. THE SOURCES. LITERARY CRITICISM AND THE HISTORY OF THE TRADITIONS[1]

OUR ONLY source of information about the settlement in central Palestine is the book of Joshua. What is interesting in this connection is that in all that follows Joshua occupies so little space in the biblical tradition. He is mentioned only once in 1 Kings 16:34, which refers to Jos 6:26, once in 1 Chron 7:27 in the genealogy of Ephraim and once in Neh 8:17. He is mentioned too, in the eulogy of the ancestors of Israel written by Ben Sirach (Ecclus 46:1–6). Joshua was a figure associated with the northern kingdom. He was buried at Timnath-serah in the hill country of Ephraim, where he had been given an estate (Jos 24:29–31; cf. Jos 19:49–50 and Judges 2:8–9). With the exception of the Deuteronomist, the Judaeans were not concerned with him.

The Deuteronomist made use of the northern tradition concerning Joshua in order to begin his history with the story of the conquest and the partition of the Promised Land. Joshua 1 is entirely the work of the Deuteronomist and is linked with the deuteronomistic introduction of Deut 1–4, in which Joshua is introduced as Moses' successor and the conqueror of the Promised Land (Deut 1:38; 3:21, 28). The account of the conquest in the book of Joshua ends with a recapitulation of the kings conquered east and west of the Jordan (Jos 12). At least one attempt has been made in recent years to prove that the whole of Deuteronomy in its earliest form and Jos 1–11 together formed a separate work, a 'book of the conquest', composed in the northern kingdom either a little before or a little later than

---

[1] In general: A. Alt, 'Joshua', *Werden und Wesen des Alten Testaments (BZAW, 66)*, 1936, pp. 13–29 = *Kleine Schriften*, I, pp. 176–192; M. Noth, *Überlieferungsgeschichtliche Studien*, pp. 40–47; *ibid., Josua (ATD)*,[2] 1953, pp. 7–16; S. Mowinckel, *Tetrateuch–Pentateuch–Hexateuch (BZAW, 90)*, 1964, pp. 33–51; H. Schmid, 'Erwägungen zur Gestalt Josuas in Überlieferung und Geschichte', *Judaica*, 24 (1968), pp. 44–57.

[2] H. Schmid, *op cit.*, pp. 48–52.

Jehu's revolt.[3] The arguments are not entirely convincing, but it is undoubtedly true to say that the Deuteronomist made use of the northern traditions that had already been brought together by a *Sammler*, 'collector', round about 900 B.C. (M. Noth). It is more difficult to ascertain the extent to which the Deuteronomist changed this document. The story of the altar set up on Mount Ebal and the reading of the law (Jos 8:30–35) is certainly an addition, interrupting the course of events from Ai (Jos 8) to Gibeon (Jos 9) with a detour through Shechem. Noth was of the opinion that the Deuteronomist was responsible for this addition; other scholars have suggested a later date.[4] The part played by the Deuteronomist in the composition of Jos 9–11 may well be greater than Noth is prepared to acknowledge.[5]

The answer that an Old Testament scholar gives to the question whether it was an early collector or the Deuteronomist who combined the different accounts into the dominant theme of a total conquest of the entire land by all the tribes under the leadership of Joshua (which is, of course, the message of the book of Joshua in its existing form), will clearly depend on the position that he takes up. According to Noth, it was the collector of the various traditions who was responsible for the summaries of the conquest of the whole of the south of Canaan (Jos 10:40–42) and of the whole country (Jos 11:16–20), which formed the conclusion to the work of this collector. According to J. Gray, however,[6] it was the Deuteronomist who was responsible for this. Gray's reason for thinking this is a good one – the conquest was accompanied by the extermination of all the inhabitants (Jos 10:40b; 11:20) and Noth himself regarded the refrain about the ban imposed on all the towns conquered in the south as editorial (Jos 10:28–40). What is more, the extermination of the Canaanites was one of the major themes of the Deuteronomist, who was the first to enunciate the directions concerning the *herem* (see especially Deut 2:34–35; 7:2; 20:16–17).[7] This *herem* was, however, an early institution of the holy war and it is mentioned on the Moabite Stone, which tells us that Mesha carried out a *herem* against the Israelites. It was also pronounced against Jericho (Jos 6–21) and Ai (Jos 8:23–26) and both Gray and Noth regarded these texts as the work of the collector. It would seem, however, that the collector had already presented Joshua's conquest as a total conquest, involving the extermination of the inhabitants, and that the Deuteronomist simply gave emphasis to this presentation because it corresponded to his own theological position regarding the Promised Land and the need to keep the chosen people from all

---

[3] A. C. Tunyogi, 'The Book of the Conquest', *JBL*, 84 (1965), pp. 374–380.

[4] J. L'Hour, 'L'alliance de Schem', *RB*, 69 (1962), pp. 178–181.

[5] J. Gray, *Joshua, Judges and Ruth (The Century Bible)*, 1967, pp. 20–21.

[6] J. Gray, *op. cit.*

[7] A. C. Tunyogi, *op. cit.*, pp. 376–377.

contact with the Canaanites.[8]

Whatever interpretation is placed on this problem, the fact remains that all the traditions which presented the conquest as incomplete or partial and carried out by each tribe in isolation and acting on its own account were eliminated, ignored or changed by the collector. Some of these traditions have been preserved in Judges 1, which is concerned with the conquest of the south of Canaan, but which also contains some of the traditions gathered together by the collector, as, for example, the tradition concerning Bethel (Judges 1:22–26). This would seem to point to the fact that the two groups of traditions were not transmitted in the same environments. The traditions found in Judges 1, which relate above all to the occupation of the south of Canaan, were preserved at Jerusalem, whereas the traditions of the book of Joshua which are grouped around the person of Joshua the Ephraimite, were collected together in the northern kingdom.[9]

Among this second group of traditions, the most important position is occupied by a description of the events that took place along the route from Jericho to Gibeon (Jos 2–9, less the addition, Jos 8:30–35, see above). These include the sending of spies to Jericho, the capture of Ai and the treaty with the Gibeonites. These events are linked to each other in the narrative. The story of Rahab acts as a link between the account of the sending of the spies (Jos 2) and the capture and destruction of Jericho (see Jos 6:17b, 22–25) although the story of the crossing of the Jordan and the sanctuary at Gilgal comes in between (Jos 3–4:14). The story of Achan (Jos 7), connects the story of the taking of Jericho (Jos 6) with the capture of Ai (Jos 8). The taking of Jericho and Ai is the reason why the Gibeonites ask for a treaty between them and the Israelites (Jos 9).

The geographical framework of this long narrative includes the territory of Benjamin, from the Jordan to Gibeon. The story of Achan, however, goes beyond this framework and is enacted in the plain of Achor, which was in Judah, just south of the frontier with Benjamin. The centre of the operations in Canaan was Gilgal. The Israelites camped at Gilgal after crossing the Jordan (Jos 4:19). It was from Gilgal that they set out to attack Jericho (Jos 6:11, 14). The Gibeonites came to Gilgal to submit to Joshua (Jos 9:6). Gilgal was also the sanctuary where the ark was placed (Jos 4:18–19; 6:6 ff), where the Israelites were circumcised (Jos 5:2–9) and where the first Passover was celebrated in Canaan (Jos 5:10–12). This sanctuary became very popular during the early period of the monarchy. According to one tradition concerning the institution of the monarchy, it was at Gilgal that Saul was proclaimed king before Yahweh (1 Sam 11:15), that

---

[8] S. Mowinckel, *Tetrateuch, op. cit.,* p. 34.

[9] I believe this in opposition to M. Noth, who thought that the collector was a Judaean, basing his opinion on the aetiology of Makkedah and the summary of the conquest of the south (Jos 10:16–38).

he was rejected by Samuel (1 Sam 13:7–15; 15:12–23), that Judah waited for David's return from Transjordan (2 Sam 19:16) and that Judah and Israel disputed over the king (2 Sam 19:41). Gilgal remained as a place of pilgrimage until the eighth century B.C. (Hos 4:15;12:12; Amos 4:4; 5:5).

We may therefore conclude that the combined traditions brought together in Jos 2–9 were originally Benjaminite and that they were first recited in the sanctuary at Gilgal.[10] We must now consider each of these traditions separately.

II. THE SENDING OF THE SPIES AND THE STORY OF RAHAB [11]
(Jos 2 and 6:22–25)

A Canaanite clan known as the *bêth rāhābh* or 'house of Rahab' lived on the ruined site of Jericho or in a neighbouring oasis during the period of the Judges or at the beginning of the age of the kings ('until now', Jos 6:25). To explain the presence of this Canaanite group among the Israelites, the following story is narrated in the book of Joshua.

Before crossing the Jordan, Joshua sent two spies from Shittim to reconnoitre the land. They went into the house of a prostitute, Rahab, or into an inn belonging to Rahab. The king of Jericho, warned that they had come, sent messengers to seize them, but Rahab hid them, got rid of the king's messengers by lying to them and let the spies escape through the window of her house, which was built against the wall of the city. The spies promised Rahab that she would be spared and told her to tie a red cord to her window as a sign. They hid for three days in the hills, then crossed the Jordan and returned to Joshua, reporting that Yahweh had delivered the whole country into their hands (Jos 2:24). As a reward for what she had done, Rahab and her family were spared when Jericho was taken (Jos 6:22–25).

This story is not in accordance with the account of the fall of Jericho in Jos 6. In that account, it was by the power of God that the walls of the city collapsed (Jos 6:5, 20) and, as it was built against the city wall, Rahab's house would certainly have fallen as well. There was clearly no reason for

[10] I am convinced that these conclusions are correct, despite what Y. Kaufmann has said in *The Biblical Account of the Conquest of Palestine*, Jerusalem, 1953, pp. 67–69. I am rather more hesitant with regard to the story of Ai and its capture; see p.564.

[11] The most recent study has been written by W. L. Moran, 'The Repose of Rahab's Israelite Guests', *Studi sull'Oriente e la Bibbia (Volume G. Rinaldi)*, Genoa, 1967, pp. 273–284 (a study on style), which contains a full bibliography of previous works. See also D. J. Wiseman, 'Rahab of Jericho', *Tyndale House Bulletin*, Cambridge, 14 (1964), pp. 8–11 (see also *JSS*, 9 (1964), p. 359), who believes that, according to the Akkadian parallels, Rahab was an inn-keeper rather than a prostitute; S. Wagner, 'Die Kundschaftergeschichten im Alten Testament', *ZAW*, 76 (1964), pp. 255–269.

displaying the red cord as a sign that Rahab's house should not be plundered and destroyed (Jos 2:18) and this is why it is not mentioned at the end of this account (Jos 6:22–25).[12]

According to this tradition, it would seem as though Jericho had been taken because Rahab had betrayed the city. This is paralleled in the story of the taking of Bethel (Judges 1:22–26), but there is also a more general parallel, since Jos 2 clearly belongs to the literary *genre* of spy stories associated with the accounts of the conquest.[13] For example, Moses sent scouts or envoys from Kadesh (Num. 13–14). There is also a reference to his sending men to reconnoitre the land of Jazer (Num 21:32). Joshua sent spies to Jericho (Jos 2) and men to Ai (Jos 7:2–3). The Danites sent men to Laish (Judges 18:2–10).[14] In those cases where the story is in a good state of preservation, what the scouts report is very much the same as the returning spies told Joshua: 'Yahweh has delivered the whole country into your hands' (Jos 2:24). These spy stories are also usually followed by an attack against the territory or town reconnoitred and the Israelites' victory. In the case of Laish, the Danites were successful (Judges 18:27). The Israelites were first driven back by the townsmen of Ai (Jos 7:4–5), but conquered the town when the sacrilege had been expiated (Jos 8). As we have already seen, the story of the scouts sent out from Kadesh to reconnoitre Canaan concluded with the conquest of the land under the leadership of Caleb. The tradition of Jos 2 ought therefore to be followed by an account of an armed attack against Jericho and its capture. The memory of this attack and capture is preserved in Jos 24:11: 'Those who held Jericho fought against you ... but I put them all in your power'.

It would be wrong to regard this other representation of the conquest of Jericho as profane, in contrast to the idea of the holy war, in which Yahweh assured the victory of his people by working wonders. This representation also expresses a religious idea. In particular, the verb in the perfect should be noted: 'Yahweh has delivered ... ' The part that the scouts have to play, in other words, is to confirm and proclaim Israel's faith in God's promise which has already been fulfilled. Victory is *already* assured even before the fighting begins. The formula 'Yahweh has delivered into your hands' is a formula of the holy war.[15] This conclusion to the story of the spies and of Rahab (Jos 2) was suppressed in order to give prominence to the account of

---

[12] For these two traditions, see W. Rudolph, *Der 'Elohist' von Exodus bis Josua (BZAW*, 68), 1938, p. 169; K. Möhlenbrink, 'Die Landnahmesagen des Buches Josua', *ZAW*, 56 (1938), especially pp. 258–259; M. Noth, *Josua (HAT)*,[2] pp. 22–23, 29–31; J. Gray, *op. cit.*, pp. 53–54; M. Weippert, *Die Landnahme der israelitischen Stämme*, Göttingen, 1967, pp. 32–34.

[13] S. Wagner, *op. cit.* (note 11).

[14] For this last text, see A. Malamat, 'The Danite Migration and the Pan-Israelite Exodus-Conquest: A Biblical Narrative Pattern', *Bib*, 51 (1970), pp. 1–16.

[15] G. von Rad, *Der heilige Krieg im alten Israel*, Zürich, 1951, pp. 7–8; C. J. McCarthy, 'Some Holy War Vocabulary in Joshua 2', *CBQ*, 33 (1971), pp. 228–230.

the miracle of the collapse of the walls of Jericho (Jos 6). All that was preserved of this conclusion was a simplified account of the sparing of Rahab and her family.

In the opinion of certain authors,[16] this tradition about Rahab is without any basis in history and is simply an aetiology explaining the survival of a Canaanite group known as the 'house of Rahab' at Jericho. This is, however, too negative an interpretation of the tradition. Other scholars have regarded the tradition of the miraculous collapse of the walls of Jericho and the taking of the city as an aetiology provided by the authors of the story of Rahab to explain the ruins that they saw were left.

I would not deny the aetiological character of these two stories. What is clear, however, is that the aetiology is connected with the circumstances surrounding the fact in each case, not with the fact itself. The first story explains the survival of a Canaanite clan at Jericho as the *consequence* of the fact that the city was captured. The second story explains the presence of the ruined wall by the *way in which* the city fell because of the power of the Israelites. Both stories, however, presuppose that the capture of Jericho was accepted as a fact by both those who told the stories and those who heard them. The clan of Rahab on the one hand and the ruins of Jericho on the other are used to establish not the fact, but rather the memory that Jericho was really captured by the Israelites.

The tradition of Rahab is undoubtedly the earlier of the two, the tradition of the collapse of the walls of the city having been, as we shall see later, influenced by cultic practice. It is very difficult to justify the existence of two different traditions, both connected with the same place and concerned with different circumstances surrounding the same event if they have no historical foundation. The historian is justified in concluding from the story of Rahab (Jos 2 and 6:22–25), taken together with the information given in Jos 6:1 and the independent datum provided in Jos 24:11, that the Israelites did in fact conquer Jericho. When we come later in this chapter to study the second account (Jos 6), we shall consider what this conquest consisted of and how our conclusion accords with the archaeological evidence. In the meantime, however, we must turn our attention to the crossing of the Jordan.

III. THE CROSSING OF THE JORDAN AND THE SOJOURN AT GILGAL [17]
(Jos 3–5)

1. *Attempts made in literary criticism and the history of the traditions*

The literary analysis of these three chapters of the book of Joshua and es-

[16] See especially Alt and Noth and also W. Rudolph, *Der 'Elohist'*, op. cit. (note 12), p. 169.
[17] Recent works include P. P. Saydon, 'The Crossing of the Jordan, Jos 3–4', *CBQ*, 12

pecially of chapter 4 has proved extremely difficult. No satisfactory results have been obtained from the attempts made to recover the sequence of the sources in the Pentateuch within the framework of a Hexateuch. A new breakthrough has been achieved in the study of the history of traditions, especially in M. Noth's[18] recognition, behind the editorial work and the additions of the Deuteronomist, of the hand of the *Sammler*, a 'collector'; and his theory that the basis of the story consists of two aetiologies. One of the aetiologies explains the stone circle as having been formed of stones brought from the Jordan when it was crossed by Israel's ancestors (Jos 4:20 ff). The other aetiology is an explanation of the stones that could be seen in the middle of the Jordan on the bed of the river. These were the stones on which those who carried the ark across the river had stood (Jos 4:9). These were Benjaminite traditions concerning the sanctuary at Gilgal and Joshua the Ephraimite had nothing to do with it. The leading part played by the ark can be explained, Noth argued, by the fact that it was the cultic object of the amphictyony of the twelve tribes. Noth and others[19] also thought that Gilgal was, at least for a time, the place where the ark rested and was therefore the central sanctuary of the tribes.

This hypothesis was accepted by S. Mowinckel,[20] who believed, however, that the early aetiology was concerned with the stones of Gilgal and that the stones on the bed of the Jordan, which could not be seen most of the time, were a secondary theme of the story. He was also of the opinion that the crossing of the Jordan was simply a copy in prose of the crossing of the Red Sea. Mowinckel, however, insisted that the fact of the Israelites having crossed the Jordan was not an invention on the part of tradition.

J. Dus[21] distinguished five stages in the editorial process, abandoning the double tradition of the stones in the Jordan and the stones at Gilgal. These hypothetical stages are: (1) an aetiology of the stones in the Jordan, understood as the stones that supported the ark while the people were crossing

---

(1950), pp. 194–207. H.-J. Kraus, 'Gilgal. Ein Beitrag zur Kultusgeschichte Israels', *VT*, 1 (1951), pp. 181–199; J. Dus, 'Die Analyse zweier Ladeerzählungen des Josuabuches (Jos. 3–4 und 6)', *ZAW*, 72 (1960), pp. 107–134; H.-J. Kraus, *Gottesdienst in Israel,*[2] Munich, 1962, pp. 179–187; J. Maier, *Das altisraelitische Ladeheiligtum (BZAW,* 93), 1965, pp. 18–39; A. R. Hulst, 'Der Jordan in den alttestamentlichen Uberlieferungen', *OTS*, 14 (1965), pp. 162–188, especially 168–184; E. Vogt, 'Die Erzählung vom Jordanübergang, Josua 3–4', *Bib*, 46 (1965), pp. 125–148; R. Schmid, 'Meerwunder- und Landnahme-Traditionen', *TZ*, 21 (1965), pp. 260–268; J. A. Soggin, 'Gilgal, Passah und Landnahme. Eine neue Untersuchung des kultischen Zusammenhangs der Kap. III-VI des Josuabuches', *Volume du Congrès. Genève* (*SVT*, 15), 1966, pp. 263–277; F. Langlamet, *Gilgal et les récits de la traversée du Jourdain*, Paris, 1969.

[18] M. Noth, *Josua (HAT),*[2] 1953, pp. 31–39.

[19] Especially H.-J. Kraus, *VT*, 1 (1951), pp. 181 ff.

[20] S. Mowinckel, *Tetrateuch – Pentateuch – Hexateuch*, p. 35.

[21] J. Dus. *op. cit.* (note 17).

the river; (2) an aetiology of the stones of Gilgal, soon added to the preceding aetiology; (3) the introduction by the collector of the person of Joshua; (4) a deuteronomistic editing, which exalts the ark and the part played by the priests who carried it; (5) a priestly narrative, transferring from Chapter 3 to Chapter 4 the material concerning the stones of the Jordan. This literary analysis is not without merit, but it is unfortunately overshadowed by the author's unacceptable theory of the cultic movements of the ark.[22]

The theory of the amphictyony and the hypothesis of the central sanctuary of the ark at Gilgal were rejected by J. Maier.[23] He followed the same method of analysis, however, and suggested five stages of composition: (1) The earliest narrative was an aetiology of the stones of the Jordan. (2) To this was joined an aetiology of the stones of Gilgal. (3) The figure of Joshua was, according to Maier, introduced during the period of the Judges, when the Benjaminite tradition was taken over by the Ephraimites. Joshua was then 'nationalised', in other words, extended to apply to the whole of Israel at the beginning of the monarchy at Jerusalem. (4) Much later, the ark was introduced, by analogy with the story of the ark in the books of Samuel. (5) The last stage is the Deuteronomist's narrative. What is new in Maier's analysis is the late stage at which he places the ark.

One is bound to ask whether this literary analysis has really produced more positive results than the earlier literary criticism based on the theory of a Hexateuch. A new beginning, however, was made some years ago by H.-J Kraus,[24] who interpreted this narrative as a cultic legend concerning the sanctuary at Gilgal, while at the same time accepting Noth's analysis of the composition. Kraus believes that a feast was celebrated there in which the crossing of the sea (the exodus) and the entry into the Promised Land were re-enacted and made present liturgically. This was an annual ceremony expressing the faith of the little historical creed of Deut 26:5–9: 'Yahweh brought us out of Egypt . . . and gave us this land'. It was during a feast at Shechem that the events of Sinai and the covenant were commemorated. The crossing of the sea is, moreover, explicitly called to mind in Jos 4–23. The text describes a cultic procession which sets off from the east bank of the Jordan. The people, purified by this sacred action, follow the ark, which is carried by the priests, at a respectful distance, cross the Jordan behind the ark and continue as far as Gilgal, where a circumcision is celebrated and the Passover is kept with unleavened bread. The aetiologies of the stones and the name of Gilgal and the traditions concerning the sanctuary there are added to this analysis.

Kraus' theory has not been widely accepted, at least in its entirety. H.

[22] J. Dus, *TZ*, 17 (1961), p. 15.
[23] J. Maier, *op. cit.* (note 17).
[24] First outlined in *VT*, 1 (1951), then in *Gottesdienst in Israel.*[2]

Wildberger[25] has accepted most of it, but he denies the presence of the ark in the original narrative and believes that the feast was a feast of Israel's election by God, which was connected with the feast of massôth or Unleavened Bread and was the occasion when Israel's election was proclaimed (Ex 19:4–6). C. A. Keller[26] has retained certain aspects of Kraus' theory, but he criticised Kraus for not having taken the literary analysis of the passage and the different levels of tradition sufficiently into account. H. W. Hertzberg[27] thinks that Jos 3–4 was a 'legend' recited or read at a feast at Gilgal and regards it as no more than a possibility that it was made present in a procession. M. Noth[28] raised three objections to Kraus' theory: first, that it was difficult to see how the procession with the ark could have crossed the Jordan; secondly, that the reference to the crossing of the sea is (Jos 4:23) accidental; and thirdly, that the literary difficulties in Jos 3–4 have not been solved. O. Kaiser[29] rejected the theory for the same reasons as Noth, but has added a further objection, namely that it is not in accordance with the religious position occupied by the ark and Gilgal itself before the reign of Saul.

A. R. Hulst[30] has also criticised Kraus' theory quite severely. No more than a recitation of the events, he believes, would have been necessary to make the exodus from Egypt and the entry into the Promised Land present and actual. The Jordan, moreover, could hardly be crossed in procession and a procession leaving and coming back to Gilgal would mean two crossings. Hulst has also pointed out that it would have been impossible to commemorate the essential aspect of the crossing, that is, crossing dry-shod, because the miracle could not have been repeated annually. This ceremony could, furthermore, have taken place only if the ark had stayed at Gilgal, and it was only there at the beginning of the period when the Israelites were settling in Canaan. Finally, Hulst insists that it has not been proved that this cultic renewal of the crossing of the Jordan was a way of making the crossing of the sea present and actual, especially since the Jordan tradition was originally independent of the exodus tradition.

All these objections that have been made to Kraus' theory are to some extent valid, but it cannot be denied that the cultic aspect of the story in Jos 3–4 is very clear, the crossing of the Jordan and the arrival of the Israelites at Gilgal being described as a liturgical procession. Attempts have therefore been made to take this liturgical character of the story seriously into ac-

[25] H. Wildberger, *Jahwes Eigentumsvolk*, Zürich and Stuttgart, 1960, pp. 55–61.

[26] C. A. Keller, 'Über einige alttestamentliche Heiligtumslegenden', II, *ZAW*, 68 (1956), pp. 85–97.

[27] H. W. Hertzberg, *Die Bücher Josua, Richter, Ruth (ATD)*,[4] 1969, p. 31.

[28] M. Noth, *Josua (HAT)*,[2] p. 33.

[29] O, Kaiser, *Die mythische Bedeutung des Meeres in Ägypten, Ugarit und Israel (BZAW*, 78), 1959, pp. 137–138.

[30] A. S. Hulst, *op. cit.* (note 17).

count while at the same time avoiding the criticisms that have been made of Kraus' theory. The result has been a certain modification of his ideas.

J. A. Soggin[31] believes that Gilgal was in fact an amphictyonic sanctuary, at least during the reign of Saul, and that it was used throughout the period of the monarchy. There are so many points of similarity between the crossing of the Jordan and the crossing of the sea that they must, in Soggin's opinion, have been combined in cult. Finally, he does not think that any serious objections can be made to the idea of cultic procession if this was at least partly symbolic. In Soggin's view, the priests and the people only had to touch the waters of the Jordan with their feet, which is in fact what is said in Jos 3:8, 13, 15; 4:18.

E. Vogt[32] had taken this idea of cultic symbolism still further. He has distinguished in Jos 3–4 an account which he has called 'historical', in that it is a sober narrative of the military expedition. It is found in Jos 3:1, 14a, 16; 4:10b, 13, 19b and in the editorial additions of the Deuteronomist, 3:7; 4:12, 14, and describes the march from the camp at Shittim to the camp at Gilgal. It continues the story of the scouts and Rahab and can be extended as far as Jos 6:1, which describes how the gates of Jericho were closed against the advance of the Israelites. This was followed by a story of the battle. The memory of this has, Vogt thinks, been preserved in Jos 24:11, but the story itself was replaced by the account of the miraculous collapse of the walls of Jericho.

A cultic account in two parts was, in Vogt's opinion, superimposed on the battle story. The first part, A, describes the journey from the camp at Shittim as far as the Jordan and the standing still of the waters (proclaimed in Jos 1:10–11), This part of the account is contained in Jos 3:2–6, 8–11, 14b–15. The second part of the account describes the crossing of the Jordan itself and the setting up of the stones and there are, according to Vogt, two parallel versions of this. B describes the stones in the Jordan (Jos 3:12, 17; 4:4–7, 9–10a) and B¹ describes the stones at Gilgal (Jos 4:1b–3, 8, 11, 20–24). Finally, there are two late additions (Jos 3:15b; 4:15–19a). This cultic account is liturgical, the whole ceremony taking place at Gilgal itself, where the stones commemorated the crossing of the Jordan. From the point of view of the liturgical celebration of the crossing, 'Jordan' and 'Gilgal' were the same and the fact that the ark was present was enough to symbolise the drying of the waters of the Jordan.

Vogt's outline of the ceremony can therefore be reconstructed in the following way. The pilgrims went in procession from their camp to the circle of stones at Gilgal. This is the ceremony that Vogt has called A. The ark stopped at Gilgal and twelve men took a stone each. The procession crossed ahead of them and they each placed their stones in front of the twelve stelae

[31] J. A. Soggin, *op. cit.* (note 17).
[32] E. Vogt, *op. cit.* (note 17).

at Gilgal. (The explanation of this rite is given in Jos 4:6–7, 9.) This is ceremony B. Later, this ceremony was changed in order to make it more expressive. In this modified ceremony B¹, the twelve men took their stones to the pilgrims' camp and then, when all the people had 'crossed', they took the stones back to Gilgal and placed them in front of the stelae. (The explanation of ceremony B¹ is given in Jos 4:21–24).

F. Langlamet's study is not only the most recent, but also the most profound.[33] He has preserved what he believes are the most important and authentic elements in all these theories and is particularly indebted to Dus and Vogt. In his analysis, he has divided the early elements and the editorial material in Jos 3–4 into nine sub-divisions. These are (1) an Israelitic version, without the figure of Joshua, of the aetiology of the stones of Gilgal; (2) a 'Shittim-Gilgal' story; (3) an 'ark' story; (4) an aetiology of the stones in the Jordan; (5) a version containing the figure of Joshua of the aetiology of the stones of Gilgal; (6) two catechetic instructions on Gilgal; (7) a first editorial revision carried out by the Deuteronomist; (8) the texts of the deuteronomistic historian or of his school and (9) several short, later additions.

According to the 'Shittim-Gilgal' story, Gilgal was not a sanctuary, but the camp outside Jericho from which the attack against the city was made. Unlike Vogt, however, Langlamet does not think that this was simply a story of a military expedition. It was rather the religious account of a holy war. It is therefore very close to the Yahwistic traditions and this lends support to the attempts made to interpret these chapters in the book of Joshua by the earlier literary critics. Kraus' theory is also to some extent justified by the fact that the 'ark' story would make an excellent 'legend' for a feast at Gilgal. This cultic story was not, however, necessarily accompanied by liturgical action, since the stones of Gilgal were not in themselves a memorial and it was not even necessary for the ark to be present. In general, Langlamet's theory can be accepted All that we have now to do is to apply his conclusions to what we already know about the sanctuary and then to try to interpret the story as a whole in the historical perspective.

2. The Gilgal cult

It has proved impossible to locate Gilgal. The only datum provided by the Bible is that it was at the eastern limit (of the territory) of Jericho (Jos 4:19). All attempts to arrive at a more precise location[34] have come to nothing and it would probably be futile to look for any archaeological

---

[33] F. Langlamet, op. cit. (note 17).
[34] See O. Bächli, 'Zur Lage des alten Gilgal', *ZDPV*, 83 (1967), pp. 64-71 and M. Weippert, *Die Landnahme der israelitischen Stämme*, p. 30, together with his bibliography.

evidence of Gilgal, since this was certainly originally and very probably always an open-air sanctuary, as its name shows, a circle of raised stones.

It was, moreover, probably also a Canaanite sanctuary which was adopted later by the Israelites. It was not only a sanctuary used by Benjamin, situated in the land that belonged to Benjamin, but also a sanctuary of Ephraim. Both the Benjaminites and the Ephraimites shared a common tradition concerning the conquest of Canaan, the tradition that is used in Jos 2–9. Gilgal was not used as a sanctuary by the whole of Israel until the time of Samuel and Saul (1 Sam 7:16; 11:15; 13:7–15; 15:12–23). It is mentioned during the reign of David (2 Sam 19:16, 41) and then does not appear again in the historical books of the Old Testament. It continued, however, to be used during the eighth century B.C., but the prophets condemned the cult there (Amos 4:4; 5:5; Hos 4:15; 12:12).

The 'feast' of Gilgal that has been reconstructed on the basis of Jos 3–4 is a feast celebrated by all twelve tribes and using the two traditions of the twelve stones. It could therefore only have been celebrated when Gilgal had already become a sanctuary shared by all the tribes, in other words, during the period of Samuel and Saul or during the reign of David. The ark must, however, have played an essential part in this ceremony and, at the time of Samuel and Saul, it was with the Philistines and later at Kiriath-jearim and during David's reign, it was at Jerusalem. We are therefore bound to conclude that the liturgy that has been suggested by Vogt and others could never have been celebrated at Gilgal.

Although the account in Jos 3–4 is undoubtedly cultic in character, it is not a liturgy, but rather a sacred discourse which was recited at Gilgal where the twelve stones were displayed, set up as a memorial. Kraus was mistaken in his conviction that the two crossings, of the Jordan and of the sea, were both commemorated at Gilgal,[35] because the crossing of the sea is only mentioned incidentally in Jos 3–4. What is more, the account of the crossing of the sea did not, as some scholars have contended, influence the story of the crossing of the Jordan. On the contrary, the description of the crossing of the river influenced that of the crossing of the sea in Ex 14.[36] We may go even further and reaffirm what we have already said in this work, namely that the account of the crossing of the Jordan was transferred to the tradition of the exodus, which originally consisted only of the miracle of the destruction of the Egyptian army in the sea and did not contain the Israelites' crossing of the sea.[37]

[35] Kraus was followed in this opinion by Wildberger and Soggin in the works mentioned in notes 17 and 25. See also F. M. Cross, 'The Divine Warrior in Israel's Early Cult', *Biblical Motifs*, ed. A. Altmann, Cambridge, Mass., 1966, pp. 25–27; W. F. Albright, *Yahweh and the Gods of Canaan*, London, 1968, p. 40.

[36] R. Schmid, *TZ*, 21 (1965), pp. 266–267; A. R. Hulst, *OTS*, 14 (1965), pp. 179–184; O. Coats, *VT*, 17 (1967), pp. 260–261.

[37] See above, pp. 385–387.

What this cultic account contained in Jos 3–4 commemorated above all was the crossing of the Jordan which marked the entry of the Israelites into the Promised Land and the beginning of a new era. This character is emphasised by the three short accounts in Jos 5, all of which are situated at Gilgal and are cultic.[38]

(a) *The circumcision* (Jos 5:2–9). At Gilgal there was a small hill known as the Hill of Foreskins, on which Joshua is said to have circumcised the Israelites with knives made of flint (verses 2–3). The reason for this ceremony is given in verses 4–8. Literary analysis has shown that these verses are composite and they are different in the Hebrew and the Greek. Their purpose is to explain why the Israelites had arrived in Canaan without having been circumcised. In verse 9, a rather forced argument is given to explain the name Gilgal, that Yahweh made the shame of Egypt roll *(gālal)* away from the Israelites. The deeper meaning would seem to be that the people were consecrated as they entered the Promised Land. It is also possible that the rite of circumcision at Gilgal performed with knives of flint was an ancient one and that what lies behind this tradition and the rite described is an accurate memory that circumcision was not practised by the Israelites until they arrived in Canaan.

(b) *The first Passover in the Promised Land* (Jos 5:10–12). These verses have been regarded as late and have, moreover, been ascribed to P.[39] The underlying tradition must, however, have been early.[40] It must, furthermore, have been a tradition that was peculiar to Gilgal and it may have been adapted from a pre-Israelitic rite. The unleavened bread and the roasted ears of corn have been added in this account to the Passover; they certainly did not form part of the Israelite Passover rite. They are, however, prescribed as an oblation of first-fruits (Lev 2:14) and they are also mentioned in connection with the offering of the first sheaf (Lev 23:14), which was not practised before the entry into the Promised Land, a fact that is explicitly stated in Lev 23:10. The novelty of eating the produce of the land of Canaan for the first time and of ceasing to eat manna, which no longer fell, is stressed in Jos 5:10–12. This too marks the end of the exodus and the beginning of a new era.

(c) *The theophany* (Jos 5:13–15). This episode describing the appearance of the leader of the heavenly army may also have been connected with the Gilgal cult,[41] although several authors have regarded it as an introduction

[38] A. George, 'Les récits de Gilgal en Josué (v, 2–15)', *Mémorial J. Chaine*, Lyons, 1950, pp. 169–186.

[39] G. Fohrer, *Geschichte der israelitischen Religion*, Berlin, 1969, p. 90.

[40] M. Noth, *Josua (HAT)*,[2] *in loco*; H. Wildberger, *Jahwes Eigentumsvolk*, pp. 51 ff; H.–J. Kraus, *Gottesdienst in Israel*,[2] pp. 189–191; R. de Vaux, *Institutions*, pp. 487–488.

[41] A. George, *op. cit.* (note 38); F.–M. Abel, *Miscellanea Biblica et Orientalia . . . A. Miller*, Rome, 1951, pp. 109–113.

to the story of the capture of Jericho.[42] This little story, however, has no link at all with what follows. The theophany takes place 'at Jericho', which has not yet been taken, and the phrase should no doubt be understood in the sense of 'near Jericho'. The text would seem to be the remnant of a longer account describing the setting up of a sanctuary. The need to erect this sanctuary was confirmed by an appearance of God, as in the case of Bethel (Gen 28:16), and the sanctuary itself may, of course, have been the sanctuary of Gilgal.

3. *Historical interpretation*

As we have seen, these chapters in the book of Joshua contain traditions concerning the crossing of the Jordan and the first halting-place in Canaan which were recited at Gilgal (Jos 3–4); also the memory of the rites that were celebrated in the sanctuary there, the circumcision and the Passover (Jos 5:2–12). As the result of theological reflection, the entry into the Promised Land was presented as the antithesis of the exodus from Egypt. The two events occurred at the same time of year. The Passover celebrated in Egypt was followed by the crossing of the sea and the crossing of the Jordan was followed similarly by the first Passover celebrated in the Promised Land. The period spent in the desert began and ended with a miracle of water. The manna on which the Israelites had fed in the desert ceased to fall when they arrived in the Promised Land. Finally, the theophany described in Jos 5:13–15 corresponds closely to the theophany of the Burning Bush, to such an extent that the same words occur in Jos 5:15 and Ex 3:5. This appearance of the leader of Yahweh's army looks forward to the successful conquest of the land of Canaan. It is clear, then, that, from every point of view, a new era was beginning for Israel.

Not only is this presentation in the book of Joshua true from the theological point of view – it also has an authentic basis in history, in that it describes how elements of the future people of Israel, who had come to Canaan from Egypt, bearing with them their faith in Yahweh, crossed the Jordan at a point opposite the city of Jericho. There is no good reason for denying that Joshua originally featured in this tradition, which was a tradition belonging to Benjamin and also to Ephraim, which was at that time not distinct from Benjamin and was very closely associated with it.[43]

---

[42] G. Del Olmo Lete, 'La conquista de Jerico y la leyenda ugaritica de Krt', *Sefarad*, 25 (1965), pp. 3–15.

[43] I believe this, contrary to the opinions of Alt, Noth and others; see the recent work by O. Eissfeldt, 'Israels Führer in der Zeit vom Auszug aus Ägypten bis zur Landnahme', *Studia Biblica et Semitica (Festschrift Vriezen)*, Wageningen, 1966, especially pp. 67–70 = *Kleine*

There was no need for a miracle to enable the Israelites to cross the Jordan, which could be very easily forded. The spies sent out by Joshua (Jos 2) crossed the river twice. It was also possible for a large number of people, even an army, to cross the Jordan. In the course of history, it was in fact crossed by all the armies both of Israel, when they left Palestine to fight beyond the Jordan, and of Israel's enemies coming from beyond the Jordan to attack Israel. Before the time of the Arabs, there was no bridge over the river.[44] The fording of the river presented no problems unless the fords were guarded, as they were by Gilead in the episode in Judges 12:5. This was not the case in Jos 6:1.

An event, however, did take place which was interpreted as a miracle – the crossing by the Israelites who remained 'dry-shod', a miracle which is stressed by the addition in Jos 3:15, according to which the Jordan was at that time in flood. This miracle may, of course, have been a natural event interpreted in this way. We have already mentioned, when we compared the miracle of the sea with the crossing of the Jordan previously in the present work in our discussion of the exodus from Egypt, the report by the Arab chronicler Nowairi that, on the night of the 7 and 8 December 1267, the dunes upstream of the bridge at Damieh collapsed, causing the river to cease flowing from midnight until ten o'clock in the morning.[45] In his report of this event, Nowairi only mentions the fact that the Jordan ceased to flow as a circumstance that led to the repair of the bridge at Damieh, but we should accept his description as authentic, above all because the geographical situation is favourable to such a natural event. Nowairi's account is, moreover, very similar to that in Jos 3:16, which belongs to a very early level and is also extremely sober: 'the waters coming from above rose up into one mass, very far, near the city of Adam, which is close to Zarethan, and the waters which flowed into the Sea of the 'Arabah, the Salt

---

Schriften, IV, pp. 302–304; H. Schmid, 'Erwägungen zur Gestalt Josuas in Überlieferung und Geschichte', Judaica, 24 (1968), especially pp. 52–54.

[44] M. Noth, 'Der Jordan in der alten Geschichte Palästinas', ZDPV, 72 (1956), especially pp. 134–146.

[45] Nowairi, Vie de Bibars, fol. 31ᵛ. The text has also been translated by Quatremère in a footnote in his translation of Maqrizi's Histoire des Sultans Mamluks, I, 2, p. 26, note 29; see also PEFQS, 1895, p. 253 ff. F.–M. Abel has made use of the text in his Géographie de la Palestine, I, p. 481 and in other works. According to J. Garstang, Joshua, Judges: The Foundations of Bible History, London, 1931, p. 137, a similar event took place in July 1927 – an earthquake caused the dunes at Damieh to collapse and this apparently obstructed the river and prevented the waters from flowing for twenty-one and a half hours. Garstang quoted witnesses who claimed to have crossed the bed of the river several times 'dry-shod'. As this story has been repeated more than once by very different authors, including those with a serious purpose, it must be said that it is an invention. It has, moreover, not been confirmed by any description of an earthquake based on eye-witness accounts; see F.–M. Abel, RB, 36 (1927), pp. 571–578; A. J. Braver, 'Yerushalayim'. Journal of the Jewish Palestine Exploration Society, 1928, pp. 316–325; M. Blanckenhorn, ZDPV, 50 (1927), pp. 288–296.

Sea, disappeared entirely'. The Israelites may have observed a phenomenon similar to the one described by Nowairi in the thirteenth century A.D. and have made use of their experience in their description of their ancestors' crossing of the Jordan. On the other hand, however, their ancestors may themselves have experienced a phenomenon of this kind and have regarded it as a miraculous intervention on the part of their God. There is no good reason for believing that this second hypothesis is invalid.

IV. THE TAKING OF JERICHO [46]
(Jos 6)

The Hebrew text of Jos 6 is longer than that of the Septuagint, which leaves out the repetitions, but both texts presuppose the same literary and pre-literary history, which is very complicated. Joshua speaks at one time to the warriors and at another to the priests. The order given to the people to remain silent until they are told to raise the war cry (verse 10) is certainly not in keeping with the order given several times to blow the trumpets. Sometimes the soldiers blow the trumpets and sometimes it is the priests. The principal theme is, of course, that of going round the walls of the town. One circuit is made on the first day (verse 11) and, on the seventh day, seven circuits are made (verse 15). According to verses 3 and 14, however, one circuit was made each day between the first day and the seventh. The priests blow their trumpets during the seven circuits made on the seventh day (verse 4), or only on the seventh circuit (verses 5 and 16) or during all the circuits made on all seven days (verses 8, 9, 13). The fact that the town is placed under a ban (verses 17–19, 22–25) makes it possible for the story of Rahab to be resumed (Jos 2) and for the way to be prepared for the story of Achan (Jos 7). Similarly, the curse pronounced against anyone who rebuilds Jericho (Jos 6:26) also prepares the way for the information given in 1 Kings 16:34, concerning Hiel's rebuilding of the town at the price of the death of his two sons. This incident is, however, the work of the Deuteronomist and does not belong to the early tradition.

The whole text is so entangled that it is almost impossible to distinguish all the different literary levels with any precision. An analysis of the different levels of tradition is in itself very difficult. M. Noth[47] has

---

[46] See, apart from the commentaries, J. Dus, 'Die Analyse zweier Ladeerzählungen des Josuabuches', *ZAW*, 72 (1960), especially pp. 107–121; S. Gevirtz, 'Jericho and Shechem: a Religio-Literary Aspect of City Destruction', *VT*, 13 (1963), pp. 52–62; G. del Olmo Lete, 'La conquista de Jerico y la leyanda ugaritica de Krt', *Sefarad*, 25 (1965), pp. 3–15; J. Maier, *Das altisraelitische Ladeheiligtum (BZAW*, 93), pp. 32–39; M. Weippert, *Die Landnahme der israelitischen Stämme*, pp. 32–34, 54–55. None of these books or articles deal with the archaeological problem.

[47] M. Noth, *Josua (HAT)*,[2] *in loco*.

distinguished an aetiological legend concerning the ruined walls of Jericho, claiming that the collector was responsible for introducing the figure of Joshua and the Deuteronomist for adding, at several levels, the ark and the priests. J. Dus[48] has followed this analysis fairly closely, but he thinks that the ark belongs to the first stage and that the whole story describes a cultic action in which the ark was carried in procession each year to commemorate the taking of Jericho. Hertzberg[49] and Kraus[50] also favoured a cultic explanation, but this interpretation of the story as a liturgical action seems to me to be as unconvincing as the liturgical explanation of Jos 3–4. Finally, J. Maier[51] has suggested the following analysis. (1) There was originally a conclusion to the story of Rahab, of which nothing remains. (2) This was followed by an Ephraimite editorial addition introducing the figure of Joshua. (3) The collector then 'nationalised' the story by extending the tradition to cover all twelve tribes. (4) A first revision including the ark was followed by (5) a second revision including the ark and finally by (6) an editing by the Deuteronomist.

With some reservations, I would like to suggest the following analysis. There was originally a local aetiology, a tradition of the sanctuary at Gilgal, which explained how the walls of Jericho had come to be ruined as the result of the first operation in the war of Yahweh in Canaan. The following is a reconstruction with the parallels in the other stories of the holy war.

Verse 2 (cf. verse 16): Yahweh announces that he has delivered (the verb is in the perfect!) Jericho to Joshua (cf. Jos 8:1; Judges 4:7, 14; 7:9).

Verses 3–10: The Israelites go round the town once in silence and then return to the camp. According to verse 11, they take the ark with them. It is the sign of the presence of Yahweh the warrior (cf. Num 10:35–36; 1 Sam 4; 2 Sam 11:11).

Verse 15: On the seventh day, the people go round the town seven times. There is no parallel which can be quoted in this case. The figure 7 is also characteristic of the story – there are seven days, seven circuits of the town, seven priests and seven trumpets.

Verse 16: On the seventh time round, the trumpets are blown. This trumpet, *sôphār*, is a ram's horn, *yôbhēl* (cf. verse 13). For sophar, cf. Judges 7:19–22. The war cry is raised (cf. Judges 7:20). This war cry is the *t'rû'āh* (cf. Jos 6:5) and is paralleled in 1 Sam 4:5, alongside *sôphār* (cf. Amos 2:2). ˙

Verse 20: 'The people shouted, the trumpets sounded. When they heard the sound of the trumpet, the people raised a mighty war cry *(t'rû'āh)* and the wall collapsed then and there. At once the people stormed the town,

[48] J. Dus, *op. cit.* (note 46).
[49] H. W. Hertzberg, *Die Bücher Josua, Richter, Ruth (ATD),*[4] 1969, *in loco.*
[50] H.–J. Kraus, *Gottesdienst in Israel,*[2] pp. 187–188.
[51] J. Maier, *op. cit.* (note 46).

every man going straight ahead; and they captured the town.' The holy war is a victory on the part of Yahweh, who fights for Israel (cf. Jos 10:14;11:6). The Israelites themselves did nothing at all, as when Yahweh destroyed the Egyptians in the miracle of the sea (Ex 14:14).

Verse 21: The ḥerem is imposed. This marks the end of the holy war.

There is also, in my opinion, no good reason for believing that Joshua did not figure originally in this story, as in the case of the account of the crossing of the Jordan.

The ark was, however, a cultic object which was entrusted to the priests; the sôphār became an instrument of liturgical music and the t'rû'āh became a cultic cry, a jubilation or yôbhēl. This aetiological account, which was at the same time a type of the story of the holy war of conquest, was transformed into a cultic account by a series of additions which emphasised the part played by the priests. It eventually became a description of a procession with a fanfare which had lost the mysterious grandeur of the early account, a description that expressed a theological truth, namely that it was Yahweh who had given to Israel the land that he had promised to the people.

This early narrative that we have tried to reconstruct is, however, not a historical account. Its climax is the collapse of the walls of Jericho at the sound of the trumpet and the war cry of the Israelites. If the Israelites really took the town, however, the historical event of its capture certainly did not take that form, which is undoubtedly simply an aetiological explanation of the ruins that were seen in that place. But, as we have seen, an aetiology may well be concerned, not with an essential fact, but rather with a circumstance. The Israelites, then, may have taken Jericho, but in a different way.

This brings us to the archaeological evidence.[52] Excavations carried out at Jericho have shown that Israelites who arrived at the end of the thirteenth century B.C. could not have taken Jericho for the simple reason that the town was not inhabited at that time. The Middle Bronze town had been destroyed round about 1550 and had then been abandoned. It was occupied again, although the population remained small, in the fourteenth century. Evidence of this reoccupation is fourteenth-century pottery found in Middle Bronze tombs that were used again in the fourteenth century and a house containing a mid-fourteenth-century jug. Nothing can be attributed to the thirteenth century. There are no signs of Late Bronze fortifications. Miss Kenyon has concluded from this that it is not possible to associate a destruction of Jericho with an entry of the Israelites into Canaan at the end of the thirteenth century B.C. The town could have been destroyed by a previous wave of invaders and if so, the dramatic account of the siege and

[52] K. M. Kenyon, *Digging up Jericho*, London, 1957, pp. 256–265; 'Jericho', *Archaeology and Old Testament Study*, ed. D. Winton Thomas, Oxford, 1967, especially pp. 272–274; H. J Franken, 'Tell es-Sultan and Old Testament Jericho', *OTS*, 14 (1965), pp. 189–200.

the sack of Jericho must have been aetiological. These conclusions have been received with favour by all those who believe that the account is purely aetiological and that the Israelites settled peacefully in Canaan.[53]

Nonetheless, it is important to bear in mind that a lack of archaeological evidence cannot be used as an argument against textual evidence, especially when it can be explained. W. F. Albright[54] has discussed Miss Kenyon's dates and has himself dated certain Mycenaean vases and imitations of such vases that have been found in previous excavations in a tomb at the site of ancient Jericho as belonging to the beginning of the thirteenth century. This, however, is of secondary importance and is insufficient evidence. It is of greater importance to consider the prevailing local conditions.

The tell of Jericho has been seriously eroded[55] and, although it is quite certain that the city was occupied during the fourteenth century, there is only one point where evidence of this occupation has been found. The very dense occupation during the Middle Bronze Age has resulted in only a few traces of archaeological evidence at the top of the tell. There is no trace at all at the height of the period of reoccupation during the Iron Age, of which there is textual evidence in 1 Kings 16:34, telling of the rebuilding of Jericho by Hiel of Bethel during the reign of Ahab. There is evidence of a fairly dense population during the seventh century, consisting of a few ruins in one part of the tell – a building on the slope, two tombs and a number of fragments in the wash at the summit of the tell. The fact that there were no walls at this time is not significant, because they may have been eroded. The Late Bronze inhabitants of Jericho may also have used the Middle Bronze city walls, as happened elsewhere, for example, at Tell Beit Mirsim or the northern site of Tell el-Fār'ah. Nor is the absence of tombs at the end of the Late Bronze Age of decisive importance – it is, after all, possible that they have not been discovered. W. F. Albright, for example, did not find a single tomb at Tell Beit Mirsim, nor was I able to find an Iron Age tomb at Tell el Fār'ah. Miss Kenyon, on the other hand, excavated a tomb at Tell es-Sultan, the site of Jericho, which dates back to the end of the tenth century, that is, before the period of Ahab.[56]

Does this therefore mean that the oasis was sparsely inhabited, but that the tell was not occupied? According to the Bible, it would seem that Jericho was not entirely abandoned between the period of Joshua and that of Ahab. In the first place, there is the story of the clan of Rahab which survived the destruction of Jericho and the memory of Rahab's house built

[53] M. Weippert, *Die Landnahme der israelitischen Stämme*, pp. 54–55.

[54] See his *Recent Discoveries in Bible Lands*,[2] New York, 1955, p. 87; *The Biblical Period*,[3] New York, 1963, pp. 28–29 and note 59, p. 100.

[55] K. M. Kenyon, *Digging up Jericho*, has insisted again and again on the extent of this erosion at different periods.

[56] Tomb A 85 in K. M. Kenyon, *Jericho*, II, London, 1965, pp. 479–490.

against the city wall. Secondly, according to Judges 3:13, Eglon the Moabite seized the 'city of palms', which can only be Jericho. Eglon moreover had a house there with an upper room, in which he was murdered by Ehud. Finally, according to 2 Sam 10:5, the messengers whom David sent to the king of the Ammonites stayed at Jericho until their beards, which, to their shame, had been cut off, had grown again.

We cannot therefore say, on the basis of archaeological evidence, that Jericho was not occupied when the Israelites arrived in Canaan. There is also the isolated text of Jos 24:1, which preserves the memory of a tradition which was different from that of Jos 6: 'Those who held Jericho fought against you ... but I put them all in your power'. We have linked this memory to the story of Rahab, which would normally have been followed immediately by an account of the taking of Jericho. I would therefore accept the fact that the aetiology which is at the basis of Jos 6 is not an aetiology pure and simple, but rather a story based on a historical memory of the taking of Jericho. Jericho itself must at this time have been a poor settlement, with little or no fortifications to protect it from attack. On the other hand, however, the town had to be conquered before the Israelites could penetrate as far as the highlands. This first 'conquest' in the Promised Land was given epic proportions and a sacral character by the biblical tradition.

V. THE TAKING OF AI[57]

(Jos 7–8)

The story of the taking of Ai is presented in a way which is quite different from that of the capture of Jericho. In the form in which we have it now in the Bible, it is linked to the story of Jericho's capture by the story of Achan, who defied the ban imposed on the town and was held responsible, because of his action, for the failure of the first attack made against Ai and was stoned to death (Jos 7:1, 5b–26). This link is, however, an artificially constructed one, because the story of Achan was originally quite independent of the accounts of the taking of Jericho and of Ai. Achan was, it will be recalled, a Judaean and the 'Vale of Achor' (= the plain of el-Buqeʻah) where the 'great cairn was reared over him, which is still there today' (Jos 7:26) is a long way from Ai and nowhere near Jericho. This

---

[57] See the recent studies by J. M. Grintz, ' "Ai which is beside Beth Aven". A Re-examination of the Identity of Ai', Bib, 42 (1961), pp. 210–216; G. Lombardi, 'Ai, la fortezza di Beth-el', Liber Annuus, 13 (1962–1963), pp. 278–286; W. M. W. Roth, 'Hinterhalt und Scheinflucht. Der stammespolemische Hintergrund von Jos 8', ZAW, 75 (1963), pp. 296–304; M. Weippert, Die Landnahme der israelitischen Stämme, pp. 34–36; J. A. Callaway, 'New Evidence on the Conquest of Ai', JBL, 87, (1968), pp. 312–320.

plain is on the frontier of the land which belonged to Benjamin, but inside the territory of Judah. As we have already seen,[58] this was a special tradition, either Judaean or else Benjaminite and therefore hostile to Judah.

Without this secondary element, the story of the taking of Ai is basically a well-presented report of a military expedition. As a result of the over-optimistic report brought back by the scouts sent to reconnoitre Ai (Jos 7:2–5a; *cf.* Jos 2 for Jericho and the parallels that we have mentioned), the small force dispatched to occupy the town was driven back and decimated. Joshua therefore had recourse to a stratagem (Jos 8). He placed a troop of picked men in a concealed position to the west of the town, between Ai and Bethel, and camped with the rest of his men in full view of the enemy. The king of Ai set out with his men to do battle and Joshua and the Israelites retreated, allowing the enemy to pursue them a long way from the town. The men in ambush entered the town and lit a fire there as a signal to the main force. These turned back and attacked the men of Ai, massacring them.

The fact that this is an episode in the holy war of conquest is indicated clearly in Jos 8:1: 'Be fearless now . . . I will put into your power the king of Ai, his people, his town and his territory' (*cf.* Jos 6:2 and the parallel texts mentioned in this context). It is also indicated in verse 18, in which Yahweh tells Joshua: 'Point your scimitar towards Ai; for I am about to put the town in your power' and similarly in verse 26, according to which Joshua did not let his arm fall until the battle was over (*cf.* Ex 17:8–16, which tells of Moses' outstretched arm enabling the Israelites to achieve victory in battle with the Amalekites). Finally, the character of holy war in this account is emphasised by the ban under which the conquered town is placed (Jos 8:27). Otherwise, it is clearly an account of a profane war.

It is also obviously a Benjaminite tradition, because Ai is in Benjaminite territory and the topographical details with which the story is studded point to a local tradition. I cannot be sure that M. Noth is right in saying that it is a tradition that was preserved at the sanctuary at Gilgal,[59] because Ai was a long way from Gilgal and above all because this story lacks the cultic aspects that characterise the accounts of the crossing of the Jordan and the taking of Jericho, both of which were certainly connected with the sanctuary at Gilgal. Since Ai was near Bethel, it has been suggested[60] that the tradition was preserved in the sanctuary of Bethel and I think that this is more probable. J. Gray[61] believes that it was connected both with the sanctuary of Bethel and with the pilgrimage to Gilgal, since the pilgrims going from Bethel to Gilgal would have passed through Ai.

---

[58] See above, pp. 545–546.

[59] M. Noth, *Josua (HAT)*,[2] 1953, p. 49.

[60] W. H. Hertzberg, *Die Bücher Josua, Richter, Ruth (ATD)*,[4] 1969, p. 60.

[61] J. Gray, *Joshua, Judges and Ruth (The Century Bible)*, 1967, *in loco*.

This is the most detailed of all the stories of the conquest of Canaan and it seems to be the most probable, especially since it contains no miraculous elements. Unfortunately, however, the story is not supported by archaeological evidence. Ai has been sited at Khirbet et-Tell, about a mile to the south-east of Bethel and this situation is certainly in accordance with the datum provided in Jos 7:2: 'east of Bethel' and confirmed in Jos 8:9: Bethel is 'to the west of Ai' (cf. 8:12). The name Ai, 'ay, is clearly related to 'iy (plural 'iyyîm), meaning a ruin or a heap of ruins. The Arab name is a translation of this – et-Tell means 'hill of ruins'. According to Jos 8:28, Joshua made Ai a tēl 'ôlam, a 'ruin for evermore'. Finally, the description of the battle, with the ambush and pretence of flight, can easily be applied to the site at Khirbet et-Tell.

Et-Tell has been excavated by two different groups of archaeologists,[62] but the results are similar. During the Early Bronze Age, et-Tell was a large town, the name of which is unknown to us. This town was destroyed in the course of Early Bronze III, round about 2400 B.C. The site was abandoned until after 1200 B.C, when a poor and unfortified village was founded on part of the ruined site. This village continued to be inhabited until the beginning of the tenth century B.C. at the latest, when the site was finally abandoned. At the time when the Israelites arrived in Canaan, there was certainly no town at Ai, nor was there a king of Ai. All that existed there was an ancient ruin of a town destroyed about 1200 years before. The Israelites only knew the site by the name hā-'ay, 'the Ruin', always prefixed by the article.

Several theories have been put forward in an attempt to resolve this contradiction between textual and archaeological evidence.

(1) Some scholars have maintained that Ai was not situated at et-Tell,[63] despite the serious arguments in favour of this site that have been summarised above. On the other hand, there is no site in the region to the east of Bethel (and this location cannot be excluded because of Jos 7:2) which was occupied at the end of the Late Bronze Age and where Ai can be situated.[64] Khirbet Haiyān, less than a mile to the south-east of et-Tell, has been suggested as the site of Ai, but was not occupied before the Roman period.[65] This means that the town of Aiath (Isa 10:28), Aija (Neh 11:31)

[62] The first expedition was made in 1933–1935 by Judith Marquet-Krause, Les fouilles de 'Ay (et-Tell), Paris, 1949. The second was made from 1964 onwards by J. A. Callaway; see J. A. Callaway, BASOR, 178 (April 1965), pp. 13–40; RB, 72 (1965), pp. 409–415; K. Schoonover, RB, 75 (1968), pp. 243–247; 76 (1969), pp. 423–426; J. A. Callaway, BASOR, 196 (Dec. 1969), pp. 2–16; RB, 77 (1970), pp. 390–393.

[63] See the recent works by J. Simons, The Geographical and Topographical Texts of the Old Testament, Leiden, 1959, p. 270. J. M. Grintz, op. cit. (note 57).

[64] J. A. Callaway, JBL, 87 (1968), p. 315; W. F. Albright, The Biblical Period,³ p. 29.

[65] H. Donner, ZDPV, 81 (1965), pp. 16–18; J. A. Callaway and M. B. Nicol, 'A Sounding at Khirbet Haiyān', BASOR, 183 (October, 1966), pp. 12–19.

and Ayyah (I Chron 7:28; the text is uncertain), which, it has been suggested, succeeded Ai at the end of the Israelitic period,[66] also cannot be located at Khirbet Haiyān. The site of this Aiath/Aija is not known. The site of Ai is not Khirbet Haiyān, but et-Tell.

(2) Another suggested solution to the problem is that the ruins of Ai were used as a fortified camp by the people of Bethel and the surrounding district in their attempt to check the Israelites' advance. This theory was put forward by L.-H. Vincent.[67] It is reinforced by the fact that Jos 8:17 speaks of men of Ai *and* Bethel, which would clearly explain the optimistic tone of the reconnaissance report, the failure of the first attack and the success of the stratagem, which is in any case so well suited to the lie of the land.[68]

Vincent's theory was recently taken up again by G. Lombardi,[69] who had recourse to a textual correction, suggesting that the text in the list of kings conquered by the Israelites, 'the king of Ai near *(miṣṣad)* Bethel' (Jos 12:9), should be read as 'Ai which is the fortress *(mᵉṣad)* of Bethel'. There is, however, no justification for this correction, which is certainly not supported by the reference to the king of Ai in verse 9 and the separate reference to the king of Bethel in verse 16b (although this is, in any case, missing from the major Greek manuscripts):

Any argument based on Jos 8:17 is bound to lack conviction, in the first place because the words 'and Bethel' are absent from the more important Greek manuscripts and from the Syro-hexaplar and, in the second place – and this is more decisive – because the preposition that is required in Hebrew grammar is not repeated before 'Bethel'. The text containing 'Bethel' should therefore read 'the men of Ai and *of* Bethel', but in the existing text, 'the men of Ai and Bethel', the word 'Bethel' gives the impression of being an addition. There is also another reason why this theory is unconvincing – it does not explain the fundamental problem of the inhabited town ruled by a king which figures in the biblical account.

(3) W. F. Albright[70] suggested a third solution, namely that the story originally described the taking of Bethel and that this description had been transferred to Ai. The two towns, Albright and those who have followed

[66] W. F. Albright, *AASOR*, IV (1924), pp. 137–144; J. Simons, *op. cit.*, p. 481; Y. Aharoni, *The Land of the Bible*, p. 372 and map 32, with a question mark. For Isa. 10:28, see especially H. Donner, 'Der Feind aus dem Norden. Topographische und archäologische Erwägungen zu Jes. 10 27b–34', *ZDPV*, 84 (1968), especially pp. 48–54.

[67] L.-H. Vincent, *RB*, 46 (1937), pp. 258–266.

[68] J. Gray seems to have combined this explanation with the explanation outlined below under (3) in his 1967 commentary, p. 92 and his commentary on Judges 1:22–26, *ibid.*, p. 251.

[69] G. Lombardi, *op. cit.* (note 57).

[70] Originally in *BASOR*, 56 (December 1934), p. 11, and frequently afterwards, especially in *BASOR*, 74 (April 1939), p. 17; *The Biblical Period,*³ p. 29. This theory was taken up again by G. E. Wright, *Biblical Archaeology*, Philadelphia, 1957, p. 80; J. Bright, *History*, p. 119. It was accepted as a possibility by W. H. Hertzberg in his commentary, p. 51 and by O. Eissfeldt, *CAH*, II, XXXIV, 1965, p. 10.

him have argued, were so close to each other that they formed a single territorial unit. The biblical evidence for this is found in Jos 12: 9, 'Ai near Bethel', Ezra 2:28 and Neh 7:32, where the people of Bethel and Ai who returned from exile are counted together, and Jos 8:17, in which the reference to Bethel as well as to Ai was regarded by Albright as original. The taking of Bethel is not narrated in the book of Joshua, but Albright has pointed to the archaeological evidence of the destruction of the town in the thirteenth century, probably by the Israelites. Because Bethel was immediately reoccupied by the invaders and all traces of the destruction were removed, the story of this conquest was, Albright concluded, transferred to the neighbouring ruin of Ai.

This theory does not really explain anything at all. Ai is distinguished from Bethel in the story, which only narrates the taking of Ai. The movements of troops during the battle and the details of the local geography only apply to Ai and not to Bethel. Finally, if Albright's theory is accepted, this presupposes an acceptance of the invention of the story by the inhabitants of Bethel and of their application of it to Ai, 'the Ruin', which they regarded as the precursor of their own town, Bethel. I am not in any way convinced that this interpretation adds anything to our understanding of the text, nor do I think that it can be historically authentic.

I am all the more convinced that this theory is unacceptable because there is in fact a story of the taking of Bethel in Judges 1:22–26. According to this account, the town of Bethel, which used to be known as Luz, was conquered by the house of Joseph after an inhabitant of the city had shown the scouts a way in. The Israelites were therefore able to enter the city, take it by surprise and massacre all the inhabitants, although they spared their informer and his family. This tradition must have been preserved at the sanctuary of Bethel. It can also be regarded as a possible parallel to the story of Rahab and the taking of Jericho.

The text itself says that the early name of the town was Luz. This can be compared with the information given in Gen 28:19, in which the change of name is ascribed to Jacob. In fact, the two names seem to have been originally applied to two different places. According to the outline of the territory belonging to the house of Joseph in Jos 16:1–2, Bethel and Luz were two points along the boundary. Bethel was an ancient Canaanite sanctuary taken over by the Israelites and may have been situated at Burj Beitīn, a little to the east of Beitīn, the probable site of Luz. Having occupied Luz, the Israelites gave it the same name as the neighbouring sanctuary. This assimilation of names took place at the time of the Yahwist, but the sanctuary remained outside the town (Gen 12:8; cf. Gen 13:3, according to which Abraham had set up an altar between Bethel to the west and Ai to the east).

If we wish to find archaeological confirmation of this capture of Bethel by the Israelites, it is clear from the excavations made at Beitīn[71] that the town was destroyed at the end of the Late Bronze Age. It is, however, not possible to date this destruction exactly by using the pottery of the last layer of the Late Bronze Age, when imports were reduced to a few fragments.[72] On the other hand, it should not be forgotten that the biblical account of the taking of Bethel in Judges 1:22-26 does not mention its destruction. It is, moreover, quite a different story from that of the capture of Ai in Jos. 8, which could not have been an authentic account of the taking of Bethel transferred to Ai. In any case, according to this theory, if the Israelites took Luz-Bethel, they did not take Ai.

(4) The archaeologist responsible for the most recent excavation of Ai, J. A. Callaway,[73] has put forward another theory. In his opinion, the life of the early Iron Age village at Khirbet et-Tell can be divided into two phases. The first village was inhabited by a group of people who were not Israelites, but possibly, Callaway thinks, Hivites, who settled there at the end of the Late Bronze Age. This village was destroyed by Israelites during the twelfth century and this conquest forms the historical basis of the account in Jos 8.

I find this explanation difficult to accept for four main reasons. First, it does not do justice to the historical aspect of the biblical account. Secondly, it has very little archaeological support. According to the description provided by the archaeologist himself, the second phase of occupation is marked by only very minor modifications and the only building of the first phase which was destroyed by fire was not rebuilt during the second phase and bears witness only to a limited catastrophe. Thirdly, there can be no historical basis for claiming that there were other immigrants into this part of Canaan at this period apart from the Sea Peoples and the Israelites. Certainly there is no historical evidence for the arrival of Hivites. Fourthly, the dates which Callaway gives to the pottery of the Iron Age village seem too early. His theory might be applicable to an episode at the period of the Judges, but it cannot be applied to an action which took place during the 'conquest'.

All these theories have been put forward in an attempt to safeguard a degree of historical authenticity in the account given in Jos 8. We are, however, bound to conclude that they do not succeed at all in confirming the historicity of that account, because all that they show is that the Israelites did not conquer a Canaanite city on the site of Khirbet et-Tell = Ai, for the simple reason that this city did not exist at the end of the thirteenth century B.C.

[71] The definitive work on this excavation is by J. K. Kelso, *The Excavation of Bethel, 1934–1960* (*AASOR*, **XXXIX**), 1968.

[72] The date 'between c. 1240:1235 B.C.' suggested by Kelso, *op. cit*, is quite unjustified.

[73] J. A. Callaway, *op. cit.* (note 57).

We must therefore consider the aetiological interpretation of this story suggested by A. Alt and M. Noth.[74] An explanation was sought for the existence of the ruins of a large town, the name of which was not known and which was called *ha-ay*, the 'Ruin'. According to the biblical tradition, Joshua had conquered this town, set fire to it and made it a 'ruin for evermore', *tēl ʿôlam*, a 'desolate place', *šʿmāmāh*, 'even today' (Jos 8:28). At the entrance to the gate of the ruined town, there was a great cairn and it was under this heap of stones, 'that is still there today', that the corpse of the king of the 'Ruin' had been placed after he had been taken down from the tree on which he had been hanged (Jos 8:29). It is even possible that the tree itself was also pointed out.

The first point to notice is that these two aetiologies are provided at the end of the story. They presuppose the abandonment of the Iron Age village itself. In its present form, the story could not have existed before the tenth century B.C. The second point to notice is that these aetiologies are only concerned with two circumstances – the total destruction of the town and the fate of its king. What is not explained is the story of the battle itself – the ambush, the pretence at flight and the return to confront the enemy.

This stratagem was practised quite frequently elsewhere in the ancient world,[75] but there is a very close parallel in Judges 20, which describes the taking of Gibeah by all the tribes of Israel united aganst Benjamin as a punishment for the crime committed against the concubine of the Levite of Ephraim. The first attack made by the Israelites was repelled by the Benjaminites (Judges 20:19–21; *cf.* Jos 7:4–5). A second attack also resulted in defeat (Judges 20:22–25). This second encounter has no parallel in Joshua. The text is moreover not clear and must in fact be a repetition. The people consequently went to Bethel, where the ark was, and wept in Yahweh's presence. Yahweh's reply was: 'March; for tomorrow I shall deliver him into your power' (Judges 20:26–28; *cf.* Jos 7:6–9, the prayer in front of the ark, and Jos 8:1, Yahweh's reply: 'I will put into your power the king of Ai'). The Israelites therefore prepared an ambush to the west of Gibeah (Judges 20:29 and 33, corrected according to the versions; *cf.* Jos 8:3 and 9). The Benjaminites were drawn a long way from the town (Judges 20:31–32, 39; *cf.* Jos 8:6 and 16, with the same terms). The Israelites who were in ambush meanwhile entered the town and lit a fire there (Judges 20:37–38); *cf.* Jos 8:19) and the Benjaminites saw the town burning (Judges 20:40; *cf.* Jos 8:20); Thereupon the Israelites turned round and massacred the Ben-

[74] A. Alt, 'Josua', *Werden und Wesen des Alten Testaments (BZAW,* 66), 1936, pp. 13–29 = *Kleine Schriften,* I, pp. 176–192, especially p. 183; M. Noth, 'Bethel und Ai', *PJB,* 31 (1935), pp. 7–29; *Josua (HAT),* [2] 1953, pp. 47–51; M. Weippert, *Die Landnahme der israelitischen Stämme,* 1967, pp. 34–36.

[75] F.–M. Abel has collected a number of examples of this stratagem as practised by the Romans and the Carthaginians; see 'Les stratagèmes dans le livre de Josuè', *RB,* 56 (1949), pp. 321–339, especially pp. 331–332.

jaminites who were caught between them and the men who had been in ambush and had meanwhile gone into Gibeah (Judges 20:42; cf. Jos 8:21–22).

There is quite obviously a connection between these two stories. The events are narrated in the same order in both accounts and the words used are very similar. However, the story in Judges was not, as has been claimed from time to time, derived from Joshua. Judges 19–21 form an appendix to the book of Judges consisting of early traditions which had been left out by the deuteronomic editor of the book and were included in the editorial revision which took place after the Exile. These early traditions, which have a firm historical basis,[76] may have contained the account of the battle outlined above.

It is generally accepted that two different traditions are combined in these post-exilic chapters of the book of Judges. The first is a tradition of the sanctuary at Mizpah and the other is a Bethel tradition. There can be little doubt that the accounts of the first defeat of the Israelites, the prayer to Yahweh, the promise of victory and, in my opinion, also the ambush [77] came from Bethel. It will be recalled that the story of the taking of Ai was, in my view, connected with the sanctuary at Bethel. We may therefore conclude that the account of the capture of Ai had been inspired by the story of the taking of Gibeah, which was narrated at the same sanctuary of Bethel.

It may also be necessary to go a stage further and regard this transference of the description of one battle in which the Benjaminites were shamefully defeated to another battle in which a victory was achieved in their tribal territory as a case of polemics between the tribes.[78] Benjamin may naturally have wished to remove all traces of the shame attached to their defeat at Gibeah by using the story to narrate the glorious conquest at Ai which was to their credit. It is possible that this was so, especially as we have already encountered a similar example of such tribal polemics. The insertion of the story of Achan between the accounts of the capture of Jericho and the taking of Ai may express a certain hostility towards Judah.[79]

The only conclusion that can be drawn from the story of the taking of Ai is that it is not historically authentic, apart from the fact that the settlement of the Israelites in Canaan was partly achieved by military conquest. In other words, it was because certain other towns were conquered by force of arms that the idea arose that the ruins at Ai could also be explained in this way. The direct inspiration for this story was the account of the taking of Gibeah in Judges 20.

[76] See the recent commentaries and M. Noth, *History*, pp. 94–95; K.–D. Schunck, *Benjamin*, (*BZAW*, 86), 1963, p. 68.

[77] See A. Besters, 'Le sanctuaire central dans Jud. xix-xxi', *ETL*, 41 (1965), pp. 20–41.

[78] W. M. W. Roth, *op. cit.* (note 57).

[79] See above, pp. 545–546.

We must finally consider in this section the story of the altar built by Joshua on Mount Ebal and the reading of the Mosaic law there. This account was inserted in this position, between the story of the taking of Ai and that of the treaty concluded with the Gibeonites (Jos 9) by the Deuteronomic editor. It therefore interrupts the course of the story by taking us from Ai northwards to Shechem and then back to Gilgal at Jos 9:6. It should be noted that this account of the altar and the reading of the law on Mount Ebal (Jos 8:30–35) is inserted between Jos 9:2 and 9:3 in the Septuagint, but that it still interrupts the narrative in this position. J. A. Soggin[80] has compared this passage with Gen 35:1–5, which he interpreted, as Alt had done,[81] as a pilgrimage from Shechem to Bethel. Seen in this light, Jos 8:30–35 can be interpreted as giving the route of a pilgrimage from Bethel to Shechem and back to Bethel if it is taken within the context of the story of the taking of Ai and that of the treaty with the Gibeonites which follows, but this leaves out of account the fact that it is certainly a late text. Despite certain modifications and the use of a later vocabulary, its basic inspiration is Deut 11, 27 and 31. It is therefore post-deuteronomistic[82] and was perhaps composed at the same time as the final editing of the Pentateuch, that is, the period of Ezra. If this is so, then its purpose would have been to show that the entire law read at Jerusalem also applied to the ancient northern kingdom (cf. Neh 8:3 and Jos 8:35).[83]

Why, then, was this addition placed precisely here in the book of Joshua? W. H. Hertzberg has suggested[84] that, after the story of the taking of Ai, the story that would be naturally expected would be one concerning Bethel, which was, after all, very near to Ai and at which the story of the capture of Ai was narrated, and concerning the taking over of the sanctuary there by the Israelites. This is what happens in the case of the story of the crossing of the Jordan, which is followed, Hertzberg has pointed out, by an account of the appropriation of the sanctuary at Gilgal (Jos 5). This taking over of the sanctuary of Bethel, which had been condemned, seemed offensive, Hertzberg believes, to the final editor and the incident was therefore replaced by the present story based on Shechem, which was fully supported by the biblical tradition.

[80] J. A. Soggin, 'Zwei umstrittene Stellen aus dem Überlieferungskreis um Schechem', ZAW, 73 (1961), pp. 78–87.

[81] A. Alt, 'Die Wallfahrt von Sichem nach Bethel', In piam memoriam A. von Bulmerincq, Riga, 1938, pp. 218–230 = Kleine Schriften, I, pp. 79–88.

[82] J. L'Hour, 'L'alliance de Sichem', RB, 69 (1962), especially pp. 178–181.

[83] See J. G. Vink, 'The date and origin of the Priestly Code in the Old Testament', OTS, 15 (1969), especially pp. 77–80.

[84] See his commentary, pp. 63–64. For Jos 8:30–35 and the parallel texts, see O. Eissfeldt, 'Gilgal or Shechem?' Proclamation and Presence. Old Testament Essays in Honor of G. Henton Davies, ed. J. D. Durham and J. R. Porter, London, 1970, pp. 90–101.

VI. THE TREATY WITH THE GIBEONITES [85]
(Jos 9)

This account bears clear signs of having been edited by the Deuteronomist.[86] The most obvious of these are verses 1–2, 9b–10, 24aβ–25 and the last words of verse 27. The pre-deuteronomistic material, however, is very complex. On the one hand, there are the inhabitants of Gibeon or the *ḥiwwî* (the 'Hivites', collectively) and, on the other, Joshua or the 'man of Israel' (used collectively) or else the *b'nê yiśrā'ēl*, the 'sons of Israel', the princes, *n'śî'îm*, or the princes or leaders of the community, *'ēdhāh*. The man of Israel questions the Hivites in verse 7, but they reply in verse 8 to Joshua. Verse 9 repeats verse 6 and verses 12–13 repeat verses 4–5. According to verse 15, it is Joshua who concludes the treaty with the Gibeonites, but according to verse 18, it is the princes. According to verse 21, it is the princes who decide that the Gibeonites are to be wood-cutters and water-carriers for the community, but, according to verses 23 and 27, it is Joshua who binds them to serve the house of God in this way or to wait on God's altar. No attempt that has so far been made to distribute this text among different written sources, whether pentateuchal or other documents, has proved to be completely satisfactory. It is equally difficult to make any distinction between different traditions or levels of tradition. K. Möhlenbrink[87] has distinguished a Gilgal tradition without Joshua and a Shiloh tradition. M. Noth[88] has also distinguished an early Gilgal tradition, into which the collector introduced the figure of Joshua. According to H. W. Hertzberg,[89] the original story was of the sanctuary at Gibeon and this did not, of course, contain any element that was hostile to Gibeon. During the reign of Solomon, however, the anti-Gibeonite elements, the ruse and the punishment of the Gibeonites, were added. J. Blenkinsopp[90] has suggested a similar solution, but he ascribed the anti-Gibeonite element to an editorial revision which took place after the reign of Solomon, but before the Deuteronomist. J. Liver[91] believed that the anti-Gibeonite aspect of the

[85] See J. Dus, 'Gibeon – eine Kultstätte des Sms und die Stadt des benjaminitischen Schicksals', *VT*, 10 (1960), pp. 353–374; M. Haran, 'The Gibeonites, Nethinim and the Sons of Solomon's Servants', *VT*, 11 (1961), pp. 159–169; J. Liver, 'The Literary History of Joshua ix', *JSS*, 8 (1963), pp. 227–243; F. C. Fensham, 'The Treaty Between Israel and The Gibeonites', *BibArch*,[27] (1964), pp. 96–100; J. Blenkinsopp. 'Are There Traces of the Gibeonite Covenant in Deuteronomy?' *CBQ*, 28 (1966), pp. 207–219; J. M. Grintz, 'The Treaty of Joshua with the Gibeonites', *JAOS*, 86 (1966), pp. 113–126.

[86] See J. Blenkinsopp, *op. cit.* (note 85).

[87] K. Möhlenbrink, 'Die Landnahmesagen des Buches Josua', *ZAW*, 56 (1938), especially pp. 241–245.

[88] M. Noth, *Josua*,[2] *in loco*.

[89] *Die Bücher Josua, Richter und Ruth (ATD)*,[4] *in loco*.

[90] *op. cit.* (note 85).

[91] *op. cit.* (note 85).

story went back to the period of Saul and J. M. Grintz[92] has tried to reconcile these contrasts in a single account.

The very fact that scholars who have concerned themselves with Jos 9 have come to such different conclusions points to the complexity of the problems of literary criticism and the history of traditions. What is of greatest interest to us here, however, is what historical conclusions can be drawn. M. Noth believed that there were none at all and that the account, which originated at Gilgal (Jos 9:6), was entirely aetiological.[93] It includes, in his view, two elements. The first aspect of the story is an attempt to explain why the four towns of the Gibeonite federation belonged to Benjamin and the second is an explanation of the fact that the Gibeonites cut wood and carried water at the sanctuary of Gilgal 'down to the present day' (Jos 9:27).

The story certainly had a Benjaminite origin and it is quite possible that it was originally narrated at Gilgal, but Noth's purely aetiological interpretation of the story is unjustified. In the first place, this treaty with the Gibeonites is given in Jos 10:1–15[94] as the reason why the five Canaanite kings formed a coalition against Gibeon and why the Israelites intervened in this conflict. Noth himself acknowledges the historical basis of this episode.[95] Secondly, and even more important, however, this treaty is confirmed by a strong, independent tradition, that of 2 Sam 21:1–14, according to which Saul had violated this treaty and the Gibeonites demanded that David should make amends for this. The expression 'down to the present day' is not used, in connection with the Gibeonites who served as water-carriers and wood-cutters at the sanctuary, in an aetiological sense. It is used by the narrator or the editor to support his story by recalling the continued existence at his own time of a situation that arose because of an event in the past.[96]

There is, however, one element which it is difficult to regard as historical. This is the amusing episode of the Gibeonites' ruse, resulting from this, their punishment being made to serve at the sanctuary. It is certainly difficult to believe that the Israelites could have been deceived by this ruse[97] and the narrator hardly seems to have believed in it himself (see verse 7). To reassure themselves that the Gibeonites were speaking the truth, the princes tasted their dry bread (verses 12 and 14), an action which, in the primitive tradition, would have referred to the shared meal which

[92] op. cit. (note 85)₂.

[93] M. Noth, Josua,² pp. 53–59; Geschichte, p. 135.

[94] J. Liver, op. cit. (note 85), pp. 234–235.

[95] M. Noth, Geschichte, p. 137, note 2.

[96] B. Childs, 'A Study of the Formula "Until This Day"', JBL, 82 (1963), pp. 279–292, especially p. 289.

[97] J. Liver, op cit. (note 85), p. 232.

sealed the treaty. What is more, if the Gibeonites had come from a long way away, they would not have required protection from the Israelites.[98] If, on the other hand, they came from nearby, then the Israelites could not have concluded a treaty with them (see verse 7b).

This, however, gives us a clue to the solution of the problem. This treaty concluded with inhabitants of Canaan is astonishing because it was quite different from the other stories which refer to imposing a ban or to destruction of the Canaanites' towns. Examples of this are the accounts of the taking of Jericho and Ai and verse 27 in this story. It was contrary to the rules of the holy war, but these rules were only applicable in Canaan. It is an idea that is also found in the purely theoretical precepts of Deut 10–18. According to this law, if a town which was a long way away and did not belong to the nations near Israel accepted the peace terms offered and opened its gates to the Israelites, all its inhabitants had to do corvée labour. On the other hand, no one living in the towns in Canaan was allowed to remain alive. In the final form of the story in Jos 9, there is an explanation given for the peace treaty made with the Gibeonites. The treaty was concluded because they said that they had come from a great distance. When the Israelites realised that they had lied, they were not able to break the oath that they had sworn, but they were able to reduce the Gibeonites to the state of wood-cutters and water-carriers.

There are, then, two historical facts in this story: the treaty with the Gibeonites and the fact that the Gibeonites were forced to serve at a sanctuary of Yahweh. With regard to the second, it is clear that the pre-Deuteronomistic editor knew that there were Gibeonites serving at a sanctuary of Yahweh 'down to the present day' (Jos 9:27). What is not certain, however, is that this was the sanctuary at Gilgal. Unlike Noth, I think that it may have been another sanctuary, that of Gibeon itself, which was, at the time of Solomon, 'the greatest of the high places' (1 Kings 3:4), and probably located at Nebī Samwīl. It was at Gibeon that, during the reign of David, the Gibeonites carried out an act of revenge on the descendants of Saul, following a rite which was certainly not an Israelitic rite (2 Sam 21:1–14; verse 6 is corrected according to the Greek version; the Hebrew has 'Gibeah of Saul').[99] These Gibeonites who served at the sanctuary disappeared quite early. They were not the same as the temple slaves mentioned in later texts, the nᵉthînîm who, according to Ezra 2:43 and 8:20, were first appointed by David, or 'Solomon's slaves' whose descendants came back with the nᵉthînîm from exile and were regarded, with the nᵉthînîm, as subordinate members of the temple staff (Ezra 2:58).[100] All of these were, however, similar in that they were all public slaves in the service of a

[98] J. Blenkinsopp. *op. cit.*, p. 211.
[99] H. Cazelles, 'David's Monarchy and the Gibeonite Claim', *PEQ*, 1955, pp. 165–175.
[100] M. Haran, *op. cit.* (note 85); B. A. Levine, 'The Neṯînîm', *JBL*, 82 (1963), pp. 207–212.

sanctuary, which was an institution that existed throughout the Ancient Near East.

The Gibeonites were employed to cut wood and to carry water. There is no need for us to look for any precise definition of their functions in connection with a particular sanctuary or cult. The words express the lowly status to which they had been reduced. A parallel exists in Deut 29:9–10, in which the different groups of the community are listed. This list ends with 'and the stranger too who is in your camp, whether he cuts wood or draws water for you' and the same verbs are used.[101] This was not originally a punishment, as it appears to be in the story in its present form, for the story of the Gibeonites' ruse is later. On the contrary, the Gibeonites themselves accepted and indeed asked for this socially inferior status: 'We are your servants; so make a b'rîth with us' (verse 11). This can be compared with verse 15: 'Joshua granted them šālôm, peace, and made a b'rîth with them guaranteeing their lives, and the leaders of the community ratified it by oath'.

There is an interesting Hittite parallel to this story. In the fourteenth century, Mursilis II waged war against the Kashka,[102] a people living in Asia Minor and governed democratically without a king, like the Gibeonites. In his annals, Mursilis tells how he captured, plundered and burnt several of their towns, just as Joshua took and set fire to Jericho and Ai (see Jos 9:3). The Hittite king continues: 'The people of Taptina, Hurshama and Pikurzi then came to meet me. They fell at my feet and spoke in this way: "Our Lord! Do not annihilate us! Take us in bondage and make us your soldiers and carriers!"'.[103]

Mursilis did not, however, conclude a treaty with the Kashka. Is it possible to speak of a covenant treaty between the Israelites and the Gibeonites? The treaties concluded by the Israelites have certainly been compared with the Hittite vassalage treaties, but many scholars have gone too far in this.[104] It is, after all, an exaggeration to say that groups of Israelites who were still

---

[101] At Ugarit, 'woodcutters' and 'water-carriers' are in parallel in *Krt* I, 111–114 = 214–217; for this text, see J. C. Greenfield, *Eretz-Israel*, 9 *(Albright Volume)*, 1969, p. 63. The water-carriers were the most numerous and there were half as many men providing wood (as well as half as many providing vegetables and fish) among the staff involved in providing food and other supplies to the workers at the royal necropolis at Deir el-Medineh in Egypt. The water-carriers had an inferior social status. See L. A. Christophe, 'Les porteurs d'eau de Deir el-Médineh pendant le règne de Ramsès III', *Bulletin de l'Institut d'Egypte*, 36 (1955), pp. 381–399.

[102] E. von Schuler, *Die Kaškäer. Ein Beitrag zur Ethnographie des Alten Kleinasien*, Berlin, 1965.

[103] A. Goetze, 'Die Annalen des Muršiliš', *MVÄG*, 38 (1933), pp. 129 ff; for the people of Dukkamma and Azzin, *ibid.*, pp. 135, 139.

[104] See Fensham, Blenkinsopp and Grintz in the works mentioned in note 85.

leading a semi-nomadic life could have imposed a treaty on the Gibeonites in the same way as the great Hittite kings imposed treaties on their vassals. The most that can be said is that this is a case of international law in the Ancient Near East. The word *b'rîth* has been wrongly translated as 'covenant' here, where it clearly preserves its basic meaning of an oath containing a promise.[105] In fact, the text insists again and again that there was an oath (verses 15, 18, 19–20; *cf.* 2 Sam 21:2). This oath is moreover accompanied by a meal (verse 14). The situation described in Jos 9 can be compared with the oath and the *b'rîth* between Abraham and Abimelech (Gen 21: 24, 27), the oath, *b'rîth* and meal between Isaac and Abimelech (Gen 26:28, 30) and the oath and the meal between Isaac and Laban (Gen 31:53–54). What Joshua promised the Gibeonites was that they would be left alive. This was the peace, *šālôm,* that he granted them (Jos 9:15). This can be compared with Yahweh's covenant with Levi in Mal 2:5: 'My *b'rîth* was with him; it stood for life, *hayyîm,* and peace, *šālôm,* and these were what I gave him'.[106] 'make peace' also means 'to conclude a treaty'.[107]

This treaty made the Gibeonites part of Israel, but their status was lower. They had made peace with the Israelites and were 'in the midst of them' (Jos 10:1; *cf.* Deut 29:10: 'in the middle of the camp'). They remained strangers, however, like the *gêrîm* of Deut 29:10 and they did not possess every right (see 2 Sam 21:4, which may mean 'we do not have the right to carry out blood vengeance against the Israelites').[108] This act of submission at the same time meant that the Gibeonites were protected by the Israelites. When they were attacked by the Canaanite kings because of their treaty with Joshua, they called for his help and he rescued them (Jos 10:6). This can be compared with the clause in the Hittite treaties of vassalage according to which the Hittite ruler pledged himself to come to the rescue of his vassal if he was attacked.[109] It is, of course, true that the Gibeonites were in a different position – unlike many royal towns which had not been conquered by the Israelites even until the time of David and Solomon, they were not a Canaanite enclave, but a people incorporated into Israel. They had not, however, been assimilated by Israel and remained a foreign group inside Israel. 'In his zeal for the Israelites and for Judah' (2 Sam 21:2), in other words, in order to achieve ethnic and religious unity in Israel, Saul had tried to eliminate the Gibeonites. This, however, was a violation of the oath

---

[105] N. Lohfink, *Die Landverheißung als Eid. Eine Studie zu Gn 15,* Stuttgart, 1967, especially pp. 101–113.

[106] See 'peace and life' in the Karatepe inscription, III, 2–3, *KAI,* No. 26.

[107] See the Alalah text No. 58, which can perhaps be translated as 'the year when Irkabtum concluded a treaty (instead of 'made peace') with the Habiru soldiers'.

[108] H. Cazelles, *op. cit.* (note 85).

[109] V. Korosec, *Hethitische Staatsverträge,* Leipzig, 1931, p. 90, note 1.

and led to the great famine, which was explained as a punishment inflicted by Yahweh (2 Sam 21:1). The plague which ravaged Asia Minor during the reign of Mursilis II was similarly explained by the violation of a treaty.[110]

There is no doubt that this incident concerning the Gibeonites was extremely important for the history of the settlement of the Israelites in Canaan.[111] The Gibeonites were Hivites (Jos 9:7; cf. 11:19). They should not be identified with the Hurrians.[112] It is not known to which racial group the Gibeonites belonged or when they settled in Palestine, but they undoubtedly had an organisation which was different from that of the other city-dwellers in Canaan. Above all, they had no king and were ruled by elders (Jos 9:11).[113] They lived in four towns, Gibeon, Chephirah, Beeroth and Kiriath-jearim (Jos 9:17 is the only text in which they are listed). Two of these Gibeonite towns have been located with great certainty. Chephirah is Tell Kefîreh to the west of Qubeibeh and Kiriath-jearim was undoubtedly at Deir el-Azhar near el-Qiryeh on the road from Jerusalem to Tel Aviv. The other two Gibeonite towns have not been located with the same degree of certainty.[114] The view that Gibeon is to be found at el-Jib has been greatly reinforced by the excavations that have been made there, but the arguments in favour of el-Bîreh for Beeroth are not convincing. In any case, these Gibeonite towns covered quite a large area, about twelve by ten miles, the land belonging to Benjamin and stretching towards the west, with access to the Shephelah. The most important aspect of this story, however, is that it is an example of an Israelite settlement without force of arms. According to Jos 11:19, this was the only example of such a settlement, but there must, of course, have been others, especially at Shechem and the surrounding district, where the Hivites lived as well, at least according to Gen 34.

---

[110] A. Malamat, 'Doctrines of Causality in Hittite and Biblical Historiography. A Parallel', *VT*, 5 (1955), pp. 1–12.

[111] J. Blenkinsopp, *op. cit.* (note 85), with some reservation.

[112] R. de Vaux, 'Les Hurrites de l'histoire et les Horites de la Bible', *RB*, 74 (1967). pp. 481–503, especially p. 497 ff.

[113] Z. Kallai and H. Tadmor, 'Bit Ninurta = Beth Horon. On the History of the Kingdom of Jerusalem in the Amarna Period', *Eretz-Israel*, 9 *(Albright Volume)*, 1969, pp. 138–147 (Hebrew with an English summary. These authors point out that the government of the Gibeonites was not really a 'primitive democracy'. It was the result of their having belonged for a very long time to the kingdom of Jerusalem, which stretched as far south as the southern limit of the highlands of Ephraim and was broken up after the Amarna period.

[114] See the discussion, with references, in M. Weippert, *Die Landnahme der israelitischen Stämme*, pp. 21–22 (note).

VII. THE BATTLE OF GIBEON AND THE CAVE AT MAKKEDAH
(Jos 10)

The consequences of the treaty which the Israelites concluded with the Gibeonites are outlined in Jos 10. The Gibeonites were attacked by a coalition of five Canaanite kings who wanted to punish them for having made peace with the Israelites. The Gibeonites at once asked Joshua to help them. Joshua came up from Gilgal, defeated the forces of the coalition and pursued them down the descent of Beth-horon as far as Makkedah (verses 1–10). This military action was helped by an intervention on the part of Yahweh, who threw enormous hailstones down on to the fugitives (verse 11) and made the sun and the moon stand still (verses 12–14). Joshua went back to Gilgal (verse 15), while the five kings sought refuge in a cave at Makkedah. Joshua came up again from Gilgal, prevented the kings from leaving the cave in which they were hiding and routed the armies of the coalition. Joshua then made the five kings come out of the cave, put them to death and hanged them from five trees. Afterwards, he had their corpses taken down from the trees and thrown into the cave, the mouth of which he had closed with stones 'and these,' the story concludes, 'are still there to-day' (verses 16–27). Joshua then conquered Makkedah, Libnah, Lachish and Eglon (verses 28–35) and finally Hebron and Debir. After having conquered the whole country – the hill country, the Negeb, the lowlands and the coastal plain – in one great expedition, he returned to Gilgal (verses 36–43).

In the form in which we have it in Jos 10, this story does not hold water. Joshua's return to Gilgal between the battle of Gibeon and the affair of the five kings at Makkedah seems highly unlikely, if the same five kings were involved in each case. What is more, Joshua's conquest of the towns listed in verses 28–38 is contradictory, as far as Hebron and Debir at least are concerned, with what is said in Judges 1 and the other texts that we have considered. G. E. Wright, however,[115] has defended the unity of this chapter and its basic historical authenticity and has tried to reconcile its data with those given in Judges 1. Joshua's return to Gilgal (verse 15) raises no problem for Wright, because the verse is missing in the Greek Old Testament (or more strictly in a part of the Greek Bible) and must have been added. (It is worth noting here that it is more probable that it was suppressed in the Septuagint because of the difficulty that it caused.) Wright

---

[115] G. E. Wright, 'The Literary and Historical Problem of Joshua 10 and Judges 1', *JNES*, 5 (1946), pp. 105–114.

also regarded Joshua's great military expedition as credible from the geographical and strategic points of view, believing that Joshua struck at all these Canaanite towns in the region in a lightning campaign. The excavations at Lachish and Tell Beit Mirsim, which he identified with Debir, in his opinion confirmed his theory. Judges 1 does not contradict Joshua 10, but describes the battles that Judah had to fight in order to gain possession of his territory, a series of conflicts which was continued after the death of Joshua (Judges 1:1). This, then, is Wright's hypothesis, but it will be clear that we cannot, on the basis of our commentary on Judges 1 and our consideration of the settlement in the south of Palestine, accept his attempt to harmonise Judges 1 and Jos 10 without taking seriously into account either the results of literary criticism or those of the history of traditions.

More recently, K-D. Schunck [116] made an attempt to safeguard the greater part of this chapter. He regards verses 29–35 as the continuation of verses 1–10 and is of the opinion that these two passages, taken as a continuous whole, form the early basis of the chapter. The historical fact that is reported in it is the victorious expedition of the group of Ephraim and Benjamin under the leadership of Joshua. The story of the cave at Makkedah (verses 16–17) comes, Schunck thinks, from another tradition. Verses 11–14 describe Yahweh's miraculous intervention. Verse 15 is an addition. Verse 28 and verses 36–39, which contradict Jos 14:6 ff; 15:13 ff and Judges 1, as well as the final verses 40–43 were, in Schunck's view, supplied by the Deuteronomist, who wanted to complete a list of five towns corresponding to the five kings in verses 1–10 and 16–27. Schunck's solution is more satisfactory than Wright's, but it is still not convincing. Verse 28 probably additional as he suggests, but he is not right in making a distinction between verses 29–35 and verses 36–39.

A third explanation has been suggested by K. Elliger, [117] who divided the story into three distinct elements – verses 1–15, the battle of Gibeon; verses 16–27, the story of Makkedah; verses 29–39, the conquest of the towns. These three elements were connected to each other by the biblical tradition. One link is the mention of Makkedah after the reference to Azekah in verse 10. Verse 28 forms another link between the story of Makkedah and the conquest of the towns. A historical memory, Elliger believed, was at the basis of this third element. Joshua played no part in the conquest of these Canaanite towns, which was in fact carried out by the Calebites (Kenizzites) who, in Elliger's opinion, came up along the coastal plain, but were checked in their movement northwards, turned towards the east and south-east and eventually, after sacking Libnah, Lachish and Eglon on the way, arrived at Hebron and Debir. It is at this point that the story of the

[116] K.–D. Schunck, *Benjamin (BZAW,* 86), 1963, pp. 28–39.
[117] K. Elliger, 'Josua in Judäa', *PJB,* 30 (1934), pp. 47–71.

Calebites-Kenizzites joins that of Judges 1. Elliger's theory is interesting, but he did not give any special attention to the battle of Gibeon and the story of Makkedah.

According to M. Noth,[118] Jos 10 does not contain three elements, but only two. The first is the story of the battle of Gibeon, which ends with Joshua's return to Gilgal (verse 15). The second element is the aetiological account of the cave at Makkedah, which is followed by a story of the conquest of five towns. In Noth's view, verse 28 was a later addition and the five towns conquered were those of the five kings in the cave at Makkedah. These kings, he was convinced, were different from those mentioned in the story of the battle of Gibeon. The list of these kings given in verses 3 and 5b is later, according to Noth, as is the reference to the king of Jerusalem as the leader of the coalition. All that the early text contained was: 'the five Amorite kings living in the mountains', as in verse 6. After having been included in verses 3 and 5, the names of these kings or their towns entered the story of Makkedah (verse 23), where they replaced the names of the kings of the five towns in verses 28–39.

Noth's analysis of Jos 10 is more convincing than the other three that are outlined above, although it is by no means decisive and does nothing to explain certain points, especially the origin of the names of the five towns and their kings (verses 3, 5, 23). What is most important in this context, however, is the historical criticism of this chapter in which three elements have to be distinguished: the battle of Gibeon, the cave at Makkedah and the conquest of the southern towns. I propose to consider them in the reverse order.

(1) *The conquest of the southern towns of Canaan.* We have already considered this question when we discussed the settlement of the tribe of Judah. This conquest cannot have been carried out by Joshua. The towns of Hebron and Debir were taken by Caleb and Othniel (Judges 1:10–15). Verse 28, which mentions the taking of Makkedah, is an editorial addition. The names of three other towns, Libnah, Lachish and Eglon, appear in the editorial list of conquered kings (Jos 12) and in the later list of the towns of Judah (Jos 15), but nowhere else in the book of Joshua. Eglon is, moreover, never mentioned again in the whole of the Old Testament, Libnah is not mentioned again until the reign of Jehoram (2 Kings 8:22) and Lachish does not occur until the reign of Amaziah (2 Kings 14:19). These towns only became the possession of the Israelites after the period of Israel's settlement in Canaan. We have, after all, already seen that archaeological research, even the ex-

[118] M. Noth, 'Die fünf Könige in der Höhle von Makkeda', *PJB*, 33 (1937), pp. 22–36; *Josua,*[2] pp. 60–67. The essential aspects of Noth's theory are accepted by J. Gray, *Joshua (The Century Bible)*, 1967, pp. 104–106. V. Fritz, *ZDPV*, 85 (1969), pp. 137–140, thinks that the names of the five towns in Jos. 10: 3, 5, 23 come from the same document as Jos. 12.

cavations carried out at Tell ed-Duweir = Lachish, has been unable to provide any clear evidence in favour of a conquest by the Israelites at the time that they were settling in Canaan. Elliger's theory that these towns were destroyed by the Calebites-Kenizzites is entirely unfounded. Y. Aharoni[119] believes that the excavations at Lachish point to a decisive battle there which also resulted in the defeat of the neighbouring towns. He regards the reference to the king of Gezer who, according to Jos 10:33, came to help Lachish in this battle, not as an invention, but rather as a confirmation of his hypothesis. In my opinion, there is no historically authentic fact in Jos 10:28–29 that can be retained, at least with regard to the period when Israel was settling in Canaan.

(2) *The story of Makkedah.* According to A. Alt and M. Noth,[120] this was a local aetiological legend, describing and explaining the existence at Makkedah of a cave with its entrance blocked by large stones which 'are still there today' (verse 27, at the end of the story) and of five trees nearby. Two explanations are in fact preserved in this story, at least in outline. According to the first, the mouth of the cave was closed so that the kings imprisoned inside would die of hunger (verse 18). According to the second explanation, the kings were buried in the cave after having been hanged from the five trees (verse 27). This can be compared with the similar hanging and burial under a cairn of the king of Ai (Jos 8:29).

I accept the aetiological basis of this story, but it is difficult to decide whether it was invented in order to explain the presence of the stones and the trees or whether the aetiology was simply attached to these details in a story which might have had a historical basis. There were, of course, numerous caves in Palestine, with their entrances blocked or fallen in and with trees growing near them, so that it is not easy to know why this story should have been attached to a site which, apart from this chapter, is only mentioned in the list of Judaean towns in the Shephelah district (Jos 15:41) and nowhere else in the whole of the Old Testament. Where, then, was this story preserved and where was it narrated? We have already compared the fate of the king of Ai with that of the five kings at Makkedah and the aetiological character of the account of the taking of Ai seems to be beyond dispute. But Ai was different from Makkedah in that it was a great field of ruins and a well-known site which was often visited and was near the sanctuary at Bethel where the story was told. None of these factors applied to Makkedah and this is precisely why I believe that the story of Makkedah has a historical basis. I do not, however, know what this historical

---

[119] Y. Aharoni, *The Land of the Bible*, p. 198.

[120] A. Alt, 'Josua', *Werden und Wesen des Alten Testaments (BZAW,* 66), 1936, p. 19 = Kleine Schriften, I, p. 183; M. Noth, *PJB,* 33 (1937), p. 23 ff. and *Josua,*[2] pp. 60–61, has discussed the question in greater detail.

background is. The site of Makkedah is unknown. It is not possible to conclude from Jos 10:10 that it was near Azekah = Tell Zakarīyeh, because the reference here is purely an editorial addition. All that can be concluded from Jos 15:41 is that it was in the same district as Eglon and Lachish. In any case, it was a long way from Gibeon, so that we may conclude that the two stories are distinct.

3. *The battle of Gibeon.* Although they both believed that the treaty with the Gibeonites is an aetiology, Alt and Noth were convinced that the battle of Gibeon was a historical event. According to Alt,[121] it was in fact the only military action in the whole book of Joshua which could be ascribed to Joshua himself as a historical person. The battle itself took place at Gibeon, in Benjaminite territory, but it continued along the descent of Beth-horon in Ephraimite territory and Joshua was later to be buried at Timnath-serah = Khirbet Tibneh, in the hill country of Ephraim. Noth does not go so far as Alt,[122] believing that Joshua was introduced later into this story as he was into the story that precedes it and the story that follows. His figure may have replaced a Benjaminite or an Ephraimite hero, Noth thinks, but this victory achieved at Gibeon by the group of Benjamin-Ephraim against the Canaanite kings was, in his opinion, historically authentic.

I think that it is possible to be even more explicit here. Joshua's part in the battle and the treaty concluded with the Gibeonites can be regarded as historical facts.[123] By this treaty, the Israelites gained control of the roads leading up from the Shephelah and especially the Beth-horon road, which had always been the main access from the plain to the highlands coming from Aijalon, since the time of the Philistine campaigns (1 Sam 14:23 – Greek – and 31) until the wars of the Maccabees (1 Mac 3:16, 24). It is to be expected that this new situation should have given rise to a sharp reaction on the part of the Canaanites, who were naturally anxious to separate the Gibeonites from the Israelites. They were, however, beaten in battle and pursued down the descent of Beth-horon as far as Azekah (Makkedah being an addition here). All this is in accordance with the geography of the region and the account is sober and brief, occupying only one verse (Jos 10:10). It should be noted that there is no question here of only one town being taken or of a whole territory being conquered The story is plausible historically.

It is more difficult to decide precisely who the aggressors were. According to verse 1, it was the king of Jerusalem, Adoni-zedek, who took the initiative and called on the kings of Hebron, Jarmuth, Lachish and Eglon. It is true that the king of Jerusalem might well have felt threatened by the settlement of the Israelites to the north of his land in the country around

---

[121] A. Alt, *Kleine Schriften*, I, pp. 187–188.
[122] M. Noth, *Josua*,[2] p. 61; *Geschichte*, p. 137.
[123] See K.–D. Schunck, *Benjamin*, p. 28 ff.

Gibeon, but Hebron was a long way off and probably already in the hands of the Calebites. What is more, these two allies would certainly not have retreated along the Beth-horon road. The enemy must have come from the west, not from the south. Jarmuth = Khirbet Yarmuk, near Tell Zakarîyeh = Azekah, is well placed at the end of the line of pursuit, but Lachish and Eglon were much farther south. The names of the five kings do not appear elsewhere and at least one of them is doubtful (Debir, the name of the king of Eglon, is the name of a town). It is probable, as Noth has said, that the primitive tradition only spoke of Amorite kings (see verse 6). We may therefore conclude that Israel's enemies in this particular encounter were minor kings who had come up from the lowlands, but precisely who they were we cannot say.

In the biblical tradition, a miraculous intervention on Yahweh's part, the hurling of enormous hailstones from the sky (verse 11), was added to the memory of this victory against the kings. There is no need for us to ask, as some Old Testament scholars have done,[124] how it was possible for the Israelites to carry on pursuing their enemies during such a hailstorm or how it was that only the Canaanites were killed by the hailstones. This great hailstorm is no more than a graphic representation or visible expression of the help given by Yahweh, which is already announced in verse 10, according to which it was Yahweh who drove the Canaanites headlong. The verb used here is *hāmam*, a word which forms part of the vocabulary of the holy war (see also Ex 14:24; 23:27; Judges 4:15). The episode of the hailstones can moreover be compared with the store of hail which God is said to keep 'for days of battle and war' (Job 38:22–23). There is the same relationship between verses 10 and 11 of this story of the battle of Gibeon as there is between the prose account of the battle of Kishon (Judges 4:15, in which the same verb *hāmam* is used) and the poetic Song of Deborah (Judges 5:20), according to which the stars fought from high in heaven against Israel's enemy.

Another addition to the memory of the defeat of the Canaanites is the miracle of the sun (verses 12–14). This miracle has been the centre of a great deal of apologetic literature, but the results cannot be taken very seriously because the approach to the problem has been from the wrong direction. It is first and foremost a problem of literary criticism. These verses form a single unit which is connected editorially to the preceding account of the miracle of the hailstones by the particle *'āz*, 'then'. The divine intervention narrated in these verses is different from the one narrated in verse 11, which explained why the Canaanites were in a state of panic – Yahweh had caused it with his hailstones. In this second case (verses 12–14), the Israelites

---

[124] A. Fernández, *Commentarius in Librum Josue*, Paris, 1938, p. 143; M. J. Gruenthaner, 'Two Sun Miracles of the Old Testament', *CBQ*, 10 (1948), pp. 271–290, especially p. 274.

ask for and obtain a miracle simply in order that they should have time to win their victory.

The nucleus of verses 12–14 is a quotation from the 'Book of the Just', *sēpher hayyāšār*, which is quoted again in 2 Sam 1:18, in David's elegy over Saul and Jonathan and in 1 Kings 8:13, in Solomon's dedication of the temple (1 Kings 8:13), if the Septuagint (1 Kings 8:53) is to be believed. According to these texts, this book was a collection of pieces of poetry attributed to Israel's heroes, Joshua, David and Solomon. The introduction to this passage in the book of Joshua (verse 12a) must also come from this Book of the Just, probably in a more simple form: 'Joshua said, on the day that Yahweh delivered the Amorites to the sons of Israel', just as, in 2 Sam 1:17, there is a short introduction: 'David made this lament over Saul and his son Jonathan' and, in 1 Kings 8:53 (Greek), 'Solomon said over the temple, when he had finished building it'. What we have here, then, is an early independent tradition concerning the battle of Gibeon confirming the Israelites' victory, the nature of their enemies and the part played by Joshua.

There is some doubt, however, about what Joshua in fact said in these verses. Critics have not reached agreement about the meaning of the two key verbs in this passage. The verb *dāmām*, describing what the sun did, may mean either 'stand still' or 'remain silent', and *'āmadh*, applied to the moon, may mean 'take up a position', 'be there' or again 'stand still'. There is also little agreement regarding the hoped for result – did Joshua ask for the sun not to go down, as the prose commentary in verse 13b says? Or did he ask for the sun not to rise,[125] so that the Israelites would be able to go up by night from Gilgal or to pursue the enemy more easily? What part, then, did the moon play in this? And how can this violation of the laws of nature be explained? Many different solutions have been suggested, some possible and others not, on the basis of astronomy (an eclipse, for example, or a change of the orbit of Venus) and meteorology (clouds, mist or refraction).

None of these explanations have proved ultimately satisfactory, but a new approach has been opened up by J. Heller.[126] The sun and the moon were, Heller suggested, not the planets, but two deities of the sky. Joshua tells the sun to 'be silent' *in* Gibeon and the moon to 'be quiet' *in* the plain of Aijalon. The name of of this place. *'ayyālôn*, is derived from *'ayyāl*, meaning 'stag', and the hind was an animal consecrated to Artemis, the goddess of the moon. There was therefore, Heller has argued, a sanctuary of the moon at Aijalon and there must also have been a sanctuary of the sun at Gibeon. Joshua ordered these two deities to keep quiet to prevent them from giving a favourable oracle: in other words, from acting on behalf of those who believed in them. This is an interesting explanation of verses

---

[125] See Hab. 3:11, according to which 'the sun and the moon stay, *'āmadh*, in their houses'.

[126] J. Heller, *ArOr*, 26 (1958), pp. 653–655. This theory has been taken up again by J. Dus, *op cit.* (note 85).

12–13, but there are two serious difficulties. First, there is nothing to indicate the presence of these cults at Aijalon and Gibeon and, secondly, Gibeon was not an enemy town. On the contrary, Joshua was fighting to defend it.

The last explanation that is worth considering here has been suggested by J. S. Holladay.[127] It is clear from the title of his article that, apart from Heller, all those who have tried to solve this problem, including that of verse 13b, have forgotten the moon. The Assyrians made astronomical forecasts for the fourteenth, fifteenth and sixteenth days of the month, that is, the time of the full moon, when the sun and the moon were both visible together. According to these omens, if the sun and the moon appeared at the proper time and place, everything would be favourable, but if the moon was late in appearing or disappeared too soon, everything would go badly. Heller believes these ideas were not necessarily confined to the Babylonian astronomers. They may have been shared by the inhabitants of Palestine – the peasants of all the countries of the Near East had sayings about the moon. According to this theory, then, Joshua was asking for the sun to the east of Gibeon and the moon to the west of Aijalon to be in a position which would herald a favourable outcome for the Israelites in the battle or else he was trying to make sure that this would happen by means of an incantation. All that these two verses indicate is that this was the case.

This theory would make a considerable step forward and overcome all difficulties in connection with the text, except for the fact that it is precisely the text that it does not take sufficiently into account. One can accept Joshua's asking for a favourable omen and the fact that the sun and the moon were in their respective positions at the required time, but the consequence was that they *remained* there until revenge had been taken on the enemy. There is no parallel to this situation in any of the Assyrian texts. The difficulties are therefore in no way eliminated. What is more, the Deuteronomistic editor did not see the saying in this light : what he saw in it was a very great miracle: 'there was never a day like that before or since' (verses 13b–14).

All these explanations are ultimately unconvincing and have to be rejected. I believe that, like the hailstorm in verse 11, the little poem in verses 12–13 is an expression, in poetry, of the supernatural help that Israel received. The prose account of the exodus from Egypt (Ex 14), can, for example, be compared with the Song of Moses (Ex 15), in which the exodus is given epic proportions, and the prose account of the battle against Sisera (Judges 4) with the Song of Deborah (Judges 5), which tells how 'from high in heaven fought the stars, fought from their orbits against Sisera' (verse 20). The editor of verses 13b–14 took this poetic expression literally in his desire to exalt Yahweh who 'was fighting for Israel' (verse 14b) and

[127] J. S. Holladay, 'The Day(s) the Moon Stood Still', *JBL*, 87 (1968), pp. 166–178.

in his wish – which is apparent throughout the whole of the book – to exalt his hero, Joshua. This was the only time that Yahweh had obeyed the word of a man (verse 14a) and thereafter the editor added 'Joshua spoke to Yahweh' (verse 12a) to the introduction to this passage, which was much earlier.

Whatever may be the case, this 'miracle of the sun' is without historical foundation. The battle of Gibeon and the Israelites' victory are historical realities, but their importance should not be exaggerated. As we have already seen, they were not connected with a conquest of the south of Palestine by Joshua. They do not even point to an extension of the land held by Israel beyond the limits of the Gibeonite tetrapolis. The text says nothing about this. This Israelite victory did, however, mean that Israel came to possess this particular territory in the face of a reaction on the part of the Canaanites and that was quite important.

VIII. The Settlement in the Highlands of Ephraim

The account of the battle of Gibeon (Jos 10) is followed immediately in the book of Joshua by the story of the battle of the waters of Merom in Upper Galilee (Jos 11). Nothing, in other words, is said about the Israelites' conquering the whole of central Palestine. This is all the more extraordinary in that it is in the book of Joshua that the traditions of the tribes of central Palestine are presented, culminating in the account of the assembly at Shechem (Jos 24). What is more, Joshua himself plays a leading part throughout the book and his land and his tomb were in the hill country of Ephraim (Jos 24:30).

On the other hand, in the geographical part of the book, there is an account which clearly comes from early sources and which was inserted after the descriptions of the lands possessed by the tribes of Ephraim and Manasseh (Jos 17:14–18).[128] In this short text, two versions of the same tradition are placed side by side. The earlier version appears in verses 16–18 – the people of the house of Joseph complain that they have insufficient room in the highlands and that they cannot expand because of the Canaanites, who have iron chariots and are stronger. Joshua tells them that the hill country is covered with woods, but that they only have to clear it. In this earlier version, there is no reference to the Josephites' moving into a new territory, as there is in the later version (verses 14–15).[129]

---

[128] Apart from the commentaries, see A. Alt, *Kleine Schriften*, I, pp. 147–148; E. Nielsen, *Shechem. A Traditio-Historical Investigation*, Copenhagen, 1955, p. 141.
[129] M. Noth, *Josua*,[2] p. 107, who says that this was Transjordania; this is, however, not certain, according to E. Nielsen, *op. cit.* S. Mittmann, *Beiträge, op. cit.* (note 88, p. 585), p. 209ff, 213ff, favours an Ephraimite colonisation of Gilead.

This is, of course, the same hill country in which they settled and in which they had, by hard work, to win themselves more land that could be cultivated. This was a peaceful form of colonisation. The peaceful character of the occupation of the land is emphasised by the explicit statement that there is to be no confrontation with the Canaanites. It is therefore possible to conclude from the fact that there is no reference to armed conflict in this episode and in the other accounts of the conquest that central Palestine was occupied without the use of arms.

This can also be explained at least partly by the human geography and partly by the political geography of the region. The region is divided into two distinct parts. There is the mountainous zone stretching south of Shechem and known as the highlands or hill country of Ephraim in the Old Testament and there is also the more complex zone of hills and valleys extending northwards from Shechem to the plain of Jezreel. The hill country of Ephraim was a region of forest, woodland or brushwood which was only very slowly cleared. Cypress and pinewood were used to build the first citadel at Tell el-Ful during the Iron Age as there were great trees in the district, but almond wood was used for the restoration during the second period of the Iron Age. The account in Jos 17 provides evidence of this deforestation. Because it was so thickly wooded, this region was at first only sparsely inhabited – the Amarna letters, for example, do not refer to any towns between Jerusalem and Aijalon in the south and Shechem in the north. Very few people lived there even during the Israelitic period. Only two relatively important towns between Bethel and Shechem are mentioned in the Bible – Shiloh and Tappuah. From the final account of the excavations of Shiloh,[130] it is clear that the site was heavily occupied during Middle Bronze II. There is, however, very little evidence of occupation during the Late Bronze Age and at the beginning of the Iron Age and no trace at all of any destruction that can be attributed to the Israelites. If Sheikh Abū Zarad is in fact the site of Tappuah, then the Israelites' settlement must have been quite unimportant, since there are no traces of it. There is both archaeological and literary evidence (in the Amarna letters) of Canaanite occupation to the north of Shechem, but this is no longer the hill country of Ephraim. There is in fact a gradual descent towards the plain of Jizreel, where there were many Canaanite towns that were not conquered by the Israelites – Ibleam, Beth-shan, Taanach and Megiddo (see Judges 1:27).

There remains Shechem and its surrounding region. Three important sites have been excavated there – Tell Balātah = Shechem; Tell el-Fār‘ah = Tirzah and Tell Dōtān = Dothan. Shechem was an important town during the Middle and Late Bronze Ages and suffered no major destruction

[130] M.–L. Buhl and S. Holm-Nielsen, *Shiloh. The Danish Excavations at Tell Sailûn, Palestine, 1926, 1929, 1932 and 1963*, Copenhagen, 1969.

between the middle of the sixteenth and the end of the twelfth centuries, at the time of Abimelech (Judges 9). No destruction took place that can be ascribed to Joshua or his period. The same conclusions can be drawn from the excavations that have been made at Dothan, where one large tomb in particular was used without interruption from about 1400 until about 1100 B.C. It is not possible to determine with any degree of certainty from a study of the strata at Tell el-Fār'ah precisely when the Late Bronze Canaanite city was destroyed and the occupation by the Israelites began. Apart from the list of kings conquered by Joshua (Jos 12: 9–24), there is no reference to any conquest of this part of Palestine and, as we have seen, this list is of little use to the historian. The first part is basically a collection of the names of towns mentioned in Jos 1–11 and the second part lists towns which do not appear in any account of the conquest, either in the book of Joshua or anywhere else. Taanach and Megiddo, which were not conquered (see Judges 1), are included in this second part of the list and the last city to be mentioned is Tirzah, almost as if it has been forgotten. Shechem and Dothan are simply not named. According to a recent theory, Jos 12 was used, apart from the stories of the conquest (in the case of Jericho and Ai), as a list of towns at the time of Solomon.[131]

Apart from the references to the town in the book of Joshua, there is also an enigmatic text in Gen 48: 22 which refers to Shechem.[132] Just before he dies, Israel tells Joseph: 'I give you a *s'khem* above (or more than) your brothers, the one I took from the Amorites with my sword and my bow'. This text is very early and it is placed in the book of Genesis just before the chapter of Jacob's blessings (Gen 49), the will and testament which he made before dying in Egypt. This text is, however, clearly the remnant of another testament of Jacob when he was about to die (see verse 21), since he was supposed to have died in the region of Shechem, where the tradition of Israel-Jacob was preserved and where Joseph was believed to have had his tomb (see Jos 24:32). The word *s'khem* means both shoulders and *s'khem* is also the name of the town that was situated between the two 'shoulders' of mounts Ebal and Gerizim. Because of the adjective of number which is used, it can be translated here as one or 'a shoulder', one slope of the mountain, and this usage can be compared with that of *kātheph*, 'shoulder'. It is clearly an allusion to the land that Jacob had acquired near Shechem (Gen 33: 19; Jos 24:32). It is, however, generally agreed that there is at least some word-play here with the name of the town of Shechem, so that it is also possible to translate the text as 'I give you Shechem as the one above your

[131] V. Fritz, 'Die sogennante Liste der besiegten Könige in Josua 12', *ZDPV*, 85 (1969), pp. 136–161.

[132] For this text, apart from the commentaries, especially G. von Rad's and E. Speiser's, see E. Nielsen, *Shechem*, pp. 283–286; H. Seebass, *Der Erzvater Israel* (*BZAW*, 98), 1966, pp. 27–28; A. de Pury, 'Genèse xxiv et l'histoire', *RB*, 76 (1969), pp. 5–49, especially pp. 11–14.

brothers',[133] which clearly points to Joseph's privileged position and is in accordance with the dreams in Gen 37:5–10, a text which also reflects a tradition from the region of Dothan and Shechem (cf. 37:19–20). This tradition of a conquest of Shechem – or of the slope of a neighbouring mountain – is, however, unique. It cannot simply be an echo of Gen 34 and it is quite different from Gen 33:19= Jos 24:32, according to which Jacob *bought* his field. It would seem too that this reference to a conquest by the sword and the bow is recognised in Jos 24:12b and rejected in that text. Various attempts have been made to reconcile these contradictions. Nielsen at first suggested that Jacob acquired Shechem *at the price of* his sword and his bow, in other words, by hiring himself as a mercenary to the Amorites, but later rejected this idea. A. de Pury[134] was in favour of this solution to the problem, believing it to be in accordance with the practices of the Apiru during the Amarna period. Like Nielsen, however, he too ultimately abandoned it, since the text insists on a conquest by force of arms. Neither de Pury nor Speiser was able to find any historically authentic explanation of this text.

There is one explanation which is in accordance with the other texts, biblical history and archaeology. What is presupposed in Gen 48:22 is that Shechem was a separate, additional portion and that the giving of Shechem took place later than the general distribution of lands to the tribes. According to the text, moreover, the patriarch addresses not Manasseh, but Joseph, who is 'above' his brothers. There is therefore also a presupposition that the 'house of Joseph' was a generally recognised entity which enjoyed a privileged position above the other tribes. As we shall see, this points to a period later than that of Joshua. Only one conquest of Shechem by the Israelites is mentioned in the Old Testament and that is the conquest by Abimelech (Judges 9). Furthermore, there is archaeological evidence of only one destruction of the town throughout the whole of this period and this took place in the twelfth century B.C., before which Shechem must have been a Canaanite town. According to the tradition of Gen 48:22, what was done by the remote descendants of Israel-Jacob was reputed to have been done by the ancestor himself. The objection has been raised that a text as early as this one cannot refer to such a late event. I am not convinced by this objection. The text may be an attempt to justify Abimelech's action a little time after the event itself and an affirmation that Shechem was possessed by the Israelites because Israel's ancestor Jacob had conquered it. But, even before Abimelech's violent action at Shechem, the Israelites had been living in the country around the city. They had in fact been living there since the time of the settlement of the tribes and it is clear from the story of Abimel-

---

[133] See Speiser and Seebass.
[134] *op. cit.* (note 132), p. 14.

ech, who was the son of Jerubbaal and a Shechemite woman, that the Canaanites and the Israelites were living together in a kind of symbiosis.

This brings us to another aspect of the settlement of the tribes in this part of Palestine — its political geography. Gen 34 provides us with a certain amount of information about the political situation at Shechem during the age of the patriarchs, the Amarna letters give some details concerning the fourteenth century B.C. and the story of Abimelech supplies political data with regard to the end of the period of the Judges. According to Gen 34, Shechem was inhabited by the Hivites and the town had no king. Hamor, its ruler, was a *nāśī'* or 'prince' (verse 2) and probably an elected leader whose authority was limited by that held by the townsmen (verse 20). In the Amarna letters,[135] Shechem is mentioned only once, in a reference to a certain Lab'ayu 'who gave the land of Shechem to the 'Apīru'. According to the other letters written by him or referring to him, this man Lab'ayu did in fact have relationships with the 'Apīru and he was able to gain control of the whole country from the plain of Jizreel to the frontiers of the kingdom of Jerusalem with the help of the 'Apīru. This is, of course, precisely the region with which we are concerned here. Lab'ayu's two sons continued to exercise the same power.[136]

Lab'ayu's own position is difficult to ascertain. He was never called the king of Shechem and it would seem as though he never in fact was king. He may himself have been an 'Apīru' and even the 'chief of the 'Apīru' referred to in one of the Amarna letters.[137] The fact that much of the land that he controlled was covered with forest is an argument in favour of M. B. Rowton's thesis that these Apiru were people who lived and fought in the brushwood.[138] H. Reviv[139] has discussed Lab'ayu's relationships with Shechem and has attempted to show that he did not originally come from the town, but exercised authority there from elsewhere, by means of a treaty with the inhabitants, who were themselves in charge of the internal administration of the town. Under the terms of the treaty, Reviv has argued, Lab'ayu had the task of defending the people of Shechem and of extending their land.

The situation that prevailed at the time of Abimelech (Judges 9) was very

---

[135] *EA*, 289, 22–23. The letters referring to Shechem and Lab'ayu have been collected together and supplied with a commentary by E. F. Campbell in G. E. Wright, *Shechem. The Biography of a Biblical City*, New York and Toronto, 1965, pp. 191–207.

[136] A. Alt, *Kleine Schriften*, I, pp. 108–110; W. F. Albright, 'The Amarna Letters from Palestine', *CAH*, II, XX, 1966, pp. 18–20.

[137] Published by F. Thureau-Dangin, *RA*, 19 (1922), p. 106 = *ANET*, p. 487.

[138] M. B. Rowton, 'The Topological Factor in the Hapiru Problem', *Studies in Honor of B. Landsberger*, Chicago, 1964, pp. 375–387.

[139] H. Reviv, 'The Government of Shechem in the El-Amarna Period and in the Days of Abimelech', *IEJ*, 16 (1966), pp. 252–257; see also 'Regarding the History of the Territory of Shekhem in the El-Amarna Period', *Tarbiz*, 33 (1963/1964), pp. 1–7 (Hebrew).

similar. Abimelech was the son of Jerubbaal of Ophrah, but his mother was a Shechemite. There was no king of Shechem, but the leaders or 'lords of Shechem', *ba°lē škhem*, are mentioned several times in the text. These lords of Shechem gave Abimelech money to recruit 'worthless scoundrels' ('Apīru perhaps?) and the same lords proclaimed Abimelech king. Abimelech did not, however, take up residence at Shechem. He appointed a representative, Zebul, known as his *pāqîdh* (verse 28) or his governor or leader (*śar*, verse 30). According to verse 28, Abimelech and Zebul were in the service of the Shechemites and it is also possible to conclude from verses 2 and 17 that the situation had been the same at the time of Abimelech's father, Jerubbaal of Ophrah. Lab'ayu and his sons were also, it will be recalled, Shechem's 'protectors'.

One further factor may be added here. During the Amarna period, the hill country of Ephraim was inhabited to a great extent by 'Apiru and Abimelech's 'worthless scoundrels' whom he recruited as his followers certainly resemble the 'Apiru. During the reign of Saul (1 Sam 14:21), there were *'ibh°rîm* = Hebrews in the highlands of Ephraim who had been in the service of the Philistines and who went over to the Israelites after Saul's victory.

It is clear, therefore, that there are striking similarities between the situation during the Amarna period and the period of the Judges. This would lead us to believe that similar conditions prevailed during the intermediate period when the Israelites were settling in central Palestine. There is a close parallel here in the treaty with the Gibeonites, who were, like the people of Shechem, Hivites without a king. The Gibeonites made a treaty with Joshua, who agreed to give them military protection, as the Shechemites probably did with Lab'ayu in the fourteenth century B.C. and were to do later with Jerubbaal and Abimelech. This does not, of course, mean that the situations in Gibeon and in Shechem were identical. They were, however, similar and it is very likely that there was a treaty between the Israelites and the Shechemites, who preserved their autonomy while maintaining good neighbourly relationships with the Israelites. This situation is undoubtedly presupposed in the purely Israelite assembly at Shechem (Jos 24) which was held outside, but not far from, the town.

IX. The Origins of the Tribe of Benjamin [140]

The stories in Jos 1–9 are usually ascribed to the Benjaminite tradition, whereas the story of the battle of Gibeon (Jos 10) and possibly the account

---

[140] See especially K.–D. Schunck, *Benjamin. Untersuchungen zur Entstehung und Geschichte eines israelitischen Stammes (BZAW)*, 86), 1963; H.–J., Zobel, *Stammesspruch und Geschichte (BZAW*, 95), 1965, especially pp. 107–112.

of the treaty with the Gibeonites (Jos 9) are attributed to the Ephraimite tradition. All the territory in central Palestine that we have considered so far in this chapter, then, was to be in the possession of the tribes of Benjamin, Ephraim and Manasseh. Some attempt must therefore be made to trace the origin of these tribes.

The explanation given in Gen 35:18 for the name Benjamin is 'son of the right hand', so that it was regarded as a name of good omen. The primitive meaning, however, is 'son of the south' (yāmîn). A very close parallel exists in the Mari texts of the seventeenth century B.C., in which a tribe called the 'sons (written ideographically and with the plural sign) of Yamina' (south) and another tribe known as 'sons of Shimal' (north) are both mentioned. Each of these two names corresponded to the place where each group lived.[141] It is, however, generally accepted that these Benjaminites of Mari had only their name in common with the Israelitic tribe.

This name is, however, interesting in itself. Although it is possible that this group of Israelites was already known as the tribe of Benjamin before it settled in Palestine, it is much more probable that it received the name of Benjamin in Palestine itself. This group settled, we know, in land south of the territory of the other group of Israelites who entered Canaan at the same time and, as we shall see, this other group, the Ephraimites, took the name of the region in which they settled. This presupposes that the tribe of Benjamin was formed as a tribe after the settlement.

This is clearly indicated in the biblical traditions concerning Benjamin, who was the last of Jacob's twelve sons and Rachel's second and last son. He was also the only one, according to the biblical tradition, to have been born in Palestine.[142] The story of the birth of Benjamin, which caused the death of his mother (Gen 35:16–20, E) is quite different from the stories of the birth of his brothers. What is more, his birth is separated from the others in space and time. Benjamin was born while Jacob was on the way to Ephrathah = Bethlehem and Rachel was buried at Ramah = er-Rām (see 1 Sam 10:2; Jer 31:15). The birth of Joseph as the last son Jacob had in Mesopotamia (Gen 30:24) marks the end of one story and verse 25 is a conclusion. At the beginning of the story of Joseph (Gen 37), everything – and particularly his father's special love for his son Joseph and Joseph's dreams – points to the fact that, in one form of the tradition at least, Joseph was Jacob's last son. This in turn points to the fact that Benjamin was a late tribe.

Leaving aside the group of Judah, which, as we have seen, settled in a

[141] For the Benjaminites of Mari, see G. Dossin, 'Benjaminites dans les Textes de Mari', Mélanges Syriens . . . R. Dussaud, II, Paris, 1939, pp. 982–996; J.–R. Kupper, Les nomades en Mésopotamie au temps des rois de Mari, Paris, 1957, pp. 47–81.
[142] J. Muilenberg, 'The Birth of Benjamin', JBL, 75 (1956), pp. 194–201; J. A. Soggin, 'Die Geburt Benjamins', VT, 11 (1961), pp. 432–440.

special way in Canaan, Benjamin was the southernmost tribe of the group which settled in central Palestine. It was because of this that it was called Benjamin, 'son of the south', although this does not mean that the groups of Israelites which formed this tribe did not come from outside Palestine and indeed from east of the Jordan, as the tradition of Jos 1–9 insists, or that there was not already a certain tribal unity before the entry into Canaan.

These pre-Benjaminite elements did not, however, cross the Jordan alone. Benjamin was closely associated with Joseph. They were both Rachel's sons. They are intimately connected with each other in the story of Joseph and his brothers in Egypt. They occupied neighbouring territories in Canaan and finally, they entered the Promised Land together. In this case, however, we should not think of the 'house of Joseph', which, as we shall show later in this chapter, was formed at a later period, but of one of its constituent elements, Ephraim. We have already seen how Benjaminite and Ephraimite traditions were merged together in Jos 1–10 and how they were preserved in two sanctuaries – the Benjaminite traditions at Gilgal and the Ephraimite traditions at Bethel. These were in fact traditions which were common to both groups and which became separated only after the two groups had settled in Palestine. We have therefore no need to ask whether the figure of Joshua the Ephraimite was introduced later into the stories in Jos 1–10. Joshua clearly belongs to the early common tradition. He was the leader of the groups of Israelites who crossed the Jordan and the part that he plays in the stories in Jos 1–10 is fundamentally historical. The continuation of the story of Benjamin belongs to the period of the Judges.

X. THE HOUSE OF JOSEPH
EPHRAIM – MANASSEH – MACHIR

Joseph was one of Jacob's twelve sons who were the ancestors of the twelve tribes of Israel. He had two sons, Ephraim and Manasseh, and Machir was the son of Manasseh. This is, in brief, the biblical genealogy and, of course, it is the basis on which the classical view is constructed,[143] namely that the ancient tribe of Joseph or a 'house of Joseph' was divided into two tribes, Ephraim and Manasseh, one of the clans of Manasseh being Machir. It is, however, clear from what we have already said about Machir and Manasseh in connection with the settlement in Transjordan that the situation is more complex. The 'house of Joseph' raises certain difficult problems.

Joseph was the name of a person and we have no reason to doubt that Joseph himself was a historical figure. Although the name might have become the name of a tribe, there is no corresponding noun in Hebrew

[143] See, for example, E. Meyer, *Die Israeliten und ihre Nachbarstämme*, Halle, 1906, pp. 287–293, 510; M. Noth, *History*, p. 59–61.

denoting an ethnic group, in other words, 'the Josephite' does not exist. There is also no 'tribe of Joseph' except in two late and doubtful texts. These are Num 13:11 in which the 'tribe of Joseph' appears side by side with the 'tribe of Manasseh' and Num 36:5, in which the 'tribe of the sons of Joseph' is mentioned. The term 'sons of Joseph' occurs in a number of late texts (Num 1:10; 26:28; 34:23; 36:1, which are all P, and 1 Chron 7:29). It also appears in a series of D texts (Jos 14:4; 16:1 ff; 17:14; 18:11; 24:32). On the other hand, in Jos 14:4 and 16:4, the 'sons of Joseph' appear in the order 'Manasseh and Ephraim', which is a clear sign that the text is early, although it does not mean that the term 'sons of Joseph' is early. We have already studied Jos 17:14–18, in which the 'sons of Joseph' as well as the 'house of Joseph' are both mentioned. Verses 14–15 were, as we have seen, a later version of verses 16–18, but verse 14 contains the expression 'the sons of Joseph', whereas the earlier verse 17 has the 'house of Joseph', 'Ephraim and Manasseh', which immediately follows, being an addition. As M. Noth suggests, the term 'sons of Joseph' at the beginning of verse 16 should either be corrected or else it forms an editorial link with the preceding verses 14–15. The term 'house of Joseph' also occurs in Jos 18:5, in a passage which is editorially very mixed.

This term 'house of Joseph' is to be found, however, above all in early texts such as Judges 1:22–23 and 35 and 2 Sam 19:21, where the phrase 'the first of all the house of Joseph' ought probably to be translated as 'before all the house of Joseph', since Shimei was a Benjaminite; and 1 Kings 11:28, according to which Jeroboam the Ephraimite was placed in charge of the corvée labour of the house of Joseph.[144] The term 'house of Joseph' is earlier than the terms 'sons of Joseph' and 'tribe of Joseph', but it does not go back to a period earlier than the beginning of the monarchy (when Judges 1:22–23 was edited). 'House of Joseph' was, at this time, parallel with 'house of Judah' and the latter term appears for the first time in the story of David's election as king at Hebron (2 Sam 2:7, 10, 11) and, what is more, repeatedly in that account. This term marks the end of a development and describes, as we have seen, the whole complex of groups integrated into or assimilated by the tribe of Judah. It is therefore reasonable to conclude that the 'house of Joseph' was formed at the same period and in the same way by a combination of groups which were originally independent of each other. So it does not mark the beginning, but the end of a development.

1. The house of Joseph in the sayings about the tribes

The story of the house of Joseph is to be found above all in the three early

---

[144] For these texts, see E. Täubler, *Biblische Studien*, 1958, pp. 197–200.

poems dealing with the tribes, the Blessings of Jacob and of Moses and the Song of Deborah.[145]

(a) *The blessings of Jacob* (Gen 49). The section of this poem devoted to Joseph (verses 22–26) is as long as that devoted to Judah (verses 8–12) and much longer than any of the sections dealing with the other tribes. It is also more clearly a blessing than the section devoted to Judah. H.–J. Zobel has distinguished different levels in this account, but it is difficult to accept these. Whereas it is said that Judah's brothers will bow before him and that Judah himself will hold the sceptre, it is said of Joseph that the blessings of fertile land will descend on him and that he is apart or consecrated, *nāzîr*, among his brothers (verses 25–26). His special position is due, according to this account, to the fact that God gave him victory over his enemies and especially against the bowmen who attacked him (verses 23–24). The date presupposed must be, at the earliest, the end of the period of the Judges, after the war waged by Ephraim against Benjamin (Judges 19–21). The earliest date of the oracle about Judah is the reign of David; it seems hardly necessary to date it as late as the period after the reign of Solomon. As we have seen, the terms 'house of Joseph' and 'house of Judah' appeared at the beginning of the monarchy. Ephraim and Manasseh are not mentioned in Gen 49.

(b) *The blessings of Moses* (Deut 33:13–17). This is the longest of the three poems and it has many points of similarity with Gen 49, especially the blessing of the land belonging to Joseph, the emphasis on Joseph as consecrated or *nāzîr* among his brother and this tossing of the peoples with his horns. The historical situation presented in this passage cannot be very different from that outlined in Gen 49 and it too must go back, at the earliest, to the end of the period of the Judges. Joseph is not mentioned explicitly in verses 13–16 and verse 17, which says 'such are the myriads of Ephraim, such are the thousands of Manasseh', is an addition. The two elements of the 'house of Joseph', which are not mentioned in Gen 49, are therefore mentioned in this passage, but priority is given to Ephraim, although Manasseh was the elder son. This addition clearly reflects the change which is expressed in another way in Gen 48, to which we shall return later.

(c) *The Song of Deborah* (Judges 5:14). This is the earliest text. It does not mention Joseph or Manasseh, but Ephraim, to which Benjamin is attached, and Machir. At this time, Manasseh had not taken the place of Machir and the house of Joseph had not been formed.

It is possible to add a few details to this outline. As we have seen, the occupation described in Jos 1–10 was carried out by Benjaminite and Ephraimite groups and the tribe of Benjamin took this name only after it had settled in the south of the conquered land. The same can be said of

---

[145] H.–J. Zobel, *Stammesspruch und Geschichte* (*BZAW*, 95), 1965, especially pp. 112–126.

Ephraim, which was, according to its form, originally not a personal, but a geographical name.[146] Just as Judah took its name from the highlands of Judah, so did Ephraim take its name from the hill country of Ephraim. The name may point to the whole mountainous region in central Palestine (see 1 Kings 4:8; Jos 20:7; 21:21), but originally it must have applied to a more limited region. According to 2 Sam 13:23, Baal-hazor = Jebel 'Asūr, five miles to the north-east of Bethel, was 'near Ephraim', which therefore must point to a precise place, probably a village. The suggestion has been made that this village was situated near 'Ain Sāmiyeh, about two miles to the north-east of Taibeh.[147] This, then, was probably the original Ephraim, from which the Ephraimites took their name, and the geographical name of Ephraim was extended, as the Ephraimites themselves expanded, to cover the whole mountainous region.

Manasseh was certainly a personal name. It occurred for the first time as the name of a tribe in the story of Gideon (Judges 6:15); according to this text, Gideon's clan was the weakest clan in Manasseh. The location of Ophrah, Gideon's homeland, is not certain. Until recently, it has been generally accepted that it was at Taibeh, some seven miles north of Beth-shan, but some years ago 'Affūleh in the plain of Jezreel was suggested as a possible site. Both, however, are a long way from the highlands of Ephraim and from Shechem, which was to be allocated to Manasseh when the land was distributed. Nothing precise is known about the origins and the early history of the tribe of Manasseh and it is only possible to suggest hypotheses.

2. Ephraim and Manasseh in Gen 48

We will take as our point of departure the story of the dying Jacob's adoption and blessing of Joseph's two sons, Ephraim and Manasseh.[148] In this story, verses 3–7 are certainly from the priestly source and the other verses combine the two earlier traditions, since there are two blessings of the sons of Joseph (verses 15–16 and 20). Both J and E are recognisable, but it is almost impossible to divide the whole account between the two sources. It would seem, moreover, that the story in Gen 48 is in any case an addition to the story of Joseph, since it is clearly not the continuation of

---

[146] M. Noth, *History*, p. 60; E. Täubler, *Biblische Studien*, pp. 177–187.
[147] H. Seebass, 'Ephraim in 2 Sam xiii 23', *VT*, 14 (1964), pp. 497–500, thought that Ephraim was the name of a district rather than that of a village; this is improbable, but does not affect our thesis.
[148] O. Kaiser, 'Stammesgeschichtliche Hintergründe der Josephgeschichte', *VT*, 10 (1960), pp. 1–15; E. C. Kingsbury, 'He set Ephraim before Manasseh', *HUCA*, 38 (1967), pp. 129–136.

Gen 47:29–31.[149] Basically, two elements can be distinguished. The first of these is the adoption of the sons of Joseph by Jacob-Israel and the second is the preference given to Ephraim rather than to the elder son, Manasseh. We shall consider each of these elements in turn.

(a) The adoption of Joseph's sons[150] is clearly expressed in verses 5–6, according to which Ephraim and Manasseh were to be Jacob's in the same way as Reuben and Simeon and Joseph's sons were to be his. This is a formula of adoption and it is attributable to P. Very much the same is said in a different way in the earlier verse 12, according to which Joseph takes his two sons whom he had placed on his father's knees. This is also a rite of adoption for which there are parallels elsewhere. Bilhah's children were born on Rachel's knees and thus became her children (Gen 30:3) and the children of Machir, the son of Manasseh 'were born in Joseph's lap' (Gen 50:23). Naomi also adopted her grandson, Ruth's son, by putting him on her knees or against her bosom (Ruth 4:16). The term 'may my name live on in them' in the blessing in verse 16 is also an adoption formula. These formulae are parall⟨e⟩ed in the Babylonia laws, although in this case the person adopted was a stranger to the family. In the cases in the Old Testament which are quoted above, the adoption was always within the family, a grandfather or grandmother adopting a grandchild. There is an exact parallel to this at Ugarit, where a man adopted his daughter's son as his own son and transferred all his property to him.[151]

According to the laws of the Ancient Near East, Ephraim and Manasseh had the same rights as Jacob's other sons when he adopted them. In terms of tribal history, this means that the tribes of Ephraim and Manasseh were recognised as Israelitic tribes in the full legal sense, which of course points to the fact that this was not the case before. The classical explanation[152] is the number 'twelve' in the case of the tribes (the twelve sons of Jacob) had to be preserved at all costs and because Levi had ceased to be a political

---

[149] A. Jepsen, *Wissenschaftliche Zeitschrift der Karl Marx-Universität Leipzig*, 3 (1953–1954). *Festschrift Alt*, p. 141.

[150] In connection with the problem of Ephraim and Manasseh and the examples of adoption which we have chosen to compare with the case of the sons of Joseph, H. Donner, 'Adoption oder Legitimation? Erwägungen zur Adoption im Alten Testament auf dem Hintergrund der altorientalischen Rechte', *OrAnt*, 8 (1969), pp. 87–119, especially pp. 108–109, believes that these were not cases of adoption and prefers to speak of a 'legitimation' with the consequences that this entails in family law. The beneficiary was in fact a descendant in the direct line. I also insisted, in my *Institutions*, I, pp. 85–87, that these were not cases of adoption in the strict sense. With this reservation, there seems no reason for not using the word 'adoption'.

[151] *Cf* I. Mendelsohn, 'A Ugaritic Parallel to the Adoption of Ephraim and Manasseh', *IEJ*, 9 (1959), pp. 180–183; F. Vattioni, 'L'adozione di Efraim e di Manasse e Ugarit', *Rivista Biblica*, 8 (1960), pp. 69–70.

[152] This explanation is also accepted by M. Noth, *History*, p. 85 and J. Bright, *History*, p. 143.

tribe, the tribe of Joseph had to be divided into two tribes. As we shall see later, however, current opinions about the twelve-tribe system must be revised and we have already seen that the 'tribe of Joseph' occurs only in two late texts. The explanation that has up till now been generally accepted is therefore unsatisfactory.

We are bound to ask whether this adoption of Ephraim and Manasseh by Jacob does not mean that the two groups originally had nothing to do with the groups of Jacob. Does it consequently also not mean perhaps that Joseph was not a Jacobite? We are bound to ask this question, but it cannot be answered directly and has to be approached from different directions.

(1) *Joseph as the first-born.* In one tradition at least, Joseph was regarded as Jacob's last son and Benjamin was not known. In other texts, however, Joseph is given both the position and the title of first-born.

According to 1 Chron 5:1–2, Reuben was the first-born, but, after committing incest, he forfeited his birthright and it was given to Joseph, son of Israel. It is clear from this text at least that Judah had priority and it is certain that David, a prince, was a descendant of Judah, but that the birthright was Joseph's. Joseph was given Shechem as a portion more than his brothers according to a text that we have already considered in some detail (Gen 48:22). Does this simply mean, as we have said, that Shechem was acquired at a later date by Israel? Or does it perhaps mean that Joseph received preferential treatment as the first-born, who, according to the laws of the Ancient Near East and that of Deut 21:17, had to be given a double share of the inheritance?[153] According to these Near Eastern parallels, a father could give the birthright and a double share of the inheritance to another son who was not the eldest and the father in Israel was only deprived of this right by the law of Deut 21:15–16. We may therefore conclude that the texts of 1 Chron 5 and Gen 48 can only point to this preference, which in turn pointed to the position of great importance that the house of Joseph came to assume in Israel. It may also be an expression of the frequent biblical theme that the youngest son was preferred to the eldest, a theme that is apparent, for example, in the stories of Cain and Abel, Jacob and Esau, and Joseph (his dreams and his conflicts with his brothers, Gen 37).

There are, however, other texts which have also to be taken into account. In Gen 46:4 (E), God tells Jacob that Joseph will close his eyes and, in Gen 47:29–31 (J), Jacob calls Joseph in order to confide his last wishes to him. These are both privileges of the eldest son. Finally, there is the obscure text of Deut 33:17a in Moses' blessing of Joseph. It is possible to translate the Hebrew as 'the first-born of his bull (which is a term denoting manly strength), the glory is in him' or else as 'his first-born bull . . . ' and regard it as a reference to Ephraim, who is the subject of the following verse. It is

---

[153] I. Mendelsohn, 'On the Preferential Status of the Eldest Son', *BASOR*, 156 (December 1959), pp. 38–40.

Joseph, however, who is addressed in this oracle and both Ephraim and Manasseh are mentioned only in the addition at the end of the verse. None of the versions, moreover, has the possessive pronoun; they all have either 'first-born bull' or else 'first-born of the bull'. Whichever may be chosen, in both cases it is clearly a name for Joseph.

None of these texts can be regarded, however, as decisive in itself. All the texts taken together, on the other hand, would seem to point to the existence of a tradition of Joseph as the first-born, particularly as they all come from different sources. But this raises another question – whose first-born son was Joseph?

(2) *Rachel-Leah.* Joseph was in fact Rachel's first-born. Afterwards, Rachel gave birth to Benjamin and died. This is, of course, not strictly relevant to our problem, since the birthright is connected with the father's line. It is, however, quite important to consider this maternal line. According to Gen 30, Jacob's other wife, Leah, had six children. The first four sons to be born were Reuben, Simeon, Levi and Judah and then, after a time, Issachar and Zabulun. Jacob's four other sons were born either to Rachel's or to Leah's slave-girl. Taking this as their point of departure, modern exegetes speak of the groups or tribes of Leah and the groups or tribes of Rachel. They are, however, not agreed about the authenticity of this grouping of the tribes. To mention only two recent but differing opinions,[154] those of S. Mowinckel and O. Eissfeldt, Mowinckel believed that this division of the twelve tribes between Jacob's wives and concubines was entirely without historical authenticity. It was, he claimed, later than the settlement of the tribes in Palestine and the result of a mixture of different traditions, of practical circumstances – the occupied territories – and of political theory. The second of these scholars to express a view, Eissfeldt, thinks that the grouping together on the one hand of Reuben, Simeon, Levi and Judah (Leah's sons) and, on the other, of Joseph and Benjamin (Rachel's sons) points to two different historical situations. In Eissfeldt's opinion there were two groups with different histories, a Jacob-Leah group and a Jacob-Rachel group.

(3) *Israel-Rachel.* It is, however, difficult to accept Mowinckel's view that there was no historical basis for the difference between Leah's and Rachel's group. In fact it is possible to go a stage further. The ancestor of the twelve tribes had two names, Jacob and Israel.[155] According to Gen 32:29, his name was changed in Transjordania, but this episode seems to have been introduced later into the struggle between Jacob and the spirit of the Jabbok.

---

[154] S. Mowinckel, 'Rahelstämme und Leastämme', *Von Ugarit nach Qumran. Festschrift O. Eissfeldt (BZAW, 77)*, 1958, pp. 129–150; O. Eissfeldt, 'Jakob-Lea und Jakob-Rahel', *Gottes Wort und Gottes Land. Festschrift H. W. Hertzberg*, Göttingen, 1965, pp. 50–55 = *Kleine Schriften*, IV, pp. 170–175.

[155] See above, p. 172.

According to Gen 35:9–13, Jacob's name was changed to Israel when God appeared to him at Bethel.

Despite this change of name, both names, Jacob and Israel, are used more or less equally in the chapters of Genesis that follow and to attribute Jacob to the Elohist and Israel to the Yahwist is hardly justifiable. What is more important is that the name Israel occurs most frequently of all in the story of Joseph and especially in Gen 48, where it is used seven times, Jacob appearing only once. It would therefore seem that the name Israel was especially connected with the tradition concerning Joseph and his 'house'. It was, however, also connected with Shechem, where 'Jacob' set up an altar to 'El, God of Israel' (Gen 33:20). This is, in fact, the first time the name Jacob is used since Gen 32:29, where it was, as we have seen, probably late. It is also only a little before the change of the name Jacob to Israel in Gen 35:10. It was also at Shechem that Joshua proclaimed the words of 'Yahweh, the God of Israel' (Jos 24:2). Finally, the story of Joseph begins in the region of Shechem (Gen 37). The name Israel remained linked to central Palestine, both during the reign of Saul and later, when there was conflict with Judah.

Jacob and Israel are both personal names. The fact that the two names were applied to the same individual points to the merging of two originally independent traditions, one acknowledging an ancestor known as Jacob and the other an ancestor Israel. Various recent authors have apparently established the existence of a distinct tradition concerning a patriarch known as Israel.[156] This tradition was connected with a district occupied by the 'house of Joseph'. It was also in this region that Benjamin was born, according to the biblical tradition, and his mother Rachel's tomb was situated. It is therefore preferable to speak, not of a Jacob-Rachel group as Eissfeldt does, but of an Israel-Rachel group, alongside a Jacob-Leah group. According to this tradition, Joseph was the first-born son of Israel and Rachel and this does justice to the texts that we studied earlier in this chapter.

Our conclusion, then, is that the change of name from Jacob to Israel and Jacob's adoption of Ephraim and Manasseh, Joseph's sons, point to the merging together of different traditions and to the association of originally independent groups.

(4) *Joseph and Machir*. We may go back even further in the traditions about Joseph. The story of Joseph begins in the region of Shechem and Dothan and it is precisely in this region that Machir, which was an important group at the time of Deborah, lived, at least in our opinion. One explanation of the name Machir, 'sold' (*mākhîr*), is that they were mercenaries in the service of Canaan or Egypt, but another possible explanation is that the Machirites, the ones 'sold', who formed part of the early group of Israel,

---

[156] V. Maag, 'Der Hirte Israels', *Schweizerische Theologische Umschau*, 28 (1958), pp. 2–28; notably H. Seebass, *Der Erzvater Israel (BZAW*, 98), 1966, especially pp. 1–5, 25–34; A. de Pury, 'Genèse xxiv et l'histoire', *RB*, 76 (1969), pp. 5–49, especially pp. 39–48.

regarded themselves as the descendants of Joseph who had been 'sold' in Egypt.[157] It may even be this very early Israel which is mentioned on the so-called 'Israel' stele of Mer-ne-Ptah.

(b) *Ephraim preferred to Manasseh.* The second element that we have to consider in Gen 48 is the preference given to Ephraim rather than to his elder brother Manasseh in Jacob's blessing. This clearly reflects a change in the situation in which the two groups were placed. According to a recent study,[158] Ephraim acquired predominance in the cult when the central sanctuary of the tribes was transferred from Shechem to Bethel during the period of the Judges. There is, however, another view, which is in our opinion preferable, namely that Ephraim was more powerful politically at the beginning of the period of the monarchy at least. After Saul had died, Abner made Saul's son Ishbaal king 'over Gilead, over the Ashurites, over Jezreel and Ephraim and Benjamin and indeed over all Israel', (2 Sam 2:9). Jezreel was, of course, part of the land of Manasseh; Ephraim included the rest of this land and the 'hill country of Ephraim' extended at that time as far as the plain of Jezreel. This hill country of Ephraim, in the widest sense, was later to be Solomon's first administrative district (1 Kings 4:8) and Shechem, a town of Manasseh, is said, in 1 Kings 12: 25, to be in the hill country of Ephraim. Manasseh is not mentioned at all in the book of Hosea, but Ephraim is named twenty-seven times, either in parallel with Israel (Hos 5:3, 5; 6:10; 7:10; 10:11) or as a name for the northern kingdom as a whole in contrast with the kingdom of Judah (Hos 4:17; 5:10–13; 8:14). Thus, from the beginning of the period of the monarchy, Manasseh seems not to have played any political rôle at all. It is, however, necessary to go back even further in the history of Israel and, if we are to justify what is said in Gen 48, we must try to ascertain whether Ephraim was in fact given priority over Manasseh.

(1) *Manasseh, Joseph's first-born.* The pre-eminence of Manasseh over Ephraim is clearly expressed in the genealogy. Asenath, Joseph's Egyptian wife, bore him two sons, first Manasseh and then Ephraim (Gen 41:50–51, JE; *cf.* 46:20, P). According to another text (Gen 48:6, P), Joseph had other sons after Manasseh and Ephraim, but nothing is known about them. In the distribution of land, the fact that Manasseh was the first-born is recalled in Jos 17:1 and, in Jos 14:4; 16:4, the two tribes are listed in the order Manasseh-Ephraim, although, in Jos 17:7ff, the territory of Ephraim is mentioned before that of Manasseh.[159] In both contexts (Jos 16:9; 17:9), towns are mentioned which are in Manasseh, but which belong to Ephraim.

---

[157] See above, pp. 312–313, 586.

[158] E. C. Kingsbury, *op. cit.* (note 148).

[159] K. Elliger, *ZDPV*, 53 (1930), p. 267, believes that the order in the early document was Manasseh-Ephraim.

Clearly, the editor found it necessary to reconcile the data in his documents which pointed to situations in different periods.[160]

One of these documents clearly had the order Manasseh-Ephraim, which is, of course, also the order followed in the census of the tribes in Num 26:28–37. On the other hand, in the census in Num 1:32–35, Ephraim is listed before Manasseh. It is also useful to compare the figures in the two census lists. The total of adult men for Manasseh in Num 26 is 52,700, but this figure falls to 32,200 in Num 1. For Ephraim, on the other hand, the figure increases from 32,500 (Num 26) to 40,500 (Num 1). However these figures are interpreted,[161] they certainly point clearly to a change in the situation and to the ascendancy of Ephraim. The census list in Num 26 is the earlier of the two.[162]

(2) *Manasseh-Machir*. However, Manasseh was not originally pre-eminent in this way. In the third quarter of the twelfth century B.C., when the Song of Deborah (Judges 5) was composed, Manasseh was not known, since it is not mentioned in the text, but Machir was. As we have seen, Machir, which must have been an important group at that time, later crossed the Jordan, while Manasseh took its place west of the Jordan. Either Manasseh had forced Machir to emigrate into Transjordania or it was a clan of Machir which had remained on the west bank of the Jordan and expanded there.[163] The second hypothesis would seem to be the more probable of the two. Whatever the reason may be, however, it is clear that Manasseh took the place of Machir and this is expressed in a genealogical connection – Manasseh was Machir's father.

Manasseh gradually became more important. At the time of Gideon-Jerubbaal, for example, it was Manasseh who predominated (Judges 6–8). Gideon himself was a Manassite from Ophrah and, in his struggle against the Midianites, he called on Manasseh, Asher, Zebulun and Naphtali (Judges 6:35). He mustered men 'from Naphtali, Asher and all Manasseh' (Judges 7:23) and after his victory he was asked to be king, but refused. As we have said in connection with the story of Shechem, Gideon controlled the whole region. The predominance of Manasseh continued during the reign of Gideon's son Abimelech (Judges 9), who accepted the

---

[160] M. Noth, *ZDPV*, 58 (1935), pp. 203–208, provides an explanation based on the ground that the 'house of Joseph' preceded the tribes, which were differentiated from it. It is not possible to accept this theory.

[161] See G. E. Mendenhall, 'The Census Lists of Numbers 1 and 26', *JBL*, 77 (1958), pp. 52–66.

[162] See M. Noth, *Das System der zwölf Stämme Israels*, Stuttgart, 1930, pp. 23–25. On the other hand, in his commentary on Numbers, *ATD*, 1966, p. 177, he was in favour of the opposite solution. G. Medenhall also thought that Num. 1 was early, but agreed that the figures for Manasseh are difficult to accept.

[163] See above, p. 584

kingship with unfortunate consequences. This was perhaps the decisive event leading to the decline of Manasseh.

(3) *The rise of Ephraim.* In the story of Gideon, Ephraim clearly occupies a subordinate position to that held by Manasseh. Gideon ordered the Ephraimites to fight the Midianites and the Ephraimites brought back the heads of the defeated Midianite leaders, Oreb and Zeeb, to Gideon the Manassite (Judges 7:24–25). The Ephraimites, however, were clearly not happy in this secondary position, because they criticised Gideon for having failed to call on them at the very beginning so that they might have taken a full part in the campaign against the Midianites (Judges 8:1-3). They also made similar claims later, when Jephthah was judge (Judges 12:1–6). They reproached him also for not having summoned them to take part in the struggle against the Ammonites. The consequence of this was that Jephthah enlisted the Gileadites' support and with them defeated the Ephraimites.

Nonetheless, the Ephraimites asserted their superiority in the end. The evidence of this is in the spread of the name of Ephraim to part of the land of Manasseh and in the possession of so many towns in Manasseh by the Ephraimites. There is further evidence in the text contained in Moses' blessings which speaks of the 'myriads of Ephraim' compared with the 'thousands of Manasseh' (Deut 33:17) and in the order Ephraim-Manasseh in the list of tribes. Ephraim also played the leading part in the war against Benjamin (Judges 19–21). It was, in this case, to avenge the crime committed against a Levite of Ephraim that the tribes decided to take up arms and it was at a sanctuary of Ephraim, Bethel, that they came together to prepare for the attack. The pre-eminence of Ephraim was finally established with the setting up of the sanctuary at Shiloh and Samuel's action.

3. Conclusion

With certain reservations, I would suggest the following conclusions with regard to the constitution of the house of Joseph:

Joseph was orginally a hero of Machir.

When Machir was replaced by Manasseh, the tradition concerning Joseph became a Manassite tradition.[164] Manasseh became the first-born of Joseph and Joseph was said to have adopted the son of Machir, the son of Manasseh. (Gen 50:23, E). This is an integration similar to the integration of Ephraim and Manasseh, the son of Joseph, by Jacob.

When Ephraim became pre-eminent and the territory was extended at the expense of the land of Manasseh, the Joseph tradition became common to both Ephraim and Manasseh. This changed situation is explained in Gen 48.

[164] See A. Jepsen, *Festschrift Alt,* quoted in note 149, p. 142.

– It was then that it became normal to speak of a 'house of Joseph' in the early texts (Jos 17:17; Judges 1:22–23 and 35; 2 Sam 19:21). This 'house of Joseph' included both Machir-Manasseh and Ephraim and the members of the house were called the 'sons of Joseph'.

Chapter Twenty

THE SETTLEMENT IN THE NORTH OF PALESTINE
ASHER, NAPHTALI, ZEBULUN AND ISSACHAR

I. THE BATTLE OF THE WATERS OF MEROM AND THE TAKING OF HAZOR
(Jos 10)

1. *Literary analysis*

The structure of Jos 11 is parallel to that of Jos 10:

Jos 11:1–5: Jabin, the king of Hazor, heads a coalition of the kings of northern Palestine in order to fight Israel.	Jos 10–1–5: A coalition is formed between five kings of southern Canaan in order to fight Gibeon, Israel's ally.
6: Yahweh tells Joshua: 'Have no fear of these men'.	8: Yahweh tells Joshua: 'Do not be afraid of these men'.
7–9: caught unawares, the kings are defeated at the waters of Merom.	9–11: caught unawares, the kings are defeated at Gibeon and along the descent of Beth-horon.
10–15: the taking of Hazor and other northern towns.	28–39: the taking of the southern towns (after the insertion of the text on the sun standing still and the Makkedah tradition (verses 12–27).
16–20: summary of the conquest, which includes both the south and the north.	40–42: summary of the conquest of the south.

This is an intentional parallelism, a fact which is emphasised by the use of the same formulae in both chapters. Taken together, the parallel chapters provide us with a picture of the conquest of the whole of the north and the whole of the south of Canaan seen as two military expeditions conducted by Joshua as the leader of the whole of Israel. The composition is the work of the pre-Deuteronomistic 'collector'. The Deuteronomistic editor added various elements, including the list of the early inhabitants of Canaan (verse

3), which is repeated from elsewhere in the book of Joshua (Jos 9:1; 12:8 etc.). This list also contains the Jebusites of Jerusalem, who play no part here.

2. *Exegesis*

Just as the battle of Gibeon forms an authentic historical basis to Jos 10, so too is the memory of a historical event, the victory at the waters of Merom, preserved in Jos 11. Our problem, however, is: when did this victory take place and who achieved it?

This story has a different geographical setting. The waters of Merom, where the battle took place, were not Lake Hūleh, as most scholars believed in the past, but the spring or springs providing water for the town of Merom. The term 'waters of Merom' can be compared with the 'waters of Megiddo' (Judges 5:19), the 'waters of Nephtoah' (Jos 15:9) and elsewhere in the Old Testament the 'waters of Nimrim' (Isa 15:6; Jer 48:34). The town of Merom is mentioned in the geographical lists made in Egypt during the reigns of Thut-mose III and Ramses II and in the account of the campaign conducted by Tiglath-pileser III in Galilee in 733–732 B.C. It has been suggested that the site of Merom is Meirōn at the foot of Jebel Jermak, but this site does not go back before the Hellenistic period. Y. Aharoni thinks that it may have been situated in Jebel Marūn or at Marūn er-Rās and that the precise site was Tell el-Kureibeh, about ten miles to the west of Hazor.[1] Late Bronze pottery has been found there and the site is well-placed strategically at a meeting-point of roads and on a high tableland, permitting the use of chariots in the battle. (The story mentions several times that horses and chariots were prominent in the battle; see Jos 11:4, 6, 9.) The defeated enemy fled over the tableland north-west towards Sidon and north-east towards the Vale of Mizpah. This has been sited as the depression of Merj'oyūn, but it is difficult to be sure of this.[2] Apart from Merom itself, Hazor plays an important part in the story and this town has been sited with certainty at Tell el-Qedah to the south-west of Lake Hūleh. This site has been excavated and we shall come back to it later in this chapter.

The Israelites' enemies named in Jos 11:1 are Jabin, the king of Hazor, and Jobab, the king of Madon. Madon has been sited at Qarn Hattūn, although there is not sufficient justification for this site, and more precisely at the nearby Khirbet Midyān. Madon, however, occurs only in Jos 11:1 and in the list in Jos 12:19, where it is absent in the Septuagint, which has Merom instead, a more probable reading. The kings of Shimron (or

[1] Y. Aharoni, *The Settlement of the Israelite Tribes in Upper Galilee,* Jerusalem, 1957, pp. 95–97 (Hebrew); *The Land of the Bible,* p. 206.

[2] For this and especially for Misrephoth-maim, see N. H. Tur-Sinai, *BIES,* 24 (1960), pp. 33–35; Y. Aharoni, *The Land of the Bible,* pp. 215–216.

Shimon in the Greek) and Achshaph are also mentioned in Jos 11:1, although they are not named and finally, without any precise details given, there is reference to the kings of the 'northern highlands', the plain opposite Chinneroth, the 'lowlands' and the region of Dor. The editor may have extended an early text which mentioned only the kings of Hazor and Merom by name and no others. The kings of Shimron and Achshaph may have been taken from the list of conquered kings (Jos 12:19). It may itself have been traditional – as we shall see, there is both archaeological and extrabiblical support for the affirmation in verse 10, according to which 'Hazor in earlier days was at the head of all these kingdoms'.

The reference to horses and chariots in verses 4, 6 and 9 is interesting. This is the only place in any account of fighting in the whole book of Joshua where they are mentioned, in striking contrast with the statement that the Israelites were not able to stand up against the Canaanites' chariots in Jos 17:16; Judges 1:19. These chariots must clearly have belonged to an early tradition.

Finally, it would be futile to look for aetiologies in this account, one to explain the battle and the other to elucidate the origin of the ruins of Hazor.[3] What we have here is obviously a historical event and we have now to try to ascertain its authenticity.

II. The Relationship between Joshua 11 and Judges 4–5

There is clearly a close relationship between the battle of the waters of Merom (Jos 11) and that of the waters of Megiddo (Judges 4–5), in that in both cases the main adversary of the Israelites is Jabin, the king of Hazor. This obviously has a bearing on our problem. In Jos 11, Jabin personally takes part in the action, whereas in Judges 4 he sends Sisera, the general in command of his army. The battle described in Jos 11 takes place at the time of Joshua, in contrast to the battle of the waters of Megiddo (Judges 4), which takes place at the time of the judge Barak and the prophetess Deborah.

Various solutions have been suggested. The first theory, that there were two kings of Hazor with the same name, is not worthy of serious consideration.[4] Another is that the only historically authentic event was the victory of Barak during the period of the Judges and that the memory of

---

[3] A. Alt suggested this solution rather hesitantly in his *Kleine Schriften*, I, p. 102, note 7 and M. Noth put it forward, at least implicitly, in the case of the destruction of Hazor, in *Josua*,[2] p. 69.

[4] W. F. Albright did not accept this theory, but suggested that the confusion apparent in Judges 4 was caused by an identification of Jabin of Hazor at the time of Joshua with a Canaanite king of the same name at the time of Deborah; see *The Biblical Period*,[3] 1963, p. 102, note 83.

that one victory was divided into two in order to complete the picture of Joshua's conquests.[5] This theory is untenable, however, because the geographical setting is different in each case – the battle of Judges 4 is described as taking place on the plain of Jezreel, whereas the battle of Jos 11 was fought in Upper Galilee. According to a recent hypothesis, both battles were historically authentic and Jabin of Hazor originally featured in both accounts, but the order of the two battles in time should be reversed. The battle of the waters of Merom, in other words, took place after Barak's victory and therefore dates back to the time of the Judges.[6] The victory of Barak-Deborah, which was achieved by the Israelites and resulted in the defeat of Sisera, Jabin's commander, and his allies, was not accompanied by a conquest of Canaanite towns, but it certainly destroyed the power of the Canaanites in the north of Palestine. According to this theory, this victory was followed by another battle in Upper Galilee, the battle of the waters of Merom, which also took place during the reign of Jabin. This second victory enabled the Israelites to control the whole region. Hazor was unable to hold its own and was consequently destroyed. Before this took place, the Israelites had settled in Upper Galilee, where Aharoni has discovered several small sites with remains of the coarse pottery of the beginning of the Iron Age. We must therefore consider the texts in conjunction with the archaeological evidence before turning our attention more closely to this theory and suggesting our own solution to the problem.

III. HAZOR ACCORDING TO THE TEXTS AND ARCHAEOLOGY [7]

According to Jos 11:10, 'Hazor in earlier days was at the head of all these kingdoms' and Judges 4:2 speaks of 'Jabin the king of Canaan who reigned at Hazor'. This is the only biblical text in which a king of Canaan and not only a king of a town of Canaan is mentioned. The exceptional importance of Hazor is confirmed by non-biblical texts and by archaeological evidence.

[5] O. Eissfeldt accepted this as a possibility; see 'Die Eroberung Palästinas durch Altisrael', *WO*, 2 (1955), especially p. 168; *CAH*, II, XXXIV, 1965, pp. 9–10.

[6] This is the solution suggested by B. Mazar, *HUCA*, 24 (1952/1953), pp. 83–84 and developed more fully by Y. Aharoni, 'Problems of the Israelite Conquest in the Light of Archaeological Discoveries', *Antiquity and Survival*,[2] (1957), especially pp. 142–150; *The Land of the Bible*, pp. 200–208; 'New Aspects of the Israelite Occupation in the North', *Near Eastern Archaeology in the Twentieth Century. Essays in Honor of Nelson Glueck*, ed. J. A. Sanders, Garden City, N.Y., 1970, pp. 254–265.

[7] Final reports on the excavations; Y. Yadin and others, *Hazor I*, Jerusalem, 1958; *Hazor II*, 1960; *Hazor III-IV* (plates only), 1961. Summary by Y. Yadin, 'Hazor', *Archaeology and Old Testament Study*, ed. D. Winton Thomas, Oxford, 1967, pp. 245–263. More recent excavations: Y. Yadin, *IEJ*, 19 (1969), pp. 1–19. For the Canaanite Hazor, see A. Malamat, 'Hazor "the Head of All those Kingdoms" ', *JBL*, 79 (1960), pp. 12–19; F. M. Tocci, 'Hazor

The first reference to Hazor is in the Egyptian execration texts of the nineteenth century B.C. The town is also mentioned several times in the Mari letters (eighteenth century B.C.).[8] Hazor was clearly an important town at that time, since the official correspondence refers to ambassadors from Hazor passing through Mari on their way to Babylon or travellers coming from Babylon or other Mesopotamian towns and going to Hazor. The messengers from Hazor and four kings of Amurru came to Mari and tin was sent from Mari to Hazor. In another text, there is reference to various objects that the king of Hazor sent to Caphtor (Crete) and Mari. It is clear that Hazor was situated on an important trade route. In an Assyrian itinerary,[9] Hazor is mentioned as a stopping-place on the road from Lower Mesopotamia to Syria; this route passed through Mari, Qatna and Hazor. The Hazor road is also mentioned in a papyrus dating from the end of the reign of Ramses II.[10] Hazor is included among the towns conquered by Thut-mose III and Amen-hotep II. The town is also mentioned in a list of messengers sent to Egypt at this time by towns in northern Palestine,[11] appearing alongside Chinneroth, Achshaph and Shimron, which are, of course, precisely the places listed together with Hazor in Jos 11. In the fourteenth century Amarna letters,[12] the king of Pihil (Pella) accused the king of Hazor of having taken three of his towns and the king of Tyre wrote to the pharaoh, Amen-hotep III, to inform him that the king of Hazor had left his city and had sought refuge among the 'Apīru. At the same time there are two letters from the king of Hazor himself, in which he declares his loyalty to the pharaoh. It is clearly important that, in contrast to the general practice in the Amarna letters, the king of Hazor is given the title of *šarrum* and, what is even more remarkable, that he himself assumes this title in his letters to the pharaoh. This is unique in the whole of the Amarna correspondence. It is obvious, then, from the prominent place occupied by Hazor in these letters, that Hazor was still exceptionally important in Canaan in the fourteenth century. This is in accordance with the evidence in Jos 11:10 and Judges 4:2.

---

nell'età del medio e tardo bronzo', *RSO*, 37 (1962), pp. 59–64; A. Malamat, 'Hazor and its Northern Neighbours in New Mari Documents', *Eretz-Israel*, 9 (*Albright Volume*), 1969, pp. 102–108 (Hebrew). For Hazor in the Bible, see F. Maass, 'Hazor und das Problem der Landnahme', *Von Ugarit nach Qumran. Festschrift O. Eissfeldt*, (*BZAW*, 77), 1958, pp. 105–117; A. Rolla, 'Gli scavi di Hazor e la Bibbia', *Rivista Biblica*, 7 (1959), pp. 364–368; J. Gray, 'Hazor', *VT*, 16 (1966), pp. 26–52.

[8] See A. Malamat's two articles and the article by F. M. Tocci mentioned in note 7.

[9] A. L. Oppenheim, *The Interpretation of Dreams in the Ancient Near East*, Philadelphia, 1956, pp. 268, 312, 313; W. W. Hallo, *JCS*, 18 (1964), p. 86 and the map on p. 87.

[10] Papyrus Anastasi, I, *ANET*, p. 477b.

[11] Papyrus Golénischeff; see C. Epstein, 'A New Appraisal of Some Lines from a Long-known Papyrus', *JEA*, 49 (1963), pp. 49–56.

[12] See F. M. Tocci's article, quoted in note 7.

The same picture emerges from the excavations made at the site of Hazor, the biggest in the whole of Palestine. It consists of an acropolis and a lower town extending over an area of more than 3275 x 2300 feet, which is more than ten times greater than the area of Megiddo. The acropolis was occupied during the third millennium and during Early Bronze Ages II and III. This period was followed by a gap, after which the site was re-occupied by semi-nomadic people in the twentieth century and at the beginning of the nineteenth century B.C. This occupation was followed by another possible gap, which was in turn succeeded by a period of urban occupation at the beginning of Middle Bronze II B, during the eighteenth century B.C. This was the most flourishing period in the town's history and corresponds to the position that it occupied throughout the Late Bronze Age, especially during the Amarna period, until it was destroyed just before the end of the thirteenth century B.C. When Jos 11:10 says that Hazor was 'in earlier days' at the head of all these kingdoms, this is not simply a reflection of a memory of earlier glory during the Mari period;[13] it is a description of Hazor as it still was when the Israelites arrived.[14]

The town was, however, destroyed and set on fire. The best chronological evidence of this is the presence of Mycenaean III B pottery which has been found in considerable quantities at stratum XIII, the level of the destruction. It has unfortunately not yet been possible to give a certain date to this pottery and all that we can say is that Hazor was destroyed in the second half of the thirteenth century. The lower town was never rebuilt. Above the level of the destruction, there is, however, evidence of a settlement dating back to the beginning of the Iron Age on the acropolis. This is stratum XII and it bears witness to a semi-nomadic occupation with storage pits, dwellings, the foundations of huts and places for tents. Twelfth-century pottery similar to that found in the poorer Iron Age I settlements in Upper Galilee has been discovered at this stratum. Stratum XI has not been found everywhere on the acropolis. It shows evidence of limited occupation without any city walls, but of a stable kind, with several solid buildings including a sanctuary. The ceramic ware dates back to the eleventh century B.C. The Hazor of stratum X was clearly an important town with walls and fortifications. This was Solomon's Hazor (see 1 Kings 9:15).

IV. HISTORICAL INTERPRETATION[15]

When we considered other sites that were destroyed at the end of the thirteenth century B.C., we concluded that they were probably destroyed by

---

[13] A. Malamat, op. cit., (note 7), p. 19.

[14] See Y. Yadin, Archaeology and Old Testament Study, p. 261, note 12.

[15] See especially the works by F. Maass and J. Gray mentioned in note 7.

the Sea Peoples, the Egyptians or other Canaanites rather than by the Israelites. In the case of Hazor, however, the destruction was more probably the work of the Israelites. Because of its dominant position in Canaan, it is unlikely that Hazor fell in a struggle between Canaanite cities. It would seem too that the Sea Peoples never penetrated as far as Hazor and that there could not have been any Egyptian intervention at this time. On the other hand, the archaeological evidence is apparently completely in accordance with the biblical evidence, in that, according to the Old Testament, the Israelites seized Hazor and set fire to the city (Jos 11:10–11), the biblical text adding that the city was burnt (Jos 11:13). The abandonment of Hazor after its destruction followed by a more sparse occupation attested by strata XII and XI is also in accordance with the earliest period of the Israelite settlement, when the people were leaving their semi-nomadic way of life behind and gradually adapting themselves to a more urban pattern.

On the basis of archaeological evidence the destruction of Hazor has been dated at the end of the thirteenth century. This rules out the last of the solutions which we considered above and according to which the battle of the waters of Merom and the taking of Hazor were later than the victory of Barak and Deborah, which has generally been dated round about the middle of the twelfth century.[16] At that time, there was no town at Hazor. The inhabitants were the semi-nomadic people of stratum XII and these people were not Canaanites. The only way in which this theory can be rendered credible is to make the whole of the chronology of the Israelite settlement earlier and to place Deborah in the thirteenth century, which would, of course, be impossible.

There is also no archaeological justification for the other theory, according to which the battle of the waters of Merom and the taking of Hazor were in fact memories of the victory of Barak and Deborah, which took place during the period of the Judges, projected into the period of Joshua. The truth is that Hazor was destroyed during the period which is generally accepted to be that of Joshua and the settlement of the Israelites. To this may be added the textual evidence of Judges 1: 27–33, which is regarded as closer to the historical truth than the stories in the book of Joshua. Hazor is not included among the Canaanite towns in the north of Canaan listed in this passage as not conquered.

The problem, however, still remains – how did the Israelites manage to defeat this Canaanite coalition with its chariot troops, when they did not dare to stand up to the Canaanite chariots elsewhere? How too were they able to take this very strong town of Hazor, which was at the head of all the northern Canaanite kingdoms?

---

[16] A. D. H. Mayes, 'The Historical Context of the Battle against Sisera', *VT*, 19 (1969), pp. 353–360 has suggested the eleventh century, but his reasons are not convincing.

What is remarkable is that the story does not describe a siege or an attack – Hazor is simply taken, according to the text in the book of Joshua, as the consequence of the battle of the waters of Merom, where the decisive action took place. It is also remarkable that this battle of the waters of Merom is not described. All that is said is that the Israelites took the Canaanites by surprise when they were encamped in the open (verse 7). It seems likely that the Israelites' cutting the horses' hamstrings and burning the chariots (verse 9; *cf.* verse 6) was not in fact the consequence of their victory, but rather the stratagem which enabled them to defeat the Canaanites. The enemy, deprived of horses and chariots, took flight and the Israelites were able to seize Hazor, which was without troops, and set fire to it.

Finally, this victory must have involved a large number of groups acting together. According to Jos 11, the action was carried out by the whole of Israel, under the leadership of Joshua. This, however, seems impossible to accept. As we have already seen, the various groups of Israelites which settled in central Palestine did so peacefully for the most part. They halted before the Canaanite towns on the plain of Jezreel, and in the valley of Nahr el-Jalud and Megiddo, Taanach, Beth-shan; these and other towns were not conquered (Judges 1:27). What happened at the waters of Merom and at Hazor took place thirty miles north of this barrier. Other groups were involved in this action and it forms part of a different history. In my opinion, it was clearly an episode in the settlement of the northern tribes. The history of these tribes was different from that of the house of Joseph, just as the southern tribes and the Transjordan tribes also had their own special histories. As we shall see, however, there was a connection with the settlement of the house of Joseph and the person of Joshua.

V. The Northern Tribes

Leaving aside Dan, which did not reach its territory at the sources of the Jordan until much later, after having been driven out of central Palestine (see Jos 19:47; Judges 1:34; 17–18), we have to include among the northern tribes Naphtali, Dan's brother (they were both sons of Bilhah, Rachel's slave), Asher, the son of Zilpah, Leah's slave-girl (Asher's brother Gad settled in Transjordan), and Issachar and Zebulun, who were both Leah's sons, What is most striking in the case of these tribes is that nothing explicit is said in the Old Testament about their settlement, with the result that we can do no more than conjecture.

As we have said,[17] the distribution of the ancestors of the tribes of Israel among Jacob's wives and concubines must to some extent be historically

[17] See above, p. 648.

authentic, but other circumstances could also have played an important part. Naphtali and Dan may well have been half-brothers on the mother's side, since their lands were adjoining. On the other hand, although they lived a long way apart, Asher and Gad were half-brothers with the same mother and some part may have been played here by the analogy of their names, both of which are formed from a divine name. What is more important, however, is that all these four tribes descended from concubines. This may indicate that they were not of pure blood or that they did not participate in the same early history. It may, on the other hand, point to both factors, and this would certainly seem to be the case − far more than the other tribes, these four tribes undoubtedly became mixed with Canaanites and none of them took part either in the descent into Egypt or in the exodus from Egypt.

Issachar and Zebulun were both sons of Leah, but the story of their birth (Gen 30:17–20) is narrated separately from the story of the birth of Leah's other four sons (Gen 29:32–35). Their territory was in Lower Galilee and closest to the land that Leah's other two sons, Simeon and Levi, had in the country around Shechem and were unable to keep (see Gen 34). These four groups may have had a common origin or they may at least have been closely associated originally. Later, Zebulun and Issachar may have remained where they were, while Simeon and Levi were obliged to emigrate to the south of Palestine.

Issachar and Zebulun were in any case very closely linked. A blessing is devoted to them in Deut 33:18–19, which mentions their shared holy mountain. This was undoubtedly Mount Tabor. The boundaries of Issachar's land are not properly defined in Jos 19:17–23, which provides only a list of towns, and, in the outline of countries not conquered by the Israelites in Judges 1:22–33, Zebulun is mentioned, but Issachar is not. According to these texts, then, it would seem as though Issachar and Zebulun were closely associated as a pair of tribes, but that Issachar had originally been part of Zebulun.

The ending -ûn would seem to indicate that Zebulun, z^{e}bhûlûn, was originally a geographical name, and zbl is a place name in a Ugaritic text. The name Issachar has been explained as 'îš śakhār, 'the man who receives a salary'.[18] This name and the origin of the tribe are explained in one of the Amarna letters, in which the king of Megiddo informs the pharaoh, Amen-hotep III, that he is making sure that the land in the region of the town of Shunama is being cultivated by 'men of the corvée' (mazza) brought from the towns of Japhia and Nuribda.[19] A. Alt recognised that

[18] W. F. Albright, on the other hand, has explained the name as Yasaskir, 'may (God) grant favour' and by recourse to the names common in the eighteenth century B.C.; see AOS, 74 (1954), p. 227.

[19] F. Thureau-Dangin, RA, 19 (1922), pp. 97–98; ANET, p. 485b; EA, 365, in A. E.

this text could tell us something about the Issachar.[20] The fertile land around Shunama had been laid waste by Lab'ayu and had become the property of the Egyptian crown, although its cultivation was placed in the hands of Canaanite vassals, who recruited the men to work on the land. Shunama or Shunem was included among Issachar's towns (Jos 19:19). The site of Nuribda is not known, but Yapu, where the other workers came from, is undoubtedly Japhia in the hills of Lower Galilee, which was, according to Jos 19:12, a town belonging to Zebulun. The eastern part of the plain of Jezreel must therefore have been colonised by groups of people coming from Zebulun, who chose to live as serfs on good land rather than as shepherds or herdsmen in a poorer district. This is, of course, what is said in Gen 49:14–15: 'Issachar is a strong ass, lying down in the midst of the sheepfolds. He saw how good it was to take his ease, how pleasant was the country, so he bowed his shoulders for the load, he became a slave to forced labour (mas, corvée).' If this interpretation is correct, the group of Issachar probably formed round about 1400 B.C. (the year, approximately, of the king of Megiddo's letter outlined above) when it separated from Zebulun, which had settled in Lower Galilee at an uncertain date, probably when Simeon and Levi, two more of Leah's sons, were in the Shechem district. According to Gen 49:13, however, Zebulun lived 'by the shore of the sea' and was 'a sailor on board the ships'. Since Zebulun's land never stretched as far as the sea, this can only be explained if we think of the people of Zebulun hiring themselves in service to the coastal cities.

The same may also be said about Asher. According to Jos 19:24–31, the land allotted to Asher extended as far as Carmel and the sea and, according to Judges 5:17b, Asher 'kept by the sea coast ... within his harbours'. North of Acco, however, the Israelites never succeeded in penetrating beyond the mountainous hinterland. A possible explanation of this reference to the sea and harbours is that the Asherites also served there as hired men. It has also been suggested that the name Asher occurs in the Egyptian texts of the fourteenth and thirteenth centuries B.C.[21] This may be the case, but it is no more than a possibility. The attempt that has been made to identify the name Asher with a word in the Ras Shamrah texts, however, has to be rejected. W. F. Albright has suggested that Asher can be compared with certain personal names occurring in the eighteenth century B.C.[22] The genealogy of 1 Chron. 7:30–40 contains several names that can

---

Rainey, *El Amarna Tablets 359-379* (*Alter Orient und Altes Testament,* 8), Neukirchen and Vluyn, 1970, pp. 24–27.

[20] A. A. Alt. 'Neues über Palästina aus dem Archiv Amenophis' IV', *PJB.* 20 (1924), pp. 22–41 = *Kleine Schriften,* III, pp. 158–175, especially pp. 169–174; E. Täubler, *Biblische Studien. Die Epoche der Richter,* Tübingen, 1958, pp. 101–107.

[21] This reference can be found in A. Gardiner, *Ancient Egyptian Onomastica,* I, Oxford, 1947, pp. 192*–193*.

[22] W. F. Albright, *JAOS,* 74 (1954), pp. 229–231, under No. 23; see also S. Yeivin, 'The

be located in the south of the hill country of Ephraim. This may be a memory of an early settlement of certain Asherite groups before they moved northwards,[23] as the Danites did. In view of the date of this text, it is more probable that these were northern groups of Asherites, who came to settle in the lands of the tribes of Ephraim and Benjamin, with which they eventually became integrated.[24]

Naphtali was probably in the first place a geographical name. Jos 20:7 lists the highlands of Naphtali, Ephraim and Judah and the history of the name of Naphtali may well be parallel to that of the names Ephraim and Judah. According to Jos 19:32–39, the land allotted to Naphtali was extremely large and lay to the north of Zebulun and to the east of Asher. It included the heights overlooking Lake Tiberias and the upper Jordan. It is not known precisely when Naphtali settled in this hilly, wooded Galilean country. It is possible that the description 'Naphtali is a free hind' (Gen 49:21) is an allusion to this. There are no signs of Canaanite occupation of this hilly region – these are only found when the hills become lower north of the Jebel Jermak and the fertile tableland begins.[25]

It was in this more densely populated region that the battle of the waters of Merom took place (Jos 11) and Naphtali is the Israelite group that was nearest to Hazor. Naphtali certainly played a part and perhaps even the most important part in this expedition. This theory would seem to be confirmed by the statement in Judges 5:18:[26] 'The tribe of Zebulun fronted death, Naphtali too, on rising ground'. This verse in the Song of Deborah is constructed like the sayings in Gen 49 and Deut 33. Its rhythm is different from that of the rest of the Song of Deborah, and it is furthermore the only text in this Song in which the name of a tribe occurs for a second time – Zebulun is mentioned in verse 14 and it is probable that Naphtali was also mentioned before in verse 15, where the Hebrew has Issachar twice. What is more, the action which took place 'on rising ground' is out of place in the battle described in Judges 4–5, which was fought on level ground. Finally, the formula used for this 'rising ground', 'al m'rômê śādheh, would appear to be an allusion to the name Merom. All these factors entitle us to think that this is an early saying about Zebulun and Naphtali which referred to the battle of the waters of Merom and was inserted into the Song of Deborah between the list of those who did or did not take part (verses 13–17) and the description of the battle itself (verses 19–31).

Either at the level of tradition or at the level of editing, two battles are

---

Israelite Settlement in Galilee and the Wars with Jabin of Hazor', *Mélanges Bibliques* . . . A. Robert, Paris, 1957. p. 98.

[23] A. Malamat, *JAOS*, 82 (1962), pp. 145–146.
[24] Y. Aharoni, *The Land of the Bible*, p. 223.
[25] Y. Aharoni, in the works mentioned in note 6.
[26] H.–J. Zobel, *Stammesspruch und Geschichte (BZAW, 95)*, 1965, pp. 51–52, 80–81.

similarly combined in the prose account in Judges 4, which is independent
of the Song of Deborah (Judges 5). This combination was made easier by
the fact that Barak was a man of Naphtali (Judges 4:6) and that he summoned Zebulun and Naphtali (Judges 4:6 and 10). The enemy was Sisera of
Harosheth-ha-goiim, who was probably a leader of the Sea Peoples. Only
Sisera is named in the Song of Deborah and there is nobody above him. In
the prose account, Sisera is called the commander of the army of Jabin, the
king of Hazor (Judges 4:7, 17), although Jabin himself takes no part in the
action. Within the editorial framework of Deuteronomy, Jabin finally
became the oppressor of the Israelites (Judges 4:1–2 and 23–24). This is the
solution which we seem to be impelled to accept in connection with the
relationship between the accounts in Jos 11 and Judges 4–5.

The battle of the waters of Merom, then, was different from and prior to
the battle of the waters of Megiddo. It was an event which took place at the
time of the settlement of the Israelites in Canaan. It is entirely in accordance
with the history of the northern tribes as we have outlined it and with the
human and political geography of the region.[27] For as long as the Israelite
groups confined themselves to the wooded districts or served the Canaanites
as hired men, the Canaanites did not object to their presence in the land. As
soon as they showed a desire to expand northwards, however, into more
fertile lands and nearer to the roads which led to the Phoenician coast and
the Syrian Beqā', the Canaanites were bound to react and among the
Canaanites affected most directly by this northwards expansion was the
king of Hazor, who controlled the whole region. According to Judges 5:18,
which does not, in our opinion, really belong to the Song of Deborah,
because it describes the battle of the waters of Merom, the victory was
gained in that battle by Zebulun and Naphtali, which were the most important groups. Their action was probably also accompanied by a revolt on
the part of the serfs working for the Egyptians in the Shunem region under
the direction of the Canaanite kings living on the plain of Jezreel. At the
end of the eighteenth century B.C., Egypt was incapable of demanding and
exacting taxes – it was in this way that Issachar probably became independent. In this particular case, then, I accept the theory suggested by G.
Mendenhall,[28] who explained the settlement in Canaan as a peasant revolt.
This historical reconstruction may also be in accordance with the results of
archaeological exploration in Upper Galilee. It should not surprise us that
evidence has been found at Hazor of settlements at the beginning of the
Iron Age I before the first Israelite occupation of the town.[29] Naphtali had,
after all, already settled there before the battle of the waters of Merom and

---

[27] Although I have certain serious reservations, I am mainly indebted here to J. Gray,
'Hazor', *VT*, 16 (1966), especially pp. 49–52.

[28] G. Mendenhall, 'The Hebrew Conquest of Palestine', *BibArch*, 25 (1962), pp. 66–87.

[29] Y. Aharoni in the works mentioned in note 6.

the taking of Hazor. This victory, then, broke the Canaanite hegemony in the north of the country and enabled the Israelite tribes to settle independently. It also made possible the victory of Barak and Deborah, in which Naphtali played a leading part. In this way, everything can be reasonably accounted for in the historical framework.

It was, however, not a victory gained by Joshua or by the house of Joseph, but a victory gained by Naphtali and Zebulun (and Issachar). Does this mean, then, that this victory had no connection with anything that took place in the southern part of Canaan? It must have been more or less contemporary with what was happening further south, since it took place before the migration of Dan and the victory of Barak and Deborah, which occurred early in the period of the Judges. Moreover, it was the groups that came with Joshua which brought Yahwism and the idea of the holy war of Yahweh with them. This element is found in Jos 11, which contains Yahweh's assurance of victory before the battle (verse 6) and the ban imposed after the victory (verses 11–14). This may, of course, have been the work of the pre-Deuteronomistic collector who, as we saw at the beginning of this chapter, constructed Jos 11 as a parallel with Jos 10, in which the idea of the holy war conducted by Yahweh emerges clearly. It is, however, also possible and even probable that the arrival of Joshua's groups with the new faith which they brought with them caused the northern groups of Israelites to move. We shall try to show in the last section of this chapter that Joshua appealed to precisely these groups and commended Yahwism to them at the time of the assembly at Shechem (Jos 24). If the battle of the waters of Merom and the taking of Hazor took place before this assembly, the tribes would certainly have been able to come together more easily and there would have been a good reason for the assembly. If, on the other hand, the victory at Merom followed the assembly at Shechem, then the northern tribes must have been inspired by their new faith in Yahweh. The chronological question is difficult to answer, but it is clear that, in both cases, there were good reasons for the editor of the book of Joshua to include the story of the conquest of the north of Canaan in his general outline of the settlement of the Israelites under Joshua.

VI. The Assembly at Shechem[30]
(Jos 24)

Chapter 24 of the book of Joshua has recently been the subject of considerable interest among scholars. From the historical point of view, it is

[30] Apart from the commentaries, see the following more recent works: G. Mendenhall, *Law and Covenant in Israel and the Ancient Near East*, Pittsburgh, Pa, 1955, especially pp. 1–44; E. Nielsen, *Shechem. A Traditio-Historical Investigation*, Copenhagen, 1955, pp. 86–134;

regarded as the charter which established the league of the twelve tribes or the amphictyony, as it has been called. From the theological point of view, there is a close relationship between the covenant of Shechem and that of Sinai and a formal relationship at least between it and the Hittite vassal treaties. Finally, from the cultic point of view, it provides evidence, according to some scholars, of the existence of a regular feast renewing the covenant.

We must begin our study of the assembly at Shechem with literary criticism. Jos 23 contains the farewell discourse delivered to Israel by Joshua when he was 'old, far advanced in years' (verse 2). In the form in which we have them now, this discourse and its conclusion, describing Joshua's sending away the people, his death and his burial (Judges 2: 6–9), are the work of the Deuteronomist. Jos 24 was added in a second editorial revision which took place during the Exile, although it is based on an early tradition. Those scholars who favour the idea of a Hexateuch believe that it belonged originally to the Elohistic source, whereas others lay greater emphasis on the style, which is that of the Deuteronomist editor, whose contribution is difficult to determine, but must have been considerable.

Having summoned all the people of Israel to Shechem (verse 1), Joshua delivers to them a message that he has received from Yahweh, the God of Israel, who recalls all the interventions that he has made in history in favour of his people (verse 2–13). This is, of course, a historical confession of faith similar to those historical creeds that we have already considered (Deut 26:5–9; 6:21–24), but more fully developed and beginning like Neh 9:7–25, with the departure from Mesopotamia. Points of contact with other passages in the Pentateuch are not lacking, but there are important differences. What is said here, for example, about Balak and Balaam (Jos 24:9–10) is not entirely in accordance with the account in Numbers. Again, it is reported in verse 11 that the people of Jericho fought against the Israelites, which is certainly different from the story in Jos 6. Finally, it is rather surprising that there is no mention at all, in this discourse which was presumably – according to the intention of the editor – delivered at the end of the conquest, of the events narrated in Jos 2–10. It is therefore clear that an independent tradition lies behind this chapter.

This historical prologue is followed by Joshua's appeal to the people to give up the gods that they served 'beyond the River' (and 'in Egypt', which

J. Muilenburg, 'The Form and Structure of the Covenantal Formulations', VT, 9 (1959), pp. 347–365, especially pp. 357–360; K. Baltzer, Das Bundesformular, Neukirchen and Vluyn, 1960, 2nd edn. 1964, especially pp. 29–37; J. L'Hour, 'L'Alliance de Sichem', RB, 69 (1962), pp. 5–36, 161–184, 350–368; H.-J. Kraus, Gottesdienst in Israel,[2] Munich, 1962, especially pp. 160–172; D. McCarthy, Treaty and Covenant, Rome, 1963, especially pp. 145–149; C. H. Giblin, 'Structural Patterns in Jos 24 1–25', CBQ, 26 (1964); pp. 50–69; G. Schmitt, Der Landtag von Sichem, Stuttgart, 1964; V. Maag, 'Sichembund und Vätergötter', Hebräische Wortforschung. Festschrift Baumgartner (SVT, 16), 1967, pp. 205–218.

is missing in the parallels, verses 2 and 15, and is clearly an addition) and to serve Yahweh (verse 14). If they refuse to serve Yahweh, Joshua tells them, they must then serve the gods that their ancestors served beyond the River or the gods of the Amorites, in whose country they were living. Joshua concludes this statement of a remarkable choice with the words: 'As for me and my House, we will serve Yahweh' (verse 15).

It is quite exceptional that a choice should have been offered to the people in this way – elsewhere and in the first place at Sinai, the exclusive service of Yahweh is not simply suggested to the people but imposed on them. It is even more remarkable if those to whom Joshua was speaking, 'This is all the tribes of Israel' (v. 1), had taken part in the exodus and in the event at Sinai and had therefore already decided to choose Yahweh. The only possible explanation of these two verses, which are at the centre of the chapter, is that they represent a very early tradition concerning the assembly at Shechem and that this tradition, which apparently departs from the norm, was not retained in the first Deuteronomistic edition of the book of Joshua. An echo of this early tradition was taken back to the patriarchal era and appears in Gen 35:2–4 (E), according to which Jacob, returning from 'beyond the River', tells his family and all those who were with him to get rid of the foreign gods that they had in their midst.[31]

We may therefore conclude that Joshua was addressing a group of Israelites who had not yet accepted the religion of Yahweh. Their answer is given in verses 16–18, but it is long and full of memories of the exodus and the entry into Canaan from the books of Exodus and Deuteronomy. The editor clearly elaborated on the theme of the early tradition, which possibly contained no more than the final words of this passage: 'We too will serve Yahweh, for he is our God', which are found at the end of verse 15. Verses 19–22 are basically a commentary which make it clear, in the later vocabulary and the theological understanding of Deuteronomy, that the Israelites would be punished severely if they abandoned Yahweh. This second group of verses also seems to be the work of the editor. The early narrative is resumed in all probability in verses 23–24.

Verses 25–28 are also basically early, since they describe how Joshua concluded a b'rîth for the people, laid down a statute and a law for them and set up a stone under the oak of the sanctuary of Yahweh as a witness to the covenant.

Serious attempts have been made to find in this 'covenant of Shechem' the elements forming the Hittite treaties of vassalage. These include:
  an historical prologue
  stipulations

---

[31] See A. Alt, 'Die Wallfahrt von Sichem nach Bethel', *In Piam Memoriam A. v. Bulmerincq*, Riga, 1938, pp. 218–230 = *Kleine Schriften*, I, pp. 79–88; J. A. Soggin, 'Zwei umstrittene Stellen aus dem Überlieferungskreis um Shechem', *ZAW*, 73 (1961), pp. 78–87.

a clause about the preservation of the document of the treaty in a temple
also concerning the public reading of the treaty at regular intervals
a list of gods called as witnesses
blessings and curses.

The only elements that are in fact present in Jos 24 are the historical
prologue and the document itself (the stele). Attempts have been made [32] to
reconstruct the framework by relating Jos 24 to Jos 8:30–35 and Deut 27,
where accounts are found of the law written on stones and read in public
and the blessings and curses are present. The stipulations, the statute and the
ordinance mentioned in Jos 24:25 are to be found, it has been claimed, in
the Book of the Covenant (Ex 21–23), a body of laws which was kept
separate to avoid competition with the Mosaic Law. The Book of the
Covenant, it has been suggested, was taken back to the event at Sinai. The
weakness of this hypothesis is that it appeals to too many uncertain factors
and does not take sufficiently into account the earliest form of the tradition
underlying Jos 24 and especially its essential characteristic, namely that the
people were able to choose to serve Yahweh. In the treaties of vassalage,
service of this kind was not open to choice – it was simply imposed.

These texts (that is, Jos 24; Jos 8:30–35 and Deut 27, together with Deut
31:9–13, a passage outlining the need to read the law at the feast of Tabernacles during the sabbatical year) have also been brought together in an
attempt to reconstruct a feast of the Renewal of the Covenant which, it has
been conjectured, was celebrated as part of a great autumnal feast at
Shechem.[33] There is, however, no evidence, either in the historical texts or
in the religious calendars, that any such feast was ever celebrated.[34]

It is generally accepted by Old Testament scholars that a historical event
was at the basis of Jos 24, but little agreement has been reached as to the
precise nature of that event. H. H. Rowley[35] was of the opinion that an
event going back to the age of the patriarchs was applied to the period of
the conquest. In this context, he has pointed to the group of traditions connected with Shechem. Jacob built an altar at Shechem (Gen 33:20), he concluded a matrimonial alliance with the Shechemites, which was soon
broken (Gen 34) and he buried the images of the foreign gods under the
oak tree at Shechem (Gen 35:2–4). Rowley claimed that the covenant of Jos
24 was connected with these Jacob traditions and was a treaty concluded

---

[32] J. L'Hour, op. cit. (note 30).

[33] G. von Rad, Das formgeschichtliche Problem des Hexateuch, Stuttgart, 1938 = Gesammelte
Studien zum Alten Testament, Munich, 1958, especially p. 44ff; H.–J. Kraus, Gottesdienst in
Israel,[2] pp. 161–171; G. Schmitt, Der Landtag von Sichem, Chapter 3.

[34] See the criticisms made by G. Fohrer, Geschichte der israelitischen Religion, Berlin, 1969, p.
56.

[35] H. H. Rowley, From Joseph to Joshua, London, 1950, p. 126 ff; Worship in Ancient Israel,
London, 1967, p. 58.

between the Israelites' ancestors (perhaps Simeon and Levi) and the Canaanites. This, however, is impossible, since it is explicitly stated in verses 14 and 15 that Joshua's partners in the treaty of Shechem were not Canaanites.

Other scholars confine themselves to the period of the settlement of the tribes for the historical basis of Jos 24. According to G. Fohrer,[36] who is convinced that the words 'my House' in verse 15 have to be understood in the narrow sense, it was simply a question of Joshua's own tribe accepting Yahwism. This explanation does not, however, go far enough, since the whole of Joshua's group, not simply his 'House', believed in Yahweh.

According to E. Nielsen,[37] this religious covenant was concluded between Ephraim, which was Joshua's group, and the group of Machir/ Manasseh. This is more likely to be true, but, in view of our interpretation of the origins of Machir/Manasseh and the relationships between this group and that of Ephraim, we cannot accept it.

E. Sellin[38] believes that faith in Yahweh was suggested, in Jos 24, by the newcomers to Canaan who already practised Yahwism to groups of non-Canaanite people living in the country. M. Noth accepted this theory and developed it further[39] and it has often been revived since his time. In his view, the covenant concluded at Shechem marked the beginning of the federation of the twelve tribes, the founding of the 'amphictyony' and the setting up of Shechem as the central sanctuary where a periodic renewal of the ceremony of the covenant took place. It is, however, obvious that, taken on its own, Jos 24 cannot be used as a basis for conclusions of this kind. It is in fact only possible to draw such conclusions on the basis of other textual evidence elsewhere and, as we shall see, the system of the twelve tribes was constructed after the period of the settlement, the tribes never had an 'amphictyonic' relationship with each other and there was no central sanctuary at the time of the Judges.

If we confine ourselves to the information provided by the early parts of the text of Jos 24, we find that Joshua's partners in the covenant were not Canaanites, but people who had come from 'beyond the River' and were living among the Amorites. They had an origin similar to that of Joshua's group, but they were not acquainted with Yahwism – they had therefore

---

[36] G. Fohrer, 'Altes Testament – "Amphiktyonie" und "Bund"?' *TLZ*, 91 (1966), especially col. 810; in his *Geschichte der israelitischen Religion*, pp. 77 and 81, he gave a little more light and shade to his opinion, concluding that the 'House' was Joshua's tribe and probably the group of tribes in southern Palestine.

[37] E. Nielsen, *op. cit.* (note 30), pp. 126–128.

[38] E. Sellin, 'Seit welcher Zeit verehrten die nordisraelitischen Stämme Yahwe?' *Oriental Studies . . . P. Haupt*, Baltimore, 1926, pp. 124–134, and *Geschichte des israelitisch-jüdischen Volkes*, I, Leipzig, 1924, p. 98 ff.

[39] *Das System der Zwölf Stämme Israels*, Stuttgart, 1930, pp. 65–75; *History*, pp. 91–92, 99–100.

not taken part in the exodus and had not been at Sinai. They were groups of people who were originally related to Joshua's group and with whom Joshua's group came into contact at this point in history, because they were already living in territory bordering the land in which Joshua's group had settled. They accepted Yahwism at this time, with the result that they became associated with Joshua's group, at least in observing certain religious and moral laws.

The only groups which answer to this description are the northern tribes which were to become part of Israel, the people of Yahweh, which did not go down into Egypt, which had immigrated into Canaan and which had the same ethnic origin as Joshua's group. The question that arises in this context is whether the four northern tribes were present at the assembly at Shechem, whether the only tribes to take part in the assembly were the nearest to Shechem, Zebulun-Issachar, or whether those which had joined in the battle of the waters of Merom, Zebulun-Issachar and Naphtali, attended the assembly. This question is interesting, but it is purely of secondary importance. Of first importance is that, once it had been introduced into the north of Palestine, Yahwism quickly spread there. It is, as we have already observed, quite possible that the impetus for Zebulun's and Naphtali's rejection of Canaanite domination was provided by the assembly at Shechem. It is more than possible, indeed it is certain, that the assembly at Shechem prepared the way for the victory of Barak and Deborah half a century later.

The whole viewpoint was, however, changed in the final editing of Jos 24, according to which all the tribes of Israel, not simply the northern or some of the northern groups, took part in the assembly. All these tribes assembled at Shechem had participated in the events of the exodus, Sinai and the conquest (see verses 2–13 and 17–18a), at least according to the editor. On the other hand, there are elements in the editor's references to Yahweh's interventions which are different from the tradition canonised by the Pentateuch and the book of Joshua and there are also omissions. It is therefore justifiable to ask whether the early tradition concerning the assembly at Shechem did not contain a summary of Yahweh's great deeds, precisely in order to convince the northern tribes of their need to accept Yahweh as their God.

Chapter Twenty-One

GENERAL SURVEY OF THE SETTLEMENT IN CANAAN

THERE are, as we have seen, two main theories concerning the settlement of the Israelites in Canaan. The first proposition is based primarily on the historical geography of the territories and also on literary criticism of the biblical texts and an analysis of traditions. Those who support this thesis have concluded that there was no real 'conquest', but that the semi-nomadic tribes infiltrated peacefully into uninhabited or sparsely inhabited territories and into the gaps between the Canaanite cities at a time when no firm control was being exercised by Egypt. This peaceful occupation or taking possession of the land *(Landnahme)* was followed by a period of consolidation *(Landesausbau)*, when, in settling in and developing the country, the tribes came into conflict with the Canaanites. The Israelites' settlement in Canaan, then, took quite a long time and it was characterised by various displacements of people and geographically distinct movements. According to this argument, stories of the conquest of the land in the book of Joshua are aetiological and Joshua himself played practically no historical part at all in them.

The second thesis is based above all on archaeological evidence, which is used principally to resolve the uncertainty that frequently prevails in our understanding of the biblical traditions. In the light of excavations made at the sites, it is clear that several of the Palestinian towns that can be identified with those mentioned in the book of Joshua were destroyed in the second half of the thirteenth century B.C. and were reoccupied shortly afterwards at the beginning of the Iron Age, when a distinctively new culture commenced. The negative archaeological evidence of the excavations at Jericho and Ai has been variously explained. Most scholars have concluded that the biblical account must ultimately be trusted. This points clearly to a conquest, lasting a relatively short time and carried out by the groups of Israelites who came from Egypt with Joshua as their leader. Joshua himself therefore played an important historical part in the settlement of the Israelites in Canaan, according to this theory.

Our aim in this volume has been to try to find a more balanced view. To this end, we have combined the two approaches. Nonetheless, we have given precedence to textual study and have regarded literary criticism and the criticism of traditions as more important than archaeological evidence. The historian's primary source must, after all, always be the texts themselves. Criticism of the texts prepares the way for a historical understanding which is bound to take into account both the territorial situation and external evidence. The most important external evidence in our case is, of course, that provided by archaeology. We have, moreover, followed a geographical order which is more or less in accordance with that followed in the biblical narratives themselves and which is also more or less in accordance with the chronological order of the stages in the occupation of Palestine.

Two general remarks which have often been made are worth recalling here:

(1) The traditions concerning the settlement in Canaan were 'nationalised' when the first written documents appeared and the events were applied to the 'whole of Israel' when in fact they were accomplished by only a part of what was to become the whole of Israel. Nonetheless, certain traditions that were peculiar to certain groups have been preserved and we are able, by means of literary criticism, to discover those who played an active part in the events.

(2) The biblical texts speak of the tribes as already formed and use the names by which they were known when they had been constituted. We are, of course, bound to do the same, but it has to be borne in mind that these tribes only acquired their identity and often only received their names after they had become settled in a territory.

1. *The settlement in the south of Palestine*

There was a movement of peoples into Canaan from the south, that is from the Kadesh district and the 'Arabah. The most important part in this movement was played by groups which only later became integrated into Israel — the Calebites above all, but also the Kenizzites of Othniel, the Jerahmeelites and the Kenites. Two other groups which came with them were the Simeonites and a part of the Levites, who were later to become a priestly tribe. It is also probable that the original group of Judah accompanied these groups. These elements of Simeon, Levi and Judah had probably also been in Egypt, which they no doubt left at a time and by a route which were different from those of the group led by Moses. In any case, the two groups must have made contact with each other at Kadesh because they had in common the faith that had been brought to them by Moses. Later, however, they became separated.

This settlement in the south took place by means of a peaceful infiltration into Canaan. When the immigrants reached the hill country of Judah, which was occupied by settled Canaanites, however, military force had to be used. The chief military operations in the south were the conquest of Hormah, which we have ascribed to Simeon, the conquest of Hebron by Caleb and the conquest of Debir by Othniel. There were also defeats, the most notable being that to the north of Hormah.

It is more difficult to trace the history of the settlement of the group of Judah. The original element of this group was the clan of Ephrathah, which settled at Bethlehem. In all probability, this group also came up from the south at the same time as the Simeonites, taking its name from the hill country in which it settled. The group spread into the west of the highlands of Judah and into the Shephelah helped by covenants with the Canaanites, the three leading clans of Judah stemming from Judah's marriage with a Canaanite woman (the clan of Shelah) and from Judah's incest with another Canaanite woman, Tamar (the clans of Perez and Zerah). No conquest can be ascribed to Judah. It was only during David's reign that the tribe of Judah was finally constituted when the Simeonites became integrated into Judah and the non-Israelite Calebites, Kenizzites and Jerahmeelites were absorbed.

2. The settlement in Transjordania

It is almost impossible to reconstruct the route followed by Moses' group from Kadesh to Moab. The only element of the early tradition that has been retained is that the group was refused right of way by Edom and had therefore to follow the route of the Gulf of 'Aqabah and skirt round Edom by the eastern desert route. The first event that took place in the conquest was the war against Sihon, the king of Heshbon. The Israelites' victory opened the way to the Jordan Valley. This was a historical event, which is not the case with the war against Og, the king of Bashan. The oracles of Balaam and the story of the Baal of Peor point to a situation at the time of the Judges.

It is probable that Reuben played the most important part in the victory gained over Sihon. It was in any case undoubtedly this group which settled in the conquered territory, which stretched from the Arnon to north of Heshbon. It was here that the Reubenites came into contact with the Gadites, who occupied the early territory of Gilead and may have settled there peacefully as early as the patriarchal period. (The treaty between Jacob and Laban may be evidence of this.) They certainly did not go down into Egypt. They accepted Yahwism when the group led by Moses arrived. During the period of the Judges and either during the attacks made by the

Moabites or during the course of the struggles against Gad, or perhaps during both, Reuben became less and less important and was ultimately absorbed by Gad. Neither Reuben nor Gad took part in the conquest of Canaan to the west of the Jordan.

The half-tribe of Manasseh did not settle in the territory between the Jabbok and the Yarmuk before the second part of the period of the Judges. When this settlement took place, it was carried out by the early tribe of Machir coming from the west. It was, at least in part, a conquest by force of arms.

3. The settlement in central Palestine

The stories in Jos 2–9 are in the main based on traditions concerning the sanctuary at Gilgal. This accounts for the cultic elements in the accounts in the stories describing the crossing of the Jordan and the taking of Jericho. The cultic legend of the fall of Jericho obscured the early tradition, which, to judge from the story of Rahab and the spies, described how the town was attacked and taken by the Israelites. This tradition cannot be rejected simply because of the absence of archaeological evidence, nor can the crossing of the Jordan and the taking of Jericho be explained simply as aetiologies. The story of the capture of Ai, on the other hand, is a pure aetiology, without any basis in history, establishing, in the ruins of Ai, the (precise) memory that Canaan was (partially) conquered by force of arms. The details of the story of the taking of Ai come from those of the taking of Gibeah. The fact that there is no archaeological evidence to support the story is very much in accordance with the conclusions drawn from the analysis of traditions.

The treaty between the Israelites and the Gibeonites is historically authentic. It played an important part in the Israelites' settlement in central Palestine and is an example of the way in which their peaceful infiltration of this part of Palestine may also have taken place elsewhere. The victory at Gibeon is also historically authentic, but the extension of the campaign to the whole of southern Palestine, which is in contradiction with the date of the early tradition of Judges 1, is without any historical basis.

The traditions of Jos 2–9 have generally been regarded as Benjaminite traditions and those of Jos 10, which outline the battle of Gibeon, as Ephraimite. In fact, these traditions were common to both tribes, since the two tribes of Benjamin and Ephraim became separate and took their names only after they had settled in the lands in Canaan. One important consequence of this is that Joshua, who was of the tribe of Ephraim, may now be regarded as having played a historical part in all these traditions as the leader of the Benjaminite-Ephraimite groups which crossed the Jordan.

The Israelites settled peacefully in the wooded and sparsely inhabited hill country of Ephraim. Settlement in the land around Shechem, on the other hand, was made possible by means of a treaty with the inhabitants. This can be compared with the treaty concluded with the Gibeonites.

It was Manasseh who settled in the Shechem region. According to the biblical tradition, Manasseh was Ephraim's brother and Joseph's son. Joseph and Benjamin were both Rachel's sons and Rachel's group was connected with the figure of the patriarch Israel. It was the group of Israel-Rachel, which was different from the group of Jacob-Leah, which settled in the whole of central Palestine. Ephraim's pre-eminence over Manasseh and Benjamin became marked only during the period of the Judges and was given cultic recognition when the sanctuary was established at Shiloh. Towards the end of the period of the Judges, the term 'house of Joseph' came to be used, just as in the south of the country there was reference to a 'house of Judah'.

4. The settlement in the north

The history of the Israelite settlement of northern Palestine has to be regarded as quite distinct. The tribes involved in this settlement were Zebulun and Issachar, the sons of Leah, and Asher and Naphtali, the sons of Jacob's concubines. These groups had been settled in the north for an unknown period of time and had not gone down into Egypt. Issachar was part of the tribe of Zebulun and colonised the eastern section of the plain of Jezreel, where they at first served as serfs subject to Egypt. Zebulun and Asher served as hired men with the Canaanites living in the coastal region. Naphtali remained independent, living in the hill country to the east of Lake Tiberias and the upper reaches of the Jordan as well as the wooded hills of Upper Galilee. Naphtali came into conflict with the Canaanites only when an attempt was made to penetrate further north into more fertile territory. This movement may have been accompanied by a revolt against their Canaanite masters on the part of groups of people who were related to Naphtali. The decisive event was the battle of the waters of Merom. In it, Naphtali and Zebulun at least were victorious, defeating a Canaanite coalition led by Jabin, the king of Hazor. This victory was followed by the capture and destruction of Hazor. This event, for which there is clear archaeological evidence, was different from the victory of Barak and Deborah on the plain of Jezreel and preceded it.

Joshua played no direct part in this history. It is, however, possible that the settlement of Rachel's group in the land immediately to the south of the plain of Jezreel gave an impetus to this movement on the part of the northern tribes. Certainly faith in Yahweh and the teaching (and practice) of the holy war of Yahweh were brought by this group of Rachel, led by

Joshua. The battle of the waters of Merom and its consequences are presented as a holy war of Yahweh.

At the assembly of Shechem, Joshua proclaimed faith in Yahweh to groups of Israelites whose origin was the same as his own, but who had not gone down into Egypt. We may conclude that the 'covenant' of Shechem was a religious pact between the northern tribes and the group that had just settled in central Palestine. Both this pact and the part played in it by Joshua himself may be regarded as historically authentic.

5. Infiltration and conquest

If our conclusions are compared with the two theses summarised at the beginning of this chapter, two further conclusions can be drawn:

(1) We accept, as the propounders of the first thesis accept, that the Israelites settled in Palestine partly by infiltrating peacefully into sparsely inhabited regions or else by means of treaties or agreements with the inhabitants. We also recognise that they settled independently and in different ways, according to the territories and the individual groups themselves.

Nonetheless, we insist that there were military operations in each of these regions. The Israelites had to fight against Hormah, Hebron and Debir in the south, against Heshbon in Transjordania, against Jericho and at Gibeon in central Palestine and against Jabin of Hazor in the north. Except in this last case (Hazor), in which pre-Israelite groups had already been settled for a long time in the country, the active warfare is not to be seen as a second stage of consolidation, later than the stage of peaceful penetration; they are two concurrent aspects of the settlement. Those scholars who have insisted on the aetiological character of the stories of the settlement have not always taken sufficiently into account the aspect of conquest, with the possible exception of the story of the conquest of Ai. An aetiological explanation can certainly be justified in many cases, but it ought to be confined to the details of the stories in question rather than extended to the story as a whole. The part played by Joshua in the settlement in central Palestine from the crossing of the Jordan to the assembly at Shechem must above all be regarded as historically well founded.

(2) With regard to the second thesis, which gives such prominence to archaeological evidence, we too have accorded a suitable place to the extrabiblical texts and to the conclusions drawn from surface explorations and excavations made at the sites. These archaeological findings, taken together with textual evidence outside the Bible, are extremely valuable in providing information about the population of Palestine both before and after the arrival of the Israelites. They have helped, for example, to explain the absence of information in the Bible concerning a 'conquest' of the hill

country of Ephraim, the special features of the settlement in the Shechem district and the situation of the northern tribes. They have confirmed the existence of the Canaanite kingdom of Heshbon and the nature of that kingdom. As a final example, we may take the story of the taking of Ai, the purely aetiological character of which has been confirmed by archaeologists.

Nonetheless, we regard it as wrong to overestimate the archaeological evidence and have consequently tried to avoid the error of ascribing all the signs of destruction at archaeological sites to the Israelites. After all, there are very few cases where a precise date has been found for any demolition, and some may, in any case, have been caused by enemies who were not Israelites.

6. *Chronology*

Any chronology of the settlement in Canaan can only be approximate. We can in the first place leave aside the northern groups and the group of Gad which, according to our theory, had already been settled for a long time in part of their lands. We are therefore above all concerned with Joshua's group, which settled in central Palestine after the exodus from Egypt with Moses and before the coming of the Sea Peoples, who are not mentioned in the book of Joshua. The exodus from Egypt took place during the reign of Ramses II, and the Sea Peoples (the Philistines) settled on the coast of Palestine after the Egyptian victory in the eighth year of Ramses III's reign. We have accepted the dates 1290–1224 for the reign of Ramses II, so that the exodus might have taken place round about 1250 or a little earlier. If the biblical tradition concerning a sojourn in the desert for a whole generation is accepted, then the earliest possible date when Joshua's group crossed the Jordan and entered Canaan would be 1225 B.C. The invasion of the Sea Peoples in the eighth year of the reign of Ramses III has, in the light of the most recent studies, been dated at 1175, at least to within one or two years on either side. This allows sufficient time for the Israelites to settle in central Palestine during Joshua's generation.

It is not possible to determine the precise date when the groups related to the Israelites settled in the Kadesh region in the south, although this certainly took place before the exodus. The fact that these groups moved northwards and occupied the highlands of Judah, however, where they established faith in Yahweh, presupposes that they were in contact with Moses' group and were therefore later than the exodus. As a pure hypothesis, it is possible to say that these groups penetrated into the south of Palestine a generation before Joshua's group, which approached Palestine via Transjordania, entered the land.

As far as the north of Palestine is concerned, if there was a connection between the conflict with the Canaanites and the battle of the waters of Merom on the one hand and the assembly at Shechem on the other and if the assembly took place at Shechem at the end of the settlement of the Israelites in central Palestine, then all these events must have occurred round about 1200 B.C. This is the latest date that archaeologists can accept for the destruction of Hazor and it is certainly not out of the question.

The different stages in the settlement in Canaan would therefore seem to have been spaced out in the second half of the thirteenth century B.C. between approximately 1250 in the case of the southern groups and about 1200 in the case of the northern groups, with the occupation of central Palestine taking place from about 1250 onwards. These dates can be no more than an indication and it is certain that some of the tribes of Israel continued to move for some time afterwards. The tribe of Gad, for example, extended its territory by taking land from Reuben. The half-tribe of Manasseh did not become settled in northern Gilead until quite late in the period of the Judges. As we have seen, it is also possible that Asherite groups continued to move for an undefined period. Finally, there is the tribe of Dan. We have more information about the movements of this tribe than about any other and we shall consider them when we come to study more fully the period of the Judges.

PART IV

The Period of The Judges

Chapter Twenty-Two

THE BIBLICAL SOURCES. THE BOOK OF JUDGES

WHAT is known as the 'period of the Judges' is the time between the 'conquest' of Canaan and the institution of the monarchy. Historically, it covers slightly less than two centuries, from the beginning of the twelfth century until approximately 1020 B.C. This is certainly the period according to the biblical tradition, which extends it to include Samuel's farewell discourse (1 Sam 12). This serves to conclude the period of the Judges just as Joshua's farewell discourse (Jos 23) ended the story of the conquest of Canaan. It is followed at once by the story of the kings, which begins (1 Sam 13:1) with a formula similar to those used to introduce all the reigns in Israel and Judah until the fall of Jerusalem. In 1 Sam 12:3–5, Samuel receives confirmation from the people that he has been an impartial judge. In 1 Sam 12:11, he is named together with Jerubbaal and Jephthah as a liberator of the people. Finally, in 1 Sam 7, Samuel's prayer is regarded as bringing about a victory over the Philistines and the passage concludes with the statement that 'Samuel was judge over Israel as long as he lived' (verse 15). Samuel, then, was the last of the judges.

The story of Samuel is, however, enriched by accounts of his childhood and youth (1 Sam 1–3), of the ark in the hands of the Philistines (1 Sam 4–6) and of the part played by Samuel in the institution of the monarchy (1 Sam 8–11). As a result in the book of Judges the story of Samuel became divided from the final arrangement of the historical books and it is therefore quite legitimate for the modern historian to discuss under separate headings the story of the Judges on the one hand and the account of Samuel and the institution of the monarchy on the other. Our only source for the first part of this story is the Book of Judges. First of all, we must consider the difficult problems of literary criticism and of the history of traditions with which this book confronts us.

I. CONTENTS

Although the Book of Judges opens with an editorial note: 'After the death of Joshua' (Judges 1:1), it is not with the period of the Judges, but rather with the conquest of Canaan that the beginning of the book (Judges 1:1–2:5) is still concerned. This introduction consists of a collection of traditions which are independent of those in the Book of Joshua. This passage and the preceding one at the end of the Book of Joshua on the assembly at Shechem (Jos 24) intervene and Judges 2:6 follows directly after the end of Joshua's farewell discourse (Jos 23:16).

The true introduction to the story of the Judges, which suggests that it should be interpreted in a religious sense, is found in Judges 2:6–3:6. The body of the book is taken up with the various narratives which fill the central chapters (Judges 3:7–16:31). There are also two additions in Chapters 17–21. These are independent of each other and are also separate from the story of the Judges. The first (Judges 17–18) deals with the migration of the Danites and the foundation of the sanctuary of Dan. The second of these additions (Judges 19–21) describes the crime at Gibeah and the war against Benjamin. The presence of these two additions in the Book of Judges is justified by the fact that these two episodes belong to the history of the tribes before the setting up of the monarchy (see, for example, Judges 17:6; 18:1; 21:25, 'there was no king in Israel').

Most commentators and historians have distinguished, in the central section of the book, six 'great' Judges – Othniel, Ehud, Barak (and Deborah), Gibeon, Jephthah and Samson – and six 'lesser' Judges – Shamgar, Tola, Jair, Ibzan, Elon and Abdon. Whereas there are more detailed accounts of the 'great' Judges, very little information is given about the 'lesser' Judges. This distinction, however, is not made in the Hebrew text and the criterion used is not valid in every case. In the case of one of the 'great' Judges, for instance, Othniel, the relevant passage (Judges 3:7–11a), apart from the editorial framework, contains no more than a brief reference, without any details, to his victory over the enigmatic figure Cushan-rishataim. What is more, this same Othniel, son of Kenaz, Caleb's brother, also appears in Jos 15:16–19 and Judges 1:12–15 and, if his victory over the oppressor Cushan-rishataim is based on historical fact, then it must have taken place, not during the period of the Judges, but at the time of the settlement of the tribes.[1] Among the 'lesser' Judges, moreover, Shamgar (Judges 3:31), is an intruder, the verse in which he is mentioned having been inserted at a later stage between the passage on Ehud and that on Barak (see Judges 4:1 and the end of 3:31, 'he *too* was a saviour of Israel'). It is very likely that this Shamgar, who is also mentioned in the Song of Deborah (Judges 5:6), was not even an Israelite. The name Shamgar would seem to be Hurrian and the second name 'son of Anath' may indicate that he was a worshipper of the great goddess 'Anat, a Canaanite deity, unless it should be understood in the sense that he came from the Galilean town of Beth-anath, which the Israelites

---

[1] See pp. 545–546.

were unable to conquer (Judges 1:33). From another point of view, however, it is possible to justify the distinction between 'great' and 'lesser' Judges. The former were clearly heroes who saved Israel or who at least, like Samson, attacked Israel's enemies. Apart from Shamgar, who can, as we have seen, in any case be regarded as an intruder, none of the 'lesser' Judges performed any comparable action. Furthermore, different formulae are used for each group. Later on, we shall see the significance of these differences with regard to the literary composition of the book and its historical interpretation.

The stories of the 'great' Judges are also different from each other. The account of the Benjaminite Ehud, who delivers Israel from oppression by Eglon, the king of Moab (Judges 3:11b-30), is unified, whereas the story of the victory achieved by Barak and Deborah over a coalition of Canaanite kings on the Plain of Jezreel is composite and includes a prose account and a song of victory (Judges 4 and 5 respectively). In the prose account, the leading part is played first by Deborah, a prophetess of Ephraim, then by Barak, who came from Naphthali, and finally by Jael, the wife of Heber the Kenite. The main theme in the story of Gideon (Judges 6–8)[2] is the victory achieved by the Manassite Gideon, who is also known as Jerubbaal, over the Midianites (Judges 7) and his pursuit of the conquered enemy beyond the Jordan (Judges 8). Added to this theme, however, are several traditions concerning Gideon – the building of an altar to Yahweh (6:11–24), the destruction of the altar and the sacred post of Baal (6:25–32), the making of an ephod (8:24–27), the oracle of the fleece (6:36–40) and the choosing of the three hundred warriors (7:2–8). Finally, to the story of Gideon is added that of Abimelech and his brief reign at Shechem (Judges 9), with the inserted fable of Jotham (9:8–15).

The list of the 'lesser' Judges (10:1–5; 12:8–15) is interrupted by the story of Jephthah (10:6–12:7).[3] The story itself is preceded by a long introduction which serves as a preface to the accounts of both Jephthah and Samson, the Philistines being named in verses 6 and 7 alongside the Ammonites. In the main narrative, Jephthah the Gileadite is brought back from exile and leads the Israelites to victory over the Ammonites who have been oppressing them (10:17 to 11:11, 29, 32–33). This story is combined with the account of Jephthah's vow and an aetiology of the practice for the daughters of Israel to commemorate the death of Jephthah's daughter every year by lamenting (11:30–31, 34–40) and also with the account of a war between Gilead and Ephraim (12:1–6). The negotiations between Jephthah and the Ammonites are reported in an addition (11:12–28) which is clearly inspired

[2] C. F. Whitley, 'The Sources of Gideon Stories', *VT*, 7 (1957), pp. 157–164; W. Beyerlin, 'Geschichte und heilsgeschichtliche Traditionsbildung im Alten Testament (Richter VI-VIII)', *VT*, 13 (1963), pp. 1–25.
[3] W. Richter, 'Die Überlieferungen um Jephtah', *Bib*, 47 (1966), pp. 485–556.

by Num 20–21 and which raises the question of the territorial rights of Moab rather than those of Ammon. The final verse in the story of this Judge connects Jephthah to the list of the 'lesser' Judges (12:7).

Several different episodes which are independent of each other are included within the story of Samson (13:1–16:31).[4] These are the birth of Samson, his marriage, the destruction of the Philistines' crops, the donkey's jawbone, with a first conclusion (15:20), followed by the episode of the gates of Gaza, the account of Samson and Delilah, the death of Samson and finally a second conclusion (16:31). Although both these conclusions say that Samson 'judged' Israel, he lacks the character both of a 'great' and of a 'lesser' Judge. He is not shown in the biblical story as carrying out the function of a judge or ruler or as liberating Israel. He appears simply as a man who 'resists', in the modern sense of the word, the Philistine oppressors and who was possessed by the Spirit of God. It is these two characteristics which account for his inclusion among the 'great' Judges of Israel, but his story is at once a parallel and an antithesis to the story of Samuel. Like Samson, Samuel was the son of a barren mother and, again like Samson, he was also consecrated to God and 'judged' Israel (1 Sam 7:15–17).

II. COMPOSITION[5]

This analysis of the book of Judges shows that its definitive form was acquired only at the end of a long literary development. Frequent attempts have been made to explain the book as a continuation and a combination of the same sources as those found in the Pentateuch. In recent years, the authors whose writings have most closely reflected this tendency are O. Eissfeldt,[6] G. Hölscher[7] and C. A. Simpson.[8] They are not in agreement about the precise division of the book of Judges according to its sources,[9]

---

[4] J. Blenkinsopp, 'Structure and Style in Judges 13–16' JBL, 82 (1963), pp. 65–76.

[5] A critical review of recent publications in this sphere, that is, between 1940 and 1960, has been carried out by E. Jenni in 'Zwei Jahrzehnte Forschung an den Büchern Josua bis Könige', Theologische Rundschau, 27 (1961), pp. 1–32, 97–146, especially pp. 97–118, 129–136.

[6] O. Eissfeldt, Die Quellen des Richterbuches, Leipzig, 1925; Einleitung, pp. 342–357 (The Old Testament, An Introduction, Oxford, 1965) and the articles and books mentioned in note 9 below.

[7] G. Hölscher, Die Anfänge der hebräischen Geschichtsschreibung (Sitzungsberichte der Heidelberger Akademie der Wissenschaften, Phil.–hist. Klasse, 1941–1942, 3), 1942; ibid., Geschichtsschreibung in Israel, Lund, 1952.

[8] C. A. Simpson, Composition of the Book of Judges, Oxford, 1957.

[9] See O. Eissfeldt, Die ältesten Traditionen Israels (BZAW, 71), 1950, in which the author criticises C. A. Simpson, The Early Traditions of Israel, Oxford, 1948; O. Eissfeldt, Geschichtsschreibung im Alten Testament, Berlin, 1948, in which he criticises G. Hölscher (and M. Noth); C. A. Simpson, Composition, op. cit., pp. 149–196, in which the author criticises O. Eissfeldt.

but this disagreement is not so great that the entire method should be condemned, since those who advocate other solutions agree no better between themselves. It has been more important to show that we cannot trace and follow parallel lines of traditions in the narratives in the book of Judges as we do in the Pentateuch; and this seems to have been definitively established by W. Richter's analysis.[10]

A decisive turning point was reached when M. Noth put forward his theory of a great deuteronomistic history, beginning with the book of Deuteronomy and ending with Kings, composed in the middle of the sixth century B.C. and making use of various sources.[11] For the period of the Judges, two groups of early traditions were used by the Deuteronomist, the first dealing with celebrated liberators belonging to different tribes and the second concerned with a number of men invested with the task of governing in a confederation of tribes; it is this second group of men whom we know as the 'lesser' Judges. Since Jephthah was included in the list of these 'lesser' Judges and a very detailed memory of the part that he played as a liberator of Israel was preserved, the author would have merged the two series of traditions together and extended the title of 'Judge' to the tribal heroes and given these a position of importance in the whole of Israel. Noth suggests that he also integrated all these figures into a chronological system and put forward his own theological interpretation of the period both in his general introduction and within the framework of each narrative. His book probably did not contain the story of Samson and certainly did not contain the appendices in Chapters 17–21.

M. Noth's hypothesis has been widely accepted by scholars and many recent commentators have been inspired by it.[12] Others, however, have hesitated to regard the history of the Judges in the form in which it has come down to us as the work of a single author and have preferred to think of it as the fruit of a continuing current of tradition related to Deuteronomy. Among those scholars who tend towards this view is W. Richter, whose work marks an important new step forward.[13] He claims to have established the existence of a 'book of liberators' containing at least the stories of Ehud, Deborah-Barak and Gideon (and Abimelech) and composed in the Northern Kingdom during the dynasty of Jehu. This book was, he believes, revised (perhaps during the reign of Josiah?) by a first

[10] W. Richter, *Traditionsgeschichtliche Untersuchungen zum Richterbuch (Bonner Biblische Beiträge*, 18), Bonn, 1963.

[11] M. Noth, *Überlief. Studien*, pp. 3–110, especially pp. 47–61, which deal with the period of the Judges.

[12] H. W. Hertzberg, *Die Bücher Josua, Richter, Ruth (ATD)*, 1953, 4th edn, 1969; J. Gray, *Joshua, Judges and Ruth (The Century Bible)*, 1967.

[13] W. Richter, *Traditionsgeschichtliche Untersuchungen, op. cit.*, note 10; *Die Bearbeitungen des 'Retterbuches' in der deuteronomischen Epoche (Bonner Biblische Beiträge*, 21), Bonn, 1964.

editor, who introduced the formulae framing the narratives relating to each hero. At that time, the story of Abimelech was also radically modified. A second editor was, in Richter's opinion, probably responsible for the short section on Othniel, which was introduced as a type or example. This revised 'book of liberators' did not contain the story of Jephthah, which has its own introduction and makes use of different formulae. This story did, however, come from the same background.[14] Richter believed that there was also a third editor, who corresponds broadly to the author of Noth's deuteronomistic history and who had the most important part of all. It was he who was responsible for the theological orientation of the book as a whole, the introductions, the combination with the list of the 'lesser' Judges and the chronological framework. Finally, Richter does not include the story of Samson (Judges 13–16) and the appendices (17–21) in his 'book of liberators'.

Despite all these efforts however, there has been no critical placing of the book of Judges which is completely satisfying. Very different analyses of the introductions to the book have been suggested.[15] It is generally recognised that the descriptions of the 'lesser' Judges are based on early information, but whereas some scholars believe that these descriptions were combined at a very early period with the traditions of the liberator heroes,[16] others are of the opinion that they were added to the deuteronomistic book.[17] Here we shall consider only those results which seem to be most assured and which are of the greatest significance for the historical use of the book.

It is clear that there were certain traditions concerning heroes of the period preceding the monarchy who had 'saved' their clan, their tribe or several tribes from attacks by the Canaanites or by other neighbouring peoples. These traditions were originally handed down orally and frequently in different forms, but quite early during the period of the kings they became the common property of the whole of Israel and were collected together into what may be called a 'book of liberators'. This book con-

---

[14] W. Richter, 'Die Überlieferungen um Jephtah,' *op. cit.,* note 3.

[15] E. O'Doherty, 'The Literary Problem of Judges 1:1–3:6', *CBQ,* 18 (1956), pp. 1–7; A. Penna, 'L'introduzione al libro dei Giudici (1:1–3:6)', *Miscelánea Biblica A. Fernández,* Madrid, 1961, pp. 521–529; W. Beyerlin, 'Gattung und Herkunft des Rahmens im Richterbuch', *Tradition und Situation (Festschrift A. Weiser),* Göttingen, 1963, pp. 1–29; A. Rofe, 'The Composition of the Introduction of the Book of Judges', *Tarbiz,* 35 (1965–1966), pp. 201–213 (Hebrew); N. Stemmer, 'The Introduction to Judges, 2, 1–3, 4', *JQR,* 57 (1966–1967), pp. 239–241; M. Weinfeld, 'The Period of the Conquest and of the Judges as Seen by the Earlier and the Later Sources', *VT,* 17 (1967), pp. 93–113.

[16] W. Vollborn, *Festschrift Fr. Baumgärtel,* Erlangen, 1959, p. 193.

[17] Recent authors who incline towards this view are A. Weiser, *Einleitung in das Alte Testament,*[5] Göttingen, 1963, p. 139; E. Sellin and G. Fohrer, *Einleitung in das Alte Testament,*[10] Heidelberg, 1965, p. 231 (*Introduction to the Old Testament,* London).

tained the stories of Ehud, Barak and Deborah and Gideon with the episode of Abimelech. It probably also contained the story of Jephthah and may have included an editorial framework which clarified the religious significance of these narratives for the whole people. Quite separately, a list of 'Judges' who carried out their special function in certain towns in Israel at certain fixed times was also preserved. The hero Jephthah had been one of these Judges and so he served as a link between the two groups of men and stories. The merging of the two groups was carried out by 'deuteronomistic' editors who added, at various stages which are difficult to define and to date, the passage dealing with Othniel (Judges 3:7–11), which was given as a type-example at the beginning of the stories of the liberators, the composite introduction of Judges 2:6–3:6 and the accounts of Samson, first those in Judges 13–15 and then those in Chapter 16. Since this editorial work is connected with that in the Book of Joshua and goes beyond the Book of Judges to include the books of Samuel and Kings, it is possible to speak of a 'deuteronomistic history', although this cannot be ascribed to a single 'author', as M. Noth has suggested. The deuteronomistic Book of Judges therefore comprises the section of the Book of Judges as we have it from 2:6 to 16:31. At the time of the Exile or during the post-exilic period, various early traditions that had been ignored or rejected by the deuteronomistic editors were added. These were, at the beginning of the Book of Judges, certain traditions concerning the earliest stages of the settlement in Canaan (1:1–2:5) and, at the end, traditions concerning the tribes of Dan (17–18) and Benjamin (19–21), prior to the monarchy.

III. CHRONOLOGY

As we have seen, it was the last and chief editor in this series of deuteronomistic editors who gave the Book of Judges its chronological framework. There are frequent references to time in the book and these profess to comprise a continuous chain. They can, however, be divided into several groups:

1. Periods of oppression:

Cushan-rishataim, 3:8	8
Eglon, 3:14	18
Jabin, 4:3	20
Midian, 6:1	7
Ammon, 10:8	18
Philistines, 13:1	40
	111 years

2. Periods of 'peace' after liberation by a 'great' Judge:

Othniel, 3:11	40
Ehud, 3:30	80
Deborah, 5:31	40
Gideon, 8:28	40
Samson, 15:20; 16:31	20
	220 years

3. Periods of office of the 'lesser' Judges:

Tola, 10:2	23
Jair, 10:3	22
Ibzan, 12:9	7
Elon, 12:11	10
Abdon, 12:14	8
	70 years

To which must be added:

Time of Jephthah, 12:7	6
Reign of Abimelech, 9:22	3
	9 years

It would seem, therefore, that the period of the Judges covered 410 years. The figures of which this total is made up, however, are not all of the same nature. The editor who was responsible for this chronology clearly found precise figures in his sources for the 'lesser' Judges and perhaps also for the periods of oppression, or at least for some of them. He did not, however, find exact figures for the spells of peace which resulted from the actions of Israel's liberators. These are round figures which he himself ascribed to these periods. 40 years is the span of one generation or, more exactly, the length of the active life of an individual. The period of rest of 80 years after Israel's liberation by Ehud clearly also covers the period of Shamgar, for which no figure is given.

This chronology moreover forms part of a much larger structure which includes other historical books. According to the deuteronomistic revision of 1 Kings 6:1, 480 years elapsed between the exodus from Egypt and the beginning of the building of the temple in the fourth year of Solomon's reign. This presupposes that the following data were added to the figures given in the Book of Judges:

Sojourn in the desert and conquest, Jos 14:10	45
Time of Eli, 1 Sam 4:18b	40
Sojourn of the ark at Kiriath-jearim, 1 Sam 7:2	20
Saul's reign, 1 Sam 13:1	2
David's reign, 1 Kings 2:11	40
Beginning of Solomon's reign, 1 Kings 6:1	4
	151 years

If, however, these 151 years are added to the 410 years of the period of the Judges, a total of 561 years is obtained. Frequent attempts have been made to reconcile this figure with that of 480 years given in 1 Kings 6:1. Some exegetes have suggested that the 70 years of the 'lesser' Judges who, they believe, were not originally included within the deuteronomistic book should be taken away from the total number of years. We do not, however, accept this view of the book and the subtraction of 70 years from the total still leaves it too high.

Three recent solutions deserve to be considered here. The first has been suggested by M. Noth,[18] who has rejected the 40 years of Eli's period of office as a post-deuteronomistic addition. He also proposes that the 40 years of Philistine domination extended as far as the liberation of Israel by Samuel according to 1 Sam 7:11ff and that this period can be divided into two equal halves – the 20 years ascribed to Samson (if the story of Samson in fact formed part of the deuteronomistic book) and the 20 years during which the ark was at Kiriath-jearim. If these two periods of 40 years are taken away from the total of 561 years, we are left with a total of 481. The difference of one year between this total and the 480 given in 1 Kings 6:1 can be explained, Noth suggests, if the deuteronomist, bearing in mind the anticipated consecration of Solomon (1 Kings 1), identified the first year of Solomon's reign with the last year of David's.

A similar solution has been put forward by W. Vollborn,[19] who keeps the datum concerning the period of office of Eli found in 1 Sam 4:18b, but prefers the reading in the Greek version, which reduces the period to 20 years. Since neither Samson nor Eli set Israel free from the Philistines, the 20 years of Samson and the 20 years of Eli together make up the 40 years of the Philistine domination and these figures could not therefore have been added. Finally, the 20 years during which the ark was at Kiriath-jearim cannot be included because this exile of the ark does not form part of the history of salvation as such. In this way, which is different from Noth's, W. Vollborn has reached the figure 481. He explains the difference of one year in the same way as Noth explains it.

[18] M. Noth, *Überlief. Studien*, pp. 18–27.
[19] W. Vollborn, 'Die Chronologie des Richterbuches', *Festschrift Fr. Baumgärtel*, Erlangen,

A third solution has been worked out by W. Richter.[20] This scholar has arranged the chronological data in accordance with the formulae used by the editor and varying with the different periods. Going back in time, this method produces the following result: the reigns of Solomon (4), David (40) and Saul (2), a total of 46 years; the periods of Eli, Samson, Jephthah and the five 'lesser' Judges, a total of 136, years; the period of the liberators of Israel, which includes both the periods of peace after liberation by Gideon, Barak, Ehud and Othniel, in all 200 years, and the periods of oppression by Midian, Jabin, Eglon and Cushan-rishataim, in all 53 years, making a total of 253 years; finally the time between the exodus from Egypt and the blessing of Caleb, Othniel's uncle (Jos 14:10), that is, 45 years. Richter has in this way obtained the following table:

Exodus and conquest	45
Period of the liberators	253
Period of the Judges	136
Period of the Kings	46
	480 years

W. Richter rejects the 3 years of Abimelech, the 40 years of the Philistine domination and the 20 years when the ark was at Kiriath-jearim, because these data are expressed in different formulae and are not found in the institutional framework of the other dates. He also rejects the 18 years of the Ammonite oppression, because he regards Judges 10:8 as an addition.

Although this solution is perhaps the best of the three that we have considered here, it is probably not definitive. It is, however, a problem which is of greater interest to the exegete than to the historian. Some of the figures may come from a good source, but the system within which they have been integrated is undoubtedly an editor's construction and it is therefore necessary to use other means in order to establish the chronology of the period of the Judges.

IV. HISTORICAL VALUE

We have just seen of how little use the historical framework which the deuteronomist gave to the Book of Judges is to the historian. The artificial nature of the calculation of the number of years is clear from the recurrence of the figure 40 (four times), the figure 80, which is twice 40 (once), and the figure 20, which is half 40 (twice). It is moreover impossible that the

1959, pp. 192–196.
[20] W. Richter, *Die Bearbeitungen des 'Retterbuches'*, *op. cit.*, note 13, pp. 132–140.

period of the Judges covered as much as 410 years; in fact it lasted less than two centuries.

The Judges – both the 'great' and the 'lesser' Judges – are shown in the book as following one another consecutively and without any interruption, and their activity or authority is presented as extending over the whole of Israel. According to the early accounts, however, it is clear that this was not the case either with the oppressions or with the liberations of Israel. In both cases, the actions reported were obviously very limited in geographical area and involved only one tribe or at the most a few tribes. The great Judges had already gained the stature of national heroes in the 'book of liberators' and it is probable that the order in which these figures were presented there was respected by the deuteronomistic editor. We have, however, no certain way of knowing whether this order was also the historically chronological order. Since the stories of Samson and the two appendices were added at different stages in the composition of the Book of Judges, their position in the book cannot help us to date the events reported in them. The list of the 'lesser' Judges is also based on very early data, but it is is difficult to decide whether these figures possessed an authority which extended beyond their own town and whether or not an editor was responsible for arranging the texts dealing with them in chronological order.

In view of all these uncertainties, it is not possible to write a well-ordered history of the period of the Judges. Despite this, however, the book has considerable historical value. Both the deuteronomistic editorial work and the final editing with the appendices have preserved genuine traditions concerning this period during which the people of Israel was formed and for which the Book of Judges is our only source of information. In it, we are aware of the tribes becoming more firmly settled in the possession of their territories, defending them against pressure from their enemies in the land or against invasion from abroad, fighting amongst themselves to establish a hegemony and preparing the way for the unity which was eventually to be brought about by the setting up of the monarchy. We are also confronted with the social and political crises caused by the people's change from a semi-nomadic way of life to the urban life of Canaan. This encounter with Canaanite institutions also took place in the religious sphere and the Book of Judges shows us how the Yahwism of the semi-nomadic life of the desert was preserved and yet at the same time became adapted to a settled way of life in Canaan and how its institutions developed there. The task of reconstructing this history is both fascinating and difficult.

Chapter Twenty-Three

THE TWELVE TRIBES OF ISRAEL

L IKE the settlement in Canaan, the period of the Judges is presented
by the biblical sources as the common story of the twelve tribes
which had descended from the twelve sons of Jacob and which
formed the people of Israel. The contemporary historian is confronted with
the fundamental question of establishing how this grouping was formed, by
what bonds its members were united and by what institutions this unity was
maintained. The answers given to these questions will be no more
than probable.

THE THEORY OF THE 'ISRAELITE AMPHICTYONY'*

I. THE HISTORY OF THE QUESTION

More than a century ago, H. Ewald gathered together, in connection
with the twelve sons of Jacob, all the references to the twelve tribes, peoples
or cities that he found in the Bible and in Greek or Latin literature and
suggested that a similar grouping might possibly have existed since the time
of the patriarchs.[1] More recently, the sociologist M. Weber described Israel
at the period of the Judges as a warlike confederation with its social order
guaranteed and its prosperity assured by Yahweh. 'Israel', he suggested, was
the name of a cultic league which may have had 'amphictyonic' rites.[2] This
would seem to be the first time that this term was used in this context. It
was, however, employed a little later by A. Alt, who spoke of an 'amphictyony' of Mamre.[3]

---

* This chapter has already been published in 'Studies in Memory of Paul Lapp', HTR, 64
1971), pp. 415-436.
[1] H. Ewald, Geschichte des Volkes Israel, I³, Göttingen, 1864, p. 519 ff.
[2] M. Weber, Gesammelte Aufsätze zur Religionssoziologie, III, Das antike Judentum,²
Tübingen, 1923, pp. 90 ff and 98.
[3] A. Alt, Der Gott der Väter, Stuttgart, 1929, p. 59 = Kleine Schriften, I, p. 55. After the

Making use of converging lines of thought, M. Noth was able to give this theory its definitive form.[4] A study of the various lists of the tribes in the Bible has revealed that, despite certain changes, the figure 12 was always retained and that, within this figure, the six tribes of Leah, the first to settle in Canaan, formed a constant group. The Greek amphictyonies and the Italic leagues provide us with an analogy that we cannot afford to ignore. In these characteristic groupings, twelve (or six) peoples or cities were united by an oath around a common sanctuary, where they gathered periodically for religious feasts. The individual members of these leagues preserved their political autonomy, but their representatives had the task of ensuring that certain rules were observed and of deciding on joint action against any member violating the oath.

According to M. Noth, these elements were found in Israel during the period of the Judges, 'Israel' being the name of a league of twelve tribes with a central sanctuary where the ark was kept. This sanctuary was first at Shechem, then at Bethel, Gilgal and finally Shiloh. It was at Shechem where, according to Jos 24, the tribes acknowledged Yahweh to be their God, where they were united with each other and with God by a pact and where they were given a statute and an ordinance. When they came together each year for the religious feasts at the central sanctuary, the affairs common to the twelve tribes were discussed by their representatives, the twelve n'śî'îm, the list of whom is given several times in the book of Numbers. The tribes were, in Noth's opinion, subjected to an amphictyonic law, which may be represented by part of the Book of the Covenant (Ex 21–23) and to a common law. Transgressions were punished and the action taken by the tribes against Benjamin after the crime at Gibeah (Judges 19–20) should be interpreted as an amphictyonic war.

Noth also extended his theory to cover other aspects of the history of Israel. The task performed by the 'lesser' Judges, the list of whom is given in Judges 10:1–5 and 13:7–15, within this league of tribes was of central importance.[5] The pre-exilic laws of the Pentateuch originated in the amphictyonic law.[6] The whole of the Pentateuch, in which 'Israel' is

---

publication of M. Noth's book, *Das System der zwölf Stämme Israels* (see the following note), Alt described the twelve tribes as a sacred league constituted in the manner of the amphictyonies of Greece and Italy; see his *Die Staatenbildung der Israeliten in Palästina*, Leipzig, 1930, p. 11 = *Kleine Schriften*, II, p. 8. These two studies have been recently republished in A. Alt, *Grundfragen der Geschichte des Volkes Israel*, ed. S. Herrmann, Munich, 1970.

[4] M. Noth, *Das System der zwölf Stämme Israels*, Stuttgart, 1930. *Geschichte*, pp. 83–104 (*History*, pp. 85–108). It must be pointed out that Noth himself says that his theory cannot be proved mathematically, but that it can be accepted if it throws light on the history of Israel and its institutions; see *Das System, op. cit.*, pp. 59–60. He is more cautious in what he says about this theory in his *Geschichte*, p. 88 (*History*, p. 90).

[5] M. Noth, 'Das Amt des "Richters Israels" ', *Festschrift A. Bertholet*, Tübingen, 1950, pp. 404–417 = *Gesammelte Studien zum Alten Testament*, II, Munich, 1969, pp. 71–85.

regarded as a unity, is, Noth believes, a development of the profession of faith in 'Yahweh who brought Israel out of Egypt' and it expresses above all the ideas and convictions which inspired the league of the twelve tribes and which ensured that the league remained united.[7] Noth therefore took this league of the twelve tribes of Israel as the point of departure for his history of Israel, going back from this point to the traditions preserved by the league concerning its origins – the exodus from Egypt, Sinai and the patriarchs.[8]

Noth's views have had a considerable influence on Old Testament studies generally and his theory has become classical. It has been used, often with far less caution than he himself exercised, to throw light on Israel's religion, worship, law and institutions.[9] The way in which this theory has been expounded and in which it explains, or at least seems to explain, a very obscure period and so many aspects of the life of Israel makes it very attractive. In recent years, however, doubts have been expressed about the soundness of the structure set up by Noth. These doubts were hesitant at first, but more recently quite lively objections have been raised, resulting in a need to review the entire question.[10]

II. Greek Amphictyonies and Italic Leagues

In Greece, an 'amphictyony' was, according to the meaning of the word, a league of those who were 'settled around' a common sanctuary.[11] There

[6] M. Noth, *Die Gesetze im Pentateuch. Ihre Voraussetzungen und ihr Sinn*, Halle, 1940, especially pp. 22 ff = *Gesammelte Studien zum Alten Testament*, I, Munich, 1957, p. 42 ff.

[7] M. Noth, *Überlieferungsgeschichte*, especially p. 50 ff, 272 ff.

[8] M. Noth, *Geschichte (History)*, the whole of the first part.

[9] Examples have been provided by S. Herrmann, *TLZ*, 87 (1962), col. 565; G. Fohrer, *BZAW*, 115, 1969, pp. 87–88; in general, see J. Bright, *History*, pp. 141–151; J. A. Soggin, *When the Judges Ruled*, London, 1965, especially pp. 20–22, 33–34, 70–73.

[10] H. M. Orlinsky, 'The Tribal System of Israel and Related Groups in the Period of the Judges' *OrAnt*, I, 1962, pp. 11–20 = *Studies and Essays in Honor of Abraham A. Neuman*, Leiden, 1962, pp. 375–387; C. H. J. de Geus, 'De Rechters van Israël', *NTT*, 20 (1965–1966), pp. 81–100; B. D. Rahtjen, 'Philistine and Hebrew Amphictyonies', *JNES*, 24 (1965), pp. 100–104; G. Fohrer, 'Altes Testament – "Amphiktyonie" und "Bund"?', *Studien zur alttestamentlichen Theologie und Geschichte (BZAW, 115)*, 1969, pp. 84–119, first published in *TLZ*, 91 (1966), col. 801–816, 893–904; *ibid.*, *Geschichte der israelitischen Religion*, Berlin, 1969, pp. 78–83; G. W. Anderson, 'Israel: Amphictyony: 'AM; KAHAL; 'EDAH', *Translating and Understanding the Old Testament. Essays in Honor of Herbert G. May*, Nashville and New York, 1970, pp. 135–151.

[11] The important works dealing with this subject are F. Cauer, 'Amphiktyonia', *PW*, I, 1894, col. 1904–1935; G. Busolt and H. Swoboda, *Griechische Staatskunde (Handbuch der Alterumswissenschaft*, IV, I, I), II,[3] 1925, pp. 1280–1309. For the Pylaeo-Delphic amphictyony, which is the best documented, there has been no full study since that made by H. Bürgel, *Die Pylaeisch-delphische Amphiktyonie*, Munich, 1877.

must clearly have been many of these groupings, but only a few are mentioned explicitly in the early sources and only a little information is given about them. Strabo (IX II 33) refers to the amphictyony of Onchestos in Boeotia gathered around a sanctuary of Poseidon, but we do not know how many members this amphictyony contained. According to the same author (VIII VI 14), there were seven maritime towns in the amphictyony of Calauria, an island in the gulf of Aegina, also grouped around a sanctuary of Poseidon.[12] Delos, the sacred island of Apollo, was the centre of an amphictyony. What we know above all about this amphictyony is the part that it played in the imperialist policy of Athens.

The best known and the most important of the Greek amphictyonies is the Pylaeo-Delphic amphictyony. Its origins are obscure. It was first set up by certain towns around the sanctuary of Demeter at Anthēla, at Thermopylae. It may not have been before the beginning of the sixth century B.C. that this amphictyony included Delphi, the prestige of which was assured by the sanctuary of Apollo and the oracle of the Pythia. At that time it certainly consisted of twelve peoples from central Greece, each of which sent two representatives or sacred recorders (hieromnēmon) to the amphictyonic council, the presidents of which were the Thessalian representatives. The composition of this amphictyony was not constant, but, until the time of the changes imposed by the Roman Empire, there were always twelve members. The council met twice each year at Thermopylae and Delphi. Its main task was to protect and maintain the two federal sanctuaries. The members of the league took an oath 'agreeing not to destroy any town of the amphictyonic league, not to cut off the waters supplying the towns either in times of war or in times of peace and, if anyone violated these prescriptions, to march against him and to overthrow his towns and, if anyone plundered the treasures of the god or was an accomplice in any act of profanation or tried to lay hands on the sacred things, to join their hands, feet, voices and all their strength to punish him'.[13] The amphictyonic law of 380 B.C. that was discovered at Delphi instructed the sacred recorders to pass the most just sentences in any trials, but, in the text that follows, what is stressed is the limited and strictly religious nature of their powers. They had to keep guard over the sacred plain and punish anyone who attempted to cultivate it, take care of the cultic statues, keep the temples of Apollo and Athēna Pronoia in a good condition, see to the upkeep of the roads and bridges that enabled the pilgrims to reach Delphi and manage the god's finances.

In the case of the Pylaeo-Delphic amphictyony, which is the best documented, certain fundamental aspects of the Greek amphictyonic system can be distinguished. These amphictyonies were above all local or regional

---

[12] J. Penrose-Harland, 'The Calaurian Amphictyony', AJA, 29 (1925), pp. 160–171.
[13] Aeschines, Amb. 115.

institutions with an essentially religious character. They only took either in-direct or occasional political action when they were used to further the am-bitions of one or other of their more powerful members. At no time did they ever form a stage on the way to setting up a wider political unity than that of the city.

Although in the early sources the name 'amphictyony' is not used of the leagues of certain Greek cities in Asia Minor that were grouped around a common sanctuary, there is a similarity between these leagues and the Greek amphictyonies proper. The most important is the league of ten Ionian cities set up in the eighth century B.C. The number of member cities in this league was increased to twelve with the inclusion of the islands of Chios and Samos. The central sanctuary of Melia, dedicated to Poseidon, became the federal sanctuary and was given the name of Panionion.[14] Further to the north, twelve cities of the Aeolic were grouped around the sanctuary of Apollo at Grynion. Their number was reduced to eleven when Smyrna fell into the hands of the Ionians.[15] To the south, at Rhodes and along the neighbouring coast, six Dorian towns were united in the worship of Apollo at Cape Triopion. Their number was reduced to five when Halicarnassus was excluded from the league.[16] Unfortunately, we possess little information about the history of these leagues or about the way in which they functioned.

In Italy,[17] a comparable league was that formed by the twelve little states of southern Etruria, the *duodecim populi Etruriae*.[18] The representatives of these states met each year at the sanctuary of the goddess Voltumna, which was probably on the territory of Volsinii.[19] They formed the *concilium Etruriae* and elected a leader who was first called the 'king' and then the 'priest'. None of the ancient authors has provided us with the list of these twelve peoples. We know nothing about the way in which the league functioned. Evidence has, however, been provided by Livy that the member states met at the sanctuary of Voltumna between 434 and 389 B.C. (IV, 23, 5 and VI, 2, 2). The origin of the league was undoubtedly cultic. One after another the Etruscan towns fell and were subjugated by Rome and, when, at the time of the Roman Empire, references to the *praetor* and

---

[14] L. Ziehen, 'Paniônia', *PW*, XVIII, 3, 1949, col. 601–605; H. Bengtson, *Griechische Geschichte (Handbuch der Altertumswissenschaft, II, 4),*[2] Munich, 1960, pp. 56–57; J. M. Cook, *The Greeks in Ionia and the East*, London, 1962, p. 34.

[15] J. M. Cook, *op. cit.*, p. 26.

[16] J. M. Cook, *op. cit.*, p. 30.

[17] V. Bellini, 'Sulla genesi e la struttura delle leghe nell' Italia arcaica', *RIDA*, IIIe series, 7 1960), pp. 273–305; 8 (1961), pp. 167–227; II (1964), pp. 95–120.

[18] For the Etruscan league, apart from the first article by V. Bellini in note 17 above, see A. Pallottino, *La civilisation étrusque*, Paris, 1949, pp. 134–138; Luisa Banti, *Die Welt der Etrusker*, Stuttgart, 1960, pp. 130–132; R. Bloch, *The Etruscans*, London, 1965, pp. 116–117.

[19] W. Eisenhut, 'Voltumna', *PW*, IX, A, I, 1961, col. 850–851.

to the 'fifteen (sic) peoples of Etruria' survived, these were no more than memories of a distant past. The 'twelve peoples' of Padanian Etruria and the 'twelve peoples' of Etruscan Campania are also mentioned by the ancient authors, but we know nothing about them. In pre-Roman southern Italy, Latin authors mention in passing the 'twelve peoples' of Brutium, the Iapygi, the Messaepians and the Poediculi, but we know nothing of the religious or political nature of these groupings or of their reality. There are also vague references to the 'thirty peoples' of the Latium.

It is also possible to draw parallels with other parts of the world and other periods of history. Scandinavia provides us with such possibilities. Before the arrival of the Vikings, for example, there were, in Sweden, leagues of 'ten regions', joined in a federation and with a central sanctuary at Uppsala, where the members met every nine years and solemnly renewed their union. This was certainly an institution with a religious basis and supreme authority was exercised by a priest. The equivalent is also found in ancient Iceland, Norway and Denmark.[20]

What we have here, then, is clearly an institution which seems to have been widespread among the Indo-European peoples, although it took different forms. The earliest examples known to us, however, are all later than the beginning of the first millennium before our era. The system of the twelve tribes of Israel belongs to a very different ethnic and cultural environment and it is also earlier. What is more, the information that we possess concerning these amphictyonies or leagues is uneven and on the whole very incomplete. There is only one of these groupings for which we have relatively good information about its history and the way in which it functioned and that is the Pylaeo-Delphic amphictyony; and even then our knowledge is confined to the period from the sixth century B.C. onwards. It would therefore be unwise to take this privileged example of a different civilisation and of a different period as a means of explaining the grouping of the twelve tribes of Israel and of reconstructing an Israelite 'amphictyony' on the Greek model.

III. THE TWELVE TRIBES DID NOT FORM AN AMPHICTYONY

Many different kinds of political institution existed in the great Semitic world, but there was never anything resembling a Greek amphictyony.[21]

---

[20] M. Scovazzi, 'L'ordinamento gentilizio dei populi nordici e la prima costituzione di stati territoriali nell'Alto Medio Evo', *Dalla tribù allo stato (Problemi attuali di scienza e di cultura*, Accademia Nazionale dei Lincei), Rome, 1962, pp. 83–121. The author calls these federations 'amphictyonies'.

[21] G. Fohrer, *BZAW* 115 (see above, note 10), p. 92; G. W. Anderson (see also note 10), p. 144.

There have certainly been allusions in recent years to a 'Sumerian amphictyony' — it has been pointed out that, during the Third Dynasty of Ur, at the end of the third millennium, the cities of Sumer and Akkad had in turn to provide for the needs of the sanctuaries of Nippur, the national religious centre, for twelve months of the year. The list and the order of those who had to contribute to the provisioning of the sanctuaries changed, however, from one year to the next and smaller cities shared the task during the same month, whereas larger cities contributed alone for two months or more.[22] This practice is clearly not in accordance with the definition of an amphictyony. On the contrary, it recalls the monthly provisions that the twelve administrators appointed by Solomon had to supply to the king's palace (1 Kings 4:7; 5:7–8). It has also been claimed that the league of five Philistine cities was more like an amphictyony than the twelve tribes of Israel.[23] This argument, however, is not very convincing, because the Philistine league was basically an ethnic and military federation and there is no evidence at all that it had a religious character, which is an essential element in any amphictyony. The fact that the ark was put by the Philistines in the temple of Dagon at Ashdod (1 Sam 5:1) does not provide us with enough evidence to call this temple a central sanctuary and in any case Dagon was not a Philistine god. It is more important to stress that the Phoenician cities never joined together to form an amphictyony. There would, of course, have been every reason for them to form such an amphictyony, on the model of towns on the coasts of Greece and Asia Minor, if the institution had become established in the Semitic world.

One objection that has been raised against Noth's hypothesis is that there was no word in Hebrew to denote this presumed amphictyony and that the name 'Israel' cannot be regarded as a sufficient substitute.[24] This argument, however, cannot be viewed as in any sense decisive, since the frequently used terms 'the tribes of Israel' or 'all Israel' and the less commonly employed expressions 'the twelve tribes' or 'the twelve tribes of Israel' are parallel to the name *duodecim populi Etruriae*, which was of course the name of the Etruscan league, in which characteristics similar to those of the amphictyonies have been recognised and perhaps over-estimated.

The question of the name is, however, of secondary importance and it is much more valuable to find out whether the comparisons that have been drawn between the twelve tribes and the Greek amphictyonies or their equivalents in Italy can be regarded as valid.

[22] W. W. Hallo, 'A Sumerian Amphictyony', *JCS*, 14 (1960), pp. 88–96; 'Royal Hymns and Mesopotamian Unity', *ibid.*, 17 (1963), pp. 112–118.
[23] B. D. Rahtjen, 'Philistine and Hebrew Amphictyonies', *JNES*, 24 (1965), pp. 100–104.
[24] G. Fohrer, *BZAW* 115, pp. 90–91 and, with certain special emphases, G. W. Anderson, *op. cit.* (note 10), pp. 142 and 150–151.

1. *The figure twelve*

The whole of Noth's hypothesis was based originally on the occurrence of the figure twelve, but it must be pointed out that this lacks the importance that he and even more, his followers have attributed to it. Among the leagues that are explicitly called amphictyonies in the texts, it is only the Delphic amphictyony which kept strictly, from the sixth century B.C. until the Roman period, to the figure twelve in spite of the many difficulties that this entailed as a result of historical changes. The original nuclear amphictyony of Anthela, however, began with only a few members. There were only seven members of the amphictyony of Calauria, and the composition of the other amphictyonies is not known to us. In Asia Minor, the Ionian league began with ten members, the Dorian league had six and then five, and the Aeolian league had twelve and then eleven. At a much later date, in Scandinavia, the Swedish league formed a federation of groups of ten, eight and four members. As for Italy, we do not know which were the 'twelve peoples' of the Etruscan league or of the other leagues and it is quite possible that 'twelve' simply had a symbolic value in this case. The figure twelve, which is the number of the months of the year and of the signs of the zodiac, after all expresses fullness.[25] In Greece, groups of twelve people, animals or things are found frequently in literature, in legends and in the public worship of the people. Aeolus, for example, had twelve children, twelve cows were dedicated to Athena and twelve bulls to Poseidon, Hercules performed twelve labours, there were twelve Titans and twelve great gods of Olympus. In Rome, there were also twelve great gods in the Pantheon, the twelve Arval brothers, twelve Luperci, the law of the Twelve Tablets and so on.

Closer parallels to the twelve sons of Jacob and the twelve tribes of Israel can, of course, be found in the Semitic world and the Bible itself. There are, for instance, twelve Aramaean tribes, named after the twelve 'sons' of Nahor. Eight of these sons were born to Nahor's wife Milcah and four to his concubine Reumah (Gen 22:20–34). Ishmael had twelve sons, who are said to be 'twelve chiefs of as many tribes' (Gen 25:12–16). Esau also had twelve descendants (Gen 36:10–14), excluding Amalek (verse 12). Apart from these very close parallels, the figure twelve is used elsewhere in the Old Testament with the same symbolic value as in Greece and Rome. There are many examples of this. On Solomon's temple, for instance, there were 'twelve oxen beneath the sea' (1 Kings 7:44) and, in the temple, 'twelve lions on either side of the six steps' of the throne (1 Kings 10:20). Elisha

---

[25] There is unfortunately no recent work dealing with the figure twelve. As far as classical antiquity is concerned, O. Weinreich has provided a very full documentation in the introduction to his article 'Zwölfgötter', in W. H. Roscher's *Ausführliches Lexikon für griechischen und römischen Mythologie*, VI, 1924–1937, especially col. 765–772.

ploughed behind twelve yoke of oxen (1 Kings 19:19). Twelve of Benjamin's men and twelve men from David's following fought near the Pool of Gibeon (2 Sam 2:15). Finally, the figure 12,000 occurs frequently in the Old Testament. There are Solomon's 12,000 horses (1 Kings 5:6; 10:26) and many references to 12,000 warriors (Jos 8:25; Judges 21:10; 2 Sam 10:6; 17:1; Ps 60:2). Without leaving the Semitic world, it is also possible to add to this list examples drawn from the New Testament – especially the Apocalypse[26] – and from Jewish writings.[27]

2. The amphictyonic pact

It has been suggested that the pact which brought the Israelite amphictyony into being was concluded at the assembly of Shechem (Jos 24). This hypothesis was put forward by E. Sellin, long before the term 'amphictyony' became fashionable,[28] and later taken up and developed by M. Noth.[29] The historical memory which is preserved in the pan-Israelite editing of this chapter of the book of Joshua is, however, not one that is common to all twelve tribes. According to the most probable interpretation, the pact was concluded between the northern tribes, those which had not taken part in the exodus and in the experience of Sinai, and Joshua's group. It was Joshua, as leader of this group, who proposed faith in Yahweh. It is, of course, true that it was above all a religious pact (verses 23–24) and that it included the imposition of a statute and an ordinance (verse 25). Not all the twelve tribes were involved in it, however, since they had not all been finally constituted by this time and their representatives were not all present at Shechem. What is more, this pact does not display any of the specific characteristics of an amphictyony.

3. The central sanctuary

One necessary condition of an amphictyony is the existence of a central sanctuary. It must be in existence before the amphictyony itself comes into being. It also explains why the amphictyony was established and justifies its

---

[26] See K. H. Rengstorf's article δώδεκα in *TWNT*, II, Stuttgart, 1935, pp. 321–328; A. Jaubert, 'La symbolique des Douze', *Hommages à André Dupont-Sommer*, Paris, 1971, pp. 453–460.

[27] See L. Ginzberg, *The Legends of the Jews*, VII, *Index*, Philadelphia, 1938, under 'Twelve'.

[28] E. Sellin, 'Seit welcher Zeit verehrten die nordisraelitischen Stämme Jahwe?', *Oriental Studies . . . P. Haupt*, Baltimore, 1926, pp. 121–134; see also Sellin's *Geschichte des israelitisch-jüdischen Volkes*, I, Leipzig, 1924, p. 98 ff.

[29] M. Noth, *Das System der zwölf Stämme Israels, op. cit.*, pp. 65–75; *Das Buch Josua (HAT)*[2], 1953, p. 139; *Geschichte*, pp. 90–91, 96–97 (*History*, pp. 92–93, 99–100).

existence and even its name. It was 'clustered round' this sanctuary that the amphictyony was formed. The communal religious feasts were celebrated at the sanctuary and the amphictyonic council met there. The normal function of this council was the maintenance of the sanctuary and its police guard. In the case of the hypothesis that we are considering, that suggested by M. Noth, the central sanctuary of the Israelite 'amphictyony' was the one where the ark, the symbol of the presence of Yahweh, the God of the covenant, was placed and where the cultic expression of that covenant was celebrated. The ark was moved from time to time, with the result that the central sanctuary was in turn at Shechem, where the amphictyony was first founded, Bethel, Gilgal and finally Shiloh.[30] Although Noth's hypothesis has been widely accepted and even developed,[31] it has also been criticised quite severely.[32]

Having a central sanctuary of this kind, which changed its site periodically, the Israelite 'amphictyony' would be different from all the other amphictyonies known to us. The Pylaeo-Delphic amphictyony is not a valid comparison – the amphictyonic sanctuary did not move from Thermopylae to Delphi; on the contrary, the sanctuary at Delphi was added to that at Anthela, with the result that this is also a unique case. This general objection, however, is not the most serious one, since it is possible to demonstrate that none of the sanctuaries included in Noth's list ever played the part of a central sanctuary for all the tribes.

Shechem. We know nothing about the possible presence of the ark at Shechem. The ark is not mentioned in Jos 24, the passage dealing with the setting up of the 'amphictyony'. It is in fact only mentioned in connection with Shechem (or, to be more precise, in connection with Mount Gerizim and Mount Ebal), in Jos 8:33 which forms part of a post-deuteronomistic addition. The purpose of this text is to show that Joshua carried out Moses' orders, as reported in Deut 11:29–30; 27:4–8; 27:11–13. These three texts, in which the ark is not mentioned, are, however, both secondary and composite. The description of the carrying out of these orders ought to come immediately after the account of the crossing of the Jordan and the entry into Canaan, in which the Gilgal region is indicated (Gilgal is explicitly

[30] M. Noth, *Das System der zwölf Stämme Israels, op. cit.*, pp. 94–97, 116; *Geschichte*, pp. 88–94 (*History*, pp. 91–95).

[31] See especially K.–H. Bernhardt, *Gott und Bild*, Berlin, 1956, pp. 134–144; H.–J. Kraus, *Gottesdienst in Israel,*[2] Munich, 1962, pp. 149–209. J. Dus has suggested that there were very many places where the ark rested and that it was moved every seven years before finally resting at Shiloh; see his 'Der Brauch der Ladewanderung im alten Israel', *TZ*, 17 (1961), pp. 1–16 and 'Noch zum Brauch der "Ladewanderung"', *VT*, 13 (1963), pp. 126–132.

[32] See especially R. Smend, *Jahwekrieg und Stämmebund*, Göttingen, 1963, pp. 56–70; W. H. Irwin, 'Le sanctuaire central israélite avant l'établissement de la monarchie', *RB*, 72 (1965), pp. 161–184; M. H. Woudstra, *The Ark of the Covenant from Conquest to Kingship*, Philadelphia, 1965, pp. 126–133; G. Fohrer, *BZAW* 115 (see above, note 10), pp. 94–98.

mentioned in Deut 11:30). The reference to Gerizim and Ebal is not compatible with this other geographical datum and must therefore be in accordance with a different intention.[33] What is more, a ceremony such as is described in Jos 8:30–35 as taking place at Shechem could not have occurred at a time when Israel had not even settled in the district. We are therefore bound to conclude that it is not possible to use these texts in conjunction with Jos 24 in order to prove that a feast of the renewal of the covenant was celebrated at the beginning of the period of the Judges. It has been suggested that this feast took place at the time of the Feast of Tabernacles,[34] but the latter is not mentioned in any of these texts and there is no proof of the existence of an annual feast of the renewal of the covenant during the early period, either at Shechem or elsewhere.[35] What is certain is that the neighbouring sanctuary of Shechem was a meeting-place for the northern tribes – the pact described in Jos 24 was concluded there among these tribes and the political schism took place there between them after the death of Solomon (1 Kings 12). Only one historical datum, however, is connected with the sanctuary of Shechem between these two events – the proclamation of Abimelech as king by the Canaanite inhabitants of Shechem (Judges 9:1–6). This Canaanite environment would have been the worst possible choice to make in any attempt to prove the existence of a central sanctuary common to all the Israelite tribes. We may therefore conclude that Shechem, where, as we have seen, the ark never rested, at least according to the evidence at our disposal, was never either the central sanctuary of Israel or an 'amphictyonic' sanctuary.

Bethel. Noth and others have suggested that the central sanctuary and the ark were transferred from Shechem to Bethel, possibly after the episode of Abimelech.[36] Certainly there is reference to the presence of the ark at Bethel, where it was guarded by Phinehas, the son of Eleazer, who was in turn the son of Aaron, in Judges 20:27b–28a. This is, however, without any doubt an addition. It may well preserve an early memory, but it is much more likely that the aim of the writer of this gloss was really to justify the

---

[33] See O. Eissfeldt, 'Gilgal or Shechem?' in *Proclamation and Presence (G. Henton Davies Volume)*, London, 1970, pp. 90–101.

[34] G. von Rad, *Das formgeschichtliche Problem des Hexateuchs*, Stuttgart, 1938, pp. 33–37 = *Gesammelte Studien zum Alten Testament*, Munich, 1958, pp. 44–48; H.–J. Kraus, *Gottesdienst in Israel*,[2] pp. 161–171.

[35] See E. Kutsch, 'Feste und Feier', *RGG*,[3] II, 1958, col. 915–916. G. Fohrer, *Geschichte der israelitischen Religion*, p. 56. The text which is usually quoted in this connection is Deut 31:9–13. According to this text, the law had to be read publicly to the whole of Israel every seven years in the year of remission. The Feast of Tabernacles was no more than the time when this proclamation of the law took place and Shechem is not even mentioned in the text. In Judaism, the commemoration of the covenant was incorporated into the Feast of Weeks, not the Feast of Tabernacles.

[36] M. Noth, *Geschichte*, p. 91 (*History*, p. 94).

religious part played by the sanctuary at Bethel, which was later condemned in orthodox circles, in this story (Judges 20:18, 26–28; 21:2), by
stressing the presence there of the ark and of a Levite descended from an
authentic family of Levites. What is more, these texts referring to Bethel do
not form part of the earliest layer in the narrative, according to which Israel
came together, united in the struggle against Benjamin, at Mizpah (Judges
20:1–3; 21:1–5, 8).[37] Finally, we should not be deceived by the pan-Israelite
editing of this story – it would seem that, in history, it was only the tribe of
Ephraim which was opposed to Benjamin.[38]

A memory of the transference of the central sanctuary from Shechem to
Bethel can be found, they tell us, in Gen 35:1–7, a passage in which Jacob
and his family are presented as going from Shechem to Bethel. Their
journey begins with a cultic act (verse 2) and ends with the building of an
altar (verse 7). This transference was, according to these authors, commemorated later by a pilgrimage.[39] The 'divine terror' which accompanied
this movement (verse 5) can be taken as a clear sign that the ark took part.[40]
If, however, such a pilgrimage ever took place, this would prove that the
two sanctuaries were in use at the same time, but not that Bethel became the
central sanctuary. As far as the 'divine terror' is concerned, this was certainly not connected exclusively with the presence of the ark.[41] There is in fact
no real evidence at all that Bethel was at any time during the period of the
Judges the central sanctuary of Israel or that an 'amphictyonic' cult was ever
celebrated there.

Gilgal. On the other hand, however, the ark certainly rested, at least for
some time, at the sanctuary of Gilgal, since there is no other way of explaining how the accounts in Jos 3–4 could have been composed. These accounts, however, with the double aetiology of the twelve stones, also
presuppose that there was a cult which united the twelve tribes. The conclusion that has been drawn from this is that Gilgal became the 'amphic-

[37] A. Besters, 'Le sanctuaire central dans Jud., XIX–XXI', *ETL*, 41 (1965), pp. 20–41. We
cannot accept the hypothesis put forward by J. Dus in 'Bethel und Mispa in Jdc. 19–21 und
Jdc. 10–12', *OrAnt*, 3 (1964), pp. 227–243, according to which Bethel was at that time the
central sanctuary and Mizpah was introduced at a later stage into this account. Dus also
suggested that the cultic object of this central sanctuary at Bethel was not the ark, but an image of a bull; see his 'Ein richterzeitliches, Stierbildheiligtum zu Bethel?' *ZAW*, 77 (1965),
pp. 268–286.
[38] O. Eissfeldt, 'Der geschichtliche Hintergrund der Erzählung von Gibeas Schandtat'
Festschrift G. Beer, Stuttgart, 1935, pp. 19–40 =   *Kleine Schriften*, II, pp. 64–80. See also
below, p. 714.
[39] M. Noth, *Geschichte*, pp. 91–92 (*History*, p. 94). Noth based his hypothesis in this
instance on A. Alt, 'Die Wallfahrt von Sichem nach Bethel', *In piam memoriam A. von
Bulmerincq*, Riga, 1938, pp. 218–230 =   *Kleine Schriften*, I, pp. 79–88.
[40] J. A. Soggin, 'Zwei umstrittene Stellen aus dem Überlieferungskreis um Schechem'
ZAW (1961), pp. 78–87.
[41] R. Smend, *Jahwekrieg und Stämmebund, op. cit.* (see note 32), p. 69.

tyonic' sanctuary after Shechem (and Bethel).[42] Certain serious difficulties are, however, encountered in this hypothesis. Gilgal was certainly the first sanctuary used by the Israelite groups when they entered Canaan after crossing the Jordan and the first place where the ark rested, if we accept that this cultic object was in fact brought into Canaan by the groups coming from the desert. Gilgal cannot, however, have been at that time the central sanctuary of the twelve tribes of Israel, since these were not then united. No part at all is played by Gilgal in the whole of the book of Judges.[43] It was in fact not until the reign of Saul that Gilgal figured as the privileged place where the tribes met together (1 Sam 10:8; 11:14–15; 13, *passim*; 15:12, 21–33). At that time, however, the ark was at Kiriath-jearim, under the control of the Philistines.[44]

Shiloh. More serious claims can be made for Shiloh, the final place where the ark rested according to M. Noth, as a possible central sanctuary for the whole of Israel, and some authors are of the opinion that it was in fact the only central sanctuary during the period of the Judges.[45] The situation is, however, less clear than it seems at first.[46] There is evidence that the ark was at Shiloh in the two independent accounts of the childhood of Samuel (1 Sam 3:3) and the story of the ark contained in 1 Sam 4:1–7:1. It was taken from Shiloh to the battlefield at Aphek, where it was captured by the Philistines (1 Sam 4:3–6, 11, 17). At Shiloh, it was placed in a sanctuary or *hêkhāl* (1 Sam 1:9; 3:3), the 'house of Yahweh' (1 Sam 1–7,24; 3:15). This was a specially constructed sanctuary with a door (1 Sam 1:9) which was opened in the morning (1 Sam 3:15). This was in fact the first of Yahweh's temples.[47] Unlike Shechem and Bethel, however, Shiloh was not connected

[42] M. Noth, *Geschichte*, p. 92 (*History*, pp. 94–95); H.–J. Kraus, *Gottesdienst in Israel*,[2] pp. 179–193.

[43] The name itself appears only twice, in the introductions to Judges (Judges 2:1 and 3:19), and then only as a geographical landmark.

[44] See J. A. Soggin, 'Gilgal, Passah und Landnahme', *Volume du Congrès, Genève (SVT* 15), 1966, pp. 263:277, especially p. 269; F. Langlamet, *Gilgal et les récits de la traversée du Jourdain* (*Cahiers de la RB* 11), pp. 16–17, 121–122.

[45] W. F. Albright, *Archaeology and the Religion of Israel*,[2] Baltimore, 1946, pp. 103–105; *ibid.*, *Archaeology, Historical Analogy and Early Biblical Tradition*, Baton Rouge, 1966, pp. 55–56; E. Nielsen, *Shechem. A Traditio-Historical Investigation*, Copenhagen, 1955, p. 36, note 1; M. H. Woudstra, *The Ark of the Covenant, op. cit.* (see note 32), pp. 126–128 and 133.

[46] W. H. Irwin (see note 32), pp. 176–178.

[47] This hypothesis is not accepted by M. Haran, 'Shilo and Jerusalem', *JBL*, 81 (1962) pp. 14–24. This author believes that Shiloh was a 'tabernacle' which may have served as a model for the priestly description in Exodus. He places too much confidence in the late texts which will be discussed later in the present chapter and feels obliged to reject the texts that have just been mentioned as well as Jer 7:12–14. His acceptance of Nathan's prophecy (2 Sam 7:6–7), on which he bases his argument, can be explained differently – the prophet objected to the building of a Canaanite type of temple, but he knew that there was a 'house of Yahweh' at Shiloh and that the ark had rested in Abinadab's house at Kiriath-jearim (1 Sam 7:1) and later at Obed-edom's house (2 Sam 6:11–12). See also A. Weiser, 'Die Tempelbaukrise unter

with any patriarchal tradition and we do not know when this sanctuary was first set up. According to Jos 18:1 (see also 19:51), the Tent of Meeting was erected at Shiloh immediately after the conquest of Canaan and lots were cast 'before Yahweh' for the territory to be apportioned to the seven tribes which had not by that time received their share (Jos 18:8–10) and for the cities set aside for the Levites (Jos 21:1–8). It was also at Shiloh that the Transjordanian tribes took leave of the remainder of Israel (Jos 22:9) and that the whole community of Israel gathered in order to make war on these tribes because they had built an altar beside the Jordan (Jos 22:12). All these texts, however, form part of a priestly editing of the book of Joshua which took place after the exile.[48] In Judges 21:19–21, there is, moreover, reference to an annual feast including a pilgrimage to Shiloh during which the daughters of the country danced in the vineyards. This 'feast of Yahweh' may have been the great autumnal feast prescribed in Ex 23:16, but it is above all reminiscent of the Canaanite feast of the harvest of the vineyards at Shechem (Judges 9:27). In any case, the episode certainly presupposes the existence of a sanctuary at Shiloh, possibly quite early during the period of the Judges, although we cannot be sure when it was founded.

In fact, this sanctuary at Shiloh only appears relatively clearly at the end of this period. It was administered by a levitical family, Eli and his two sons Hophni and Phinehas.[49] It was at this sanctuary that the minister gave oracles (1 Sam 1:17) and that God revealed himself to Samuel (1 Sam 3). Sacrifices were also offered there (1 Sam 1, passim; 2:12–17, 19), Samuel's father came there every year with his family (1 Sam 1:3, 22) and, according to Judges 21:19–21, there was, as we have seen, an annual pilgrimage to Shiloh. Neither the ark, the levitical priesthood, the oracles, the sacrifices nor the pilgrimage, however, can be regarded as sufficient to make Shiloh the central sanctuary of an 'amphictyony'.[50] The annual visit made by Elkanah and his family was not connected with any religious feast bringing all the tribes together. It was rather a private or family devotion,[51] which Elkanah made to a sanctuary that was well-known to this tribe – Shiloh was, after all, in Ephraim and Elkanah was an Ephraimite (1 Sam 1:1). The story in Judges 21:15–23 can only be understood if it is thought of as describing a local feast, in which the dancers are the daughters of Shiloh and the Benjaminites are not pilgrims, but have come to abduct them after emerging from hiding. In the story of the Philistine war, the ark is taken to

---

David', ZAW, 77 (1965), pp. 153–168, especially pp. 158–159; R. de Vaux, 'Jérusalem et les prophètes', RB, 73 (1965), pp. 481–509, especially pp. 486–487.

[48] The reference to Shiloh in Judges 21:12 is a gloss of the same period.

[49] A. Cody, A History of Old Testament Priesthood, Rome, 1969, pp. 65–72.

[50] W. H. Irwin (see above, note 32); A. Besters (see above, note 37).

[51] M. Haran, Zebah hayyamîm', VT, 19 (1969), pp. 11–22.

Shiloh after the Israelites have suffered a first defeat (1 Sam 4:3–4). It was not taken by the army and there is no evidence at all to indicate that the army was first concentrated at Shiloh. It is therefore in no way justifiable to say that Shiloh was at that time the centre, if not of an amphictyony, then at least of a military league formed against the Philistines.[52] Leaving aside the obvious gloss, Judges 21:12, it is clear that there is no evidence pointing to Shiloh as a place where the tribes met at the time of the Judges. According to this whole story (Judges 19–21), Mizpah has a better claim to be seen in this light. It was, after all, at Mizpah that all the Israelites gathered in the presence of Yahweh and took a solemn vow (Judges 20:1–3; 21:1–5, 8) and that Samuel summoned the whole of Israel (1 Sam 7:5–12). On that occasion, the Israelites offered a libation to Yahweh, fasted and offered a holocaust, while Samuel 'judged' Israel. According to 1 Sam 10:17 ff, it was at Mizpah, too, that Saul was chosen to be king by lot and by consulting Yahweh. On the other hand, the ark never rested at Mizpah and it is this that has always been regarded as the central object of worship in the Israelite 'amphictyony'.[53]

It is therefore not possible to prove beyond doubt that there was a central sanctuary common to all the tribes during the period of the Judges. On the contrary, it is quite striking how many different places of cult there were at that time. In the first place, there were Shechem and Bethel, to which may be added Beersheba (see 1 Sam 8:2), where the memory of the patriarchs was preserved. There was also Gilgal, where the memory of the entry into Canaan was preserved. In addition, there were Shiloh, Mizpah and even Ramah (see 1 Sam 7:17; 9:12–25), with its obscure origin. Two other places of worship that can be mentioned in this context are Ophrah and Dan, the foundation of the latter being narrated in some detail in Judges 6 and 18. Finally, there must have been many others, quite apart from the purely household shrines such as Micah's (see Judges 17). A special importance may have been given to one or other of these sanctuaries by the presence of the ark, the geographical location of the place or the memories connected with it and believers may have been attracted to the sanctuary in question from considerable distances. It is also quite likely that some of these sanctuaries were visited by several tribes. Parallels can easily be found. In pre-Islamic Arabia, for example, pilgrims from different tribes gathered in the great sanctuaries and not simply at Mecca, as the later tradition would have us believe.[54] There is also possible evidence of this phenomenon in

---

[52] This has been suggested by J. Maier, *Das altrisraelitische Ladeheiligtum* (*BZAW* 93), 1965, p. 58; G. Fohrer, *BZAW* 115 (see above, note 10), pp. 97–98.

[53] J. Dus, has, however, suggested, in *OrAnt*, 3 (1964), (see above, note 37), especially pp. 236–242, the unlikely hypothesis that the ark was left at Mizpah during the period when Jephthah was judge, claiming that the dates in Judges 10:17; 11; 11b and 34 apply to Mizpah in Benjamin and not to Mizpah in Gilead, as in the case of Judges 11:29.

Palestine itself, revealed by archaeological finds going back to a period before the Israelites settled in the country. These include Late Bronze temples excavated at Amman and on the slopes of Mount Gerizim [55] and the excavations at Deir 'Alla on the eastern bank of the Jordan.[56] These may well have been sanctuaries which were used by different groups of semi-nomadic peoples living in the region, although it must be pointed out that we know nothing about the extent of the territories inhabited by these groups or about any organisation in leagues. As far as Israel is concerned, none of the sanctuaries mentioned at the period of the Judges can be designated as the central, 'amphictyonic' sanctuary of all the tribes.

4. The amphictyonic council

The representatives of the tribes at the council of the Israelite 'amphictyony' were, Noth believed, the $n^e\acute{s}\hat{i}\,\hat{i}m$, a word that is usually, though inaccurately, translated as 'princes'. According to one possible etymology $(n\hat{a}\acute{s}a'\ q\hat{o}l)$, they were those who 'lifted up the voice', in other words, they were the spokesmen. One of these men represented each tribe and lists of their names are given in Num 1:5–16, cf. 2:3–29; 7:12–83; 10:13–27; 13:2–15; 34:17–29. As representatives of the tribes of Israel, they corresponded to the *hieromnenons* of the Greek amphictyonies.[57] This comparison does not, however, seem to be at all justified.[58]

The word $n\hat{a}\acute{s}\hat{i}'$ is used most frequently in Ezekiel and in the priestly passages in the Pentateuch, in Exodus and above all in the book of Numbers. In the first of these books, Ezekiel, the word has a special meaning and importance and a distinction is made between $n\hat{a}\acute{s}\hat{i}'$ and *melekh*, 'king'. It is this title – and never 'king' – which the author always gives to the future leader of Israel.[59] His use of the word seems to have influenced

---

[54] J. Wellhausen, *Reste arabischen Heidentums*,[2] Berlin, 1897, pp. 84–94; this author even uses the term 'amphictyons' in connection with Mecca (p. 85), although this is going too far. See also H. Lammens, 'Les sanctuaires préislamites dans l'Arabie occidentale', *MUSJ*, 11 (1926), pp. 36–173, especially p. 154 ff; M. Gaudefroy-Demombynes, *Mahomet*, Paris, 1957, pp. 34–35.

[55] E. F. Campbell and G. E. Wright, 'Tribal League Shrines in Amman and Shechem', *BibArch*, 32 (1969), pp. 104–116.

[56] H. J. Franken, 'Excavations at Deir 'Alla. Season 1964', *VT*, 14 (1964), pp. 417–422, especially pp. 419 and 422.

[57] M. Noth, *Das System der zwölf Stämme Israels*, pp. 151–162; *Geschichte*, p. 95 (*History*, p. 98). J. Bright, *History*, p. 144.

[58] J. van der Ploeg, 'Les chefs du peuple d'Israël et leurs titres', *RB*, 57 (1950), pp. 40–61, especially pp. 47–54; E. A. Speiser, 'Background and Function of the Biblical *naśi'* ', *CBQ*, 25 (1963), pp. 111–117, an article which is also included in the author's *Oriental and Biblical Studies*, Philadelphia, 1967, pp. 113–122.

[59] See W. Zimmerli, *Ezechiel (BKAT)*, 1969, pp. 915–918, 1227–1230, 1244–1246.

Lev 4:22; Ezr 1:8 and the present text of 1 Kings 11:34. Nonetheless, he modified an earlier meaning of the word. In Numbers, the nᵉśîʾîm are the twelve chiefs or leaders of the tribes. The word can also be used for the leaders of less important subdivisions – according to Num 3:24, 30, 35, each of the three levitical clans had its own nāśîʾ and, according to Num 16:2, there were two hundred and fifty nᵉśîʾîm or leaders of the community.⁶⁰ According to the Old Testament, this title was not confined to the Israelites. In Gen 25:13–16, the names of the twelve nᵉśîʾîm of the Ishmaelites are given, there is reference in Num 25:18 to a nāśîʾ of the Midianites and, in Jos 13:21, the five nᵉśîʾîm of the Midianites, called 'kings' in Num 31:8, are listed. All these are later texts, but they are based on early traditions and the term nāśîʾ was inherited from a period prior to the monarchy. According to the Book of the Covenant, the Israelite was forbidden to 'revile God' and to 'curse a nāśîʾ of the people' (Ex 22:27). It is interesting to compare this with 1 Kings 21:10, according to which Naboth was accused of having 'cursed God and the king'. Like the king during the period of the monarchy and in spite of the sacral character given to all those in authority in Israel, the nāśîʾ was a secular, not a religious leader. In Gen 34:2, Hamor is said to be the nāśîʾ of the Shechem region, the population and the constitution of which were different from those of the little Canaanite kingdoms – they were Hivites and did not have a king and, according to verse 20 in the same chapter, the nāśîʾ did not possess unlimited authority. Indeed, the word seems to have had, not the active significance given to it by Noth, but rather a passive meaning – in other words, the nāśîʾ was the man who was 'lifted up' or 'raised' by or in the assembly. This meaning is reinforced by the use of the composite term: those called in the assembly, the nᵉśîʾîm of their patriarchal tribes (see Num 1:16). This text can be compared with the nᵉśîʾîm of the assembly (Num 4:34, etc.), the nᵉśîʾîm in the assembly (Ex 34:31) and others. These references certainly point to some king of choice or election.⁶¹

In view of this evidence, we may therefore conclude that the nāʾśîʾ was not originally a religious leader in Israel and that he was also not a prince, but rather the chief chosen by a tribe or a sub-division of a tribe. The best equivalent that can be found in a similar social environment is the Arab sheikh, who rules his tribe or his subdivision of the tribe in common with the heads of other families. He is also chosen for his personal worth, even though the function usually remains within the same family. According to the pan-Israelite view presented in the books of Exodus (Ex 16:22; 34:31; 35:27) and Numbers (see the texts quoted above and Num 7:2 ff; 10:4; 17:17, 21; 27:2; 31:13; 36:1) as well as Joshua (Jos 9:15–21; 17:4; 22:14, 30,

---

⁶⁰ This text is, however, composite according to M. Noth, *Das System der zwölf Stämme Israels*, p. 155; *Das vierte Buch Mose. Numeri (ATD)*, 1966, p. 107.

⁶¹ E. A. Speiser, *CBQ, op. cit.* (note 58), pp. 117–118.

32), these tribal leaders represent the whole of the people and act collectively. In none of these texts, however, are they given the functions of
hieromnemons, as in the Greek amphictyonies. The only passages in which
they are named in the context of the sanctuary are Ex 35:27–28 and Num
7 and here it is clear that, although they bring offerings to the sanctuary,
they do not act as ministers. What is more, they play no part at all in the
assembly at Shechem (Jos 24), which is claimed to be the act which constituted the Israelite amphictyony, nor are they mentioned anywhere in the
book of Judges, which, it has been said, covers the whole of the period of
this amphictyony.[62] The *nᵉśî'îm,* then, cannot be regarded as the members of
an amphictyonic council.

5. The amphictyonic law

According to the theory that we are considering here, Israel had an
amphictyonic law. This was partly preserved in the Book of the Covenant,
especially in the 'religious and moral prohibitions'[63] contained in Ex
22:17–23:9, and its influence can also be found in certain later collections,
especially the deuteronomic law (Deut 12–26) and the Law of Holiness
(Lev 17–26). This law was regularly proclaimed whenever the tribes met at
the central sanctuary, the 'Judge of Israel' being responsible for making it
known, explaining it and making sure that it was observed, while at the
same time adapting it to the changing circumstances. A list of these Judges
is, according to Noth and others, preserved in Judges 10:1–5 and 12:8–15.[64]
It is undoubtedly true that the Book of the Covenant does provide us with
the laws and customs of the tribes that had settled in Canaan and been
united in the same faith in Yahweh. This does not, however, mean that it
had the character of an amphictyonic law. We might, of course, be tempted
to associate this Book of the Covenant with Shechem, where Joshua laid
down 'a statute and an ordinance', written in a 'Book of the Law' (Jos
24:25–26), but, as we have already seen, not all the tribes were involved in
the pact made at Shechem, this pact was not the action by which an
amphictyony was established and Shechem was not the central sanctuary of
the Israelite tribes. Noth himself has observed that the cultic laws of the

[62] This comment was made by H. M. Orlinsky, *op. cit.* (see above, note 10), p. 14, note 7;
see also G. W. Anderson, *op. cit.* (see also above, note 10), p. 147.

[63] This name was given by A. Jepsen, *Untersuchungen zum Bundesbuch (BWANT,* III, 5),
Stuttgart, 1927, pp. 87:90.

[64] M. Noth, *Das System der zwölf Stämme Israels, op. cit.,* pp. 97–100; *Die Gesetze im
Pentateuch,* Halle, 1940, especially pp. 22–29 = Gesammelte Studien, I, pp. 42–43; 'Das Amt
des "Richters Israels"', *Festschrift A. Bertholet,* Tübingen, 1950, pp. 404–417 = *Gesammelte
Studien,* II, pp. 71–85; A. Alt, *Die Ursprünge des israelitischen Rechts,* Leipzig, 1934, pp. 31–33
= *Kleine Schriften,* I, pp. 300–302.

Book of the Covenant, which should themselves have been the special object of an amphictyonic law, had in mind not a central sanctuary, but rather various local sanctuaries.[65] There is moreover no evidence pointing to the fact that the authority of the 'lesser' Judges, any more than that of the 'great' Judges, extended to the whole of Israel[66] and that they had any connection with an amphictyonic institution or assumed what Noth called 'the central office in the Israelites' twelve-tribe society'.[67] In this particular instance, then, the comparison with the Greek amphictyonies seems especially weak.[68] A magistrate similar to a 'Judge of Israel' cannot be found in any of them. The *hieromnemons* exercised some judiciary power, but they did not judge offences against the sanctuary or the god.[69] What is more, it is not really possible to speak of an amphictyonic law even in Greece, where one law common to several cities never in fact existed.

6. Amphictyonic action

In Greece, it was possible for an amphictyony to take collective action against an offending member or enemies of the sanctuary. The possibility of such activity was provided for in the amphictyonic oath[70] and throughout the history of Greece there were several of these 'holy wars', in which the religious motive was no more than a pretext, concealing fundamentally political aims. According to Noth, the war conducted by the tribes against Benjamin in punishment of the crime at Gibeah (Judges 19–21) is a close parallel to these amphictyonic wars in Greece; it was, in his opinion, the story of an amphictyonic war against a member of the amphictyony which had openly broken the amphictyonic law.[71] G. von Rad also believed that all the 'holy wars' that took place during the period of the Judges were in principle a reaction on the part of the amphictyony, even if not all the tribes participated in them.[72] He also used the term 'amphictyonic army'.[73] More recently, the lamentation of the Israelites following the war against Ben-

---

[65] M. Noth, *Das System der zwölf Stämme Israels, op. cit.*, pp. 97–98.

[66] G. W. Anderson, *op. cit.* (note 10), p. 148.

[67] M. Noth, *Geschichte*, p. 98 (*History*, p. 101).

[68] M. Noth was himself aware of this; see *Geschichte*, p. 99 (*History*, pp. 102–103).

[69] See above, p. 698.

[70] See above, p. 698.

[71] M. Noth, *Das System der zwölf Stämme Israels, op. cit.*, pp. 100–106; 168–170; the quotation will be found on p. 170; see also *Geschichte*, pp. 100–101 (*History*, pp. 104–105).

[72] G. von Rad, *Der Heilige Krieg im alten Israel*, Zürich, 1951, pp. 25–26; see also E. Nielsen's criticism in 'La Guerre considérée comme une religion et la Religion comme une Guerre', *ST*, 15 (1961), p. 100 and R. Smend's (see above, note 76).

[73] G. von Rad, *op. cit.* (see the previous note), p. 26, note 43.

jamin (Judges 21:3) has been described as a fragment of 'amphictyonic poetry'.[74]

In all these cases, the word 'amphictyony' is wrongly applied. There was no war during the period of the Judges in which either the whole or even the majority of the tribes took part. According to the Song of Deborah (Judges 5), six tribes took part in the battle of Kishon, yet the prose account of the same battle, it should be noted, explicitly mentions only two tribes, Zebulun and Naphthali (see Judges 4). The wars that occurred during the period of the Judges were certainly 'holy wars',[75] but they did not have an amphictyonic character.[76] With the exception of the war against Benjamin, they were not waged against a member of the 'amphictyony', they were not decided upon by a council of the tribes, they did not have any religious motive and, in the case of the war against Benjamin, they were not conducted with the aim of defending the privileges of a central sanctuary. It is remarkable that Noth, who regarded this war against Benjamin as a typical case of amphictyonic war, derived his main argument from the pan-Israelite form given to the story by an editor.[77] In fact, the account describes an episode in Ephraim's struggle for supremacy (as in Judges 8:1–3 and 12:1–6.) The reason – or rather pretext – for this war was a sexual offence committed by the men of Gibeah, an 'infamy in Israel' or n'bhālāh (Judges 20:6, 10), but there is no justification for us to regard it as a crime condemned by an 'amphictyonic law'. There are other cases in the Old Testament of crimes presented as having had political consequences, without the question of possible 'amphictyonic' action being raised. One example is the rape of Dinah, another n'bhālāh in Israel (Gen 34:7), which led to the attack against Shechem by the sons of Jacob. A further n'bhālāh in Israel, Amnon's raping of his sister Tamar (2 Sam 13:12–13) led directly to the murder of Amnon by Absalom, but the latter was also trying to make sure that he succeeded David.

An appeal could be made on better grounds to the story in Jos 22. According to this story, the whole community, 'edhāh, of Israel assembled at Shiloh, after learning that the Reubenites and the Gadites had erected an altar near to the Jordan, in order to make war on those two tribes, and sent the priest Phinehas and the n'si'im of the ten other tribes to them to accuse them of rebelling against Yahweh. According to Noth, Shiloh was the

---

[74] J. Dus 'Die altisraelitische amphiktyonische Poesie', *ZAW*, 75 (1963), pp. 45–47.

[75] M. Noth acknowledged that the battle of Kishon was a 'holy war' (*Geschichte*, p. 139; *History*, pp. 149–150), but did not use it in his amphictyonic theory because the list of tribes in the Song of Deborah did not correspond to his 'twelve-tribe system' (see *Das System der zwölf Stämme Israels*, pp. 5–6, 36).

[76] R. Smend, *Jahwekrieg und Stämmebund*, Göttingen, 1963, pp. 10–32.

[77] O. Eissfeldt, 'Der geschichtliche Hintergrund der Erzählung von Gibeas Schandtat', *Festschrift G. Beer*, Stuttgart, 1935, pp. 19–40 = *Kleine Schriften*, II, pp. 64–80, especially the author's criticism of M. Noth, p. 68.

amphictyonic sanctuary and the n'śī'îm were the representatives of the tribes belonging to the amphictyony. One would think, then, that the story dealt with a case in which a fundamental law of the amphictyony was broken, that of the central sanctuary, and it would be impossible to think of a better example of an 'amphictyonic war', although this was in fact avoided by means of a compromise.[78] Nonetheless, he did not, after all, make use of this story and he was right not to do so, since all the 'amphictyonic' aspects were, he pointed out, derived from a priestly editing of the text.[79]

All my examination of the evidence therefore leads me to the same ultimate conclusion, namely that any comparison between the group of Israelite tribes and the Greek amphictyonies is completely unjustified. To begin with, the difference between the two environments makes any similarity of this kind unlikely. The essential elements of an amphictyony cannot be found in Israel. It is not possible to establish the existence of either a central sanctuary or a council of representatives from the tribes in Israelite society. There is no single example in the history of Israel of joint action undertaken by all the tribes. These tribes observed the same laws and customs, but not an amphictyonic law. It might be possible to prove that there was a central Judge for all the tribes, but such a figure was unknown in the Greek amphictyonies. The use of the word 'amphictyony' in connection with Israel can only cause confusion and give a wrong impression of the mutual relationships between the different tribes. It should be abandoned.

[78] K. Möhlenbrink thought that this was a case of conflict between two 'amphictyonies', one at Shiloh and the other at Gilgal; see *ZAW*, 56 (1938), pp. 246–250.
[79] M. Noth, *Das Buch Josua (HAT)*,² 1953, p. 133.

Chapter Twenty-Four

THE 'TWELVE–TRIBE SYSTEM'

A S WE have seen in the previous chapter, various attempts have been made to explain the 'twelve-tribe system' of Israel by means of a hypothesis that there was an Israelite amphictyony. Indeed, M. Noth himself entitled his classic work 'The Twelve-Tribe, System of Israel'. We, however, felt bound, by our examination of the evidence, to reject this amphictyonic explanation and in this chapter propose to outline an alternative explanation for this 'system'.

We must make an important preliminary comment. The two terms 'the twelve tribes of Israel' and 'the twelve tribes' are commonly used by scholars, but they are both exceptional in the Old Testament itself. The expression 'the twelve tribes of Israel' can be found only once in its literal form, namely in Ex 24:4, a text which is generally regarded as Elohistic. According to this text, Moses erected twelve stelae 'for the twelve tribes of Israel'. It also occurs again in an equivalent form in Gen 49:28 at the editorial conclusion to the so-called 'Testament of Jacob': 'All these [that is, the sons of Jacob] make up the tribes of Israel, twelve in number'. Again, the term 'the twelve tribes' occurs only twice in the Hebrew Old Testament, namely in Ex 28:21 and 39:14. In these parallel passages in the priestly narrative, the twelve stones of the priest's pectoral are to be engraved 'each with the name of one of the twelve tribes'. To these two texts in which the term 'the twelve tribes' is used, we can add only Ecclus 44:26, according to which the land was shared out 'among the twelve tribes'. Finally, there are, of course, other texts which refer to the 'twelve' sons of Jacob (Gen 35:22; 42:13, 32), who were the ancestors of the tribes, those which speak of 'twelve' men, one from each tribe (Deut 1:23; Jos 4:2 and 4) and the various lists of tribes based on the number twelve. We shall study the latter in some detail later in this chapter.

At a certain period in their history, which we shall attempt to establish at a later stage in this chapter, the Israelites became aware of the fact that their people consisted of twelve tribes. There can be no doubt that this awareness corresponded to a historical reality. These tribes must have been connected with each other by certain blood-ties outside the true or presumed community. These blood-ties, however, never resulted in a unity which might have become known as 'the twelve tribes' or 'the twelve tribes of Israel'. If that had been the case, then these two terms would not have occurred either so rarely or only – with the exception of Ex 24:4 – in late texts. It is therefore only with considerable reservations that it is possible to speak of a 'twelve-tribe system'. These reservations are even more important in that several 'systems' are presented in the texts. They can be classified under three different headings, which may conveniently be called the 'genealogical' system, the tribal system and the 'territorial' system.[1]

I. THE GENEALOGICAL SYSTEM

The whole of the people of Israel is presumed to have descended from the pattern of the 'twelve sons of Jacob'. Even if some of these sons bore the names of individuals who really existed at the beginning of certain groups, their only significance is that they were heroes who gave their names to the tribes. This is something that is generally accepted. In the texts that we shall be studying here, however, the part that they played in personifying the various tribes is of less importance than their supposed relationship with the patriarch Jacob-Israel. These texts are based on the genealogical principles by which Israel had systematised the traditions that were preserved about the people's origins. The archetypal account of this system is the story of the birth of the sons of Jacob (Gen 29:31–30:24 and 35:16–20).[2]

1. Gen 29–30 and 35

The story of the birth of the first eleven sons of Jacob in Mesopotamia is generally regarded as a combination of Yahwistic and Elohistic sources,

[1] The most important work is undoubtedly that of M. Noth, *Das System der zwölf Stämme Israels*, Stuttgart, 1930, especially pp. 3–60. It is also necessary, however, to consider in this context B. Luther, 'Die israelitischen Stämme, *ZAW*, 21 (1901), pp. 1–76, especially pp. 33–53; E. Meyer, *Die Israeliten und ihre Nachbarstämme*, Halle a. S., 1906, pp. 472–561; R. Kittel, *Geschichte des Volkes Israel*, I,[7] Stuttgart, 1932, pp. 296–305; II,[7] 1925, pp. 8–19; in addition to the above mentioned book by Noth, see also his *Geschichte*, pp. 83–104 (*History*, pp. 85–108); J. Bright, *History*, pp. 142–146; J. Hoftijzer, 'Enige opmerkingen rond het Israëlitische 12–stammensysteem', *NTT*, 14 (1959–1960), pp. 241–263; S. Mowinckel, *Israels opphav og eldste historie*, Oslo, 1967, pp. 94–100, 171–184; G. Fohrer, *Studien zur alttestamentlichen Theologie und Geschichte (BZAW* 115), 1969, pp. 100–103.

[2] Apart from the commentaries on Genesis, see S. Lehming, 'Zur Erzählung von der Geburt der Jakobsöhne', *VT*, 13 (1963), pp. 74–81; O. Eissfeldt, 'Jakob-Lea und Jakob-Rachel', *Gottes Wort und Gottes Land. Festschrift H.–W. Hertzberg*, Göttingen, 1965, pp. 50–55 = *Kleine Schriften*, IV, pp. 170–175.

both of which were very similar in this case. It is above all a family story. Unlike Gen 49, Deut 33 and Judges 5, no reference is made in it to the tribes bearing the names of the sons of Jacob, nor is any mention made of the history of those tribes. The etymological explanations given in the text for each of the names simply express the mother's feelings when each son was born. The narrator has, by his art, contrived to turn this genealogy into a dramatic story of rivalry between Leah and Rachel, the two sisters married to Jacob. This is, of course a theme that is found in other family stories in Genesis (Sarah and Hagar). From the birth of the first son to Leah, the unloved wife, through the various interventions first of Rachel's servant and then of Leah's and the return of Leah herself to the scene, the drama moves on towards its climax in the birth of Joseph, the son so long awaited by Rachel, the wife whom Jacob loved.[3] The story must have been given its form in central Palestine, in the 'house of Joseph'.

The order in which the births are recorded may have been the result, not of the primitive tradition, but rather of literary art, since the rivalry between Jacob's two wives is sharpened and the listener or reader waits with heightened expectation for the end of the story because of the division of Leah's sons into two groups separated by the birth of sons to Bilhah and Zilpah, while Rachel remains without them. It is not possible to draw any conclusion from this order of birth regarding the successive stages through which the tribe passed in its development. It is not followed by the genealogical lists given in Gen 35:23–26; 46:8–25. Even though the same distribution of the sons among Jacob's wives and concubines is preserved in these lists, both of them present Leah's sons first. The same applies to the lists of the tribal system. This priority of the group of Leah over that of Rachel is one unvarying aspect of the whole tradition. When seen as part of the history of the people, the sons of the slave-girls Bilhah and Zilpah are the ancestors of groups regarded as less authentic because their blood was more mixed, the place where they lived was more remote or their history was different – or even all three at the same time.

What is remarkable is that this story includes the birth of a daughter, Dinah, to Leah and that it is in this way that the figure of twelve is obtained for the children of Jacob in Mesopotamia. It would, however, be mistaken to conclude from this[4] that there was also a tribe of Dinah and that the earliest 'twelve-tribe system', which did not include Benjamin, is to be found in Gen 29–30. This Dinah is not mentioned in the genealogy of Jacob until Gen 46:15, which is dependent on our text, and her name is the only one that is not given an etymological explanation. Dinah was in fact mentioned here in order to prepare for the story in Gen 34, in which she plays

---

[3] In addition to Lehming, *op. cit.* (see the previous note), see C. Westermann, *Forschung am Alten Testament. Gesammelte Studien*, Munich, 1964, p. 88.

[4] As G. Fohrer did, *BZAW*, 115, pp. 100–101.

an important part as the sister of Simeon and Levi, Leah's sons, and, in this independent tradition, it seems unlikely that Dinah ought to be interpreted as representing a clan.[5]

In fact, the list of the twelve sons of Jacob is completed by the story of Benjamin's birth in Canaan (Gen 35:16–20), which is regarded as an Elohistic text without any Yahwistic parallel.[6] This narrative was not separated from that of Benjamin's eleven brothers by an editor who wanted to change it nor did it replace another story of the birth of Benjamin which was suppressed in Gen 29–30. This fine story always concluded with the birth of Joseph, an ending which provided a perfect dénouement. There was never any doubt that Benjamin was one of Jacob's sons and the ancestor of one of the twelve tribes, but there was a memory of his having had a special history and his birth was traditionally linked with the death of his mother Rachel, whose tomb was venerated on the territory belonging to the tribe of Benjamin. The composition of the story contained in Gen 29–30 presupposes that the birth of Benjamin had already been determined in this way. It is therefore not possible to situate his birth in Mesopotamia.[7]

The same genealogical system of Jacob's twelve sons is also found in the priestly lists, although the order is different: Gen 35:23–26 (Leah, Rachel, Bilhah, Zilpah); Gen 46:8–25 (Leah, Zilpah, Rachel, Bilhah); Ex 1:2–5 (as in Gen 35, but without the names of the mothers and, of course, without Joseph, who was, according to this account, already in Egypt). The same order as in Gen 35 and Ex 1 is also followed in 1 Chron 2:1–2, with the exception of Dan, who is placed in a different position, no doubt by some textual accident.

2. Gen 49

The Testament or Blessings of Jacob has also to be included within the genealogical system (Gen 49:2–27). According to the framework given to this passage by the priestly editor (verses 1 and 28) and according to the introduction (verse 2), Jacob-Israel addresses his twelve sons in this text and their names are the same as in Gen 29–30 and 35. They are also grouped according to maternal origin. This poetic composition is not in accordance with any of the sources known to us in the Pentateuch. It has been suggested that it was collected or compiled by the Yahwist, who used early

[5] See E. Nielsen, *Shechem. A Traditio-Historical Investigation*, Copenhagen, 1955, p. 246; S. Lehming, 'Zur Uberlieferungsgeschichte von Gen. 34', *ZAW*, 70 (1958), pp. 228–250, especially p. 234.

[6] J. Muilenburg, 'The Birth of Benjamin', *JBL*, 75 (1956), pp. 194–201; J. A. Soggin, 'Die Geburt Benjamins, Genesis **XXXV**, 16–20 (21)', *VT*, 11 (1961), pp. 432–440.

[7] This is, however, what is done in the priestly genealogy provided in Gen 35:23–26.

poetical fragments, but the arguments supporting this hypothesis are not convincing. It is in fact a collection of sayings or proverbs about the tribes. These are early, although they date back to different periods and have different origins. It is also difficult to interpret them. This composition as a whole cannot be dated earlier than David's reign because Joseph and Judah play such an important part in it. The historical data concerning each individual tribe that can be deduced from this account is not what interests us principally in this context.[8] At the same time, we are not primarily preoccupied with the environment from which these sayings came or their possible connection with cultic practice.[9] Our basic concern here is rather to examine the evidence provided by the poem for our understanding of the twelve-tribe system.

Leah's six sons appear at the beginning and Rachel's two sons are placed at the end. The four sons of the slave-girls are inserted between these two groups. This is essentially the same order as in Gen 29-30. The slave-girls' sons, however, form only one block, Dan and Naphthali (Bilhah's sons) being separated by Gad and Asher (Zilpah's sons). This order is unique and no satisfactory explanation has been provided for it – as we shall see later, the respective order of the four sons of the slave-girls was never established by tradition.

Although it is for this reason and also because of its editorial framework connected with the genealogical system of the twelve sons of Jacob, this passage in fact represents a transition from this system to the tribal system of the twelve tribes of Israel. There are, on the one hand, individual characteristics in some of the sayings – Reuben, the first-born, mounted his father's bed, which is an allusion to Gen 35:22, and Simeon and Levi, for example, acted violently, which expresses a tradition that is parallel with, but not exactly the same as, the tradition of Gen 34. On the other hand, the punishments are collective – Reuben loses the first place and Simeon and Levi are scattered among Israel. As far as the rest are concerned, there are no individual characteristics[10] – the sayings are applied only to tribes. This is, of course, precisely what is said in the editorial framework. In verse 1, Jacob tells his sons what will happen to them in the course of time and, in verse 28, we read: 'All these make up the tribes of Israel'.

---

[8] See, for this question, H.–J. Zobel, *Stammesspruch und Geschichte* (*BZAW* 95), 1965.

[9] A. H. J. Gunneweg, 'Über den Sitz im Leben der sog. Stammessprüche', *ZAW*, 76 (1964), pp. 245–255.

[10] I find it impossible to accept the explanation of the saying about Judah by a reference to the story of Tamar (Gen 38), which has been suggested by E. M. Good, *JBL*, 82 (1963), pp. 427–432 and C. M. Carmichael, *JBL*, 88 (1969), pp. 435–444.

3. Deut 33

Before we go on to discuss the tribal type of system, we must compare the Testament of Jacob with a poetical fragment of the same kind – the Blessings of Moses (Deut 33).[11] Like Gen 49, this passage is also independent of the pentateuchal sources. It was added to the book of Deuteronomy before the account of Moses' death and put into the mouth of the dying Moses (verse 1), in the same way as Gen 49 was presumed to be a report of the last words of Jacob.

Two distinct elements are present in these Blessings of Moses – on the one hand, a psalm (verses 2–5, 26–29) and, on the other, several oracles enclosed within the framework of the psalm.[12] The psalm is one of the oldest fragments of poetry in the whole of the Old Testament, dating from before the monarchy, and the oracles are inserted into it.[13] These oracles are different in kind from those of Gen 49 – they are all favourable, they have a religious flavour and, in several cases, they refer to Yahweh and take the form of prayers. They were brought together and combined with the psalm in northern Israel and the composition took place later than that of Gen 49, but before the ruin of Samaria. It is not possible to be more precise than this. The oracles are given in the following order: Reuben, Judah, Levi (the sons of Leah), Benjamin and Joseph (the sons of Rachel), Zebulun and Issachar (the sons of Leah), Gad, Dan, Naphthali and Asher (the sons of the slave-girls, not in order). This, of course, is neither the order of birth as given in Gen 29–30, nor the grouping according to maternal origin as in Gen 49. The geneaological type of system does not apply here. Levi is certainly mentioned in this list, but has already become the priestly tribe (see verses 8–11). Zebulun and Issachar are combined in the same oracle (see verses 18–19). The oracle about Joseph concludes with a reference to Ephraim and Manasseh (see verse 17b), which must be an addition borrowed from the tribal system.[14] If this is set aside, what we have left are the names of the eleven 'sons of Israel' (see the title, verse 1), to whom the ten oracles are addressed. These 'sons of Israel' are not, however, the sons of Jacob, but rather the tribes which descended from the latter. It should also

[11] Apart from H.–J. Zobel and A. H. J. Gunneweg (see above, notes 8 and 9), see especially F. M. Cross and D. N. Freedman, 'The Blessings of Moses', *JBL*, 67 (1948), pp. 191–210; R. Tournay, 'Le Psaume et les Bénédictions de Moise', *RB*, 65 (1958), pp. 181–213; I. L. Seeligmann, 'A Psalm from Pre-Regal Times', *VT*, 14 (1964), pp. 75–92.
[12] I. L. Seeligmann, *op. cit.* (see the previous note), has dissociated verse 21b from the blessing of Gad and added it to this.
[13] The unity of the poem has, on the other hand, been defended by several authors, in particular R. Tourney, *op. cit.* (see note 11).
[14] B. Luther, *ZAW*, 21 (1901), p. 31; M. Noth, *Das System der zwölf Stämme Israels*, pp. 21–23. It is not certain whether this may be in order to obtain a total of twelve names (as B. Luther believed).

be noted that one name is missing from this list – Simeon's. In Gen 49, this name only appeared together with that of Levi and both were condemned to be scattered in Israel. The absence of Simeon from the Blessings of Moses may be explained either by the fact that it had disappeared as a tribe, having become completely integrated into Judah[15] or simply by the fact that the oracle concerning this tribe was not known to the compiler of the passage.[16] In any case, this list of the tribes descended from the sons of Jacob, which is neither complete nor in order, clearly points to the fact that the 'twelve-tribe system' was not given the canonical authority that it might have had if it had represented a living institution.

Two other texts have finally to be considered as connected with this system of the 'twelve sons of Jacob'. In the blessings and curses in Deut 27:12–13, the tribes are divided into two groups: Simeon, Levi, Judah, Issachar, Joseph and Benjamin are said to stand on Mount Gerizim, while Reuben, Gad, Asher, Zebulun, Dan and Naphthali stand on Mount Ebal. The principle underlying the division of the tribes in this way has not yet been elucidated.[17] The second of these two texts forms the final paragraph of the book of Ezekiel (Ezek 48:31–34). It is an addition describing the gates of the future city of Jerusalem, named after the twelve sons of Jacob.[18] The three gates in the north are those of Reuben, Judah and Levi (the three most distinguished sons of Leah), in the east are Joseph, Benjamin and Dan (Rachel's two sons and the first son of her slave-girl Bilhah), in the south are Simeon, Issachar and Zebulun (Leah's other three sons) and finally on the west side are the gates of Gad, Asher and Naphthali (the slave-girls' other three sons). The principle behind this naming is genealogical.

II. The Tribal System

The second system is based not on the names of the eponymous heroes of the tribes, the twelve sons of Jacob, but on the groups of the people of Israel which were independent and in possession of their own territory either at the time or in the past. This is the system of the 'twelve tribes of Israel'. One striking characteristic of this system is that it does not include Levi, which had become a priestly tribe without political autonomy and geographical links. The total of twelve is, however, preserved in that Joseph is divided

---

[15] During the reign of David according to the reference in 1 Chron 4:31b. See above, p. 529.

[16] M. Noth, *Das System der zwölf Stämme Israels*, p. 22.

[17] See, for example, the argument put forward by E. Nielsen, *Shechem, A Traditio-Historical Investigation*, pp. 69–72. This author defends the geographical principle and believes that the list originated in Judah.

[18] H. Gese, *Der Verfassungsentwurf des Ezechiel (Kap. 40–48) traditionsgeschichtlich untersucht*, Tübingen, 1957, p. 107.

between the two tribes which descended from him, Ephraim and Manasseh. This system is found exclusively in the book of Numbers, where the evidence is contained in seven texts and in two slightly different forms.[19]

1. Num 1:5–16; 13:4–15

The first of these two forms is found particularly in Num 1:5–16. According to this text, Moses and Aaron were helped in taking a census of Israel by the twelve *n'śî'îm* or leaders of the tribes. In the list provided, their names are given after the names of the tribe which they represent. The order in which these tribes appear reveals the continuing influence of the genealogical principle – Leah's five sons come first (Levi is not included), followed by the group of Rachel, in which Ephraim and Manasseh replace Joseph (this is why the words 'the sons of Joseph' are added at the beginning of verse 10) and finally the sons of the slave-girls, in an order which is different from that of the other lists. What is interesting in this context is that the census itself (verses 20–42) is in the other form of the system which we shall consider next and which includes Gad in a different position. The list of leaders named as Moses' and Aaron's helpers is moreover connected imperfectly to verse 4, the continuation of which is found in verse 17. We may conclude from this that the priestly editor inserted an independent list of the *n'śî'îm* of the twelve tribes, but it has not, however, been established beyond doubt that this list is an early one.[20]

The only other example of this form of the tribal system can be found in a second list of *n'śî'îm* in the book of Numbers. This is the list of the men who were sent out from Kadesh into Canaan to reconnoitre the land (Num 13:4–15). In this list, the names of the leaders are different, but the order is the same if verses 10–11 are moved back to a position before verse 8. This was certainly the original place, if the beginning of verse 11 is taken into account, that is, 'the tribe of Joseph' (*cf.* the 'sons of Joseph', Num 1:10), announcing not only Manasseh in the same verse, but also Ephraim in verse 8. It is also interesting to note that the order Manasseh-Ephraim is not the same as in Num 1:5–16, but is the same as in Num 26:28ff. The order of the four sons of the slave-girls is once again different in this list and the word 'tribe', which appears before each member makes the nature of the system quite explicit – it is a tribal system. The passage also belongs to a later stratum in the priestly editing and it would seem to have been constructed

---

[19] See especially M. Noth, *Das System der zwölf Stämme Israels*, pp. 14–20 and his commentary on Numbers *(ATD)*, 1966.

[20] M. Noth believed that it was early (see his commentary); cf. D. Kellermann, *Die Priesterschaft von Numeri 1, 1 bis 10 (BZAW 120)*, 1970, pp. 5–6. This form is, according to Kellermann, later in date than Num 1:20–43; *ibid.*, pp. 15–17.

artificially rather than to preserve an early list.

2. Num 1:20–43; 2:2–31; 7:10–88; 10:13–27; 26:5–51

The second of these forms is that of two cases of a census taken of the tribes, at the beginning and at the end of their sojourn in the desert (Num 1:20–43 and 26:5–51).[21] In both of these lists, the numbers given for the members of each tribe are so great that they cannot be regarded as valid either for the period of the Judges or for the time spent in the desert.[22] All that really concerns us here, however, is the list and the order of the tribes. In Num 26, Reuben, Simeon, Gad, Judah, Issachar and Zebulun are listed first (these constitute the Leah group). Manasseh, Ephraim and Benjamin (the group of Rachel) follow. The list concludes with Dan, Asher and Naphthali (the group of the concubines). The situation is the same in Num 1, the only difference being that the order is Ephraim-Manasseh instead of Manasseh-Ephraim. M. Noth gives priority to Num 26. He was of the opinion that the figures were of a later date, but that in this list of the tribes the priestly editor had provided an authentic and early document, certainly dating back to the period of the Judges after Deborah and before David. According to Noth, the details of the clans of each tribe given in this list – details which, in his view, influenced the genealogies given in Gen 46:8–27 and 1 Chron 2–8 – can only be explained satisfactorily if the list dates back to a period when these subdivisions were still significant, in other words, a period before the new administrative organisation of the monarchy. According to another hypothesis, some of these Israelite clans bore the names of Canaanite cities or enclosures which were not destroyed until the reign of David. Neither of these two arguments is at all convincing[23] and there are serious objections to them. Quite apart from the figures and the details add-

[21] For this second text in particular, see M. Noth, *Das System der zwölf Stämme Israels, Exkurs I*, pp. 122–132.

[22] Three explanations – all of them equally improbable – have been suggested for this. The first is that the figures are historically important, but that they reflect a later census made at the time of David. This view is held by W. F. Albright, 'The Administrative Divisions of Israel and Judah', *JPOS*, 5 (1925), pp. 17–54, especially pp. 22–25. The second explanation is that they were obtained by means of gematria; see G. Fohrer, *Einleitung in das Alte Testament*, Heidelberg, 1965, p. 200 (*Introduction to the Old Testament*,); or by means of a mathematical combination; see M. Barnouin, 'Remarques sur les tableaux numériques du Livres des Nombres', *RB*, 76 (1969), pp. 351–364. Finally, according to the third explanation that has been offered, the word *eleph* does not mean a 'thousand', but a squad of ten men; see G. E. Mendenhall, 'The Census Lists of Numbers 1 and 26', *JBL*, 77 (1958), pp. 52–66, cf. M. Noth, in his commentary, *ATD*, pp. 22–23 and 177.

[23] See S. Mowinckel, ' "Rahelstämme" und "Leastämme" ', *Von Ugarit nach Qumran. Festschrift O. Eissfeldt (BZAW, 77)*, 1958. pp. 129–150, especially pp. 139–142; J. Hoftijzer, *NTT*, 14 (1959–1960) (see above, note 1), p. 259.

ed in the case of certain tribes, it is most unlikely that this list reflects a document dating back to the period of the Judges. It would be difficult to explain why it was edited at all and how it came to have been preserved for such a long time considering that – according to Noth himself – it no longer had any real practical value. The purpose of the list was apparently to provide a census of Israel as taken by Moses on the plains of Moab, but this is without any doubt a fiction. The obvious conclusion, then, is that the list itself may well be fictitious and it is possible and even probable that authentic early traditions are used in it. It is not, however, a piece of authentic evidence of a 'twelve-tribe system' dating back to the period before the institution of the monarchy.

The most striking aspect of this tribal system is the different position occupied by Gad, which occurs third, in the place taken by Levi in the system of the twelve sons of Jacob. According to Noth, this change of position can be explained by a desire to maintain, after Levi had been suppressed, a group of six tribes of Leah (Gad was the son of Leah's slave-girl Zilpah).[24] It is, however, not at all certain whether there was, at an early stage, an established group of six sons of Leah – a first 'amphictyony of the six tribes' as it has been called. We shall return to this question later; in the meantime, it can be said that this does not explain either the choice of Gad or the exact place given to this tribe. This change of position can be better explained[25] as a division of the twelve tribes into four groups of three each. If an attempt is made to divide in the same way the list as it is given in the other form of the system (see Num 1:5–15), Judah has to be placed in the third position in the group of Reuben and the three tribes of Rachel are shared between two groups. If Gad is placed in the position occupied by Levi, Judah then has to be placed at the beginning of a group and the group of Rachel remains unchanged. If, on the other hand, Gad was chosen to take Levi's place, this must have been because of the tribe's geographical and historical connections with Reuben in the group in which it was placed, with the secondary advantage that the three other sons of the concubines also formed a closely connected group from the geographical point of view – they were, after all, the three southernmost tribes.[26] These manipulations provide another clear example of the artificial character of this 'system'.

The same division of the tribes into four groups of three tribes each is also found in the order of the tribes in the camp given in Num 2:2–31 and the marching order given in Num 10:13–27. In both of these lists, there is the

---

[24] M. Noth, *Geschichte*, p. 86 (*History*, pp. 88–89).

[25] This opinion was expressed by J. Hoftijzer, *NTT*, 14 (1959–1960), pp. 259–260; D. Kellermann, *BZAW* 120 (see above, note 20), pp. 11–17.

[26] The geographical argument is, however, not enough to account for this order, which seems also to have been determined by the arrangement of the camp in Num 2:2–31; see the following note.

same inversion of Ephraim-Manasseh as in Num 1 and the same position at the beginning of the group led by Judah. The order of the tribes in the camp is as follows:[27]

On the east side: Judah, Issachar and Zebulun;
On the south side: Reuben, Simeon and Gad;
On the west side: Ephraim, Manasseh and Benjamin;
On the north side: Dan, Asher and Naphthali.

In the order of march, the 'camps' move off one after the other under the standards of Judah, Reuben, Ephraim and Dan.

It was also in this order that the leaders of the twelve tribes brought their offerings for the dedication of the altar over a period of twelve successive days (Num 7:10–88). This text belongs to a late priestly level and is dependent on Num 2 and 10. In this form, the ties with the genealogical system of the twelve tribes of Jacob and these with the tradition of Gen. 29–30 are completely broken.

III. THE TERRITORIAL LISTS

As we have already pointed out, the twelve-tribe system was applied to autonomous human groups, each one with its own territory. One would expect to find the same system in the territorial lists which are included in the great geographical description occupying the whole of the middle of the book of Joshua (Jos 13–19), in the account of the arrangements made by Moses for the sharing of the Promised Land (Num 34) and in the outline of the geography of the Israel of the future given in Ezek 48.

1. Jos 13–19

After recalling the division of Transjordania between the tribes of Reuben and Gad and the half-tribe of Manasseh (Jos 13:8–33), the book of Joshua proceeds to describe the territories allocated to the three great tribes to the west of the Jordan – Judah (and Caleb), Ephraim and the other half of Manasseh (Jos 14–17). The rest of the country was shared out by lot between the seven other tribes at an assembly held at Shiloh, portions being awarded in turn to Benjamin, Simeon, Zebulun, Issachar, Asher, Naphthali and Dan (Jos 18–19). According to this text, then, there were thirteen

---

[27] In this arrangement according to the points of the compass, Judah is given the place of honour in the east, where the entrance to the Tent of Meeting was; the order of the other groups derives from this; see A. Kuschke, 'Die Lagervorstellung der priesterschriftlichen Erzählung. Eine Überlieferungsgeschichtliche Studie', *ZAW*, 63 (1951), pp. 74–105, especially pp. 96–98; D. Kellermann, *BZAW* 120 (see above note 20), pp. 17–32.

territories – or fourteen, if the share awarded by lot to Caleb, which is discussed separately (Jos 14:6–15; 15:13–19), is included – although there were only twelve tribes (Manasseh being divided into two), those of the tribal system of Numbers. Levi had no territory of its own according to this account (Jos 13:33; 14:4; 18:7), but the Levites received the tenure of a number of towns in the territories of all the tribes (Jos 21). Various reminders of the genealogical system of the twelve sons of Jacob are found in the notes (Jos 14:4 and 16:4) on the sons of Joseph forming the two tribes of Manasseh and Ephraim and on the 'house of Joseph' (Jos 17:14 ff). Despite this, however, the order is not the same as that of the tribal system or that of the genealogical system. On the contrary, it follows the stages of the settlement of the tribes – first Transjordania and then Canaan on the west bank of the Jordan, in the first place the territories claimed by the great tribes (Jos 14:6; 17:14) and then the territories which had been 'conquered', but were not 'occupied' (Jos 18:3) and which had been distributed among the other tribes.

A. Alt[28] made a distinction between two elements in this geographical outline – a description of the frontiers of the different tribes, based on a document dating from the end of the period of the Judges, before the reign of David, and certain lists of towns reflecting the administrative divisions existing at the time of Josiah. More recent studies have resulted in these lists being given an earlier date, but these do not concern us here. As far as the definition of the tribal frontiers is concerned, M. Noth, who has developed Alt's thesis, was of the opinion that they were based on a document prior to the monarchy and listing only the 'frontier points', which an editor put into connected sentences.[29]

This analysis has, however, been criticised by S. Mowinckel,[30] who was of the opinion that the whole of this passage in the book of Joshua was composed by the priestly author after the Exile. This author did not, Mowinckel claimed, use written 'documents', but constructed his description from oral traditions and memories of the situation that existed before the Exile. Y. Kaufmann has also raised serious objections to this theory, although his conclusions were different.[31] According to this scholar, Jos 13–19 was an early text; it was, he believed, a book describing the distribu-

---

[28] A. Alt, Das System der Stammesgrenzen im Buche Josua. Festschrift E. Sellin, Leipzig, 1927, pp. 13–24 = Kleine Schriften, I, pp. 193–202.

[29] M. Noth 'Studien zu den historisch-geographischen Dokumenten des Josuabuches', ZDPV, 58 (1935), pp. 185–255, especially pp. 185–201; Das Buch Josua (HAT),[2] 1953, pp. 13–15.

[30] S. Mowinckel, Zur Frage nach dokumentarischen Quellen in Josua 13–19, Oslo, 1946; Tetrateuch-Pentateuch-Hexateuch (BZAW 90), 1964, pp. 51–75. M. Noth's reply to the former book is in 'Überlieferungsgeschichtliches zur zweiten Hälfte des Josuabuches', Alttestamentliche Studien. Festschrift Fr. Nötscher (BBB 1), 1950, pp. 152–167.

[31] Y. Kaufmann, The Biblical Account of the Conquest of Palestine, Jerusalem, 1953, pp. 7–57.

tion of the land that had been conquered or remained to be conquered between the members of the federation of the tribes, a Utopian document dating back to the time of Joshua himself.

Kaufmann's theory can be set aside without further comment, but Mowinckel's calls for closer consideration. Several authors of Introductions to the Old Testament published in recent years have supported the thesis that this entire section of Joshua was post-deuteronomistic and priestly in origin,[32] whereas the thesis put forward by Alt and Noth is generally accepted by historians and geographers. The essential elements of the latter can be retained and the date of the editorial work can be left open. If certain aspects simply represent an ideal – and this is especially the case with the extension of the tribal frontiers to the Mediterranean coastline, a point which they never reached – there are also complicated frontier outlines which could never have been simply invented nor could they represent a situation existing after the time of David. The editor certainly did not find these data in a 'document' in which the frontiers of all the tribes were defined. He undoubtedly drew on several early traditions.[33] The tribes were in fact dealt with in a very unequal way.[34]

Alt had already observed that the frontiers of three tribes – Issachar, Dan and Simeon – on the west of the Jordan were left undefined. The territories allotted to the tribes in Transjordania are named in the description, but the precise frontiers are not given. The frontiers in the south, east and west of the territory allotted to Judah are, in the passage that we are considering here, no more than the general limits of the land of Canaan. Only the northern frontier is defined and, while this is defined more precisely than that of the other tribes, it is at the same time the southern frontier of the territory given to Benjamin and appears to reflect the situation at the time of David. The description of the frontiers is therefore only really effective in the case of six of the tribes, which are presented in this order: Ephraim, Manasseh, Benjamin, Zebulun, Asher and Naphthali. These, it should be noted, are the same tribes – and, what is more, the only ones – that are found in Judges 1 in the list of towns which had not been conquered in verse 21, Benjamin and, in verses 27–33, Manasseh, Ephraim, Zebulun, Asher and Naphthali. The same list is found again, in a more or less complete form, in the story of Gideon (Judges 6:35; 7:23–24); Manasseh, Asher, Zebulun, Naphthali and the highlands of Ephraim (which might include Benjamin). It is also the same list of tribes which, according to the Song of

[32] O. Eissfeldt, A. Weiser and G. Fohrer.

[33] K.–D. Schunk, *Benjamin, Untersuchungen zur Entstehung und Geschichte eines israelitischen Stammes (BZAW* 86), 1963, pp. 141–143.

[34] For what follows, see Y. Aharoni, *The Land of the Bible*, London, 1967, pp. 227–239, *ibid.*, 'New Aspects of the Israelite Occupation in the North', *Near Eastern Archaeology in the Twentieth Century. Essays in Honor of Nelson Glueck*, Garden City, N.Y., 1970, especially pp. 260–262.

Deborah (Judges 5), took part in the battle: Ephraim, Benjamin, Machir, Zebulun, Issachar and Naphthali. This list is different only in that Machir replaces Manasseh and Issachar takes Asher's place. We shall be returning to this text, but in the meantime it is important to compare it here with the definition of the tribal frontiers given in Jos 13–19 and the list provided in Judges 1– there was a grouping of the central and northern tribes before the institution of the monarchy which was different from the 'twelve-tribe system'. The latter, which is reflected in the passage in Jos 13–19 describing the territories of all the tribes, does not seem to go back to a period before the reign of David. As we have already pointed out, the lists of towns reflect a still later period.

2. Num 34

This chapter of the book of Numbers begins with a description of Canaan, the Promised Land to the west of the Jordan, and a definition of its frontiers (Num 34:1–12). This is followed by a reminder of the lands allotted to Reuben, Gad and the half-tribe of Manasseh in Transjordania (Num 34:13–15). Finally, there is a list of the leaders or *n'ši'îm* who were to divide the country between the nine other tribes and the other half of Manasseh (Num 34:16–29). The order in which they are placed is from south to north, although Dan is placed beside Benjamin because the learned editor remembered the first settlement of Dan before the tribe migrated towards the north (Jos 19:40–47; Judges 18). The passage belongs to a comparatively late stratum in the priestly editing.

3. Ezek 48

One last territorial list is provided by Ezekiel, in his description of the sharing of the territory between the tribes of the renewed Israel of the future.[35] The new land of Israel was to be entirely to the west of the Jordan, in accordance with the description given in Ezek 47:13–23. Consequently all the tribes, including those of Transjordania, were to be regrouped in this new Holy Land. According to the prophet's description, the country was to be divided into parallel strips running from the east to the west and on both sides of the territory set aside for Yahweh, the *t'rûmah;* this was to be divided between the sanctuary with its priests and Levites, the city

---

[35] W. Zimmerli, *Ezechiel (BKAT)*, 1969, pp. 1226–1235; M. Greenberg, 'Idealism and Practicality in Numbers 35:4–5 and Ezekiel 48', *JAOS*, 88 (1968), pp. 59–66; G. C. Macholz, 'Noch einmal: Planungen für den Wiederaufbau nach der Katastrophe von 587', *VT*, 19 (1969), pp. 322–352, especially pp. 330–336.

(Jerusalem) and the prince or *nāśî* (verses 23–28). Seven tribes were to have their portion to the north of this sacred territory (verses 1–7) and five to the south (verses 23–28). This unequal division of the land appears to take the far from central position of Jerusalem into account. The order in which the tribes are given in this passage again is from south to north, but it is difficult to find a complete explanation for every detail of it. The tribes descended from the slave-girls are, in this list, given land at the extremities of the country and farthest from the sanctuary, whereas those descended from Leah and Rachel are nearest to the sanctuary. On each side of the part set aside for the sanctuary are Judah and Benjamin, the chosen portion of the new Israel. Reuben is placed next to Judah because of the early pre-eminence of the tribe and possibly because Reuben's incest was remembered – it took place in this region. The presence of Reubenite elements from Transjordania in this part of the country may also account for its having been allocated to this tribe. The transference of the territories of Issachar and Zebulun to the south can perhaps be explained as an attempt to create a balance between the two groups of seven and five tribes. It is more difficult to account for the placing of Judah to the north and Benjamin to the south of Jerusalem, which is, after all, contrary to the historical geographical position. It may be due to an attempt to place Benjamin closer to the sanctuary, which was situated in the northern part of the *t'rûmāh*.[36] On the other hand, it may reflect an influence exerted by the basic meaning of the name Benjamin (*ben-yāmîn*, 'son of the south').

This Utopian geographical arrangement at least reflects a vision of the future tribal system without Levi and with Ephraim and Manasseh divided. At the same time, the placing of the tribes according to their presumed maternal origin and the gloss in Ezek 47:13b connect this territorial system with the genealogical system.

IV. THE MIXED LISTS

Before concluding our outline of these systems, it is necessary to mention two late lists. These are the lists of the various contingents of tribes which came to Hebron to proclaim David king (1 Chron 12:25–38) and the list of the leaders of the tribes at the time of David (1 Chron 27:16–22). These two passages are, like their contexts, additions to the Chronicler's work.

1. *1 Chron 12:25–38*

This list includes the Cisjordanian tribes listed from south to north and the Transjordanian tribes given as a block. Levi is reported in this list as

---

[36] G. C. Macholz, *op. cit.* (see the preceding note).

coming with its own contingent, together with those of the Aaronites and of Zadok. Ephraim and Manasseh are listed separately and Manasseh is further divided into two half-tribes coming from both sides of the Jordan. There are therefore thirteen tribes included in this list, but only twelve contingents, since only one comes from Transjordania. The list is a free composition which falsifies the tribal and territorial system by adding the name of Levi in order to satisfy the interests of the levitical circles from which the list came.[37]

2. 1 Chron 27:16–22

In this list of the tribal leaders during the reign of David, the six tribes of the genealogical group of Leah are mentioned first of all in the same order as Gen 29–30, including Levi, but adding to Levi the Aaronites with their own leader Zadok, as though Aaron were a tribe (see the beginning of verse 16). These are followed by the group of Rachel: Ephraim, the two halves of Manasseh, Benjamin and, on each side of the latter, Naphthali and Dan, the sons of Bilhah, Rachel's slave-girl. If Levi and Aaron are counted as one and the two halves of Manasseh are kept separate or if Levi and Aaron are kept separate and the two halves of Manasseh are counted as one, a total of twelve tribes is obtained, but Gad and Asher, the two sons of Zilpah, Leah's slave-girl, are missing. The list therefore does not correspond with any of the known systems. It is neither genealogical nor tribal and the inclusion of Levi reflects, as it does in the first of these two lists (1 Chron 12), the preoccupations of the circle of priests and Levites. It preserves the figure twelve, but in order to do this it has to omit two tribes. There is, moreover, no evidence of the existence of most of the names of the leaders outside the book of Chronicles. It is undoubtedly a late composition.

V. THE DATE OF THE 'SYSTEMS'

A number of conclusions can be drawn from this study of the texts with regard to the date of the various systems.

1. *Literary criticism*

The genealogical system is the one found in the earliest texts. The tradition of the sons of Jacob (Gen 29–30; 35:16–20) has already been traced

[37] The historical importance of this list has, however, been defended by G. E. Mendenhall in the article quoted above in note 22, pp. 62–63. According to J. M. Myers, *I Chronicles*

back to the period during which the Yahwist was working, at the time of David or Solomon. The passage containing the Blessings or Testament of Jacob (Gen 49) was not written before the reign of David, but it cannot, on the other hand, have been written much later than this. The incomplete list in Deut 33, the lists contained in Deut 27:12–13 and Ezek 48:31–34 and the priestly genealogies in Gen 35:23–26; 46:8–25; Ex 1:2–5 and 1 Chron 2:1–2 are all derived from this genealogical type and testify to its persistence throughout the whole of the Old Testament tradition.

The second type, that is, the tribal system without Levi, is found only in the priestly editing of the book of Numbers. A form in which the genealogical grouping is maintained is present in the two lists of the leaders of the tribes (Num 1:5–16; 13:4–15). The other form, in which Gad appears in the place occupied by Levi in the genealogical system, is found in the two examples of a census (Num 1–20–43 and 26:5–51) and, together with the change of position of the three tribes led by Judah, in the order of the tribes in the camp (Num 2:2–31) and the order of march (Num 10:13–28), on which Num 7:10–83 is based. Considered as the product of editors the form of Num 1:5–16 is later than that of Num 1:20–43 and 26; the first of these texts may have been an attempt to correct the latter by replacing Gad in the position that it occupied in the genealogical system.

The third type, the territorial system, is found in the geographical description given in Jos 13–19, the editing of which is post-deuteronomistic. In the literary criticism of this long passage, however, a distinction has been made between a general description of the tribal territories as they were at the time of David and an earlier definition of the boundaries of the six central and northern tribes preserved within this general description. The territorial list in Num 34 is a late work of the priestly editor, whereas the geographical outline provided by Ezek 48 is clearly Utopian.

2. History of traditions

It is clear from this literary analysis that the latest system is the tribal type as exemplified in the book of Numbers. It is, as we have already said, unlikely that 'documents' were used by the priestly editor of these texts. This tribal system belongs rather to the same tradition as Jos 13–19, since it contains the same number of tribes and the same names. As we have also pointed out, the boundaries of the tribal territories which are the framework of this geographical outline reflect the situation that existed dur-

---

(*Anchor Bible*), Garden City, N.Y., 1965, pp. 95–96, it was not a pure fabrication composed after the Exile. According to F. Michaeli, *Les Livres des Chroniques, d'Esdras et de Néhémie*, Neuchâtel, 1967, p. 84, it was based on an early tradition.

ing the reign of David. The tribal system therefore goes back to this period at least. This is the same date to which we were led by our literary analysis of the genealogical system of Gen 29–30 and Gen 49. What we are bound to ask now is whether we can use traditio-historical means to go back further into the past and determine which system is the earlier – the genealogical system of the twelve sons of Jacob, including Levi and Joseph, or the system of the twelve tribes of Israel, without Levi and Joseph, but including Ephraim and Manasseh.

According to M. Noth,[38] the earlier system was undoubtedly that of the twelve eponymous sons of Jacob, since it included a profane tribe of Levi and in the case of Joseph did not make any division into the two tribes of Ephraim and Manasseh. This system dated from the beginning of the period of the Judges, the time of the founding of the 'amphictyony'. The second system was, in Noth's opinion, later than the disappearance of the profane tribe of Levi and later than the Song of Deborah, in which Manasseh was not yet recognized, but it was earlier than the monarchy.

Although A. H. J. Gunneweg[39] believed that there was never a profane tribe of Levi, he accepted the order of the systems proposed by Noth and claimed that the genealogical system included the twelve members of the 'amphictyony' and that Levi formed part of this, not as a political 'tribe', but as a constitutive part of 'Israel'. In his opinion, the tribal system was an adaptation of this amphictyonic system to new geographical and political conditions – Levi, being without territory, was no longer represented in the amphictyony and Joseph had given way to the two tribes Ephraim and Manasseh, which had become consolidated. It is clear from this that both Noth and Gunneweg based their views on the idea of an amphictyony of Israel, and we have already shown how untenable this idea is.

G. Fohrer[40] rejected this thesis, but accepted Noth's dating of both the genealogical system of Gen 49 and the tribal system. On the other hand, he believed that there was an even earlier system without Benjamin, but containing a tribe of Dinah which soon disappeared. This system could be dated either at the end of the settlement in Canaan or right at the beginning of the period of the Judges. We have rejected this hypothesis.[41]

Later dates and the opposite order were claimed by J. Hoftijzer.[42] This scholar believed that the tribal system without Levi reflected the situation as it existed at the end of the period of the Judges and as consolidated into a

---

[38] M. Noth, *Das System der zwölf Stämme Israels, op. cit.*, pp. 28–39, 66–74; *Geschichte*, pp. 83–84 (*History*, pp. 85–86).

[39] A. H. J. Gunneweg, *Leviten und Priester. Hauptlinien der Traditionsbildung und Geschichte des israelitisch-jüdischen Kultpersonals*, Göttingen, 1965, pp. 52–64.

[40] G. Fohrer, *BZAW*, 115, quoted above in note 1, pp. 100–103.

[41] See above, p. 719–720.

[42] J. Hoftijzer, *NTT*, 14 (1959–1960), quoted above in note 1, especially pp. 261–262.

'system' by the activity of the newly established monarchy to centralise the administration. The system of the twelve sons of Jacob, which was, in Hoftijzer's opinion, later, was an attempt to include the group of levitical priests in the list of the twelve tribes, with its firmly established number of twelve, by uniting Ephraim and Manasseh under the name of Joseph.

A review of the opinions of these different scholars shows clearly how difficult the problem of dating these systems is. It is, of course, possible that it has not been correctly posed. In the previous chapter, we attempted to banish the spell cast by the amphictyonic thesis and some of the arguments used there can be taken even further. During the whole of the period of the Judges, for instance, there is no evidence at all of any communal action taken by all twelve tribes or of the existence of a council of all the tribes or of any intertribal political organisation. This would seem to point to the fact that no 'twelve-tribe system' ever functioned as an institution during the whole of this period. This conclusion is certainly borne out by the variants in the lists – although the figure twelve is constant, the names and the order in which they appear are variable, changing from one system to another and even within different lists in the same system. These variations do not reflect historical changes to which an institution that was founded at an earlier date would have had to adapt itself. On the contrary, they are in accordance with special intentions underlying the compositions of the lists. The tribal system and the territorial system are really only two different forms of the twelve-tribe system of Israel seen either in its political aspect in the case of the first or in its geographical aspect in the case of the second. The ancestors who gave their names to the tribes and who were all presumed to have been the sons of Jacob-Israel are set out on a genealogical table in the system of the twelve sons of Jacob. Since these two forms are based on different principles and neither the one nor the other has any corresponding institution or function, they may well have been contemporary and no more than two different ways of expressing the unity of the people of Israel in the plurality of its many aspects.

Both of these two forms were later than the settlement in Canaan.[43] They presuppose this settlement as an event in the past and some of the tribes already bear the names of the territories in which they have settled – the hill country of Judah, the hill country of Ephraim and perhaps even the hill country of Naphthali. The probable explanation of the name Benjamin is the location of this group in the country south of Ephraim, the tribe with which it crossed the Jordan and entered central Palestine. On the other hand, both forms are prior to the reign of Solomon, who divided Israel into twelve districts. The list of these districts is given in the early document of 1

[43] In this paragraph, some of the conclusions drawn in Part III, 'The Traditions concerning the Settlement in Canaan', are repeated.

736 IV: THE PERIOD OF THE JUDGES

Kings 4:7–19.[44] Judah had a special administration and only four of the administrative districts in Solomon's kingdom bore the name of a tribe. These were Naphthali, Issachar, Benjamin and Asher. The last, however, also included Zebulun and this name can be restored to verse 16 ('in the highlands'). The 'hill country of Ephraim' is a geographical name which includes Ephraim and Manasseh. Even if the name 'Gad' is read – as in the Greek version – instead of Gilead in verse 19, the 'land of Gad' is also a geographical term and the rest of Transjordania is divided into two districts named after their administrative centres – Ramoth-gilead and Mahanaim. The other four of these administrative districts group together towns in the coastal region and on the Plain of Jezreel, in Canaanite territories which were not conquered until the reign of David. Although it takes into account the fact that certain of the tribes belonged to it, this administrative division marks a clear break with the political and geographical system of the twelve tribes in the lists contained in the book of Numbers and in Jos 13–19.

It is possible to give fairly precise dates between these two limits, that is, the settlement in Canaan and the reign of Solomon. As far as the twelve-tribe system is concerned, the territorial description provided in Jos 13–19, which includes both Judah and Israel, is in accordance with the united kingdom of David. The twelve-tribe system itself may have existed before this one kingdom, but certainly not much before. It included Judah and Simeon, which are not mentioned in the Song of Deborah. Simeon was not integrated into Judah fully and definitively until the reign of David, but, on the other hand, the tribe of Judah itself does not, in our opinion, seem to have achieved full individuality before the time of Saul and does not, moreover, seem to have reached its full stature as a tribe until David came to power at Hebron.[45] The twelve-tribe system, we may therefore conclude, seems not to have existed before the end of the period of the Judges or the very beginning of the monarchy.

The system of the twelve sons of Jacob was, it seems, no earlier than this,[46] since, in this system, Judah is given a place of honour among the eponyms. The fact that Levi and Joseph also have a place in this list cannot be used as an argument against this dating. In Gen 49, Levi appears as a profane tribe, but according to the oracle it was to be 'scattered among

[44] A. Alt, 'Israels Gaue unter Salomo', *Alttestamentliche Studien R. Kittel ... dargebracht*, Leipzig, 1913, pp. 1–19 = *Kleine Schriften*, II, pp. 76–89; R. de Vaux, *Institutions*, I, pp. 206–208 (*Ancient Israel. Its Life and Institutions*, pp. 133–135); Y. Aharoni, *The Land of the Bible*, London, 1967, pp. 273–280; G. E. Wright, 'The Provinces of Solomon', *Eretz-Israel*, 8 (*E.L. Sukenik Memorial Volume*), 1967, pp. 58*–68*.
[45] See above, pp. 546–550.
[46] G. Wallis, *ZAW*, 81 (1969), p. 28 believed that this system certainly represented the situation as it was at the time of David's united kingdom.

Israel'. At the time when this oracle was composed, Levi was in no sense a political unity. In view of this situation, a place could not be given to Levi in the political and geographical system of the twelve tribes found in Numbers and Jos 13–19, but the tribe could be included in the genealogical system. It is quite possible to assume, as I have done, that there was a profane tribe of Levi which, after it had been 'scattered among Israel', became a priestly tribe. Another possibility is that there was a profane tribe of Levi, but that the priestly tribe of the same name had not really descended from the profane tribe. On the other hand, there may never have been a profane tribe of Levi at all. Whichever hypothesis is accepted, however, it is clear that despite their special position the Levites regarded themselves and were regarded by those around them as an authentic element of the people of Israel and as the descendants of one of the sons of Jacob, their ancestor Levi having a special place in a list of eponyms.

As far as Joseph is concerned, we may be quite certain that there never was a tribe of this name. There is no mention of Joseph in the earliest literary text dealing with the tribes, the Song of Deborah, which lists only Ephraim, to which is joined Benjamin, and Machir (Manasseh). Ephraim and Manasseh were not branches of a tribe of Joseph which was presumably divided into two, but rather tribes joined together under a common eponym. Terms such as the 'tribe of Joseph' (once), the 'tribe of the sons of Joseph' (once) and the 'sons of Joseph' (several times) occur only in later texts. The term the 'house of Joseph' is earlier – it occurs, for example, in the Yahwistic text Judges 1:22–23 and in 2 Sam 19:21 – but it presupposes the existence of Ephraim and Manasseh and, on the basis of these texts, we cannot go back earlier than the reign of David. It was then that a 'house of Joseph' was mentioned for the first time as including Ephraim and Manasseh, just as there was a tendency, when David was made king at Hebron (2 Sam 2:7, 10, 11), to speak of a 'house of Judah' as the name for the tribe of Judah and the various groups assimilated by it.[47] Our conclusion is therefore that the genealogical system of the twelve sons of Jacob can be given the same date as that given to the system of the twelve tribes. In this way, our dates are very close to those suggested by scholars who have based their dates on a literary analysis of the earliest evidence of the two systems.

The two systems, then, are contemporary. They are different from each other because they are constructed according to different principles, but it is precisely because of this difference that we can be sure that neither is representative of an institution that ever really functioned. They are both artificial, but only partially.[48] On the one hand, it is certain that each of the

[47] See above, pp. 443–510.
[48] This was clearly perceived by M. Noth, *Das System der zwölf Stämme Israels*, op. cit., pp. 39–41, *Geschichte*, pp. 84–85 (*History*, pp. 86–87), but it does not strengthen the amphictyonic theory.

twelve tribes belonging to the tribal system existed as an autonomous group at a certain time. On the other hand, however, it is equally certain that the members of each of these groups regarded themselves as united by blood and as the descendants of one of the eponyms of the system of the twelve sons of Jacob. It would be quite wrong to deprive the early traditions of the Pentateuch and the books of Joshua and Judges of all their historical basis. The sayings about the tribes recorded in Gen 49 are early and the description of the apportioning of territories to the tribes in Jos 13–19 reflects a real situation. However, the two lists each begin with the tribes of Reuben and Simeon, both of which soon became unimportant; whereas the insignificant tribe of Dan is retained in the lists, the southern groups, which played an important part at the time of the settlement, and Caleb in particular, are not included. Zebulun and Issachar, which occupied adjoining and rather restricted territories with badly defined frontiers, are treated in both systems as different groups and placed on the same level as the great tribes. The two halves of Manasseh, which possessed much larger territories, separated by the Jordan, formed only one tribe, however, at least according to these lists. Historical reasons can, of course, be given for each of these choices, but the fact remains that the choices were made. The motive for this was to arrive at the figure of twelve for the number of tribes, this being the only element common to the two systems and present even in the mixed lists of 1 Chron 12 and 27. Since the comparison with the twelve members of the Pylaeo-Delphic amphictyony and the Etruscan league has, however, proved to be a totally insufficient reason for preserving this number we are bound to look for another explanation.

VI. Tribal Federations in the Semitic World

One objection that has been raised against the hypothesis of an Israelite 'amphictyony' is that the group formed by the twelve tribes of Israel was compared with certain institutions in an entirely different ethnic and social environment. There are in fact closer parallels among the Semitic peoples leading, or having led in the past, a semi-nomadic way of life as shepherds or herdsmen similar to the life of the Israelites at the beginning of their history. We propose to examine a number of examples of this, beginning with the modern era and going back in history.

The camel-breeding tribes of Syria and Mesopotamia are represented above all by two great, rival groups, the 'Aneze and the Shammar, both of which go back to the pre-Islamic era.[49] The 'Aneze arrived from Arabia in

[49] For the 'Aneze and the Shammar, see Max Freiherr von Oppenheim, *Die Beduinen*, I, Leipzig, 1939, pp. 62–165. For the 'Aneze, see E. Gräf, 'Anaza', *Encyclopédie de l'Islam*,

several migrations. The various groups had different origins, but they all acknowledge a common ancestor, 'Annaza. From about A.D. 1700 or even earlier, the pattern of their tribal organisation begins to emerge and they now form six tribes, each with its own territory for grazing. These tribes are the Ruwalā, the Sba'a, the 'Amarāt, the Fed'ān, the Wald 'Ali and the Hesene. These six tribes are also grouped into two rival branches, each connected with an intermediate ancestor – on the one hand, the Hesene, the Wald 'Ali and the Ruwalā, and, on the other, the Fed'ān, the Sba'a and the 'Amarāt. Each tribe preserves its independence, but all the tribes are conscious of their common origin and of the solidarity uniting them. The hereditary enemies of the 'Aneze are the Shammar. The latter arrived from Arabia in two successive waves. They form a confederation of tribes of different origin, grouped into two branches, one – the Shammar-Nejd – in northern Arabia and the other – the Shammar-Jerba – in Jezireh (northern Syria). Unlike the 'Aneze, they all acknowledge the authority of a supreme sheikh.

In the region of the Middle Euphrates, there is a group of small sheep-raising tribes which came from Arabia at least two centuries ago and are known as the 'Agedāt, a word meaning the 'confederates'. They are, however, also believed to have descended from a common ancestor. They are both nomadic and settled people at the same time and are divided into about twenty different groups, each with its own sheikh, chosen by the heads of families. Although they lack a central organisation they are conscious of their mutual solidarity, dating from their migration together from Arabia and their shared conquest of the valley.[50]

In Transjordania, several tribes which are in the process of becoming settled have joined together in a covenant known as the ben'ame.[51] The etymological significance of the name is that these people have become 'cousins'. Neighbouring tribes are joined together by an oath in this covenant, which is both defensive and offensive and includes clauses promising mutual assistance and special rules regarding blood vengeance.

This modern practice is a survival of an earlier Islamic institution, generally known as the hilf.[52] This hilf was always concluded with solemnity. It did not in any way encroach on the autonomy or the equality of the individual tribes, but aimed to bring about a state of lasting peace between them and to unite them in certain important matters. These in-

---

Leiden, I, 1960, pp. 496–498. For the Shammar, see L. Stein, *Die Sammar-Gerba, Beduinen im Übergang vom Nomadismus zur Seßhaftigkeit*, Berlin, 1967.

[50] H. Charles, *Tribus moutonnières du Moyen-Euphrate* (*Documents d'Etudes Orientales*, 8), Institut Français de Damas, 1939.

[51] A. Jaussen, *Coutumes des Arabes au pays de Moab*, Paris, 1908, pp. 149–162.

[52] I. Goldziher, *Muhammedanische Studien*, I, Halle, 1889, pp. 63–69; E. Tyan, 'Hilf', *Encyclopédie de l'Islam*,[2] III, 1971, p. 401.

cluded common defence, joint action in the case of raids or blood-feuds, mutual assistance of various kinds and the possession of grazing land. A frequent consequence of the *hilf* was the merging together of different groups, confirmed by the adoption of a common ancestor who may have been real or fictitious. Many of the great Arabian tribes were in fact formed in this way.

Unfortunately, we have little useful information about this question in the first millennium before the present era. What we do know comes mainly from the annals of the kings of Assyria. Sargon II, for example, boasted of his conquest of four tribes and gave the names of these people who were remote Arabs living in the desert. He had nothing to say, however, about their organisation.[53] Ashurbanipal conducted a campaign in Arabia against Uaite, a king of the Arabs, and it is probable that he was leading a confederation of tribes, although we have no details about this.[54] The Aramaean tribes of Lower Mesopotamia are mentioned more frequently,[55] Tiglath-pileser III listing thirty-five[56] and Sargon II twelve.[57] We know nothing, however, about their organisation.

It has been possible to gain earlier information from the Mari texts, which date back to the eighteenth century B.C. Partly-settled nomadic tribes from the Syrian desert and Upper Mesopotamia are frequently mentioned in these texts.[58] The vocabulary dealing with their social units, tribes, branches and clans as well as their leaders is large, as is that of the Arabs today and the Israelites of the Old Testament, but it is noteworthy that there are also even wider groupings. In a list of those receiving rations, four and nine clans or tribes, *gâyûm,* are mentioned, all of the Haneans.[59] Yahdun-Lim, the king of Mari, boasted of having conquered a coalition of seven 'kings', the 'Fathers of Hana'.[60] The semi-nomadic Benjaminites were divided into four tribes, bearing early personal names.[61] Their 'kings' are mentioned, always in the plural and, as Kupper pointed out, 'the Benjaminites formed a confederation of tribes, each drawn up behind a sheikh. It was natural, in times of war, that certain leaders were recognised because of their personal influence or the strength of the military contingents following them ... As soon as this need ceased to exist, each tribe

[53] *ARAB,* II, § 17.

[54] *ARAB,* II, § 817–834. Both here and elsewhere in Luckenbill's book (§§ 869, 940) there is reference to the 'people of Arabia'.

[55] S. Schiffer, *Die Aramäer,* Leipzig, 1911, pp. 1-6.

[56] *ARAB,* I, § 788.

[57] *ARAB,* II, § 54.

[58] J.–R. Kupper, *Les nomades en Mésopotamie au temps des rois de Mari,* Paris, 1957.

[59] J.–R. Kupper, *op. cit.,* p. 20. For the meaning of *gâyûm,* see A. Malamat, 'Aspects of Tribal Societies in Mari and Israel', *XVme Rencontre Assyriologique Internationale 1966,* Liège, 1967, pp. 133–135.

[60] J.–R. Kupper, *op. cit.,* pp. 32–33.

[61] *ibid.,* pp. 49–52 and 71.

withdrew to its own side and each sheikh resumed his full powers.'[62] Various connections were established between these tribal groupings – in several texts, Benjaminites are associated with Haneans and, in two texts in particular, it is said explicitly that the Benjaminites and the Rabbeans were 'brothers'. This may point to a blood relationship, but it may, on the other hand, indicate a fictitious relationship based on a covenant,[63] as in the case of the Arabs. At the beginning of the second millennium, then, the principles were already evident which were to be of first importance in the grouping together of the Israelite tribes and their association with other groups of 'brothers'.

It is with these 'brotherly' groupings between the Israelites and others that we find – according to the evidence in the Old Testament itself – the closest parallels to the twelve-tribe system. Genesis, for example, contains several genealogical lists in which the groups forming an established people are presented as the 'sons' of an ancestor who was himself connected to the great genealogical tree to which Israel belonged.[64] Such an ancestor was usually introduced proportionately earlier into the common line in the genealogical tree if the 'brotherly' group was living in territory that was geographically remote from that of Israel. In the 'table of peoples' (Gen 10:26–30, J), there is a list of the sons of Joktan, the brother of Peleg, who was also Abraham's ancestor, to the fifth generation (Gen 11:18–26). These were tribes in southern Arabia. Thirteen names are given in the list, but it is possible that one of them (Ophir) was added later and that, in the original tradition, there were only twelve sons of Joktan.[65] Another example can be found elsewhere in Genesis. The northern Arabs were the descendants of Ishmael, who was Isaac's brother and Abraham's son. This Ishmael had twelve sons (Gen 25:13–16, P), whose names are given in order of birth (see Gen 29–30) and who were twelve leaders or $n^e\hat{s}\hat{i}\hat{i}m$, according to the tribes or 'ummôth.[66] Again, according to Gen 25:1–4 (J), Abraham had six sons by Keturah, who represent other groups in Arabia. One of these sons was Midian, who himself had five sons. The five 'kings' of Midian are listed in Num 31:8, but they are called $n^e\hat{s}\hat{i}\hat{i}m$ in Jos 13:21 and, in Num 25:15, one of them is named as the 'chief of a clan ('ummôth)'. The Midianites, then, clearly formed a federation of five tribes.[67] Nahor, Abraham's brother, we

---

[62] *ibid.*, p. 59.

[63] *ibid.*, pp. 72–73; A. Malamat, *op. cit.*, p. 137.

[64] For the first of these genealogies studied in this chapter, that is, Joktan, Keturah and Ishmael, see F. V. Winnett, 'The Arabian Genealogies in the Book of Genesis', *Translating and Understanding the Old Testament. Essays in Honor of H. G. May*, Nashville and New York, 1970, pp. 171–196. The author's position with regard to literary criticism is a special one in that he attributes these texts to a 'second Yahwist' active in the sixth century B.C.

[65] F. V. Winnett, *op. cit.*, pp. 185–186.

[66] For the meaning of *'ummāh*, see above, p. 239.

[67] For the political influence, see the hypothesis suggested by O. Eissfeldt in 'Protektorat

read in another genealogy, had twelve sons who were the ancestors of the Aramaean tribes (Gen 22:20–24, J). Eight of these sons were born to Hanor's wife Milcah and four to his concubine Reumah. This is, of course, reminiscent of the division of Jacob's sons between his two wives and their slave-girls. Finally, in Gen 36, there are several lists relating to Edom. In one of them (Gen 36:9–14, J), the genealogy of Esau, the 'father of Edom', is provided.[68] According to this list, Esau had three wives. The first, Adah, bore him a son, Eliphaz, who had five sons and a bastard, Amalek, The second wife, Basemath, gave him a son Reuel, who had four sons; and the third wife, Oholibamah, gave him three sons. Esau therefore had twelve descendants, from different mothers and divided into two generations. This is very similar to the twelve-tribe system, which includes Ephraim and Manasseh. Amalek, the son of a concubine of Eliphaz (see verse 12a), was added later and the reference to him interrupts the list and introduces a different ethnic element. The same names appear again, including that of Amalek, in the list that follows (Gen 36:15–19), giving the chiefs or clans of Edom.[69]

These are all very early lists, even though one of them (Gen 25:13–16) is only found in the priestly material. They are very similar to the twelve-tribe system, following the same genealogical principle in every case and several times making the same distinction according to maternal origin. In the case of Hanor and Ishmael the figure twelve appears quite clearly as the number of descendants. It is less clear in the primitive Edomite list and it is probable in the case of Joktan's descendants. It is, however, unlikely that this figure twelve represented a historical reality in all these cases. Like the system of the twelve tribes of Israel, these other systems are partly arbitrary. Alongside names representing groups or territories known in the Bible or in extrabiblical sources, these lists also contain names which cannot be identified – the names of tribes which were quite insignificant or which had disappeared. The figure twelve was, however, retained, because, in the Semitic world as in Greece and Rome,[70] twelve expressed fullness. There are very many examples, in the Bible alone, of this meaning of the figure twelve: the twelve loaves of burnt offering (Lev 24:5). the 'twelve oxen beneath the sea' on the temple (1 Kings 7:44); the 'twelve lions on either side of the six steps' of Solomon's throne in the temple (1 Kings 10:20); Elisha's ploughing behind twelve yoke of oxen (1 Kings 19:19); twelve of Benjamin's men and twelve of David's fighting near the Pool of Gibeon (2 Sam 2:15) and Solomon's 12,000 horses (1 Kings 5:6; 10:26). Finally, in the

---

der Midianiter über ihre Nachbarn im letzten Viertel des 2. Jahrtausends v. Chr.', *JBL*, 87 (1968), pp. 383–393.

[68] E. Meyer, *Die Israeliten und ihre Nachbarstämme*, Halle, 1906, pp. 345–353.

[69] The meaning of *'allûph* is obscure.

[70] See also above, p. 702.

Old Testament the figure 12,000 recurs again and again in connection with 'warriors' (Jos 8:25; Judges 21:10; 2 Sam 10:6; 17:1; Ps 60:2). There are also cases of the recurrence of the figure twelve within the Semitic environment of the New Testament – examples can be found especially in the Apocalypse[71] – and in the rabbinical writings.[72]

These parallels are in fact so striking that it is possible for us to ask whether they do not constitute evidence of the fact that the Israelites' idea of the structure of the neighbouring peoples was based on the image of their own people, the Israel of twelve tribes. It is, of course, not possible to reply to this question with absolute assurance. It should, however, be noted that this system was not applied to the Midianites or to the sons of Keturah; that, apart from the case of Ishmael's descendants, there is no explicit reference to the figure twelve and that the addition of a thirteenth name to the list of Joktan's descendants and to that of Esau's may point to the fact that there was no longer any consciousness that the lists were related to the twelve-tribe system. It is therefore probable that these lists reflect national traditions which were alien to Israel. If they were invented, they are at least evidence of the fact that the Israelites based their conception of the formation of other peoples on that of their own people and that this genealogical principle rather than some 'amphictyonic' idea underlay the twelve-tribe system.

Another objection can be raised if the independent value of these parallels is accepted. They are provided by the nomadic and semi-nomadic peoples and would seem to point to an earlier date for the creation of the twelve-tribe system of Israel, that is, a date earlier than that of the end of the period of the Judges, after more than a century of settled life. This difficulty is, however, merely apparent. The fact that all these genealogical lists contain geographical names at least shows that there were certain links with definite territories and, at the time when these lists were known in Israel, the Edomites and the Aramaeans were without doubt already well advanced on the way towards becoming fully settled. The same can undoubtedly be said of other peoples which have provided us with more remote parallels for the formation of a tribal league – the present-day Arab tribes of the Middle Euphrates and Transjordania or the Benjaminites of the Mari period. On the other hand, however, the Israelites tribes only became settled progressively. The movements of the different tribes continued throughout the whole period of the Judges. Dan, for example, moved towards the north, part of Manasseh settled in Transjordania and Judah spread out into the Shephelah. For a long time after the settlement the tribes preserved semi-nomadic habits and attitudes. The real problem confronting us is, when and how did these tribes become conscious of the fact that they formed only one single people, the people of twelve tribes?

[71] See K. H. Rengstorf, ' δώδεκα ', *TWNT*, II, 1935, pp. 321–328.
[72] L. Ginzberg, *The Legends of the Jews*, VII, *Index*, Philadelphia, 1938, under 'Twelve'.

VII. THE FORMATION OF THE PEOPLE OF ISRAEL

In the accounts of the births of Jacob's sons (Gen 29–30 and 35:16–20), Israel's ancestors are divided according to their maternal origin: the sons of Leah – Reuben, Simeon, Levi, Judah, Zebulun and Issachar; the sons of Rachel – Joseph and Benjamin; the sons of the slave-girls divided into the sons of Bilhah – Dan and Naphthali – and the sons of Zilpah – Gad and Asher. This grouping is found in the Blessings or Testament of Jacob (Gen 29) and is preserved, with certain modifications, as we have noted, in the tribal system of the book of Numbers. Because of this consistent pattern, modern authors have tended to speak of a group of the 'tribes of Leah' and a group of the 'tribes of Rachel'.

Once again, however, it is worth pointing out that these terms are never used in the Bible itself. With the exception of the cycle of stories about Jacob and Laban (Gen 29–33) and a number of texts which are dependent on these stories, the only references to the two ancestresses in the book of Genesis are in fact references to the places where they were buried – Leah in the cave of Machpelah (Gen 49:31) and Rachel near Ephratha (Gen 35:19–20). Bilhah and Zilpah are not mentioned again, apart from the genealogical lists. Nonetheless, attempts have been made to read into this division according to maternal origin a history of the tribes of Israel and their grouping.[73] M. Noth himself[74] believed that the tribes of Leah, which were the earliest to settle in the land, had formed a first 'amphictyony' of six tribes, the same figure that is sometimes encountered in the leagues of Greek cities and which is also the number of Keturah's sons in Gen 25:1–4. S. Mowinckel, on the other hand,[75] regarded this connection between Jacob's sons and four different mothers as artificial and thought that historians could not draw any useful conclusions from it. More recently, O. Eissfeldt[76] suggested that the genealogical system presupposed a merging together of two Jacob groups which were originally independent of each other – a group of Jacob-Leah in the south of Palestine with Reuben, Simeon, Levi and Judah and a group of Jacob-Rachel in central Palestine and east of the Jordan with the 'house of Joseph'. The traditions of the first group (Jacob-Leah) were, in Eissfeldt's opinion, preserved in the cycle of Jacob and Esau, while those of the second (the Jacob-Rachel group) were

[73] See especially C. Steurnagel, *Die Einwanderung der israelitischen Stämme in Kanaan*, Berlin, 1901, pp. 1–49.

[74] M. Noth, *Das System der zwölf Stämme Israels, op. cit.*, pp. 75–85; *Geschichte*, pp. 86–87 (*History*, pp. 88–89).

[75] S. Mowinckel, ' "Rahelstämme" und "Leastämme" ', *Von Ugarit nach Qumran. Festschrift O. Eissfeldt (BZAW 77)*, 1958, pp. 129–150.

[76] O. Eissfeldt, 'Jakob-Lea und Jakob-Rahel', *Gottes Wort und Gottes Land. Festschrift H.–W. Hertzberg*, Göttingen, 1965, pp. 50–55 = *Kleine Schriften*, IV, pp. 170–175; *ibid.*, *CAH*, II, XXXIV, 1965, pp. 12–17.

preserved in the cycle of stories about Jacob and Laban. The account of the births of Jacob's sons in Gen 29–30 was the result of a process of development based on historical foundations that were, Eissfeldt believed, difficult to determine.

None of these explanations is really satisfactory. It must be said definitely that not all the features of the twelve-tribe system are entirely artificial; for instance, the classification of the 'sons of Jacob' according to different mothers, the distinction among Aramaean tribes between the sons of Nahor's wife and those of his concubine, and in the Edomite tribes between Esau's three wives. These distinctions are no more arbitrary than the division of the Shammar in the modern era into two groups each connected with an intermediate ancestor. What is, however, arbitrary in the parallels between the twelve-tribe system and those outside Israel itself is the genealogical telescoping of historical memories extending over a long space of time. It is simply not possible to reduce to the same level the six tribes of Leah – the profane tribe of Levi disappeared very early, Issachar became separated from Zebulun before the time of Joshua, Reuben and Simeon became unimportant during the period of the Judges and Judah's development was only gradual. The different composition of the so-called Rachel group provided in the two types of system, the Joseph-Benjamin and the Ephraim-Manasseh-Benjamin types, reflects a historical development, and the process by which Benjamin, Ephraim and Manasseh became individual tribes was later than the entry of the group of tribes led by Joshua into Canaan.

It is certainly not possible to understand how the twelve-tribe system was built up and how the people of Israel came to be formed if the entire prehistory of Israel and the historical continuity between the patriarchal traditions and those of the exodus from Egypt, the settlement in Canaan and the period of the Judges is not taken into account. The explanation that is offered in the following paragraphs must, however, remain purely hypothetical because of the uncertainty of every interpretation of these early traditions.

The first movement into Canaan of the groups of semi-nomadic peoples who were ancestors of the Israelites can be traced back to the great migrations that took place at the beginning of the second millennium B.C. We do not know what names these groups had at that time since our knowledge of these distant origins of Israel is confined to the family histories of the three great ancestors preserved by tradition – Abraham, Isaac and Jacob. The groups of Asher and Naphthali may perhaps have stopped in the north of Palestine and the group of Gad may have already been settled in Transjordania. The group of Dan may perhaps have become integrated into Israel at a very late stage. None of these groups went down into Egypt. Their remote territory and their special history can be explained if they are regarded as having descended from Jacob's concubines. Two other groups which did not go down into Egypt were Zebulun and Issachar and their connection with Leah can be explained by the early relationships which they had with Simeon and Levi. The latter groups occupied a territory neighbouring that of Zebulun and Issachar in the Shechem region (see Gen 34) in the patriarchal period. When Simeon and Levi were forced to migrate to the south, Zebulun and Issachar were isolated and it is tempting, although perhaps rather too daring, to regard the narrative in Gen 29–30, in which the birth of Zebulun and Issachar is separated from those of Leah's other sons, as a memory of this fact. The migration of Simeon and Levi is connected with that of the other groups of Jacob, which may be represented by the tribe of Reuben and the nucleus of the tribe of Judah. There was, however, another group which claimed another ancestor, Israel. The double name Israel/Jacob presupposes the merging together of various traditions concerning two different ancestors and there are good reasons for associating Israel with Rachel, as there are for linking Jacob with Leah.[77] The eponymous heroes of this group of Israel-Rachel were Joseph and Benjamin. It is very probable that the elements of the three groups of the genealogical system, the sons of Leah, the sons of Rachel and the sons of the slave-girls, were already in existence, at least in some form, at the time of the patriarchs.

There can, moreover, be no doubt that some of Israel's ancestors stayed in Egypt. The story of Joseph, however romanticised it may be, certainly points to the fact that the Rachel group went down into Egypt. The part played by Reuben and Simeon in this story and the levitical circle surrounding Moses also indicated that elements of the group of Leah went to Egypt as well. There is evidence both inside the Bible (the story of Abraham in Egypt) and outside it pointing to the ease with which semi-nomadic groups of shepherds and herdsmen moved from the south of Palestine to the Nile delta. There must therefore have been several entries into Egypt and several cases of exodus from the country. There are moreover two ways in which the exodus is presented, the first as an expulsion and the second as a flight from Egypt and the two routes followed by the Israelites, the first towards the north and the second towards the east and the south-east,[78] are in accordance with these two modes of exodus. One of the routes might have led the clans of Simeon (and perhaps Judah) and part of the group of Levi to Kadesh. The other route was followed by the group led by Moses and including the clans of Levi, the Rachel group and possibly Reuben. This group continued to lead a nomadic life in the Sinai desert and the wilderness of Transjordania and finally reached the Jordan opposite Jericho.

[77] See above, pp. 648–649.
[78] See above, pp. 371ff.

The settlement in Canaan took place in several phases. The groups of Simeon-Judah and some of the clans of Levi entered the country directly from the south at the same time as other semi-nomadic groups which later became integrated into Judah. These were the Calebites, the Jerahmeelites and the Kenizzites. Reuben settled in Transjordania next to the clan of Gad who had already installed themselves there, possibly long before. The Rachel group, led by Joshua, penetrated into central Palestine as far as the Shechem region, where it became the neighbour of tribes which had not gone down into Egypt.

The period that followed was that of the Judges. During this period, the tribes consolidated their possession of the territories that they had occupied and so gained their definitive identity – for example, Ephraim-Manasseh-Benjamin within the group of Rachel – or else lost that identity; when, for example, a weaker tribe was absorbed by a tribe that had become stronger, as in the case of Reuben, which became merged with Gad, or Simeon, which was integrated into Judah. At the same time, however, a movement in the opposite direction was taking place and leading to a closer union between these scattered elements which had passed, and were still passing, through different historical experiences. Many factors contributed to this closer reunion. There was, for example, a strong feeling of belonging together ethnically and therefore of sharing a common origin, expressed in terms of kinship. There was also – and this was an even more effective bond, since it insulated the various elements of Israel from the surrounding peoples – the sharing of a faith in the same God. This faith, Yahwism, was both a continuation of the old religion of the god of the fathers and a new religion. It had been carried by the group that Moses led out of Egypt, and handed on to the southern groups at the time that they were all at Kadesh. The group led by Joshua had received the faith inherited by Moses and had introduced Yahwism into central Palestine. At Shechem, the new faith had been suggested to the northern tribes and accepted by them. Various traditions of a special kind, handed down by the elders of each tribe and shared in the sanctuaries frequented by several tribes, gathered round this faith and the historical tradition on which it was based. The struggles that took place at the time of the conquest of Canaan were wars of Yahweh, and those conducted later in order to defend territories acquired were also wars of Yahweh. A final factor contributing towards unity between the different elements was the need that they felt to combine against common enemies. The need to be free from the menace of the Philistines led ultimately to unity, which was achieved in two stages, the first during the reign of Saul, the second during that of David.

The first Israelite groups had also prepared for this unity and for the same reason. The earliest text that we have dealing with a union of the tribes is the Song of Deborah (Judges 5), which dates back to the middle of the period of the Judges or thereabouts. We are not concerned here either with the literary genre of this poem or with its historical context. All that interests us at present is the information that it provides about the tribes. Six tribes are mentioned in it: Ephraim, to which Benjamin is connected, Machir, Zebulun, Issachar and Naphthali. Four tribes did not, according to the poem, respond to the call – Reuben, Gilead, Dan and Asher. This is the earliest list that is in our possession and it is different from all the others, in that it contains no more than ten tribes. Judah and Simeon are not included and two new names occur in it: Machir and Gilead. It is understandable that M. Noth refused to take it into account in considering his 'twelve-tribe system'.[79] The reasons that he gave were that it was not in accordance with the prose account in Judges 4, in which only Zebulun and Naphthali are mentioned and that it was clearly based on an arbitrary choice made by the poet. Noth's explanation has not been accepted, however, and with good reason. The intention of the author of this Song was undoubtedly to provide a list of the tribes of which Israel was composed at the time and that list must have been complete.[80] It does not include the profane tribe of Levi, which was no longer in existence, or the tribes of Judah and Simeon. Machir is there in place of Manasseh, by which it was to be absorbed. Gilead is often interpreted as the name of a tribe which had disappeared, replaced by Gad.[81] It is, however, more probable that, here as elsewhere, Gilead should be seen as a geographical name, the primitive Gilead where Gad had its territory. In the Song of Deborah, then, the tribe of Gad is called by the name of the territory that it occupied.[82]

In this way, ten tribes are obtained and as a result of this certain authors have spoken about a first 'amphictyony' of ten tribes, without Judah and Simeon.[83] The same objections that we have already raised to the amphictyonic hypothesis in general can, however, also be raised against this theory. The Song of Deborah points nonetheless to the fact that a certain grouping of tribes existed in Israel. This grouping included at least the six tribes which are listed in the Song as having been present and almost the same tribes can also be found in the story of Gideon (Judges 6:35; 7:23–24): Manasseh (Machir), Asher, Zebulun, Naphthali and the 'highlands of Ephraim', which could also include Benjamin. A similar grouping can also

[79] M. Noth, Das System der zwölf Stämme Israels, op. cit., pp. 5, 36; ibid. Geschichte, p. 139, note 4 (History, p. 151).

[80] J. Hoftijzer, NTT, 14 (1959–1960), pp. 241–263, especially pp. 252–253; M. Ottosson, Gilead, Tradition and History, Lund, 1969, pp. 136–143.

[81] J. Hoftijzer, op. cit., pp. 245–252; H.–J. Zobel, BZAW 95, pp. 97–98.

[82] See above, pp. 574–576.

[83] S. Mowinckel, Zur Frage nach dokumentarischen Quellen in Josua 13–19, Oslo, 1946, pp. 20 ff. ibid., BZAW 77, especially p. 137; A. Weiser, ZAW, 71 (1959), p. 96; K.–D. Schunck, Benjamin (BZAW 86), 1963, pp. 48–57.

be found, as we have already seen, in a part of the description of the tribal territories in Jos 13–19.[84] There was therefore a union, which was always unstable, of the central and northern tribes. It is also possible that the four tribes in Judges 5 which did not respond to the call in the Song of Deborah did not at that time form part of the league, but that there was a general desire for their participation.[85]

The dominant element in this federation of tribes was the Rachel group and the three tribes forming this group are mentioned first in Judges 5. We have suggested that they should be connected with the patriarch Israel. It is also remarkable how many times the name 'Israel' appears in the Song of Deborah. It occurs eight times in the first twelve verses alone: the 'warriors of Israel', 'Israel's chieftains', Deborah, 'a mother in Israel' and finally Yahweh, the 'God of Israel' and 'Israel, Yahweh's people'. From the literary point of view, Judges 5 is the earliest text in which Israel is defined as a people uniting the ten tribes listed in the Song, or at least desirous of doing so. This is in fact the meaning which the name 'Israel' was to have until the period of Saul and of David, when the terms 'Israel' and 'Judah' came to be distinguished from each other. When David returned from Transjordania, the elders of Israel said to the men of Judah: 'We have ten shares in the king' (2 Sam 19:44). The prophet Ahijah of Shiloh also said to Jeroboam: 'This is what Yahweh, the God of Israel, says: "I am going to give *the* ten tribes to you"' (1 Kings 11:31). Although they were united under the personal power of David, Israel and Judah remained separate, both as military and as administrative units, and David was the king of Israel *and* of Judah.

The twelve-tribe system, uniting the tribes in the same genealogical or tribal list, was, during the reign of David, the ideal structure of a 'great Israel' which never in fact existed as a political organisation.[86] The same faith in Yahweh, the God of Israel, was, however, shared by Judah and it was with this religious significance that the word was finally used until the last period described in the Old Testament, and so it has been since.

---

[84] See above, p. 730.

[85] S. Herrmann, *TLZ*, 87 (1962), col. 567–568.

[86] S. Mowinckel, *BZAW* 77, p. 149; S. Herrmann, *TLZ*, 87 (1962), col. 573; G. H. J. de Geus, 'De rechteren van Israël', *NTT*, 20 (1965–1966), pp. 81–100.

Chapter Twenty-Five

THE JUDGES OF ISRAEL

I N USING the expression 'the period of the Judges' for the time between the settlement in Canaan and the establishment of the monarchy, the historian is certainly following a biblical practice. The story of Ruth, for example, took place 'in the days of the Judges' (Ruth 1:1). According to the Second Book of the Kings, 'the days when the Judges ruled Israel' preceded 'the period of the kings of Israel and the kings of Judah' (2 Kings 23:22). This period of the Judges was the time when Yahweh 'appointed Judges over his people Israel' (2 Sam 7:11; cf. 7:7; text corrected according to 1 Chron 17:6 [1]). Again, according to the introduction to the Book of Judges (Judges 2:16–18), these men were God's chosen agents, appointed to rescue the people. On the other hand, however, it is remarkable that in the body of the book itself the noun 'Judge' never appears in the plural and occurs only once in the singular, when it is applied to Yahweh (Judges 11:27). The verb 'to judge' is, however, applied to the 'lesser Judges', the list of whom is given in Judges 10:1–5 and 12:8–15. Each of these men 'judged' Israel. The same verb is also used in connection with Othniel (3:10), Deborah (4:4), Jephthah (12:7), Samson (15:20; 16:31), Eli (1 Sam 4:18) and Samuel (1 Sam 7:15). It would therefore seem that in his editing the Deuteronomist ascribed to the liberators of Israel whose stories he collected and whom we know as the 'great Judges', a title and a function that they did not possess in the early traditions. He clearly arranged all these 'Judges' in a chronological order which, although interrupted by periods of oppression, stretched continuously from the death of Joshua until the eclipse of Samuel by the king whom he had instituted. This, then, was the 'age of the Judges' according to the deuteronomistic editing. It is, of course, an artificial pattern [2] and was possible only because there was no memory of any other public office

---

[1] The Massoretic text has, however, been defended by P. de Robert, 'Juges ou tribus en 2 Samuel VII 7?', *VT*, 21 (1971), pp. 116–118; see also Z. W. Falk, in the article mentioned below in Note 18.

[2] See above, 724–725.

in Israel throughout the whole of this period, apart from that mentioned in the early list of the 'lesser Judges'. We must therefore investigate the problem of who these 'Judges' were and what their function was.

I. THE STATE OF THE PROBLEM

This problem has often been discussed in the past forty years in connection with the hypothesis of the twelve tribes. The suggestion has been made that the 'Judge of Israel' was a functionary and indeed the main official of the amphictyony.

A. Alt, elaborating a theory proposed by A. Klostermann,[3] compared the list of the 'lesser Judges' with the 'orators of the law' in mediaeval Iceland, whose main function was to proclaim each year to the assembled people the law that had been received from Norway but who were also able to make decisions in certain legal cases. The function of the 'Judge of Israel' was, in Alt's opinion, to make sure that the law of cases derived from Canaan was transmitted and observed by the league of tribes.[4] O. Grether accepted this view and attempted to explain how the title of these Judges had been applied to the liberator heroes.[5] M. Noth went even further in maintaining that the authority of these Judges extended to all twelve tribes of Israel. They were appointed for life and succeeded each other, Noth believed, but the way in which they were chosen was not known – the years when they held office may possibly have been used in ancient Israel to establish dates. Their function in the amphictyony was, in Noth's opinion, of central importance. Their task was to proclaim, explain and adapt, not the law borrowed from Canaan, as Alt claimed, but rather the 'law of God', which was the amphictyonic law.[6] Noth even suggested that this central office continued during the period of the monarchy; the 'Judge of Israel' is found in Micah (Mic 4:14), and there was a supreme Judge to whom an appeal was made in difficult cases, according to Deut 17:8–13.[7]

Noth's hypothesis has certainly had an effect on later studies. H. W. Hertzberg, for example, added to the list of 'lesser Judges' Othniel, Deborah, Gideon, Abimelech, Jephthah, Samuel and possibly Eli as a

[3] A. Klostermann, *Der Pentateuch. Neue Folge*, Leipzig, 1907, pp. 419–421.
[4] A. Alt, *Die Ursprünge des israelitischen Rechts*, Leipzig, 1934, pp. 31–33 = *Kleine Schriften*, I, pp. 300–302.
[5] O. Grether, 'Die Bezeichnung "Richter" für die charismatischen Helden der vorstaatlichen Zeit', *ZAW*, 57 (1939), pp. 110–121.
[6] M. Noth, 'Das Amt des "Richters Israels"', *Festschrift A. Bertholet*, Tübingen, 1950, pp. 404–417 = *Gesammelte Studien zum Alten Testament*, II, Munich, 1969, pp. 71–85; *ibid., Geschichte*, pp. 97–99 (*History*, pp. 99–102).
[7] M. Noth, *Gesammelte Studien zum Alten Testament, op. cit.*, II, pp. 83–85; Noth discarded this theory, however, in his *History*.

twelfth Judge. According to this scholar, their function was to make legal decisions in accordance with a traditional law – the 'law of God' – which they proclaimed and explained.[8] H.–J. Kraus accepted Noth's definition of the Judges and regarded them as the successors of Moses, the charismatic leader who proclaimed the law. Like him they carried out this prophetic task in the religious assemblies of the tribes that took place each year and they also acted as supreme judges in everyday life.[9] H. C. Thomson took as his point of departure the examples of Deborah, who was both a prophetess and a Judge, and Gideon, who possessed God's spirit and obtained answers from God. The conclusion that Thomson drew from this was that the Judge was the source of decisions which came from God and which were of interest to the whole or part of the amphictyony; there was therefore less difference than has generally been claimed between the 'lesser' and the 'great' Judges.[10] J. Dus compared the 'lesser' and the 'great' Judges of Israel with the suffetes of Carthage and concluded that the league of twelve tribes had a republican constitution borrowed from the Canaanites, the elders of the people – six for each tribe (Num 11:24, 26) – sending a representative to the college of the twelve chiefs of each tribe, who chose the Judge. According to Dus, Israel was already a state – and, what is more, a republican state, before the establishment of the monarchy.[11] K.-D. Schunck also rejected the distinction between the 'great' and the 'lesser' Judges and compiles a list of twelve Judges, including Joshua, Othniel, Ehud, Gideon, Tola, Jair, Jephthah, Ibzan, Elon, Abdon, Samson and Samuel. This list, he believed, was established during the royal period and its inspiration was the twelve-tribe system. It was partly artificial (Othniel and Samson) but it represented a real succession of central power in the league of ten, then twelve tribes. The Judge of Israel resided at the centre of the amphictyony, at Shiloh, and his authority extended beyond the law and into the political and military spheres.[12] Finally, there is the most recent theory of D. A. McKenzie, who is convinced that the Judges of Israel were judges in the real sense of the word and the fact that this term was applied to the heroes who liberated Israel means that the Deuteronomist rightly or wrongly regarded them as having exercised a judiciary function. The authority of these Judges, then, McKenzie concludes, extended to the whole federation of tribes. Their function was not inherited: they were appointed for life and

---

[8] H. W. Hertzberg, 'Die kleinen Richter', *TLZ*, 79 (1954), col. 285–290 = *Beiträge zur Traditionsgeschichte und Theologie des Alten Testaments*, Göttingen, 1962, pp. 118–125.

[9] H.–J. Kraus, *Die prophetische Verkündigung des Rechts in Israel*, Zollikon, 1957, p. 18.

[10] H. C. Thomson, 'Shophet and Mishpat in the Book of Judges', *Glasgow University Oriental Society. Transactions*, 19 (1961–1962), 1963, pp. 74–85.

[11] J. Dus, 'Die "Sufeten Israels" ', *ArOr*, 31, (1963), pp. 444–469.

[12] K.-D. Schunck, 'Die Richter Israels und ihr Amt', *Volume du Congrès, Genève* (*SVT* 15), 1966, pp. 252–262.

they succeeded each other without interruption. The last of these Judges was, in McKenzie's opinion, Samuel.[13]

All these authors have made use of the hypothesis first put forward by A. Alt and M. Noth and they have frequently drawn conclusions that would not have been acceptable to Alt or Noth. But contrary opinions are heard: these have taken into account, on the one hand, some of the doubts which have been raised against the amphictyonic hypothesis in general and, on the other, recent semantic studies of the root š-p-ṭ, 'to judge'. R. Smend was of the opinion that the interpretation of the Judges of Israel as amphictyonic officials or functionaries was open to serious doubts, since no parallel was provided by the Greek amphictyonies. He insisted also that the distinction between the 'great' Judges, who represented the war of Yahweh, and the 'lesser' Judges, who represented the league of tribes, should be preserved.[14] At the same time, several scholars have given a great deal of attention to the study of the root š-p-ṭ. O. Grether, for example, rejected the theory that has often been suggested, that this root might have the double meaning of 'judge' and 'rule', maintaining that the second meaning of 'rule' only appears rarely in texts that are of late date or that are open to a different interpretation.[15] F. C. Fensham, on the other hand, has pointed out that this double meaning is in accordance with the usage of the same root in Akkadian, Ugaritic and Phoenician and that the function of the 'lesser' Judges of Israel has therefore to be interpreted in the light of this double meaning.[16] The conclusion that A. van Selms has drawn from this is that the Deuteronomistic historian was right to regard the Judges as the forerunners of the kings of Israel.[17] Z. W. Falk has suggested that šēbheṭ, 'tribe' was the early form of šōpheṭ, 'judge', and that both words indicated the chief, who carried the rod or šēbheṭ, as the sign that he was the ruler.[18] W. Schmidt has, independently of this, pointed out that ṭpṭ in Ugaritic had the meaning of 'to rule' and detected a Canaanite influence in the use in Hebrew of this root with this meaning, especially in certain psalms.[19]

[13] D. A. McKenzie, 'The Judge of Israel', *VT*, 17 (1967), pp. 118–121.

[14] R. Smend, *Jahwekrieg und Stämmebund*, Göttingen, 1963, pp. 33–35. This author deals with the subject in the light of his main thesis that there was a difference between the idea of the war of Yahweh and that of the institution of the league of tribes.

[15] O. Grether, *op. cit.* (see above, note 5).

[16] F. C. Fensham, 'The Judges and Ancient Israelite Jurisprudence', *Die Ou Testamentiese Werkgemeenskap in Suid-Afrika*, 2nd Meeting, 1959, pp. 15–22.

[17] A. van Selms, *ibid.*, pp. 41–50.

[18] Z. W. Falk, 'Ruler and Judge', *Lešonenu*, 30 (1965–1966), pp. 243–247 (Hebrew). S. E. Loewenstamm, 'Ruler and Judge Reconsidered', *ibid.*, 32 (1967–1968), pp. 272–274, has replied to Falk, claiming that the two words were derived from different proto-Semitic roots, švbṭ and ṭpṭ.

[19] W. Schmidt, *Königtum Gottes in Ugarit und Israel* (*BZAW* 80), 1961, pp. 27–34; cf. I. H. Eybers, 'The Stem š-p-ṭ in the Psalms', *Die Ou Testamentiese Werkgemeenskap in Suid-Afrika*, 6th Meeting, 1963, pp. 58–63.

Finally, we are bound to mention two important recent works by authors who are in agreement about the doubtful nature of the amphictyonic theory and who have combined research into comparative philology with a study of literary and historical criticism in order to provide us with a new image of the 'Judge of Israel'. The first of these scholars, W. Richter, has taken as his point of departure the list of the lesser Judges, the basic outline of which is found, in a much earlier form, in connection with Samuel. This outline moreover was derived, in Richter's opinion, from that in the books of Kings. In this list, Richter believed, the word 'Israel' does not point to an amphictyony of twelve tribes, but is rather a political geographical concept, with the result that the emphasis is placed in this list not on the tribes, but on the towns and the territories. The placing of these 'Judges' in order of time is, in Richter's opinion, of secondary importance. Their function cannot be limited simply to the administration of justice – they were also men who governed and that meant not only responsibility for justice, but also carrying out the whole of civic administration. This meaning of the word is borne out by the usage of the root in Ugaritic, Phoenician and Punic as well as in the Mari texts, to which Richter devoted a great deal of attention. He believed that the title of 'Judge' may have had a nomadic origin. The conclusion to which this scholar has come is that the Judges of Israel represented a transitional stage between tribal government and government of the city type. They were given this task by the tribal elders of the civic and judiciary administration of a town and of the territory dependent on it.[20] Turning now to the second of these authors, C. H. J. de Geus, we find that he does not deny the existence of an amphictyony or a twelve-tribe system at the time of the Judges. In his view, the root $š$-p-t was Canaanite and its meaning in Ugaritic and Phoenician was 'to exercise power', which was often synonymous with 'to rule', which clearly included the administration of justice. The Judge was a local chief, whose authority was derived from the council of the elders of the town. Some of these chiefs acquired – above all through their military exploits – a reputation which went beyond the confines of their own towns. No precise distinction can be made between the 'great' and the 'lesser' Judges. Finally, de Geus has suggested that the Deuteronomist's list of these Judges was as follows: (Othniel), Ehud, (Barak), Gideon, Jephthah, Tola, Jair, Ibzan, Elon, Abdon, Eli and Samuel. They prepared the way for the institution of the monarchy.[21]

II. THE LIST OF THE 'LESSER' JUDGES

It is clear from this brief survey of more recent opinions that the problem

[20] W. Richter, 'Zu den "Richtern Israels" ', *ZAW*, 77 (1965), pp. 40–72.
[21] C. H. J. de Geus, 'De rechteren van Israël', *NTT*, 20 (1965–1966), pp. 81–100.

is stated in terms which are very different from those in which it was posed forty years ago. It is, however, also obvious that it has by no means been solved. Before attempting to find a solution, it is necessary to reconsider its various elements.

The list of the 'lesser' Judges (Judges 10:1–5; 12:8–15) is divided into two parts by the insertion of the story of Jephthah. The brief data about each of the Judges follow a pattern which is quite different from that of the liberator Judges. The formula is: 'After him, X (name and origin) judged Israel. He judged Israel for Y years. Then X died and was buried at Z (place name)'. There are, however, certain variants of this basic formula. In the case of the first two Judges, Tola and Jair, the first 'judged Israel' is replaced by 'rose'. There is also additional information in the case of Jair, Ibzan and Abdon about their families and this is in each case of the same kind. Jair 'had thirty sons who rode on thirty donkeys' colts and they possessed thirty towns' (Judges 10:4). Ibzan 'had thirty sons and thirty daughters'. He sent the thirty daughters outside in marriage and brought in thirty young women from outside for his sons to marry (Judges 12:9). Finally, Abdon 'had forty sons and thirty grandsons who rode on seventy donkeys' colts' (Judges 12:14). These additions, which are remarkable because of their very similar contents and their round figures, would appear to be a stereotyped way of expressing the wealth and the prestige enjoyed by these Judges in their own environments. Finally, in the case of Jair, a gloss (10:4b) identifies the thirty towns with the duars or 'encampments' of Jair known to us in other texts.

There are certain difficulties in connection with the names of these Judges. The first Judge is called Tola, son of Puah, but, according to Gen 46:13 (P), Tola and Puah were two 'sons' of Issachar, in other words, two clans of Issachar according to Num 26:23 (cf. 1 Chron 7:1). Jair has also been interpreted as the name of a clan of Manasseh, to which the conquest of the duars or 'encampments' of Jair were attributed (Num 32:41). The name of the last Judge but one, Elon, is also the name of a clan of Zebulun (Gen 46:14; Num 26:26). The marriages of the sons and daughters of Ibzan also point to covenants between different groups. The conclusion that has been drawn from this is that these five 'lesser' Judges were not historical persons but personifications of clans and that these data had been added to the book of Judges in order to obtain the figure of twelve Judges, representing the twelve tribes of Israel.[22] All these names might, however, be the names of individuals – those of Jair and Abdon, for example, were the names of other Israelites as well – and it is more reasonable to think of them all as representing real historical persons.[23]

[22] C. F. Burney, *The Book of Judges*, London, 1918, pp. 289–290.
[23] M. Noth, *Gesammelte Studien zum Alten Testament, op. cit.,* II (see above, note 6), pp. 76–79.

With regard to the origins of these 'lesser' Judges, Tola was clearly a man from Issachar, Jair was a Gileadite, Ibzan came from Bethlehem and probably this was Bethlehem in Zebulun (Jos 19:15) rather than Bethlehem in Judah, if the isolation of Judah during the whole of the period of the Judges is borne in mind; Elon was a Zebulunite and finally Abdon was an inhabitant of Pirathon (see 2 Sam 23:30). In the case of one of these 'lesser' Judges, Tola of Issachar, we are told that he lived at a place that was different from the place where he originated – he 'lived at Shamir in the mountain country of Ephraim' (Judges 10:1) and was also buried there. Jair was buried at Kamon, which was in Gilead the country of his origin. Ibzan of Bethlehem was buried at Bethlehem and Abdon of Pirathon was buried at Pirathon which, we are told, was also in the mountain country of Ephraim.[24] Elon the Zebulunite was buried at Aijalon in the country of Zebulun, but only one Aijalon is known to us – the place in the Shephelah, and the similarity between the name of the Judge and that of his tomb (the consonants are the same) eliminates all doubts.

Only two of these Judges are said to belong to a tribe. These are Tola, who 'belonged to Issachar', and Elon, who was a Zebulunite. The other Judges are designated by the towns in which they originated – Ibzan from Bethlehem and Abdon from Pirathon – or by the region from which they came – Jair, for example, coming from Gilead. On the other hand, in each case, the town is always mentioned in connection with the tomb – Tola is said to have been buried at Shamir, in the hill country of Ephraim, Jair at Kamon, Ibzan at Bethlehem, Elon at Aijalon in Zebulun and Abdon at Pirathon in the hill country of Ephraim. Membership of a tribe is clearly subordinated to membership of a territory or a town in this list, which cannot go back to an official document emanating from a league of tribes, to say nothing of a system of twelve tribes.[25] On the other hand, however, all the towns mentioned in the list are unimportant, if the Bethlehem listed here is identified with the town in Zebulun and if the information given in the text about Aijalon in Zebulun is accepted. None of these small towns or large villages was ever the centre of a Canaanite principality, none is mentioned elsewhere in the book of Judges and none played any part at all in the period of the monarchy. If the Judges exercised their authority only within these very small towns, then it is quite remarkable that their names should ever have been preserved and it would be impossible to maintain that the government of the 'lesser' Judges was a preparation for the institution of the monarchy.[26]

[24] The addition to the text, 'in the mountain country of the Amalekites' is not meaningful and the Greek 'in the land of Sellem' (Shalim of 1 Sam 9:4?) is no clearer.

[25] I believe this in opposition to M. Noth.

[26] My view here is therefore contrary to those of C. H. J. de Geus and W. Richter as well as that held by G. Fohrer, *Studien zur alttestamentlichen Theologie und Geschichte (BZAW* 115), 1969, pp. 117–118.

Despite these obviously local connections, however, these men, we are told, judged 'Israel'. This cannot have been the 'great Israel' of the twelve tribes, the late and ideal character of which we have already discussed. The word has a political geographical meaning which we must try to ascertain. The territory covered by these geographical references is restricted. It includes Zebulun and Issachar, the hill country of Ephraim and Gilead in Transjordania and it is difficult to say exactly what is meant here by this land of Gilead. The territory from which the 'lesser' Judges came, then, was the Plain of Jezreel, central Palestine and the parts of Transjordania that were their dependencies. It is, of course, possible that we have only part of the original list, but it is remarkable that this provides us with a group that is very similar to that found in various other tribal and territorial lists that we have examined.[27] For example, the presence of certain tribes is praised in the Song of Deborah (Judges 5), which at the same time stresses the fact that they belong to 'Israel'. In Judges 6:35; 7:23–24 various tribes are mentioned in the story of Gideon: Manasseh, Asher, Zebulun, Naphthali and the hill country of Ephraim. All of these are called 'men of Israel'. To this can be added the description in 2 Sam 2:9 of Ishbaal's being made king over Gilead, the Ashurites, Jezreel, Ephraim and Benjamin (Saul's tribe) 'and indeed over all Israel'. The Israel which features in the list of the 'lesser' Judges, then, may possibly represent this group, which only gradually became extended and cohesive.

Finally, it is important to point out that the list is very general in character. The brief data about the 'lesser' Judges are linked to each other, in that each description begins with the words 'After him . . . ', each gives the exact number of years during which each Judge was in office (23, 22, 7, 10 and 8 years) and each ends with a reference to the death of the Judge and his place of burial. The purpose of this list is therefore to provide a record of the uninterrupted succession of 'Judges', each one of whom was in office alone until his death. This series of formulae has been compared with that used as a chronological framework for the history of the kings – Saul (1 Sam 13:1), David (1 Kings 2:10–12) and Solomon (1 Kings 11:42–43). It has also been compared with the synchronic history of the kings of Israel and Judah at the beginning and the end of each reign: 'in the eighteenth year of King Jeroboam, son of Nebat, Abijam became king of Judah and reigned for three years in Jerusalem . . . Then Abijam slept with his ancestors and they buried him in the citadel of David; his son Asa succeeded him. In the twentieth year of Jeroboam, king of Israel, Asa became king of Judah and reigned for forty-one years in Jerusalem, etc . . .' (1 Kings 15:1, 8:9–10). W. Richter attempted to prove that the series of formulae used in the Book of Judges was derived from that in the Book of the

---

[27] See above, pp. 747–749.

Kings and that the 'lesser' Judges were put in order of succession at a later date.[28] His arguments are, however, not convincing. At the same time, an attempt to show that the opposite was the case, that is, that the formulae used in the Book of the Kings were dependent on those found in Judges,[29] is equally unconvincing. The two sets of formulae may, after all, be independent of each other, since the terms used are not the same in each case and, in any attempt to describe a succession of men occupying the same office, the same or similiar formulae have to be used.

It is more fruitful to compare the list of the 'lesser' Judges with the list of the first eight kings of Edom in Gen 36:31–39.[30] This list begins in the following way: 'In Edom there ruled Bela son of Beor; his city was called Dinhabah. Bela died and Jobab, son of Zerah, from Bozrah, succeeded. Jobab died and Husham of the land of the Temanites succeeded, etc.' All that is added to these formulae is a reference to the victory gained by one of these kings against the Midianites (verse 35) and the name of another king's wife (verse 39). Although this list is even more of a skeleton framework than that of the 'lesser' judges, it resembles it closely in its essential details – the kings of Edom are all specified according to their origin, town or region, which is different in each case, and, although they succeed each other without interruption, none of them is the son or the kinsman of his predecessor.

The historical interpretation of this list of Edomite kings raises as many difficulties as that of the 'lesser' Judges and as we shall see it is not possible to explain the one by reference to the other and in this way, to arrive at a solution that is common to both. With regard to the list of the 'lesser' Judges, we should note that the personal and geographical names contained in it are so striking and the figures given in it so precise that it would be very difficult to accept that it was simply invented. One is also inclined to accept that the order in which these Judges appear in sequence of time is authentic. The list can therefore be seen as representing an early tradition about various persons who followed each other in succession – not necessarily, however, uninterruptedly (it should be noted that 'after him' is used instead of 'succeeded' in the list of Edomite kings) – in an office which they carried out within this group which was known as Israel and which we have tried to define. Nothing is said in the text itself about the nature of their activities. All that is said is that they 'judged'. If we are to discover precisely what their function was, we must extend our enquiry to include the other persons who were called 'Judges of Israel' and we must also look more closely at the semantics of the root š-p-ṭ, 'to judge'.

[28] W. Richter, op. cit. (see above, note 20), pp. 43–45.

[29] See, for example, C. H. J. de Geus, op. cit. (see above, note 21), p. 95.

[30] For the difficulties contained in this list. see J. R. Bartlett, 'The Edomite King-List of Genesis XXXVI. 31–39 and 1 Chron. I. 43–50', JTS, New Series 16 (1965), pp. 301–314.

III. The Other 'Judges of Israel'

There were, of course, other persons in the history of Israel before the period of the monarchy who were among those who apparently 'judged Israel'. The easiest case to assess is that of Jephthah, whose story ends with the words: 'Jephthah was judge in Israel for six years. Then Jephthah the Gileadite died, and was buried in the town of Gilead' (Judges 12:7). The end of this verse is corrupt and, according to the Septuagint, the words 'in his own town of Gilead' at least have to be corrected. According to the rest of the story, this town might have been Mizpah and some exegetes, basing their argument on certain Greek miniscule texts and on Josephus, have introduced the name of this town here. Be this as it may, however, this concluding formula is exactly the same as the one which is used to conclude each of the short texts on the 'lesser' Judges and it is moreover perfectly in accordance with what follows: 'After him, [that is, Jephthah] Ibzan of Bethlehem was judge in Israel . . . ' (Judges 12:8). What is quite certain is that Jephthah is included in the list of the Judges. There was also, however, a story about him inserted by the editor (Judges 10:6–12:6) which eliminated the beginning of the primitive text. This would have been: 'After him, Jephthah the Gileadite judged Israel' and it would have followed the short text on Jair (Judges 10:5). This is the only possible satisfactory explanation for the unusual position of the story of Jephthah, which divides the list of the 'lesser' Judges in two.

Jephthah was an inhabitant of Gilead, which is without any doubt the primitive Gilead to the south of the Jabbok, where Mizpah in Gilead (Judges 10:17; 11:11) was situated and where the Israelites shared their frontier with the Ammonites. The fact that Jephthah originated in this primitive Gilead does not affect the conclusions to which we came with regard to the remainder of the list of the 'lesser' Judges. Jephthah is, however, the only one of these Judges whose story is narrated and this story may perhaps throw light on the way in which the Judges were chosen as well as on the nature of their functions.[31]

According to the earliest account (Judges 11:1–11*), Jephthah had been driven out by his brothers because of his illegitimate birth and sought refuge in the land of Tob, where he became the leader of a gang. It was apparently on this basis that the elders of Gilead invited him to become their 'commander' (qāṣîn, verse 6), then, when he hesitated, promised to make him the 'leader', rôš, of all the inhabitants of Gilead (verse 8). In his reply, Jephthah seems to have regarded this title of 'leader' as less important

---

[31] For the literary analysis and the history of traditions concerning Jephthah, see, in addition to the various commentaries, E. Täubler, *Biblische Studien. Die Epoche der Richter,* Tübingen, 1958, pp. 283–297; W. Richter, 'Die Überlieferungen um Jephthah. Ri 10, 17–12 6', *Bib* 47 (1966), pp. 485–556.

than his victory over the Ammonites, but the elders call on Yahweh to bear witness to this promise (verse 10). Their promise is then confirmed by the people of Israel at the sanctuary at Mizpah, where Jephthah is appointed *qāṣîn* and *rôš* even before embarking on the campaign against the Ammonites (verse 11).

Several comments have to be made about this account. Jephthah is, for instance, not called a 'Judge' in it, but is given the general title *rôš* and the much rarer one of *qāṣîn*, which is a much more precise title for a military leader, as in Jos 10:24 (Joshua's officers), Isa 22:3 (the battle context), Dan 11:18 (with reference to the consul L. Cornelius Scipio, who was victorious over Antiochus III). Elsewhere, however, the word usually means no more than 'Leader'.[32] It should also be noted that it is only at the end of the account, at the point where it is re-attached to the list of the 'lesser' Judges, that Jephthah is said to have 'judged Israel'.

Israel itself is not even mentioned in the early account and is in fact only found in the passages belonging to the later editing of the story (Judges 10:17. 11:4–5a; 11:13–27). The whole episode is purely Gileadite – the messengers sent to Jephthah are the elders of Gilead, Jephthah becomes the leader of all the inhabitants of Gilead and he is acknowledged by the people in a Gileadite sanctuary. The military action is confined to Gilead [33] and the independent tradition of the war with Ephraim (Judges 12:1–6) presupposes that the Gileadites were the only ones who took part in the war against Ammon.

There is, however, nothing that might point in all this to the existence of an amphictyony or even – on a more restricted scale – a league of tribes. What is more, this choice of a leader in Gilead is given the religious sanction of an oath sworn by the elders and is acknowledged by the people in a sanctuary. The reasons for the choice, however, are purely human. According to Judges 11:29, 'the spirit of Yahweh came upon Jephthah', but, even if these words do form part of the early source – and this is open to doubt – this descent of the spirit took place later than the choice of Jephthah by the elders and the people. Nonetheless, this leader of Gilead was also a Judge of Israel. It is possible that he became a Judge after his victory over the Ammonites,[34] but we do not know how he was raised to this status or by whom.

[32] J. van der Ploeg, 'Les chefs du peuple d'Israël et leurs titres', *RB*, 57 (1950), especially p. 52. There is evidence that the word existed at Ugarit as a proper name: *qsn* and *bn qsn*. It has been compared with the Arabic *qâḍî*, 'judge', but this is open to doubt. Certainly there was no established sense of the noun 'judge' in Hebrew, according to P. Joüon, *MUSJ*, 10 (1925), p. 41. It cannot be concluded from the single example of Jephthah that *qāṣîn* was the title of the 'Judges' of Israel.

[33] For this difficult text, see S. Mittmann, 'Aroer, Minnith und Abel Keramin (Jdc. 11. 33)', *ZDPV*, 85 (1969), pp. 63–75.

[34] This has been proposed by R. Smend, *Jahwekrieg und Stämmebund*, (note 14), p. 39;

762   IV: THE PERIOD OF THE JUDGES

There are two references to the fact that Samson 'judged Israel' (Judges 15:20; 16:31), but these can be set aside, since they are intended to provide an explanation for the insertion of the stories of the Danite hero and possibly also to act as an element in a chronological system. The reference to Othniel (Judges 3:10) can also be discounted, because the brief text dealing with him is a deuteronomistic composition and forms a typical example, combining characteristics both of the 'great' and of the 'lesser' Judges.

It is important, however, to take the figure of Deborah into account. In Judges 4:4–5, she is presented as 'a prophetess, the wife of Lappidoth' and 'at this time . . . a judge in Israel'. The text goes on to say that 'she used to sit under Deborah's palm between Ramah and Bethel in the highlands of Ephraim and the Israelites would come to her to have their disputes decided', that is, for judgement or *miš'pāṭ*. It has therefore been suggested that Deborah should be added to the list of the 'lesser' Judges.[35] According to the Song of Deborah, she is from Issachar (Judges 5:15), but she passes judgement in the hill country of Ephraim, like the 'lesser' Judge Tola, who was also from Issachar,but who lived at Shamir in the highlands of Ephraim (Judges 10:11). It is possible, then, that Deborah combined the function of a Judge with the charisma of a prophetess and held a permanent office in Israel. People consulted her and her decisions carried weight in matters of great importance for 'Israel'. On behalf of God, Deborah appointed Barak to lead the war against Sisera.

It is, of course, true that Judges 4:4b–5 is very similar to the brief texts on the lesser Judges, but at the same time it is also similar to a parenthesis and an addition,[36] in that verse 6 is clearly the normal continuation of verse 4a, the prophetess Deborah calling on Barak to tell him what God had said. What is more, Deborah's function as a judge is not mentioned in any other place, either in the prose account in Chapter 4 or in the poetical account in Chapter 5. In both of these accounts, all that is emphasised is Deborah's character as an inspired person urging the people on (see, for example, Judges 4:6–10, 14; 5:7, 12, 15). It would therefore appear that the memory of another Deborah, Rebekah's nurse, was added to this tradition concerning the prophetess Deborah (Judges 4:4b–5). It is in fact very difficult to avoid associating[37] Deborah's palm tree situated between Ramah and Bethel (Judges 4:5) and other trees, including especially the Oak of Tears below Bethel, under which Deborah, Rebekah's nurse, was buried (Gen

C. H. J. de Geuss, *NTT*, 20 (1965–1966), p. 97.

[35] H. W. Hertzberg, *TLZ*, 79 (1954), col. 286ff; H. C. Thomson, *op. cit.* (see above, note 10), pp. 76–77; R. Smend, *Jahwekrieg und Stämmebund, op. cit.*, pp. 42–45, in which Deborah's function as a judge is simply admitted as a possibility.

[36] W. Richter, *Traditionsgeschichtliche Untersuchungen zum Richterbuch* (*BBB* 18), Bonn. 1963, pp. 37–42.

[37] I expressed myself with some reserve about this in my *Institutions*, II, p. 100 (*Ancient Israel*, London, 1973, pp. 278–279) and in *La Genèse (BJ)*, note on Gen 35–8.

35:8) and the Oak of Tabor on the road to Bethel, which is mentioned in 1 Sam 10:3 and which, it has often been suggested, should be corrected to read the 'Oak of Deborah'. In the same district of Bethel, there was a sacred tree with which a memory of Rebekah's nurse was associated and with which a tradition concerning Deborah, the prophetess of Issachar, who had nothing to do with this district, was connected at a later date. On the other hand, it was a common practice to come to such places to find God's replies or decisions under the sacred tree there. Near Shechem, there was, for example, an 'Oak of the Teacher' (Gen 12:8), which was also known as the 'Oak of the Diviners' (Judges 9:37), to which it was the practice to go in order to ask a prophetess like Deborah for replies, *mišpaṭim*, to certain questions. All this made it possible for the memory of Deborah, originally from Issachar, to be taken to Ephraim and for her to be accorded the function of a judge. This, however, took place at a later stage, during the period of the deuteronomistic editing.[38] Deborah has therefore to be removed from the list of the judges.

There is finally no person, apart from those whom we have considered here, who is said in the Book of Judges to have 'judged Israel'. This, however, is said of Eli in 1 Sam 4:18 and of Samuel in 1 Sam 7:15–17. We will look first at the case of Samuel and then briefly at that of Eli.

The complexity of the traditions concerning Samuel (see p. xxviii)

In the Deuteronomist's account, Samuel is presented as the last of the Judges. The formulae found in the Book of Judges occur in Chapter 7 of 1 Sam in an attempt to attribute a great victory over the Philistines to Samuel's intercession with God. At the end of the chapter, moreover, there is a brief text which is similar to those dealing with the 'lesser' Judges (1 Sam 7:15–17). In Chapter 12, Samuel gives way to the king whom he has appointed. Following Stade and Wellhausen, many scholars have regarded this transformation of Samuel from a 'seer' into a 'judge' as an invention on the part of the editors of the Books of Samuel. It has, after all, to be recognised that a great victory over the Philistines at the time of Samuel is not in accordance with the historical facts, since the war of liberation did not begin until the time of Saul (1 Sam 13–14) and was not won until David became king (2 Sam 5:17–25; 8:1). It is, however, clear that the Deuteronomist dared not present Samuel either as a military leader or as a liberator, but only as one who interceded with God. This, is, of course, in no way contradictory to the tradition, according to which he was a Judge in the sense of the 'lesser' Judges.[39] This tradition is expressed in 1 Sam

[38] This is the conclusion reached by W. Richter, see above, note 36, and C. H. J. de Geus, *NTT*, 20 (1965-1966), p. 94.

[39] This tradition is accepted by quite a large number of recent authors, who nonetheless

7:15–17a: 'Samuel was judge over Israel as long as he lived. Each year he went on circuit through Bethel and Gilgal and Mizpah and judged Israel in all these places. He would then return to Ramah, for his home was there; there too he judged Israel'. If the data concerning Samuel's death and burial, given separately in 1 Sam 25:1, are added to this information, then what we have are the major elements that are provided in the case of the 'lesser' Judges, although these elements are presented differently in the case of Samuel. There was, then, a tradition concerning Samuel as Judge which was independent of the list of the 'lesser' Judges.

The geographical details given in verses 16–17a (Bethel, Gilgal, Mizpah and Ramah) certainly provide a different geographical outline from that within which the list of the 'lesser' Judges was placed, namely Benjamin and the south of Ephraim according to our hypothesis. It is, of course, possible that the names of the sanctuaries mentioned in the story of Samuel were added to the tradition. Samuel, after all, judged 'Israel' and the name 'Israel' must clearly have here the same meaning as the one which we have tried to determine, namely that of a group of tribes. The elders of Israel who came to ask for a king (1 Sam 8:4) therefore represent something more than just Ephraim and Benjamin.

A recognition of Samuel as having the function of a Judge does not imply a denial of his rôle as a seer and as someone who was inspired. In fact, the prestige that he enjoyed because he possessed these charismatic gifts was probably the determining factor in his choice as Judge. On the other hand, however, the function that he carried out in Israel was permanent. There is one passage, 1 Sam 12:1–5, which above all throws light on the nature of this permanent function. According to this text, when he gave way to the king whom he had appointed, Samuel asked the people to acquit him of maladministration: 'Whose ox have I taken? Whose donkey have I taken? Have I ever wronged or oppressed anyone? Have I ever taken a bribe from anyone, so that I should close my eyes? [40] If so I will requite you'. The people replied: 'You have neither wronged nor oppressed us, nor accepted a bribe from anyone'. There is obviously nothing in this text which suggests

interpret Samuel's function as a judge very diversely. See, for example, H. W. Hertzberg, *TLZ*, 79 (1954), col. 288; H. Wildberger, 'Samuel und die Entstehung des israelitischen Königtums', *TZ*, 13 (1957), especially pp. 463–466; J. Bright, *History*, p. 166; A. Weiser, *Samuel. Seine geschichtliche Aufgabe und religiöse Bedeutung*, Göttingen, 1962, pp. 9–11, 83; J. Dus, *ArOr*, 31 (1963) p. 463; R. Smend, *Jahwekrieg und Stämmebund, op. cit.*, pp. 45–53; W. Richter, *ZAW*, 77 (1965), pp. 47–49; H. Seebass, 'Traditionsgeschichte von 1 Sam 8; 10, 17ff und 12', *ZAW*, 77 (1965), especially p. 292 and note 15; C. H. J. de Geus, *NTT*, 20 (1965–1966), pp. 93, 98; K.–D. Schunck, 'Die Richter Israels und ihr Amt', *Volume du Congrès. Genève (SVT*, 15), 1966, especially pp. 254–255; F. Langlamet, 'Les récits de l'institution de la royauté (1 Sam., VII-XII)', *RB*, 77 (1970), especially pp. 172–175.

[40] Instead of 'so that I should close my eyes', the Greek version has 'or a pair of sandals? Answer me!' and it is difficult to choose between these two readings.

that Samuel had the function of interpreting the law – the function which Alt and Noth believed was that of a Judge of Israel – or that Samuel's task was limited to the sphere of judging. It cannot be denied that what is said in this passage could be applied to an unjust or corrupt judge, but it could also equally well be applied to an old ruler with other functions apart from administering justice. The passage can profitably be compared with Samuel's denunciation of the abuses which the king would commit (1 Sam 8:11–7) and even with the text in which Moses defends himself (Num 16:15). What is more, Samuel presents himself as a ruler: 'I have led you from my youth until this day', he declares and now 'it is the king who will lead you' (1 Sam 12:2). This clearly means that he was their 'leader'.

When the elders of Israel came to ask Samuel to appoint a king, they addressed him not as a prophet, but as their leader (1 Sam 8:4–5) – they wanted a king because he was too old and his sons were not following his example. Verses 1–3 can be regarded as preparing the way for this – when he was old, Samuel appointed his two sons Joel and Abijah as judges at Beersheba, but they took bribes and allowed the law to be perverted. The names of Samuel's two sons and the name of the place where they lived do not seem to have been invented, but the story is nonetheless very difficult for various reasons. The function of a Judge for instance, was not a hereditary one. Another novelty in this account is the division of the office of Judge between two men, both, however, living in the same place. This place, moreover, was in the extreme south of the country of Judah, which would mean that it was remote from the centre of the communal life of Israel. Finally, they were not judges in the same way as Samuel was a Judge – rather they were judges in the strict sense of the word. The whole story, then, is difficult to accept. One is tempted to ask whether it is not an invented story, based on the account of the two wicked sons of Eli (1 Sam 2:12–17, 22–25). In any case, this tradition was not known to the editor of 1 Sam 12:2, since, if Samuel was intent on making his honesty known, he would not have mentioned his sons if they had such a bad reputation.

If this story is to be preserved as true, we can say that there is no question here of a succession. What in fact happened is that Samuel, when he was old, delegated to his sons part of his functions: those which he carried out at Beersheba, where, through Judah, very early connections had been maintained with the north. It is also possible to see in this story the end of an institution which was in decline, Samuel being the last of the Judges and the first of the kings.

At this point, we must briefly consider the story of Eli and ask whether he too was a Judge. The statement is added to the story of Eli's death: 'He had judged Israel for forty years' ['twenty years' in the Septuagint] (1 Sam 4:18b). Almost the only Old Testament scholar to have seriously believed that Eli was really a Judge was Hertzberg,[41] who claimed that his

priesthood could not be regarded as an objection and that it is also possible
to attribute to him the function of a Judge because of the part he played in
the important sanctuary at Shiloh. In 1 Sam 2–3, moreover, Samuel appears
as Eli's chosen successor. On the other hand, Eli is presented neither as a
liberator nor as a Judge and 1 Sam 4:18b is undoubtedly an editorial insertion, though it is difficult to decide whether it is a later addition [42] or
whether the Deuteronomist regarded Eli as one of the Judges and incorporated him into his chronological plan.[43] From the historical point of
view, however, it is clear that Eli cannot be included in the list of the
Judges.[44]

Up till now, we must conclude, our investigation has proved disappointing. We have been able to add only two names to the five 'lesser' Judges in
the list contained in Judges 10 and 12 – Jephthah, who was certainly one of
the 'lesser' Judges and Samuel, who was very probably one. So far, then,
we have learnt a little about the origin and the functions of these Judges,
but we must now continue further with our investigation and make use of
the analogical method.

IV. THE MEANING OF THE ROOT Š P Ṭ

1. *In Hebrew*

In his article 'Die Bezeichnung "Richter" für die charismatischen Helden
der vorstaatlichen Zeit', in *ZAW*, 57 (1939), pp. 110–121, O. Grether
attempted to prove that the basic meaning of this root in Hebrew was 'to
judge' and that it also had certain variants: to settle a case, pass sentence, do
justice to (help, rescue) or the opposite, mete out justice to = condemn.
Out of about two hundred cases where the root is used, Grether found only
three in which it was employed in the sense of 'to rule'. His conclusions
were accepted by Alt and Noth, who made use of them in their hypothesis
of an amphictyonic judge. They were also accepted, with certain
refinements, by J. van der Ploeg in his article on *šāphat* and *mišᵖāṭ* in *OTS*, 2
(1943), pp. 144–155. In the light of our present knowledge of other Semitic
languages, however, Grether's conclusions have to be reconsidered.

[41] H. W. Hertzberg, *TLZ*, 79 (1954), col. 288; *Die Samuelbücher (ATD)*,[4] 1968, p. 36.
[42] M. Noth, *Überlieferungsgeschichtliche Studien*, pp. 22–23, was of this opinion.
[43] See W. Richter, *Die Bearbeitungen des 'Retterbuches' in der deuteronomischen Epoche (BBB
21)*, 1964, pp. 117, 133–134; C. H. J. de Geus, *NTT*, 20 (1965–1966), pp. 91–92.
[44] See K.–D. Schunck, *SVT* 15, 1966, p. 255 and note 6.

2. In Phoenician and Punic

Ahiram's inscription at Byblos, which dates back to about 1000 B.C., contains a malediction: 'May the sceptre of his mišpaṭ be broken and may the throne of his royalty be overthrown'.[45] Here the word has the meaning of 'government' or 'authority'. During the fourth and third centuries B.C., in Cyprus, the participle špṭ pointed to a function, the precise nature of which eludes us.[46] The same applies to an inscription of Pireus dating back to the third century B.C.[47] There is never reference to anyone except to kings in the Phoenician inscriptions of the metropolis, but Josephus points out, in his treatise against Apion (C. Ap. I, 157), that, after Nebuchadnezzar's siege of Tyre, the city was ruled, not by kings, but by judges: 'Eknibal, the son of Baslekh, judged for two months; Chelbes, the son of Abdeus, for ten months; the high priest Abbar for three months; Myttynos and Gerastrates, the sons of Abdelimus, were judges for six years'. After this period of government by judges, there was a return to the monarchy. This is clearly a 'list of lesser Judges', of Tyre, who replaced the kings during a time of anarchy following a national disaster.

Carthage was ruled by suffetes,[48] špṭm, mentioned in the Punic inscriptions from the fourth century B.C. onwards. In the writings of Greek and Latin authors, these suffetes are called 'kings', βασιλεῖς, reges, but some authors use a transcription of the original word – sufes, in the plural sufetes – and compare their functions to those of the Roman consuls. There was a period in the history of Carthage when there were two suffetes. They were elected for one year and that year was named after them. It is, however, possible that this was a result of an influence emanating from Rome. Suffetes were also present in the Carthaginian colonies in the Mediterranean at Gades in Spain and at Tharros in Sardinia. After the fall of Carthage and even until the third century A.D., suffetes practised as municipal magistrates in certain towns in northern Africa. We know very little about the origin of this institution in Carthage or about the election and the functions of these suffetes. Only a few names are given on the Punic inscriptions and we are bound to suspect that the Greek and Latin authors who wrote about the suffetes identified this institution inevitably with those which were familiar to them in their own environment. Because we are so badly informed about

[45] KAI, 1, 2.

[46] CIS I 47 = KAI 36.

[47] CIS I 118 = KAI 58.

[48] For the suffetes, see S. Gsell, Histoire ancienne de l'Afrique du Nord, II, Paris, 1920, pp. 193–201, 290–292; Ehrenberg, 'Sufeten', PW, IV A 1, 1931, col. 643–651; C. Poinssot, Karthago, 10 (1959–1960), pp. 124–127; L. Teutsch, RIDA, 3rd series, 8 (1961), pp. 286–288; G. C. Picard, 'Les sufètes de Carthage chez Tite-Live et Cornelius Nepos', Revue des Etudes Latines, 41 (1963), pp. 269–281; W. Seston, 'Des "portes" de Thugga à la "Constitution" de Carthage', Revue Historique, 237 (1967–A), pp. 277–294.

the suffetes and because of the geographical remoteness and the distance in time, any comparison between them and the Judges of Israel must be of limited value only.[49] What is certain in any case is that these suffetes were not only or even mainly 'judges'. They were clearly rulers and this fact may throw some light on the meaning of the corresponding Hebrew word and on the functions of the Judges of Israel.

3. In Ugaritic

The root *tpt* has two meanings: to do justice to, and to rule.[50] Of the hero Danel, it is said that 'he judges the judgement *(idn dn)* of the widow; he does justice *(itpt tpt)* to the orphan' (2 Aq v 7s. = 1 Aq I 23–25). The king's son Keret criticises his aged father: 'you do not judge the judgement *(ltdn dn)* of the widow; you do not do justice *(lttpt tpt)* to the oppressed' (Gordon, 127, 33–34, repeated in 46–47). It will be noted in both cases that it is the task of a king to carry out justice in this way.

The noun *mtpt* seems to have had the meaning of 'decision' (or perhaps 'oracle') in a recently discovered Ras Shamrah text[51] and this has been compared with the meaning of the Hebrew *miš'pāṭ* in Num 27:21; Prov 16:33 and the 'pectoral of *miš'pāṭ*' in Ex 28:15, 29, 30.

In a text of the Baal cycle which is parallel to the inscription of Ahiram cited above, however, the word *mtpt* has the meaning of 'government' or 'authority': '(El) will overthrow the throne of your royalty; he will break the sceptre of your government'.[52]

The participle-noun *tpt* also has the meaning of 'leader' or 'ruler'. What is more, *tpt* is also in parallel with *zbl*, 'prince', as a title of the god Yam (frequently): 'our *tpt*' is used in parallel with 'our king'.[53]

4. At Mari[54]

In the eighteenth century, the Mari texts contained a word *šiptu*, which

---

[49] I have already mentioned (see above, note 11), J. Dus' exaggerated study, 'Die "Sufeten Israels"', *ArOr*, 31 (1963), pp. 444–469. See also the reservations expressed by H. M. Orlinsky, *OrAnt*, I (1962), p. 13, note 6.

[50] F. C. Fensham, 'The Judges and Ancient Israel Jurisprudence', *op. cit.*, (note 16); W. Schmidt, *Königtum Gottes in Ugarit und Israel, op. cit.* (note 19), pp. 27–34; W. Richter, *ZAW*, 77 (1965), pp. 59–61; C. H. Gordon, *Ugaritic Textbook*, Rome, 1965, glossary No. 2727; J. Aistleitner, *Wörterbuch der ugaritischen Sprache*, Berlin,² 1965, No. 2921.

[51] *Ugaritica*, V, No. 6, p. 564; see also J. C. de Moor, *Ugarit-Forschungen*, 2 (1970), pp. 303–305.

[52] Gordon, 49, VI 28–29; cf. 129, 17–18 = I AB, VI 28–29; III AB, C 17–18.

[53] Gordon, 51, IV 44 = II AB, IV-V, 44; Gordon, 'nt V 40 = V AB, E 40.

[54] W. Richter, *ZAW*, 77 (1965), pp. 61–68.

has been interpreted as 'reprimand' or 'rebuke',[55] but which probably meant 'ordinance', 'edict' or 'decision'.[56] This is, of course, the same meaning as the Hebrew *miš'pāṭ*, which is often found together with *ḥôq*, 'law' or 'decree', and the expression *šiptam nadânu (šakânu)* is parallel to the Hebrew phrase *śîm ḥôq w'miš'pāṭ*, 'to give a law and an ordinance', which is said of Moses (Ex 15:25) and of Joshua (Jos 24:25) and David (1 Sam 30:25).

The noun *'sapitu* was only known to us in Mari lexicons and in two contracts of the land of Hana, which was near to Mari[57] and where the word meant the magistrate who was responsible for carrying out the contract in question. Now, however, several uses of this noun have come to light at Mari itself,[58] confirming that the word was western Semitic, as the root *'špt* itself probably was. There is one text in which the word really means 'judge' in the strict sense. This is a legal text recording a sentence, *dinu*, passed by a *'sapitu*.[59] Elsewhere, the more general meaning would seem to be more suitable and in some texts it would seem to point to an important official appointed by the king. Certainly his responsibilities went beyond the purely legal sphere.[60]

It has been suggested that the word and the institution itself might have originated in the nomadic or semi-nomadic tribal society.[61] The word is clearly parallel to *abu bîti*, 'family chiefs', in *ARM*, I, 73, 52; VII, 214, 6. What is more, in *ARM*, II, 98, there is reference to an intervention by the *'sapitu* in connection with the movements of the nomadic Haneans. The *suqaqu* or sheikhs are also mentioned in the same context. This is, of course, possible, but, in the Mari texts, the *'sapitu* forms part of the royal administration.

---

[55] F. Thureau-Dangin, 'Le terme siptum dans les lettres de Mâri', in *Or*, 12 (1943), pp. 10–112, on *ARM*, II, 13, 24–33; 92, 6, followed by J.-R. Kupper, *ARM*, III, 12, 22; 30, 25.

[56] This view is held by G. Dossin on *ARM*, I, 6, 14–15, 20; 83, 27 (but, in *ARM*, IV, 16, 2', he translates *šiptam nadânu* as 'sermonise'). W. Richter, *ZAW*, 77 (1965), p. 63; A. Malamat, 'The Ban in Mari and in the Bible', *Biblical Essays 1966. 9th Meeting of Die Ou Testament. Werkgemeenskap in Suid-Afrika*, p. 45 (with a new translation of *ARM*, II, 13, pp. 44–45).

[57] F. Thureau-Dangin, *JA*, Dixième série, 14 (1909–B), pp. 149–155; cf. A. Walther, *Das altbabylonische Gerichtswesen (Leipziger Semitistische Studien*, VI, 4–6), Leipzig, 1917, pp. 106–107.

[58] *ARM*, I, 62, 9'; 73, 52; II, 32, 16; 98, 12'; VII, 214, 6'; VIII, 6, 17; 84, 4. See also A. Finet, *Répertoire analytique, ARM*, XV, under the word *'sapitu*, and H. B. Huffmon, *Amorite Personal Names in the Mari Texts*, 1965, p. 268.

[59] *ARM*, VIII, 84, 4; see also G. Boyer's commentary, *ibid.*, p. 238.

[60] M. Noth, *Die Ursprünge des alten Israel im Lichte neuer Quellen*, Cologne, 1961, keeps to the meaning of 'judge', which is, of course, in accordance with his interpretation of the judge of Israel'.

[61] J. Bottéro, *ARM*, VII, pp. 241–242; A. Malamat, *op. cit.* (note 56), p. 45; W. Richter, *op. cit.*, p. 68.

V. An Attempt at a Solution

It is therefore clear that, at Mari and at Ugarit as well as in Phoenician and in Punic, the root špṭ had a much wider meaning than simply that of 'administering justice to'. There is evidence of this latter meaning at Mari and Ugarit, but the basic meaning is 'to rule' or 'to command'. 'To administer justice' is a duty and a privilege of the leader and this is the secondary or later meaning which the root came to have. This secondary sense became the ordinary meaning in Hebrew. Despite this, however, the word is encountered in certain texts outside the book of Judges with the meaning of 'to rule', especially in the Psalms[62] and the accounts of the institution the monarchy. In Ps 2:10, šôphēt is parallel to king; in Ps 148:11, it appears alongside king (melekh) and prince (śar). In Pss 96:13 and 98:9, the verb špṭ probably has the meaning of 'to rule' rather than that of 'to judge'.[63] In Ps 82:8, the meaning of the verb is quite clear: 'Rise God, and rule (špṭ) the earth, for you are the master of all the nations'.[64] This use of the verb can be explained by the Canaanite influence on the poetry of Israel. The verb špṭ = to rule can also be found in the accounts of the institution of the monarchy. It is difficult to avoid translating špṭ in 1 Sam 8:5 as 'to rule': 'Give us a king to rule over us, like the other nations' and also in verse 6 and 1 Sam 8:20: 'So that we in our turn can be like other nations; our king shall rule us and be our leader and fight our battles.' As we have already pointed out, however, the title 'judge' which was given to Samuel meant that he was more than an administrator of justice – he was a ruler. The institution of the monarchy brought a change in the type of government. Before the time of the kings, Israel was ruled by the Judges. The same texts indicate the nature of this change – Israel wanted to be 'like other nations' and therefore adopted what amounted to a foreign type of government, the Canaanite monarchy.

This difference between the king and the Judge is clearly illustrated in the story of Gideon (Jerubbaal) and Abimelech. The literary analysis and the criticism of traditions of Judges 6–9 is extremely difficult.[65] Gideon is also

---

[62] W. Schmidt, *Königtum Gottes in Ugarit und Israel, op. cit.* (note 19), pp. 30–34.

[63] See M. Dahood, *Psalms I; II (Anchor Bible)*, in loco; H.–J. Kraus (*BKAT*), however, believes that the verb should be translated by 'to judge'.

[64] A. Gonzalez, 'Le Psaume LXXXII', *VT*, 13 (1963), pp. 293–309; M. Dahood, *Psalms II* 1968, p. 271.

[65] W. Richter, *Traditionsgeschichtliche Untersuchungen zum Richterbuch (BBB 18)*, 1963, pp 112–318; W. Beyerlin, 'Geschichte und heilsgeschichtliche Traditionsbildung im Alten Testament (Richter VI–VIII)', *VT*, 13 (1963), pp. 1–25; B. Lindars, 'Gideon and Kingship' *JTS*, New Series 16 (1965), pp. 315–326; H. Haag, 'Gideon – Jerubbaal – Abimelek' *ZAW*, 79 (1967), pp. 305–314; H. Schmid, 'Die Herrschaft Abimelechs (Jdc 9)', *Judaica*, 26 (1970), pp. 1–11.

[N.B. In his text – in the margin of this paragraph – Roland de Vaux had made the obser

known as Jerubbaal and the reason why he was given this name is given in Judges 6:25–32, the story of the destruction of the altar of Baal. Some scholars[66] are of the opinion that these two names point to the existence of two different traditions which became merged together at an early date. They are not, however, in agreement as to what has to be attributed to Gideon and what to Jerubbaal. According to Haag, Gideon was a man of Manasseh, a member of the clan of Abiezer and the hero of the struggle against the Midianites. The story of his victory was linked with the legend of the sanctuary at Ophrah, but this connection is not a primitive one. The story of Gideon was associated with that of Jerubbaal-Abimelech, which belongs to the Shechem cycle. Gideon thus became the father of Abimelech. According to Noth, Kutsch and Schmid, Gideon and Jerubbaal were assimilated because both of them originated at Ophrah. Although this hypothesis is quite probable, it is, in my opinion, impossible to separate the text now between the two traditions. What is of interest to us in this context is that Gideon-Jerubbaal refused the kingship that was offered to him (Judges 8:22–23), but that his son Abimelech sought and obtained that kingship from the Shechemites.

According to Judges 8:22–23,[67] after his victory over the Midianites, the 'men of Israel' asked Gideon to 'become their master (māšal)', he himself, his son and his grandson. He replied that Yahweh, not he, would be their master or māšal. This text can be compared with 1 Sam 8:7, according to which Yahweh told Samuel: 'It is not you they have rejected; they have rejected me, and no longer want me to rule (mlk) over them' and 12:12: 'Yahweh your God is your king (melekh)'. The passage in Judges 8:22–23 may therefore reflect the theology of the Deuteronomist. This is even more likely in that Gideon in fact wields power – he takes charge of the spoils taken from the Midianites (8:24–27) and after his death Abimelech said to the leaders of the Shechemites (9:2): 'Which is better for you? To be ruled by seventy – I mean all the sons of Jerubbaal – or to be ruled by one?' It is, however, possible to regard Judges 8:22–23 as an early text if it is interpreted not as a refusal, but rather as a polite acceptance containing an element of reserve (in this case, the desire to maintain God's law). This is the way in which it has been interpreted by G. H. Davies and J. Gray in *Joshua, Judges and Ruth (The Century Bible)*, 1967, p. 227.

I myself believe that it is a historical fact that Israel, that is to say, the group of tribes including Manasseh, Ephraim, Asher and Zebulun (see

---

vation: 'Revise, making a distinction between Gideon, hero and lesser Judge, "Judge of Israel", and Jerubbaal'; see below, p. 801.]

[66] M. Noth, *Geschichte*, p. 141, note 1 (*History*, p. 152, note 1); E. Kutsch, *RGG* under 'Gideon' (II, col. 1570); Richter, Lindars, Haag and Schmid, all quoted in the previous note (No. 65).

[67] In addition to Lindars, *op. cit.*, see also G. Henton Davies, *VT*, 13 (1963), pp. 151–157.

Judges 6:35; 7:23–24) offered authority to Gideon-Jerubbaal after his victory over the Midianites – this can be compared with the case of Jephthah, who became a Judge after his victory – and that Gideon accepted this authority and exercised it until he died. The word 'king', it should be noted, is never used in this context. This authority was to be handed down to Gideon's son and grandson (8:22); however, this would be to adopt the dynastic monarchy of the little Canaanite states, and Gideon would not accept this.

In addition to exercising this authority over Israel, that is, the group of tribes as defined above, Gideon also had authority over Shechem, which was Canaanite. This is in fact a repetition of the situation that existed during the Amarna period,[68] when Shechem was subject to Lab'ayu and his sons.

Abimelech, who was the son of Gideon's Shechemite concubine, was himself half a Canaanite-Shechemite. When Gideon died, Abimelech had himself proclaimed 'king' by the Shechemite leaders (9:6). He remained king for three years, but was eventually killed in a revolt by his Canaanite subjects. The territory over which he had power is not known, but we can be sure that the episode of Abimelech was of little importance in the history of Israel, since the people were not ready for government by monarchy.

The story of Gideon-Jerubbaal concludes in this way (8:30–32): 'Gideon had seventy sons begotten by him, for he had many wives. His concubine, who lived in Shechem, bore him a son too, whom he called Abimelech. Gideon son of Joash was blessed in his old age; he died and was buried in the tomb of Joash his father, at Ophrah of Abiezer.' This text is, of course, strongly reminiscent of the formulae used in the case of the 'lesser' Judges,[69] as is the round number indicating numerous descendants. Even though the word 'judge' is not to be found in any of the stories about Gideon-Jerubbaal, the latter may be regarded as a judge of Israel[70] and be associated with a group of tribes representing the Israel of the period.

During the period of the Judges, then, there was an instrument of government known as the 'Judge'. The biblical list of the 'lesser' Judges is in no sense complete, nor were all the 'great' Judges really 'Judges' (a typical case is Othniel; Samson). Bearing in mind the list of the 'lesser' Judges and the formula: 'after him, . . , was judge', it is clear that the office was filled continuously. As for the 'great' Judges, their periods of office were separated by gaps, namely during times of oppression. It is, of course, possible that the strictly continuous succession of Judges may have been the work of an editor or that the words 'after him' (instead of 'succeeded him', which is

---

[68] See H. Reviv, 'The Government of Shechem in the El-Amarna Period and in the Days of Abimelech', *IEJ*, 16 (1966), pp. 252–257.

[69] See Lindars, *op. cit.*, p. 324.

[70] See De Geus, *NTT*, 20 (1965–1966), p. 94.

found in the formulae used of the kings) may be explained as allowing for a succession with some gaps in between the Judges. The tribes led independent existences: 'there was no king in Israel and every man did as he pleased' (Judges 17:6; 18:1; 19:1; 21:25). When danger threatened all the tribes, groups were formed and a leader or 'judge' was chosen, but as soon as the danger passed, each tribe became autonomous again. This situation can be compared with that of the Benjaminites of Mari, of whom Kupper said: 'they formed a confederation of tribes, each drawn up behind a sheikh. It was natural, in times of war, that certain leaders were recognised because of their personal influence or the strength of the military contingents following them ... As soon as this need ceased to exist, each tribe withdrew to its own side and each sheikh resumed his full powers'.[71]

[71] J.–R. Kupper, *Les nomades en Mésopotamie au temps des rois de Mari*, Paris, 1957, p. 59.

Chapter Twenty-Six

THE LIFE OF THE TRIBES

THE book of Judges does not provide us with a full history of this period. All that it does is to provide episodes involving only one clan, one tribe or one group of tribes. We cannot be certain that these episodes took place in the order in which they are presented in the book itself and they are undoubtedly only one part of the history of the tribes. Nonetheless, because of these stories we are able to imagine the kind of life led by the tribes at this period. On the one hand, it is clear that there was a continuation of the conditions that prevailed at the time of the settlement of the tribes, when various groups were moving from one place to another and acquiring new territories, and relationships with the Canaanites still preserved the double aspect of peaceful mutual understanding on the one hand and armed conflict on the other. On the other hand, however, new problems arose at this time – above all it became necessary to defend territories when they were attacked by neighbours and this gave rise to a struggle between certain tribes for predominance.

I. MOVEMENTS OF TRIBES OR CLANS

1. *Dan*

It was, of course, only very gradually that the tribes found their definitive territories and a number of tribal movements certainly took place during the period of the Judges. It is only about the Danites that we possess any fairly detailed information and our knowledge of the movements of this tribe comes from an appendix to the book of Judges, Chapters 17–18.[1] This

---

[1] Apart from the commentaries, see C. Hauret, 'Aux origines du sacerdoce danite. A propos de Jud., 1, 30–31', *Mélanges Bibliques ... A. Robert*, Paris, 1957, pp. 105–113; E. Täubler, *Biblische Studien. Die Epoche der Richter*. Tübingen, 1958, pp. 43–99; M. Noth, 'The Background of Judges 17–18', *Israel's Prophetic Heritage. Essays in Honor of J. Muilenburg*, ed. B. W. Anderson and W. Harrelson, New York, 1962, pp. 68–85; Y. Yadin, ' "And Dan, why did he remain in ships?" ', *The Australian Journal of Biblical Archaeology*, I 1 (1968), pp. 9–23; A. Malamat, 'The Danite Migration and the Pan-Israelite Exodus-Conquest: A Biblical Narrative Pattern', *Bib* 51 (1970), pp. 1–16.

is an early tradition which had been either overlooked or else rejected by the Deuteronomist in his editing of the Book of Judges, not only because he found its theology disturbing, but also because it did not fit in with his plan to provide the story of a saving Judge. It was in fact introduced into the post-exilic edition of the book. In the literary criticism of these chapters, a distinction has often been made between two different sources, but it is quite possible to view the chapters as a literary unity, apart from a few additions. According to A. Malamat, the account is, especially in the case of Dan, in complete conformity with the plan of the stories of the pan-Israelite conquest, which begin with the sending out of men to reconnoitre the land (Num 13–14). This structural analysis does not, however, prejudice our historical interpretation of the story. It is above all a Danite tradition. According to Noth, it is more than this, being a tradition concerning the priests of the royal sanctuary established by Jeroboam I, who was scornful of the ancient tribal sanctuary with its priest and its idol of doubtful origin. The story is especially important in any study of the levitical tradition and the religious situation at the time of the Judges. What is of chief interest to us here, however, is that it is in the context of the establishment of this sanctuary that the story of the Danite migration is narrated (Judges 18).

No territory, it will be remembered, had been allocated to the Danites. They therefore sent five men from Zorah and Eshtaol to look for a place where they would be able to settle. On their reconnaissance, these men reached Laish, at the source of the Jordan, and this country seemed to them to be fertile and its inhabitants isolated and defenceless. When they heard this news, six hundred men of the clan left Zorah and Eshtaol with the families and their animals. On their way through the hill country of Ephraim, they took the idol, the ephod and the teraphim from Micah's house, where he had a sanctuary, and at the same time took the priest with them. They then marched against Laish, killing all the inhabitants and setting fire to the town. Then they rebuilt the town, called it Dan and set up the idol there, appointing priests to minister to it. The memory of this migration was preserved in the geographical name, maḥ'neh-dān, the 'Camp of Dan', the first encampment of the emigrants to the west of Kiriath-jearim according to Judges 18:12 and situated between Zorah and Eshtaol in the story of Samson (Judges 13:25). These two statements may, however, come to the same thing.

The data in this story must, of course, be compared with those contained in other texts. According to Judges 1:34, the Amorites forced the Danites to retreat into the highlands and did not allow them to reach the plain. According to Jos 19:47, the territory of the Danites resisted them, so that they went up and attacked Leshem and seized it. They consequently settled in Leshem and renamed it Dan after the name of their ancestor. The name 'Leshem' is encountered nowhere else. It is in fact an error in transcription and is meant to represent Laish, a name known to us in the Egyptian execration texts, the Mari texts and also in a geographical list of Thutmose III. In spite of this, however, a list of seventeen towns which are said to have been allocated to Dan at the time of the apportioning of the land among the tribes is given in Jos 19:40–46. This list, however, includes such towns as Aijalon and Sha-alabbin, which, according to Judges 1:35, remained Amorite, and others such as Timnah, Ekron and Gibbethon, which were Philistine towns. This territory also includes the Jaffa region and therefore shows how the land belonging to the Israelites had extended during the reigns of David[2] and Solomon.[3] Nothing is known about the extent of the new territory of the Danites around the ancient town of Laish.

Did the whole of the tribe of Dan emigrate or was the movement confined to only a part of the tribe? It was, after all, a very small tribe. In the introduction to the account, Judges 18:1, Dan is called a *sēbhet* or 'tribe', but in the story itself only a *mišʿpāhah* or 'clan' in verses 2 and 11, but both a *sēbhet* and a *misʿpāhah* in verse 19. In the story of Samson, Dan is called a 'clan' or *mišʿpāhah* (Judges 13:2). In the genealogical table of the family of Jacob (Gen 46–23), Dan is said to have only one son, Hushim. In the census of the tribes in Num 26:42, the Danites form only one clan, that of Shuham (Shuham and Hushim are the same name transmitted in different forms). It is true that in this census 64,400 men are attributed to Dan, whereas in the census of Num 1:39, the Danites are said to number 62,700 and, in the list of warriors who made David king at Hebron, there are 28,600 Danites (1 Chron 12:36). One explanation that has been suggested for these fantastic figures[4] is that they represented not 'thousands' but much more restricted military units, so that, in the census of Num 26:42, there were 64 units forming a total of 400 men, in the list of Num 1:39, there were 62 units with a total of 700 men and, in the list contained in 1 Chron 12:36, there were 28 units totalling 600 men. According to Judges 18:11, 16, 17, there were 600 armed men of the 'tribe of Dan' who set off on their migration. The census figures make Dan appear to be a strong and numerous tribe, but this was simply not the case at all, either historically or in the account that we are considering here. Nothing useful can therefore be concluded from the figures.[5] The impression gained from the whole chapter, however, is of a mass departure, the whole of Dan emigrating.

There are nonetheless certain difficulties. If the whole of the tribe of Dan

[2] Y. Aharoni, *The Land of the Bible*, London, 1967, p. 266.

[3] B. Mazar, 'The Cities and the Territory of Dan', *IEJ*, 10 (1960), pp. 65–77; according to Z. Kallai, 'The Town Lists of Judah, Simeon, Benjamin and Dan', *VT*, 8 (1958), pp. 134–160, especially pp. 144–148; *ibid.*, *The Northern Boundaries of Judah*, Jerusalem, 1960 (Hebrew), pp. 27–28; this list corresponds to the second of Solomon's districts.

[4] G. Mendenhall, 'The Census Lists of Numbers 1 and 26', *JBL*, 77 (1958), pp. 52–66.

[5] According to A. Malamat, *Bib* 51 (1970), p. 9, note 3 and G. Mendenhall, *JBL*, 77 (1958), *op cit.*, (note 4), p. 62, it was also a figure representing a large military unit.

emigrated, the story of the Danite hero Samson, which is set in this precise region of Zorah and Eshtaol (Judges 13:2), at *maḥᵃnēh-dān,* the 'Camp of Dan' between Zorah and Eshtaol (Judges 13:25), must be prior to the migration itself.[6] Israel's enemies at that time, however, were the Philistines; these are undoubtedly the people mentioned in Judges 18 and only the Amorites are mentioned in Judges 1:34.[7] It took some time for the Philistines to extend their influence as far as the Shephelah, but, according to the story in Judges 18 and the reference in Judges 1:34, these events took place very soon after the settlement in Canaan. On the other hand, the stories concerning Samson, which contain so many allusions to local topography, could only have been handed down and preserved within a Danite environment on the spot. It is therefore more likely that the migration was not a complete one and that it was confined to this region of Danite families which had become merged with other tribes, especially with Judah (Zorah and Eshtaol are regarded as towns belonging to Judah in Jos 15:33) or with Benjamin (the name Hushim is also found in the list of Benjamin's descendants, 1 Chron 8:8, 11, but as the name of a woman).

It is also difficult to date the Danite migration.[8] It took place after the battle of the waters of Merom and the capture of Hazor (Jos 11), because it is clear that the little tribe of Dan could not possibly have reached Laish while the king of Hazor was still in power in the region. Dan must also have been already settled in the north when the saying recorded in Deut 33:22 was composed: 'Dan is a lion cub leaping from Bashan'. This is certain, not only because Bashan is mentioned in this text, but also because Laish means 'lion'. Dan was probably already in the north according to the text of Gen 49:17: 'Dan is a serpent on the road'.[9]

It is even more difficult to ascertain whether the migration of the Danites took place before or after the victory of Barak-Deborah over Sisera. Opinions are very divided about this and for the most part depend on the interpretation given to the text: 'Why is Dan in the ships of strangers?' (Judges 5:17). Dan is included among the four tribes which did not answer the call, after Reuben and Gilead (Gad) in Transjordania and before Asher. The closeness of Asher would seem to point to the fact that Dan had already

---

[6] This is one opinion among others; see A. T. Olmstead, *History of Palestine and Syria,* New York and London, 1931, p. 272ff; T. H. Robinson, *A History of Israel,* I, Oxford, 1932, p. 156; M. Noth, *Geschichte,* p. 150 (*History,* pp. 162–163); O. Eissfeldt, 'The Hebrew Kingdom', *CAH,* II, XXXIV, 1965, p. 23.

[7] The 'Amorites' can be regarded as a general name for the early inhabitants of the region, including the Philistines who had subjugated them; see M. Noth, *Geschichte,* p. 67, note 1 (*History,* p. 68, note 1).

[8] H, H. Rowley, *From Joseph to Joshua,* London, 1950, pp. 81–86; H.–J. Zobel, *Stammesspruch und Geschichte* (*BZAW,* 95), 1965, pp. 88–96.

[9] Zobel, *op. cit,* places Gen. 49, 17 (excluding verse 16), however, before the Danite migration.

settled in the north. It is furthermore no longer possible to explain the reference to the ships by speaking, as has been done in the past,[10] about sailing on Lake Huleh. The Danites might, however, have served the Canaanites of the coastal region as hired men, as the men of Asher did. We are, after all, told that the inhabitants of Laish, whom the Danites replaced, lived like the Sidonians (Judges 18:7). This is the view that has been frequently expressed in recent commentaries, such as those by A. Vincent and H. W. Hertzberg, in BJ and ATD as well as in the articles and books of E. Täubler,[11] S. Mowinckel,[12] J. Bright[13] and O. Eissfeldt.[14]

However, it is by no means certain that the Song of Deborah follows a geographical order – or that particular geographical order – in its list of tribes and, if the Sidonians are meant in Judges 18:7, the same text adds at once that the people of Laish lived a long way away from the Sidonians, even though they had the same customs. The connection between the Danites and the ships can apply equally well – or equally inadequately – to Dan still in the south and to Dan already settled in the north,[15] since Zorah and Eshtaol were no further from the Mediterranean coast than Laish-Dan was. Before they migrated, the Danites might have served the ship-owners on the coast in the Jaffa region as hired men. In one of the Amarna letters, the sender of which unfortunately cannot be identified,[16] there is reference to people from the interior of the country who were sent to Jaffa to serve the pharaoh. Their work would probably have been to load and unload the pharaoh's ships. The Danites were no doubt forced to leave because of pressure from the Amorites (see Judges 1:34), but the Amorites themselves were driven back by the Philistines. It has therefore been suggested that the migration took place in the decades following Barak's victory.[17]

In both cases, the text is difficult to explain and attempts have been made to correct it. Budde has suggested, for example, that n‘ōthāw, 'his pastures', should be read in this verse instead of ᵒnîyyôth, 'ships'. Rowley cautiously proposed gē’ayôth, 'valleys'.[18] The best suggestion, however, has been made by J. Gray,[19] who has compared the text with the Ugaritic gr ’an ‘rm and has

[10] J. Garstang, Joshua Judges, London, 1931, p. 305.

[11] E. Täubler, op. cit. (note 1), pp. 89–92.

[12] S. Mowinckel, Von Ugarit nach Qumran. Festschrift Eissfeldt (BZAW 77), 1958, p. 137.

[13] J. Bright, History, p. 80.

[14] O. Eissfeldt, CAH, II, XXXIV, 1965, p. 23.

[15] See H. H. Rowley and H.-J. Zobel, above (note 8).

[16] EA, 294, 18–20. It has been attributed to a prince of Gezer, but cf. E. F. Campbell, The Chronology of the Amarna Letters, Baltimore, 1964, pp. 101, note 73, and 126. A. Alt linked this letter with Judges 5:17; see PJb, 10 (1924), p. 35 = Kleine Schriften, III, p. 169, note 6.

[17] See H. H. Rowley and H.-J. Zobel, above (note 8), and Y. Yadin, whose hypothesis will be discussed.

[18] H. H. Rowley, op. cit. (note 8), p. 83.

[19] J. Gray, Joshua, Judges and Ruth (The Century Bible), 1967, p. 288.

translated it as: 'he dwelt quietly in the town', in accordance with the Arabic *'ana,* 'to be at ease', 'to be quiet'. Together with others, Gray has suppressed the 'why', which breaks the prosody and he believed that 'Dan dwells quietly' or 'at ease', *"nîyyôth,* possibly with different vowels, was an adverbial accusative. In this way, the resulting sentence is similar to that applied to Gilead previously and Asher immediately afterwards.

Judges 18:38 has been cited in support of an early date for the Danite migration.[20] According to this text, the first priest at the sanctuary of Dan was a man called Jonathan, son of Gershom, son of Manasseh. In the last of these three names, the *nûn* is written above the line, in other words, it is 'hanging'. There has clearly been a correction for 'Moses,' which must have been the reading in the original text. The correction was a pious one, made in an attempt to eliminate the memory of Moses from this heterodox sanctuary. This Jonathan, then, was a grandson of Moses. Certain scholars have regarded this datum as being very early and as having considerable historical value.[21] Even if this is accepted, it is clear that the genealogy may be incomplete – Moses certainly had a son, Gershom, but the only other son known to us, apart from Gershom, is not Jonathan, but Shebuel (1 Chron 23:15; *cf.* 26:24). Above all, as a result of literary analysis, verse 30b has come to be regarded as an addition.[22] This Jonathan was clearly the unnamed Levite dealt with in the history of Israel at some length; it would seem to be abnormal for his name to appear only at the end of this account. Attempts have even been made to read the name Gershom into Judges 17:7, but they have come to nothing. It is, however, possible that Jonathan or Jonathan ben Gershom was a recurrent name in the priesthood of Dan. In order to wash away the stain of the latter's doubtful origin, an attempt was made to connect the Danite priesthood with Moses, but at a later stage this seemed to the copyists to be an insult and they therefore corrected the name Moses, making it 'Manasseh', the name of the wicked king of Judah. In any case, nothing can be derived from this text which would help us to date the Danite migration.

Nor do the recent excavations at Dan assist us in any way to arrive at a decision.[23] The last town of the late Bronze Age, Str. VII, was destroyed by fire. At the next level, Str. VI, there is a pottery in which Late Bronze shapes are mixed with those dating back to the beginning of the Iron Age. This level merges without any gap into the next level, Str. V, although it is

[20] See Burney in his commentary (1918), pp. 415–416.
[21] A. Cody, *A History of the Old Testament Priesthood,* Rome, 1969, p. 51, note 50, with references to earlier books and articles.
[22] E. Täubler, *op. cit.* (note 1), pp. 55–58; M. Noth, *op. cit.* (Note 1), pp. 70. note 6, 83–84; A. H. J. Gunneweg, *Leviten und Priester,* Göttingen, 1965, pp. 20–23.
[23] A. Biran, 'Chronique Archéologique', *RB,* 75 (1968), pp. 380–381; 77 (1969), p. 403; *Bible et Terre Sainte,* No. 125 (Nov. 1970), p. 11.

separated from the later level by slight traces of fire. This later level (Str. V)
ended in a conflagration. It is difficult to establish the exact dates of these
levels and to determine which of them represents the arrival of the Danites.
According to the archaeologists, the sixth level (Str. VI) represents the last
Canaanite town of Laish, which was destroyed by the Danites, who at once
rebuilt the town of Str. V. According to this archaeological evidence, then,
the Danite migration took place at the end of the twelfth or the beginning
of the eleventh century B.C. and in any case after Barak's victory.

In his hypothesis, Y. Yadin has thrown a completely new light on the
question of the migration of the Danites.[24] According to Gen 49:16, Dan
was 'judge of his people as of any one of the tribes of Israel', which, Yadin
believes, meant that Dan had not always been recognised as a tribe of Israel,
a belief that is reinforced by the statement in Judges 18: 1 that Dan had not
yet received any territory among the tribes of Israel. In the genealogical
system, Dan had, as we have seen, no descendants, only a son (or clan) being mentioned. The statement in Judges 5:17 that Dan lived in ships cannot
be satisfactorily explained by Dan's settlement in the south or by a settlement in the north – it must refer to a period when the Danites lived beside
the sea and led a seafaring life. The stories of Samson show how closely the
Danites were connected with the Philistines, although certain problems are,
of course, raised by Samson and it has been suggested that he has some of
the characteristics of the Greek sun heroes.

Apart from the Philistines who according to the Bible were settled
along the coast to the south of Jaffa, and the Tjeker or Zakkala who were,
according to the Egyptian story of Wen-Amon, settled at Dor, the Egyptian documents also mention another Sea People, the Denen or Danuna,
who are represented in a dress similar to that of the Philistines and the
Zakkala. These Danuna are exactly the same as the Danaioi of the Greeks.
The eponym of the Danaioi was Danaos and their heroes were Perseus and
Mopsos. According to the Greek sources, Danaos came from the east to
found Argos in Greece. Perseus, the founder of Tirynthus (or Mycenae according to another tradition), was linked in legend with Jaffa – it was, for
example, near Jaffa that he saved Andromeda from the sea monster. Mopsos
travelled in Asia Minor, Phoenicia and Palestine and conquered Ashkelon.
His people settled along the coasts of Cilicia, Syria and Phoenicia, at least
according to Strabo. He became famous because of the riddles which he
asked (cf. Samson).

In a comparison which he has made of these two sets of evidence, Yadin
has put forward the hypothesis that the Danaeans settled on the coast in
territory between that of the Philistines and that of the Zakˡˤala. He believes
that they founded Tell Qasīleh, near Jaffa, basing his theory on the fact that

[24] Y. Yadin, *The Australian Journal of Biblical Archaeology*, II (1968), pp. 9–23.

Str. XII, the earliest level, contains Philistine pottery. Since this stratum had been destroyed about 1100 B.C., it is remarkable that the next stratum should also contain Philistine pottery. According to Yadin, the Danaeans were driven out by another Sea People, possibly the Shardans. The Danites were, he concludes, these Danaeans, who clearly emigrated towards the north about the year 1100 B.C.; they were converted to Yahwism and for this reason took possession of the furnishings of the sanctuary of Micah together with its priest. They were finally incorporated into the league of the tribes of Israel and Dan, who had not had any inheritance among the tribes, became a Judge, like one of the tribes of Israel.

Although this is a clever and in many ways attractive hypothesis,[25] I am hesitant to accept it, because it is based on too many uncertain factors and is not in accordance with all the biblical texts. It is not possible to find, either in the stories of Samson or in those of the migration, any reference to a non--Israelite origin of the Danites (similar to that of the Calebites, for instance, who later became integrated into Israel). The stories of Samson provide us with evidence of the close contacts that existed between the Danites and the Philistines as well as of the differences between them and their opposition to each other. The Philistines are not mentioned, however, in the story of the Danite migration and, according to Judges 1:34, it was the Amorites who drove the Danites back into the highlands. It is also difficult to accept that the theft of the furnishings of the shrine of Micah and the taking away of the priest were really indicative of a conversion to Yahwism. One of Yadin's main arguments is based on the text in the Song of Deborah: 'Why is Dan in the ships of strangers?' (Judges 5:17) and this text can better be used as an argument against Yadin's theory, since it appears to point to Dan as one of the tribes which did not respond to the call and which therefore effectively or at least potentially formed part of the league of tribes. None of this, however, can be applied to the Danaeans, a Sea People living along the coastline and not integrated into Israel, before the migration of the Danites which, according to Yadin, took place about the year 1100 B.C., after the time that the Song of Deborah was composed.

We have still to consider in this context the text of Gen 49:16: 'Dan is judge of his people like each one of the tribes of Israel'. This is a play of words on the name of the tribe: *dan yadin*. There are several cases, both explicit and implicit, of such wordplay in this passage containing Jacob's blessings.[26] This ought to be enough to account for the text, but I believe that it contains rather more than this and points in fact to a change in the situation in which Dan found itself, having become equal to the other

---

[25] Yadin's view is at least partly shared by C. H. Gordon, *Congress Volume. Bonn* (*SVT* 9), 1963, pp. 21–22.

[26] A. H. J. Gunneweg, 'Über den Sitz im Leben der sog. Stammessprüche', *ZAW*, 76, (1964), pp. 245–255, especially pp. 248–250.

tribes. This, however, can be explained in a way which is different from Yadin's explanation. According to Zobel,[27] Dan had first been made the subject of foreign masters and had then freed itself from this domination and had become an independent tribe. I am, however, reluctant to make use of the reference to Dan in the Song of Deborah (Judges 5:17), since the meaning of this text and even the text itself are, as we have seen, uncertain. I am in favour of a different solution. This is that Dan was only a clan or *miš'pāḥāh*[28] and was acknowledged to be an autonomous tribe only after its migration and the conquest of Laish. Dan was originally a clan of Benjamin (see 1 Chron 8:8 and 11?) which was checked in its movement westward by the Canaanites (see Judges 1:34) and looked elsewhere for a place to settle. This would explain why no territory was allotted to Dan and why Dan was regarded as the son of Bilhah, Rachel's slave-girl and the mother of Benjamin. This was how the groups that had emigrated were commonly presented, namely as the descendants of wives of second rank or concubines. Examples of this practice are Ishmael, who was the son of the slave-girl Hagar (Gen 21:8–20) and the sons of Abraham's concubines (Gen 25:6) as well as the geographical distribution of Nahor's sons by his wife and his concubine (Gen 22:20–24).[29] Apart from the position occupied by Dan in the extreme north of the land, which served to mark off the land of Israel 'from Dan to Beersheba', and the choice of this territory by Jeroboam for the site of his second golden calf (1 Kings 12:28), Dan and the Danites played no part in the history of Israel. The Danite migration was in fact a very minor affair. A much more important event was the movement of part of the tribe of Manasseh into Transjordania.

2. *Eastern Manasseh*[30] (see p. xxviii)

Another migration took place during the period of the Judges, but this has to be inferred from the texts which refer to the settlement during the time of Joshua.

According to Num 32:33, half of the tribe of Manasseh was allotted land in Transjordania at the same time as Reuben and Gad. This same half-tribe of Manasseh would seem, therefore, to have taken part, like Reuben and Gad, in the conquest of Canaan (Jos 1:12; 4:12) and to have returned

[27] H.–J. Zobel, *op. cit.* (note 8), p. 96.
[28] See above, p. 777.
[29] According to A. Malamat, 'Aspects of Tribal Societies in Mari and Israel', *XV Rencontre Assyriologique Internationale, 1966*, Liège, 1967, pp. 129–138, especially pp. 129–130.
[30] A. Bergman, 'The Israelite Tribe of Half-Manasseh', *JPOS*, 16 (1936), pp. 224–254; M. Noth, 'Beiträge zur Geschichte des Ostjordanlandes, III', *ZDPV*, 68 (1946–1951), pp. 1–50, especially 2–18; E. Täubler, *Biblische Studien*, 1958, pp. 176–203, 246–252; H.–J. Zobel, *Stammesspruch und Geschichte*, 1965, pp. 112–126.

afterwards to Transjordania (Jos 22:1, 9). According to Jos 13:30 and Deut 3:13, the territory of Manasseh included the whole of Gilead to the north of the Jabbok and the whole of Bashan.

On the other hand, according to Num 32:39–42, it was Machir, the son of Manasseh who conquered Gilead. Another of Manasseh's sons, Jair, took the *hawwôth,* the 'encampments' and gave them his own name, while Nobah took the town of Kenath and called it after himself. According to Deut 3:14–15, Jair, Manasseh's son, seized the encampments bearing his name and Machir received Gilead (see also Jos 13:31; 17:1).

The settlement of part of the tribe of Manasseh in northern Transjordania is therefore ascribed to two of Manasseh's 'sons' – Machir and Jair. I propose to leave out of this discussion Nobah, who is mentioned only in Num 32:42 and who is said to have conquered only a town.

In the genealogies, Machir is described as the son of Manasseh and the father of Gilead (Num 26:29; 27:1; 1 Chron 2:21–23, etc.). Manasseh is, however, not named in the Song of Deborah. In the list of tribes who responded to the call, on the other hand, Machir is mentioned between Ephraim-Benjamin and Zebulun-Issachar-Naphthali. Assuming that this list follows the geographical order of the tribes, Machir was clearly settled in territory to the west of the Jordan between Ephraim and Zebulun. This district to the north and north-west of Shechem was the place where the story of Joseph began, at Dothan (Gen 37), and Machir had special links with Joseph – according to Gen 50:23, Machir's children were born in Egypt on Joseph's lap, that is to say, they were adopted by their grandfather. This territory corresponds to that belonging to Manasseh, but it should not be inferred from this that Machir was an important group settled to the west of the Jordan during the period of Deborah and that Manasseh no longer existed at that time as a tribal unit.

According to all the other texts which refer to Machir, however, the territory of the latter was in Transjordania (see Num 32:39–40; Deut 3:15; Jos 12:31; 17:1). All these are later texts than the Song of Deborah. According to Num 32:39, Machir occupied Gilead by driving out the Amorites who were there previously and the warlike nature of Machir is emphasised in Jos 17:1. That is a possibility, but this conquest must on the other hand have been an easy one, since only one royal city to the east of the Jordan is mentioned in the Amarna letters and that is Pehel = Pella, which was on the edge of the valley. The other Canaanite towns were to the north of the Yarmuk and were not conquered by the Israelites. The most recent archaeological discoveries have shown[31] that the sites occupied in the Late Bronze Age were very rare. Those of Iron Age I are much more numerous,

---

[31] N. Glueck, *Explorations in Eastern Palestine,* IV = *ASSOR,* 25–28 (1951); S. Mittmann, *Beiträge zur Siedlungs- und Territorialgeschichte des nördlichen Ostjordanlandes (Abhandlungen des deutschen Palästinavereins),* Wiesbaden, 1970.

but it is impossible to say whether or not they were in existence when the Machirites arrived.

In Cisjordania, the name Machir was replaced by that of Manasseh and this name was extended to include the groups which emigrated into Transjordania, reference being made to the other half of the tribe of Manasseh. In the genealogies, Machir thus became the son of Manasseh and, because he was settled in Gilead, he became the father of Gilead. What, however, were the original relationships between Machir and Manasseh and why did the migration take place? One possibility is that the two groups were quite distinct from each other and that the Machirites were forced to emigrate because of pressure from the stronger Manassites or perhaps in order to escape from being dominated by them.[32] It is more probable, however, that Manasseh was a clan of Machir which remained in Cisjordania, became more important and gave its name to the whole group.[33] The reason for this conquest was that this expanding tribe had not enough territory for its needs. It was at this time that Manasseh became important. At the time of Gideon, as we have already seen, Manasseh was the leading tribe of a group in the north and Ephraim had a subordinate place. This, then, was the period during which Manasseh was predominant over Ephraim and, according to the genealogies, it was Manasseh who was Joseph's first-born (Gen 41:50–51; cf. Jos 17:1). Sometimes both tribes are mentioned together, but in the order Manasseh-Ephraim (Jos 14:4; 16:4; Num 26:28 ff). When Ephraim came to the fore, the change was explained in the account of the blessings of Jacob, in which the latter gives priority to the younger of the two sons, Ephraim (Gen 48). The migration of Machir and the settlement of the half-tribe in Gilead date back to the period during which Manasseh became important, that is, after Deborah and before Gideon.

It has been suggested that Jos 17:14–18 contains a reference to a movement to the east on the part of Manasseh. According to this text, the house of Joseph had insufficient space in its own territory and asked Joshua for an additional portion of land. The story is presented in two different variants; according to the first (verses 14–15), Joshua sent the members of the house of Joseph to clear the forest region of the country of the Perizzites and the Rephaim, whereas according to the second variant (verses 16–18), he gave them the mountain and told them to clear it of trees. The interpretation of the whole passage is therefore difficult. According to some scholars,[34] the second variant, which is the earlier version, refers to an expansion to the west of the Jordan into the hill region of Ephraim. The first variant, which is later, refers, these authors believe, to an expansion into Transjordania, the Rephaim being the early inhabitants of northern Transjordania (Deut

---

[32] See H.-J. Zobel, op. cit., pp. 114–115.
[33] See M. Noth, Geschichte, pp. 61–62 and 71, note 3 (History, pp. 61–62, 72, note 3).
[34] M. Noth, Josua (ATD),² p. 107 and others.

3:4, according to which Og was the last of the Rephaim, and Deut 3:13, according to which his kingdom was the land of the Rephaim). According to this theory, then, Manasseh received the land of the Rephaim. Other scholars, however, have rejected this suggested reference to Transjordania, claiming that the Perizzites and the Rephaim are said equally often to have been to the west as to the east of the Jordan and that the words 'the country of the Perizzites and the Rephaim' are absent from G.[35] Finally, it has also been suggested that both variants refer to Transjordania, the 'mountain' or 'highlands' being those overlooking the valley of the Jordan on the east.[36]

Jair's settlement was closely connected with that of Machir. According to Num 32:41, Deut 3:14 and 1 Kings 4:13, he was the son of Manasseh, but, according to 1 Chron 2:18–22, he was the son of Segub, the son of Hezron the Judaean, and of Machir's daughter. In these genealogies, Jair is clearly a clan of Machir-Manasseh. Jair is also, however, the name of a person.[37]

According to Num 32:41, this same Jair seized 'their *hawwôth*', *hwthyhm*, which can be corrected into 'the *hawwôth* of Ham' (see Gen 14–5), just under five miles south of Irbid,[38] and called them by his own name. *Hawwôth* is a word meaning 'tents' or 'encampment'. According to Deut 3:14, these 'encampments of Jair' are the same as the *hebhel* of Argob (cf. 1 Kings 4:13). The meaning of this word *hebhel* is not clear; it may mean a strip of land, a portion marked out by a line or a confederation. The encampments of Jair (= Argob) were, we may therefore assume, the district situated between the highlands of 'Ajlūn and the Yarmuk, the most northerly region reached by the Israelites, who did not cross the Yarmuk, and the occupation of this district must have taken place late in the period of the Judges, the movement into the region beginning from the territory of Machir.

It is not easy to determine the precise relationship between this Jair – the clan or individual – and Jair the lesser Judge who originated in Gilead (Judges 10:3–5).[39] They are identified with each other in this biblical text, according to which the Judge had thirty sons who rode on thirty donkeys and lived in thirty towns called *hawwôth yā'ir*. This reference to the 'encampments of Jair', however, is undoubtedly an addition. In general, all

---

[35] H. W. Hertzberg, *Die Bücher Josua, Richter, Ruth (ATD)*,[4] 1969, p. 104; J. Gray, *Joshua, Judges and Ruth (The Century Bible)*, 1967, p. 151.

[36] S. Mittmann, *op. cit.*, pp. 209–211.

[37] Y. Aharoni, *The Land of the Bible*, pp. 191–192, following Mazar, has compared the clan of Jair with a group known as the Yauri, which, according to the Assyrian texts (*ARAB*, I, § 73) lived in the thirteenth century along the Euphrates. These non-Israelites who settled in Transjordania had, Aharoni believes, become integrated into Eastern Manasseh.

[38] A. Bergman, *JPOS*, 54 (1934), p. 176; D. Leibel, *BIES*, 24 (1959–1960), p. 55.

[39] M. Noth, 'Das Amt des "Richters Israels" ', *Festschrift A. Bertholet*, Tübingen, 1950, pp. 404–417 = *Gesammelte Studien zum Alten Testament*, II, Munich, 1969, pp. 71–85, especially pp. 77–78.

historical connection between the two names has been rejected. The two views that have most commonly been proposed are that the lesser Judge was invented and given the name of the clan or that he was in fact a historical person bearing the same name as the eponym of the clan. Noth, on the other hand, believed that Jair originated in primitive Gilead south of the Jabbok and that he existed before the settlement of the 'encampments of Jair' in the north.

I wonder, however, whether it is not possible to accept the fact that both names point to the same person. There is no evidence at all of the Judge Jair originating in primitive Gilead south of the Jabbok. He was buried at Kamon (Judges 10:5), which was probably also the place where he originated. This place Kamon has been identified by Abel (Géographie, II, p. 412) and Aharoni with Qamm, which is about seven miles to the west-north-west of Irbid, but this site was not occupied at the beginning of the Iron Age. More recently, Kamon has been identified with a site known as Hanzire, five miles to the east of Pella, and this would also correspond to the Kamon mentioned by Polybius near Pella. Potsherds dating back to the Iron Age (I) and to the Hellenistic period have been found there.[40] It is to the north of the Jabbok. The expansion towards the north which has been ascribed to Jair the Machirite-Manassite by some scholars may have taken place at the same time as Jair the Gileadite was Judge at Kamon. In other words, is it not possible that there was only one Jair, who was made the Judge of Israel after the taking of the encampments of Jair, just as Jephthah was made Judge after his victory over the Ammonites?

3. Were Ephraim and Benjamin in Transjordania?

In Judges 12:1–6, the Ephraimites blame Jephthah for not having called on them to go with him to fight the Ammonites, and they tell the Gilead-ites, who followed Jephthah (verse 4): 'You are no more than deserters (pālît) from Ephraim, you Gileadites in the heart of Ephraim and Manas-seh'. M. Noth[41] has claimed that this is sufficient proof that part of Ephraim migrated into Transjordania and settled in primitive Gilead to the south of the Jabbok. This would, of course, be the Gilead mentioned in the Song of Deborah and if this theory is true, the migration must have taken place before that of Machir. It must, however, be pointed out that this sentence is missing from part of the Greek tradition and that pālît does not mean 'deserter' – the word required to satisfy the hypothesis – but 'survivor'. The sentence is in fact a repetition of part of verse 5, in which the same words recur: 'When the survivors of Ephraim said . . . ' The doublet, it has been

---

[40] S. Mittmann, op. cit., pp. 227–228 and p. 45, note 104.

[41] M. Noth, Geschichte, p. 61 (History, pp. 60–61). S. Mittmann, op. cit., p. 213 ff.

argued, had to be completed at all costs and the result was an incomprehensible list.[42]

Another indication which might possibly point to an Ephraimite colonisation in Transjordania is the existence of a 'Forest of Ephraim', the battleground where Absalom was killed (2 Sam 18:6).[43] This, it has been claimed, was the name given to the land occupied by the Ephraimites to the north of the Jabbok. Ephraim, however, was originally a geographical name and it was only later that it became the name of a tribe, the one that occupied the hill country of Ephraim. Like other geographical names, the name Ephraim can be found in Transjordania without any connection with the tribe of the same name.[44]

Scholars have also suggested that elements of Benjamin migrated into Transjordania.[45] This theory has been based mainly on the close links between Benjamin and Jabesh-gilead; see Judges 21:6–14 (legendary); 1 Sam 11:1–11; 31:11–13, (historical), which can be understood only if Jabesh-gilead was a foundation of Benjaminite emigrants. A satisfactory explanation, however, for both the legend and the history is that there were family relationships between the inhabitants of Jabesh and those of Benjamin. An explanation has been suggested for the enmity existing between the people of Succoth and Penuel on the one hand and Gideon on the other (Judges 8:4ff), namely that this was a conflict between the Benjaminite columns and the members of another Israelite tribe. Finally, the suggestion has been made that Mahanaim was chosen as the residence of the son and successor of Saul the Benjaminite after the disaster at Gilboa (2 Sam 2:8) because Mahanaim was a Benjaminite colony.[46] All these arguments, however, seem to be unsatisfactory.

4. A migration of Asher?

In 1 Chron 7:30–40, there is an astonishingly well developed geneaology of Asher, which was, after all, a tribe of little importance. This genealogy has as its basis the text of Gen 46:17 (cf. Num 26:44–47 for the first two generations; the continuation however, is peculiar to the Chronicler).

---

[42] W. Richter, Bib, 47 (1966), p. 519; J. Gray, op .cit. (note 35), p. 340.

[43] H. W. Hertzberg, Die Samuelbücher (ATD),⁴ 1968, p. 295; S. Mittmann, op. cit., pp. 221–224.

[44] M. Noth, Geschichte, p. 60 (History, p. 60); D. Leibel, in 'Mount Rephaim – The Wood of Ephraim?', Yediot, 31 (1967), pp. 136–139 (Hebrew), has suggested the reading 'the Forest of Rephaim'.

[45] M. Noth, PJb, 37 (1941), p. 77, regarded this as a possibility and the idea was developed by S. Mittmann, op. cit., pp. 214–217.

[46] K.-D. Schunk, 'Erwägungen zur Geschichte und Bedeutung von Mahanaim', ZDMG, 113 (1963), pp. 34–40.

Several of these clans of Asher lived not in the territory allotted to Asher in the north of Palestine, but rather in the land apportioned to Ephraim and Benjamin.[47] A grandson of Asher, Malchiel, is said in this genealogy to be the father of Birzaith, which is now Birzeit to the north of Jerusalem. His brother Heber had, according to this list, a son called Japhlet; this is the clan of the Japhletites who lived on the boundary between Benjamin and Ephraim (Jos 16:3). Shemer/Shomer can also be compared with the clan of Shemer and Benjamin (1 Chron 8:12: LXX). The name of one of the sons of Asher, Beriah, can also be found in the genealogy of Ephraim (1 Chron 7.23) as well as in the genealogy of Benjamin (1 Chron 8:13). Among the more distant descendants of Asher are found Shual and Shilshah (1 Chron 7:36, 37) and these have obviously to be connected with the land of Shual (1 Sam 13:17) and the land of Shalishah (1 Sam 9:4) in the south of the territory of Ephraim. From these data, the conclusion has sometimes been drawn that Asher had spent some time in central Palestine and later emigrated towards the north, as Dan did,[48] or that the tribe had in fact settled in both parts of the land.[49] It is, however, more probable that Asherite families came in the course of time to settle in this region and that they became merged with the tribes of Ephraim or Benjamin.[50]

II. RELATIONSHIPS WITH THE CANAANITES

The tribes became consolidated in Canaan by a double process similar to that which had taken place during their settlement in the land – on the one hand, by armed conflict and, on the other, by peaceful infiltration and agreement.

1. The battle of Kishon

The only battle about which we have a good deal of information is the one fought on the Plain of Jezreel between a Canaanite coalition and the Israelites led by Barak and urged on by the prophetess Deborah.

[47] F.–M. Abel, 'Une mention biblique de Birzeit', *RB*, 46 (1937), pp. 217–224; S. Yeivin, *Encyclopaedia Biblica* (Hebrew), I, Jerusalem, 1950, art. *'āšer*, col. 777–786; A. Malamat, *JAOS*, 82 (1962), pp. 145–146; Y. Aharoni, *The Land of the Bible*, p. 223.

[48] Following C. Steuernagel, *Die Einwanderung der israelitischen Stämme in Kanaan*, 1901, pp. 30–31.

[49] S. Yeivin, 'The Israelite Settlement in Galilee and the Wars with Jabin of Hazor', *Mélanges Bibliques ... A. Robert*, Paris, 1957, pp. 95–104, especially pp. 99–100.

[50] Y. Aharoni, *op. cit.* Relationships existed between Asher and the south. According to 2 Chron 30:11, some men of Asher came to Jerusalem for the Passover of Hezekiah. At the time of Jesus, the prophetess Anna belonged to the tribe of Asher (see Luke 2:36).

There are two different accounts of this battle – a story in prose (Judges 4) and a poem entitled the Song of Deborah (Judges 5).[51] These two passages are in no way dependent on each other, the Song having been inserted at a later date into the book of Judges. This is clear from the fact that the final verse of Judges 4, that is verse 24, is continued in the last words of Judges 5. Several different traditions are combined in the prose account – the main person involved is first of all Deborah, then Barak and finally Jael, the wife of Heber the Kenite. The poem is moreover not the work of Deborah, since her name is interpolated in verses 7 and 12. It is undoubtedly a very early poem and was written very soon after the events had taken place, but its literary genre is uncertain. A. Weiser and after him J. Gray.[52] have both regarded it as an amphictyonic liturgy, in which the victory of Zebulun and Naphthali was celebrated by the assembled tribes (or by the tribes which ought to have met together) at a feast of the covenant. This, however, is too hypothetical in my opinion. I believe that it is a song of victory, very similar to the songs of victory sung by the nomadic Arabs.[53]

The fact that the Song of Deborah is a song or a composition in poetry means that it was less likely than the prose account to be modified or to have additions. This, on the other hand, does not necessarily mean that it is any closer to the historical reality, because poetry after all modifies reality. In any historical interpretation of the events, then, the prose story must also be taken into account. Certain difficulties are, however, raised in any comparison of the two passages.

Jabin and Sisera

In the prose account, the oppressor is Jabin, the king of Hazor (Judges 4:2). The leader of Jabin's army is Sisera of Harosheth-ha-Goiim (4:2, 7). In the poetic account, on the other hand, there is only one oppressor and that is Sisera, who is said to be a king (Judges 5:26–30). Jabin, the king of Hazor, is also the same king who was defeated at the battle of the waters of Merom (Joshua II), which took place during the period of Joshua.

The easy solution, namely that there were two kings of Hazor, Jabin I and Jabin II, has to be rejected, since, according to Jos 11, the Canaanite city of Hazor was destroyed and there never was a Jabin II. The only his-

---

[51] For the criticism of traditions and the literary analysis of these two passages, see W. Richter, *Traditionsgeschichtliche Untersuchungen zum Richterbuch* (BBB 18), 1963, pp. 29–112; summarised in *ibid.*, *Die Bearbeitungen des 'Retterbuches' in der deuteronomischen Epoche* (BBB 21), pp. 6–9.

[52] A. Weiser, 'Das Deboralied', *ZAW*, 71 (1959), pp. 67–97; J–Gray. *op. cit.*, (note 35), pp. 221, 275.

[53] M. S. Seale, 'Deborah's Ode and the Ancient Arabian Qasida', *JBL*, 81 (1962), pp. 343–347.

torical event during the period of the Judges that has been retained as certain is the victory of Barak, whose name is no doubt repeated in order to complete the picture of Joshua's conquests. The destruction of Hazor and the end of Jabin should no doubt be dated in the period of the Judges,[54] but the two battles took place in different geographical environments, the events described in Judges 4 being located in the Plain of Jezreel, those described in Jos 11 in Upper Galilee.

According to Aharoni,[55] the victory of Barak-Deborah over Sisera, Jabin's commander, and his allies was not followed by a conquest of the Canaanite towns, although it did effectively end the Canaanite power in the north. It was followed, Aharoni believes, by another battle in Upper Galilee which also took place during the reign of Jabin, namely the battle of the waters of Merom. As a result of this second victory over the Canaanites, the Israelites gained control of the whole region. Hazor, unable to hold out, was destroyed. The victory of Deborah-Barak therefore must have taken place at the very beginning of the period of the Judges and the destruction of Hazor must have taken place later. From the archaeological point of view, however, it is not possible to date the destruction of Hazor later than 1200 B.C. This means that Deborah has to be put back to the thirteenth century B.C. and this would throw out the entire chronology of the conquest of Canaan.

The solution in my opinion is that Jabin of Hazor was in fact an intruder into the account in Judges 4. He plays no active part in the account and is found only in the editorial framework (Judges 4:1–3, 23–24) and the addition (Judges 4:17b). The reference to him in verse 7 is also an addition. The combination of Sisera and Jabin is also found in 1 Sam 12:9; Ps 83:10. The Song of Deborah is therefore correct in saying that Israel's adversary was Sisera.

Why, then, was Jabin introduced at all into the account? I am of the opinion that it is because the two victories were in fact ascribed mainly to the same two tribes. According to the prose account, Barak was from Naphthali (Judges 4:6) and he called together Naphthali and Zebulun (Judges 4:6, 10). In the Song (Judges 5) verse 18 especially praises Zebulun and Naphthali, who braved death on 'rising ground' in the country. This verse is nonetheless an addition to the Song.[56] It has a different rhythm from the rest of the Song, one that can be related to that of the sayings about the tribes found in Gen 49 and Deut 33. It is also the only text in which the name of a tribe occurs for a second time – Zebulun is mentioned in verse 14

[54] See also O. Eissfeldt, *CAH*, II, XXXIV, 1965, pp. 9–10.

[55] Y. Aharoni, *The Land of the Bible*, pp. 200–208; see also *ibid.*, 'New Aspects of the Israelite Occupation in the North', *N. Glueck Volume*, Garden City, N.Y., 1970, pp. 254–267.

[56] H.–J. Zobel, *Stammesspruch und Geschichte*, pp. 51–52, 80–81; see also above, p. 665.

and Naphthali was probably also quoted in verse 15 (where Issachar occurs twice in the Hebrew). These events taking place on 'rising ground' are not in accordance with the geographical framework presented in Judges 4–5, namely level ground. Finally, the term employed here is *'al m'rômê śadheh*, which would appear to be an allusion to the waters of Merom. In my opinion, what we have here is a saying which is much earlier than the rest of the Song and which refers to the battle of the waters of Merom (Jos 11). It was in fact inserted into Judges because Naphthali and Zebulun also play ed an important part in the battle of Kishon. The two battles were combined at the level of tradition because they appeared in the two independent sources of the prose account and the Song of Deborah.

Israel's opponent, then, was Sisera. This is not a Semitic name. A. Alt has compared it with the Illyrian names in –ero, which is in accordance with his theory that the Philistines and other related groups had an Illyrian origin.[57] Another scholar, W. F. Albright,[58] has compared it with the name Zi-za-ru-wa, a prince of northern Syria during the fourteenth century, quoted in the Ras Shamrah texts.[59] The name, Albright believes, was Luwian and the Philistines' language was, in his opinion, Luwian.[60] In both cases, Sisera was a leader of the Sea Peoples and, Albright maintains, confirmation of this fact is to be found in the name of the place where he lived, namely Harosheth-ha-goiim, which is generally located in the extreme west of the Plain of Jezreel. The name means 'the wooden region of the nations'. These *gôyim* were, it is believed, immigrating Sea Peoples.[61] This is quite probable, but it must be remembered that there is no reference to the Sea Peoples in the prose account and that the confusion with the battle of the waters of Merom presupposes that Israel's opponents in this case too were the Canaanites; and that there is explicit reference to the kings of Canaan in the Song of Deborah (Judges 5:19). Aharoni has gone so far as to suggest that the end of the recapitulatory list of conquered kings in Jos 12:10–23 may not in fact contain the names of the kings who took part in this battle.[62] This would account for the number of nine hundred iron-plated chariots which Sisera was able to muster (Judges 4:3). This

[57] A. Alt, *ZAW*, 60 (1944), p. 78, note 3 = *Kleine Schriften*, I, p. 266, note 3.

[58] W. F. Albright, *Yahweh and the Gods of Canaan*, London, 1968, p. 218 and note 127; *ibid.*, 'Prologomenon' to the new edition of C. F. Burney's *The Book of Judges*, New York. 1970, p. 15.

[59] *PRU*, IV, p. 286.

[60] W. F. Albright, *CAH*, II, XXXIII, 1966, p. 30. In *Die Personennamen der Texte aus Ugarit*, Rome, 1967. p. 306, however, F. Gröndahl has listed the name among those with an unknown linguistic origin.

[61] According to Y. Aharoni, *The Land of the Bible*, pp. 201–203, this is the name of the wooded regions of Galilee. He consequently sees no reason for associating Sisera or Harosheth-ha-goiim with the Sea Peoples. According to Judges 4:16 and even Judges 4:13, Harosheth-ha-goiim is a specific place-name and not a region.

[62] Y. Aharoni, *op. cit.*, pp. 203 and 210–211.

would certainly seem to be true, broadly speaking, for the battle of the waters of Merom (see Jos 11:1–2), but it is not true in the case of the battle of Kishon, although, as we have seen, Aharoni connected the two battles. Is it therefore necessary to assume that there was a coalition between the groups of Sea Peoples who had settled in the Plain of Acco, Jezreel and as far as Beth-shean (Sisera) and the Canaanites, and that it was against them that the Israelites fought for possession of the Plain?

Who took part in the struggle on the Israelite side? This at once raises another difficulty. Only Naphthali and Zebulun are mentioned in the prose account (Judges 4:6 and 10), whereas Ephraim and Benjamin, Machir, Zebulun, Issachar and Naphthali (the latter has to be inserted into verse 15, in place of Issachar, which appears twice) are said to have responded to the call in the Song (verses 14, 15). According to M. Noth, it was only Naphthali and Zebulun who fought, as is stated in the prose account. The list in the poem was a later composition, the poet listing the names of tribes chosen purely subjectively.[63] In my opinion, Noth's hypothesis is very improbable. Our difficulty did not exist at all for A. Weiser,[64] who regarded the Song of Deborah as belonging to a feast to which the tribes in the confederation of tribes had been called in order to celebrate the victory of Zebulun and Naphthali. Weiser's interpretation of the poem is, however, as improbable as Noth's hypothesis and cannot be accepted if, as we have seen, verse 18 is not original, but was an addition. The Song may, of course, have been right and the prose account wrong – a certain number of tribes had been engaged in the action, but Barak, who himself came from Naphthali, had given the most important part to Naphthali and the neighbouring tribe of Zebulun, a fact which was preserved in the prose account.

No precise locality is given for the place at which the battle took place. Led by Barak, the Israelites encamped on Mount Tabor (Judges 4:6, 12) and Sisera took his troops from Harosheth-ha-goiim to Kishon (4:13). The battle was fought near Kishon (4:7; 5:21) and the Israelites were sure of winning because a storm whipped up the wadi Kishon, which overflowed its banks and swept away Sisera's chariots (5:20–21; cf. 4:15). That Yahweh strikes fear into Sisera, all his chariots and the whole of his army is a clear mark that this is a holy war. In the Song, verse 19, we also read that the battle took place at Taanach, by Megiddo's waters. This points to a more precise location for the battle, the marshy district which stretched out opposite Taanach and Megiddo before the installation of a modern system

---

[63] M. Noth, *Das System der zwölf Stämme Israels*, Stuttgart, 1930, p. 5; see also *Geschichte*, p. 39, note 4 (*History*, pp. 150–151).
[64] A. Weiser, 'Das Deboralied', *ZAW*, 71 (1959), pp. 67–97.

of drainage.[65] This place would not have been possible when the wadi Kishon was overflowing its banks.

This victory did not necessarily result in the taking of a town, but it was important from many points of view. In the first place, if our interpretation is correct, it was above all an action undertaken jointly by a group of tribes which certainly strengthened their unity. It was moreover a victory which was achieved on a plain against the greatly feared Canaanite chariots (Judges 4:13; cf. Jos 17:16–18; Judges 1:19). Finally, this victory destroyed the Canaanite hegemony in this region and thus it allowed the tribes to settle in the plains and enabled the tribes in the centre of the land to maintain contact more easily with those in the north.

What was the date of this battle?

Albright has tried to establish this date by means of archaeological data. In his opinion, the statement made in verse 19 of the Song of Deborah – 'at Taanach, by Megiddo's waters' – means that Taanach was inhabited at that time and that Megiddo was uninhabited, with the result that the battle took place before the Israelites had settled at Megiddo. This would mean that the battle was fought between strata VII and VI of Megiddo, stratum VI being the first Israelite stratum.[66] All this points to a date about 1150 B.C.[67] This argument has often been accepted,[68] but it is very uncertain. There are several reasons for this:

1) There is in the first place no certainty regarding the stratigraphy of Megiddo and the dates of the various levels. These are Yadin's final conclusions.[69]

Str. VIIa: during the reign of Ramses III – Ramses VI. Egyptian with an incursion of Sea Peoples in Palestine.

Str. VIb: very difficult; not very important. Philistine pottery. Beginning between 1150 and 1220 B.C. Did not last long. (Not Israelite.)

Str. VIa: heavy occupation. Abundance of metal; Philistine pottery. Second half of eleventh century. Probably destroyed by David.

Str. Vb: poor open village.

Stra. Va–IVb: Solomon.

[65] D. Baly, *The Geography of the Bible*, New York, 1957, p. 152.
[66] W. F. Albright, 'The Song of Deborah in the Light of Archaeology', *BASOR*, 62 (April 1936), pp. 26–31; see also 68 (December 1937), p. 25; *ibid., The Biblical Period*,[4] 1963, pp. 39 ff and note 82.
[67] This was W. F. Albright's last word on the question; see his *Yahweh and the Gods of Canaan*, London, 1968, p. 11 and note 35. Previously, he hesitated between 1150 and 1125 B.C.
[68] See the history of this question in V. Vilar Hueso, 'La batalla del Quisón y su problema cronológico (Ju 4–5)', *Miscelánea Bíblica Andrés Fernández*, Madrid, 1961, pp. 531–536.
[69] Y. Yadin, *Bib Arch*, 33 (1970), p. 93; A. D. H. Mayes, *VT*, 19 (1969), pp. 353–354.

2) New excavations at Taanach have shown that the history of Taanach and that of Megiddo were not, as Albright believed, complementary, but parallel. There were two periods of occupation during the twelfth century, both ending in destruction; the first was at the beginning of the twelfth century and the second about 1125. After this, the site remained unoccupied for at least a century.[70] This is certainly in accordance with Str. VIIa and VIb of Megiddo.

3) No conclusion with regard to the date of the battle can be drawn from these archaeological data. P. Lapp[71] was inclined to attribute the destruction of Taanach and Megiddo to the Israelites led by Barak in 1125. Neither of the two accounts, however, has anything to say on this score and it was only during the reign of David that both sites were occupied by the Israelites.

Nor is it possible to agree with Aharoni's theory[72] that the battle has to be dated at a period when Taanach and Megiddo were flourishing cities, because of the reference to the two cities in Judges 5, that is, before 1125. We reject this hypothesis because Taanach and Megiddo occur in the poem only as geographical indications and whether they were occupied or not makes no difference.

A much more sure way of dating this battle would be to compare it with other known historical data, but there are unfortunately very few such facts which are certain. We have already rejected Aharoni's hypothesis[73] that the battle took place at the very beginning of the period of the Judges, even before the battle of the waters of Merom and the taking of Hazor. At the other extreme, A. D. H. Mayes has suggested that the battle of Kishon was fought in the second half of the eleventh century B.C., shortly before the defeat of Aphek (1 Sam 4), the war waged by the Philistines against Israel being a reaction to the Israelite victory over Sisera. It would, however, seem to be out of the question to give such a late date to this battle, at the very end of the period of the Judges.

This battle presupposes that the tribes had already settled in Canaan and that their settlement there had become fully consolidated. It could not, in other words, have taken place at the very beginning of the period of the Judges. Nonetheless, I am inclined to place it quite early during that period. Machir had not been replaced by Manasseh, so that the battle must have taken place not only before Machir's migration into Transjordania, which might well have occurred at quite an early date, but also before the appearance of Manasseh as a fully constituted tribe and therefore before Gideon. I would therefore say that it took place about the middle of the

[70] P. W. Lapp. *BibArch*, 30 (1967), pp. 8–9; *BASOR*, 185 (February 1967), p. 3.
[71] *BibArch, op. cit.*
[72] Y. Aharoni, *Volume Glueck*, p. 260.
[73] See above, p. 791 ff.

twelfth century B.C., but should not like to be more precise than this. As we have already seen, it is difficult to establish any exact chronological connection between the battle of Kishon and the Danite migration.

2. The expansion of Judah

Just as there had been during the period of the settlement of the tribes in Canaan, so too during the time of the Judges there were not only armed struggles against the Canaanites, but also a number of peaceful infiltrations which resulted in the tribal territories being enlarged. As an example of this type of peaceful expansion, I should like to discuss the activities of the tribe of Judah during this period.[74]

The nucleus of the tribe settled, peacefully it would seem, in the hill country of Judah from which it took its name, in the region surrounding Bethlehem. The development of the tribe is clearly expressed in the various genealogies. Ephrathah, who gave her name to the Judean clan of Bethlehem, married for a second time, becoming the wife of Caleb, and from this marriage came Tekoa (1 Chron 2:24). This is the name of a district between Bethlehem and Hebron which was occupied by the Calebites. This prepared the way for the merging of the two groups of Judah and Caleb, although this was not completed until the reign of David.

The descendants of Ephrathah and her first husband, Hezron, Judah's grandson, are presented in a confused form in the genealogies of 1 Chron 2 and 4, but it would seem as though Hur was among them. Among Hur's 'descendants' (1 Chron 2:50–55; 4:2–4, 16–19) there are several places situated between Bethlehem and Bethzur (Etam and Gedor, for example), to the north and north-west of Bethlehem (Nephtoah, Kiriath-jearim, the Vale of Sorek, Eshtaol and Zorah) and finally in the Shephelah (Soco and Keilah.).

Like the other genealogical lists in Chronicles, this genealogy is, in fact, a description of the process by which the territory became populated as the result of a slow movement towards the north-west and the west from the region of Bethlehem. This was, of course, the only direction in which the Judaean group could move. In the south, the movement had been halted by the Calebites of Hebron, with whom the group had entered into an agreement (the marriage between Ephrathah and Caleb; see above). In the north, the Judaeans were prevented from expanding by a line of Canaanite towns consisting of Jerusalem, Aijalon and Gezer.

This expansion took place at a later date than that of the settlement at the

---

[74] R. de Vaux, 'The Settlement of the Israelites in Southern Palestine and the Origins of the Tribe of Judah', *Translating and Understanding the Old Testament. Essays in Honor of H. G. May*, Nashville and New York, 1970, pp. 108–134. This will also be found above pp. 523–549.

time of Joshua. Kiriath-jearim had originally formed part of the Gibeonite tetrapolis (Jos 9:1) and the Vale of Zorah, Eshtaol and Zorah could have become Judaean territory only after the migration of the Danites had taken place.

With regard to the Judaean settlement in the Shephelah, there is in fact one story in the Old Testament which, although it is attached to the age of the patriarchs, must in fact be set in the period of the Judges. This is the story of Judah and Tamar, recounted by the Yahwist in Gen 38. This story not only provides us with an example of the law of levirate marriage – it also explains how the tribe of Judah grew, by means of an account of the personal adventures of the tribal ancestor. According to this story, Judah left his brothers and went down to Adullam (= esh-Sheikh Madhkur) in the Shephelah, about three miles to the south-east of Soco. He had flocks at Timnah, about four miles to the north-west of Adullam. While he was in the Shephelah, he married the daughter of a Canaanite called Shua and this wife gave him three sons, Er, Onan and Shelah. Er married Tamar, who was also in all probability a Canaanite. When Er died and Tamar became his widow, the law of levirate marriage should have been carried out, but first Onan, Er's brother, refused to give her a child and then Judah refused to let her have his third son, Shelah. Tamar succeeded in fulfilling the law, however, by means of a trick and had twins, Perez and Zerah, by her father-in-law. This story illustrates the expansion of the Judaean groups towards the plain, their family links with the Canaanites, the formation of the clans which eventually died out (Er and Onan) and that of the three clans of Judah listed in Num 26:20 – the Shelanites, the Perezzites and the Zerahites. In this way, a link is formed with the genealogies found in Chronicles, as described above. It should be added at this point that another geographical name found in the Shephelah also occurs among the descendants of Shelah, that of Mareshah (1 Chron 4:21).

The expansion outlined here would seem to have taken place peacefully. According to Jos 10:28–39, however, the conquest of a number of towns included within the territory allotted to Judah is ascribed to Joshua and to the whole of Israel. These towns are Makkedah, Libnah, Lachish, Eglon, Hebron and Debir. In the Old Testament itself, however, the conquest of Hebron is attributed to Caleb and the conquest of Debir is attributed to Othniel (Jos 15:13–19; Judges 1:12–15, 20) and the schematic list found in Jos 10:28–39 contains nothing that the historian can regard as authentic. In the same way, he is unable to accept as historically valid the statement made in Judges 1:9: 'The sons of Judah went down to attack those Canaanites living in the highlands and in the Negeb and the lowlands (= the Shephelah)'. Nor can he accept verse 10, according to which Hebron was conquered by Judah.

Archaeologists are also not in favour of the theory that Judah conquered and occupied the towns of the Shephelah, namely Libnah, Lachish and Eglon. Libnah (= Tell Bornat, which is about five miles to the south of es-Safi, with which it was until recently identified) was occupied at the end of the Late Bronze Age and at the beginning of the Iron Age, but the site has not been excavated. Eglon is now located at Tell el-Hesi. It appears that the town was destroyed at the end of the Late Bronze Age, but that it remained unoccupied for most of the period of the Judges. Lachish (= Tell ed-Duweir) has been thoroughly excavated, but its destruction cannot be exactly dated (the first years of the twelfth century if the presence of a scarab belonging to Ramses III in the destruction level is taken into account) nor can it be said for certain that the Israelites carried out this destruction. In any case, after this destruction Lachish remained unoccupied throughout the whole period of the Judges. On the basis of this archaeological evidence it would seem probable that the reference to Libnah, Eglon and Lachish in Jos 10 points to a growth on the part of Judah during the reigns of David and Solomon, parallel to the expansion mentioned in Gen 38.

3. The agreements with the Canaanites

(a) The Gibeonites

Jos 10 contains a description of a treaty concluded between Joshua and the Gibeonites,[75] the 'Hivite' inhabitants of the four towns forming the confederation of Gibeon; that is, Gibeon itself, Chephirah, Beeroth and Kiriath-jearim. As a result of this agreement, the Gibeonites were incorporated into Israel, but they enjoyed a lower status. They made peace with Israel and 'entered their community' (Jos 10:1), but they continued to be aliens and, as such, they were able to count on the support of Israel as their protector (Jos 10:6), although they did not enjoy all the rights of the Israelites themselves (2 Sam 21:4). They were obliged to serve the sanctuary (Jos 9:27), which was probably the high place of Gibeon. The situation in which these four towns found themselves was different from that of the Canaanite enclaves which continued to exist until the time of David and Solomon – they formed part of Israel and were incorporated into the community, but they were not completely assimilated and enjoyed a special status.

It would seem that this situation continued until the end of the period of the Judges. At the same time, however, it is probable that the population soon became very mixed. The probable reason for choosing Kiriath-jearim as the place where the ark was to be kept after it had been sent back by the

[75] See above, pp. 621–627.

Philistines (1 Sam 6:21) is that it would be on neutral territory in a town which, although it formed part of Israel, was not strictly Israelite and that it would also be in a place where the Philistines, who no longer wanted to have the ark on their territory, would nonetheless be able to keep it under supervision. At the same time, there was at Kiriath-jearim a good Yahwist who was also clearly an Israelite – Abinadab – and it was therefore possible for the ark to be left in his house and for his son to be appointed as priest in charge of it (1 Sam 7:1). One of David's thirty heroes also came from Beeroth (2 Sam 23:37) and another of David's champions, according to 1 Chron 12:4, was Ishmaiah of Gibeon. (This is, it should be noted, a Yahwist name.)

It was not until the reign of Saul that the crisis erupted. According to 2 Sam 21:1–14, Saul broke the oath that had been made to the Gibeonites and tried to annihilate them. This crime led to a famine lasting three years as God's punishment of the Israelites. David removed this scourge by handing Saul's descendants over to the Gibeonites, who put them to death on the high place 'before Yahweh'. They did this, however, according to a rite which was not an Israelite rite.[76] We have no details concerning this action performed by Saul. All that we know is that Saul acted 'in his zeal for the Israelites and for Judah' (2 Sam 21:2). His intention was to make sure that his kingdom was inwardly united and above all to reinforce his own power in this particular district, which bordered on Philistine territory. David's intention, in satisfying the Gibeonites, was clearly to make sure that his non-Israelite subjects would support him. Saul's violent actions must also have been felt in Beeroth. This is certainly what can be deduced from 2 Sam 4:2–3, since the two officers of Saul's army who murdered Ishbaal, Saul's son, came from Beeroth. We are told that they were Benjaminites, 'for Beeroth is regarded as belonging to Benjamin. The people of Beeroth had taken refuge in Gittaim (near Ramleh), where they have remained to this day as resident aliens.'[77]

The story contained in 2 Sam 21:1–14 and the fact that David satisfied the request of the Gibeonites show clearly that the latter had preserved their special status in spite of Saul's efforts to extinguish them. The Gibeonites are not mentioned afterwards in the Old Testament. No one has as yet suggested a convincing interpretation of the statement in Jos 9:27 that the Gibeonites were engaged in the task of serving at Yahweh's altar 'down to the present day'. It is also very unlikely that their descendants were the

[76] H. Cazelles, 'David's Monarchy and the Gibeonite Claim (II Sam. XXI, 1–14)', *PEQ*, 87 (1955), pp. 165–175; A. S. Kapelrud, 'King and Fertility. A Discussion of II Sam 21:1–14', *Interpretationes ad V.T. pertinentes . . . S. Mowinckel*, Oslo, 1955, pp. 113–122; A. Malamat, 'Doctrines of Causality in Hittite and Biblical Historiography: A Parallel', *VT*, 5 (1955), pp. 1–12; M. Haran, 'The Gibeonites, the Nethinim and the Sons of Solomon's Servants', *VT*, 11 (1961), pp. 159–169, especially pp. 161–162.

[77] See A. Malamat, *op. cit.*, p. 11.

n'thînîm, those who were 'given' and assigned to serve the Levites according to Ezra 2:43–54 and whose origin went back, according to Ezra 8:20, to David. The only similarity between the Gibeonites and the *n'thînîm* is that both were public servants assigned to the sanctuary.

In the geographical lists found in the book of Joshua, Beeroth, Chephirah and Gibeon were allotted to Benjamin (see Jos 18:25–26). According to the Greek version of Jos 18:28, Kiriath-jearim was also allotted to Benjamin, but, according to Jos 15:60 and 1 Chron 13:6 (see also the genealogy in 1 Chron 2:53), it was in Judah, and the latter is more probable.

(b) *Shechem*

It would also seem that the Israelites settled in the district of Shechem by making a covenant with the Shechemites.[78] There is in fact no reference in the Old Testament to any battle at Shechem or in the country around it or to any conquest of the town. There is, moreover, no archaeological evidence that the town might have been destroyed at the end of the Late Bronze or the beginning of the Iron Age, before the destruction which took place in the course of the twelfth century and which must have been brought about by Abimelech (Judges 9:45).[79] Before that time, Shechem was a Canaanite town, although the Israelites had a sanctuary near the town, where 'the pact at Shechem' was concluded (Jos 24:26). It was at this sanctuary that Joseph's bones were venerated; these had been brought back from Egypt and buried in the field that Jacob had bought from Hamor, Shechem's father (Gen 33:18–20; Jos 24:32). This presupposes that peaceful relationships existed between the Israelites and the Shechemites and possibly that the latter were to some extent a subject-people of the Israelites, as the Gibeonites were.

This theory is based on what we know about the history of Shechem before the Israelites came on the scene and on our knowledge of the situation that existed at the time of Jerubbaal-Abimelech. It seems that the population and the constitution of Shechem were similar to those of the Gibeonite towns. According to the patriarchal story found in Gen 34, an account of a treaty concluded between the Shechemites and Israel's ancestors and broken by the treachery of Jacob's sons, Shechem was inhabited – like the Gibeonite towns – by the Hivites, had no king – Hamor was a *nāśî'* or 'chief' (verse 2) – but decisions were taken by the townsmen (verse 20). In the Amarna letters of the fourteenth century,[80] Shechem is

---

[78] See above, pp. 636–640.

[79] G. E. Wright, *Shechem. The Biography of a Biblical City,* New York and Toronto, 1965, pp. 78, 123 ff; *ibid.,* 'Shechem', *Archaeology and Old Testament Study,* ed. D. Winton Thomas, Oxford, 1967, p. 364.

[80] The letters which refer to Shechem and Lab'ayu have been translated with a commentary by E. F. Campbell and are included in G. E. Wright, *Shechem, op. cit.,* pp

mentioned only once (*EA*, 289, 22–23) and in this one letter it is said that Lab'ayu 'gave the land of Shechem to the 'Apīru'. According to the other letters written by this same man, Lab'ayu, or referring to him, it is clear that he was in control of the whole country from the Plain of Jezreel to the boundaries of the kingdom of Jerusalem, in other words, of the entire hill country of Ephraim in the broadest sense. After Lab'ayu's death, his two sons continued to exercise the same authority. Lab'ayu was not, however, given the title of king of Shechem and it is very doubtful whether he ever was. It would seem too[81] that he did not live at Shechem; his authority was probably exercised from elsewhere by means of an agreement made with the inhabitants. The latter took care of the internal administration of the city and recognised Lab'ayu's authority as a kind of protectorate, giving him responsibility for defending and extending their territory.

The story of Jerubbaal and Abimelech points to a similar situation existing at the time of the Judges.[82] I have come to the conclusion that a distinction has to be made between Gideon, the conqueror of the Midianites and the Judge of Israel, and Jerubbaal, the father of Abimelech. Many scholars have not made this distinction and have identified Gideon and Jerubbaal, possibly because they were both from Ophrah or possibly because Gideon refused the kingship which Abimelech, the son of Jerubbaal, accepted, thus allowing a parallel to be established, in the form of an antithesis, between the two.

Abimelech was the son of Jerubbaal and a woman of Shechem. He was brought up at Shechem in a Canaanite environment, while his father Jerubbaal lived at Ophrah. (The location of Ophrah is not certain, but it was undoubtedly not far from Shechem. Aharoni has suggested 'Affūleh, which would be, in my opinion, impossible.) Jerubbaal was the leader of an important clan of Manasseh and we are bound to infer from Judges 9:2 and 16a that he exercised some authority over Shechem. We do not, however, know how he acquired this authority over the town. According to verse 17, he acquired it by virtue of his victory over the Midianites. Verses 16b–19a, however, were added by the Deuteronomist,[83] who identified Jerubbaal with Gideon and implicitly regarded the inhabitants of Shechem as Israelites. It should, however, be borne in mind that Jerubbaal was not the

---

191–207 (see above, note 79).

[81] H. Reviv, 'The Government of Shechem in the El-Amarna Period and in the Days of Abimelech', *IEJ*, 16 (1966), pp. 252–257.

[82] See especially B. Lindars, 'Gideon and Kingship', *JTS*, New Series 16 (1965), pp. 315–326; H. Haag, 'Gideon-Jerubbaal-Abimelek', *ZAW*, 79 (1967), pp. 305–314; J. A. Soggin, *Das Königtum in Israel* (*BZAW* 104), 1967, pp. 20–25; H. Schmid, 'Die Herrschaft Abimelechs (Jdc 9)', *Judaica*, 26 (1970), pp. 1–11.

[83] W. Richter, *Traditionsgeschichtliche Untersuchungen zum Richterbuch* (*BBB* 18), 1963, pp. 250–251; 313, 316.

king of Shechem and that he did not live in the town. His position was very
similar to that of Lab'ayu during the Amarna period. There was in fact no
king at Shechem, but there are frequent references in the text to the *ba̅ʿlē*
škhem, the 'Lords' or 'leading men of Shechem', who were responsible at
least for the administration of the city and formed a kind of aristocracy. Just
as Lab'ayu had handed his authority on to his sons, so too did Jerubbaal's
authority, according to Judges 9:1–2, go after his death to his sons. The
number seventy, which appears in verses 2 and 5 (*cf.* verses 24 and 56; the
editorial framework), is due to the fact that Jerubbaal is identified with
Gideon, who had seventy sons (Judges 8:30), a fact which, as we have
already seen, brings him close to the 'lesser Judges'.

Abimelech wanted above all to make it clear to the Shechemites that it
was better for them to be subjects of himself personally, since he at least half
belonged to them by blood, rather than be subjected to an entire Israelite
clan. It should be noted in this context that Abimelech does not use the
words 'king' or 'to reign' here, but rather the verb *māšal*, 'to dominate' or
'to rule'. The 'Lords of Shechem' gave him money from the treasure of the
temple of Baal-berith, with which he was able to recruit a band of
mercenaries (Judges 9:4). According to the following verse (verse 5), this
enabled him to murder Jerubbaal's family. This was, however, not the case
at all – this money was in fact the pay given to Abimelech, the *condottiere* of
the mercenary band, by the people of Shechem so that he would protect
them. This points once again to the parallel between Abimelech and
Lab'ayu and his 'Apiru mercenaries. Abimelech, however, had higher
ambitions and had himself proclaimed king, *melekh* (Judges 9:6).

Abimelech did not live at Shechem, but at Arumah (Judges 9:41 and 31,
corr.), which is Khirbet el–'Ormah, about six miles to the south-south-west
of Shechem, At Shechem, he was represented by a commissar or 'delegate'
pāqîdh (verse 28), who was also known as the 'governor' or *šar* of the city
(verse 30). This delegate or governor was Zebul, who must have been a
Shechemite. Abimelech may also have tried to persuade groups of Israelites
to acknowledge his kingship, but there can be no doubt that it continued to
be above all a Shechemite kingship. It was only later on that the editor gave
this episode a pan-Israelite importance. Examples of such additions are verse
22: 'Abimelech ruled over Israel for three years' and verse 55, which mentions the army ('the men') of Israel. Both these verses are editorial.[84]

It was perhaps this hybrid character of Abimelech's kingdom – it was
both Shechemite and Israelite – which led to its destruction. It may, on the
other hand, have been because Abimelech himself did not come up to the
expectations that the Shechemites had of him. Whatever may have been the
reason, the fact remains that there was serious discord between the 'Lords of

---

[84] W. Richter, *op. cit.*, pp. 251–252, 326. These verses cannot be regarded as early and w
are bound to refute H. Schmid's argument, *op. cit.*, p. 2.

Shechem' and Abimelech. They laid ambushes and plundered the caravans that travelled close to Shechem, which was at a junction of many roads (verse 25). Was this simply in order to create confusion and to put Abimelech in a difficult situation? Or was it to deprive him of a source of profit to which he was entitled and to show that they could do without him? In any case, there was a revolt against him, led by Gaal, the son of Ebed or Obed, who came to Shechem with his 'brothers', in other words, his troop of men (Judges 9:26 ff). Gaal was the leader of a Canaanite band and he and his men had come to Shechem to make merry at the time of the grape harvest. They cursed Abimelech, remembering that he was not a Shechemite and that both he and his appointed deputy Zebul were dependent on the Shechemites.[85] The revolt, however, was a failure. Gaal was defeated by Abimelech before Shechem and Zebul drove him and his troop of men away (verses 29–41). This revolt was followed by another armed conflict, about which we have much less information, and this resulted in the capture and destruction of Shechem (Judges 9:42–45).[86] Abimelech had thus himself destroyed the foundation of his kingship.

The episode at Thebez, where Abimelech died (Judges 9:50–55) is relevant here. There are philological reasons for rejecting an identification of Thebez with Tubas and there is, moreover, no archaeological evidence to support this. This is the only reference to Thebez in the Old Testament. Malamat has suggested that it may be an error, possibly for Tirzah (*cf.* Aharoni, *The Land of the Bible*, p. 242). It was certainly a Canaanite city with the same constitution as Shechem – it also had 'lords' or 'leading men of the town' (verse 51). Abimelech's action can be explained in two ways. On the one hand, Thebez may have been under his authority, as Shechem was, and have revolted against him. On the other hand, however, Abimelech may have wanted to extend his territory and include this Canaanite town with Manasseh. The second explanation seems the more likely.

The episode of Abimelech and the destruction of the city, then, mark the end of the special status enjoyed by Shechem and at the same time the end of this particular aspect of the relationships between the Israelites and the Canaanites. From this time onwards, Shechem was an integral part of Israel. According to Num 26:30, Shechem was one of the clans of Manasseh (Jos 17:2; 1 Chron 7:19). The town was, however, rebuilt and repopulated very slowly. According to 1 Kings 12:25, it was during the reign of Jeroboam I that the rebuilding took place.

Archaeologists have been able to give only approximate dates to the

---

[85] This is at least the most likely meaning of verse 28, which is difficult and probably corrupt.
[86] For the difference between these two struggles, see E. Täubler, *Biblische Studien*, pp. 274–275. According to W. Richter, *op. cit.*, pp. 252–259, 278–282, 316, verses 42–44 are based on verses 26–40 and prepare the way for verse 45, that is, the destruction of the town.

events at Shechem. A destruction in the twelfth century has been ascribed to Abimelech, but different dates have been given to this by different archaeologists. Their suggestions have included the first half of the twelfth century,[87] the second half of the same century,[88] a more exact date, namely between 1130 and 1100 B.C.[89] and finally during the course of the twelfth century.[90] We have to wait until the definitive publication of the material available before any certainty can be reached. If Jerubbaal, the father of Abimelech, was in fact not the same as Gideon, then the episode of Abimelech cannot be related to the Midianite incursions or to any event taking place at the time and moreover it is not possible even to outline the chronology of the episode in relation to other events. It might, in that case, have taken place at any time within the period as a whole. The date 1300–1100 would seem to be suitable. The signs of the later Israelite occupation of the site and other archaeological evidence would seem to point to a resettlement during the period of Solomon, when Shechem might have been the administrative centre of the province of Mount Ephraim.[91]

Apart from the failure of the siege of Thebez and Abimelech's death there, we have no account of any attempt on the part of the tribes during the period of the Judges to seize Canaanite cities that had not been occupied during the settlement of the tribes in Canaan. A list of these cities that had not been conquered is given in Judges 1:21, 27–35 and part of this list is repeated in the description of the territory of the tribes, in this order: Jos 15:8 = 18:16; 17:11–13; 16:10. These are towns which were within the territory of one or other of the tribes, but which continued to be inhabited by Canaanites. They were, in fact, Canaanite enclaves.[92] This is the list:

Judges 1:21: in Benjamin, Jerusalem.

Judges 1:27–28: in Manasseh, Beth-shean, Taanach, Megiddo, Dor and Ibleam, that is, the Plain of Jezreel, its southern approaches (Ibleam) and the north of Sharon (Dor).

Judges 1:29: in Ephraim, Gezer.

Judges 1:30:in Zebulun, Kitron and Nahalol (the location of these towns is not precisely known).

Judges 1:31–32: in Asher, Acco, Achzib, Aphik and Rehob; in fact the whole of the Plain of Acco as well as the Phoenician towns of Sidon and Ahlab/Hebla = Mehebel (Jos 19:29), which is present-day Khirbet el-Mahalib, a few miles to the north of Tyre. This clearly means that the

---

[87] E. F. Campbell, *BibArch*, 23 (1960), p. 107.

[88] G. E. Wright, *Shechem*, p. 78.

[89] *ibid.*, illustration on p. VIII.

[90] G. E. Wright, *Archaeology and Old Testament Study* (note 79), p. 364.

[91] G. E. Wright, *Archaeology and Old Testament Study*, *op. cit.*, p. 366.

[92] Y. Aharoni, *The Land of the Bible*, pp. 212–215 and the map on p. 213.

territory that was in theory allotted to Asher continued in fact to be, to a great extent, Canaanite. This fact is reflected in the wording of the biblical texts. In the case of Manasseh, Ephraim and Zebulun, we read: 'In those parts the Canaanites held their ground' (Judges 1:27) or 'The Canaanites went on living among them' (verses 29 and 30). In the case of Asher, the words of the biblical text are: 'The Asherites lived among the Canaanite inhabitants of the country' (verse 32).[93]

Judges 1:33: in Naphthali, Beth-shemesh and Beth-anath; the location of these towns is also uncertain, although they were probably in Upper Galilee.

Judges 1:34–35: in Dan, Har-heres, which is probably another name for Beth-shemesh, also Aijalon and Shaalbim. Although there is no mention in this text of Dan's migration to the north of Canaan, it is significant that, according to verse 35, it was the house of Joseph, not Dan, which made the inhabitants of these three towns perform forced labour.

Nothing is said in this context about Judah (and Simeon). This is because this chapter in the Book of Judges (Judges 1) is a southern tradition and entirely in favour of Judah, attributing to this tribe conquests which it did not in fact make (verses 1–17) or which were not even made by the Israelites at all, as in verse 18 (Hebrew), according to which Judah took Gaza and Ekron. The Greek text has a negative here ('Judah did not take . . .") and this is more probable. According to this chapter, Judah suffered no setbacks at all, apart from the general comment in verse 19: 'Yahweh was with Judah and Judah subdued the highlands, but they could not drive out the inhabitants of the plain, because they had iron chariots.' We have tried to be rather more precise in our study of the expansion of the tribe of Judah.

These Canaanite enclaves were in regions which were economically and strategically important – from Beth-shean to Acco, the Plain of Jezreel and the Plain of Acco, which were among the richest agricultural districts in the whole country and were crossed by international highways going from Egypt to Damascus and into Phoenicia. These Canaanite towns acted therefore as a kind of barrier between the northern tribes and those inhabiting the centre of Canaan. Another barrier, between the central tribes and Judah, was formed by the line of towns Jerusalem, Aijalon and Gezer. As far as can be assessed, this situation continued throughout the whole of the period of the Judges. If Har-heres was in fact the same as Beth-shemesh, it would have become an Israelite town before the end of the period of the Judges (see 1 Sam 6:9ff). Gezer became Israelite only when it was given to Solomon by Pharaoh (1 Kings 9:16). Generally speaking, however, it was David who finally succeeded in destroying these Canaanite enclaves in the tribal territories. This is explicitly reported in the case of

[93] See Aharoni's comment, *op. cit.*, p. 214, but it should be noted that the same is said of Naphthali in verse 33.

Jerusalem (2 Sam 5:6–9) and it was probably also the case with the towns in the Shephelah and the Plain of Jezreel. It is possible, of course, that they remained at first under the authority of the Philistines and that they became an easy prey to Israel after David had defeated the Philistines.[94]

In Judges 1, apart from the information that these towns were not conquered, it is said that 'when the Israelites became stronger, they subjected the Canaanites to forced labour, though they did not drive them out' (Judges 1:28; cf. 30, 33, 35). This statement can be compared with 1 Kings 9:20–22, according to which all the survivors of the early inhabitants of the country were subjected to slave labour, *mas obhedh*, which the Israelites did not have to perform. As this would seem to go against the data given in 1 Kings 5:20, 23, 27–28, concerning forced labour imposed on the Israelites, the texts of Judges 1 and 1 Kings 9:20–22 have often been rejected as having been influenced by the Deuteronomist. It is, however, possible that, during the reigns of David and Solomon and especially in view of the building programme carried out at that time, there was a difference in the way in which the Israelites and the inhabitants of the Canaanite cities were treated and that the Israelite rulers imposed on the Canaanites the kind of rule which they had known during the reigns of their own native kings. Forced labour was, after all, a Canaanite institution.[95]

III. THE STRUGGLE AGAINST THE ALIENS
THE ACTIVITY OF THE 'GREAT JUDGES'

What is new in Israel's history during the period of the Judges, in comparison with that of the settlement in Canaan, is that in the later period the tribes had to defend their territory against attacks by the neighbouring peoples – Edomites, Moabites, Ammonites and Midianites – or by aliens who had come into the country either with them or a little later – the Philistines. The activity of the saviours of Israel, whom we call the 'great Judges', was directed against these 'oppressors'.

1. Othniel (Judges 3:7–11)

Almost everything in this passage is expressed in the deuteronomistic formulae used in the editorial framework, and the formulae of the 'Judges'

[94] See J. Bright, *History*, p. 180. This view is also shared by T. N. D. Mettinger, *Solomonic State Officials. A Study of the Civil Government Officials of the Israelite Monarchy*, Lund, 1971, pp. 134–137.
[95] See M. Noth, *Geschichte*, p. 193 (*History*, pp. 209–210); *Könige I (BKAT)*, 1968, pp 216–218.

are combined with those of the 'saviours' (see verses 10a and 11b). The Deuteronomist's aim was clearly to head the list of the Judges with a typical example of both these categories in combination, in other words that of a saviour who was at the same time a Judge.[96] At the same time, he also wanted to give a place to the tribe of Judah in this gallery of Judge-saviours.

This, however, does not necessarily mean that this passage was entirely invented. It may well preserve a historical memory. Outside this framework, all that is contained in the passage is that for eight years the Israelites were enslaved by Cushan-rishathaim, the king of Aram Naharaim, and that they were set free by Othniel, the son of Kenaz, who was Caleb's younger brother. Othniel the Kenizzite, who was Caleb's nephew and who became his son-in-law, is known to us – he is the Othniel who conquered Debir and settled there (Jos 15:16–19; Judges 1:12–15). This Othniel, however, did not belong to the period of the Judges, but to that of the settlement of the tribes.

The name of Israel's oppressor in this instance has either been invented or changed. It means 'Cushan of double wickedness' and the bearer of this name is said to be the king of Aram Naharaim, which is, of course, Upper Mesopotamia, the land 'of the two rivers'. Attempts have been made to identify this king with another king of the same region, the Mitanni, called Tushratta, who reigned in the fourteenth century B.C.[97] but this theory is contrary to all our chronological and philological evidence. Another and very ingenious theory has been put forward by A. Malamat,[98] who accepted Aram Naharaim, but identified Cushan-rishataim with an Asiatic called Irsu who seized power in Egypt and remained in power for a certain time, possibly for exactly eight years, about the year 1200 B.C. Irsu was overthrown by the first pharaoh of the Twentieth Dynasty, Set-nakht, the father of Ramses III.[99] Irsu and Rishataim, then, were two different and uncertain transcriptions, Malamat has suggested, of a name that was foreign both to the Israelites and to the Egyptians. In opposition to this theory, however, it has to be pointed out, in the first place, that there is evidence at Ras Shamrah that Irsu was a Semitic name and, in the second place, that Irsu was, in the Egyptian texts, possibly a nickname, meaning 'the usurper' or 'the self-made man'. It might in fact have been another name for the great chancellor Bay, who was not an Egyptian by birth and who exercised a

[96] W. Richter, *Die Bearbeitungen des 'Retterbuches' in der deuteronomischen Epoche* (BBB 21), 1964, pp. 23–26, 61.

[97] H. Hänslar, 'Der historische Hintergrund von Richter 3, 8–10', *Bib*, 11 (1930), pp. 391–418; 12 (1931), pp. 3–26; 271–296, 395–410.

[98] A. Malamat, 'Cushan and the Decline of the Near East Around 1200 B.C.', *JNES*, 13 (1954), p. 231–242.

[99] *ANET*, p. 260a.

certain authority at the end of the Nineteenth Dynasty.[100] This Irsu, then, is almost as enigmatic as Cushan-rishaitaim.[101]

It is in any case true to say that oppression by such a distant enemy – from Upper Mesopotamia – would certainly have been a unique occurrence in the period of the Judges, and intervention by a saviour coming from the southernmost part of country would have been even more unlikely. Far more acceptable here is an early hypothesis that has been taken up again by several recent commentators,[102] that is, that the name of the country 'of the two rivers' was incorrectly preserved. In other words, 'rm is an error for 'dm, as in other places, and this error led to the addition of Naharaim, as in Gen 24:10, etc. In the second reference to Aram, in verse 10, the world Naharaim does not appear. In the case of Cushan, this name can be compared with that of the tribe Cushan which is mentioned in parallel with Midian in Hab 3:7 and Moses's 'Cushite' wife (Num 12:1). In Egypt, there is the geographical name Qšnrm = Qushān-Rōm, which occurs in the geographical list of Ramses II and was taken up again by Ramses III,[103] and the name kušn in the execration texts. The location of this group in the south of Transjordania or the south of Palestine is based simply on the biblical tribe of Cushan which was associated with the Midianites.[104]

Certain scholars have gone even further and have identified this kwšn ršʿtym with the third king of Edom according to the list given in Gen 36:34, hšm m'rshtymny.[105] This may, of course, be going much too far, but it does seem likely that Edomite elements as well as the tribes of Israel tried to settle in southern Palestine. They seem to have controlled the copper mines in the 'Arabah, the place from which the Kenites-Kenizzites came up, at least according to Judges 1:16. Othniel is said to have driven back these invaders and the Deuteronomist, it is believed, is here repeating a tradition concerning the Kenizzites which goes back to the period of the settlement. It does not therefore belong to the period of the Judges.

---

[100] See above, pp. 300, 492, 536.

[101] Cushan-rishataim may, it has been suggested, have been a nomadic Aramaean leader who caused trouble about the year 1200 B.C.; see M. F. Unger, *Israel and the Aramaeans of Damascus*, London, 1957, pp. 40–41.

[102] R. Tamisier, 1949; A. Vincent, 1952; H. W. Hertzberg, 1953; J. Gray, 1967.

[103] List XXIII, 13; XXVII, 89 in J. Simons, *Handbook for the Study of Egyptian Topographical Lists*, 1937. It is not located, but quoted in connection with one of Ramses II's campaigns in Syria; see M. Noth, *ZDPV*, 64 (1941), p. 60; W. F. Albright, *op. cit.*, note 104 below.

[104] W. F. Albright, *Archaeology and the Religion of Israel*, p. 205, note 49; B. Maisler (Mazar), *Revue de l'Histoire Juive en Egypte*, 1 (1947), pp. 37–78.

[105] A. Klostermann, *Geschichte des Volkes Israel*, 1896, p. 119; Klostermann's theory is accepted by A. Vincent and J. Gray.

2. Ehud (Judges 3:12–30)[106]

The Israelites were enslaved by Eglon, the king of Moab, for eighteen years and were delivered by a Benjaminite, Ehud of the clan of Gera, who murdered Eglon treacherously when he was on a mission to take the Israelites' tribute to the Moabite king. After killing Eglon, Ehud called on the people living in the hill country of Ephraim to bear arms against Moab. They blocked the fords of the Jordan and inflicted a serious defeat on the Moabites.

Although it is no longer customary now to distinguish two different sources in this story,[107] exegesis of the passage is still very difficult, especially the geographical interpretation. According to Judges 3:13, Eglon seized hold of the 'city of palms'. This is, of course, Jericho, which is also called the 'city of palm trees' in Deut 34:3 and 2 Chron 28:15. The identification of this 'city of palm trees' is reinforced by the references in the text to the Moabites, the Benjaminites, Gilgal and the fords of the Jordan. However, there is a 'city of palms' in Judges 1:16 as well and this is identified with Tamar, a town to the south of the Dead Sea; Auerbach[108] believed that the 'city of palms' in Judges 3:13 was also Tamar and that the Moabites must have made a wide turning movement when they marched against Israel. This, in Auerbach's opinion, explains why they took the Amalekites as their allies (verse 13). What is more, the expedition was made, he believed, not against Benjamin, but against Judah. It was the first editor, probably the Yahwist, who transposed the story to Jericho and who made Ehud a Benjaminite. As a result of this, Auerbach continued, the 'idols' in the early story were situated at Gilgal, the passes of the 'Arabah became the fords of the Jordan and the men of the hill country of Ephraim were called to arms. This theory of Auerbach's is, however, quite unconvincing and it is no longer accepted by anyone.

The fact that Jericho is not named in the passage calls, however, for an explanation. In the two other passages (Deut 34:3; 2 Chron 28:15) the 'city of palm trees' is combined, in apposition, with Jericho, which is named. According to the Old Testament, Jericho remained in a state of ruin from the period of Joshua (Jos 6) until the time of Ahab (1 Kings 16:34). There is no archaeological evidence of a reoccupation of the site before the seventh century B.C. but there is a tomb dating back to the end of the tenth and the beginning of the ninth century, in other words, a little earlier than Ahab's

---

[106] Apart from the commentaries, see also E. Auerbach, 'Ehud', *ZAW*, 51 (1933), pp. 47–51; E. G. Kraeling, 'Difficulties in the Story of Ehud', *JBL*, 54 (1935), pp. 205–210; E. Täubler, *Biblische Studien*, 1958, pp. 21–42; A. H. van Zyl, *The Moabites*, Leiden, 1960, pp. 125–130; W. Richter, *Traditionsgeschichtliche Untersuchungen*, 1963, pp. 1–29.

[107] See the history of the exegesis of this passage in W. Richter.

[108] E. Auerbach, *op. cit.* (note 106 above).

reign.[109] All the same, even if the site of Jericho remained unoccupied, the oasis at least continued to be inhabited (see the beginning of our text, the story of David's ambassadors, 2 Sam 10:5). Included among the inhabitants of this oasis were people belonging to the clan of Rahab, who had been spared by Joshua and had 'dwelt among Israel until now' (Jos 6:25). We may therefore legitimately ask whether the term 'city of palms' does not point to this oasis and its settlement rather than to the town of Jericho.

A more difficult geographical question to answer is where Ehud brought the tribute and where he murdered Eglon. It is customary to think here of Jericho, where Eglon is supposed to have had quite a luxurious residence (verses 20–23). In fact, however, after the king had been murdered, the Israelites cut off the Moabites' retreat by occupying the fords of the Jordan (verse 28); This was the view of the last editor of the text, but the text does not say that the 'city of palms' was Eglon's residence or that it was the place where he was murdered. There is, moreover, a further difficulty, namely that, having handed over the tribute, Ehud went off with his companions, yet, when the p'sîlîm which were near Gilgal had been reached, he went back alone, claiming that he had to give Eglon a message from God (verse 19). He then murdered him, fled, passed the p'sîlîm and escaped to Seirah (verse 26) This place cannot be identified,[110] but the article preceding the name, haśś'îrah, may indicate that it was a district rather than a town – 'the undergrowth' or 'the wooded region'. The p'sîlîm were carved stakes or 'idols'. Those mentioned in this text were 'near Gilgal' and they are not mentioned elsewhere.

If, however, Ehud murdered Eglon at Jericho and if Gilgal was in fact situated between Jericho and the Jordan, then Ehud must have fled in the direction of Moab, which is very unlikely. The two references to the p'sîlîm and the reference to Gilgal in verses 19 and 26 presuppose that Eglon's residence was on the other side of the Jordan.[111] Various suggestions have been made, including Medeba[112] and Heshbon.[113] A choice between Medeba or Heshbon would, however, be purely arbitrary and neither one nor the other was ever the capital city of Moab. It would, moreover, be curious to say the least if in a description of the route followed by Ehud there was no mention of crossing the Jordan. The narrative presupposes that there was no great distance between the p'sîlîm (and therefore Gilgal) and Eglon's residence and this is justified if his residence was in fact at Jericho. The difficulty that has been raised in connection with Gilgal, however, is

[109] K. M. Kenyon, in *Archaeology and Old Testament Study, op. cit.* (note 79 above), p. 274; *ibid., Jericho*, II, pp. 482–489 (Tomb A 85).
[110] E. Täubler, *op. cit.*, pp. 24–25: 'the land of the ś'îrîm' or 'demons', that is, the Ghōr.
[111] W. Richter, *op. cit.*, pp. 9–10;
[112] E. G. Kraeling, *op. cit.* (note 106), p. 205.
[113] E. Täubler, *op. cit.*, p. 32.

eliminated or at least very much reduced if Gilgal was, as various authors have suggested in recent years, only a few miles to the north or north-west of Jericho.[114] In that case, Ehud would have made hardly any detour at all and may indeed have followed the normal way. Finally it is reasonable to suggest that the handing over of the tribute coincided with a visit by Eglon to the country which was subject to him. I therefore regard it as very likely that all these events took place at Jericho itself.[115]

From the historical point of view too, the story is very interesting.[116] The northern frontier of the Moabites' territory was theoretically the Arnon, but they were always extending their territory further in that direction. Sihon of Heshbon had thrown them back to the Arnon (Num 21:26) and his place was taken by the Israelites (Reuben?) (Num 21:25). The Moabites, however, soon regained the ascendancy. The prophecies of Balaam (Num 22–24) provide us with an outline of the situation after the conquest, in which Reuben was weak and obliged to give up some of its territory. Balak, the king of Moab, took the soothsayer Balaam along the edge of the plateau of Transjordania from the north of the Dead Sea as far as Mount Nebo, so that he would curse the Israelites occupying the plain.[117] The Moabites were, after all, masters of the plateau. They encountered the Israelites at the sanctuary of the Baal of Peor (Num 25).

This plain to the north-east of the Dead Sea between the Jordan and the highlands is known in the Old Testament as 'ar'bôth mô'ābh. This name is not found in the early sources. It occurs only in the priestly passages of Numbers (eight times), Deuteronomy (Deut 34; twice) and Joshua (Jos 13:32 = P, at least according to the protagonists of the Hexateuch; it is, in any case, a very late text). The name must certainly go back to a period when this plain was in the possession of the Moabites, in other words, to a time before David but after Balaam. This is undoubtedly the situation presupposed by the story of Ehud. The Moabites went even further – their king Eglon, who is mentioned nowhere else in the Bible, crossed the Jordan, occupied the oasis of Jericho and subjected the Israelites to tribute. According to Judges 3:13, Eglon's allies in this expedition were the Ammonites and the Amalekites, the latter being nomads living in the south of Palestine and certainly not in this region. Apparently a deuteronomistic

---

[114] See the bibliography in M. Weippert, *Die Landnahme der israelitischen Stämme*, Göttingen, 1967, p. 30, note 1.

[115] Many recent commentators have also expressed themselves in favour of this theory – Hertzberg, Gray, O. Eissfeldt, *CAH*, II XXXIV, 1965, p. 20; A. H. van Zyl, *op. cit.* (note 106), pp. 128–129. M. Noth, *Geschichte*, p. 145 (*History*, p. 156), does not try to solve the problem.

[116] M. Noth, 'Israelitische Stämme zwischen Ammon und Moab', *ZAW*, 60 (1944), pp. 11–57, especially p. 17 ff; *Geschichte*, pp 144–145 (*History*, pp. 156–157.)

[117] M. Noth, *op. cit.* (note 116 above), pp. 26–30, believed that the Israelites settled to the north and north-west of the place referred to by Balaam.

editor of the Book of Judges took pleasure in making the Amalekites intervene everywhere. They also appear in Judges 6:3, 33; 7:12 (Gideon) and 10:12 (the introduction to the story of Jephthah). The Ammonites may possibly have helped the Moabites, but this too may be an editorial addition.

The event was of limited dimensions as far as the Israelites were concerned. There is nothing to indicate that the Moabite occupation extended beyond the oasis of Jericho. It was, moreover, an individual action on the part of the Benjaminite Ehud which brought about the liberation of the Israelites, and despite the pan-Israelite statements made in the editorial framework and verse 27, it is unlikely that any others apart from Benjaminites were involved in the military campaign which followed. Ehud made a call to arms in the highlands of Ephraim (verse 27), but this is not a tribal name here, but rather a geographical name for the mountainous region, the southern part of which was occupied by Benjamin. This whole military action was, moreover, restricted to an operation in which the occupying troops were cut off and prevented from retreating (verse 28). These troops may also have been no more than an armed escort accompanying the king of Moab on his visit.

The Benjaminites did not pursue the Moabites beyond the Jordan. They were satisfied with having driven them out of their territory. In the same way, the tribes of Transjordania did not intervene. The Reubenites had been overwhelmed by the Moabites. What, then, had happened to the Gadites? What we have here is an example of the individualism that was prevalent among the tribes. This was a special aspect of the tribes in Transjordania, which led very independent lives. We shall return to this question when we discuss the cases of Gideon and Jephthah below. In the meantime, we are bound to say that it is possible that the murder of Eglon initiated a period of anarchy in Moab and that the Gadites took advantage of this situation to reoccupy the territory to the north of the Arnon. They possessed this territory during the reign of David (2 Sam 24:5) and, in the ninth century, Mesha, the king of Moab, said, in his inscription (on the so-called Moabite stone, 1:10): 'the men of Gad had always dwelt in the land of Ataroth' (near Machaerus). Dibon, just north of the Arnon, is mentioned by Mesha in his inscription as one of his capitals, and, in Num 33:45, is given the name Dibon-gad.

The story of Ehud, then, must be placed quite early in the period of the Judges, before Gad had expanded at the expense of Reuben and Moab and before Benjamin had been weakened in the struggle with Ephraim.

3. Gideon (Judges 6–8)

We have already tried to show that Gideon was a 'Judge of Israel' and have pointed out that he may have been recognised as a 'Judge' after his victory over the Midianites. Like Jephthah, the 'Judge' Gideon was originally a 'Saviour' of Israel, in that he delivered Israel from the Midianites (Judges 6–8). From the literary and traditio-historical points of view, these chapters are very complicated.[118] Here, however, we shall confine ourselves to what is important in our historical interpretation of the passage.

The situation is outlined in the verses introducing the story of Gideon, that is, verses 1–6 of Judges 6. According to these verses, the Midianites invaded the country every year with their tents, camels and flocks, sending these out to pasture in the fields where the Israelites had sowed seed. They destroyed everything, like locusts. In verse 4, we read that they went as far as Gaza and this, of course, is not in accordance with the very restricted district in which this activity is described as having taken place. We also read in verse 3 (cf. Judges 6:33 and 7:12) that the Midianites were accompanied by the Amalekites and the b'nê qedhem, the 'sons of the East', although this is probably an editorial addition. We have already seen that the Amalekites were probably added to the Moabites in the story of Ehud (Judges 3:13). The title b'nê qedhem is moreover a vague one, given to the nomadic peoples of the eastern desert. In Judges 8:10, it is used as a synonym for the 'Midianites'.

At a later period, 'the land of Midian' indicates north-west of Arabia, but the Midianites were in fact nomadic and in the Old Testament texts they are found in very remote places – Joseph, for example, was found at Dothan by a caravan of Midianite traders, who took him to Egypt (Gen 37:28, 36) and Moses went to the land of Midian and married there (Ex 2:15–22). After the exodus, there were further connections betwen Israel and the Midianites (see Ex 18; Num 10:29–31). All these events took place, in my opinion, not in northern Arabia, but in the Sinai peninsula.

The Midianites, however, reappear later in an unfavourable light. The elders of Midian, for example, joined with the elders of Moab and went out to ask the soothsayer Balaam to curse Israel (Num 22:4, 7). With the daughters of Moab, the daughter of a Midianite leader persuaded the Israelites to take part in the cult of the Baal of Peor (Num 25:6–18). The presence of the Midianites alongside the Moabites is confirmed by a text in Genesis concerning the fourth king in the list of Edomite kings: 'Hadad, son

---

[118] C. F. Whitley, 'The Sources of the Gideon Stories', VT, 7 (1957), pp. 157–164; W. Beyerlin, 'Geschichte und heilsgeschichtliche Traditionsbildung im Alten Testament. Ein Beitrag zur Traditionsgeschichte von Richter VI–VIII', VT, 13 (1963), pp. 1–25; W. Richter, Traditionsgeschichtliche Untersuchungen, 1963, pp. 112–246.

of Bedad, succeeded; he defeated the Midianites in the country of Moab'
(Gen 36:35).[119] The story of the Baal of Peor is followed by an account of a
holy war waged against the people of Midian (Num 31). This chapter
belongs to a later level of P, although Eissfeldt has recently tried to establish
its historical validity,[120] claiming that, taken together with the information
provided in Num 22 and 25, it points to the fact that the Midianites ruled
Edom and Moab as protectorates. I find it, however, impossible to accept
this hypothesis.[121] All that we are really able to conclude from the biblical
evidence is that there were Midianite groups in Transjordania.

These groups undoubtedly made incursions into the country to the west
of the Jordan. These may have taken two forms. There may, on the one
hand, have been seasonal migrations, the Midianites coming as nomadic
shepherds and herdsmen, who, in the spring, took their flocks and herds
into cultivated land and trampled the crops underfoot. This is what would
appear to be indicated in the text (Judges 6:1–6), which refers, in verses
3–4a, to the regularity of these incursions and the fact that they always took
place during the same season and, in verse 5a, to the cattle and the tents. On
the other hand, however, they may have been raids – short, rapid incursions made with the aim of taking booty. Such raids would not have involved the flocks or herds of the Midianites. This would seem to be the type
of incursion indicated in verse 4b and verse 5b, which describe the
Midianites as arriving on camels and laying the country waste, leaving
Israel without a single head of cattle.

The editing of verses 3–5 is obviously clumsy and attempts have been
made to distinguish two different sources in it. I believe, however, that the
same editor has brought together two different traditions concerning the
Midianite incursions, one presenting the incursions as seasonal migrations
and the other presenting them as raids. Seen from the historical point of
view, there may well have been two traditions. In the accounts of Gideon's
campaigns, there is never any question either of flocks or herds on the one
hand – as opposed to the story of the war against the Midianites (Num 31)
and the booty taken – or of camels on the other (7:12 is an addition,
repeating what is said in 6:3 and 5[122]), with the exception, in the latter case,
of the half-verse in 8:21b (and the story of the ephod made from the booty,
8:27). The description of the battle fought near En-harod and of the pursuit
that followed (7:1–25) would seem to indicate that both the Midianites and

---

[119] According to J. R. Bartlett, *JTS*, New Series 16 (1965), p. 304, Hadad was a local
prince of Moab.

[120] O. Eissfeldt, 'Protektorat der Midianiter über ihre Nachbarn im letzten Viertel des 2.
Jahrtausends v. Chr.', *JBL*, 87 (1968), pp. 383–393.

[121] Despite the support given to this theory by W. F. Albright, 'Midianite Donkey
Caravan', *Translating and Understanding the Old Testament. Essays in Honor of H. G. May*,
Nashville and New York, 1970, pp. 197–205. See also above, p. 569.

[122] W. Richter, *op. cit.*, p. 169.

the Israelites fought on foot. The same is presupposed in the description of the further pursuit into Transjordania (Judges 8), since it is obviously impossible to catch up with men fleeing on camels if one is on foot.

I am afraid that too much importance has been attached to these camels of the Midianites.[123] According to several scholars, and especially Albright, this is the first historical evidence of the use of the domestic camel. It is, of course, true that the intensive raising of domestic camels and their use in caravans and in war began to spread only at the end of the second millennium. It is also probable that the Midianites whom Gideon fought had camels and that they made use of them during their incursions into Israelite territory, but apart from a brief reference to them at the beginning of the story of Gideon and occasional references later, these camels are little more than a vague memory. A century later the memory is recorded in a much more concrete and lively way in the story of David's pursuit of the Amalekite raiders who had destroyed Ziklag (1 Sam 30). In that account, all the details that are lacking in the verses in Judges 6 are present – the booty is recovered, the Israelites massacre the raiders and only those who flee on camels escape.

These incursions into Israelite territory by nomads from Transjordania point not only to the growing strength of these groups gained from their possession of camels, but also to the fact that there was no other group powerful enough to oppose them and to prevent them from laying waste their territories. They crossed the Jordan and passing through Beth-shean spread out over the Plain of Jezreel. This expansion would have been impossible if the Egyptians had been in control of the country at the time, since Beth-shean was an Egyptian garrison during the reign of Ramses II and perhaps even until the reign of Ramses VI in the second half of the twelfth century.[124] It would also have been impossible if the Canaanite cities on the Plain had been strong enough to resist the nomads. This presupposes, then, that Gideon's conflict with the Midianites took place after the battle of Barak and Deborah. Manasseh had become an important tribe and had replaced the Machir of the Song of Deborah. The Egyptians no longer controlled the country and the Israelites on the one hand and the Sea Peoples on the other had both entered and seized territory. This had led to the destruction of all authority in the country and the nomads took advantage of this disorder.

Gideon's liberation of the country is described in two stages, the first being a description of his campaign to the west of the Jordan (Judges 6:33–7:25), the second an account of a pursuit into Transjordania (8:4–21). It is obvious that the two accounts are independent of each other. In the first, the two Midianite chieftains, śar, are Oreb and Zeeb and these two

[123] M. Noth, Geschichte, p. 149 (History, pp. 160–161); J. Bright, History, p. 158.
[124] W. A. Ward, in F. W. James, The Iron Age at Beth Shan, 1966, pp. 172–179.

men are taken prisoner and killed (7:25). That closes the story. In the second story, however, the two kings, *melekh*, are Zebah and Zalmunna and these too are taken prisoner, but the story goes on to describe how the people of Succoth and Penuel refused to supply Gideon's men with food (8:5), arguing that Zebah and Zalmunna were not yet in his power. This reply would not have been possible if Gideon had in fact just gained a great victory to the west of the Jordan and was passing through Succoth and Penuel in pursuit of the defeated Midianites. The second story, however, is not, like the first, an account of Israel's liberation, as announced in the story of Gideon's call (6:13ff). It is a story of personal revenge – Gideon's brothers had been killed by Zebah and Zalmunna (8:17–19). This is, in other words, a case of blood-revenge. This fact is emphasised by Gideon's asking his son to carry out the act (verse 20).

One explanation for the refusal of the people of Succoth and Penuel to give food to Gideon's troop (8:5–8) is that they feared reprisals from the Midianites when Gideon had crossed the Jordan again. Another is that it was an expression of tribal jealousies – both towns were, it has been suggested, inhabited either by Machirites (Machir had been supplanted by Manasseh) [125] or by Benjaminites, who were the enemies of Ephraim (and Manasseh). [126] All this is, of course, purely conjectural. It should be pointed out that Succoth was regarded as a Gadite town (Jos 13:27) when Gad extended its territory towards the north in the Jordan valley. The inhabitants of Succoth (and Penuel), then, were presumably Gadites. It is therefore important to know whether these two towns were Israelite towns at that time. Penuel (= Tulūl edh-Dhahab) is situated on the Jabbok at the point where the river enters the Jordan valley and it is not connected with any tribe in the lists in the book of Joshua; it was in fact not until the reign of Jeroboam I that it appeared as an Israelite town (see 1 Kings 12:25). The site has not been excavated. Succoth is generally located at Tell Deir 'Allah, north of the Jabbok. The site has been excavated by H. Franken. Aharoni believes that Gideon may have been responsible for the destruction of the sanctuary that was there in the twelfth century. [127] This is, in my opinion, impossible and I would give three reasons for my view. First, the sanctuary was destroyed not by military action but by an earthquake. Secondly, the text (Judges 8:16) refers to Gideon's punishment of the inhabitants of Succoth, but not to his destruction of the town itself, as in the case of Penuel, where he is said (verse 17) to have destroyed the tower. Thirdly, it is almost certain that Succoth was not Deir 'Allah. It was a sanctuary frequented by semi-nomadic peoples which was later surrounded by a village, but Deir

[125] E. Täubler, *Biblische Studien*, p. 247.

[126] See above, pp. 787–788; K.–D. Schunk, *ZDMG*, 113 (1963), p. 37; S. Mittmann, *Beiträge zur Siedlungs- und Territorialgeschichte, op. cit.*, 1970, p. 216, note 22.

[127] Y. Aharoni, *The Land of the Bible*, p. 241, note 174.

'Allah was never a town.[128] It is, moreover, difficult to say exactly when Deir 'Allah was occupied by the Israelites. The fact that Penuel and Succoth may have been not Israelite towns but Canaanite enclaves in Transjordania cannot be ruled out. H. Reviv[129] has attempted to point out that the constitution of these two towns, the 'people of Succoth' and the 'people of Penuel', is more similar to that of Canaanite cities than to that of Israelite towns and that the 'princes' or 'chieftains' of Succoth (verses 6 and 14) were a later addition. Reviv's argument is not convincing, however, and I still believe that Succoth and Penuel were occupied at that time by Gadites.

In any case, the tradition of Judges 8:4–21 was a local Transjordanian one which was clearly in touch with the topography of the country.[130] From Succoth (Deir 'Allah or nearby), Gideon 'went up' to Penuel (Tulūl edh-Dhahab) and then he went up the 'way' of those who lived in tents, a caravan route, to the west of Nobah and Jogbehah. We do not know the site of Nobah,[131] but Jogbehah is now Ajebehat, a group of ruins on the road from es-Salt to Amman. Gideon then reached Zebah and Zalmunna at Karkor, where the latter were camping. Karkor has sometimes been identified with Qarqar in the Wadi Sirhan,[132] but as it is about a hundred and fifty miles from Jogbehah, it is much too far away. It is possible that the name is a descriptive one – several of the derivatives from the Arabic *qrqr* are used to name certain types of country. Gideon returned by the 'ascent of the sun god' (Judges 8:13), a road coming down from Tell Hejaj (Mahanaim) above Tulūl edh-Dhahab (Penuel) and ending at the outskirts of Deir 'Allah (Succoth). This is the outline of a Roman road.[133]

The blood revenge carried out by Gideon against the two nomadic chieftains concerned only his own clan. The fantastic figures of the enemy and the reference to the battle (8:10 and 13) are editorial.[134] The episode was of no importance for Israel and it would be very mistaken to interpret Gideon's reprisals against the people of Succoth and Penuel as indicating that he exercised some power over this district in Transjordania and that this might have added weight to the request made to him to become king.[135]

The really important event was the one that took place to the west of the Jordan (Judges 6:33–7:25). This event seems to have set a whole group of

[128] H. J. Franken, *CAH*, II XXVI (b), 1968, p. 8. We can disregard what is said by G. Sauer, 'Die Tafeln von Deir Alla', *ZAW*, 81 (1969), pp. 145–156, about Judges 6–8, pp. 151–154.

[129] H. Reviv, 'Two Notes to Judges VIII, 4–17', *Tarbiz*, 38 (1968–1969), pp. 309–317.

[130] R. de Vaux, *Bible et Orient*, 1967, p. 134.

[131] It cannot be compared with the personal name Nobah (Num. 32. 42) and located in the north of Transjordania, as J. Gray has attempted to do, *in loco*.

[132] Y. Aharoni, *The Land of the Bible*, p. 241, following A. Musil and others.

[133] S. Mittmann, 'Die Steige des Sonnengottes (Ri. 8. 13)', *ZDPV*, 81 (1965), pp. 80–87.

[134] W. Richter, *op. cit.*, pp. 230–232.

[135] G. Sauer, *ZAW*, 81 (1969), p. 154.

tribes in movement[136] Gideon had behind him not only his clan of Abiezer (6:34), but also the whole of Manasseh and contingents of Asher, Zebulun and Naphthali (6:35). After routing the Midianites, the men of Naphthali, Asher and Manasseh pursued them and all the men of Ephraim cut off their retreat at the fords of the Jordan (7:23–24). What is strange, however, is that after he had called on everyone to fight the Midianites, Gideon told the cowards to turn back (cf. Deut 22) and twenty-two thousand men went away. Ten thousand men remained, but of them Gideon retained only three hundred, choosing them by the way in which they drank water from a stream (7:1–7). Attempts have been made to establish military reasons for taking these steps,[137] but a better reason – a theological one – is given in the text itself for these reductions in the number of men. This theological reason is that Yahweh is the one who was delivering Midian into the hands of Israel and that it was not for Israel to be glorified. It was, in other words, a holy war in which three hundred men, the warriors who were retained, represented the whole of Israel. It can, therefore, be a story belonging to the history of salvation, but, from the historical point of view, it is unlikely. It is also improbable that, after the Midianites had been routed in the attack made by the three hundred men, the contingents from all the tribes would have joined together once again in the pursuit (7:23). An action of this sort would undoubtedly have taken more time.

It would therefore seem that, seen from the historical point of view – and in the first stage of the tradition – it was only Gideon's clan, Abiezer, which was involved in the action (6:34).[138] The figure given in the text of three hundred warriors is probable – six hundred Danites set out from Zorah and Eshtaol (Judges 18:11). The victory that was gained by these three hundred men of Abiezer, however, was of benefit to the whole group of tribes threatened by the incursions into the Plain of Jezreel by the Midianites and it therefore soon became a communal tradition. A very similar situation arose, as we have seen, in the case of the battle of Kishon. In the prose account of this action (Judges 4), only Naphthali and Zebulun take part, whereas, in the Song of Deborah, many groups are listed as participants: Ephraim and Benjamin, Machir (Manasseh), Zebulun, Issachar and Naphthali; in other words, a grouping of tribes similar to that of Gideon.

The geographical framework of the battle against the Midianites is quite clear. The Midianites were on the Plain of Jezreel (6:33), encamped at the foot of the hill of Moreh (7:1), which is the present-day Jebel Dahi or 'Little Hermon', with Shunem at its foot. Gideon's forces camped further south at En-harod ('Ain Jalūd) (Judges 7:1). The route followed by the

---

[136] For what follows, see W. Beyerlin, VT, 13 (1963), especially pp. 2–5.

[137] A. Malamat, 'The War of Gideon and Midian. A Military Approach', PEQ, 85 (1953), pp. 61–65.

[138] W. Beyerlin; J. Gray, op. cit. (see above, note 35), pp. 225 and 301.

Midianites when they retreated is less clear. According to 7:22, they fled as far as Beth-shittah in the direction of Zererah (which should probably be read as Zarethan), going as far as the bank of Abel-meholah, facing Tabbath. This text is, of course, overloaded with details and the sites of the places mentioned are either unknown or else subject to discussion. [139]

According to Judges 7:24, the Ephraimites were sent to cut off the Midianites' retreat by occupying the water-points as far as Beth-barah, the site of which is not known to us. They captured and killed Oreb and Zeeb and the text gives an explanation of the place-names (7:25), which is clearly an aetiological tradition of Ephraim. Gideon replied to the Ephraimites' criticism that he had not summoned them when he went to fight the Midianites by saying that the gleaning of Ephraim's grapes, in other words, the capture of the two Midianite chieftains, was worth more than the vintage of Abiezer, that is, Gideon's victory. If this story which is probably Abiezerite, has a historical basis, then it is probably a confirmation of what we have already said, namely, that the struggle against the Midianites at first involved no more than the clan of Abiezer. It is in any case clear evidence of Ephraim's claims to supremacy and can be compared with the story of Jephthah (Judges 12:1–6) and the whole of the war against Benjamin (Judges 19–20). Whatever may be the case, we may safely say that Gideon's intervention put an end to the Midianite incursions into Israelite territory. In recognition of what he had done, the Israelites wanted to offer him the kingship, but he refused this title (8:22–23), although, as we have already seen, he probably carried out the function of a Judge of Israel, at least over the group of tribes in the north and in central Palestine. Traditionally, his exploits were placed at the same level as the victory achieved by Deborah and Barak (Ps 83:10–12). Yahweh's action in striking Midian at the rock of Oreb is in parallel with the miracle of the exodus from Egypt (Is 10:26). In another place in the book of Isaiah, the 'day of Midian' is the symbol of Israel's deliverance from oppression (Is 9:3).

4. Jephthah (Judges 10:6–12:7) [140]

The literary analysis of this part of the Book of Judges is quite complex. As we have already pointed out, it constitutes an interruption in the story of the 'lesser' Judges. The basic content of the main account (see G. Fohrer, Einleitung; cf. also W. Richter, whose analysis is more complicated, and Täubler, whose analysis is simpler) is to be found in 11:1–11, 29, 32b–33a and 12:7. To this basic content various elements have been added – the

[139] See H.–J. Zobel, 'Abel-Mehola', ZDPV, 82 (1966), pp. 83–108.
[140] E. Täubler, Biblische Studien, pp. 283–297; W. Richter, 'Die Überlieferungen um Jephthah, Ri 10, 17–12, 6', Bib, 47 (1966), pp. 485–556.

story of Jephthah's vow and an aetiology of the lament commemorating the death of his daughter (11:30–31, 34–40), the story of a war between Gilead and Ephraim (12:1–6) and the negotiations between Jephthah and the Ammonites which deal more with the territorial rights of Moab than with those of Ammon (11:12–28). There is also a long theological introduction (10:1–16) which acts as a preface both to the stories of Jephthah and to those about Samson. (It should be noted that the Philistines are also mentioned together with the Ammonites in verses 6 and 7.) Finally, the conclusion of the whole passage (Judges 12:7) links the story of Jephthah to the list of the lesser Judges.

According to 11:1, Jephthah was a Gileadite, but, despite Judges 5:17,[141] there never was a tribe of Gilead. The name was that of a region – this is clearly indicated in verse 8, which mentions the 'inhabitants of Gilead'. The Gilead in question is the primitive Gilead, south of the Jabbok, which was where Israel shared a frontier with the Ammonites. It is noteworthy that Mizpah in Gilead (= Khirbet Jel'ad or thereabouts, south of the Jabbok) plays an important part in the account.

Jephthah was exiled to the land of Tob and it was there that the elders of Gilead went to look for him (11:3–5). In 2 Sam 10:6–8, the men of Tob are presented, together with other Aramaean groups, as allies of the Ammonites. Tob has often been identified with the T-b-y found in the list of Thutmose III and with the Tubu occurring in the Amarna list and it has been located at et-Ṭayībeh on the way between Busra and Der'a.[142] This location of Tob may be valid for the period of David – Tob was a city then alongside other principalities of the Aramaeans in the district of Damascus – but it is not necessarily also valid for the period of the Judges. In particular, it is a long way from the primitive Gilead where Jephthah originated. This 'land of Tob' where Jephthah sought refuge and raised the men with whom he made his expeditions was more probably a sparsely inhabited district to the north or north-west of the Jabbok.[143]

The only military operation described in this basic story is that included in 11:33: 'He (Jephthah) harassed them (the Ammonites) from Aroer almost to Minnith, twenty towns, and to Abel-keramim'. This Aroer is not the town on the Arnon, which is mentioned in the addition, Judges 11:12–28, at verse 26. It is another Aroer, near Rabbah of the Ammonites (Jos 13:25). F.–M. Abel has suggested that it was situated at Khirbet es-Safra, five miles to the east of 'Ammān.[144] S. Mittmann[145] has suggested Khirbet el-Beder, a

---

[141] For both the meanings of Gilead in this story, see M. Noth, *ZDPV*, 75 (1959), pp. 34–38.

[142] See, for example, Abel, Simons and Aharoni.

[143] This is the view held by M. Noth, *Geschichte*, p. 146, note 2 (*History*, p. 156, note 2).

[144] F.–M. Abel, *Géographie*, II, p. 250.

[145] S. Mittmann, 'Aroer, Minnith und Abel Keramim', *ZDPV*, 85 (1969), pp. 63–75; *ibid.*, *Beiträge*, pp. 236–237.

tell about three miles to the north of the citadel of 'Ammān, from where it can be seen, with walls and many potsherds dating back to the period between the eleventh and the eighth centuries B.C. Abel-keramim may well be Kim Yajuz, about two miles to the north of Khirbet el-Beder. Minnith has not been located. The 'twenty towns' may possibly represent villages in this district.

This first conflict between the Ammonites and Israel was not important. It would seem as though it took place very early in the period of the Judges. Gilead here is mentioned in its primitive sense, as it probably is also in the Song of Deborah,[147] and the formulations are therefore not yet fully established. The Ammonites, who became a settled people later than the Edomites and the Amorites, were at this time thinking of extending their territory towards the west. Jephthah drove them back and, if the location of Aroer and Abel-keramim is exact, he repelled them to a point very close to 'Ammān. The frontier of Ammon, however, was to be established on the western side of the Beqā' (the small forts)[148] at the foot of Mount Gilead, at what was to be regarded as the traditional frontier of Israel. (See the story of Jacob and Laban, in which Gilead appears as a frontier.)

This event was magnified by tradition and Judges 11:12–28 goes so far as to report an exchange of messages between Jephthah and the king of the Ammonites, according to which the whole territory from the Jabbok to the Arnon was under discussion, in other words, the land of the Amorites (Sihon), who had been dispossessed by the Israelites. This land was claimed by the Ammonites as their own. It would even seem here to be more concerned with the Moabites and indeed to be mainly a question of Chemosh, the god of the Moabites, who had replaced Milcom, the god of the Ammonites.[149] This whole passage is, of course, an addition, a fragment of historical theology based on Num 20–21. It is, however, earlier in date than the Deuteronomist's editing of the book and may go back to the period of Jeremiah (cf. Jer 49:1–5; Moab against Ammon).[150] It is possible that it may have come about as a result of the reference to Aroer (near 'Ammān) in the primitive account (11:33), which would no doubt have been confused with the other Aroer (on the Arnon). In 11:26 (Heb.), this is corrected

---

[146] E. Täubler, *Biblische Studien*, p. 289; M. Noth, *ZDPV*, 75 (1959), pp. 37 and 40. The introduction (10:9) cannot be taken into account here; according to this introduction, the Ammonites had crossed the Jordan and fought Judah, Benjamin and Ephraim.

[147] M. Noth, *ZDPV*, 68 (1946–1951), pp. 39–40; J. Bright, *History*, p. 169, on the other hand, placed the episode at the end of the period.

[148] See R. de Vaux, *Bible et Orient*, 1967, p. 137.

[149] It is surprising that Albright should say, in the *Prolegomenon* of the new edition of Burney's commentary, 1970, p. 21, that the same deity was probably worshipped under these two different names by both the Moabites and the Ammonites, this deity being equivalent to Nergal or Resheph.

[150] W. Richter, *Bib*, 47 (1966), pp. 522–547.

(Jerusalem Bible) according to the Vulgate and part of the Greek Old Testament into Jazer and Jordan.

The war between Jephthah and Ephraim (12:1–6) is also an addition on the same theme as 8:1–3, that is, the sensitivity of Ephraim and its claim to pre-eminence. The story must, however, have some historical basis,[151] but one that is much wider than that of the Ammonite war. It may have been the choice of Jephthah as Judge after his victory (Judges 12:7). Ephraim would not have favoured the choice of a Transjordanian Judge.[152]

Finally, the story of Jephthah's vow (11:30–31, 34–40) is clearly a cultic aetiology and only arbitrarily linked to the main story of Jephthah.

5. The Philistines

At the end of the period of the Judges, during the reigns of Eli, Samuel and Saul, the Philistines constituted a very serious danger for Israel. They had, however, already been in the country for a considerable time. They had settled there after Ramses III's victory over the Peoples of the Sea, that is, in 1175 B.C. according to our present chronology. It is indeed remarkable that the Philistines feature so little in the Book of Judges. They are in fact mentioned only in the stories of Samson at the end of the book. Chapters 13–16, and in the verse dealing with the Judge Shamgar at the beginning of the book, namely Judges 3:31. I propose to discuss this reference first.

Shamgar: the reference is clearly an addition, since verse 4:1 (the death of Ehud) is a continuation of verse 3:30, without any allusion at all to Shamgar.[153] It was probably added to the text by the main deuteronomistic editor and may have included the figure eighty instead of forty for the period of rest after Ehud, this figure covering both Ehud and Shamgar. The words 'he *too* was a deliverer of Israel' emphasise the fact that it was an addition. It was probably inserted at this point in the text because Shamgar is mentioned in the Song of Deborah (Judges 5:6) together with Jael and he was regarded as one who had delivered Israel.

The name: attempts have been made in recent years to explain the name as Semitic,[154] Shamgar being a *shafel* from a root *mgr*, or even as an Egyptian-Canaanite composite name, *gar = gêr* and Sham being the transcription of the Egyptian *sm3* into Canaanite. The latter is a very strange

---

[151] Despite the view held by Täubler, *op. cit.*, p. 293 ff.

[152] This has been suggested by H. W. Hertzberg, *Die Bücher Josua, Richter, Ruth, op. cit.* (note 35), p. 218.

[153] W. Richter, *Die Bearbeitungen des 'Retterbuches' in der deuteronomischen Epoche* (BBB 21), 1964, pp. 92–97.

[154] A. van Selms, 'Judge Shamgar', *VT*, 14 (1964), pp. 294–309.

explanation.[155] The most convincing explanation was provided many years ago, namely that it is a Hurrian name, *ši—mi—ga—ri*.[156]

Although it can be accepted that Shamgar is a Hurrian name, it is clear that it was also assimilated and given a Semitic form. This is especially clear from the second name, *ben-ʿanath,* 'son of Anath.' Different interpretations have been suggested for this. One theory is quite impossible and has to be rejected at once – that of F. C. Fensham, that Shamgar was a descendant of the Hanaeans found in the Mari texts.[157] 'Anat is, of course, the name of a Canaanite goddess and, since she was a goddess of war, the name 'son of Anath' has been explained as a laudatory title given to Shamgar because of his successful exploits.[158] It is, however, more probable that the name showed that he was an inhabitant of Beth-anath, a town with a sanctuary to the goddess and mentioned in Judges 1:33 and Jos 19:38 as one of the towns not conquered by Naphthali. According to this hypothesis, Shamgar may even have been the prince of this town.[159] It is, however, certainly true that Ben-Anath was also a personal name – there is evidence of it in cuneiform, Ugaritic and Egyptian documents.[160] The most likely explanation, then, is that the name was simply Shamgar (son of) Ben-Anath. He was in any case not an Israelite, but a Canaanite with a Hurrian ancestry.

This Shamgar Ben-Anath is, moreover, certainly the same as the person of the same name in the Song of Deborah (Judges 5:6). The latter is named in a very obscure context: 'In the days of Shamgar the son of Anath, in the days of Jael, every highroad was forsaken; those who went forth on their travels through by-ways took their way. Dead, dead were Israel's villages, until you rose up, O Deborah'. In this context, Shamgar would seem to have been a person living before the time of Deborah and Israel's enemy. But who, then, was Jael? Attempts have been made to correct the text, on the basis of early corruption and the supposition that, since Jael helped Israel, Shamgar must have been Israel's ally. He was regarded as responsible for an exploit against the Philistines of the same kind as the exploits carried out by David's heroes (see especially 2 Sam 23:11–13: Shamma alone against the Philistines).

If, however, Shamgar is dissociated from Beth-anath, then we cannot tell where this episode took place, although, according to the Song of Deborah, the tradition of Shamgar is certainly a northern tradition. But, in that case, how did the Philistines come to play a part in this tradition? According to Aharoni,[161] the 'Philistines' were 'Sea Peoples' who had settled at Beth-

[155] E. Danelius, 'Shamgar ben 'Anath', *JNES,* 22 (1963), pp. 191–193.
[156] B. Maisler (Mazar), *PEFQS,* 1934, pp. 192–194.
[157] F. C. Fensham, 'Shamgar ben 'Anath', *JNES,* 20 (1961), pp. 197–198.
[158] A. van Selms, *op. cit.* (note 154), pp. 303–304.
[159] B. Maisler, *op. cit;* A. Alt, *Kleine Schriften,* I, p. 262; J. Bright, *History,* p. 157.
[160] J. T. Milik, *BASOR,* 143 (Oct. 1956), p. 5.
[161] Y. Aharoni, 'New Aspects of the Israelite Occupation in the North', *Volume Glueck,*

shean and it was Shamgar who is said to have destroyed Beth-shean (level VII) at the end of the thirteenth century B.C. This hypothesis is, however, very much open to doubt.

1970, pp. 254–267, especially pp. 255–259 and 264.

ADDENDA

(Additional information to be considered where there is an asterisk in the text or at the end of a footnote.)

p. 45, n. 38: G. E. Wright, 'The Significance of Ai in the Third Millennium B.C.', in *Archäologie und Altes Testament. Festschrift K. Galling*, eds A. Kuschke and E. Kutsch, Tübingen, 1970, pp. 299–319.

p. 47, n. 40: R. Amiran, 'The Beginnings of Urbanization in Canaan', in *Near Eastern Archaeology in the Twentieth Century: Essays in Honor of Nelson Glueck*, ed. J. A. Sanders, Garden City, N.Y., 1970, pp. 83–100.

p. 52, n. 55: See also J. Monnet-Saleh, 'Forteresses ou villes-protégées thinites?', *BIFAO*, 67, (1969), pp. 173–187.

p. 55, n. 1: H. Klengel, *Geschichte Syriens im 2. Jahrtausend v.u.Z. – Teil 1: Nordsyrien*, Berlin, 1965; *Teil 2: Mittel- und Sudsyrien*, Berlin, 1969; *Teil 3: Historische Geographie und allgemeine Darstellung*, Berlin, 1970.

p. 55, n. 2: W. G. Dever, 'The "Middle Bronze I" Period in Syria and Palestine', in *Near Eastern Archaeology in the Twentieth Century*, ed. J. A. Sanders, pp. 132–163.

p. 77, n. 67: H. te Velde, *Seth, God of Confusion*, Leiden, 1967, especially pp. 109–151; J. Vandier, 'Le dieu Seth au Nouvel Empire', *MDAI*, 25 (1969), pp. 188–197.

p. 77, n. 68: M. Bietak, 'Vorläufiger Bericht über die dritte Kampagne der österreichischen Ausgrabungen auf Tell ed-Dab'a . . . 1968', *MDAI*, 26 (1970), pp. 15–42. Importations of Palestinian origin started at the beginning of the Middle Bronze Age (MB II A according to Albright, MB I following K. M. Kenyon) under the XIII Dynasty, which supports the theory of an infiltration of Semitic Palestinians into the eastern Delta region that was at least initially peaceful.

p. 78, n. 72: M. Bietak, *MDAI*, 26 (1970), p. 39.

p. 83, n. 2: H. Klengel, *Geschichte Syriens im 2. Jahrtausend v.u.Z. – Teil 3: Historische Geographie und allgemeine Darstellung*, Berlin, 1970, pp. 156–179.

p. 86, n. 7: The bones are definitely those of domesticated donkeys and not those of horses, J. Boessneck, *MDAI*, 26 (1970), p. 42.

p. 89, n. 24: H. Klengel, *Geschichte Syriens im 2.Jahrtausend v.u.Z. – Teil 3*, pp. 179–194; K. M. Kenyon, 'Palestine in the Time of the Eighteenth Dynasty', *CAH*, II XI. 1971

p. 94, before the last paragraph: The Amarna letters published after the edition of J. A. Knudtzon, *Die El-Amarna-Tafeln*, Leipzig, 1908–1915 (abbrev. *EA*) have been edited and revised in A. F. Rainey, *El Amarna Tablets 359–379* (*Alter Orient und Altes Testament* 8), Neukirchen and Vluyn, 1970.

p. 94, n. 44: H. Klengel, *Geschichte Syriens im 2.Jahrtausend v.u.Z.* – *Teil 3*, pp. 195–203.

p. 96, n. 54: A. Malamat, 'Northern Canaan and the Mari Texts', *Near Eastern Archaeology in the Twentieth Century*, ed. J. A. Sanders, pp. 164–177.

p. 99, n. 73: Ph. H. J. Houwink ten Cate, *The Records of the Early Hittite Empire, c. 1450–1380 B.C.* (*Publications de l'Institut historique et archéologique de Stamboul*, 26), Istanbul, 1970.

p. 100, n. 74: E. Laroche, 'Fragments hittites du traité mitannien de Suppiluliuma I', *Ugaritica VI*, Paris, 1969, pp. 369–373.

p. 111, n. 139: R. Giveon, *Les bédouins Shosou des documents égyptiens*, Leiden, 1971, especially pp. 267–271.

p. 119, n. 171: On the maritime trade between Syria and Egypt, see also R. de Vaux, 'La Phénicie et les Peuples de la Mer', *MUSJ*, 45 (1969) = *Mélanges offerts à M. Dunand*, I, pp. 481–498, especially p. 492; W. Helck, 'Ein Indiz früher Handelsfahrten syrischer Kaufleute', *Ugarit-Forschungen*, 2 (1970), pp. 35–37.

p. 122, n. 179: provisionally: A. Biran, 'Laish-Dan', *Qadmoniot*, 4 (1971), pp. 2–10; V. Karageorghis, 'Notes on the Mycenean Charioteer Vase from Tel Dan', *ibid.*, pp. 11–13 (in Hebrew); A. Biran, 'A Mycenean Charioteer Vase from Tel Dan', *IEJ*, 20 (1970), pp. 92–94.

p. 138, n. 52: Shamgar was a Canaanite leader according to Y. Aharoni, 'New Aspects of the Israelite Occupation in the North', *Near Eastern Archaeology in the Twentieth Century*, ed. J. A. Sanders, pp. 254-267.

p. 139, n. 55: M. Dietrich and O. Loretz, 'Die soziale Struktur von Alalah und Ugarit', *WO*, 3/3 (1966), pp. 188–205; 5/1 (1969), pp. 57–93.

p. 141, n. 59: J. Gray, 'Sacral Kingship in Ugarit', *Ugaritica VI*, Paris, 1969, pp. 289–302.

p. 145, n. 80: H. Cazelles, 'Essai sur le pouvoir de la divinité à Ugarit et en Israël', *Ugaritica VI*, Paris, 1969, pp. 25–44; M. J. Mulder, 'Accentverschuiving bij de karakterisering van enige kanaänitische goden', *NTT*, 24 (1969–70), pp. 401–420; J. C. de Moor, 'The Semitic Pantheon of Ugarit', *Ugarit-Forschungen*, 2 (1970), pp. 187–228; H. Gese in H. Gese, Maria Höfner, K. Rudolph, *Die Religion Altsyriens, Altarabiens und Mandäer*, Stuttgart, 1970, pp. 1–232.

p. 147, n. 83: On El in Arabia, see also U. Oldenburg, 'Above the Stars of El. El in Ancient South Arabic Religion', *ZAW*, 82, (1970), pp. 187–208.

p. 147, n. 85: J. C. de Moor, *The Seasonal Pattern in the Ugaritic Myth of Ba'lu* (*Alter Orient und Altes Testament* 16), Neukirchen and Vluyn, 1971.

PART ONE

p. 195, n. 50: At Chagar Bazar also, text 39, 24: O. Loretz, 'Texte aus Chagar Bazar', *lišān mithurti. Festschrift W. von Soden* (*Alter Orient und Altes Testament* 1), Neukirchen and Vluyn, 1969, p. 216.

p. 199, n. 83: Texts 42 III 12; 45 III 4; 63, 4, O. Loretz, *op. cit.*, pp. 199–260.

p. 205, n. 132: See however G. Garbini, *Studi aramaici 1–2*, in *Annali dell'Istituto Orientale di Napoli*, n.s. 19 (1969), pp. 1–8.

p. 220, n. 190: See also the criticism by J. A. Emerton, 'Some False Clues in the Study of Genesis XXIV', *VT*, 21 (1971), pp. 24–47, where he contends also that Gen 24 refers to a poetic text (thus specifically opposing Albright) or to a cuneiform document (thus specifically opposing Speiser). On the Chedor-laomer texts, see also, more recently, N. Stokholm, 'Zur Überlieferung von Heliodor, Kuturnahhunte und anderen missglückten Tempelräubern', *ST*, 22 (1968), pp. 1–28, especially 8–14; J. A. Brinkman, *A Political History of Post-Kassite Babylonia, 1158–722 B.C.*, Rome, 1968, especially pp. 19 and 80–82.

p. 227, n. 29: More probably a young dog and a goat, *hazzu*, M. Held, 'Philological Notes on the Mari Covenant Rituals', *BASOR*, 200 (Dec. 1970), pp. 32–40; see also W. von Soden, *Akkadisches Handwörterbuch*, I, 1965, p. 339b.

p. 241, n. 79: J. J. Finkelstein, 'The Laws of Ur-Nammu', *JCS*, 22 (1968–69), pp. 66–82.

p. 242, n. 83: J. J. Finkelstein, 'The Edict of Ammisaduqa: A New Text', *RA*, 63 (1969), pp. 45–64, 189–190.

p. 242, n. 87: V. Souček, 'Zur Sprache der hethitischen Gesetze', *ArOr*, 38 (1970), pp. 269–276.

PART TWO

p. 291, n. 1: D. B. Redford, *A Study of the Biblical Story of Joseph, Genesis 37–50*, (*SVT* 20), 1970.

p. 292, n. 2: N. Lohfink, 'Zum "Kleinen geschichtlichen Credo", Dtn 26, 5–9', *Theologie und Philosophie*, 46 (1971), pp. 19–39.

p. 334, n. 59: R. Giveon, *Les bédouins Shosou des documents égyptiens*, Leiden, 1971, pp. 27–28, 76.

p. 339, end of section: On the motives behind this priestly tradition, see N. Lohfink, 'Die priesterschriftliche Abwertung der Tradition von der Offenbarung des Jahwenamens an Mose', *Bib*, 49 (1968), pp. 1–8; M. Oliva, 'Revelación del nombre de Yahweh en la "Historia sacerdotal": Ex 6, 2–8', *Bib.*, 52 (1971), pp. 1–19.

p. 340, n. 82: A date at the return from the Exile seems more likely to J. C. L. Gibson, *Textbook of Syrian Semitic Inscriptions*, I, *Hebrew and Moabite Inscriptions*, Oxford, 1971, p. 57.

p. 347, n. 123: Following G. Wallis, 'Die Sesshaftwerdung Alt-Israels und das Gottesdienstverständnis des Jahwisten im Lichte der elohistischen Kritik', *ZAW*, 83 (1971), pp. 1–15.

p. 360, n. 2: L. Pomerance, *The Final Collapse of Santorini (Thera), 1400 B.C. or 1200 B.C.?* (*Studies in Mediterranean Archaeology* 26), Gothenburg, 1970, especially pp. 19–20: Ex 15 renders an eye-witness account of the tidal wave caused by the eruption of Santorini, 1180–1170 B.C.

p. 366, n. 19: P. Laaf, *Die Pascha-Feier Israels*, Bonn, 1970; H. Haag, *Vom alten zum neuen Pascha. Geschichte und Theologie des Osterfestes*, Stuttgart, 1971.

p. 376, n. 38: M. Haran, 'The Exodus Routes in the Pentateuchal Sources', *Tarbiz*, 40 (1970–71), pp. 113–143 (in Hebrew with an English summary). He discerns three different routes, one for each of the sources J, E and P, corresponding to established natural routes across the isthmus and the Sinai peninsula. The author's present concern is with the entire journey across the desert, right up to the arrival in Moab.

p. 432, n. 121: The interpretation of a volcanic eruption has been criticised by Th. V. Mann, 'The Pillar of Cloud in the Red Sea Narrative', *JBL*, 90 (1971), pp. 15–30.

p. 441, n. 144: With the next two paragraphs, compare L. Perlitt, *Bundestheologie im Alten Testament*, Neukirchen and Vluyn, 1969, chapter 4: 'Der Bundestheologie in der Sinaiperikope', pp. 156–238.

p. 450, n. 180: W. Zimmerli, 'Erwägungen zum "Bund". Die Aussagen über die Jahwe-*b'rît* in Ex 19–34', *Wort-Gebot-Glaube. Festschrift W. Eichrodt*, Zürich, 1970, pp. 171–190.

p. 450, n. 181: E. Kutsch, 'Sehen und Bestimmen. Die Etymologie von *b'rît*', *Archäologie und Altes Testament. Festschrift K. Galling*, Tübingen, 1970, pp. 165–178.

p. 467, n. 41: J. Gutmann, 'The History of the Ark', *ZAW*, 83 (1971), pp. 22–30; R. J. Clifford, 'The Tent of El and the Israelite Tent of Meeting', *CBQ*, 33 (1971), pp. 221–227.

PART THREE

p. 481, n. 8: F. Golka, 'Zur Erforschung der Ätiologien im Alten Testament', *VT*, 20 (1970), pp. 90–98.

p. 497, n. 37: H. G. Güterbock, 'The Predecessors of Suppiluliuma Again', *JNES*, 20 (1970), pp. 73–77. On the whole subject, E. O. Forrer, 'Der Untergang des Hatti-Reiches', *Ugaritica VI*, Paris, 1969, pp. 207–228, and above all G. A. Lehmann, 'Der Untergang des hethitischen Grossreiches und die neuen Texte aus Ugarit', *Ugarit-Forschung*, 2 (1970), pp. 39–73.

p. 501, n. 55: See also the criticism of G. A. Lehmann, *Ugarit-Forschung*, 2 (1970) pp. 66–72.

p. 504, n. 70: G. Neumann, 'Zum Forschungsstand beim Diskos von Phaistos', *Kadmos*, 7 (1968), pp. 27–44 with bibliography; W. Nahm, 'Zur Struktur der Sprache des Diskos von Phaistos', *Kadmos*, 8 (1969), pp. 110–119; I. Pini, 'Zum Diskos von Phaistos', *Kadmos*, 9 (1970), p. 93. On the coiffure of the Philistines and other Peoples of the Sea, K. Galling, 'Die Kopfzier der Philister in den Darstellung von Medinet Habu', *Ugaritica VI*, Paris, 1969, pp. 248–265; F. Schachermeyr, 'Hörnerhelme und Federkronen als Kopfbedeckungen bei den "Seevölkern" der ägyptischen Reliefs', *ibid.*, pp. 451–459.

p. 508, n. 79: P. Dikaios, *Enkomi, Excavations 1948–1958*, Mainz, 1969, III a, frontispiece and plate 187 19.

p. 511, n. 92: The name Sisera has more recently been compared with *Sisaruwa*, a name attested at Ras Shamra which would be of Luvite origin: following W. F. Albright, *Yahweh and the Gods of Canaan*, London, 1968, p. 218.

p. 511, n. 93: Y. Aharoni, 'New Aspects of the Israelite Occupation in the North', *Near Eastern Archaeology in the Twentieth Century*, ed. J. A. Sanders, pp. 254–265, especially pp. 257–259.

p. 519, n. 122: The names of the Edomite tribes which contained the name of the national deity Qaus may perhaps be found in the geographical lists of Ramses II and Ramses III, B. Oded, 'Egyptian References to the Edomite Deity Qaus', *Andrews University Seminary Studies*, 9 (1971), pp. 47–50.

p. 531, n. 31: V. Fritz, *Israël in der Wüste. Traditionsgeschichtliche Untersuchungen der Wüstenüberlieferung des Jahwisten*, Marburg, 1970, pp. 48–55.

ARCHAEOLOGICAL PERIODS

	B.C.
Early Palaeolithic (Old Stone Age), beginning in ...	?
Middle Palaeolithic, beginning before	60 000
Galilean Man, ca. 60 000	
Carmel Men, average date 45 000	
Late Palaeolithic, beginning about	35 000
Mesolithic (Middle Stone Age); Natufian culture	9000-7000
Neolithic (New Stone Age); Pre-Pottery culture	7000-6000
	gap
Pottery Neolithic; dark burnished pottery, beginning about	5000
Pottery Neolithic; culture of Jericho etc., beginning about	4500
Lower Chalcolithic (Copper-Stone Age); Ghassulian-culture	3600-3200
Upper Chalcolithic (Proto-Urban Age)	3400–3100
Early Bronze	3100-2200
Early Bronze I	3100–2800
Early Bronze II	2800–2500
Early Bronze III	2500–2200
Intermediate Period (Early Bronze IV – Middle Bronze I)	2200–1900
Middle Bronze	1900–1550
Middle Bronze I (Middle Bronze II A)	1900–ca.1800
Middle Bronze II (Middle Bronze II B-C)	ca.1800–1550
Late Bronze	1550–1200
Late Bronze I	1550–1400
Late Bronze II	1400–1300
Late Bronze II B	1300–1200
Iron I	1200–1100

	EGYPT		ASIA MINOR	SYRIA
2100	**XI Dynasty** *1st Intermediate Period*			
2050				Infiltration of Hurrians and movements of Amorites
2000	*Middle Kingdom* **XII Dynasty** Amen-em-het I	1991–1962		
	Sesostris I	1971–1928		
1950				
	Amen-em-het II	1929–1895		
1900	Sesostris II	1897–1878	Assyrian colonies	
	Sesostris III	1878–1843	in	**Mari**
1850	Amen-em-het III	1842–1797	Cappadocia	Yaggid-Lim Yahdun-Lim 1825-1810
			Pithana, king of Kussar	Yasmah-Addu (Assyrian interregnum)
1800	Amen-em-het IV	1798–1790		
	Sobkineferu	1789–1786	Anitta	
	XIII Dyn. 1786–1633	**XIV Dyn.** 1786–1603 (Xoïs)		Zimri-Lim 1782–1759
1750				
	2nd Intermediate Period Beginning of Hyksos			Hurrian Expansion
1700			*Early Hittite Empire* Labarnas	
	XV Dyn. 1660	**XVI Dyn.** 1670–1552	Hattusilis I	
1650	–1552 Hyksos	**XVII Dyn.** (Thebes) 1640–1552		
	Khyan		Mursilis I	
1600	Apophis I		Hantilis I	
	Apophis II			
		Seqnen-Re Ka-mose	Zidanta I	**Mitanni**
1550	*Late Kingdom*			Suttarna I
	Amosis	1552–1527	Ammuna	

PALESTINE	ASSYRIA	BABYLONIA	
Eclipse of urban civilisation		**III Dynasty of Ur**	– 2100
		Shu-Sin 2048–2039 Ibbi-Sin 2039–2015	– 2050
Settlement of Amorites	Puzur-ashur I	**Dyn. of Isin and Larsa** Ishbi-Irra Naplanum	– 2000
	Erishum I 1940–1901		– 1950
Middle Bronze I (MB II A)		continuing until Hammurabi **I Dynasty of Babylonia** Sumui-abum 1894–1881 Sumu-la-el 1880–1845	– 1900
Campaign of Sesostris III Execration texts		Sabium 1844–1831 Apil-Sin 1830–1813	– 1850
Beginning of 'Patriarchal Period'	Shamshi-adad I 1814–1782	Sinmuballit 1812–1793	– 1800
Middle Bronze II (MB II B–C)	Ishme-dagan 1781–1742 Anarchy	Hammurabi 1792–1750 Samsu-Iluna 1749-1712	– 1750
	Adasi	**Cassites** Abieshuh Agum I 1711–1684 Kashtiliash I	– 1700
	Sharma-adad I	Ammiditana 1683–1647	
Descent of Pre-Israelite groups into Egypt	Kidin-ninua Sharma-adad II Shamshi-adad II	Ammisaduga 1646–1626 Kashtiliash II Samsuditana 1625–1595 Raid of Mursilis I	– 1650 – 1600
Late Bronze I	Shamshi-adad III	Agum II Burnaburiash I	– 1550

	EGYPT		ASIA MINOR		SYRIA
	Late Kingdom				**Mitanni**
1550	**XVIII Dynasty**				
	Amosis	1552–1527	Ammuna		Suttarna I
	Amen-hotep	1527–1506			
			Huzziya I		
					Parattarna
1500	Thut-mose I	1506–1494	Telepinus		
	Hat-shepsut	1490–1468			
					Saustatar
	Thut-mose (personal reign)				
		1468–1436			
1450			*Late Hittite Empire*		
	Amen-hotep II	1438–1412	Tudhaliyas I		
			Arnuwandas I		
			Tudhaliyas II		Artatama I
	Thut-mose IV	1412–1402	Hattusilis II		
1400	Amen-hotep III	1402–1364			Suttarna II
			Tudhaliyas III		Tusratta
					Amurru
	Amen-hotep IV		Suppiluliumas I	1370–1336	'Abdu-Ashirta
	Akh-en-Aten	1364–1347			
1350					Aziru
	Tut-ankh-Amon	1347–1338	Arnuwandas II	1335–1300	Artatama II
	Aye	1338–1334	Mursilis II		Mattiwaza
	Hor-em-heb	1334–1306			Duppi-Tessub
	XIX Dynasty				
1300	Seti I	1304–1290	Muwatallis	1285	Sattuara I Benteshina
	Ramses II	1290–1224	Urhi-Tessub	1285–1278	
	Battle of Kadesh 1286		Hattusilis III	1278–1250	
	Hittite Treaty 1269		Egyptian treaty 1269		Sattuara II
1250			Tudhaliyas IV	1250–1220	Shaushgamuwa
	Mer-ne-Ptah	1224–1204	Arnuwandas III		
1200	Seti II	1200–1194	Suppiluliumas II		
	Ta-Usert	1194–1186			
	XX Dynasty				
	Ramses III	1184–1153			
	Defeat of Sea Peoples 1172				
1150	Ramses IV				
	Ramses VI				
	Ramses IX				
1100	Ramses XI	1099–1070			

PALESTINE	ASSYRIA	BABYLONIA	
Late Bronze I			–1550
		Burnaburiash I	
	Puzur-ashur III		
		Kashtiliash III	–1500
Battle of Megiddo 1468 Conquests of Thut-mose III		Ulamburiash	
	Ashurnadinahhe I	Agum III	–1450
Campaign of Amen-hotep II Taanach tablets	Ashurnirari II 1426–1420	Karaindash	
Late Bronze II A	Ashurnadinahhe II Eriba-adad I 1392–1366	Kurigalzu I	–1400
Amarna Letters		Kadashman-Enlil I Burnaburiash II 1375–1347	
	Ashuruballit I 1365–1330		
			–1350
		Kurigalzu II 1345–1324	
	Arikdenilu 1318–1307	Nazimaruttash 1325–1298	
	Adadnirari I 1307–1275		
Late Bronze II B Campaigns of Seti I		Kadashman-Turgu	–1300
Campaigns of Ramses II		Kadashman-Enil II	
	Shalmaneser I 1274–1245		
Exodus of Moses' group Settlement of southern	Tukulti-Ninurta I		–1250
tribes	1244–1208	Kashtiliash IV 1242–1233	
Settlement of central		Assyrian interregnum	
tribes		Adadshumusur 1220–1190	
	Ashurnadinapli 1207–1204		
Battle of the Waters	Ashurnirari III 1203–1198		–1200
of Merom		Melishihu 1190–1175	
Iron I	Ashurdan I 1179–1133		
Settlement of Philistines			
Deborah-Barak			–1150
	Ashurreshishi 1132–1115		
		Nebuchadnezzar I	
	Tiglath-pileser I	1126–1104	
	1115–1070		
Machir in Transjordania			–1100

BIBLICAL INDEX
(The more important references are in bold)

HISTORICAL INDEX

Aaron, 470; family, 318, 327; group of – (and 1 Chron 27), 732; exodus from Egypt, 402; at Meribah, 421, 525; at Sinai, 414; – and Jethro, 338; tomb, 553, 561.
Aaronites (in 1 Chron 12), 732.
Aba(AD)-rama/ -ramu/ -rame, 196-7.
Abam-ram/râma, 196.
Abbael, king of Aleppo, 65.
Abbar, high priest and judge of Tyre, 767.
Abdon, lesser Judge, 684, 690, 753, 755-6; of Pirathon and Ephraim, 757.
Abiezer, Gideon's clan, 771, 818.
Abdu-Ashirta, Amorite leader, 95, 102.
Abdu-Heba, king of Jerusalem, 87, 104-5, 138.
Abel and Cain, 144, 169n.
Abihu, son of Aaron, 444.
Abimelech, king of Gerar; covenant with Abraham and Isaac, 167, 232, 335-6, 338; – and Sarah and Rebekah, 245-6; 'king of the Philistines', 503.
Abimelech (Judges 9), 638-40, 651-2.
Abinadab, and the ark, 707n., 799.
Abijah, son of Samuel, 765.
Abijam, king of Judah, 758.
Abiram, Reubenite, 318, 420.
Abiramu, 197.
Abi-shar/Ibsha, 62, 316.
Abi-shemu, king of Byblos, 72-3.
Abraham:
Abraham (Isaac) cycle, 166-9, 179; – and Jacob cycle, 174-7, 266.
Name, 197-200, 264.
Family: wives, 237-8, 244-6; Isaac, 167-8, 225, 283;

Ishmael, 245; Lot, 168-9, 240, 254.
Migration from Ur, 187-92, 260-1, 262-3, 273, 451; – and Haran/Aram Naharaim, 154, 176-7, 192-3, 195-6, 214, 263; sojourn in Egypt, 245-6, 316, 320, 371, 375, 533. – at Mamre, 167, 280; cave of Machpelah, 255-6; Abraham and Abimelech, 234, 245-6; – and the four great kings of the East, 181, 216-20, 258, 260-1.
Date, 259-63. Ethnic environment (Amorite), 262, 264-5; social environment (shepherd), 224-5, 228, 231-3; family type, 235; adoption, 236-7, 249.
Religion: the 'god of Abraham', 268-70, 272-3, 349; the promises, 154, 162, 166, 174, 179, 273-4, 280, 452, 456; the covenant, 396-7, 411, 412, 451-2; sacred trees, 285-6; circumcision, 287, 395; sacrifice of Isaac, 283-4.
Abram/Abiram, 196-8, 264.
Absalom, 714, 788.
abu bîti, 769.
Aburahana, 198, 264.
Achan and the taking of Ai, 318, 482, 546, 579, 612-13, 619.
Achaeans (= Ahhiyawa ?), 498-9.
Achish, prince of Gath, 505.
Adadnirari I, king of Assyria, 100, 201.
Adah, Esau's wife, 742.
Adoni-bezek/Adoni-zedek, king of Jerusalem, 541, 631.
Aeolus, – had twelve children, 702.
'Agedat, Arab tribes, 183, 739.

Ahab, and Jericho, 809.
Ahhiyawa (= Achaeans ?), 498, 502-3, 510.
Ahijah of Shiloh, 749.
Ahiman, son of Anak, 138.
Ahimelech, 134-5.
Ahiram, inscription of –, 767.
Ahi-yami/Ahi-yawi, 341n.
Ahlamu/Aramaeans, 200-3, 207-8, 521; – and the Sutaeans, 207-8.
Aitakama, king of Kadesh, 87, 102.
Akhthoes III, king of Egypt, 62.
'allûf, 742n.
Almatu, Sutaean clan, 111.
Alyattes and the name Goliath, 506; – and the name Maduwatta, 489.
Amalek, son of Eliphaz, 702, 742.
Amalekites, 392, 422-3, 461, 527; allies of Eglon, 809, 811-12; – and Gideon, 813; – and David, 549, 815; battle in Exod 17, 384, 422, 460, 527. 'Amarat, tribe of –, 739.
Amen-em-hēt I, king of Egypt, 62.
Amen-em-het II, 72-3.
Amen-em-het III, 72-3, 349, 528.
Amen-em-het IV, 72-3.
Amen-hotep I, 89.
Amen-hotep II, 'beloved of Horeb', 118; and Habiru, 108, 215, 326; and Hittites, 95; and Palestine, 93, 97-8, 126, 127; and Hurrians, 88; and Taanach tablets, 89, 96n.
Amen-hotep III, 94; mention of Aramaeans ?, 204, 341n; Soleb list, 117n., 127n., 334n.
Amen-hotep IV (Akh-en-aten) 97-8, 100-3, 299, 464.
Amminadab, Aaron's father--in-law, 318.
Ammisaduga, king of Baby-

GEOGRAPHICAL INDEX

INDEX OF AUTHORS